arihant

SUCCESS AND NOTHING LESS

ARIHANT PRAKASHAN (SERIES), MEERUT

AF814411

Skills in Mathematics

JEE Main & Advanced

Integral Calculus

Amit M Agarwal

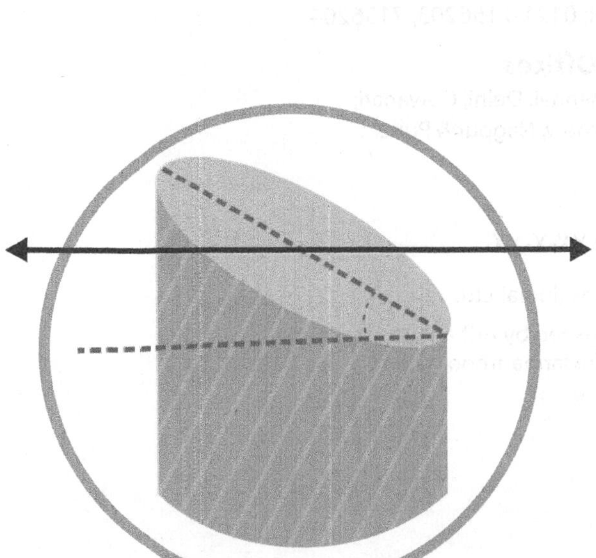

arihant
SUCCESS AND NOTHING LESS

Arihant Prakashan (Series), Meerut

Administrative & Production Offices

Regd. Office

'Ramchhaya' 4577/15, Agarwal Road, Darya Ganj, New Delhi -110002
Tele: 011- 47630600, 43518550

Head Office

Kalindi, TP Nagar, Meerut (UP) - 250002 Tel: 0121-7156203, 7156204

Sales & Support Offices

Agra, Ahmedabad, Bengaluru, Bareilly, Chennai, Delhi, Guwahati, Hyderabad, Jaipur, Jhansi, Kolkata, Lucknow, Nagpur & Pune.

PRICE:

PO No : TXT-XX-XXXXXXX-X-XX

Published by Arihant Publications (India) Ltd.

For further information about the books published by Arihant, log on to www.arihantbooks.com or e-mail at info@arihantbooks.com

Follow us on

Preface

It is a matter of great pride and honour for me to have received such an overwhelming response to the previous editions of this book from the readers. In a way, this has inspired me to revise this book thoroughly as per the changed pattern of JEE Main & Advanced. I have tried to make the contents more relevant as per the needs of students, many topics have been re-written, a lot of new problems of new types have been added. All possible efforts are made to remove all the printing errors that had crept in previous editions. The book is now in such a shape that the students would feel at ease while going through the problems, which will in turn clear their concepts too.

A Summary of changes that have been made in Revised & Enhanced Edition

- Theory has been completely updated so as to accommodate all the changes made in JEE Syllabus & Pattern in recent years.
- The most important point about this new edition is, now the whole text matter of each chapter has been divided into small milestones with practice exercise in each milestones. This will help reader in step by step learning
- Theory of each milestone is more precise with **JEE focus Points** and **JEE Spike**.
- **JEE Scanners** are incorporated in theory for more synced learning with JEE Main and Advanced PYQs.
- Just after completion of theory, Solved Examples of all JEE types have been given, providing the students a complete understanding of all the formats of JEE questions & the level of difficulty of questions generally asked in JEE.
- Along with exercises given with each Milestone, following three exercises have been given at the end of each chapter.
- Practice Milestone 1- JEE Main Pattern Exercises.
- Practice Milestone 2- JEE Advanced Pattern Exercises.
- Practice Milestone 3- Challenging Problems Exercises.
- Previous Years questions asked in JEE Main and Advanced have been incorporated in all the exercises.

However I have made the best efforts and put my all teaching experience in revising this book. Still I am looking forward to get the valuable suggestions and criticism from my own fraternity i.e. the fraternity of JEE teachers. I strongly believe that

"YOU CAN DO ANYTHING IF YOU SET YOUR MIND FOR IT. I ALWAYS BELIEVE THE MOST IMPORTANT FORMULA IS

COURAGE + DREAMS = SUCCESS"

I would also like to motivate the students to send their suggestions or the changes that they want to be incorporated in this book. All the suggestions given by you all will be kept in prime focus at the time of next revision of the book.

Amit M Agarwal

Enhanced Features

JEE Focus Points

- $\int f(x)\,dx = g(x) + C$, where C is constant
  $[\because (g(x)+C)' = g'(x) = f(x)]$
  and C is called constant of integration.
- $\frac{d}{dx}\left(\int f(x)\,dx\right) = f(x)$
- $\int f'(x)\,dx = \int\left[\frac{d}{dx}(f(x))\right]dx = f(x)$
- $\int f(g(x))\,d(g(x)) = F(g(x)) + C$, where $F'(x) = f(x)$

Concept Inside Video

A collection of Key Points/Results prime from JEE Preparation point of View. These are further elaborated with support videos.

Seggregated most valuable Pointers for JEE preparation

JEE SPIKE

The above theorem is also true, if we have e^{kx} in place of e^x
i.e. $\int e^{kx}\{f(kx) + f'(kx)\}\,dx = e^{kx} f(kx) + C$

JEE SCANNER

Example Similar to PYQ Asked in JEE Main 2022

The integral $\int e^x\left(\frac{1-x}{1+x^2}\right)^2 dx$ *is equal to*

(a) $\frac{e^x}{1+x^2}+C$ (b) $\frac{e^{2x}}{1+x^2}+C$

(c) $\frac{-e^x}{1+x^2}+C$ (d) $\frac{e^x}{1-x^2}+C$

Sol. (a) $I = \int e^x\left(\frac{1-x}{1+x^2}\right)^2 dx = \int e^x \frac{(1-2x+x^2)}{(1+x^2)^2}\,dx$

$= \int e^x\left\{\frac{1+x^2}{(1+x^2)^2} - \frac{2x}{(1+x^2)^2}\right\}dx$

$= \int e^x\left\{\frac{1}{1+x^2} - \frac{2x}{(1+x^2)^2}\right\}dx$

$\therefore\ I = \frac{e^x}{1+x^2}+C$ $\left[\text{as } \frac{d}{dx}\left(\frac{1}{1+x^2}\right) = -\frac{2x}{(1+x^2)^2}\right]$

Skill Builder

The integral $\int e^{\sin^2 x}(\cos x \sin 2x - \sin x)\,dx$ is equal to

(a) $e^{\sin x}\cos^2 x + C$ (b) $e^{\sin^2 x}\cos x + C$

(c) $e^{\sin x}\cos x + C$ (d) $e^{\cos^2 x}\sin x + C$

For Sol.

- **For more practice** See Q.22 of Milestone Practice 1.4.

Unmatched Concept elevation tool helpful in syncing recent JEE Main & Advanced PYQs with theory and provide additional practice through Skill Builders.

Contents

Syllabus

JEE Main

Integral Calculus

Integral as an anti - derivative. Fundamental integrals involving algebraic, trigonometric, exponential and logarithmic functions. Integration by substitution, by parts and by partial fractions. Integration using trigonometric identities.

Evaluation of simple integrals of the type

$$\int \frac{dx}{x^2 \pm a^2}, \quad \int \frac{dx}{\sqrt{x^2 \pm a^2}}, \quad \int \frac{dx}{a^2 - x^2}, \quad \int \frac{dx}{\sqrt{a^2 - x^2}},$$

$$\int \frac{dx}{ax^2 + bx + c}, \quad \int \frac{dx}{\sqrt{ax^2 + bx + c}}, \quad \int \frac{(px + q)\, dx}{ax^2 + bx + c},$$

$$\int \frac{(px + q)\, dx}{\sqrt{ax^2 + bx + c}}, \quad \int \sqrt{a^2 \pm x^2}\, dx \quad \text{and} \quad \int \sqrt{x^2 - a^2}\, dx$$

Fundamental Theorem of Calculus. Properties of definite integrals. Evaluation of definite integrals, determining areas of the regions bounded by simple curves in standard form.

Differential Equations

Ordinary differential equations, their order and degree. Solution of differential equations by the method of separation of variables, solution of homogeneous and linear differential equations of the type $\frac{dy}{dx} + p(x)y = q(x)$

JEE Advanced

Integral Calculus

Integration as the inverse process of differentiation, indefinite integrals of standard functions, definite integrals as the limit of sums, definite integral and their properties, fundamental theorem of integral calculus.

Integration by parts, integration by the methods of substitution and partial fractions, application of definite integrals to the determination of areas bounded by simple curves. Formation of ordinary differential equations, solution of homogeneous differential equations of first order and first degree, separation of variables method, linear first order differential equations.

1

By integration we mean the process of achieving unity of effort among the various subsystems in the accomplishment of the organization's tasks.

-Paul R Lawrence

Indefinite Integral

Learning Milestones

Milestone 1 Fundamentals of Indefinite Integral
- Integration
- Fundamentals of Indefinite Integral

Milestone 2 Integration by Substitution
- Methods of Integration
- Integration by Substitution

Milestone 3 Some Special Integrals
- Some Special Integrals
- Trigonometric Integrals

Milestone 4 Integration by Parts
- Some More Special Types of Integrals

Milestone 5 Integration Using Partial Fraction

Milestone 6 Indirect and Derived Substitutions
- Indirect Substitution
- Derived Substitution

Milestone 7 Euler's Substitution, Reduction Formula and Integration Using Differentiation
- Integration Using Euler's Substitution
- Reduction Formulae
- Integration Using Differentiation

Practice Milestones

Practice Milestone 1- JEE Main Pattern
Practice Milestone 2 - JEE Advanced Pattern
Practice Milestone 3 - Challenging Problems

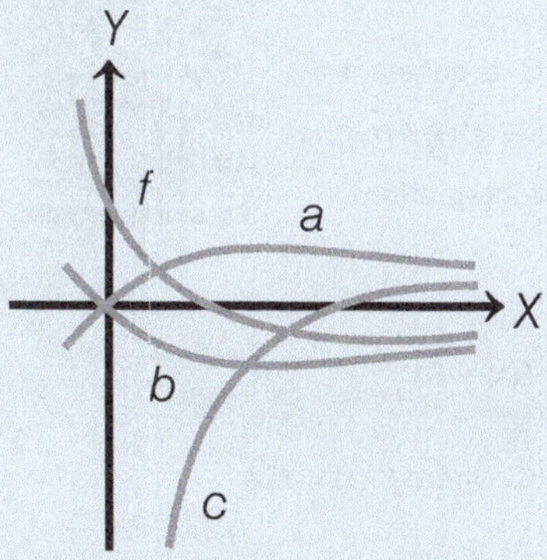

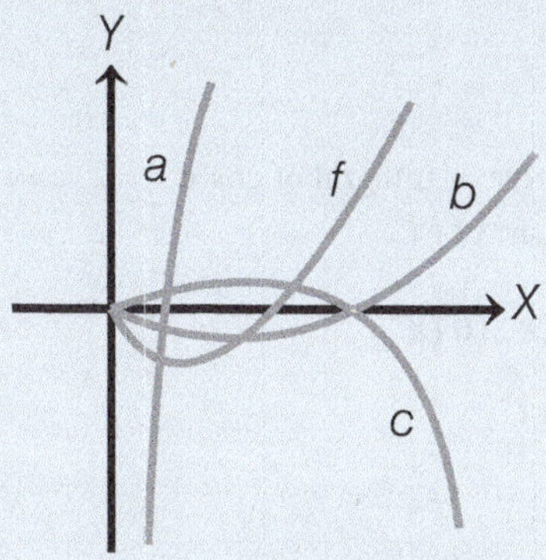

Milestone 1 Fundamentals of Indefinite Integral

• Integration • Fundamentals of Indefinite Integral

It was in this aspect that the process of integration was treated by Leibnitz, the symbol of $\int$ being regarded as the initial letter of the word sum, in the same way as the symbol of differentiation d is the initial letter in the word difference.

1.1 Integration

We know that differentiation is the process of finding the derivative of the function and integration is the process of finding the anti-derivative of a function.

So, these processes are inverse of each other.

So, we can say that integration is the inverse process of differentiation or *vice-versa.*

Let $g(x)$ be differentiable function of x such that

$$\frac{d(g(x)+C)}{dx}=f(x)$$

Then, $$\int f(x)dx=g(x)+C$$

Thus, $g(x)$ is called a **primitive** or **anti-derivative** or an **indefinite integral** or **simply integral of $f(x)$** with respect to x, where $f(x)$ is called the **integrand** and C is called the **constant of integration**.

Geometrical Interpretation of Constant of Integration

By adding C means the graph of function would shift in upward or downward direction along Y-axis as C is +ve or – ve, respectively.

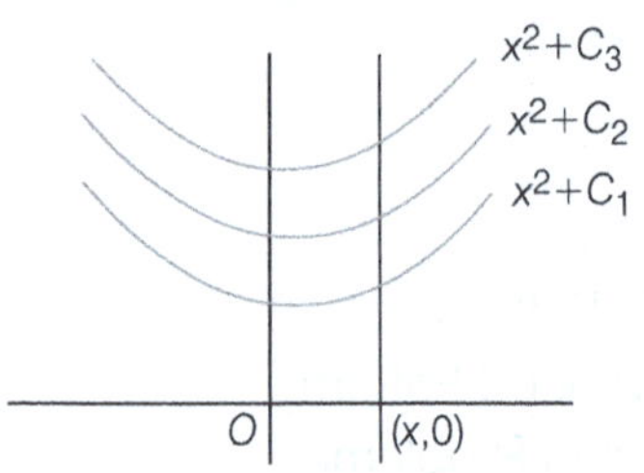

e.g. $$y=\int x\,dx=\frac{x^2}{2}+C$$

$\therefore$ $$y=\int f(x)\,dx=F(x)+C$$

$\Rightarrow$ $$F'(x)=f(x);\ F'(x_1)=f(x_1)$$

Hence, $y=\int f(x)\,dx$ denotes a family of curves such that the slope of the tangent at $x=x_1$ on every member is same

i.e $F'(x_1)=f(x_1)$ [when x_1 lies in the domain of $f(x)$]

Hence, anti-derivative of a function is not unique. If $g_1(x)$ and $g_2(x)$ are two anti-derivatives of a function $f(x)$ on $[a, b]$, then they differ only by a constant.

i.e. $$g_1(x)-g_2(x)=C$$

Anti-derivative of a continuous function is differentiable.

JEE Focus Points

Concept Inside Video

- $\int f(x)\,dx = g(x) + C$, where C is constant $[\because (g(x)+C)' = g'(x) = f(x)]$ and C is called constant of integration.
- $\frac{d}{dx}\left(\int f(x)\,dx\right) = f(x)$
- $\int f'(x)\,dx = \int\left[\frac{d}{dx}(f(x))\right]dx = f(x) + C$
- $\int f(g(x))\,d(g(x)) = F(g(x)) + C$, where $F'(x) = f(x)$

Example 1. If $\frac{d}{dx}(\sin x + C) = \cos x$, then find $\int \cos x\,dx$.

Sol. As, $\frac{d}{dx}(\sin x + C) = \cos x$

$\Rightarrow$ $\sin x + C$ is anti-derivative or integral of $\cos x$.

$\therefore$ $$\int \cos x\,dx = (\sin x) + C$$

Example 2. Evaluate $\int \cos(x^2)\,d(x^2)$.

Sol. $\int \cos(x^2)d(x^2)=\sin(x^2)+C$

1.2 Fundamentals of Indefinite Integral

Since, $\dfrac{d}{dx}\{g(x)\} = f(x) \Leftrightarrow \int f(x)\,dx = g(x) + C$

Therefore, based upon this definition and various standard differentiation formulae, we obtain the following integration formulae.

(i) $\dfrac{d}{dx}\left(\dfrac{x^{n+1}}{n+1}\right) = x^n, n \neq -1$

$\Rightarrow \int x^n\,dx = \dfrac{x^{n+1}}{n+1} + C, n \neq -1$

(ii) $\dfrac{d}{dx}(\log|x|) = \dfrac{1}{x}$

$\Rightarrow \int \dfrac{1}{x}\,dx = \log|x| + C$, when $x \neq 0$

(iii) $\dfrac{d}{dx}(e^x) = e^x \Rightarrow \int e^x\,dx = e^x + C$

(iv) $\dfrac{d}{dx}\left(\dfrac{a^x}{\log_e a}\right) = a^x, a > 0, a \neq 1 \Rightarrow \int a^x\,dx = \dfrac{a^x}{\log_e a} + C$

(v) $\dfrac{d}{dx}(-\cos x) = \sin x \Rightarrow \int \sin x\,dx = -\cos x + C$

(vi) $\dfrac{d}{dx}(\sin x) = \cos x \Rightarrow \int \cos x\,dx = \sin x + C$

(vii) $\dfrac{d}{dx}(\tan x) = \sec^2 x \Rightarrow \int \sec^2 x\,dx = \tan x + C$

(viii) $\dfrac{d}{dx}(-\cot x) = \operatorname{cosec}^2 x$

$\Rightarrow \int \operatorname{cosec}^2 x\,dx = -\cot x + C$

(ix) $\dfrac{d}{dx}(\sec x) = \sec x \tan x$

$\Rightarrow \int \sec x \tan x\,dx = \sec x + C$

(x) $\dfrac{d}{dx}(-\operatorname{cosec} x) = \operatorname{cosec} x \cot x$

$\Rightarrow \int \operatorname{cosec} x \cot x\,dx = -\operatorname{cosec} x + C$

(xi) $\dfrac{d}{dx}(\log|\sin x|) = \cot x$

$\Rightarrow \int \cot x\,dx = \log|\sin x| + C$

(xii) $\dfrac{d}{dx}(-\log|\cos x|) = \tan x$

$\Rightarrow \int \tan x\,dx = -\log|\cos x| + C$

(xiii) $\dfrac{d}{dx}(\log|\sec x + \tan x|) = \sec x$

$\Rightarrow \int \sec x\,dx = \log|\sec x + \tan x| + C$

$= \log\left|\tan\left(\dfrac{\pi}{4} + \dfrac{x}{2}\right)\right| + C$

(xiv) $\dfrac{d}{dx}(\log|\operatorname{cosec} x - \cot x|) = \operatorname{cosec} x$

$\Rightarrow \int \operatorname{cosec} x\,dx = \log|\operatorname{cosec} x - \cot x| + C$

$= \log\left|\tan\dfrac{x}{2}\right| + C$

(xv) $\dfrac{d}{dx}\left(\sin^{-1}\dfrac{x}{a}\right) = \dfrac{1}{\sqrt{a^2 - x^2}}$

$\Rightarrow \int \dfrac{dx}{\sqrt{a^2 - x^2}} = \sin^{-1}\left(\dfrac{x}{a}\right) + C$

(xvi) $\dfrac{d}{dx}\left(\cos^{-1}\dfrac{x}{a}\right) = \dfrac{-1}{\sqrt{a^2 - x^2}}$

$\Rightarrow \int \dfrac{-1}{\sqrt{a^2 - x^2}}\,dx = \cos^{-1}\left(\dfrac{x}{a}\right) + C$

(xvii) $\dfrac{d}{dx}\left(\dfrac{1}{a}\tan^{-1}\dfrac{x}{a}\right) = \dfrac{1}{a^2 + x^2}$

$\Rightarrow \int \dfrac{dx}{a^2 + x^2} = \dfrac{1}{a}\tan^{-1}\left(\dfrac{x}{a}\right) + C$

(xviii) $\dfrac{d}{dx}\left(\dfrac{1}{a}\cot^{-1}\dfrac{x}{a}\right) = \dfrac{-1}{a^2 + x^2}$

$\Rightarrow \int \dfrac{-1}{a^2 + x^2}\,dx = \dfrac{1}{a}\cot^{-1}\left(\dfrac{x}{a}\right) + C$

(xix) $\dfrac{d}{dx}\left(\dfrac{1}{a}\sec^{-1}\dfrac{x}{a}\right) = \dfrac{1}{x\sqrt{x^2 - a^2}}$

$\Rightarrow \int \dfrac{dx}{x\sqrt{x^2 - a^2}} = \dfrac{1}{a}\sec^{-1}\left(\dfrac{x}{a}\right) + C$

(xx) $\dfrac{d}{dx}\left(\dfrac{1}{a}\operatorname{cosec}^{-1}\dfrac{x}{a}\right) = \dfrac{-1}{x\sqrt{x^2 - a^2}}$

$\Rightarrow \int \dfrac{-dx}{x\sqrt{x^2 - a^2}} = \dfrac{1}{a}\operatorname{cosec}^{-1}\left(\dfrac{x}{a}\right) + C$

(xxi) $\int |f(x)|\,dx = \operatorname{sgn} f(x) \cdot \int f(x)\,dx$

Basic Properties of Indefinite Integration

1. $\int k\, f(x)\, dx = k \int f(x)\, dx$, where k is constant.
   i.e. the integral of the product of a constant and a function = the constant × integral of the function
2. $\int \{f_1(x) \pm f_2(x) \pm \ldots \pm f_n(x)\}\, dx$
   $$= \int f_1(x)\, dx \pm \int f_2(x)\, dx \pm \ldots \pm \int f_n(x)\, dx$$
   i.e. the integral of the sum or difference of a finite number of functions is equal to the sum or difference of the integrals of the individual functions.
3. If $f(x)$ is continuous, then
   $$\int f(x)\, dx = F(x) + C \Rightarrow F'(x) = f(x)$$
   $\Rightarrow F'(x)$ always exists and is continuous.
4. If integral is discontinuous at $x = x_1$, then its anti-derivative at $x = x_1$ need not be discontinuous.
   e.g. $\int x^{-1/3} dx$
   Here, $x^{-1/3}$ is discontinuous at $x = 0$. But
   $\int x^{-1/3} dx = \frac{3}{2} x^{2/3} + C$ is continuous at $x = 0$.
5. Anti-derivative of a periodic function need not be a periodic function.
   e.g. $f(x) = \cos x + 1$ is periodic but
   $\int (\cos x + 1)\, dx = \sin x + x + C$ is not periodic.
6. The signum function has an anti-derivative on any interval which doesn't contain the point $x = 0$ and does not possess an anti-derivative on any interval which contain the point $x = 0$.
7. The anti-derivative of every odd function is an even function and *vice-versa*.

Example 3. Evaluate

(i) $\int \left(\frac{x^3 + 5x^2 + 4x + 1}{x^2}\right) dx$ (ii) $\int \left(\sqrt{x} + \frac{1}{\sqrt{x}}\right)^3 dx$

(iii) $\int \frac{x^3 - x^2 + x - 1}{x - 1} dx$

Sol. (i) Let $I = \int \frac{x^3 + 5x^2 + 4x + 1}{x^2} dx$

$$= \int \left(\frac{x^3}{x^2} + \frac{5x^2}{x^2} + \frac{4x}{x^2} + \frac{1}{x^2}\right) dx = \int \left(x + 5 + \frac{4}{x} + \frac{1}{x^2}\right) dx$$

$$= \int x dx + \int 5 dx + \int \frac{4}{x} dx + \int x^{-2} dx$$

$$= \frac{x^2}{2} + 5x + 4 \log|x| - \frac{1}{x} + C$$

(ii) Let $I = \int \left(\sqrt{x} + \frac{1}{\sqrt{x}}\right)^3 dx$

$$= \int \left((\sqrt{x})^3 + \left(\frac{1}{\sqrt{x}}\right)^3 + 3(\sqrt{x})^2 \left(\frac{1}{\sqrt{x}}\right) + 3\sqrt{x}\left(\frac{1}{\sqrt{x}}\right)^2\right) dx$$

$$= \int \left(x^{\frac{3}{2}} + x^{\frac{-3}{2}} + 3(x)^{\frac{1}{2}} + 3x^{\frac{-1}{2}}\right) dx$$

$$= \int x^{\frac{3}{2}} dx + \int x^{\frac{-3}{2}} dx + 3\int x^{\frac{1}{2}} dx + 3\int x^{\frac{-1}{2}} dx$$

$$= \frac{x^{\frac{5}{2}}}{\frac{5}{2}} + \frac{x^{\frac{-1}{2}}}{\frac{-1}{2}} + \frac{3x^{\frac{3}{2}}}{\frac{3}{2}} + \frac{3x^{\frac{1}{2}}}{\frac{1}{2}} + C$$

$$= \frac{2}{5} x^{\frac{5}{2}} - 2x^{\frac{-1}{2}} + 2x^{\frac{3}{2}} + 6x^{\frac{1}{2}} + C$$

$$= \frac{2}{5} x^{\frac{5}{2}} + 2x^{\frac{3}{2}} - \frac{2}{\sqrt{x}} + 6\sqrt{x} + C$$

(iii) Let $I = \int \frac{x^3 - x^2 + x - 1}{x - 1} dx$

$$= \int \frac{x^2(x-1) + 1(x-1) dx}{x - 1} = \int \frac{(x^2+1)(x-1)}{x-1} dx$$

$$= \int (x^2 + 1) dx = \int x^2 dx + \int 1 dx = \frac{x^3}{3} + x + C$$

Example 4. Evaluate

(i) $\int 5^{\log_e x} dx$ (ii) $\int 2^{\log_4 x} dx$

(iii) $\int \left(\frac{e^{7\log_e x} - e^{6\log_e x}}{e^{4\log_e x} - e^{3\log_e x}}\right) dx$ (iv) $\int \frac{2^{x+1} - 5^{x-1}}{10^x} dx$

Sol. (i) Let $I = \int 5^{\log_e x} dx$

$$= \int x^{\log_e 5} dx \qquad [\text{using } a^{\log_c b} = b^{\log_c a}]$$

$$= \frac{x^{\log_e 5 + 1}}{(\log_e 5 + 1)} + C$$

$$\therefore \int 5^{\log_e x} dx = \frac{x^{\log_e 5 + 1}}{\log_e 5 + 1} + C$$

(ii) Let $I = \int 2^{\log_4 x} dx = \int 2^{\log_{2^2} x} dx = \int 2^{(1/2)\log_2 x} dx$

$$\left[\text{using } \log_{b^n} x = \frac{1}{n} \log_b x\right]$$

$$= \int 2^{\log_2 \sqrt{x}} dx = \int \sqrt{x}\, dx \qquad [\text{using } a^{\log_a b} = b]$$

$$= \frac{x^{3/2}}{3/2} + C$$

$$\therefore \int 2^{\log_4 x} dx = \frac{2}{3} x^{3/2} + C$$

(iii) Let $I = \int \left(\frac{e^{7 \log_e x} - e^{6 \log_e x}}{e^{4 \log_e x} - e^{3 \log_e x}} \right) dx$

$$= \int \left(\frac{e^{\log_e x^7} - e^{\log_e x^6}}{e^{\log_e x^4} - e^{\log_e x^3}} \right) dx = \int \left(\frac{x^7 - x^6}{x^4 - x^3} \right) dx$$

$$= \int \frac{x^6(x-1)}{x^3(x-1)} dx = \int x^3 dx = \frac{x^4}{4} + C$$

(iv) Let $I = \int \frac{2^{x+1} - 5^{x-1}}{10^x} dx$

$$= \int \left[2\left(\frac{1}{5}\right)^x - \frac{1}{5}\left(\frac{1}{2}\right)^x \right] dx = 2 \frac{\left(\frac{1}{5}\right)^x}{\ln\left(\frac{1}{5}\right)} - \frac{1}{5} \cdot \frac{\left(\frac{1}{2}\right)^x}{\ln\left(\frac{1}{2}\right)} + C$$

$$= -\frac{2}{5^x \ln 5} + \frac{1}{5 \cdot 2^x \ln 2} + C$$

Example 5. Evaluate

(i) $\int \frac{x^4 + x^2 + 1}{x^2 - x + 1} dx$ (ii) $\int \left[\frac{y+1}{y^{\frac{2}{3}} - y^{\frac{1}{3}} + 1} - \frac{y-1}{y - y^{\frac{1}{2}}} \right] dy$

(iii) $\int \frac{\sqrt{x^4 + x^{-4} + 2}}{x^3} dx$ (iv) $\int \frac{1 + 2x^2}{x^2(1 + x^2)} dx$

Sol. (i) $I = \int \frac{x^4 + x^2 + 1}{x^2 - x + 1} dx$

$$= \int \frac{(x^2 + 1 + x)(x^2 + 1 - x)}{x^2 - x + 1} dx$$

$$= \int (x^2 + x + 1)\, dx = \frac{x^3}{3} + \frac{x^2}{2} + x + C$$

(ii) $I = \int \left[\frac{y+1}{y^{\frac{2}{3}} - y^{\frac{1}{3}} + 1} - \frac{y-1}{y - y^{\frac{1}{2}}} \right] dy$

$$= \int \left[\frac{\left(y^{\frac{1}{3}} + 1\right)\left(y^{\frac{2}{3}} - y^{\frac{1}{3}} + 1\right)}{\left(y^{\frac{2}{3}} - y^{\frac{1}{3}} + 1\right)} - \frac{\left(y^{\frac{1}{2}} - 1\right)\left(y^{\frac{1}{2}} + 1\right)}{y^{\frac{1}{2}}\left(y^{\frac{1}{2}} - 1\right)} \right] dy$$

$$\left[\because y + 1 = \left(y^{\frac{1}{3}}\right)^3 + 1^3 = \left(y^{\frac{1}{3}} + 1\right)\left(y^{\frac{2}{3}} - y^{\frac{1}{3}} + 1\right) \right]$$

$$= \int \left[\left(y^{\frac{1}{3}} + 1\right) - \left(1 + y^{-\frac{1}{2}}\right) \right] dy$$

$$= \int \left(y^{\frac{1}{3}} - y^{-\frac{1}{2}}\right) dy = \frac{3}{4} y^{\frac{4}{3}} - 2y^{\frac{1}{2}} + C$$

(iii)

> **Decoding the Question**
>
> Use the identity $x^4 + \frac{1}{x^4} = \left(x^2 + \frac{1}{x^2}\right)^2 - 2$

$$I = \int \frac{\sqrt{x^4 + x^{-4} + 2}}{x^3} dx$$

$$= \int \frac{1}{x^3} \sqrt{x^4 + \frac{1}{x^4} + 2}\, dx = \int \frac{1}{x^3}\left(x^2 + \frac{1}{x^2}\right) dx$$

$$= \int \left(\frac{1}{x} + \frac{1}{x^5} \right) dx = \ln|x| - \frac{1}{4x^4} + C$$

(iv) $I = \int \frac{1 + 2x^2}{x^2(1 + x^2)} dx = \int \frac{1 + x^2 + x^2}{x^2(1 + x^2)} dx$

$$= \int \frac{1 + x^2}{x^2(1 + x^2)} dx + \int \frac{x^2}{x^2(1 + x^2)} dx$$

$$= \int \frac{1}{x^2} dx + \int \frac{1}{1 + x^2} dx$$

$$= -\frac{1}{x} + \tan^{-1} x + C$$

Integral of the Form $\int \frac{f(x)}{g(x)} dx$

Where $f(x)$ and $g(x)$ be two polynomial such that degree of $f(x) \geq$ degree of $g(x)$. Simply divide the numerator by denominator and use result of integration.

Example 6. Evaluate

(i) $\int \frac{x^3}{x+2} dx$ (ii) $\int \frac{x^2}{x^2 + 5} dx$

Sol. (i) We have, $\int \frac{x^3}{x+2} dx$

Here, degree of numerator is greater than denominator.

$\therefore$ We divide numerator by denominator by long division method, we get

$$\frac{x^3}{x+2} = (x^2 - 2x + 4) - \frac{8}{x+2}$$

$$\therefore \quad \int \frac{x^3}{x+2} dx = \int \left[(x^2 - 2x + 4) - \frac{8}{x+2} \right] dx$$

$$= \int (x^2 - 2x + 4) dx - 8 \int \frac{dx}{x+2}$$

$$= \frac{x^3}{3} - \frac{2x^2}{2} + 4x - 8 \log|x + 2| + C$$

$$= \frac{x^3}{3} - x^2 + 4x - 8 \log|x + 2| + C$$

(ii) $I=\int \frac{x^2}{x^2+5}dx=\int \frac{x^2+5-5}{x^2+5}dx=\int\left(\frac{x^2+5}{x^2+5}-\frac{5}{x^2+5}\right)dx$

$=\int\left(1-\frac{5}{x^2+5}\right)dx=x-5\int\frac{dx}{x^2+(\sqrt{5})^2}$

$=x-\frac{5}{\sqrt{5}}\tan^{-1}\left(\frac{x}{\sqrt{5}}\right)+C=x-\sqrt{5}\tan^{-1}\left(\frac{x}{\sqrt{5}}\right)+C$

Example 7. Evaluate

(i) $\int\frac{x^6-1}{x^2+1}dx$ (ii) $\int\frac{x^7}{x+1}dx$

Sol. (i) $\int\frac{x^6-1}{x^2+1}dx$

Here, degree of numerator is greater than denominator. We divide numerator by denominator using long division method, we get

$$\frac{x^6-1}{x^2+1}=x^4-x^2+1-\frac{2}{x^2+1}$$

$$\Rightarrow\int\frac{x^6-1}{x^2+1}dx=\int\left(x^4-x^2+1-\frac{2}{x^2+1}\right)dx$$

$$=\frac{x^5}{5}-\frac{x^3}{3}+x-2\tan^{-1}x+C$$

(ii)

Decoding the Question

First convert $\frac{x^7}{x+1}$ in the form of $\frac{x^7-(-1)^7}{x-(-1)}-\frac{1}{x+1}$, then apply formula $\frac{x^n-a^n}{x-a}=x^{n-1}+x^{n-2}a+x^{n-3}a^2+\ldots+xa^{n-2}+a^{n-1}$.

After simplification, integrate the result.

$I=\int\frac{x^7}{x+1}dx=\int\frac{(x^7+1)-1}{x+1}dx$

$=\int\frac{x^7-(-1)^7}{x-(-1)}dx-\int\frac{1}{x+1}dx$

$=\int(x^6-x^5+x^4-x^3+x^2-x+1)\,dx-\int\frac{1}{x+1}dx$

$\left[\because \frac{x^n-a^n}{x-a}=x^{n-1}+x^{n-2}a+x^{n-3}a^2+\ldots+xa^{n-2}+a^{n-1}\right]$

$=\frac{x^7}{7}-\frac{x^6}{6}+\frac{x^5}{5}-\frac{x^4}{4}+\frac{x^3}{3}-\frac{x^2}{2}+x-\log|x+1|+C$

Example 8. Evaluate

(i) $\int\frac{(\sqrt{x}+1)(x^2-\sqrt{x})}{x\sqrt{x}+x+\sqrt{x}}dx$

(ii) $\int\sqrt{1+x\sqrt{1+(x+1)\sqrt{1+(x+2)(x+4)}}}\,dx$

Sol. (i) Here, $I=\int\frac{(\sqrt{x}+1)\cdot\sqrt{x}(x^{3/2}-1)}{\sqrt{x}(x+\sqrt{x}+1)}dx$

$=\int\frac{(\sqrt{x}+1)[(\sqrt{x})^3-1^3]}{(x+\sqrt{x}+1)}dx$

$=\int\frac{(\sqrt{x}+1)(\sqrt{x}-1)(x+\sqrt{x}+1)}{(x+\sqrt{x}+1)}dx$

[using $a^3-b^3=(a-b)(a^2+ab+b^2)$]

$=\int(x-1)\,dx=\frac{x^2}{2}-x+C$

(ii) Here, $I=\int\sqrt{1+x\sqrt{1+(x+1)\sqrt{1+(x+2)(x+4)}}}\,dx$

$=\int\sqrt{1+x\sqrt{1+(x+1)\sqrt{x^2+6x+9}}}\,dx$

$=\int\sqrt{1+x\sqrt{1+(x+1)(x+3)}}\,dx$

$=\int\sqrt{1+x\sqrt{x^2+4x+4}}\,dx$

$=\int\sqrt{1+x^2+2x}\,dx$

$=\int(x+1)dx=\frac{x^2}{2}+x+C$

Example 9. Evaluate

$$\int\left(\frac{x^{-6}-64}{4+2x^{-1}+x^{-2}}\cdot\frac{x^2}{4-4x^{-1}+x^{-2}}-\frac{4x^2(2x+1)}{1-2x}\right)dx.$$

Sol. Here,

$I=\int\left(\frac{x^{-6}-64}{4+2x^{-1}+x^{-2}}\cdot\frac{x^2}{4-4x^{-1}+x^{-2}}-\frac{4x^2(2x+1)}{1-2x}\right)dx$

$=\int\left(\frac{\frac{1-64x^6}{x^6}}{\frac{4x^2+2x+1}{x^2}}\cdot\frac{x^2}{\frac{4x^2-4x+1}{x^2}}-\frac{4x^2(2x+1)}{(1-2x)}\right)dx$

$=\int\left(\frac{1-(4x^2)^3}{x^6\cdot(4x^2+2x+1)}\cdot\frac{x^6}{(4x^2-4x+1)}-\frac{4x^2(2x+1)}{(1-2x)}\right)dx$

$=\int\left(\frac{(1-4x^2)(1+4x^2+16x^4)}{(4x^2+2x+1)(4x^2-4x+1)}-\frac{4x^2(2x+1)}{(1-2x)}\right)dx$

$=\int\left(\frac{(1-4x^2)\cdot(4x^2+2x+1)(4x^2-2x+1)}{(4x^2+2x+1)(2x-1)^2}-\frac{4x^2(2x+1)}{(1-2x)}\right)dx$

[using $16x^4+4x^2+1=16x^4+8x^2+1-4x^2$
$=(4x^2+1)^2-(2x)^2$
$=(4x^2+1+2x)(4x^2-2x+1)$]

$=\int\left(\frac{(1-2x)(1+2x)(4x^2-2x+1)}{(1-2x)^2}-\frac{4x^2(2x+1)}{(1-2x)}\right)dx$

$=\int\left(\frac{(1+2x)\cdot(4x^2-2x+1)}{(1-2x)}-\frac{4x^2(2x+1)}{(1-2x)}\right)dx$

$=\int\frac{(2x+1)\{4x^2-2x+1-4x^2\}\,dx}{1-2x}$

$=\int\frac{(2x+1)(1-2x)}{(1-2x)}dx=\int(2x+1)\,dx=x^2+x+C$

Integration of Trigonometric Functions Using Identity

Example 10. Evaluate

(i) $\int \tan^2 x\, dx$ (ii) $\int \frac{dx}{\sin^2 x \cos^2 x}$

(iii) $\int \frac{\sin^6 x + \cos^6 x}{\sin^2 x \cos^2 x} dx$ (iv) $\int \frac{\cos x - \cos 2x}{1 - \cos x} dx$

Sol. (i) $I = \int \tan^2 x\, dx = \int (\sec^2 x - 1)\, dx$

$= \int \sec^2 x\, dx - \int 1\, dx$ [using $\int \sec^2 x dx = \tan x + C$]

$= \tan x - x + C$

(ii) **Decoding the Question**
Here, 1 is replaced by $\sin^2 x + \cos^2 x$

$I = \int \frac{1}{\sin^2 x \cos^2 x} dx$

$= \int \frac{\sin^2 x + \cos^2 x}{\sin^2 x \cos^2 x} dx$ [using $\sin^2 x + \cos^2 x = 1$]

$= \int \frac{\sin^2 x}{\sin^2 x \cos^2 x} dx + \int \frac{\cos^2 x}{\sin^2 x \cos^2 x} dx$

$= \int \sec^2 x\, dx + \int \text{cosec}^2 x\, dx = \tan x - \cot x + C$

(iii) $I = \int \frac{\sin^6 x + \cos^6 x}{\sin^2 x \cos^2 x} dx = \int \frac{(\sin^2 x)^3 + (\cos^2 x)^3}{\sin^2 x \cos^2 x} dx$

[using $(a+b)^3 = a^3 + b^3 + 3ab(a+b)$]

$= \int \frac{(\sin^2 x + \cos^2 x)^3 - 3\sin^2 x \cos^2 x(\sin^2 x + \cos^2 x)}{\sin^2 x \cos^2 x} dx$

$= \int \frac{1 - 3\sin^2 x \cos^2 x}{\sin^2 x \cos^2 x} dx = \int \frac{1}{\sin^2 x \cos^2 x} dx - \int 3 dx$

$= \int \frac{(\sin^2 x + \cos^2 x)}{\sin^2 x \cos^2 x} dx - 3x + C$

$= \int \sec^2 x\, dx + \int \text{cosec}^2 x\, dx - 3x + C$

$= \tan x - \cot x - 3x + C$

(iv) $I = \int \frac{\cos x - \cos 2x}{1 - \cos x} dx = \int \frac{\cos x - (2\cos^2 x - 1)}{1 - \cos x} dx$

[using $\cos 2x = 2\cos^2 x - 1$.]

$= \int \frac{-2\cos^2 x + \cos x + 1}{1 - \cos x} dx$

$= \int \frac{-(2\cos x + 1)(\cos x - 1)}{-(\cos x - 1)} dx$

[as $-2\cos^2 x + \cos x + 1 = -(2\cos x + 1)\cdot(\cos x - 1)$]

$\Rightarrow I = \int (2\cos x + 1)\, dx$

$\therefore I = 2\sin x + x + C$

Milestone Practice 1.1

Evaluate the following integration.

1. $\int \cos(e^x) \cdot d(e^x)$
2. If $\int x^{26}(x-1)^{17}(5x-3)\, dx = \frac{x^{27}(x-1)^{18}}{K} + C$, where C is a constant of integration, then find the value of K.
3. If $g(x) = \left(4\cos^4 x - 2\cos 2x - \frac{1}{2}\cos 4x - x^7\right)^{1/7}$, then find $\int g(g(x))dx$.
4. $\int \frac{1}{\sqrt{x+1} - \sqrt{x}} dx$
5. $\int \frac{(1+x)^2}{x(1+x^2)} dx$
6. $\int \frac{\sqrt[3]{x + \sqrt{2 - x^2}} \cdot \sqrt[6]{1 - x\sqrt{2 - x^2}}}{\sqrt[3]{1 - x^2}} dx$
7. $\int 2^x \cdot e^x dx$
8. $\int \frac{e^{3x} + e^{5x}}{e^x + e^{-x}} dx$
9. $\int \cos^3 x\, dx$
10. $\int \frac{\sin 2x - \sin 2K}{\sin x - \sin K + \cos x - \cos K} dx$
11. $\int \left(\frac{\cos 2x - \cos 2\alpha}{\sin x - \sin\alpha}\right) dx$
12. If $f'(\sin x) = \cos^2 x$, $\forall\ x \in R$, $f(1) = 1$, then find $f(x)$.
13. $\int \frac{dx}{1 + \sin x}$

Answer Key

1. $\sin(e^x) + C$ 2. $K = 9$ 3. $\frac{x^2}{2} + C$ 4. $\frac{2}{3}[(x+1)^{3/2} + x^{3/2}] + C$ 5. $\ln|x| + 2\tan^{-1} x + C$ 6. $2^{\frac{1}{6}} x + C$

7. $\frac{2^x e^x}{1 + \ln 2} + C$ 8. $\frac{e^{4x}}{4} + C$ 9. $\frac{\sin 3x}{12} + \frac{3}{4}\sin x + C$ 10. $\sin x - \cos x + x(\sin k + \cos k) + C$

11. $2\cos x - 2x\sin\alpha + C$ 12. $x - \frac{x^3}{3} + \frac{1}{3}$ 13. $\tan x - \sec x + C$

For Detailed Solution

Milestone 2 Integration by Substitution

• Methods of Integration • Integration by Substitution

1.3 Methods of Integration

If the integral is not a derivative of a simple function, then the corresponding integrals cannot be found directly. In order to find the integral of complex problems.

We use different methods of integration.

Some Integrals which Cannot be Found

Any function continuous on an interval (a, b) has an anti-derivative in that interval.

In other words, there exists a function $F(x)$ such that $F'(x) = f(x)$.

However, not every anti-derivative $F(x)$, even when it exists, is expressible in closed form in terms of elementary functions such as polynomials, trigonometric, logarithmic, exponential functions etc. Then, we say that such anti-derivatives or integrals "cannot be found''.

Some typical examples are

(i) $\int \frac{\sin x}{x} dx$ (ii) $\int \frac{\cos x}{x} dx$

(iii) $\int \frac{1}{\log x} dx$ (iv) $\int \sqrt{1-k^2 \sin^2 x}\, dx$

(v) $\int \sqrt{\sin x}\, dx$ (vi) $\int \sin(x^2)\, dx$

(vii) $\int \cos(x^2)\, dx$ (viii) $\int x \tan x\, dx$

(ix) $\int e^{-x^2} dx$ (x) $\int e^{x^2} dx$

(xi) $\int \frac{x^2}{1+x^5} dx$ (xii) $\int \sqrt[3]{1+x^2}\, dx$

(xiii) $\int \sqrt{1+x^3}\, dx$ etc.

1.4 Integration by Substitution

If $g(x)$ is a continuously differentiable function, then to evaluate integrals of the form, $I = \int f(g(x)) \cdot g'(x)\, dx$, we substitute $g(x) = t$ and $g'(x)\, dx = dt$

The substitution reduces the integral to $\int f(t)\, dt$. After evaluating this integral we substitute back the value of t.

Example 11. Prove that

$$\int (ax+b)^n dx = \frac{(ax+b)^{n+1}}{(n+1)a} + C, n \neq 1.$$

Sol. Putting, $ax + b = t$, we get

$$adx = dt \text{ or } dx = \frac{1}{a} dt$$

$$\therefore I = \int (ax+b)^n dx = \int t^n \cdot \frac{dt}{a} = \frac{1}{a} \cdot \frac{t^{n+1}}{n+1} + C$$

$$= \frac{(ax+b)^{n+1}}{a(n+1)} + C$$

Concept Inside Video

JEE Focus Points

- If $\int f(x)\, dx = g(x) + C$, then $\int f(ax+b)\, dx = \frac{1}{a} g(ax+b) + C$
- If $\int \frac{1}{x} dx = \log|x| + C$, then $\int \frac{1}{ax+b} dx = \frac{1}{a} \log|ax+b| + C$

Thus, in any fundamental integral formulae given in article fundamental integration formulae if in place of x we have $(ax + b)$, then same formula is applicable but we must divide by coefficient of x or derivative of $(ax + b)$ i.e. a.

Here is the List of Some of Frequently Used Formulae

(i) $\int (ax+b)^n\, dx = \frac{(ax+b)^{n+1}}{a(n+1)} + C, n \neq -1$

(ii) $\int \frac{1}{ax+b}\, dx = \frac{1}{a} \log|ax+b| + C$

(iii) $\int e^{ax+b}\, dx = \frac{1}{a} e^{ax+b} + C$

(iv) $\int a^{bx+c}\, dx = \frac{1}{b} \cdot \frac{a^{bx+c}}{\log a} + C$

(v) $\int \sin(ax+b)\, dx = -\frac{1}{a} \cos(ax+b) + C$

(vi) $\int \cos(ax+b)\,dx = \frac{1}{a}\sin(ax+b)+C$

(vii) $\int \sec^2(ax+b)\,dx = \frac{1}{a}\tan(ax+b)+C$

(viii) $\int \text{cosec}^2(ax+b)\,dx = -\frac{1}{a}\cot(ax+b)+C$

(ix) $\int \sec(ax+b)\tan(ax+b)\,dx = \frac{1}{a}\sec(ax+b)+C$

(x) $\int \text{cosec}(ax+b)\cot(ax+b)\,dx$

$= -\frac{1}{a}\text{cosec}(ax+b)+C$

(xi) $\int \tan(ax+b)\,dx = -\frac{1}{a}\log|\cos(ax+b)|+C$

(xii) $\int \cot(ax+b)\,dx = \frac{1}{a}\log|\sin(ax+b)|+C$

(xiii) $\int \sec(ax+b)dx = \frac{1}{a}\log|\sec(ax+b)+\tan(ax+b)|+C$

(xiv) $\int \text{cosec}(ax+b)\,dx = \frac{1}{a}\log|\text{cosec}(ax+b)-\cot(ax+b)|+C$

(xv) $\int \frac{1}{\sqrt{1-(ax+b)^2}}\,dx = \frac{1}{a}\sin^{-1}(ax+b)+C$

or $-\frac{1}{a}\cos^{-1}(ax+b)+C$

(xvi) $\int \frac{1}{1+(ax+b)^2}\,dx = \frac{1}{a}\tan^{-1}(ax+b)+C$

or $-\frac{1}{a}\cot^{-1}(ax+b)+C$

(xvii) $\int \frac{1}{|ax+b|\sqrt{(ax+b)^2-1}}\,dx = \frac{1}{a}\sec^{-1}(ax+b)+C$

or $-\frac{1}{a}\text{cosec}^{-1}(ax+b)+C$

Types of Substitution

TYPE 1

When integrand is the product of two factors such that one is the derivative of the others i.e. $I = \int f(x)f'(x)dx$

In this case, we put $f(x)=t$ and convert it into a standard integral.

Example 12. Evaluate

(i) $\int \frac{x^2\tan^{-1}x^3}{1+x^6}dx$ (ii) $\frac{d(\ln x)}{\cos^2(1+\ln x)}$

Sol. (i) $I = \int \frac{x^2\tan^{-1}x^3}{1+x^6}dx$

On putting $\tan^{-1}x^3 = t$

$\Rightarrow \frac{1}{1+(x^3)^2}\cdot 3x^2\,dx = dt$

$\Rightarrow \frac{x^2}{1+x^6}dx = \frac{dt}{3}$

$\therefore I = \frac{1}{3}\int t\,dt = \frac{1}{3}\left(\frac{t^2}{2}\right)+C$

$= \frac{1}{6}(\tan^{-1}x^3)^2+C$

(ii) $I = \int \frac{d(\ln x)}{\cos^2(1+\ln x)}$

$= \int \sec^2(1+\ln x)\,d(\ln x)$

On putting $\ln x = t \Rightarrow d(\ln x) = dt$

$\therefore I = \int \sec^2(1+t)dt$

$= \tan(1+t)+C$

$= \tan(1+\ln x)+C$

Example 13. Evaluate $\int 3^{3^{3^x}}\cdot 3^{3^x}\cdot 3^x dx$.

Sol. (i) $I = \int 3^{3^{3^x}}\cdot 3^{3^x}\cdot 3^x\,dx$

On putting $3^{3^{3^x}} = t$

$\Rightarrow (3^{3^{3^x}}\cdot \ln 3)\cdot(3^{3^x}\cdot\ln 3)\,(3^x\ln 3)\,dx = dt$

$\Rightarrow 3^{3^{3^x}}\cdot 3^{3^x}\cdot 3^x\,dx = \frac{dt}{(\ln 3)^3}$

$\therefore I = \frac{1}{(\ln 3)^3}\int dt = \frac{1}{(\ln 3)^3}t + C = \frac{3^{3^{3^x}}}{(\ln 3)^3}+C$

Example 14. Evaluate

(i) $\int \frac{10x^9+10^x\ln 10}{\sqrt{10^x+x^{10}+7}}dx$ (ii) $\int \frac{1}{x(x+1)\ln^2\left(\frac{x}{x+1}\right)}dx$

Sol. (i) $I = \int \frac{(10x^9+10^x\ln 10)}{\sqrt{10^x+x^{10}+7}}dx$

On putting $10^x+x^{10}+7 = t$

$\Rightarrow (10^x\ln 10+10x^9)dx = dt$

$\therefore I = \int \frac{dt}{\sqrt{t}} = 2\sqrt{t}+C$

$= 2\sqrt{10^x+x^{10}+7}+C$

(ii) We have, $I = \int \frac{1}{x(x+1)\ln^2\left(\frac{x}{x+1}\right)}\,dx$

On putting $\ln\left(\frac{x}{x+1}\right) = t$

$$\Rightarrow \frac{1}{\left(\frac{x}{x+1}\right)} \cdot \frac{(x+1)\cdot 1 - x}{(x+1)^2}\,dx = dt$$

$$\Rightarrow \frac{1}{x(x+1)}\,dx = dt$$

$$\therefore \quad I = \int \frac{1}{t^2}\,dt = -\frac{1}{t} + C = -\frac{1}{\ln\left(\frac{x}{x+1}\right)} + C$$

TYPE 2

Integral of a function of the form

$$\int \frac{f'(x)}{f(x)}\,dx = \log|f(x)| + C$$

In this case, we put $f(x) = t$ and $f'(x)dx = dt$, we get

$$I = \int \frac{1}{t}\,dt = \log|t| + C = \log|f(x)| + C$$

Example 15. Evaluate $\int \frac{\sin 2x}{a^2 \sin^2 x + b^2 \cos^2 x}\,dx.$

Sol. Put $a^2 \sin^2 x + b^2 \cos^2 x = t$

$$(a^2(2\sin x \cos x) + b^2(-2\sin x \cos x))dx = dt$$

$$(2\sin x \cos x)(a^2 - b^2)dx = dt$$

$$\sin 2x\,dx = \frac{dt}{a^2 - b^2}$$

$$\therefore \quad I = \int \frac{dt}{(a^2 - b^2)t} = \frac{1}{a^2 - b^2}\int \frac{dt}{t}$$

$$= \frac{1}{a^2 - b^2}\log|t| + C$$

$$= \frac{1}{a^2 - b^2}\log|a^2 \sin^2 x + b^2 \cos^2 x| + C$$

Example 16. Evaluate $\int \frac{1}{x \cdot \ln x \cdot \ln(\ln x) \cdot \ln(\ln(\ln x))}\,dx.$

Sol. We have, $I = \int \frac{1}{x \cdot \ln x \cdot \ln(\ln x) \cdot \ln(\ln(\ln x))}\,dx$

On putting $\ln(\ln(\ln x)) = t$

$$\Rightarrow \frac{1}{\ln(\ln x)} \cdot \frac{1}{\ln x} \cdot \frac{1}{x}\,dx = dt$$

$$\therefore \quad I = \int \frac{1}{t}\,dt = \ln t + C = \ln(\ln(\ln(\ln x))) + C$$

JEE SCANNER

Example Similar to PYQ Asked in JEE Main 2023

The integral $\int \left(\left(\frac{x}{e}\right)^x + \left(\frac{e}{x}\right)^x\right) \ln x\,dx$ *is equal to*

(a) $\left(\frac{x}{e}\right)^x + \left(\frac{e}{x}\right)^x + C$ (b) $\left(\frac{x}{e}\right)^x - \left(\frac{e}{x}\right)^x + C$

(c) $\left(\frac{x}{e}\right)^x \log\left(\frac{x}{e}\right) + C$ (d) $\left(\frac{x}{e}\right)^x \log\left(\frac{e}{x}\right) + C$

Sol. (b) We have, $I = \int \left(\left(\frac{x}{e}\right)^x + \left(\frac{e}{x}\right)^x\right) \ln x\,dx$

On putting $\left(\frac{x}{e}\right)^x = t \Rightarrow x\ln\left(\frac{x}{e}\right) = \ln t$

$$\Rightarrow \quad x(\ln x - \ln e) = \ln t$$

$$\Rightarrow \quad x(\ln x - 1) = \ln t$$

$$\Rightarrow \quad \left[1\cdot(\ln x - 1) + x\left(\frac{1}{x}\right)\right]dx = \frac{dt}{t}$$

$$\Rightarrow \quad \ln x\,dx = \frac{dt}{t}$$

$$\therefore \quad I = \int \left(t + \frac{1}{t}\right)\frac{dt}{t} = \int \left(1 + \frac{1}{t^2}\right)dt$$

$$= t - \frac{1}{t} + C = \left(\frac{x}{e}\right)^x - \left(\frac{e}{x}\right)^x + C$$

Skill Builder

The integral $\int \left[\left(\frac{x}{3}\right)^x + \left(\frac{3}{x}\right)^x\right] \log\left(\frac{xe}{3}\right) dx$ is equal to

(a) $\left(\frac{x}{3}\right)^x + \left(\frac{3}{x}\right)^x + C$ (b) $\left(\frac{x}{3}\right)^x \log\left(\frac{x}{3}\right) + C$

(c) $\left(\frac{x}{3}\right)^x - \left(\frac{3}{x}\right)^x + C$ (d) $\left(\frac{x}{3}\right)^x \log\left(\frac{3}{x}\right) + C$

For Sol.

- **For more practice** See Q.7 of Milestone Practice 1.2.

Example 17. Evaluate $\int \frac{1}{\sin(x-a)\cos(x-b)}\,dx$

Sol. $I = \int \frac{1}{\sin(x-a)\cos(x-b)}\,dx$

$$= \frac{\cos(a-b)}{\cos(a-b)} \cdot \int \frac{dx}{\sin(x-a)\cos(x-b)}$$

$$= \frac{1}{\cos(a-b)} \cdot \int \frac{\cos\{(x-b)-(x-a)\}}{\sin(x-a)\cos(x-b)}\,dx$$

$$= \frac{1}{\cos(a-b)} \cdot \int \left\{\frac{\cos(x-b)\cdot\cos(x-a)}{\sin(x-a)\cos(x-b)} + \frac{\sin(x-b)\cdot\sin(x-a)}{\sin(x-a)\cos(x-b)}\right\}dx$$

$$= \frac{1}{\cos(a-b)} \int \{\cot(x-a) + \tan(x-b)\}\, dx$$

$$= \frac{1}{\cos(a-b)} \{\log|\sin(x-a)| - \log|\cos(x-b)|\} + C$$

$$= \frac{1}{\cos(a-b)} \log\left|\frac{\sin(x-a)}{\cos(x-b)}\right| + C$$

TYPE 3

Integral of the form $\int \frac{dx}{\sqrt{ax \pm b} \pm \sqrt{ax \pm d}}$.

Simplify, rationalise the denominator and integrate.

Example 18. Evaluate $\int \frac{1}{\sqrt{3x+4} - \sqrt{3x+1}}\, dx$.

Decoding the Question

First use rationalisation to reduce the denominator in constant term and then use the standard formula,

$$(ax+b)^n\, dx = \frac{(ax+b)^{n+1}}{(n+1)a} + C.$$

Sol. Here, $I = \int \frac{dx}{\sqrt{3x+4} - \sqrt{3x+1}}$

$$= \int \frac{(\sqrt{3x+4} + \sqrt{3x+1})}{(\sqrt{3x+4} - \sqrt{3x+1})(\sqrt{3x+4} + \sqrt{3x+1})}\, dx$$

$$= \int \frac{(\sqrt{3x+4} + \sqrt{3x+1})}{(3x+4) - (3x+1)}\, dx$$

$$= \frac{1}{3} \int \sqrt{3x+4}\, dx + \frac{1}{3} \int \sqrt{3x+1}\, dx$$

$$= \frac{1}{3} \left\{\frac{(3x+4)^{3/2}}{(3/2) \times 3}\right\} + \frac{1}{3} \left\{\frac{(3x+1)^{3/2}}{(3/2) \times 3}\right\} + C$$

$$\left[\text{using } \int (ax+b)^n\, dx = \frac{(ax+b)^{n+1}}{(n+1)\, a} + C\right]$$

$$= \frac{2}{27} [(3x+4)^{3/2} + (3x+1)^{3/2}] + C$$

Time Saving Technique

$$\int \frac{dx}{\sqrt{ax+b} - \sqrt{ax+d}} = \frac{2}{3a(b-d)} ((ax+b)^{3/2} + (ax+d)^{3/2}) + C$$

$$\therefore \int \frac{dx}{\sqrt{3x+4} - \sqrt{3x+1}} = \frac{2}{3 \times 3(4-1)} ((3x+4)^{3/2} + (3x+1)^{3/2}) + C$$

$$= \frac{2}{27} [(3x+4)^{3/2} + (3x+1)^{3/2}] + C$$

TYPE 4

Integral of the form

$$\int \frac{cx+d}{(ax+b)^n}\, dx,\ \int (cx+d)(ax+b)^n\, dx$$

In this case, put $ax + b = t$

$$x = \frac{t-b}{a} \Rightarrow dx = \frac{dt}{a}$$

Example 19. Evaluate

(i) $\int \frac{8x+13}{\sqrt{4x+7}}\, dx$ (ii) $\int (7x-2)\sqrt{3x+2}\, dx$

Sol. (i) We have, $I = \int \frac{8x+13}{\sqrt{4x+7}}\, dx$

Put $4x + 7 = t \Rightarrow x = \frac{t-7}{4} \Rightarrow dx = \frac{dt}{4}$

$$\therefore \quad I = \frac{1}{4} \int \frac{8\left(\frac{t-7}{4}\right) + 13}{\sqrt{t}}\, dt$$

$$= \frac{1}{16} \int \frac{8t-4}{\sqrt{t}}\, dt$$

$$= \frac{8}{16} \int \frac{t\,dt}{\sqrt{t}} - \frac{4}{16} \int \frac{1}{\sqrt{t}}\, dt$$

$$= \frac{1}{2} \int (t)^{\frac{1}{2}}\, dt - \frac{1}{4} \int t^{\frac{-1}{2}}\, dt$$

$$= \frac{1}{2} \times \frac{2}{3} t^{\frac{3}{2}} - \frac{1}{4} \times 2t^{\frac{1}{2}} + C = \frac{1}{3} t^{\frac{3}{2}} - \frac{1}{2} t^{\frac{1}{2}} + C$$

$$= \frac{1}{3}(4x+7)^{\frac{3}{2}} - \frac{1}{2}(4x+7)^{\frac{1}{2}} + C$$

$$= \frac{1}{6}(8x+11)\sqrt{4x+7} + C$$

Alternate Solution

Here, $I = \int \frac{8x+13}{\sqrt{4x+7}}\, dx = \int \frac{8x+14-1}{\sqrt{4x+7}}\, dx$

$$= \int \frac{2(4x+7)-1}{\sqrt{4x+7}} dx = 2\int \frac{4x+7}{\sqrt{4x+7}}\, dx - \int \frac{dx}{\sqrt{4x+7}}$$

$$= 2\int (\sqrt{4x+7})dx - \int (4x+7)^{-1/2} dx$$

$$= 2\left(\frac{(4x+7)^{3/2}}{3/2 \times 4}\right) - \left(\frac{(4x+7)^{1/2}}{1/2 \times 4}\right) + C$$

$$= \frac{1}{3}(4x+7)^{3/2} - \frac{1}{2}(4x+7)^{1/2} + C$$

$$= \frac{1}{6}(8x+11)\sqrt{4x+7} + C$$

(ii) Here, $I = \int (7x-2)\sqrt{3x+2}\, dx$

$$= 7\int \left(x - \frac{2}{7}\right)\sqrt{3x+2}\, dx$$

$$= \frac{7}{3}\int \left(3x - \frac{6}{7}\right)\sqrt{3x+2}\, dx$$

$$= \frac{7}{3}\int \left(3x + 2 - 2 - \frac{6}{7}\right)\sqrt{3x+2}\, dx$$

$$= \frac{7}{3}\int (3x+2)\sqrt{3x+2}\, dx - \frac{20}{3}\int \sqrt{3x+2}\, dx$$

$$= \frac{7}{3}\int (3x+2)^{3/2}\,dx - \frac{20}{3}\int \sqrt{3x+2}\,dx$$

$$= \frac{7}{3}\left(\frac{(3x+2)^{5/2}}{\frac{5}{2}\times 3}\right) - \frac{20}{3}\left(\frac{(3x+2)^{3/2}}{\frac{3}{2}\times 3}\right) + C$$

$$= \frac{14}{45}(3x+2)^{5/2} - \frac{40}{27}(3x+2)^{3/2} + C$$

TYPE 5

Integral of the form

$\int \sin^2 x\,dx$, $\int \cos^2 x\,dx$, $\int \sin^3 x\,dx$, $\int \cos^3 x\,dx$.

In this case, use the following trigonometric identities.

(i) $\sin^2 x = \frac{1-\cos 2x}{2}$ (ii) $\cos^2 x = \frac{1+\cos 2x}{2}$

(iii) $\sin 3x = 3\sin x - 4\sin^3 x$ (iv) $\cos 3x = 4\cos^3 x - 3\cos x$

Example 20. Evaluate

(i) $\int \sin^3 x \cdot \cos^3 x\,dx$ (ii) $\int \cos^4 x\,dx$

Sol. (i) $I = \int \sin^3 x \cdot \cos^3 x\,dx$

$$= \frac{1}{8}\int (2\sin x \cdot \cos x)^3 dx = \frac{1}{8}\int \sin^3 2x\,dx$$

$$= \frac{1}{8}\int \frac{3\sin 2x - \sin 3(2x)}{4}\,dx$$

$$= \frac{1}{32}\int (3\sin 2x - \sin 6x)\,dx$$

$$= \frac{1}{32}\left[3\left(-\frac{\cos 2x}{2}\right) - \left(-\frac{\cos 6x}{6}\right)\right] + C$$

$$= \frac{-3}{64}\cos 2x + \frac{1}{192}\cos 6x + C$$

(ii) $I = \int \cos^4 x\,dx = \int (\cos^2 x)^2\,dx$

$$= \int \left(\frac{1+\cos 2x}{2}\right)^2 dx$$

$$= \frac{1}{4}\int (1+\cos^2 2x + 2\cos 2x)\,dx$$

$$= \frac{1}{4}\int \left[1 + \frac{1+\cos 4x}{2} + 2\cos 2x\right] dx$$

$$= \frac{1}{4}\int \left[\frac{3}{2} + \frac{1}{2}\cos 4x + 2\cos 2x\right] dx$$

$$= \frac{3}{8}\int dx + \frac{1}{8}\int \cos 4x\,dx + \frac{1}{2}\int \cos 2x\,dx$$

$$= \frac{3}{8}x + \frac{1}{8}\left(\frac{\sin 4x}{4}\right) + \frac{1}{2}\left(\frac{\sin 2x}{2}\right) + C$$

$$= \frac{3}{8}x + \frac{1}{32}\sin 4x + \frac{1}{4}\sin 2x + C$$

TYPE 6

Integral of the form

$\int \sin mx \cos nx\,dx$, $\int \sin mx \sin nx\,dx$, $\int \cos mx \cos nx\,dx$

While solving product of trignometric, it is expedient to use the following trigonometric identities

1. $\sin mx \cos nx = \frac{1}{2}\{\sin(m-n)x + \sin(m+n)x\}$
2. $\cos mx \sin nx = \frac{1}{2}\{\sin(m+n)x - \sin(m-n)x\}$
3. $\sin mx \sin nx = \frac{1}{2}\{\cos(m-n)x - \cos(m+n)x\}$
4. $\cos mx \cos nx = \frac{1}{2}\{\cos(m-n)x + \cos(m+n)x\}$

Example 21. Evaluate $\int \cos x \cos 2x \cos 5x\,dx$.

Decoding the Question
When calculating such integrals it is advisable to use the trigonometric product formulae.

Sol. $\int \cos x \cos 2x \cos 5x\,dx$,

We have, $(\cos x \cos 2x)\cos 5x = \frac{1}{2}(\cos x + \cos 3x)\cos 5x$,

[using $\cos mx \cdot \cos nx = \frac{1}{2}\{\cos(m-n)x + \cos(m+n)x\}$]

$$= \frac{1}{4}\{2\cos x\cos 5x + 2\cos 3x\cos 5x\}$$

$$= \frac{1}{4}\{(\cos 4x + \cos 6x) + (\cos 2x + \cos 8x)\}$$

$\therefore$ $\cos x\cos 2x\cos 5x = \frac{1}{4}\{\cos 2x + \cos 4x + \cos 6x + \cos 8x\}$

$\therefore$ $I = \int (\cos x\cos 2x\cos 5x)\,dx$

$$= \frac{1}{4}\int (\cos 2x + \cos 4x + \cos 6x + \cos 8x)\,dx$$

$$= \frac{\sin 2x}{8} + \frac{\sin 4x}{16} + \frac{\sin 6x}{24} + \frac{\sin 8x}{32} + C$$

TYPE 7

Integral of the form $\int \tan^m x \sec^n x\,dx$ m,where $n \in N$.

Case I When n is even, put $\tan x = t$

Example 22. Evaluate $\int \tan^2 x \sec^4 x\,dx$.

Sol. Let $I = \int \tan^2 x \sec^4 x\,dx$

Put $\tan x = t$, $\sec^2 x\,dx = dt$

$$\therefore \quad I = \int t^2(\sec^2 x)dt = \int t^2(1 + \tan^2 x)dt$$
$$= \int t^2(1 + t^2)dt = \int (t^2 + t^4)dt$$
$$= \frac{t^3}{3} + \frac{t^5}{5} + C = \frac{\tan^3 x}{3} + \frac{\tan^5 x}{5} + C$$

Case II **When m and n both are odd, put $\sec x = t$.**

Example 23. Evaluate $\int \sec^5 x \tan^3 x\, dx$.

Sol. Let $I = \int \sec^5 x \tan^3 x\, dx$

Put $\sec x = t \Rightarrow \sec x \tan x\, dx = dt$

$$\therefore \quad I = \int \sec^4 x \tan^2 x \sec x \tan x\, dx$$
$$= \int t^4(t^2 - 1)dt = \int (t^6 - t^4)dt$$
$$= \frac{t^7}{7} - \frac{t^5}{5} + C = \frac{\sec^7 x}{7} - \frac{\sec^5 x}{5} + C$$

TYPE 8

Integral of the form

$\int \sin^m x \cos^n x\, dx$, where m and n are rational numbers.

Case I **When m is odd and n is even, put $\cos x = t$.**

Example 24. Evaluate $\int \sin^3 x \cos^2 x\, dx$.

Sol. Put $\cos x = t \Rightarrow -\sin x\, dx = dt$

$$\therefore \quad I = \int \sin^2 x \cos^2 x (\sin x) dx$$
$$= \int (1 - \cos^2 x)\cos^2 x \sin x\, dx = -\int (1 - t^2)t^2 dt$$
$$= \int (t^4 - t^2)dt = \frac{t^5}{5} - \frac{t^3}{3} + C$$
$$= \frac{\cos^5 x}{5} - \frac{\cos^3 x}{3} + C$$

Case II **When m is even and n is odd, put $\sin x = t$.**

Example 25. Evaluate $\int \sin^2 x \cos^5 x\, dx$.

Sol. Put $\sin x = t \Rightarrow \cos x\, dx = dt$

$$\therefore \quad I = \int t^2 \cos^4 x\, dt = \int t^2(1 - \sin^2 x)^2 dt$$
$$= \int t^2(1 - t^2)^2 dt$$
$$= \int t^2(1 - 2t^2 + t^4)dt$$
$$= \int (t^2 - 2t^4 + t^6)dt$$
$$= \frac{t^3}{3} - \frac{2t^5}{5} + \frac{t^7}{7} + C$$
$$= \frac{\sin^3 x}{3} - \frac{2\sin^5 x}{5} + \frac{\sin^7 x}{7} + C$$

Case III **When m and n both are odd, put either $\sin x = t$ or $\cos x = t$.**

Example 26. Evaluate $\int \sin^3 x\, e^{\log \cos x}\, dx$.

Sol. Let $I = \int \sin^3 x\, e^{\log \cos x} dx$

$$= \int \sin^3 x \cos x\, dx \qquad [\because e^{a \log x} = x^a]$$

Putting $\sin x = t \Rightarrow \cos x\, dx = dt$

$$\therefore \quad I = \int t^3 dt = \frac{t^4}{4} + C$$
$$= \frac{\sin^4 x}{4} + C$$

Case IV **When $m + n$ is a negative even integer i.e $m + n = -2k$ (say), where $k \in N$.**

In this case,

(i) Divide the numerator and denominator by $\cos^{2k} x$.

(ii) Put $\tan x = t$

JEE SCANNER

Example Similar to PYQ Asked in JEE Main 2019

The integral $\int \operatorname{cosec}^{3/2} x \sec^{5/2} x\, dx$ *is equal to*

(a) $\frac{2}{3}\tan^{3/2} x + 2\sqrt{\tan x} + C$ (b) $\frac{2}{3}\tan^{3/2} x - 2\sqrt{\tan x} + C$

(c) $\frac{2}{3}\tan^{3/2} x - \frac{2}{\sqrt{\tan x}} + C$ (d) $\frac{2}{3}\tan^{3/2} x + \frac{2}{\sqrt{\tan x}} + C$

Sol. (c) Let $I = \int \operatorname{cosec}^{3/2} x \sec^{5/2} x\, dx = \int \frac{1}{\sin^{3/2} x \cos^{5/2} x} dx$

Here, $m + n = \frac{3}{2} + \frac{5}{2} = \frac{8}{2} = 4$ is even integer.

Divide numerator and denominator by $\cos^4 x$.

$$\therefore \quad I = \int \frac{\sec^4 x\, dx}{\tan^{3/2} x}$$

Put $\tan x = t \Rightarrow \sec^2 x\, dx = dt$

$$\therefore \quad I = \int \frac{\sec^2 x dt}{t^{3/2}} = \int \frac{(1 + \tan^2 x)dt}{t^{3/2}} = \int \frac{(1 + t^2)dt}{t^{3/2}}$$
$$= \int (t^{-3/2} + t^{1/2})dt = \frac{t^{\frac{-3}{2}+1}}{\frac{-3}{2}+1} + \frac{t^{\frac{1}{2}+1}}{\frac{1}{2}+1} + C$$
$$= -2t^{-1/2} + \frac{2}{3}t^{3/2} + C = \frac{-2}{\sqrt{\tan x}} + \frac{2}{3}\tan^{3/2} x + C$$

Skill Builder

$\int (\operatorname{cosec}^{1/2} x \sec^{3/2} x)\, dx$ is equal to

For Sol.

(a) $2(\tan x)^{1/2} + C$ (b) $2(\tan x)^{3/2} + C$

(c) $-2(\tan x)^{-1/2} + C$ (d) $2(\tan x)^{-3/2} + C$

- **For more practice** See Q.23 of Milestone Practice 1.2.

Case V When *m* and *n* both are even.

In this case, we shall use the following formula

$$1+\cos 2x = 2\cos^2 x \text{ or } 1-\cos 2x = 2\sin^2 x$$

Example 27. Evaluate $\int \sin^2 x \cos^4 x\, dx$.

Sol. Let $I = \int \sin^2 x \cos^4 x\, dx = \int \sin^2 x (\cos^2 x)^2\, dx$

$$= \int \left(\frac{1-\cos 2x}{2}\right)\left(\frac{1+\cos 2x}{2}\right)^2 dx$$

$$= \int \left(\frac{1-\cos^2 2x}{4}\right)\left(\frac{1+\cos 2x}{2}\right) dx$$

$$= \frac{1}{8}\int [1+\cos 2x - \cos^2 2x - \cos^3 2x]\, dx$$

$$= \frac{1}{8}\int \left[1+\cos 2x - \frac{(1+\cos 4x)}{2} - \frac{(\cos 6x + 3\cos 2x)}{4}\right] dx$$

$$= \frac{1}{32}\int (4+4\cos 2x - 2 - 2\cos 4x - \cos 6x - 3\cos 2x)\, dx$$

$$= \frac{1}{32}\int (2+\cos 2x - 2\cos 4x - \cos 6x)\, dx$$

$$= \frac{1}{32}\left[2x + \frac{\sin 2x}{2} - \frac{\sin 4x}{2} - \frac{\sin 6x}{6}\right] + C$$

Milestone Practice 1.2

Evaluate the following integration.

1. $\int (3x+4)^3 + (2x+5)^{\frac{1}{3}} dx$
2. $\int \frac{1}{3-4x} + \frac{3}{\sqrt{2x-3}}\, dx$
3. $\int x^2 \sin x^3 dx$
4. $\int \frac{dx}{\sqrt{x}(4+3\sqrt{x})^2}$
5. $\int \frac{dx}{x^2(1+x^4)^{\frac{3}{4}}}$
6. $\int \frac{\sqrt{1+\sin(\log x)}}{x}\, dx$
7. $\int \left[\left(\frac{x}{5}\right)^x + \left(\frac{5}{x}\right)^x\right] \log\left(\frac{xe}{5}\right) dx$
8. $\int \frac{x^x(1+\log x)}{x^x+1}\, dx$
9. $\int \frac{\sin^3 x}{(\cos^4 x + 3\cos^2 x + 1)\tan^{-1}(\sec x + \cos x)}\, dx$
10. $\int \frac{dx}{\sqrt{2x+3} - \sqrt{2x-3}}$
11. $\int \frac{\sin^2 x \cos^2 x}{(\sin^5 x + \cos^3 x \sin^2 x + \sin^3 x \cos^2 x + \cos^5 x)^2}\, dx$
12. $\int \frac{2x^{12} + 5x^9}{(x^5 + x^3 + 1)^3}\, dx$
13. $\int \frac{e^{2x}+1}{e^{2x}-1}\, dx$
14. $\int \frac{3x+5}{\sqrt{7x+9}}\, dx$
15. $\int \sin^3 4x\, dx$
16. $\int \frac{dx}{\sqrt{\sin^3 x \sin(x+\alpha)}}$
17. If $\int \frac{(1+\log x)^2}{1+\log x^{x+1} + (\log x^{\sqrt{x}})^2}\, dx = \log|f(x)| + C$, then find $f(2)$.
18. $\int \frac{dx}{\sin(x+a)\sin(x+b)}$
19. $\int \sin 3x \cos 5x\, dx$
20. $\int \frac{\sin 2x}{\sin 5x \sin 3x}\, dx$
21. $\int \sin^3 x \cos^4 x\, dx$
22. $\int \sin^4 x \cos^2 x\, dx$
23. $\int \frac{dx}{\sin^{1/2} x \cos^{7/2} x}$
24. $\int \tan^5 x \sec^4 x\, dx$
25. $\int \sec^5 x \tan^3 x\, dx$

Answer Key

For Detailed Solution

1. $\frac{1}{12}(3x+4)^4 + \frac{3}{8}(2x+5)^{4/3} + C$
2. $-\frac{1}{4}\log|3-4x| + 3\sqrt{2x-3} + C$
3. $-\frac{1}{3}\cos x^3 + C$
4. $\frac{-2}{3(4+3\sqrt{x})} + C$
5. $-\left(1+\frac{1}{x^4}\right)^{1/4} + C$
6. $2\left(\sin\left(\frac{1}{2}\log|x|\right) - \cos\left(\frac{1}{2}\log|x|\right)\right) + C$
7. $\left(\frac{x}{5}\right)^x - \left(\frac{5}{x}\right)^x + C$
8. $\log|x^x + 1| + C$
9. $\log \tan^{-1}|\sec x + \cos x| + C$
10. $\frac{1}{18}[(2x+3)^{3/2} + (2x-3)^{3/2}] + C$
11. $\frac{-1}{3(1+\tan^3 x)} + C$
12. $\frac{x^{10}}{2(x^5+x^3+1)^2} + C$
13. $\log|e^x - e^{-x}| + C$
14. $\frac{2(7x+17)(7x+9)^{1/2}}{49} + C$
15. $\frac{-3}{16}\cos 4x + \frac{\cos 12x}{48} + C$
16. $\frac{-2}{\sin\alpha}\sqrt{\frac{\sin(x+\alpha)}{\sin x}} + C$
17. $\log 4e$
18. $\frac{1}{\sin(a-b)}\log\left|\frac{\sin(x+b)}{\sin(x+a)}\right| + C$
19. $\frac{1}{2}\left(\frac{-\cos 8x}{8} + \frac{\cos 2x}{2}\right) + C$
20. $\frac{1}{3}\log\sin 3x - \frac{1}{5}\log\sin 5x + C$
21. $\frac{\cos^7 x}{7} - \frac{\cos^5 x}{5} + C$
22. $\frac{1}{192}[12x - 21\sin 2x - 3\sin 4x + \sin 6x] + C$
23. $2\sqrt{\tan x} + \frac{2}{5}(\tan x)^{5/2} + C$
24. $\frac{\tan^6 x}{6} + \frac{\tan^8 x}{8} + C$
25. $\frac{\sec^7 x}{7} - \frac{\sec^5 x}{5} + C$

Milestone 3 Some Special Integrals

- Some Special Integrals • Trigonometric Integrals

1.5 Some Special Integrals

(i) $\int \frac{dx}{x^2 - a^2} = \frac{1}{2a} \log \left| \frac{x-a}{x+a} \right| + C$

(ii) $\int \frac{dx}{a^2 - x^2} = \frac{1}{2a} \log \left| \frac{a+x}{a-x} \right| + C$

(iii) $\int \frac{dx}{x^2 + a^2} = \frac{1}{a} \tan^{-1} \left(\frac{x}{a} \right) + C$

(iv) $\int \frac{dx}{\sqrt{a^2 - x^2}} = \sin^{-1} \left(\frac{x}{a} \right) + C$

(v) $\int \frac{dx}{\sqrt{a^2 + x^2}} = \log | x + \sqrt{x^2 + a^2} | + C$

(vi) $\int \frac{dx}{\sqrt{x^2 - a^2}} = \log | x + \sqrt{x^2 - a^2} | + C$

Proof

(i) Let $I = \int \frac{dx}{x^2 - a^2} = \int \frac{1}{(x-a)(x+a)} \times \frac{2a}{2a} dx$

[multiplying numerator and denominator by $2a$]

$$= \frac{1}{2a} \int \frac{(x+a) - (x-a)}{(x-a)(x+a)} dx$$

$$= \frac{1}{2a} \int \left[\frac{1}{(x-a)} - \frac{1}{(x+a)} \right] dx$$

$$= \frac{1}{2a} \left[\int \frac{1}{(x-a)} dx - \int \frac{1}{(x+a)} dx \right]$$

$$= \frac{1}{2a} [\log |x-a| - \log |x+a|] + C$$

$$= \frac{1}{2a} \log \left| \frac{x-a}{x+a} \right| + C$$

(ii) We can prove this formula as done in (i).

(iii) Now, put $x = a \tan\theta$ and $dx = a \sec^2 \theta d\theta$ in $\int \frac{dx}{x^2 + a^2}$, we get

$$\int \frac{dx}{x^2 + a^2} = \int \frac{a \sec^2 \theta}{a^2 \tan^2 \theta + a^2} d\theta$$

$$= \int \frac{a \sec^2 \theta}{a^2 (\sec^2 \theta)} d\theta \quad [\because \sec^2 \theta = \tan^2 \theta + 1]$$

$$= \frac{1}{a} \int d\theta = \frac{1}{a} \theta + C$$

$$\Rightarrow \quad \int \frac{dx}{x^2 + a^2} = \frac{1}{a} \tan^{-1} \frac{x}{a} + C$$

$$\left[\because x = a \tan\theta \Rightarrow \tan\theta = \frac{x}{a} \Rightarrow \theta = \tan^{-1} \frac{x}{a} \right]$$

Similarly, we can prove other formulae by using following substitutions

(iv) Put $x = a \sin\theta$

(v) Put $x = a \tan\theta$

(vi) Put $x = a \sec\theta$

Example 28. Evaluate

(i) $\int \frac{dx}{4x^2 - 25}$ (ii) $\int \frac{x dx}{3x^4 + 4}$ (iii) $\int \frac{1}{\sqrt{1 - e^{2x}}} dx$

Sol. (i) Let $I = \int \frac{dx}{4x^2 - 25}$

Put $2x = t \Rightarrow 2dx = dt$

$$\therefore \quad I = \frac{1}{2} \int \frac{dt}{t^2 - 25} = \frac{1}{2} \int \frac{dt}{t^2 - (5)^2}$$

$$= \frac{1}{2} \left[\frac{1}{2} \times \frac{1}{5} \log \left| \frac{t-5}{t+5} \right| + C \right] = \frac{1}{20} \log \left| \frac{2x-5}{2x+5} \right| + C_1,$$

where $C_1 = \left(\frac{1}{2} \right) C$

(ii) Let $I = \int \frac{x dx}{3x^4 + 4}$

Put $\sqrt{3} x^2 = t \Rightarrow 2\sqrt{3} x \, dx = dt$

$$\therefore \quad I = \frac{1}{2\sqrt{3}} \int \frac{dt}{t^2 + (2)^2} = \frac{1}{2\sqrt{3}} \times \frac{1}{2} \tan^{-1} \left(\frac{t}{2} \right) + C$$

$$= \frac{1}{4\sqrt{3}} \tan^{-1} \left(\frac{\sqrt{3} x^2}{2} \right) + C$$

(iii) Here, $I = \int \frac{dx}{\sqrt{1 - e^{2x}}}$

Let $\quad 1 - e^{2x} = t^2$

Then, $-2e^{2x}dx = 2t\,dt \Rightarrow dx = -\dfrac{t\,dt}{e^{2x}} = \dfrac{t\,dt}{t^2-1}$

$$\therefore \quad I = \int\left(\frac{1}{\sqrt{t^2}}\cdot\frac{t}{t^2-1}\right)dt = \int\frac{dt}{t^2-1}$$

$$= \frac{1}{2\cdot 1}\log\left|\frac{t-1}{t+1}\right| + C = \frac{1}{2}\log\left|\frac{\sqrt{1-e^{2x}}-1}{\sqrt{1+e^{2x}}+1}\right| + C$$

Example 29. Evaluate

(i) $\displaystyle\int \frac{a^x}{\sqrt{1-a^{2x}}}dx$ (ii) $\displaystyle\int\sqrt{\frac{x}{a^3+x^3}}dx$

Sol. (i) Here, $I = \displaystyle\int\frac{a^x}{\sqrt{1-a^{2x}}}dx$

Let $a^x = t$

$\therefore\ a^x \log a\,dx = dt \Rightarrow a^x\,dx = \dfrac{dt}{\log a}$

$$\therefore \quad I = \int\frac{1}{\sqrt{1-t^2}}\cdot\frac{dt}{\log a} = \frac{1}{\log a}\cdot\sin^{-1}(t) + C$$

$$I = \frac{1}{\log a}\sin^{-1}(a^x) + C$$

(ii) Here, $I = \displaystyle\int\sqrt{\frac{x}{a^3+x^3}}dx = \int\frac{x^{1/2}\,dx}{\sqrt{(a^{3/2})^2+(x^{3/2})^2}}$

Let $x^{3/2} = t \Rightarrow \dfrac{3}{2}x^{1/2}\,dx = dt \Rightarrow x^{1/2}\,dx = \dfrac{2}{3}dt$

$$\therefore \quad I = \int\frac{\frac{2}{3}dt}{\sqrt{(a^{3/2})^2+(t)^2}}$$

$$= \frac{2}{3}\log|t+\sqrt{a^3+t^2}| + C$$

$$= \frac{2}{3}\log|x^{3/2}+\sqrt{a^3+x^3}| + C$$

Some Important Substitutions

Expression	Substitution
a^2+x^2	$x = a\tan\theta$ or $a\cot\theta$
a^2-x^2	$x = a\sin\theta$ or $a\cos\theta$
x^2-a^2	$x = a\sec\theta$ or $a\,\text{cosec}\,\theta$
$\sqrt{\frac{a-x}{a+x}}$ or $\sqrt{\frac{a+x}{a-x}}$	$x = a\cos 2\theta$
$\sqrt{\frac{x+\alpha}{\beta-x}}$ or $\sqrt{(x-\alpha)(\beta-x)}$	$x = \alpha\cos^2\theta + \beta\sin^2\theta$
$\sqrt{\frac{x-\alpha}{x-\beta}}$ or $\sqrt{(x-\alpha)(x-\beta)}$	$x = \alpha\sec^2\theta - \beta\tan^2\theta$

Example 30. Evaluate $\displaystyle\int x\sqrt{\frac{a^2-x^2}{a^2+x^2}}dx$

Sol. Let $I = \displaystyle\int x\sqrt{\frac{a^2-x^2}{a^2+x^2}}dx$

Put $x^2 = t \Rightarrow 2x\,dx = dt$

$$\therefore \quad I = \int\sqrt{\frac{a^2-t}{a^2+t}}\cdot\frac{dt}{2}$$

$$= \frac{1}{2}\int\sqrt{\frac{a^2-t}{a^2+t}\cdot\frac{a^2-t}{a^2-t}}\,dt = \frac{1}{2}\int\frac{a^2-t}{\sqrt{a^4-t^2}}dt$$

$$= \frac{1}{2}a^2\int\frac{dt}{\sqrt{(a^2)^2-(t)^2}} - \frac{1}{2}\int\frac{t\,dt}{\sqrt{a^4-t^2}}$$

$$= \frac{1}{2}a^2\cdot\sin^{-1}\left(\frac{t}{a^2}\right) + \frac{1}{4}\int\frac{du}{\sqrt{u}},$$

[where $a^4 - t^2 = u \Rightarrow -2t\,dt = du$]

$$= \frac{1}{2}a^2\cdot\sin^{-1}\left(\frac{t}{a^2}\right) + \frac{1}{4}\cdot\left(\frac{u^{1/2}}{1/2}\right) + C$$

$$= \frac{1}{2}a^2\cdot\sin^{-1}\left(\frac{x^2}{a^2}\right) + \frac{1}{2}\cdot\sqrt{a^4-x^4} + C$$

[where $t = x^2$ and $u = a^4 - x^4$]

Integral of the Types $\displaystyle\int\frac{dx}{ax^2+bx+c}$, $\displaystyle\int\frac{dx}{\sqrt{ax^2+bx+c}}$

Suppose given integral is of the form $\displaystyle\int\frac{dx}{ax^2+bx+c}$, then to evaluate such integrals, we use the following steps :

I. Firstly, take a common from denominator to make coefficient of x^2 unity i.e. $I = \displaystyle\int\frac{dx}{a\left(x^2+\frac{b}{a}x+\frac{c}{a}\right)}$

II. Add and subtract $\left(\dfrac{b}{2a}\right)^2$ from denominator and try to write denominator in the form $X^2 \pm k^2$ or $k^2 \pm X^2$ where, $X^2 = \left(x \pm \dfrac{b}{2a}\right)^2$ and $k^2 = \left(\dfrac{c}{a} - \dfrac{b^2}{4a^2}\right)$.

III. Substitute $x \pm \dfrac{b}{2a} = t$ and reduce the integral obtained in Step II into one of the form $\dfrac{1}{a}\displaystyle\int\frac{dt}{t^2 \pm k^2}$ or $\dfrac{1}{a}\displaystyle\int\frac{dt}{k^2-t^2}$.

IV. In the integral $\int \frac{dx}{\sqrt{ax^2 + bx + c}}$ will be formed $\frac{1}{a}\int \frac{dt}{\sqrt{t^2 \pm k^2}}$ or $\frac{1}{a}\int \frac{dt}{\sqrt{k^2 - t^2}}$, which can be integrated by using suitable formulae.

Example 31. Evaluate

(i) $\int \frac{1}{9x^2+6x+5}\,dx$ (ii) $\int \frac{1}{2x^2+x-1}\,dx$

Sol. (i) Let $I = \int \frac{1}{9x^2+6x+5}\,dx = \frac{1}{9}\int \frac{1}{x^2+\frac{2}{3}x+\frac{5}{9}}\,dx$

[take 9 common from denominator]

$$= \frac{1}{9}\int \frac{1}{x^2+2\cdot\frac{1}{3}\cdot x+\left(\frac{1}{3}\right)^2+\frac{5}{9}-\left(\frac{1}{3}\right)^2}\,dx$$

$\left[\text{here } a = 9 \text{ and } b = 6, \text{ adding and subtracting } \left(\frac{b}{2a}\right)^2 = \left(\frac{6}{2\times 9}\right)^2 = \left(\frac{1}{3}\right)^2 \text{ from denominator}\right]$

$$= \frac{1}{9}\int \frac{1}{x^2+\frac{2}{3}x+\left(\frac{1}{3}\right)^2+\frac{5}{9}-\frac{1}{9}}\,dx$$

$$= \frac{1}{9}\int \frac{1}{\left(x+\frac{1}{3}\right)^2+\left(\frac{2}{3}\right)^2}\,dx$$

$$= \frac{1}{9}\left(\frac{1}{2/3}\right)\tan^{-1}\left(\frac{x+1/3}{2/3}\right)+C$$

$\left[\because \int \frac{dx}{a^2+x^2} = \frac{1}{a}\tan^{-1}\left(\frac{x}{a}\right)+C\right]$

$$= \frac{1}{6}\tan^{-1}\left(\frac{3x+1}{2}\right)+C$$

(ii) We have, $I = \int \frac{1}{2x^2+x-1}\,dx = \frac{1}{2}\int \frac{1}{x^2+\frac{x}{2}-\frac{1}{2}}\,dx$

$$= \frac{1}{2}\int \frac{1}{x^2+\frac{x}{2}+\frac{1}{16}-\frac{1}{16}-\frac{1}{2}}\,dx$$

$$= \frac{1}{2}\int \frac{dx}{\left(x+\frac{1}{4}\right)^2-\frac{9}{16}} = \frac{1}{2}\int \frac{dx}{\left(x+\frac{1}{4}\right)^2-\left(\frac{3}{4}\right)^2}$$

$$= \frac{1}{2}\cdot\frac{1}{2(3/4)}\log\left|\frac{x+\frac{1}{4}-\frac{3}{4}}{x+\frac{1}{4}+\frac{3}{4}}\right|+C$$

$\left[\text{using } \int \frac{dx}{x^2-a^2} = \frac{1}{2a}\log\left|\frac{x-a}{x+a}\right|+C\right]$

$$= \frac{1}{3}\log\left|\frac{x-1/2}{x+1}\right|+C$$

$$\therefore\ I = \frac{1}{3}\log\left|\frac{2x-1}{2(x+1)}\right|+C$$

Example 32. Evaluate

(i) $\int \frac{dx}{\sqrt{3-x+x^2}}$ (ii) $\int \frac{e^x}{\sqrt{5-4e^x-e^{2x}}}\,dx$

Sol. (i) Let $I = \int \frac{dx}{\sqrt{3-x+x^2}} = \int \frac{dx}{\sqrt{x^2-x+3}}$

$$= \int \frac{dx}{\sqrt{x^2-2\times x\times\frac{1}{2}+\left(\frac{1}{2}\right)^2-\left(\frac{1}{2}\right)^2+3}}$$

$\left[\text{here } a = 1, b = -1, \text{ adding and subtracting } \left(\frac{b}{2a}\right)^2 = \left(\frac{-1}{2}\right)^2 = \left(\frac{1}{2}\right)^2 \text{ from denominator}\right]$

$$= \int \frac{dx}{\sqrt{\left(x-\frac{1}{2}\right)^2+3-\frac{1}{4}}} = \int \frac{dx}{\sqrt{\left(x-\frac{1}{2}\right)^2+\frac{11}{4}}}$$

Now, put $x-\frac{1}{2} = t \Rightarrow dx = dt$

$$\therefore\ I = \int \frac{dt}{\sqrt{t^2+\left(\frac{\sqrt{11}}{2}\right)^2}} = \log\left|t+\sqrt{t^2+\left(\frac{\sqrt{11}}{2}\right)^2}\right|+C$$

$\left[\because \int \frac{dx}{\sqrt{x^2+a^2}} = \log|x+\sqrt{x^2+a^2}|+C\right]$

$$= \log\left|\left(x-\frac{1}{2}\right)+\sqrt{\left(x-\frac{1}{2}\right)^2+\left(\frac{\sqrt{11}}{2}\right)^2}\right|+C$$

$\left[\because t = x-\frac{1}{2}\right]$

Hence, $I = \log\left|\left(x-\frac{1}{2}\right)+\sqrt{3-x+x^2}\right|+C$

(ii) Let $I = \int \frac{e^x}{\sqrt{5-4e^x-e^{2x}}}\,dx$

Now, put $e^x = t \Rightarrow e^x dx = dt$

$$\therefore\ I = \int \frac{dt}{\sqrt{5-4t-t^2}} = \int \frac{dt}{\sqrt{-(t^2+4t-5)}}$$

$$= \int \frac{dt}{\sqrt{9-(t+2)^2}} = \int \frac{dt}{\sqrt{(3)^2-(t+2)^2}}$$

$$= \sin^{-1}\left(\frac{t+2}{3}\right) + C \quad \left[\because \int \frac{dx}{\sqrt{a^2 - x^2}} = \sin^{-1}\frac{x}{a} + C\right]$$

$$= \sin^{-1}\left(\frac{e^x + 2}{3}\right) + C \quad [\because t = e^x]$$

JEE SCANNER

Example Similar to PYQ Asked in JEE Main 2020

The integral $\int \frac{\cos x}{\sqrt{\sin^2 x - 2\sin x - 3}} dx$ *is equal to*

(a) $\log|(\sin x + 1) + \sqrt{\sin^2 x - 2\sin x - 3}| + C$

(b) $\log|(\sin x - 1) + \sqrt{\sin^2 x - 2\sin x - 3}| + C$

(c) $\log|(\sin x + 2) + \sqrt{\sin^2 x - 2\sin x - 3}| + C$

(d) $\log|(\sin x - 2) + \sqrt{\sin^2 x - 2\sin x - 3}| + C$

Sol. (b) Let $I = \int \frac{\cos x\, dx}{\sqrt{\sin^2 x - 2\sin x - 3}}$

Put $\sin x = t \Rightarrow \cos x\, dx = dt$

$$\therefore \quad I = \int \frac{dt}{\sqrt{t^2 - 2t - 3}} = \int \frac{dt}{\sqrt{t^2 - 2t + 1 - 1 - 3}}$$

$$= \int \frac{dt}{\sqrt{(t-1)^2 - (2)^2}}$$

$$= \log|(t-1) + \sqrt{(t-1)^2 - (2)^2}| + C$$

$$\therefore \quad I = \log|(\sin x - 1) + \sqrt{\sin^2 x - 2\sin x - 3}| + C$$

Skill Builder

$\int \frac{e^x}{\sqrt{e^{2x} - 2e^x - 8}} dx$ is equal to

(a) $\log|(e^x + 1) + \sqrt{e^{2x} - 2e^x - 8}| + C$

(b) $\log|(e^x - 1) + \sqrt{e^{2x} - 2e^x - 8}| + C$

(c) $\log|(e^x + 2) + \sqrt{e^{2x} - 2e^x - 8}| + C$

(d) $\log|(e^x - 2) + \sqrt{e^{2x} - 2e^x - 8}| + C$

For Sol.

■ **For more practice** See Q.14 of Milestone Practice 1.3.

Integral of the Type $\int \frac{px+q}{ax^2+bx+c} dx$ and $\int \frac{px+q}{\sqrt{ax^2+bx+c}} dx$

To evaluate such integrals, we firstly write the numerator as

$$px + q = A\left\{\frac{d}{dx}(ax^2 + bx + c)\right\} + B = A(2ax + b) + B$$

Then, find A and B by comparing the coefficients of like powers of x from both sides.

Now, put the resultant value of $(px + q)$ in given integral and then given integral is reduced to one of the known forms which can be integrate easily.

Example 33. Evaluate $\int \frac{x+2}{2x^2 + 6x + 5} dx.$

Sol.

Decoding the Question

First, make numerator as the sum of derivative of denominator and constant term and then integrate both part of integral using formulae

(i) $\int \frac{f'(x)}{f(x)} dx = \ln|f(x)| + C$

(ii) $\int \frac{dx}{x^2 + a^2} = \frac{1}{a}\tan^{-1}\left(\frac{x}{a}\right) + C$

Let $(x + 2) = A\frac{d}{dx}(2x^2 + 6x + 5) + B$

$$\Rightarrow (x + 2) = A(4x + 6) + B \quad \text{...(i)}$$

On equating the coefficients of x and constant term from both sides, we get

$$1 = 4A \text{ and } 6A + B = 2 \Rightarrow A = \frac{1}{4} \text{ and } B = \frac{1}{2}$$

$\therefore$ From Eq. (i), we get

$$(x + 2) = \frac{1}{4}(4x + 6) + \frac{1}{2}$$

Now, the given integral can be written as

$$I = \int \frac{(x+2)}{2x^2 + 6x + 5} = \int \frac{\frac{1}{4}(4x + 6) + \frac{1}{2}}{2x^2 + 6x + 5} dx$$

$$= \frac{1}{4}\int \frac{4x + 6}{2x^2 + 6x + 5} dx + \frac{1}{2}\int \frac{dx}{2x^2 + 6x + 5}$$

$$\Rightarrow \quad I = \frac{1}{4}I_1 + \frac{1}{2}I_2 \quad \text{...(ii)}$$

where, $I_1 = \int \frac{4x + 6}{2x^2 + 6x + 5} dx$ and $I_2 = \int \frac{dx}{2x^2 + 6x + 5}$

Now, consider $I_1 = \int \frac{4x + 6}{2x^2 + 6x + 5} dx$

Now, put $2x^2 + 6x + 5 = t \Rightarrow (4x + 6)\, dx = dt$

$$\therefore \quad I_1 = \int \frac{dt}{t} = \log|t| + C_1 = \log\left|2x^2 + 6x + 5\right| + C_1$$

and $I_2 = \int \frac{dx}{2x^2 + 6x + 5} = \frac{1}{2}\int \frac{dx}{x^2 + 3x + \frac{5}{2}}$

$$= \frac{1}{2}\int \frac{dx}{x^2 + 2\cdot\frac{3}{2}\cdot x + \left(\frac{3}{2}\right)^2 - \left(\frac{3}{2}\right)^2 + \frac{5}{2}}$$

$$= \frac{1}{2}\int \frac{dx}{\left(x + \frac{3}{2}\right)^2 + \left(\frac{1}{2}\right)^2} = \frac{1}{2}\cdot\frac{1}{\left(\frac{1}{2}\right)}\tan^{-1}\left(\frac{x + \frac{3}{2}}{\frac{1}{2}}\right) + C_2$$

$$= \frac{1}{2} \cdot 2 \tan^{-1}(2x+3) + C_2 = \tan^{-1}(2x+3) + C_2$$

Now, substitute the value of I_1 and I_2 in Eq. (ii).

$$I = \frac{1}{4} \log |2x^2 + 6x + 5| + \frac{1}{2} \tan^{-1}(2x+3) + \frac{1}{4} C_1 + \frac{1}{2} C_2$$

$$= \frac{1}{4} \log \left| 2x^2 + 6x + 5 \right| + \frac{1}{2} \tan^{-1}(2x+3) + C$$

where, $C = \frac{1}{4} C_1 + \frac{1}{2} C_2$

Integrals of the Type $\int \frac{ax^2 + bx + c}{(px^2 + qx + r)} dx$ and $\int \frac{(ax^2 + bx + c)}{\sqrt{px^2 + qx + r}} dx$

In above cases, substitute

$$ax^2 + bx + c = \lambda (px^2 + qx + r) + \mu \left\{ \frac{d}{dx} (px^2 + qx + r) \right\} + \gamma.$$

Find λ, μ and γ. These integrations reduces to integration of three independent functions.

Example 34. Evaluate $\int \frac{x^2 + x + 3}{x^2 - x - 2} dx.$

Sol. Let $I = \int \frac{x^2 + x + 3}{x^2 - x - 2} dx$

$$\therefore \quad I = \int \left(1 + \frac{2x+5}{x^2 - x - 2} \right) dx$$

$$= \int 1\, dx + \int \frac{2x+5}{x^2 - x - 2} dx = x + \int \frac{2x+5}{x^2 - x - 2} dx$$

Put, $2x + 5 = \lambda \left\{ \frac{d}{dx} (x^2 - x - 2) \right\} + \mu.$

Then, obtaining $2x + 5 = \lambda (2x - 1) + \mu$, comparing the coefficients of like terms, we get

$$2 = 2\lambda \text{ and } 5 = \mu - \lambda$$

$$\therefore \quad \lambda = 1 \text{ and } \mu = 6$$

$$\therefore \quad I = x + \int \frac{\lambda (2x-1) + \mu}{x^2 - x - 2} dx$$

$$= x + \int \frac{2x-1}{x^2 - x - 2} dx + 6 \int \frac{1}{x^2 - x - 2} dx$$

$$= x + \int \frac{1}{t} dt + 6 \int \frac{1}{x^2 - x + \frac{1}{4} - \frac{1}{4} - 2}$$

[where $t = x^2 - x - 2$]

$$= x + \log |t| + 6 \int \frac{dx}{(x - 1/2)^2 - (3/2)^2} dx$$

$$= x + \log |x^2 - x - 2| + 6 \cdot \frac{1}{2(3/2)} \log \left| \frac{x - \frac{1}{2} - \frac{3}{2}}{x - \frac{1}{2} + \frac{3}{2}} \right| + C$$

$$= x + \log |x^2 - x - 2| + 2 \cdot \log \left| \frac{x-2}{x+1} \right| + C$$

Example 35. Evaluate $\int \frac{2x^2 + 5x + 4}{\sqrt{x^2 + x + 1}} dx.$

Sol. Let $I = \int \frac{2x^2 + 5x + 4}{\sqrt{x^2 + x + 1}} dx$

Put $2x^2 + 5x + 4 = \lambda (x^2 + x + 1) + \mu \left\{ \frac{d}{dx} (x^2 + x + 1) \right\} + \gamma$

or $2x^2 + 5x + 4 = \lambda (x^2 + x + 1) + \mu (2x + 1) + \gamma$

Comparing the coefficients of like terms, we get

$$2 = \lambda, \quad 5 = \lambda + 2\mu, \quad 4 = \lambda + \mu + \gamma$$

$$\therefore \quad \lambda = 2, \quad \mu = 3/2, \quad \gamma = 1/2$$

Hence, the above integral reduces to

$$I = \int \frac{2x^2 + 5x + 4}{\sqrt{x^2 + x + 1}} dx$$

$$= \int \left(2 \cdot \frac{(x^2 + x + 1)}{\sqrt{x^2 + x + 1}} + \frac{3}{2} \cdot \frac{(2x+1)}{\sqrt{x^2 + x + 1}} + \frac{1}{2} \cdot \frac{1}{\sqrt{x^2 + x + 1}} \right) dx$$

$$= 2 \int \sqrt{x^2 + x + 1}\, dx + \frac{3}{2} \int \frac{dt}{\sqrt{t}} + \frac{1}{2} \int \frac{dx}{\sqrt{x^2 + x + 1}}$$

[where $t = x^2 + x + 1$]

$$= 2 \int \sqrt{(x + 1/2)^2 + (\sqrt{3}/2)^2}\, dx + \frac{3}{2} \cdot \frac{t^{1/2}}{1/2} + \frac{1}{2} \int \frac{dx}{\sqrt{(x + 1/2)^2 + (\sqrt{3}/2)^2}}$$

$$= 2 \left[\frac{1}{2} \left(x + \frac{1}{2} \right) \sqrt{x^2 + x + 1} + \frac{1}{2} \cdot \frac{3}{4} \cdot \log \left| \left(x + \frac{1}{2} \right) + \sqrt{x^2 + x + 1} \right| \right]$$

$$+ 3 \sqrt{x^2 + x + 1} + \frac{1}{2} \log \left| \left(x + \frac{1}{2} \right) + \sqrt{x^2 + x + 1} \right| + C$$

$$\therefore I = \left(x + \frac{1}{2} \right) \sqrt{x^2 + x + 1} + \frac{3}{4} \log \left\{ \left(x + \frac{1}{2} \right) + \sqrt{x^2 + x + 1} \right\}$$

$$+ 3 \sqrt{x^2 + x + 1} + \frac{1}{2} \log \left\{ \left(x + \frac{1}{2} \right) + \sqrt{x^2 + x + 1} \right\} + C$$

$$= \left(x + \frac{7}{2} \right) \sqrt{x^2 + x + 1} + \frac{5}{4} \log \left\{ \left(x + \frac{1}{2} \right) + \sqrt{x^2 + x + 1} \right\} + C$$

$$\left[\because \int \sqrt{x^2 + a^2}\, dx = \frac{x}{2} \sqrt{x^2 + a^2} + \frac{a^2}{2} \log (x + \sqrt{x^2 + a^2}) + C \right]$$

Integrals of the Form $\int \frac{k(x)}{ax^2 + bx + c} dx$, where $k(x)$ is a Polynomial of Degree Greater than 2

To evaluate this type of integrals we divide the numerator by denominator and express the integral as

$Q(x) + \frac{R(x)}{ax^2 + bx + c}$, where $R(x)$ is a linear function of x.

Example 36. Evaluate $\int \frac{2x^3+6x^2+6x+2}{2x^2+6x+5}\,dx$.

Sol. Let $I = \int \frac{2x^3+6x^2+6x+2}{2x^2+6x+5}\,dx$

$$= \int \left(x + \frac{x+2}{2x^2+6x+5}\right) dx = \int x\,dx + \int \frac{x+2}{2x^2+6x+5}\,dx$$

$$= \int x\,dx + \frac{1}{4}\int \frac{4x+6}{2x^2+6x+5}\,dx + \frac{1}{2}\int \frac{1}{2x^2+6x+5}\,dx$$

$$= \int x\,dx + \frac{1}{4}\int \frac{4x+6}{2x^2+6x+5}\,dx + \frac{1}{4}\int \frac{1}{\left(x+\frac{3}{2}\right)^2+\left(\frac{1}{2}\right)^2}\,dx$$

$$= \frac{x^2}{2} + \frac{1}{4}\log|2x^2+6x+5| + \frac{1}{4}\times\frac{1}{\left(\frac{1}{2}\right)}\tan^{-1}\left(\frac{x+\frac{3}{2}}{\frac{1}{2}}\right) + C$$

$$= \frac{x^2}{2} + \frac{1}{4}\log|2x^2+6x+5| + \frac{1}{2}\tan^{-1}(2x+3) + C$$

1.6 Trigonometric Integrals

(a) Integrals of the Form

$$\int \frac{1}{a\cos^2 x + b\sin^2 x}\,dx,\ \int \frac{1}{a+b\sin^2 x}\,dx,$$

$$\int \frac{1}{a+b\cos^2 x}\,dx,\ \int \frac{1}{(a\sin x + b\cos x)^2}\,dx,$$

$$\int \frac{1}{a+b\sin^2 x + c\cos^2 x}\,dx$$

To evaluate this type of integrals, divide numerator and denominator both by $\cos^2 x$, replace $\sec^2 x$, if any, in denominator by $(1+\tan^2 x)$ and put $\tan x = t$.

So that $\sec^2 x\,dx = dt$.

Example 37. Evaluate

(i) $\int \frac{1}{4\sin^2 x + 9\cos^2 x}\,dx$ (ii) $\int \frac{\sin x}{\sin 3x}\,dx$

Sol. (i) Let $I = \int \frac{dx}{4\sin^2 x + 9\cos^2 x}$

Here, dividing numerator and denominator by $\cos^2 x$, we get

$$I = \int \frac{\sec^2 x}{4\tan^2 x + 9}\,dx$$

Put $\tan x = t \Rightarrow \sec^2 x\,dx = dt$

$$\therefore I = \int \frac{dt}{4t^2+9} = \frac{1}{4}\int \frac{dt}{t^2+(3/2)^2}$$

$$= \frac{1}{4}\cdot\frac{1}{3/2}\tan^{-1}\left(\frac{t}{3/2}\right) + C = \frac{1}{6}\tan^{-1}\left(\frac{2\tan x}{3}\right) + C$$

(ii) Let $I = \int \frac{\sin x}{\sin 3x}\,dx = \int \frac{\sin x}{3\sin x - 4\sin^3 x}\,dx$

$$I = \int \frac{dx}{3 - 4\sin^2 x}$$

Dividing numerator and denominator by $\cos^2 x$, we get

$$I = \int \frac{\sec^2 x\,dx}{3\sec^2 x - 4\tan^2 x}$$

$$= \int \frac{\sec^2 x\,dx}{3(1+\tan^2 x) - 4\tan^2 x} = \int \frac{\sec^2 x\,dx}{3-\tan^2 x}$$

Let $\tan x = t \Rightarrow \sec^2 x\,dx = dt$

$$\therefore \quad I = \int \frac{dt}{(\sqrt{3})^2 - (t)^2} = \frac{1}{2\sqrt{3}}\log\left|\frac{\sqrt{3}+t}{\sqrt{3}-t}\right| + C$$

$$= \frac{1}{2\sqrt{3}}\log\left|\frac{\sqrt{3}+\tan x}{\sqrt{3}-\tan x}\right| + C$$

(b) Integrals of the Form

$$\int \frac{1}{a\sin x + b\cos x}\,dx,\ \int \frac{1}{a+b\sin x}\,dx,$$

$$\int \frac{1}{a+b\cos x}\,dx,\ \int \frac{1}{a\sin x + b\cos x + c}\,dx$$

To evaluate this type of integrals we put

$\sin x = \frac{2\tan x/2}{1+\tan^2 x/2}$ and $\cos x = \frac{1-\tan^2 x/2}{1+\tan^2 x/2}$ and replace $\tan x/2 = t$, by performing these steps the integral reduces to the form $\int \frac{1}{at^2+bt+c}\,dt$ which can be evaluated by methods discussed earlier.

Example 38. Evaluate $\int \frac{dx}{2+\sin x+\cos x}$.

Sol. (i) Let $I = \int \frac{dx}{2+\sin x+\cos x}$

$$= \int \frac{dx}{2 + \frac{2\tan x/2}{1+\tan^2 x/2} + \frac{1-\tan^2 x/2}{1+\tan^2 x/2}}$$

$$= \int \frac{\sec^2 \frac{x}{2}\,dx}{2 + 2\tan^2\frac{x}{2} + 2\tan\frac{x}{2} + 1 - \tan^2\frac{x}{2}}$$

$$= \int \frac{\sec^2 \frac{x}{2}\,dx}{\tan^2\frac{x}{2} + 2\tan\frac{x}{2} + 3}$$

Put $\tan\frac{x}{2} = t \Rightarrow \frac{1}{2}\sec^2\frac{x}{2}\,dx = dt$

$$= \int \frac{2\,dt}{t^2+2t+3} = 2\int\frac{dt}{t^2+2t+1+2}$$

$$= 2\int\frac{dt}{(t+1)^2+(\sqrt{2})^2} = 2\cdot\frac{1}{\sqrt{2}}\tan^{-1}\left(\frac{t+1}{\sqrt{2}}\right)+C$$

$$I = \sqrt{2}\tan^{-1}\left(\frac{\tan x/2+1}{\sqrt{2}}\right)+C$$

(c) Alternative Method to Evaluate the Integrals of the Form

$$\int\frac{1}{a\sin x + b\cos x}\,dx$$

To evaluate this type of integrals we substitute $a = r\cos\theta$, $b = r\sin\theta$ and so

$$r = \sqrt{a^2+b^2},\quad \theta = \tan^{-1}\left(\frac{b}{a}\right)$$

$\therefore\quad a\sin x + b\cos x = r\sin(x+\theta)$

So, $\int\frac{1}{a\sin x+b\cos x}\,dx = \frac{1}{r}\int\frac{1}{\sin(x+\theta)}\,dx$

$$= \frac{1}{r}\int\operatorname{cosec}(x+\theta)\,dx = \frac{1}{r}\log\left|\tan\left(\frac{x}{2}+\frac{\theta}{2}\right)\right|+C$$

$\therefore\quad \int\frac{1}{a\sin x + b\cos x}\,dx$

$$= \frac{1}{\sqrt{a^2+b^2}}\log\left|\tan\left(\frac{x}{2}+\frac{1}{2}\tan^{-1}\frac{b}{a}\right)\right|+C$$

Example 39. Evaluate $\int\frac{1}{\sqrt{3}\sin x+\cos x}\,dx$.

Sol. Let $\sqrt{3} = r\cos\theta$ and $1 = r\sin\theta$.

Then, $r = \sqrt{(\sqrt{3})^2+(1)^2} = 2$ and $\tan\theta = \frac{1}{\sqrt{3}} \Rightarrow \theta = \frac{\pi}{6}$

$$\therefore I = \int\frac{1}{\sqrt{3}\sin x+\cos x}\,dx$$

$$= \int\frac{1}{r\cos\theta\sin x + r\sin\theta\cos x}\,dx$$

$$= \frac{1}{r}\int\frac{dx}{\sin(x+\theta)} = \frac{1}{r}\int\operatorname{cosec}(x+\theta)\,dx$$

$$= \frac{1}{r}\log\left|\tan\left(\frac{x}{2}+\frac{\theta}{2}\right)\right|+C = \frac{1}{2}\log\left|\tan\left(\frac{x}{2}+\frac{\pi}{12}\right)\right|+C$$

Time Saving Technique

On dividing numerator and denominator by 2, we get

$$I = \frac{1}{2}\int\frac{1}{\frac{\sqrt{3}}{2}\sin x+\frac{1}{2}\cos x}\,dx = \frac{1}{2}\int\frac{1}{\sin\left(x+\frac{\pi}{6}\right)}\,dx$$

$$= \frac{1}{2}\int\operatorname{cosec}\left(x+\frac{\pi}{6}\right)dx = \frac{1}{2}\log\left|\tan\left(\frac{x}{2}+\frac{\pi}{12}\right)\right|+C$$

(d) Integrals of the Form

$$\int\frac{p\cos x+q\sin x+r}{a\cos x+b\sin x+c}\,dx,\ \int\frac{p\cos x+q\sin x}{a\cos x+b\sin x}\,dx$$

Rule for (i) In this integral, express numerator as

λ (denominator) $+\mu$ (diff. of denominator) $+\gamma$.

Find λ, μ and γ by comparing coefficients of $\sin x, \cos x$ and constant term and split the integral into sum of three integrals.

$$\lambda\int dx + \mu\int\frac{\text{d.c.of (denominator)}}{\text{denominator}}\,dx + \gamma\int\frac{dx}{a\sin x + b\cos x + c}$$

Rule for (ii) Express numerator as λ (denominator) $+\mu$ (differentiation of denominator) and find λ and μ as above.

Example 40. Evaluate $\int\frac{(2+3\cos x)}{\sin x+2\cos x+3}\,dx$.

Sol. Write the numerator $= \lambda$ (denominator) $+\mu$ (d.c. of denominator) $+\gamma$

$\Rightarrow 2+3\cos x = \lambda(\sin x+2\cos x+3)+\mu(\cos x-2\sin x)+\gamma$

Comparing the coefficients of $\sin x$, $\cos x$ and constant terms, we get $0 = \lambda - 2\mu,\ 3 = 2\lambda+\mu,\ 2 = 3\lambda+\gamma$

$\Rightarrow\quad \lambda = 6/5,\ \mu = 3/5,\ \gamma = -8/5$

Hence, $I = \frac{6}{5}\int 1\,dx + \frac{3}{5}\int\frac{\cos x - 2\sin x}{\sin x+2\cos x+3}\,dx - \frac{8}{5}\int\frac{dx}{\sin x + 2\cos x + 3}$

$$= \frac{6}{5}\cdot x + \frac{3}{5}\log|\sin x + 2\cos x + 3| - \frac{8}{5}I_3 \quad \text{...(i)}$$

where, $I_3 = \int\frac{dx}{\sin x+2\cos x+3}$

$$= \int\frac{dx}{\frac{2\tan x/2}{1+\tan^2 x/2}+\frac{2(1-\tan^2 x/2)}{1+\tan^2 x/2}+3}$$

$$= \int\frac{\sec^2\frac{x}{2}\,dx}{2\tan\frac{x}{2}+2-2\tan^2\frac{x}{2}+3+3\tan^2\frac{x}{2}}$$

$$= \int\frac{\sec^2\frac{x}{2}\,dx}{\tan^2\frac{x}{2}+2\tan\frac{x}{2}+5}$$

Let $\tan\frac{x}{2} = t \Rightarrow \frac{1}{2}\sec^2\frac{x}{2}\,dx = dt$

$$\therefore\quad I_3 = \int\frac{2dt}{t^2+2t+5} = 2\int\frac{dt}{(t+1)^2+2^2}$$

$$= 2\cdot\frac{1}{2}\cdot\tan^{-1}\left(\frac{t+1}{2}\right) = \tan^{-1}\left(\frac{\tan\frac{x}{2}+1}{2}\right) \quad \text{...(ii)}$$

From Eqs. (i) and (ii), we get

$$I = \frac{6}{5}x+\frac{3}{5}\log|\sin x+2\cos x+3| - \frac{8}{5}\tan^{-1}\left|\left(\frac{\tan\frac{x}{2}+1}{2}\right)\right|+C$$

Milestone Practice 1.3

Evaluate the following integrals

1. $\int \frac{x\,dx}{9-16x^4}$
2. $\int \frac{x^3\,dx}{16x^8-25}$
3. $\int \sqrt{\frac{x^4}{a^6+x^6}}\,dx$
4. $\int \frac{1}{4e^{-x}+9e^x}\,dx$
5. $\int \frac{2^x}{\sqrt{4^x-25}}\,dx$
6. $\int \frac{8x-11}{\sqrt{5+2x-x^2}}\,dx$
7. $\int \frac{\sin 4\theta\,d\theta}{\sqrt{2\cos^4\theta+\sin^2\theta}}\,d\theta$
8. $\int \frac{(x\cos\theta-1)}{x^2-2x\cos\theta+1}\,dx$
9. $\int \frac{\sqrt{x}\,dx}{\sqrt{2x+3}}$
10. $\int \sqrt{\frac{1-\sqrt{x}}{1+\sqrt{x}}}\frac{dx}{x}$
11. $\int \sqrt{\frac{a-x}{x-b}}\,dx$
12. $\int \frac{dx}{5-8x-x^2}$
13. $\int \frac{1}{\sqrt{x^2-4x}}\,dx$
14. $\int \frac{\sin x\,dx}{\sqrt{\cos^2 x-4\cos x-5}}\,dx$
15. $\int \frac{x^2+2x+3}{\sqrt{x^2+x+1}}\,dx$
16. $\int \frac{x^2-x+2}{x^2+1}\,dx$
17. $\int \frac{dx}{\sin^2 x+9\cos^2 x}$
18. $\int \frac{dx}{1+\sin x+\cos x}$
19. $\int \frac{dx}{\sin x+\sqrt{3}\cos x}$
20. $\int \frac{2\sin x+3\cos x}{3\sin x+4\cos x}\,dx$

Answer Key

1. $\frac{1}{48}\log\left|\frac{3+4x^2}{3-4x^2}\right|+C$
2. $\frac{1}{160}\log\left|\frac{4x^4-5}{4x^4+5}\right|+C$
3. $\frac{1}{3}\log|x^3+\sqrt{a^6+x^6}|+C$
4. $\frac{1}{6}\tan^{-1}\left(\frac{3e^x}{2}\right)+C$
5. $\frac{1}{\log 2}\log\,|2^x+\sqrt{4^x-25}|+C$
6. $-8\sqrt{5+2x-x^2}-3\sin^{-1}\left(\frac{x-1}{\sqrt{6}}\right)+C$
7. $-2\sqrt{2\cos^4\theta-\cos^2\theta+1}+\frac{1}{\sqrt{2}}\log\left|\cos^2\theta-\frac{1}{4}+\sqrt{2\cos^4\theta-\cos^2\theta+1}\right|+C$
8. $\frac{\cos\theta}{2}\log|x^2-2x\cos\theta+1|-\sin\theta\tan^{-1}\left(\frac{x-\cos\theta}{\sin\theta}\right)+C$
9. $\frac{1}{4}\sqrt{2x^2+3x}-\frac{3}{4\sqrt{2}}\log\left|\left(x+\frac{3}{4}\right)+\sqrt{x^2+\frac{3x}{2}}\right|+C$
10. $\log\left|\frac{1-\sqrt{1-x}}{1+\sqrt{1-x}}\right|-2\sin^{-1}\sqrt{x}+C$
11. $(b-a)\left[\tan^{-1}\sqrt{\frac{a-x}{x-b}}-\frac{\sqrt{(a-x)(x-b)}}{a-b}\right]+C$
12. $\frac{1}{2\sqrt{21}}\log\left|\frac{\sqrt{21}+x+4}{\sqrt{21}-x-4}\right|+C$
13. $\log\,|(x-2)+\sqrt{x^2-4x}|+C$
14. $-\log\,|(\cos x-2)+\sqrt{\cos^2 x-4\cos x-5}\,|+C$
15. $\frac{2x+5}{4}\sqrt{x^2+x+1}+\frac{15}{8}\log\left|\frac{2x+1}{2}+\sqrt{x^2+x+1}\right|+C$
16. $=x-\frac{1}{2}\log\,|x^2+1|+\tan^{-1}x+C$
17. $\frac{1}{3}\tan^{-1}\left(\frac{\tan x}{3}\right)+C$
18. $\log\left|\tan\frac{x}{2}+1\right|+C$
19. $\frac{1}{2}\log\left|\tan\left(\frac{x}{2}+\frac{\pi}{6}\right)\right|+C$
20. $\frac{18}{25}x+\frac{1}{25}\log[3\sin x+4\cos x]+C$

For Detailed Solution

Milestone 4 Integration by Parts

- Some More Special Types of Integrals

Theorem If u and v are two functions of x, then

$$\int uv\,dx = u\int v\,dx - \int\left\{\frac{du}{dx}\int v\,dx\right\}dx$$

i.e. The integral of product of two functions = (first function) × (integral of second function) − integral of (differential of first function × integral of second function).

Proof For any two functions $f(x)$ and $g(x)$, we have

$$\frac{d}{dx}\{f(x)\cdot g(x)\} = f(x)\cdot\frac{d}{dx}\{g(x)\} + g(x)\cdot\frac{d}{dx}\{f(x)\}$$

$$\therefore \int\left(f(x)\cdot\frac{d}{dx}\{g(x)\}+g(x)\cdot\frac{d}{dx}\{f(x)\}\right)dx = \int\left(\frac{d}{dx}\{f(x)\cdot g(x)\}\right)dx$$

$$\Rightarrow \int\left(f(x)\cdot\frac{d}{dx}\{g(x)\}\right)dx + \int\left(g(x)\cdot\frac{d}{dx}\{f(x)\}\right)dx = f(x)\cdot g(x)$$

$$\Rightarrow \int\left(f(x)\cdot\frac{d}{dx}\{g(x)\}\right)dx = f(x)\cdot g(x) - \int\left(g(x)\cdot\frac{d}{dx}\{f(x)\}\right)dx$$

Let $\quad f(x) = u \quad$ and $\quad \frac{d}{dx}\{g(x)\} = v$

So that $g(x) = \int v\,dx$

$$\therefore \int uv\,dx = u\cdot\int v\,dx - \int\left\{\frac{du}{dx}\cdot\int v\,dx\right\}\cdot dx$$

Concept Inside Video

JEE Focus Points

While applying the above rule, care has to be taken in the selection of first function (u) and selection of second function (v). Normally we use the following methods :

- If in the product of the two functions, one of the functions is not directly integrable (e.g. $\log|x|$, $\sin^{-1}x$, $\cos^{-1}x$, $\tan^{-1}x$, ..., etc.) Then, we take it as the first function and the remaining function is taken as the second function. i.e. In the integration of $\int x\tan^{-1}x\,dx$, $\tan^{-1}x$ is taken as the first function and x as the second function.
- If there is no other function, then unity is taken as the second function. e.g. In the integration of $\int \tan^{-1}x\,dx$, $\tan^{-1}x$ is taken as first function and 1 as the second function.
- If both of the function are directly integrable, then the first function is chosen in such a way that the derivative of the function thus obtained under integral sign is easily integrable.

Usually we use the following preference order for selecting the first function. (Inverse, Logarithmic, Algebraic, Trigonometric, Exponent).

In above stated order, the function on the left is always chosen as the first function. This rule is called as **ILATE**.

Example 41. Evaluate

(i) $\int \sin^{-1}x\,dx$ (ii) $\int \log_e|x|\,dx$

(iii) $\int x\cos x\,dx$ (iv) $\int x^2\cos x\,dx$

Sol. (i) $I = \int \underset{\text{I}}{\sin^{-1}x}\cdot\underset{\text{II}}{1}\,dx$

Here, we know by definition of integration by parts that order of preference is taken according to ILATE. So, '$\sin^{-1}x$' should be taken as first and '1' as the second function to apply by parts.

Applying integration by parts, we get

$$I = \sin^{-1}x\cdot(x) - \int\frac{1}{\sqrt{1-x^2}}\cdot x\,dx$$

Let $1-x^2 = t \Rightarrow -2x\,dx = dt \Rightarrow x\,dx = -\frac{1}{2}dt$

$$= x\cdot\sin^{-1}x + \frac{1}{2}\int\frac{dt}{t^{1/2}}$$

$$\therefore \quad I = x\sin^{-1}x + \frac{1}{2}\cdot\frac{t^{1/2}}{1/2} + C$$

$$= x\sin^{-1}x + \sqrt{1-x^2} + C$$

$$\therefore \int\sin^{-1}x\,dx = x\sin^{-1}x + \sqrt{1-x^2} + C$$

(ii) $I = \int \underset{\text{I}}{\log_e|x|}\cdot\underset{\text{II}}{1}\,dx$

Applying integration by parts, we get

$$= \log|x|\cdot x - \int\frac{1}{x}\cdot x\,dx = x\log|x| - \int 1\,dx$$

$$I = x\log|x| - x + C$$

(iii) $I = \int \underset{\text{I}}{x}\,\underset{\text{II}}{\cos x}\,dx$

Applying integration by parts,

$$I = x\left(\int\cos x\,dx\right) - \int\left\{\frac{d}{dx}(x)\right\}\left\{\int(\cos x)\,dx\right\}dx$$

$$I = x\sin x - \int 1\cdot\sin x\,dx = x\sin x + \cos x + C$$

(iv) $I = \int \underset{\text{I}}{x^2} \underset{\text{II}}{\cos x}\, dx$

Applying integration by parts,

$$I = x^2 \left(\int \cos x\, dx\right) - \int \left\{\frac{d}{dx}(x^2)\right\} \cdot \left\{\int \cos x\right\} dx$$

$$= x^2 \sin x - \int 2x \cdot (\sin x)\, dx$$

$$= x^2 \sin x - 2 \int x (\sin x)\, dx$$

We again have to integrate $\int x \sin x\, dx$ using integration by parts,

$$I = x^2 \cdot \sin x - 2 \int \underset{\text{I}}{x} \cdot \underset{\text{II}}{\sin x}\, dx$$

$$= x^2 \sin x - 2 \left\{ x \left(\int \sin x\, dx\right) - \int \frac{d}{dx}(x) \left(\int \sin x\, dx\right) dx \right\}$$

$$= x^2 \sin x - 2\{- x \cos x - \int 1 \cdot (- \cos x)\, dx\}$$

$$= x^2 \sin x + 2x \cos x - 2 \sin x + C$$

Example 42. Evaluate $\int \dfrac{\sin^{-1} \sqrt{x} - \cos^{-1} \sqrt{x}}{\sin^{-1} \sqrt{x} + \cos^{-1} \sqrt{x}}\, dx.$

Sol. Let $I = \int \dfrac{\sin^{-1} \sqrt{x} - \cos^{-1} \sqrt{x}}{\sin^{-1} \sqrt{x} + \cos^{-1} \sqrt{x}}\, dx$

$$= \int \frac{\sin^{-1} \sqrt{x} - (\pi / 2 - \sin^{-1} \sqrt{x})}{\pi / 2}\, dx$$

$[\because \sin^{-1} \theta + \cos^{-1} \theta = \pi / 2]$

$$= \frac{2}{\pi} \int (2 \sin^{-1} \sqrt{x} - \pi / 2)\, dx$$

$$= \frac{4}{\pi} \int \sin^{-1} \sqrt{x}\, dx - \int 1\, dx$$

$$= \frac{4}{\pi} \int \sin^{-1} \sqrt{x}\, dx - x + C \quad \text{...(i)}$$

Let $x = \sin^2 \theta$, then $dx = 2 \sin \theta \cos \theta\, d\theta = \sin 2\theta\, d\theta$

$\therefore \quad \int \sin^{-1} \sqrt{x}\, dx = \int \underset{\text{I}}{\theta} \cdot \underset{\text{II}}{\sin 2\theta}\, d\theta$

Applying integration by parts

$$\int \sin^{-1} \sqrt{x} dx = - \theta \cdot \frac{\cos 2\theta}{2} + \int \frac{1}{2} \cos 2\theta\, d\theta$$

$$= \frac{-\theta}{2} \cdot \cos 2\theta + \frac{1}{4} \sin 2\theta$$

$$= \frac{-1 \cdot \theta}{2} \cdot (1 - 2 \sin^2 \theta) + \frac{1}{2} \cdot \sin \theta \cdot \sqrt{1 - \sin^2 \theta}$$

$$= \frac{-1}{2} \sin^{-1} \sqrt{x}\, (1 - 2x) + \frac{1}{2} \cdot \sqrt{x}\, \sqrt{1 - x} \quad \text{...(ii)}$$

From Eqs. (i) and (ii), we get

$$I = \frac{4}{\pi} \left\{ \frac{-1}{2} (\sin^{-1} \sqrt{x}) (1 - 2x) + \frac{1}{2} \sqrt{x} \sqrt{1 - x} \right\} - x + C$$

$$= \frac{2}{\pi} \{\sqrt{x - x^2} - (1 - 2x) \sin^{-1} \sqrt{x}\} - x + C$$

Example 43. If $\cos\theta > \sin\theta > 0$, then evaluate

$$\int \left\{ \ln \left(\frac{1 + \sin 2\theta}{1 - \sin 2\theta} \right)^{\cos^2 \theta} + \ln \left(\frac{\cos 2\theta}{1 + \sin 2\theta} \right) \right\} d\theta.$$

Sol. $I = \int \left\{ \ln \left(\dfrac{\cos\theta + \sin\theta}{\cos\theta - \sin\theta} \right)^{2 \cos^2 \theta} + \ln \left(\dfrac{\cos^2 \theta - \sin^2 \theta}{(\cos\theta + \sin\theta)^2} \right) \right\} d\theta$

$$= \int \left\{ 2\cos^2 \theta \cdot \ln \left(\frac{\cos\theta + \sin\theta}{\cos\theta - \sin\theta} \right) + \ln \left(\frac{\cos\theta - \sin\theta}{\cos\theta + \sin\theta} \right) \right\} d\theta$$

$$= \int \left\{ 2\cos^2 \theta \cdot \ln \left(\frac{\cos\theta + \sin\theta}{\cos\theta - \sin\theta} \right) - \ln \left(\frac{\cos\theta + \sin\theta}{\cos\theta - \sin\theta} \right) \right\} d\theta$$

$$= \int \left\{ (2\cos^2 \theta - 1) \cdot \ln \left(\frac{\cos\theta + \sin\theta}{\cos\theta - \sin\theta} \right) \right\} d\theta$$

$$= \int \cos 2\theta \cdot \ln \left(\frac{\cos\theta + \sin\theta}{\cos\theta - \sin\theta} \right) d\theta$$

Applying integration by parts, we get

$$= \ln \left(\frac{\cos\theta + \sin\theta}{\cos\theta - \sin\theta} \right) \cdot \frac{\sin 2\theta}{2} - \int \left(\frac{2}{\cos 2\theta} \cdot \frac{\sin 2\theta}{2} \right) d\theta$$

$$= \frac{\sin 2\theta}{2} \ln \left(\frac{\cos\theta + \sin\theta}{\cos\theta - \sin\theta} \right) + \frac{1}{2} \log |\cos 2\theta| + C$$

Example 44. Evaluate $\int \operatorname{cosec}^3 x\, dx$.

Sol. $I = \int \operatorname{cosec}^3 x\, dx = \int \underset{\text{I}}{\operatorname{cosec} x} \cdot \underset{\text{II}}{\operatorname{cosec}^2 x}\, dx$

$$= \operatorname{cosec} x \int \operatorname{cosec}^2 x\, dx - \int \left(-\operatorname{cosec} x \cdot \cot x \int \operatorname{cosec}^2 x\, dx\right) dx$$

$$= - \operatorname{cosec} x \cdot \cot x - \int \operatorname{cosec} x \cot^2 x\, dx$$

$$= - \operatorname{cosec} x \cdot \cot x - \int \operatorname{cosec} x (\operatorname{cosec}^2 x - 1) dx$$

$$= - \operatorname{cosec} x \cdot \cot x - \int \operatorname{cosec}^3 x\, dx + \int \operatorname{cosec} x\, dx$$

$$= - \operatorname{cosec} x \cdot \cot x - I + \ln |\operatorname{cosec} x - \cot x|$$

or $2I = - \operatorname{cosec} x \cdot \cot x + \ln |\operatorname{cosec} x - \cot x|$

$\therefore \quad I = -\dfrac{1}{2} [\operatorname{cosec} x \cdot \cot x - \ln |\operatorname{cosec} x - \cot x|] + C$

Example 45. Evaluate $\int \sin^{-1} \left\{ \dfrac{2x + 2}{\sqrt{4x^2 + 8x + 13}} \right\} dx.$

Sol. Here, $I = \int \sin^{-1} \left(\dfrac{2x + 2}{\sqrt{4x^2 + 8x + 13}} \right) dx$

$$= \int \sin^{-1} \left(\frac{2x + 2}{\sqrt{(2x + 2)^2 + 3^2}} \right) dx$$

Put $2x + 2 = 3 \tan \theta \Rightarrow 2\, dx = 3 \sec^2 \theta\, d\theta$

$$= \int \sin^{-1} \left(\frac{3 \tan \theta}{3 \sec \theta} \right) \frac{3}{2} \sec^2 \theta\, d\theta = \frac{3}{2} \int \theta \sec^2 \theta\, d\theta$$

$$= \frac{3}{2} \{\theta \tan \theta - \int \tan \theta\, d\theta\} = \frac{3}{2} \{\theta \tan \theta - \log |\sec \theta|\} + C'$$

$$\Rightarrow I=\frac{3}{2}\left[\frac{2x+2}{3}\tan^{-1}\left(\frac{2x+2}{3}\right)-\log\left(\sqrt{1+\left(\frac{2x+2}{3}\right)^2}\right)\right]+C'$$

$$=\frac{3}{2}\left\{\frac{2}{3}(x+1)\tan^{-1}\left(\frac{2}{3}(x+1)\right)-\log\sqrt{4x^2+8x+13}\right\}+C',$$

where $C=C'+\frac{3}{2}\log 3$

$$\Rightarrow I=(x+1)\tan^{-1}\left(\frac{2}{3}(x+1)\right)-\frac{3}{4}\log(4x^2+8x+13)+C$$

Example 46. Find the value of

$$\int\sqrt{\frac{3-x}{3+x}}\cdot\sin^{-1}\left(\frac{1}{\sqrt{6}}\sqrt{3-x}\right)dx.$$

Sol. Here, $I=\int\sqrt{\frac{3-x}{3+x}}\cdot\sin^{-1}\left(\frac{1}{\sqrt{6}}\sqrt{3-x}\right)dx$

Put $x=3\cos 2\theta \Rightarrow dx=-6\sin 2\theta\, d\theta$

$$\therefore\ I=\int\sqrt{\frac{3-3\cos 2\theta}{3+3\cos 2\theta}}\cdot\sin^{-1}\left(\frac{1}{\sqrt{6}}\sqrt{3-3\cos 2\theta}\right)(-6\sin 2\theta)d\theta$$

$$=\int\frac{\sin\theta}{\cos\theta}\cdot\sin^{-1}(\sin\theta)\cdot(-6\sin 2\theta)\,d\theta$$

$$=-6\int\theta\cdot(2\sin^2\theta)\,d\theta=-6\int\theta(1-\cos 2\theta)\,d\theta$$

$$=-6\left\{\frac{\theta^2}{2}-\int\theta\cos 2\theta\, d\theta\right\}$$

$$=-6\left\{\frac{\theta^2}{2}-\left(\theta\frac{\sin 2\theta}{2}-\int 1\cdot\left(\frac{\sin 2\theta}{2}\right)d\theta\right)\right\}$$

$$=-3\theta^2+6\left\{\frac{\theta\sin 2\theta}{2}+\frac{\cos 2\theta}{4}\right\}+C$$

$$=\frac{1}{4}\left\{-3\left(\cos^{-1}\left(\frac{x}{3}\right)\right)^2+2\sqrt{9-x^2}\cdot\cos^{-1}\left(\frac{x}{3}\right)+2x\right\}+C$$

Example 47. Find the value of $\int\frac{\sec x(2+\sec x)}{(1+2\sec x)^2}dx$.

Sol. Let $I=\int\frac{\sec x(2+\sec x)}{(1+2\sec x)^2}dx=\int\frac{2\cos x+1}{(\cos x+2)^2}dx$

$$=\int\frac{\cos x(\cos x+2)+\sin^2 x}{(2+\cos x)^2}dx$$

$$=\int\frac{\cos x}{2+\cos x}dx+\int\frac{\sin^2 x}{(2+\cos x)^2}dx$$

$$=\int\underset{\text{II}}{\cos x}\cdot\underset{\text{I}}{\frac{1}{(2+\cos x)}}dx+\int\frac{\sin^2 x}{(2+\cos x)^2}dx$$

Applying integration by parts to first by taking $\cos x$ as second function, keeping $\int\frac{\sin^2 x}{(2+\cos x)^2}dx$ as it is.

$$\therefore\quad I=\frac{1}{2+\cos x}\cdot(\sin x)-\int\sin x\cdot\frac{\sin x}{(2+\cos x)^2}dx+\int\frac{\sin^2 x}{(2+\cos x)^2}dx$$

$$\therefore\quad I=\frac{\sin x}{2+\cos x}+C$$

JEE SCANNER

Example Similar to PYQ Asked in JEE Main 2023

The integral $\int\frac{x^2(x\sec^2 x+\tan x)\,dx}{(x\tan x+1)^2}$ *is equal to*

(a) $\frac{x^2}{x\tan x+1}+2\log|x\sin x+\cos x|+C$

(b) $\frac{x^2}{x\tan x+1}-2\log|x\sin x+\cos x|+C$

(c) $-\frac{x^2}{x\tan x+1}+2\log|x\sin x+\cos x|+C$

(d) $-\frac{x^2}{x\tan x+1}-2\log|x\sin x+\cos x|+C$

Sol. (c) Here, $I=\int x^2\cdot\frac{x\sec^2 x+\tan x}{(x\tan x+1)^2}dx$

$$=x^2\left(-\frac{1}{(x\tan x+1)}\right)-\int 2x\cdot\left(-\frac{1}{(x\tan x+1)}\right)dx+C\quad\text{...(i)}$$

$$\left[\text{using }\int\frac{x\sec^2 x+\tan x}{(x\tan x+1)^2}dx=\int\frac{dt}{t^2}=-\frac{1}{t}=-\frac{1}{(x\tan x+1)}\right]$$

$$\Rightarrow I=-\left(\frac{x^2}{x\tan x+1}\right)+\int\frac{2x(\cos x)}{x\sin x+\cos x}dx+C$$

[put, $x\sin x+\cos x=u$

$\Rightarrow(x\cos x+\sin x-\sin x)\,dx=du$]

$$=-\frac{x^2}{(x\tan x+1)}+2\int\frac{du}{u}+C$$

$$=-\frac{x^2}{x\tan x+1}+2\log|u|+C$$

$$=-\frac{x^2}{x\tan x+1}+2\log|x\sin x+\cos x|+C$$

Skill Builder

The integral $\int\frac{x^2[(-x\operatorname{cosec}^2 x)+\cot x]}{(x\cot x-1)^2}dx$ is equal to

(a) $-\left(\frac{x^2}{x\cot x-1}\right)-2\log|x\cos x-\sin x|+C$

(b) $-\left(\frac{x^2}{x\cot x-1}\right)+2\log|x\cos x-\sin x|+C$

(c) $\left(\frac{x^2}{x\cot x-1}\right)-2\log|x\cos x-\sin x|+C$

(d) $\left(\frac{x^2}{x\cot x-1}\right)+2\log|x\cos x-\sin x|+C$

For Sol.

■ **For more practice** See Q.21 of Milestone Practice 1.4.

Integral of Form $\int e^x\{f(x)+f'(x)\}dx$

Theorem Prove that

$$\int e^x\{f(x)+f'(x)\}\,dx = e^x f(x)+C$$

Proof We have, $\int e^x\{f(x)+f'(x)\}\,dx$

$$= \int \underset{\text{II}}{e^x}\cdot f(x)\,dx + \int e^x\cdot \underset{\text{I}}{f'(x)}\,dx$$

$$= f(x)\cdot e^x - \int f'(x)\cdot e^x dx + \int e^x\cdot f'(x)\,dx + C$$

$$= f(x)\cdot e^x + C$$

Thus, to evaluate the integrals of the type $\int e^x\{f(x)+f'(x)\}\,dx$, we first express the integral as the sum of two integrals $\int e^x f(x)\,dx$ and $\int e^x f'(x)\,dx$ and then integrate the integral involving $e^x f(x)$ as integral by parts taking e^x as second function.

JEE SPIKE

The above theorem is also true, if we have e^{kx} in place of e^x

i.e. $\int e^{kx}\{f(kx)+f'(kx)\}\,dx = e^{kx} f(kx)+C$

General Concept

$$\int e^{g(x)}\{f(x)g'(x)+f'(x)\}\,dx$$

Proof $I = \int \underbrace{e^{g(x)}}_{\text{II}}\underbrace{f(x)}_{\text{I}}\underbrace{g'(x)}_{\text{II}}\,dx + \underbrace{\int e^{g(x)} f'(x)\,dx}_{\text{as it is}}$

Using $\int e^{g(x)}\cdot g'(x)\,dx = e^{g(x)}$, we get

$$= f(x)\cdot e^{g(x)} - \int f'(x)\cdot e^{g(x)}dx + \int e^{g(x)}\cdot f'(x)\,dx$$

$$= f(x)\cdot e^{g(x)} + C$$

Example 48. Evaluate $\int e^x\left(\dfrac{1+\sin x\cos x}{\cos^2 x}\right)dx$.

Sol. $$I = \int e^x\left(\frac{1+\sin x\cos x}{\cos^2 x}\right)dx$$

$$= \int e^x\left\{\frac{1}{\cos^2 x}+\frac{\sin x\cos x}{\cos^2 x}\right\}dx$$

$$= \int e^x\{\tan x+\sec^2 x\}\,dx$$

$$= \int \underset{\text{II}}{e^x}\cdot \underset{\text{I}}{\tan x}\,dx + \int e^x(\sec^2 x)\,dx$$

$$= \tan x\cdot e^x - \int \sec^2 x\cdot e^x\,dx + \int e^x\cdot\sec^2 x\,dx + C$$

$$= e^x\tan x + C$$

JEE SCANNER

Example Similar to PYQ Asked in JEE Main 2022

The integral $\int e^x\left(\dfrac{1-x}{1+x^2}\right)^2 dx$ *is equal to*

(a) $\dfrac{e^x}{1+x^2}+C$ (b) $\dfrac{e^{2x}}{1+x^2}+C$

(c) $\dfrac{-e^x}{1+x^2}+C$ (d) $\dfrac{e^x}{1-x^2}+C$

Sol. (a) $I = \int e^x\left(\dfrac{1-x}{1+x^2}\right)^2 dx = \int e^x\dfrac{(1-2x+x^2)}{(1+x^2)^2}dx$

$$= \int e^x\left\{\frac{1+x^2}{(1+x^2)^2}-\frac{2x}{(1+x^2)^2}\right\}dx$$

$$= \int e^x\left\{\frac{1}{1+x^2}-\frac{2x}{(1+x^2)^2}\right\}dx$$

$$\therefore\ I = \frac{e^x}{1+x^2}+C \qquad \left[\text{as } \frac{d}{dx}\left(\frac{1}{1+x^2}\right) = -\frac{2x}{(1+x^2)^2}\right]$$

Skill Builder

The integral $\int e^{\sin^2 x}(\cos x\sin 2x-\sin x)\,dx$ is equal to

For Sol.

(a) $e^{\sin x}\cos^2 x+C$ (b) $e^{\sin^2 x}\cos x+C$

(c) $e^{\sin x}\cos x+C$ (d) $e^{\cos^2 x}\sin x+C$

■ **For more practice** See Q.22 of Milestone Practice 1.4.

Example 49. Find the value of $\int e^x\left(\dfrac{x^4+2}{(1+x^2)^{5/2}}\right)dx$.

Sol. Let $I = \int e^x\left(\dfrac{x^4+2}{(1+x^2)^{5/2}}\right)dx$

$$= \int e^x\left(\frac{1}{(1+x^2)^{1/2}}+\frac{1-2x^2}{(1+x^2)^{5/2}}\right)dx$$

$$= \int e^x\left(\frac{1}{(1+x^2)^{1/2}}-\frac{x}{(1+x^2)^{3/2}}+\frac{x}{(1+x^2)^{3/2}}+\frac{1-2x^2}{(1+x^2)^{5/2}}\right)dx$$

$$= \frac{e^x}{(1+x^2)^{1/2}}+\frac{xe^x}{(1+x^2)^{3/2}}+C$$

$$= \frac{e^x\{1+x^2+x\}}{(1+x^2)^{3/2}}+C$$

Example 50. Find the value of

$$\int e^{(x\sin x+\cos x)}\cdot\left(\frac{x^4\cos^3 x - x\sin x+\cos x}{x^2\cos^2 x}\right)dx.$$

Sol. Let $I = \int e^{(x \sin x + \cos x)} \cdot \left(\frac{x^4 \cos^3 x - x \sin x + \cos x}{x^2 \cos^2 x} \right) dx$

$$= \int (x \cdot e^{(x \sin x + \cos x)} \cdot x \cos x)\, dx - \int e^{(x \sin x + \cos x)} \cdot \left(\frac{x \sin x - \cos x}{(x \cos x)^2} \right) dx$$

Applying integration by parts

$$= \{x \cdot e^{(x \sin x + \cos x)} - \int e^{(x \sin x + \cos x)}\, dx\} - \left\{ e^{(x \sin x + \cos x)} \cdot \frac{1}{x \cos x} - \int e^{(x \sin x + \cos x)}\, dx \right\}$$

$$= e^{(x \sin x + \cos x)} \left(x - \frac{1}{x \cos x} \right) + C$$

Integrals of the Form $\int e^{ax} \sin bx\, dx, \int e^{ax} \cos bx\, dx$

Let $\quad I = \int e^{ax} (\sin bx)\, dx$

Then, $I = \int \underset{\text{I}}{\sin bx} \cdot \underset{\text{II}}{e^{ax}}\, dx$

$$= \sin bx \cdot \left(\frac{e^{ax}}{a} \right) - \int b \cos bx \cdot \frac{e^{ax}}{a}\, dx$$

$$= \frac{1}{a} \sin bx \cdot e^{ax} - \frac{b}{a} \left\{ \cos bx \cdot \frac{e^{ax}}{a} - \int (-b \sin bx) \cdot \frac{e^{ax}}{a}\, dx \right\}$$

$$= \frac{1}{a} \sin bx \cdot e^{ax} - \frac{b}{a^2} \cos bx \cdot e^{ax} - \frac{b^2}{a^2} \int \sin bx \cdot e^{ax}\, dx$$

$$I = \frac{1}{a} \sin bx \cdot e^{ax} - \frac{b}{a^2} \cos bx \cdot e^{ax} - \frac{b^2}{a^2} I$$

$$\therefore \quad I + \frac{b^2}{a^2} I = \frac{1 \cdot e^{ax}}{a^2} \cdot (a \sin bx - b \cos bx)$$

$$\Rightarrow \quad I \left(\frac{a^2 + b^2}{a^2} \right) = \frac{e^{ax}}{a^2} (a \sin bx - b \cos bx)$$

or $\quad I = \frac{e^{ax}}{a^2 + b^2} (a \sin bx - b \cos bx) + C$

Thus, $\int e^{ax} \sin bx\, dx = \frac{e^{ax}}{a^2 + b^2} (a \sin bx - b \cos bx) + C$

Similarly, $\int e^{ax} \cos bx\, dx = \frac{e^{ax}}{a^2 + b^2} (a \cos bx + b \sin bx) + C$

Alternate Solution

Use Euler's equation

Let $P = \int e^{ax} \cos bx\, dx$ and $Q = \int e^{ax} \sin bx\, dx$

Hence, $P + iQ = \int e^{ax} \cdot e^{ibx}\, dx = \int e^{(a + ib)x}\, dx$

$$P + iQ = \frac{1}{a + ib} e^{(a + ib)x} = \frac{a - ib}{a^2 + b^2} e^{ax} (\cos bx + i \sin bx)$$

$$= \frac{(ae^{ax} \cos bx + be^{ax} \sin bx) - i\,(ae^{ax} \sin bx - be^{ax} \cos bx)}{a^2 + b^2}$$

$$\therefore \quad P = \frac{e^{ax} (a \cos bx + b \sin bx)}{a^2 + b^2},\ Q = \frac{e^{ax} (a \sin bx - b \cos bx)}{a^2 + b^2}$$

Example 51. Evaluate

(i) $\int e^{3x} (\sin 2x)\, dx$ $\qquad$ (ii) $\int e^{2x} \cos 5x\, dx$

Sol. (i) Let $I = \int \underset{\text{I}}{\sin 2x} \cdot \underset{\text{II}}{e^{3x}}\, dx$

$$= \sin 2x \left(\frac{e^{3x}}{3} \right) - \int 2 \cos 2x \cdot \frac{e^{3x}}{3}\, dx$$

$$= \frac{1}{3} \sin 2x \cdot e^{3x} - \frac{2}{3} \left\{ \cos 2x \frac{e^{3x}}{3} - \int (-2 \sin 2x) \frac{e^{3x}}{3}\, dx \right\}$$

$$= \frac{1}{3} \sin 2x \cdot e^{3x} - \frac{2}{9} \cos 2x \cdot e^{3x} - \frac{4}{9} \int \sin 2x \cdot e^{3x}\, dx$$

$$\Rightarrow I = \frac{1}{3} \sin 2x \cdot e^{3x} - \frac{2}{9} \cos 2x \cdot e^{3x} - \frac{4}{9} I$$

$$\Rightarrow \quad I + \frac{4}{9} I = \frac{1}{3} \sin 2x \cdot e^{3x} - \frac{2}{9} \cos 2x \cdot e^{3x}$$

$$\Rightarrow \quad \frac{13}{9} I = \frac{e^{3x}}{9} (3 \sin 2x - 2 \cos 2x)$$

$$\therefore \quad I = \frac{e^{3x}}{13} (3 \sin 2x - 2 \cos 2x) + C$$

(ii) Let $I = \int \underset{\text{I}}{\cos 5x} \cdot \underset{\text{II}}{e^{2x}}\, dx$

$$= \cos 5x \left(\frac{e^{2x}}{2} \right) - \int (-5 \sin 5x) \cdot \frac{e^{2x}}{2}\, dx$$

$$= \frac{1}{2} \cos 5x \cdot e^{2x} + \frac{5}{2} \int \sin 5x \cdot e^{2x}\, dx$$

$$= \frac{1}{2} \cos 5x \cdot e^{2x} + \frac{5}{2} \left\{ \sin 5x \cdot \frac{e^{2x}}{2} - \int 5 \cos 5x \cdot \frac{e^{2x}}{2}\, dx \right\}$$

$$= \frac{1}{2} \cos 5x \cdot e^{2x} + \frac{5}{4} \sin 5x \cdot e^{2x} - \frac{25}{4} \int \cos 5x \cdot e^{2x}\, dx$$

$$\Rightarrow \quad I = \frac{1}{2} \cos 5x \cdot e^{2x} + \frac{5}{4} \sin 5x \cdot e^{2x} - \frac{25}{4} I$$

$$\Rightarrow \quad \frac{29}{4} I = \frac{1}{4} (2 \cos 5x \cdot e^{2x} + 5 \sin 5x \cdot e^{2x}) + C$$

$$\therefore \quad I = \frac{e^{2x}}{29} (2 \cos 5x + 5 \sin 5x) + C$$

1.7 Some More Special Types of Integrals

Here, we will discuss some more special types of integrals, which can be proved by using integration by parts and directly used to evaluate the given integrals.

(i) $\int \sqrt{x^2 - a^2}\, dx = \frac{x}{2} \sqrt{x^2 - a^2} - \frac{a^2}{2} \log |x + \sqrt{x^2 - a^2}| + C$

(ii) $\int \sqrt{x^2+a^2}\, dx = \frac{x}{2}\sqrt{x^2+a^2} + \frac{a^2}{2}\log|x+\sqrt{x^2+a^2}| + C$

(iii) $\int \sqrt{a^2-x^2}\, dx = \frac{x}{2}\sqrt{a^2-x^2} + \frac{a^2}{2}\sin^{-1}\frac{x}{a} + C$

Proof

(i) Let $I = \int \underset{\text{I}}{\sqrt{x^2-a^2}} \times \underset{\text{II}}{1}\, dx$ ...(i)

$$= \sqrt{x^2-a^2}\int 1dx - \int\left[\frac{d}{dx}(\sqrt{x^2-a^2})\int 1dx\right]dx$$

$$\left[\because \int \underset{\text{I}}{u}\cdot\underset{\text{II}}{v}\, dx = u\int v dx - \int\left(\frac{d}{dx}(u)\int v dx\right)dx\right]$$

$$= \sqrt{x^2-a^2}\times x - \int\left[\frac{1}{2\sqrt{x^2-a^2}}\times 2x\right]x\, dx$$

$$= x\sqrt{x^2-a^2} - \int \frac{x^2}{\sqrt{x^2-a^2}}dx$$

$$= x\sqrt{x^2-a^2} - \int \frac{x^2-a^2+a^2}{\sqrt{x^2-a^2}}dx$$

[adding and subtracting a^2]

$$= x\sqrt{x^2-a^2} - \int\sqrt{x^2-a^2}\,dx - \int\frac{a^2 dx}{\sqrt{x^2-a^2}}$$

$$\Rightarrow I = x\sqrt{x^2-a^2} - I - a^2\int\frac{1\,dx}{\sqrt{x^2-a^2}}$$

$$\Rightarrow 2I = x\sqrt{x^2-a^2} - a^2[\log|x+\sqrt{x^2-a^2}|]$$

$$\left[\because \int\frac{1}{\sqrt{x^2-a^2}}dx = \log|x+\sqrt{x^2-a^2}|\right]$$

$$\Rightarrow I = \frac{x}{2}\sqrt{x^2-a^2} - \frac{a^2}{2}[\log|x+\sqrt{x^2-a^2}|] + C$$

Similarly, we can prove other formulae given above.

Example 52. Evaluate

(i) $\int\sqrt{1-4\tan^2 x}\sec^2 x\,dx$

(ii) $\int\frac{\sqrt{9(\log x)^2+4}}{x}dx$

Sol. (i) Let $I = \int\sqrt{1-4\tan^2 x}\sec^2 x\,dx$

Put $2\tan x = t \Rightarrow 2\sec^2 x dx = dt$

$$\therefore\quad I = \frac{1}{2}\int\sqrt{1-t^2}\,dt = \frac{1}{2}\left[\frac{t}{2}\sqrt{1-t^2}+\frac{1}{2}\sin^{-1}t\right]+C$$

$$= \frac{1}{2}\left[\frac{2\tan x}{2}\sqrt{1-4\tan^2 x}+\frac{1}{2}\sin^{-1}(2\tan x)+C\right]$$

$$= \left[\frac{1}{2}\tan x\sqrt{1-4\tan^2 x}+\frac{1}{4}\sin^{-1}(2\tan x)+C\right]$$

(ii) Let $I = \int\frac{\sqrt{9(\log x)^2+4}}{x}dx$

Put $3\log x = t \Rightarrow \frac{3}{x}dx = dt$

$$\therefore\quad I = \frac{1}{3}\int\sqrt{t^2+4}\,dt$$

$$= \frac{1}{3}\left[\frac{t}{2}\sqrt{t^2+4}+\frac{4}{2}\log|t+\sqrt{t^2+4}|+C\right]$$

$$= \frac{1}{3}\left[\frac{3\log x\sqrt{9(\log x)^2+4}}{2} + 2\log|3\log x+\sqrt{9(\log x)^2+4}|\right]+C$$

$$= \frac{1}{2}\log x\sqrt{9(\log x)^2+4}+\frac{2}{3}\log|3\log x + \sqrt{9(\log x)^2+4}|+C$$

Integrals of Type $\int\sqrt{ax^2+bx+c}\,dx$

To evaluate this type of integral, we use following steps

I. Firstly, take a common from integrand to make coefficient of x^2 unity

i.e. $I = \int\sqrt{a\left(x^2+\frac{b}{a}x+\frac{c}{a}\right)}\,dx$

II. Add and subtract $\left(\frac{b}{2a}\right)^2$ from integrand inside the square root and convert it in the form $\sqrt{X^2\pm k^2}$ or $\sqrt{k^2-X^2}$

where, $X^2 = \left(x\pm\frac{b}{2a}\right)^2$ and $k^2 = \left(\frac{c}{a}\mp\frac{b^2}{4a^2}\right)$.

III. Substitute $x\pm\frac{b}{2a} = t$ and reduce the integral obtained from Step II into one of the form

$$\int\sqrt{t^2\pm k^2}\,dt \text{ or } \int\sqrt{k^2-t^2}\,dt$$

Then, apply suitable formula to integrate.

Example 53. Evaluate $\int \sqrt{2x^2 - 3x + 1}\, dx$

Sol. $I = \int (\sqrt{2x^2 - 3x + 1})\, dx$

$$= \sqrt{2} \int (\sqrt{x^2 - 3x/2 + 1/2})\, dx$$

$$= \sqrt{2} \int (\sqrt{x^2 - 3x/2 + 9/16 - 9/16 + 1/2})\, dx$$

$$= \sqrt{2} \int (\sqrt{(x - 3/4)^2 - 1/16})\, dx$$

$$= \sqrt{2} \left\{ \begin{array}{l} \frac{1}{2}(x - 3/4)\sqrt{(x - 3/4)^2 - 1/16} \\ - \frac{1}{16 \times 2} \log |(x - 3/4) + \sqrt{(x - 3/4)^2 - 1/16}| \end{array} \right\} + C$$

$$= \sqrt{2} \left\{ \begin{array}{l} \frac{1}{8}(4x - 3)\sqrt{x^2 - 3x/2 + 1/2} \\ - \frac{1}{32} \log |(x - 3/4) + \sqrt{x^2 - 3x/2 + 1/2}| \end{array} \right\} + C$$

Integral of Type $\int (px + q)\sqrt{ax^2 + bx + c}\, dx$

To evaluate such integrals, we firstly write $(px + q)$ as

$$px + q = A \frac{d}{dx}(ax^2 + bx + c) + B$$

$$= A(2ax + b) + B.$$

Then, find A and B by comparing the coefficient of like powers of x from both sides.

Now, put this value of $(px + q)$ in the given integral and then given integral is reduce to one of the known forms which can be integrate easily.

Example 54. Evaluate $\int (x + 1)\sqrt{1 - x - x^2}\, dx.$

Sol. Let $I = \int (x + 1)\sqrt{1 - x - x^2}\, dx$

Put $(x + 1) = \lambda \cdot \left(\frac{d}{dx}(1 - x - x^2)\right) + \mu$

Then, $(x + 1) = \lambda(-1 - 2x) + \mu$ comparing the coefficients of like powers of x, we get

$$-2\lambda = 1 \text{ and } \mu - \lambda = 1$$

$$\Rightarrow \quad \lambda = -1/2 \text{ and } \mu = 1/2.$$

$$\therefore \quad (x + 1) = -\frac{1}{2}(-1 - 2x) + \frac{1}{2}$$

So, $\int (x + 1)\sqrt{1 - x - x^2}\, dx = \int \left\{-\frac{1}{2}(-1 - 2x) + \frac{1}{2}\right\} \sqrt{1 - x - x^2}\, dx$

$$= -\frac{1}{2}\int (-1 - 2x)\sqrt{1 - x - x^2}\, dx + \frac{1}{2}\int \sqrt{1 - x - x^2}\, dx$$

$$= -\frac{1}{2}\int (-1 - 2x)\sqrt{1 - x - x^2}\, dx + \frac{1}{2}\int \sqrt{\left\{1 - \left(x^2 + x + \frac{1}{4} - \frac{1}{4}\right)\right\}}\, dx$$

$$= -\frac{1}{2}\int \sqrt{t}\, dt + \frac{1}{2}\int \sqrt{(\sqrt{5}/2)^2 - (x + 1/2)^2}\, dx$$

[where, $t = 1 + x - x^2$]

$$= -\frac{1}{2}\left(\frac{t^{3/2}}{3/2}\right) + \frac{1}{2}\left\{\frac{1}{2}\left(x + \frac{1}{2}\right)\sqrt{1 - x - x^2} + \frac{1}{2} \cdot \frac{5}{4} \sin^{-1}\left(\frac{x + 1/2}{\sqrt{5}/2}\right)\right\} + C$$

$$= -\frac{1}{3}(1 - x - x^2)^{3/2} + \frac{1}{8}(2x + 1)\sqrt{1 - x - x^2} + \frac{5}{16}\sin^{-1}\left(\frac{2x + 1}{\sqrt{5}}\right) + C$$

Milestone Practice 1.4

Evaluate the following.

1. $\int x^3 \cdot e^x dx$
2. $\int x^2 \sin x\, dx$
3. $\int \cos\sqrt{x}\, dx$
4. $\int (\log x)^2 dx$
5. $\int (\tan^{-1} x)\, dx$
6. $\int (\sec^{-1} x)\, dx$
7. $\int x\tan^{-1} x\, dx$
8. $\int \frac{\log x}{x^2} dx$
9. $\int \frac{x - \sin x}{1 - \cos x} dx$
10. $\int \ln(x + \sqrt{x^2 + a^2})\, dx$
11. $\int e^{\cos^{-1} x} \cdot \frac{(x+1) + \sqrt{1 - x^2}}{(x+1)^2 \sqrt{1 - x^2}} dx$
12. $\int e^x \left\{\frac{1 + \sin x \cos x}{\cos^2 x}\right\} dx$
13. $\int \left(\log(\log x) + \frac{1}{(\log x)^2}\right) dx$
14. $\int \frac{e^x \cdot (2 - x^2)}{(1 - x)\sqrt{1 - x^2}} dx$
15. $\int e^{ax} \cdot \cos(bx + c)\, dx$
16. $\int \sec^3 x\, dx$
17. $\int (\sin^{-1} x)^2 dx$
18. $\int \cot^{-1}(1 - x + x^2)\, dx$
19. $\int \sin^{-1}\sqrt{\frac{x}{a + x}}\, dx$
20. $\int \frac{\sqrt{x^2 + 1}\{\log(x^2 + 1) - 2\log x\}}{x^4} dx$
21. $\int \frac{\cos^2 x + \sin 2x}{(2\cos x - \sin x)^2} dx$
22. $\int e^{\sin x}\left(\frac{x\cos^3 x - \sin x}{\cos^2 x}\right) dx$
23. $\int \frac{x^2 + n(n - 1)}{(x\sin x + n\cos x)^2} dx$

Answer Key

1. $e^x(x^3 - 3x^2 + 6x - 6) + C$
2. $-x^2 \cos x + 2(x\sin x + \cos x) + C$
3. $2\sqrt{x}\sin\sqrt{x} + 2\cos\sqrt{x} + C$
4. $x(\log x)^2 - 2x\log x + 2x + C$
5. $x\tan^{-1} x - \frac{1}{2}\log|1 + x^2| + C$
6. $x\sec^{-1} x - \log|x + \sqrt{x^2 - 1}| + C$
7. $\frac{x^2}{2}\tan^{-1} x - \frac{1}{2}(x - \tan^{-1} x) + C$
8. $-\frac{1}{x}(1 + \log x) + C$
9. $-x\cot\frac{x}{2} + C$
10. $x\ln(x + \sqrt{x^2 + a^2}) - \sqrt{x^2 + a^2} + C$
11. $-\frac{e^{\cos^{-1} x}}{1 + x} + C$
12. $e^x \tan x + C$
13. $x\log(\log x) - \frac{x}{\log x} + C$
14. $e^x\sqrt{\frac{1 + x}{1 - x}} + C$
15. $\frac{e^{ax}}{a^2 + b^2}[a\cos(bx + c) + b\sin(bx + c)] + C$
16. $\frac{1}{2}\sec x \cdot \tan x + \frac{1}{2}\ln|\sec x + \tan x| + C$
17. $x(\sin^{-1} x)^2 + 2\sqrt{1 - x^2}\sin^{-1} x - 2x + C$
18. $x\cot^{-1}(1 - x + x^2) - \tan^{-1}(1 - x) - \frac{1}{2}\log(1 + x^2) - \frac{1}{2}\log(x^2 - 2x + 2) + C$
19. $x\sin^{-1}\sqrt{\frac{x}{a + x}} - \sqrt{a}\left(\sqrt{x} - \sqrt{a}\tan^{-1}\sqrt{\frac{x}{a}}\right) + C$
20. $-\frac{1}{3}\left(1 + \frac{1}{x^2}\right)^{3/2}\log\left(1 + \frac{1}{x^2}\right) + \frac{2}{9}\left(1 + \frac{1}{x^2}\right)^{3/2} + C$
21. $\frac{\cos x}{2\cos x - \sin x} - \frac{x}{5} - \frac{2}{5}\log|2\cos x - \sin x| + C$
22. $e^{\sin x}(x - \sec x) + C$
23. $\frac{-x\sec x}{x\sin x + n\cos x} + \tan x + C$

For Detailed Solution

Milestone 5 Integration Using Partial Fraction

This section deals with the integration of general algebraic rational functions, of the form $\frac{f(x)}{g(x)}$, where $f(x)$ and $g(x)$ are both polynomials. We already have seen some examples of this form. For example, we know how to integrate functions of the form $\frac{1}{Q(x)}$ or $\frac{L(x)}{Q(x)}$ or $\frac{P(x)}{Q(x)}$ where $L(x)$ is a linear factor, $Q(x)$ is a quadratic factor and $P(x)$ is a polynomial of degree $n \geq 2$. We intend to generalise that previous discussion in this section.

We are assuming the scenario where $g(x)$ (the denominator) is decomposible into linear or quadratic factors. These are the only cases relevant to us right now. Any linear or quadratic factor in $g(x)$ might also occur repeatedly.

Thus, $g(x)$ could be of the following general forms.

- $g(x) = L_1(x)L_2(x)\ldots L_n(x)$ (n linear factors)
- $g(x) = L_1(x)\ldots L_r^k(x)\ldots L_n(x)$ (n linear factors; the rth factor is repeated k times)
- $g(x) = L_1^{k_1}(x)L_2^{k_2}(x)\ldots L_n^{k_n}(x)$ (n linear factors, the ith factor is repeated k_i times)
- $g(x) = L_1(x)L_2(x)\ldots L_n(x)Q(x)Q_2(x)\ldots Q_m(x)$ (n linear factors and m quadratic factors)
- $g(x) = \ldots Q_r^k(x)\ldots$ (a particular quadratic factor repeats more than once)
- A combination of any of the above

Suppose that the degree of $g(x)$ is n and that of $f(x)$ is m. If $m \geq n$, we can always divide $f(x)$ by $g(x)$ to obtain a quotient $q(x)$ and a remainder $r(x)$ whose degree would be less than n.

$$\frac{f(x)}{g(x)} = q(x) + \frac{r(x)}{g(x)} \qquad \ldots\text{(i)}$$

If $m < n$, $\frac{f(x)}{g(x)}$ is termed a proper rational function.

The partial fraction expansion technique says that a proper rational function can be expressed as a sum of simpler rational functions each possessing one of the factors of $g(x)$. The simpler rational functions are called partial fractions.

From now on, we consider only proper rational functions. If $\frac{f(x)}{g(x)}$ is not proper, we make it proper $\left(\frac{r(x)}{g(x)}\right)$ by the procedure described in (1) above. Let us consider a few examples.

Case I

Let $g(x)$ be a product of non-repeated, linear factors :

$$g(x) = L_1(x)L_2(x)\ldots L_n(x)$$

Then, we can expand $\frac{f(x)}{g(x)}$ in terms of partial fractions as

$$\frac{f(x)}{g(x)} = \frac{A_1}{L_1(x)} + \frac{A_2}{L_2(x)} + \ldots + \frac{A_n}{L_n(x)}$$

where the $A_i's$ are all constants that need to be determined.

Suppose $f(x) = x + 1$ and $g(x) = (x-1)(x-2)(x-3)$. Let us write down the partial fraction expansion of $\frac{f(x)}{g(x)}$:

$$\frac{f(x)}{g(x)} = \frac{x+1}{(x-1)(x-2)(x-3)} = \frac{A}{x-1} + \frac{B}{x-2} + \frac{C}{x-3}$$

We need to determine A, B and C. Cross multiplying in the expression above, we obtain :

$$(x+1) = A(x-2)(x-3) + B(x-1)(x-3) + C(x-1)(x-2)$$

A, B, C can now be determined by comparing coefficients on both sides.

More simply since this relation that we have obtained should held true for all x,we substitute those values of x that would straight way give us the required values of A, B and C. These values are obviously the roots of $g(x)$.

$x = 1 \Rightarrow 2 = A(-1)(-2) + B(0) + C(0)$
$\Rightarrow A = 1$

$x = 2 \Rightarrow 3 = A(0) + B(1)(-1) + C(0)$
$\Rightarrow B = -3$

$x = 3 \Rightarrow 4 = A(0) + B(0) + C(2)(1)$
$\Rightarrow C = 2$

Thus, $A = 1$, $B = -3$ and $C = 2$.

We can therefore write $\dfrac{f(x)}{g(x)}$ as a sum of partial fractions.

$$\frac{f(x)}{g(x)} = \frac{1}{x-1} - \frac{3}{x-2} + \frac{2}{x-3}$$

Integrating $\dfrac{f(x)}{g(x)}$ is now a simple matter of integrating the partial fractions. This was our sole motive in writing such an expansion, so that integration could be carried out easily. In the example above :

$$\int \frac{f(x)}{g(x)}\,dx = \ln(x-1) - 3\ln(x-2) + 2\ln(x-3) + C$$

Now, suppose that $g(x)$ contains all linear factors, but a particular factor, say $L_1(x)$, is repeated k times.

Thus, $\quad g(x) = L_1^k(x) L_2(x) \dots L_n(x)$

$\dfrac{f(x)}{g(x)}$ can now be expanded into partial fractions as follows

$$\frac{f(x)}{g(x)} = \underbrace{\frac{A_1}{L_1(x)} + \frac{A_2}{L_1^2(x)} + \frac{A_3}{L_1^3(x)} + \dots + \frac{A_k}{L_1^k(x)}}_{k \text{ partial fractions corresponding to } L_1(x)} + \frac{B_2}{L_2(x)} + \dots + \frac{B_n}{L_n(x)}$$

This means that we will have k terms corresponding to $L_1(x)$. The rest of the linear factors will have single corresponding terms in the expansion. Here are some examples.

$\dfrac{1}{(x-1)^2(x-2)}$ can be expanded as

$$\frac{A}{x-1} + \frac{B}{(x-1)^2} + \frac{C}{x-2}$$

$\dfrac{1}{(x-1)^3(x-2)(x-3)}$ can be expanded as

$$\frac{A}{x-1} + \frac{B}{(x-1)^2} + \frac{C}{(x-1)^3} + \frac{D}{(x-2)} + \frac{C}{(x-3)}$$

$\dfrac{1}{(x-1)^2(x+5)^3}$ can be expanded as

$$\frac{A}{x-1} + \frac{B}{(x-1)^2} + \frac{C}{(x+5)} + \frac{D}{(x+5)^2} + \frac{E}{(x+5)^3}$$

Example 55. $\dfrac{2x+1}{(x+1)(x-2)}$ into partial fractions

Sol. Here, $\dfrac{2x+1}{(x+1)(x-2)}$ has $Q(x) = (x+1)(x-2)$ i.e linear and non-repeated roots.

$$\therefore \quad \frac{2x+1}{(x+1)(x-2)} = \frac{A}{x+1} + \frac{B}{x-2}$$

$$\Rightarrow \quad (2x+1) = A(x-2) + B(x+1)$$

On putting, $x = 2$ we get

$$5 = A(0) + B(3)$$

$$\Rightarrow \quad B = \frac{5}{3}$$

Again, let $\quad x = -1$

$$\Rightarrow \quad 2(-1) + 1 = A(-1-2) + B(0)$$

$$\therefore \quad A = \frac{1}{3}$$

$$\therefore \quad \frac{2x+1}{(x+1)(x-2)} = \frac{1/3}{x+1} + \frac{5/3}{x-2}$$

Example 56. Resolve $\dfrac{1}{(x-1)(x+2)(2x+3)}$ into partial fractions.

Sol. Let $\dfrac{1}{(x-1)(x+2)(2x+3)} = \dfrac{A}{x-1} + \dfrac{B}{x+2} + \dfrac{C}{2x+3}$,

where A, B and C are constants.

$$1 = A(x+2)(2x+3) + B(x-1)(2x+3) + C(x-1)(x+2) \quad \dots(i)$$

For finding A, let $x - 1 = 0$ or $x = 1$ in Eq. (i), we get

$$1 = A(1+2)(2+3) + B(0) + C(0)$$

$$\therefore \quad A = \frac{1}{15}$$

Similarly, for getting B, let $x + 2 = 0$ or $x = -2$ in Eq. (i), we get

$$1 = A(0) + B(-2-1)(-4+3) + C(0)$$

$$\Rightarrow \quad B = \frac{1}{3}$$

For getting C, let $2x + 3 = 0$ or $x = -3/2$ in Eq. (i), we get

$$1 = A(0) + B(0) + C\left(-\frac{3}{2} - 1\right)\left(-\frac{3}{2} + 2\right)$$

$$\Rightarrow \quad C = -\frac{4}{5}$$

Hence, $\dfrac{1}{(x-1)(x+2)(2x+3)} = \dfrac{1}{15(x-1)} + \dfrac{1}{3(x+2)} - \dfrac{4}{5(2x+3)}$

Example 57. Resolve $\dfrac{3x^3 + 2x^2 + x + 1}{(x+1)(x+2)}$ into partial fractions.

> **Decoding the Question**
> The given fraction is not proper fraction as degree of numerator > degree of denominator. So, first convert it into proper fraction, then solve by partial fraction.

Sol. Now, $\quad 3x^3 + 2x^2 + x + 1 = 3x(x^2 + 3x + 2) - 7(x^2 + 3x + 2) + (16x + 15)$

So, the given polynomial

$$\frac{3x^3 + 2x^2 + x + 1}{(x+1)(x+2)} = (3x - 7) + \frac{(16x + 15)}{(x+1)(x+2)} \quad \dots(i)$$

Now, the second term is proper fraction hence it can be expressed as a sum of partial fractions.

$$\frac{16x+15}{(x+1)(x+2)}=\frac{A}{x+1}+\frac{B}{x+2}$$

To find A put $x+1=0$, i.e. $x=-1$ in the fraction except in the factor $(x+1)$.

$$\therefore \quad \frac{16(-1)+15}{(-1+2)}=A \Rightarrow A=-1 \quad \text{...(ii)}$$

To find B put $x+2=0$, i.e. $x=-2$ in the fraction except in the factor $(x+2)$.

$$\therefore \quad \frac{16(-2)+15}{(-2+1)}=B \Rightarrow B=17 \quad \text{...(iii)}$$

$\Rightarrow$ The given expression $=(3x-7)-\dfrac{1}{x+1}+\dfrac{17}{x+2}$

[using Eqs. (i), (ii) and (iii)]

Example 58. Evaluate $\displaystyle\int \frac{1}{\sin x-\sin 2x}dx$.

Sol. Let $I=\displaystyle\int \frac{1}{\sin x-\sin 2x}dx=\int \frac{1}{\sin x-2\sin x\cos x}dx$

$$=\int \frac{1}{\sin x(1-2\cos x)}dx=\int \frac{\sin x}{\sin^2 x(1-2\cos x)}dx$$

$$=\int \frac{\sin x}{(1-\cos^2 x)(1-2\cos x)}dx$$

[put $\cos x=t \Rightarrow -\sin x\,dx=dt$]

$$\therefore \quad I=\int \frac{-dt}{(1-t^2)(1-2t)}=\int \frac{-1}{(1-t)(1+t)(1-2t)}dt \quad \text{...(i)}$$

Here, in Eq. (i) we have linear and non-repeated factors thus we use partial fractions

$$\frac{-1}{(1-t)(1+t)(1-2t)}=\frac{A}{(1-t)}+\frac{B}{(1+t)}+\frac{C}{(1-2t)}$$

or $-1=A(1+t)(1-2t)+B(1-t)(1-2t)+C(1-t)(1+t)$ ...(ii)

Putting $(t+1)=0$ or $t=-1$, we get

$$-1=B(2)(1+2) \Rightarrow B=-\frac{1}{6}$$

Putting $(1-t)=0$ or $t=1$, we get

$$-1=A(2)(-1) \Rightarrow A=\frac{1}{2}$$

Putting $(1-2t)=0$ or $t=1/2$, we get

$$-1=C\left(1-\frac{1}{2}\right)\left(1+\frac{1}{2}\right) \Rightarrow C=-\frac{4}{3}$$

$$\therefore \quad \frac{-1}{(1-t)(1+t)(1-2t)}=\frac{1}{2(1-t)}-\frac{1}{6(1+t)}-\frac{4}{3(1-2t)}$$

So, Eq. (i) reduces to

$$I=\frac{1}{2}\int \frac{1}{1-t}dt-\frac{1}{6}\int \frac{1}{1+t}dt-\frac{4}{3}\int \frac{1}{1-2t}dt$$

$$=-\frac{1}{2}\log|1-t|-\frac{1}{6}\log|1+t|-\frac{4}{3}\times\left(-\frac{1}{2}\right)\log|1-2t|+C$$

$$=-\frac{1}{2}\log|1-\cos x|-\frac{1}{6}\log|1+\cos x|$$

$$+\frac{2}{3}\log|1-2\cos x|+C$$

JEE SCANNER

Example Similar to PYQ Asked in JEE Main 2023

Let $f(x)=\displaystyle\int \frac{e^x dx}{(e^x+1)(e^x+3)}$. *If* $f(0)=\dfrac{1}{2}\log\dfrac{1}{2}$, *then* $f(\log 2)$ *is*

(a) $\dfrac{1}{2}\log\dfrac{5}{3}$ (b) $\dfrac{1}{2}\log\dfrac{1}{4}$

(c) $\dfrac{1}{2}\log\dfrac{3}{5}$ (d) $\dfrac{1}{2}\log\left|\dfrac{e^2+1}{e^2+3}\right|$

Sol. (c) We have, $f(x)=\displaystyle\int \frac{e^x dx}{(e^x+1)(e^x+3)}$

Put $e^x=t \Rightarrow e^x dx=dt$

$$f(x)=\int \frac{dt}{(t+1)(t+3)}$$

Let $\dfrac{1}{(t+1)(t+3)}=\dfrac{A}{t+1}+\dfrac{B}{t+3} \Rightarrow 1=A(t+3)+B(t+1)$

When $t=-1$, then $A=\dfrac{1}{2}$; When $t=-3$, then $B=-\dfrac{1}{2}$

$$\because \quad f(x)=\frac{1}{2}\int \frac{dt}{t+1}-\frac{1}{2}\int \frac{dt}{t+3}$$

$$f(x)=\frac{1}{2}|\log(t+1)-\log(t+3)|+C=\frac{1}{2}\log\left|\frac{t+1}{t+3}\right|+C$$

$$f(x)=\frac{1}{2}\log\left|\frac{e^x+1}{e^x+3}\right|+C$$

Now, $f(0)=\dfrac{1}{2}\log\left|\dfrac{1+1}{1+3}\right|+C$

$$\Rightarrow \quad \frac{1}{2}\log\frac{1}{2}=\frac{1}{2}\log\frac{1}{2}+C$$

$$C=0$$

$$\because \quad f(\log(2))=\frac{1}{2}\log\left|\frac{e^{\log 2}+1}{e^{\log 2}+3}\right|$$

$$=\frac{1}{2}\log\left|\frac{2+1}{2+3}\right|=\frac{1}{2}\log\frac{3}{5}$$

Skill Builder

Let $f(x)=\displaystyle\int \frac{\sec^2 x\,dx}{(\tan x+1)(\tan x+3)}$, if $f(0)=\dfrac{1}{2}\log\left(\dfrac{1}{3}\right)$, then $f\left(\dfrac{\pi}{4}\right)$ is equal to

(a) $\dfrac{1}{2}\log\left(\dfrac{1}{3}\right)$ (b) $\dfrac{1}{2}\log\left(\dfrac{1}{2}\right)$

(c) $\dfrac{1}{2}\log\left(\dfrac{1}{4}\right)$ (d) $\dfrac{1}{2}\log\left(\dfrac{2}{3}\right)$

For Sol.

■ **For more practice** See Q.5 of Milestone Practice 1.5.

Case II

When the denominator $g(x)$ is expressible as the product of the linear factors such that some of them are repeating. (Linear and Repeated)

Let $Q(x)=(x-a)^k (x-a_1)(x-a_2)\ldots(x-a_r)$. Then, we assume that

$$\frac{P(x)}{Q(x)}=\frac{A_1}{(x-a)}+\frac{A_2}{(x-a)^2}+\ldots+\frac{A_k}{(x-a)^k}+\frac{B_1}{(x-a_1)}+\frac{B_2}{(x-a_2)}+\ldots+\frac{B_r}{(x-a_r)}$$

Example 59. Expression $\frac{x+5}{(x-2)^2}$ has repeated (twice) linear factors in denominator, so find partial fractions.

Sol. Let $\frac{x+5}{(x-2)^2}=\frac{A}{(x-2)}+\frac{B}{(x-2)^2}$

$\therefore \quad (x+5)=A(x-2)+B$

Comparing the like terms, $A=1, -2A+B=5$ or $B=7$

$$\therefore \quad \frac{x+5}{(x-2)^2}=\frac{1}{(x-2)}+\frac{7}{(x-2)^2}$$

Example 60. Resolve $\frac{3x-2}{(x-1)^2(x+1)(x+2)}$ into partial fractions.

Sol. Let $\frac{3x-2}{(x-1)^2(x+1)(x+2)}$

$$=\frac{A}{(x-1)}+\frac{B}{(x-1)^2}+\frac{C}{(x+1)}+\frac{D}{(x+2)}$$

$$\therefore\ 3x-2=A(x-1)(x+1)(x+2)+B(x+1)(x+2)+C(x-1)^2(x+2)+D(x-1)^2(x+1)$$

Putting $(x-1)=0$, we get $B=1/6$,

Putting $(x+1)=0$, we get $C=-5/4$

Putting $(x+2)=0$, we get $D=8/9$

Now, equating the coefficient of x^3 on both the sides, we get

$$0=A+C+D \Rightarrow A=\frac{5}{4}-\frac{8}{9}=\frac{13}{36}$$

$$\therefore \quad \frac{3x-2}{(x-1)^2(x+1)(x+2)}=\frac{13}{36(x-1)}+\frac{1}{6(x-1)^2}-\frac{5}{4(x+1)}+\frac{8}{9(x+2)}$$

Case III

When some of the factors in denominator are quadratic but non-repeating. Corresponding to each quadratic factor ax^2+bx+c, we assume the partial fraction of the type $\frac{Ax+B}{ax^2+bx+c}$, where A and B are constants to be determined by comparing coefficients of similar powers of x in numerator of both the sides.

Example 61. Resolve $\frac{2x+7}{(x+1)(x^2+4)}$ into partial fractions.

Sol. Let $\frac{2x+7}{(x+1)(x^2+4)}=\frac{A}{x+1}+\frac{Bx+C}{x^2+4}$

$\therefore \quad 2x+7=A(x^2+4)+(Bx+C)(x+1)$

Put $\quad x=-1$

$\therefore \quad 5=5A$ or $A=1$

Comparing the terms, $0=A+B \Rightarrow B=-1$

$7=4A+C \Rightarrow C=3$

$$\therefore \quad \frac{2x+7}{(x+1)(x^2+4)}=\frac{1}{x+1}+\frac{(-x+3)}{x^2+4}$$

> **Alternate Solution**
>
> To obtain values of A, B and C from
>
> $2x+7=A(x^2+4)+(Bx+C)(x+1)$
>
> i.e. $\quad 2x+7=(A+B)x^2+(B+C)x+4A+C$
>
> Equating the coefficients of identical powers of x, we get
>
> $A+B=0, B+C=2$ and $4A+C=7$.
>
> Solving, we get $A=1, B=-1, C=3$

Example 62. Find the partial fraction

$$\frac{2x+1}{(3x+2)(4x^2+5x+6)}.$$

Sol. Let $\frac{2x+1}{(3x+2)(4x^2+5x+6)}=\frac{A}{(3x+2)}+\frac{Bx+C}{(4x^2+5x+6)}$, then

$2x+1=A(4x^2+5x+6)+(Bx+C)(3x+2)$

where A, B, C are constants.

For A, let $\quad 3x+2=0$,

i.e. $\quad x=-2/3$

$$2\left(-\frac{2}{3}\right)+1=A\left\{4\cdot\frac{4}{9}-\frac{10}{3}+6\right\}+\left\{B\left(-\frac{2}{3}\right)+C\right\}(0)$$

$$-\frac{1}{3}=A\left(\frac{40}{9}\right) \Rightarrow A=-\frac{3}{40}$$

Comparing coefficients of x^2 and constant term on both the sides for B and C, we get

$4A+3B=0$,

$$\therefore \quad B=-\frac{4}{3}A \Rightarrow B=\frac{1}{10}$$

and $\quad 6A+2C=1$

$$\therefore \quad C=\frac{1-6A}{2} \Rightarrow C=\frac{29}{40}$$

$$\therefore \quad \frac{2x+1}{(3x+2)(4x^2+5x+6)}=\frac{-3}{40(3x+2)}+\frac{\left(x+\frac{29}{4}\right)}{10(4x^2+5x+6)}$$

Example 63. Evaluate $\int \frac{(1 - x\sin x)\,dx}{x(1 - x^3 e^{3\cos x})}$.

Sol. Here, $I = \int \frac{(1 - x\sin x)\,dx}{x(1 - (xe^{\cos x})^3)}$

Put $xe^{\cos x} = t$

$\Rightarrow (xe^{\cos x} \cdot (-\sin x) + e^{\cos x})\,dx = dt$

$$\therefore \quad I = \int \frac{dt}{t(1-t^3)}$$

$$= \int \frac{dt}{t(1-t)(1+t+t^2)}$$

$$= \int \left(\frac{A}{t} + \frac{B}{1-t} + \frac{Ct + D}{1+t+t^2}\right) dt$$

Let $\frac{1}{t(t-1)(1+t+t^2)} = \frac{A}{t} + \frac{B}{t-1} + \frac{Ct+D}{1+t+t^2}$

Comparing coefficients, we get

$$A = 1,\ B = \frac{1}{3},\ C = -\frac{2}{3},\ D = -\frac{1}{3}$$

$$\therefore \quad I = \int \frac{dt}{t} + \frac{1}{3}\int \frac{dt}{1-t} + \int \frac{\left(-\frac{2}{3}t - \frac{1}{3}\right)}{1+t+t^2}\,dt$$

$$= \log|t| - \frac{1}{3}\log|1-t| - \frac{1}{3}\log|1+t+t^2| + C$$

[where, $t = xe^{\cos x}$]

Case IV

When some of the factors of the denominator are quadratic and repeating. For every quadratic repeating factor of the type $(ax^2 + bx + c)^k$, we assume :

$$\frac{A_1 x + A_2}{ax^2 + bx + c} + \frac{A_3 x + A_4}{(ax^2 + bx + c)^2} + \ldots + \frac{A_{2k-1}x + A_{2k}}{(ax^2 + bx + c)^k}$$

Example 64. Resolve $\frac{2x^4 + 2x^2 + x + 1}{x(x^2+1)^2}$ into partial fractions.

Sol. Let $\frac{2x^4 + 2x^2 + x + 1}{x(x^2+1)^2} = \frac{A}{x} + \frac{Bx + C}{x^2+1} + \frac{Dx + E}{(x^2+1)^2}$

or $2x^4 + 2x^2 + x + 1 = A(x^2+1)^2 + (Bx + C)x(x^2+1) + (Dx + E)x$

Comparing coefficients of x^4, x^3, x^2, x and constant term

$\therefore \quad A + B = 2, C = 0, 2A + D + B = 2, E + C = 1, A = 1$

$\therefore$ We get $A = 1, B = 1, C = 0, D = -1, E = 1$

Hence, the partial fraction,

$$\frac{2x^4 + 2x^2 + x + 1}{x(x^2+1)^2} = \frac{1}{x} + \frac{x}{1+x^2} + \frac{1-x}{(1+x^2)^2}$$

Example 65. Evaluate the following integrals:

(i) $\int \frac{(1 - x^2)\,dx}{x(1-2x)}$ (ii) $\int \frac{x^2 + x + 1}{x^2(x+2)}\,dx$

Sol. (i) Let $\frac{1-x^2}{x(1-2x)} = \frac{1}{2} + \frac{A}{x} + \frac{B}{(1-2x)}$

$$\Rightarrow \quad (1 - x^2) = \frac{1}{2}x(1-2x) + A(1-2x) + B(x)$$

On putting $x = 0$ and $x = \frac{1}{2}$, we get

$$1 = A \text{ and } 1 - \frac{1}{4} = B \cdot \frac{1}{2}$$

$$\Rightarrow \quad A = 1,\ B = \frac{3}{2}$$

$$\therefore \int \frac{1-x^2}{x(1-2x)}\,dx = \int \left(\frac{1}{2} + \frac{1}{x} + \frac{3}{2(1-2x)}\right) dx$$

$$= \frac{1}{2}x + \log|x| + \frac{3}{2}\frac{\log|1-2x|}{-2} + C$$

$$= \frac{1}{2}x + \log|x| - \frac{3}{4}\log|1-2x| + C.$$

(ii) Let $\frac{x^2 + x + 1}{x^2(x+2)} = \frac{A}{x} + \frac{B}{x^2} + \frac{C}{x+2}$

$$\Rightarrow \quad x^2 + x + 1 = Ax(x+2) + B(x+2) + C(x^2) \quad \ldots\text{(i)}$$

On putting, $x = -2$ and $x = 0$ in Eq. (i), we get

$$C = 3/4 \text{ and } B = 1/2$$

On equation Coefficient of x^2 on both sides of (i), we get $1 = A + C \Rightarrow A = 1/4$.

$$\therefore \int \frac{x^2 + x + 1}{x^2(x+2)}\,dx = \int \left(\frac{1/4}{x} + \frac{1/2}{x^2} + \frac{3/4}{x+2}\right) dx$$

$$= \frac{1}{4}\log|x| - \frac{1}{2x} + \frac{3}{4}\log|x+2| + C$$

Milestone Practice 1.5

Evaluate the following integrals :

1. $\int \frac{x^2}{(x-1)(x-2)(x-3)} dx$

2. $\int \frac{dx}{1+x^3}$

3. $\int \frac{(x^3+2)}{(x-1)(x-2)^3} dx$

4. $\int \frac{dx}{x(x^n+1)}$

5. $\int \frac{2x}{(x^2+1)(x^2+3)} dx$

6. $\int \frac{\cos x}{(1+\sin x)(2+\sin x)} dx$

7. $\int \frac{1}{\sin x(3+2\cos x)} dx$

8. $\int \frac{\sec x}{1+\operatorname{cosec} x} dx$

9. $\int \frac{\tan x+\tan^3 x}{1+\tan^3 x} dx$

10. $\int \frac{dx}{x[6(\log x)^2+7\log x+2]}$

11. $\int \frac{\tan^{-1} x}{x^4} dx$

12. $\int \frac{1}{(e^x-1)^2} dx$

13. Evaluate $\int \frac{f(x)}{x^3-1} dx$, where $f(x)$ is a polynomial of degree 2 in x such that $f(0)=f(1)=3f(2)=-3$.

Answer Key

1. $\frac{1}{2}\log|x-1|-4\log|x-2|+\frac{9}{2}\log|x-3|+C$

2. $\frac{1}{3}\log|1+x|-\frac{1}{6}\log|x^2-x+1|+\frac{1}{\sqrt{3}}\tan^{-1}\left|\frac{2x-1}{\sqrt{3}}\right|+C$

3. $-3\ln|x-1|+4\ln|x-2|-\frac{2}{x-2}-\frac{5}{(x-2)^2}+C$

4. $\frac{1}{n}\ln\left|\frac{x^n}{x^n+1}\right|+C$

5. $\frac{1}{2}\ln\left|\frac{x^2+1}{x^2+3}\right|+C$

6. $\ln\left|\frac{\sin x+1}{\sin x+2}\right|+C$

7. $I=\frac{1}{10}\ln|\cos x-1|-\frac{1}{2}\ln|\cos x+1|+\frac{2}{5}\ln|3+2\cos|+C$

8. $\frac{1}{4}\ln\left|\frac{1+\sin x}{1-\sin x}\right|+\frac{1}{2(1+\sin x)}+C$

9. $-\frac{1}{3}|\ln|1+\tan x|+\frac{1}{6}\ln|\tan^2 x-\tan x+1|+\frac{1}{\sqrt{3}}\tan^{-1}\left(\frac{2\tan x-1}{\sqrt{3}}\right)+C$

10. $\log\left|\frac{2\log x+1}{3\log x+2}\right|+C$

11. $-\frac{\tan^{-1}x}{(3x^3)}+\frac{1}{6}\left(\log\left|\frac{x^2+1}{x^2}\right|-\frac{1}{x^2}\right)+C$

12. $\frac{1}{1-e^x}-\log|e^x-1|+x+C$

13. $\log\left|\frac{(x^2+x+1)}{(x-1)}\right|+\frac{2}{\sqrt{3}}\tan^{-1}\left(\frac{2x+1}{\sqrt{3}}\right)+C$

For Detailed Solution

Milestone 6 Indirect and Derived Substitutions

- Indirect Substitution • Derived Substitution

1.8 Indirect Substitution

If the integral is of the form $f(x) \cdot g(x)$, where $g(x)$ is a function of the integral of $f(x)$, then put integral of $f(x) = t$.

Example 66. If $\int \frac{(\sqrt{x})^5}{(\sqrt{x})^7 + x^6} dx = a \log\left(\frac{x^k}{1+x^k}\right) + C$, then find a and k.

Sol. Here, $I = \int \frac{(\sqrt{x})^5}{(\sqrt{x})^7 + x^6} dx = \int \frac{dx}{(\sqrt{x})^2 + (\sqrt{x})^7}$

$$= \int \frac{dx}{x^{7/2}\left\{1 + \frac{1}{x^{5/2}}\right\}}$$

Put $\frac{1}{x^{5/2}} = y \Rightarrow -\frac{5}{2x^{7/2}} dx = dy$

$\therefore \quad I = -\frac{2}{5} \int \frac{dy}{1+y}$

$$= -\frac{2}{5} \log|1+y| + C = \frac{2}{5} \log\left|\frac{1}{1+y}\right| + C$$

$$= \frac{2}{5} \log\left|\frac{x^{5/2}}{x^{5/2}+1}\right| + C \quad \text{...(i)}$$

where, $I = a \log\left(\frac{x^k}{1+x^k}\right) + C$ (given) ...(ii)

$\therefore$ From Eqs. (i) and (ii), we get

$$a \log\left(\frac{x^k}{1+x^k}\right) + C = \frac{2}{5} \log\left(\frac{x^{5/2}}{1+x^{5/2}}\right) + C$$

$$\Rightarrow \quad a = \frac{2}{5} \text{ and } k = \frac{5}{2}$$

Example 67. For any natural number m, evaluate $\int (x^{3m} + x^{2m} + x^m)(2x^{2m} + 3x^m + 6)^{1/m} dx, x > 0$

Sol. Here, $I = \int (x^{3m} + x^{2m} + x^m)(2x^{2m} + 3x^m + 6)^{1/m} dx$

$$= \int (x^{3m} + x^{2m} + x^m) \frac{(2x^{3m} + 3x^{2m} + 6x^m)^{1/m}}{x} dx$$

$$= \int (x^{3m-1} + x^{2m-1} + x^{m-1})(2x^{3m} + 3x^{2m} + 6x^m)^{1/m} dx \quad \text{...(i)}$$

Put $2x^{3m} + 3x^{2m} + 6x^m = t$

$\Rightarrow 6m(x^{3m-1} + x^{2m-1} + x^{m-1}) dx = dt$

$\therefore$ Eq. (i) becomes,

$$I = \int t^{1/m} \frac{dt}{6m} = \frac{1}{6m} \cdot \frac{t^{(1/m)+1}}{(1/m)+1} + C$$

$$I = \frac{1}{6(m+1)} \{2x^{3m} + 3x^{2m} + 6x^m\}^{\frac{m+1}{m}} + C$$

JEE SCANNER

Example Similar to PYQ Asked in JEE Main 2021

If $f(x) = \int \frac{5x^4 + 4x^5}{(x^5 + x + 1)^2} dx$, $x \geq 0$, $f(0) = 0$ and $f(1) = \frac{1}{k}$, then the value of k is ....

Sol. Here, $f(x) = \int \frac{5x^4 + 4x^5}{(x^5 + x + 1)^2} dx = \int \frac{x^4(5+4x)}{x^{10}\left(1 + \frac{1}{x^4} + \frac{1}{x^5}\right)^2} dx$

$$= \int \frac{5/x^6 + 4/x^5}{\left(1 + \frac{1}{x^4} + \frac{1}{x^5}\right)^2} dx$$

Put $1 + \frac{1}{x^4} + \frac{1}{x^5} = t \Rightarrow \left(-\frac{4}{x^5} - \frac{5}{x^6}\right) dx = dt$

$$\therefore \quad f(x) = \int -\frac{dt}{t^2} = \frac{1}{t} + C = \frac{1}{1 + \frac{1}{x^4} + \frac{1}{x^5}} + C$$

$$= \frac{x^5}{x^5 + x + 1} + C$$

$\Rightarrow f(0) = 0 + C \Rightarrow C = 0$

$\because f(1) = \frac{1}{1+1+1} = \frac{1}{3}$

$\therefore \quad k = 3$

Skill Builder

If $f(x) = \int \frac{6x^5 + 5x^6}{(x^6 + x + 1)^2} dx$, $x \geq 0$, $f(0) = 0$ and $f(2) = \frac{64}{k}$, then the value of k is ....

For Sol.

- **For more practice** See Q.1 of Milestone Practice 1.6.

Example 68. Evaluate $\int \frac{x\,dx}{\sqrt{1+x^2+\sqrt{(1+x^2)^3}}}$.

Sol. Let $I=\int \frac{x\,dx}{\sqrt{1+x^2+\sqrt{(1+x^2)^3}}}$

$$=\int \frac{xdx}{\sqrt{(1+x^2)+(1+x^2)\sqrt{1+x^2}}}=\int \frac{x\,dx}{\sqrt{(1+x^2)}\sqrt{1+\sqrt{1+x^2}}}$$

Put $1+\sqrt{1+x^2}=t^2 \Rightarrow \frac{2x}{2\sqrt{1+x^2}}dx=2t\,dt$

$$\therefore \quad \frac{x\,dx}{\sqrt{1+x^2}}=2t\,dt$$

$$\therefore \quad I=\int \frac{2t\,dt}{t}=2t+C=2\sqrt{1+\sqrt{1+x^2}}+C$$

Example 69. Evaluate $\int \frac{(2x+1)}{(x^2+4x+1)^{3/2}}dx$.

Sol. $\int \frac{2x+1}{(x^2+4x+1)^{3/2}}dx=\int \frac{2x+1}{x^3\left(1+\frac{4}{x}+\frac{1}{x^2}\right)^{3/2}}dx$

$$=\int \frac{2x^{-2}+x^{-3}}{\left(1+\frac{4}{x}+\frac{1}{x^2}\right)^{3/2}}dx$$

Now, put $\frac{1}{x^2}+\frac{4}{x}+1=t^2 \Rightarrow \left(-\frac{2}{x^3}-\frac{4}{x^2}\right)dx=2t\,dt$

$$\therefore \quad I=\int \frac{-t\,dt}{t^3}=\frac{1}{t}+C=\frac{x}{\sqrt{x^2+4x+1}}+C$$

Example 70. Evaluate $\int \frac{p\,x^{p+2q-1}-qx^{q-1}}{x^{2p+2q}+2x^{p+q}+1}dx$.

Sol. Here, $I=\int \frac{px^{p+2q-1}-qx^{q-1}}{x^{2p+2q}+2x^{p+q}+1}$

$$\int \frac{px^{p+2q-1}-qx^{q-1}}{(x^{p+q}+1)^2}dx=\int \frac{px^{p-1}-qx^{-q-1}}{(x^p+x^{-q})^2}dx$$

Taking x^q common from denominator and take it in numerator.

Put $x^p+x^{-q}=t \Rightarrow (px^{p-1}-qx^{-q-1})\,dx=dt$

$$\therefore \quad I=\int \frac{dt}{t^2}=-\frac{1}{t}+C=-\left(\frac{x^q}{x^{p+q}+1}\right)+C$$

Example 71. Evaluate $\int \frac{x^2\,(1-\ln x)}{\ln^4 x-x^4}dx$.

Sol. Here, $I=\int \frac{x^2(1-\ln x)}{\ln^4 x-x^4}$

$$I=\int \frac{x^2\,(1-\ln x)}{x^4\left(\left(\frac{\ln x}{x}\right)^4-1\right)}dx=\int \frac{1-\ln x}{x^2\left(\left(\frac{\ln x}{x}\right)^4-1\right)}dx$$

Put $\frac{\ln x}{x}=t \Rightarrow \frac{1-\ln x}{x^2}=dt$

$$\therefore \quad I=\int \frac{dt}{(t^4-1)}=\int \frac{dt}{(t^2+1)(t^2-1)}$$

$$=\frac{1}{2}\int \frac{(t^2+1)-(t^2-1)}{(t^2+1)(t^2-1)}dt$$

$$=\frac{1}{2}\left(\int \frac{dt}{t^2-1}-\int \frac{dt}{t^2+1}\right)=\frac{1}{2}\left(\frac{1}{2}\ln\frac{t-1}{t+1}-\tan^{-1}t\right)+C$$

$$=\frac{1}{4}\ln\left(\frac{\ln x-x}{\ln x+x}\right)-\frac{1}{2}\tan^{-1}\left(\frac{\ln x}{x}\right)+C$$

Example 72. Evaluate $\int \frac{x^2-1}{x^3\sqrt{2x^4-2x^2+1}}dx$.

Sol. Let $I=\int \frac{x^2-1}{x^3\sqrt{2x^4-2x^2+1}}dx$

$$=\int \frac{x^2-1}{x^5}\cdot\frac{dx}{\sqrt{2-\frac{2}{x^2}+\frac{1}{x^4}}}=\frac{1}{4}\int \frac{\frac{4}{x^3}-\frac{4}{x^5}}{\sqrt{2-\frac{2}{x^2}+\frac{1}{x^4}}}dx$$

$$=\frac{1}{4}\cdot 2\sqrt{2-\frac{2}{x^2}+\frac{1}{x^4}}+C \qquad \left[\because \int \frac{f'(x)}{\sqrt{f(x)}}dx=2\sqrt{f(x)}+C\right]$$

$$=\frac{\sqrt{2x^4-2x^2+1}}{2x^2}+C$$

Example 73. Let $f(x)=\frac{x}{(1+x^n)^{1/n}}$ for $n\geq 2$ and $g(x)=\underbrace{fofo\ldots of}_{n \text{ times}}(x)$, then find $\int x^{n-2}\,g(x)\,dx$.

Sol. $\because \quad f(x)=\frac{x}{(1+x^n)^{1/n}}$

$$\therefore \quad f(f(x))=\frac{y}{(1+y^n)^{1/n}},\text{ where } y=\frac{x}{(1+x^n)^{1/n}}$$

$$=\frac{x}{(1+2x^n)^{1/n}}$$

Similarly, $f(f(f(x)))=\frac{x}{(1+3x^n)^{1/n}}$

and $\underbrace{(fofofo\ldots of)}_{n\text{ times}}(x)=g(x)=\frac{x}{(1+nx^n)^{1/n}}$

$$\therefore \quad \int x^{n-2}g(x)\,dx=\int \frac{x^{n-1}}{(1+nx^n)^{1/n}}dx$$

$$=\frac{1}{n^2}\int n^2\cdot x^{n-1}\cdot(1+nx^n)^{-1/n}\,dx$$

$$=\frac{1}{n^2}\cdot\frac{(1+nx^n)^{1-\frac{1}{n}}}{1-\frac{1}{n}}+C=\frac{(1+nx^n)^{1-\frac{1}{n}}}{n(n-1)}+C$$

Example 74. Evaluate $\int \sqrt{x+\sqrt{x^2+2}}\, dx$.

Sol. $I = \int \sqrt{x+\sqrt{x^2+2}}\, dx$

Let $x+\sqrt{x^2+2} = t \Rightarrow (\sqrt{x^2+2} - x) = \dfrac{2}{\sqrt{x^2+2}+x} = \dfrac{2}{t}$

$\Rightarrow \quad 2x = t - \dfrac{2}{t} \Rightarrow x = \dfrac{t}{2} - \dfrac{1}{t} \Rightarrow dx = \left(\dfrac{1}{2}+\dfrac{1}{t^2}\right)dt$

$\therefore \quad I = \int \sqrt{t}\left(\dfrac{1}{2}+\dfrac{1}{t^2}\right)dt = \dfrac{1}{2}\cdot\dfrac{2}{3}t^{\frac{3}{2}} + \left(\dfrac{-2}{\frac{1}{t^{2}}}\right) + C$

$= \dfrac{1}{3}(x+\sqrt{x^2+2})^{\frac{3}{2}} - \dfrac{2}{(x+\sqrt{x^2+2})^{\frac{1}{2}}} + C$

1.9 Derived Substitutions

Some times it is useful to write the integral as a sum of two related integrals which can be evaluated by making suitable substitutions.

Examples of such integrals are

Type I

(a) **Algebraic Twins**

$$\int \frac{2x^2}{x^4+1}dx = \int \frac{x^2+1}{x^4+1}dx + \int \frac{x^2-1}{x^4+1}dx$$

$$\int \frac{2}{x^4+1}dx = \int \frac{x^2+1}{x^4+1}dx - \int \frac{x^2-1}{x^4+1}dx$$

$$\int \frac{2x^2}{x^4+1+kx^2}dx, \int \frac{2}{(x^4+1+kx^2)}dx$$

(b) **Trigonometric Twins**

$$\int \sqrt{\tan x}\, dx, \int \sqrt{\cot x}\, dx,$$

$$\int \frac{1}{(\sin^4 x+\cos^4 x)}dx, \int \frac{1}{\sin^6 x+\cos^6 x}dx,$$

$$\int \frac{\pm \sin x \pm \cos x}{a+b\sin x\cos x}dx$$

Method of evaluating these integral are illustrated by mean of the following examples :

Integral of the Form

1. $\int f\left(x+\dfrac{1}{x}\right)\left(1-\dfrac{1}{x^2}\right)dx$

Put $x+\dfrac{1}{x} = t \Rightarrow \left(1-\dfrac{1}{x^2}\right)dx = dt$

2. $\int f\left(x-\dfrac{1}{x}\right)\left(1+\dfrac{1}{x^2}\right)dx.$

Put $x-\dfrac{1}{x} = t \Rightarrow \left(1+\dfrac{1}{x^2}\right)dx = dt$

3. $\int \dfrac{x^2+1}{x^4+kx^2+1}dx.$

Divide numerator and denominator by x^2.

4. $\int \dfrac{x^2-1}{x^4+kx^2+1}dx$

Divide numerator and denominator by x^2.

Example 75. Evaluate $\int \dfrac{1}{x^4+5x^2+1}dx$.

Sol. Let $I = \dfrac{1}{2}\int \dfrac{2}{x^4+5x^2+1}dx$

$= \dfrac{1}{2}\int \dfrac{1+x^2}{x^4+5x^2+1}dx + \dfrac{1}{2}\int \dfrac{1-x^2}{x^4+5x^2+1}dx$

$= \dfrac{1}{2}\int \dfrac{1+1/x^2}{x^2+5+1/x^2}dx - \dfrac{1}{2}\int \dfrac{1-1/x^2}{x^2+5+1/x^2}dx$

[dividing numerator and denominator by x^2]

$= \dfrac{1}{2}\int \dfrac{(1+1/x^2)}{(x-1/x)^2+7}dx - \dfrac{1}{2}\int \dfrac{(1-1/x^2)}{(x+1/x)^2+3}dx$

$= \dfrac{1}{2}\int \dfrac{dt}{t^2+(\sqrt{7})^2} - \dfrac{1}{2}\int \dfrac{du}{u^2+(\sqrt{3})^2}$

where $t = x - \dfrac{1}{x}$ and $u = x + \dfrac{1}{x}$

$\therefore \quad I = \dfrac{1}{2}\cdot\dfrac{1}{\sqrt{7}}\left(\tan^{-1}\dfrac{t}{\sqrt{7}}\right) - \dfrac{1}{2}\cdot\dfrac{1}{\sqrt{3}}\left(\tan^{-1}\dfrac{u}{\sqrt{3}}\right) + C$

$= \dfrac{1}{2}\left[\dfrac{1}{\sqrt{7}}\tan^{-1}\left(\dfrac{x-1/x}{\sqrt{7}}\right) - \dfrac{1}{\sqrt{3}}\tan^{-1}\left(\dfrac{x+1/x}{\sqrt{3}}\right)\right] + C$

Example 76. Evaluate $\int \sqrt{\tan x}\, dx$.

Sol. Here, $I = \int \sqrt{\tan x}\, dx$

Put $\tan x = t^2 \Rightarrow \sec^2 x\, dx = 2t\, dt$

$\Rightarrow dx = \dfrac{2t\, dt}{1+\tan^2 x} \Rightarrow dx = \dfrac{2t\, dt}{1+t^4}$

$\therefore \quad I = \int t\cdot\dfrac{2t}{1+t^4}dt = \int \dfrac{2t^2}{t^4+1}dt = \int \dfrac{t^2+1}{t^4+1}dt + \int \dfrac{t^2-1}{t^4+1}dt$

$= \int \dfrac{1+1/t^2}{t^2+1/t^2}dt + \int \dfrac{1-1/t^2}{t^2+1/t^2}dt$

$= \int \dfrac{1+1/t^2}{(t-1/t)^2+2}dt + \int \dfrac{1-1/t^2}{(t+1/t)^2-2}dt$

$= \int \dfrac{ds}{s^2+(\sqrt{2})^2} + \int \dfrac{dr}{r^2-(\sqrt{2})^2} \quad \left[s = t - \dfrac{1}{t} \text{ and } r = t + \dfrac{1}{t}\right]$

$$=\frac{1}{\sqrt{2}}\tan^{-1}\left(\frac{s}{\sqrt{2}}\right)+\frac{1}{2\sqrt{2}}\log\left|\frac{r-\sqrt{2}}{r+\sqrt{2}}\right|+C$$

$$=\frac{1}{\sqrt{2}}\left[\tan^{-1}\left(\frac{t-1/t}{\sqrt{2}}\right)+\frac{1}{2}\log\left(\frac{t+\frac{1}{t}-\sqrt{2}}{t+\frac{1}{t}+\sqrt{2}}\right)\right]+C$$

[where, $t=\sqrt{\tan x}$]

Example 77. Evaluate $\int\frac{4}{\sin^4 x+\cos^4 x}dx$.

Sol. Let $I=4\int\frac{dx}{\sin^4 x+\cos^4 x}$

Dividing numerator and denominator by $\cos^4 x$, we get

$$I=4\int\frac{\sec^4 x}{\tan^4 x+1}dx=4\int\frac{\sec^2 x\,(1+\tan^2 x)}{1+\tan^4 x}dx$$

Put $\tan x=t\Rightarrow \sec^2 x\,dx=dt$

$$\therefore I=4\int\frac{t^2+1}{t^4+1}dt=4\int\frac{1+1/t^2}{t^2+1/t^2}dt=4\int\frac{1+1/t^2}{(t-1/t)^2+2}dt$$

Again, put $z=t-\frac{1}{t}\Rightarrow dz=\left(1+\frac{1}{t^2}\right)dt$

$$\therefore\quad I=4\int\frac{dz}{z^2+2}=\frac{4}{\sqrt{2}}\tan^{-1}\left(\frac{z}{\sqrt{2}}\right)+C$$

$$I=2\sqrt{2}\tan^{-1}\left(\frac{\tan x-1/\tan x}{\sqrt{2}}\right)+C$$

Example 78. Find the value of $\int\frac{(ax^2-b)\,dx}{x\sqrt{c^2x^2-(ax^2+b)^2}}$.

Sol. Here, $I=\int\frac{(ax^2-b)\,dx}{x\sqrt{c^2x^2-(ax^2+b)^2}}=\int\frac{\left(a-\frac{b}{x^2}\right)dx}{\sqrt{c^2-\left(ax+\frac{b}{x}\right)^2}}$

Put $ax+\frac{b}{x}=t$

$$\therefore\quad\left(a-\frac{b}{x^2}\right)dx=dt$$

$$I=\int\frac{dt}{\sqrt{c^2-t^2}}=\sin^{-1}\left(\frac{t}{c}\right)+k=\sin^{-1}\left(\frac{ax+b/x}{c}\right)+k$$

Example 79. $\int\frac{x^x\,(x^{2x}+1)\,(\ln x+1)}{x^{4x}+1}dx$.

Sol. Here, $I=\int\frac{x^x\,(x^{2x}+1)(\ln x+1)}{x^{4x}+1}dx$

Put $x^x=y\Rightarrow x^x(\ln x+1)\,dx=dy$

$$\therefore\quad I=\int\frac{y^2+1}{y^4+1}dy=\int\frac{1+\frac{1}{y^2}}{y^2+\frac{1}{y^2}}dy=\int\frac{1+\frac{1}{y^2}}{\left(y-\frac{1}{y}\right)^2+2}dy$$

Put $y-\frac{1}{y}=t\Rightarrow\left(1+\frac{1}{y^2}\right)dy=dt$

$$\therefore\quad I=\int\frac{dt}{t^2+2}=\frac{1}{\sqrt{2}}\left(\tan^{-1}\frac{t}{\sqrt{2}}\right)+C$$

$$=\frac{1}{\sqrt{2}}\tan^{-1}\left(\frac{y-\frac{1}{y}}{\sqrt{2}}\right)+C=\frac{1}{\sqrt{2}}\tan^{-1}\left(\frac{x^x-\frac{1}{x^x}}{\sqrt{2}}\right)+C$$

JEE SCANNER

Example Similar to PYQ Asked in JEE Main 2024

The integral $\int\frac{(x^2-1)\,dx}{(x^4+3x^2+1)\tan^{-1}\left(x+\frac{1}{x}\right)}$ *equal to*

(a) $\frac{1}{2}\log\tan^{-1}\left(x+\frac{1}{x}\right)+C$ (b) $\log|\tan^{-1}\left(x+\frac{1}{x}\right)|+C$

(c) $\left(\tan^{-1}\left(x+\frac{1}{x}\right)\right)^2+C$ (d) $2\log\tan^{-1}\left(x+\frac{1}{x}\right)+C$

Sol. (b) Here $I=\int\frac{(x^2-1)}{(x^4+3x^2+1)\tan^{-1}\left(x+\frac{1}{x}\right)}$

The given integral can be written as

$$I=\int\frac{(1-1/x^2)\,dx}{(x^2+3+1/x^2)\tan^{-1}\left(x+\frac{1}{x}\right)}$$

[dividing numerator and denominator by x^2]

$$I=\int\frac{(1-1/x^2)\,dx}{\{(x+1/x)^2+1\}\tan^{-1}\left(x+\frac{1}{x}\right)}$$

Put, $x+\frac{1}{x}=t\Rightarrow\left(1-\frac{1}{x^2}\right)dx=dt$

$$\therefore\quad I=\int\frac{dt}{(t^2+1)\cdot\tan^{-1}(t)}\quad\text{...(i)}$$

Now, make one more substitution $\tan^{-1}t=u$.

Then, $\frac{dt}{t^2+1}=du$

$\therefore$ Eq. (i) becomes, $I=\int\frac{du}{u}=\log|u|+C$

$\Rightarrow I=\log|\tan^{-1}t|+C=\log|\tan^{-1}\left(x+\frac{1}{x}\right)|+C$

Skill Builder

For Sol.

The integral $\int\frac{x^4-x^2}{(x^6+3x^4+x^2)\cot^{-1}\left(x+\frac{1}{x}\right)}dx$ is equal to

(a) $\log\left|\tan^{-1}\left(x-\frac{1}{x}\right)\right|+C$ (b) $-\log\left|\tan^{-1}\left(x+\frac{1}{x}\right)\right|+C$

(c) $\log\left|\cot^{-1}\left(x+\frac{1}{x}\right)\right|+C$ (d) $-\log\left|\cot^{-1}\left(x+\frac{1}{x}\right)\right|+C$

■ **For more practice** See Q.3 of Milestone Practice 1.6.

Example 80. Evaluate

$$I=\int \frac{(x-1)\sqrt{x^4+2x^3-x^2+2x+1}}{x^2\,(x+1)}\,dx.$$

Sol. Here, $I=\int \frac{(x^2-1)\sqrt{x^4+2x^3-x^2+2x+1}}{x^2\,(x+1)^2}\,dx$

$$=\int \frac{\left(1-\frac{1}{x^2}\right)\sqrt{x^2\left(x^2+2x-1+\frac{2}{x}+\frac{1}{x^2}\right)}}{\frac{x^2\,(x^2+2x+1)}{x^2}}\,dx$$

$$=\int \frac{\left(1-\frac{1}{x^2}\right)\sqrt{\left(x^2+\frac{1}{x^2}\right)+2\left(x+\frac{1}{x}\right)-1}}{\left(x+\frac{1}{x}+2\right)}\,dx$$

Put $x+\frac{1}{x}=t \Rightarrow \left(1-\frac{1}{x^2}\right)dx=dt$

$$=\int \frac{\sqrt{(t^2-2)+2t-1}}{(t+2)}\,dt=\int \frac{\sqrt{t^2+2t-3}}{(t+2)}\,dt$$

$$=\int \frac{t^2+2t-3}{(t+2)\sqrt{t^2+2t-3}}\,dt$$

$$=\int \frac{t(t+2)}{(t+2)\sqrt{t^2+2t-3}}\,dt-3\int \frac{dt}{(t+2)\sqrt{t^2+2t-3}}$$

$$I=I_1-3I_2 \qquad \text{...(i)}$$

where, $I_1=\int \frac{t\,dt}{\sqrt{t^2+2t-3}}$ and $I_2=\int \frac{dt}{(t+2)\sqrt{t^2+2t-3}}$

$\therefore \quad I_1=\int \frac{t\,dt}{\sqrt{(t+1)^2-4}}$

Put $t+1=z$ and $dt=dz$

$$\therefore \quad I_1=\int \frac{(z-1)\,dz}{\sqrt{z^2-2^2}}=\int \frac{z dz}{\sqrt{z^2-2^2}}-\int \frac{dz}{\sqrt{z^2-2^2}}$$

$$=\sqrt{z^2-2^2}-\log|z+\sqrt{z^2-4}|$$

$$=\sqrt{t^2+2t-3}-\log|(t+1)+\sqrt{t^2+2t+3}| \qquad \text{...(ii)}$$

Put $t+2=\frac{1}{y}$ and $dt=-\frac{1}{y^2}dy$

Also, $I_2=\int \frac{-dy}{y^2\cdot\frac{1}{y}\sqrt{\left(\frac{1}{y}-2\right)^2+2\left(\frac{1}{y}-2\right)-3}}$

$$=\int \frac{-dy}{\sqrt{1-2y-3y^2}}=\frac{-1}{\sqrt{3}}\int \frac{dy}{\sqrt{\left(\frac{2}{3}\right)^2-\left(y+\frac{1}{3}\right)^2}}$$

$$=\frac{-1}{\sqrt{3}}\sin^{-1}\left(\frac{y+\frac{1}{3}}{\frac{2}{3}}\right)=\frac{-1}{\sqrt{3}}\sin^{-1}\left(\frac{5+t}{2(2+t)}\right) \qquad \text{...(iii)}$$

$$\therefore \quad I=\sqrt{t^2+2t-3}-\log(t+1+\sqrt{t^2+2t-3})+\sqrt{3}\sin^{-1}\left(\frac{t+5}{2(2+t)}\right)+C$$

where, $t=x+\frac{1}{x}$

Type II

Integration of Some Special Irrational Algebraic Functions

In this case we shall discuss integrals of the form

$\int \frac{\phi(x)}{P\sqrt{Q}}\,dx$, where P and Q are polynomial functions of x

and $\phi(x)$ is polynomial in x.

(a) Integrals of the Form $\int \frac{\phi(x)}{P\sqrt{Q}}\,dx$, where P and Q are both linear of x

To evaluate this type of integrals we put $Q=t^2$, i.e. to evaluate integrals of the form $\int \frac{1}{(ax+b)\sqrt{cx+d}}\,dx$, put $cx+d=t^2$.

The following examples illustrate the procedure :

Example 81. Evaluate $\int \frac{1}{(x+1)\sqrt{x-2}}\,dx$.

Sol. Let $I=\int \frac{1}{(x+1)\sqrt{x-2}}\,dx$

Here, P and Q both are linear, so we put $Q=t^2$

i.e. $\quad x-2=t^2$

So that $dx=2t\,dt$

$$\therefore \quad I=\int \frac{1}{(t^2+2+1)\sqrt{t^2}}\cdot 2t\,dt=2\int \frac{dt}{t^2+3}$$

$$=2\times\frac{1}{\sqrt{3}}\tan^{-1}\left(\frac{t}{\sqrt{3}}\right)+C$$

$$\therefore \quad I=\frac{2}{\sqrt{3}}\tan^{-1}\left(\frac{\sqrt{x-2}}{\sqrt{3}}\right)+C$$

(b) Integrals of the Form $\int \frac{\phi(x)}{P\sqrt{Q}}\,dx$, where P is a quadratic expression and Q is a linear expression

To evaluate this type of integrals we put $Q=t^2$ i.e. to evaluate the integrals of the form

$$\int \frac{1}{(ax^2+bx+c)\sqrt{px+q}}\,dx$$

put $px+q=t^2$.

Example 82. Evaluate $\int \frac{x+2}{(x^2+3x+3)\sqrt{x+1}}\,dx.$

Sol. Let $I = \int \frac{x+2}{(x^2+3x+3)\sqrt{x+1}}\,dx$

Put $x+1 = t^2 \Rightarrow dx = 2t\,dt$

$$\therefore \quad I = \int \frac{(t^2-1)+2}{\{(t^2-1)^2+3(t^2-1)+3\}\sqrt{t^2}}\cdot(2t)\,dt$$

$$= 2\int \frac{t^2+1}{t^4+t^2+1}\,dt = 2\int \frac{1+1/t^2}{t^2+1+1/t^2}\,dt$$

$$= 2\int \frac{1+1/t^2}{(t-1/t)^2+(\sqrt{3})^2}\,dt$$

$$\left[\text{where } u = t - \frac{1}{t} \Rightarrow du = \left(1+\frac{1}{t^2}\right)dt\right]$$

$$\therefore \quad I = 2\int \frac{du}{u^2+(\sqrt{3})^2} = \frac{2}{\sqrt{3}}\tan^{-1}\left(\frac{u}{\sqrt{3}}\right)+C$$

$$\therefore \quad I = \frac{2}{\sqrt{3}}\tan^{-1}\left(\frac{t^2-1}{\sqrt{3}t}\right)+C$$

$$= \frac{2}{\sqrt{3}}\tan^{-1}\left(\frac{x}{\sqrt{3(x+1)}}\right)+C$$

(c) Integral of the Form $\int \frac{1}{(ax+b)}\cdot\frac{dx}{\sqrt{px^2+qx+r}}$, **where in** $\int \frac{dx}{P\sqrt{Q}}$, **P is linear and Q is a quadratic. Put** $ax+b = \frac{1}{t}$.

Example 83. Evaluate $\int \frac{dx}{(x-1)\sqrt{x^2+x+1}}$.

Sol. Let $I = \int \frac{dx}{(x-1)\sqrt{x^2+x+1}}$

Put $x-1 = \frac{1}{t} \Rightarrow dx = -\frac{1}{t^2}dt$

$$\therefore \quad I = \int \frac{-1/t^2\,dt}{(1/t)\sqrt{\left(\frac{1}{t}+1\right)^2+\left(\frac{1}{t}+1\right)+1}}$$

$$= -\int \frac{dt}{\sqrt{3t^2+3t+1}} = -\frac{1}{\sqrt{3}}\int \frac{dt}{\sqrt{\left(t+\frac{1}{2}\right)^2+\frac{1}{12}}}$$

$$= -\frac{1}{\sqrt{3}}\log|(t+1/2)+\sqrt{(t+1/2)^2+1/12}|+C$$

$$= -\frac{1}{\sqrt{3}}\log\left|\left(\frac{1}{x-1}+\frac{1}{2}\right)+\sqrt{\frac{12\left(\frac{1}{x-1}+\frac{1}{2}\right)^2+1}{12}}\right|+C$$

(d) Integrals of the Form $\int \frac{dx}{P\sqrt{Q}}$, **where P and Q both are pure quadratic expression in x i.e.** $P = ax^2+b$ **and** $Q = cx^2+d$ **i.e.** $\int \frac{dx}{(ax^2+b)\sqrt{cx^2+d}}$.

To evaluate this type of integrals of the form we put $x = \frac{1}{t}$

Example 84. Evaluate $\int \frac{dx}{(1+x^2)\sqrt{1-x^2}}$.

Sol. Let $I = \int \frac{dx}{(1+x^2)\sqrt{1-x^2}}$

Put $x = \frac{1}{t}$, so that $dx = -\frac{1}{t^2}dt$

$$\therefore \quad I = \int \frac{-1/t^2\,dt}{(1+1/t^2)\sqrt{1-1/t^2}} = -\int \frac{t\,dt}{(t^2+1)\sqrt{t^2-1}}$$

Again, $t^2 = u \Rightarrow 2t\,dt = du$

$$= -\frac{1}{2}\int \frac{du}{(u+1)\sqrt{u-1}},$$

which reduces to the form $\int \frac{dx}{P\sqrt{Q}}$ where both P and Q are linear.

So, that we put $u-1 = z^2$, so that $du = 2z\,dz$

$$\therefore \ I = -\frac{1}{2}\int \frac{2z\,dz}{(z^2+1+1)\sqrt{z^2}} = -\int \frac{dz}{(z^2+2)}$$

$$= -\frac{1}{\sqrt{2}}\tan^{-1}\left(\frac{z}{\sqrt{2}}\right)+C = -\frac{1}{\sqrt{2}}\tan^{-1}\left(\frac{\sqrt{u-1}}{\sqrt{2}}\right)+C$$

$$= -\frac{1}{\sqrt{2}}\tan^{-1}\left(\frac{\sqrt{t^2-1}}{\sqrt{2}}\right)+C$$

$$= -\frac{1}{\sqrt{2}}\tan^{-1}\left(\frac{\sqrt{1-x^2}}{\sqrt{2}x}\right)+C$$

Alternate Solution

Put $x = \cos\theta$, $dx = -\sin\theta\,d\theta$

$$\therefore \quad I = -\int \frac{\sin\theta\,d\theta}{(1+\cos^2\theta)\sin\theta} = -\int \frac{d\theta}{1+\cos^2\theta}$$

$$= -\int \frac{\sec^2\theta\,d\theta}{\sec^2\theta+1} = -\int \frac{\sec^2\theta\,d\theta}{\tan^2\theta+2}$$

Put $\tan\theta = t \Rightarrow \sec^2\theta\,d\theta = dt$

$$\therefore \quad I = -\int \frac{dt}{t^2+2} = -\frac{1}{\sqrt{2}}\tan^{-1}\left(\frac{t}{\sqrt{2}}\right)+C$$

$$= -\frac{1}{\sqrt{2}}\tan^{-1}\left(\frac{\tan\theta}{\sqrt{2}}\right)+C = -\frac{1}{\sqrt{2}}\tan^{-1}\left(\frac{\sqrt{1-x^2}}{\sqrt{2}\,x}\right)+C$$

$$\left[\because \ \cos\theta = x \Rightarrow \sin\theta = \sqrt{1-x^2} \quad \therefore \ \tan\theta = \frac{\sqrt{1-x^2}}{x}\right]$$

JEE SCANNER

Example Similar to PYQ Asked in JEE Main 2020

If $f(x)=\int \frac{dx}{(1+2x^2)\sqrt{2-x^2}}, |x|<\sqrt{2}$. *If* $f(0)=0$ *and* $f(1)=\frac{1}{\alpha}\tan^{-1}(\alpha), \alpha, \beta>0$, *then* $5\alpha^2$ *is equal to* ....

Sol. Put $x=\sqrt{2}\sin\theta \Rightarrow dx=\sqrt{2}\cos\theta\, d\theta$

$$\because \quad f(\theta)=\int \frac{\sqrt{2}\cos\theta\, d\theta}{(1+4\sin^2\theta)\sqrt{2-2\sin^2\theta}}$$

$$f(\theta)=\int \frac{\sqrt{2}\cos\theta\, d\theta}{\sqrt{2}\cos\theta(1+4\sin^2\theta)}$$

$$f(\theta)=\int \frac{d\theta}{1+4\sin^2\theta}$$

Divide Nr and Dr by $\cos^2\theta$, we get

$$f(\theta)=\int \frac{\sec^2\theta\, d\theta}{\sec^2\theta+4\tan^2\theta}$$

$$=\int \frac{\sec^2\theta\, d\theta}{1+5\tan^2\theta}$$

Put $\tan\theta=t \Rightarrow \sec^2\theta\, d\theta=dt$

$$f(t)=\int \frac{dt}{1+5t^2}=\frac{1}{\sqrt{5}}\tan^{-1}(\sqrt{5}t)+C$$

$$\Rightarrow \quad f(\theta)=\frac{1}{\sqrt{5}}\tan^{-1}(\sqrt{5}\tan\theta)+C$$

$$f(x)=\frac{1}{\sqrt{5}}\tan^{-1}\left(\frac{\sqrt{5}x}{\sqrt{2-x^2}}\right)+C$$

$$f(0)=0$$

$$\Rightarrow \quad C=0$$

$$f(1)=\frac{1}{\sqrt{5}}\tan^{-1}(\sqrt{5})+C$$

$$\because \quad \alpha=\sqrt{5}$$

$$\Rightarrow \quad 5\alpha^2=5(5)=25$$

Skill builder

If $f(x)=\int \frac{dx}{(1+3x^2)(\sqrt{3-x^2})}, |x|<\sqrt{3}$ and if $f(0)=0$ and $f(1)=\frac{1}{\sqrt{\alpha}}\tan^{-1}\left(\sqrt{\frac{\alpha}{\beta}}\right)$, $\alpha,\beta>0$, then value of $\alpha\beta$ is ....

For Sol.

■ **For more practice** See Q.6 of Milestone Practice 1.6.

(e) Integrals of the Form $\int \frac{dx}{(x-k)^r\sqrt{ax^2+bx+c}}$, **where** $r\geq 2$ **and** $r\in I$

Here, we substitute, $x-k=\frac{1}{t}$

Example 85. Evaluate $\int \frac{dx}{(x-3)^3\sqrt{x^2-6x+10}}$.

Sol. Substitute $(x-3)=\frac{1}{t} \Rightarrow dx=-\frac{1}{t^2}dt$, we get

$$\int \frac{dx}{(x-3)^3\sqrt{x^2-6x+10}}$$

$$=\int \frac{-1/t^2\, dt}{1/t^3\sqrt{(1/t+3)^2-6(1/t+3)+10}}$$

$$=-\int \frac{t^2\, dt}{\sqrt{1+t^2}}$$

$$=\int \frac{dt}{\sqrt{1+t^2}}-\int \sqrt{1+t^2}\, dt$$

$$=\log|t+\sqrt{1+t^2}|-\frac{t}{2}\sqrt{1+t^2}-\frac{1}{2}\log|t+\sqrt{1+t^2}|+C$$

$$=\frac{1}{2}\log|t+\sqrt{1+t^2}|-\frac{t}{2}\sqrt{1+t^2}+C$$

$$=\frac{1}{2}\left[\log\left|\frac{1+\sqrt{x^2-6x+10}}{|x-3|}\right|-\frac{\sqrt{x^2-6x+10}}{|x-3|^2}\right]+C$$

(f) If the integral is a rational function of x and fractional power of ratio of two linear expression i.e. $\frac{ax+b}{px+q}$, then the suitable substitution is $\frac{ax+b}{px+q}=t^m$ where m has the same sense as above.

Example 86. Evaluate $\int \frac{dx}{\sqrt[3]{(x-1)^2(x+4)^4}}$.

Sol. Here, $\sqrt[3]{(x-1)^2(x+4)^4}=(x+4)^2\left(\frac{x-1}{x+4}\right)^{2/3}$

$$\text{Put } \left(\frac{x-1}{x+4}\right)=t^3$$

$$=\frac{(x+4)(1)-(x-1)(1)}{(x+4)^2}dx=3t^2dt$$

$$=\frac{5}{(x+4)^2}dx=3t^2dt$$

$$\because \quad I=\frac{3}{5}\int \frac{t^2dt}{t^2}=\frac{3}{5}\int dt=\frac{3}{5}t+C$$

$$\therefore \quad I=\frac{3}{5}\sqrt[3]{\frac{x-1}{x+4}}+C$$

JEE SCANNER

Example Similar to PYQ Asked in JEE Main 2021

The integral $\int \dfrac{dx}{(x+4)^{5/4}(x-3)^{3/4}}$ is equal to

(a) $\dfrac{4}{7}\left(\dfrac{x-3}{x+4}\right)^{1/4}$ (b) $\dfrac{1}{7}\left(\dfrac{x-1}{x+4}\right)^{3/4}$

(c) $\dfrac{4}{7}\left(\dfrac{x-3}{x+4}\right)^{1/4}$ (d) None of these

Sol. $I=\displaystyle\int \frac{dx}{(x+4)^2\left(\frac{x-3}{x+4}\right)^{3/4}}$

Put $\dfrac{x-3}{x+4}=t \Rightarrow \dfrac{7}{(x+4)^2}dx=dt$

$\because \quad I=\dfrac{1}{7}\displaystyle\int \frac{dt}{(t)^{3/4}}=\frac{1}{7}\frac{t^{-\frac{3}{4}+1}}{-3/4+1}+C=\frac{4}{7}t^{1/4}+C$

$\therefore \quad I=\dfrac{4}{7}\left(\dfrac{x-3}{x+4}\right)^{1/4}+C$

Skill Builder

For Sol.

The integral $\int \dfrac{dx}{(x+8)^{7/4}(x-7)^{1/4}}$ is equal to

(a) $\dfrac{4}{3}\left(\dfrac{x-7}{x+8}\right)^{3/4}+C$ (b) $\dfrac{3}{4}\left(\dfrac{x-7}{x+8}\right)^{3/4}+C$

(c) $\dfrac{4}{45}\left(\dfrac{x-7}{x+8}\right)^{3/4}+C$ (d) $\dfrac{4}{45}\left(\dfrac{x+8}{x-7}\right)^{3/4}+C$

- **For more practice** See Q.7 of Milestone Practice 1.6.

(g) Integrals of the Form $\displaystyle\int \frac{ax^2+bx+c}{(dx+e)\sqrt{fx^2+gx+h}}\,dx$

Here, we write

$$ax^2+bx+c=A_1(dx+e)(2fx+g)+B_1(dx+e)+C_1$$

Where A_1, B_1 and C_1 are constants which can be obtained by comparing the coefficients of like terms on both the sides.

Example 87. Evaluate $\displaystyle\int \frac{2x^2+5x+9}{(x+1)\sqrt{x^2+x+1}}\,dx$.

Sol. Let $2x^2+5x+9=A(x+1)(2x+1)+B(x+1)+C$

or $2x^2+5x+9=x^2(2A)+x(3A+B)+(A+B+C)$

$\Rightarrow \quad A=1, B=2, C=6$

Thus, $\displaystyle\int \frac{2x^2+5x+9}{(x+1)\sqrt{x^2+x+1}}\,dx$

$$=\int \frac{(x+1)(2x+1)}{(x+1)\sqrt{x^2+x+1}}\,dx+2\int \frac{x+1}{(x+1)\sqrt{x^2+x+1}}\,dx+6\int \frac{dx}{(x+1)\sqrt{x^2+x+1}}$$

$$=\int \frac{2x+1}{\sqrt{x^2+x+1}}\,dx+2\int \frac{dx}{\sqrt{x^2+x+1}}+6\int \frac{dx}{(x+1)\sqrt{x^2+x+1}}$$

$$=\int \frac{du}{\sqrt{u}}+2\int \frac{dx}{\sqrt{(x+1/2)^2+(3/4)}}+6\int \frac{-dt}{\sqrt{t^2-t+1}}$$

$\left[\text{where } u=x^2+x+1 \text{ and } \dfrac{1}{t}=x+1\right]$

$$=2\sqrt{x^2+x+1}+2\cdot 1\log|(x+1/2)+\sqrt{x^2+x+1}|-6\int \frac{dt}{\sqrt{(t-1/2)^2+3/4}}$$

$$=2\sqrt{x^2+x+1}+2\log\left|\left(x+\frac{1}{2}\right)+\sqrt{x^2+x+1}\right|-6\log\left|\left(t-\frac{1}{2}\right)+\sqrt{t^2-t+1}\right|+C$$

$$=2\sqrt{x^2+x+1}+2\log\left|\left(x+\frac{1}{2}\right)+\sqrt{x^2+x+1}\right|-6\log\left|\frac{1-x+2\sqrt{x^2+x+1}}{2(x+1)}\right|+C$$

Type III

Integrals of the Form $\int x^m(a+bx^n)^P\,dx$

Case I If $P\in N$. We expand using binomial and integrate.

Case II If $P\in I^-$ (*ie*, negative integer), write $x=t^k$, where k is the LCM of m and n.

Case III If $\dfrac{m+1}{n}$ is an integer and P belongs to fraction, put $(a+bx^n)=t^k$, where k is denominator of the fraction P.

Case IV If $\left(\dfrac{m+1}{n}+P\right)$ is an integer and $P\in$ fraction.

We put $(a+bx^n)=t^k x^n$, where k is denominator of the fraction P.

Example 88. Evaluate $\int x^{1/3}(2+x^{1/2})^2\,dx$.

Sol. $I=\int x^{1/3}(2+x^{1/2})^2\,dx$

Since, P is natural number.

$\therefore \quad I=\int x^{1/3}(4+x+4x^{1/2})\,dx=\int(4x^{1/3}+x^{4/3}+4x^{5/6})\,dx$

$$=\frac{4x^{4/3}}{4/3}+\frac{x^{7/3}}{7/3}+\frac{4x^{11/6}}{11/6}+C$$

$$=3x^{4/3}+\frac{3}{7}x^{7/3}+\frac{24}{11}x^{11/6}+C$$

Example 89. Evaluate $\int x^{-2/3}(1+x^{2/3})^{-1}\,dx$.

Sol. If we substitute $x = t^3$ (as we know $P \in$ negative integer)

$\therefore$ Let $x = t^k$, where k is the LCM of m and n.

$$\therefore \quad x = t^3 \Rightarrow dx = 3t^2\,dt$$

$$\text{or} \quad I = \int \frac{3t^2}{t^2(1+t^2)}\,dt = 3\int \frac{dt}{t^2+1} = 3\tan^{-1}(t) + C$$

$$\Rightarrow \quad I = 3\tan^{-1}(x^{1/3}) + C$$

Example 90. Evaluate $\int x^5(1+x^3)^{2/3}\,dx$.

Sol. Here, $\int x^5(1+x^3)^{2/3}\,dx$ have $m = 5$, $n = 3$ and $p = \frac{2}{3}$

$$\therefore \quad \frac{m+1}{n} = \frac{6}{3} = 2 \quad \text{[an integer]}$$

So, we substitute $1 + x^3 = t^3$ and $x^2\,dx = t^2 dt$

$$\therefore \int x^5(1+x^3)^{2/3}dx = \int x^3(1+x^3)^{2/3}x^2dx$$

$$= \int (t^3-1)(t^3)^{2/3}\,t^2dt$$

$$= \int (t^3-1)\,t^4dt = \int (t^7-t^4)\,dt = \frac{1}{8}t^8 - \frac{1}{5}t^5 + C$$

$$= \frac{1}{8}(1+x^3)^{8/3} - \frac{1}{5}(1+x^3)^{5/3} + C$$

Example 91. Evaluate $\int \frac{1}{\sqrt[3]{x}+\sqrt[4]{x}}\,dx$.

Sol. Let $I = \int \frac{1}{\sqrt[3]{x}+\sqrt[4]{x}}\,dx$

Put $x^{1/12} = t$, $\Rightarrow x = t^{12}$ and $dx = 12t^{11}\,dt$

$$\therefore \quad I = \int \frac{1}{t^4+t^3}\cdot 12\,t^{11}dt = 12\int \frac{t^8}{t+1}\,dt$$

Again put $(t+1) = y$

$$\therefore\ dt = dy \Rightarrow 12\int \frac{(y-1)^8}{y}\,dy$$

$$= 12\int \frac{(y^8 - 8y^7 + 28y^6 - 56y^5 + 70y^4 - 56y^3 + 28y^2 - 8y + 1)}{y}\,dy$$

[using binomial]

$$= 12\int (y^7 - 8y^6 + 28y^5 - 56y^4 + 70y^3 - 56y^2 + 28y - 8 + 1/y)\,dy$$

$$= 12\begin{pmatrix} \dfrac{y^8}{8} - \dfrac{8y^7}{7} + \dfrac{28y^6}{6} - \dfrac{56y^5}{5} + \dfrac{70y^4}{4} \\ -\dfrac{56y^3}{3} + \dfrac{28y^2}{2} - 8y + \log|y| \end{pmatrix} + C$$

where, $y = x^{1/12} + 1$

Milestone Practice 1.6

Evaluate the following integrals

1. $\int \frac{2x^{12}+5x^9}{(x^5+x^3+1)^3}dx$
2. $\int \frac{dx}{(1+\sqrt{x})\sqrt{x-x^2}}$
3. $\int \frac{(x+2)\,dx}{(x^2+3x+3)\sqrt{x+1}}$
4. $\int \frac{dx}{(x+1)^{1/3}+(x+1)^{1/2}}$
5. $\int \frac{dx}{(x+a)^{8/7}(x-b)^{6/7}}$
6. $\int \frac{dx}{(1+5x^2)(\sqrt{5-x^2})}dx$
7. $\int \frac{dx}{(x+1)^{3/4}(x-2)^{5/4}}$
8. $\int \frac{\cos x dx}{1+\sin^4 x}$
9. $\int \frac{\sec x \cdot dx}{\sqrt{\sin(2x+A)+\sin A}}$
10. $\int (x^2+a^2)(x^4+a^2x^2+a^4)^{-1}\,dx$
11. $\int \frac{(1+x^2)}{1-2x^2\cos\alpha+x^4}dx$
12. $\int \frac{dx}{(x^3+3x^2+3x+1)\sqrt{x^2+2x-3}}$

Answer Key

1. $\frac{x^{10}}{2(x^5+x^3+1)^2}+C$
2. $-2\sqrt{\frac{1-\sqrt{x}}{1+\sqrt{x}}}+C$
3. $\frac{2}{\sqrt{3}}\tan^{-1}\left(\frac{x}{\sqrt{3}\sqrt{x+1}}\right)+C$
4. $2t^3-3t^2+6t-6\log(t+1)+C$
5. $\frac{7}{(a+b)}\left(\frac{x-b}{x+a}\right)^{1/7}+C$
6. $\frac{1}{\sqrt{26}}\tan^{-1}\left(\frac{\sqrt{26}x}{\sqrt{5-x^2}}\right)+C$
7. $-\frac{4}{3}\left(\frac{x+1}{x-2}\right)^{1/4}+C$
8. $\frac{1}{2\sqrt{2}}\tan^{-1}\left(\frac{t^2-1}{\sqrt{2}t}\right)-\frac{1}{4\sqrt{2}}\left(\frac{t^2-\sqrt{2}t+1}{t^2+\sqrt{2}t+1}\right)+C$
9. $\sqrt{2}\sec A\sqrt{\tan x\cos A+\sin A}+C$
10. $\frac{\tan^{-1}\left(\frac{2x+a}{\sqrt{3}a}\right)+\tan^{-1}\left(\frac{2x-a}{\sqrt{3}a}\right)}{\sqrt{3}\,a}+C$
11. $\frac{1}{2}\operatorname{cosec}\frac{\alpha}{2}\tan^{-1}\left(\frac{x^2-1}{2x\sin\frac{\alpha}{2}}\right)+C$
12. $\frac{1}{16}\cos^{-1}\left(\frac{2}{x+1}\right)+\frac{\sqrt{x^2+2x-3}}{8(x+1)^2}+C$

For Detailed Solution

Milestone 7 Euler's Substitution, Reduction Formula and Integration Using Differentiation

• Integration Using Euler's Substitutions • Reduction Formulae • Integration Using Differentiation

1.10 Integration Using Euler's Substitution

Integrals of the form $\int f(x)\sqrt{ax^2+bx+c}\,dx$ are calculated with the aid of one of the three Euler's substitutions

(i) $\sqrt{ax^2+bx+c}=t\pm x\sqrt{a}$, if $a>0$.

(ii) $\sqrt{ax^2+bx+c}=tx\pm\sqrt{c}$, if $c>0$.

(iii) $\sqrt{ax^2+bx+c}=(x-\alpha)\,t$, if $ax^2+bx+c=a(x-\alpha)(x-\beta)$, i.e. If α is real root of (ax^2+bx+c).

JEE SPIKE

The Euler's substitutions often lead to rather cumbersome calculations, therefore they should be applied only when it is difficult to find another method for calculating a given integral.

Example 92. Evaluate $I=\int\frac{x\,dx}{(\sqrt{7x-10-x^2})^3}$.

Sol. In this case $a<0$ and $c<0$.

Therefore, neither (I) nor (II) Euler's Substitution is applicable. But the quadratic $7x-10-x^2$ has real roots $\alpha=2,\beta=5$.

$\therefore$ We use the substitution (III)

i.e. $\sqrt{7x-10-x^2}=\sqrt{(x-2)(5-x)}=(x-2)\,t$

Where $(5-x)=(x-2)\,t^2$ or $5+2t^2=x(1+t^2)$

$$\therefore \quad x=\frac{5+2t^2}{1+t^2}$$

$$(x-2)\,t=\left(\frac{5+2t^2}{1+t^2}-2\right)t=\frac{3t}{1+t^2}$$

$$\therefore \quad dx=\frac{-6t}{(1+t^2)^2}\,dt$$

Hence, $$I=\int\frac{x\,dx}{(\sqrt{7x-10-x^2})^3}=\int\frac{\left(\frac{5+2t^2}{1+t^2}\right)\cdot\frac{-6t}{(1+t^2)^2}\,dt}{\left(\frac{3t}{1+t^2}\right)^3}$$

$$=\frac{-6}{27}\int\frac{5+2t^2}{t^2}\,dt$$

$$=\frac{-2}{9}\int\left(\frac{5}{t^2}+2\right)dt=\frac{-2}{9}\left[\frac{-5}{t}+2t\right]+C$$

$$\therefore \int\frac{x\,dx}{(\sqrt{7x-10-x^2})^3}=\frac{-2}{9}\left(\frac{-5}{t}+2t\right)+C,$$

where, $t=\frac{\sqrt{7x-10-x^2}}{x-2}$

Example 93. Evaluate $\int\frac{dx}{x+\sqrt{x^2-x+1}}$.

Sol. Since, here $c=1$, we can apply the second Euler's Substitution.

$$\sqrt{x^2-x+1}=tx-1$$

Therefore, $(2t-1)\,x=(t^2-1)\,x^2 \Rightarrow x=\frac{2t-1}{t^2-1}$

$$\therefore \quad dx=-\frac{2(t^2-t+1)\,dt}{(t^2-1)^2} \text{ and } x+\sqrt{x^2-x+1}=\frac{t}{t-1}$$

$$\therefore \quad I=\int\frac{dx}{x+\sqrt{x^2-x+1}}=\int\frac{-2t^2+2t-2}{t(t-1)(t+1)^2}\,dt$$

Using partial fractions, we have

$$\frac{-2t^2+2t-2}{t(t-1)(t+1)^2}=\frac{A}{t}+\frac{B}{t-1}+\frac{C}{(t+1)}+\frac{D}{(t+1)^2}$$

or $$(-2t^2+2t-2)=A(t-1)(t+1)^2+Bt(t+1)^2+C(t-1)(t+1)t+Dt(t-1)$$

we get $A=2,\quad B=-1/2,\quad C=-3/2,\quad D=-3$

Hence, $$I=2\int\frac{dt}{t}-\frac{1}{2}\int\frac{dt}{t-1}-\frac{3}{2}\int\frac{dt}{(t+1)}-3\int\frac{dt}{(t+1)^2}$$

$$=2\log_e|t|-\frac{1}{2}\log_e|t-1|-\frac{3}{2}\log_e|t+1|+\frac{3}{(t+1)}+C$$

$$\left[\text{where } t=\frac{\sqrt{x^2-x+1}+1}{x}\right]$$

Introduction of Reduction Formulae (a recursive relation) Over Indefinite Integrals

Reduction formulae makes it possible to reduce an integral depending on the index $n > 0$, called the order of the integral, to an integral of the same type with smaller index (i.e. To reduce the integrals into similar integrals of order less than or greater than given integral).

Application of reduction formula is given with the help of some examples.

Reduction Formula for $\int \sin^n x\,dx$

Let $I_n = \int \sin^n x\,dx = \int \underset{\text{I}}{\sin^{n-1} x}\,\underset{\text{II}}{\sin x}\,dx$

$$= -\sin^{n-1} x \cos x + \int (n-1)\sin^{n-2} x \cos^2 x\,dx$$

$$= -\sin^{n-1} x \cos x + (n-1)\int \sin^{n-2} x(1-\sin^2 x)\,dx$$

$$= -\sin^{n-1} x \cos x + (n-1)\int (\sin^{n-2} x - \sin^n x)\,dx$$

$$= -\sin^{n-1} x \cos x + (n-1) I_{n-2} - (n-1) I_n$$

$\therefore \quad n I_n = -\sin^{n-1} x \cos x + (n-1) I_{n-2}$

$\Rightarrow \quad I_n = -\dfrac{\sin^{n-1} x \cos x}{n} + \dfrac{n-1}{n} I_{n-2}$

Thus, $\displaystyle\int \sin^n x\,dx = \frac{-\sin^{n-1} x \cos x}{n} + \frac{n-1}{n}\int \sin^{n-2} x\,dx$

Reduction Formula for $\int \cos^n x\,dx$

Let $I_n = \int \cos^n x\,dx = \int \underset{\text{I}}{\cos^{n-1} x}\,\underset{\text{II}}{\cos x}\,dx$

$$= \cos^{n-1} x \sin x + \int (n-1)\cos^{n-2} x \sin^2 x\,dx$$

$$= \cos^{n-1} x \sin x + (n-1)\int \cos^{n-2} x\,(1-\cos^2 x)\,dx$$

$$= \cos^{n-1} x \sin x + (n-1) I_{n-2} - (n-1) I_n$$

$\therefore \quad nI_n = \cos^{n-1} x \sin x + (n-1) I_{n-2}$

or $\displaystyle\int \cos^n x\,dx = \frac{\cos^{n-1} x \sin x}{n} + \frac{n-1}{n}\int \cos^{n-2} x\,dx$

Reduction Formula for $\int \tan^n x\,dx$

Let $I_n = \int \tan^n x\,dx$

$\Rightarrow \quad I_n = \int \tan^{n-2} x \tan^2 x\,dx = \int \tan^{n-2} x\,(\sec^2 x - 1)\,dx$

$$= \int \tan^{n-2} x \sec^2 x - I_{n-2} = \int t^{n-2}\,dt - I_{n-2}$$

where, $\tan x = t \Rightarrow \sec^2 x\,dx = dt$

$$I_n = \frac{t^{n-1}}{n-1} - I_{n-2}$$

$\therefore \quad I_n = \dfrac{\tan^{n-1} x}{n-1} - I_{n-2}$

$\Rightarrow \quad \displaystyle\int \tan^n x\,dx = \frac{\tan^{n-1} x}{n-1} - \int \tan^{n-2} x\,dx$

Reduction Formula for $\int \operatorname{cosec}^n x\,dx$

Let $I_n = \int \operatorname{cosec}^n x\,dx = \int \underset{\text{I}}{\operatorname{cosec}^{n-2} x}\,\underset{\text{II}}{\operatorname{cosec}^2 x}\,dx$

$$= \operatorname{cosec}^{n-2} x\,(-\cot x) - \int (n-2)\operatorname{cosec}^{n-2} x\,(\operatorname{cosec}^2 x - 1)\,dx$$

$$= -\operatorname{cosec}^{n-2} x \cot x - (n-2)\int (\operatorname{cosec}^n x - \operatorname{cosec}^{n-2} x)\,dx$$

$$= -\operatorname{cosec}^{n-2} x \cot x - (n-2) I_n + (n-2) I_{n-2}$$

$\therefore \quad (n-1) I_n = -\operatorname{cosec}^{n-2} x \cot x + (n-2) I_{n-2}$

or $\quad I_n = -\dfrac{\operatorname{cosec}^{n-2} x \cot x}{n-1} + \dfrac{n-2}{n-1} I_{n-2}$

$\therefore \quad \displaystyle\int \operatorname{cosec}^n x\,dx = -\frac{\operatorname{cosec}^{n-2} x \cot x}{n-1} + \frac{n-2}{n-1}\int \operatorname{cosec}^{n-2} x\,dx$

Reduction Formula for $\int \sec^n x\,dx$

Let $I_n = \int \sec^n x\,dx = \int \underset{\text{I}}{\sec^{n-2} x}\,\underset{\text{II}}{\sec^2 x}\,dx$

$$= \sec^{n-2} x \tan x - \int (n-2)\sec^{n-3} x\,\sec x \tan x \cdot \tan x\,dx$$

$$= \sec^{n-2} x \tan x - (n-2)\int \sec^{n-2} x\,(\sec^2 x - 1)\,dx$$

$$= \sec^{n-2} x \tan x - (n-2) I_n + (n-2) I_{n-2}$$

$\Rightarrow \quad (n-1) I_n = \sec^{n-2} x \tan x + (n-2) I_{n-2}$

or $\quad I_n = \dfrac{\sec^{n-2} x \tan x}{(n-1)} + \dfrac{(n-2)}{(n-1)} I_{n-2}$

$\therefore \quad \displaystyle\int \sec^n x\,dx = \frac{\sec^{n-2} x \tan x}{(n-1)} + \frac{(n-2)}{(n-1)}\int \sec^{n-2} x\,dx$

Reduction Formula for $\int \cot^n x\,dx$

Let $I_n = \int \cot^n x\,dx = \int \cot^{n-2} x \cot^2 x\,dx$

$$= \int \cot^{n-2} x\,(\operatorname{cosec}^2 x - 1)\,dx$$

$$= \int \cot^{n-2} x \operatorname{cosec}^2 x\,dx - \int \cot^{n-2} x\,dx$$

$$= -\int t^{n-2}\, dt - I_{n-2}, \qquad \text{[where } t = \cot x\text{]}$$

$$I_n = -\frac{\cot^{n-1} x}{n-1} - I_{n-2}$$

$$\therefore \quad \int \cot^n x\, dx = -\frac{\cot^{n-1} x}{n-1} - \int \cot^{n-2} x\, dx$$

Reduction Formula for $\int \sin^m x \cos^n x\, dx$

Let $A = \sin^{m-1} x \cos^{n+1} x$

$$\therefore \quad \frac{dA}{dx} = (m-1)\sin^{m-2} x \cos^{n+2} x - (n+1)\sin^m x \cos^n x$$

$$= (m-1)\sin^{m-2} x \cos^n x (1-\sin^2 x) - (n+1)\sin^m x \cos^n x$$

$$= (m-1)\sin^{m-2} x \cos^n x - (m-1+n+1) \sin^m x \cos^n x$$

$$= (m-1)\sin^{m-2} x \cos^n x - (m+n)\sin^m x \cos^n x$$

Integrating with respect to x on both the sides, we get

$$A = (m-1)\int \sin^{m-2} x \cos^n x\, dx - (m+n) \int \sin^m x \cos^n x\, dx$$

$$\Rightarrow \quad (m+n)\int \sin^m x \cos^n x\, dx = (m-1) \int \sin^{m-2} x \cos^n x\, dx - A$$

$$\Rightarrow \quad \int \sin^m x \cos^n x\, dx = \frac{(m-1)}{(m+n)}\int \sin^{m-2} x \cos^n x\, dx - \frac{\sin^{m-1} x \cos^{n+1} x}{m+n}$$

or $$I_{(m,n)} = \frac{(m-1)}{(m+n)} I_{(m-2,n)} - \frac{\sin^{m-1} x \cos^{n+1} x}{(m+n)}$$

Reduction Formula for $\int \cos^m x \sin nx\, dx$

Let $I_{(m,n)} = \int \underset{\text{I}}{\cos^m x}\ \underset{\text{II}}{\sin nx}\, dx$

$$= -\frac{\cos^m x \cos nx}{n} - \frac{m}{n}\int \cos^{m-1} x \sin x \cos nx\, dx$$

$$= -\frac{\cos^m x \cos nx}{n} - \frac{m}{n}\int \cos^{m-1} x \{\sin nx \cos x - \sin(n-1)x\}\, dx$$

[using $\sin(n-1)x = \sin nx \cos x - \cos nx \sin x$

$\Rightarrow \sin x \cos nx = \sin nx \cos x - \sin(n-1)x$]

$$= -\frac{\cos^m x \cos nx}{n} - \frac{m}{n}\int \cos^m x \sin nx\, dx + \frac{m}{n}\int \cos^{m-1} x \sin(n-1)x\, dx$$

$$\Rightarrow \quad I_{(m,n)} = -\frac{\cos^m x \cos nx}{n} - \frac{m}{n} I_{(m,n)} + \frac{m}{n} I_{(m-1,n-1)}$$

$$\Rightarrow \quad \frac{m+n}{n} I_{(m,n)} = -\frac{\cos^m x \cos nx}{n} + \frac{m}{n} I_{(m-1,n-1)}$$

or $$I_{(m,n)} = -\frac{\cos^m x \cos nx}{m+n} + \frac{m}{m+n} I_{(m-1,n-1)}$$

JEE Focus Points

Concept Inside Video

Similarly, we can show

- $\int \sin^m x \cos^n x\, dx = \frac{\sin^{m+1} x \cos^{n+1} x}{m+n} + \frac{n-1}{m+n}\int \sin^m x \cos^{n-2} x\, dx$
- $\int \sin^m x \cos^n x\, dx = \frac{\sin^{m+1} x \cos^{n+1} x}{m+1} + \frac{m+n+2}{m+1}\int \sin^{m+2} x \cos^n x\, dx$
- $\int \sin^m x \cos^n x\, dx = \frac{\sin^{m+1} x \cos^{n+1} x}{n+1} + \frac{m+n+2}{n+1}\int \sin^m x \cos^{n+2} x\, dx$
- $\int \sin^m x \cos^n x\, dx = -\frac{\sin^{m-1} x \cos^{n+1} x}{n+1} + \frac{m-1}{n+1}\int \sin^{m-2} x \cos^{n+2} x\, dx$
- $\int \sin^m x \cos^n x\, dx = \frac{\sin^{m+1} x \cos^{n-1} x}{m+1} + \frac{n-1}{m+1}\int \sin^{m+2} x \cos^{n-2} x\, dx$
- $\int \cos^m x \cos nx\, dx = \frac{\cos^m x \sin nx}{m+n} + \frac{m}{m+n}\int \cos^{m-1} x \cos(n-1)x\, dx$
- $\int \sin^m x \sin nx\, dx = \frac{n \sin^m x \cos nx}{m^2-n^2} - \frac{m \sin^{m-1} x \cos x \cos nx}{m^2-n^2} + \frac{m(m-1)}{m^2-n^2}\int \sin^{m-2} x \sin nx\, dx$
- $\int \sin^m x \cos nx\, dx = \frac{n \sin^m x \sin nx}{m^2-n^2} - \frac{m \sin^{m-1} x \cos x \cos nx}{m^2-n^2} + \frac{m(m-1)}{m^2-n^2}\int \sin^{m-2} x \cos nx\, dx$

Reduction Formula for $\int \frac{dx}{(x^2+a^2)^n}$

Let $I_n = \int \frac{dx}{(x^2+a^2)^n} = \int \frac{1}{(x^2+a^2)^n}\cdot 1\, dx$

Applying integration by parts, we get

$$= \frac{1}{(x^2+a^2)^n}\cdot x - \int \frac{(2x)}{(x^2+a^2)^{n+1}}\cdot(-n)\cdot(x)\, dx$$

$$= \frac{x}{(x^2+a^2)^n} + 2n\int \frac{x^2}{(x^2+a^2)^{n+1}}\,dx$$

$$= \frac{x}{(x^2+a^2)^n} + 2n\int \frac{x^2+a^2-a^2}{(x^2+a^2)^{n+1}}\,dx$$

$$\therefore \quad I_n = \frac{x}{(x^2+a^2)^n} + 2n\int \frac{1}{(x^2+a^2)^n}\,dx - 2a^2 n\int \frac{dx}{(x^2+a^2)^{n+1}}$$

$$I_n = \frac{x}{(x^2+a^2)^n} + 2n\,I_n - 2n\,a^2\,I_{n+1}$$

$$\therefore \quad 2n\,a^2\,I_{n+1} = \frac{x}{(x^2+a^2)^n} + (2n-1)\,I_n$$

or
$$I_{n+1} = \frac{1}{2n\,a^2}\cdot\frac{x}{(x^2+a^2)^n} + \frac{(2n-1)}{2n}\cdot\frac{1}{a^2}\,I_n$$

JEE SPIKE

Above obtained formula reduces the calculations of the integral I_{n+1} to the calculations of the integral I_n and consequently, allows us to calculate completely an integral with natural index, as

$$I_1 = \int \frac{dx}{x^2+a^2} = \frac{1}{a}\tan^{-1}\left(\frac{x}{a}\right) + C$$

Concept Inside Video

$\therefore$ From above formula,

Let $n = 1$

$$I_2 = \int \frac{dx}{(x^2+a^2)^2} = \frac{1}{2a^2}\cdot\frac{x}{x^2+a^2} + \frac{1}{2a^2}\cdot I_1$$

$$= \frac{1}{2a^2}\cdot\frac{x}{x^2+a^2} + \frac{1}{2a^2}\cdot\frac{1}{a}\cdot\tan^{-1}\left(\frac{x}{a}\right) + C$$

$$= \frac{1}{2a^2}\cdot\frac{x}{x^2+a^2} + \frac{1}{2a^3}\cdot\tan^{-1}\left(\frac{x}{a}\right) + C$$

Let $n = 2$

$$I_3 = \int \frac{dx}{(x^2+a^2)^3} = \frac{1}{4a^2}\cdot\frac{x}{(x^2+a^2)^2} + \frac{3}{4a^2}\,I_2$$

$$= \frac{1}{4a^2}\cdot\frac{x}{(x^2+a^2)^2} + \frac{3}{8a^4}\cdot\frac{x}{x^2+a^2} + \frac{3}{8a^5}\tan^{-1}\left(\frac{x}{a}\right) + C$$

...and so on.

Example 94. Derive reduction formula for

$$I_{(n,\,m)} = \int \frac{\sin^n x}{\cos^m x}\,dx.$$

Sol. Using integration by parts for $I_{(n,\,m)}$, we get

$$I_{(n,\,m)} = \int \underset{\text{I}}{\sin^{n-1} x}\;\underset{\text{II}}{\frac{\sin x}{\cos^m x}}\,dx$$

$$= \sin^{n-1} x\cdot\frac{(\cos x)^{-m+1}}{(m-1)} - \int (n-1)\sin^{n-2} x\,\cos x\cdot\frac{(\cos x)^{-m+1}}{(m-1)}\,dx$$

$$= \frac{1}{m-1}\cdot\frac{\sin^{n-1} x}{\cos^{m-1} x} - \frac{(n-1)}{(m-1)}\cdot\int \frac{\sin^{n-2} x}{\cos^{m-2} x}\,dx$$

$$I_{(n,\,m)} = \frac{1}{(m-1)}\cdot\frac{\sin^{n-1} x}{\cos^{m-1} x} - \frac{(n-1)}{(m-1)}\cdot I_{(n-2,\,m-2)}$$

is required reduction formula.

1.11 Integration Using Differentiation

In $\int \frac{dx}{(a+b\cos x)^2}$, $\int \frac{dx}{(a+b\sin x)^2}$, $\int \frac{dx}{(\sin x + a\sec x)^2}$, $\int \frac{a+b\sin x}{(b+a\sin x)^2}\,dx, \ldots$ we follow the following method.

1. Let $A = \frac{\sin x}{a+b\cos x}$ or $A = \frac{\cos x}{a+b\sin x}$ according to the integral to evaluated is of the form $\int \frac{dx}{(a+b\cos x)^2}$ or $\int \frac{dx}{(a+b\sin x)^2}$
2. Find $\frac{dA}{dx}$ and express it in terms of $\frac{1}{a+b\cos x}$ or $\frac{1}{a+b\sin x}$ as the case may be.
3. Integrate both the sides of the expression obtained in step 2 to obtain the value of the required integral.

Example 95. Evaluate $\int \frac{dx}{(5+4\cos x)^2}$.

Sol. Here, $A = \frac{\sin x}{5+4\cos x}$, then

$$\frac{dA}{dx} = \frac{(5+4\cos x)(\cos x) - \sin x\,(-4\sin x)}{(5+4\cos x)^2}$$

$$\Rightarrow \quad \frac{dA}{dx} = \frac{5\cos x + 4}{(5+4\cos x)^2} = \frac{\frac{5}{4}(4\cos x + 5) + 4 - \frac{25}{4}}{(5+4\cos x)^2}$$

$$\Rightarrow \quad \frac{dA}{dx} = \frac{5}{4}\cdot\frac{1}{(5+4\cos x)} - \frac{9}{4}\cdot\frac{1}{(5+4\cos x)^2}$$

Integrating both the sides w.r.t. 'x', we get

$$A = \frac{5}{4}\int \frac{dx}{5+4\cos x} - \frac{9}{4}\int \frac{dx}{(5+4\cos x)^2}$$

$$\Rightarrow \quad \frac{9}{4}\int \frac{dx}{(5+4\cos x)^2} = \frac{5}{4}\int \frac{dx}{5+4\cos x} - A$$

$$= \frac{5}{4}\int \frac{dx}{5+4\,\frac{(1-\tan^2 x/2)}{(1+\tan^2 x/2)}} - \frac{\sin x}{(5+4\cos x)}$$

$$\Rightarrow \int \frac{dx}{(5+4\cos x)^2} = \frac{5}{9}\int \frac{1+\tan^2 x/2}{9+\tan^2 x/2}\,dx - \frac{4}{9}\cdot\frac{\sin x}{5+4\cos x}$$

$$\Rightarrow \int \frac{dx}{(5+4\cos x)^2} = \frac{5}{9}\int \frac{2\,dt}{9+t^2} - \frac{4}{9}\cdot\frac{\sin x}{5+4\cos x}$$

[where $\tan x/2 = t$]

$$\Rightarrow \int \frac{dx}{(5+4\cos x)^2} = \frac{10}{9}\cdot\frac{1}{3}\tan^{-1}\left(\frac{t}{3}\right) - \frac{4}{9}\cdot\frac{\sin x}{5+4\cos x}$$

$$\Rightarrow \int \frac{dx}{(5+4\cos x)^2} = \frac{10}{27}\tan^{-1}\left(\frac{\tan x/2}{3}\right) - \frac{4}{9}\left(\frac{\sin x}{5+4\cos x}\right) + C$$

Example 96. Evaluate $\int \frac{dx}{(\sin x + a\sec x)^2}$, when $|a| > 1/2$.

Sol. Here, $I = \int \frac{dx}{(\sin x + a\sec x)^2}$ or $I = \int \frac{\cos^2 x\, dx}{(\sin x\cos x + a)^2}$

$$= \int \frac{\cos^2 x\, dx}{a^2 + 2a\sin x\cos x + \sin^2 x\cos^2 x}$$

$$= \int \frac{\cos^2 x\, dx}{a^2 + a\sin 2x + \frac{1}{4}\sin^2 2x}$$

$$= \int \frac{4\cos^2 x\, dx}{(4a^2 + 4a\sin 2x + \sin^2 2x)} = 2\int \frac{(1+\cos 2x)\, dx}{(2a+\sin 2x)^2}$$

$$= 2\int \frac{dx}{(2a+\sin 2x)^2} + 2\int \frac{\cos 2x\, dx}{(2a+\sin 2x)^2}$$

$$= 2I_1 + \int \frac{dt}{t^2}$$

[where $(2a+\sin 2x) = t$, $(2\cos 2x)\,dx = dt$]

$$= 2I_1 - \frac{1}{(2a+\sin 2x)} + C$$

where $I_1 = \int \frac{dx}{(2a+\sin 2x)^2}$ ...(i)

Put $A = \frac{\cos 2x}{2a+\sin 2x}$

$$\Rightarrow \frac{dA}{dx} = \frac{(2a+\sin 2x)(-2\sin 2x) - \cos 2x\,(2\cos 2x)}{(2a+\sin 2x)^2}$$

$$\Rightarrow \frac{dA}{dx} = \frac{-4a\sin 2x - 2}{(2a+\sin 2x)^2}$$

$$\Rightarrow \frac{dA}{dx} = \frac{-4a(\sin 2x + 2a) - 2 + 8a^2}{(2a+\sin 2x)^2}$$

$$\Rightarrow \frac{dA}{dx} = -\frac{4a}{(2a+\sin 2x)} + \frac{(8a^2-2)}{(2a+\sin 2x)^2}$$

Integrating both the sides w.r.t. 'x', we get

$$A = -4a\int \frac{dx}{(2a+\sin 2x)} + (8a^2-2)\, I_1$$

$$\Rightarrow (8a^2-2)\, I_1 = A + 4a\int \frac{\sec^2 x\, dx}{2a + 2\tan x + 2a\tan^2 x}$$

$$= A + \frac{4a}{2a}\int \frac{dt}{t^2 + \frac{t}{a} + 1}$$

$$= A + 2\int \frac{dt}{\left(t + \frac{1}{2a}\right)^2 + \left(1 - \frac{1}{4a^2}\right)}$$

$$= A + 2\frac{(2a)}{\sqrt{4a^2-1}}\tan^{-1}\left(\frac{(2at+1)}{\sqrt{4a^2-1}}\right)$$

$$\Rightarrow (8a^2-2)\, I_1 = \frac{\cos 2x}{2a+\sin 2x} + \frac{4a}{\sqrt{4a^2-1}}\tan^{-1}\left(\frac{(2a\tan x+1)}{\sqrt{4a^2-1}}\right) \quad \text{...(ii)}$$

From Eqs. (i) and (ii), we get

$$I = \frac{1}{(4a^2-1)}\cdot\frac{\cos 2x}{(2a+\sin 2x)} + \frac{4a}{(4a^2-1)^{3/2}}\tan^{-1}\left(\frac{2a\tan x+1}{\sqrt{4a^2-1}}\right) - \frac{1}{(2a+\sin 2x)} + C$$

Milestone Practice 1.7

1. Evaluate $\int \frac{dx}{1+\sqrt{x^2+2x+2}}$.

2. If $\int \frac{dx}{x^3\sqrt{x^2-1}} = \frac{1}{m}\left[\frac{\sqrt{x^2-1}}{x^2} + \tan^{-1}\sqrt{x^2-1}\right] + C$, then find the value of m.

3. Evaluate $\int \frac{\sin^6 x}{\cos^4 x}\, dx$.

4. Evaluate $\int \frac{a+b\sin x}{(b+a\sin x)^2}\, dx$.

5. Evaluate $\int \frac{dx}{(\sin x + 2\sec x)^2}$.

6. Evaluate $\int \sec^7 x\, dx$.

Answer Key

1. $\ln|x+1+\sqrt{x^2+2x+2}| + \frac{2}{x+2+\sqrt{x^2+2x+2}} + C$

2. 2

3. $\tan x + \frac{\tan^3 x}{3} - 3\tan x + \frac{5}{2}x - \frac{1}{4}\sin 2x + C$

4. $-\frac{\cos x}{b+a\sin x} + C$

5. $\frac{8}{15\sqrt{15}}\left[\tan^{-1}\frac{2\sqrt{2}}{\sqrt{15}}\left(\sqrt{2}\tan x + \frac{1}{2\sqrt{2}}\right) + \frac{1}{2}\sin\left(2\tan^{-1}\left(\frac{2\sqrt{2}}{\sqrt{15}}\sqrt{2}\tan x + \frac{1}{2\sqrt{2}}\right)\right)\right] + C$

6. $\frac{1}{6}\sec^5 x\cdot\tan x + \frac{5}{24}\sec^3 x\cdot\tan x + \frac{15}{48}[(\sec x\cdot\tan x) + \log|\sec x + \tan x|] + C$

For Detailed Solution

JEE Pattern EXAMPLES

Single Option Correct Type Questions

Example 1 *The value of* $\int \frac{dx}{\cos^6 x + \sin^6 x}$, *is equal to*

(a) $\tan^{-1}(2\cot 2x) + C$ (b) $\tan^{-1}(\cot 2x) + C$

(c) $\tan^{-1}\left(\frac{1}{2}\cot 2x\right) + C$ (d) $\tan^{-1}(-2\cot 2x) + C$

> **Decoding the Question**
> First convert denominator of the given integration into $\tan x$ and then let $\tan x = t$. After solving it, we get the result in form of $t - \frac{1}{t}$, then again we let it as z and solve accordingly.

Sol. (d) Let $I = \int \frac{dx}{\cos^6 x + \sin^6 x}$

$$= \int \frac{\sec^6 x\, dx}{1 + \tan^6 x} = \int \frac{(1+\tan^2 x)^2 \cdot \sec^2 x}{1 + \tan^6 x} dx$$

Put $\tan x = t \Rightarrow \sec^2 x\, dx = dt$

$$\therefore\ I = \int \frac{(1+t^2)^2}{1+t^6} dt = \int \frac{(1+t^2)^2}{(1+t^2)(1-t^2+t^4)} dt$$

$$= \int \frac{1+t^2}{1-t^2+t^4} dt = \int \frac{(1+1/t^2)\,dt}{(1/t^2 - 1 + t^2)} = \int \frac{\left(1+\frac{1}{t^2}\right)dt}{(t-1/t)^2 + 1}$$

Put $t - \frac{1}{t} = z \Rightarrow \left(1 + \frac{1}{t^2}\right) dt = dz$

$$\therefore\ I = \int \frac{dz}{z^2+1}$$

$$= \tan^{-1}(z) + C = \tan^{-1}\left(\frac{t^2-1}{t}\right) + C$$

$$= \tan^{-1}\left(\frac{\tan^2 x - 1}{\tan x}\right) + C$$

$$= \tan^{-1}(-2\cot 2x) + C$$

Example 2 *Let* $I = \int \frac{e^x}{e^{4x} + e^{2x} + 1} dx$ *and*

$$J = \int \frac{e^{-x}}{e^{-4x} + e^{-2x} + 1} dx.$$

Then, for an arbitrary constant C, the value of $J - I$ *equals to*

(a) $\frac{1}{2}\log\left(\frac{e^{4x} - e^{2x} + 1}{e^{4x} + e^{2x} + 1}\right) + C$

(b) $\frac{1}{2}\log\left(\frac{e^{2x} + e^{x} + 1}{e^{2x} - e^{x} + 1}\right) + C$

(c) $\frac{1}{2}\log\left(\frac{e^{2x} - e^{x} + 1}{e^{2x} + e^{x} + 1}\right) + C$

(d) $\frac{1}{2}\log\left(\frac{e^{4x} + e^{2x} + 1}{e^{4x} - e^{2x} + 1}\right) + C$

Sol. (c) $J = \int \frac{e^{3x}}{1 + e^{2x} + e^{4x}} dx$

$$J - I = \int \frac{(e^{3x} - e^x)}{1 + e^{2x} + e^{4x}} dx = \int \frac{(u^2-1)}{1+u^2+u^4} du$$

[put $u = e^x \Rightarrow du = e^x dx$]

$$= \int \frac{\left(1 - \frac{1}{u^2}\right)du}{1 + \frac{1}{u^2} + u^2} = \int \frac{\left(1 - \frac{1}{u^2}\right)du}{\left(u + \frac{1}{u}\right)^2 - 1} = \int \frac{dt}{t^2 - 1}$$

$\left[\text{put } t = u + \frac{1}{u} \Rightarrow dt = 1 - \frac{1}{u^2} du\right]$

$$= \frac{1}{2}\log\left|\frac{t-1}{t+1}\right| + C = \frac{1}{2}\log\left|\frac{u^2-u+1}{u^2+u+1}\right| + C$$

$$= \frac{1}{2}\log\left|\frac{e^{2x} - e^x + 1}{e^{2x} + e^x + 1}\right| + C$$

Example 3 *Integral of* $\sqrt{1 + 2\cot x(\cot x + \operatorname{cosec} x)}$ *w.r.t. x, is*

(a) $2\ln\cos\frac{x}{2} + C$ (b) $2\ln\sin\frac{x}{2} + C$

(c) $\frac{1}{2}\ln\cos\frac{x}{2} + C$ (d) $\ln\sin x - \ln(\operatorname{cosec} x - \cot x) + C$

Sol. (b) $I = \int \sqrt{1 + 2\operatorname{cosec} x \cot x + 2\cot^2 x}\, dx$

$$= \int \sqrt{\operatorname{cosec}^2 x + 2\operatorname{cosec} x \cot x + \cot^2 x}\, dx$$

$$= \int (\operatorname{cosec} x + \cot x)\, dx$$

$$= \int \frac{1 + \cos x}{\sin x} dx = \int \cot\left(\frac{x}{2}\right) dx = 2\log\left|\sin\frac{x}{2}\right| + C$$

JEE SCANNER

Example 4 Similar to PYQ Asked in JEE Main 2024

The integral $\int \frac{(x^8 - x^2)\,dx}{(x^{12}+3x^6+1)\cot^{-1}\left(x^3+\frac{1}{x^3}\right)}$ *is*

(a) $\log_e\left(\left|\cot^{-1}\left(x^3+\frac{1}{x^3}\right)\right|\right)+C$

(b) $\log_e\left(\left|\cot^{-1}\left(x^3+\frac{1}{x^3}\right)\right|\right)^{1/2}+C$

(c) $\log_e\left(\left|\cot^{-1}\left(x^3+\frac{1}{x^3}\right)\right|\right)^{1/3}+C$

(d) $\log_e\left(\left|\cot^{-1}\left(x^3+\frac{1}{x^3}\right)\right|\right)^{-1/3}+C$

Sol. (d) Let $I = \int \frac{(x^8 - x^2)dx}{(x^{12}+3x^6+1)\cot^{-1}\left(x^3+\frac{1}{x^3}\right)}$

Put $\cot^{-1}\left(x^3+\frac{1}{x^3}\right) = t \Rightarrow -\frac{1}{1+\left(x^3+\frac{1}{x^3}\right)^2}\times\left(3x^2-\frac{3}{x^4}\right)dx = dt$

$$\Rightarrow \quad -\frac{1}{1+\left(\frac{x^6+1}{x^3}\right)^2}\times\left(\frac{3x^6-3}{x^4}\right)dx = dt$$

$$\Rightarrow \quad \frac{-(x^3)^2}{(x^3)^2+(x^{12}+1+2\times1\times x^6)}\times\frac{3(x^6-1)}{x^4}dx = dt$$

$$\Rightarrow \quad \frac{-x^6\times3(x^6-1)}{x^4(x^6+x^{12}+1+2x^6)}dx = dt$$

$$\Rightarrow \quad -\frac{(x^8-x^2)}{(x^{12}+3x^6+1)}dx = \frac{1}{3}dt$$

So, $I = -\frac{1}{3}\int\frac{1}{t}dt = -\frac{1}{3}\log_e|t|+C = -\frac{1}{3}\log_e\left(\left|\cot^{-1}\left(x^3+\frac{1}{x^3}\right)\right|\right)+C$

Hence, $I = \log_e\left(\left|\cot^{-1}\left(x^3+\frac{1}{x^3}\right)\right|\right)^{-1/3}+C$

Skill Builder

The integral $\int \frac{(x^5 - x)\,dx}{(x^8+3x^4+1)\tan^{-1}\left(x^2+\frac{1}{x^2}\right)}$ is equal to

(a) $\log_e\left(\left|\tan^{-1}\left(x^2+\frac{1}{x^2}\right)\right|\right)+C$

(b) $\log_e\left(\left|\tan^{-1}\left(x^2+\frac{1}{x^2}\right)\right|\right)^{-1/2}+C$

(c) $\log_e\left(\left|\tan^{-1}\left(x^2+\frac{1}{x^2}\right)\right|\right)^{1/2}+C$

(d) $\log_e\left(\left|\tan^{-1}\left(x^2+\frac{1}{x^2}\right)\right|\right)^{1/3}+C$

For Sol.

Example 5 *The value of* $\int \frac{dx}{\sqrt{(x-a)(b-x)}}$*, is*

(a) $2\sin^{-1}\sqrt{\frac{x-a}{b-a}}+C$ (b) $2\sin^{-1}\sqrt{\frac{x-b}{b-a}}+C$

(c) $\sin^{-1}\sqrt{\frac{x-a}{b-a}}+C$ (d) None of these

Sol. (a) Let $x = a\cos^2\theta + b\sin^2\theta$ in the given integral.

So that, $dx = a\,(2\cos\theta)(-\sin\theta) + b\,(2\sin\theta)(\cos\theta)\,d\theta$

$$dx = 2\,(b-a)\sin\theta\cos\theta\,d\theta$$

$$\therefore\ I = \int \frac{2\,(b-a)\sin\theta\cos\theta\,d\theta}{\sqrt{(a\cos^2\theta+b\sin^2\theta-a)\,(b-a\cos^2\theta-b\sin^2\theta)}}$$

$$= 2\,(b-a)\int\frac{\sin\theta\cos\theta\,d\theta}{\sqrt{(b\sin^2\theta-a\sin^2\theta)\,(b\cos^2\theta-a\cos^2\theta)}}$$

$$= 2\,(b-a)\int\frac{\sin\theta\cos\theta\,d\theta}{(b-a)\sin\theta\cos\theta} = 2\int 1\,d\theta$$

$$= 2\theta + C = 2\sin^{-1}\sqrt{\frac{x-a}{b-a}}+C$$

Example 6 *The value of* $\int \frac{(x-1)}{(x+1)\sqrt{x^3+x^2+x}}dx$*, is*

(a) $2\tan^{-1}\sqrt{\frac{x+1}{x}}+C$ (b) $\tan^{-1}\sqrt{\frac{x^2+x+1}{x}}+C$

(c) $2\tan^{-1}\sqrt{\frac{x^2+x+1}{x}}+C$ (d) None of these

Sol. (c) Let $I = \int\frac{(x-1)}{(x+1)\sqrt{x^3+x^2+x}}dx$

$$= \int\frac{(x^2-1)}{(x+1)^2\sqrt{x^3+x^2+x}}dx$$

$$= \int\frac{x^2(1-1/x^2)}{(x^2+2x+1)\sqrt{x^3+x^2+x}}dx$$

$$= \int\frac{x^2(1-1/x^2)}{x\,(x+2+1/x)\cdot x\sqrt{x+1+1/x}}dx$$

Put $x+\frac{1}{x} = t \Rightarrow (1-1/x^2)\,dx = dt$

$$= \int\frac{dt}{(t+2)\sqrt{t+1}},$$

which reduces to $\int\frac{dx}{P\sqrt{Q}}$.

Let $t+1 = z^2 \Rightarrow dt = 2z\,dz$

$$= \int\frac{2z\,dz}{(z^2+1)\sqrt{z^2}}$$

$$= 2\int\frac{dz}{z^2+1} = 2\tan^{-1}(z)+C$$

$$= 2\tan^{-1}(\sqrt{t+1})+C = 2\tan^{-1}\sqrt{\frac{x^2+x+1}{x}}+C$$

JEE SCANNER

Example 7 Similar to PYQ Asked in JEE Main 2024

If $\int \frac{\sin^{3/2} x + \cos^{3/2} x}{\sqrt{\sin^3 x \cos^3 x \sin(x-\phi)}} dx = \lambda \sqrt{\cos\phi \tan x - \sin\phi}$ $+\mu \sqrt{\cos\phi - \sin\phi \cot x} + C$, *where C is the integration constant, then* $3(\lambda^2+\mu^2)$ *at* $\phi = \frac{\pi}{6}$ *is equal to*

(a) 64 (b) 32
(c) 128 (d) 16

Sol. (a) Let $I = \int \frac{\sin^{3/2} x + \cos^{3/2} x}{\sqrt{\sin^3 x \cdot \cos^3 x \cdot \sin(x-\phi)}} dx$

$$= \int \frac{dx}{\sqrt{\cos^3 x(\sin x \cos\phi - \cos x \sin\phi)}} + \int \frac{dx}{\sqrt{\sin^3 x(\sin x \cos\phi - \cos x \sin\phi)}}$$

$$= \int \frac{\sec^2 x dx}{\sqrt{\tan x \cos\phi - \sin\phi}} + \int \frac{\text{cosec}^2 x\, dx}{\sqrt{\cos\phi - \cot x \sin\phi}}$$

Put $\tan x = y$ and $-\cot x = z$

$\sec^2 x dx = dy$ and $\text{cosec}^2 x\, dx = dz$

$$I = \int \frac{dy}{\sqrt{y\cos\phi - \sin\phi}} + \int \frac{dz}{\sqrt{\cos\phi + z\sin\phi}}$$

$$= \frac{2\sqrt{y\cos\phi - \sin\phi}}{\cos\phi} + \frac{2\sqrt{\cos\phi + z\sin\phi}}{\sin\phi} + C$$

$$= 2\sec\phi \sqrt{\cos\phi \tan x - \sin\phi} + 2\text{cosec}\,\phi \sqrt{\cos\phi - \sin\phi \cot x} + C$$

$\therefore \lambda = 2\sec\phi$ and $\mu = 2\text{cosec}\,\phi$

So, $3(\lambda^2+\mu^2)_{\text{at } \phi = \frac{\pi}{6}} = 3(4\sec^2\phi + 4\text{cosec}^2\phi)$

$$= 3\left(\frac{4\times4}{3} + \frac{4\times4}{1}\right)$$

$$= 3\times16\left(\frac{1}{3}+1\right)$$

$$= 3\times16\times\frac{4}{3} = 64$$

Skill Builder

If $\int \frac{\sin^{3/2} x + \cos^{3/2} x}{\sqrt{\sin^3 x \cos^3 x \sin(x-\theta)}} dx = \lambda\sqrt{\cos\theta \tan x - \sin\theta}$ $+\mu \sqrt{\cos\theta - \sin\theta \cot x} + C$, where C is the integration constant, then $\left[10\left(\frac{\lambda}{\mu}\right)\right]_{\text{at } \theta = \frac{\pi}{4}}$ is equal to

(a) 5 (b) 10
(c) 20 (d) 40

For Sol.

Example 8 *The value of* $\int \frac{(1+x^2)\,dx}{(1-x^2)\sqrt{1+x^2+x^4}}$, *is*

(a) $-\frac{1}{2\sqrt{3}} \log\left|\frac{\sqrt{x^4+x^2+1}-\sqrt{3}x}{\sqrt{x^4+x^2+1}+\sqrt{3}x}\right| + C$

(b) $\frac{1}{2\sqrt{3}} \log\left|\frac{\sqrt{x^4+x^2+1}+\sqrt{2}x}{\sqrt{x^4+x^2+1}-\sqrt{2}x}\right| + C$

(c) $\frac{1}{2\sqrt{3}} \log\left|\frac{\sqrt{x^4-x^2+1}-\sqrt{3}x}{\sqrt{x^4+x^2+1}+\sqrt{3}x}\right| + C$

(d) None of the above

Sol. (a) Let $I = \int \frac{(1+x^2)\,dx}{(1-x^2)\sqrt{1+x^2+x^4}}$

$$= \int \frac{x^2\left(1+\frac{1}{x^2}\right)dx}{x\left(\frac{1}{x}-x\right)x\sqrt{\frac{1}{x^2}+1+x^2}}$$

$$= -\int \frac{(1+1/x^2)\,dx}{(x-1/x)\sqrt{(x-1/x)^2+3}}$$

Put $x - \frac{1}{x} = t = \left(1+\frac{1}{x^2}\right)dx = dt \Rightarrow -\int \frac{dt}{t\sqrt{t^2+3}}$

Again, put $t^2+3 = s^2 \Rightarrow 2t\,dt = 2s\,ds$

$$= -\int \frac{s\,ds}{s(s^2-3)} = -\int \frac{ds}{s^2-(\sqrt{3})^2} = -\frac{1}{2\sqrt{3}}\log\left|\frac{s-\sqrt{3}}{s+\sqrt{3}}\right| + C$$

$$= -\frac{1}{2\sqrt{3}}\log\left|\frac{\sqrt{t^2+3}-\sqrt{3}}{\sqrt{t^2+3}+\sqrt{3}}\right| + C$$

$$= -\frac{1}{2\sqrt{3}}\log\left|\frac{\sqrt{(x-1/x)^2+3}-\sqrt{3}}{\sqrt{(x-1/x)^2+3}+\sqrt{3}}\right| + C$$

$$= -\frac{1}{2\sqrt{3}}\log\left|\frac{\sqrt{x^2+\frac{1}{x^2}+1}-\sqrt{3}}{\sqrt{x^2+\frac{1}{x^2}+1}+\sqrt{3}}\right| + C$$

$$= -\frac{1}{2\sqrt{3}}\log\left|\frac{\sqrt{x^4+x^2+1}-\sqrt{3}x}{\sqrt{x^4+x^2+1}+\sqrt{3}x}\right| + C$$

Example 9 *The value of* $I = \int \frac{dx}{(a+bx^2)\sqrt{b-ax^2}}$, *is*

(a) $\frac{1}{\sqrt{a(a^2+b^2)}}\tan^{-1}\left(\frac{x\sqrt{a^2+b^2}}{\sqrt{a}\sqrt{b-ax^2}}\right) + C$

(b) $\frac{1}{\sqrt{(a^2+b^2)}}\tan^{-1}\left(\frac{x\sqrt{a^2+b^2}}{a\sqrt{b-ax^2}}\right) + C$

(c) $\frac{1}{\sqrt{a(a^2+b^2)}}\tan^{-1}\left(\frac{x\sqrt{a^2+b^2}}{a}\right) + C$

(d) None of the above

Sol. (a) Substituting $ax^2 = b\sin^2\theta \Rightarrow dx = \sqrt{\frac{b}{a}}\cos\theta\, d\theta$

$$\therefore \quad I = \int \frac{\sqrt{\frac{b}{a}}\cos\theta\, d\theta}{\left(a + \frac{b^2}{a}\sin^2\theta\right)\sqrt{b - b\sin^2\theta}}$$

$$= \sqrt{a}\int \frac{\cos\theta\, d\theta}{(a^2 + b^2\sin^2\theta)\cdot\cos\theta} = \sqrt{a}\int \frac{d\theta}{a^2 + b^2\sin^2\theta}$$

On dividing numerator and denominator by $\cos^2\theta$, we get

$$= \sqrt{a}\int \frac{\sec^2\theta\, d\theta}{a^2\sec^2\theta + b^2\tan^2\theta} \qquad [\text{put } \tan\theta = t \Rightarrow \sec^2\theta\, d\theta = dt]$$

$$= \sqrt{a}\int \frac{dt}{a^2(1+t^2) + b^2t^2} = \sqrt{a}\int \frac{dt}{(a^2+b^2)t^2 + a^2}$$

$$= \frac{\sqrt{a}}{a^2+b^2}\int \frac{dt}{t^2 + \frac{a^2}{a^2+b^2}}$$

$$= \frac{\sqrt{a}}{a^2+b^2}\cdot\left(\frac{\sqrt{a^2+b^2}}{a}\right)\tan^{-1}\left(\frac{t\sqrt{a^2+b^2}}{a}\right) + C$$

$$= \frac{1}{\sqrt{a(a^2+b^2)}}\cdot\tan^{-1}\left(\frac{x\sqrt{a^2+b^2}}{\sqrt{a}\sqrt{b-ax^2}}\right) + C \quad \left[\because t = \tan\theta = \frac{\sqrt{a}\,x}{\sqrt{b-ax^2}}\right]$$

Example 10 *If $y(x-y)^2 = x$, then*

$\int \frac{dx}{(x-3y)} = \frac{m}{n}\ln[(x-y)^2 - 1]$. Then, $(m+2n)$ is equal to

(a) 1 (b) 3 (c) 5 (d) 7

Sol. (c) Let $P = \int \frac{dx}{(x-3y)} = \frac{1}{2}\ln[(x-y)^2 - 1]$

$$\therefore \quad \frac{dP}{dx} = \frac{1}{x-3y} = \frac{(x-y)\left\{1 - \frac{dy}{dx}\right\}}{\{(x-y)^2 - 1\}} \qquad \text{...(i)}$$

Given, $y(x-y)^2 = x$, on differentiating both the sides, we get

$$\frac{dy}{dx} = \frac{1 - 2y(x-y)}{(x-y)(x-3y)} \qquad \text{...(ii)}$$

$$\therefore \quad \frac{dP}{dx} = \frac{(x-y)\left\{1 - \frac{1-2y(x-y)}{(x-y)(x-3y)}\right\}}{\{(x-y)^2 - 1\}}$$

$$= \frac{(x-y)(x-3y) - 1 + 2y(x-y)}{(x-3y)\{(x-y)^2 - 1\}}$$

$$= \frac{(x-y)^2 - 1}{(x-3y)\{(x-y)^2 - 1\}}$$

$$\therefore \quad \frac{dP}{dx} = \frac{1}{(x-3y)} \qquad \text{...(iii)}$$

which is true as given.

$$\therefore \quad \int \frac{dx}{(x-3y)} = \frac{1}{2}\log\{(x-y)^2 - 1\},$$

$$\therefore \quad m = 1, n = 2 \Rightarrow m + 2n = 5$$

JEE SCANNER

Example 11 Similar to PYQ Asked in JEE Main 2023

If $\int \sqrt{\sec 2x - 1}\, dx$

$$= \lambda \log_e|\cos 2x + \mu + \sqrt{\cos 2x\left(1 + \cos\frac{1}{\mu}x\right)}| + C,$$

then $|4\lambda\mu|$ is equal to ......

(a) 1 (b) 2 (c) 4 (d) $\frac{1}{2}$

Sol. (a) $I = \int \sqrt{\sec 2x - 1}\, dx = \int \sqrt{\frac{1-\cos 2x}{\cos 2x}}\, dx = \int \frac{\sqrt{2}\sin x}{\sqrt{2\cos^2 x - 1}}\, dx$

Let $\sqrt{2}\cos x = t \Rightarrow -\sqrt{2}\sin x\, dx = dt$

Then, $I = \int \frac{-1}{\sqrt{t^2-1}}\, dt = -\ln|t + \sqrt{t^2-1}| + A$

Put $t = \sqrt{2}\cos x$

$$\therefore \quad I = -\ln|\sqrt{2}\cos x + \sqrt{2\cos^2 x - 1}| + A$$

$$= -\frac{1}{2}\ln|(\sqrt{2}\cos x + \sqrt{\cos 2x})^2| + A$$

$$= -\frac{1}{2}\ln|2\cos^2 x + \cos 2x + 2\sqrt{2}\sqrt{\cos 2x}\sqrt{\frac{1+\cos 2x}{2}}| + A$$

$$= -\frac{1}{2}\ln|1 + \cos 2x + \cos 2x + 2\sqrt{\cos 2x(1+\cos 2x)}| + A$$

$$= -\frac{1}{2}\log_e|\cos 2x + \frac{1}{2} + \sqrt{\cos 2x(1+\cos 2x)}| + C,$$

where $C = A - \frac{1}{2}\log_e 2$

So, $\lambda = -\frac{1}{2}$ and $\mu = \frac{1}{2}$ Hence, $|4\lambda\mu| = \left|4\times\left(-\frac{1}{2}\right)\times\frac{1}{2}\right| = 1$

Skill Builder

If $I(x) = \int \sqrt{\sec 2x + 1}\, dx$ and $I(0) = 0$, then the value of $\frac{4}{\pi}I\left(\frac{\pi}{4}\right)$ is equal to

(a) 1 (b) 2 (c) 4 (d) 1/2

For Sol.

Example 12 *If $\int (x + \sqrt{1+x^2})^n\, dx$*

$$= \frac{1}{a(n+1)}\{x + \sqrt{1+x^2}\}^{n+1} + \frac{1}{b(n-1)}\{x + \sqrt{1+x^2}\}^{n-1} + C$$

Then, $(a+b)$ is equal to

(a) 2 (b) 3 (c) 4 (d) 5

Sol. (c) Let $I = \int (x + \sqrt{1+x^2})^n\, dx$

$$\text{Put} \quad x + \sqrt{1+x^2} = t \qquad \text{...(i)}$$

$$\Rightarrow \left(1 + \frac{1}{2\sqrt{1+x^2}}\cdot 2x\right)dx = dt \Rightarrow \left(\frac{\sqrt{1+x^2}+x}{\sqrt{1+x^2}}\right)dx = dt \qquad \text{...(ii)}$$

We know, $t = x + \sqrt{1+x^2} = x + \sqrt{1+x^2} \times \frac{x - \sqrt{1+x^2}}{x - \sqrt{1+x^2}}$

$$t = \frac{-1}{x - \sqrt{1+x^2}} \Rightarrow -\frac{1}{t} = x - \sqrt{1+x^2}$$

Subtracting, we get

$$2\sqrt{1+x^2} = t + \frac{1}{t} \quad \text{or} \quad \frac{1}{\sqrt{1+x^2}} = \frac{2t}{t^2+1} \qquad \text{...(iii)}$$

From Eqs. (i), (ii) and (iii), we get $dx = \dfrac{t^2+1}{2t^2}\, dt$

$$\therefore \quad I = \int t^n \cdot \frac{t^2+1}{(2t^2)}\, dt = \frac{1}{2}\int (t^n + t^{n-2})\, dt$$

$$= \frac{1}{2}\left[\frac{t^{n+1}}{n+1} + \frac{t^{n-1}}{n-1}\right] + C$$

$$\Rightarrow \quad I = \frac{1}{2(n+1)}[x + \sqrt{(1+x^2)}]^{n+1} + \frac{1}{2(n-1)}(x + \sqrt{(1+x^2)})^{n-1} + C \quad \text{...(iv)}$$

Then, comparing the values of a and b by Eq. (iv), we get

$$a = 2, b = 2$$

$$\therefore \quad (a+b) = (2+2) = 4$$

Example 13 *Let* $f(x) = \lim\limits_{n \to \infty} n^2\left(x^{\frac{1}{n}} - x^{\frac{1}{n+1}}\right), x > 0$, *then* $\displaystyle\int \frac{f(x+1) - f(x)}{x(x+1)}\, dx$ *equal to*

(a) $-\dfrac{1}{2}\left[\log\left(1+\dfrac{1}{x}\right)\right]^2 + C$ (b) $\dfrac{1}{2}\log\left(1+\dfrac{1}{x}\right)^2 + C$

(c) $\dfrac{1}{2}\log\left(1-\dfrac{1}{x}\right)^2 + C$ (d) $\dfrac{1}{2}\left[\log\left(1-\dfrac{1}{x}\right)\right]^2 + C$

Sol. (a) $f(x) = \lim\limits_{n \to \infty} n^2\left(x^{\frac{1}{n}} - x^{\frac{1}{n+1}}\right), x > 0$

$$= \lim_{n \to \infty} \frac{x^{\frac{1}{n+1}}\left(x^{\left(\frac{1}{n} - \frac{1}{n+1}\right)} - 1\right)}{\frac{1}{n^2}} = \lim_{n \to \infty} \frac{x^{\frac{1}{n+1}}\left(x^{\frac{1}{n(n+1)}} - 1\right)}{\frac{1}{n(n+1)} \cdot \frac{n(n+1)}{n^2}}$$

$$= \log x$$

$$\left[\because x^{\frac{1}{n(n+1)}} = 1 + \frac{1}{n(n+1)}\log x + \left(\frac{1}{n(n+1)}\right)^2 \cdot \frac{1}{2!}(\log x)^2 + \ldots \infty\right]$$

$$\therefore \quad f(x+1) = \log(1+x)$$

$$\therefore \int \frac{f(1+x) - f(x)}{x(x+1)}\, dx = \int \frac{\log(1+x) - \log x}{x(x+1)}\, dx$$

$$= \int \frac{\log\left(1+\frac{1}{x}\right)}{x^2\left(1+\frac{1}{x}\right)}\, dx = -\int \frac{\log t}{t}\, dt \quad \left[\text{put } 1 + \frac{1}{x} = t \Rightarrow -\frac{1}{x^2}\, dx = dt\right]$$

$$= -\frac{1}{2}(\log t)^2 + C = -\frac{1}{2}\left(\log\left(1+\frac{1}{x}\right)\right)^2 + C$$

JEE SCANNER

Example 14 Similar to PYQ Asked in JEE Main 2024

For $x \in \left(-\dfrac{\pi}{2}, \dfrac{\pi}{2}\right)$, if

$$y(x) = \int \frac{\sec x + \cos x}{\sec x \cdot \operatorname{cosec} x + \cot x \cos^2 x}\, dx$$

and $\lim\limits_{x \to (0)^-} y(x) = 0$, then $y\left(\dfrac{\pi}{3}\right)$ is equal to

(a) $\dfrac{1}{\sqrt{2}}\tan^{-1}\left(\dfrac{3}{2\sqrt{2}}\right)$ (b) $\dfrac{1}{\sqrt{2}}\tan^{-1}\left(-\dfrac{3}{2\sqrt{2}}\right)$

(c) $-\dfrac{1}{\sqrt{2}}\tan^{-1}\left(-\dfrac{3}{2\sqrt{2}}\right)$ (d) $-\dfrac{1}{\sqrt{2}}\tan\left(\dfrac{3}{2\sqrt{2}}\right)$

Sol. (c) Given, $y(x) = \displaystyle\int \frac{\frac{1}{\cos x} + \cos x}{\frac{1}{\cos x} \cdot \frac{1}{\sin x} + \frac{\cos x}{\sin x} \cdot \cos^2 x}\, dx$

$$= \int \frac{(1 + \cos^2 x)\sin x}{1 + \cos^4 x}\, dx$$

On putting $\cos x = t \Rightarrow -\sin x\, dx = dt$

$$y(x) = -\int \frac{1+t^2}{1+t^4}\, dt = -\int \frac{t^2\left(\frac{1}{t^2} + 1\right)}{t^2\left(\frac{1}{t^2} + t^2\right)}\, dt$$

$$= -\int \frac{\left(\frac{1}{t^2} + 1\right)}{\frac{1}{t^2} + t^2 - 2 + 2}\, dt = -\int \frac{\left(1 + \frac{1}{t^2}\right)}{\left(t - \frac{1}{t}\right)^2 + (\sqrt{2})^2}\, dt$$

Put $t - \dfrac{1}{t} = z \Rightarrow \left(1 + \dfrac{1}{t^2}\right)dt = dz$

$$= -\int \frac{dz}{z^2 + (\sqrt{2})^2} = -\frac{1}{\sqrt{2}}\tan^{-1}\left(\frac{z}{\sqrt{2}}\right) + C$$

$$= -\frac{1}{\sqrt{2}}\tan^{-1}\frac{\left(t - \frac{1}{t}\right)}{\sqrt{2}} + C$$

When $x = 0$, then $t = 1$

$$\therefore \quad C = 0$$

Hence, $y\left(\dfrac{\pi}{3}\right) = -\dfrac{1}{\sqrt{2}}\tan^{-1}\left(-\dfrac{3}{2\sqrt{2}}\right)$

Skill Builder

For $x \in \left(-\dfrac{\pi}{2}, \dfrac{\pi}{2}\right)$, if $y(x) = \displaystyle\int \frac{\operatorname{cosec} x + \sin x}{\operatorname{cosec} x \sec x + \tan x \sin^2 x}\, dx$

and $\lim\limits_{x \to \left(\frac{\pi}{2}\right)^-} y(x) = 0$, then $y\left(\dfrac{\pi}{6}\right)$ is equal to

(a) $\dfrac{1}{\sqrt{2}}\tan^{-1}\left(\dfrac{1}{\sqrt{2}}\right)$ (b) $\dfrac{1}{\sqrt{2}}\tan^{-1}\left(-\dfrac{3}{2\sqrt{2}}\right)$

(c) $\dfrac{1}{\sqrt{2}}\tan^{-1}\left(-\dfrac{1}{2\sqrt{2}}\right)$ (d) $\dfrac{1}{\sqrt{2}}\tan^{-1}\left(\dfrac{3}{2\sqrt{2}}\right)$

For Sol.

Example 15 *The value of the integral* $\int \frac{\sin^3 x + \sin^5 x}{\cos^2 x + \cos^4 x} dx$ *is*

(a) $-\cos x + 2(\cos x)^{-1} + 6\tan^{-1}(\cos x) + C$

(b) $\cos x - 2(\cos x)^{-1} + 4\tan^{-1}(\cos x) + C$

(c) $\cos x - 2(\cos x)^{-1} + \tan^{-1}(\cos x) + C$

(d) None of the above

Sol. (a) $I = \int \frac{\sin^3 x + \sin^5 x}{\cos^2 x + \cos^4 x} dx$

$$= \int \frac{\sin x(\sin^2 x + \sin^4 x)}{(\cos^2 x + \cos^4 x)} dx$$

$$= \int \frac{\sin x[1 - \cos^2 x + (1 - \cos^2 x)^2]}{\cos^2 x + \cos^4 x} dx$$

Put $\cos x = t \Rightarrow -\sin x dx = dt$

$$I = -\int \frac{[(1-t^2) + (1-t^2)^2]}{t^2 + t^4} dt = -\int \frac{2 - 3t^2 + t^4}{t^2 + t^4} dt$$

$$= -\int \frac{(t^4 + t^2) + 2 - 4t^2}{(t^2 + t^4)} dt = -\int dt - \int \frac{2 - 4t^2}{t^2(t^2+1)} dt$$

$$= -\int dt - \int \left(\frac{2}{t^2} - \frac{6}{t^2+1}\right) dt$$

$$= -t + \frac{2}{t} + 6\tan^{-1} t + C$$

$$= -\cos x + 2(\cos x)^{-1} + 6\tan^{-1}(\cos x) + C$$

Example 16 *The value of* $\int \frac{x^2 - 1}{(x^2+1)\sqrt{x^4+1}} dx$*, is equal to*

(a) $\frac{1}{\sqrt{2}} \sec^{-1}\left(\frac{x^2+1}{\sqrt{2}x}\right) + C$ (b) $\sqrt{2} \sec^{-1}\left(\frac{x^2+1}{\sqrt{2}x}\right) + C$

(c) $\frac{1}{\sqrt{2}} \text{cosec}^{-1}\left(\frac{x^2+1}{\sqrt{2}x}\right) + C$ (d) $\sqrt{2} \text{cosec}^{-1}\left(\frac{x^2+1}{\sqrt{2}x}\right) + C$

Sol. (a) Let $I = \int \frac{(x^2-1)}{(x^2+1)\sqrt{x^4+1}} dx = \int \frac{x^2(1 - 1/x^2)\,dx}{x^2\left(x + \frac{1}{x}\right)\sqrt{x^2 + \frac{1}{x^2}}}$

$$= \int \frac{(1 - 1/x^2)\,dx}{\left(x + \frac{1}{x}\right)\sqrt{\left(x + \frac{1}{x}\right)^2 - 2}}$$

Put $x + \frac{1}{x} = t \Rightarrow \left(1 - \frac{1}{x^2}\right) dx = dt$

$$= \int \frac{dt}{t\sqrt{t^2 - 2}} = \frac{1}{\sqrt{2}} \sec^{-1}\left(\frac{t}{\sqrt{2}}\right) + C$$

$$= \frac{1}{\sqrt{2}} \sec^{-1}\left(\frac{x^2+1}{\sqrt{2}x}\right) + C$$

Example 17 *Let* $\int \tan^{-1}\left(\frac{\tan x}{2}\right) dx = \alpha$*, then the value of* $\int \tan^{-1}\left(\frac{\tan x - 2\cot x}{3}\right) dx$ *equals to* $\left(\text{where } 0 < x < \frac{\pi}{2}\right)$

(a) $\alpha + \frac{\pi x}{2} + \frac{x^2}{2} + C$ (b) $\alpha - \frac{\pi x}{2} + \frac{x^2}{2} + C$

(c) $-\alpha - \frac{\pi x}{2} + \frac{x^2}{2} + C$ (d) $-\alpha + \frac{\pi x}{2} - \frac{x^2}{2} + C$

Sol. (b) $\int \tan^{-1}\left(\frac{\tan x - 2\cot x}{3}\right) dx = \int \tan^{-1}\left(\frac{\tan x - 2\cot x}{1 + 2\tan x \cot x}\right) dx$

$$\int [\tan^{-1}(\tan x) - \tan^{-1}(2\cot x)]\, dx$$

$$= \frac{x^2}{2} - \int \left[\frac{\pi}{2} - \cot^{-1}\left(\frac{2}{\tan x}\right)\right] dx = \frac{x^2}{2} - \frac{\pi x}{2} + \int \left[\tan^{-1}\left(\frac{\tan x}{2}\right)\right] dx$$

$$= \frac{x^2}{2} - \frac{\pi x}{2} + \alpha + C \qquad \left[\because \text{ given } \int \tan^{-1}\left(\frac{\tan x}{2}\right) dx = \alpha\right]$$

Example 18 $\int \frac{\cos^6 x\, dx}{\sin^4 x(\cos^7 x + \sin^7 x)^{\frac{4}{7}}}$ *is equal to*

(a) $\frac{-1}{3}(1 + \cot^7 x)^{\frac{3}{7}} + C$ (b) $\frac{-1}{3}(1 + \cot^7 x)^{\frac{7}{3}} + C$

(c) $\frac{-1}{21}(1 + \cot^7 x)^{\frac{7}{3}} + C$ (d) $\frac{1}{21}(1 + \cot^7 x)^{\frac{7}{3}} + C$

Decoding the Question

First convert the given integration in form of $\tan x$ and then let the obtained result $(1 + \tan x)^{-7} = t$, then solve it accordingly.

Sol. (a) $\int \frac{\cos^6 x}{\sin^4 x(\cos^7 x + \sin^7 x)^{\frac{4}{7}}} dx$

$$= \int \frac{\cos^6 x}{\sin^4 x \cdot \cos^4 x(1 + \tan^7 x)^{\frac{4}{7}}} dx$$

$$\therefore \quad I = \int \frac{\sec^2 x\, dx}{\tan^4 x \cdot (1 + \tan^7 x)^{\frac{4}{7}}}$$

$$= \int \frac{\sec^2 x\, dx}{\tan^8 x \cdot (1 + \tan^{-7} x)^{\frac{4}{7}}} = \int \frac{\sec^2 x \cdot (\tan x)^{-8}}{(1 + (\tan x)^{-7})^{\frac{4}{7}}} dx$$

Let $1 + (\tan x)^{-7} = t \Rightarrow -7(\tan x)^{-8} \sec^2 x\, dx = dt$

$$\Rightarrow (\tan x)^{-8} \cdot \sec^2 x\, dx = \frac{-1}{7} dt$$

$$\therefore \quad I = \frac{-1}{7}\int \frac{dt}{t^{\frac{4}{7}}} = \frac{-1}{7}\left[\frac{t^{1-\frac{4}{7}}}{1 - \frac{4}{7}}\right] + C$$

$$= \frac{-1}{7} \cdot \frac{7}{3} t^{\frac{3}{7}} = \frac{-1}{3} \cdot [1 + (\tan x)^{-7}]^{\frac{3}{7}} + C$$

$$\therefore \quad I = \frac{-1}{3}[1 + (\cot x)^7]^{\frac{3}{7}} + C$$

Example 19 *If* $\int \frac{\sec^2 x\, dx}{(\tan^{101} x + \tan x)} = g(x) + C$, *where* $g\left(\frac{\pi}{4}\right) = -\frac{\ln 2}{100}$, *then* $\lim_{x \to \frac{\pi}{2}} g(x)$ *is equal to*

(a) 0 (b) 1 (c) −1 (d) 2

Sol. (a) Given, $\int \frac{\sec^2 x\, dx}{(\tan^{101} x + \tan x)} = g(x) + C$

Let $1 + (\tan x)^{-100} = t$

$\Rightarrow -100(\tan x)^{-101} \sec^2 x\, dx = dt$

$$\Rightarrow \quad -\int \frac{dt}{100t} = -\frac{1}{100} \ln t + C$$

$$= -\frac{1}{100} \ln\left[1 + \frac{1}{(\tan x)^{100}}\right] + C$$

$$\Rightarrow \quad g(x) = -\frac{1}{100} \ln\left[1 + \frac{1}{(\tan x)^{100}}\right]$$

$$\Rightarrow \quad \lim_{x \to \frac{\pi}{2}} g(x) = -\frac{1}{100} \ln(1) = 0$$

Example 20 $\int \frac{e^{\tan^{-1} x}}{(1 + x^2)} \left[(\sec^{-1} \sqrt{1 + x^2})^2 + \cos^{-1}\left(\frac{1 - x^2}{1 + x^2}\right)\right] dx$, $(x > 0)$ *is equal to*

(a) $e^{\tan^{-1} x} \cdot \tan^{-1} x + C$

(b) $\frac{e^{\tan^{-1} x} \cdot (\tan^{-1} x)^2}{2} + C$

(c) $e^{\tan^{-1} x} \cdot (\sec^{-1}(\sqrt{1 + x^2}))^2 + C$

(d) $e^{\tan^{-1} x} \cdot (\operatorname{cosec}^{-1}(\sqrt{1 + x^2}))^2 + C$

Sol. (c) Note that

$\sec^{-1} \sqrt{1 + x^2} = \tan^{-1} x$; $\cos^{-1}\left(\frac{1 - x^2}{1 + x^2}\right) = 2 \tan^{-1} x$,

For $x > 0$, $I = \int \frac{e^{\tan^{-1} x}}{1 + x^2} \{(\tan^{-1} x)^2 + 2 \tan^{-1} x\}\, dx$,

Put $\tan^{-1} x = t \Rightarrow dt = \frac{dx}{1 + x^2}$

$$= \int e^t (t^2 + 2t)\, dt = e^t \cdot t^2 + C = e^{\tan^{-1} x} (\tan^{-1} x)^2 + C$$

$$= e^{\tan^{-1} x} (\sec^{-1}(\sqrt{1 + x^2}))^2 + C$$

Example 21 *If* $\int \frac{dx}{(x^2 + a^2)^2} = \frac{1}{ka^2} \left\{\frac{x}{x^2 + a^2} + \frac{1}{a} \tan^{-1} \frac{x}{a}\right\} + C.$

Then, the value of k, *is*

(a) 1 (b) 2 (c) 3 (d) 4

Decoding the Question

In this, apply integration by part which Ist term is $\frac{1}{x^2 + a^2}$ and IInd term is 1.

Sol. (b) Here, we know

$$\int \frac{dx}{x^2 + a^2} = \frac{1}{a} \tan^{-1} \frac{x}{a} + C \quad \text{...(i)}$$

Also, $\int \frac{1}{x^2 + a^2} \cdot 1\, dx = \frac{1}{x^2 + a^2}\, x - \int \frac{-2x}{(x^2 + a^2)^2}\, x\, dx$

$$= \frac{x}{x^2 + a^2} + 2 \int \frac{x^2 + a^2 - a^2}{(x^2 + a^2)^2}\, dx$$

I II

$$\int \frac{dx}{x^2 + a^2} = \frac{x}{x^2 + a^2} + 2 \int \frac{dx}{x^2 + a^2} - 2a^2 \int \frac{dx}{(x^2 + a^2)^2} \quad \text{...(ii)}$$

From Eqs. (i) and (ii), we get

$$\frac{1}{a} \tan^{-1} \frac{x}{a} = \frac{x}{x^2 + a^2} + 2\, \frac{1}{a} \tan^{-1} \frac{x}{a} - 2a^2 \int \frac{dx}{(x^2 + a^2)^2}$$

$$\Rightarrow 2a^2 \int \frac{dx}{(x^2 + a^2)^2} = \frac{x}{x^2 + a^2} + \frac{1}{a} \tan^{-1} \frac{x}{a}$$

or $\int \frac{dx}{(x^2 + a^2)^2} = \frac{1}{2a^2} \left\{\frac{x}{x^2 + a^2} + \frac{1}{a} \tan^{-1} \frac{x}{a}\right\} + C$

$$= \frac{1}{ka^2} \left\{\frac{x}{x^2 + a^2} + \frac{1}{a} \tan^{-1} \frac{x}{a}\right\} + C$$

$\therefore \quad k = 2$

Example 22 *If* $\int e^{1 - \cos x} (1 + x \sin x)\, dx = f(x) \cdot e^{1 - g(x)} + C$, *then find the number of solutions of the equation* $|f(x)| = g(x)$.

(a) 1 (b) 2 (c) 3 (d) Zero

Decoding the Question

Number of solutions of the equation $|f(x)| = g(x)$ is the number of intersection points of $f(x)$ and $g(x)$.

Sol. (b) $\int e^{1 - \cos x} (1 + x \sin x)\, dx = \int e^{1 - \cos x}\, dx + \int e^{1 - \cos x} x \sin x\, dx$

$$= x e^{1 - \cos x} - \int x (e^{1 - \cos x} \sin x) dx + \int e^{1 - \cos x} x \sin x\, dx + C$$

$$= x e^{1 - \cos x} + C$$

$$= f(x) \cdot e^{1 - g(x)} + C$$

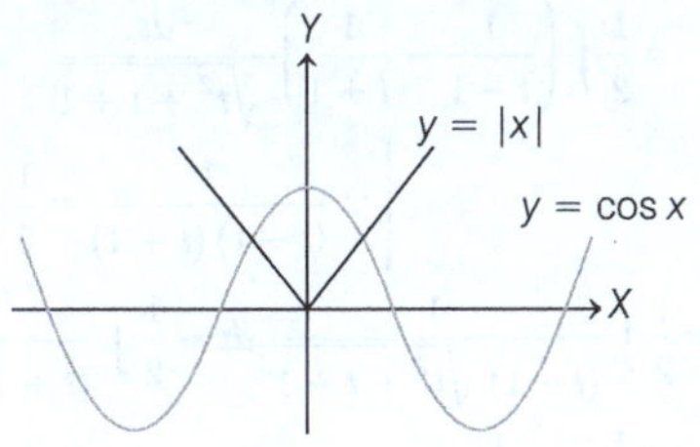

$f(x) = x, g(x) = \cos x$

$|f(x)| = g(x)$

$\Rightarrow |x| = \cos x$ has two solutions.

Example 23 *Let* $A = 2^{\frac{-\log_{10}\left(\frac{100}{x}-1\right)}{\log_{10} 2}}$*, then* $\int \ln 10 \cdot \log_{10}\left(\frac{1}{A}\right) dx$ *is equal to*

(a) $(x - 100)\ln(100 - x) - x\ln x + C$
(b) $(x - 100)\ln(100 - x) + x\ln x + C$
(c) $(100 - x)\ln(100 - x) - x\ln x + C$
(d) $(100 - x)\ln(100 - x) + x\ln x + C$

Sol. (a) $A = 2^{\frac{-\log_{10}\frac{100-x}{x}}{\log_{10} 2}} \Rightarrow A = 2^{\left[\log_2\left(\frac{x}{100-x}\right)\right]}$

$$\Rightarrow A = \frac{x}{100-x} \Rightarrow \frac{1}{A} = \frac{100-x}{x}$$

$$I = \int \log_e 10 \cdot \log_{10}\left(\frac{100-x}{x}\right) dx = \int (\ln(100-x) - \ln x)\, dx$$

$$= (x - 100)\ln(100 - x) + (100 - x) - x\ln x + x + C_1$$

$$= (x - 100)\ln(100 - x) - x\ln x + C,$$

where $C = 100 + C_1$

Example 24 *The value of*

$$I = \int \frac{dx}{2x\sqrt{1-x}\sqrt{(2-x)+\sqrt{1-x}}}$$

$$= -\frac{1}{2}\left\{\log\left(z + \frac{3}{2} + \sqrt{z^2+3z+3}\right)\right\} + \frac{1}{2}\left|\log\left(s - \frac{1}{2} + \sqrt{s^2-s+1}\right)\right| + C$$

and $s - z = \frac{k}{x}$*, then value of k, is*

(a) 1 (b) 2 (c) 3 (d) 4

Sol. (b) Here, $I = \int \frac{dx}{2x\sqrt{1-x}\sqrt{(2-x)+\sqrt{1-x}}}$,

Put $(1 - x) = t^2 \Rightarrow -dx = 2t\, dt$

$$= -\int \frac{2t\, dt}{2(1-t^2)\cdot t\sqrt{1+t^2+t}}$$

$$= -\int \frac{dt}{(1-t^2)\sqrt{t^2+t+1}}$$

$$= \int \frac{dt}{(t-1)(t+1)\sqrt{t^2+t+1}}$$

$$= \frac{1}{2}\int \left(\frac{1}{t-1} - \frac{1}{t+1}\right)\cdot \frac{dt}{\sqrt{t^2+t+1}}$$

$$\left[\because \frac{1}{(t-1)(t+1)} = \frac{1}{2}\left(\frac{1}{t-1} - \frac{1}{t+1}\right)\right]$$

$$= \frac{1}{2}\int \frac{1}{(t-1)\sqrt{t^2+t+1}}\, dt - \frac{1}{2}\int \frac{1}{(t+1)\sqrt{t^2+t+1}}\, dt$$

Let $I = \frac{1}{2} I_1 - \frac{1}{2} I_2$ ...(i)

where, $I_1 = \int \frac{dt}{(t-1)\sqrt{t^2+t+1}}$ and $I_2 = \int \frac{dt}{(t+1)\sqrt{t^2+t+1}}$

For I_1, put $(t - 1) = \frac{1}{z} \Rightarrow dt = -\frac{1}{z^2} dz$

$$I_1 = \int \frac{-1/z^2\, dz}{\frac{1}{z}\sqrt{\left(1+\frac{1}{z}\right)^2 + \left(1+\frac{1}{z}\right) + 1}} = -\int \frac{dz}{\sqrt{\left(z+\frac{3}{2}\right)^2 + \left(\frac{\sqrt{3}}{2}\right)^2}}$$

$$= -\log\left|\left(z + \frac{3}{2}\right) + \sqrt{z^2+3z+3}\right| \quad \text{...(ii)}$$

For I_2, put $(t + 1) = \frac{1}{s} \Rightarrow dt = -\frac{1}{s^2} ds$

$$I_2 = -\int \frac{ds}{\sqrt{\left(s-\frac{1}{2}\right)^2 + \frac{3}{4}}} = -\log\left|\left(s - \frac{1}{2}\right) + \sqrt{s^2-s+1}\right| \quad \text{...(iii)}$$

$$\therefore \quad I = -\frac{1}{2}\log\left|z + \frac{3}{2} + \sqrt{z^2+3z+3}\right| + \frac{1}{2}\log\left|\left(s-\frac{1}{2}\right) + \sqrt{s^2-s+1}\right| + C$$

where, $z = \frac{1}{\sqrt{1-x}-1}$ and $s = \frac{1}{\sqrt{1-x}+1}$

$$\therefore \quad s - z = \frac{1}{\sqrt{1-x}+1} - \frac{1}{\sqrt{1-x}-1} = \frac{2}{x} \Rightarrow k = 2$$

Example 25 *The value of* $\int \frac{(1+x)}{x(1+xe^x)^2} dx$*, is equal to*

(a) $\log\left|\frac{x}{1+xe^x}\right| + \frac{1}{(1+xe^x)} + C$

(b) $\log\left|\frac{xe^x}{1+xe^x}\right| + \frac{1}{1+xe^x} + C$

(c) $\log\left|\frac{xe^x}{1+e^x}\right| + \frac{1}{1+xe^x} + C$

(d) None of the above

Sol. (b) Let $I = \int \frac{(1+x)}{x(1+xe^x)^2} dx = \int \frac{(1+x)e^x}{(xe^x)(1+xe^x)^2} dx$

On putting $1 + xe^x = t$, we get

$$(1+x)e^x\, dx = dt \Rightarrow \int \frac{dt}{(t-1)\cdot t^2}$$

On applying partial fraction, we get

$$\frac{1}{(t-1)t^2} = \frac{A}{t-1} + \frac{B}{t} + \frac{C}{t^2}$$

$$\Rightarrow \quad 1 = A(t^2) + Bt(t-1) + C(t-1)$$

For $t = 1 \Rightarrow A = 1$

For $t = 0 \Rightarrow C = -1$ and $B = -1$

$$\therefore \quad I = \int \left\{\frac{1}{t-1} - \frac{1}{t} - \frac{1}{t^2}\right\} dt = \log|t-1| - \log|t| + \frac{1}{t} + C$$

$$= \log|xe^x| - \log|1+xe^x| + \frac{1}{1+xe^x} + C$$

$$= \log\left|\frac{xe^x}{1+xe^x}\right| + \frac{1}{1+xe^x} + C$$

JEE SCANNER

Example 26 Similar to PYQ Asked in JEE Main 2023

Let $I(x) = \int \frac{(x+1)}{x(2+xe^x)^2} dx$, $x > 0$. If $\lim_{x\to\infty} I(x) = 0$, then $I(1)$ is equal to

(a) $\frac{e+2}{4(2+e)} - \frac{1}{4}\ln(2+e)$ (b) $\frac{e+2}{4(2+e)} + \frac{1}{4}\ln(2+e)$

(c) $\frac{e+4}{4(2+e)} + \frac{1}{4}\ln(2+e)$ (d) $\frac{e+4}{4(2+e)} - \frac{1}{4}\ln(2+e)$

Sol. (d) $I(x) = \int \frac{x+1}{x(2+xe^x)^2} dx = \int \frac{(x+1)e^x\, dx}{xe^x(2+xe^x)^2}$

Let $2 + xe^x = t \Rightarrow (x+1)e^x dx = dt \Rightarrow I(x) = \int \frac{dt}{(t-2)(t)^2}$ ...(i)

$$\therefore\ I(x) = \int \left(-\frac{1}{4t} - \frac{1}{2t^2} + \frac{1}{4(t-2)}\right) dt$$

$$= -\frac{1}{4}\ln(t) + \frac{1}{2t} + \frac{1}{4}\ln(t-2) + C$$

$$= \frac{1}{2(2+xe^x)} + \frac{1}{4}\ln\left(\frac{xe^x}{2+xe^x}\right) + C$$

Now, for $x \to \infty$, $I(x) \to 0$

$$\therefore\ \lim_{x\to\infty} I(x) = \lim_{x\to\infty} \frac{1}{2(2+xe^x)} + \lim_{x\to\infty} \frac{1}{4}\ln\left(\frac{xe^x}{2+xe^x}\right) + C = 0$$

$$\Rightarrow\ 0 + 0 + C = 0 \Rightarrow C = 0$$

$$\text{Now, } I(1) = \frac{1}{2(2+e)} + \frac{1}{4}\ln\left(\frac{e}{2+e}\right) = \frac{1}{4+2e} + \frac{1}{4}(1 - \ln(2+e))$$

$$= \frac{e+4}{4(2+e)} - \frac{1}{4}\ln(2+e)$$

Skill Builder

Let $I(x) = \int \frac{(x+1)}{x(3+xe^x)^2} dx$, $x > 0$. If $\lim_{x\to\infty} I(x) = 0$, then $I(2)$ is equal to

(a) $\frac{1}{3(3+2e^2)} - \frac{1}{9}\ln\left(\frac{2e^2}{3+2e^2}\right)$

(b) $\frac{1}{3(3+2e^2)} + \frac{1}{9}\ln\left(\frac{2e^2}{3+2e^2}\right)$

(c) $\frac{1}{3+2e^2} - \frac{1}{9}\ln\left(\frac{2e^2}{3+2e^2}\right)$

(d) $\frac{1}{3+2e^2} + \frac{1}{9}\ln\left(\frac{2e^2}{3+2e^2}\right)$

For Sol.

Example 27 *If $I_n = \int \cot^n x\, dx$, then $I_0 + I_1 + 2(I_2 + I_3 + \ldots + I_8) + I_9 + I_{10}$ equals to (where $u = \cot x$)*

(a) $u + \frac{u^2}{2} + \ldots + \frac{u^9}{9}$ (b) $-\left(u + \frac{u^2}{2} + \ldots + \frac{u^9}{9}\right)$

(c) $-\left(u + \frac{u^2}{2!} + \ldots + \frac{u^9}{9!}\right)$ (d) $\frac{u}{2} + \frac{2u^2}{3} + \ldots + \frac{9u^9}{10}$

Sol. (b) $I_n = \int \cot^n x\, dx = \int \cot^{n-2} x \cdot (\operatorname{cosec}^2 x - 1)\, dx$

$$I_n = -\frac{u^{n-1}}{n-1} - I_{n-2} \quad \text{or} \quad I_n + I_{n-2} = -\frac{u^{n-1}}{n-1}$$

[put $n = 2, 3, 4, \ldots, 10$]

$$I_2 + I_0 = -\frac{u}{1}$$

$$I_3 + I_1 = -\frac{u^2}{2}$$

$$I_4 + I_2 = -\frac{u^3}{3}$$

....

....

$$I_{10} + I_8 = -\frac{u^9}{9}$$

Adding, $I_0 + I_1 + 2(I_2 + I_3 + \ldots + I_8) + I_9 + I_{10}$

$$= -\left(u + \frac{u^2}{2} + \ldots + \frac{u^9}{9}\right)$$

More than One Correct Option Type Questions

Example 28 $\int \frac{\sqrt{4+x^2}}{x^6} dx = \frac{A(4+x^2)^{3/2}(Bx^2-6)}{x^5} + C$, *then*

(a) $A = \frac{1}{120}$ (b) $B = 1$ (c) $A = -\frac{1}{120}$ (d) $B = -1$

Decoding the Question

First convert the given integral as $\int \frac{\sqrt{1+\frac{4}{x^2}}}{x^5} dx$, then let $\sqrt{1+\frac{4}{x^2}} = t$ and then solve it accordingly.

Sol. (a, b) Here, $I = \int \frac{\sqrt{4+x^2}}{x^6} dx = \int \frac{\sqrt{1+\frac{4}{x^2}}}{x^5} dx = \int \frac{\sqrt{1+\frac{4}{x^2}}}{x^2 \cdot x^3} dx$

Put $t = \sqrt{1+\frac{4}{x^2}} \Rightarrow t^2 = 1 + \frac{4}{x^2}$

$$\therefore\ 2t\, dt = -\frac{8}{x^3} dx$$

$$\Rightarrow\ I = \frac{1}{16}\int (t^2 - t^4)\, dt = \frac{1}{16}\left\{\frac{t^3}{3} - \frac{t^5}{5}\right\} + C$$

$$= \frac{1}{120} \cdot \frac{(4+x^2)^{3/2}}{x^5}(x^2 - 6) + C$$

$$A = \frac{1}{120},\ B = 1$$

Example 29 *If $I = \int (\sqrt{\tan x} + \sqrt{\cot x})\, dx = f(x) + C$, then $f(x)$ is equal to*

(a) $\sqrt{2}\sin^{-1}(\sin x - \cos x)$

(b) $\frac{\pi}{\sqrt{2}} - \sqrt{2}\cos^{-1}(\sin x - \cos x)$

(c) $\sqrt{2}\tan^{-1}\left(\frac{\tan x - 1}{\sqrt{2}\sqrt{\tan x}}\right)$

(d) None of the above

Sol. (a, b, c) $I = \int (\sqrt{\tan x} + \sqrt{\cot x})\, dx = \int \sqrt{2} \cdot \frac{\sin x + \cos x}{\sqrt{2 \sin x \cos x}} dx$

If $\sin x - \cos x = p$, then $(\cos x + \sin x)\, dx = dp$

$$I = \sqrt{2} \int \frac{dp}{\sqrt{1 - p^2}} = \sqrt{2} \sin^{-1} p + C$$

According to the question,

$f(x) + C = \sqrt{2} \sin^{-1} (\sin x - \cos x) + C$

$$f(x) = \frac{\pi}{\sqrt{2}} - \sqrt{2} \cos^{-1} (\sin x - \cos x)$$

$$= \sqrt{2} \tan^{-1} \left(\frac{\sin x - \cos x}{\sqrt{1 - (\sin x - \cos x)^2}} \right)$$

$$= \sqrt{2} \tan^{-1} \left(\frac{\sin x - \cos x}{\sqrt{2 \sin x \cos x}} \right)$$

$$= \sqrt{2} \tan^{-1} \left(\frac{\tan x - 1}{\sqrt{2 \tan x}} \right)$$

Example 30 *Suppose, $J = \int \frac{\sin^2 x + \sin x}{1 + \sin x + \cos x} dx$ and $K = \int \frac{\cos^2 x + \cos x}{1 + \sin x + \cos x} dx$. If C is an arbitrary constant of integration, then which of the following is/are correct?*

(a) $J = \frac{1}{2}(x - \sin x + \cos x) + C$

(b) $J = K - (\sin x + \cos x) + C$

(c) $J = x - K + C$

(d) $K = \frac{1}{2}(x - \sin x + \cos x) + C$

Sol. (b, c) $J + K = \int \frac{1 + \sin x + \cos x}{1 + \sin x + \cos x} dx = x + C$

$$J - K = \int \frac{\sin^2 x + \sin x - \cos^2 x - \cos x}{1 + \sin x + \cos x} dx$$

$$= \int \frac{(\sin x - \cos x)(1 + \sin x + \cos x)}{1 + \sin x + \cos x} dx$$

$$= \int (\sin x - \cos x) dx$$

$$= -\cos x - \sin x + C$$

$\therefore \quad 2J = x - \sin x - \cos x + C$

and $\quad 2K = x + \cos x + \sin x + C$

Example 31 *The value of the integral $\int e^{\sin^2 x} (\cos x + \cos^3 x) \sin x\, dx$ is*

(a) $\frac{1}{2} e^{\sin^2 x} (3 - \sin^2 x) + C$

(b) $e^{\sin^2 x} \left(1 + \frac{1}{2} \cos^2 x\right) + C$

(c) $e^{\sin^2 x} (3 \cos^2 x + 2 \sin^2 x) + C$

(d) $e^{\sin^2 x} (2 \cos^2 x + 3 \sin^2 x) + C$

Sol. (a, b) Put $t = \sin^2 x$

The integral reduces to

$$I = \frac{1}{2} \int e^t (2 - t)\, dt = \frac{3}{2} e^t - \frac{t e^t}{2} + C$$

$$= \frac{1}{2} e^{\sin^2 x} (3 - \sin^2 x) + C \qquad \text{[option (a)]}$$

$$= e^{\sin^2 x} \left(1 + \frac{1}{2} \cos^2 x\right) + C \qquad \text{[option (b)]}$$

Example 32 *Let $f(x) = \int \frac{e^{\sin x}}{2 \sin^3 x} (\sin x - 2) \cos x\, dx$ such that $f\left(\frac{\pi}{2}\right) = \frac{e}{2}$, then*

(a) $\lim_{x \to 0} \frac{2 \sin^2 x (f(x)) - 1}{\tan\left(\frac{x}{2}\right)} = 2$

(b) If $g'(x) = f(x)$, then $g : R - [n\pi] \to R$ is an injective function.

(c) $\lim_{x \to 0} x f(x)$ is not defined.

(d) $\lim_{x \to 0} x f(x) = 1$

Sol. (a, b, c) $f(x) = \int \frac{e^{\sin x}}{2 \sin^3 x} (\sin x - 2) \cos x\, dx$

Put $\sin x = t \Rightarrow \cos x\, dx = dt$

$$= \int \frac{e^t}{2t^3} (t - 2)\, dt = \int e^t \left(\frac{1}{2t^2} - \frac{1}{t^3} \right) dt = \frac{e^t}{2t^2} + C$$

$$\Rightarrow \quad f(x) = \frac{e^{\sin x}}{2 \sin^2 x} + C \Rightarrow f\left(\frac{\pi}{2}\right) = \frac{e}{2} \Rightarrow \frac{e}{2} = \frac{e}{2} + C$$

$$\Rightarrow \quad C = 0$$

$$\lim_{x \to 0} \frac{2 \sin^2 x (f(x)) - 1}{\tan\left(\frac{x}{2}\right)} = \lim_{x \to 0} \frac{2 \sin^2 x \frac{e^{\sin x}}{2 \sin^2 x} - 1}{\tan\left(\frac{x}{2}\right)}$$

$$= \lim_{x \to 0} \frac{e^{\sin x} - 1}{\sin x} \cdot \frac{\sin x}{\tan \frac{x}{2}} = 2$$

$$g'(x) = f(x) = \frac{e^{\sin x}}{2 \sin^2 x} > 0,$$

$g(x)$ is $\lim_{x \to 0} x f(x) = \lim_{x \to 0} \frac{x e^{\sin x}}{2 \sin^2 x} = \lim_{x \to 0} \frac{e^{\sin x}}{2} \left(\frac{x}{\sin x} \right)^2 \frac{1}{x}$

is not injective function.

Example 33 *If $\int \frac{3 \cot 3x - \cot x}{\tan x - 3 \tan 3x} dx = p\, f(x) + q\, g(x) + C$, where C is a constant of integration, then*

(a) $p = 1; q = \frac{1}{\sqrt{3}}; f(x) = x; g(x) = \ln \left| \frac{\sqrt{3} - \tan x}{\sqrt{3} + \tan x} \right|$

(b) $p = 1; q = -\frac{1}{\sqrt{3}}; f(x) = x; g(x) = \ln \left| \frac{\sqrt{3} - \tan x}{\sqrt{3} + \tan x} \right|$

(c) $p = 1; q = -\frac{2}{\sqrt{3}}; f(x) = x; g(x) = \ln \left| \frac{\sqrt{3} + \tan x}{\sqrt{3} - \tan x} \right|$

(d) $p = 1; q = -\frac{1}{\sqrt{3}}; f(x) = x; g(x) = \ln \left| \frac{\sqrt{3} + \tan x}{\sqrt{3} - \tan x} \right|$

Sol. (a, d) $I = \int \dfrac{(3\tan x - \tan 3x)\,dx}{\tan x \tan 3x(\tan x - 3\tan 3x)}$

$$\Rightarrow \quad I = \int \frac{3\tan x - \left(\dfrac{3\tan x - \tan^3 x}{1 - 3\tan^2 x}\right)}{\tan x\left(\dfrac{3\tan x - \tan^3 x}{1-3\tan^2 x}\right)\left[\tan x - 3\left(\dfrac{3\tan x - \tan^3 x}{1 - 3\tan^2 x}\right)\right]}$$

$$\Rightarrow \quad I = \int \frac{(1-3\tan^2 x)(-8\tan^3 x)}{\tan^2 x(3-\tan^2 x)(-8\tan x)}dx$$

Simplifying gives $I = \int \dfrac{(1-3\tan^2 x)\sec^2 x}{(3-\tan^2 x)(1+\tan^2 x)}dx$

Put $\tan x = t \Rightarrow \sec^2 x\,dx = dt$

$$\therefore I = \int \frac{1-3t^2}{(3-t^2)(1+t^2)}dt = \int\left(\frac{1}{1+t^2} - \frac{2}{3-t^2}\right)dt$$

$$= \tan^{-1} t + \frac{1}{\sqrt{3}}\ln\left|\frac{\sqrt{3}-t}{\sqrt{3}+t}\right| + C$$

$$= x + \frac{1}{\sqrt{3}}\ln\left|\frac{\sqrt{3}-\tan x}{\sqrt{3}+\tan x}\right| + C$$

Passage Based Questions

Passage I

(Ex. Nos. 34 and 35)

Consider two differential functions $f(x), g(x)$ satisfying $6\int f(x)\,g(x)\,dx = x^6 + 3x^4 + 3x^2 + C$ and $2\int \dfrac{g(x)\,dx}{f(x)} = x^2 + C$, where $f(x) > 0, \forall\, x \in R$.

Example 34 $\int \{g(x) - f(x)\}\,dx$ *is equal to*

(a) $\dfrac{x^4}{4} - \dfrac{x^2}{2} + x + C$ (b) $\dfrac{x^4}{4} + \dfrac{x^2}{2} - \dfrac{x^3}{3} - x + C$

(c) $\dfrac{x^4}{4} - \dfrac{x^3}{3} + \dfrac{x^2}{2} - x + C$ (d) $\dfrac{x^4}{4} + \dfrac{x^3}{3} + C$

Example 35 $\lim\limits_{x\to 0} \dfrac{\log\{f(x)\}}{g(x)}$ *is equal to*

(a) e (b) 2 (c) 3 (d) 0

Sol. (Ex. Nos. 34 and 35)

We have, $6\int f(x)g(x)\,dx = x^6 + 3x^4 + 3x^2 + C$

On differentiating both sides, we get

$$6f(x)\,g(x) = 6x^5 + 12x^3 + 6x$$

$$\therefore \quad f(x)\,g(x) = x^5 + 2x^3 + x \quad \text{...(i)}$$

$$2\int \frac{g(x)\,dx}{f(x)} = x^2 + C$$

On differentiating both sides, we get

$$\frac{g(x)}{f(x)} = x \quad \text{...(ii)}$$

On multiplying Eqs. (i) and (ii), we get

$$\{g(x)\}^2 = x^6 + 2x^4 + x^2$$

$$\{g(x)\}^2 = (x^3 + x)^2$$

$$\therefore \quad g(x) = x^3 + x$$

$$\therefore \quad f(x) = x^2 + 1, \text{ as } f(x) > 0$$

34. (b) Now, $\int \{g(x) - f(x)\}\,dx$

$$= \int (x^3 + x - x^2 - 1)\,dx$$

$$= \frac{x^4}{4} + \frac{x^2}{2} - \frac{x^3}{3} - x + C$$

35. (d) $\lim\limits_{x\to 0}\dfrac{\log\{f(x)\}}{g(x)} = \lim\limits_{x\to 0}\dfrac{\log(1+x^2)}{x+x^3}$

$$= \lim_{x\to 0}\frac{\log(1+x^2)}{x^2}\cdot\frac{x^2}{x+x^3}$$

$$= \lim_{x\to 0}\frac{x}{1+x^2} = 0$$

Stem Based Questions

Stem I

(Ex. Nos. 36 and 37)

Let $f(x)$, $g(x)$, $h(x)$ be three differentiable functions satisfying $\int (f(x) + g(x))dx = \dfrac{x^3}{3} + C_1$,

$\int (f(x) - g(x))\,dx = x^2 - \dfrac{x^3}{3} + C_2$ and

$\int \dfrac{f(x)}{h(x)}\,dx = -\dfrac{1}{x} + C_3$ (where C_1, C_2, C_3 are integration constants).

The number of points of non-differentiability of function $\phi(x) = \min\{f(x), f(x) + g(x), h(x)\}$ is p and number of distinct terms in the expansion of

$\left((1 + f(x)) + \left(\dfrac{f(x)+g(x)}{h(x)}\right)\right)^{\Sigma n}$, $(n \in N)$ is 31. Then,

Example 36 *The value of p is equal to ....*

Example 37 *The value of* $\dfrac{n+p}{4}$ *is equal to ....*

Sol. (Ex. Nos. 36 and 37)

36. $\int (f(x) + g(x))\,dx = \dfrac{x^3}{3} + C_1$

On differentiating, we get

$$f(x) + g(x) = x^2 \quad \text{...(i)}$$

$$\int (f(x) - g(x))dx = x^2 - \frac{x^3}{3} + C_2$$

$$\Rightarrow \quad f(x) - g(x) = 2x - x^2 \quad \text{...(ii)}$$

From Eqs. (i) and (ii), we get

$$f(x) = x, \; g(x) = x^2 - x$$

$$\int \frac{f(x)}{h(x)} dx = -\frac{1}{x} + C_3$$

On differentiating, we get

$$\frac{f(x)}{h(x)} = \frac{1}{x^2} \Rightarrow h(x) = x^3$$

$$\Rightarrow \phi(x) = \min\{f(x), f(x) + g(x), h(x)\} = \min(x, x^2, x^3)$$

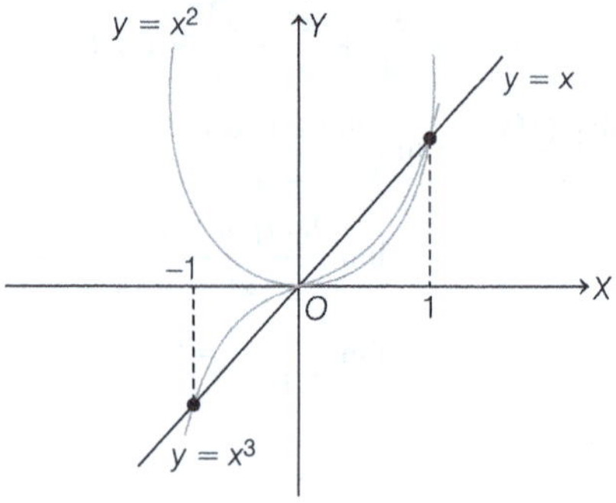

$\phi(x)$ is not differentiable at $x = -1, 0, 1$

Hence, $p = 3$

37. $$\left((1 + f(x)) + \left(\frac{f(x) + g(x)}{h(x)}\right)\right)^{\Sigma n} = \left(1 + x + \frac{x^2}{x^3}\right)^{\Sigma n} = \left(1 + x + \frac{1}{x}\right)^{\Sigma n}$$

Total number of terms in $\left(1 + x + \frac{1}{x}\right)^{\Sigma n}$

$$= \text{Total number of terms in } \left(2 + x + \frac{1}{x}\right)^{\Sigma n}$$

$$= \text{Total number of terms in } \left(\sqrt{x} + \frac{1}{\sqrt{x}}\right)^{2\Sigma n} = 2\Sigma n + 1$$

$\Rightarrow \quad 2\Sigma n + 1 = 31$ [given]

$\Rightarrow \quad \Sigma n = 15 \Rightarrow n(n+1) = 30 \Rightarrow n = 5$

$\therefore \quad \frac{n + p}{4} = \frac{5 + 3}{4} = 2$

Single Integer Answer Type Questions

Example 38 *If the primitive of the function* $f(x) = \frac{x^{2009}}{(1 + x^2)^{1006}}$ *w.r.t. x is equal to* $\frac{1}{n}\left(\frac{x^2}{1 + x^2}\right)^m + C$*, then* $\frac{n}{m}$ *is equal to ......*

> **Decoding the Question**
> First let $1 + x^2 = t$ and then solve it accordingly.

Sol. (2) $$f(x) = \int \frac{x^{2009}}{(1 + x^2)^{1006}} dx$$

Put $1 + x^2 = t \Rightarrow 2x\, dx = dt$

$$\therefore \quad I = \frac{1}{2}\int \frac{(t-1)^{1004}\, dt}{t^{1006}} = \frac{1}{2}\int \left(1 - \frac{1}{t}\right)^{1004} \cdot \frac{1}{t^2} dt$$

Put $1 - \frac{1}{t} = y \Rightarrow \frac{1}{t^2} dt = dy$

$$\therefore \quad I = \frac{1}{2}\int y^{1004} dy = \frac{1}{2} \cdot \frac{y^{1005}}{1005} + C$$

$$= \frac{1}{2010} \cdot \left(\frac{t-1}{t}\right)^{1005} + C = \frac{1}{2010} \cdot \left(\frac{x^2}{1 + x^2}\right)^{1005} + C$$

$$\Rightarrow \quad m = 1005, n = 2010 \Rightarrow \frac{n}{m} = \frac{2010}{1005} = 2$$

Example 39 *Suppose* $\begin{vmatrix} f'(x) & f(x) \\ f''(x) & f'(x) \end{vmatrix} = 0$*, where* $f(x)$ *is continuous differentiable function with* $f'(x) \neq 0$ *and satisfies* $f(0) = 1$ *and* $f'(0) = 2$*, then* $f(x) = e^{\lambda x} + k$*, then* $\lambda + k$ *is equal to ....*

Sol. (2) $f'(x) \cdot f'(x) - f(x) \cdot f''(x) = 0$ or $\frac{[f'(x)]^2 - f(x) f''(x)}{[f'(x)]^2} = 0$

$$\frac{d}{dx}\left[\frac{f(x)}{f'(x)}\right] = 0$$

On integrating, we get

$$\frac{f(x)}{f'(x)} = C \quad \text{...(i)}$$

Put $x = 0$, $\frac{f(0)}{f'(0)} = C \Rightarrow C = \frac{1}{2}$.

Hence, $$\frac{f(x)}{f'(x)} = \frac{1}{2} \quad \text{...(ii)}$$

From Eq. (i), $2f(x) = f'(x)$

$$\therefore \quad \frac{f'(x)}{f(x)} = 2$$

Again, integrating, $\ln[f(x)] = 2x + k$

Put $x = 0$ to get, $k = 0$

$$f(x) = e^{2x} \Rightarrow \lambda + k = 2 + 0 = 2$$

Example 40 $\int \{\sin(101x) \cdot \sin^{99} x\}\, dx = \frac{\sin(100x)(\sin x)^\lambda}{\mu}$, *then* $\frac{\lambda}{\mu}$ *is equal to ......*

Sol. (1) $I = \int \{\sin(100x + x) \cdot (\sin x)^{99}\}\, dx$

$$= \int \{\sin(100x)\cos x + \cos 100x \sin x\}(\sin x)^{99} dx$$

$$= \int \underbrace{\sin(100x)}_{\text{I}} \underbrace{\cos x \cdot (\sin x)^{99}}_{\text{II}} dx + \int \cos(100x) \cdot (\sin x)^{100} dx$$

$$= \frac{\sin(100x)(\sin x)^{100}}{100} - \frac{100}{100}\int \cos(100x)(\sin x)^{100} dx + \int \cos(100x)(\sin x)^{100} dx$$

$$= \frac{\sin(100x)(\sin x)^{100}}{100} + C$$

$$\Rightarrow \lambda = 100, \mu = 100 \Rightarrow \frac{\lambda}{\mu} = \frac{100}{100} = 1$$

Example 41 *If* $\int (x^6 + 7x^5 + 6x^4 + 5x^3 + 4x^2 + 3x + 1)e^x dx$ *is equal to* $\sum_{k=1}^{\alpha} \beta x^k \cdot e^x + C$ *(where C is constant of integration), then* $(\alpha + \beta)$ *is equal to ....*

Sol. (7) $\int \{(x^6 + 6x^5) + (x^5 + 5x^4) + (x^4 + 4x^3) + (x^3 + 3x^2) + (x^2 + 2x) + (x + 1)\} e^x dx$

$$= (x^6 + x^5 + x^4 + x^3 + x^2 + x)e^x + C$$

$$= \sum_{k=1}^{6} x^k e^x + C \qquad [\because \int e^x (f(x) + f'(x))dx = e^x f(x) + C]$$

$\Rightarrow \quad \alpha = 6, \ \beta = 1 \Rightarrow (\alpha + \beta) = 7$

Numerical Value Type Questions

Example 42 *If* $\int \dfrac{(1 + x\cos x - \sin x)dx}{(x + \sin x + \cos x)^{\frac{1}{2}} (x - \sin x + \cos x)^{\frac{3}{2}}}$

$= (x + l\sin x + m\cos x)^n \cdot (x + p\sin x + q\cos x)^r + C$

(where C is constant of integration and l, n > 0), then $\left(\dfrac{l+m}{n}\right)^2 (p-q)^2 r^2$ *is equal to ....*

Sol. (16) Let $I = \int \dfrac{(1 + x\cos x - \sin x)dx}{\sqrt{\dfrac{x + \sin x + \cos x}{x - \sin x + \cos x}} \cdot (x - \sin x + \cos x)^2}$

Put $\dfrac{x + \sin x + \cos x}{x - \sin x + \cos x} = t^2$

$\Rightarrow \quad \dfrac{2(1 + x\cos x - \sin x)\, dx}{(x - \sin x + \cos x)^2} = 2t\, dt$

$\Rightarrow \quad I = \int \dfrac{t\, dt}{t} = t = \sqrt{\dfrac{x + \sin x + \cos x}{x - \sin x + \cos x}} + C$

$l = 1, \ m = 1, n = \dfrac{1}{2}; p = -1, q = 1, r = -\dfrac{1}{2}$

$\left(\dfrac{l+m}{n}\right)^2 (p-q)^2 r^2 = 4^2(-2)^2 \left(\dfrac{-1}{2}\right)^2 = 16$

Example 43 *Let* $f(x)$ *be a function satisfying* $f(0) = 2, \ f'(0) = 3, \ f''(x) = f(x), \ f(4) = \dfrac{k(5e^8 - 1)}{e^4}$, *then k is equal to ....*

Sol. (0.5) $f''(x) = f(x)$

$\Rightarrow \quad 2f'(x)\, f''(x) = 2f(x) \cdot f'(x)$

$\Rightarrow \quad \dfrac{d}{dx}[(f'(x))^2] = \dfrac{d}{dx}[(f(x))^2] \Rightarrow [f'(x)]^2 = [f(x)]^2 + C$

gives $f(0) = 2, \ f'(0) = 3, \ C = 5$

$\therefore \quad (f'(x))^2 = (f(x))^2 + 5$

$\Rightarrow \quad f'(x) = \sqrt{5 + (f(x))^2} \Rightarrow \dfrac{f'(x)}{\sqrt{5 + (f(x))^2}} = 1$

On integrating,

$\Rightarrow \quad \int \dfrac{d(f(x))}{\sqrt{(\sqrt{5})^2 + (f(x))^2}} = x + C_1$

$\Rightarrow \log(f(x) + \sqrt{5 + (f(x))^2}) = x + C_1$

$f(0) = 2 \Rightarrow C_1 = \log 5$

$\Rightarrow \log(f(x) + \sqrt{5 + (f(x))^2}) = x + \log 5$

$\Rightarrow \quad f(x) + \sqrt{5 + (f(x))^2} = 5e^x$

$\therefore \quad 2f(x) = (5e^x - e^{-x}) \Rightarrow f(4) = \dfrac{1}{2}(5e^4 - e^{-4}) = \dfrac{1}{2}\dfrac{(5e^8 - 1)}{e^4}$

$\therefore \quad k = \dfrac{1}{2} = 0.5$

Example 44 *If*

$$f(x) = \lim_{n \to \infty} \left[\sin^n\left(\frac{2\pi n}{3n+1}\right) + \frac{x^n - x^{-n}}{x^n + x^{-n}} (x > 1)\right]$$

and $\int \dfrac{x\, f(x) \cdot \log(x + \sqrt{1+x^2})}{\sqrt{1+x^2}} dx$ *is* $t[\sqrt{1+x^2} \log(x + \sqrt{1+x^2}) - x] + C$. *Then,* $\dfrac{t}{2}$ *is equal to ....*

Sol. (0.5) $f(x) = \lim\limits_{n \to \infty} \sin^n\left(\dfrac{2\pi n}{3n+1}\right) + \lim\limits_{n \to \infty} \dfrac{1 - x^{-2n}}{1 + x^{-2n}} = 0 + 1 = 1$

$$I = \int \frac{x\log(x + \sqrt{1 + x^2})dx}{\sqrt{1 + x^2}}$$

$$= \log(x + \sqrt{1 + x^2})\sqrt{1 + x^2} - \int dx$$

$$= \sqrt{1 + x^2} \log(x + \sqrt{1 + x^2}) - x + C$$

Therefore, $t = 1$

So, $\dfrac{t}{2} = 0.5$

Example 45 $\int \dfrac{2x^2}{2x\cos 2x + (x^2 - 1)\sin 2x} dx$

$= \ln\left|\tan\left(\dfrac{\pi}{4} + \dfrac{f(x)}{2}\right)\right| + C$. *Then,* $\dfrac{[f(1)]^3}{3}$ *is equal to ....*

Sol. (2.66) We know that $a\cos\theta + b\sin\theta = \sqrt{a^2 + b^2} \cos(\theta - \alpha)$

where, $\alpha = \tan^{-1}\left(\dfrac{b}{a}\right)$

$$I = \int \frac{\dfrac{2x^2}{x^2 + 1}dx}{\cos\left(2x - \tan^{-1}\dfrac{1}{2}\left(x - \dfrac{1}{x}\right)\right)}$$

$\left[\because 2x\cos 2x + (x^2 - 1)\sin 2x = (x^2 + 1) \cos\left(2x - \tan^{-1}\dfrac{1}{2}\left(x - \dfrac{1}{x}\right)\right)\right]$

Let $t = 2x - \tan^{-1}\frac{1}{2}\left(x - \frac{1}{x}\right)$

$$dt = \left[2 - \frac{1}{1 + \frac{1}{4}\left(x - \frac{1}{x}\right)^2} \times \frac{1}{2}\left(1 + \frac{1}{x^2}\right)\right] dx$$

$$= \left[2 - \frac{4x^2}{4x^2 + (x^2 - 1)^2} \times \frac{1}{2x^2}(1 + x^2)\right] dx$$

$$\Rightarrow dt = \frac{2x^2}{x^2 + 1} dx$$

$$\therefore \quad I = \int \frac{dt}{\cos t} = \ln\left|\tan\left(\frac{\pi}{4} + \frac{t}{2}\right)\right| + C$$

where, $t = f(x)$

$\because \quad f(1) = 2$

$\therefore \quad \frac{[f(1)]^3}{3} = \frac{8}{3}$

Matching Type Questions

Example 46 *Match the following.*

	Column I		Column II
(A)	If $\int \frac{\sqrt{x^2 + 1}}{x^4} dx = -\frac{1}{3}\frac{(1 + x^2)^{3/2}}{x^k}$, then k is equal to	(p)	3
(B)	If $\int \frac{2 + \sqrt{x}}{(x + \sqrt{x} + 1)^2} dx = \frac{\lambda x}{x + \sqrt{x} + 1} + C$, then λ is equal to	(q)	2
(C)	If $\int \frac{\sqrt{x^{10} + 2}}{x^{16}} dx = -\frac{1}{30}\frac{(x^{10} + 2)^{3/2}}{x^m} + C$, then m is equal to	(r)	15
(D)	If $\int \frac{dx}{x + \sqrt{x}} = n \log(1 + \sqrt{x}) + C$, then n is equal to	(s)	5

Sol. (A) → (p); (B) → (q); (C) → (r); (D) → (q)

(A) Let $I = \int \frac{\sqrt{x^2 + 1}}{x^4} dx$

On putting $x = \tan\theta$,

then $I = \int \frac{\sec\theta \cdot \sec^2\theta}{\tan^4\theta} d\theta = \int \frac{\cos\theta}{\sin^4\theta} d\theta$

$$= \int t^{-4} dt, \text{ where } t = \sin\theta$$

$$= \frac{t^{-4+1}}{-4+1} + C = -\frac{1}{3}t^{-3} + C$$

$$= -\frac{1}{3}\frac{1}{\sin^3\theta} + C = -\frac{1}{3}\left(\frac{1}{(\sin^2\theta)^{3/2}}\right) + C$$

$$= -\frac{1}{3}(\text{cosec}^2\theta)^{3/2} + C = -\frac{1}{3}(1 + \cot^2\theta)^{3/2} + C$$

$$= -\frac{1}{3}\left(1 + \frac{1}{x^2}\right)^{3/2} + C = -\frac{1}{3}\frac{(x^2 + 1)^{3/2}}{x^3} + C$$

Therefore, $k = 3$

(B) We have, $I = \int \frac{2 + \sqrt{x}}{(x + \sqrt{x} + 1)^2} dx$

$$= \int \frac{2 + \sqrt{x}}{x^2\left(1 + \frac{1}{\sqrt{x}} + \frac{1}{x}\right)^2} dx = \int \frac{\frac{2}{x^2} + \frac{1}{x\sqrt{x}}}{\left(1 + \frac{1}{\sqrt{x}} + \frac{1}{x}\right)^2} dx$$

On putting, $1 + \frac{1}{\sqrt{x}} + \frac{1}{x} = t$

$$\Rightarrow \left(-\frac{1}{2x\sqrt{x}} - \frac{1}{x^2}\right) dx = dt \Rightarrow \left(\frac{2}{x^2} + \frac{1}{x\sqrt{x}}\right) dx = -2dt$$

Therefore, $I = \int \frac{1}{t^2}(-2dt) = \frac{2}{t} + C$

$$= \frac{2}{\frac{1}{x} + \frac{1}{\sqrt{x}} + 1} + C = \frac{2x}{1 + \sqrt{x} + x} + C$$

Therefore, $\lambda = 2$

(C) We have, $I = \int \frac{\sqrt{x^{10} + 2}}{x^{16}} dx$

$$= \int \frac{\sqrt{x^{10} + 2}}{x^{11} \cdot x^5} dx = \int \frac{\sqrt{1 + \frac{2}{x^{10}}}}{x^{11}} dx$$

On putting $1 + \frac{2}{x^{10}} = t^2 \Rightarrow \frac{-20}{x^{11}} dx = 2t\,dt \Rightarrow \frac{dx}{x^{11}} = -\frac{1}{10}t\,dt$

Therefore, $I = \int t\left(-\frac{1}{10}\right) t\,dt$

$$= -\frac{t^3}{30} + C = -\frac{1}{30}\left(1 + \frac{2}{x^{10}}\right)^{3/2} + C$$

$$= -\frac{1}{30}\frac{(x^{10} + 2)^{3/2}}{x^{15}} + C$$

So, $m = 15$

(D) We have, $I = \int \frac{dx}{x + \sqrt{x}} = \int \frac{dx}{\sqrt{x}(\sqrt{x} + 1)}$

On putting $\sqrt{x} = t \Rightarrow \frac{1}{2\sqrt{x}} dx = dt$

Therefore, $I = \int \frac{2}{t + 1} dt$

$$= 2\log(t + 1) + C$$

$$= 2\log(\sqrt{x} + 1) + C$$

So, $n = 2$

Example 47 *If $x \in (0, 1)$, then match the entries of Column I with Column II considering 'C' as an arbitrary constant of integration.*

Column I	Column II
(A) $\int \tan\left(2\tan^{-1}\sqrt{\dfrac{\sqrt{1+\sqrt{x}}-1}{\sqrt{1+\sqrt{x}}+1}}\right)dx$	(p) $\dfrac{4}{3}x^{3/4}+C$
(B) $\int \cot\left(2\tan^{-1}\sqrt{\dfrac{\sqrt{1+\sqrt{x}}-\sqrt[4]{x}}{\sqrt{1+\sqrt{x}}+\sqrt[4]{x}}}\right)dx$	(q) $\dfrac{4}{5}x^{5/4}+C$
(C) $\int\left(\dfrac{1-\tan\left(\frac{1}{2}\sin^{-1}\left(\frac{1-\sqrt{x}}{1+\sqrt{x}}\right)\right)}{1+\tan\left(\frac{1}{2}\sin^{-1}\left(\frac{1-\sqrt{x}}{1+\sqrt{x}}\right)\right)}\right)dx$	(r) $\dfrac{2}{3}x^{3/4}+C$
(D) $\int\sqrt{x}\tan\left(2\tan^{-1}\left(\dfrac{\sqrt{\sqrt{1+\sqrt{x}}+1}-\sqrt{\sqrt{1+\sqrt{x}}-1}}{\sqrt{\sqrt{1+\sqrt{x}}+1}+\sqrt{\sqrt{1+\sqrt{x}}-1}}\right)\right)dx$	(s) $\dfrac{2}{5}x^{5/4}+C$

Sol. (A) → (q); (B) → (q); (C) → (q); (D) → (q)

Let $\sqrt{x}=\tan^2\theta$

$$x=\tan^4\theta \Rightarrow \tan\theta = x^{1/4}$$

$\therefore$ $dx = 4\tan^3\theta\sec^2\theta\,d\theta$ $\left[\begin{array}{l}\because x\in(0,1)\\ \therefore \theta\in(0,\pi/4)\end{array}\right]$

$\therefore \sqrt{1+\sqrt{x}}=\sec\theta$

(A) $I=\int\tan\left(2\tan^{-1}\sqrt{\dfrac{\sqrt{1+\sqrt{x}}-1}{\sqrt{1+\sqrt{x}}+1}}\right)dx$

$$\Rightarrow \tan\left(2\tan^{-1}\sqrt{\frac{\sqrt{1+\sqrt{x}}-1}{\sqrt{1+\sqrt{x}}+1}}\right)=\tan\left(2\tan^{-1}\sqrt{\frac{\sec\theta-1}{\sec\theta+1}}\right)$$

$$=\tan\left(2\tan^{-1}\left(\tan\frac{\theta}{2}\right)\right)=\tan\theta$$

$$\therefore \quad I=\int\tan\theta\cdot 4\tan^3\theta\sec^2\theta\,d\theta$$

$$=\frac{4}{5}\tan^5\theta+C=\frac{4}{5}(x^{5/4})+C$$

(B) $I=\int\cot\left(2\tan^{-1}\sqrt{\dfrac{\sqrt{1+\sqrt{x}}-\sqrt[4]{x}}{\sqrt{1+\sqrt{x}}+\sqrt[4]{x}}}\right)dx$

$$\therefore \cot\left(2\tan^{-1}\sqrt{\frac{\sqrt{1+\sqrt{x}}-\sqrt[4]{x}}{\sqrt{1+\sqrt{x}}+\sqrt[4]{x}}}\right)$$

$$=\cot\left(2\tan^{-1}\sqrt{\frac{\sec\theta-\tan\theta}{\sec\theta+\tan\theta}}\right)$$

$$=\cot\left(2\tan^{-1}\sqrt{(\sec\theta-\tan\theta)^2}\right)$$

$$=\cot\left(2\tan^{-1}\frac{1-\sin\theta}{\cos\theta}\right)$$

If $\theta\in(0,\pi/4)$, then $\sec\theta-\tan\theta>0$

$$=\cot\left(2\tan^{-1}\tan\left(\frac{\pi}{4}-\frac{\theta}{2}\right)\right)=\cot\left(\frac{\pi}{2}-\theta\right)=\tan\theta$$

$$\therefore I=\int\tan\theta\cdot 4\tan^3\theta\sec^2\theta\,d\theta$$

$$=\frac{4}{5}\tan^5\theta+C=\frac{4}{5}(x^{5/4})+C$$

(C) Put $\sqrt{x}=\tan^2\theta \Rightarrow dx=4\tan^3\theta\sec^2\theta\,d\theta$

$$\therefore \frac{1}{2}\sin^{-1}\left(\frac{1-\sqrt{x}}{1+\sqrt{x}}\right)=\frac{1}{2}\sin^{-1}\left(\frac{1-\tan^2\theta}{1+\tan^2\theta}\right)$$

$$=\frac{1}{2}\sin^{-1}(\cos 2\theta)=\frac{1}{2}\sin^{-1}\sin\left(\frac{\pi}{2}-2\theta\right)=\frac{\pi}{4}-\theta$$

$$\therefore \int\left(\frac{1-\tan\left(\frac{1}{2}\sin^{-1}\left(\frac{1-\sqrt{x}}{1+\sqrt{x}}\right)\right)}{1+\tan\left(\frac{1}{2}\sin^{-1}\left(\frac{1-\sqrt{x}}{1+\sqrt{x}}\right)\right)}\right)dx$$

$$=\int\frac{1-\tan\left(\frac{\pi}{4}-\theta\right)}{1+\tan\left(\frac{\pi}{4}-\theta\right)}4\tan^3\theta\sec^2\theta\,d\theta$$

$$=\int\tan\left(\frac{\pi}{4}-\left(\frac{\pi}{4}-\theta\right)\right)4\tan^3\theta\sec^2\theta\,d\theta$$

$$=\int 4\tan^4\theta\sec^2\theta\,d\theta=\frac{4}{5}\tan^5\theta+C=\frac{4}{5}(x^{5/4})+C$$

(D) Let $\sqrt{x}=\tan^2\theta$

$\Rightarrow$ $x=\tan^4\theta$

$\therefore$ $dx=4\tan^3\theta\sec^2\theta\,d\theta$ $\left[\begin{array}{l}\because x\in(0,1)\\ \therefore \theta\in(0,\pi/4)\end{array}\right]$

$\therefore \sqrt{1+\sqrt{x}}=\sec\theta$

$$I=\int\sqrt{x}\tan\left(2\tan^{-1}\left(\frac{\sqrt{\sqrt{1+\sqrt{x}}+1}-\sqrt{\sqrt{1+\sqrt{x}}-1}}{\sqrt{\sqrt{1+\sqrt{x}}+1}+\sqrt{\sqrt{1+\sqrt{x}}-1}}\right)\right)dx$$

$$\therefore \sqrt{x}\tan\left(2\tan^{-1}\left(\frac{\sqrt{\sqrt{1+\sqrt{x}}+1}-\sqrt{\sqrt{1+\sqrt{x}}-1}}{\sqrt{\sqrt{1+\sqrt{x}}+1}+\sqrt{\sqrt{1+\sqrt{x}}-1}}\right)\right)$$

$$=\tan^2\theta\cdot\tan\left(2\tan^{-1}\left(\frac{\sqrt{\sec\theta+1}-\sqrt{\sec\theta-1}}{\sqrt{\sec\theta+1}+\sqrt{\sec\theta-1}}\right)\right)$$

$$=\tan^2\theta\cdot\tan\left(2\tan^{-1}\left(\frac{\cos\frac{\theta}{2}-\sin\frac{\theta}{2}}{\cos\frac{\theta}{2}+\sin\frac{\theta}{2}}\right)\right)$$

$$=\tan^2\theta\cdot\tan\left(2\tan^{-1}\tan\left(\frac{\pi}{4}-\frac{\theta}{2}\right)\right)$$

$$=\tan^2\theta\cdot\tan\left(\frac{\pi}{2}-\theta\right)=\tan^2\theta\cdot\cot\theta=\tan\theta$$

$$\therefore I=\int\tan\theta\cdot 4\tan^3\theta\sec^2\theta\,d\theta=\frac{4\tan^5\theta}{5}+C=\frac{4}{5}(x^{5/4})+C$$

EXERCISE 1

JEE Main Pattern

Single Option Correct Type Questions

1. Let $f(x)=\int \frac{x^2}{(1+x^2)(1+\sqrt{1+x^2})}dx$ and $f(0)=0$. Then, $f(1)$ is equal to

(a) $\log_e(1+\sqrt{2})$ (b) $\log_e(1+\sqrt{2})-\frac{\pi}{4}$

(c) $\log_e(1+\sqrt{2})+\frac{\pi}{4}$ (d) None of these

2. $\int \log(\sqrt{1-x}+\sqrt{1+x})\,dx$ is equal to

(a) $x\log(\sqrt{1-x})+\sin^{-1}x+C$

(b) $x\log(\sqrt{1-x}+\sqrt{1+x})+x+\sin^{-1}x+C$

(c) $x\log(\sqrt{1-x}+\sqrt{1+x})-x+\sin^{-1}x+C$

(d) $\log(\sqrt{1-x}+\sqrt{1+x})+\sin^{-1}\frac{x}{2}+C$

3. Let $F(x)$ be the primitive of $\frac{3x+2}{\sqrt{x-9}}$ w.r.t. x. If $F(10)=60$, then the value of $F(13)$ is

(a) 66 (b) 132 (c) 248 (d) 264

4. $\int (x^x)^x\,(2x\log_e x+x)\,dx$ is equal to

(a) $x^{(x^x)}+C$ (b) $(x^x)^x+C$

(c) $x^2\cdot\log_e x+C$ (d) None of these

5. The value of $\int x\log x(\log x-1)\,dx$ is equal to

(a) $2(x\log x-x)^2+C$ (b) $\frac{1}{2}(x\log x-x)^2+C$

(c) $(x\log x)^2+C$ (d) $\frac{1}{2}(x\log x)^3+C$

6. $\int \tan^4 x\,dx = A\tan^3 x+B\tan x+f(x)$, then

(a) $A=\frac{1}{3}, B=-1, f(x)=x+C$

(b) $A=\frac{2}{3}, B=-1, f(x)=x+C$

(c) $A=\frac{1}{3}, B=1, f(x)=x+C$

(d) $A=\frac{2}{3}, B=1, f(x)=-x+C$

7. If the anti-derivative of $\int \frac{\sin^4 x}{x}dx$ is $f(x)$, then $\int \frac{\sin^4\{(p+q)x\}}{x}dx$ in terms of $f(x)$ is

(a) $f\{(p+q)x\}$ (b) $\frac{f\{(p+q)x\}}{p+q}$

(c) $f\{(p+q)x\}(p+q)$ (d) None of these

8. Let $x^2\neq n\pi-1, n\in N$. Then, the value of $\int x\sqrt{\frac{2\sin(x^2+1)-\sin 2(x^2+1)}{2\sin(x^2+1)+\sin 2(x^2+1)}}\,dx$ is equal to

(a) $\log\left|\frac{1}{2}\sec(x^2+1)\right|+C$ (b) $\log\left|\sec\left(\frac{x^2+1}{2}\right)\right|+C$

(c) $\frac{1}{2}\log|\sec(x^2+1)|+C$ (d) None of these

9. $\int \frac{dx}{\cos 2x\cos 4x}$ is equal to

(a) $\frac{1}{2\sqrt{2}}\log\left|\frac{1+\sqrt{2}\sin 2x}{1-\sqrt{2}\sin 2x}\right|-\frac{1}{2}(\log|\sec 2x+\tan 2x|)+C$

(b) $\frac{1}{2\sqrt{2}}\log\left|\frac{1+\sqrt{2}\sin 2x}{1+\sqrt{2}\sin x}\right|-\frac{1}{2}(\log|\sec 2x+\tan 2x|)+C$

(c) $\frac{1}{\sqrt{2}}\log\left|\frac{1+\sqrt{2}\sin 2x}{1-\sqrt{2}\sin 2x}\right|-\frac{1}{2}(\log|\sec 2x-\tan 2x|)+C$

(d) None of the above

10. $\int \frac{\sin^3 x}{(\cos^4 x+3\cos^2 x+1)\tan^{-1}(\sec x+\cos x)}dx$ is equal to

(a) $\tan^{-1}(\sec x+\cos x)+C$

(b) $\log_e|\tan^{-1}(\sec x+\cos x)|+C$

(c) $\frac{1}{(\sec x+\cos x)^2}+C$

(d) None of the above

11. Given, $f(x)=\begin{vmatrix} 0 & x^2-\sin x & \cos x-2 \\ \sin x-x^2 & 0 & 1-2x \\ 2-\cos x & 2x-1 & 0 \end{vmatrix}$, then $\int f(x)\,dx$ is equal to

(a) $\frac{x^3}{3}-x^2\sin x+\sin 2x+C$

(b) $\frac{x^3}{3}-x^2\sin x-\cos 2x+C$

(c) $\frac{x^3}{3}-x^2\cos x-\cos 2x+C$

(d) None of the above

12. $I=\int\left(\log_2\left(\left(\left(\frac{\sin[x]\pi}{x^2+x+1}\right)+\text{sgn}(x^2+x+1)+1\right)\right)\right)dx$ is equal to (where $[\cdot]$ denotes GIF)

(a) $x+C$

(b) $\cos x+x+C$

(c) $\sin x+\text{sgn}(x^2+x+1)+x+C$

(d) $-x+C$

13. $\int\frac{3+\sqrt{x}}{(x+2\sqrt{x}+3)^2}dx$ is equal to

(a) $\frac{2x}{(x+2\sqrt{x}+3)^2}+C$ (b) $\frac{2x}{x+2\sqrt{x}+3}+C$

(c) $\frac{x}{(x+2\sqrt{x}+3)^2}+C$ (d) $\frac{x}{x+2\sqrt{x}+3}+C$

14. $\int\frac{2e^{5x}+e^{4x}-4e^{3x}+4e^{2x}+2e^x}{(e^{2x}+4)(e^{2x}-1)^2}dx$ is equal to

(a) $\tan^{-1}\left(\frac{e^x}{2}\right)-\frac{1}{e^{2x}-1}+C$ (b) $\tan^{-1}(e^x)-\frac{1}{2(e^{2x}-1)}+C$

(c) $\tan^{-1}\left(\frac{e^x}{2}\right)-\frac{1}{2(e^{2x}-1)}+C$ (d) $1-\tan^{-1}\left(\frac{e^x}{2}\right)+\frac{1}{2(e^{2x}-1)}+C$

15. $\int(x^4+1)^{1/3}\cdot x^7dx=k(x^4+1)^{4/3}(4x^4-3)+C$, where k is equal to

(a) $\frac{1}{112}$ (b) $\frac{1}{28}$ (c) $\frac{3}{112}$ (d) $\frac{1}{56}$

16. $\int x^{-6}(1+2x^3)^{2/3}dx$ is equal to

(a) $-\frac{1}{5}(2+x^{-3})^{5/3}+C$ (b) $\frac{1}{5}(x^{-3}+2)^{5/3}+C$

(c) $\frac{3}{5}(2+x^{-3})^{5/3}+C$ (d) $\frac{-3}{5}(x^{-3}+2)^{-5/3}+C$

17. $\int\frac{x}{\sqrt{1+x^2+\sqrt{(1+x^2)^3}}}dx$ is equal to

(a) $\frac{1}{2}\ln(1+\sqrt{1+x^2})+C$ (b) $\frac{-2}{3(1+\sqrt{1+x^2})^{3/2}}+C$

(c) $2(1+\sqrt{1+x^2})+C$ (d) $2\sqrt{1+\sqrt{1+x^2}}+C$

18. Let $I_n=\int\tan^n x\,dx(n>1)$. $I_4+I_6=a\tan^5x+bx^5+C$, where C is a constant of integration, then the ordered pair (a, b) is equal to

(a) $\left(-\frac{1}{5}, 0\right)$ (b) $\left(-\frac{1}{5}, 1\right)$

(c) $\left(\frac{1}{5}, 0\right)$ (d) $\left(\frac{1}{5}, -1\right)$

19. If $\int\frac{\sin^4 x}{\cos^8 x}dx=a\tan^5x+b\tan^7x+C$, then

(a) $7a=5b$ (b) $5a=7b$

(c) $7a+5b=0$ (d) $5a+7b=0$

20. If $\int f(x)\,dx=F(x)$, then $\int x^3f(x^2)\,dx$ is equal to

(a) $\frac{1}{2}[x^2\{F(x)\}^2-\int\{F(x)\}^2\,dx]$

(b) $\frac{1}{2}[x^2F(x^2)-\int F(x^2)\,d(x^2)]$

(c) $\frac{1}{2}[x^2F(x)-\frac{1}{2}\int\{F(x)\}^2\,dx]$

(d) None of the above

21. $\int\frac{e^{(x^2+4\ln x)}-x^3e^{x^2}}{x-1}dx$ is equal to

(a) $\left(\frac{e^{3\ln x}-e^{\ln x}}{2x}\right)e^{x^2}+C$ (b) $\frac{(x-1)\,xe^{x^2}}{2}+C$

(c) $\frac{(x^2-1)}{2x}-e^{x^2}+C$ (d) None of these

22. $\int\frac{1-7\cos^2 x}{\sin^7 x\cos^2 x}dx=\frac{f(x)}{(\sin x)^7}+C$, then $f(x)$ is equal to

(a) $\sin x$ (b) $\cos x$ (c) $\tan x$ (d) $\cot x$

23. The primitive of the function $f(x)=x|\cos x|$, when $\frac{\pi}{2}<x<\pi$ is given by

(a) $\cos x+x\sin x+C$ (b) $-\cos x-x\sin x+C$

(c) $x\sin x-\cos x+C$ (d) None of these

24. The primitive of the function $f(x)=(2x+1)|\sin x|$, when $\pi<x<2\pi$ is

(a) $-(2x+1)\cos x+2\sin x+C$

(b) $(2x+1)\cos x-2\sin x+C$

(c) $(x^2+x)\cos x+C$

(d) None of the above

25. If $\int f(x)dx=g(x)$ and $f'(x)$ is differentiable, then $\int f^{-1}(x)dx$ is equal to

(a) $g^{-1}(x)+C$ (b) $xf^{-1}(x)+C$

(c) $xf^{-1}(x)-g(f^{-1}(x))+C$ (d) $f^{-1}(x)+C$

26. $\int\frac{dx}{\sqrt{(x-p)^3(x-q)}}$ is equal to

(a) $\frac{2}{(p-q)}\sqrt{\left(\frac{x-p}{x-q}\right)}+C$ (b) $-\frac{2}{(p-q)}\sqrt{\left(\frac{x-q}{x-p}\right)}+C$

(c) $\frac{2}{\sqrt{(x-p)(x-q)}}+C$ (d) None of these

27. $\int\frac{x^4+1}{x^6+1}dx$ is equal to

(a) $\tan^{-1}x-\frac{1}{3}\tan^{-1}(x^3)+C$

(b) $\tan^{-1}x+\frac{1}{3}\tan^{-1}(x^3)+C$

(c) $\tan^{-1}x+\frac{1}{2}\tan^{-1}(x^2)+C$

(d) $\tan^{-1}x-\frac{1}{2}\tan^{-1}(x^2)+C$

28. $\int \frac{1}{\sin x \cos x(\tan^9 x+1)} dx$ is equal to

(a) $\log\left|\frac{\cos^9 x}{\sin^9 x+\cos^9 x}\right|+C$

(b) $\frac{1}{9}\log\left|\frac{\sin^9 x}{\sin^9 x+\cos^9 x}\right|+C$

(c) $\frac{1}{9}\log\left|\frac{\sin^9 x+\cos^9 x}{\sin^9 x}\right|+C$

(d) $\frac{1}{9}\log\left|\frac{\cos^9 x}{\sin^9 x+\cos^9 x}\right|+C$

Numerical Value Type Questions

29. If $\int \frac{2\sin x+3\cos x}{3\sin x+4\cos x} dx = 18kx + k\log|3\sin x+4\cos x|+C$, then the value of $\frac{1}{k}$ is ....

30. If $\int \frac{dx}{\sqrt{\sin^3 x\cos^5 x}} = a\sqrt{\cot x}+b\sqrt{\tan^3 x}+C$, then the value of $\frac{a^2}{b^2}$ is ....

31. If $\int \frac{\sqrt{x^{10}+2}}{x^{16}} dx = -\frac{1}{30}\frac{(x^{10}+2)^{3/2}}{x^m}+C$, then the value of m is ....

32. If $\int e^{(x^3+x^2-1)}(3x^4+2x^3+2x)\,dx = f(x)+C$, then the value of $f(1)\times f(-1)$ is ....

33. If $\int \frac{1-(\cot x)^{2023}}{\tan x+(\cot x)^{2024}} = \frac{1}{k}\log|\sin^k x+\cos^k x|+C$, then the value k is ....

34. If $\int \frac{2x+5}{\sqrt{9x^2+6x+2}} dx = a\sqrt{9x^2+6x+2}$ $+ b\log|3x+1+\sqrt{9x^2+6x+2}|+C$, then $9(a+b)$ is equal to ....

35. If $\int \frac{dx}{x^{2024}+x} = \frac{1}{p}\log\left|\frac{x^q}{1+x^r}\right|+C$, where $p, q, r \in N$ and need not be distinct, then the value of $(p+q+r)$ is ......

36. If $\int \frac{(2x+3)dx}{x(x+1)(x+2)(x+3)+1} = C-\frac{1}{f(x)}$, where $f(x)$ is a quadratic polynomial, then the value of $f(2)$ is ....

37. If $\int \frac{dx}{\cos^3 x-\sin^3 x} = A\tan^{-1}(f(x))$

$$+B\log\left|\frac{\sqrt{2}+f(x)}{\sqrt{2}-f(x)}\right|+C,$$

where $f(x)=\sin x+\cos x$, then the value of $(12A+9\sqrt{2}\,B)$ is ....

38. If $\int (x^6+x^4+x^2)\sqrt{2x^4+3x^2+6}\,dx$ $= \frac{(\alpha x^6+\beta x^4+\gamma x^2)^{3/2}}{18}+C$, then the value of $(\alpha^2+\beta^2+\gamma^2)$ is ....

39. Let $\int \sec^{-1}[-\sin^2 x]dx = f(x)+C$, where $[y]$ denotes the largest integers $\le y$, then the value of $\left[f\left(\frac{8}{\pi x}\right)\right]''$ at $x=2$ is ....

40. If $\int x^{23}(1-x)^{31}(3-7x)dx = \frac{x^p(1-x)^q}{r}+C$, where $p, q, r \in N$, then gcd of (p, q, r) is ....

41. Let $\int \frac{4x^3(1+(x^4)^{2023})}{(1+x^4)^{2025}} dx = f(x)+C$, the value of $f(1)-f(0)=\frac{m}{n}$, where m and n are relatively prime positive integer, then the value of $m+n$ is ....

42. If $\int \frac{x+(\cos^{-1}(3x))^2}{\sqrt{1-9x^2}} dx$

$$=\frac{1}{\lambda}\left(\sqrt{1-9x^2}-\frac{1}{9}(\cos^{-1}(3x))^{\mu}\right)+C,$$

then the value of $\lambda^2+\mu^2$ is ....

43. If $\int \frac{(x-1)\,dx}{(x+x\sqrt{x}+\sqrt{x})(\sqrt{\sqrt{x}(x+1)})} = 4\tan^{-1}(g(x))+C$, then the value of $g^2(4)$ is ....

Previous Years Questions

44. If $\int \frac{1}{a^2\sin^2 x+b^2\cos^2 x} dx = \frac{1}{12}\tan^{-1}(3\tan x)+$ constant, then the maximum value of $a\sin x+b\cos x$, is

[Single Correct Type, 2024 Main]

(a) $\sqrt{42}$
(b) $\sqrt{41}$
(c) $\sqrt{40}$
(d) $\sqrt{39}$

45. If $\int \frac{\sin^{3/2} x+\cos^{3/2} x}{\sqrt{\sin^3 x\cos^3 x\sin(x-\theta)}} dx$

$$= A\sqrt{\cos\theta\tan x-\sin\theta}+B\sqrt{\cos\theta-\sin\theta\cot x}+C,$$

where C is the integration constant, then AB is equal to

[Single Correct Type, 2024 Main]

(a) $4\ \text{cosec}\,(2\theta)$
(b) $4\sec\theta$
(c) $8\ \text{cosec}\,(2\theta)$
(d) $2\sec\theta$

46. For $x \in \left(-\frac{\pi}{2}, \frac{\pi}{2}\right)$, if

$y(x) = \int \frac{\text{cosec } x + \sin x}{\text{cosec } x \sec x + \tan x \sin^2 x} dx$ and

$\lim_{x \to \left(\frac{\pi}{2}\right)^-} y(x) = 0$, then $y\left(\frac{\pi}{4}\right)$ is equal to

[Single Correct Type, 2024 Main]

(a) $\frac{1}{2}\tan^{-1}\left(\frac{1}{\sqrt{2}}\right)$ (b) $\frac{1}{\sqrt{2}}\tan^{-1}\left(-\frac{1}{2}\right)$

(c) $\tan^{-1}\left(\frac{1}{\sqrt{2}}\right)$ (d) $-\frac{1}{\sqrt{2}}\tan^{-1}\left(\frac{1}{\sqrt{2}}\right)$

47. The integral $\int \frac{(x^8 - x^2)dx}{(x^{12} + 3x^6 + 1)\tan^{-1}\left(x^3 + \frac{1}{x^3}\right)}$ is equal to **[Single Correct Type, 2024 Main]**

(a) $\log_e\left(\left|\tan^{-1}\left(x^3 + \frac{1}{x^3}\right)\right|\right) + C$

(b) $\log_e\left(\left|\tan^{-1}\left(x^3 + \frac{1}{x^3}\right)\right|\right)^{1/2} + C$

(c) $\log_e\left(\left|\tan^{-1}\left(x^3 + \frac{1}{x^3}\right)\right|\right)^3 + C$

(d) $\log_e\left(\left|\tan^{-1}\left(x^3 + \frac{1}{x^3}\right)\right|\right)^{1/3} + C$

48. If $I(x) = \int e^{\sin^2 x}(\cos x \sin 2x - \sin x)dx$ and $I(0) = 1$, then $I\left(\frac{\pi}{3}\right)$ is equal to

[Single Correct Type, 2023 Main]

(a) $e^{\frac{3}{4}}$ (b) $-e^{\frac{3}{4}}$ (c) $\frac{1}{2}e^{\frac{3}{4}}$ (d) $-\frac{1}{2}e^{\frac{3}{4}}$

49. Let $I(x) = \int \frac{(x+1)}{x(1 + xe^x)^2} dx$, $x > 0$. If $\lim_{x \to \infty} I(x) = 0$, then $I(1)$ is equal to **[Single Correct Type, 2023 Main]**

(a) $\frac{e+2}{e+1} - \log_e(e+1)$ (b) $\frac{e+2}{e+1} + \log_e(e+1)$

(d) $\frac{e+1}{e+2} + \log_e(e+1)$ (d) $\frac{e+1}{e+2} - \log_e(e+1)$

50. Let $I(x) = \int \frac{x^2(x\sec^2 x + \tan x)}{(x\tan x + 1)^2} dx$. If $I(0) = 0$, then $I\left(\frac{\pi}{4}\right)$ is equal to

[Single Correct Type, 2023 Main]

(a) $\log_e \frac{(\pi+4)^2}{16} - \frac{\pi^2}{4(\pi+4)}$

(b) $\log_e \frac{(\pi+4)^2}{16} + \frac{\pi^2}{4(\pi+4)}$

(c) $\log_e \frac{(\pi+4)^2}{32} + \frac{\pi^2}{4(\pi+4)}$

(d) $\log_e \frac{(\pi+4)^2}{32} - \frac{\pi^2}{4(\pi+4)}$

51. Let f and g be twice differentiable functions on R such that

$$f''(x) = g''(x) + 6x$$
$$f'(1) = 4g'(1) - 3 = 9$$
$$f(2) = 3g(2) = 12$$

Then, which of the following is not true?

[Single Correct Type, 2023 Main]

(a) There exists $x_0 \in \left(1, \frac{3}{2}\right)$ such that $f(x_0) = g(x_0)$

(b) $g(-2) - f(-2) = 20$

(c) If $-1 < x < 2$, then $|f(x) - g(x)| < 8$

(d) $|f'(x) - g'(x)| < 6 \Rightarrow -1 < x < 1$

52. Let $f(x) = \int \frac{2x}{(x^2+1)(x^2+3)} dx$. If

$f(3) = \frac{1}{2}(\log_e 5 - \log_e 6)$, then $f(4)$ is equal to

[Single Correct Type, 2023 Main]

(a) $\frac{1}{2}(\log_e 19 - \log_e 17)$ (b) $\frac{1}{2}(\log_e 17 - \log_e 19)$

(c) $\log_e 19 - \log_e 20$ (d) $\log_e 17 - \log_e 18$

53. Let $f(x) = \int \frac{dx}{(3 + 4x^2)\sqrt{4 - 3x^2}}$, $|x| < \frac{2}{\sqrt{3}}$. If $f(0) = 0$ and $f(1) = \frac{1}{\alpha\beta}\tan^{-1}\left(\frac{\alpha}{\beta}\right)$, $\alpha, \beta > 0$, then $\alpha^2 + \beta^2$ is equal to ....

[Numerical Value Type, 2023 Main]

54. Let $I(x) = \int \sqrt{\frac{x+7}{x}} dx$ and $I(9) = 12 + 7\log_e 7$. If $I(1) = \alpha + 7\log_e(1 + 2\sqrt{2})$, then α^4 is equal to ....

[Numerical Value Type, 2023 Main]

55. If $\int \sqrt{\sec 2x - 1}dx = \alpha \log_e$

$\left|\cos 2x + \beta + \sqrt{\cos 2x\left(1 + \cos\frac{1}{\beta}x\right)}\right|$ + constant, then

$\beta - \alpha$ is equal to .... **[Numerical Value Type, 2023 Main]**

56. For $I(x) = \int \frac{\sec^2 x - 2022}{\sin^{2022} x} dx$, if $I\left(\frac{\pi}{4}\right) = 2^{1011}$, then

[Single Correct Type, 2022 Main]

(a) $3^{1010} I\left(\frac{\pi}{3}\right) - I\left(\frac{\pi}{6}\right) = 0$ (b) $3^{1010} I\left(\frac{\pi}{6}\right) - I\left(\frac{\pi}{3}\right) = 0$

(c) $3^{1011} I\left(\frac{\pi}{3}\right) - I\left(\frac{\pi}{6}\right) = 0$ (d) $3^{1011} I\left(\frac{\pi}{6}\right) - I\left(\frac{\pi}{3}\right) = 0$

57. $\int \frac{(x^2+1)e^x}{(x+1)^2} dx = f(x)e^x + C$, where C is a constant, then $\frac{d^3 f}{dx^3}$ at $x = 1$ is equal to

[Single Correct Type, 2022 Main]

(a) $-\frac{3}{4}$ (b) $\frac{3}{4}$ (c) $-\frac{3}{2}$ (d) $\frac{3}{2}$

58. If $\int \frac{\sin x}{\sin^3 x + \cos^3 x} dx = \alpha \log_e |1 + \tan x|$ $+ \beta \log_e |1 - \tan x + \tan^2 x| + \gamma \tan^{-1}\left(\frac{2\tan x - 1}{\sqrt{3}}\right) + C,$ where C is constant of integration, then the value of $18(\alpha + \beta + \gamma^2)$ is ......

[Numerical Value Type, 2022 Main]

59. For real numbers α, β and γ and δ, if

$$\int \frac{(x^2 - 1) + \tan^{-1}\left(\frac{x^2+1}{x}\right)}{(x^4 + 3x^2 + 1)\tan^{-1}\left(\frac{x^2+1}{x}\right)} dx$$

$= \alpha \log_e \left(\tan^{-1}\left(\frac{x^2+1}{x}\right)\right) + \beta \tan^{-1}\left(\frac{\gamma(x^2-1)}{x}\right)$ $+ \delta \tan^{-1}\left(\frac{x^2+1}{x}\right) + C$, where C is an arbitrary constant, then the value of $10(\alpha + \beta\gamma + \delta)$ is equal to ....

[Numerical Value Type, 2021 Main]

60. If $\int \frac{\cos\theta}{5 + 7\sin\theta - 2\cos^2\theta} d\theta = A \log_e |B(\theta)| + C$, where C is a constant of integration, then $\frac{B(\theta)}{A}$ can be

[Single Correct Type, 2020 Main]

(a) $\frac{2\sin\theta + 1}{\sin\theta + 3}$

(b) $\frac{2\sin\theta + 1}{5(\sin\theta + 3)}$

(c) $\frac{5(\sin\theta + 3)}{2\sin\theta + 1}$

(d) $\frac{5(2\sin\theta + 1)}{\sin\theta + 3}$

61. Let $f(x) = \int \frac{\sqrt{x}}{(1+x)^2} dx \ (x \geq 0)$. Then, $f(3) - f(1)$ is equal to

[Single Correct Type, 2020 Main]

(a) $-\frac{\pi}{6} + \frac{1}{2} + \frac{\sqrt{3}}{4}$ (b) $-\frac{\pi}{12} + \frac{1}{2} + \frac{\sqrt{3}}{4}$

(c) $\frac{\pi}{6} + \frac{1}{2} - \frac{\sqrt{3}}{4}$ (d) $\frac{\pi}{12} + \frac{1}{2} - \frac{\sqrt{3}}{4}$

EXERCISE 2

JEE Advanced Pattern

Single Option Correct Type Questions

1. If n is an odd positive integer, then $\int |x^n| dx$ is equal to

(a) $\left|\frac{x^{n+1}}{n+1}\right| + C$ (b) $\frac{x^{n+1}}{n+1} + C$

(c) $\frac{|x|^n x}{n+1} + C$ (d) None of these

2. Let $f(x)$ be a polynomial satisfying $f(0) = 2$, $f'(0) = 3$ and $f''(x) = f(x)$. Then, $f(4)$ is equal to

(a) $\frac{5(e^8+1)}{2e^4}$ (b) $\frac{5e^8 - 1}{2e^4}$ (c) $\frac{2e^4}{5(e^8-1)}$ (d) $\frac{2e^4}{5(e^8+1)}$

3. $\int \left(\frac{\sin\theta}{\cos 3\theta} + \frac{\sin 3\theta}{\cos 9\theta} + \frac{\sin 9\theta}{\cos 27\theta}\right) d\theta$ is equal to

(a) $\frac{1}{2}\log\left|\frac{\sec 27\theta}{\sec\theta}\right| + C$ (b) $\frac{1}{2}\log\left|\frac{\sec\theta}{\sec 27\theta}\right| + C$

(c) $\frac{1}{2}\log\left|\frac{\sqrt[27]{\sec 27\theta}}{\sec\theta}\right| + C$ (d) None of these

4. Let $A = \begin{bmatrix} x^2 & 6 & 0 \\ 1 & -5 & 1 \\ 2 & 0 & x \end{bmatrix}$ and $B = \begin{bmatrix} 4 & 0 & 0 \\ 0 & 1 & 0 \\ 0 & 0 & 8 \end{bmatrix}$. If a function is defined as $f(x) = \text{trace}(AB)$, then $\int \frac{3dx}{f(x)}$ is equal to

(a) $\frac{1}{4}\ln\left|\frac{2x-1}{2x+5}\right| + C$ (b) $\frac{1}{4}\ln\left|\frac{2x+5}{2x-1}\right| + C$

(c) $\frac{1}{3}\ln\left|\frac{1-2x}{2x+5}\right| + C$ (d) $\frac{1}{3}\ln\left|\frac{1-2x}{2x+3}\right| + C$

5. $\int \frac{(\sin 2x)^{\frac{1}{3}} d((\tan x)^{\frac{1}{3}})}{\sin^{\frac{2}{3}} x + \cos^{\frac{2}{3}} x}$ is equal to

(a) $\ln|1 + \cot^{\frac{1}{3}} x| + C$ (b) $2^{\frac{1}{3}} \ln|1 + \tan^{\frac{2}{3}} x| + C$

(c) $\frac{1}{2^{\frac{2}{3}}} \ln|1 + \tan^{\frac{1}{3}} x| + C$ (d) $\frac{1}{2^{\frac{2}{3}}} \ln|1 + \tan^{\frac{2}{3}} x| + C$

6. If $\int \frac{x\,dx}{\sqrt[2012]{(1+x^2)^{1012}(2+x^2)^{3012}}} = \frac{\alpha}{\beta}(1-f(x))^{\frac{1000}{2012}} + K,$ then which is true ?

(a) $\alpha = 503, \beta = 500, f(\sqrt{2}) = \frac{1}{\beta-\alpha}$

(b) $\alpha = 503, \beta = 250, f(\sqrt{2}) = \frac{1}{\alpha-\beta}$

(c) $\alpha = 503, \beta = 500, f(1) = \frac{1}{\alpha-\beta}$

(d) $\alpha = 503, \beta = 225, f(\sqrt{3}) = \frac{1}{\alpha-\beta}$

7. $I = \int \tan\left[2\tan^{-1}\left(\sqrt{\frac{\sqrt{1+\sqrt{x}}-1}{\sqrt{1+\sqrt{x}}+1}}\right)\right] dx$ and $x \in (0, 1)$ is equal to

(a) $\frac{4}{5}x^{5/4} + C$ (b) $\frac{5}{4}x^{4/5} + C$

(c) $\frac{1}{2}\sqrt{x} + C$ (d) None of these

8. $\int \frac{x}{(x^2-3x+2)\sqrt{x^2-4x+3}}\,dx$ is equal to

(a) $-2\sin^{-1}\frac{1}{x-2} + \frac{\sqrt{x^2-4x+3}}{x-1} + C$

(b) $2\sin^{-1}\frac{1}{x-2} + \frac{\sqrt{x^2-4x+3}}{x-1} + C$

(c) $-2\sin^{-1}\frac{1}{x-2} - \frac{\sqrt{x^2-4x+3}}{x-1} + C$

(d) $2\sin^{-1}\frac{1}{x-2} - \frac{\sqrt{x^2-4x+3}}{x-1} + C$

9. The integral $\int \left(\frac{x}{x\sin x + \cos x}\right)^2 dx$ is equal to (where, C is a constant of integration)

(a) $\tan x + \frac{x\sec x}{x\sin x + \cos x} + C$

(b) $\tan x - \frac{x\sec x}{x\sin x + \cos x} + C$

(c) $\sec x + \frac{x\tan x}{x\sin x + \cos x} + C$

(d) $\sec x - \frac{x\tan x}{x\sin x + \cos x} + C$

10. $\int \frac{e^{(x^2+4\ln x)} - x^3 e^{x^2}}{x-1}\,dx$ is equal to

(a) $\left(\frac{x^3-x}{2}\right)e^{x^2} + C$ (b) $\frac{(x-1)xe^{x^2}}{2} + C$

(c) $\left(\frac{x^2-1}{2x}\right)e^{x^2} + C$ (d) $\frac{(x^2-1)e^{x^2}}{2} + C$

11. $\int \left(1 + 2x^2 + \frac{1}{x}\right) e^{\left(x^2 - \frac{1}{x}\right)} dx$ is equal to

(a) $-xe^{x^2-\frac{1}{x}} + C$ (b) $xe^{x^2-\frac{1}{x}} + C$

(c) $(2x-1)e^{x^2-\frac{1}{x}} + C$ (d) $(2x+1)e^{x^2-\frac{1}{x}} + C$

12. $\int \left(\frac{\ln x \cdot \ln(x \cdot \ln x)\ln(x \cdot \ln(x\ln x)) + 1 + \ln x}{\ln x \cdot \ln(x\ln x)}\right) dx$ is equal to

(a) $x\ln x - x\ln(\ln(x\ln x)) + x + C$

(b) $x\ln x - x\ln(\ln(x\ln x)) - x + C$

(c) $x\ln x + x\ln(\ln(x\ln x)) - x + C$

(d) None of the above

13. In a determinant (D), if elements of third row are $a_{31} = e^x, a_{32} = e^x f(x), a_{33} = -1$ and their corresponding minors are $f(x), -f'(x), e^x(f(x)f'(x) + f''(x))$ respectively, then $\int D\,dx$ is equal to

(a) $e^x(f(x) + f''(x)) + C$ (b) $e^x(f(x) - f''(x)) + C$

(c) $e^x(f(x) - f'(x)) + C$ (d) $e^x(f(x) + f'(x)) + C$

14. The value of $\int \frac{1-\cos x}{\cos x(1+\cos x)}\,dx$ is

(a) $\ln|\sin x| - 2\tan\frac{x}{2} + C$

(b) $\ln|\sec x + \tan x| - \tan\frac{x}{2} + C$

(c) $\ln|\sec x + \tan x| - 2\tan\frac{x}{2} + C$

(d) $\ln|\sec x + \tan x| + C$

15. $\int \frac{dx}{\sin x + \sin 2x} = A\log(1-\cos x) + B\log(1+\cos x) + C\log(1+2\cos x) + K$, then $6(A+B+C)$ is

(a) 0 (b) 1 (c) 5 (d) 2

16. $\int \frac{1 + x\cos x}{x(1 - x^2 e^{2\sin x})}\,dx$ is equal to

(a) $\log|xe^{\sin x}| + \frac{1}{2}\log|1 + x^2e^{2\sin x}| + C$

(b) $\log|xe^{\sin x}| - \frac{1}{2}\log|1 - x^2e^{2\sin x}| + C$

(c) $\frac{1}{2}\{\log|xe^{\sin x}| - \log|1 - x^2e^{2\sin x}|\} + C$

(d) None of the above

More than One Correct Option Type Questions

17. $\int \frac{dx}{(x+1)(x-2)} = A\log(x+1) + B\log(x-2) + C$, where

(a) $A + B = 0$ (b) $AB = 0$

(c) $A/B = -1$ (d) None of these

18. If $\int \frac{dx}{(x^2+1)(x^2+4)} = k\tan^{-1}x + l\tan^{-1}\left(\frac{x}{2}\right) + C$, then

(a) $k = \frac{1}{3}$ (b) $l = \frac{2}{3}$

(c) $k = -\frac{1}{3}$ (d) $l = -\frac{1}{6}$

19. If $\int x\log(1+x^2)\,dx = \phi(x)\log(1+x^2) + x(\psi) + C$, then

(a) $\phi(x) = \frac{1+x^2}{2}$ (b) $\psi(x) = \frac{1+x^2}{2}$

(c) $\psi(x) = -\frac{1+x^2}{2}$ (d) $\phi(x) = -\frac{1+x^2}{2}$

20. If $\int \frac{4e^x + 6e^{-x}}{9e^x - 4e^{-x}}\,dx = Ax + B\log_e(9e^{2x} - 4) + C$, then

(a) $A = \frac{3}{2}$ (b) $B = \frac{35}{36}$

(c) C is indefinite (d) $A + B = -\frac{19}{36}$

21. If $\int \tan^5 x\,dx = A\tan^4 x + B\tan^2 x + g(x) + C$, then

(a) $A = \frac{1}{4}, B = -\frac{1}{2}$ (b) $g(x) = \ln|\sec x|$

(c) $g(x) = \ln|\cos x|$ (d) $A = -\frac{1}{4}, B = \frac{1}{3}$

22. If $\int \frac{x^2+3}{x^4+x^3-x^2-3x+9}\,dx$

$$= \frac{m}{\sqrt{n}}\tan^{-1}\left(\frac{m(x-\alpha)(x-\beta)}{\sqrt{n}\,x}\right) + C,$$

where $\alpha > \beta$ and $\alpha, \beta \in R$ and m and n are prime numbers, then (where C is constant of integration)

(a) $n - m$ is a prime number

(b) $n + m$ is a prime number

(c) $m + \beta = 0$

(d) $|\alpha + \beta| = m^{-1}$

23. Let $f(x)$ be a function such that $f''(x) = f(x)$ and $f'(0) = f(0) = 0$. Then, the value of $\int \frac{f(x)}{4 - f(x)}\,dx$ is equal to

(a) $\log_e(4 - f(x)) + C$ (b) $-\log_e(4 - f(x)) + C$

(c) $\log_e\left(\frac{1+f(x)}{4-f(x)}\right) + C$ (d) $-\log_e\left(\frac{1+f(x)}{4-f(x)}\right) + C$

24. If $\int \frac{dx}{\cos^3 x - \sin^3 x} = A\tan^{-1}(\sin x + \cos x)$

$$+ B\ln\left|\frac{\cos x + \sin x - \sqrt{2}}{\cos x + \sin x + \sqrt{2}}\right| + C,\text{ then}$$

(a) $A = \frac{2}{3}$ (b) $B = \frac{-2}{3\sqrt{2}}$ (c) $A = \frac{-2}{3}$ (d) $B = -\frac{1}{3\sqrt{2}}$

25. If $\int \frac{x^x(x^{4x}+1)(\log x + 1)}{1 + x^{6x}}\,dx = \sum_{r=1}^{3} a_r \tan^{-1} x^{rx} + C$, then

(a) $a_1a_2a_3 = 0$ (b) $a_2 < a_3 < a_1$

(c) $\sum_{r=1}^{3} ra_r = 2$ (d) $a_1a_3 > 0$

26. If $\int \frac{4x^3 + 3x^2}{x^8 + 2x^7 + x^6 + 4x^4 + 4x^3 + 13}\,dx$

$$= \frac{K}{K_1}\tan^{-1}(Ax^4 + Bx^3 + C) + D,\text{ then}$$

(a) $K_1 + K = 4$ (b) $A + B = C$

(c) $K_1 + K = 3$ (d) $A + B = 2C$

27. If $f(x) = ax^3 + bx^2 + cx + d$ such that $f(0) = 1, f(1) = 2$. Also, $x = 0$ is stationary point but not a point of extrema. If $\int \frac{(x^2+x+1)f(x)}{x+1}\,dx = \frac{x}{a_1} + \frac{x^3}{b_1} + \frac{x^5}{c_1} + K$, then

(a) a_1, b_1, c_1 are in AP (b) HCF of $(b_1, c_1) = 1$

(c) $a_1 + b_1^2 = 2c_1$ (d) $a_1 < b_1 < c_1$

28. Let $f: R \to R$ and $g: R \to R$ be two non-constant differentiable functions. If $f'(x) = (e^{(f(x) - g(x))})\,g'(x)$ for all $x \in R$ and $f(1) = g(2) = 1$, then which of the following statement(s) is (are) TRUE?

(a) $f(2) < 1 - \log_e 2$ (b) $f(2) > 1 - \log_e 2$

(c) $g(1) > 1 - \log_e 2$ (d) $g(1) < 1 - \log_e 2$

Passage Based Questions

Passage I

(Q. Nos. 29 and 30)

- Let us consider the integral of the following forms

$$f(x_1, \sqrt{mx^2 + nx + p})^{1/2}$$

Case I If $m > 0$, then put $\sqrt{mx^2 + nx + C} = u \pm x\sqrt{m}$

Case II If $p > 0$, then put $\sqrt{mx^2 + nx + C} = ux \pm \sqrt{p}$

Case III If quadratic equation $mx^2 + nx + p = 0$ has real roots α and β there put $\sqrt{mx^2 + nx + p} = (x - \alpha)\,u$ or $(x - \beta)\,u$.

29. $\int \frac{(x + \sqrt{1+x^2})^{15}}{\sqrt{1+x^2}}\,dx$ is equal to

(a) $\frac{(x+\sqrt{1+x^2})^{16}}{10} + C$ (b) $\frac{1}{15(\sqrt{1+x^2}+x)} + C$

(c) $\frac{15}{(\sqrt{1+x^2}-x)} + C$ (d) $\frac{(x+\sqrt{1+x^2})^{15}}{15} + C$

30. To evaluate $\int \frac{dx}{(x-1)\sqrt{-x^2+3x-2}}$ one of the most suitable substitution could be

(a) $\sqrt{-x^2+3x-2}=u$

(b) $\sqrt{-x^2+3x-2}=(ux\sqrt{2})$

(c) $\sqrt{-x^2+3x-2}=u(1-x)$

(d) $\sqrt{-x^2+3x-2}=u(x+2)$

Passage II

(Q. Nos. 31 and 32)

- Let $I_{(n,m)}=\int \sin^n x\cos^m x\,dx$. Then, we can relate $I_{(n,m)}$ with each of the following :

(i) $I_{(n-2,m)}$ (ii) $I_{(n+2,m)}$ (iii) $I_{(n,m-2)}$

(iv) $I_{(n,m+2)}$ (v) $I_{(n-2,m+2)}$ (vi) $I_{(n+2,m-2)}$

Suppose we want to establish a relation between $I_{(n,m)}$ and $I_{(n,m-2)}$, then we get

$$P(x)=\sin^{n+1}x\cos^{m-1}x \quad \text{...(i)}$$

In $I_{(n,m)}$ and $I_{(n,m-2)}$ the exponent of cos x is m and $m-2$ respectively, the minimum of the two is $m-2$, adding 1 to the minimum we get $m-2+1=m-1$.

Now, choose the exponent $m-1$ of cos x in $P(x)$.

Similarly, choose the exponent of sin x for

$P(x)=(nH)\sin^n x\cos^m x-(m-1)\sin^{n+2}x\cos^{m-2}x$.

Now, differentiating both the sides of Eq. (i), we get

$$=(n+1)\sin^n x\cos^m x-(m-1)\sin^n x\,(1-\cos^2 x)\cos^{m-2}x$$

$$=(n+1)\sin^n x\cos^m x-(m-1)\sin^n x\cos^{m-2}x+(m-1)\sin^n x\cos^n x$$

$$=(n+m)\sin^n x\cos^m x-(m-1)\sin^n x\cos^{m-2}x$$

Now, integrating both the sides, we get

$$\int \sin^{n+1}x\cos^{m-1}x\,dx=(n+m)\,I_{(n,m)}-(m-1)\,I_{(n,m-2)}$$

Similarly, we can establish the other relations.

31. The relation between $I_{(4,2)}$ and $I_{(6,2)}$ is

(a) $I_{(4,2)}=\frac{1}{5}(\sin^5 x\cos^3 x+8\,I_{(6,2)})$

(b) $I_{(4,2)}=\frac{1}{5}(-\sin^5 x\cos^3 x+8\,I_{(6,2)})$

(c) $I_{(4,2)}=\frac{1}{5}(\sin^5 x\cos^3 x-8I_{(6,2)})$

(d) $I_{(4,2)}=\frac{1}{6}(\sin^5 x\cos^3 x+8I_{(6,2)})$

32. The relation between $I_{(4,2)}$ and $I_{(4,4)}$ is

(a) $I_{(4,2)}=\frac{1}{3}(\sin^5 x\cos^3 x+8\,I_{(4,4)})$

(b) $I_{(4,2)}=\frac{1}{3}(-\sin^5 x\cos^3 x+8\,I_{(4,4)})$

(c) $I_{(4,2)}=\frac{1}{3}(\sin^5 x\cos^3 x-8I_{(4,4)})$

(d) $I_{(4,2)}=\frac{1}{3}(\sin^5 x\cos^3 x+6I_{(4,4)})$

Passage III

(Q. Nos. 33 to 34)

- If $f: R\to(0,\infty)$ be a differentiable function $f(x)$ satisfying $f(x+y)-f(x-y)=f(x)\cdot\{f(y)-f(y)-y\}$, $\forall\, x,y\in R$, $(f(y)\neq f(-y)$ for all $y\in R)$ and $f'(0)=2010$.

Now, answer the following questions.

33. Which of the following is true for $f(x)$

(a) $f(x)$ is one-one and into

(b) $\{f(x)\}$ is non-periodic, where $\{\cdot\}$ denotes fractional part of x.

(c) $f(x)=4$ has only two solutions.

(d) $f(x)=f^{-1}(x)$ has only one solution.

34. Let $g(x)=\log_e(\sin x)$, and $\int f(g(x))\cos x\,dx=h(x)+C$, (where C is constant of integration), then $h\left(\frac{\pi}{2}\right)$ is equal to

(a) 0 (b) $\frac{1}{2010}$

(c) 1 (d) $\frac{1}{2011}$

Passage IV

(Q. Nos. 35 to 36)

- Let $f: R\to R$ be a function as $f(x)=(x-1)(x+2)(x-3)(x-6)-100$. If $g(x)$ is a polynomial of degree ≤ 3 such that $\int \frac{g(x)}{f(x)}dx$ does not contain any logarithm function and $g(-2)=10$. Then,

35. The minimum value of $f(x)$ is

(a) -136 (b) -100

(c) -84 (d) -68

36. $\int \frac{g(x)}{f(x)}dx$, equals

(a) $\tan^{-1}\left(\frac{x-2}{2}\right)+C$ (b) $\tan^{-1}\left(\frac{x-1}{1}\right)+C$

(c) $\tan^{-1}(x)+C$ (d) None of these

Stem Based Questions

Stem I

(Q. Nos. 37 to 38)

- If $\int \frac{x(x-1)}{(x^2+1)(x+1)\sqrt{x^3+x^2+x}}dx$
$$= \frac{1}{2}\ln\left|\frac{\sqrt{f(x)}-1}{\sqrt{f(x)}+1}\right| - \tan^{-1}\sqrt{f(x)} + C$$
and $\lim_{x\to\infty} \tan^{-1}\sqrt{f(x)} = \frac{m}{n}$, then

37. The value of $f(1)$ is ....

38. The value of $[m+n]$ is .... (where $[\cdot]$ denotes GIF)

Stem II

(Q. Nos. 39 to 40)

- Let $\int \frac{\ln(x+\sqrt{1+x^2})}{\sqrt{1+x^2}}dx = fog(x)+C$, where f and g are functions of x and C is an arbitrary constant. If $\int f(x)\cdot g(x)\,dx = ax^3 g(x) + b(1+x^2)^{3/2} + d(1+x^2)^{1/2} + e$ and $\int e^{g(x)}\,dx = k\cdot x\cdot e^{g(x)} + kg(x) + k_1$, then

39. The value of $a+d-12b$ is ....

40. The value of $4k$ is ....

Single Integer Type Questions

41. If $\int \frac{(2x+3)\,dx}{x(x+1)(x+2)(x+3)+1} = C - \frac{1}{f(x)}$, where $f(x)$ is of the form of ax^2+bx+c, then $(a+b+c)$ equals to ....

42. Let $F(x)$ be the primitive of $\frac{3x+2}{\sqrt{x-9}}$ w.r.t. x. If $F(10)=60$, then the sum of digits of the value of $F(13)$, is ....

43. Let $u(x)$ and $v(x)$ are differentiable function such that $\frac{u(x)}{v(x)}=7$. If $\frac{u'(x)}{v'(x)}=p$ and $\left(\frac{u(x)}{v(x)}\right)'=q$, then $\frac{p+q}{p-q}$ has the value equal to ....

44. If $\int \frac{1}{(x^2-1)}\ln\left(\frac{x-1}{x+1}\right)dx = 6A\left[\ln\left(\frac{x-1}{x+1}\right)\right]^2 + C$, then find $24A$.

45. If $\int \frac{e^x(2-x^2)}{(1-x)\sqrt{1-x^2}}dx = \mu e^x\left(\frac{1+x}{1-x}\right)^{\lambda} + C$, then $2(\lambda+\mu)$ is equal to ....

46. If $\int \frac{\cos x - \sin x + 1 - x}{e^x + \sin x + x}dx = \ln\{f(x)\} + g(x) + C$, where C is the constant of integrating and $f(x)$ is positive, then $\frac{f(x)+g(x)}{e^x+\sin x}$ is equal to ....

47. Suppose $A = \int \frac{dx}{x^2+6x+25}$ and $B = \int \frac{dx}{x^2-6x-27}$.
If $12(A+B) = \lambda\cdot\tan^{-1}\left(\frac{x+3}{4}\right) + \mu\cdot\ln\left|\frac{x-9}{x+3}\right| + C$, then the value of $(\lambda+\mu)$ is .... .

48. If $\int \frac{\cos 6x + \cos 9x}{1-2\cos 5x}dx = -\frac{\sin 4x}{k} - \sin x + C$, then the value of k is ....

49. The value of $\int \frac{\tan x}{1+\tan x+\tan^2 x}dx$
$$= x - \frac{2}{\sqrt{A}}\tan^{-1}\left(\frac{2\tan x+1}{\sqrt{A}}\right) + C$$, then the value of A is......... .

50. $\int \sin^{5/2} x\cos^3 x\,dx = 2\sin^{A/2} x\left[\frac{1}{B} - \frac{1}{C}\sin^2 x\right] + C$, then the value of $(A+B)-C$ is equal to ....

51. If $\int (x^{2010} + x^{804} + x^{402})(2x^{1608} + 5x^{402} + 10)^{1/402}\,dx$
$= \frac{1}{10a}(2x^{2010} + 5x^{804} + 10x^{402})^{a/402}$. Then, $(a-400)$ is equal to ....

52. If $\int e^{x^3+x^2-1}(3x^4+2x^3+2x)\,dx = h(x)+c$ Then, the value of $\ln|h(1)|$, is ....

53. If $\int \tan^9 x\,dx = f(x) + \log|\cos x|$, where $f(x)$ is a polynomial of degree n in $\tan x$, then the value of n is ....

Numerical Value Type Questions

54. Let $f(x)$ be a polynomial satisfying $f(0)=3$, $f'(0)=4$ and $f''(x)=f(x)$, $f(7)=k\left(e^{14}-\frac{1}{7}\right)e^{-7}$, then the value of k is ....

55. If $f(x) = \lim_{n\to\infty}[2x+4x^3+..+2nx^{2n-1}]$, where $(0<x<1)$ and $\int f(x)\,dx = \frac{P}{Q+Rx^2}+C$, then $\frac{P}{Q-R}$ is ....

56. If $I = \int \frac{\sqrt{x}\,dx}{(\sqrt{x}\sin\sqrt{x}+\cos\sqrt{x})\sqrt{(1+x)}}$
$$= 2\ln\left|\tan\frac{f(x)}{2}\right| + C$$, then $f(1)$ is equal to ....

57. Let $\frac{d}{dx}(f(x)) = \frac{(\sin^{12} x - \cos^{12} x)}{(\sin^2 x - \cos^2 x)(1 - 3\sin^2 x \cos^2 x)}$ be such that $f(0) = 0$, then $f\left(\frac{\pi}{2}\right)$ equal $k\pi$. Then, the value of k is ....

58. If $\int \frac{[f'(x)g(x) - g'(x)f(x)]\,dx}{[f(x) + g(x)]\sqrt{g(x)(f(x) - g(x))}}$ is equal to $\sqrt{m}\tan^{-1}\left(\sqrt{\frac{f(x) - g(x)}{ng(x)}}\right) + C$, where $m, n \in R$ and C is constant of integration $(g(x) > 0)$, then $(m + n)^2$ is equal to ....

59. Let $f : R \to R$ be a differentiable function with $f(0) = 1$ and satisfying the equation
$f(x + y) = f(x) f'(y) + f'(x) f(y)$ for all $x, y \in R$.
Then, the value of $5\log_e(f(4))$ is ....

60. Let $f(x)$ be a cubic polynomial with leading coefficient unity such that $f(0) = 1$ and all the roots of $f'(x) = 0$ are also root of $f(x) = 0$, if $\int f(x)\,dx = g(x) + C$, where $g(0) = \frac{1}{4}$ and C is constant of integration, then $g(3) - g(1)$ is equal to ....

61. If $\int \frac{(1 + x^4)\,dx}{(1 - x^4)^{3/2}} = f(x) + C_1$, where $f(0) = 0$ and $\int f(x)\,dx = g(x) + C_2$ with $g(0) = 0$ if $g\left(\frac{1}{\sqrt{2}}\right) = \frac{\pi}{k}$, then the value of k is ....

Matching Type Questions

62. Match the following

Column I		Column II
(A) If $I = \int \frac{\sin x - \cos x}{\lvert \sin x - \cos x \rvert}\,dx$, where $\frac{\pi}{4} < x < \frac{3\pi}{8}$, then I is equal to	(p)	$\sin x$
(B) If $\int \frac{x^2}{(x^3 + 1)(x^3 + 2)}\,dx = \frac{1}{3} f\left(\frac{x^3 + 1}{x^3 + 2}\right) + C$, then $f(x)$ is equal to	(q)	$x + C$
(C) If $\int \sin^{-1} x \cdot \cos^{-1} x\,dx = f^{-1}(x)\left[\frac{\pi}{2}x - xf^{-1}(x) - 2\sqrt{1 - x^2}\right] + \frac{\pi}{2}\sqrt{1 - x^2} + 2x + C$, then $f(x)$ is equal to	(r)	$\ln \lvert x \rvert$
(D) If $\int \frac{dx}{xf(x)} = f(f(x)) + C$, then $f(x)$ is equal to	(s)	$\sin^{-1} x$

63. Match the following

Column I		Column II
(A) If $\int \left(\frac{x^2 + \cos^2 x}{1 + x^2}\right)\text{cosec}^2 x\,dx = A\cot^{-1} x + B\frac{\text{cosec}\, x}{\sec x}$, then	(p)	$A = 1$
(B) If $\int \sqrt{x + \sqrt{x^2 + 2}}\,dx = \frac{A}{3}(x + \sqrt{x^2 + 2})^{3/2} - \frac{B}{(x + \sqrt{x^2 + 2})}$, then	(q)	$B = -1$
(C) If $\int \frac{\sqrt{2 - x - x^2}}{x^2}\,dx = A\frac{\sqrt{2 - x - x^2}}{x} + \frac{B}{4\sqrt{2}}\log\left(\frac{4 - x + \sqrt{2 - x - x^2}}{4x}\right) - \sin^{-1}\left(\frac{2x + 1}{3}\right)$, then	(r)	$B = 2$
(D) If $\int \frac{\sin 2x}{\sin^4 x + \cos^4 x}\,dx = B\cot^{-1}(\tan^2 x)$, then	(s)	$A = -1$

Previous Years Questions

64. Let b be a non-zero real number. Suppose $f : R \to R$ is a differentiable function such that $f(0) = 1$. If the derivative f' of f satisfies the equation
$f'(x) = \frac{f(x)}{b^2 + x^2}$ for all $x \in R$, then which of the following statements is/are true?

[More Than One Correct, 2020 Adv.]

(a) If $b > 0$, then f is an increasing function
(b) If $b < 0$, then f is a decreasing function
(c) $f(x)f(-x) = 1, \forall\, x \in R$
(d) $f(x) - f(-x) = 0, \forall\, x \in R$

65. Let $f : R \to R$ and $g : R \to R$ be functions satisfying $f(x + y) = f(x) + f(y) + f(x) f(y)$ and $f(x) = xg(x)$ for all $x, y \in R$. If $\lim_{x \to 0} g(x) = 1$, then which of the following statements is/are true?

[More Than One Correct, 2020 Adv.]

(a) f is differentiable at every $x \in R$
(b) If $g(0) = 1$, then g is differentiable at every $x \in R$
(c) The derivative $f'(1)$ is equal to 1
(d) The derivative $f'(0)$ is equal to 1

EXERCISE 3

Challenging Problems

1. If I_n denotes $\int z^n e^{1/z}\, dz$, then show that $(n+1)!\, I_n = I_0 + e^{1/z}(1!\, z^2 + 2!\, z^3 + \ldots + n!\, z^{n+1})$.

2. If $I_n = \int x^n \sqrt{a^2 - x^2}\, dx$, prove that $I_n = -\dfrac{x^{n-1}(a^2 - x^2)^{3/2}}{(n+2)} + \dfrac{(n-1)}{(n+2)} a^2 I_{n-2}$.

3. If $I_m = \int (\sin x + \cos x)^m\, dx$, then show that $mI_m = (\sin x + \cos x)^{m-1} \cdot (\sin x - \cos x) + 2(m-1) I_{m-2}$.

4. If $I_{m,n} = \int \cos^m x \cdot \cos nx\, dx$, show that $(m+n) I_{m,n} = \cos^m x \cdot \sin nx + m I_{(m-1, n-1)}$.

5. Evaluate $\displaystyle\int \frac{\tan\left(\frac{\pi}{4} - x\right)}{\cos^2 x \sqrt{\tan^3 x + \tan^2 x + \tan x}}\, dx$.

6. Evaluate $\int x^2 \log(1 - x^2)\, dx$, and hence prove that $\dfrac{1}{1\cdot 5} + \dfrac{1}{2\cdot 7} + \dfrac{1}{3\cdot 9} + \ldots = \dfrac{2}{3}\log 2 - \dfrac{8}{9}$.

7. Evaluate $\displaystyle\int \frac{a + b\sin x}{(b + a\sin x)^2}\, dx$.

8. Evaluate $\displaystyle\int \frac{dx}{(x-1)^{3/4}(x+2)^{5/4}}$.

Answer Key

Exercise 1

1. (b)	2. (c)	3. (b)	4. (b)	5. (b)	6. (a)	7. (a)	8. (b)	9. (a)	10. (b)
11. (d)	12. (a)	13. (d)	14. (c)	15. (c)	16. (a)	17. (d)	18. (c)	19. (b)	20. (b)
21. (a)	22. (c)	23. (b)	24. (b)	25. (c)	26. (b)	27. (b)	28. (b)	29. (25)	30. (9)
31. (15)	32. (1)	33. (2025)	34. (41)	35. (6069)	36. (11)	37. (11)	38. (49)	39. (2)	40. (8)
41. (2025)	42. (90)	43. (2.5)	44. (c)	45. (c)	46. (b)	47. (d)	48. (c)	49. (a)	50. (d)
51. (c)	52. (b)	53. (28)	54. (64)	55. (1)	56. (a)	57. (b)	58. (3)	59. (6)	60. (d)
61. (d)									

Exercise 2

1. (c)	2. (b)	3. (c)	4. (a)	5. (d)	6. (c)	7. (a)	8. (c)	9. (b)	10. (d)
11. (b)	12. (c)	13. (c)	14. (c)	15. (a)	16. (b)	17. (a,c)	18. (a,d)	19. (a,c)	20. (b,c,d)
21. (a,b)	22. (a,c,d)	23. (a,b)	24. (a,d)	25. (a,b,c,d)	26. (a,b)	27. (a,b,c,d)	28. (b,c)	29. (d)	30. (c)
31. (a)	32. (b)	33. (b)	34. (d)	35. (c)	36. (a)	37. (3)	38. (5)	39. (1)	40. (2)
41. (5)	42. (6)	43. (1)	44. (1)	45. (3)	46. (1)	47. (4)	48. (4)	49. (3)	50. (3)
51. (3)	52. (1)	53. (8)	54. (3.5)	55. (0.5)	56. (1.78)	57. (0.4375)	58. (16)	59. (10)	60. (60)

61. (12)
62. (A) → (q), (B) → (r), (C) → (p), (D) → (r)
63. (A) → (p,q), (B) → (p,r), (C) → (r,s), (D) → (q)
64. (a,c)
65. (a,b,d)

Solutions

Exercise 1 - JEE Main Pattern

1. Let $I = \int \frac{x^2 \cdot dx}{(1 + x^2)(1 + \sqrt{1 + x^2})}$

Put $x = \tan\theta \Rightarrow dx = \sec^2\theta\, d\theta$

$$I = \int \frac{\tan^2\theta}{1 + \sec\theta}\, d\theta = \int (\sec\theta - 1)\, d\theta$$

$$= \log(\sec\theta + \tan\theta) - \theta + C$$

$$f(x) = \log_e(x + \sqrt{x^2 + 1}) - \tan^{-1} x + C$$

$$f(0) = 0 \Rightarrow C = 0$$

$$\Rightarrow \quad f(1) = \log_e(1 + \sqrt{2}) - \tan^{-1} 1 = \log_e(1 + \sqrt{2}) - \frac{\pi}{4}$$

2. **Decoding the Question**

Here, we have only one function. This can be solved easily by applying integration by parts taking unity as second function.

If we take $u = \log(\sqrt{1 - x} + \sqrt{1 + x})$ as the first function and $v = 1$ as the second function.

Then, $I = \int 1 \cdot \log(\sqrt{1 - x} + \sqrt{1 + x})\, dx$

$$= \{\log(\sqrt{1 - x} + \sqrt{1 + x})\} \cdot x - \int \frac{1}{\sqrt{1 - x} + \sqrt{1 + x}} \left(-\frac{1}{2\sqrt{1 - x}} + \frac{1}{2\sqrt{1 + x}}\right) \cdot x\, dx$$

$$= x \log(\sqrt{1 - x} + \sqrt{1 + x}) - \frac{1}{2} \int \frac{\sqrt{1 - x} - \sqrt{1 + x}}{\sqrt{1 - x} + \sqrt{1 + x}} \cdot \frac{1}{\sqrt{1 - x^2}} \cdot x\, dx$$

$$= x \log(\sqrt{1 - x} + \sqrt{1 + x}) - \frac{1}{2} \int \frac{(1 - x) + (1 + x) - 2\sqrt{1 - x^2}}{(1 - x) - (1 + x)} \cdot \frac{1}{\sqrt{1 - x^2}} \cdot 2x\, dx$$

$$= x \log(\sqrt{1 - x} + \sqrt{1 + x}) - \int \frac{\sqrt{1 - x^2} - 1}{\sqrt{1 - x^2}}\, dx$$

$$= x \log(\sqrt{1 - x} + \sqrt{1 + x}) - \int 1\, dx + \int \frac{1}{\sqrt{1 - x^2}}\, dx$$

$$= x \log(\sqrt{1 - x} + \sqrt{1 + x}) - x + \sin^{-1} x + C$$

3. $F(x) = \int \frac{3x + 2}{\sqrt{x - 9}}\, dx.$

Let $x - 9 = t^2 \Rightarrow dx = 2t\, dt$

$$\therefore \quad F(x) = \int \left(\frac{3(t^2 + 9) + 2}{t} \cdot 2t\right) dt$$

$$= 2 \int (29 + 3t^2)\, dt = 2[29t + t^3] + C$$

$$F(x) = 2[29\sqrt{x - 9} + (x - 9)^{3/2}] + C$$

Given, $F(10) = 60 = 2[29 + 1] + C \Rightarrow C = 0$

$$\therefore \quad F(x) = 2[29\sqrt{x - 9} + (x - 9)^{3/2}]$$

$$F(13) = 2[29 \times 2 + 4 \times 2] = 132$$

4. We have, $\int (x^x)^x (2x \log_e x + x)\, dx$

$$= \int x^{x^2} (2x \log_e x + x)\, dx$$

$$= \int 1 \cdot d(x^{x^2}) = x^{x^2} + C = (x^x)^x + C$$

5. We have, $\int x \log x (\log x - 1)\, dx$

$$= \int \log x (x \log x - x)\, dx$$

$$= \int (x \log x - x)\, d(x \log x - x)$$

$$= \frac{(x \log x - x)^2}{2} + C$$

6. $\int \tan^4 x\, dx = \int (\tan^2 x \sec^2 x - \sec^2 x + 1)\, dx$

$$= \frac{\tan^3 x}{3} - \tan x + x + C$$

$$\Rightarrow \quad A = \frac{1}{3}, B = -1 \text{ and } f(x) = x + C$$

7. $\int \frac{\sin^4 x}{x}\, dx = f(x) \Rightarrow \int \frac{\sin^4 (p + q)x}{(p + q)x}\, dx = \frac{f\{(p + q)x\}}{p + q}$

$$\int \frac{\sin^4 (p + q)x}{x}\, dx = f\{(p + q)x\}$$

8. We have, $\int x \sqrt{\frac{2\sin(x^2 + 1) - \sin 2(x^2 + 1)}{2\sin(x^2 + 1) + \sin 2(x^2 + 1)}}\, dx$

$$= \int x \sqrt{\frac{2\sin(x^2 + 1) - 2\sin(x^2 + 1)\cos(x^2 + 1)}{2\sin(x^2 + 1) + 2\sin(x^2 + 1)\cos(x^2 + 1)}}\, dx$$

$$= \int x \sqrt{\frac{1 - \cos(x^2 + 1)}{1 + \cos(x^2 + 1)}}\, dx$$

$$= \int x \tan\left(\frac{x^2 + 1}{2}\right) dx = \int \tan\left(\frac{x^2 + 1}{2}\right) d\left(\frac{x^2 + 1}{2}\right)$$

$$= \log\left|\sec\left(\frac{x^2 + 1}{2}\right)\right| + C$$

9. $\int \frac{\sin(4x - 2x)\, dx}{\sin(2x)\cos(2x)\cos(4x)} = \int \frac{\sin(4x)\, dx}{\sin(2x)\cos(4x)} - \int \sec 2x\, dx$

$$= 2\int \frac{\cos 2x\, dx}{\cos 4x} - \frac{1}{2}(\log|\sec 2x + \tan 2x|)$$

$$= 2\int \frac{\cos 2x}{(1 - 2\sin^2 2x)}\, dx - \frac{1}{2}(\log|\sec 2x + \tan 2x|)$$

$$= \frac{2}{2\sqrt{2}}\left[\frac{1}{2 \times 1} \log\left|\frac{1 + \sqrt{2}\sin 2x}{1 - \sqrt{2}\sin 2x}\right|\right] - \frac{1}{2}\log|\sec 2x + \tan 2x| + C$$

$$= \frac{1}{2\sqrt{2}}\left[\log\left|\frac{1 + \sqrt{2}\sin 2x}{1 - \sqrt{2}\sin 2x}\right|\right] - \frac{1}{2}\log|\sec 2x + \tan 2x| + C$$

10. We have, $\int \frac{\sin^3 x}{(\cos^4 x + 3\cos^2 x + 1)\tan^{-1}(\sec x + \cos x)} dx$

$$= \int \frac{\frac{\sin^3 x}{\cos^2 x}}{(\cos^2 x + 3 + \sec^2 x)\tan^{-1}(\sec x + \tan x)} dx$$

$$= \int \frac{1}{1 + (\sec x + \cos x)^2} \times \frac{\sin x(1 - \cos^2 x)}{\cos^2 x} \times \frac{1}{\tan^{-1}(\sec x + \tan x)} dx$$

$$= \int \frac{1}{\tan^{-1}(\sec x + \cos x)} \times \frac{1}{1 + (\sec x + \cos x)^2} (\tan x \sec x - \sin x)\, dx$$

$$= \int \frac{1}{\tan^{-1}(\sec x + \cos x)} d\,|\tan^{-1}(\sec x + \cos x)|$$

$$= \log_e |\tan^{-1}(\sec x + \cos x)| + C$$

11. We have, $f(x) = \begin{vmatrix} 0 & x^2 - \sin x & \cos x - 2 \\ \sin x - x^2 & 0 & 1 - 2x \\ 2 - \cos x & 2x - 1 & 0 \end{vmatrix}$

$$\Rightarrow \quad f(x) = \begin{vmatrix} 0 & \sin x - x^2 & 2 - \cos x \\ x^2 - \sin x & 0 & 2x - 1 \\ \cos x - 2 & 1 - 2x & 0 \end{vmatrix}$$

[interchanging rows and columns]

$$\Rightarrow \quad f(x) = (-1)^3 \begin{vmatrix} 0 & x^2 - \sin x & \cos x - 2 \\ \sin x - x^2 & 0 & 1 - 2x \\ 2 - \cos x & 2x - 1 & 0 \end{vmatrix}$$

[taking (– 1) common from each column]

$$\Rightarrow \quad f(x) = -f(x)$$

$$\Rightarrow \quad f(x) = 0 \Rightarrow \int f(x)\,dx = C$$

12. $I = \int (\log_2(0 + 1 + 1))\,dx$

$$= \int (\log_2 2)\,dx$$

$$= \int dx$$

$$= x + C$$

13. $\int \frac{3 + \sqrt{x}}{(x + 2\sqrt{x} + 3)^2} dx = \int \frac{\frac{3}{x^2} + \frac{1}{x\sqrt{x}}}{\left(1 + \frac{2}{\sqrt{x}} + \frac{3}{x}\right)^2} dx$

$$\Rightarrow \quad 1 + \frac{2}{\sqrt{x}} + \frac{3}{x} = t$$

$$\Rightarrow \left(-\frac{1}{x\sqrt{x}} - \frac{3}{x^2}\right) dx = dt$$

$$\Rightarrow \quad \int -\frac{dt}{t^2} = \frac{1}{t} + C = \frac{1}{1 + \frac{2}{\sqrt{x}} + \frac{3}{x}} + C$$

$$= \frac{x}{(x + 2\sqrt{x} + 3)} + C$$

14. $I = \int \frac{2e^{5x} + e^{4x} - 4e^{3x} + 4e^{2x} + 2e^x}{(e^{2x} + 4)(e^{2x} - 1)^2} dx$

On putting $e^x = t$, we get

$$I = \int \frac{(2t^4 - 4t^2 + 2)}{(t^2 + 4)(t^2 - 1)^2} dt + \int \frac{(t^3 + 4t)}{(t^2 + 4)(t^2 - 1)^2} dt$$

$$= 2\int \frac{dt}{t^2 + 4} + \frac{1}{2}\int \frac{2t\,dt}{(t^2 - 1)^2}$$

$$= \tan^{-1}\left(\frac{t}{2}\right) - \frac{1}{2(t^2 - 1)} + C$$

$$= \tan^{-1}\left(\frac{e^x}{2}\right) - \frac{1}{2(e^{2x} - 1)} + C$$

15. Let $I = \int (x^4 + 1)^{1/3} x^7\,dx$

On putting $x^4 + 1 = t^3$

So, $4x^3 dx = 3t^2 dt$

$$\therefore \quad I = \int t \cdot (t^3 - 1)\frac{3}{4} t^2 dt$$

$$= \frac{3}{4}\int (t^6 - t^3)\,dt$$

$$= \frac{3}{4}\left[\frac{t^7}{7} - \frac{t^4}{4}\right] + C$$

$$= \frac{3}{112} t^4 (4t^3 - 7) + C$$

$$= \frac{3}{112}(x^4 + 1)^{4/3}[4(x^4 + 1) - 7] + C$$

$$= \frac{3}{112}(x^4 + 1)^{4/3}(4x^4 - 3) + C$$

Hence, $k = \frac{3}{112}$

16. Here, $m = -6$, $n = 3$ and $p = \frac{2}{3}$, so that

$$\frac{m + 1}{n} + p = -\frac{5}{3} + \frac{2}{3} = -1 \text{ (integer)}$$

On putting $1 + 2x^3 = x^3 t^3$

$$\Rightarrow \quad x^3(t^3 - 2) = 1$$

$$\Rightarrow \quad x = (t^3 - 2)^{-1/3}$$

$$\Rightarrow \quad dx = -\frac{1}{3}(t^3 - 2)^{-4/3}(3t^2)dt$$

$$\Rightarrow \quad dx = -t^2(t^3 - 2)^{-4/3} dt$$

Hence, $I = \int [(t^3 - 2)^2 \{(t^3 - 2)^{-1} t^3\}^{2/3} (-t^2)(t^3 - 2)^{-4/3}]\,dt$

$$= -\int t^4 (t^3 - 2)^{2 - \frac{2}{3} - \frac{4}{3}} dt$$

$$= -\int t^4 dt$$

$$= -\frac{t^5}{5} + C = -\frac{1}{5}\left(\frac{1 + 2x^3}{x^3}\right)^{5/3} + C$$

$$= -\frac{1}{5}(2 + x^{-3})^{5/3} + C$$

17. Let $I = \int \frac{x}{\sqrt{1 + x^2 + \sqrt{(1 + x^2)^3}}} dx$

Let $(1 + x^2) = t^2 \Rightarrow xdx = t\,dt$

$\therefore \quad I = \int \frac{t}{\sqrt{t^2 + t^3}} dt = \int \frac{1}{\sqrt{1 + t}} dt = 2\sqrt{1 + t} + C$

$\Rightarrow \quad I = 2\sqrt{1 + \sqrt{1 + x^2}} + C$

18. We have, $I_n = \int \tan^n x\,dx$

$\Rightarrow \quad I_4 + I_6 = \int (\tan^4 x + \tan^6 x)\,dx$

$= \int \tan^4 x(1 + \tan^2 x)dx = \int \tan^4 x \sec^2 x\,dx$

Let $\tan x = t \Rightarrow \sec^2 x\,dx = dt$

$= \int t^4 dt = \frac{t^5}{5} + C = \frac{\tan^5 x}{5} + C$

$\therefore \quad a = \frac{1}{5}$ and $b = 0$

$\Rightarrow \quad (a, b) = \left(\frac{1}{5}, 0\right)$

19.

> **Decoding the Question**
>
> First convert the given integral in terms of $\tan x$ and $\sec x$ then let $\tan x = t$. After substituting the values, integrate it accordingly.

Let $I = \int \frac{\sin^4 x}{\cos^8 x} dx$

$\Rightarrow \quad I = \int \frac{\tan^4 x}{\cos^4 x} dx = \int \tan^4 x \sec^4 x\,dx$

$\Rightarrow \quad I = \int \tan^4 x \cdot (1 + \tan^2 x)\sec^2 x\,dx$

Let $\tan x = t \Rightarrow \sec^2 x\,dx = dt$

$\Rightarrow \quad I = \int t^4(1 + t^2)\,dt \Rightarrow I = \int (t^4 + t^6)\,dt$

$\Rightarrow \quad I = \frac{t^5}{5} + \frac{t^7}{7} + C \Rightarrow I = \frac{1}{5}\tan^5 x + \frac{1}{7}\tan^7 x + C$

$\therefore \quad a = \frac{1}{5}$ and $b = \frac{1}{7} \Rightarrow 5a = 7b$

20. We have, $\int f(x)\,dx = F(x)$

$\therefore \quad \int x^3 f(x^2)\,dx = \frac{1}{2}\int \underbrace{x^2}_{\text{I}}\, \underbrace{f(x^2)}_{\text{II}} d(x^2)$

$= \frac{1}{2}[x^2 F(x^2) - \int F(x^2)\,d(x^2)]$

21. We have,

$\int \frac{e^{x^2 + 4\ln x} - x^3 e^{x^2}}{x - 1} dx = \int \frac{e^{x^2} \cdot x^4 - x^3 e^{x^2}}{x - 1} dx$

$= \int x^3 e^{x^2} dx = \frac{1}{2}\int t e^t dt \quad$ [where $t = x^2$]

$= \frac{1}{2}(t - 1)\,e^t + C = \frac{1}{2}(x^2 - 1)\,e^{x^2} + C$

$= \frac{1}{2x}(e^{3\ln x} - e^{\ln x})\,e^{x^2} + C$

22. $\int \frac{1 - 7\cos^2 x}{\sin^7 x \cos^2 x} dx = \int \left(\frac{\sec^2 x}{\sin^7 x} - \frac{7}{\sin^7 x}\right) dx$

$= \int \frac{\sec^2 x}{\sin^7 x} dx - \int \frac{7}{\sin^7 x} dx = I_1 + I_2$

Now, $\quad I_1 = \int \frac{\sec^2 x}{\sin^7 x} dx$

$= \frac{\tan x}{\sin^7 x} - 7\int \frac{\tan x \cdot \cos x}{\sin^8 x} dx$

$= \frac{\tan x}{\sin^7 x} - I_2$

$\therefore \quad I_1 + I_2 = \frac{\tan x}{\sin^7 x} + C$

$\Rightarrow \quad f(x) = \tan x$

23. We have, $f(x) = x\,|\cos x|, \frac{\pi}{2} < x < \pi$

$\Rightarrow \quad f(x) = -x\cos x \quad [\because \cos x < 0 \text{ for } x \in (\pi/2, \pi)]$

Hence, required primitive is given by

$\int f(x)\,dx = -\int x\cos x\,dx + C = -x\sin x - \cos x + C$

24. We have, $f(x) = (2x + 1)\,|\sin x|, \pi < x < 2\pi$

$\Rightarrow \quad f(x) = -(2x + 1)\sin x$

Hence, required primitive is given by

$-\int \underset{\text{I}}{(2x + 1)} \underset{\text{II}}{\sin x}\,dx = -[-(2x + 1)\cos x + 2\sin x] + C$

$= (2x + 1)\cos x - 2\sin x + C$

25. $I = \int f^{-1}(x)dx = f^{-1}(x) \cdot x - \int x \cdot ((f^{-1}(x))'dx$

On putting $f^{-1}(x) = t$, we get

$I = f^{-1}(x) \cdot x - \int f(t) \cdot dt$

$= f^{-1}(x) \cdot x - g(t) + C = x \cdot f^{-1}(x) - g(f^{-1}(x)) + C$

26. Let $\quad I = \int \frac{dx}{\sqrt{(x - p)^3 (x - q)}}$

$= \int \frac{dx}{(x - p)^{3/2}(x - q)^{1/2}}$

$= \int \frac{dx}{(x - p)^2 \left[\frac{(x - q)}{(x - p)}\right]^{1/2}}$

Let $\frac{(x - q)}{(x - p)} = t$

$\Rightarrow \quad \left[\frac{(x - p) \cdot 1 - (x - q) \cdot 1}{(x - p)^2}\right] dx = dt$

$\Rightarrow \quad \frac{dx}{(x - p)^2} = \frac{dt}{(q - p)}$

$\therefore \quad I = \frac{1}{(q - p)}\int \frac{dt}{t^{1/2}}$

$= \frac{1}{(q - p)} \times 2\sqrt{t} + C$

$= \frac{2}{(q - p)}\sqrt{\frac{x - q}{x - p}} + C$

27. Let $I = \int \frac{x^4+1}{x^6+1}\,dx$

$$= \int \frac{x^4+1}{(x^2+1)(x^4-x^2+1)}\,dx$$

$$= \int \frac{(x^4-x^2+1)+x^2}{(x^2+1)(x^4-x^2+1)}\,dx$$

$$= \int \frac{dx}{x^2+1} + \int \frac{x^2}{x^6+1}\,dx$$

$$= \tan^{-1}x + \frac{1}{3}\int \frac{3x^2}{(x^3)^2+1}\,dx$$

$$= \tan^{-1}x + \frac{1}{3}\int \frac{dt}{1+t^2}, \text{ where } t = x^3$$

$$= \tan^{-1}x + \frac{1}{3}\tan^{-1}t + C$$

$$= \tan^{-1}x + \frac{1}{3}\tan^{-1}(x^3) + C$$

28. $I = \int \frac{1}{\sin x \cos x(\tan^9 x+1)}\,dx$

$$= \int \frac{1}{\tan x \cos^2 x(\tan^9 x+1)}\,dx$$

$$= \int \frac{\sec^2 x}{\tan x(\tan^9 x+1)}\,dx$$

$$= \int \frac{dt}{t(t^9+1)} \qquad [\because \tan x = t]$$

$$= \frac{1}{9}\int \frac{9t^8 dt}{(t^9)(t^9+1)} \qquad [\because t^9 = y]$$

$$= \frac{1}{9}\int \frac{dy}{y(y+1)}$$

$$= \frac{1}{9}\int\left[\frac{1}{y} - \frac{1}{y+1}\right]dy = \frac{1}{9}\log\left|\frac{y}{y+1}\right| + C$$

$$= \frac{1}{9}\log\left|\frac{(\tan x)^9}{(\tan x)^9+1}\right| + C = \frac{1}{9}\log\left|\frac{\sin^9 x}{\sin^9 x + \cos^9 x}\right| + C$$

29. Let $I = \int \frac{2\sin x + 3\cos x}{3\sin x + 4\cos x}\,dx$

Let $2\sin x + 3\cos x = \lambda(3\sin x + 4\cos x) + \mu\,\frac{d}{dx}(3\sin x + 4\cos x)$

$\Rightarrow$ $2\sin x + 3\cos x = \lambda(3\sin x + 4\cos x) + \mu\,(3\cos x - 4\sin x)$

Now, equating the coefficient of $\sin x$ and $\cos x$, we get

$$3\lambda - 4\mu = 2,\ 4\lambda + 3\mu = 3$$

On solving these equations, we get

$$\lambda = \frac{18}{25} \text{ and } \mu = \frac{1}{25}$$

$$\therefore \quad I = \int \frac{18}{25}dx + \frac{1}{25}\int \frac{3\cos x - 4\sin x}{3\sin x + 4\cos x}\,dx$$

$$= \frac{18}{25}x + \frac{1}{25}\log|3\sin x + 4\cos x| + C$$

$$\because \quad k = \frac{1}{25} \Rightarrow \frac{1}{k} = 25$$

30. Let $I = \int \frac{dx}{\sin^{3/2} x \cos^{5/2} x}$

Divide numerator and denominator by $\cos^4 x$, we get

$$I = \int \frac{\sec^4 x dx}{\tan^{3/2} x}$$

Put $\tan x = t \Rightarrow \sec^2 x dx = dt$

$$I = \int \frac{(1+t^2)dt}{t^{3/2}}$$

$$I = \int t^{-3/2} + t^{1/2}\,dt = \frac{-2}{\sqrt{t}} + \frac{2}{3}t^{3/2} + C$$

$$= -2\sqrt{\cot x} + \frac{2}{3}\sqrt{\tan^3 x} + C$$

$$\therefore \quad a = -2 \text{ and } b = \frac{2}{3}$$

$$\because \quad \frac{a^2}{b^2} = \frac{4}{4/9} = 9$$

31.

Decoding the Question

First convert the given integral $\int \frac{\sqrt{x^{10}+2}}{x^{16}}dx$ into $\int \frac{\sqrt{1+\frac{2}{x^{10}}}}{x^{11}}dx$ and then let $1+\frac{2}{x^{10}} = t$ and then solve it accordingly.

Let $I = \int \frac{\sqrt{x^{10}+2}}{x^{16}}dx = \int \frac{x^5\sqrt{1+\frac{2}{x^{10}}}}{x^{16}}dx = \int \frac{\sqrt{1+\frac{2}{x^{10}}}}{x^{11}}dx$

Put $1 + \frac{2}{x^{10}} = t \Rightarrow -\frac{20}{x^{11}}dx = dt$

$$\because \quad I = -\frac{1}{20}\int \sqrt{t}\,dt$$

$$I = -\frac{1}{20}\frac{t^{3/2}}{3/2} + C = -\frac{1}{30}(t)^{3/2} + C$$

$$I = -\frac{1}{30}\left(1 + \frac{2}{x^{10}}\right)^{3/2} + C$$

$$I = -\frac{1}{30}\frac{(x^{10}+2)^{3/2}}{x^{15}} + C$$

$$\therefore \quad m = 15$$

32. Let $I = \int e^{x^3+x^2-1}(3x^4 + 2x^3 + 2x)dx$

$$= \int e^{x^3+x^2-1}(3x^4 + 2x^3)dx + \int e^{x^3+x^2-1}(2x)dx$$

$$= \int \underset{\text{I}}{x^2}\,\underset{\text{II}}{e^{x^3+x^2-1}(3x^2+2x)}dx + \int e^{x^3+x^2-1}(2x)dx$$

$$= x^2 e^{x^3+x^2-1} - \int 2xe^{x^3+x^2-1}dx + \int 2xe^{x^3+x^2-1}dx$$

$$= x^2 e^{x^3+x^2-1} + C$$

$$\because \quad f(x) = x^2 e^{x^3+x^2-1}$$

$$f(1)\cdot f(-1) = (1)e^{1+1-1}\cdot(1)e^{-1+1-1}$$

$$= e \times \frac{1}{e} = 1$$

33. Let $I = \int \frac{1-\cot^{2023} x}{\tan x + \cot^{2024} x} dx$

$$= \int \left(\frac{\sin^{2023} x - \cos^{2023} x}{\sin^{2025} x + \cos^{2025} x} \right) \sin x \cos x \, dx$$

Put $\sin^{2025} x + \cos^{2025} x = t$

$(2025 \sin^{2024} x \cos x - 2025 \cos^{2024} x \sin x) dx = dt$

$\Rightarrow \quad 2025 \sin x \cos x (\sin^{2023} x - \cos^{2023} x) dx = dt$

$\Rightarrow \quad I = \frac{1}{2025} \int \frac{dt}{t} = \frac{1}{2025} \log |\sin^{2025} x + \cos^{2025} x| + C$

$\therefore \quad k = 2025$

34. Let $I = \int \frac{2x+5}{\sqrt{9x^2+6x+2}} dx$

Let $2x + 5 = \lambda \left(\frac{d(9x^2+6x+2)}{dx} \right) + \mu$

$\Rightarrow \quad 2x + 5 = \lambda(18x+6) + \mu$

Equating the coefficient of x and constant term, we get

$$\lambda = \frac{1}{9}, \mu = \frac{13}{3}$$

$\because \quad I = \frac{1}{9} \int \frac{18x+6}{\sqrt{9x^2+6x+2}} dx + \frac{13}{3} \int \frac{dx}{\sqrt{(3x+1)^2+1}}$

$$= \frac{2}{9}\sqrt{9x^2+6x+2} + \frac{13}{3} \log |3x+1+\sqrt{9x^2+6x+2}| + C$$

$\because \quad a = \frac{2}{9}$

and $\quad b = \frac{13}{3}$

$$9(a+b) = 9\left(\frac{2}{9} + \frac{13}{3} \right) = 41$$

35. Let $I = \int \frac{dx}{x^{2024} + x}$

$$= \int \frac{dx}{x^{2024}\left(1 + \frac{1}{x^{2023}}\right)}$$

Put $\left(1 + \frac{1}{x^{2023}}\right) = t \Rightarrow -\frac{2023}{x^{2024}} dx = dt$

$\therefore \quad I = -\frac{1}{2023} \int \frac{dt}{t} = -\frac{1}{2023} \log |t| + C$

$$= \frac{1}{2023} \log \left| \frac{1}{t} \right| + C = \frac{1}{2023} \log \left| \frac{1}{1 + \frac{1}{x^{2023}}} \right| + C$$

$$= \frac{1}{2023} \log \left| \frac{x^{2023}}{1 + x^{2023}} \right| + C$$

$\because \quad p = q = r = 2023$

$\Rightarrow \quad p + q + r = 2023 + 2023 + 2023 = 6069$

36. Let $I = \int \frac{(2x+3)dx}{x(x+1)(x+2)(x+3)+1}$

$$= \int \frac{(2x+3)dx}{(x^2+3x)(x^2+3x+2)+1}$$

Put $x^2 + 3x = t \Rightarrow (2x+3)dx = dt$

$$I = \int \frac{dt}{t(t+2)+1} = \int \frac{dt}{t^2+2t+1} = \int \frac{dt}{(t+1)^2}$$

$\Rightarrow \quad I = -\frac{1}{t+1} + C$

$$= -\frac{1}{x^2+3x+1} + C$$

Here $f(x) = x^2 + 3x + 1$

$$f(2) = (2)^2 + 3(2) + 1 = 4 + 6 + 1 = 11$$

37. Let $I = \int \frac{dx}{\cos^3 x - \sin^3 x}$

$$= \int \frac{dx}{(\cos x - \sin x)(1 + \sin x \cos x)}$$

$$= 2 \int \frac{(\cos x - \sin x) dx}{(\cos x - \sin x)^2 (2 + (\sin x + \cos x)^2 - 1)}$$

$$= 2 \int \frac{(\cos x - \sin x) dx}{((\sin^2 x + \cos^2 x) - 2 \sin x \cos x)(1 + (\sin x + \cos x)^2)}$$

$$= 2 \int \frac{(\cos x - \sin x) dx}{(2 - (\sin x + \cos x)^2)(1 + (\sin x + \cos x)^2)}$$

Put $\sin x + \cos x = t \Rightarrow (\cos x - \sin x) dx = dt$

$\therefore \quad I = \int \frac{dt}{(2-t^2)(1+t^2)}$

$$= \frac{2}{3} \int \frac{1}{1+t^2} dt + \frac{2}{3} \int \frac{dt}{2-t^2}$$

$$= \frac{2}{3} \tan^{-1} t + \frac{1}{3\sqrt{2}} \log \left| \frac{\sqrt{2}+t}{\sqrt{2}-t} \right| + C$$

Here, $A = \frac{2}{3}, b = \frac{1}{3\sqrt{2}}$

$\because \quad 12A + 9\sqrt{2}B = 12 \times \frac{2}{3} + 9\sqrt{2} \times \frac{1}{3\sqrt{2}}$

$$= 8 + 3 = 11$$

38. Let $I = \int (x^5 + x^3 + x)\sqrt{2x^6 + 3x^4 + 6x^2}$

Put $2x^6 + 3x^4 + 6x^2 = t^2 \Rightarrow 12(x^5 + x^3 + x) dx = 2t \, dt$

$\because \quad I = \frac{1}{12} \int 2t^2 \, dt$

$$I = \frac{1}{6}\left(\frac{t^3}{3} \right) + C = \frac{1}{18}(2x^6 + 3x^4 + 6x^2)^{3/2} + C$$

$\therefore \quad \alpha = 2, \beta = 3, \gamma = 6$

Now, $\alpha^2 + \beta^2 + \gamma^2 = 2^2 + 3^2 + 6^2 = 49$

39. We have, $\int \sec^{-1}[-\sin^2 x] dx = f(x) + C$

$$-1 \le -\sin^2 x \le 0$$

$\therefore \quad [-\sin^2 x] = -1$ or 0

$\Rightarrow \quad \sec^{-1}[-\sin^2 x] = \sec^{-1}(-1)$ or $\sec^{-1}(0)$

$= \pi$, $\sec^{-1}(0)$ is not defined

$\because \quad \int \sec^{-1}[-\sin^2 x] dx = \int \pi \, dx = \pi x + C$

$$f(x) = \pi x$$

$$f\left(\frac{8}{\pi x}\right)=\pi\frac{8}{\pi x}=\frac{8}{x}$$
$$f'\left(\frac{8}{\pi x}\right)=-\frac{8}{x^2}$$
$$f''\left(\frac{8}{\pi x}\right)=\frac{16}{x^3}$$
$$\therefore \quad f''\left(\frac{8}{\pi x}\right) \text{ at } x=2 \text{ is } \frac{16}{2^3}=\frac{16}{8}=2$$

40. Let $I=\int x^{23}(1-x)^{31}(3-7x)dx$
$$=\int x^{23}(1-x)^{31}(3(1-x)-4x]dx$$
$$=\int (3x^{23}(1-x)^{32}-4x^{24}(1-x)^{31})dx$$
Put $x^{24}(1-x)^{32}=t$
$$(24x^{23}(1-x)^{32}-32x^{24}(1-x)^{31})dx=dt$$
$$\Rightarrow 8(3x^{23}(1-x)^{32}-4x^{24}(1-x)^{31})dx=dt$$
$$\therefore \quad I=\frac{1}{8}\int dt=\frac{t}{8}+C$$
$$I=\frac{1}{8}x^{24}(1-x)^{32}+C$$
$\because \quad p=24, q=32, r=8$

GCD of (24, 32, 8) is 8.

41. We have, $\int \frac{4x^3(1+(x^4)^{2023})}{(1+x^4)^{2025}}dx=f(x)+C$

Put $x^4=t \Rightarrow 4x^3dx=dt$
$$\because \quad \int \frac{1+(t)^{2023}}{(1+t)^{2025}}dt=\int \frac{1}{(1+t)^{2025}}+\frac{t^{2023}}{(1+t)^{2025}}dt$$
$$=\int \frac{1}{(1+t)^{2025}}dt+\int \frac{1}{t^2\left(1+\frac{1}{t}\right)^{2025}}dt$$
$$=\frac{(1+t)^{-2024}}{-2024}+\frac{\left(1+\frac{1}{t}\right)^{-2024}}{2024}+C$$
$$\because \quad f(x)=\frac{(1+x^4)^{-2024}}{-2024}+\frac{\left(1+\frac{1}{x^4}\right)^{-2024}}{2024}$$
$$f(1)-f(0)=-\frac{1}{2024}\left[\left[\frac{1}{2^{2024}}-\frac{1}{2^{2024}}\right]-1-0\right]=\frac{1}{2024}$$
$\because \quad m+n=1+2024=2025$

42. Let $I=\int \frac{x+(\cos^{-1}(3x))^2}{\sqrt{1-9x^2}}dx$
$$=\int \frac{x}{\sqrt{1-9x^2}}dx+\int \frac{(\cos^{-1}(3x))^2}{\sqrt{1-9x^2}}dx$$
Let $I_1=\int \frac{xdx}{\sqrt{1-9x^2}}$ and $I_2=\int \frac{(\cos^{-1}(3x))^2}{\sqrt{(1-9x^2)}}dx$

Put $1-9x^2=t \Rightarrow -18xdx=dt$
$$\therefore \quad I_1=-\frac{1}{18}\int \frac{dt}{\sqrt{t}}=-\frac{1}{9}\sqrt{1-9x^2}$$
$$I_2=\int \frac{(\cos^{-1}(3x))^2}{\sqrt{1-9x^2}}dx$$
Put $(\cos^{-1}(3x))=y \Rightarrow \frac{-3}{\sqrt{1-9x^2}}dx=dy$
$$I_2=-\frac{1}{3}\int y^2dy=-\frac{y^3}{9}+C$$
$$\Rightarrow \quad I=-\frac{1}{9}\sqrt{1-9x^2}-\frac{1}{9}(\cos^{-1}3x)^3+C$$
$\because \quad \lambda=-9$

$\mu=3$
$$\therefore \quad \lambda^2+\mu^2=(-9)^2+(3)^2=81+9=90$$

43. Let $I=\int \frac{(x-1)dx}{(x+x\sqrt{x}+\sqrt{x})(\sqrt{\sqrt{x}(x+1)}}$

Put $x=t^2 \Rightarrow dx=2t\,dt$
$$\because \quad I=2\int \frac{(t^2-1)t}{(t^2+t^3+t)\sqrt{t(t^2+1)}}dt$$
$$\Rightarrow I=2\int \frac{t(t^2-1)dt}{t(t+t^2+1)t\sqrt{t+\frac{1}{t}}} \Rightarrow I=2\int \frac{1-\frac{1}{t^2}}{\left(t+\frac{1}{t}+1\right)\sqrt{t+\frac{1}{t}}}$$
Put $t+\frac{1}{t}=y^2 \Rightarrow \left(1-\frac{1}{t^2}\right)dt=2y\,dy$
$$\therefore \quad I=4\int \frac{y\,dy}{(y^2+1)y}=4\tan^{-1}y+C$$
$$I=4\tan^{-1}\sqrt{t+\frac{1}{t}}+C=4\tan^{-1}\sqrt{\sqrt{x}+\frac{1}{\sqrt{x}}}+C$$
Here, $g(x)=\sqrt{\sqrt{x}+\frac{1}{\sqrt{x}}}$
$$g(4)=\sqrt{\sqrt{4}+\frac{1}{\sqrt{4}}}=\sqrt{2+\frac{1}{2}}=\sqrt{\frac{5}{2}}$$
$$g^2(4)=\frac{5}{2}=2.5$$

44. Let $I=\int \frac{dx}{a^2\sin^2 x+b^2\cos^2 x}$

Dividing numerator and denominator by $\cos^2 x$
$$I=\int \frac{\sec^2 x\,dx}{a^2\tan^2 x+b^2}$$
Now, let $\tan x=t \Rightarrow \sec^2 x\,dx=dt$
$$I=\int \frac{dt}{a^2t^2+b^2} \Rightarrow I=\frac{1}{a^2}\int \frac{dt}{t^2+\left(\frac{b}{a}\right)^2}$$
Using identity, $\int \frac{1}{x^2+P^2}dx=\frac{1}{P}\tan^{-1}\frac{x}{P}+C$

So, $$I=\frac{1}{a^2\left(\frac{b}{a}\right)}\tan^{-1}\left(\frac{t}{b/a}\right)+C$$
$$\Rightarrow \quad I=\frac{1}{ab}\tan^{-1}\left(\frac{a}{b}\tan x\right)+C$$

Comparing with RHS,

$$ab = 12 \text{ and } \frac{a}{b} = 3$$

Solving both, $b^2 = 4$ and $a^2 = 36$

Now, maximum value of $a \sin x + b \cos x$ is

$$\sqrt{a^2 + b^2} = \sqrt{36 + 4} = \sqrt{40}$$

45. $$\int \frac{\sin^{\frac{3}{2}} x + \cos^{\frac{3}{2}} x}{\sqrt{\sin^3 x \cdot \cos^3 x \cdot \sin(x - \theta)}} dx$$

$$= A\sqrt{\cos\theta \cdot \tan x - \sin\theta} + B\sqrt{\cos\theta - \sin\theta \cot x} + C$$

Let $$I = \int \frac{\sin^{\frac{3}{2}} x + \cos^{\frac{3}{2}} x}{\sqrt{\sin^3 x \cdot \cos^3 x \cdot \sin(x - \theta)}} dx$$

$$= \int \frac{dx}{\sqrt{\cos^3 x(\sin x \cos\theta - \cos x \sin\theta)}} + \int \frac{dx}{\sqrt{\sin^3 x(\sin x \cos\theta - \cos x \sin\theta)}}$$

$$= \int \frac{\sec^2 x \, dx}{\sqrt{\tan x \cos\theta - \sin\theta}} + \int \frac{\operatorname{cosec}^2 x \, dx}{\sqrt{\cos\theta - \cot x \sin\theta}}$$

Put $\tan x = y$ and $-\cot x = z$

$\sec^2 x \, dx = dy$, $\operatorname{cosec}^2 x \, dx = dz$

$$= \int \frac{dy}{\sqrt{y \cos\theta - \sin\theta}} + \int \frac{dz}{\sqrt{\cos\theta + z \sin\theta}}$$

$$= \frac{2\sqrt{y\cos\theta - \sin\theta}}{\cos\theta} + \frac{2\sqrt{\cos\theta + z\sin\theta}}{\sin\theta}$$

$$= 2\sec\theta\sqrt{\cos\theta \tan x - \sin\theta} + 2\operatorname{cosec}\theta\sqrt{\cos\theta - \sin\theta \cot x} + C$$

$\therefore \quad A = 2\sec\theta, B = 2\operatorname{cosec}\theta$

$AB = 2\sec\theta \cdot 2\operatorname{cosec}\theta$

$$= \frac{4}{\sin\theta \cos\theta} = \frac{8}{\sin 2\theta} = 8\operatorname{cosec} 2\theta$$

46. Given, $$y(x) = \int \frac{\operatorname{cosec} x + \sin x}{\operatorname{cosec} x \sec x + \tan x \sin^2 x} dx$$

$$= \int \frac{(1 + \sin^2 x)\cos x}{1 + \sin^4 x} dx$$

On putting, $\sin x = t \Rightarrow \cos x \, dx = dt$

$$= \int \frac{1 + t^2}{t^4 + 1} dt = \frac{1}{\sqrt{2}} \tan^{-1}\left[\frac{\sqrt{2}t}{1 - t^2}\right] + C$$

$$y(x) = \frac{1}{\sqrt{2}} \tan^{-1}\left[\frac{\sqrt{2}\sin x}{\cos x}\right] + C$$

Use $\lim_{x \to \left(\frac{\pi}{2}\right)^{-1}} y(x) = 0$, we get

$$C = -\frac{\pi}{2\sqrt{2}}$$

Now, $$y\left(\frac{\pi}{4}\right) = \frac{1}{\sqrt{2}}\left[\tan^{-1}(2) - \frac{\pi}{2}\right] = \frac{1}{\sqrt{2}}\left[\tan^{-1}\left(-\frac{1}{2}\right)\right]$$

47. Let $$I = \int \frac{(x^8 - x^2)dx}{(x^{12} + 3x^6 + 1)\tan^{-1}\left(x^3 + \frac{1}{x^3}\right)}$$

Put $\tan^{-1}\left(x^3 + \frac{1}{x^3}\right) = z$

$$\Rightarrow \frac{1}{1 + \left(x^3 + \frac{1}{x^3}\right)^2} \times \left(3x^2 - \frac{3}{x^4}\right) dx = dz$$

$$\Rightarrow \frac{1}{1 + \left(\frac{x^6 + 1}{x^3}\right)^2} \times \left(\frac{3x^6 - 3}{x^4}\right) dx = dz$$

$$\Rightarrow \frac{(x^3)^2}{(x^3)^2 + (x^{12} + 1 + 2 \times 1 \times x^6)} \times \frac{3(x^6 - 1)}{x^4} dx = dz$$

$$\Rightarrow \frac{x^6 \times 3(x^6 - 1)}{x^4 [x^6 + x^{12} + 1 + 2x^6]} dx = dz$$

$$\Rightarrow \frac{(x^8 - x^2)}{(x^{12} + 3x^6 + 1)} dx = \frac{1}{3} dz$$

So, $$I = \frac{1}{3}\int \frac{1}{z} dz = \frac{1}{3} \ln|z| + C = \frac{1}{3}\log_e\left(\left|\tan^{-1}\left(x^3 + \frac{1}{x^3}\right)\right|\right) + C$$

$$\Rightarrow I = \log_e\left(\left|\tan^{-1}\left(x^3 + \frac{1}{x^3}\right)\right|\right)^{1/3} + C$$

48. Given, $I(x) = \int e^{\sin^2 x}(\cos x \sin 2x - \sin x) \, dx$

$$= \int e^{\sin^2 x} \cdot \cos x \cdot \sin 2x dx - \int \sin x e^{\sin^2 x} dx$$

$$= \int \underset{\text{I}}{[(\cos x)} \; \underset{\text{II}}{e^{\sin^2 x} \cdot \sin 2x]} dx - \int \sin x \cdot e^{\sin^2 x} dx$$

$$= \cos x \cdot e^{\sin^2 x} - \int(-\sin x)e^{\sin^2 x} dx - \int \sin x e^{\sin^2 x} dx$$

$$= \cos x \cdot e^{\sin^2 x} + \int \sin x \, e^{\sin^2 x} \cdot dx - \int \sin x \cdot e^{\sin^2 x} dx + C$$

$$I(x) = e^{\sin^2 x} \cdot \cos x + C$$

Given, $I(0) = 1 \Rightarrow C = 0$

So, $I(x) = e^{\sin^2 x} \cdot \cos x \Rightarrow I(\pi/3) = e^{3/4} \cdot \frac{1}{2} = \frac{e^{3/4}}{2}$

49.

> **Decoding the Question**
>
> First let $1 + xe^x = t$ and then solve the integral. After the substitutes $x \to \infty$, $I(x) \to 0$, then find the value of constant of integration and then find the value of $I(x)$ at $x = 1$.

$$I(x) = \int \frac{x + 1}{x(1 + xe^x)^2} dx = \int \frac{(x + 1)e^x \, dx}{xe^x(1 + xe^x)^2}$$

Let $1 + xe^x = t \Rightarrow (x + 1)e^x \, dx = dt$

$$I(x) = \int \frac{dt}{(t - 1)t^2} \quad \text{...(i)}$$

$$\therefore I(x) = \int\left(\frac{-1}{t} + \frac{-1}{t^2} + \frac{1}{t - 1}\right) dt = -\ln(t) + \frac{1}{t} + \ln(t - 1) + K$$

$$I(x) = \frac{1}{1 + xe^x} + \ln\left(\frac{xe^x}{1 + xe^x}\right) + K$$

Now, for $x \to \infty$ $I(x) \to 0$

$$\therefore \lim_{x \to \infty} I(x) = \lim_{x \to \infty} \frac{1}{1 + xe^x} + \lim_{x \to \infty} \ln\left(\frac{xe^x}{1 + xe^x}\right) + K = 0$$

$$\Rightarrow 0 + 0 + K = 0 \Rightarrow K = 0$$

Now, $$I(1) = \frac{1}{1 + e} + \ln\left(\frac{e}{1 + e}\right) = \frac{1}{1 + e} + 1 - \ln(1 + e)$$

$$= \frac{2 + e}{1 + e} - \ln(e + 1)$$

50. We have, $I(x) = \int \frac{x^2(x\sec^2 x + \tan x)}{(x\tan x + 1)^2}\,dx$

$$= x^2 \int \frac{x\sec^2 x + \tan x}{(x\tan x+1)^2}\,dx - \int\left\{\frac{d}{dx}(x^2)\int \frac{x\sec^2 x + \tan x}{(x\tan x+1)^2}\right\}dx$$

Integration by parts

$$= x^2\left(\frac{-1}{x\tan x + 1}\right) + \int \frac{2x}{x\tan x + 1}\,dx$$

Now, let $I_1 = 2\int \frac{x}{x\tan x + 1}\,dx$

$$= 2\int \frac{x\cos x}{x\sin x + \cos x}\,dx$$

On putting $x\sin x + \cos x = t$

$\Rightarrow (x\cos x + \sin x - \sin x)\,dx = dt$

$\Rightarrow \quad x\cos x\,dx = dt$

$\therefore \quad I_1 = 2\int \frac{dt}{t} = 2\log t + c$

$= 2\log(x\sin x + \cos x) + C$

$\therefore \; I(x) = \frac{-x^2}{x\tan x + 1} + 2\log(x\sin x + \cos x) + C$ ...(i)

When $x = 0$,

then $I(0) = 0 + 2\log(1) + C = 0$

$\Rightarrow \quad C = 0$

$\therefore \quad I(x) = \frac{-x^2}{x\tan x + 1} + 2\log(x\sin x + \cos x)$

$$\Rightarrow I\left(\frac{\pi}{4}\right) = \frac{-\frac{\pi^2}{16}}{\frac{\pi}{4}+1} + 2\log\left(\frac{\pi}{4}\times\frac{1}{\sqrt{2}} + \frac{1}{\sqrt{2}}\right)$$

$$= \log\left(\frac{(\pi+4)^2}{32}\right) - \frac{\pi^2}{4(\pi+4)}$$

51. Given that $f''(x) = g''(x) + 6x$

$f'(1) = 4g'(1) - 3 = 9$

$f(2) = 3g(2) = 12$

Here, $f''(x) = g''(x) + 6x$

On integrating both side, we get

$f'(x) = g'(x) + 3x^2 + C_1$ ...(i)

Again, integrating both sides, we get

$f(x) = g(x) + x^3 + C_1 x + C_2$ ...(ii)

Now, use $f'(1) = 4g'(1) - 3 = 9$ in Eq. (i), we get

$9 = 3 + 3 + C_1 \Rightarrow C_1 = 3$

Again, use $f(2) = 3g(2) = 12$ in Eq. (ii), we get

$12 = 4 + 8 + 6 + C_2$

$\Rightarrow \quad C_2 = -6$

So, $f(x) = g(x) + x^3 + 3x - 6$

Now, $f(x) - g(x) = x^3 + 3x - 6$

Let at $x = x_0$, $f(x_0) = g(x_0)$

So, $x_0^3 + 3x_0 - 6 = 0$

Now, let $h(x) = x^3 + 3x - 6$

In the interval $(1, 3/2)$,

$h(1) = -2(-\text{ve})$

$h\left(\frac{3}{2}\right) = \frac{15}{8}(+\text{ve})$

So, $h(x)$ has a root between $\left(1, \frac{3}{2}\right)$.

$\Rightarrow \; f(x_0) \in \left(1, \frac{3}{2}\right)$

such that $f(x_0) = g(x_0)$

Option (a) is true.

$h(-2) = f(-2) - g(-2) = -20 \Rightarrow g(-2) - f(-2) = 20$

Option (b) is true.

Now, $|f'(x) - g'(x)| < 6$

$\Rightarrow \quad |3x^2 + 3| < 6 \Rightarrow 3x^2 + 3 < 6$

$\Rightarrow \quad x^2 - 1 < 0 \Rightarrow x \in (-1, 1)$

Option (d) is true.

52. Given, $f(x) = \int \frac{2x}{(x^2+1)(x^2+3)}\,dx$

On putting $x^2 = t \Rightarrow 2x\cdot dx = dt$

$$\therefore \quad f(x) = \int \frac{dt}{(t+1)(t+3)} = \frac{1}{2}\int \frac{1}{t+1} - \frac{1}{t+3}\,dt$$

$$f(x) = \frac{1}{2}(\ln|t+1| - \ln|t+3|) + C$$

$$f(x) = \frac{1}{2}\ln\left|\frac{t+1}{t+3}\right| + C = \frac{1}{2}\ln\left|\frac{x^2+1}{x^2+3}\right| + C$$

$$f(3) = \frac{1}{2}\ln\left|\frac{9+1}{9+3}\right| + C = \frac{1}{2}\ln\frac{5}{6} + C$$

$$\frac{1}{2}(\ln 5 - \ln 6) = \frac{1}{2}(\ln 5 - \ln 6) + C$$

$$C = 0$$

So, $f(x)$ becomes

$$f(x) = \frac{1}{2}\ln\left|\frac{x^2+1}{x^2+3}\right|$$

$$f(4) = \frac{1}{2}\ln\left(\frac{17}{19}\right) = \frac{1}{2}(\log_e 17 - \log_e 19)$$

53. Given, $f(x) = \int \frac{dx}{(3+4x^2)\sqrt{4-3x^2}}, |x| < \frac{2}{\sqrt{3}}$

On putting $x = \frac{1}{t} \Rightarrow dx = -\frac{1}{t^2}\,dt$

$$\therefore \; f(x) = \int \frac{\left(-\frac{1}{t^2}\right)dt}{\left(3+\frac{4}{t^2}\right)\sqrt{4-\frac{3}{t^2}}} = \int \frac{-t\,dt}{(3t^2+4)\sqrt{4t^2-3}}$$

Put $4t^2 - 3 = z^2 \Rightarrow 8t\,dt = 2z\,dz$

$$\Rightarrow \quad t\,dt = \frac{1}{4} z\,dz \Rightarrow \int \frac{\left(-\frac{1}{4} z\,dz\right)}{\left[3\left(\frac{z^2+3}{4}\right)+4\right]z}$$

$$= -\frac{1}{4}\int \frac{4\,dz}{3z^2+25} = -\int \frac{dz}{3\left\{z^2+\frac{25}{3}\right\}}$$

$$= -\frac{1}{3}\int \frac{dz}{(z)^2+\left(\frac{5}{\sqrt{3}}\right)^2}$$

$$= -\frac{1}{3}\cdot\frac{\sqrt{3}}{5}\tan^{-1}\left(\frac{z}{5/\sqrt{3}}\right)+C$$

$$= \frac{-1}{5\sqrt{3}}\tan^{-1}\left(\frac{\sqrt{3}}{5}\sqrt{4t^2-3}\right)+C$$

$$\therefore \quad f(x) = -\frac{1}{5\sqrt{3}}\tan^{-1}\left(\frac{\sqrt{3}}{5}\sqrt{\frac{4-3x^2}{x^2}}\right)+C$$

Since, $f(0)=0 \Rightarrow c = \dfrac{\pi}{10\sqrt{3}}$

$$\therefore \quad f(x) = -\frac{1}{5\sqrt{3}}\tan^{-1}\left(\frac{\sqrt{3}\,\sqrt{4-3x^2}}{5\quad x}\right)+\frac{\pi}{10\sqrt{3}}$$

$$\therefore \quad f(1) = -\frac{1}{5\sqrt{3}}\tan^{-1}\left(\frac{\sqrt{3}}{5}\right)+\frac{\pi}{10\sqrt{3}}$$

$$= \frac{1}{5\sqrt{3}}\left(\frac{\pi}{2}-\tan^{-1}\left(\frac{\sqrt{3}}{5}\right)\right)$$

$$= \frac{1}{5\sqrt{3}}\cot^{-1}\left(\frac{\sqrt{3}}{5}\right)$$

$$f(1) = \frac{1}{5\sqrt{3}}\tan^{-1}\left(\frac{5}{\sqrt{3}}\right) = \frac{1}{\alpha\beta}\tan^{-1}\left(\frac{\alpha}{\beta}\right) \quad \text{[given]}$$

So, $\alpha = 5, \beta = \sqrt{3}$ $\quad [\because \alpha, \beta > 0]$

$\therefore \alpha^2+\beta^2 = (5)^2+(\sqrt{3})^2 = 25+3 = 28$

54. $I(x) = \int \sqrt{\dfrac{x+7}{x}}\,dx = \int \sqrt{1+\dfrac{7}{x}}\,dx$

Let $\sqrt{1+\dfrac{7}{x}} = \sec\theta \Rightarrow 1+\dfrac{7}{x} = \sec^2\theta$

$$\Rightarrow \quad x = 7\cot^2\theta$$

$$\Rightarrow \quad dx = -14\cot\theta\cdot(\text{cosec}^2\theta)d\theta$$

$$= -14\cot\theta\,\text{cosec}^2\theta\,d\theta$$

$$\therefore \quad I(\theta) = -14\int \sec\theta\cdot\cot\theta\,\text{cosec}^2\theta\,d\theta$$

$$= -14\int \text{cosec}^3\theta\,d\theta$$

$$= 14\begin{pmatrix} -\frac{1}{2}\ln\left|\frac{1-\cos\theta}{\sin\theta}\right| \\ +\frac{1}{2}\text{cosec}\theta\cot\theta \end{pmatrix}+C$$

$$= -7\ln\left|\frac{1-\cos\theta}{\sin\theta}\right| + \frac{7\cos\theta}{\sin^2\theta}+C$$

$$\sec\theta = \sqrt{\frac{x+7}{x}} \Rightarrow \cos\theta = \sqrt{\frac{x}{x+7}}$$

$$\Rightarrow \sin^2\theta = 1-\cos^2\theta = 1-\frac{x}{x+7} = \frac{7}{x+7}$$

$$\Rightarrow \sin\theta = \frac{\sqrt{7}}{\sqrt{x+7}}$$

$$\therefore \quad I(x) = -7\ln\left|\frac{1-\frac{\sqrt{x}}{\sqrt{x+7}}}{\left(\frac{\sqrt{7}}{\sqrt{x+7}}\right)}\right| + \frac{\left(\frac{7\sqrt{x}}{\sqrt{x+7}}\right)}{\left(\frac{7}{x+7}\right)}+C$$

$$\Rightarrow \quad I(x) = -7\ln\left|\frac{\sqrt{x+7}-\sqrt{x}}{\sqrt{7}}\right| + \sqrt{x(x+7)}+C$$

$$I(9) = 12+\ln 7$$

$$\Rightarrow -7\ln\left(\frac{\sqrt{9+7}-\sqrt{9}}{\sqrt{7}}\right)+\sqrt{9(9+7)}+c = 12+7\ln 7$$

$$\Rightarrow \quad 7\ln(\sqrt{7})+12+c = 12+7\ln(7)$$

$$\Rightarrow \quad \frac{7}{2}\ln(7)+c = 7\ln(7)$$

$$\Rightarrow \quad c = \frac{7}{2}\ln(7)$$

Now, $I(1) = \alpha + 7\ln(2\sqrt{2}+1)$

$$\Rightarrow -7\ln\left(\frac{\sqrt{1+7}-\sqrt{1}}{\sqrt{7}}\right)+\sqrt{1(1+7)}+\frac{7}{2}\ln(7)$$

$$= \alpha + 7\ln(2\sqrt{2}+1)$$

$$\Rightarrow -7\ln\left(\frac{2\sqrt{2}-1}{\sqrt{7}}\right)+2\sqrt{2}+7\ln(\sqrt{7})-7\ln(2\sqrt{2}+1) = \alpha$$

$$\Rightarrow \quad \alpha = 2\sqrt{2}+7\ln\left(\frac{\sqrt{7}\times\sqrt{7}}{(2\sqrt{2}-1)(2\sqrt{2}+1)}\right)$$

$$\Rightarrow \quad \alpha = 2\sqrt{2}+7\ln\left(\frac{7}{8-1}\right) = 2\sqrt{2}+7\ln(1)$$

$$\Rightarrow \quad \alpha = 2\sqrt{2} \Rightarrow \alpha^4 = 64$$

55. $I = \int \sqrt{\sec 2x - 1}\,dx$

$$= \int \sqrt{\frac{1-\cos 2x}{\cos 2x}}\,dx$$

$$= \int \frac{\sqrt{2}\sin x}{\sqrt{2\cos^2 x-1}}\,dx$$

Let $\sqrt{2}\cos x = t \Rightarrow -\sqrt{2}\sin x\cdot dx = dt$

Then $I = \int \dfrac{-1}{\sqrt{t^2-1}}\,dt = -\ln|t+\sqrt{t^2-1}|+C$

Put $t = \sqrt{2}\cos x$

$$I = -\ln|\sqrt{2}\cos x+\sqrt{2\cos^2 x-1}|+C$$

$$= -\frac{1}{2}\ln|(\sqrt{2}\cos x+\sqrt{\cos 2x})^2|+C$$

$$= -\frac{1}{2}\ln\left|2\cos^2 x+\cos 2x+2\sqrt{2}\sqrt{\cos 2x}\sqrt{\frac{1+\cos 2x}{2}}\right|+C$$

$$= -\frac{1}{2}\ln|1 + \cos 2x + \cos 2x + 2\sqrt{\cos 2x(1 + \cos 2x)}| + C$$

$$= -\frac{1}{2}\log_e\left|\begin{matrix}\cos 2x + \frac{1}{2} \\ + \sqrt{\cos 2x(1 + \cos 2x)}\end{matrix}\right| + C$$

So, $\alpha = -\frac{1}{2},\ \beta = \frac{1}{2}$

$$\beta - \alpha = \frac{1}{2} - \left(-\frac{1}{2}\right) = 1$$

56. Given integral is

$I(x) = \int \sec^2 x \cdot \sin^{-2022} x\, dx - 2022 \int \sin^{-2022} x dx$

Applying by parts,

$$= \tan x(\sin x)^{-2022} + \int (2022) \tan x \cdot (\sin x)^{-2023}$$

$$\cos x\, dx - 2022 \int (\sin x)^{-2022}\, dx$$

$I(x) = (\tan x)(\sin x)^{-2022} + C$ ...(i)

At, $x = \frac{\pi}{4},\ 2^{1011} = \left(\frac{1}{\sqrt{2}}\right)^{-2022} + C$ [constant]

so, $C = 0$

Hence, $I(x) = \frac{\tan x}{(\sin x)^{2022}}$

On putting $x = \frac{\pi}{6}$ and $x = \frac{\pi}{3}$ in the above expression, we get

$$I\left(\frac{\pi}{6}\right) = \frac{1}{\sqrt{3}\left(\frac{1}{2}\right)^{2022}} = \frac{2^{2022}}{\sqrt{3}}$$

$$I\left(\frac{\pi}{3}\right) = \frac{\sqrt{3}}{\left(\frac{\sqrt{3}}{2}\right)^{2022}} = \frac{2^{2022}}{(\sqrt{3})^{2021}} = \frac{1}{3^{1010}} I\left(\frac{\pi}{6}\right)$$

Thus, $3^{1010} I\left(\frac{\pi}{3}\right) = I\left(\frac{\pi}{6}\right)$

57. Given integral is

$$\int\left(\frac{x^2 + 1}{(x + 1)^2}\right) e^x\, dx = \int\left(\frac{x^2 - 1 + 2}{(x + 1)^2}\right) e^x\, dx$$

$$= \int\left(\frac{x - 1}{x + 1} + \frac{2}{(x + 1)^2}\right) e^x dx$$

$[\because \int (f(x) + f'(x))\, e^x dx = f(x)\, e^x + C \text{ (constant)}]$

After comparing the integral the function is $f(x) = \frac{x - 1}{x + 1}$

Then, $f'(x) = \frac{2}{(x + 1)^2}$

On differentiating both sides w.r.t. x, we get

$$f''(x) = \frac{-4}{(x + 1)^3} \Rightarrow f'''(x) = \frac{12}{(x + 1)^4}$$

On putting $x = 1$ in above equation, we get

$$f'''(1) = \frac{12}{16} = \frac{3}{4}$$

58. Let $I = \int \frac{\frac{\sin x}{\cos^3 x}}{1 + \tan^3 x}\, dx$

$$= \int \frac{\tan x \cdot \sec^2 x}{(\tan x + 1)(1 + \tan^2 x - \tan x)}\, dx$$

Let $\tan x = t \Rightarrow \sec^2 x\, dx = dt$

$$= \int \frac{t}{(t + 1)(t^2 - t + 1)}\, dt$$

Let $\frac{t}{(t + 1)(t^2 - t + 1)} = \frac{A}{t + 1} + \frac{B(2t - 1)}{t^2 - t + 1} + \frac{C}{t^2 - t + 1}$

$\Rightarrow A(t^2 - t + 1) + B(2t - 1)(t + 1) + C(t + 1) = t$

$\Rightarrow t^2(A + 2B) + t(-A + B + C) + A - B + C = t$

$\therefore \quad A + 2B = 0$ ...(i)

$-A + B + C = 1$ ...(ii)

$A - B + C = 0$ ...(iii)

$\Rightarrow \quad C = \frac{1}{2}$

$\Rightarrow \quad A - B = -\frac{1}{2}$ ...(vi)

Solving Eqs. (i) and (iv), we get

$$B = \frac{1}{6},\ A = -\frac{1}{3}$$

$$\therefore\ I = -\frac{1}{3}\int\frac{dt}{1 + t} + \frac{1}{6}\int\frac{2t - 1}{t^2 - t + 1}\, dt + \frac{1}{2}\int\frac{dt}{t^2 - t + 1}$$

$$= -\frac{1}{3}\log_e|(1 + \tan x)| + \frac{1}{6}\log_e|\tan^2 x - \tan x + 1| + \frac{1}{2}\cdot\frac{2}{\sqrt{3}}\tan^{-1}\left(\frac{\left(\tan x - \frac{1}{2}\right)}{\frac{\sqrt{3}}{2}}\right)$$

$$= -\frac{1}{3}\log_e|(1 + \tan x)| + \frac{1}{6}\log_e|\tan^2 x - \tan x + 1| + \frac{1}{\sqrt{3}}\tan^{-1}\left(\frac{2\tan x - 1}{\sqrt{3}}\right) + C$$

Now, comparing, we get

$$\alpha = -\frac{1}{3}, \beta = \frac{1}{6}, \gamma = \frac{1}{\sqrt{3}}$$

So, $18(\alpha + \beta + \gamma^2) = 18\left(-\frac{1}{3} + \frac{1}{6} + \frac{1}{3}\right) = 3$

59. Let $I = \int \frac{x^2 - 1}{(x^4 + 3x^2 + 1)\tan^{-1}\left(\frac{x^2 + 1}{x}\right)}\, dx + \int \frac{1}{x^4 + 3x^2 + 1}\, dx$

$I = I_1 + I_2$ [let] ...(i)

For I_1, let $\tan^{-1}\frac{x^2 + 1}{x} = t$, then

$$\frac{x^2 - 1}{x^4 + 3x^2 + 1}\, dx = dt$$

$I_1 = \int \frac{1}{t}\, dt = \log t = \log\left|\tan^{-1}\left(\frac{x^2 + 1}{x}\right)\right| + C_1$ [constant] ...(ii)

$$I_2 = \frac{1}{2}\int \frac{(x^2+1)-(x^2-1)}{x^4+3x^2+1}$$

$$= \frac{1}{2}\int \frac{x^2+1}{x^4+3x^2+1} - \frac{1}{2}\int \frac{x^2-1}{x^4+3x^2+1}$$

Divide numerator and denominator by x^2, we get

$$\frac{1}{2}\int \frac{1+\frac{1}{x^2}}{\left(x-\frac{1}{x}\right)^2+5} - \frac{1}{2}\int \frac{1-\frac{1}{x^2}}{\left(x+\frac{1}{x}\right)^2+1}$$

$$= \frac{1}{2\sqrt{5}}\tan^{-1}\left(\frac{x^2-1}{\sqrt{5}x}\right) - \frac{1}{2}\tan^{-1}\left(\frac{x^2+1}{x}\right) + C_2$$

[constant] ...(iii)

$$\text{Thus, } I = \log\left|\tan^{-1}\left(\frac{x^2+1}{x}\right)\right| + \frac{1}{2\sqrt{5}}\tan^{-1}\left(\frac{x^2-1}{\sqrt{5}x}\right) - \frac{1}{2}\tan^{-1}\left(\frac{x^2+1}{x}\right) + C,$$

where $C = C_1 + C_2$

Now comparing, we get,

$$\alpha = 1, \beta = \frac{1}{2\sqrt{5}}, \gamma = \frac{1}{\sqrt{5}}, \delta = -\frac{1}{2}$$

$$\text{So, } 10(\alpha + \beta\gamma + \delta) = 10\left(1 + \frac{1}{2\sqrt{5}} \times \frac{1}{\sqrt{5}} - \frac{1}{2}\right)$$

$$= 10\left(1 + \frac{1}{10} - \frac{1}{2}\right) = 6$$

60. Since, $I = \int \frac{\cos\theta}{5+7\sin\theta-2\cos^2\theta}\,d\theta$

$$= \int \frac{\cos\theta}{3+7\sin\theta+2\sin^2\theta}\,d\theta$$

Let $\sin\theta = t \Rightarrow \cos\theta\,d\theta = dt$

$$\therefore \quad I = \int \frac{dt}{2t^2+7t+3} = \frac{1}{2}\int \frac{dt}{t^2+\frac{7}{2}t+\frac{3}{2}}$$

$$= \frac{1}{2}\int \frac{dt}{\left(t+\frac{7}{4}\right)^2+\left(\frac{3}{2}-\frac{49}{16}\right)}$$

$$= \frac{1}{2}\int \frac{dt}{\left(t+\frac{7}{4}\right)^2-\left(\frac{5}{4}\right)^2}$$

$$= \frac{1}{2}\times\frac{1}{2\times\frac{5}{4}}\log_e\left|\frac{t+\frac{7}{4}-\frac{5}{4}}{t+\frac{7}{4}+\frac{5}{4}}\right| + C'$$

$$= \frac{1}{5}\log_e\left|\frac{2t+1}{2t+6}\right| + C'$$

$$= \frac{1}{5}\log_e\left|\frac{2\sin\theta+1}{\sin\theta+3}\right| + C,$$

where $C = C' - \frac{1}{5}\log_e 2$

On comparing with $A\log_e|B(\theta)| + C,$ [given]

$$\therefore \quad \frac{B(\theta)}{A} = \frac{5(2\sin\theta+1)}{(\sin\theta+3)}$$

61. It is given that,

$$f(x) = \int \frac{\sqrt{x}}{(1+x)^2}\,dx, (x \ge 0)$$

Let $x = \tan^2 t \Rightarrow dx = 2\tan t\sec^2 t\,dt$

$$\therefore \quad f(x) = \int \frac{2\tan^2 t\sec^2 t}{\sec^4 t}\,dt$$

$$= \int 2\sin^2 t\,dt$$

$$= \int (1-\cos 2t)dt \qquad [\because 2\sin^2 x = 1-\cos 2x]$$

$$= t - \frac{\sin 2t}{2} + C$$

$$\text{So, } f(x) = t - \frac{\tan t}{1+\tan^2 t} + C$$

$$= \tan^{-1}\sqrt{x} - \frac{\sqrt{x}}{1+x} + C$$

$$\therefore f(3) - f(1) = \left(\tan^{-1}\sqrt{3} - \frac{\sqrt{3}}{1+3} + C\right) - \left(\tan^{-1}(1) - \frac{1}{1+1} + C\right)$$

$$= \frac{\pi}{3} - \frac{\sqrt{3}}{4} - \frac{\pi}{4} + \frac{1}{2}$$

$$= \frac{\pi}{12} + \frac{1}{2} - \frac{\sqrt{3}}{4}$$

Exercise 2 - JEE Advanced Pattern

1. We have the following cases :

Case I When $x \ge 0$

In this case, we have

$$\int |x^n|\,dx = \int |x|^n\,dx = \int x^n\,dx \qquad [\because |x| = x]$$

$$= \frac{x^{n+1}}{n+1} + C$$

$$= \frac{|x|^n x}{n+1} + C \qquad [\because x \ge 0 \Rightarrow |x| = x]$$

Case II When $x \le 0$

In this case, we have $|x| = -x$

$$\therefore \quad \int |x^n|\,dx = \int |x|^n\,dx$$

$$= \int (-x)^n\,dx$$

$$= -\int x^n\,dx \qquad [\because n \text{ in odd}]$$

$$= -\frac{x^{n+1}}{n+1} + C$$

$$= \frac{(-x)^n x}{n+1} + C$$

$$= \frac{|x|^n x}{n+1} + C$$

$$\text{Hence, } \int |x^n|\,dx = \frac{|x|^n x}{n+1} + C$$

2. We have, $f''(x) = f(x)$

$$\Rightarrow 2f'(x)\, f''(x) = 2f(x)\, f'(x)$$

$$\Rightarrow \frac{d}{dx}\{f'(x)\}^2 = \frac{d}{dx}\{f(x)\}^2$$

$$\Rightarrow \{f'(x)\}^2 = \{f(x)\}^2 + C \quad \text{...(i)}$$

Now, $f(0) = 2$ and $f'(0) = 3$.

Therefore, from Eq. (i), we get

$$\{f'(0)\}^2 = \{f(0)\}^2 + C$$

$$\Rightarrow 9 = 4 + C$$

$$\Rightarrow C = 5$$

$$\therefore \{f'(x)\}^2 = \{f(x)\}^2 + 5$$

$$\Rightarrow f'(x) = \sqrt{5 + \{f(x)\}^2}$$

$$\Rightarrow \int \frac{1}{\sqrt{(\sqrt{5})^2 + \{f(x)\}^2}}\, d\{f(x)\} = \int dx$$

$$\Rightarrow \log\left| f(x) + \sqrt{5 + \{f(x)\}^2} \right| = x + C_1$$

$$\therefore f(0) = 2$$

$$\Rightarrow \log|2 + 3| = C_1$$

$$\Rightarrow C_1 = \log 5$$

$$\therefore \log|f(x) + \sqrt{5 + \{f(x)\}^2}| = x + \log 5$$

$$\Rightarrow \log\left\{\frac{f(x) + \sqrt{5 + \{f(x)\}^2}}{5}\right\} = x$$

$$\Rightarrow f(x) + \sqrt{5 + \{f(x)\}^2} = 5e^x$$

$$\Rightarrow \sqrt{5 + \{f(x)\}^2} + f(x) = 5e^x$$

$$\Rightarrow f(x) = \frac{5}{2}e^x - \frac{1}{2}e^{-x}$$

$$\Rightarrow f(4) = \frac{5}{2}e^4 - \frac{1}{2}e^{-4}$$

$$\Rightarrow f(4) = \frac{5e^8 - 1}{2e^4}$$

3. On solving, $\dfrac{\sin\theta}{\cos 3\theta} = \dfrac{1}{2}[\tan 3\theta - \tan\theta]$

$$\frac{\sin 3\theta}{\cos 9\theta} = \frac{1}{2}[\tan 9\theta - \tan 3\theta]$$

$$\frac{\sin 9\theta}{\cos 27\theta} = \frac{1}{2}[\tan 27\theta - \tan 9\theta]$$

$$\therefore \int\left(\frac{\sin\theta}{\cos 3\theta} + \frac{\sin 3\theta}{\cos 9\theta} + \frac{\sin 9\theta}{\cos 27\theta}\right) d\theta = \frac{1}{2}\int(\tan 27\theta - \tan\theta)\, d\theta$$

$$= \frac{1}{2}\left\{\frac{1}{27}\log(\sec 27\theta) - \log(\sec\theta)\right\} + C$$

$$= \frac{1}{2}\log\left|\frac{\sqrt[27]{\sec 27\theta}}{\sec\theta}\right| + C$$

4. $A = \begin{bmatrix} x^2 & 6 & 0 \\ 1 & -5 & 1 \\ 2 & 0 & x \end{bmatrix}$, $B = \begin{bmatrix} 4 & 0 & 0 \\ 0 & 1 & 0 \\ 0 & 0 & 8 \end{bmatrix}$

$$AB = \begin{bmatrix} 4x^2 & \dots & \dots \\ \dots & -5 & \dots \\ \dots & \dots & 8x \end{bmatrix}$$

$$f(x) = \text{trace of } AB = 4x^2 - 5 + 8x$$

$$\int \frac{3\,dx}{f(x)} = \int \frac{3\,dx}{4x^2 + 8x - 5}$$

$$= \frac{3}{4}\int \frac{dx}{x^2 + 2x - \frac{5}{4}} = \frac{3}{4}\int \frac{dx}{(x+1)^2 - \left(\frac{3}{2}\right)^2}$$

$$= \frac{3}{4}\cdot\frac{1}{2\left(\frac{3}{2}\right)}\ln\left|\frac{x + 1 - \frac{3}{2}}{x + 1 + \frac{3}{2}}\right| + C$$

$$= \frac{1}{4}\ln\left|\frac{2x - 1}{2x + 5}\right| + C$$

5. $I = \displaystyle\int \frac{(2\sin x\cos x)^{\frac{1}{3}}\, d(\tan x)^{\frac{1}{3}}}{\sin^{\frac{2}{3}} x + \cos^{\frac{2}{3}} x}$

$$= \int \frac{2^{\frac{1}{3}}\, d((\tan x)^{\frac{1}{3}})}{\dfrac{\sin^{\frac{2}{3}} x + \cos^{\frac{2}{3}} x}{\sin^{\frac{1}{3}} x \cdot \cos^{\frac{1}{3}} x}} = 2^{\frac{1}{3}}\int \frac{d((\tan x)^{\frac{1}{3}})}{(\tan x)^{\frac{1}{3}} + \dfrac{1}{(\tan x)^{\frac{1}{3}}}}$$

Now, $(\tan x)^{\frac{1}{3}} = t$

$$\therefore I = 2^{\frac{1}{3}}\int \frac{dt}{t + \frac{1}{t}} = \frac{2^{\frac{1}{3}}}{2}\int \frac{2t}{1 + t^2}\, dt$$

$$= \frac{1}{2^{\frac{2}{3}}}\ln(1 + t^2) + C$$

$$= \frac{1}{2^{\frac{2}{3}}}\ln(1 + \tan^{2/3} x) + C$$

6. $I = \displaystyle\int \frac{x}{(1 + x^2)^2\left(\dfrac{2 + x^2}{1 + x^2}\right)^{\frac{3012}{2012}}}\, dx$

Let $\dfrac{2 + x^2}{1 + x^2} = t$

$$\Rightarrow \frac{(1 + x^2)2x - (2 + x^2)2x}{(1 + x^2)^2}\, dx = dt$$

$$\Rightarrow \frac{-2x}{(1 + x^2)^2}\, dx = dt$$

$$\therefore \quad I = -\int \frac{dt}{2t^{\left(\frac{3012}{2012}\right)}}$$

$$= -\frac{1}{2}\left[\frac{t^{\left(\frac{-3012}{2012}+1\right)}}{-\frac{3012}{2012}+1}\right] + C$$

$$= \frac{1}{2}\left(\frac{1+x^2}{2+x^2}\right)^{\frac{1000}{2012}} \cdot \frac{2012}{1000} + C$$

$$= \frac{1006}{1000}\left(\frac{1+x^2}{2+x^2}\right)^{\frac{1000}{2012}} + C$$

$\Rightarrow \quad \alpha = 503$ and $\beta = 500$

$$f(x) = \frac{1}{2+x^2} \Rightarrow f(1) = \frac{1}{3} = \frac{1}{\alpha - \beta}$$

7. We have, $I = \int \tan\left[2\tan^{-1}\left(\sqrt{\frac{\sqrt{1+\sqrt{x}}-1}{\sqrt{1+\sqrt{x}}+1}}\right)\right] dx$

Let $\sqrt{x} = \tan^2\theta$,

$$x \in (0, 1), \theta \in \left(0, \frac{\pi}{4}\right)$$

$$x = \tan^4\theta \Rightarrow \tan\theta = x^{1/4}$$

$$\therefore \quad dx = 4\tan^3\theta\sec^2\theta\, d\theta$$

Also, $\sqrt{1+\sqrt{x}} = \sec\theta$

$$\text{Now, } \tan\left(2\tan^{-1}\sqrt{\frac{\sqrt{1+\sqrt{x}}-1}{\sqrt{1+\sqrt{x}}+1}}\right) = \tan\left(2\tan^{-1}\sqrt{\frac{\sec\theta-1}{\sec\theta+1}}\right)$$

$$= \tan\left\{2\tan^{-1}\left(\tan\frac{\theta}{2}\right)\right\} = \tan\theta$$

$$\text{Now,} \quad I = \int \tan\theta \cdot 4\tan^3\theta \cdot \sec^2\theta\, d\theta$$

$$= \frac{4}{5}\tan^5\theta + C$$

$$= \frac{4}{5}(x)^{5/4} + C$$

8. Let $\quad I = \int \frac{x}{(x^2-3x+2)\sqrt{x^2-4x+3}}\, dx$

$$= \int \frac{x}{(x-2)(x-1)\sqrt{x^2-4x+3}}\, dx$$

$$= \int \left(\frac{2}{x-2} - \frac{1}{x-1}\right)\frac{dx}{\sqrt{x^2-4x+3}}$$

Therefore,

$$I = 2\underbrace{\int \frac{dx}{(x-2)\sqrt{x^2-4x+3}}}_{I_1} - \underbrace{\int \frac{dx}{(x-1)\sqrt{x^2-4x+3}}}_{I_2} \quad \ldots\text{(i)}$$

Let $\quad I_1 = \int \frac{dx}{(x-2)\sqrt{x^2-4x+3}}$

$$= \int \frac{dx}{(x-2)\sqrt{(x-2)^2-1}}$$

$$= \int \frac{\frac{1}{(x-2)^2}}{\sqrt{1-\left(\frac{1}{x-2}\right)^2}}\, dx = -\sin^{-1}\left(\frac{1}{x-2}\right) + C$$

Now, let $I_2 = \int \frac{dx}{(x-1)\sqrt{x^2-4x+3}}$

$$= \int \frac{dx}{(x-1)^{3/2}(x-3)^{1/2}}$$

$$= \int \frac{dx}{\left(\frac{x-1}{x-3}\right)^{3/2}(x-3)^2}$$

On putting $\frac{x-1}{x-3} = t^2$

$$\Rightarrow \quad x = \frac{1-3t^2}{1-t^2} = 3 - \frac{2}{1-t^2}$$

$$\Rightarrow \quad x - 3 = \frac{-2}{1-t^2}$$

Therefore, $dx = \frac{-4t}{(1-t^2)^2}\, dt$

This gives, $I_2 = \int \frac{1}{t^3\left(\frac{4}{(1-t^2)^2}\right)} \cdot \frac{-4t}{(1-t^2)^2}\, dt$

$$\Rightarrow \quad I_2 = -\int \frac{1}{t^2}\, dt \Rightarrow I_2 = \frac{1}{t}$$

$$\Rightarrow \quad I_2 = \sqrt{\frac{x-3}{x-1}}$$

$$\Rightarrow \quad I_2 = \frac{\sqrt{x^2-4x+3}}{x-1} + C$$

On substituting the values of I_1 and I_2 in Eq. (i), we get

$$I = -2\sin^{-1}\left(\frac{1}{x-2}\right) - \frac{\sqrt{x^2-4x+3}}{x-1} + C$$

9. Let $\quad I = \int \left(\frac{x}{x\sin x + \cos x}\right)^2 dx$

$$I = \int \frac{x}{\cos x} \cdot \frac{x\cos x}{(x\sin x + \cos x)^2}\, dx$$

$$= \frac{x}{\cos x}\int \frac{x\cos x}{(x\sin x + \cos x)^2}\, dx$$

$$-\int \left(\frac{\cos x + x\sin x}{\cos^2 x}\int \frac{x\cos x}{(x\cos x + \cos x)^2}\, dx\right) dx \quad \ldots\text{(i)}$$

Let $\quad I_1 = \int \frac{x\cos x}{(x\sin x + \cos x)^2}\, dx$

Let $x\sin x + \cos x = t$

$\Rightarrow (x\cos x + \sin x - \sin x)\, dx = dt \Rightarrow x\cos x\, dx = dt$

$$\therefore \quad I_1 = \int \frac{1}{t^2} dt = -\frac{1}{t} = -\frac{1}{x\sin x + \cos x}$$

From Eq. (i),

$$I=\frac{x}{\cos x}\left(-\frac{1}{x\sin x+\cos x}\right)-\int\frac{\cos x+x\sin x}{\cos^2 x}\times\left(-\frac{1}{x\sin x+\cos x}\right)dx$$

$$=\frac{x}{\cos x}\left(-\frac{1}{x\sin x+\cos x}\right)+\int\sec^2 x\,dx$$

$$=\frac{-x\sec x}{x\sin x+\cos x}+\tan x+C$$

$$=\tan x-\frac{x\sec x}{x\sin x+\cos x}+C$$

10. Let $I=\int\frac{e^{(x^2+4\ln x)}-x^3e^{x^2}}{x-1}dx$

$$=\int\frac{e^{x^2}\cdot x^4-x^3\cdot e^{x^2}}{x-1}dx$$

$$=\int\frac{x^3\cdot e^{x^2}(x-1)}{x-1}dx$$

$$=\int x^3\cdot e^{x^2}dx$$

On putting $x^2=t \Rightarrow 2x\,dx=dt$

$$\therefore\quad I=\frac{1}{2}\int te^t dt$$

$$=\frac{1}{2}\left[t\cdot e^t-\int e^t dt\right]$$

$$=\frac{1}{2}[te^t-e^t]+C$$

$$=\frac{1}{2}(t-1)e^t+C$$

$$=\frac{1}{2}(x^2-1)e^{x^2}+C$$

11. Let $I=\int\left(1+2x^2+\frac{1}{x}\right)e^{\left(x^2-\frac{1}{x}\right)}dx$

$$=\int\left[e^{x^2-\frac{1}{x}}+x\left(2x+\frac{1}{x^2}\right)e^{x^2-\frac{1}{x^2}}\right]dx$$

$$=xe^{x^2-\frac{1}{x}}-\int e^{x^2-\frac{1}{x}}\left(2x+\frac{1}{x^2}\right)x\,dx+\int x\left(2x+\frac{1}{x^2}\right)e^{x^2-\frac{1}{x}}dx$$

$$=xe^{x^2-\frac{1}{x}}+C$$

12. $I=\int(\ln x+\ln(\ln(x\cdot\ln x)))\,dx+\int\left(\frac{1+\ln x}{\ln x\cdot\ln(x\ln x)}\right)dx$

$$=x\ln x-x+\int(\underbrace{1}_{\text{II}}\cdot\underbrace{\ln(\ln(x\ln x))}_{\text{I}})\,dx+\int\frac{1+\ln x}{\ln x\cdot\ln(x\ln x)}dx$$

$$=x\ln x-x+\ln(\ln(x\ln x))\cdot x-\int\left(\frac{1}{\ln(x\ln x)}\cdot\frac{1}{x\ln x}(1+\ln x)\int 1\,dx\right)dx+\int\frac{1+\ln x}{\ln x\cdot\ln(x\ln x)}dx$$

$$=x\ln x-x+\ln(\ln(x\ln x))\,x-\int\frac{1+\ln x}{\ln x\cdot\ln(x\ln x)}dx+\int\frac{1+\ln x}{\ln x\cdot\ln(x\ln x)}dx$$

$$=x\ln x-x+\ln(\ln(x\ln x))\cdot x+C$$

13. $D=a_{31}C_{31}+a_{32}C_{32}+a_{33}C_{33}$

$$=a_{31}m_{31}-a_{32}m_{32}+a_{33}m_{33}$$

$$=e^x f(x)+e^x f(x)f'(x)-e^x(f(x)f'(x)+f''(x))$$

$$=e^x(f(x)-f''(x))$$

Then, $\int D\,dx=\int e^x(f(x)-f''(x))\,dx$

$$=\int e^x(f(x))+f'(x))dx-\int e^x(f''(x)+f'(x))dx$$

$$=e^x f(x)-e^x f'(x)+C$$

$$=e^x(f(x)-f'(x))+C$$

14. Let $I=\int\frac{1-\cos x}{\cos x(1+\cos x)}dx$

Let $\cos x=y$

Then, $\frac{1-\cos x}{\cos x(1+\cos x)}=\frac{1-y}{y(1+y)}$

By partial fraction,

$$=\frac{1}{y}-\frac{2}{1+y}$$

$$=\frac{1}{\cos x}-\frac{2}{1+\cos x}$$

$$\therefore\quad I=\int\frac{1-\cos x}{\cos x(1+\cos x)}dx$$

$$=\int\frac{1}{\cos x}dx-\int\frac{2}{1+\cos x}dx$$

$$=\int\sec x\,dx-\int\frac{2}{2\cos^2\frac{x}{2}}dx$$

$$=\ln|\sec x+\tan x|-\int\sec^2\frac{x}{2}dx$$

$$\Rightarrow\quad I=\ln|\sec x+\tan x|-2\tan\frac{x}{2}+C$$

15. Let $I=\int\frac{dx}{\sin x+\sin 2x}$

$$=\int\frac{\sin x}{\sin^2 x(1+2\cos x)}dx$$

$$=\int\frac{\sin x\,dx}{(1-\cos^2 x)(1+2\cos x)}$$

$$=\int\frac{\sin x\,dx}{(1-\cos x)(1+\cos x)(1+2\cos x)}$$

Let $\cos x=t \Rightarrow -\sin x\,dx=dt$

$\therefore\ I = -\int \frac{dt}{(1-t)(1+t)(1+2t)}$

Split into partial fractions, we get

$$= -\int \left[\frac{1}{6(1-t)} - \frac{1}{2(1+t)} + \frac{4}{3(1+2t)}\right] dt$$

$$= \int \left[\frac{-1}{6(1-t)} + \frac{1}{2(1+t)} - \frac{4}{3}\frac{1}{(1+2t)}\right] dt$$

$$= \frac{1}{6}\log(1-\cos x) + \frac{1}{2}\log(1+\cos x) - \frac{2}{3}\log(1+2\cos x) + K$$

So, $A = \frac{1}{6}$, $B = \frac{1}{2}$ and $C = -\frac{2}{3}$

$$\therefore\quad 6(A+B+C) = 6\left(\frac{1}{6}+\frac{1}{2}-\frac{2}{3}\right) = 6\left(\frac{1+3-4}{6}\right) = 0$$

16. Let $I = \int \frac{1+x\cos x}{x(1-x^2e^{2\sin x})}\,dx$

On putting $xe^{\sin x} = t \Rightarrow (xe^{\sin x}\cos x + e^{\sin x})\,dx = dt$

$\Rightarrow\quad e^{\sin x}(x\cos x + 1)\,dx = dt$

$$\therefore\quad I = \int \frac{dt}{t(1-t^2)} = \int \frac{dt}{t(1-t)(1+t)}$$

Using partial fraction

$$= \int \left(\frac{1}{t} + \frac{1}{2(1-t)} - \frac{1}{2(1+t)}\right) dt$$

$$= \log|t| - \frac{1}{2}\log|1-t| - \frac{1}{2}\log|1+t| + C$$

$$= \log|t| - \frac{1}{2}\log|1-t^2| + C$$

$$= \log|xe^{\sin x}| - \frac{1}{2}\log|1 - x^2e^{2\sin x}| + C$$

17. $\int \frac{dx}{(x+1)(x-2)} = \int \left(-\frac{1}{3(x+1)} + \frac{1}{3(x-2)}\right) dx$

$$= -\frac{1}{3}\log(x+1) + \frac{1}{3}\log(x-2) + C$$

$$\therefore\quad A = -\frac{1}{3},\ B = \frac{1}{3}$$

$$\therefore\quad A + B = 0 \Rightarrow \frac{A}{B} = \frac{-\frac{1}{3}}{\frac{1}{3}} = -1$$

18. $\frac{1}{3}\int\left(\frac{1}{x^2+1} - \frac{1}{x^2+4}\right) dx$

$$\Rightarrow \frac{1}{3}\tan^{-1}x - \frac{1}{6}\tan^{-1}\frac{x}{2} = k\tan^{-1}x + l\tan^{-1}\frac{x}{2}$$

$$\therefore\quad k = \frac{1}{3} \text{ and } l = -\frac{1}{6}$$

19. $I = \int \underset{\text{II}}{x}\ \underset{\text{I}}{\log(1+x^2)}\,dx = \log(1+x^2)\cdot\frac{x^2}{2} - \int \frac{1}{1+x^2}\cdot 2x\cdot\frac{x^2}{2}\,dx$

$$= \frac{x^2}{2}\log(1+x^2) - \int \frac{x^3}{x^2+1}\,dx$$

$$I = \left(\frac{x^2+1}{2}\right)\log(1+x^2) - \left(\frac{x^2+1}{2}\right) + C$$

$$\therefore\quad \phi(x) = \frac{x^2+1}{2},\ \psi(x) = -\left(\frac{1+x^2}{2}\right)$$

20. $I = \int \frac{4e^x + 6e^{-x}}{9e^x - 4e^{-x}}\,dx$

$I = \int \frac{4e^{2x}+6}{9e^{2x}-4}\,dx$, put $9e^{2x} - 4 = z \Rightarrow 18e^{2x}dx = dz$

Then, $I = \int \frac{1}{z}\left\{4\cdot\frac{z+4}{9} + 6\right\}\frac{1}{18}\frac{dz}{\frac{z+4}{9}}$

$$= \int \frac{1}{z(z+4)}\left\{\frac{2z+8}{9} + 3\right\} dz$$

$$= \frac{1}{9}\int \frac{2z+35}{z(z+4)}\,dz = \frac{1}{9}\int \frac{2(z+4)+27}{z(z+4)}\,dz$$

$$= \frac{2}{9}\int\frac{dz}{z} + \frac{3}{4}\int\left(\frac{1}{z} - \frac{1}{z+4}\right) dz$$

$$= \left(\frac{2}{9}+\frac{3}{4}\right)\log z - \frac{3}{4}\log(z+4) + C$$

$$= \frac{35}{36}\log(9e^{2x}-4) - \frac{3}{4}\log(9e^{2x}) + C$$

$$= -\frac{3}{2}x + \frac{35}{36}\log(9e^{2x}-4) + C$$

On comparing with $Ax + B\log_e(9e^{2x}-4) + C$, we get

$$A = -\frac{3}{2},\ B = \frac{35}{36} \text{ and } A + B = -\frac{19}{36}$$

21. $\int \tan^3 x(\sec^2 x - 1)\,dx = \int \tan^3 x\sec^2 x\,dx - \int \tan^3 x\,dx$

$$I_1 = \int \tan^3 x\sec^2 x\,dx = \frac{\tan^4 x}{4} + C_1$$

$$I_2 = \int \tan x(\sec^2 x - 1)\,dx$$

$$= \frac{\tan^2 x}{2} - \ln|\sec x| + C_2$$

$$\therefore\ \int \tan^5 x\,dx = \frac{\tan^4 x}{4} - \frac{1}{2}\tan^2 x + \ln|\sec x| + C$$

On comparing with $4\tan^4 x + B\tan^2 x + g(x) + C$, we get

$$A = \frac{1}{4},\ B = -\frac{1}{2} \text{ and } g(x) = \ln|\sec x|$$

22. $\int \frac{\left(1+\frac{3}{x^2}\right)dx}{\left(x-\frac{3}{x}\right)^2 + x - \frac{3}{x} + 5} = \int \frac{dy}{y^2+y+5}$, where $y = x - \frac{3}{x}$

$$= \int \frac{dy}{\left(y+\frac{1}{2}\right)^2 + \left(\frac{\sqrt{19}}{2}\right)^2} = \frac{2}{\sqrt{19}}\tan^{-1}\left(\frac{2y+1}{\sqrt{19}}\right) + C$$

$$= \frac{2}{\sqrt{19}}\tan^{-1}\left[\frac{2(x+2)\left(x-\frac{3}{2}\right)}{\sqrt{19}x}\right] + C$$

$\therefore\ \alpha = \frac{3}{2}$ and $\beta = -2$ and $m = 2$ and $n = 19$

Now, put the values of α, β, m and n in given options to find the correct option(s).

23. $f''(x) = f(x)$

$$\Rightarrow \quad f''(x)f'(x) = f'(x)\, f(x)$$

$$\Rightarrow \quad \int f''(x)f'(x)dx = \int f'(x)f(x)\, dx$$

$$\Rightarrow \quad (f'(x))^2 = (f(x))^2$$

$$\Rightarrow \quad f'(x) = f(x)$$

$$\Rightarrow \quad f'(x) = -f(x) \qquad [\because f(0) = f'(0) = 0]$$

$$\Rightarrow \quad \int \frac{f(x)}{4 - f(x)}\, dx = \int \frac{\pm f'(x)}{4 - f(x)}\, dx$$

$$= \log_e(4 - f(x)) + C \text{ or } -\log_e(4 - f(x)) + C$$

24. $$\int \frac{dx}{\cos^3 x - \sin^3 x} = \frac{dx}{(\cos x - \sin x)\left(1 + \frac{\sin 2x}{2}\right)}$$

$$= \int \frac{(\cos x - \sin x)dx}{(1 - \sin 2x)\left(1 + \frac{\sin 2x}{2}\right)}$$

Let $\cos x + \sin x = t \Rightarrow (\cos x - \sin x)dx = dt$

$$= \int \frac{2dt}{(2 - t^2)(t^2 + 1)}$$

$$= \frac{2}{3}\int \frac{dt}{2 - t^2} + \frac{2}{3}\int \frac{dt}{t^2 + 1}$$

$$= \frac{2}{3}\frac{1}{2\sqrt{2}} \ln\left|\frac{\sqrt{2} + t}{\sqrt{2} - t}\right| + \frac{2}{3}\tan^{-1} t$$

$$= \frac{2}{3}\tan^{-1}(\sin x + \cos x) - \frac{1}{3\sqrt{2}} \ln\left|\frac{\cos x + \sin x - \sqrt{2}}{\cos x + \sin x + \sqrt{2}}\right| + C$$

25. Given, $\int \frac{x^x(x^{4x} + 1)(\log x + 1)}{1 + x^{6x}}dx$

$$= \int \frac{t^4 + 1}{1 + t^6}\, dt \qquad [\because x^x = t]$$

$$= \int \frac{(t^4 - t^2 + 1) + t^2}{(t^2 + 1)(t^4 - t^2 + 1)}\, dt$$

$$= \int \frac{dt}{1 + t^2} + \int \frac{t^2}{1 + t^6}\, dt$$

$$= \tan^{-1} t + \frac{1}{3}\tan^{-1} t^3 + C$$

$$= \tan^{-1} x^x + \frac{1}{3}\tan^{-1} x^{3x} + C$$

$$= \sum_{r=1}^{3} a_r \tan^{-1} x^{rx} + C \qquad \text{[given]}$$

$$= \tan^{-1} x^x + \frac{1}{3}\tan^{-1} x^{3x} + C$$

$$= a_1 \tan^{-1} x^x + a_2 \tan^{-1} x^{2x} + a_3 \tan^{-1} x^{3x} + C$$

On comparing, we get

$$a_1 = 1, a_2 = 0 \text{ and } a_3 = \frac{1}{3}$$

$\therefore \; a_1a_2a_3 = 1 \cdot 0 \cdot \frac{1}{3} = 0$

Also, $a_2 < a_3 < a_1$

and $\sum_{r=1}^{3} ra_r = 1 \cdot a_1 + 2 \cdot a_2 + 3 \cdot a_3 = 1 \cdot 1 + 2 \cdot 0 + 3\left(\frac{1}{3}\right) = 2$

26. $$\int \frac{4x^3 + 3x^2}{x^8 + 2x^7 + x^6 + 4x^4 + 4x^3 + 13}\, dx$$

$$= \frac{K}{K_1}\tan^{-1}(Ax^4 + Bx^3 + C) + D,$$

$$= \int \frac{(4x^3 + 3x^2)\, dx}{(x^4 + x^3)^2 + 4(x^4 + x^3) + 13}$$

$$= \int \frac{d(x^4 + x^3)}{(x^4 + x^3)^2 + 4(x^4 + x^3) + 13}$$

$$= \int \frac{dt}{t^2 + 4t + 13}, \qquad [t = x^4 + x^3]$$

$$= \int \frac{dt}{(t + 2)^2 + 3^2}$$

$$= \frac{1}{3}\tan^{-1}\left(\frac{t + 2}{3}\right)$$

$$= \frac{1}{3}\tan^{-1}\left(\frac{x^4 + x^3 + 2}{3}\right) + D$$

$$= \frac{K}{K_1}\tan^{-1}(Ax^4 + Bx^3 + C) + D$$

$\therefore \; K = 1, K_1 = 3, A = \frac{1}{3}, B = \frac{1}{3}, C = \frac{2}{3}$

$\therefore \; A + B = \frac{1}{3} + \frac{1}{3} = \frac{2}{3} = C, K_1 + K = 4$

27. Given, $f(x) = ax^3 + bx^2 + cx + d$ ...(i)

$\therefore \; f(0) = 1 \Rightarrow d = 1$ [by putting $x = 0$ in Eq. (i)]

Again, $f(1) = a + b + c + d \Rightarrow a + b + c = 1$

[using $d = 1$ and $f(1) = 2$]

Again, $f(x) = ax^3 + bx^2 + cx + d$

$\Rightarrow \quad f'(x) = 3x^2 + 2bx + c$ and $f''(x) = 6ax + 2b$

As, $x = 0$ is stationary point.

$\therefore \; f'(0) = f''(0) = 0$

$\Rightarrow \quad c = 0$ and $b = 0$

$\therefore \; a + b + c = 1 \Rightarrow a = 1$

$\therefore \quad f(x) = x^3 + 1$

Thus, $$\int \frac{(x^2 + x + 1)f(x)}{(x + 1)}\, dx = \frac{x}{a_1} + \frac{x^3}{b_1} + \frac{x^5}{c_1} + K$$

$$\Rightarrow \int \frac{(x^2 + x + 1)(x^3 + 1)}{(x + 1)}\, dx = \frac{x}{a_1} + \frac{x^3}{b_1} + \frac{x^5}{c_1} + K$$

$$\Rightarrow \quad \int (x^4 + x^2 + 1)\, dx = \frac{x}{a_1} + \frac{x^3}{b_1} + \frac{x^5}{c_1} + K$$

$$\Rightarrow \quad \frac{x^5}{5} + \frac{x^3}{3} + \frac{x}{1} = \frac{x}{a_1} + \frac{x^3}{b_1} + \frac{x^5}{c_1}$$

$$\Rightarrow \quad a_1 = 1, b_1 = 3, c_1 = 5$$

As, $(a_1, b_1, c_1) = 1, 3, 5$

$\Rightarrow \quad a_1, b_1, c_1 \in$ AP

HCF $(b_1, c_1) = 1$ and $b_1^2 + a_1 = 9 + 1 = 10 = 2c_1$

Also, $a_1, b_1, c_1 = 1, 3, 5$

i.e. $a_1 < b_1 < c_1$.

28. We have, $f'(x) = e^{(f(x) - g(x))}\, g'(x)\ \forall\ x \in R$

$\Rightarrow \quad f'(x) = \dfrac{e^{f(x)}}{e^{g(x)}}\, g'(x)$

$\Rightarrow \quad \dfrac{f'(x)}{e^{f(x)}} = \dfrac{g'(x)}{e^{g(x)}}$

$\Rightarrow \quad e^{-f(x)} f'(x) = e^{-g(x)}\, g'(x)$

On integrating both side, we get

$$e^{-f(x)} = e^{-g(x)} + C$$

At $x = 1$,

$$e^{-f(1)} = e^{-g(1)} + C$$

$$e^{-1} = e^{-g(1)} + C \qquad [\because f(1) = 1] \ \ldots(\text{i})$$

At $x = 2$,

$$e^{-f(2)} = e^{-g(2)} + C$$

$$\Rightarrow \quad e^{-f(2)} = e^{-1} + C \qquad [\because g(2) = 1] \ldots(\text{ii})$$

From Eqs. (i) and (ii), we get

$$e^{-f(2)} = 2e^{-1} - e^{-g(1)} \qquad \ldots(\text{iii})$$

$\Rightarrow \quad e^{-f(2)} < 2e^{-1}$

$\therefore \quad -f(2) < \log_e 2 - 1$

$\Rightarrow \quad f(2) > 1 - \log_e 2$

$$e^{-g(1)} + e^{-f(2)} = 2e^{-1} \qquad [\text{from Eq. (iii)}]$$

$\Rightarrow \quad e^{-g(1)} < 2e^{-1}$

$\Rightarrow \quad -g(1) < \log_e 2 - 1$

$\Rightarrow \quad g(1) > 1 - \log_e 2$

29. Here, as per notations given, we can substitute

$$\sqrt{1 + x^2} = (u - x)$$

As $m = 1 > 0$ and $p = 1 > 0$

$\Rightarrow \quad I = \int \dfrac{u^{15}}{u}\, du = \int u^{14} du = \dfrac{1}{15} u^{15} + C$

$$= \frac{1}{15}(x + \sqrt{1 + x^2})^{15} + C$$

30. Here, $\quad m = -1 < 0$

$$p = -2 < 0$$

Also, $-x^2 + 3x - 2 = -(x - 1)(x - 2)$

We can use case III

$\Rightarrow$ Putting, $\sqrt{-x^2 + 3x - 2} = u(x - 2)$

or $\quad (x - 1)u \quad$ or $\quad u(1 - x)$

31. Let $P = \sin^5 x \cos^3 x$

$\therefore \quad \dfrac{dP}{dx} = 5 \sin^4 x \cos^4 x - 3 \sin^6 x \cos^2 x$

$$= 5 \sin^4 x (1 - \sin^2 x) \cos^2 x - 3\sin^6 x \cos^2 x$$

$$= 5 \sin^4 x \cos^2 x - 8\sin^6 x \cos^2 x$$

$\therefore \quad P = 5I_{4,2} - 8I_{6,2}$

$\therefore \quad I_{4,2} = \dfrac{1}{5}(P + 8I_{6,2})$

32. Let $P = \sin^5 x \cos^3 x$

$\therefore \quad \dfrac{dP}{dx} = 5 \sin^4 x \cos^4 x - 3\sin^6 x \cos^2 x$

$$= 5 \sin^4 x \cos^4 x - 3 \sin^4 x (1 - \cos^2 x) \cos^2 x$$

$$= 8\sin^4 x \cos^4 x - 3\sin^4 x \cos^2 x$$

$\therefore \quad P = 8I_{4,4} - 3I_{4,2}$

$\therefore \quad I_{4,2} = \dfrac{1}{3}(-P + 8I_{4,4})$

33. Here, $2f'(x) = \lim\limits_{h \to 0} \left(\dfrac{f(x + h) - f(x)}{h} + \dfrac{f(x - h) - f(x)}{-h} \right)$

$$= \lim_{h \to 0} \left(\frac{f(x + h) - f(x - h)}{h} \right) \qquad \ldots(\text{i})$$

$\therefore \quad 2f'(0) = \lim\limits_{h \to 0} \left(\dfrac{f(h) - f(0)}{h} + \dfrac{f(-h) - f(0)}{-h} \right)$

$$= \lim_{h \to 0} \frac{f(h) - f(-h)}{h} \qquad \ldots(\text{ii})$$

Now by given relation, we have

$$f(h) - f(-h) = \frac{f(x + h) - f(x - h)}{-h} \text{ and } f(0) = 1$$

From Eqs. (i) and (ii), we have

$$\frac{f'(x)}{f(x)} = 2010$$

$\Rightarrow \quad f(x) = e^{2010x}, f(0) = 1$

$\therefore \ \{f(x)\}$ is non-periodic.

34. Here, $\int f(g(x)) \cos x\, dx = \int f(\log(\sin x)) . \cos x\, dx$

$$= \int e^{2010 \log (\sin x)} . \cos x\, dx$$

$$= \int (\sin x)^{2010} . \cos x\, dx$$

$$= \int (\sin x)^{2010} . \cos x\, dx$$

$$= \frac{(\sin x)^{2011}}{2011} + C$$

$\therefore \quad h(x) = \dfrac{(\sin x)^{2011}}{2011}$

$\Rightarrow \quad h\left(\dfrac{\pi}{2}\right) = \dfrac{1}{2011}$

Sol. (Q.Nos. 35 to 36)

Here, $f(x) = (x - 1)(x + 2)(x - 3)(x - 6) - 100$

$$= (x^2 - 4x + 3)(x^2 - 4x - 12) - 100$$

$$= (x^2 - 4x)^2 - 9(x^2 - 4x) - 136$$

$$= (x^2 - 4x + 8)(x^2 - 4x - 17)$$

35. $f(x) = (x^2 - 4x - 17)(x^2 - 4x + 8)$

$$= \{((x - 2)^2 - 21\}\{(x - 2)^2 + 4\}$$

$\because \quad (f(x))_{\min} = (-21)(4) = -84$

which occurs at $x = 2$

36. $\because \quad \int \frac{g(x)}{f(x)} = \frac{g(x)}{(x^2-4x-17)(x^2-4x+8)}$

$$= \frac{Ax+B}{x^2-4x-17} + \frac{Cx+D}{x^2-4x+8}$$

Clearly, A, B and C must be zero.

$$\therefore \quad \frac{g(x)}{(x^2-4x-17)(x^2-4x+8)} = \frac{D}{x^2-4x+8}$$

$$\therefore \quad g(x) = D(x^2-4x-17)$$

$$\Rightarrow \quad g(-2) = D(4+8-17) = -10 \qquad \text{[given]}$$

$$\Rightarrow \quad \frac{g(x)}{f(x)} = \frac{2(x^2-4x-17)}{(x^2-4x-17)(x^2-4x+8)} = \frac{2}{x^2-4x+8}$$

$$\therefore \quad \int \frac{g(x)}{f(x)}dx = \int \frac{2}{x^2-4x+8}dx = 2\int \frac{dx}{(x-2)^2+(2)^2}$$

$$= 2\cdot\frac{1}{2}\tan^{-1}\left(\frac{x-2}{2}\right) + C = \tan^{-1}\left(\frac{x-2}{2}\right) + C$$

37. Let $I = \int \frac{x(x-1)}{(x^2+1)(x+1)\sqrt{x^3+x^2+x}}dx$

$$= \int \frac{x(x-1)}{(x^2+1)(x+1)x\sqrt{x+1+\frac{1}{x}}}dx$$

$$= \int \frac{(x^2-1)}{(x^2+1)(x+1)^2\sqrt{x+1+\frac{1}{x}}}dx$$

$$= \int \frac{\left(1-\frac{1}{x^2}\right)}{\left(x+\frac{1}{x}\right)\left(x+2+\frac{1}{x}\right)\sqrt{x+1+\frac{1}{x}}}dx$$

On putting $x + \frac{1}{x} + 1 = t^2$, we get

$$I = \int \frac{2t\,dt}{(t^2-1)(t^2+1)\,t}$$

$$= 2\int \frac{dt}{(t^2-1)(t^2+1)}$$

$$= \int \frac{(t^2+1)-(t^2-1)}{(t^2-1)(t^2+1)}dt$$

$$= \int \left(\frac{1}{t^2-1} - \frac{1}{t^2+1}\right)dt$$

$$= \frac{1}{2}\log\left|\frac{t-1}{t+1}\right| - \tan^{-1}t + C$$

$$= \frac{1}{2}\log\left|\frac{\sqrt{x+\frac{1}{x}+1}-1}{\sqrt{x+\frac{1}{x}+1}+1}\right| - \tan^{-1}\sqrt{x+\frac{1}{x}+1} + C$$

$$\Rightarrow \quad f(x) = x + \frac{1}{x} + 1$$

$$\therefore \quad f(1) = 3$$

38. $\lim_{x\to\infty} \tan^{-1}\sqrt{f(x)} = \tan^{-1}(\infty) = \frac{\pi}{2}$

$$\therefore \quad [m+n] = 5$$

Sol. (Q.Nos. 39 to 40)

$$I = \int \frac{\ln(x+\sqrt{1+x^2})}{\sqrt{1+x^2}}dx$$

On putting $\ln(x+\sqrt{1+x^2}) = t$, we get

$$\frac{1}{(x+\sqrt{1+x^2})}\left(1+\frac{1}{2\sqrt{1+x^2}}\cdot 2x\right)dx = dt$$

$$\Rightarrow \quad \frac{1}{\sqrt{1+x^2}}dx = dt$$

$$\therefore \quad I = \int t\,dt = \frac{t^2}{2} + C$$

$$= \frac{1}{2}[\ln(x+\sqrt{1+x^2})]^2 + C = fog(x) + C$$

$$\Rightarrow f(x) = \frac{1}{2}x^2$$

and $g(x) = \ln(x+\sqrt{1+x^2})$

39. $\int f(x)\cdot g(x)\,dx = \int \frac{1}{2}x^2\ln(x+\sqrt{1+x^2})\,dx$

$$= \frac{1}{2}\left[\ln(x+\sqrt{1+x^2})\frac{x^3}{3} - \int \frac{1}{\sqrt{1+x^2}}\cdot\frac{x^3}{3}dx\right]$$

$$= \frac{1}{2}\left[\frac{1}{3}x^3\ln(x+\sqrt{1+x^2}) - \frac{1}{3}\int \frac{x^2\cdot x}{\sqrt{1+x^2}}dx\right]$$

$$[\because 1+x^2 = t^2 \Rightarrow 2x\,dx = 2t\,dt]$$

$$= \frac{1}{2}\left[\frac{1}{3}x^3\ln(x+\sqrt{1+x^2}) - \frac{1}{3}\int (t^2-1)\,dt\right]$$

$$= \frac{1}{6}x^3\ln(x+\sqrt{1+x^2}) - \frac{1}{6}\left(\frac{t^3}{3} - t\right) + e$$

$$= \frac{1}{6}x^3\ln(x+\sqrt{1+x^2}) - \frac{1}{18}(1+x^2)^{3/2} + \frac{1}{6}(1+x^2)^{1/2} + e$$

$$\Rightarrow a = \frac{1}{6}, b = -\frac{1}{18}, d = \frac{1}{6}$$

$$\therefore a + d - 12b = \frac{1}{6} + \frac{1}{6} - 12\left(-\frac{1}{18}\right)$$

$$= \frac{1}{3} + \frac{2}{3} = 1$$

40. $\int e^{g(x)}dx = \int e^{\ln(x+\sqrt{1+x^2})}dx = \int (x+\sqrt{1+x^2})\,dx$

$$= \frac{x^2}{2} + \left(\frac{x}{2}\sqrt{1+x^2} + \frac{1}{2}\ln(x+\sqrt{1+x^2}) + K_1\right)$$

$$= \frac{x}{2}(x+\sqrt{1+x^2}) + \frac{1}{2}g(x) + K_1$$

$$= \frac{1}{2}x\cdot e^{g(x)} + \frac{1}{2}g(x) + K_1$$

$$\Rightarrow K = \frac{1}{2}$$

$$\therefore \quad 4K = 2$$

41. $\int \frac{2x+3}{(x^2+3x)(x^2+3x+2)+1}\,dx$

Put $x^2+3x=t \Rightarrow (2x+3)\,dx=dt$

$$\int \frac{dt}{t(t+2)+1}=\int \frac{dt}{(t+1)^2}=C-\frac{1}{t+1}=C-\frac{1}{x^2+3x+1}$$

$\Rightarrow \quad a=1, b=3, c=1 \Rightarrow a+b+c=5$

42. $F(x)=\int \frac{3x+2}{\sqrt{x-9}}\,dx.$

Let $\quad x-9=t^2 \Rightarrow dx=2t\,dt$

$\therefore\ F(x)=\int \left(\frac{3(t^2+9)+2}{t}\cdot 2t\right)dt=2\int (29+3t^2)\,dt=2[29t+t^3]$

$F(x)=2[29\sqrt{x-9}+(x-9)^{3/2}]+C$

Given, $\quad F(10)=60=2[29+1]+C \Rightarrow C=0$

$\therefore \quad F(x)=2[29\sqrt{x-9}+(x-9)^{3/2}]$

$F(13)=2[29\times 2+4\times 2]=4\times 33=132$

Hence, sum of digits $=1+3+2=6$

43. $u(x)=7v(x) \Rightarrow u'(x)=7v'(x)$

$\Rightarrow \quad p=7 \quad$ [given]

Again, $\quad \frac{u(x)}{v(x)}=7 \Rightarrow \left(\frac{u(x)}{v(x)}\right)'=0 \Rightarrow q=0$

Now, $\quad \frac{p+q}{p-q}=\frac{7+0}{7-0}=1$

44. Let $t=\ln\left(\frac{x-1}{x+1}\right) \Rightarrow \frac{dt}{dx}=\frac{2}{x^2-1}$

$\therefore\ I=\int \frac{1}{2}t\,dt=\frac{1}{4}t^2+C \Rightarrow I=\frac{1}{4}\left[\ln\left(\frac{x-1}{x+1}\right)\right]^2+C$

$\Rightarrow \quad 6A=\frac{1}{4} \Rightarrow 24A=1$

45. $I=\int e^x\left(\frac{1}{(1-x)\sqrt{1-x^2}}+\sqrt{\frac{1+x}{1-x}}\right)dx$

As, $\quad \frac{d}{dx}\left(\sqrt{\frac{1+x}{1-x}}\right)=\frac{1}{(1-x)\sqrt{1-x^2}}$

$\therefore \quad I=e^x\sqrt{\frac{1+x}{1-x}}+C \Rightarrow I=e^x\left(\frac{1+x}{1-x}\right)^{1/2}+C$

$\Rightarrow \quad \mu=1, \lambda=\frac{1}{2}$

$\Rightarrow \quad 2(\mu+\lambda)=2\left(1+\frac{1}{2}\right)=2\times\frac{3}{2}=3$

46. $I=\int \frac{(e^x+\cos x+1)-(e^x+\sin x+x)}{e^x+\sin x+x}\,dx$

$=\ln(e^x+\sin x+x)-x+C$

$\therefore \quad f(x)=e^x+\sin x+x$ and $g(x)=-x$

$\Rightarrow \quad f(x)+g(x)=e^x+\sin x$

$\Rightarrow \quad \frac{f(x)+g(x)}{e^x+\sin x}=1$

47. On solving given integral, we get

$$A=\frac{1}{4}\tan^{-1}\frac{x+3}{4} \text{ and } B=\frac{1}{\sqrt{2}}\ln\left|\frac{x-9}{x+3}\right|$$

Now, $12(A+B)=12\left[\frac{1}{4}\tan^{-1}\frac{x+3}{4}+\frac{1}{2\cdot 6}\ln\left|\frac{x-9}{x+3}\right|\right]$

$=3\tan^{-1}\left(\frac{x+3}{4}\right)+\ln\left|\frac{x-9}{x+3}\right|$

$\Rightarrow \quad \lambda=3, \mu=1$

$\Rightarrow \quad \lambda+\mu=4$

48. $\frac{2\cos\frac{15}{2}x\cos\frac{3}{2}x}{1-2\left(2\cos^2\frac{5x}{2}-1\right)}=\frac{2\left(4\cos^3\frac{5x}{2}-3\cos\frac{5x}{2}\right)\cos\frac{3x}{2}}{3-4\cos^2\frac{5x}{2}}$

$=-2\cos\frac{5x}{2}\cos\frac{3x}{2}$

$=-(\cos 4x+\cos x)$

On integrating both sides, we get

$$I=-\frac{\sin 4x}{4}-\sin x+C$$

$\therefore \quad k=4$

49. $I=\int \frac{\tan x}{1+\tan x+\tan^2 x}\,dx=\int \frac{\frac{\sin x}{\cos x}}{\frac{1}{\cos^2 x}+\frac{\sin x}{\cos x}}\,dx$

$=\int \frac{\sin 2x}{2+\sin 2x}\,dx=\int dx-2\int \frac{dx}{2+\sin 2x}$

$=x-2\int \frac{\sec^2 x}{2\sec^2 x+2\tan x}\,dx$

Let $t=\tan x \Rightarrow dt=\sec^2 x\,dx$

$$=x-\frac{2}{2}\int \frac{dt}{t^2+t+1}=x-\int \frac{dt}{\left(t+\frac{1}{2}\right)^2+\left(\frac{\sqrt{3}}{2}\right)^2}$$

$$I=x-\frac{2}{\sqrt{3}}\tan^{-1}\left(\frac{2\tan x+1}{\sqrt{3}}\right)+C$$

50. $\int \sin^{5/2}x\cos^3 x\,dx=\int \sin^2 x\sin^{1/2}x\cos^2 x\cos x\,dx$

$=\int \sin^2 x\sin^{1/2}x(1-\sin^2 x)\cos x\,dx$

$=\int t^2 t^{1/2}(1-t^2)\,dt=\int [t^{5/2}-t^{9/2}]dt \quad$ [put $\sin x=t$]

$=\int t^{5/2}dt-\int t^{9/2}dt=\frac{t^{7/2}}{7/2}-\frac{t^{11/2}}{11/2}+C$

$=\frac{2}{7}t^{7/2}-\frac{2}{11}t^{11/2}+C=\frac{2}{7}\sin^{7/2}x-\frac{2}{11}\sin^{11/2}x+C$

$=2\sin^{7/2}x\left[\frac{1}{7}-\frac{1}{11}\sin^2 x\right]+C$

$\Rightarrow \quad A=7, B=7, C=11$

$\Rightarrow \quad (A+B)-C=(7+7)-11=3$

51. Let $I = \int (x^{2010} + x^{804} + x^{402})(2x^{1608} + 5x^{402} + 10)^{1/402} dx$

$$= \int x(x^{2009} + x^{803} + x^{401}) \cdot (2x^{1608} + 5x^{402} + 10)^{1/402} dx$$

$$= \int (x^{2009} + x^{803} + x^{401}) \cdot (2x^{2010} + 5x^{804} + 10x^{402})^{1/402} dx$$

Put $2x^{2010} + 5x^{804} + 10x^{402} = t$

$\Rightarrow 4020(x^{2009} + x^{803} + x^{401})\, dx = dt$

$$\therefore \quad I = \int \frac{1}{4020} \cdot (t)^{1/402} dt = \frac{1}{4020} \cdot \frac{t^{1/402 + 1}}{1/402 + 1}$$

$$= \frac{1}{4020} \cdot \frac{t^{403/402}}{403/402}$$

$$= \frac{1}{4030}(2x^{2010} + 5x^{804} + 10x^{402})^{403/402}$$

$\therefore\ a - 400 = 3$

52. Let $e^{x^3 + x^2 - 1}(3x^4 + 2x^3 + 2x)\, dx$

$$= \int \underset{\text{I}}{x^2} \cdot \underset{\text{II}}{e^{x^3 + x^2 - 1} \cdot (3x^2 + 2x)}\, dx + \int e^{x^3 + x^2 - 1} \cdot (2x)\, dx$$

Applying by parts in first integral, we get

$$I = x^2 e^{x^3 + x^2 - 1} - \int 2x \cdot e^{x^3 + x^2 - 1} dx + \int e^{x^3 + x^2 - 1}(2x)\, dx$$

$$= x^2 \cdot e^{x^3 + x^2 - 1} + C = h(x) + C$$

$\therefore \quad h(x) = x^2 \cdot e^{x^3 + x^2 - 1}$

Now, $\ln|h(x)| = 2 \ln x + x^3 + x^2 - 1$

$\therefore \quad \ln|h(1)| = 1$

53. Let $I_9 = \int \tan^9 x\, dx = \int \tan^7 x (\sec^2 x - 1)\, dx$

i.e. $I_9 = \dfrac{\tan^8 x}{8} - I_7$

Similarly, $I_7 = \dfrac{\tan^6 x}{6} - I_5$

....
....
....

$$I_3 = \frac{\tan^2 x}{2} - I_1 = \frac{\tan^2 x}{2} - \int \tan x\, dx$$

$$= \frac{\tan^2 x}{2} + \log|\cos x|$$

$\therefore\ I_9 =$ (a polynomial of degree 8 in $\tan x$) + $\log|\cos x| + C$

54. Given, $\quad f''(x) = f(x)$

$$\therefore \quad 2f'(x)\, f''(x) = 2f'(x) f(x) \Rightarrow \frac{d}{dx}(f'(x))^2 = \frac{d}{dx}(f(x))^2$$

On integrating, we get

$$(f'(x))^2 = (f(x))^2 + A_1 \qquad \text{...(i)}$$

$\Rightarrow \quad (f'(0))^2 = (f(0))^2 + A_1 \qquad [\because x = 0]$

$\Rightarrow \quad 16 = 9 + A_1 \qquad [\because f'(0) = 4, f(0) = 3]$

$\therefore \quad A_1 = 7$

Now, by Eq. (i), we get

$$(f'(x))^2 = (f(x))^2 + 7$$

$$\therefore \quad f'(x) = \sqrt{7 + (f(x))^2} \Rightarrow \frac{f'(x)}{\sqrt{(\sqrt{7})^2 + (f(x))^2}} = 1$$

Again, on integrating, we get

$$\log[f(x) + \sqrt{7 + (f(x))^2}] = x + A_2 \qquad \text{...(ii)}$$

$\Rightarrow \quad \log[f(0) + \sqrt{7 + (f(0))^2}] = A_2$

$\Rightarrow \quad \log(3 + 4) = A_2$ i.e. $A_2 = \log 7$

Again, by Eq. (ii), we have

$$f(x) + \sqrt{7 + (f(x))^2} = 7e^x$$

$\Rightarrow \quad 7 + (f(x))^2 = (7e^x - f(x))^2$

$\Rightarrow \quad 2f(x)e^x = 7\left(e^{2x} - \dfrac{1}{7}\right)$

$\therefore \quad f(x) = \dfrac{7}{2}\left(e^{2x} - \dfrac{1}{7}\right)e^{-x}$

$\therefore \quad f(7) = \dfrac{7}{2}\left(e^{14} - \dfrac{1}{7}\right)e^{-7} = k\left(e^{14} - \dfrac{1}{7}\right)e^{-7}$

$\therefore \quad k = \dfrac{7}{2} = 3.5$

55. For $0 < x < 1$

$$f(x) = \lim_{n \to \infty} (2x + 4x^3 + \ldots + 2n \cdot x^{2n - 1})$$

$$= 2x(1 \cdot 1 + 2 \cdot x^2 + 3 \cdot x^2 + \ldots \infty)$$

$$= 2x\left[\frac{1}{1 - x^2} + \frac{1 \cdot x^2}{(1 - x^2)^2}\right] = 2x\left[\frac{1}{(1 - x^2)^2}\right]$$

$$\int f(x)\, dx = \int \frac{2x}{(x^2 - 1)^2} dx = \frac{-1}{x^2 - 1} + C = \frac{P}{Q + R^{x^2}} + C$$

Therefore, $\dfrac{P}{Q - R} = \dfrac{-1}{-1 - (1)} = \dfrac{1}{2} = 0.5$

56. $\sqrt{x} \sin\sqrt{x} + \cos\sqrt{x}$

$$= \sqrt{1 + x}\left[\frac{\sqrt{x}}{\sqrt{1 + x}} \sin\sqrt{x} + \frac{1}{\sqrt{1 + x}} \cos\sqrt{x}\right]$$

$$= \sqrt{1 + x}\left[\sin\left(\sqrt{x} + \tan^{-1}\frac{1}{\sqrt{x}}\right)\right]$$

Let $t = \sqrt{x} + \tan^{-1}\dfrac{1}{\sqrt{x}}$

$$\Rightarrow dt = \left[\frac{1}{2\sqrt{x}} + \frac{1}{1 + \frac{1}{x}} \times \left(\frac{-1}{2}\right) \times \frac{1}{x\sqrt{x}}\right] dx$$

$$= \frac{1}{2\sqrt{x}}\left[1 - \frac{1}{1 + x}\right] dx = \frac{\sqrt{x}}{2(1 + x)} dx$$

$$\therefore \quad I = \frac{\sqrt{x + 1}\, \frac{\sqrt{x}}{x + 1} dx}{(\sqrt{x} \sin\sqrt{x} + \cos\sqrt{x})}$$

$$= \int \frac{2\, dt}{\sin t} = 2 \ln\left|\tan\frac{t}{2}\right| + C,$$

where $t = \sqrt{x} + \cos^{-1}\sqrt{\dfrac{x}{x + 1}} = f(x)$

$$f(1) = 1 + \frac{\pi}{4} = 1 + 0.78 = 1.78$$

57. Let

$$f(x)=\int \frac{(\sin^{12}x-\cos^{12}x)}{(\sin^2 x-\cos^2 x)((\sin^2 x+\cos^2 x)^3-3\sin^2 x\cos^2 x)}dx$$

$$=\int \frac{\sin^{12}x-\cos^{12}x}{(\sin^2 x-\cos^2 x)((\sin^2 x+\cos^2 x)^3-3\sin^2 x\cos^2 x)}dx$$

$$=\int \frac{(\sin^6 x-\cos^6 x)(\sin^6 x+\cos^6 x)}{(\sin^2 x-\cos^2 x)(\sin^6 x+\cos^6 x)}dx$$

$$=\int \frac{(\sin^2 x-\cos^2 x)(\sin^4 x+\cos^4 x+\sin^2 x\cos^2 x)\,dx}{(\sin^2 x-\cos^2 x)}$$

$$=\int (\sin^4 x+\cos^4 x+\sin^2 x\cos^2 x)dx$$

$$=\int (1-\sin^2 x\cos^2 x)\,dx$$

$$=\int \left(1-\frac{1}{4}\sin^2 2x\right)dx$$

$$=\int \left(1-\frac{1}{8}(1-\cos 4x)\right)dx$$

$$=\int \left(\frac{7}{8}+\frac{1}{8}\cos 4x\right)dx=\frac{7}{8}x+\frac{1}{32}\sin 4x+C$$

As, $f(0)=0 \Rightarrow C=0$

$\therefore\ f(x)=\frac{7}{8}x+\frac{1}{32}\sin 4x$

Hence, $f\left(\frac{\pi}{2}\right)=\frac{7}{16}\pi=\frac{k\pi}{16}$, so $k=\frac{7}{16}=0.4375$

58. $I=\int \frac{[f'(x)\,g(x)-g'(x)\,f(x)]\,dx}{[f(x)+g(x)]\sqrt{g(x)(f(x)-g(x))}}$

$$=\int \frac{\left(\frac{f'(x)g(x)-g'(x)\,f(x)}{(g(x))^2}\right)}{\left(\frac{f(x)}{g(x)}+1\right)\sqrt{\frac{f(x)}{g(x)}-1}}dx$$

Let $\frac{f(x)}{g(x)}-1=t^2 \Rightarrow \frac{f'(x)\,g(x)-g'(x)\,f(x)}{(g(x))^2}dx=2t\,dt$

$\therefore I=\int \frac{2t\,dt}{(t^2+2)\cdot t}=\frac{2}{\sqrt{2}}\tan^{-1}\left(\frac{t}{\sqrt{2}}\right)+C$

$=\sqrt{2}\tan^{-1}\left\{\sqrt{\frac{f(x)}{2g(x)}-\frac{1}{2}}\right\}+C$

$\Rightarrow m=2$ and $n=2$

$\therefore (m+n)^2=(4)^2=16$

59. Given, $f(x+y)=f(x)\,f'(y)+f'(x)f(y), \forall x,y\in R$

and $f(0)=1$

On putting $x=y=0$, we get

$$f(0)=f(0)\,f'(0)+f'(0)\,f(0)$$

$\Rightarrow\ 1=2f'(0)$

$\Rightarrow\ f'(0)=\frac{1}{2}$

On putting $x=x$ and $y=0$, we get

$$f(x)=f(x)\,f'(0)+f'(x)\,f(0)$$

$\Rightarrow\ f(x)=\frac{1}{2}f(x)+f'(x)$

$\Rightarrow\ f'(x)=\frac{1}{2}f(x)$

$\Rightarrow\ \frac{f'(x)}{f(x)}=\frac{1}{2}$

On integrating, we get

$$\log f(x)=\frac{1}{2}x+C$$

$\Rightarrow\ f(x)=Ae^{\frac{1}{2}x}$,

where $e^C=A$

If $f(0)=1$, then $A=1$

Hence, $f(x)=e^{\frac{1}{2}x}$

$\Rightarrow\ \log_e f(x)=\frac{1}{2}x$

$\Rightarrow\ \log_e f(4)=\frac{1}{2}\times 4=2$

Hence, $5\log_e(f(4))=10$

60. We have, $f(x)=(x+1)^3$

$\therefore\ \int (x+1)^3 dx=\frac{(x+1)^4}{4}+C$

$$g(x)=\frac{(x+1)^4}{4}$$

$$g(3)-g(1)=\frac{(4)^4}{4}-\frac{(2)^4}{4}=64-4=60$$

61. Let $I=\int \frac{1+x^4}{(1-x^4)^{3/2}}dx$

$$I=\int \frac{1+x^4}{x^3\left(\frac{1}{x^2}-x^2\right)^{3/2}}dx$$

$$I=\int \frac{x+\frac{1}{x^3}}{\left(\frac{1}{x^2}-x^2\right)^{3/2}}dx$$

Put $\frac{1}{x^2}-x^2=t \Rightarrow \left(-\frac{2}{x^3}-2x\right)dx=dt$

$\because\ I=-\frac{1}{2}\int \frac{dt}{t^{3/2}}=\frac{1}{\sqrt{t}}+C=\frac{x}{\sqrt{1-x^4}}+C$

$\therefore\ f(x)=\frac{x}{\sqrt{1-x^4}}$

Now, $\int \frac{x}{\sqrt{1-x^4}}dx=\frac{1}{2}\sin^{-1}x^2+C_2$

$\therefore\ g(x)=\frac{1}{2}\sin^{-1}x^2$

$$g\left(\frac{1}{\sqrt{2}}\right)=\frac{1}{2}\sin^{-1}\left(\frac{1}{\sqrt{2}}\right)^2=\frac{1}{2}\sin^{-1}\left(\frac{1}{2}\right)=\frac{1}{2}\times\frac{\pi}{6}=\frac{\pi}{12}$$

$\therefore\ k=12$

62. (A) If $\frac{\pi}{4} < x < \frac{3\pi}{8}$, then $\sin x > \cos x$

$$\therefore \int \frac{\sin x - \cos x}{|\sin x - \cos x|}\,dx = \int 1\,dx = x + C$$

(B) $$\int \frac{x^2 dx}{(x^3+1)(x^3+2)} = \frac{1}{3}\int 3x^2\left(\frac{1}{x^3+1} - \frac{1}{x^3+2}\right)dx$$

$$= \frac{1}{3}\ln\left|\frac{x^3+1}{x^3+2}\right| + C$$

(C) $$\int \sin^{-1}x\cos^{-1}x\,dx = \int\left[\frac{\pi}{2}\sin^{-1}x - (\sin^{-1}x)^2\right]dx$$

$$\Rightarrow \frac{\pi}{2}(x\sin^{-1}x + \sqrt{1-x^2}) - \{x(\sin^{-1}x)^2$$

$$+ \sin^{-1}x\,\sqrt[2]{1-x^2} - 2x\} + C \quad \text{[by parts]}$$

$$\Rightarrow \sin^{-1}x\left[\frac{\pi}{2}x - x\sin^{-1}x - 2\sqrt{1-x^2}\right] + \frac{\pi}{2}\sqrt{1-x^2} + 2x + C$$

$$\therefore \quad f^{-1}(x) = \sin^{-1}x,\ f(x) = \sin x$$

(D) $$\int \frac{dx}{x\ln|x|} = \ln|\ln|x|| + C$$

$$\therefore \quad f(x) = \ln|x|$$

63. (A) $$I = \int\left(\frac{x^2+\cos^2 x}{1+x^2}\right)\cdot \operatorname{cosec}^2 x\,dx$$

$$= \int\left(\frac{x^2+1-\sin^2 x}{1+x^2}\right)\cdot \operatorname{cosec}^2 x\,dx$$

$$= \int\left(\operatorname{cosec}^2 x - \frac{1}{1+x^2}\right)dx = -\cot x + \cot^{-1}x + k$$

$$\Rightarrow \quad A = 1,\ B = -1$$

(B) $$I = \int\sqrt{x+\sqrt{x^2+2}}\,dx$$

Put $\sqrt{x^2+2} + x = t \Rightarrow \sqrt{x^2+2} - x = \frac{2}{t}$

$$\therefore \quad 2x = t - \frac{2}{t} \Rightarrow 2\,dx = \left(1+\frac{2}{t^2}\right)dt$$

$$= \frac{1}{2}\int\left(\sqrt{t} + \frac{2}{t^{3/2}}\right)dt$$

$$\Rightarrow \quad I = \frac{1}{2}\cdot\frac{t^{3/2}}{\frac{3}{2}} + \frac{1}{-\frac{1}{2}t^{1/2}} + k$$

$$= \frac{1}{3}(x+\sqrt{x^2+2})^{3/2} - \frac{2}{\sqrt{x+\sqrt{x^2+2}}} + k$$

$$\Rightarrow \quad A = 1 \text{ and } B = 2$$

(C) $$I = \int\frac{2-x-x^2}{x^2\sqrt{2-x-x^2}}\,dx$$

$$= -\int\frac{dx}{\sqrt{2-x-x^2}} + 2\int\frac{dx}{x^2\sqrt{2-x-x^2}} - \int\frac{dx}{x\sqrt{2-x-x^2}}$$

$$= -\int\frac{dx}{\sqrt{\frac{9}{4}-\left(x+\frac{1}{2}\right)^2}} + 2\int -\frac{dt}{\sqrt{2-\frac{1}{t}-\frac{1}{t^2}}} + \int\frac{\frac{1}{t}dt}{\sqrt{2-\frac{1}{t}-\frac{1}{t^2}}}$$

$$\left(\text{put } x = \frac{1}{t}\right)$$

$$= -\sin^{-1}\left(\frac{2x+1}{3}\right) - \frac{1}{2}\int\frac{(4t-1)dt}{\sqrt{2t^2-t-1}} + \frac{1}{2}\int\frac{dt}{\sqrt{2t^2-t-1}}$$

$$= -\sin^{-1}\left(\frac{2x+1}{3}\right) - \frac{1}{2}\frac{\sqrt{2t^2-t-1}}{\frac{1}{2}} + \frac{1}{2\sqrt{2}}\int\frac{dt}{\sqrt{t^2-\frac{t}{2}-\frac{1}{2}+\frac{1}{16}-\frac{1}{16}}}$$

$$= -\sin^{-1}\left(\frac{2x+1}{3}\right) - \frac{\sqrt{2-x-x^2}}{x} + \frac{1}{2\sqrt{2}}\log\left|\left(t-\frac{1}{4}\right) + \sqrt{2t^2-t-1}\right| + K$$

$$= -\frac{\sqrt{2-x-x^2}}{x} + \frac{1}{2\sqrt{2}}\log\left|\frac{(4-x)+\sqrt{2-x-x^2}}{4x}\right| - \sin^{-1}\left(\frac{2x+1}{3}\right) + K$$

$$\therefore A = -1,\ B = 2$$

(D) $\int\frac{\sin 2x}{\sin^4 x + \cos^4 x}\,dx$, dividing N^r and D^r by $\cos^4 x$

$$I = \int\frac{2\tan x\cdot\sec^2 x}{\tan^4 x + 1}dx, \text{ put } \tan^2 x = t$$

$$\Rightarrow 2\tan x\cdot\sec^2 x\,dx = dt = \int\frac{dt}{t^2+1} = -\cot^{-1}(t) + C$$

$$\Rightarrow \quad -\cot^{-1}(\tan^2 x) + C$$

$$\therefore\ B = -1$$

64. Given that $f'(x) = \frac{f(x)}{b^2+x^2}$

$$\int\frac{f'(x)}{f(x)}dx = \int\frac{dx}{x^2+b^2} \quad \text{[taking integration on both sides]}$$

$$\Rightarrow \quad \ln|f(x)| = \frac{1}{b}\tan^{-1}\left(\frac{x}{b}\right) + C$$

Now, $\quad f(0) = 1$

$\therefore \quad C = 0$

$$\therefore \quad |f(x)| = e^{\frac{1}{b}\tan^{-1}\left(\frac{x}{b}\right)}$$

$$\Rightarrow \quad f(x) = \pm e^{\frac{1}{b}\tan^{-1}\left(\frac{x}{b}\right)}$$

$\because \quad f(0) = 1$

$$\therefore \quad f(x) = e^{\frac{1}{b}\tan^{-1}\left(\frac{x}{b}\right)}$$

$$\because \quad f'(x) = e^{\frac{1}{b}\tan^{-1}\frac{x}{b}} \times \frac{1}{b^2+x^2} > 0$$

for all the value of b.

$\therefore$ $f(x)$ is increasing function for all value of b.

So, option (a) is true.

$$f(-x) = e^{-\frac{1}{b}\tan^{-1}\left(\frac{x}{b}\right)}$$

$$\therefore \quad f(x)\cdot f(-x) = e^0 = 1$$

65. $\lim_{x\to 0} f(x) = \lim_{x\to 0} x \cdot \lim_{x\to 0} g(x) = 0 \quad [\because \lim_{x\to 0} g(x) = 1 \text{ given}]$

$$\because \quad f'(x) = \lim_{h\to 0}\frac{f(x+h)-f(x)}{h}$$

$$\Rightarrow \quad f'(x) = \lim_{h\to 0}\frac{f(x)+f(h)+f(x)\cdot f(h)-f(x)}{h}$$

$$\Rightarrow \quad f'(x) = \lim_{h\to 0}\frac{f(h)}{h}(1+f(x)) \left[\because \lim_{h\to 0}\frac{f(h)}{h} = \lim_{h\to 0}\frac{hg(h)}{h} = 1\right]$$

$$\Rightarrow \quad f'(x) = 1 + f(x)$$

$$\Rightarrow \quad \frac{f'(x)}{1+f(x)} = 1$$

$$\Rightarrow \int \frac{f'(x)}{1+f(x)}\,dx = \int dx$$

$$\Rightarrow \quad \ln(1+f(x)) = x + c$$

$$\Rightarrow \quad 1 + f(x) = e^{x+c} \qquad [\because f(0) = 0 \Rightarrow c = 0]$$

$$\Rightarrow \quad f(x) = e^x - 1$$

$$\Rightarrow \quad f'(x) = e^x$$

So, $f(x)$ is differentiable at every $x \in R$

$$f'(0) = e^0 = 1 \qquad [\text{put } x = 0]$$

$$g(x) = \frac{f(x)}{x} = \begin{cases} \dfrac{e^x - 1}{x}; & x \neq 0 \\ 1; & x = 0 \end{cases}$$

$\therefore g(x)$ is differentiable at every $x \in R$.

So, option a, b, d are correct.

Exercise 3 - Challenging Problems

1. $I_n = \int z^n e^{1/z}\,dz$,

Applying integration by parts taking $e^{1/z}$ as first function and z^n as second function.

We get,

$$I_n = \frac{e^{1/z}\cdot z^{n+1}}{(n+1)} - \int e^{1/z}\left(-\frac{1}{z^2}\right)\cdot\frac{z^{n+1}}{n+1}\,dz$$

$$= \frac{e^{1/z}\cdot z^{n+1}}{(n+1)} + \frac{1}{(n+1)}\int e^{1/z}\cdot z^{n-1}\,dz$$

$$I_n = \frac{e^{1/z}\cdot z^{n+1}}{(n+1)} + \frac{I_{n-1}}{(n+1)}$$

$$= \frac{e^{1/z}\cdot z^{n+1}}{(n+1)} + \frac{1}{(n+1)}\left[\frac{e^{1/z}\cdot z^n}{n} + \frac{1}{n}I_{n-2}\right]$$

$$= \frac{e^{1/z}(z)^{n+1}}{(n+1)} + \frac{e^{1/z}\cdot(z)^n}{(n+1)\,n} + \frac{1}{(n+1)\,n}I_{n-2}$$

$$= \frac{e^{1/z}\cdot(z)^{n+1}}{(n+1)} + \frac{e^{1/z}\cdot(z)^n}{(n+1)n} + \frac{e^{1/z}\cdot(z)^{n-1}}{(n+1)n\cdot(n-1)} + \frac{1}{(n+1)n(n-1)}I_{n-3}$$

… …

… …

$$= \frac{e^{1/z}\cdot(z)^{n+1}}{n+1} + \frac{e^{1/z}\cdot(z)^n}{(n+1)\,n} + \ldots + \frac{e^{1/z}\cdot(z)^1}{(n+1)\,n\ldots 3\cdot 2} + \frac{1}{(n+1)\,n\,(n-1)\ldots 3\cdot 2}I_0$$

Multiplying both the sides by $(n+1)!$, we get

$$(n+1)!\,I_n = (e^{1/z}\cdot z^{n+1}\cdot n! + e^{1/z}\cdot z^n\,(n-1)! + \ldots + \ldots + e^{1/z}\cdot z^3\cdot(2)! + e^{1/z}\cdot z^2\cdot 1!) + I_0$$

$$\Rightarrow \quad I_n\,(n+1)! = I_0 + e^{1/z}\,(1!\,z^2 + 2!\,z^3 + \ldots + n!\,z^{n+1})$$

Hence Proved.

2. $I_n = \int x^n\sqrt{a^2-x^2}\,dx = \int \underset{\text{I}}{x^{n-1}}\cdot\{\underset{\text{II}}{x\sqrt{a^2-x^2}}\}\,dx$

Applying integration by parts, we get

$$I_n = x^{n-1}\cdot\left\{-\frac{(a^2-x^2)^{3/2}}{3}\right\} + \int (n-1)\,x^{n-2}\cdot\left\{-\frac{(a^2-x^2)^{3/2}}{3}\right\}dx$$

$$= -\frac{x^{n-1}(a^2-x^2)^{3/2}}{3} + \frac{(n-1)}{3}\int x^{n-2}\cdot(a^2-x^2)\sqrt{a^2-x^2}\,dx$$

$$= -\frac{x^{n-1}(a^2-x^2)^{3/2}}{3} + \frac{(n-1)\,a^2}{3}I_{n-2} - \frac{(n-1)}{3}I_n$$

$$\therefore \quad I_n + \frac{(n-1)}{3}I_n = -\frac{x^{n-1}(a^2-x^2)^{3/2}}{3} + \frac{(n-1)\,a^2}{3}I_{n-2}$$

$$\left(\frac{n+2}{3}\right)I_n = -\frac{x^{n-1}(a^2-x^2)^{3/2}}{3} + \frac{(n-1)\,a^2}{3}I_{n-2}$$

$$I_n = -\frac{x^{n-1}(a^2-x^2)^{3/2}}{(n+2)} + \frac{(n-1)\,a^2}{(n+2)}I_{n-2}$$

Hence Proved.

3. $\because I_m = \int(\sin x + \cos x)^m\,dx$

$$= \int(\sin x + \cos x)^{m-1}\cdot(\sin x + \cos x)\,dx,$$

Applying integration by parts

$$I_m = (\sin x + \cos x)^{m-1}(\sin x - \cos x) - \int(m-1)(\sin x + \cos x)^{m-2}\cdot(\cos x - \sin x)\cdot(\sin x - \cos x)\,dx$$

$$= (\sin x + \cos x)^{m-1}(\sin x - \cos x) + (m-1)\int(\sin x + \cos x)^{m-2}(\sin x - \cos x)^2\,dx$$

As we know, $(\sin x + \cos x)^2 + (\sin x - \cos x)^2 = 2$,

$$\therefore I_m = (\sin x + \cos x)^{m-1}(\sin x - \cos x) + (m-1)\int(\sin x + \cos x)^{m-2}\cdot\{2 - (\sin x + \cos x)^2\}\,dx$$

$$= (\sin x + \cos x)^{m-1}(\sin x - \cos x) + (m-1)\int 2(\sin x + \cos x)^{m-2}\,dx - (m-1)\int(\sin x + \cos x)^m\,dx$$

$$I_m = (\sin x + \cos x)^{m-1}(\sin x - \cos x) + 2(m-1)I_{m-2} - (m-1)I_m$$

or $(m-1)I_m + I_m = (\sin x + \cos x)^{m-1}(\sin x - \cos x) + 2(m-1)I_{m-2}$

or $\quad m\,I_m = (\sin x + \cos x)^{m-1}(\sin x - \cos x) + 2(m-1)I_{m-2}$

Hence Proved.

4. We have, $I_{(m,n)} = \int \underset{\text{I}}{\cos^m x} \cdot \underset{\text{II}}{\cos nx}\, dx$

$$= (\cos^m x)\left[\frac{\sin nx}{n}\right] - \int m\cos^{m-1} x(-\sin x)\cdot\frac{\sin nx}{n}\,dx$$

$$= \frac{1}{n}\cos^m x\cdot\sin nx + \frac{m}{n}\int \cos^{m-1} x\,\{\sin x\cdot\sin nx\}\,dx$$

As we have, $\cos(n-1)x = \cos nx\cos x + \sin nx \sin x$

$$\therefore\ I_{m,n} = \frac{1}{n}\cos^m x\cdot\sin x + \frac{m}{n}\int \cos^{m-1} x\,\{\cos(n-1)x - \cos nx\cdot\cos x\}\,dx$$

$$= \frac{1}{n}\cos^m x\cdot\sin x + \frac{m}{n}\int \cos^{m-1} x\cdot\cos(n-1)x\,dx - \frac{m}{n}\int\cos^m x\cdot\cos nx\,dx$$

$$= \frac{1}{n}\cos^m x\cdot\sin nx + \frac{m}{n}I_{(m-1,n-1)} - \frac{m}{n}I_{(m,n)}$$

$$I_{(m,n)} + \frac{m}{n}I_{(m,n)} = \frac{1}{n}[\cos^m x\cdot\sin nx + m\,I_{(m-1,n-1)}]$$

$$\left(\frac{m+n}{n}\right)I_{(m,n)} = \frac{1}{n}[\cos^m x\cdot\sin nx + m\,I_{(m-1,n-1)}]$$

$$(m+n)\,I_{(m,n)} = \cos^m x\cdot\sin nx + m\,I_{(m-1,n-1)}$$

5. $$I = \int\frac{\tan\left(\frac{\pi}{4}-x\right)dx}{\cos^2 x\sqrt{\tan^3 x + \tan^2 x + \tan x}}$$

$$= \int\frac{(1-\tan^2 x)\,dx}{(1+\tan x)^2\cos^2 x\sqrt{\tan^3 x + \tan^2 x + \tan x}}$$

$$I = \int\frac{-\left(1-\frac{1}{\tan^2 x}\right)\sec^2 x\,dx}{\left(\tan x + 2 + \frac{1}{\tan x}\right)\sqrt{\tan x + 1 + \frac{1}{\tan x}}}$$

Let $\quad y = \sqrt{\tan x + 1 + \frac{1}{\tan x}}$

$$\Rightarrow 2y\,dy = \left(\sec^2 x - \frac{1}{\tan^2 x}\cdot\sec^2 x\right)dx$$

$$\therefore\quad I = \int\frac{-2y\,dy}{(y^2+1)\cdot y} = -2\int\frac{dy}{1+y^2} = -2\tan^{-1}y + C$$

$$= -2\tan^{-1}\left(\sqrt{\tan x + 1 + \frac{1}{\tan x}}\right) + C$$

6. We know, $\log(1-x) = -\left\{x + \frac{x^2}{2} + \frac{x^3}{3} + \frac{x^4}{4} + \dots\infty\right\}$

Put x^2 instead of x in the above identity,

$$\Rightarrow\quad \log(1-x^2) = -\left\{x^2 + \frac{x^4}{2} + \frac{x^6}{3} + \frac{x^8}{4} + \dots\infty\right\}$$

$$\Rightarrow\quad x^2\log(1-x^2) = -\left\{x^4 + \frac{x^6}{2} + \frac{x^8}{3} + \frac{x^{10}}{4} + \dots\infty\right\}$$

Integrating both the sides, we get

$$\int x^2\log(1-x^2)\,dx = -\left\{\frac{x^5}{1\cdot5} + \frac{x^7}{2\cdot7} + \frac{x^9}{3\cdot9} + \dots\infty\right\} + C$$

Now, to find constant of integration, put $x = 0$

$$\Rightarrow\qquad 0 = 0 + C \Rightarrow C = 0$$

$$\therefore\quad \int \underset{\text{II}}{x^2}\,\underset{\text{I}}{\log(1-x^2)}\,dx = -\left\{\frac{x^5}{1\cdot5} + \frac{x^7}{2\cdot7} + \frac{x^9}{3\cdot9} + \dots\infty\right\}$$

Applying integration by parts, and taking limits 0 to 1 for LHS

$$= \left(\frac{x^3}{3}\log(1-x^2)\right)_0^1 - \int_0^1\frac{x^3}{3}\cdot\frac{1(-2x)}{1-x^2}\,dx$$

$$= \left(\frac{x^3}{3}\log(1-x^2)\right)_0^1 + \frac{2}{3}\left(-\frac{x^3}{3} - x + \frac{1}{2}\log\left|\frac{1+x}{1-x}\right|\right)_0^1$$

Taking $\log(1-x^2) = \log(1+x) + \log(1-x)$

and $\log\left(\frac{1+x}{1-x}\right) = \log(1+x) - \log(1-x)$

$$\Rightarrow\ \frac{1}{3}\log 2 + \frac{1}{3}\log 2 - \frac{2}{3} - \frac{2}{9} + \lim_{x\to1}\left(\frac{x^3}{3} - \frac{1}{3}\right)\log(1-x)$$

$$\left[\because \lim_{x\to1}(x^3-1)\log(1-x) = 0\right]$$

$$\Rightarrow\qquad \frac{2}{3}\log 2 - \frac{8}{9} = \text{RHS}$$

$$\therefore\quad \frac{1}{1\cdot5} + \frac{1}{2\cdot7} + \frac{1}{3\cdot9} + \dots = \frac{2}{3}\log(2) - \frac{8}{9}$$

7. Here, $I = \int\frac{a + b\sin x}{(b + a\sin x)^2}\,dx = \frac{b}{a}\int\frac{\frac{a^2}{b} - b + (b + a\sin x)}{(b + a\sin x)^2}\,dx$

$$I = \frac{a^2 - b^2}{a}\int\frac{dx}{(b + a\sin x)^2} + \frac{b}{a}\int\frac{dx}{(b + a\sin x)}\qquad\dots\text{(i)}$$

Now, let $A = \frac{\cos x}{b + a\sin x}$

$$\Rightarrow\qquad \frac{dA}{dx} = \frac{-b\sin x - a}{(b + a\sin x)^2}$$

$$\Rightarrow\qquad \frac{dA}{dx} = -\frac{b}{a}\left\{\frac{a\sin x + b + \frac{a^2}{b} - b}{(b + a\sin x)^2}\right\}$$

$$\Rightarrow\qquad \frac{dA}{dx} = -\frac{b}{a}\left\{\frac{1}{b + a\sin x} + \frac{a^2 - b^2}{b\,(b + a\sin x)^2}\right\}$$

Integrating both the sides w.r.t. 'x', we get

$$A = -\frac{b}{a}\int\frac{dx}{b + a\sin x} - \frac{(a^2 - b^2)}{a}\int\frac{dx}{(b + a\sin x)^2}$$

$$\Rightarrow\qquad \frac{a^2 - b^2}{a}\int\frac{dx}{(b + a\sin x)^2} = -\frac{b}{a}\int\frac{dx}{b + a\sin x} - A\qquad\dots\text{(ii)}$$

From Eqs. (i) and (ii), we get

$$I = -\frac{b}{a}\int\frac{dx}{(b + a\sin x)} - A + \frac{b}{a}\int\frac{dx}{(b + a\sin x)}$$

$$\Rightarrow\ I = -A + C\ \Rightarrow\ I = -\left(\frac{\cos x}{b + a\sin x}\right) + C$$

8. Let $I = \int\frac{dx}{(x-1)^{3/4}(x+2)^{5/4}} = \int\frac{dx}{(x+2)^2\left(\frac{(x-1)}{(x+2)}\right)^{3/4}}$

Let $\frac{x-1}{x+2} = t$ so that $\frac{3}{(x+2)^2}\,dx = dt$

$$\therefore\ I = \int\frac{dt}{3\,t^{3/4}} = \frac{1}{3}\int t^{-3/4}\,dt = \frac{1}{3}\cdot\frac{t^{1/4}}{1/4} + C = \frac{4}{3}\left(\frac{x-1}{x+2}\right)^{1/4} + C$$

2

> *Mathematics knows no races or geographic boundaries; for Mathematics, the cultural world is one country.*
>
> **-David Hilbert**

Definite Integral

Learning Milestones

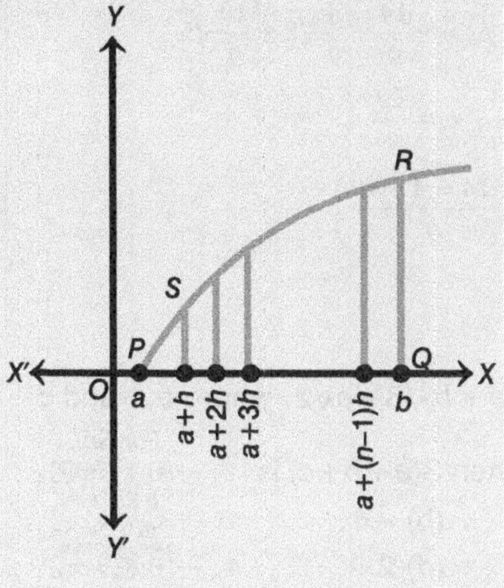

Practice Milestones

Milestone 1 Evaluation of Definite Integrals by Substitution

• Introduction • Geometrical Interpretation of Definite Integral • Evaluation of Definite Integrals by Substitution

2.1 Introduction

The definite integral has a unique value. The definite integral is introduced either as limit of a sum or as anti-derivative in the given integral.

Let f be a function of x defined in the closed interval $[a, b]$ and ϕ be another function, such that $\phi'(x) = f(x)$ for all x in the domain of f, then

$$\int_a^b f(x)\, dx = [\phi(x) + c]_a^b = \phi(b) - \phi(a)$$

is called the definite integral of the function $f(x)$ over the interval $[a, b]$, a and b are called the limits of integration, a is called the lower limit and b is called the upper limit.

JEE Focus Points

Concept Inside Video

- In definite integrals, constant of integration is never present.
- If f is continuous on $[a, b)$ and has infinite discontinuity at b, then $\int_a^b f(x)\, dx = \lim_{x \to b^-} F(x) - F(a)$, provided limit exist.
- If f is continuous on $(a, b]$ and has infinite discontinuity at a, then $\int_a^b f(x)\, dx = F(b) - \lim_{x \to a^+} F(x)$
- If f is not defined at $x = a, b$, then $\int_a^b f(x)\, dx = \lim_{x \to b^-} F(x) - \lim_{x \to a^+} F(x)$, where $F(x)$ is an arbitrary anti-derivative of $f(x)$.

Working Rules

To evaluate definite integral $\int_a^b f(x)\, dx$.

1. First evaluate the indefinite integral $\int f(x)\, dx$ and suppose the result is $g(x)$.
2. Next find $g(b)$ and $g(a)$.
3. Finally, the value of the definite integral is obtained by subtracting $g(a)$ from $g(b)$.

Thus, $\int_a^b f(x)\, dx = [g(x)]_a^b = g(b) - g(a)$

JEE SCANNER

Example Similar to PYQ Asked in JEE Main 2022

If $\int_0^1 \frac{dx}{\sqrt{4+x} + \sqrt{1+x}} = a + b\sqrt{2} + c\sqrt{5}$, *where a, b and c are rational number, then* $9(a + b + c)$ *is*

(a) 8 (b) −8

(c) 4 (d) −4

Sol. (b) Let $I = \int_0^1 \frac{dx}{\sqrt{4+x} + \sqrt{1+x}} = \int_0^1 \frac{(4+x)^{1/2} - (1+x)^{1/2}}{(4+x) - (1+x)}\, dx$

$$= \frac{1}{3}\int_0^1 ((4+x)^{1/2} - (1+x)^{1/2})\, dx$$

$$= \frac{1}{3}\left[\frac{2}{3}(4+x)^{3/2} - \frac{2}{3}(1+x)^{3/2}\right]_0^1$$

$$= \frac{2}{9}[(5^{3/2} - 4^{3/2}) - (2^{3/2} - 1^{3/2})]$$

$$= \frac{2}{9}[(5\sqrt{5} - 8) - (2\sqrt{2} - 1)]$$

$$= \frac{2}{9}(5\sqrt{5} - 8 - 2\sqrt{2} + 1)$$

$$= \frac{2}{9}[5\sqrt{5} - 2\sqrt{2} - 7] = -\frac{14}{9} - \frac{4}{9}\sqrt{2} + \frac{10}{9}\sqrt{5}$$

Here, $a = -\frac{14}{9}$, $b = -\frac{4}{9}$, $c = \frac{10}{9}$

$$\therefore \quad 9(a + b + c) = 9\left(\frac{-14 - 4 + 10}{9}\right) = -8$$

Skill Builder

If $\int_0^1 \frac{dx}{\sqrt{3+x} + \sqrt{x+1}} = a + b\sqrt{3} + c\sqrt{2}$, where a, b and c are rational number, then $3(a + b + c)$ is

(a) 8 (b) − 4

(c) 4 (d) 2

For Sol.

■ **For more practice** See Q.5 of Milestone Practice 2.1.

Example 1. Evaluate

(i) $\int_0^1 \frac{1}{3+4x}\,dx$ (ii) $\int_0^{\pi/2} \sin^4 x\,dx$

Sol. (i) Here, $I = \int_0^1 \frac{1}{3+4x}\,dx = \left[\frac{\ln(3+4x)}{4}\right]_0^1$

$$= \frac{1}{4}[\ln 7 - \ln 3] = \frac{1}{4}\ln\left(\frac{7}{3}\right)$$

(ii) Let $I = \int_0^{\pi/2} \sin^4 x\,dx$

$$= \frac{1}{4}\int_0^{\pi/2} (2\sin^2 x)^2\,dx = \frac{1}{4}\int_0^{\pi/2} (1-\cos 2x)^2\,dx$$

$$= \frac{1}{4}\int_0^{\pi/2} (1 - 2\cos 2x + \cos^2 2x)\,dx$$

$$= \frac{1}{4}\int_0^{\pi/2} \left(1 - 2\cos 2x + \frac{1+\cos 4x}{2}\right) dx$$

$$= \frac{1}{4}\int_0^{\pi/2} \left(\frac{3 - 4\cos 2x + \cos 4x}{2}\right) dx$$

$$= \frac{1}{8}\left[3x - \frac{4}{2}\sin 2x + \frac{\sin 4x}{4}\right]_0^{\pi/2}$$

$$= \frac{1}{8}\left[\left(\frac{3\pi}{2} - 2\sin\pi + \frac{1}{4}\sin 2\pi\right) - 0\right]$$

$$= \frac{1}{8}\left(\frac{3\pi}{2} - 0 + 0\right) = \frac{3\pi}{16}$$

Example 2. Find all the values of a for which $\int_1^2 \{a^2 + (4-4a)x + 4x^3\}dx \le 12$

Sol. We have,

$$\int_1^2 \{a^2 + (4-4a)x + 4x^3\}dx \le 12$$

$$\Rightarrow \quad [a^2 x + (2-2a)x^2 + x^4]_1^2 \le 12$$

$$\Rightarrow a^2(2-1) + (2-2a)(4-1) + (2^4 - 1^4) \le 12$$

$$\Rightarrow \quad a^2 + 3(2-2a) + 15 \le 12$$

$$\Rightarrow \quad a^2 - 6a + 9 \le 0 \Rightarrow (a-3)^2 \le 0$$

$$\therefore \quad a = 3$$

Example 3. Evaluate $\int_0^1 \ln x\,dx$.

Sol. The function $\ln x$ is not defined at $x = 0$ and defined at $x = 1$.

$$I = \int_0^1 \ln x\,dx$$

$$= [x\ln x - x]_0^1$$

$$= (\ln 1 - 1) - \lim_{x\to 0^+} (x\ln x - x)$$

[using by parts]

$$= -1 - 0 = -1$$

2.2 Geometrical Interpretation of Definite Integral

In general, $\int_a^b f(x)\,dx$ represents the algebraic sum of the areas of the figures bounded by the curve $y = f(x)$, the X-axis and the straight lines $x = a$ and $x = b$.

The areas above X-axis are taken with plus sign and the areas below X-axis are taken with minus sign,

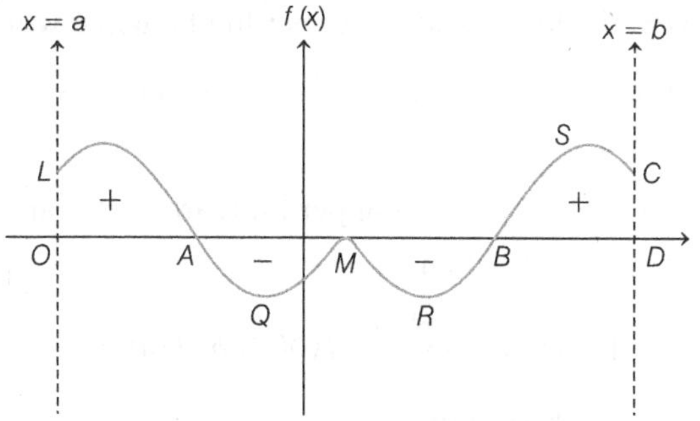

i.e. $\int_a^b f(x)\,dx = \text{Area}(OLA) - \text{Area}(AQM) - \text{Area}(MRB)$
$+ \text{Area}(BSCD)$

JEE SCANNER

Example Similar to PYQ Asked in JEE Main 2022

Evaluate $\int_{-1}^{1} \min\{|x|, |x-1|, |x+1|\}\,dx$.

Sol. The graph of $f(x) = \min\{|x|, |x-1|, |x+1|\}$ is shown in figure.

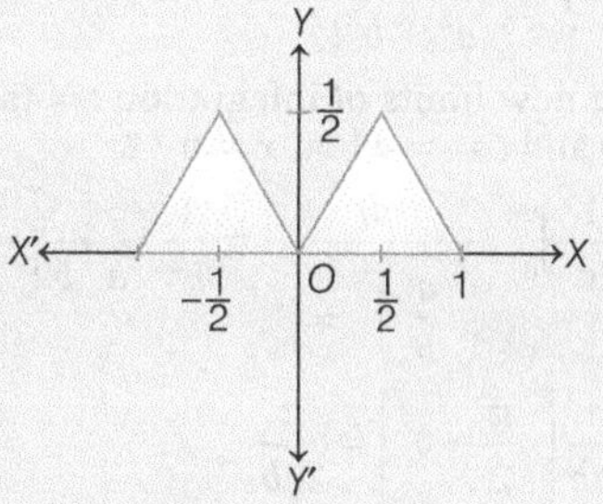

$\therefore \int_{-1}^{1} \min\{|x|, |x-1|, |x+1|\}\,dx$

Area of shaded region $= 2 \times \frac{1}{2} \times 1 \times \frac{1}{2}$

$= \frac{1}{2}$ sq unit

Skill Builder

Evaluate $\int_{-2}^{2} \min\{x-[x], -x-[-x]\}\,dx$, where [·] denotes the greatest integer function.

For Sol.

■ **For more practice** See Q.12 of Milestone Practice 2.1.

2.3 Evaluation of Definite Integrals by Substitution

Sometimes, the indefinite integral may need substitution, say $x = \phi(t)$. Then, in that case don't forget to change the limits of integration a and b corresponding to the new variable t. The substitution $x = \phi(t)$ is not valid, if it is not continuous in the interval $[a, b]$.

By the substitution $x = \phi(t)$ in the definite integral $\int_a^b f(x)\,dx$, the lower and the upper limit change when $x \to a$, then $\phi(t) \to a \Rightarrow t \to \phi^{-1}(a)$ and when $x \to b$, then $\phi(t) \to b \Rightarrow t \to \phi^{-1}(b)$.

Hence, the new lower and upper limit are $\phi^{-1}(a)$ and $\phi^{-1}(b)$ respectively, then

$$\int_a^b f(x)\,dx = \int_{\phi^{-1}(a)}^{\phi^{-1}(b)} f(\phi(t))\,\phi'(t)\,dt$$

Example 4. Show that

$$\int_0^{\pi/2} \frac{dx}{a^2\cos^2 x + b^2\sin^2 x} = \frac{\pi}{2ab};\ a, b > 0.$$

Sol. Let $$I = \int_{x=0}^{x=\pi/2} \frac{dx}{a^2\cos^2 x + b^2\sin^2 x}$$

$$= \int_{x=0}^{x=\pi/2} \frac{\sec^2 x\,dx}{a^2 + b^2\tan^2 x}$$

[divide numerator and denominator by $\cos^2 x$]

Put $\tan x = t \Rightarrow \sec^2 x\,dx = dt$

$$\therefore \quad I = \int_{t=0}^{t=\infty} \frac{dt}{a^2 + b^2t^2}$$

We find the new limits of integration $t = \tan x \Rightarrow t = 0$ when $x = 0$ and $t = \infty$ when $x = \pi/2$.

$$\Rightarrow \quad I = \frac{1}{b^2}\int_0^\infty \frac{dt}{\left(\frac{a}{b}\right)^2 + t^2} = \frac{1}{b^2}\cdot\frac{1}{a/b}\left[\tan^{-1}\frac{bt}{a}\right]_0^\infty$$

$$= \frac{1}{ab}\left[\frac{\pi}{2} - 0\right] = \frac{\pi}{2ab}$$

Example 5. The value of

$$\int_0^{e-1} \frac{e^{\frac{x^2+2x-1}{2}}}{(x+1)}\,dx + \int_1^e x\log x\cdot e^{\frac{x^2-2}{2}}\,dx \text{ is equal to}$$

Sol. Let $$I = \int_0^{e-1} \frac{e^{\frac{x^2+2x-1}{2}}}{(x+1)}\,dx + \int_1^e x\log x\cdot e^{\frac{x^2-2}{2}}\,dx$$

Put $x + 1 = t$ in first integral

$$\therefore I = \int_1^e \frac{e^{\frac{t^2-2}{2}}}{t}\,dt + \int_1^e x\log x\cdot e^{\frac{x^2-2}{2}}\,dx$$

$$= \int_1^e e^{\frac{t^2-2}{2}}\left\{\frac{1}{t} + t\cdot\log t\right\}dt = \left(\log t\cdot e^{\frac{t^2-2}{2}}\right)_1^e$$

$$= (\sqrt{e})^{e^2-2}$$

JEE SCANNER

Example Similar to PYQ Asked in JEE Main 2022

If the value of definite integral $\int_1^a x\cdot a^{-[\log_a x]}\,dx$, where $a > 1$ and $[x]$ denotes the greatest integer, is $\frac{e-1}{2}$, then the value of a equals to

(a) $\sqrt{e}$ (b) e (c) $\sqrt{e+1}$ (d) $e-1$

Sol. (a) Let $I = \int_1^a x\cdot a^{-[\log_a x]}\,dx$

Put $\log_a x = t \Rightarrow a^t = x$

$$\therefore \quad I = \ln a\cdot\int_0^1 (a^t\cdot a^{-[t]}\cdot a^t)\,dt$$

$$= \ln a\cdot\int_0^1 (a^{t-[t]}\cdot a^t)\,dt$$

$$= \ln a\cdot\int_0^1 (a^{\{t\}}\cdot a^t)\,dt = \ln a\cdot\int_0^1 a^{2t}\,dt$$

[as $\{t\} = t$, if $t \in (0,1)$]

$$= \left[\frac{\ln a}{2}\cdot\frac{a^{2t}}{\ln a}\right]_0^1 = \frac{1}{2}(a^2 - 1)$$

$$\therefore \quad \frac{1}{2}(a^2-1) = \frac{e-1}{2} \Rightarrow a = \sqrt{e}$$

Skill Builder

If the value of definte integral $\int_1^e x\cdot e^{-[\log_e x]}dx$, where $e > 1$ and $[x]$ denotes the greatest integer is $\frac{a^2-1}{2}$, then the value of e equals to

(a) $\sqrt{a}$ (b) a^2
(c) $a-1$ (d) a

For Sol.

■ **For more practice** See Q.18 of Milestone Practice 2.1.

Example 6. Let $a_n = \int_0^{\pi/2} (1-\sin t)^n \sin 2t\,dt$, then evaluate $\lim_{n\to\infty}\sum_{n=1}^{n}\frac{a_n}{n}$.

Sol. We have, $a_n = \int_0^{\pi/2} (1-\sin t)^n \sin 2t\,dt$

Let $1 - \sin t = u \Rightarrow -\cos t\,dt = du$

When $t = 0$, then $u = 1$ and when $t = \frac{\pi}{2}$, then $u = 0$

$$\therefore \quad a_n = -2\int_1^0 u^n(1-u)\,du = -2\left(\int_1^0 u^n\,du - \int_1^0 u^{n+1}\,du\right)$$

$$= 2\left(\frac{1}{n+1} - \frac{1}{n+2}\right)$$

Therefore, $\frac{a_n}{n} = 2\left(\frac{1}{n(n+1)} - \frac{1}{n(n+2)}\right)$

$$\therefore \lim_{n \to \infty} \sum_{n=1}^{n} \frac{a_n}{n} = 2\left[\sum\left(\frac{1}{n} - \frac{1}{n+1}\right) - \frac{1}{2}\sum\left(\frac{1}{n} - \frac{1}{n+2}\right)\right]$$

$$= 2\sum_{n=1}^{n}\left(\frac{1}{n} - \frac{1}{n+1}\right) - \sum_{n=1}^{n}\left(\frac{1}{n} - \frac{1}{n+2}\right)$$

$$= 2(1) - \left[\left(1 - \frac{1}{3}\right) + \left(\frac{1}{2} - \frac{1}{4}\right) + \left(\frac{1}{3} - \frac{1}{5}\right) + \dots\right] = 2 - \frac{3}{2} = \frac{1}{2}$$

Example 7. Let $f(x)$ be a continuous function satisfying $\int_0^1 f(x)\,(4x^2 - f(x))\,dx = \frac{4}{5}$, then find $f(3)$.

Sol. $$\int_0^1 f(x)(4x^2 - f(x))\,dx = \frac{4}{5}$$

$$\Rightarrow \int_0^1 \{[f(x)]^2 - 2 \cdot 2x^2 f(x) + (2x^2)^2 - 4x^4\}\,dx = -\frac{4}{5}$$

$$\Rightarrow \int_0^1 (f(x) - 2x^2)^2\,dx - 4\int_0^1 x^4\,dx = -\frac{4}{5}$$

$$\Rightarrow \int_0^1 (f(x) - 2x^2)^2\,dx - \frac{4}{5} = -\frac{4}{5}$$

$$\Rightarrow \int_0^1 (f(x) - 2x^2)^2\,dx = 0$$

$$\Rightarrow f(x) - 2x^2 = 0$$

$$\Rightarrow f(x) = 2x^2$$

$$\Rightarrow f(3) = 18$$

JEE SPIKE

As, integral of a non-negative continuous function is zero, then function is zero function i.e. $\int_a^b f^2(x)\,dx = 0$, then $f(x) = 0$

Milestone Practice 2.1

Directions (Q.Nos. 1 to 11) Evaluate the following.

1. $\int_0^{\pi/4} \cos^2 x\,dx$ **2.** $\int_0^{\pi/2} \frac{dx}{1+\cos x}$

3. $\int_1^2 \ln(x-1)\,dx$ **4.** $\int_0^{\pi/6} \sin 2x \cdot \cos x\,dx$

5. $\int_1^2 \frac{dx}{\sqrt{x} - \sqrt{x-1}}$ **6.** $\int_0^{\pi/4} \frac{(\sin x + \cos x)}{9 + 16\sin 2x}\,dx$

7. $\int_a^b \frac{1}{\sqrt{(x-a)(b-x)}}\,dx, b > a$ **8.** $\int_a^b \sqrt{\frac{x-a}{b-x}}\,dx$

9. $\int_0^{\pi/4} \sqrt{\tan x}\,dx$ **10.** $\int_0^{\pi} \cos 2x \cdot \log(\sin x)\,dx$

11. $\int_0^{\pi/4} e^{\sin x}\left(\frac{x\cos^3 x - \sin x}{\cos^2 x}\right)dx$

12. If $f(x) = \min\left(|x|, 1-|x|, \frac{1}{4}\right) \forall x \in R$, then find the value of $\int_{-1}^{1} f(x)\,dx$.

13. If $f(x)$ is a function satisfying $f\left(\frac{1}{x}\right) + x^2 f(x) = 0$ for all non-zero x, then find $\int_{\sin\theta}^{\operatorname{cosec}\theta} f(x)\,dx$.

14. The value of $\int_0^1 \left(\prod_{r=1}^{n}(x+r)\right)\left(\sum_{k=1}^{n}\frac{1}{x+k}\right)dx$ equals to

(a) n (b) $n!$ (c) $(n+1)!$ (d) $n \cdot n!$

15. If $I_1 = \int_0^1 (1 - x^{10})^{20}\,dx$ and $I_2 = \int_0^1 (1 - x^{10})^{19}\,dx$, then find $I_1 : I_2$.

16. Let $f(x)$, $f'(x)$ and $f''(x)$ are continuous on $[0, \ln 2]$ and $f(0) = 0$, $f'(0) = 3$, $f'(\ln 2) = 4$, $f(\ln 2) = 6$ and $\int_0^{\ln 2} e^{-2x} \cdot f(x)\,dx = 3$, then find the value of $\int_0^{\ln 2} e^{-2x} f''(x)\,dx$.

17. If $\int_0^{\pi/4} \frac{\ln(\cot x)}{[(\sin x)^{2009} + (\cos x)^{2009}]^2} (\sin 2x)^{2008}\,dx = \frac{a^b \ln a}{c^2}$ [where a, b, c are in their lowest terms], then find the value of $(a + b + c)$.

18. Show that the value of the definite integral $\int_{-\infty}^{a} \frac{(\sin^{-1} e^x + \sec^{-1} e^{-x})}{(\tan^{-1} e^a + \tan^{-1} e^x)(e^x + e^{-x})}, (a \in R)$ is independent of a.

Answer Key

1. $\frac{1}{4} + \frac{\pi}{8}$ **2.** 1 **3.** -1 **4.** $2\left(\frac{1}{3} - \frac{\sqrt{3}}{8}\right)$ **5.** $\frac{4\sqrt{2}}{3}$ **6.** $\frac{\log 9}{40}$ **7.** π **8.** $\frac{\pi}{2}(b-a)$ **9.** $\frac{\pi}{2\sqrt{2}} + \frac{1}{2\sqrt{2}}\log\left|\frac{\sqrt{2}-1}{\sqrt{2}+1}\right|$

10. $-\frac{\pi}{2}$ **11.** $e^{1/\sqrt{2}}\left(\frac{\pi}{4} + \sqrt{2}\right) - 1$ **12.** $\frac{3}{8}$ sq unit **13.** 0 **14.** (d) **15.** $\frac{200}{201}$ **16.** 13

17. 4019 **18.** $I = \frac{\pi}{2}\ln 2$, independent of a

For Detailed Solution

Milestone 2 Properties of Definite Integral

Properties of Definite Integrals

PROPERTY I $\int_a^b f(x)\,dx = \int_a^b f(t)\,dt$

i.e. The integration is independent of the change of variable.

Proof Let $\phi(x)$ be a primitive of $f(x)$, then

$$\frac{d}{dx}[\phi(x)] = f(x) \Rightarrow \frac{d}{dt}[\phi(t)] = f(t)$$

Therefore, $\int_a^b f(x)\,dx = [\phi(x)]_a^b = \phi(b) - \phi(a)$ ...(i)

and $\int_a^b f(t)\,dt = [\phi(t)]_a^b = \phi(b) - \phi(a)$ ...(ii)

From Eqs. (i) and (ii), we have

$$\int_a^b f(x)\,dx = \int_a^b f(t)\,dt$$

PROPERTY II $\int_a^b f(x)\,dx = -\int_b^a f(x)\,dx$

i.e. if the limits of definite integral are interchanged, then its value changes by minus sign only.

Proof Let $\phi(x)$ be a primitive of $f(x)$, then

$$\int_a^b f(x)\,dx = \phi(b) - \phi(a)$$

and $-\int_b^a f(x)\,dx = -[\phi(a) - \phi(b)] = \phi(b) - \phi(a)$

$\therefore$ $\int_a^b f(x)\,dx = -\int_b^a f(x)\,dx$

Example 8. Suppose f is such that $f(-x) = -f(x)$ for every real x and $\int_0^1 f(x)dx = 5$. Then, find the value of $\int_{-1}^0 f(t)dt$.

Sol. Given, $I = \int_0^1 f(x)dx = 5$

put $x = -t \Rightarrow dx = -dt$

$\therefore$ $I = \int_0^{-1} f(-t)(-dt) = \int_0^{-1} f(t)dt$ $[\because f(-x) = -f(x)]$

$= -\int_{-1}^0 f(t)dt = -5$

PROPERTY III $\int_0^a f(x)\,dx = \int_0^a f(a-x)\,dx$

Proof On RHS put $(a - x) = t$, so that $dx = -dt$

Also, when $x = 0$, then $t = a$

and when $x = a$, then $t = 0$

$\therefore$ $\int_0^a f(a-x)\,dx = -\int_a^0 f(t)\,dt = \int_0^a f(t)\,dt = \int_0^a f(x)\,dx$

$\therefore$ $\int_0^a f(a-x)\,dx = \int_0^a f(x)\,dx$

JEE SPIKE

This property is useful to evaluate a definite integral without first finding the corresponding indefinite integrals which may be difficult or sometimes impossible to find.

Geometrically $\int_0^a f(x)\,dx = \int_0^a f(a-x)\,dx$

This property says that when integrating from 0 to a, we will get the same result whether we use the function $f(x)$ or $f(a-x)$. The justification for this property will become clear from the figures below :

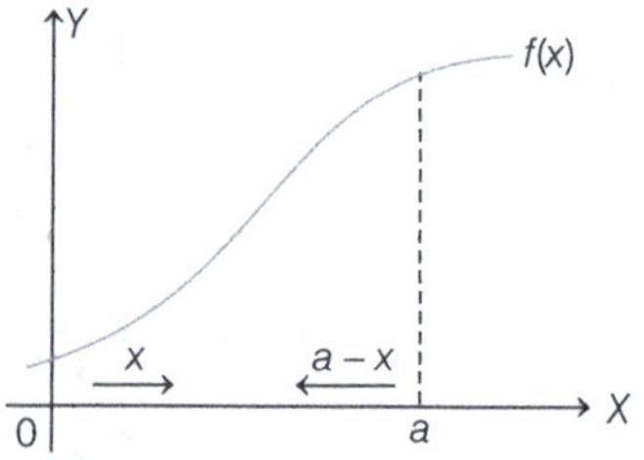

As x progresses from 0 to a, the variable $a - x$ progresses from a to 0. Thus, whether we use x or $a - x$, the entire interval $[0, a]$ is still covered.

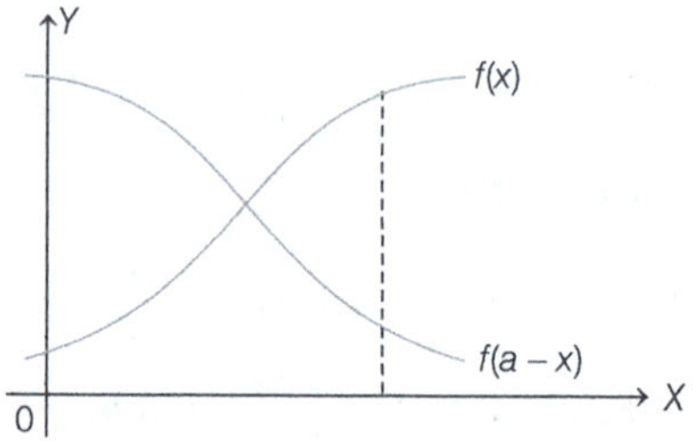

The function $f(a-x)$ can be obtained from the function $f(x)$ by first flipping $f(x)$ along the Y-axis and then shifting it right by a units. Notice that in the interval $[0, a]$, $f(x)$ and $f(a-x)$ describe precisely the same area.

There are two ways to look at the justification of this property, as described in the figures on the left and right respectively.

Example 9. Show that

(i) $\int_0^{\pi/2} f(\sin x)\, dx = \int_0^{\pi/2} f(\cos x)\, dx$

(ii) $\int_0^{\pi/2} f(\sin 2x) \sin x\, dx = \int_0^{\pi/4} \sqrt{2}\, f(\cos 2x) \cdot \cos x\, dx$
$= \int_0^{\pi/2} f(\sin 2x) \cdot \cos x\, dx$

(iii) $\int_0^{\pi} x f(\sin x)\, dx = \frac{\pi}{2} \int_0^{\pi} f(\sin x)\, dx$

Sol. (i) We know, $\int_0^{\pi/2} f(\sin x)\, dx = \int_0^{\pi/2} f\left[\sin\left(\frac{\pi}{2} - x\right)\right] dx$

$\left[\text{using } \int_0^a f(x)\, dx = \int_0^a f(a-x)\, dx\right]$

$= \int_0^{\pi/2} f(\cos x)\, dx$

$\therefore \quad \int_0^{\pi/2} f(\sin x)\, dx = \int_0^{\pi/2} f(\cos x)\, dx$

(ii) We know, $I = \int_0^{\pi/2} f(\sin 2x) \sin x\, dx$ ...(i)

$= \int_0^{\pi/2} f\left[\sin 2\left(\frac{\pi}{2} - x\right)\right] \cdot \sin\left(\frac{\pi}{2} - x\right) dx$

$\left[\text{using } \int_0^a f(x)\, dx = \int_0^a f(a-x)\, dx\right]$

$= \int_0^{\pi/2} f(\sin(\pi - 2x)) \cos x\, dx$

$I = \int_0^{\pi/2} f(\sin 2x) \cos x\, dx$ ...(ii)

Adding Eqs. (i) and (ii), we get

$2I = \int_0^{\pi/2} f(\sin 2x)(\sin x + \cos x)\, dx$

$= \sqrt{2} \int_0^{\pi/2} f(\sin 2x) \sin\left(x + \frac{\pi}{4}\right) dx$

Put $x + \frac{\pi}{4} = \left(\frac{\pi}{2} - \theta\right)$ $\left[\text{i.e. } x = \frac{\pi}{4} - \theta\right]$

$\Rightarrow \quad 2I = -\sqrt{2} \int_{\pi/4}^{-\pi/4} f(\cos 2\theta) \cos\theta\, d\theta$

$= \sqrt{2} \int_{-\pi/4}^{\pi/4} f(\cos 2\theta) \cos\theta\, d\theta$

$= 2\sqrt{2} \int_0^{\pi/4} f(\cos 2\theta) \cos\theta\, d\theta$

[since it is even]

$\therefore \quad I = \sqrt{2} \int_0^{\pi/4} f(\cos 2\theta) \cos\theta\, d\theta$

$\Rightarrow \quad I = \sqrt{2} \int_0^{\pi/4} f(\cos 2x) \cos x\, dx$

(iii) Let $I = \int_0^{\pi} x f(\sin x)\, dx$ ...(i)

Replacing x by $(\pi - x)$, we get

$I = \int_0^{\pi} (\pi - x) f(\sin(\pi - x))\, dx$

$\Rightarrow \quad I = \int_0^{\pi} (\pi - x) f(\sin x)\, dx$ ...(ii)

Adding Eqs. (i) and (ii), we get

$2I = \int_0^{\pi} \pi f(\sin x)\, dx \Rightarrow I = \frac{\pi}{2} \int_0^{\pi} f(\sin x)\, dx$

$\therefore \quad \int_0^{\pi} x f(\sin x)\, dx = \frac{\pi}{2} \int_0^{\pi} f(\sin x)\, dx$

Example 10. If f and g are continuous functions satisfying $f(x) = f(a-x)$ and $g(x) + g(a-x) = 2$, then show that $\int_0^a f(x) g(x)\, dx = \int_0^a f(x)\, dx$.

Sol. Let $I = \int_0^a f(x) g(x)\, dx = \int_0^a f(a-x) g(a-x)\, dx$

$\left[\text{using } \int_0^a f(x)\, dx = \int_0^a f(a-x)\, dx\right]$

$= \int_0^a f(x) \cdot [2 - g(x)]\, dx$

$\because \quad f(x) = f(a-x)$ and $g(a-x) + g(x) = 2$ [given]

$\therefore \quad \int_0^a f(x) \cdot g(x)\, dx = 2\int_0^a f(x)\, dx - \int_0^a f(x) \cdot g(x)\, dx$

or $2\int_0^a f(x) \cdot g(x)\, dx = 2\int_0^a f(x)\, dx$

$\Rightarrow \quad \int_0^a f(x) g(x)\, dx = \int_0^a f(x)\, dx$

Example 11. Evaluate

(i) $\int_0^{\pi/2} \frac{dx}{1 + \sqrt{\tan x}}$ (ii) $\int_0^{\pi/2} \log(\tan x)\, dx$

(iii) $\int_0^{\pi/2} \frac{\sin x - \cos x}{1 + \sin x \cos x}\, dx$

Sol. (i) Let $I = \int_0^{\pi/2} \frac{dx}{1 + \sqrt{\tan x}} = \int_0^{\pi/2} \frac{\sqrt{\cos x}}{\sqrt{\cos x} + \sqrt{\sin x}}\, dx$ ...(i)

Then, $I = \int_0^{\pi/2} \frac{\sqrt{\cos(\pi/2 - x)}}{\sqrt{\cos(\pi/2 - x)} + \sqrt{\sin(\pi/2 - x)}}\, dx$

$= \int_0^{\pi/2} \frac{\sqrt{\sin x}}{\sqrt{\sin x} + \sqrt{\cos x}}\, dx$ ...(ii)

On adding Eqs. (i) and (ii), we get

$2I = \int_0^{\pi/2} \frac{\sqrt{\sin x}}{\sqrt{\sin x} + \sqrt{\cos x}}\, dx + \int_0^{\pi/2} \frac{\sqrt{\cos x}}{\sqrt{\sin x} + \sqrt{\cos x}}\, dx$

$= \int_0^{\pi/2} \frac{\sqrt{\sin x} + \sqrt{\cos x}}{\sqrt{\sin x} + \sqrt{\cos x}}\, dx = \int_0^{\pi/2} 1\, dx$

$= [x]_0^{\pi/2} = \frac{\pi}{2} - 0 \Rightarrow 2I = \frac{\pi}{2} \Rightarrow I = \frac{\pi}{4}$

(ii) Let $I = \int_0^{\pi/2} \log(\tan x)\, dx$ ...(i)

Then, $I = \int_0^{\pi/2} \log\left\{\tan\left(\frac{\pi}{2} - x\right)\right\} dx$

$\Rightarrow \quad I = \int_0^{\pi/2} \log(\cot x)\, dx$ ...(ii)

On adding Eqs. (i) and (ii), we get

$2I = \int_0^{\pi/2} \log(\tan x)\, dx + \int_0^{\pi/2} \log(\cot x)\, dx$

$= \int_0^{\pi/2} (\log \tan x + \log \cot x)\, dx$

$= \int_0^{\pi/2} \log(\tan x \cdot \cot x)\, dx = \int_0^{\pi/2} \log(1)\, dx$

$\Rightarrow 2I = 0$

$\Rightarrow I = 0$

(iii) Let $I = \int_0^{\pi/2} \frac{\sin x - \cos x}{1 + \sin x \cos x} dx$ ...(i)

Then, $I = \int_0^{\pi/2} \frac{\sin\left(\frac{\pi}{2} - x\right) - \cos\left(\frac{\pi}{2} - x\right)}{1 + \sin\left(\frac{\pi}{2} - x\right) \cos\left(\frac{\pi}{2} - x\right)} dx$

$\Rightarrow \quad I = \int_0^{\pi/2} \frac{\cos x - \sin x}{1 + \cos x \cdot \sin x} dx$ ...(ii)

On adding Eqs. (i) and (ii), we get

$$2I = \int_0^{\pi/2} \frac{\sin x - \cos x}{1 + \sin x \cos x} dx + \int_0^{\pi/2} \frac{\cos x - \sin x}{1 + \sin x \cos x} dx$$

$\Rightarrow 2I = 0 \Rightarrow I = 0$

JEE SCANNER

Example Similar to PYQ Asked in JEE Main 2024

The value of $\int_0^{\pi} \frac{\sin x}{(1 + \cos^2 x)(1 + e^{\cos x})} dx$ is

(a) $\frac{\pi}{3}$ (b) $\frac{\pi}{2}$ (c) $\frac{\pi}{4}$ (d) $\frac{\pi}{6}$

Sol. (c) $I = \int_0^{\pi} \frac{\sin x}{(1 + \cos^2 x)(1 + e^{\cos x})} dx$ ...(i)

Using property

$\int_0^a f(x)\, dx = \int_0^a f(a - x)\, dx$

$I = \int_0^{\pi} \frac{e^{\cos x} \sin x}{(1 + \cos^2 x)(1 + e^{\cos x})} dx$ ...(ii)

On adding Eqs. (i) and (ii), we get

$$2I = \int_0^{\pi} \frac{\sin x}{1 + \cos^2 x} dx$$

On putting $\cos x = t \Rightarrow -\sin x\, dx = dt$

$$2I = \int_1^{-1} \frac{(-dt)}{1 + t^2} = -[\tan^{-1} t]_1^{-1}$$

$$= -[\tan^{-1}(-1) - \tan^{-1}(1)]$$

$$= -\left(-\frac{\pi}{4} - \frac{\pi}{4}\right)$$

$\Rightarrow \quad 2I = \frac{\pi}{2}$

$\therefore \quad I = \frac{\pi}{4}$

Skill Builder

The value of $\int_0^{\pi} \frac{\sin x}{(1 + \cos^2 x)(1 + e^{-\cos x})} dx$ is

(a) $\frac{\pi}{4}$ (b) $\frac{\pi}{2}$ (c) 2π (d) $\frac{\pi}{8}$

For Sol.

■ **For more practice** See Q.1 of Milestone Practice 2.2.

Example 12. The value of $\int_0^a \log(\cot a + \tan x)\, dx$, where $a \in (0, \pi/2)$ is equal to

(a) $a \log(\sin a)$ (b) $-a \log(\sin a)$

(c) $-a \log(\cos a)$ (d) None of these

Sol. (b) Let $I = \int_0^a \log(\cot a + \tan x)\, dx$

$$= \int_0^a \log\left(\frac{\cos a}{\sin a} + \frac{\sin x}{\cos x}\right) dx$$

$$= \int_0^a \log\left(\frac{\cos(a - x)}{\sin a \cos x}\right) dx$$

$$= \int_0^a \log[\cos(a - x)]\, dx - \int_0^a \log(\sin a)\, dx - \int_0^a \log(\cos x)\, dx$$

$$= \int_0^a \log\cos(x) dx - \int_0^a \log(\sin a) dx - \int_0^a \log(\cos x) dx$$

$\left[\text{using } \int_0^a f(x)\, dx = \int_0^a f(a - x)\, dx \text{ to first integral}\right]$

$$= -\log(\sin a) \int_0^a dx$$

$$= -a \log(\sin a)$$

PROPERTY IV $\int_a^b f(x)\, dx = \int_a^b f(a + b - x)\, dx$

Proof Put $x = a + b - t \Rightarrow dx = -dt$

Also, when $x = a$, then $t = b$ and when $x = b$, then $t = a$

$\therefore \int_a^b f(x)\, dx = \int_b^a f(a + b - t)(-dt)$

$$= -\int_b^a f(a + b - t)\, dt$$

$$= \int_a^b f(a + b - t)\, dt$$

$$= \int_a^b f(a + b - x)\, dx$$

$\therefore \int_a^b f(x)\, dx = \int_a^b f(a + b - x)\, dx$

Geometrically $\int_a^b f(x) dx = \int_a^b f(a + b - x)\, dx$

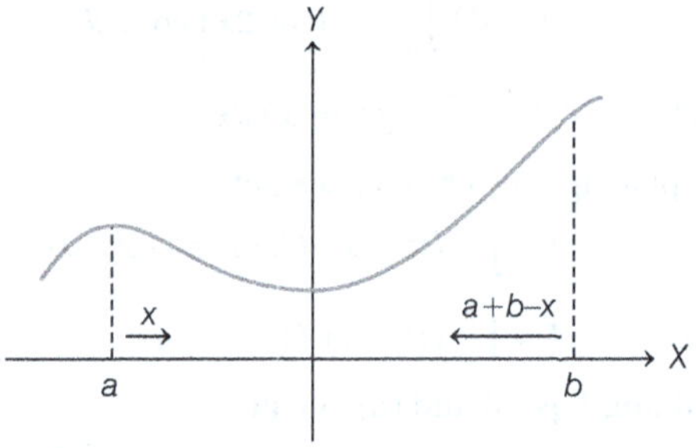

As the variable x varies from a to b, the variable $a + b - x$ varies from b to a.

Thus, whether we use x or $a+b-x$, the entire interval $[a, b]$ is covered in both the cases and the areas will be the same.

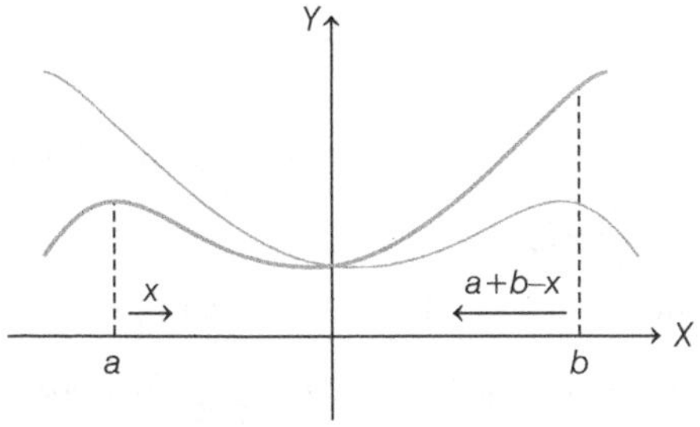

The graph of $f(a+b-x)$ can be obtained from the graph of $f(x)$ by first flipping the graph of $f(x)$ along the Y-axis and then shifting it $(a+b)$ units towards the right; the areas described by $f(x)$ and $f(a+b-x)$ in the interval $[a, b]$ are precisely the same.

Example 13. Evaluate $\int_{\pi/6}^{\pi/3} \frac{dx}{1+\sqrt{\tan x}}$.

Sol. We have, $I = \int_{\pi/6}^{\pi/3} \frac{dx}{1+\sqrt{\tan x}}$ ...(i)

$$I = \int_{\pi/6}^{\pi/3} \frac{dx}{1+\sqrt{\tan\left(\frac{\pi}{3}+\frac{\pi}{6}-x\right)}}$$

$$\left[\because \int_a^b f(x)dx = \int_a^b f(a+b-x)dx\right]$$

$$I = \int_{\pi/6}^{\pi/3} \frac{dx}{1+\sqrt{\cot x}} \Rightarrow I = \int_{\pi/6}^{\pi/3} \frac{\sqrt{\tan x}\, dx}{\sqrt{\tan x}+1} \quad \text{...(ii)}$$

On adding Eqs. (i) and (ii), we get

$$2I = \int_{\pi/6}^{\pi/3} \frac{(1+\sqrt{\tan x})dx}{1+\sqrt{\tan x}} = \int_{\pi/6}^{\pi/3} dx$$

$$2I = [x]_{\pi/6}^{\pi/3} = \frac{\pi}{3}-\frac{\pi}{6} = \frac{\pi}{6} \Rightarrow I = \frac{\pi}{12}$$

Example 14. Prove that $\int_a^b \frac{f(x)}{f(x)+f(a+b-x)} dx = \frac{b-a}{2}$.

Sol. Let $I = \int_a^b \frac{f(x)}{f(x)+f(a+b-x)} dx$ ...(i)

then, $I = \int_a^b \frac{f(a+b-x)}{f(a+b-x)+f(a+b-(a+b-x))} dx$

$$\Rightarrow \quad I = \int_a^b \frac{f(a+b-x)}{f(a+b-x)+f(x)} dx \quad \text{...(ii)}$$

On adding Eqs. (i) and (ii), we get

$$2I = \int_a^b \frac{f(a+b-x)+f(x)}{f(a+b-x)+f(x)} dx$$

$$\Rightarrow \quad 2I = \int_a^b 1\, dx = (b-a)$$

$$\Rightarrow \quad I = \frac{b-a}{2}$$

JEE SCANNER

Example Similar to PYQ Asked in JEE Main 2023

The value $\int_{-\pi}^{\pi} \frac{\cos^2 x}{1+a^x} dx$ is

(a) π (b) $\frac{\pi}{2}$ (c) 2π (d) $\frac{\pi}{4}$

Sol. (b) Let $I = \int_{-\pi}^{\pi} \frac{\cos^2 x}{1+a^x} dx$ ...(i)

$$I = \int_{-\pi}^{\pi} \frac{\cos^2(\pi-\pi-x)}{1+a^{\pi-\pi-x}} dx$$

$$\left[\because \int_a^b f(x)\, dx = \int_a^b f(a+b-x) dx\right]$$

$$I = \int_{-\pi}^{\pi} \frac{\cos^2 x}{1+a^{-x}} dx \quad \text{...(ii)}$$

On adding Eqs. (i) and (ii), we get

$$2I = \int_{-\pi}^{\pi} \cos^2 x \left(\frac{1+a^x}{1+a^x}\right) dx = \int_{-\pi}^{\pi} \cos^2 x\, dx$$

$$2I = \int_{-\pi}^{\pi} \left[\frac{1+\cos 2x}{2}\right] dx = \left[\frac{1}{2}x + \frac{\sin 2x}{4}\right]_{-\pi}^{\pi}$$

$$2I = \frac{1}{2}[\pi+\pi] + \frac{1}{4}[\sin 2\pi - \sin(-2\pi)]$$

$$2I = \pi + 0 \Rightarrow I = \frac{\pi}{2}$$

Skill Builder

The value of $\int_{-\pi}^{\pi} \frac{\sin^2 x}{1+a^{-x}} dx$ is

(a) $\frac{\pi}{4}$ (b) $\frac{\pi}{2}$ (c) π (d) 2π

For Sol.

■ **For more practice** See Q.6 of Milestone Practice 2.2.

Example 15. Solve $I = \int_{\cos^4 t}^{-\sin^4 t} \frac{\sqrt{f(z)}\, dz}{\sqrt{f(\cos 2t - z)} + \sqrt{f(z)}}$.

Sol. We have, $I = \int_{\cos^4 t}^{-\sin^4 t} \frac{\sqrt{f(z)}\, dz}{\sqrt{f(\cos 2t - z)} + \sqrt{f(z)}}$ ...(i)

$$\therefore \quad I = \int_{\cos^4 t}^{-\sin^4 t} \frac{\sqrt{f(\cos 2t - z)}\, dz}{\sqrt{f(\cos 2t - z)} + \sqrt{f(z)}} \quad \text{..(ii)}$$

$$\left[\text{using } \int_a^b f(x)\, dx = \int_a^b f(a+b-x)\, dx\right]$$

On adding Eqs. (i) and (ii), we get

$$2I = \int_{\cos^4 t}^{-\sin^4 t} dz \Rightarrow 2I = (z)_{\cos^4 t}^{-\sin^4 t}$$

$$\therefore \quad I = -\frac{1}{2}(\sin^4 t + \cos^4 t) = -\frac{1}{2}(1 - 2\sin^2 t \cos^2 t)$$

$$= -\frac{1}{2}\left(1 - \frac{1}{2}\sin^2 2t\right) = -\frac{1}{2} + \frac{1}{4}\sin^2 2t$$

Milestone Practice 2.2

1. The value of $\int_0^{\pi} \frac{e^{\cos x} \sin x}{(1+\cos^2 x)(e^{\cos x}+e^{-\cos x})} dx$ is equal to
   (a) $\frac{\pi}{3}$ (b) $\frac{\pi}{4}$ (c) $\frac{\pi}{2}$ (d) $\frac{\pi}{6}$

2. For any integer n, the value of $\int_0^{\pi} e^{\cos^2 x} \cdot \cos^3 (2n+1)\, x \cdot dx$ is equal to
   (a) 0 (b) 1
   (c) −1 (d) None of these

3. The value of $\int_2^3 \frac{\sqrt{x}}{\sqrt{5-x}+\sqrt{x}} dx$ is equal to
   (a) 1/2 (b) 1/3
   (c) 1/4 (d) None of these

4. The value of $\int_0^2 \frac{dx}{(17+8x-4x^2)(e^{6(1-x)}+1)}$ is equal to
   (a) $-\frac{1}{8\sqrt{21}} \log \left| \frac{2-\sqrt{21}}{2+\sqrt{21}} \right|$
   (b) $-\frac{1}{8\sqrt{21}} \log \left| \frac{2+\sqrt{21}}{\sqrt{21}-2} \right|$
   (c) $-\frac{1}{8\sqrt{21}} \left\{ \log \left| \frac{2-\sqrt{21}}{2+\sqrt{21}} \right| - \log \left| \frac{2+\sqrt{21}}{\sqrt{21}-2} \right| \right\}$
   (d) None of the above

5. If f is an odd function, then the value of $\int_{-a}^{a} \frac{f(\sin x)}{f(\cos x)+f(\sin^2 x)} dx$ is equal to
   (a) 0 (b) $f(\cos x)+f(\sin x)$
   (c) 1 (d) None of these

6. Find the value of $\int_{-\pi/4}^{\pi/4} \frac{\sec^2 x}{1+a^x} dx$.

7. If f, g, h be continuous functions on $[0, a]$ such that $f(a-x)=f(x)$, $g(a-x)=-g(x)$ and $3h(x)=5+4h(a-x)$, then the value of $\int_0^a f(x) \cdot g(x) \cdot h(x) dx$ is
   (a) 0 (b) 1 (c) a (d) $2a$

8. If $2f(x)+f(-x)=\frac{1}{x}\sin\left(x-\frac{1}{x}\right)$, then the value of $\int_{1/e}^{e} f(x) dx$ is
   (a) 0 (b) e (c) $1/e$ (d) $e+1/e$

9. Prove that $\int_0^{\pi} x f(\sin x) dx = \frac{\pi}{2} \int_0^{\pi} f(\sin x) dx$.

10. Evaluate $\int_0^{\pi} \frac{x^2 \sin 2x \cdot \sin\left(\frac{\pi}{2}\cos x\right) dx}{(2x-\pi)}$.

11. Number of positive continuous function $f(x)$ defined on $[0, 1]$ for which $\int_0^1 f(x) dx = 1$, $\int_0^1 x f(x) dx = 2$ and $\int_0^1 x^2 f(x) dx = 4$.

12. Let $I_1 = \int_0^1 \frac{e^x}{1+x} dx$ and $I_2 = \int_0^1 \frac{x^2}{e^{x^3}(2-x^3)} dx$.
    Then, $\frac{I_1}{I_2}$ is equal to
    (a) $\frac{3}{e}$ (b) $\frac{3}{e}$ (c) $3e$ (d) $\frac{1}{3e}$

13. If $f(x)=\frac{e^x}{1+e^x}$, $I_1=\int_{f(-a)}^{f(a)} x \cdot g\{x(1-x)\} dx$ and $I_2=\int_{f(-a)}^{f(a)} g\{x(1-x)\} dx$, then the value of $\frac{I_2}{I_1}$ is
    (a) 1 (b) −3 (c) −1 (d) 2

14. Let f be a positive function, let
    $I_1 = \int_{1-k}^{k} x \cdot f[x(1-x)]\, dx$ and
    $I_2 = \int_{1-k}^{k} f[x(1-x)]\, dx$, where $(2k-1)>0$, then compute $\frac{I_1}{I_2}$.

15. Evaluate $\int_{\sin^{-1}(x^2-4x+5)}^{\cos^{-1}(x^2-4x+5)} \frac{\sqrt{f(x)}}{\sqrt{f\left(\frac{\pi}{2}-x\right)}+\sqrt{f(x)}} dx$.

16. Evaluate $\int_{\sqrt{\ln 2}}^{\sqrt{\ln 3}} \frac{x \cdot \sin x^2}{\sin x^2 + \sin(\ln 6 - x^2)} dx$.

Answer Key

1. (b)	2. (a)	3. (a)	4. (c)	5. (a)
6. (1)	7. (a)	8. (a)	10. $\frac{8}{\pi}$	11. 0
12. (c)	13. (d)	14. $\frac{1}{2}$	15. $-\frac{\pi}{4}$	16. $\frac{1}{4}\ln\frac{3}{2}$

For Detailed Solution

Milestone 3 Applications of Piecewise Function Property

Applications of Piecewise Function Property

PROPERTY V $\int_a^b f(x)\,dx = \int_a^c f(x)\,dx + \int_c^b f(x)\,dx$, where $c \in R$

Proof Let $\phi(x)$ be primitive of $f(x)$, then

$$\int_a^b f(x)\,dx = \phi(b) - \phi(a) \quad \text{...(i)}$$

and $\int_a^c f(x)dx + \int_c^b f(x)dx = [\phi(c) - \phi(a)] + [\phi(b) - \phi(c)]$

$$= \phi(b) - \phi(a) \quad \text{...(ii)}$$

From Eqs. (i) and (ii), we get

$$\int_a^b f(x)\,dx = \int_a^c f(x)\,dx + \int_c^b f(x)\,dx$$

Generalisation Property V can be generalised into the following form

$$\int_a^b f(x)dx = \int_a^{c_1} f(x)dx + \int_{c_1}^{c_2} f(x)\,dx + \ldots + \int_{c_n}^b f(x)dx$$

where, $a < c_1 < c_2 < \ldots < c_{n-1} < c_n < b$

Example 16. Given function, $f(x) = \begin{cases} x^2, \text{for } 0 \le x < 1 \\ \sqrt{x}, \text{for } 1 \le x \le 2 \end{cases}$.

Evaluate $\int_0^2 f(x)\,dx$.

Sol. Here, $\int_0^2 f(x)\,dx = \int_0^1 f(x)\,dx + \int_1^2 f(x)\,dx$

$$\therefore \int_0^2 f(x)\,dx = \int_0^1 x^2\,dx + \int_1^2 \sqrt{x}\,dx$$

$$= \left[\frac{x^3}{3}\right]_0^1 + \left[\frac{x^{3/2}}{3/2}\right]_1^2$$

$$= \left[\frac{x^3}{3}\right]_0^1 + \left[\frac{2}{3}x\sqrt{x}\right]_1^2$$

$$= \left[\frac{1}{3} - 0\right] + \frac{2}{3}[2\sqrt{2} - 1]$$

$$= \frac{1}{3} + \frac{4\sqrt{2}}{3} - \frac{2}{3}$$

$$= \frac{4\sqrt{2}}{3} - \frac{1}{3} = \frac{1}{3}(4\sqrt{2} - 1)$$

Example 17. If $\int_{1/3}^3 |\log_e x|\,dx = \frac{m}{n}\log_e\left(\frac{n^2}{e}\right)$, find the value of $m^2 + n^2$, where m and n are coprime natural numbers.

Sol. $\int_{1/3}^3 |\ln x|\,dx = \int_{1/3}^1 (-\ln x)\,dx + \int_1^3 (\ln x)\,dx$

$$= -[x \ln x - x]_{1/3}^1 + [x \ln x - x]_1^3$$

$$= -\left[-1 - \left(\frac{1}{3}\ln\frac{1}{3} - \frac{1}{3}\right)\right] + [3\ln 3 - 3 - (-1)]$$

$$= -\frac{4}{3} + \frac{8}{3}\ln 3$$

$$= \frac{4}{3}(2\ln 3 - 1) = \frac{4}{3}\ln\left(\frac{9}{e}\right)$$

$\Rightarrow \quad m = 4, n = 3$

$\therefore \quad m^2 + n^2 = 16 + 9 = 25$

Example 18. Evaluate

(i) $\int_0^\pi |\cos x|\,dx$ (ii) $\int_0^2 |x^2 + 2x - 3|\,dx$

Sol. (i) $\int_0^\pi |\cos x|\,dx = \int_0^{\pi/2} |\cos x|\,dx + \int_{\pi/2}^\pi |\cos x|\,dx$

$$= \int_0^{\pi/2} (\cos x)\,dx - \int_{\pi/2}^\pi (\cos x)\,dx$$

$$= [\sin x]_0^{\pi/2} - [\sin x]_{\pi/2}^\pi$$

$$= (1 - 0) - (0 - 1) = 2$$

(ii) $\int_0^2 |x^2 + 2x - 3|\,dx$

$$= \int_0^1 |x^2 + 2x - 3|\,dx + \int_1^2 |x^2 + 2x - 3|\,dx \quad \text{...(i)}$$

We have, $x^2 + 2x - 3 = (x + 3)(x - 1)$

$\therefore \quad x^2 + 2x - 3 > 0$ for $x < -3$ or $x > 1$

and $x^2 + 2x - 3 < 0$ for $-3 < x < 1$

So, $|x^2 + 2x - 3|$

$$= \begin{cases} (x^2 + 2x - 3), & \text{for } x < -3 \text{ or } x > 1 \\ -(x^2 + 2x - 3), & \text{for } -3 < x < 1 \end{cases}$$

$\therefore$ Eq. (i) becomes

$$I = \int_0^1 -(x^2 + 2x - 3)\,dx + \int_1^2 (x^2 + 2x - 3)\,dx$$

$$= -\left[\frac{x^3}{3} + x^2 - 3x\right]_0^1 + \left[\frac{x^3}{3} + x^2 - 3x\right]_1^2$$

$$= 4$$

JEE SCANNER

Example Similar to PYQ Asked in JEE Main 2022

$\int_0^2 \left(|2x^2 - 3x| + \left[x - \frac{1}{2}\right]\right) dt$, where [t] is the greatest integer function, is equal to

(a) $\frac{7}{6}$ (b) $\frac{19}{12}$ (c) $\frac{31}{12}$ (d) $\frac{1}{2}$

Sol. (b) Take first modulus part of the given integral,

$$\int_0^2 |2x^2 - 3x|\, dx$$

Let $2x^2 - 3x = 0 \Rightarrow x = 0, x = \frac{3}{2}$

$$\Rightarrow \int_0^{3/2} (3x - 2x^2)\, dx + \int_{3/2}^2 (2x^2 - 3x)\, dx = \frac{19}{12}$$

Now, take greatest integer function integral.

Let $x - \frac{1}{2} = P$

$$\int_0^2 \left[x - \frac{1}{2}\right] dx = \int_{-1/2}^{3/2} [P]\, dx$$

$$= \int_{-1/2}^{0} (-1)\, dx + \int_0^1 (0)\, dx + \int_1^{3/2} (1)\, dx = 0$$

$$\int_0^2 |2x^2 - 3x|\, dx + \left[x - \frac{1}{2}\right] dx = \frac{19}{12} + 0 = \frac{19}{12}$$

Skill Builder

$\int_0^1 \left(|2x^2 - x| - \left[x - \frac{1}{3}\right]\right) dt$, where [t] is the greatest integer function, is equal to

(a) $-\frac{1}{12}$ (b) $-\frac{7}{12}$ (c) $\frac{7}{12}$ (d) $\frac{1}{12}$

For Sol.

- **For more practice** See Q.1 of Milestone Practice 2.3.

Example 19. Evaluate $\int_0^2 \{x\}\, dx$, where $\{x\}$ denotes the fractional part of x.

Sol. $\int_0^2 \{x\}\, dx = \int_0^2 (x - [x])\, dx = \int_0^2 x\, dx - \int_0^2 [x]\, dx$

$$= \left(\frac{x^2}{2}\right)_0^2 - \left(\int_0^1 [x]\, dx + \int_1^2 [x]\, dx\right)$$

$$= \frac{1}{2}(4 - 0) - \left(\int_0^1 0\, dx + \int_1^2 1\, dx\right)$$

$$= 2 - (x)_1^2 = 2 - (1) = 1$$

Example 20. Evaluate $\int_0^9 \{\sqrt{x}\}\, dx$, where $\{x\}$ denotes the fractional part of x.

Sol. $\int_0^9 \{\sqrt{x}\}\, dx = \int_0^9 \left(\sqrt{x} - [\sqrt{x}]\right) dx$

$$= \int_0^9 (x^{1/2})\, dx - \int_0^9 [\sqrt{x}]\, dx$$

$$= \frac{2}{3}(x^{3/2})_0^9 - \int_0^9 [\sqrt{x}]\, dx$$

$$= \frac{2}{3}[27] - \int_0^9 [\sqrt{x}]\, dx$$

As, $\int_0^9 [\sqrt{x}]\, dx \Rightarrow 0 \le x \le 9$ and $0 \le \sqrt{x} \le 3$

Thus, it should be divided into three parts

$$0 \le \sqrt{x} \le 1, 1 \le \sqrt{x} \le 2, 2 \le \sqrt{x} \le 3$$

i.e. $I = 2(9) - \int_0^9 [\sqrt{x}]\, dx$

$$= 18 - \left[\int_0^1 [\sqrt{x}]\, dx + \int_1^4 [\sqrt{x}]\, dx + \int_4^9 [\sqrt{x}]\, dx\right]$$

$$= 18 - \left(\int_0^1 0\, dx + \int_1^4 1\, dx + \int_4^9 2\, dx\right)$$

$$= 18 - \left(0 + (x)_1^4 + (2x)_4^9\right) = 18 - (3 + 10) = 5$$

Example 21. If the value of $\int_0^{100} [\tan^{-1} x]\, dx = \lambda - \tan\mu$ (where $[\cdot]$ denotes the greatest integer function), then find the value of $\lambda + \mu$.

Sol. Let $I = \int_0^{100} [\tan^{-1} x]\, dx$, where $[\tan^{-1} x]$ is shown as

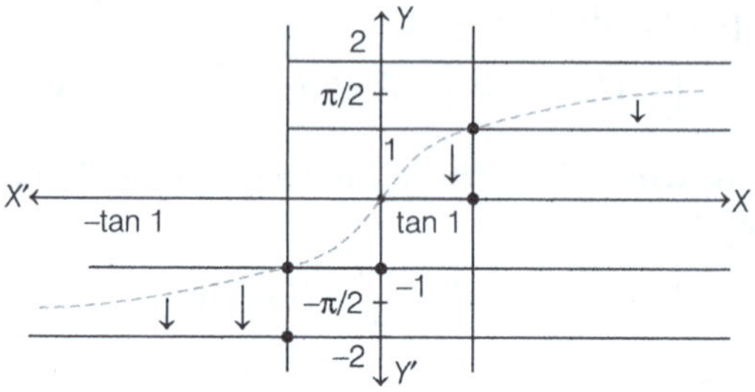

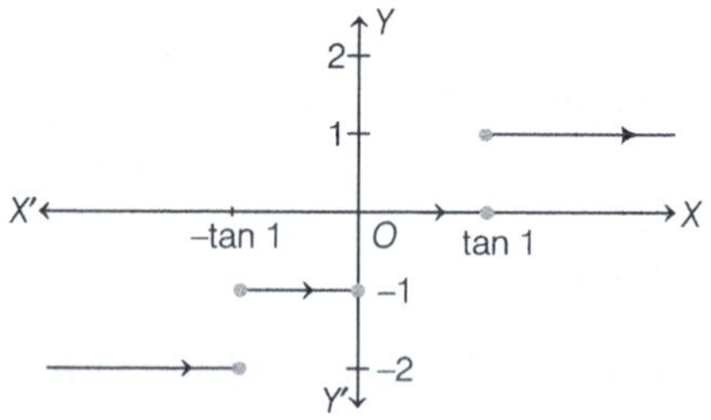

$\therefore \int_0^{100} [\tan^{-1} x]\, dx$ is shown as

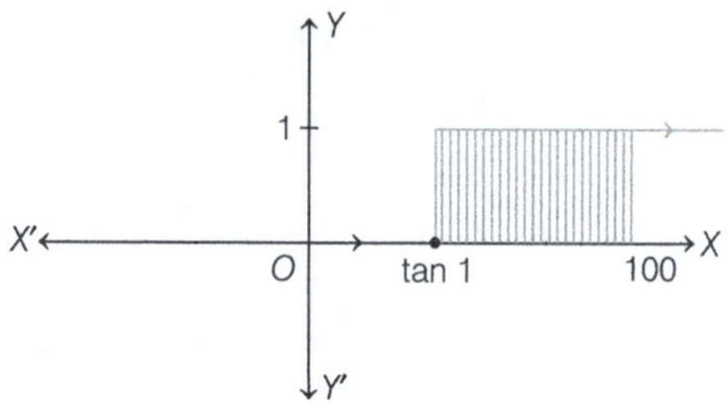

$$= 1 \times (100 - \tan 1) = 100 - \tan 1$$

$\Rightarrow$ $\lambda = 100$ and $\mu = 1$

$$\lambda + \mu = 100 + 1 = 101$$

Example 22. The value of $\int_1^2 (x^{[x^2]} + [x^2]^x)\,dx$ is equal to where $[\cdot]$ denotes the greatest integer function

(a) $\frac{5}{4} + \sqrt{3} + (2^{\sqrt{3}} - 2^{\sqrt{2}}) + \frac{1}{\log 3}(9 - 3^{\sqrt{3}})$

(b) $\frac{5}{4} + \sqrt{3} + \frac{\sqrt{2}}{3} + \frac{1}{\log 2}(2^{\sqrt{3}} - 2^{\sqrt{2}}) + \frac{1}{\log 3}(9 - 3^{\sqrt{3}})$

(c) $\frac{5}{4} + \frac{\sqrt{2}}{3} + \frac{1}{\log 2}(2^{\sqrt{3}} - 2^{\sqrt{2}}) + \frac{1}{\log 3}(9 - 3^{\sqrt{3}})$

(d) None of the above

Sol. (b) Let $I = \int_1^2 (x^{[x^2]} + [x^2]^x)\,dx$

$$= \int_1^{\sqrt{2}} (x+1)\,dx + \int_{\sqrt{2}}^{\sqrt{3}} (x^2 + 2^x)\,dx + \int_{\sqrt{3}}^{2} (x^3 + 3^x)\,dx$$

$$= \left[\frac{x^2}{2} + x\right]_1^{\sqrt{2}} + \left[\frac{x^3}{3} + \frac{2^x}{\log 2}\right]_{\sqrt{2}}^{\sqrt{3}} + \left[\frac{x^4}{4} + \frac{3^x}{\log 3}\right]_{\sqrt{3}}^{2}$$

$$= \frac{5}{4} + \sqrt{3} + \frac{\sqrt{2}}{3} + \frac{1}{\log 2}(2^{\sqrt{3}} - 2^{\sqrt{2}}) + \frac{1}{\log 3}(9 - 3^{\sqrt{3}})$$

Example 23. Find the value of $\int_0^{2\pi} [|\sin x| + |\cos x|]\,dx$.

Sol. Let $f(x) = [|\sin x| + |\cos x|]$

As, $|\sin x| \ge \sin^2 x$ and $|\cos x| \ge \cos^2 x$

$\therefore$ $|\sin x| + |\cos x| \ge 1$

and $|\sin x| + |\cos x| \le \sqrt{1^2 + 1^2}$

$\Rightarrow$ $1 \le |\sin x| + |\cos x| \le \sqrt{2}$

Thus, $[|\sin x| + |\cos x|] = 1$

$\therefore$ $\int_0^{2\pi} [|\sin x| + |\cos x|]\,dx = \int_0^{2\pi} 1\,dx = 2\pi$

Example 24. If the value of the definite integral $\int_0^{\pi/2} \sin|2x - \alpha|\,dx = f(\alpha)$, where $\alpha \in [0, \pi]$, then find the value of $(\pi/3)$.

Sol. Let $I = \int_{-\alpha}^{(\pi-\alpha)} \sin|t|\,dt$, where $2x - \alpha = t \Rightarrow dx = \frac{dt}{2}$

$$= \frac{1}{2}\int_{-\alpha}^{0} -\sin t\,dt + \frac{1}{2}\int_0^{\pi-\alpha} \sin t\,dt$$

$$= \left[\frac{1}{2}\cos t\right]_{-\alpha}^{0} - \left[\frac{1}{2}\cos t\right]_0^{\pi-\alpha}$$

$$= \frac{1}{2}[1 - \cos\alpha] - \frac{1}{2}[-\cos\alpha - 1]$$

$$= \frac{1}{2}(1 - \cos\alpha) + \frac{1}{2}(1 + \cos\alpha) = 1$$

$f(\alpha) = 1$ and $f(\pi/3) = 1$

Example 25. Find the value of $\int_0^2 f(x)\,dx$, where

$$f(x) = \begin{cases} 0, \text{ when } x = \frac{n}{n+1}, & n = 1, 2, 3 \ldots \\ 1, \text{elsewhere} \end{cases}$$

Sol. Here, $\int_0^2 f(x)\,dx = \int_0^{1/2} 1\,dx + \int_{1/2}^{2/3} 1\,dx + \int_{2/3}^{3/4} 1\,dx + \ldots$

$$+ \int_{\frac{n-1}{n}}^{\frac{n}{n+1}} 1\,dx + \int_1^2 1\,dx \quad [\because \text{ here, } n \to \infty]$$

$$= \left(\frac{1}{2}\right) + \left(\frac{2}{3} - \frac{1}{2}\right) + \left(\frac{3}{4} - \frac{2}{3}\right) + \ldots + \left(\frac{n}{n+1} - \frac{n-1}{n}\right) + 1$$

$[\because \text{ here, } n \to \infty]$

$$= \frac{n}{n+1} + 1 \quad [\because \text{ here, } n \to \infty]$$

We take, limit $n \to \infty$

We have, $\int_0^2 f(x)\,dx = \lim_{n\to\infty} \frac{n}{n+1} + 1 = 1 + 1 = 2$

JEE SCANNER

Example Similar to PYQ Asked in JEE Main 2024

For any real number x, let $[x]$ denotes the largest integer less than or equal to x. If $I = \int_0^{10} \left[\sqrt{\frac{10x}{x+1}}\right] dx$, then the value of $9I$ is.........

Sol. (182) Given, $I = \int_0^{10} \left[\sqrt{\frac{10x}{x+1}}\right] dx$ ...(i)

$$\frac{10x}{x+1} = 1 \Rightarrow 10x = x + 1 \Rightarrow x = \frac{1}{9}$$

$$\frac{10x}{x+1} = 4 \Rightarrow 10x = 4x + 4 \Rightarrow x = \frac{2}{3}$$

$$\frac{10x}{x+1} = 9 \Rightarrow 10x = 9x + 9 \Rightarrow x = 9$$

From Eq. (i), we get

$$I = \int_0^{1/9} \left[\sqrt{\frac{10x}{x+1}}\right] dx + \int_{1/9}^{2/3} \left[\sqrt{\frac{10x}{x+1}}\right] dx + \int_{2/3}^{9} \left[\sqrt{\frac{10x}{x+1}}\right] dx + \int_9^{10} \left[\sqrt{\frac{10x}{x+1}}\right] dx$$

$$= \int_0^{1/9} 0 \cdot dx + \int_{1/9}^{2/3} 1 \cdot dx + \int_{2/3}^{9} 2 \cdot dx + \int_9^{10} 3 \cdot dx$$

$$= 0 + [x]_{1/9}^{2/3} + [2x]_{2/3}^{9} + [3x]_9^{10}$$

$$= \frac{2}{3} - \frac{1}{9} + 18 - \frac{4}{3} + 30 - 27 = 21 - \frac{2}{3} - \frac{1}{9} = \frac{182}{9}$$

Hence, $9I = 182$

Skill Builder

For any real number x, let $[x]$ denotes the greatest integer less than or equal to x. If $I = \int_0^{12} \left[\sqrt{\frac{11x}{x+1}}\right] dx$, then the value of $14I$ is ....

For Sol.

- **For more practice** See Q.18 of Milestone Practice 2.3.

Milestone Practice 2.3

1. The value of $\int_{-1}^{3}\{|x-2|+[x]\}\,dx$, where [.] denotes the greatest integer function, is equal to
(a) 5 (b) 6 (c) 7 (d) None of these

2. The value of $\int_{-1}^{3}(|x|+|x-1|)\,dx$ is equal to
(a) 9 (b) 6 (c) 3 (d) None of these

3. Evaluate $\int_0^3 [2x]\,dx$, where $[\cdot]$ denotes GIF.

4. The value of $\int_0^2 [x+[x+[x]]]\,dx$ (where, [.] denotes the greatest integer function) is equal to
(a) 2 (b) 3 (c) −3 (d) None of these

5. The value of $\int_0^{[x]}\dfrac{2^x}{2^{[x]}}\,dx$ is equal to (where, [.] denotes the greatest integer function)
(a) $\dfrac{[x]}{\log 2}$ (b) $\dfrac{[x]}{2\log 2}$ (c) $\dfrac{[x]}{4\log 2}$ (d) None of these

6. Evaluate $\int_0^4 \text{sgn}\,(x^2-3x+2)\,dx$.

7. The value of $\int_1^4 \{x\}^{[x]}\,dx$ (where, [.] and {.} denote the greatest integer and fractional part of x) is equal to
(a) $\dfrac{11}{12}$ (b) $\dfrac{13}{12}$
(c) $\dfrac{7}{12}$ (d) $\dfrac{19}{12}$

8. The value of $\int_0^x [t+1]^3\,dt$ (where, [.] denotes the greatest integer function of x) is equal to
(a) $\left(\dfrac{[x]([x]+1)}{2}\right)^2+([x]+1)^3\{x\}$
(b) $\left(\dfrac{[x]([x]+1)}{2}\right)^3+([x]+1)^3+\{x\}$
(c) $\left(\dfrac{[x]([x]+1)}{2}\right)^3+([x]+1)^2+\{x\}$
(d) None of the above

9. The value of $\int_0^{10\pi}[\tan^{-1}x]\,dx$ (where, $[\cdot]$ denotes the greatest integer function of x) is equal to
(a) $\tan 1$ (b) 10π
(c) $10\pi-\tan 1$ (d) None of these

10. The value of $\int_0^{\infty}[2e^{-x}]\,dx$ (where, $[\cdot]$ denotes the greatest integer function of x) is equal to
(a) 1 (b) $\log_e 2$ (c) 0 (d) $\dfrac{1}{e}$

11. The value of $\int_1^{10\pi}([\sec^{-1}x]+[\cot^{-1}x])\,dx$ (where, $[\cdot]$ denotes the greatest integer function) is equal to
(a) $(\sec 1)-10\pi$ (b) $10\pi-\sec 1$
(c) $\pi-\sec 1$ (d) None of these

12. The value of $\int_{-\pi/2}^{\pi/2}[\cot^{-1}x]\,dx$ (where, $[\cdot]$ denotes greatest integer function) is equal to
(a) $\pi+\cot 1$ (b) $\pi+\cot 2$
(c) $\pi+\cot 1+\cot 2$ (d) $\cot 1+\cot 2$

13. The value of $\int_0^{\pi/4}(\tan^n(x-[x])+\tan^{n-2}(x-[x]))\,dx$ (where, $[\cdot]$ denotes greatest integer function) is equal to
(a) $\dfrac{1}{n}$ (b) $\dfrac{1}{n-1}$ (c) $\dfrac{1}{n(n-1)}$ (d) $\dfrac{1}{n(n+1)}$

14. The value of $\int_0^1[-8x^2+6x-1]\,dx$ (where $[\cdot]$ denotes GIF) is equal to
(a) −1 (b) $-\dfrac{5}{4}$ (c) $\dfrac{\sqrt{17}-13}{8}$ (d) $\dfrac{\sqrt{17}-11}{8}$

15. Evaluate $\int_0^a [x^n]\,dx$, (where, $[\cdot]$ denotes the greatest integer function).

16. Prove that $\int_0^x [x]\,dx = x[x]-\dfrac{1}{2}[x]([x]+1)$, where $[\cdot]$ denotes the greatest integer function.

17. If $f(n)=\dfrac{\int_0^n [x]\,dx}{\int_0^n \{x\}\,dx}$ (where, $[\cdot]$ and $\{\cdot\}$ denotes greatest integer and fractional part of x and $n\in N$). Then, the value of $f(4)$ is ...

18. If $f(x)=\int_0^x [\cos t]\,dt$, where $x\in\left(2n\pi, 2n\pi+\dfrac{\pi}{2}\right)$; $n\in N$ and $[\cdot]$ denotes the greatest integer function. Then, the value of $\left|f\left(\dfrac{1}{\pi}\right)\right|$ is ...

19. If $\int_0^x [x]\,dx=\int_0^{[x]} x\,dx$, $x\notin$ integer (where, $[\cdot]$ and $\{\cdot\}$ denotes the greatest integer and fractional parts respectively, then the value of $4\{x\}$ is equal to ...

Answer Key

1. (c)	2. (a)	3. 15/2	4. (b)	5. (a)	6. 2	7. (b)	8. (a)	9. (c)
10. (b)	11. (b)	12. (c)	13. (b)	14. (c)	15. $-1-2^{1/n}-3^{1/n}...-a$			
17. 3	18. 1	19. 2						

For Detailed Solution

Milestone 4 Applications of Even-Odd Property and Half the Integral Limit Property

PROPERTY VI

$$\int_{-a}^{a} f(x)\,dx = \begin{cases} 2\int_0^a f(x)\,dx, & \text{if } f(x) \text{ is an even function} \\ 0, & \text{if } f(x) \text{ is an odd function} \end{cases}$$

Proof We know,

$$\int_a^b f(x)\,dx = \int_a^c f(x)\,dx + \int_c^b f(x)\,dx, \text{if } a < c < b$$

$$\therefore \quad \int_{-a}^{a} f(x)\,dx = \int_{-a}^{0} f(x)\,dx + \int_0^a f(x)\,dx \qquad \text{...(i)}$$

Now, $\int_{-a}^{0} f(x)\,dx = \int_a^0 f(-t)(-dt)$,

where $t = -x$

$$= -\int_a^0 f(-t)\,dt = \int_0^a f(-t)\,dt$$

$$= \int_0^a f(-x)\,dx \qquad \text{[using properties I and II]}$$

$$= \begin{cases} \int_0^a f(x)\,dx, & \text{if } f(x) \text{ is even} \\ -\int_0^a f(x)\,dx, & \text{if } f(x) \text{ is odd} \end{cases} \qquad \text{...(ii)}$$

From Eqs. (i) and (ii), we get

$$\int_{-a}^{a} f(x)\,dx = \begin{cases} 2\int_0^a f(x)\,dx, & f(x) \text{ is even} \\ 0, & \text{if } f(x) \text{ is odd} \end{cases}$$

Example 26. Evaluate $\int_{-\pi/2}^{\pi/2} \sin^2 x\,dx$.

Sol. Let $f(x) = \sin^2 x$, then

$$f(-x) = \sin^2(-x)$$
$$= [\sin(-x)]^2 = (-\sin x)^2 = \sin^2 x = f(x)$$

So, $f(x)$ is an even function, hence

$$\int_{-\pi/2}^{\pi/2} (\sin^2 x)\,dx = 2\int_0^{\pi/2} (\sin^2 x)\,dx$$

$$= 2\int_0^{\pi/2} \frac{1-\cos 2x}{2}\,dx$$

$$= \left(x - \frac{\sin 2x}{2}\right)_0^{\pi/2} = \frac{\pi}{2}$$

$$\therefore \quad \int_{-\pi/2}^{\pi/2} \sin^2 x\,dx = \frac{\pi}{2}$$

Example 27. Evaluate $\int_{-1/2}^{1/2} \sec x \ln\left(\frac{1-x}{1+x}\right) dx$.

Sol. Let $I = \int_{-1/2}^{1/2} \sec x \cdot \ln\left(\frac{1-x}{1+x}\right) dx$

$$f(x) = \sec x \cdot \ln\left(\frac{1-x}{1+x}\right)$$

$$f(-x) = \sec(-x)\left(-\ln\left(\frac{1-x}{1+x}\right)\right) = -f(x)$$

$\Rightarrow f(x)$ is an odd function.

$$\therefore \quad I = 0$$

Example 28. Let $f, g : [-a, a] \to R$ be two continuous functions and f is odd and g is even, then prove

$$\int_{-a}^{a} \frac{g(x)}{1 + f(x) + \sqrt{1 + f^2(x)}}\,dx = \int_0^a g(x)\,dx$$

Sol.

$$I = \int_{-a}^{a} \frac{g(x)}{1 + f(x) + \sqrt{1 + f^2(x)}}\,dx \qquad \text{...(i)}$$

$$I = \int_{-a}^{a} \frac{g(-x)}{1 + f(-x) + \sqrt{1 + f^2(-x)}}\,dx$$

$$\left[\because \int_a^b f(x)\,dx = \int f(a+b-x)\,dx\right]$$

$$I = \int_{-a}^{a} \frac{g(x)}{(1 - f(x)) + \sqrt{1 + f^2(x)}}\,dx \qquad \text{...(ii)}$$

$$[\because g(-x) = g(x), f(-x) = -f(x)]$$

On adding Eqs. (i) and (ii), we get

$$2I = \int_{-a}^{a} \frac{2g(x)[1 + \sqrt{1 + f^2(x)}]}{[1 + \sqrt{1 + f^2(x)}]^2 - f^2(x)}\,dx$$

$$\Rightarrow \quad I = \int_{-a}^{a} \frac{g(x)[1 + \sqrt{1 + f^2(x)}]}{[1 + 1 + f^2(x) + 2\sqrt{1 + f^2(x)}] - f^2(x)}\,dx$$

$$\Rightarrow \quad I = \frac{1}{2}\int_{-a}^{a} g(x)\,dx = \frac{1}{2}\cdot 2\int_0^a g(x)\,dx$$

$$\therefore \quad I = \int_0^a g(x)\,dx$$

JEE SCANNER

Example Similar to PYQ Asked in JEE Main 2022

The value of the integral $\int_{-2}^{2} \frac{\cos x}{\left[\frac{x}{\pi}\right]+\frac{1}{2}} dx$ *is, where [x] is greatest integer function.*

(a) $\frac{\pi}{2}$ (b) 1 (c) 0 (d) $\frac{\pi}{4}$

Sol. (c) Let $I = \int_{-2}^{2} \frac{\cos x}{\left[\frac{x}{\pi}\right]+\frac{1}{2}} dx$ ...(i)

Let $f(x) = \left[\frac{x}{\pi}\right]+\frac{1}{2}$

$$f(-x) = \left[-\frac{x}{\pi}\right]+\frac{1}{2}$$

$$f(-x) = -1 - \left[\frac{x}{\pi}\right]+\frac{1}{2} = -\frac{1}{2} - \left[\frac{x}{\pi}\right]$$

$[\because [-x]+[x] = -1, x \notin I]$

$$f(-x) = -f(x)$$

$$I = \int_{-2}^{2} -\frac{\cos x}{\left[\frac{x}{\pi}\right]+\frac{1}{2}} dx \quad \text{...(ii)}$$

On adding Eqs. (i) and (ii), we get

$$2I = 0$$

$$\therefore \quad I = 0$$

Skill Builder

The value of the integral $\int_{-4}^{4} \frac{\cos^3 x}{\left[\frac{x}{\pi}\right]+\frac{1}{2}} dx$ is, where $[x]$ is greatest integer function.

For Sol.

(a) $\frac{\pi}{2}$ (b) 0 (c) 1 (d) $\frac{\pi}{4}$

■ **For more practice** See Q.9 of Milestone Practice 2.4,

Example 29. Evaluate

$$\int_{-1}^{1} \frac{x}{\sqrt{1-x^2}} \cdot \sin^{-1}(2x\sqrt{1-x^2})\, dx.$$

Sol. Let $I = \int_{-1}^{1} \frac{x}{\sqrt{1-x^2}} \cdot \sin^{-1}(2x\sqrt{1-x^2})\, dx$

$$= 2\int_{0}^{1} \frac{x}{\sqrt{1-x^2}} \cdot \sin^{-1}(2x\sqrt{1-x^2})\, dx$$

$$\left[\text{using } \int_{-a}^{a} f(x)\,dx = 2\int_{0}^{a} f(x)\,dx, \text{if } f(-x) = f(x)\right]$$

Put $x = \sin\theta \Rightarrow dx = \cos\theta\, d\theta$

$$\therefore I = 2\int_{0}^{\pi/2} \frac{\sin\theta}{\sqrt{1-\sin^2\theta}} \cdot \sin^{-1}(2\sin\theta\cos\theta) \cdot \cos\theta\, d\theta$$

$$= 2\int_{0}^{\pi/4} \sin\theta \cdot 2\theta\, d\theta + 2\int_{\pi/4}^{\pi/2} (\pi - 2\theta)\sin\theta\, d\theta$$

$$\left[\text{using } \sin^{-1}(\sin 2\theta) = \begin{cases} 2\theta, & 0<\theta<\pi/4 \\ \pi - 2\theta, & \pi/4<\theta<\pi/2 \end{cases}\right]$$

$$= 4\int_{0}^{\pi/4} \theta\cdot\sin\theta\, d\theta + 2\pi\int_{\pi/4}^{\pi/2} \sin\theta\, d\theta - 4\int_{\pi/4}^{\pi/2} \theta\cdot\sin\theta\, d\theta$$

$$= 4\{\theta(-\cos\theta)\}_0^{\pi/4} - 4\int_{0}^{\pi/4} 1\cdot(-\cos\theta)d\theta + 2\pi(-\cos\theta)_{\pi/4}^{\pi/2}$$

$$- 4\{\theta(-\cos\theta)\}_{\pi/4}^{\pi/2} + 4\int_{\pi/4}^{\pi/2} (-\cos\theta)\, d\theta$$

$$= -\frac{\pi}{\sqrt{2}} + 2\sqrt{2} + \sqrt{2}\pi - \frac{\pi}{\sqrt{2}} - 4 + 2\sqrt{2}$$

$$= 4\sqrt{2} - 4 = 4(\sqrt{2} - 1)$$

Example 30. Suppose the function $g_n(x) = x^{2n+1} + a_n x + b_n (n \in N)$ satisfies the equation $\int_{-1}^{1} (px+q) g_n(x) dx = 0$ for all linear functions $(px+q)$, then find $\left|\frac{1}{a_6}\right|$.

Sol. We have, $\int_{-1}^{1} (px+q)(x^{2n+1} + a_n x + b_n) dx = 0$

Equating the odd component to be zero and integrating, we get

$$\frac{2p}{2n+3} + \frac{2a_n p}{3} + 2b_n q = 0 \text{ for all } p, q$$

Therefore, $b_n = 0$ and $a_n = -\frac{3}{2n+3}$

$$\Rightarrow \quad a_6 = \frac{-3}{12+3} = -\frac{1}{5} \Rightarrow \left|\frac{1}{a_6}\right| = |-5| = 5$$

PROPERTY VII (a)

$$\int_{0}^{2a} f(x)\,dx = \begin{cases} 2\int_{0}^{a} f(x)\,dx, & \text{if } f(2a-x) = f(x) \\ 0, & \text{if } f(2a-x) = -f(x) \end{cases}$$

Proof We know,

$$\int_{0}^{2a} f(x)\,dx = \int_{0}^{a} f(x)\,dx + \int_{a}^{2a} f(x)\,dx \quad \text{...(i)}$$

Consider the integral $\int_{a}^{2a} f(x)\,dx$; putting $x = 2a - t$,

so that $dx = -dt$

Also, when $x = a$, then $t = a$ and when $x = 2a$, then $t = 0$.

$$\therefore \int_{a}^{2a} f(x)\,dx = \int_{a}^{0} f(2a-t)(-dt) = -\int_{a}^{0} f(2a-t)\,dt$$

$$= \int_{0}^{a} f(2a-t)\,dt = \int_{0}^{a} f(2a-x)\,dx$$

$$= \begin{cases} \int_{0}^{a} f(x)\,dx, & \text{if } f(2a-x) = f(x) \\ -\int_{0}^{a} f(x)\,dx, & \text{if } f(2a-x) = -f(x) \end{cases} \quad \text{...(ii)}$$

From Eqs. (i) and (ii), we have

$$\int_0^{2a} f(x)\,dx = \begin{cases} 2\int_0^a f(x)\,dx, & \text{if } f(2a-x) = f(x) \\ 0, & \text{if } f(2a-x) = -f(x) \end{cases}$$

Example 31. Evaluate $\int_0^{\pi} \frac{x}{1+\cos^2 x}\,dx$.

Sol. Let $I = \int_0^{\pi} \frac{x}{1+\cos^2 x}\,dx = \int_0^{\pi} \frac{(\pi - x)\,dx}{1+\cos^2(\pi - x)}$

$$= \int_0^{\pi} \frac{\pi\,dx}{1+\cos^2 x} - \int_0^{\pi} \frac{x\,dx}{1+\cos^2 x}$$

$$\therefore \quad I = \pi \int_0^{\pi} \frac{dx}{1+\cos^2 x} - I$$

$$\Rightarrow \quad 2I = \pi \int_0^{\pi} \frac{dx}{1+\cos^2 x} = 2\pi \int_0^{\pi/2} \frac{dx}{1+\cos^2 x}$$

$$\left[\text{using} \int_0^{2a} f(x)\,dx = \begin{cases} 0, & f(2a-x) = -f(x) \\ 2\int_0^a f(x)\,dx, & f(2a-x) = f(x) \end{cases}\right]$$

$$\Rightarrow \quad I = \pi \int_0^{\pi/2} \frac{\sec^2 x}{\sec^2 x + 1}\,dx$$

[dividing numerator and denominator by $\cos^2 x$]

$$I = \pi \int_0^{\pi/2} \frac{\sec^2 x}{2+\tan^2 x}\,dx$$

Put $\tan x = t \Rightarrow \sec^2 x\,dx = dt$

Also, when $x = 0$, then $t = 0$ and when $x = \pi/2$, then $t = \infty$

Hence, $I = \pi \int_0^{\infty} \frac{dt}{2+t^2} = \frac{\pi}{\sqrt{2}}\left(\tan^{-1}\frac{t}{\sqrt{2}}\right)_0^{\infty}$

$$= \frac{\pi}{\sqrt{2}}\left(\frac{\pi}{2} - 0\right) = \frac{\pi^2}{2\sqrt{2}}$$

Example 32. Prove that

$$\int_0^{\pi/2} \log(\sin x)\,dx = \int_0^{\pi/2} \log(\cos x)\,dx = -\frac{\pi}{2}\log 2.$$

Sol. Let $I = \int_0^{\pi/2} \log(\sin x)\,dx$ ...(i)

Then, $I = \int_0^{\pi/2} \log\sin(\pi/2 - x)\,dx$

$= \int_0^{\pi/2} \log(\cos x)\,dx$ ...(ii)

On adding Eqs. (i) and (ii), we get

$$2I = \int_0^{\pi/2} \log\sin x\,dx + \int_0^{\pi/2} \log\cos x\,dx$$

$$= \int_0^{\pi/2} (\log\sin x + \log\cos x)\,dx$$

$$= \int_0^{\pi/2} \log(\sin x\cos x)\,dx = \int_0^{\pi/2} \log\left(\frac{2\sin x\cos x}{2}\right)dx$$

$$= \int_0^{\pi/2} \log\left(\frac{\sin 2x}{2}\right)dx$$

$$= \int_0^{\pi/2} \log(\sin 2x)\,dx - \int_0^{\pi/2} (\log 2)\,dx$$

$$= \int_0^{\pi/2} \log\sin 2x\,dx - (\log 2)(x)_0^{\pi/2}$$

$\Rightarrow 2I = \int_0^{\pi/2} \log(\sin 2x)\,dx - \frac{\pi}{2}\log 2$ ...(iii)

Let $I_1 = \int_0^{\pi/2} \log(\sin 2x)\,dx$

$I_1 = \int_0^{\pi} \log\sin t\,\frac{dt}{2}$ [putting $2x = t$]

$$= \frac{1}{2}\int_0^{\pi} \log\sin t\,dt = \frac{1}{2}\cdot 2\int_0^{\pi/2} \log(\sin t)\,dt$$

$$\left[\text{using} \int_0^{2a} f(x)\,dx = \begin{cases} 0, & f(2a-x) = -f(x) \\ 2\int_0^a f(x)\,dx, & f(2a-x) = f(x) \end{cases}\right]$$

$$= \int_0^{\pi/2} \log(\sin x)\,dx$$

$\therefore$ Eq. (iii) becomes $2I = I - \frac{\pi}{2}\log 2$

Hence, $\int_0^{\pi/2} \log\sin x\,dx = -\frac{\pi}{2}\log 2.$

Example 33. If $f(x) = -\int_0^x \log(\cos t)\,dt$, then find

$$f(x) - 2f\left(\frac{\pi}{4}+\frac{x}{2}\right) + 2f\left(\frac{\pi}{4}-\frac{x}{2}\right).$$

Sol. Here, $f\left(\frac{\pi}{4}+\frac{x}{2}\right) = -\int_0^{\pi/4 + x/2} \log(\cos t)\,dt$

$= -\int_0^{\pi/4} \log(\cos t)\,dt - \int_{\pi/4}^{\pi/4 + x/2} \log(\cos t)\,dt$ ...(i)

$f\left(\frac{\pi}{4}-\frac{x}{2}\right) = -\int_0^{\pi/4 - x/2} \log(\cos t)\,dt$

$= -\int_0^{\pi/4} \log(\cos t)\,dt - \int_{\pi/4}^{\pi/4 - x/2} \log(\cos t)\,dt$ ...(ii)

$$\therefore \quad 2f\left(\frac{\pi}{4}+\frac{x}{2}\right) - 2f\left(\frac{\pi}{4}-\frac{x}{2}\right)$$

$$= 2\int_{\pi/4}^{\pi/4 - x/2} \log(\cos t)\,dt - 2\int_{\pi/4}^{\pi/4 + x/2} \log(\cos t)\,dt$$

Put $t = \frac{\pi}{4} - z$ in first integral and $t = \frac{\pi}{4} + z$ in second integral, we get

$$= -2\int_0^{x/2} \log\cos\left(\frac{\pi}{4} - z\right)dz - 2\int_0^{x/2} \log\cos\left(z + \frac{\pi}{4}\right)dz$$

$$= -2\int_0^{x/2} \log\left(\frac{1}{2}(\cos^2 z - \sin^2 z)\right)dz$$

$$= 2\int_0^{x/2} (\log 2)\,dz - 2\int_0^{x/2} \log(\cos 2z)\,dz$$

$$= x\log 2 - 2\int_0^{x/2} \log(\cos 2z)\,dz$$

$$\therefore \quad 2f\left(\frac{\pi}{4}+\frac{x}{2}\right) - 2f\left(\frac{\pi}{4}-\frac{x}{2}\right) = x(\log 2) - 2\int_0^{x/2} \log(\cos 2z)\,dz$$

$$\Rightarrow \quad 2f\left(\frac{\pi}{4}+\frac{x}{2}\right) - 2f\left(\frac{\pi}{4}-\frac{x}{2}\right) = x(\log 2) + f(x)$$

or $\quad f(x) - 2f\left(\frac{\pi}{4}+\frac{x}{2}\right) + 2f\left(\frac{\pi}{4}-\frac{x}{2}\right) = -x\log 2$

Example 34. If $\int_0^{\pi}\left(\frac{x}{1+\sin x}\right)^2 dx = A$, then the value for $\int_0^{\pi}\frac{2x^2\cdot\cos^2 x/2}{(1+\sin x)^2}dx$ is equal to

(a) $A+2\pi-\pi^2$ (b) $A-2\pi+\pi^2$
(c) $2\pi-A-\pi^2$ (d) None of these

Sol. (a) Let $B=\int_0^{\pi}\frac{2x^2\cos^2 x/2}{(1+\sin x)^2}dx$

$$\therefore\ B-A=\int_0^{\pi}\frac{x^2(2\cos^2 x/2-1)}{(1+\sin x)^2}dx=\int_0^{\pi}\frac{x^2\cdot\cos x}{(1+\sin x)^2}dx$$

Using by parts,

$$B-A=\left\{-\frac{x^2}{1+\sin x}\right\}_0^{\pi}+2\int_0^{\pi}\frac{x}{(1+\sin x)}dx$$

$$B-A=-\pi^2+2K \quad \text{...(i)}$$

where, $K=\int_0^{\pi}\frac{x\,dx}{1+\sin x}=\int_0^{\pi}\frac{(\pi-x)\,dx}{1+\sin x}$

$$\therefore\ K=\pi\int_0^{\pi}\frac{dx}{1+\sin x}-K,$$

$$\left[\text{using}\int_0^{2a}f(x)\,dx=\begin{cases}0, & f(2a-x)=-f(x)\\ 2\int_0^a f(x)\,dx, & f(2a-x)=f(x)\end{cases}\right]$$

$$\Rightarrow\ 2K=2\pi\int_0^{\pi/2}\frac{dx}{1+\sin x}=2\pi\int_0^{\pi/2}\frac{dx}{1+\cos x}$$

$$=2\pi\int_0^{\pi/2}\frac{1}{2}\sec^2\frac{x}{2}\,dx=2\pi\left\{\tan\frac{x}{2}\right\}_0^{\pi/2}=2\pi$$

$$\therefore\ K=\pi$$

Thus, $B-A=-\pi^2+2K\Rightarrow B=A-\pi^2+2\pi$

PROPERTY VII (b)

$$\int_a^b f(x)\,dx=(b-a)\int_0^1 f[(b-a)\,x+a]\,dx$$

Sometimes, it is convenient to change the limits of integration into some other limits. For example, suppose we have to add two definite integrals I_1 and I_2; the limits of integration of these integrals are different. if we could somehow change the limits of I_2 into those of I_1 or vice-versa, or infact change the limits of both I_1 and I_2 into a third (common) set of limits, the addition could be accomplished easily.

Suppose that $I=\int_a^b f(x)\,dx$. We need to change the limits (a to b) to (a' to b'). As x varies from a to b, we need a new variable t (in terms of x) which varies from a' to b'.

As x varies from a to b, t varies from a' to b'.

Thus, $\frac{t-a'}{x-a}=\frac{b'-a'}{b-a}$

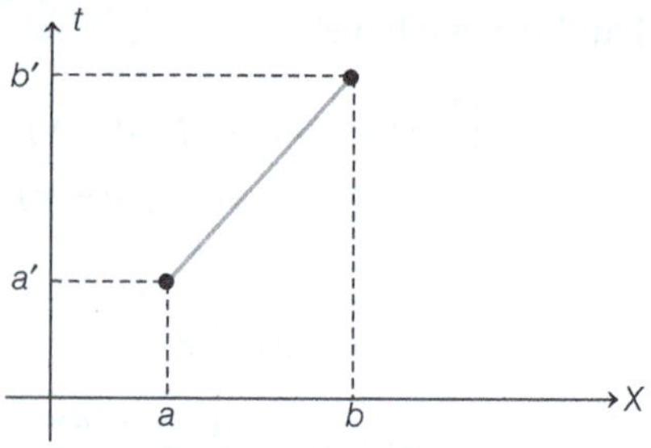

As described in the figure above, the new variable t is given by, $t=a'+\left(\frac{b'-a'}{b-a}\right)(x-a)$.

Thus, $dt=\frac{b'-a'}{b-a}dx$

$$\Rightarrow I=\int_a^b f(x)\,dx=\int_{a'}^{b'}f\left(a+\left(\frac{b-a}{b'-a'}\right)(t-a')\right)\left(\frac{b-a}{b'-a'}\right)dt$$

The modified integral has the limits (a' to b'). A particular case of this property is modifying the arbitrary integration limits (a to b) to (0 to 1) i.e. $a'=0$ and $b'=1$. For this case,

$$I=\int_a^b f(x)\,dx=(b-a)\int_0^1 f(a+(b-a)\,x)\,dx$$

Example 35. Evaluate

$$\int_{-4}^{-5}e^{(x+5)^2}dx+3\int_{1/3}^{2/3}e^{9\left(x-\frac{2}{3}\right)^2}dx.$$

Sol. Here, we know $\int e^{x^2}dx$ cannot be evaluated by indefinite integral.

Let $I_1=\int_{-4}^{-5}e^{(x+5)^2}dx=(-5+4)\int_0^1 e^{[(-5+4)x-4+5]^2}dx$

$$\therefore\ I_1=-\int_0^1 e^{(x-1)^2}dx \quad \text{...(i)}$$

Again, let $I_2=\int_{1/3}^{2/3}e^{9(x-2/3)^2}dx$

$$=\left(\frac{2}{3}-\frac{1}{3}\right)\int_0^1 e^{9\left[\left(\frac{2}{3}-\frac{1}{3}\right)x+\frac{1}{3}-\frac{2}{3}\right]^2}dx$$

$$=\frac{1}{3}\int_0^1 e^{(x-1)^2}dx=\frac{1}{3}(-I_1) \quad \text{...(ii)}$$

where, $I=I_1+3I_2=I_1+3\left(-\frac{I_1}{3}\right)=I_1-I_1=0$

$$\therefore\ \int_{-4}^{-5}e^{(x+5)^2}dx+3\int_{1/3}^{2/3}e^{9(x-2/3)^2}dx=0$$

PROPERTY VII (c)

If $f(t)$ is an odd function, then $\phi(x)=\int_a^x f(t)\,dt$ is an even function.

Proof We have, $\phi(-x)=\int_a^{-x}f(t)\,dt$

$$\Rightarrow\ \phi(-x)=\int_a^{-a}f(t)\,dt+\int_{-a}^{-x}f(t)\,dt$$

$\Rightarrow \quad \phi(-x) = 0 + \int_{-a}^{-x} f(t)\, dt$

$\left[\because f(t) \text{ is an odd function, then } \int_{-a}^{a} f(t)\, dt = 0\right]$

$\Rightarrow \quad \phi(-x) = -\int_{a}^{x} f(-y)\, dy, \text{ where } t = -y$

$\Rightarrow \quad \phi(-x) = \int_{a}^{x} f(y)\, dy$

$[\because f \text{ is an odd function, then } f(-y) = -f(y)]$

$\Rightarrow \quad \phi(-x) = \int_{a}^{x} f(t)\, dt \quad \Rightarrow \phi(-x) = \phi(x)$

Hence, $\phi(x) = \int_{a}^{x} f(t)\, dt$ is an even function, if $f(t)$ is odd.

Example 36. If $f(x) = \int_0^x \log\left(\frac{1-t}{1+t}\right) dt$, then discuss whether even or odd?

Sol. Let $\quad \phi(t) = \log\left(\frac{1-t}{1+t}\right)$

$\therefore \quad \phi(-t) = \log\left(\frac{1+t}{1-t}\right) = -\log\left(\frac{1-t}{1+t}\right) = -\phi(t)$

$\Rightarrow \quad \phi(-t) = -\phi(t)$ i.e. $\phi(t)$ is odd function

$\therefore \quad f(x) = \int_0^x \log\left(\frac{1-t}{1+t}\right) dt$ is an even function.

PROPERTY VII (d)

If $f(t)$ is an even function, then $\phi(x) = \int_0^x f(t)\, dt$ is an odd function.

Proof We have,

$$\phi(-x) = \int_0^{-x} f(t)\, dt$$

$$= -\int_0^{x} f(-y)\, dy, \text{ where } t = -y$$

$\Rightarrow \quad \phi(-x) = -\int_0^{x} f(y)\, dy$

$[\because f \text{ is even function} \Rightarrow f(-y) = f(y)]$

$\Rightarrow \quad \phi(-x) = -\int_0^{x} f(t)\, dt \Rightarrow \phi(-x) = -\phi(x)$

Hence, $\phi(x)$ is an odd function.

JEE SPIKE

If $f(t)$ is an even function, then for non-zero 'a', $\int_a^x f(t)\, dt$ is not necessarily an odd function.

It will be an odd function, if $\int_0^a f(t)\, dt = 0$,

because, if $\phi(x) = \int_a^x f(t)\, dt$, it is an odd function.

Concept Inside Video

Example 37. Prove that the function

$f(x) = \int_0^x \cos(\sin(\log(\sqrt{t^2+1}+t)))dt$ is an odd function.

Sol. Let $\phi(t) = \cos(\sin(\log(\sqrt{t^2+1}+t)))$

$$\phi(-t) = \cos(\sin(\log(\sqrt{t^2+1}-t)))$$

$$= \cos\left(\sin\left(\log\left(\frac{t^2+1-t^2}{\sqrt{t^2+1}+t}\right)\right)\right)$$

$$= \cos\left(\sin\log\left(\frac{1}{\sqrt{t^2+1}+t}\right)\right)$$

$$= \cos(-\sin\log(\sqrt{t^2+1}+t))$$

$$= \cos(\sin(\log\sqrt{t^2+1}+t)) = \phi(t)$$

is an even function.

$\therefore f(x) = \int_0^x \cos(\sin(\log(\sqrt{t^2+1}+t)))dt$ is an odd function.

Milestone Practice 2.4

1. Let $f: R \to R$ and $g: R \to R$ be continuous functions, then the value of $\int_{-\pi/2}^{\pi/2} [f(x) + f(-x)][g(x) - g(-x)]\, dx$ is equal to

(a) -1 (b) 0
(c) 1 (d) None of these

2. The value of $\int_{-1}^{1} \left(\frac{x^2 + \sin x}{1 + x^2}\right) dx$ is equal to

(a) $2 - \pi$ (b) $\pi - 2$
(c) $2 - \frac{\pi}{2}$ (d) None of these

3. The value of

$$\int_{-1/\sqrt{3}}^{1/\sqrt{3}} \frac{\cos^{-1}\left(\frac{2x}{1+x^2}\right) + \tan^{-1}\left(\frac{2x}{1-x^2}\right)}{1+e^x} dx$$

is equal to

(a) $\frac{\pi}{2}$ (b) $\frac{\pi}{\sqrt{3}}$
(c) $\frac{\pi}{2\sqrt{3}}$ (d) $\frac{\pi}{3\sqrt{3}}$

4. If $f(x)$ is an odd function, then the value of $\int_{-a}^{a} \frac{f(\sin x)}{f(\cos x) + f(\sin^2 x)} dx$ is equal to

(a) 0 (b) $f(\cos x) + f(\sin x)$
(c) 1 (d) None of these

5. The integral $\int_{-1/2}^{1/2} \left\{[x] + \log_e\left(\frac{1+x}{1-x}\right)\right\} dx$ is equal to (where, [·] denotes greatest integer function)

(a) $-\frac{1}{2}$ (b) 0
(c) 1 (d) $2\log\left(\frac{1}{2}\right)$

6. The value of $\int_{-\pi/2}^{\pi/2} \frac{1}{e^{\sin x} + 1} dx$ is equal to

(a) 0 (b) 1
(c) $\frac{\pi}{2}$ (d) $-\frac{\pi}{2}$

7. If [·] denotes greatest integer function, then the value of $\int_{-\pi/2}^{\pi/2} \left(\left[\frac{\pi}{2}\right] + 0.5\right) dx$ is

(a) π (b) $\frac{\pi}{2}$
(c) 0 (d) $-\frac{\pi}{2}$

8. The equation
$\int_{-\pi/4}^{\pi/4} \left\{a|\sin x| + \frac{b\sin x}{1+\cos^2 x} + c\right\} dx = 0$, where a, b, c are constants gives a relation between

(a) a, b and c (b) a and c
(c) a and b (d) b and c

9. The value of $\int_{-2}^{2} \frac{\sin^2 x}{\left[\frac{x}{2}\right] + \frac{1}{2}} dx$, where [·] denotes greatest integer function, is

(a) 1 (b) 0
(c) $4 - \sin 4$ (d) None of these

10. Let $f(x)$ be a continuous function such that $\int_{n}^{n+1} f(x)\,dx = n^3, n \in Z$. Then, the value of $\int_{-3}^{3} f(x)\,dx$ is

(a) 9 (b) -27 (c) -9 (d) 27

11. Let $f(x) = \frac{e^x + 1}{e^x - 1}$ and $\int_0^1 x^3 \cdot \frac{e^x+1}{e^x-1} dx = \alpha$. Then, $\int_{-1}^{1} t^3 f(t)\,dt$ is equal to

(a) 0 (b) α
(c) 2α (d) None of these

12. Let $f: R \to R$ be a continuous function given by $f(x+y) = f(x) + f(y)$ for all $x, y \in R$. if $\int_0^2 f(x)\,dx = \alpha$, then $\int_{-2}^{2} f(x)\,dx$ is equal to

(a) 2α (b) α
(c) 0 (d) None of these

13. The value of $\int_{-2}^{2} |[x]|\,dx$ is equal to

(a) 1 (b) 2 (c) 3 (d) 4

- **Directions** (Q. Nos. 14 to 16)

Let $I_n = \int_{-\pi}^{\pi} \frac{\sin x}{(1+\pi^x)\sin x} dx; n = 0, 1, 2, \ldots$

14. The value of $I_{n+2} - I_n$ is equal to

(a) $n\pi$ (b) π
(c) $-\pi$ (d) 0

15. The value of $\sum_{m=1}^{10} I_{2m+1}$ is equal to

(a) 0 (b) 5π
(c) 10π (d) None of these

16. The value of $\sum_{m=1}^{10} I_{2m}$ is equal to

(a) 0 (b) 5π
(c) 10π (d) None of these

Answer Key

1. (b)	2. (c)	3. (c)	4. (a)	5. (a)
6. (c)	7. (c)	8. (b)	9. (b)	10. (b)
11. (c)	12. (c)	13. (d)	14. (d)	15. (c)
16. (c)				

For Detailed Solution

Milestone 5 Applications of Periodic Functions and Newton-Leibnitz's Formula

PROPERTY VIII

If $f(x)$ be a periodic function with period T, then

(i) $\int_0^{nT} f(x)\,dx = n\int_0^T f(x)\,dx$

(ii) $\int_a^{a+nT} f(x)dx = n\int_0^T f(x)\,dx,\ n \in Z,\ a \in R$

(iii) $\int_{mT}^{nT} f(x)\,dx = (n-m)\int_0^T f(x)\,dx,\ m, n \in Z$

(iv) $\int_{nT}^{a+nT} f(x)\,dx = \int_0^a f(x)\,dx\ ,\ n \in Z,\ a \in R$

(v) $\int_{a+nT}^{b+nT} f(x)\,dx = \int_a^b f(x)\,dx, n \in Z,\ a, b, \in R$

Proof (i) LHS $\int_0^{nT} f(x)\,dx$

$$= \sum_{r=1}^{n} \int_{(r-1)T}^{rT} f(x)\,dx$$

Put $x = (r-1)T + y$

$$= \sum_{r=1}^{n} \int_0^T f((r-1)T + y)dy$$

Since, $f(x)$ is periodic, so $f[(r-1)T + y] = f(y)$

$$= \sum_{r=1}^{n} \int_0^T f(y)\,dy$$

$$= n\int_0^T f(y)\,dy$$

$$= n\int_0^T f(x)\,dx$$

Graphical Method

If $f(x)$ is a periodic function with period T, then the area under $f(x)$ for n periods would be n times the area under $f(x)$ for one period

i.e. $$\int_0^{nT} f(x)\,dx = n\int_0^T f(x)\,dx$$

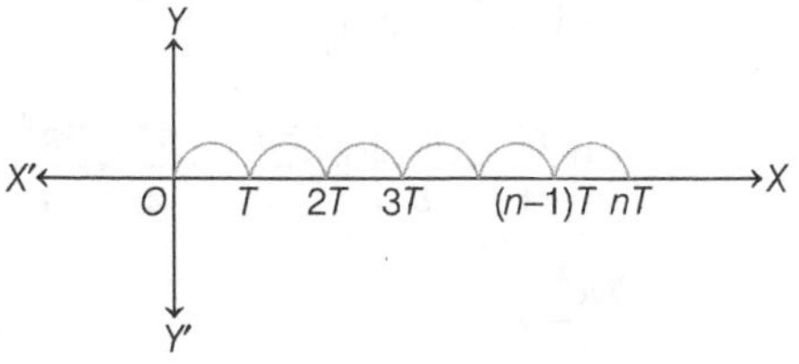

Example 38. Evaluate $\int_0^{4\pi} |\cos x|\,dx$.

Sol. Note that $|\cos x|$ is a periodic with period π.

Let $I = 4\int_0^{\pi} |\cos x|\,dx$

$$\left[\text{using property, } \int_0^{nT} f(x)\,dx = n\int_0^T f(x)\,dx\right]$$

$$= 4\left\{\int_0^{\pi/2} \cos x\,dx - \int_{\pi/2}^{\pi} \cos x\,dx\right\}$$

$$= 4\left\{\left(\sin x\right)_0^{\pi/2} - \left(\sin x\right)_{\pi/2}^{\pi}\right\} = 4\{1+1\} = 8$$

JEE SCANNER

Example Similar to PYQ Asked in JEE Main 2021

The value of $\sum_{n=1}^{25} \int_{n-1}^{n} e^{x-[x]}\,dx$, where $[x]$ is greatest integer $\le x$ is

(a) $25(e-1)$ (b) $25e$
(c) $25(1-e)$ (d) $25(1+e)$

Sol. (a) Since, $x - [x]$ is a periodic function with period one.

Therefore, $e^{x-[x]}$ has period one

$\therefore$ $I = \int_0^{25\times 1} e^{x-[x]}\,dx$

$$= 25\int_0^1 e^{x-[x]}\,dx$$

$$\left[\text{using property, } \int_0^{nT} f(x)\,dx = n\int_0^T f(x)\,dx\right]$$

$$= 25\int_0^1 e^{x-0}\,dx$$

$$= 25\,(e^x)_0^1$$

$$= 25\,(e^1 - e^0) = 25\,(e-1)$$

Skill Builder

The value of $\sum_{n=1}^{50} \int_{n-1}^{n} e^{x-[x]}\,dx$, (where $[x]$ is greatest integer $\le x$) is $\lambda(e-1)$, then the value of λ is

For Sol.

(a) 25 (b) 75 (c) 50 (d) 100

■ **For more practice** See Q.1 of Milestone Practice 2.5.

Example 39. The value of $\int_0^{2n\pi}[\sin x+\cos x]\,dx$ is equal to (where $[\cdot]$ denotes the greatest integer function)

Sol. Let $I=\int_0^{2n\pi}[\sin x+\cos x]\,dx$

We know, $\sin x+\cos x=\sqrt{2}\sin\left(x+\frac{\pi}{4}\right)$ ...(i)

$$\therefore \quad \sin x+\cos x=\begin{cases}1, & 0\le x\le \pi/2\\ 0, & \pi/2<x\le 3\pi/4\\ -1, & 3\pi/4<x\le \pi\\ -2, & \pi<x<3\pi/2\\ -1, & 3\pi/2\le x<7\pi/4\\ 0, & 7\pi/4\le x\le 2\pi\end{cases}$$

$$\therefore \int_0^{2\pi}[\sin x+\cos x]dx=\int_0^{\pi/2}(1)\,dx+\int_{\pi/2}^{3\pi/4}(0)\,dx$$

$$+\int_{3\pi/4}^{\pi}(-1)dx+\int_{\pi}^{3\pi/2}(-2)dx+\int_{3\pi/2}^{7\pi/4}(-1)dx+\int_{7\pi/4}^{2\pi}(0)\,dx$$

$$=\left(\frac{\pi}{2}\right)+(0)-\left(\pi-\frac{3\pi}{4}\right)-2\left(\frac{3\pi}{2}-\pi\right)-1\left(\frac{7\pi}{4}-\frac{3\pi}{2}\right)+0$$

$$=-\pi$$

Since, $\sin x+\cos x$ has the period 2π.

So, $I=\int_0^{2n\pi}[\sin x+\cos x]\,dx=n\int_0^{2\pi}[\sin x+\cos x]\,dx$

$$=-n\pi$$

Example 40. Find the value of $\int_{-5}^{5}f(x)\,dx$; where $f(x)=\text{minimum}(\{x+1\},\{x-1\}),\forall x\in R$ and $\{.\}$ denotes fractional part of x.

Sol. We know, $\{x+1\}=\{x-1\}=\{x\}$

Thus, $f(x)=\text{minimum}(\{x+1\},\{x-1\})=\{x\}$

$$\Rightarrow \int_{-5}^{5}f(x)\,dx=\int_{-5}^{5}\{x\}\,dx=(5-(-5))\int_0^1\{x\}\,dx$$

[as $\{x\}$ is periodic with period '1']

$$=10\int_0^1(x-[x])\,dx=10\int_0^1 x\,dx$$

$$=10\left(\frac{x^2}{2}\right)_0^1=5$$

Example 41. Evaluate $\int_{-1}^{2}e^{\{5x\}}\,dx$, (where $\{\cdot\}$ denotes FPF).

Sol. $e^{\{5x\}}$ is periodic with period $T=\frac{1}{5}$

$$I=\int_{-1}^{2}e^{\{5x\}}\,dx=\int_{-5T}^{10T}e^{\{5x\}}\,dx$$

$$=(10-(-5))\int_0^T e^{\{5x\}}\,dx$$

$$=15\int_0^{1/5}e^{\{5x\}}\,dx \quad \left(\begin{array}{l}0<x<\frac{1}{5}\Rightarrow 0<5x<1\\ \{5x\}=5x\end{array}\right)$$

$$=15\int_0^{1/5}e^{5x}\,dx$$

$$=15\left[\frac{e^{5x}}{5}\right]_0^{1/5}$$

$$=3(e-1)$$

Example 42. Show $\int_0^{n\pi+V}|\sin x|\,dx=(2n+1)-\cos V$, where n is a positive integer and $0\le V<\pi$.

Sol. $\int_0^{n\pi+V}|\sin x|\,dx=\int_0^V|\sin x|\,dx+\int_V^{n\pi+V}|\sin x|\,dx$

$$=\int_0^V\sin x\,dx+n\int_0^{\pi}|\sin x|\,dx$$

$$\left[\text{using property, }\int_a^{a+nT}f(x)dx=n\int_0^T f(x)dx\ \text{ i.e. }\int_V^{n\pi+V}|\sin x|dx=n\int_0^{\pi}|\sin x|dx\right]$$

$$=\left(-\cos x\right)_0^V+n\int_0^{\pi}\sin x\,dx$$

$$=(-\cos V+1)+n\left(-\cos x\right)_0^{\pi}$$

$$=-(\cos V)+1+n(1+1)$$

$$=(2n+1)-\cos V$$

$$\therefore \int_0^{n\pi+V}|\sin x|\,dx=(2n+1)-\cos V,$$

where n is a positive integer and $0\le V<\pi$.

Example 43. Evaluate $\int_{-2\pi}^{5\pi}\cot^{-1}(\tan x)\,dx$.

Sol. Let $I=\int_{-2\pi}^{5\pi}\cot^{-1}(\tan x)\,dx$

$$\Rightarrow I=7\int_0^{\pi}\cot^{-1}\left(\cot\left(\frac{\pi}{2}-x\right)\right)dx \qquad \text{...(i)}$$

$$\left[\because \int_{nT}^{mT}f(x)\,dx=(m-n)\int_0^T f(x)\,dx\right]$$

As we know,

$$\cot^{-1}(\cot x)=\begin{cases}x, & 0<x<\pi/2\\ \pi+x, & \pi/2<x<\pi\end{cases}$$

$$\therefore \quad I=7\left\{\int_0^{\pi/2}\left(\frac{\pi}{2}-x\right)dx+\int_{\pi/2}^{\pi}\left(\pi+\frac{\pi}{2}-x\right)dx\right\}$$

$$=7\left\{\left(\frac{\pi}{2}x-\frac{x^2}{2}\right)_0^{\pi/2}+\left(\frac{3\pi}{2}x-\frac{x^2}{2}\right)_{\pi/2}^{\pi}\right\}$$

$$=7\left\{\left(\frac{\pi^2}{4}-\frac{\pi^2}{8}\right)+\left(\frac{3\pi^2}{2}-\frac{\pi^2}{2}-\frac{3\pi^2}{4}+\frac{\pi^2}{8}\right)\right\}$$

$$=\frac{7\pi^2}{2}$$

Example 44. Let $g(x)$ be a continuous and differentiable function such that

$$\int_0^2 \left\{ \int_{\sqrt{2}}^{\sqrt{5/2}} [2x^2 - 3]\, dx \right\} \cdot g(x)\, dx = 0, \text{ then } g(x) = 0$$

when $x \in (0, 2)$ has (where, $[\cdot]$ denotes the greatest integer function)

(a) exactly one real root (b) atleast one real root
(c) no real root (d) None of these

Sol. (b) As, $1 < 2x^2 - 3 < 2, \ \forall \ x \in (\sqrt{2}, \sqrt{5/2})$

$$\Rightarrow \int_{\sqrt{2}}^{\sqrt{5/2}} [2x^2 - 3]\, dx > 0, \forall \ x \in (0, 2)$$

$\Rightarrow g(x) = 0$ should have atleast one root in $(0, 2)$.

$[\because g'(x) \neq 0]$

Hence, (b) is the correct answer.

Example 45. The value of x satisfying

$\int_0^{2[x+14]} \left\{ \frac{x}{2} \right\} dx = \int_0^{\{x\}} [x + 14]\, dx$ is equal to (where, $[\cdot]$ and $\{.\}$ denotes the greatest integer and fractional part of x)

(a) $[-14, -13)$ (b) $(0, 1)$
(c) $(-15, -14]$ (d) None of these

Sol. (a) Given, $\int_0^{2[x+14]} \left\{ \frac{x}{2} \right\} dx = \int_0^{\{x\}} [x + 14]\, dx$

$$\Rightarrow \int_0^{28 + 2[x]} \left\{ \frac{x}{2} \right\} dx = \int_0^{\{x\}} (14 + [x])\, dx$$

$$\Rightarrow \int_0^{28} \left\{ \frac{x}{2} \right\} dx + \int_{28}^{28 + 2[x]} \left\{ \frac{x}{2} \right\} dx = (14 + [x])\{x\}$$

$$\Rightarrow 14 \int_0^2 \left\{ \frac{x}{2} \right\} dx + \int_0^{2[x]} \left\{ \frac{x}{2} \right\} dx = (14 + [x])\{x\}$$

$\left[\text{using } \int_0^{nT} f(x)\, dx = n \int_0^T f(x)\, dx \text{ and } \int_a^{a+nT} f(x)\, dx = \int_0^{nT} f(x)\, dx; \text{ where } T \text{ is period of } f(x) \right]$

$$\Rightarrow 14 + [x] = (14 + [x])\{x\}$$

$$\Rightarrow (14 + [x])(1 - \{x\}) = 0$$

$$\Rightarrow [x] = -14$$

$$\Rightarrow x \in [-14, -13)$$

Hence, (a) is the correct answer.

PROPERTY IX

Leibnitz's Rule for the Differentiation under the Integral Sign

(i) If the functions $\phi(x)$ and $\psi(x)$ are defined on $[a, b]$ and are differentiable at a point $x \in (a, b)$ and $f(x, t)$ is continuous, then

$$\frac{d}{dx}\left[\int_{\phi(x)}^{\psi(x)} f(x, t)\, dt \right]$$

$$= \int_{\phi(x)}^{\psi(x)} \frac{\partial}{\partial x} f(x, t)\, dt + \left\{ \frac{d}{dx} \psi(x) \right\} f(x, \psi(x)) - \left\{ \frac{d}{dx} \phi(x) \right\} f(x, \phi(x))$$

(ii) If the functions $\phi(x)$ and $\psi(x)$ are defined on $[a, b]$ and differentiable at a point $x \in (a, b)$ and $f(t)$ is continuous, then

$$\frac{d}{dx}\left(\int_{\phi(x)}^{\psi(x)} f(t)\, dt \right) = \frac{d}{dx}\{\psi(x)\}\, f(\psi(x)) - \frac{d}{dx}\{\phi(x)\}\, f(\phi(x))$$

Example 46. Find the derivative of the following with respect to x.

(i) $\int_0^x \cos t\, dt$ (ii) $\int_0^{x^2} \cos t^2 dt$

Sol. (i) Let $f(x) = \int_0^x \cos t\, dt$

$$\therefore \frac{d}{dx}(f(x)) = \cos(x) \left\{ \frac{d}{dx}(x) \right\} - \cos 0 \cdot \left\{ \frac{d}{dx}(0) \right\} = \cos x$$

$\left[\text{using Leibnitiz's rule, } \frac{d}{dx}\int_{\phi(x)}^{\psi(x)} f(t) dt = \frac{d}{dx}\{\psi(x)\} f(\psi(x)) - \frac{d}{dx}\{\phi(x)\} f(\phi(x)) \right]$

$$\Rightarrow \frac{d}{dx}\left\{ \int_0^x \cos t\, dt \right\} = \cos x$$

(ii) Let $f(x) = \int_0^{x^2} \cos t^2\, dt$

$$\therefore \frac{d}{dx}(f(x)) = \cos(x^2)^2 \cdot \left\{ \frac{d}{dx}(x^2) \right\} - \cos(0)^2 \left\{ \frac{d}{dx}(0) \right\}$$

$$= 2x \cdot \cos x^4$$

$$\Rightarrow \frac{d}{dx}\left(\int_0^{x^2} (\cos t^2)\, dt \right) = 2x \cos x^4$$

Example 47. Find the points of maxima/minima of $\int_0^{x^2} \frac{t^2 - 5t + 4}{2 + e^t} dt$.

Sol. Let $f(x) = \int_0^{x^2} \frac{t^2 - 5t + 4}{2 + e^t} dt$

$$\therefore f'(x) = \frac{x^4 - 5x^2 + 4}{2 + e^{x^2}} \cdot 2x - 0$$

$$= \frac{(x - 1)(x + 1)(x - 2)(x + 2) \cdot 2x}{2 + e^{x^2}}$$

$-$ $+$ $-$ $+$ $-$ $+$ (sign changes at $-2, -1, 0, 1, 2$ on the number line)

From the wavy curve, it is clear that $f'(x)$ changes its sign at $x = \pm 2, \pm 1, 0$ and hence the points of maxima are $-1, 1$ (as sign changes from + ve to − ve) and of the minima are $-2, 0, 2$ (as sign changes from − ve to + ve).

JEE SCANNER

Example Similar to PYQ Asked in JEE Main 2023

If $f(x)=\frac{1}{\sqrt{x}}\int_{\pi/6}^{x}(4\sqrt{2}\sin t-3f'(t))\,dt$ $x>0$, then $f'\left(\frac{\pi}{6}\right)$ is equal to

(a) $\frac{4\sqrt{3}}{\sqrt{\pi}+6}$ (b) $\frac{4\sqrt{2}}{\sqrt{\pi}+\sqrt{6}}$ (c) $\frac{4\sqrt{3}}{\sqrt{\pi}+3\sqrt{6}}$ (d) None of these

Sol. (c) Given, $f(x)=\frac{1}{\sqrt{x}}\int_{\pi/6}^{x}(4\sqrt{2}\sin t-3f'(t))dt$

$$\sqrt{x}f(x)=\int_{\pi/6}^{x}(4\sqrt{2}\sin t-3f'(t))dt$$

On differentiating w.r.t. x both sides, we get

$$\sqrt{x}\,f'(x)+\frac{1}{2\sqrt{x}}f(x)=4\sqrt{2}\sin x-3f'(x)$$

$$f'(x)(\sqrt{x}+3)=4\sqrt{2}\sin x-\frac{1}{2\sqrt{x}}f(x)$$

$$f'\left(\frac{\pi}{6}\right)\left(\sqrt{\frac{\pi}{6}}+3\right)=4\sqrt{2}\sin\frac{\pi}{6}-\frac{1}{2\sqrt{\pi/6}}f(\pi/6)$$

$$f'\left(\frac{\pi}{6}\right)=\frac{4\sqrt{2}\times\frac{1}{2}}{\sqrt{\frac{\pi}{6}}+3}\qquad\left[\because f\left(\frac{\pi}{6}\right)=0\right]$$

$$=\frac{2\sqrt{2}\times\sqrt{6}}{\sqrt{\pi}+3\sqrt{6}}=\frac{4\sqrt{3}}{\sqrt{\pi}+3\sqrt{6}}$$

Skill Builder

If $f(x)=\frac{1}{\sqrt{x}}\int_{\pi/3}^{x}(4\cos t-2f'(t))\,dt$ $x>0$,

then $f'\left(\frac{\pi}{3}\right)$ is equal to

For Sol.

(a) $\frac{4\sqrt{3}}{\sqrt{\pi}+4\sqrt{3}}$ (b) $\frac{8\sqrt{3}}{\sqrt{\pi}+8\sqrt{3}}$ (c) $\frac{\sqrt{3}}{\sqrt{\pi}+\sqrt{3}}$ (d) $\frac{2\sqrt{3}}{\sqrt{\pi}+2\sqrt{3}}$

▪ **For more practice** See Q.8 of Milestone Practice 2.5.

Example 48. If $y=\int_0^x f(t)\sin\{K(x-t)\}\,dt$, then prove that $\frac{d^2y}{dx^2}+K^2y=Kf(x)$.

Sol. We have, $y=\int_0^x f(t)\sin\{K(x-t)\}\,dt$

On differentiating w.r.t. x, we get

$$\frac{dy}{dx}=\int_0^x\frac{\partial}{\partial x}\{f(t)\sin K(x-t)\}\,dt+\frac{d}{dx}(x)$$

$$\cdot\{f(x)\sin K(x-x)\}-\frac{d}{dx}(0)\{f(0)\sin K(x-0)\}$$

$$=K\int_0^x f(t)\cos K(x-t)\,dt+0-0$$

$$\Rightarrow\quad\frac{dy}{dx}=K\int_0^x f(t)\cos K(x-t)\,dt$$

Again, differentiating both the sides w.r.t. x, we get

$$\frac{d^2y}{dx^2}=K\left\{\int_0^x\frac{\partial}{\partial x}\{f(t)\cos K(x-t)\}\,dt\right.$$

$$+\left\{f(x)\cdot\cos K(x-x)\cdot\frac{d}{dx}(x)\right\}$$

$$\left.-\{f(0)\cos K(x-0)\cdot\frac{d}{dx}(0)\}\right\}$$

$$=K\left[-K\int_0^x f(t)\sin K(x-t)\,dt+f(x)-0\right]$$

$$=-K^2\int_0^x f(t)\sin K(x-t)\,dt+Kf(x)$$

$$\Rightarrow\quad\frac{d^2y}{dx^2}=-K^2y+Kf(x)$$

$$\Rightarrow\quad\frac{d^2y}{dx^2}+K^2y=Kf(x)$$

Example 49. Let $\frac{d}{dx}(F(x))=\frac{e^{\sin x}}{x}$, $x>0$.

If $\int_1^4\frac{2e^{\sin x^2}}{x}dx=F(K)-F(1)$, then find the value of K.

Sol. We have,

$$\frac{d}{dx}(F(x))=\frac{e^{\sin x}}{x}$$

$$\Rightarrow\quad\int\frac{e^{\sin x}}{x}dx=F(x)\qquad\text{...(i)}$$

Now, $\int_1^4\frac{2e^{\sin x^2}}{x}dx=\int_1^4\frac{e^{\sin(x^2)}}{x^2}d(x^2)$

$$=\int_1^{16}\frac{e^{\sin t}}{t}dt\qquad[\because x^2=t]$$

$$=[F(t)]_1^{16}$$

$$=F(16)-F(1)$$

$$\Rightarrow\quad K=16$$

Example 50. If $f(x)$ be a real valued function $f(x)+f(x+4)=f(x+2)+f(x+6)$, $g(x)=\int_x^{x+8}f(t)\,dt$, then find $g'(x)$.

Sol. $f(x)+f(x+4)=f(x+2)+f(x+6)$ ...(i)

Replace x by $x+2$, we get

$f(x+2)+f(x+6)=f(x+4)+f(x+8)$ ...(ii)

On adding Eqs. (i) and (ii), we get

$$f(x)=f(x+8)$$

$$g(x)=\int_x^{x+8}f(t)\,dt$$

$$\Rightarrow\quad g'(x)=f(x+8)-f(x)\quad\text{[using Leibnitz rule]}$$

$$=0$$

JEE SCANNER

Example Similar to PYQ Asked in JEE Main 2022

Let $f:(0,\infty)\to R$ and $F(x)=\int_0^x t\,f(t)\,dt$.

If $F(x^2)=x^4+x^5$, then $\sum_{r=1}^{12} f(r^2)$ is equal to

(a) 216 (b) 219 (c) 221 (d) 223

Sol. (b) Here, $F(x^2)=x^4+x^5=\int_0^{x^2} t\,f(t)\,dt$

Differentiating w.r.t. x, we get

$$x^2\,f(x^2)\cdot 2x = 4x^3+5x^4$$

$$\Rightarrow \quad f(x^2)=2+\frac{5}{2}x \Rightarrow f(r^2)=2+\frac{5}{2}r$$

$$\therefore \quad \sum_{r=1}^{n} f(r^2)=2n+\frac{5}{4}n(n+1)=\frac{n(5n+13)}{4}$$

$$\Rightarrow \quad \sum_{r=1}^{12} f(r^2)=\frac{12(60+13)}{4}=219$$

Skill Builder

For Sol.

Let $f:(0,\infty)\to R$ and $F(x)=\int_0^x t\,f(t)\,dt$. If $F(x^2)=2x^4+3x^5$, then $\sum_{r=1}^{16} f(r^2)$ is equal to

(a) 1084 (b) 271 (c) 542 (d) 1082

▪ **For more practice** See Q.11 of Milestone Practice 2.5.

Example 51. If $F(x)=\int_1^x f(t)\,dt$, where $f(t)=\int_1^{t^2}\frac{\sqrt{1+u^4}}{u}\,du$, then find the value of $(F''(2))^2$.

Sol. Here, $f'(t)=\frac{\sqrt{1+t^8}\cdot 2t}{t^2}=\frac{2\sqrt{1+t^8}}{t}$ ...(i)

Now, $F(x)=\int_1^x f(t)dt \Rightarrow F'(x)=f(x)$

$$F''(x)=f'(x) \Rightarrow F''(2)=f'(2)$$

From Eq. (i),

$$f'(2)=\sqrt{256+1}=\sqrt{257}$$

$$\Rightarrow \quad (F''(2))^2=257$$

PROPERTY X

Let a function $f(x,\alpha)$ be continuous for $a\le x\le b$ and $c\le\alpha\le d$, then for any $\alpha\in[c,d]$,

if $I(\alpha)=\int_a^b f(x,\alpha)\,dx$, then $\frac{dI(\alpha)}{d\alpha}=\int_a^b \frac{\partial f(x,\alpha)}{\partial\alpha}\,dx$

Example 52. Evaluate $I(b)=\int_0^1 \frac{x^b-1}{\ln x}\,dx;\ b\ge 0$.

Sol. We have, $I(b)=\int_0^1 \frac{x^b-1}{\ln x}\,dx$

$$\Rightarrow \frac{d}{db}(I(b))=\int_0^1 \frac{\partial}{\partial b}\left(\frac{x^b-1}{\ln x}\right)dx+0-0$$

$$=\int_0^1 \frac{x^b\ln x}{\ln x}\,dx=\int_0^1 (x^b)\,dx=\left(\frac{x^{b+1}}{b+1}\right)_0^1$$

$$=\frac{1}{b+1}[1-0]=\frac{1}{b+1}$$

$$\therefore \quad \frac{d}{db}(I(b))=\frac{1}{b+1}$$

Integrating both the sides w.r.t. b, we get

$$I(b)=\log(b+1)+C \quad \text{...(i)}$$

Given, $I(b)=\int_0^1 \frac{x^b-1}{\ln x}\,dx$

$\therefore \quad I(0)=0$ [when $b=0$] ...(ii)

Also, from Eq. (i), $I(0)=\log(1)+C$

$\therefore \quad I(0)=C$ ...(iii)

From Eqs. (ii) and (iii), $C=0$

$\Rightarrow \quad I(b)=\log(b+1)$

Example 53. If $f(x)=\int_{\ln x}^{x}\frac{dt}{x+t}$, then find $f'(1)$.

Sol. $f(x)=\int_{\ln x}^{x}\frac{dt}{x+t}$

$$\Rightarrow f'(x)=\frac{1}{x+x}(1)-\frac{1}{x+\ln x}\left(\frac{1}{x}\right)+\int_{\ln x}^{x}\frac{\partial}{\partial x}\left(\frac{1}{x+t}\right)dt$$

$$\Rightarrow f'(x)=\frac{1}{2x}-\frac{1}{x(x+\ln x)}+\int_{\ln x}^{x}\left(\frac{-1}{(x+t)^2}\right)dt$$

$$\Rightarrow f'(x)=\frac{1}{2x}-\frac{1}{x(x+\ln x)}-\int_{\ln x}^{x}\frac{dt}{(x+t)^2}$$

$$\Rightarrow f'(1)=\frac{1}{2}-\frac{1}{1(1+0)}-\int_0^1\frac{dt}{(1+t)^2}$$

$$\Rightarrow f'(1)=-\frac{1}{2}+\left[\frac{1}{1+t}\right]_0^1=-\frac{1}{2}+\frac{1}{2}-1=-1$$

Example 54. Prove that

$$\int_0^{\pi/2}\frac{dx}{(a^2\sin^2 x+b^2\cos^2 x)^2}=\frac{\pi(a^2+b^2)}{4a^3b^3}.$$

Sol. Let $I=\int_0^{\pi/2}\frac{1\,dx}{a^2\sin^2 x+b^2\cos^2 x}$

Then, $I=\int_0^{\pi/2}\frac{\sec^2 x}{a^2\tan^2 x+b^2}\,dx=\int_0^{\infty}\frac{dt}{a^2t^2+b^2}$

[where, $t=\tan x$]

$$\Rightarrow \quad I = \frac{1}{ab}\left[\tan^{-1}\left(\frac{at}{b}\right)\right]_0^{\infty} = \frac{1}{ab}\left(\frac{\pi}{2} - 0\right) = \frac{\pi}{2ab}$$

Thus, $\int_0^{\pi/2} \frac{1}{a^2 \sin^2 x + b^2 \cos^2 x}\, dx = \frac{\pi}{2ab} = f(a, b)$ ...(i)

Differentiating both the sides w.r.t. 'a', we get

$$\int_0^{\pi/2} \frac{-2a \sin^2 x}{(a^2 \sin^2 x + b^2 \cos^2 x)^2}\, dx = -\frac{\pi}{2a^2 b}$$

$$\Rightarrow \quad \int_0^{\pi/2} \frac{\sin^2 x}{(a^2 \sin^2 x + b^2 \cos^2 x)^2}\, dx = \frac{\pi}{4a^3 b} \quad \text{...(ii)}$$

Similarly, by differentiating Eq. (i) w.r.t. 'b', we get

$$\int_0^{\pi/2} \frac{\cos^2 x}{(a^2 \sin^2 x + b^2 \cos^2 x)^2}\, dx = \frac{\pi}{4ab^3} \quad \text{...(iii)}$$

On adding Eqs. (ii) and (iii), we get

$$\int_0^{\pi/2} \frac{(\sin^2 x + \cos^2 x)\, dx}{(a^2 \sin^2 x + b^2 \cos^2 x)^2} = \frac{\pi}{4a^3 b} + \frac{\pi}{4ab^3}$$

$$\Rightarrow \quad \int_0^{\pi/2} \frac{dx}{(a^2 \sin^2 x + b^2 \cos^2 x)^2} = \frac{\pi}{4a^3 b^3}(a^2 + b^2)$$

Example 55. The value of

$$\int_0^{\pi/2} \frac{\log(1 + x\sin^2\theta)}{\sin^2\theta}\, d\theta\,;\ x \ge 0 \text{ is equal to}$$

Sol. Given, $f(x) = \int_0^{\pi/2} \frac{\log(1 + x \sin^2\theta)}{\sin^2\theta}\, d\theta;\ x \ge 0$

As above integral is function of x. Thus, differentiating both the sides w.r.t. 'x', we get

$$f'(x) = \int_0^{\pi/2} \frac{1}{1 + x\sin^2\theta} \cdot \frac{\sin^2\theta}{\sin^2\theta}\, d\theta + 0 - 0$$

[using Newton-Leibnitz's formula]

$$= \int_0^{\pi/2} \frac{d\theta}{1 + x\sin^2\theta} = \int_0^{\pi/2} \frac{\operatorname{cosec}^2\theta\, d\theta}{\cot^2\theta + (1 + x)}$$

$$= \left(-\frac{1}{\sqrt{1+x}} \cdot \tan^{-1}\frac{\cot\theta}{\sqrt{1+x}}\right)_0^{\pi/2} = \frac{\pi}{2\sqrt{1+x}}$$

$$\therefore \quad f'(x) = \frac{\pi}{2\sqrt{1+x}} \Rightarrow f(x) = \pi\sqrt{1+x} + C$$

where, $f(0) = 0 \Rightarrow C = -\pi$

$$\Rightarrow \quad f(x) = \pi\sqrt{1+x} - \pi = \pi(\sqrt{1+x} - 1)$$

Milestone Practice 2.5

1. The value of $\int_{-1}^{10} \text{sgn}(x - [x])\, dx$ is equal to (where, [·] denotes greatest integer function)
   (a) 9 (b) 10 (c) 11 (d) 12

2. The value of $\frac{1}{n}\int_0^{2n\pi}\left(|\sin x| - \left[\left|\frac{\sin x}{2}\right|\right]\right) dx$ is equal to (where [·] denotes GIF)
   (a) 2 (b) 4 (c) 6 (d) 8

3. If $\int_0^{20} [x]\{x\}\, dx = k$, then $\frac{k}{19}$ equals (where [·] and {·}, respectively denotes GIF and FPF)
   (a) 5 (b) 10 (c) 15 (d) 20

4. The value of $\int_{-\pi/4}^{n\pi - \pi/4} |\sin x + \cos x|\, dx$ is equal to
   (a) $2\sqrt{2}n$ (b) $\sqrt{2}n$
   (c) $\frac{1}{2\sqrt{2}}n$ (d) None of these

5. Let $f(x) = x - [x]$ for every real number x (where, [·] denotes greatest integer function), then $\int_{-1}^{1} f(x)\, dx$ is equal to
   (a) 1 (b) 2
   (c) 0 (d) $\frac{1}{2}$

6. If $\int_0^x f(t)\, dt = x + f\int_x^1 t f(t)\, dt$, then the value of $f(1)$ is
   (a) $\frac{1}{2}$ (b) 0
   (c) 1 (d) $-\frac{1}{2}$

7. The least value of the function $\phi(x) = \int_{5\pi/4}^{x} (3\sin t + 4\cos t)\, dt$ on the interval $\left[\frac{5\pi}{4}, \frac{4\pi}{3}\right]$ is
   (a) $\sqrt{3} + \frac{3}{2}$ (b) $-2\sqrt{3} + \frac{3}{2} + \frac{1}{\sqrt{2}}$
   (c) $\frac{3}{2} + \frac{1}{\sqrt{2}}$ (d) None of these

8. If $\phi(x) = \int_1^x e^{-t^2/2}(1 - t^2)\, dt$, then $\phi'(2)$ is equal to
   (a) $-4e^{-2}$ (b) $-3e^{-2}$
   (c) $2e^2$ (d) $-3e^2$

9. If $f(x)$ is periodic function, with period T, then
   (a) $\int_a^b f(x)\,dx = \int_a^{b+T} f(x)\,dx$ (b) $\int_a^b f(x)\,dx = \int_{a+T}^{b+T} f(x)\,dx$
   (c) $\int_a^b f(x)\,dx = \int_{a+T}^{b} f(x)\,dx$ (d) $\int_a^b f(x)\,dx = \int_{a+T}^{b+2T} f(x)\,dx$

10. Let $\frac{d}{dx}(F(x)) = \frac{e^{\sin x}}{x}$, $x > 0$. If $\int_1^4 \frac{2e^{\sin x^2}}{x} dx = F(k) - F(1)$, then one of the possible value of k is

(a) 4 (b) 8 (c) 16 (d) 32

11. Let $f:(0, \infty) \to R$ and $F(x) = \int_0^x f(t)\,dt$. If $F(x^2) = x^2(1 + x)$, then $f(4)$ is equal to

(a) $\frac{5}{4}$ (b) 7 (c) 4 (d) 2

12. Let $T > 0$ be a fixed real number. Suppose f is continuous function such that $f(x + T) = f(x)$ for all $x \in R$. If $I = \int_0^T f(x)\,dx$, then the value of $\int_3^{3+3T} f(2x)\,dx$ is

(a) $\frac{3}{2}I$ (b) $2I$ (c) $3I$ (d) $6I$

13. Let $f(x) = \int_1^x \sqrt{2 - t^2}\,dt$, then the real roots of the equation $x^2 - f'(x) = 0$ are

(a) ± 1 (b) $\pm \frac{1}{\sqrt{2}}$ (c) $\pm \frac{1}{2}$ (d) $\pm \sqrt{2}$

14. $\int_{2\pi}^{2\pi + \frac{\pi}{4}} \sqrt{[\cos x + \{[\tan x] + \{\sin x\}\}]}\,dx$ is equal to (where $[\cdot]$ and $\{\cdot\}$ denotes GIF and FPF)

(a) 0 (b) $\frac{\sqrt{2}\pi}{4}$ (c) $\frac{\pi}{2}$ (d) $\frac{\pi}{4}$

15. Let $f(x)$ be an odd continuous function which is periodic with period 2. If $g(x) = \int_0^x f(t)\,dt$, then

(a) $g(x)$ is an odd function
(b) $g(n) = 0$ for all $n \in N$
(c) $g(2n) = 0$ for all $n \in N$
(d) $g(x)$ is non-periodic

16. Let $f(x)$ be a function defined by $f(x) = \int_1^x t(t^2 - 3t + 2)\,dt$, $1 \le x \le 3$. Then, the range of $f(x)$ is

(a) $[0, 2]$ (b) $\left[-\frac{1}{4}, 4\right]$
(c) $\left[-\frac{1}{4}, 2\right]$ (d) None of these

17. If $\int_0^x \frac{bt\cos 4t - a\sin 4t}{t^2}\,dt = \frac{a\sin 4x}{x}$ for all $x \ne 0$, then a and b are given by

(a) $a = \frac{1}{4}, b = 1$ (b) $a = 2, b = 2$
(c) $a = -1, b = 4$ (d) $a = 2, b = 4$

18. If $f(x) = \int_0^x \{f(t)\}^{-1}\,dt$ and $\int_0^1 \{f(t)\}^{-1} = \sqrt{2}$, then

(a) $f(x) = \sqrt{2x}$ (b) $f(x) = \sqrt{2\log_e x}$
(c) $f(x) = \sqrt{3x - 1}$ (d) None of these

19. Let f be a real valued function defined on the interval $(-1, 1)$ such that $e^{-x} f(x) = 2 + \int_0^x \sqrt{t^4 + 1}\,dt$, for all $x \in (-1, 1)$ and let f^{-1} be the inverse of f. Then, $(f^{-1})'(2)$ is equal to

(a) 1 (b) 1/3
(c) 1/2 (d) 1 / e

■ **Directions** (Q. Nos. 20 to 21) *Consider the function defined on* $[0, 1] \to R$

$$f(x) = \frac{\sin x - x\cos x}{x^2}, \text{ if } x \ne 0 \text{ and } f(0) = 0.$$

20. $\int_0^1 f(x)\,dx$ is equal to

(a) $1 - \sin(1)$ (b) $\sin(1) - 1$
(c) $\sin(1)$ (d) $-\sin(1)$

21. $\lim_{t \to 0} \frac{1}{t^2} \int_0^t f(x)\,dx$ is equal to

(a) $\frac{1}{3}$ (b) $\frac{1}{6}$
(c) $\frac{1}{12}$ (d) $\frac{1}{24}$

22. If $(f(x))^{2009} = \int_0^x (f(t))^{2008} \frac{dt}{2 + \cos t}$, then integer just greater than the value of the limit $2009\sqrt{3} \lim_{x \to \pi} f(x)$ is

(a) 4 (b) 6
(c) 8 (d) 2010

23. $\int_0^x [\sin t]\,dt$, where $x \in (2n\pi, (2n + 1)\pi)$, $n \in N$ and $[\cdot]$ denotes GIF, is equal to

(a) $-n\pi$ (b) $-(n + 1)\pi$
(c) $-2n\pi$ (d) $-(2n + 1)\pi$

Answer Key

1. (c)	2. (b)	3. (a)	4. (a)	5. (a)
6. (a)	7. (b)	8. (b)	9. (b)	10. (c)
11. (c)	12. (c)	13. (a)	14. (d)	15. (c)
16. (c)	17. (a)	18. (a)	19. (b)	20. (a)
21. (b)	22. (a)	23. (a)		

For Detailed Solution

Milestone 6 Definite Integral as the Limit of Sum

• Definite Integral as The Limit of Sum • Evaluation of the Limit of the Sum using Newton Leibnitz Formula • Applications of Inequality • Gamma Function • Beta Function • Walli's Formula • Integration Involving $f(x)$ and $f^{-1}(x)$

2.4 Definite Integral as The Limit of Sum

Let f be a continuous real function in $[a, b]$. Assume that all the values taken by the function are non-negative the graph of the function is a curve above the X-axis.

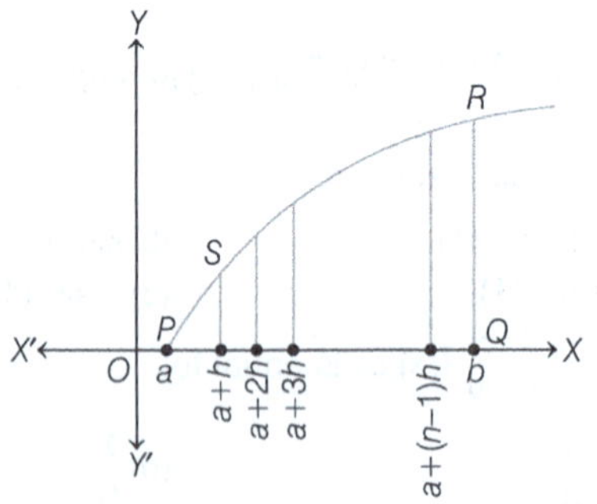

Divide the interval $[a, b]$ into n equal sub-intervals denoted by

$$[a, a+h], [a+h, a+2h], [a+2h, a+3h] \dots [a+(n-1)h, a+nh]$$

Clearly, $b = a + nh \Rightarrow nh = b - a$

$$h = \frac{b-a}{n}$$

Thus, $\int_a^b f(x)\,dx$ = Area bounded by the curve $y = f(x)$, X-axis and the coordinate $x = a$ and $x = b$.

= Area of the region $PQRSP$ between the curve, X-axis and the coordinates $x = a$ and $x = b$

$$= \lim_{h \to 0} h[f(a) + f(a+h) \dots + f(a+(n-1)h)]$$

$$= \lim_{h \to 0} h \sum_{r=0}^{n-1} f(a+rh)$$

$$= \lim_{n \to \infty} \frac{b-a}{n} \sum_{r=0}^{n-1} f\left(a + \frac{r}{n}(b-a)\right),$$

where $nh = b - a$

which is known as the first principal of integration.

Method to Express the Infinite Series as Definite Integral

(i) Express the given series in the form $\sum \frac{1}{n} f\left(\frac{r}{n}\right)$.

(ii) Then, the limit is its sum when $n \to \infty$

i.e. $\lim_{n \to \infty} \sum \frac{1}{n} f\left(\frac{r}{n}\right)$.

(iii) Replace $\frac{r}{n}$ by x and $\frac{1}{n}$ by (dx) and $\lim_{n \to \infty} \sum$ by the sign of $\int$.

(iv) The lower and the upper limit of integration are limiting values of $\frac{r}{n}$ for the first and the last term of r respectively.

2.5 Evaluation of the Limit of the Sum using Newton Leibnitz Formula

From the definition of the definite integral, we have

$$\int_a^b f(x)\,dx = \lim_{h \to 0} h \sum_{r=0}^{n} f(a+rh)$$

$$= \lim_{n \to \infty} \left(\frac{b-a}{n}\right) \sum_{r=0}^{n} f\left[a + \left(\frac{b-a}{n}\right) r\right]$$

$$= \lim_{n \to \infty} \frac{1}{n} \sum_{r=\phi(n)}^{\psi(n)} f\left(\frac{r}{n}\right), \text{ where}$$

(i) Σ is replaced by $\int$ symbol

(ii) $\frac{1}{n}$ is replaced by dx.

(iii) $\frac{r}{n}$ is replaced by x.

(iv) $a = \lim_{n \to \infty} \left(\frac{\phi(n)}{n}\right)$ and $b = \lim_{n \to \infty} \left(\frac{\psi(n)}{n}\right)$

Some particular cases of the above are

(a) $\lim_{n\to\infty} \sum_{r=1}^{n} \frac{1}{n} f\left(\frac{r}{n}\right)$

or $\lim_{n\to\infty} \sum_{r=1}^{n-1} \frac{1}{n} f\left(\frac{r}{n}\right) = \int_0^1 f(x)\,dx$

(b) $\lim_{n\to\infty} \sum_{r=1}^{Pn} \frac{1}{n} f\left(\frac{r}{n}\right) = \int_\alpha^\beta f(x)\,dx$

where, $\alpha = \lim_{n\to\infty} \frac{r}{n} = 0$ [as $r = 1$]

and $\beta = \lim_{n\to\infty} \frac{r}{n} = p$ [as $r = pn$]

Some Important Results to Remember

(i) $\sum_{r=1}^{n} r = \frac{n(n+1)}{2}$

(ii) $\sum_{r=1}^{n} r^2 = \frac{n(n+1)(2n+1)}{6}$

(iii) $\sum_{r=1}^{n} r^3 = \frac{n^2(n+1)^2}{4}$

(iv) In GP, sum of n terms, $S_n = \begin{cases} \frac{a(r^n-1)}{(r-1)}, & |r|>1 \\ na, & r=1 \\ \frac{a(1-r^n)}{(1-r)}, & |r|<1 \end{cases}$

(v) $\sin\alpha + \sin(\alpha+\beta) + \sin(\alpha+2\beta) + \ldots + \sin[\alpha + \overline{(n-1)}\beta]$

$= \frac{\sin n\beta/2}{\sin\beta/2} \cdot \sin[\alpha + (n-1)\beta/2]$

(vi) $\cos\alpha + \cos(\alpha+\beta) + \cos(\alpha+2\beta) + \ldots + \cos[\alpha + \overline{(n-1)}\beta]$

$= \frac{\sin n\beta/2}{\sin\beta/2} \cdot \cos[\alpha + (n-1)\beta/2]$

(vii) $1 - \frac{1}{2^2} + \frac{1}{3^2} - \frac{1}{4^2} + \frac{1}{5^2} - \frac{1}{6^2} + \ldots \infty = \frac{\pi^2}{12}$

(viii) $1 + \frac{1}{2^2} + \frac{1}{3^2} + \frac{1}{4^2} + \frac{1}{5^2} + \frac{1}{6^2} + \ldots \infty = \frac{\pi^2}{6}$

(ix) $1 + \frac{1}{3^2} + \frac{1}{5^2} + \ldots \infty = \frac{\pi^2}{8}$

(x) $\frac{1}{2^2} + \frac{1}{4^2} + \frac{1}{6^2} + \ldots \infty = \frac{\pi^2}{24}$

(xi) $\cos\theta = \frac{e^{i\theta} + e^{-i\theta}}{2}$, and $\sin\theta = \frac{e^{i\theta} - e^{-i\theta}}{2i}$

(xii) $\cos h\theta = \frac{e^{\theta} + e^{-\theta}}{2}$ and $\sin h\theta = \frac{e^{\theta} - e^{-\theta}}{2}$

Example 56. Evaluate the following :

(i) $\lim_{n\to\infty} \left(\frac{1}{n^2} + \frac{2}{n^2} + \frac{3}{n^2} + \ldots + \frac{n-1}{n^2}\right)$

(ii) $\lim_{n\to\infty} \left(\frac{1}{n+1} + \frac{1}{n+2} + \ldots + \frac{1}{2n}\right)$

(iii) $\lim_{n\to\infty} \frac{(1^P + 2^P + \ldots + n^P)}{n^{P+1}}, P > 0$

Sol. Let

(i) $S_n = \frac{1}{n^2} + \frac{2}{n^2} + \frac{3}{n^2} + \ldots + \frac{n-1}{n^2}$

$= \sum_{r=2}^{n} \frac{r-1}{n^2}$

$= \sum_{r=2}^{n} \frac{1}{n}\left(\frac{r-1}{n}\right)$

$\Rightarrow S = \lim_{n\to\infty} \sum_{r=2}^{n} \frac{1}{n}\left(\frac{r}{n}\right)$ $\left[\text{as } n \to \infty \Rightarrow \frac{1}{n} \to 0\right]$

$= \int_0^1 x\,dx = \frac{1}{2}$

(ii) Let $S_n = \frac{1}{n+1} + \frac{1}{n+2} + \ldots + \frac{1}{2n}$

$= \sum_{r=1}^{n} \frac{1}{n+r}$

$= \sum_{r=1}^{n} \frac{1}{n\left(1 + \frac{r}{n}\right)}$

Hence, $S = \lim_{n\to\infty} S_n = \lim_{n\to\infty} \frac{1}{n} \sum_{r=1}^{n} \frac{1}{1 + \frac{r}{n}}$

$= \int_0^1 \frac{dx}{1+x}$

$= [\log(1+x)]_0^1$

$= \log 2$

(iii) Let $S_n = \frac{1^P + 2^P + \ldots + n^P}{n^{P+1}}$

$= \sum_{r=1}^{n} \frac{r^P}{n^{P+1}} = \sum_{r=1}^{n} \frac{1}{n}\left(\frac{r}{n}\right)^P$

$\therefore S = \lim_{n\to\infty} S_n = \lim_{n\to\infty} \frac{1}{n} \sum_{r=1}^{n} \left(\frac{r}{n}\right)^P$

$= \int_0^1 x^P\,dx = \left[\frac{x^{P+1}}{P+1}\right]_0^1$

$= \frac{1}{P+1}$

JEE SCANNER

Example Similar to PYQ Asked in JEE Main 2022

$$\lim_{n\to\infty}\left[\frac{n^2}{(n^2+1)(n+1)}+\frac{n^2}{(n^2+4)(n+2)}+\frac{n^2}{(n^2+9)(n+3)}+\ldots+\frac{n^2}{(n^2+n^2)(n+n)}\right]$$ is equal to

(a) $\frac{\pi}{8}+\frac{1}{4}\log_e 2$ (b) $\frac{\pi}{4}+\frac{1}{8}\log_e 2$

(c) $\frac{\pi}{4}-\frac{1}{8}\log_e 2$ (d) $\frac{\pi}{8}+\log_e \sqrt{2}$

Sol. (a) Let $S_n=\sum_{r=1}^{n}\frac{n^2}{(n^2+r^2)(n+r)}$

$$=\sum_{r=1}^{n}\left[\frac{1}{n\left(1+\left(\frac{r}{n}\right)^2\right)\left(1+\left(\frac{r}{n}\right)\right)}\right]$$

$$\Rightarrow \quad S=\lim_{n\to\infty}S_n=\int_0^1\frac{dx}{(1+x^2)(1+x)}$$

$$=\frac{1}{2}\int_0^1\frac{1-x}{1+x^2}\,dx+\frac{1}{2}\int_0^1\frac{1}{1+x}\,dx$$

[using partial fraction]

$$=\frac{1}{2}\int_0^1\left(\frac{1}{1+x^2}-\frac{x}{1+x^2}\right)dx+\frac{1}{2}[\ln(1+x)]_0^1$$

$$=\frac{1}{2}\left[\tan^{-1}x-\frac{1}{2}\ln(1+x^2)\right]_0^1+\frac{1}{2}\ln 2$$

$$=\frac{1}{2}\left[\frac{\pi}{4}-\frac{1}{2}\ln 2\right]+\frac{1}{2}\ln 2$$

$$=\frac{\pi}{8}+\frac{1}{4}\ln 2=\frac{\pi}{8}+\frac{1}{4}\log_e 2$$

Skill Builder

$$\lim_{n\to\infty}\left[\frac{n}{(n^2+1)}+\frac{n}{(n^2+4)}+\frac{n}{(n^2+9)}+\ldots+\frac{n}{(n^2+n^2)}\right]$$

is equal to

(a) $\frac{\pi}{2}$ (b) $\frac{\pi}{8}$

(c) $\frac{\pi}{4}$ (d) π

For Sol.

- **For more practice** See Q.1 of Milestone Practice 2.6.

Example 57. Evaluate $S=\sum_{r=0}^{n-1}\frac{1}{\sqrt{4n^2-r^2}}$ as $n\to\infty$.

Sol. Let $S_n=\sum_{r=0}^{n-1}\frac{1}{\sqrt{4n^2-r^2}}=\sum_{r=0}^{n-1}\frac{1}{n\sqrt{4-(r/n)^2}}$

$$=\frac{1}{n}\sum_{r=0}^{n-1}\frac{1}{\sqrt{4-(r/n)^2}}$$

Hence, $S=\lim_{n\to\infty}S_n=\lim_{n\to\infty}\frac{1}{n}\sum_{r=0}^{n-1}\frac{1}{\sqrt{4-(r/n)^2}}$

$$=\int_0^1\frac{dx}{\sqrt{4-x^2}}$$

$$=\left[\sin^{-1}\frac{x}{2}\right]_0^1$$

$$\Rightarrow \quad S=\sin^{-1}\left(\frac{1}{2}\right)=\frac{\pi}{6}$$

$$\therefore \quad S=\frac{\pi}{6}$$

Example 58. Evaluate

$$\lim_{n\to\infty}\left(\sin\frac{\pi}{2n}\cdot\sin\frac{2\pi}{2n}\cdot\sin\frac{3\pi}{2n}\ldots\sin\frac{(n-1)\pi}{n}\right)^{1/n}$$

Sol. Let $A=\lim_{n\to\infty}\left(\sin\frac{\pi}{2n}\cdot\sin\frac{2\pi}{2n}\cdot\sin\frac{3\pi}{2n}\ldots\sin\frac{2(n-1)\pi}{2n}\right)^{1/n}$

$$\therefore \log A=\lim_{n\to\infty}\frac{1}{n}\log\left(\sin\frac{\pi}{2n}\cdot\sin\frac{2\pi}{2n}\ldots\sin\frac{2(n-1)\pi}{2n}\right)$$

$$=\lim_{n\to\infty}\frac{1}{n}\sum_{r=1}^{2(n-1)}\log\sin\frac{r\pi}{2n}$$

$$=\int_0^2\log\sin\left(\frac{\pi x}{2}\right)dx$$

$$\left[\text{using }\lim_{n\to\infty}\Sigma\frac{1}{n}f\left(\frac{r}{n}\right)=\int_a^b f(x)\,dx\right]$$

$$=\int_0^\pi\log(\sin t)\cdot\frac{2}{\pi}\,dt \qquad \left[\text{putting }\frac{\pi x}{2}=t\right]$$

$$=\frac{2\cdot 2}{\pi}\int_0^{\pi/2}\log(\sin t)\,dt$$

$$\left[\text{using }\int_0^{2a}f(x)\,dx=2\int_0^a f(x)\,dx,\text{ if }f(2a-x)=f(x)\right]$$

$$=\frac{4}{\pi}\left\{-\frac{\pi}{2}\log 2\right\}\left[\text{using}\int_0^{\pi/2}\log(\sin x)dx=-\frac{\pi}{2}\log 2\right]$$

$$=-2\log 2$$

$$\therefore \log A=\log(1/4)$$

$$\Rightarrow \quad A=1/4$$

Example 59. The interval [0, 4] is divided into n equal sub-intervals by the points $x_0, x_1, x_2, \ldots, x_{n-1}, x_n$ where $0=x_0<x_1<x_2<x_3<\ldots<x_n=4$.

If $\delta x=x_i-x_{i-1}$ for $i=1, 2, 3, \ldots, n$, then find $\lim_{\delta x\to 0}\sum_{i=1}^{n}x_i\delta x$.

Sol. $\lim_{\delta x \to 0} \delta x(x_1 + x_2 + x_3 + ... + x_n)$

$$= \lim_{n \to \infty} \frac{4}{n}\left[\frac{4}{n} + \frac{8}{n} + \frac{12}{n} + ... + 4 \cdot \frac{n}{n}\right] \qquad \left[\because \delta x = \frac{4}{n}\right]$$

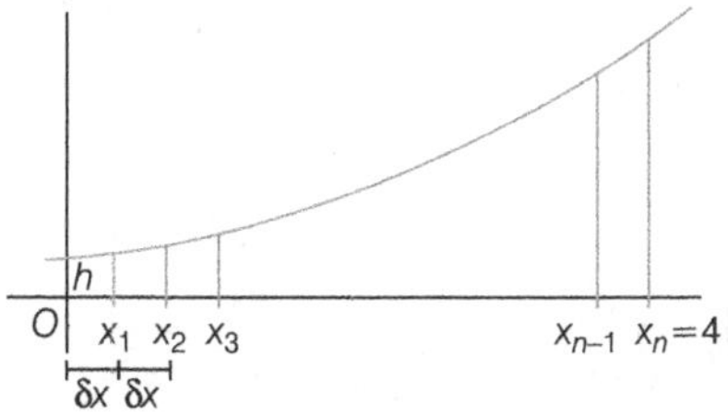

$$= \lim_{n \to \infty} \frac{16}{n^2}(1 + 2 + 3 + ... + n) = \lim_{n \to \infty} \frac{16}{n^2} \cdot \frac{n(n+1)}{2} = 8$$

JEE SCANNER

Example Similar to PYQ Asked in JEE Main 2021

Let $f:(0, 2) \to R$ be defined as $f(x) = \log_2\left(1 + \tan\left(\frac{\pi x}{4}\right)\right)$, then $\lim_{n \to \infty} \frac{2}{n}\left(f\left(\frac{1}{n}\right) + f\left(\frac{2}{n}\right) + ... + f(1)\right)$ is equal to

Sol. (1) $\lim_{n \to \infty} \frac{2}{n}\left(f\left(\frac{1}{n}\right) + f\left(\frac{2}{n}\right) + ... + f\left(\frac{n}{n}\right)\right)$

$$= \lim_{n \to \infty} \frac{2}{n} \sum_{r=1}^{n} \log_2\left(1 + \tan\frac{\pi r}{4n}\right)$$

Using integration by limit as a sum formula here,

$$I = 2\int_0^1 \log_2\left(1 + \tan\frac{\pi x}{4}\right) dx \qquad ...(i)$$

$$\Rightarrow \quad I = 2\int_0^1 \log_2\left(1 + \tan\frac{\pi}{4}(1 - x)\right) dx$$

$$\left[\because \int_0^a f(x)\, dx = \int_0^a f(a - x)\, dx\right]$$

$$\Rightarrow \quad I = 2\int_0^1 \log_2\left(\frac{2}{1 + \frac{\tan \pi x}{4}}\right) dx \qquad ...(ii)$$

On adding Eqs. (i) and (ii), we get

$$2I = 2\int_0^1 \log_2 2\, dx \Rightarrow I = \int_0^1 dx = 1 \quad [\because \log_a a = 1]$$

Skill Builder

Let $f:(0, 4) \to R$ be defined as $f(x) = \log_2\left(1 + \tan\left(\frac{\pi x}{4}\right)\right)$, then $\lim_{n \to \infty} \frac{4}{n}\left(f\left(\frac{1}{n}\right) + f\left(\frac{2}{n}\right) + ... + f(1)\right)$ is equal to ......

For Sol.

- **For more practice** See Q.7 of Milestone Practice 2.6.

2.6 Applications of Inequality

Sometimes you are asked to prove inequalities involving definite integrals or to estimate the upper and lower boundary values of definite integral, where the exact value of the definite integral is difficult to find. Under these circumstances, we use the following types

TYPE I

If $f(x)$ is defined on $[a, b]$, then

$$\left|\int_a^b f(x)\, dx\right| \le \int_a^b |f(x)|\, dx$$

Equality sign holds, where $f(x)$ is entirely of the same sign on $[a, b]$.

Example 60. Estimate the absolute value of the integral $\int_{10}^{19} \frac{\sin x}{1 + x^8} dx$.

Sol. To find, $I = \left|\int_{10}^{19} \frac{\sin x}{1 + x^8} dx\right| \le \int_{10}^{19} \left|\frac{\sin x}{1 + x^8}\right| dx \qquad ...(i)$

[using Type I]

Since, $\quad |\sin x| \le 1$

The inequality $\left|\frac{\sin x}{1 + x^8}\right| \le \frac{1}{|1 + x^8|} \qquad ...(ii)$

Also, $\quad 10 \le x \le 19$

$\Rightarrow \quad 1 + x^8 > 10^8$

$\Rightarrow \quad \frac{1}{1 + x^8} < \frac{1}{10^8}$ or $\frac{1}{|1 + x^8|} < 10^{-8} \qquad ...(iii)$

From Eqs. (ii) and (iii), $\left|\frac{\sin x}{1 + x^8}\right| < 10^{-8}$ is fulfilled.

$$\left|\int_{10}^{19} \frac{\sin x}{1 + x^8} dx\right| < \int_{10}^{19} 10^{-8}\, dx$$

$$\therefore \quad \left|\int_{10}^{19} \frac{\sin x}{1 + x^8} dx\right| < (19 - 10) \cdot 10^{-8} < 10^{-7}$$

[$\because$ the true value of integral $\approx 10^{-8}$]

Example 61. The minimum odd value of 'a' $(a > 1)$ for which $\int_{10}^{19} \frac{\sin x}{1 + x^a} dx < \frac{1}{9}$.

Sol. Let $I = \int_{10}^{19} \frac{\sin x\, dx}{1 + x^a} < \int_{10}^{19} \frac{dx}{1 + x^a}$

$$\left[\because \sin x < 1 \Rightarrow \frac{\sin x}{1 + x^a} < \frac{1}{1 + x^a}\right]$$

$$\therefore \quad I < \int_{10}^{19} \frac{dx}{1 + x^a} < \int_{10}^{19} \frac{dx}{1 + 10^a}$$

$$[\because 10 < x < 19 \Rightarrow 10^a + 1 < 1 + x^a < 19^a + 1]$$

$$\Rightarrow \quad I < \frac{9}{1+10^a}$$

$$\therefore \quad \frac{9}{1+10^a} < \frac{1}{9}$$

$$\Rightarrow \quad 1 + 10^a > 81 \quad \text{or } 10^a > 80$$

i.e. $\quad a = 2, 3, 4, 5, \ldots$

$\therefore$ Minimum odd value of 'a' is 3.

TYPE II

$$\left|\int_a^b f(x)\, g(x)\, dx\right| \le \sqrt{\left(\int_a^b f^2(x)\, dx\right)\left(\int_a^b g^2(x)\, dx\right)},$$

where $f^2(x)$ and $g^2(x)$ are integrable on $[a, b]$.

Example 62. Prove that $\int_0^1 \sqrt{(1+x)(1+x^3)}\, dx$ cannot exceed $\sqrt{15/8}$.

Sol. $\int_0^1 \sqrt{(1+x)(1+x^3)}\, dx \le \sqrt{\left(\int_0^1 (1+x)dx\right)\left(\int_0^1 (1+x^3)\, dx\right)}$

$$\le \sqrt{\left(x + \frac{x^2}{2}\right)_0^1 \left(x + \frac{x^4}{4}\right)_0^1} \le \sqrt{\frac{3}{2}\cdot\frac{5}{4}} \le \sqrt{\frac{15}{8}}$$

TYPE III

If $f(x) \ge g(x)$ on $[a, b]$, then

$\int_a^b f(x)\, dx \ge \int_a^b g(x)\, dx$. In particular, if $f(x) \ge 0$, then $\int_a^b f(x)\, dx \ge 0$.

Example 63. If $f(x)$ is a continuous function such that $f(x) \ge 0, \forall\, x \in [2, 10]$ and $\int_4^8 f(x)\, dx = 0$, then find $f(6)$.

Sol. $f(x)$ is above the X-axis or on the X-axis for all $x \in [2, 10]$. If $f(x)$ is greater than zero at any sub-interval of $[4, 8]$, then $\int_4^8 f(x)\, dx$ must be greater than zero. But

$\int_4^8 f(x)\, dx = 0$, which shows $f(x)$ can't have any value greater than zero in the sub-interval $[4, 8]$.

$\Rightarrow f(x)$ is constant in the sub-interval $[4, 8]$ and has to be zero at all points, $x \in [4, 8]$.

$$\Rightarrow \quad f(x) = 0, \quad \forall\, x \in [4, 8]$$

$$\Rightarrow \quad f(6) = 0$$

TYPE IV

For a given function $f(x)$ continuous on $[a, b]$, if you are able to find two continuous functions $f_1(x)$ and $f_2(x)$ on $[a, b]$ such that $f_1(x) \le f(x) \le f_2(x), \forall\, x \in [a, b]$, then

$$\int_a^b f_1(x)\, dx \le \int_a^b f(x)\, dx \le \int_a^b f_2(x)\, dx.$$

Example 64. Prove that $\frac{\pi}{6} \le \int_0^1 \frac{dx}{\sqrt{4 - x^2 - x^3}} \le \frac{\pi}{4\sqrt{2}}$.

Sol. Since, $4 - x^2 \ge 4 - x^2 - x^3 \ge 4 - 2x^2 > 1, \forall\, x \in [0, 1]$

$$\sqrt{4 - x^2} \ge \sqrt{4 - x^2 - x^3} \ge \sqrt{4 - 2x^2} > 1, \forall\, x \in [0, 1]$$

$$\Rightarrow \quad \frac{1}{\sqrt{4 - x^2}} \le \frac{1}{\sqrt{4 - x^2 - x^3}} \le \frac{1}{\sqrt{4 - 2x^2}}, \forall\, x \in [0, 1]$$

$$\Rightarrow \quad \int_0^1 \frac{dx}{\sqrt{4 - x^2}} \le \int_0^1 \frac{dx}{\sqrt{4 - x^2 - x^3}}$$

$$\le \int_0^1 \frac{1}{\sqrt{4 - 2x^2}}\, dx, \forall\, x \in [0, 1]$$

$$\Rightarrow \quad \left(\sin^{-1}\frac{x}{2}\right)_0^1 \le \int_0^1 \frac{dx}{\sqrt{4 - x^2 - x^3}} \le \frac{1}{\sqrt{2}}\left(\sin^{-1}\frac{x}{\sqrt{2}}\right)_0^1$$

$$\Rightarrow \quad \frac{\pi}{6} \le \int_0^1 \frac{dx}{\sqrt{4 - x^2 - x^3}} \le \frac{\pi}{4\sqrt{2}}$$

TYPE V

If m and M be global minimum and global maximum of $f(x)$ respectively in $[a, b]$, then

$$m(b-a) \le \int_a^b f(x)\, dx \le M(b-a).$$

Proof We have, $m \le f(x) \le M$ for all $x \in [a, b]$

$$\Rightarrow \quad \int_a^b m\, dx \le \int_a^b f(x)\, dx \le \int_a^b M\, dx$$

$$\Rightarrow \quad m(b-a) \le \int_a^b f(x)\, dx \le M(b-a)$$

Example 65. Prove that $4 \le \int_1^3 \sqrt{3 + x^3}\, dx \le 2\sqrt{30}$.

Sol. Since, the function $f(x) = \sqrt{3 + x^3}$ increases monotonically on the interval $[1, 3]$.

$\therefore \quad M =$ Maximum value of $\sqrt{3 + x^3} = \sqrt{3 + 3^3} = \sqrt{30}$

and $\quad m =$ Minimum value of $\sqrt{3 + x^3} = \sqrt{3 + 1^3} = 2$

$\therefore \quad m = 2, M = \sqrt{30}, b - a = 2$

Hence, $\quad 2 \cdot 2 \le \int_1^3 \sqrt{3 + x^3}\, dx \le 2\sqrt{30}$

$$\Rightarrow \quad 4 \le \int_1^3 \sqrt{3 + x^3}\, dx \le 2\sqrt{30}$$

Example 66. Prove that $1 \le \int_0^1 e^{x^2} dx \le e$.

Sol. For $0 \le x \le 1$, we have $e^0 \le e^{x^2} \le e^1$

$$\therefore\ e^0(1-0) \le \int_0^1 e^{x^2}\, dx \le e^1(1-0) \Rightarrow 1 \le \int_0^1 e^{x^2} dx \le e$$

Example 67. Prove that $1 < \int_0^{\pi/2} \frac{\sin x}{x}\, dx < \frac{\pi}{2}$.

Sol. Let $f(x) = \frac{\sin x}{x}, x \in \left(0, \frac{\pi}{2}\right)$

$$f'(x) = \left(\frac{x\cos x - \sin x}{x^2}\right) = \frac{\cos x\,(x - \tan x)}{x^2}$$

We know that $x < \tan x$, where $x \in \left(0, \frac{\pi}{2}\right)$

$$f'(x) = \frac{\cos x\,(x - \tan x)}{x^2} < 0$$

$\Rightarrow f(x)$ is strictly monotonically decreasing.

$$0 < x < \frac{\pi}{2} \Rightarrow f(0^+) > f(x) > f\left(\frac{\pi}{2}\right)$$

$$\Rightarrow \quad \lim_{x \to 0^+} \frac{\sin x}{x} > f(x) > \frac{\sin \frac{\pi}{2}}{\frac{\pi}{2}}$$

$$\Rightarrow \quad 1 > f(x) > \frac{2}{\pi}$$

$$\Rightarrow \quad \int_0^{\pi/2} 1\, dx > \int_0^{\pi/2} f(x)\, dx > \int_0^{\pi/2} \frac{2}{\pi}\, dx$$

$$\Rightarrow \quad \frac{\pi}{2} > \int_0^{\pi/2} \frac{\sin x}{x}\, dx > \frac{2}{\pi}\left(\frac{\pi}{2} - 0\right)$$

$$\therefore \quad 1 < \int_0^{\pi/2} \frac{\sin x}{x}\, dx < \frac{\pi}{2}$$

2.7 Gamma Function

If n is a positive number, then the improper integral $\int_0^\infty e^{-x} x^{n-1}\, dx$ is defined as Gamma function and is denoted by Γn.

i.e. $\quad \Gamma n = \int_0^\infty e^{-x} x^{n-1}\, dx$, where $x \in Q^+$.

Example 68. Evaluate

(i) $\Gamma 1$ (ii) $\Gamma 2$

Sol. (i) $\Gamma 1 = \int_0^\infty e^{-x} . x^{1-1}\, dx = \lim\limits_{b \to \infty} \int_0^b e^{-x}\, dx$

$$= \lim_{b \to \infty} \left[- e^{-x}\right]_0^b = \lim_{b \to \infty} (- e^{-b} + e^0)$$

$$= 0 + 1 = 1$$

(ii) $\Gamma 2 = \int_0^\infty e^{-x} x^{2-1}\, dx = \lim\limits_{b \to \infty} \int_0^b e^{-x} \cdot x\, dx$

$$= \lim_{b \to \infty} \left[- x\, e^{-x} - e^{-x}\right]_0^b$$

$$= \lim_{b \to \infty} [(- b\, e^{-b} - e^{-b}) - (0 - 1)]$$

$$= \lim_{b \to \infty} \left[\frac{-b}{e^b} - \frac{1}{e^b} + 1\right]$$

$$= \lim_{b \to \infty} \frac{-(b+1)}{e^b} + 1$$

$$= \left(\lim_{b \to \infty} -\frac{1}{e^b}\right) + 1 \qquad \text{[using L'Hospital's rule]}$$

$$= 1$$

Properties of Gamma Function

Gamma function has following properties :

(i) $\Gamma 1 = 1$, $\Gamma 0 = \infty$ and $\Gamma(n+1) = n\,\Gamma n$

e.g. $\Gamma 5 = 4\,\Gamma 4 = 4 \times 3\,\Gamma 3 = 4 \times 3 \times 2\,\Gamma 2$
$= 4 \times 3 \times 2 \times \Gamma 1 = 4 \times 3 \times 2 \times 1$

(ii) If $n \in N$, then $\Gamma(n+1) = (n)\,!$

(iii) $\Gamma(1/2) = \sqrt{\pi}$

(iv) $\int_0^{\pi/2} \sin^m x \cdot \cos^n x\, dx = \dfrac{\Gamma\left(\frac{m+1}{2}\right)\Gamma\left(\frac{n+1}{2}\right)}{2\,\Gamma\left(\frac{m+n+2}{2}\right)}$

(v) $\Gamma n\, \Gamma(1-n) = \dfrac{\pi}{\sin n\pi}, 0 < n < 1$

(vi) $\Gamma m\, \Gamma\left(m + \frac{1}{2}\right) = \dfrac{\sqrt{\pi}}{2^{2m-1}}\, \Gamma\, 2m$

(vii) $\Gamma \frac{1}{n} \Gamma\left(\frac{2}{n}\right) \ldots \Gamma\left(\frac{n-1}{n}\right) = \dfrac{(2\pi)^{\frac{n-1}{2}}}{n^{1/2}}$

Example 69. Evaluate $\int_0^\infty e^{-x} x^3\, dx$.

Sol. By definition of Gamma function,

$$\int_0^\infty e^{-x} x^3\, dx = \int_0^\infty e^{-x} x^{4-1}\, dx = \Gamma 4$$

$$\therefore \quad \int_0^\infty e^{-x} x^3\, dx = 6$$

Example 70. Evaluate $\int_0^1 \left(\log \frac{1}{x}\right)^{n-1} dx$.

Sol. Let $I = \int_0^1 \left(\log \frac{1}{x}\right)^{n-1} dx$

Put $\log \frac{1}{x} = t \Rightarrow dx = - e^{-t}\, dt$

$$\therefore \quad I = \int_\infty^0 t^{n-1} (- e^{-t})\, dt$$

$$= \int_0^\infty e^{-t}\, t^{n-1}\, dt$$

$$\therefore \quad \int_0^1 \left(\log \frac{1}{x}\right)^{n-1} dx = \Gamma n$$

2.8 Beta Function

The beta function is

$$B(m, n) = \int_0^1 x^{m-1} (1-x)^{n-1}\, dx,$$

where $m, n > 0$

Properties of Beta Function

(i) $B(m, n) = B(n, m)$, where $m, n > 0$

(ii) $B(m, n) = \dfrac{\Gamma m \Gamma n}{\Gamma(m+n)}$, where $m, n > 0$

(iii) $B(m, n) = \displaystyle\int_0^\infty \frac{x^{m-1}}{(1+x)^{m+n}}\, dx$

Example 71. Evaluate $\displaystyle\int_0^1 x^6 \sqrt{(1-x^2)}\, dx$.

Sol. Let, $I = \displaystyle\int_0^1 x^6 \sqrt{(1-x^2)}\, dx$

Put $x^2 = t$

$\Rightarrow 2x\, dx = dt$

$$\therefore \quad I = \frac{1}{2}\int_0^1 t^{5/2}\sqrt{(1-t)}\, dt$$

$$I = \frac{1}{2} B\left(\frac{7}{2}, \frac{3}{2}\right) = \frac{1}{2} \cdot \frac{\Gamma 7/2 \Gamma 3/2}{\Gamma\left(\frac{3}{2} + \frac{7}{2}\right)}$$

$$= \frac{1}{2}\,\frac{\frac{5}{2}\cdot\frac{3}{2}\cdot\frac{1}{2}\cdot\sqrt{\pi}\cdot\frac{1}{2}\cdot\sqrt{\pi}}{4\cdot 3\cdot 2\cdot 1} = \frac{5\pi}{256} \quad \left[\because \Gamma\left(\frac{1}{2}\right) = \sqrt{\pi}\right]$$

2.9 Walli's Formula

An easy way to evaluate $\displaystyle\int_0^{\pi/2} \sin^m x \cdot \cos^n x\, dx$, where $m, n \in I_+$.

We have, $\displaystyle\int_0^{\pi/2} \sin^m x \cdot \cos^n x\, dx$

$$= \int_0^{\pi/2} \sin^n x \cdot \cos^m x\, dx$$

$$= \frac{(m-1)(m-3)\ldots(1 \text{ or } 2).(n-1)(n-3)\ldots(1 \text{ or } 2)}{(m+n)(m+n-2)\ldots(1 \text{ or } 2)} \cdot \frac{\pi}{2},$$

when both m and $n \in$ even integer.

$$= \frac{(m-1)(m-3)\ldots(1 \text{ or } 2)\cdot(n-1)(n-3)\ldots(1 \text{ or } 2)}{(m+n)(m+n-2)\ldots(1 \text{ or } 2)},$$

when either of m or $n \in$ odd integer.

JEE SPIKE

If n be a positive integer, then

$$\int_0^{\pi/2} \sin^n x\, dx = \int_0^{\pi/2} \cos^n x\, dx$$

$$= \frac{n-1}{n}\cdot\frac{n-3}{n-2}\cdot\frac{n-5}{n-4}\ldots\frac{3}{4}\cdot\frac{1}{2}\cdot\frac{\pi}{2}, \; n \text{ is even.}$$

$$= \frac{n-1}{n}\cdot\frac{n-3}{n-2}\cdot\frac{n-5}{n-4}\ldots\frac{4}{5}\cdot\frac{2}{3}\cdot 1, \; n \text{ is odd.}$$

Concept Inside Video

Example 72. Evaluate $\displaystyle\int_0^{\pi/2} \sin^4 x \cdot \cos^6 x\, dx$.

Sol. Using Walli's formula, we have

$$\int_0^{\pi/2} \sin^4 x \cdot \cos^6 x\, dx = \frac{(4-1)(4-3)(6-1)(6-3)(6-5)}{10(10-2)(10-4)(10-6)(10-8)} \times \frac{\pi}{2}$$

$$= \frac{3\times1\times5\times3\times1}{10\times8\times6\times4\times2}\times\frac{\pi}{2}$$

$$= \frac{3\pi}{512}$$

Example 73. The value of $\displaystyle\int_0^\infty e^{-a^2x^2}\, dx$ is equal to

(a) $\dfrac{\sqrt{\pi}}{2a}$

(b) $\dfrac{\pi}{2a}$

(c) $\dfrac{\pi}{\sqrt{2a}}$

(d) None of these

Sol. (a) Let $I = \displaystyle\int_0^\infty e^{-a^2x^2}\, dx$

$$\therefore \quad I = \int_0^\infty e^{-t}\cdot\frac{1}{2a\sqrt{t}}\, dt \quad [\text{put } a^2x^2 = t \Rightarrow 2a^2x\, dx = dt]$$

$$= \frac{1}{2a}\int_0^\infty e^{-t}\cdot t^{-1/2}\, dt$$

$$= \frac{1}{2a}\int_0^\infty t^{1/2-1}\cdot e^{-t}\cdot dt$$

$$= \frac{1}{2a}\Gamma\left(\frac{1}{2}\right) \quad \left[\text{using } \int_0^\infty e^{-x} x^{n-1} dx = \Gamma n\right]$$

$$= \frac{1}{2a}\sqrt{\pi} \quad \left[\text{using } \Gamma\left(\frac{1}{2}\right) = \sqrt{\pi}\right]$$

2.10 Integration Involving $f(x)$ and $f^{-1}(x)$

Let $f(x)$ be increasing and bijective continuous function $f:[a, b]\to[c, d]$, then

$$\int_a^b f(x)\, dx + \int_{f(a)}^{f(b)} f^{-1}(x)\, dx = bf(b) - af(a)$$

Proof Let $f(x)$ be an increasing function for $x \in [a, b]$

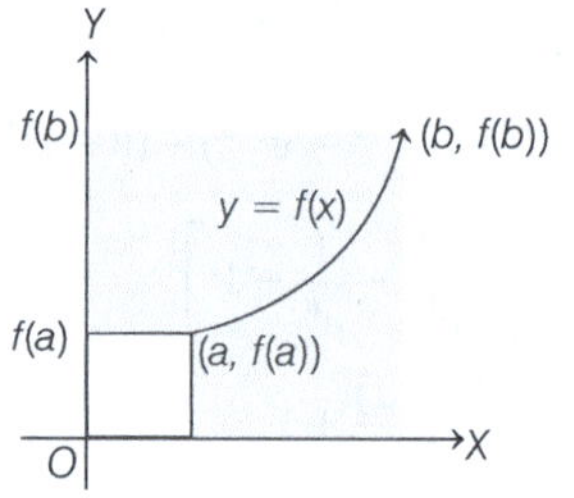

$$\int_a^b f(x)\, dx + \int_{f(a)}^{f(b)} f^{-1}(x)\, dx$$

$$= \text{Shaded area} = bf(b) - af(a)$$

Alternate As, $f(x)$ is increasing and bijective

$f(a)=c, f(b)=d$

$$\therefore \int_c^d f^{-1}(x)\,dx = \int_{f(a)}^{f(b)} f^{-1}(x)\,dx \qquad \begin{bmatrix} \text{put } f^{-1}(x)=t \\ \Rightarrow x=f(t) \\ \Rightarrow dx=f'(t)\,dt \end{bmatrix}$$

$$= \int_a^b t\, f'(t)\,dt$$

$$= [tf(t)]_a^b - \int_a^b f(t)\,dt$$

$$= [tf(t)]_a^b - \int_a^b f(x)\,dx$$

$$\Rightarrow \int_a^b f(x)\,dx + \int_c^d f^{-1}(x)\,dx = bf(b) - af(a)$$

Example 74. Let f be a one-one continuous function such that $f(2)=3$ and $f(5)=7$. Given, $\int_2^5 f(x)\,dx = 17$, then compute $\int_3^7 f^{-1}(x)\,dx$.

Sol. Let $y=f(x)$

$\Rightarrow x=f^{-1}(y)$ and $dy=f'(x)\,dx$

Let $I=\int_3^7 f^{-1}(x)\,dx$

$$=\int_3^7 f^{-1}(y)\,dy$$

$$=\int_2^5 xf'(x)\,dx$$

$$I=[xf(x)]_2^5 - \int_2^5 f(x)\,dx$$

$$=[5f(5)-2f(2)]-17$$

$$=(5\cdot 7-2\cdot 3)-17=12$$

Example 75. If $f:[0,1]\to[e,e^{\sqrt{e}}]$ be an increasing function, then $\int_0^1 e^{\sqrt{e^x}}\,dx + 2\int_e^{e^{\sqrt{e}}} \ln(\ln x)\,dx$.

Sol. As, $f(x)$ is increasing and bijective continuous function $f:[a,b]\to[c,d]$, then

$$\int_a^b f(x)\,dx + \int_{f(a)}^{f(b)} f^{-1}(x)\,dx = bf(b)-af(a) \qquad \text{...(i)}$$

Here, $f(x)=e^{\sqrt{e^x}}$, $f^{-1}(x)=\ln(\ln x)^2 = 2\ln(\ln x)$

$$a=0, b=1, f(0)=e, f(1)=e^{\sqrt{e}}$$

$$\therefore \int_0^1 e^{\sqrt{e^x}}\,dx + 2\int_e^{e^{\sqrt{e}}} \ln(\ln x)\,dx$$

$$=1\cdot e^{\sqrt{e}} - 0\cdot e \qquad \text{[from Eq. (i)]}$$

$$=e^{\sqrt{e}}$$

JEE SCANNER

Example Similar to PYQ Asked in JEE Main 2022

The greatest integer less than or equal to $\int_1^2 \log_2(x^3+1)dx + \int_1^{\log_2 9}(2^x-1)^{1/3}\,dx$ is ....

Sol. (5) $\int_1^2 \log_2(x^3+1)\,dx + \int_1^{\log_2 9}(2^x-1)^{1/3}\,dx$

Let $f(x)=y$

$\Rightarrow y=\log_2(x^3+1)$

$\Rightarrow x^3+1=2^y$

$\Rightarrow x=(2^y-1)^{1/3}$

$\Rightarrow f^{-1}(x)=(2^x-1)^{1/3}$

Using, $\int_a^b f(x)\,dx + \int_{f(a)}^{f(b)} f^{-1}(x)\,dx = bf(b)-af(a)$

So, $\int_1^2 \log_2(x^3+1)\,dx + \int_1^{\log_2 9}(2^x-1)^{1/3}\,dx$

$$=2\log_2 9 - 1\times 1$$

$$=4\log_2 3 - 1$$

$\therefore$ $[4\log_2 3 - 1]=5$

Skill Builder

The greatest integer less than or equal to $\int_0^2 \log_2(x^4+9)\,dx + \int_{\log_2 9}^{\log_2 25}(2^x-9)^{1/4}\,dx$ is ...

For Sol.

■ **For more practice** See Q.11 of Milestone Practice 2.6.

Milestone Practice 2.6

1. The value of

$$\lim_{n\to\infty}\left\{\frac{1}{1+n^4}+\frac{8}{16+n^4}+\frac{27}{81+n^4}+\dots\text{ to } n \text{ terms}\right\}$$

is equal to

(a) $\frac{1}{2}\ln 2$ (b) $\frac{1}{4}\ln 2$

(c) $\ln 2$ (d) None of these

2. The value of $\lim_{n\to\infty}\frac{1}{n}\sum_{r-1}^{n}\left(\frac{r}{n+r}\right)$ is equal to

(a) $1-\log 2$ (b) $\log 4 - 1$

(c) $\log 2$ (d) None of these

3. The value of

$$\lim_{n\to\infty}\frac{1}{n}\{(n+1)(n+2)(n+3)\dots(n+n)\}^{1/n}$$ is

equal to

(a) $4e$ (b) $\frac{e}{4}$

(c) $\frac{4}{e}$ (d) None of these

4. If $m, n \in N$, then the value of $\int_a^b (x-a)^m (b-x)^n\, dx$ is equal to

(a) $\frac{(b-a)^{m+n}\cdot m!\,n!}{(m+n)!}$ (b) $\frac{(b-a)^{m+n+1}\cdot m!\,n!}{(m+n+1)!}$

(c) $\frac{(b-a)^m\cdot m!}{m!}$ (d) None of these

5. The value of $\lim_{n\to\infty}\left(\frac{n!}{n^n}\right)^{\frac{2n^4+1}{5n^5+1}}$ is equal to

(a) e (b) $\frac{2}{e}$

(c) $\left(\frac{1}{e}\right)^{\frac{2}{5}}$ (d) None of these

6. The value of $\lim_{n\to\infty}$

$$n\left\{\frac{1}{3n^2+8n+4}+\frac{1}{3n^2+16n+16}+\dots+\text{ to } n \text{ terms}\right\}$$

is equal to

(a) $\frac{1}{2}\log\left(\frac{9}{5}\right)$ (b) $\frac{1}{3}\log\left(\frac{9}{5}\right)$

(c) $\frac{1}{4}\log\left(\frac{9}{5}\right)$ (d) None of these

7. The value of

$$\lim_{n\to\infty}\frac{1}{n^2}\left\{\sin^3\frac{\pi}{4n}+2\sin^3\frac{2\pi}{4n}+\dots+n\sin^3\frac{n\pi}{4n}\right\}$$

is equal to

(a) $\frac{\sqrt{2}}{9\pi^2}(52-15\pi)$ (b) $\frac{2}{9\pi^2}(52-15\pi)$

(c) $\frac{1}{9\pi^2}(52-15\pi)$ (d) None of these

8. If $I=\int_0^1 \frac{dx}{1+x^{\pi/2}}$, then

(a) $I > \ln 2$ (b) $I < \ln 2$

(c) $I > \frac{\pi}{4}$ (d) None of these

9. If $m, n \in N$, then $I_{m,n}=\int_0^1 x^m (1-x)^n\, dx$ is equal to

(a) $\frac{m!\,n!}{(m+n+2)!}$ (b) $\frac{2m!\,n!}{(m+n+1)!}$

(c) $\frac{m!\,n!}{(m+n+1)!}$ (d) None of these

10. The value of $I(n)=\int_0^\pi \frac{\sin^2 n\theta}{\sin^2\theta}\,d\theta$ is $(\forall\ n\in N)$

(a) $n\pi$ (b) $\frac{n\pi}{2}$

(c) $\frac{n\pi}{4}$ (d) None of these

11. If $g(x)$ is the inverse of $f(x)$ and $f(x)$ has domain $x\in[1,5]$, where $f(1)=2$ and $f(5)=10$, then the values of $\int_1^5 f(x)\,dx+\int_2^{10} g(y)\,dy$ equals

(a) 48 (b) 64

(c) 71 (d) 52

12. If $f(x)=x^3+3x+4$, then the value of $\int_{-1}^{1} f(x)\,dx+\int_0^8 f^{-1}(x)\,dx$ is equal to ....

Answer Key

1. (b)	2. (a)	3. (c)	4. (a)	5. (c)	6. (c)
7. (a)	8. (a)	9. (c)	10. (a)	11. (a)	12. (8)

For Detailed Solution

JEE Pattern EXAMPLES

Single Option Correct Type Questions

Example 1 *Let* $v_n = \int_0^{\pi/2}\frac{\sin^2 nx}{\sin^2 x}dx$. *If* $\sum_{r=1}^{100} v_r = \frac{k\pi}{2}$, *where* $k \in N$, *then k equals to*

(a) 100 (b) 2525 (c) 5050 (d) 4950

Sol. (c) Consider $(v_{n+1} - v_n) - (v_n - v_{n-1}) = 0$

$$\Rightarrow \quad 2v_n = v_{n+1} + v_{n-1}$$

$\Rightarrow v_1, v_2, v_3, \ldots$ are in AP.

Now, $v_1 = \frac{\pi}{2}$, $v_2 = \int_0^{\pi/2}\frac{\sin^2 2x}{\sin^2 x}dx$

$$= \int_0^{\pi/2} 4\cos^2 x\,dx = \pi$$

$$\therefore \quad d = \pi - \frac{\pi}{2} = \frac{\pi}{2}$$

$$S_{100} = \frac{\pi}{2}[1 + 2 + 3 + \ldots + 100]$$

$$= \frac{5050\pi}{2} = \frac{(k)\pi}{2}$$

$$\Rightarrow \quad k = 5050$$

Example 2 *The value(s) of* $\int_0^1 \frac{x^4(1-x)^4}{1+x^2}dx$ *is (are)*

(a) $\frac{22}{7} - \pi$ (b) $\frac{2}{105}$ (c) 0 (d) $\frac{71}{15} - \frac{3\pi}{2}$

Sol. (a) Let $I = \int_0^1 \frac{x^4(1-x)^4}{1+x^2}dx$

$$= \int_0^1 \frac{(x^4-1)(1-x)^4 + (1-x)^4}{(1+x^2)}dx$$

$$= \int_0^1 (x^2-1)(1-x)^4 dx + \int_0^1 \frac{(1+x^2-2x)^2}{(1+x^2)}dx$$

$$= \int_0^1 \left\{(x^2-1)(1-x)^4 + (1+x^2) - 4x + \frac{4x^2}{(1+x^2)}\right\}dx$$

$$= \int_0^1 \left((x^2-1)(1-x)^4 + (1+x^2) - 4x + 4 - \frac{4}{1+x^2}\right)dx$$

$$= \int_0^1 \left(x^6 - 4x^5 + 5x^4 - 4x^2 + 4 - \frac{4}{1+x^2}\right)dx$$

$$= \frac{1}{7} - \frac{4}{6} + \frac{5}{5} - \frac{4}{3} + 4 - 4\left(\frac{\pi}{4} - 0\right) = \frac{22}{7} - \pi$$

JEE SCANNER

Example 3 Similar to PYQ Asked in JEE Main 2024

If $\int_0^{\pi/2} 4\sin^6 x\,dx = \frac{\alpha\pi}{\beta}$, *where* α *and* β *are coprime, then* $\alpha + \beta$ *is equal to*

(a) 16 (b) 10 (c) 13 (d) 24

Sol. (c) We have,

$$I = \int_0^{\pi/2} 4\sin^6 x\,dx$$

$$= \frac{1}{4}\int_0^{\pi/2}(3\sin x - \sin 3x)^2 dx$$

$$= \frac{1}{4}\int_0^{\pi/2}(9\sin^2 x + \sin^2 3x - 6\sin x \sin 3x)dx$$

$$= \frac{1}{4}\int_0^{\pi/2}\left[\frac{9}{2}(1-\cos 2x) + \frac{1}{2}(1-\cos 6x) - 3(\cos 2x - \cos 4x)\right]dx$$

$$= \frac{9}{8}\int_0^{\pi/2}(1-\cos 2x)dx + \frac{1}{8}\int_0^{\pi/2}(1-\cos 6x)dx - \frac{3}{4}\int_0^{\pi/2}(\cos 2x)dx + \frac{3}{4}\int_0^{\pi/2}(\cos 4x)dx$$

$$= \frac{9}{8}\left[x - \frac{\sin 2x}{2}\right]_0^{\pi/2} + \frac{1}{8}\left[x - \frac{\sin 6x}{6}\right]_0^{\pi/2} - \frac{3}{4}\left[\frac{\sin 2x}{2}\right]_0^{\pi/2} + \frac{3}{4}\left[\frac{\sin 4x}{4}\right]_0^{\pi/2}$$

$$= \frac{9}{8}\left[\frac{\pi}{2} - 0\right] + \frac{1}{8}\left[\frac{\pi}{2} - 0\right] - \frac{3}{4} \times 0 + \frac{3}{4} \times 0$$

$$= \frac{9}{16}\pi + \frac{\pi}{16} = \frac{5\pi}{8}$$

Hence, $\alpha + \beta = 13$

Skill Builder

If $\int_0^{\pi/4}\sin^4 x\,dx = \frac{\alpha\pi - \beta}{\gamma}$, where α, β and γ are ratioinal numbers, then $\gamma - \alpha\beta$ is equal to

(a) 10 (b) 4

(c) 12 (d) 8

For Sol.

Example 4 *The true set of values of 'a' for which the inequality* $\int_a^0 (3^{-2x} - 2\cdot 3^{-x})\, dx \geq 0$ *is true, is*

(a) $[0, 1]$ (b) $(-\infty, -1]$ (c) $[0, \infty)$ (d) $(-\infty, -1] \cup [0, \infty)$

Decoding the Question

In this problem, first take 3^{-x} common, because it is present in both the term of integer and then let $3^{-x} = t$ and change the limit and integration in terms of t and solve it to find the inequality in a. Then, use concepts of inequality to obtain the range of a.

Sol. (d) We have, $\int_a^0 3^{-x}(3^{-x} - 2)\, dx \geq 0$

Put $3^{-x} = t \Rightarrow 3^{-x} \ln 3\, dx = -dt$

$$\Rightarrow \quad \frac{1}{\ln 3}\int_1^{3^{-a}} (t-2)\, dt \geq 0 = \left[\frac{t^2}{2} - 2t\right]_1^{3^{-a}} \geq 0$$

$$\Rightarrow \quad \left(\frac{3^{-2a}}{2} - 2\cdot 3^{-a}\right) - \left(\frac{1}{2} - 2\right) \geq 0$$

$$\Rightarrow \quad 3^{-2a} - 4\times 3^{-a} + 3 \geq 0 \Rightarrow (3^{-a} - 3)(3^{-a} - 1) \geq 0$$

$$\Rightarrow \quad 3^{-a} \geq 3^1 \Rightarrow a \leq -1 \text{ or } 3^{-a} \leq 3^0 \Rightarrow a \geq 0$$

Thus, $a \in (-\infty, -1] \cup [0, \infty)$

Example 5 *Let* $a_n = \int_0^{\pi/2} \frac{1 - \cos 2nx}{1 - \cos 2x}\, dx$, *then the value of* $\begin{vmatrix} \pi/2 & a_2 & a_3 \\ a_4 & a_5 & a_6 \\ a_7 & a_8 & a_9 \end{vmatrix}$ *equals to*

(a) 1 (b) 2 (c) 3 (d) 0

Sol. (d) Consider $a_n + a_{n+2} - 2a_{n+1} = A$ (say)

$$\therefore \quad A = \int_0^{\pi/2} \left[\frac{(1 - \cos 2nx) + 1 - \cos(2n+4)x - 2(1 - \cos(2n+2)x)}{1 - \cos 2x}\right] dx$$

$$A = \int_0^{\pi/2} \left[\frac{2\cos(2n+2)x - 2\cos(2n+2)x\cos 2x}{1 - \cos 2x}\right] dx$$

$$A = \int_0^{\pi/2} 2\cos(2n+2)x\, dx = 2\left[\frac{\sin(2n+2)x}{2n+2}\right]_0^{\pi/2} = 0$$

$\therefore$ $a_n, a_{n+1}, a_{n+2} \in$ AP, alongwith

$$a_1 = \int_0^{\pi/2} \left(\frac{1 - \cos 2x}{1 - \cos 2x}\right) dx$$

$$\therefore \quad a_1 = \frac{\pi}{2}$$

$$\begin{vmatrix} a_1 & a_2 & a_3 \\ a_4 & a_5 & a_6 \\ a_7 & a_8 & a_9 \end{vmatrix} = \begin{vmatrix} 0 & a_2 & a_3 \\ 0 & a_5 & a_6 \\ 0 & a_8 & a_9 \end{vmatrix} = 0 \qquad [C_1 \to C_1 + C_3 - 2C_2]$$

Example 6 *If* $f : [0, 1] \to [0, \infty)$ *is differentiable function with decreasing first derivative, such that* $f(0) = 0$ *and* $f'(x) > 0$, *then*

(a) $\int_0^1 \frac{dx}{f^2(x) + 1} > \frac{f(1)}{f'(1)}$ (b) $\int_0^1 \frac{dx}{f^2(x) + 1} < \frac{f(1)}{f'(1)}$

(c) $\int_0^1 \frac{dx}{f^2(x) + 1} > \frac{\tan^{-1}(f(1))}{f'(1)}$ (d) $\int_0^1 \frac{dx}{f^2(x) + 1} = \frac{f(1)}{f'(1)}$

Sol. (b) Given, $f : [0, 1] \to [0, \infty)$

Also, $f'(x)$ is decreasing function in $[0, 1]$ ...(i)

$\Rightarrow$ $f''(x) < 0$

Since, $0 \leq x \leq 1 \Rightarrow f'(1) \leq f'(x) \leq f'(0)$ [by Eq. (i)]

Now, consider $f'(1) \leq f'(x)$

$$\Rightarrow \quad \frac{f'(1)}{f^2(x) + 1} \leq \frac{f'(x)}{f^2(x) + 1}$$

$$\Rightarrow \quad \int_0^1 \frac{f'(1)}{f^2(x) + 1} dx \leq \int_0^1 \frac{f'(x)}{f^2(x) + 1} dx$$

$$\Rightarrow \quad f'(1)\int_0^1 \frac{dx}{f^2(x) + 1} \leq \int_0^1 \frac{f'(x)}{f^2(x) + 1} dx$$

$$\Rightarrow \quad f'(1)\int_0^1 \frac{dx}{f^2(x) + 1} \leq [\tan^{-1}(f(x))]_0^1$$

$$\Rightarrow \quad f'(1)\int_0^1 \frac{dx}{f^2(x) + 1} \leq \tan^{-1}(f(1)) - \tan^{-1}(f(0))$$

$$\Rightarrow \quad \int_0^1 \frac{dx}{f^2(x) + 1} \leq \frac{\tan^{-1} f(1)}{f'(1)} \quad \text{...(ii)}$$

$[\because f(0) = 0 \Rightarrow \tan^{-1}(0) = 0]$

Now, for all $x \geq 0$, $\tan^{-1} x \leq x$

$$\Rightarrow \quad \tan^{-1} f(x) \leq f(x) \Rightarrow \tan^{-1} f(1) \leq f(1)$$

$$\Rightarrow \quad \frac{\tan^{-1} f(1)}{f'(1)} \leq \frac{f(1)}{f'(1)} \quad \text{...(iii)}$$

By Eqs. (ii) and (iii), we get

$$\int_0^1 \frac{dx}{f^2(x) + 1} \leq \frac{\tan^{-1} f(1)}{f'(1)} \leq \frac{f(1)}{f'(1)}$$

Example 7 *If* $\int_0^\infty f(x)dx = \frac{\pi}{2}$ *and* $f(x)$ *is an even function, then* $\int_0^\infty f\left(x - \frac{1}{x}\right)dx$ *is equal to*

(a) $\frac{\pi}{4}$ (b) $\frac{\pi}{2}$ (c) π (d) None of these

Sol. (b) Here, $\int_0^\infty f(x)dx = \frac{\pi}{2}$

Put $x = t - \frac{1}{t} \Rightarrow dx = \left(1 + \frac{1}{t^2}\right)dt$

$$\therefore \quad \int_0^\infty f(x)dx = \int_1^\infty f\left(t - \frac{1}{t}\right)\cdot\left(1 + \frac{1}{t^2}\right)dt$$

$$= \int_1^\infty f\left(t - \frac{1}{t}\right)dt + \int_1^\infty f\left(t - \frac{1}{t}\right)\cdot\frac{1}{t^2}dt$$

$$= \int_1^\infty f\left(t - \frac{1}{t}\right)dt + \int_1^0 f\left(\frac{1}{y} - y\right)\cdot(-dy) \qquad \left[\text{put } t = \frac{1}{y}\right]$$

$$= \int_1^{\infty} f\left(t - \frac{1}{t}\right) dt - \int_1^0 f\left(y - \frac{1}{y}\right) dy \quad \text{[as } f(x) \text{ is even]}$$

$$= \int_1^{\infty} f\left(t - \frac{1}{t}\right) dt + \int_0^1 f\left(t - \frac{1}{t}\right) dt = \int_0^{\infty} f\left(t - \frac{1}{t}\right) dt$$

$$\therefore \quad \int_0^{\infty} f\left(x - \frac{1}{x}\right) dx = \int_0^{\infty} f(x) dx = \frac{\pi}{2}$$

JEE SCANNER

Example 8 Similar to PYQ Asked in JEE Main 2024

Let $g(x)$ be function satisfying $g(x) + g(2\pi - x) = 4\pi^2$, $\forall\ x \in R$. Then, $\int_0^{2\pi} g(x) \cos x\, dx$ is equal to

(a) $2\pi^2$ (b) $4\pi^2$ (c) 0 (d) 2

Sol. (c) Let $I = \int_0^{2\pi} g(x) \cos x\, dx$ ...(i)

$$= \int_0^{2\pi} g(2\pi - x) \cos(2\pi - x)\, dx$$

$$= \int_0^{2\pi} g(2\pi - x) \cos x\, dx \quad \text{...(ii)}$$

On adding Eqs. (i) and (ii), we get

$$2I = \int_0^{2\pi} [g(x) + g(2\pi - x)] \cos x\, dx$$

$$\Rightarrow \quad 2I = \int_0^{2\pi} 4\pi^2 \cos x\, dx$$

$$\therefore \quad I = 2\pi^2 [\sin x]_0^{2\pi} \Rightarrow I = 0$$

Skill Builder

Let $f(x)$ be function satisfying $f(x) - f(2\pi - x) = -1$, $\forall\ x \in R$. Then, $\int_0^{2\pi} f(x) \sin x\, dx$ is equal to

(a) 2 (b) 1 (c) − 2 (d) 0

For Sol.

Example 9 *A function $g(x)$ is given by*

$$g(x) = \frac{x}{1 + (\log_e x)(\log_e x) \ldots \infty}, \text{ where } x \in [1, \infty), \text{ then}$$

$\int_1^{2e} g(x)\, dx$ is equal to

(a) $\frac{1}{2}\left(e - \frac{1}{e}\right)$ (b) $\frac{1}{2}\left(e + \frac{1}{e}\right)$

(c) $\frac{1}{2}(e^2 - 1)$ (d) $\frac{1}{2}(e^2 + 1)$

Sol. (c) Let $f(x) = (\log_e x) \cdot (\log_e x) \ldots \infty$

$$\left.\begin{aligned} f(x) &= 0, \text{ when } 1 < x < e \\ f(x) &= 1, \text{ when } x = e \\ f(x) &= \infty, \text{ when } e < x < 2e \end{aligned}\right\}$$

$$g(x) = \begin{cases} x, & 1 < x < e \\ \frac{x}{2}, & x = e \\ 0, & e < x < 2e \end{cases}$$

$$\int_1^{2e} g(x)\, dx = \int_1^e x\, dx + \int_e^{2e} 0\, dx = \left[\frac{x^2}{2}\right]_1^e = \frac{1}{2}(e^2 - 1)$$

Example 10 *If $\sum_{i=1}^{6} (\sin^{-1} x_i + \cos^{-1} y_i) = 9\pi$, then*

$\int_{\sum_{i=1}^{6} x_i}^{\sum_{i=1}^{6} y_i} x \ln(1 + x^2) \left(\frac{e^x}{1 + e^{2x}}\right) dx$ is equal to

(a) 0 (b) $e^6 + e^{-6}$ (c) $\ln\left(\frac{37}{12}\right)$ (d) $e^6 - e^{-6}$

Sol. (a) As, $\sum_{i=1}^{6} (\sin^{-1} x_i + \cos^{-1} y_i) = 9\pi$

$$\Rightarrow (\sin^{-1} x_1 + \sin^{-1} x_2 + \ldots + \sin^{-1} x_6)$$
$$+ (\cos^{-1} y_1 + \cos^{-1} y_2 + \ldots + \cos^{-1} y_6) = 9\pi$$

which is possible only, when

$$\sin^{-1} x_i = \frac{\pi}{2} \text{ and } \cos^{-1} y_i = \pi, \forall\ i = 1, 2, \ldots, 6$$

$$\therefore \quad x_i = 1 \text{ and } y_i = -1, \forall\ i = 1, 2, \ldots, 6$$

$$\Rightarrow \quad \sum_{i=1}^{6} x_i = 6 \text{ and } \sum_{i=1}^{6} y_i = -6$$

$$\text{Now, } \int_6^{-6} x \ln(1 + x^2) \frac{e^x}{1 + e^{2x}} dx = 0$$

[$\because$ given function is an odd function]

Example 11 *The value of the definite integral $\int_0^{2n\pi} \max(\sin x, \sin^{-1}(\sin x))\, dx$ equals to (where, $n \in I$)*

(a) $\frac{n(\pi^2 - 4)}{2}$ (b) $\frac{n(\pi^2 - 4)}{4}$ (c) $\frac{n(\pi^2 - 8)}{4}$ (d) $\frac{n(\pi^2 - 2)}{4}$

Sol. (c) Let $I = \int_0^{2n\pi} \max(\sin x, \sin^{-1}(\sin x))\, dx$

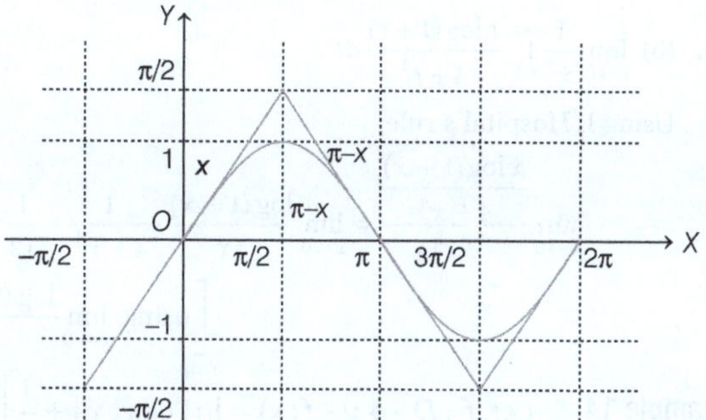

$$= n\left[\int_0^{\pi/2} x\, dx + \int_{\pi/2}^{\pi} (\pi - x)\, dx + \int_{\pi}^{2\pi} (\sin x)\, dx\right]$$

$$= n\left[\frac{\pi^2}{8} + \frac{\pi^2}{2} - \frac{1}{2}\left(\pi^2 - \frac{\pi^2}{4}\right) - 2\right]$$

$$= n\left[\frac{\pi^2}{8} + \frac{\pi^2}{2} - \frac{3\pi^2}{8} - 2\right]$$

$$= \frac{n(\pi^2 - 8)}{4}$$

JEE SCANNER

Example 12 Similar to PYQ Asked in JEE Main 2024

$$\lim_{x\to\frac{\pi}{4}} \frac{\int_2^{\sec^2 x} f(t)\,dt}{x^2-\frac{\pi^2}{16}}$$ is equal to

(a) $\frac{8}{\pi}f(2)$ (b) $\frac{2}{\pi}f(2)$ (c) $\frac{2}{\pi}f\left(\frac{1}{2}\right)$ (d) $4f(2)$

Sol. (a) $\lim_{x\to\frac{\pi}{4}} \frac{\int_2^{\sec^2 x} f(t)\,dt}{x^2-\frac{\pi^2}{16}} = \lim_{x\to\frac{\pi}{4}} \frac{f(\sec^2 x)\cdot 2\sec^2 x\tan x - 0}{2x}$

[applying L'Hospital rule]

$$= \frac{f(2)\cdot 4}{\pi/2} = \frac{8f(2)}{\pi}$$

Skill Builder

$$\lim_{x\to\frac{\pi}{2}} \left(\frac{4\int_{x^4}^{(\pi/2)^4} \cos(t^{1/4})\,dt}{\left(x-\frac{\pi}{2}\right)^2} \right)$$ is equal to

(a) $\frac{\pi^3}{2}$ (b) $\frac{\pi^3}{4}$ (c) $\frac{\pi^3}{8}$ (d) π^3

For Sol.

Example 13 *The value of* $\lim_{x\to 0} \frac{1}{x^3}\int_0^x \frac{t\ln(1+t)}{t^4+4}dt$

(a) 0 (b) $\frac{1}{12}$ (c) $\frac{1}{24}$ (d) $\frac{1}{64}$

Sol. (b) $\lim_{x\to 0} \frac{1}{x^3}\int_0^x \frac{t\log(1+t)}{4+t^4}dt$

Using L'Hospital's rule,

$$\lim_{x\to 0} \frac{\frac{x\log(1+x)}{4+x^4}}{3x^2} = \lim_{x\to 0} \frac{\log(1+x)}{3x}\cdot\frac{1}{4+x^4} = \frac{1}{12}$$

$$\left[\text{using } \lim_{x\to 0}\frac{\log(1+x)}{x} = 1\right]$$

Example 14 *Let* $f: D \to y \cdot f(x) = \ln\left[\cos|x| + \frac{1}{2}\right]$, *(where* $[\cdot]$ *represent greatest integer function), then* $\int_{x_1}^{x_2}\left(\lim_{n\to\infty}\left(\frac{(f(x))^n}{x^2+\tan^2 x}\right)\right)dx$, *where* $(x_1, x_2 \in D)$ *is*

(a) 0 (b) 1 (c) $\frac{3}{2}$ (d) 2

Sol. (a) $f(x) = \ln\left[\cos|x| + \frac{1}{2}\right]$

$$1 \le \cos|x| + \frac{1}{2} < \frac{3}{2}$$

$$\Rightarrow \left[\cos|x| + \frac{1}{2}\right] = 1,\ f(x) = 0$$

$$\int_{x_1}^{x_2}\left(\lim_{n\to\infty}\left(\frac{(f(x))^n}{x^2+\tan^2 x}\right)\right) = \int_{x_1}^{x_2} 0\,dx = 0$$

Example 15 *The value of*

$$\lim_{n\to\infty}\left(\frac{1-\cos\frac{2}{n}}{1+\cos\frac{2}{n}}\right)\left(\sum_{r=1}^{2n}\frac{n}{\sqrt{8n^2-r^2}}\right)\left(\sum_{r=1}^{3n}\frac{n}{\sqrt{18n^2-r^2}}\right)$$ *is*

equal to

(a) $\frac{\pi^2}{4}$ (b) $\frac{\pi^2}{8}$ (c) $\frac{\pi^2}{16}$ (d) $\frac{3\pi^2}{16}$

Decoding the Question

This problem contains 3 functions. In Ist function, we use $\cos 2x = 2\cos^2 x - 1 = 1 - 2\sin^2 x$ to convert it into the known limit $\lim_{x\to 0}\frac{\tan x}{x} = 1$. In IInd and IIIrd function, take n^2 common from denominator and replace $\frac{1}{n} \to dx$, $\frac{r}{n} \to x$ and $\lim_{n\to\infty}\sum \to \int$ and solve it.

Sol. (c) $\lim_{n\to\infty}\left(\frac{1-\cos\frac{2}{n}}{1+\cos\frac{2}{n}}\right)\left(\sum_{r=1}^{2n}\frac{n}{\sqrt{8n^2-r^2}}\right)\left(\sum_{r=1}^{3n}\frac{n}{\sqrt{18n^2-r^2}}\right)$

$$\lim_{n\to\infty}\left(\frac{\tan^2\frac{1}{n}}{\frac{1}{n^2}}\right)\cdot\left(\sum_{r=1}^{2n}\frac{n}{n\cdot n\sqrt{8-\frac{r^2}{n^2}}}\right)\left(\sum_{r=1}^{3n}\frac{n}{n\cdot n\sqrt{18-\frac{r^2}{n^2}}}\right)$$

$$= 1\left(\int_0^2\frac{dx}{\sqrt{8-x^2}}\right)\left(\int_0^3\frac{dx}{\sqrt{18-x^2}}\right) = \left(\sin^{-1}\frac{x}{2\sqrt{2}}\right)_0^2\left(\sin^{-1}\frac{x}{3\sqrt{2}}\right)_0^3$$

$$= \left(\sin^{-1}\frac{x}{2\sqrt{2}}\right)_0^2\left(\sin^{-1}\frac{x}{3\sqrt{2}}\right)_0^3 = \frac{\pi}{4}\cdot\frac{\pi}{4} = \frac{\pi^2}{16}$$

More than One Correct Option Type Questions

Example 16 *Let* $A_1 = \int_n^{n+1}(\min\{|x-n|, |x-(n+1)|\})\,dx$,

$$A_2 = \int_{n+1}^{n+2}(|x-n| - |x-(n+1)|)\,dx,$$

$$A_3 = \int_{n+2}^{n+3}(|x-(n+4)| - |x-(n+3)|)\,dx$$

and $g(x) = A_1 + A_2 + A_3$, *then*

(a) $A_1 + A_2 + A_3 = 9$ (b) $A_1 + A_2 + A_3 = \frac{9}{4}$

(c) $\sum_{n=1}^{100} g(x) = \frac{900}{4}$ (d) $\sum_{n=1}^{100} g(x) = 300$

Sol. (b, c) Here, min $\{|x-n|, |x-(n+1)|\}$ can be shown as

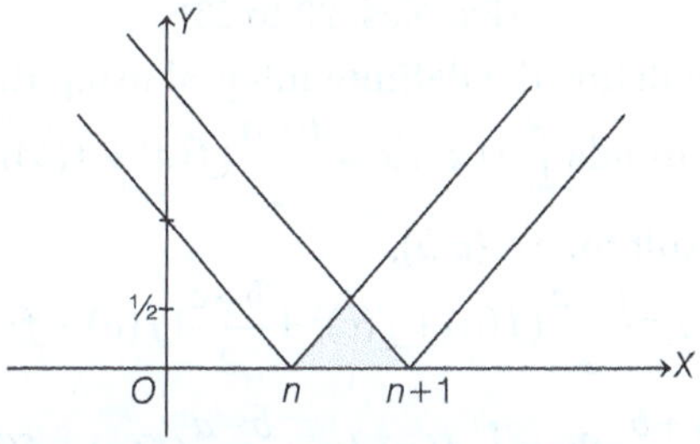

$$\therefore \quad A_1 = \int_n^{n+1} (\min\{|x-n|, |x-(n+1)|\})\, dx$$

$$= \frac{1}{2} \times 1 \times \frac{1}{2} = \frac{1}{4}$$

Now, $A_2 = \int_{n+1}^{n+2} (|x-n| - |x-(n+1)|)\, dx$

$$= \int_1^2 (|t| - |t-1|) dt \qquad \text{put } x = n+t \Rightarrow dx = dt]$$

$$= \int_1^2 (t-(t-1)) dt = \int_1^2 1 dt = (t)_1^2 = 1$$

and $A_3 = \int_{n+2}^{n+3} (|x-(n+4)| - |x-(n+3)|) dx,$

$$= \int_2^3 (|t-4| - |t-3|) dt \qquad [\text{put } x = n+t \Rightarrow dx = dt]$$

$$= \int_2^3 ((4-t)-(3-t)) dt = \int_2^3 1\, dt = 1$$

Also, $g(x) = A_1 + A_2 + A_3 = \frac{1}{4} + 1 + 1 = \frac{9}{4}$

$$\therefore \sum_{n=1}^{100} g(x) = g(1) + g(2) + g(3) + \ldots + g(100)$$

$$= \frac{9}{4} + \frac{9}{4} + \ldots + \frac{9}{4} = \frac{900}{4}$$

Example 17 *Let $f(x)$ be an even function which is mapped from $(-\pi, \pi)$. Then, the value of $\int_{-\pi}^{\pi} \left(\int_0^x f(t)\, dt + [f(x)] \right) dx$ can be (where, $[\cdot]$ denotes greatest integer function)*

(a) 0 (b) π (c) 2π (d) 4π

Sol. (c, d) As, $f(x)$ is an even function, then $\int_0^x f(x)\, dx$ is an odd function.

Also, $[f(x)] = 1, 2$ [as $1 < f(x) < 3$]

$$\therefore \quad g(x) = \int_{-\pi}^{\pi} \left(\int_0^x f(t)\, dt \right) dx + \int_{-\pi}^{\pi} [f(x)]\, dx$$

$$= 0 + \int_{-\pi}^{\pi} [f(x)]\, dx, \qquad [\because \text{since } [f(x)] = 1 \text{ or } 2]$$

$$= \int_{-\pi}^{\pi} 1\, dx \text{ or } \int_{-\pi}^{\pi} 2\, dx = 2\pi \text{ or } 4\pi$$

Example 18 *Let $L_1 = \lim_{x \to 0} \frac{1}{x^3} \int_0^x \frac{t(e^{3t}-1)\ln(1+2t)}{(t^3+3)(1-\cos\sqrt{t})} dt$ and*

$$L_2 = \lim_{x \to 0} \frac{1}{x} \left(\int_{\pi/4}^{v} \log_{\frac{1}{2}} \sin^2 t\, dt - \int_{\left(\frac{\pi}{4}+x\right)}^{v} \log_{\frac{1}{2}} \sin^2 t\, dt \right),$$

where $\pi < v < 2\pi$, then which of the following is (are) correct?

(a) $9L_1^2 + L_2^2 = 18$ (b) $3L_1 + 4L_2 = 8$

(c) $L_1 > 0$ and $L_2 < 0$ (d) $L_1 > L_2$

Decoding the Question

In this problem, L_1 will be solved by Leibnitz rule by applying L'Hospital rule and in L_2, we will use property of definite integral $\int_a^c f(x)\, dx + \int_c^b f(x)\, dx = \int_a^b f(x)\, dx$ and after that we will apply Leibnitz rule by applying L'Hospital rule.

Sol. (b, d) $L_1 = \lim_{x \to 0} \dfrac{\dfrac{x(e^{3x}-1)\ln(1+2x)}{(x^3+3)(1-\cos\sqrt{x})}}{3x^2}$

$$= \lim_{x \to 0} \frac{(e^{3x}-1)}{(1-\cos\sqrt{x})(0+3)} \cdot \frac{\ln(1+2x)}{2x} \cdot \frac{2}{3}$$

$$= \lim_{x \to 0} \frac{2}{9} \frac{3e^{3x}}{\sin\sqrt{x}} \cdot 2\sqrt{x} = \frac{4}{3}$$

$$L_2 = \lim_{x \to 0} \frac{1}{x} \left(\int_{\pi/4}^{\left(\frac{\pi}{4}+x\right)} \log_{1/2} \sin^2 t\, dt \right)$$

$$= \lim_{x \to 0} \frac{\log_{1/2} \sin^2\left(\frac{\pi}{4}+x\right) - 0}{1} = 1$$

(a) $9L_1^2 + L_2^2 = 16 + 1 = 17$

(b) $3L_1 + 4L_2 = 4 + 4 = 8$

(c) $L_1 > 0, L_2 > 0$

(d) $L_1 > L_2$

Example 19 $T_n = \sum_{r=2n}^{3n-1} \frac{r_n}{r^2+n^2}, S_n = \sum_{r=2n+1}^{rn} \frac{rn}{r^2+n^2}$, *then* $\forall\, n \in \{1, 2, 3, \ldots\}$

(a) $T_n > \frac{1}{2} \ln 2$ (b) $S_n < \frac{1}{2} \ln 2$

(c) $T_n < \frac{1}{2} \ln 2$ (d) $S_n > \frac{1}{2} \ln 2$

Sol. (a, b) Let $f(x) = \frac{x}{1+x^2}$

$$\Rightarrow \quad f'(x) = \frac{1+x^2-2x^2}{(1+x^2)^2}$$

$$f'(x) = \frac{1-x^2}{(1+x^2)^2}$$

$\Rightarrow f'(x) < 0, \forall\, x \in (1, \infty)$

$\Rightarrow f(x)$ is a decreasing function.

$$\Rightarrow \quad S_n < \int_2^3 \frac{x}{1+x^2} dx < T_n$$

$$\Rightarrow \quad S_n < \frac{1}{2} [\ln(1+x^2)]_2^3 < T_n$$

$$\Rightarrow \quad S_n < \frac{1}{2} \ln 2 < T_n$$

Passage Based Questions

Passage I

(Ex. Nos. 20 to 21)

Let the function f satisfies

$f(x)\cdot f'(-x) = f(-x)\cdot f'(x)$ for all x and $f(0) = 3$.

Example 20 *The value of $f(x)\cdot f(-x)$ for all x is*

(a) 4 (b) 9 (c) 12 (d) 16

Decoding the Question

The information given in passage can be used by rearranging into $\frac{f'(x)}{f(x)} = \frac{f'(-x)}{f(-x)}$ and this is the direct integration of logarithm by taking denominator as t and having its differentiation in numerator.

Sol. (b) Given, $f(x)\cdot f'(-x) = f(-x)\cdot f'(x)$

$$\Rightarrow \quad \frac{f'(x)}{f(x)} = \frac{f'(-x)}{f(-x)}$$

Integrating both sides, we get

$$\ln f(x) = -\log f(-x) + C$$
$$\log f(x) + \log f(-x) = C$$
$$\ln[f(x)\cdot f(-x)] = C$$
$$f(x)\cdot f(-x) = C$$

But $f(0) = 3$

$\Rightarrow \quad f^2(0) = C$

$\therefore \quad C = 9$

$\therefore \quad f(x)\cdot f(-x) = 9$

Alternate Solution

$$f(x)\cdot f'(x) - f(-x)\cdot f'(x) = 0$$

$$\Rightarrow \quad \frac{d}{dx}[f(-x)\cdot f(x)] = 0$$

Integrating both sides, we get $f(x)\cdot f(-x) =$ Constant

Hence, (b) is the correct answer.

Example 21 $\int_{-51}^{51} \frac{dx}{3+f(x)}$ *has the value equal to*

(a) 17 (b) 34 (c) 102 (d) 0

Sol. (a) Let $I = \int_{-51}^{51} \frac{dx}{3+f(x)} = \int_{-51}^{51} \frac{dx}{3+f(-x)}$

$$\left[\text{using } \int_a^b f(x)\,dx = \int_a^b f(a+b-x)\,dx\right]$$

$$2I = \int_{-51}^{51} \frac{6+f(x)+f(-x)}{[3+f(x)][3+f(-x)]}\,dx$$

$$= \int_{-51}^{51} \frac{6+f(x)+f(-x)}{9+3[f(x)+f(-x)]+f(x)\cdot f(-x)}\,dx$$

$$= \int_{-51}^{51} \frac{6+f(x)+f(-x)}{18+3[f(x)+f(-x)]}\,dx = \frac{1}{3}\int_{-51}^{51} dx = \frac{2\cdot 51}{3}$$

$$\Rightarrow \quad I = \frac{51}{3} = 17$$

Passage II

(Ex. Nos. 22 to 23)

Suppose we define the definite integral using the following formula $\int_a^b f(x)\,dx = \frac{b-a}{2}(f(a)+f(b))$, for more accurate result for $c \in (a,b)$,

$$F(c) = \frac{c-a}{2}(f(a)+f(c)) + \frac{b-c}{2}(f(b)+f(c)).$$

When $c = \frac{a+b}{2}$, then $\int_a^b f(x)\,dx = \frac{b-a}{4}(f(a)+f(b)+2f(c))$.

Example 22 $\int_0^{\pi/2} \sin x\,dx$ *is equal to*

(a) $\frac{\pi}{8}(1+\sqrt{2})$ (b) $\frac{\pi}{4}(1+\sqrt{2})$

(c) $\frac{\pi}{8\sqrt{2}}$ (d) $\frac{\pi}{4\sqrt{2}}$

Sol. (a) $\int_0^{\pi/2} \sin x\,dx = \frac{\frac{\pi}{2}-0}{4}\left(\sin(0)+\sin\left(\frac{\pi}{2}\right)+2\sin\left(\frac{0+\frac{\pi}{2}}{2}\right)\right)$

$$= \frac{\pi}{8}(1+\sqrt{2})$$

Example 23 *If $f(x)$ is a polynomial and if*

$$\lim_{t\to a} \frac{\int_a^t f(x)\,dx - \frac{(t-a)}{2}(f(t)+f(a))}{(t-a)^3} = 0 \text{ for all } a, \text{ then the}$$

degree of $f(x)$ can atmost be

(a) 1 (b) 2

(c) 3 (d) 4

Decoding the Question

In this problem, we use Leibnitz rule by applying L'Hospital rule and then apply L'Hospital rule one more time and rearrange to get required solution.

Sol. (a) Applying L' Hospital's rule,

$$\lim_{t\to a} \frac{f(t) - \frac{1}{2}(f(t)+f(a)) - \frac{(t-a)}{2}f'(t)}{3(t-a)^2} = 0$$

$$\Rightarrow \quad \lim_{t\to a} \frac{f'(t) - \frac{1}{2}(f'(t)+0) - \left(\frac{f'(t)}{2} + \left(\frac{t-a}{2}\right)f''(t)\right)}{6(t-a)} = 0$$

$$\Rightarrow \quad \lim_{t\to a} \frac{\frac{-(t-a)}{2}f''(t)}{6(t-a)} = 0$$

$$\Rightarrow \quad \lim_{t\to a} \frac{-f''(t)}{12} = 0$$

$\Rightarrow \quad f''(a) = 0$ for any a.

$\Rightarrow \quad f(a)$ is atmost of degree 1.

Stem Based Questions

Stem I

(Ex. Nos. 24 to 25)

Given, $\int_{x=a}^{x=b} f(x)\,d\alpha(x) + \int_{x=a}^{x=b} \alpha(x)\,df(x)$
$= \alpha(b)f(b) - \alpha(a)f(a)$

Example 24 $\int_0^6 (x^2 + [x])\,d\,|3-x|$ *is equal to ....*
(where $[\cdot]$ *denotes the greatest integer function)*

Sol. (63) $\int_0^6 (x^2 + [x]\,d\,|3-x|)$

$$= \int_0^3 (x^2 + [x])\,d(3-x) + \int_3^6 (x^2 + [x])\,d(x-3)$$

$$= -\int_0^3 x^2\,dx + \int_3^6 x^2\,dx - \int_0^3 [x]\,dx + \int_3^6 [x]\,dx$$

$$= -\left\{\frac{x^3}{3}\right\}_0^3 + \left\{\frac{x^3}{3}\right\}_3^6 - \int_0^3 [x]\,dx + \int_0^3 [x+3]\,dx$$

$$= -9 + (72-9) - \int_0^3 [x]\,dx + \int_0^3 [x]\,dx + 3\int_0^3 1\,dx$$

$$= 72 - 18 + 9$$

$$= 72 - 9 = 63$$

Example 25 $\int_{-2}^{3} [x]\,d\,|x|$ *is equal to ....*
(where $[\cdot]$ *denotes the greatest integer functions)*

Sol. (2) $\int_{-2}^{3} [x]\,d\,|x| = \int_{-2}^{0} [-x]\,d(-x) + \int_0^3 [x]\,dx = \int_{-2}^{0} [-x]\,dx + \int_0^3 [x]\,dx$

$$= \int_2^0 [x]\,dx + \int_0^3 [x]\,dx \qquad \text{[by property]}$$

$$= -\int_0^2 [x]\,dx + \int_0^2 [x]\,dx + \int_2^3 [x]\,dx$$

$$= \int_2^3 [x]\,dx = \int_2^3 2\cdot dx = 2(3-2) = 2$$

Single Integer Answer Type Questions

Example 26 *For any real number x, let* $[x]$ *denotes the largest integer less than or equal to x. Let f be a real valued function defined on the interval* $[-10, 10]$ *by*

$$f(x) = \begin{cases} x - [x], & \text{if } [x] \text{ is odd} \\ 1 + [x] - x, & \text{if } [x] \text{ is even} \end{cases}.$$

Then, the value of $\frac{\pi^2}{10}\int_{-10}^{10} f(x)\cos\pi x\,dx$ *is ....*

Sol. (4) We have, $f(x) = \begin{cases} x - [x], & \text{if } [x] \text{ is odd} \\ 1 + [x] - x, & \text{if } [x] \text{ is even} \end{cases}$

$f(x)$ and $\cos\pi x$ are both periodic with period 2 and are both even.

$$\therefore \int_{-10}^{10} f(x)\cos\pi x\,dx = 2\int_0^{10} f(x)\cos\pi x\,dx = 10\int_0^2 f(x)\cos\pi x\,dx$$

$$\int_0^1 f(x)\cos\pi x\,dx = \int_0^1 (1-x)\cos\pi x\,dx = -\int_0^1 u\cos\pi u\,du$$

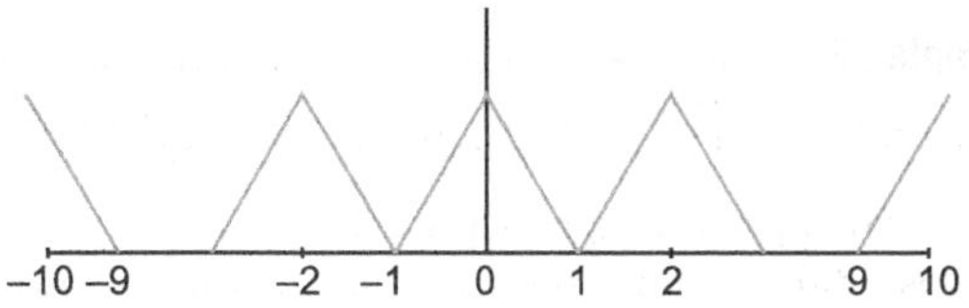

$$\int_1^2 f(x)\cos\pi x\,dx = \int_1^2 (x-1)\cos\pi x\,dx$$

$$= -\int_0^1 u\cos\pi u\,du$$

$$\therefore \int_{-10}^{10} f(x)\cos\pi x\,dx = -20\int_0^1 u\cos\pi u\,du = \frac{40}{\pi^2}$$

$$\Rightarrow \frac{\pi^2}{10}\int_{-10}^{10} f(x)\cos\pi x\,dx = 4$$

JEE SCANNER

Example 27 Similar to PYQ Asked in JEE Main 2024

Let $f(x) = \int_0^x g(t)\log_e\left(\frac{1-t}{1+t}\right)dt$*, where g is a continuous odd function. If* $\int_{-\pi/4}^{\pi/4}\left(f(x) + \frac{\sec^2 x}{1+e^x}\right)dx$ *equal to ......*

Sol. (1) Given, $f(x) = \int_0^x g(t)\log_e\left(\frac{1-t}{1+t}\right)dt$

$$\Rightarrow \quad f'(x) = g(x)\log_e\left(\frac{1-x}{1+x}\right)$$

Since, $g(x)$ and $\log_e\left(\frac{1-x}{1+x}\right)$ both are odd,

So, $f'(x)$ is an even function.

Hence, $f(x)$ is an odd function.

So, $f(x) + f(-x) = 0$

Now, let $I = \int_{-\pi/4}^{\pi/4}\left(f(x) + \frac{\sec^2 x}{1+e^x}\right)dx$

$$\therefore \quad I = \int_0^{\pi/4}\left\{f(x) + f(-x) + \sec^2 x\left(\frac{1}{1+e^x} + \frac{1}{1+e^{-x}}\right)\right\}dx$$

$$= \int_0^{\pi/4} \sec^2 x\,dx$$

$$\left[\because f(x) + f(-x) = 0 \text{ and } \frac{1}{1+e^x} + \frac{1}{1+e^{-x}} = 1\right]$$

$$= \tan x\Big|_0^{\pi/4}$$

$$= 1 - 0 = 1$$

Skill Builder

Let $f(x) = \int_0^x g(t)\log_e\left(\frac{1-t}{1+t}\right)dt$, where g is a continuous odd function. If $I = \int_{-1}^{1}\left(f(x) + \frac{x^2 e^x}{1+e^x}\right)dx$, then $9I$ is equal to ......

For Sol.

Example 28 *Let $f:R \to R$ be a continuous function which satisfies $f(x) = \int_0^x f(t)dt$. Then, the value of $f(\ln 5)$ is ....*

Sol. (0) From given integral equation, $f(0) = 0$

Also, differentiating the given integral equation w.r.t. x, we get

$$f'(x) = f(x)$$

If $\quad f(x) \neq 0$, then $\dfrac{f'(x)}{f(x)} = 1 \Rightarrow f(x) = e^c e^x$

$\because \quad f(0) = 0 \Rightarrow e^c = 0$, a contradiction

$\therefore \quad f(x) = 0, \forall\, x \in R \Rightarrow f(\ln 5) = 0$

Numerical Value Type Questions

Example 29 *Let $f(x)$ be a differentiable function satisfying $f(x) + f\left(x + \frac{1}{2}\right) = 1, \forall x \in R$ and $g(x) = \int_0^x f(t)dt$. If $g(1) = 1$,*

then the value of $\displaystyle\sum_{n=2}^{\infty}\left(\frac{8}{\sum_{k=1}^{n}(g(x+k^2) - g(x+k))}\right)$ is ....

Sol. (12) Here, $f(x) + f\left(x + \frac{1}{2}\right) = 1$

Replace x by $\left(x + \frac{1}{2}\right)$, we get $f\left(x + \frac{1}{2}\right) + f(x+1) = 1$

On subtracting, we get

$$f(x) = f(x+1) \quad \text{...(i)}$$

Also, $g(x + 1^2) = \int_0^{x+1^2} f(t)\,dt = \int_0^x f(t)\,dt + \int_x^{x+1^2} f(t)\,dt$

Since, $f(x+1) = f(x)$

$$\therefore \quad g(x+1^2) = \int_0^x f(t)\,dt + 1^2 \cdot \int_0^1 f(t)dt$$

$$g(x+2^2) = \int_0^x f(t)\,dt + 2^2 \cdot \int_0^1 f(t)dt$$

$$g(x+k^2) = \int_0^x f(t)\,dt + k^2 \cdot \int_0^1 f(t)dt \quad \text{...(ii)}$$

and $\quad g(x+k) = \int_0^x f(t)\,dt + k \cdot \int_0^1 f(t)dt \quad$ ...(iii)

Thus, $\displaystyle\sum_{k=1}^{n}(g(x+k^2) - g(x+k)) = \sum_{k=1}^{n}(k^2 - k) \cdot \int_0^1 f(t)\,dt$

$$= \sum_{k=1}^{n}(k^2 - k) \cdot g(1), \text{ given } g(x) = \int_0^x f(t)\,dt$$

$$= \left(\frac{n(n+1)(2n+1)}{6} - \frac{n(n+1)}{2}\right) \times \frac{1}{2} = \frac{n(n-1)(n+1)}{6}$$

$$\therefore \sum_{n=2}^{\infty}\frac{8}{\sum_{k=2}^{n}(g(x+k^2) - g(x+k))} = \sum_{n=2}^{\infty}\frac{8 \times 6}{(n-1)n(n+1)}$$

$$= 24\sum_{n=2}^{\infty}\left(\frac{(n+1)-(n-1)}{(n-1)\cdot n(n+1)} = \frac{1}{(n-1)n} - \frac{1}{n(n+1)}\right)$$

$$= 24\left[\left(\frac{1}{1\times 2} - \frac{1}{2\times 3}\right) + \left(\frac{1}{2\times 3} - \frac{1}{3\times 4}\right) + \ldots + \left(\frac{1}{(n-1)n} - \frac{1}{n(n+1)}\right)\right]$$

$$= 24\left(\frac{1}{2} - \frac{1}{n(n+1)}\right)_{n\to\infty} = 12$$

JEE SCANNER

Example 30 Similar to PYQ Asked in JEE Main 2024

If $\int_0^{\pi/2}\sqrt{1-\sin 2x}\,dx = \alpha(\sqrt{\alpha} + \beta)$, where α and β are rational numbers, then $10(\alpha - \beta)$ is equal to ......

Sol. (30) Let $I = \int_0^{\pi/2}\sqrt{1-\sin 2x}\,dx = \int_0^{\pi/2}\sqrt{(\sin x - \cos x)^2}\,dx$

$$= \int_0^{\pi/2}|\sin x - \cos x|\,dx$$

$$= \int_0^{\pi/4}(\cos x - \sin x)dx + \int_{\pi/4}^{\pi/2}(\sin x - \cos x)dx$$

$$= [\sin x + \cos x]_0^{\pi/4} - [\cos x + \sin x]_{\pi/4}^{\pi/2}$$

$$= \left(\frac{1}{\sqrt{2}} + \frac{1}{\sqrt{2}} - 0 - 1\right) - \left(0 + 1 - \frac{1}{\sqrt{2}} - \frac{1}{\sqrt{2}}\right)$$

$$= \sqrt{2} - 1 - 1 + \sqrt{2} = 2\sqrt{2} - 2 = 2(\sqrt{2} - 1)$$

$\therefore \quad \alpha = 2, \beta = -1$

Hence, $10(\alpha - \beta) = 10(2+1) = 30$

Skill Builder

If $\int_0^3\sqrt{x^2 - 4x + 4}\,dx = \frac{\alpha}{\beta}$, where α and β are rational numbers, then $\alpha\beta$ is equal to ...

For Sol.

Example 31 *Consider $f(x) = 3x^2 + 2x + a$, where a parameter such that $\frac{da}{dt} = 3$. Let $a = 0$, when $t = 0$ and $A(t) = \int_0^t\{f(x)\}\,dt$ (where $\{\cdot\}$ denotes fractional part function). If $A(2)$ can be expressed as sum of n integrals, then find the minimum value of n is ....*

Sol. (16) $f(x) = 3x^2 + 2x + a$

$$\frac{da}{dt} = 3$$

Let $a = 0$, when $t = 0 \Rightarrow a = 3t$

We have, $\quad f(x) = 3x^2 + 2x + 3t$

$$A(t) = \int_0^t\{f(x)\}\,dx = \int_0^t\{3x^2 + 2x + 3t\}\,dt$$

$$A(2) = \int_0^2\{3x^2 + 2x + 6\}\,dx = \int_0^t\{3x^2 + 2x\}\,dx$$

When, $x \in [0, 2]$, then $3x^2 + 2x \in [0, 16]$

As, we know that $\{\cdot\}$ is discontinuous at every integral, so integration will break minimum 16 times, so $n = 16$.

Example 32 *If $\int_0^{\pi} x\, f(\cos^2 x + \tan^4 x)\,dx = \dfrac{\pi k}{1997}\int_0^{\pi/2} f(\cos^2 x + \tan^4 x)\,dx$, then the value of k is ....*

Sol. (1997) Let $I = \int_0^{\pi} x f(\cos^2 x + \tan^4 x)\,dx$

$$= \int_0^{\pi}(\pi - x)\, f(\cos^2(\pi - x) + \tan^4(\pi - x))\,dx$$

$$= \frac{\pi}{2}\int_0^{\pi} f(\cos^2 x + \tan^4 x)\,dx$$

$$= \frac{\pi}{2}\cdot 2\int_0^{\pi/2} f(\cos^2 x + \tan^4 x)\,dx$$

Here, $k = 1997$

Example 33 *Let $f(x)$ be periodic function with fundamental period 12. If $\int_{-6}^{12} f(x)\,dx = 9$ and $\int_0^{12} f(x)\,dx = 12$, then find the value of $\left|\int_0^6 f(x)\,dx\right|$.*

> **Decoding the Question**
> Here, given that period of function is 12. So, we break limits into the –6 to 0 and 0 to 12 and we know $\int_0^{12} f(x)\,dx$, we get value of $\int_{-6}^{0} f(x)\,dx$. Now, we can convert $\int_0^{12}$ to $\int_{-6}^{6}$ and break the limit into $\int_{-6}^{0}$ and $\int_0^6$ and solve it further.

Sol. (15) $\int_{-6}^{12} f(x)\,dx = 9$

$$\Rightarrow \int_{-6}^{0} f(x)\,dx + \int_0^{12} f(x)\,dx = 9 \Rightarrow \int_{-6}^{0} f(x)\,dx = -3$$

$$\Rightarrow \int_0^{12} f(x)\,dx = \int_{-6}^{6} f(x)\,dx = 12$$

$$\Rightarrow \int_{-6}^{0} f(x)\,dx + \int_0^{6} f(x)\,dx = 12 \Rightarrow \int_0^{6} f(x)\,dx = 15$$

Example 34 *Let $f(x) = x^3 + 3x^2 - 6x + 11$, $g(x) = \ln|x|$. If $A = f(g'(-1))$, $B = g(f'(-1))$, $C = \int_{-2}^{1} f'(x)\,g'(f(x))\,dx$,*

$D = \frac{d}{dt}\int_1^{t^2} g(x)\,dx$ evaluated at $t = 3$ and $A(B + C) - D = k\ln(3)$, then the value of k^2 is ....

Sol. (70) $f(x) = x^3 + 3x^2 - 6x + 11$

$$g(x) = \ln|x| \Rightarrow g'(x) = \frac{1}{x}$$

$$f'(x) = 3x^2 + 6x - 6,\ g'(-1) = -1 \Rightarrow f'(-1) = -9$$

$$A = f(g'(-1)) = f(-1) = -1 + 3 + 6 + 11 = 19$$

$$B = g(f'(-1)) = g(-9) = \ln 9$$

$$C = \int_{-2}^{1} f'(x)\,g'(f(x))\,dx$$

$$= \int_{-2}^{1} d(g(f(x))) = g(f(1)) - g(f(-2))$$

$$= g(9) - g(27) = \ln 9 - \ln 27 = \ln\left(\frac{1}{3}\right)$$

$$D = \frac{d}{dt}\int_1^{t^2} g(x)\,dx$$

$$D = g(t^2)(2t) - 0 \text{ at } t = 3 \Rightarrow D = g(9)\cdot 6 = 6\ln 9$$

$$A(B + C) - D = 19(\ln 9 + \ln(1/3)) - 6\ln 9 = 19(\ln 3) - 12\ln 3$$

$$\Rightarrow 7\ln 3 = k(\ln 3), \text{ we get}$$

$$k = 7$$

$$\because \quad k^2 = 7^2 = 49$$

Matching Type Questions

Example 35 *Match the following.*

Column I	Column II
(A) The function $f(x) = \dfrac{e^{x\cos x} - 1 - x}{\sin x^2}$ is not defined at $x = 0$. The value of $f(0)$, so that f is continuous at $x = 0$, is	(p) -1
(B) The value of the definite integral $\int_0^1 \dfrac{dx}{\sqrt{x} + \sqrt[3]{x}}$ is equal to $a + b\ln 2$, where a and b are integers, then $(a + b)$ is equal to	(q) 0
(C) Given, $e^n \int_0^n \dfrac{\sec^2\theta - \tan\theta}{e^\theta}\,d\theta = 1$, then the value of $\tan n$ is equal to	(r) 1/2
(D) Let $a_n = \int_{\frac{1}{n+1}}^{\frac{1}{n}} \tan^{-1}(nx)\,dx$ and $b_n = \int_{\frac{1}{n+1}}^{\frac{1}{n}} \sin^{-1}(nx)\,dx$, then $\lim_{n\to\infty} \dfrac{a_n}{b_n}$ has the value equal to	(s) 1

Sol. (A) → (r), (B) → (p), (C) → (s), (D) → (r)

(A) $$\lim_{x\to 0} \frac{e^{x\cos x} - 1 - x}{x^2 \cdot \dfrac{\sin x^2}{x^2}} = \lim_{x\to 0} \frac{e^{x\cos x} - 1 - x}{x^2}$$

[applying L'Hospital's twice]

$$= \lim_{x\to 0} \frac{e^{x\cos x}\cdot(-x\sin x + \cos x) - 1}{2x}$$

$$= \lim_{x\to 0} \frac{e^{x\cos x}(-x\cos x - \sin x - \sin x) + e^{x\cos x}(-x\sin x + \cos x)}{2}$$

$$= \frac{1}{2}$$

(B) Put $x = u^6 \Rightarrow dx = 6u^5\,du$

$$\therefore\ I = \int_0^1 \frac{6u^5\,du}{u^3 + u^2} = 6\int_0^1 \frac{u^3 + 1 - 1}{u + 1}\,du = 5 - 6\ln 2$$

$$\Rightarrow a + b = 5 - 6 = -1$$

(C) $$e^n \int_0^n e^{-\theta}(\sec^2\theta - \tan\theta)\,d\theta = 1$$

Put $-\theta = t \Rightarrow d\theta = -dt$

$$-e^n \int_0^{-n} e^t(\sec^2 t + \tan t)\,dt = 1$$

[use $\int e^x(f(x) + f'(x)) = e^x f(x)$]

$$\Rightarrow -e^n[e^t \tan t]_0^{-n} = 1 \Rightarrow -e^n[-e^{-n}\tan n] = 1 \Rightarrow \tan n = 1$$

(D) $$\lim_{n\to\infty} \frac{\int_{1/n+1}^{1/n} \tan^{-1}(nx)\,dx}{\int_{1/n+1}^{1/n} \sin^{-1}(nx)\,dx}$$

Put $nx = t \Rightarrow dx = \frac{1}{n}dt$

$$\therefore\ \lim_{n\to\infty} \frac{\frac{1}{n}\int_{n/n+1}^{1} \tan^{-1}(t)\,dt}{\frac{1}{n}\int_{n/n+1}^{1} \sin^{-1}(t)\,dt} \qquad \left(\frac{0}{0}\text{ form}\right)$$

Use L'Hospital's rule, $$\lim_{n\to\infty} \frac{\tan^{-1}\left(\dfrac{n}{n+1}\right)}{\sin^{-1}\left(\dfrac{n}{n+1}\right)} = \frac{\frac{\pi}{4}}{\frac{\pi}{2}} = \frac{1}{2}$$

EXERCISE 1

JEE Main Pattern

Single Option Correct Type Questions

1. The value of $\int_0^4 \frac{(y^2 - 4y + 5)\sin(y-2)dy}{(2y^2 - 8y + 1)}$ is

(a) 0 (b) 2 (c) -2 (d) None of these

2. $\int_{\pi/2}^{x} \sqrt{(3 - 2\sin^2 t)}\, dt + \int_0^y \cos t\, dt = 0$, then $\left(\frac{dy}{dx}\right)$ at $x = \pi$ and $y = \pi$ is

(a) $\sqrt{3}$ (b) $-\sqrt{2}$ (c) $-\sqrt{3}$ (d) None of these

3. The value of the definite integral

$$\int_0^\infty \frac{dx}{(1 + x^a)(1 + x^2)}\ (a > 0) \text{ is}$$

(a) $\frac{\pi}{4}$ (b) $\frac{\pi}{2}$

(c) π (d) Some function of a

4. If $f(x) = e^{g(x)}$ and $g(x) = \int_2^x \frac{t\, dt}{1 + t^4}$, then $f'(2)$ is equal to

(a) 2/17 (b) 0

(c) 1 (d) Cannot be determined

5. If a, b and c are real numbers, then the value of

$\lim_{t \to 0} \ln\left(\frac{1}{t}\int_0^t (1 + a\sin bx)^{c/x}\, dx\right)$ equals

(a) abc (b) $\frac{ab}{c}$ (c) $\frac{bc}{a}$ (d) $\frac{ca}{b}$

6. Let $f(x) = \int_{-1}^x e^{t^2}\, dt$ and $h(x) = f(1 + g(x))$ where $g(x)$ is defined for all x, $g'(x)$ exists for all x, and $g(x) < 0$ for $x > 0$. If $h'(1) = e$ and $g'(1) = 1$, then the possible values which $g(1)$ can take

(a) 0 (b) -1 (c) -2 (d) -4

7. For $f(x) = x^4 + |x|$, let $I_1 = \int_0^\pi f(\cos x)\, dx$ and $I_2 = \int_0^{\pi/2} f(\sin x)\, dx$, then $\frac{I_1}{I_2}$ has the value equal to

(a) 1 (b) 1/2 (c) 2 (d) 4

8. Let f be a positive function.

Let $I_1 = \int_{1-k}^{k} (x)\, f(x(1-x))\, dx$;

$I_2 = \int_{1-k}^{k} f(x(1-x))\, dx$, where $2k - 1 > 0$. Then, $\frac{I_2}{I_1}$ is

(a) k (b) 1/2 (c) 1 (d) 2

9. If $f(x) = \int_0^x (f(t))^2\, dt$, $f : R \to R$ be differentiable function and $f(g(x))$ is differentiable function at $x = a$, then

(a) $g(x)$ must be differentiable at $x = a$

(b) $g(x)$ may be non-differentiable at $x = a$

(c) $g(x)$ may be discontinuous at $x = a$

(d) None of the above

10. $\lim_{n \to \infty} \sum_{k=1}^{n} \frac{n}{n^2 + k^2 x^2}$, $x > 0$ is equal to

(a) $x \tan^{-1}(x)$ (b) $\tan^{-1}(x)$

(c) $\frac{\tan^{-1}(x)}{x}$ (d) $\frac{\tan^{-1}(x)}{x^2}$

11. The set of values of 'a' which satisfy the equation $\int_0^2 (t - \log_2 a)\, dt = \log_2\left(\frac{4}{a^2}\right)$, is

(a) $a \in R$ (b) $a \in R^+$

(c) $a < 2$ (d) $a > 2$

12. $\int_0^\infty f\left(x + \frac{1}{x}\right) \cdot \frac{\ln x}{x}\, dx$ is equal to

(a) 0 (b) 1

(c) $\frac{1}{2}$ (d) Cannot be evaluated

13. The number of integral solutions of the equation $4\int_0^\infty \frac{\ln t\, dt}{x^2 + t^2} - \pi \ln 2 = 0$; $x > 0$, is

(a) 0 (b) 1

(c) 2 (d) 3

14. $\int_0^{16n^2/\pi} \cos \frac{\pi}{2}\left[\frac{x\pi}{n}\right] dx$ is equal to

(a) 0 (b) 1

(c) 2 (d) 3

15. The value of $\int_3^6 \left(\sqrt{x + \sqrt{12x - 36}} + \sqrt{x - \sqrt{12x - 36}}\right) dx$ is equal to

(a) $6\sqrt{3}$ (b) $4\sqrt{3}$

(c) $12\sqrt{3}$ (d) None of these

16. Let $I_n = \int_0^{\pi/2} \frac{\sin(2n-1)x}{\sin x}\, dx$, $J_n = \int_0^{\pi/2} \frac{\sin^2 nx}{\sin^2 x}$, $n \in N$, then

(a) $J_{n+1} - J_n = I_n$ (b) $J_{n+1} - J_n = I_{n+1}$

(c) $J_{n+1} + J_n = J_n$ (d) $J_{n+1} - J_{n+1} = J_n$

17. The value of the definite integral

$$\int_e^{e^{2010}} \frac{1}{x}\left(1+\frac{1-\log_e x}{\log_e x \log_e\left(\frac{x}{\log_e x}\right)}\right) dx \text{ equals}$$

(a) $2009-\log_e(2010-\log_e 2010)$
(b) $2010-\log_e(2009-\log_e 2009)$
(c) $2009-\log_e(2010-\log_e 2009)$
(d) $2010-\log_e(2010-\log_e 2010)$

18. The value of $\int_{-1}^{1}\{x^2+x-3\}\,dx$, where {·} denotes the fractional part of x is equal to:

(a) $\frac{1}{3}(1+3\sqrt{5})$ (b) $\frac{1}{6}(1+3\sqrt{5})$
(c) $\frac{1}{6}(3\sqrt{5}-1)$ (d) $\frac{1}{3}(3\sqrt{5}-1)$

19. Let f be a differentiable function such that $f(x)=x^2+\int_0^x e^{-t} f(x-t)\,dt$, then $f(1)+f(2)+f(3)+\ldots+f(9)$ is equal to

(a) 960 (b) 1000 (c) 1024 (d) 1126

20. Let $f(x)=\tan x$ and $g(x)=\sin x$ (where [·], {·} denotes greatest integer function, fractional part function), then

$$\int_{2\pi}^{2\pi+\frac{\pi}{4}} \sqrt{[\cos x+\{[f(x)]+\{g(x)\}\}]}\,dx$$

(a) $\frac{\pi}{4}$ (b) $\frac{3\pi}{4}$ (c) $\frac{\sqrt{2}\pi}{4}$ (d) $\frac{\pi}{2}$

21. If [·] denotes GIF and $\int_0^{\pi/3}[\sqrt{3}\tan x]\,dx=\sin^{-1}(\sqrt{k})$ $(k>0)$, then $\int_0^{2k}[\tan x]\,dx$

(a) 1 (b) −1 (c) $\frac{6}{7}-\frac{\pi}{4}$ (d) $\frac{6}{7}-\frac{\pi}{6}$

22. If $f(x)=\cos^{-1} x$ and $g(x)=[\cos(\cos x)]+[\sin(\sin x)]$, where [·] is greatest function, then the value of $\int_{-\pi}^{\pi} fog(x)\,dx$, is

(a) $\frac{3\pi^2}{2}$ (b) $\frac{3\pi^2}{4}$ (c) $\frac{5\pi^2}{2}$ (d) $\frac{\pi^2}{4}$

Numerical Value Type Questions

23. The integral $\int_{\pi/4}^{3\pi/4}\frac{dx}{1+\cos x}$ is equal to ....

24. If $\int_{\sin x}^{1} t^2 f(t)\,dt=1-\sin x, \forall x\in(0,\pi/2)$, then $f\left(\frac{1}{\sqrt{3}}\right)$ is ....

25. If $\alpha=\int_0^1 (e^{9x+3\tan^{-1}x})\left(\frac{12+9x^2}{1+x^2}\right)dx$, where $\tan^{-1} x$ takes only principal values, then the value of $\left(\log_e|1+\alpha|-\frac{3\pi}{4}\right)$ is ....

26. The value of $\int_0^1 4x^3\left\{\frac{d^2}{dx^2}(1-x^2)^5\right\}dx$ is ....

27. If $f(x)=\begin{vmatrix}\sin x+\sin 2x+\sin 3x & \sin 2x & \sin 3x\\ 3+4\sin x & 3 & 4\sin x\\ 1+\sin x & \sin x & 1\end{vmatrix}$, then the value of $\int_0^{\pi/2} f(x)\,dx$ is $\frac{1}{K}$, then the value of K is ....

28. Let [ ] denotes the greatest integer function, then the value of $\int_0^{1.5} x[x^2]\,dx$ is $\frac{p}{q}$, then $p+q$ is ....

29. Let $f:(0,2)\to R$ be defined as $f(x)=\log_2\left[1+\tan\left(\frac{\pi x}{4}\right)\right]$, then $\lim_{n\to\infty}\frac{2}{n}\left[f\left(\frac{1}{n}\right)+f\left(\frac{2}{n}\right)+\ldots+f(1)\right]$ is equal to ....

30. A function f is continuous for all x (and not everywhere zero) such that $f^2(x)=\int_0^x f(t)\frac{\cos t}{2+\sin t}\,dt$, then $f(x)$ is $\frac{1}{K}\ln\left(\frac{K+\sin x}{K}\right)$, then the value of K is ....

31. If $x\int_0^x \sin(f(t))\,dt=(x+2)\int_0^x t\sin(f(t))\,dt$, where $x>0$ then the value of $f'(x)\cot f(x)+\frac{3}{1+x}$ is ....

32. Let $f(x)=\int_1^x\sqrt{2-t^2}\,dt$. Then, the number of real roots of the equation $x^2-f'(x)=0$ is ....

33. The value of $5050\times\left[\frac{\int_0^1(1-x^{50})^{100}\,dx}{\int_0^1(1-x^{50})^{101}\,dx}\right]$ is ....

34. If $\int_0^1\cot^{-1}(1+x^2-x)\,dx=K\left(\frac{\pi}{4}-\log\sqrt{2}\right)$, then the value of K is ....

Previous Year Questions

35. If (a,b) be the orthocentre of the triangle whose vertices are (1, 2), (2, 3) and (3, 1) and $I_1=\int_a^b x\sin(4x-x^2)dx$, $I_2=\int_a^b\sin(4x-x^2)dx$, then $36\left(\frac{I_1}{I_2}\right)$ is equal to

[Single Correct Type, 2024 Main]

(a) 88 (b) 80
(c) 66 (d) 72

36. For $0 < a < 1$, the value of the integral $\int_0^{\pi} \frac{dx}{1-2a\cos x + a^2}$ is **[Single Correct Type, 2024 Main]**

(a) $\frac{\pi^2}{\pi + a^2}$ (b) $\frac{\pi^2}{\pi - a^2}$ (c) $\frac{\pi}{1 - a^2}$ (d) $\frac{\pi}{1 + a^2}$

37. If the value of the integral $\int_{-\pi/2}^{\pi/2} \left(\frac{x^2 \cos x}{1+\pi^x} + \frac{1+\sin^2 x}{1+e^{\sin x^{2023}}} \right) dx = \frac{\pi}{4}(\pi + a) - 2$, then the value of a is **[Single Correct Type, 2024 Main]**

(a) $-\frac{3}{2}$ (b) $\frac{3}{2}$ (c) 3 (d) 2

38. Let $f : R \to R$ be a function defined by $f(x) = \frac{x}{(1+x^4)^{1/4}}$ and $g(x) = f(f(f(f(x))))$. Then, $18 \int_0^{\sqrt{2\sqrt{5}}} x^2 g(x)\, dx$ is equal to **[Single Correct Type, 2024 Main]**

(a) 42 (b) 36 (c) 39 (d) 33

39. Let $f, g : (0, \infty) \to R$ be two functions defined by $f(x) = \int_{-x}^{x} (|t| - t^2) e^{-t^2} dt$ and $g(x) = \int_0^{x^2} t^{1/2} e^{-t} dt$. Then, the value of $9(f(\sqrt{\log_e 9}) + g(\sqrt{\log_e 9}))$ is equal to **[Single Correct Type, 2024 Main]**

(a) 8 (b) 10 (c) 9 (d) 6

40. If $\int_0^{\pi/3} \cos^4 x\, dx = a\pi + b\sqrt{3}$, where a and b are rational numbers, then $9a + 8b$ is equal to **[Single Correct Type, 2024 Main]**

(a) 3 (b) 1 (c) 2 (d) $\frac{3}{2}$

41. The value of $\int_0^1 (2x^3 - 3x^2 - x + 1)^{1/3} dx$ is equal to **[Single Correct Type, 2024 Main]**

(a) -1 (b) 0 (c) 2 (d) 1

42. If $\int_{-\pi/2}^{\pi/2} \frac{8\sqrt{2}\cos x\, dx}{(1+e^{\sin x})(1+\sin^4 x)} = \alpha\pi + \beta \log_e (3 + 2\sqrt{2})$, where α, β are integers, then $\alpha^2 + \beta^2$ equals .... **[Numerical Value Type, 2024 Main]**

43. If the integral $525 \int_0^{\pi/2} \sin 2x \cos^{\frac{11}{2}} x \left(1 + \cos^{\frac{5}{2}} x\right)^{1/2} dx$ is equal to $(n\sqrt{2} - 64)$, then n is equal to .... **[Numerical Value Type, 2024 Main]**

44. Let $f : R \to R$ be a function defined by $f(x) = \frac{4^x}{4^x + 2}$ and $M = \int_{f(a)}^{f(1-a)} x \sin^4 (x(1-x)) dx$, $N = \int_{f(a)}^{f(1-a)} \sin^4 (x(1-x)) dx$; $a \neq \frac{1}{2}$. If $\alpha M = \beta N$, $\alpha, \beta \in N$, then the least value of $\alpha^2 + \beta^2$ is equal to ...... **[Numerical Value Type, 2024 Main]**

45. The value of $9\int_0^9 \left[\sqrt{\frac{10x}{x+1}} \right] dx$, where $[t]$ denotes the greatest integer less than or equal to t, is .... **[Numerical Value Type, 2024 Main]**

46. If $\int_{\pi/6}^{\pi/3} \sqrt{1 - \sin 2x}\, dx = \alpha + \beta\sqrt{2} + \gamma\sqrt{3}$, where α, β and γ are rational numbers, then $3\alpha + 4\beta - \gamma$ is equal to .... . **[Numerical Value Type, 2024 Main]**

47. Let $f(x) = \int_0^x g(t) \log_e \left(\frac{1-t}{1+t} \right) dt$, where g is a continuous odd function. If $\int_{-\pi/2}^{\pi/2} \left(f(x) + \frac{x^2 \cos x}{1+e^x} \right) dx = \left(\frac{\pi}{\alpha} \right)^2 - \alpha$, then α is equal to .... **[Numerical Value Type, 2024 Main]**

48. If $\int_0^1 \frac{1}{(5+2x-2x^2)(1+e^{(2-4x)})} dx = \frac{1}{\alpha} \log_e \left(\frac{\alpha+1}{\beta} \right)$, $\alpha, \beta > 0$ then $\alpha^4 - \beta^4$ is equal to **[Single Correct Type, 2023 Main]**

(a) -21 (b) 21 (c) 0 (d) 19

49. $\int_0^{\infty} \frac{6}{e^{3x} + 6e^{2x} + 11e^x + 6} dx$ is equal to **[Single Correct Type, 2023 Main]**

(a) $\log_e \left(\frac{256}{81} \right)$ (b) $\log_e \left(\frac{64}{27} \right)$

(c) $\log_e \left(\frac{32}{27} \right)$ (d) $\log_e \left(\frac{512}{81} \right)$

50. The value of $\frac{e^{-\frac{\pi}{4}} + \int_0^{\pi/4} e^{-x} \tan^{50} x dx}{\int_0^{\pi/4} e^{-x} (\tan^{49} x + \tan^{51} x)\, dx}$ is **[Single Correct Type, 2023 Main]**

(a) 50 (b) 25

(c) 51 (d) 49

51. Let the function $f : [0, 2] \to R$ be defined as
$$f(x) = \begin{cases} e^{\min\{x^2, x - [x]\}}, & x \in [0, 1) \\ e^{[x - \log_e x]}, & x \in [1, 2] \end{cases}$$
Where, $[x]$ denotes the greatest integer less than or equal to x. Then, the value of the integral $\int_0^2 x f(x)\, dx$ is **[Single Correct Type, 2023 Main]**

(a) $2e - \frac{1}{2}$ (b) $2e - 1$ (c) $1 + \frac{3e}{2}$ (d) $(e-1)\left(e^2 + \frac{1}{2}\right)$

52. If $f : R \to R$ be a continuous function satisfying $\int_0^{\pi/2} f(\sin 2x) \sin x\, dx + \alpha \int_0^{\pi/4} f(\cos 2x) \cos x\, dx = 0$, then the value of α is **[Single Correct Type, 2023 Main]**

(a) $\sqrt{2}$ (b) $\sqrt{3}$

(c) $-\sqrt{3}$ (d) $-\sqrt{2}$

53. The value of the integral $\int_{-\log_e 2}^{\log_e 2} e^x(\log_e(e^x+\sqrt{1+e^{2x}}))\,dx$ is equal to **[Single Correct Type, 2023 Main]**

(a) $\log_e\left(\frac{(2+\sqrt{5})^2}{\sqrt{1+\sqrt{5}}}\right)+\frac{\sqrt{5}}{2}$ (b) $\log_e\left(\frac{2(2+\sqrt{5})}{\sqrt{1+\sqrt{5}}}\right)-\frac{\sqrt{5}}{2}$

(c) $\log_e\left(\frac{\sqrt{2}(3-\sqrt{5})^2}{\sqrt{1+\sqrt{5}}}\right)+\frac{\sqrt{5}}{2}$ (d) $\log_e\left(\frac{\sqrt{2}(2+\sqrt{5})^2}{\sqrt{1+\sqrt{5}}}\right)-\frac{\sqrt{5}}{2}$

54. Let f be a continuous function satisfying $\int_0^{t^2}(f(x)+x^2)\,dx=\frac{4}{3}t^3, \forall t>0$. Then, $f\left(\frac{\pi^2}{4}\right)$ is equal to **[Single Correct Type, 2023 Main]**

(a) $-\pi\left(1+\frac{\pi^3}{16}\right)$ (b) $\pi\left(1-\frac{\pi^3}{16}\right)$

(c) $-\pi^2\left(1+\frac{\pi^2}{16}\right)$ (d) $\pi^2\left(1-\frac{\pi^2}{16}\right)$

55. Let $f(x)$ be a function satisfying $f(x)+f(\pi-x)=\pi^2$, $\forall x\in R$. Then, $\int_0^{\pi} f(x)\sin x\,dx$ is equal to **[Single Correct Type, 2023 Main]**

(a) $\frac{\pi^2}{2}$ (b) $2\pi^2$ (c) π^2 (d) $\frac{\pi^2}{4}$

56. Let $\alpha\in(0,1)$ and $\beta=\log_e(1-\alpha)$. Let $P_n(x)=x+\frac{x^2}{2}+\frac{x^3}{3}+\ldots+\frac{x^n}{n}$, $x\in(0,1)$. Then, the integral $\int_0^{\alpha}\frac{t^{50}}{1-t}\,dt$ is equal to **[Single Correct Type, 2023 Main]**

(a) $P_{50}(\alpha)-\beta$ (b) $-(\beta+P_{50}(\alpha))$
(c) $\beta+P_{50}(\alpha)$ (d) $\beta-P_{50}(\alpha)$

57. Let a differentiable function f satisfy $f(x)+\int_3^x \frac{f(t)}{t}\,dt=\sqrt{x+1}$, $x\ge 3$. Then, $12f(8)$ is equal to **[Single Correct Type, 2023 Main]**

(a) 34 (b) 17 (c) 19 (d) 1

58. Let $\alpha>0$. If $\int_0^{\alpha}\frac{x}{\sqrt{x+\alpha}-\sqrt{x}}\,dx=\frac{16+20\sqrt{2}}{15}$, then α is equal to **[Single Correct Type, 2023 Main]**

(a) 4 (b) 2 (c) $\sqrt{2}$ (d) $2\sqrt{2}$

59. If $[t]$ denotes the greatest integer $\le t$, then the value of $\frac{3(e-1)}{e}\int_1^2 x^2 e^{[x]+[x^3]}\,dx$ is **[Single Correct Type, 2023 Main]**

(a) e^7-1 (b) e^8-1
(c) e^9-e (d) e^8-e

60. The value of the integral $\int_{1/2}^{2}\frac{\tan^{-1}x}{x}\,dx$ is equal to **[Single Correct Type, 2023 Main]**

(a) $\frac{1}{2}\log_e 2$ (b) $\frac{\pi}{2}\log_e 2$ (c) $\frac{\pi}{4}\log_e 2$ (d) $\pi\log_e 2$

61. The value of the integral $\int_1^2\left(\frac{t^4+1}{t^6+1}\right)dt$ is **[Single Correct Type, 2023 Main]**

(a) $\tan^{-1}2-\frac{1}{3}\tan^{-1}8+\frac{\pi}{3}$ (b) $\tan^{-1}2+\frac{1}{3}\tan^{-1}8-\frac{\pi}{3}$

(c) $\tan^{-1}\frac{1}{2}+\frac{1}{3}\tan^{-1}8-\frac{\pi}{3}$ (d) $\tan^{-1}\frac{1}{2}-\frac{1}{3}\tan^{-1}8+\frac{\pi}{3}$

62. If $f(\alpha)=\int_1^{\alpha}\frac{\log_{10}t}{1+t}\,dt, \alpha>0$, then $f(e^3)+f(e^{-3})$ is equal to **[Single Correct Type, 2023 Main]**

(a) 9 (b) $9/2$
(c) $9/\log_e(10)$ (d) $9/2\log_e(10)$

63. The minimum value of the function $f(x)=\int_0^2 e^{|x-t|}\,dt$ is **[Single Correct Type, 2023 Main]**

(a) $2(e-1)$ (b) $e(e-1)$ (c) 2 (d) $2e-1$

64. The integral $16\int_1^2\frac{dx}{x^3(x^2+2)^2}$ is equal to **[Single Correct Type, 2023 Main]**

(a) $\frac{11}{6}-\log_e 4$ (b) $\frac{11}{12}-\log_e 4$

(c) $\frac{11}{12}+\log_e 4$ (d) $\frac{11}{6}+\log_e 4$

65. For $x\in R$, let $\tan^{-1}(x)\in\left(-\frac{\pi}{2},\frac{\pi}{2}\right)$. Then, the minimum value of the function $f:R\longrightarrow R$ defined by $f(x)=\int_0^{x\tan^{-1}x}\frac{e^{(t-\cos t)}}{1+t^{2023}}\,dt$ is .... **[Numerical Value Type, 2023 Main]**

66. If $\int_{-0.15}^{0.15}|100x^2-1|\,dx=\frac{k}{3000}$, then k is equal to .... **[Numerical Value Type, 2023 Main]**

67. For $m,n>0$, let $\alpha(m,n)=\int_0^2 t^m(1+3t)^n\,dt$. If $11\alpha(10,6)+18\alpha(11,5)=p(14)^6$, then p is equal to .... **[Numerical Value Type, 2023 Main]**

68. Let $[t]$ denote the greatest integer function. If $\int_0^{2.4}[x^2]\,dx=\alpha+\beta\sqrt{2}+\gamma\sqrt{3}+\delta\sqrt{5}$, then $\alpha+\beta+\gamma+\delta$ is equal to .... **[Numerical Value Type, 2023 Main]**

69. Let $[t]$ denote the greatest integer $\le t$. Then, $\frac{2}{\pi}\int_{\pi/6}^{5\pi/6}(8[\operatorname{cosec} x]-5[\cot x])dx$ is equal to .... **[Numerical Value Type, 2023 Main]**

70. Let $f(x)=\frac{x}{(1+x^n)^{\frac{1}{n}}}, x\in R-\{-1\}, n\in N, n>2$. If $f^n(x)=(fofof\ldots \text{ upto } n \text{ times})(x)$, then $\lim_{n\to\infty}\int_0^1 x^{n-2}(f^n(x))dx$ is equal to .... **[Numerical Value Type, 2023 Main]**

71. If $\int_0^1 (x^{21}+x^{14}+x^7)(2x^{14}+3x^7+6)^{1/7}dx=\frac{1}{l}(11)^{m/n}$, where $l, m, n\in N$, m and n are coprime, then $l+m+n$ is equal to .... **[Numerical Value Type, 2023 Main]**

72. $\lim_{x\to 0}\frac{48}{x^4}\int_0^x \frac{t^3}{t^6+1}dt$ is equal to .... **[Numerical Value Type, 2023 Main]**

73. If $\int_{1/3}^{3}|\log_e x|\,dx=\frac{m}{n}\log_e(n^2/e)$, where m and n are coprime natural numbers, then m^2+n^2-5 is equal to .... **[Numerical Value Type, 2023 Main]**

74. The value of $\frac{8}{\pi}\int_0^{\pi/2}\frac{(\cos x)^{2023}}{(\sin x)^{2023}+(\cos x)^{2023}}dx$ is .... **[Numerical Value Type, 2023 Main]**

75. The value of $12\int_0^3|x^2-3x+2|\,dx$ is .... **[Numerical Value Type, 2023 Main]**

76. Let f be a differentiable function defined on $\left[0,\frac{\pi}{2}\right]$ such that $f(x)>0$ and $f(x)+\int_0^x f(t)\sqrt{1-(\log_e f(t))^2}\,dt=e$, $\forall x\in\left[0,\frac{\pi}{2}\right]$. Then, $\left(6\log_e f\left(\frac{\pi}{6}\right)\right)^2$ is equal to **[Numerical Value Type, 2023 Main]**

77. Let $I=\int_{\pi/4}^{\pi/3}\left(\frac{8\sin x-\sin 2x}{x}\right)dx$. Then, **[Single Correct Type, 2022 Main]**

(a) $\frac{\pi}{2}<I<\frac{3\pi}{4}$ (b) $\frac{\pi}{5}<I<\frac{5\pi}{12}$
(c) $\frac{5\pi}{12}<I<\frac{\sqrt{2}}{3}\pi$ (d) $\frac{3\pi}{4}<I<\pi$

78. $\int_0^2\left(|2x^2-3x|+\left[x-\frac{1}{2}\right]\right)dt$, where $[t]$ is the greatest integer function, is equal to **[Single Correct Type, 2022 Main]**

(a) $\frac{7}{6}$ (b) $\frac{19}{12}$ (c) $\frac{31}{12}$ (d) $\frac{1}{2}$

79. $\int_0^{20\pi}(|\sin x|+|\cos x|)^2\,dx$ is equal to **[Single Correct Type, 2022 Main]**

(a) $10(\pi+4)$ (b) $10(\pi+2)$
(c) $20(\pi-2)$ (d) $20(\pi+2)$

80. $\int_0^5\cos\left(\pi\left(x-\left[\frac{x}{2}\right]\right)\right)dx$, where $[t]$ denotes greatest integer less than or equal to t, is equal to **[Single Correct Type, 2022 Main]**

(a) -3 (b) -2 (c) 2 (d) 0

81. If $\int_0^2(\sqrt{2x}-\sqrt{2x-x^2})dx=$ $\int_0^1\left(1-\sqrt{1-y^2}-\frac{y^2}{2}\right)dy+\int_1^2\left(2-\frac{y^2}{2}\right)dy+I$, then I is equal to **[Single Correct Type, 2022 Main]**

(a) $\int_0^1(1+\sqrt{1-y^2})dy$ (b) $\int_0^1\left(\frac{y^2}{2}-\sqrt{1-y^2}+1\right)dy$
(c) $\int_0^1(1-\sqrt{1-y^2})\,dy$ (d) $\int_0^1\left(\frac{y^2}{2}+\sqrt{1-y^2}+1\right)dy$

82. Let $[t]$ denote the greatest integer less than or equal to t. Then, the value of the integral $\int_0^1[-8x^2+6x-1]dx$ is equal to **[Single Correct Type, 2022 Main]**

(a) -1 (b) $-\frac{5}{4}$ (c) $\frac{\sqrt{17}-13}{8}$ (d) $\frac{\sqrt{17}-16}{8}$

83. The value of $\int_0^\pi\frac{e^{\cos x}\sin x}{(1+\cos^2 x)(e^{\cos x}+e^{-\cos x})}dx$ is equal to **[Single Correct Type, 2022 Main]**

(a) $\frac{\pi^2}{4}$ (b) $\frac{\pi^2}{2}$ (c) $\frac{\pi}{4}$ (d) $\frac{\pi}{2}$

84. The value of the integral $\int_0^{\pi/2}60\frac{\sin(6x)}{\sin x}dx$ is equal to .... **[Numerical Value Type, 2022 Main]**

85. Let f be a twice differentiable function on R. If $f'(0)=4$ and $f(x)+\int_0^x(x-t)f'(t)dt=(e^{2x}+e^{-2x})\cos 2x+\frac{2}{a}x$, then $(2a+1)^5a^2$ is equal to .... **[Numerical Value Type, 2022 Main]**

86. The integral $\frac{24}{\pi}\int_0^{\sqrt{2}}\frac{(2-x^2)dx}{(2+x^2)\sqrt{4+x^4}}$ is equal to .... **[Numerical Value Type, 2022 Main]**

87. The value of the integral $\frac{48}{\pi^4}\int_0^\pi\left(\frac{3\pi x^2}{2}-x^3\right)\frac{\sin x}{1+\cos^2 x}dx$ is equal to .... **[Numerical Value Type, 2022 Main]**

88. The value of $b>3$ for which $12\int_3^b \frac{1}{(x^2-1)(x^2-4)}\,dx = \log_e\left(\frac{49}{40}\right)$, is equal to ....

[Numerical Value Type, 2022 Main]

89. The value of the integral $\int_{-1}^{1} \log(x+\sqrt{x^2+1})dx$ is

[Single Correct Type, 2021 Main]

(a) 2 (b) 0 (c) -1 (d) 1

90. The value of the definite integral $\int_{\pi/24}^{5\pi/24} \frac{dx}{1+\sqrt[3]{\tan 2x}}$ is

[Single Correct Type, 2021 Main]

(a) $\frac{\pi}{3}$ (b) $\frac{\pi}{6}$ (c) $\frac{\pi}{12}$ (d) $\frac{\pi}{18}$

91. The value of $\int_{-2}^{2} |3x^2-3x-6|\,dx$ is ....

[Numerical Value Type, 2021 Main]

92. $\int_{-\pi}^{\pi} |\pi - |x||\,dx$ is equal to

[Single Correct Type, 2020 Main]

(a) $\sqrt{2}\pi^2$ (b) $2\pi^2$

(c) π^2 (d) $\frac{\pi^2}{2}$

93. Let $[t]$ denote the greatest integer less than or equal to t. Then, the value of $\int_1^2 |2x-[3x]|\,dx$ is ....

[Numerical Value Type, 2020 Main]

EXERCISE 2

JEE Advanced Pattern

Single Option Correct Type Questions

1. Let $f(x)=x^2+ax-b$ and the only solution of the equation $f(x)=\text{minimum } f(x)$ is at $x=0$ and $f(x)=0$ has root α and β, then $\int_\alpha^\beta x^3\,dx$ is equal to

(a) $\frac{1}{4}(\beta^4+\alpha^4)$ (b) $\frac{1}{4}(a^2-b^2)$

(c) 0 (d) None of these

2. $\int_{-4}^{4} \frac{\sin^{-1}(\sin x)+\cos^{-1}(\cos x)}{(1+x^2)\left(1+\left[\frac{x^2}{17}\right]\right)}dx = \log\left(\frac{(1+x^2)}{a}\right) + b\pi\tan^{-1}\left(\frac{c-\pi}{1+c\pi}\right)$ (where, $[\cdot]$ denotes greatest integer function), then number of ways in which $a-(2b+c)$ distinct object can distributed among $\frac{a-5}{c}$ persons equally, is

(a) $\frac{9!}{(3!)^3}$ (b) $\frac{12!}{(4!)^3}$ (c) $\frac{15!}{(5!)^3}$ (d) $\frac{10!}{(6!)^3}\times 3!$

3. The value of the definite integral $\int_0^{3\pi/4} [(1+x)\sin x + (1-x)\cos x]\,dx$ is

(a) $2\tan\frac{3\pi}{8}$ (b) $2\tan\frac{\pi}{4}$

(c) $2\tan\frac{\pi}{8}$ (d) 0

4. Let $C_n = \int_{1/n+1}^{1/n} \frac{\tan^{-1}(nx)}{\sin^{-1}(nx)}dx$, then $\lim_{n\to\infty} n^2\cdot C_n$ is equal to

(a) 1 (b) 0 (c) -1 (d) $\frac{1}{2}$

5. If x satisfies the equation $\left(\int_0^1 \frac{dt}{t^2+2t\cos\alpha+1}\right)x^2 - \left(\int_{-3}^{3} \frac{t^2\sin 2t}{t^2+1}dt\right)x - 2 = 0\ (0<\alpha<\pi)$, then the value of x is

(a) $\pm\sqrt{\frac{\alpha}{2\sin\alpha}}$ (b) $\pm\sqrt{\frac{2\sin\alpha}{\alpha}}$ (c) $\pm\sqrt{\frac{\alpha}{\sin\alpha}}$ (d) $\pm 2\sqrt{\frac{\sin\alpha}{\alpha}}$

6. The value of $\lim_{n\to\infty}\sum_{r=1}^{r=4n} \frac{\sqrt{n}}{\sqrt{r}\,(3\sqrt{r}+4\sqrt{n})^2}$ is equal to

(a) $\frac{1}{35}$ (b) $\frac{1}{14}$ (c) $\frac{1}{10}$ (d) $\frac{1}{5}$

7. Let $f(x)$ be a function satisfying $f'(x)=f(x)$ with $f(0)=1$ and g be the function satisfying $f(x)+g(x)=x^2$.

The value of the integral $\int_0^1 f(x)\,g(x)\,dx$ is

(a) $e-\frac{1}{2}e^2-\frac{5}{2}$ (b) $e-e^2-3$

(c) $\frac{1}{2}(e-3)$ (d) $e-\frac{1}{2}e^2-\frac{3}{2}$

8. Let $f(x)=\int_0^{g(x)} \frac{dt}{\sqrt{1+t^2}}$, where $g(x)=\int_0^{\cos x} (1+\sin t^2)\,dt$. Also, $h(x)=e^{-|x|}$ and $f(x)=x^2\sin\frac{1}{x}$, if $x\neq 0$ and $f(0)=0$, then $f'\left(\frac{\pi}{2}\right)$ is equal to

(a) $l'(0)$ (b) $h'(0^-)$
(c) $h'(0^+)$ (d) $\lim_{x\to 0}\frac{1-\cos x}{x\sin x}$

9. Let $I(a)=\int_0^{\pi}\left(\frac{x}{a}+a\sin x\right)^2 dx$, where '$a$' is positive real. The value of 'a' for which $I(a)$ attains its minimum value, is

(a) $\sqrt{\pi\sqrt{\frac{2}{3}}}$ (b) $\sqrt{\pi\sqrt{\frac{3}{2}}}$ (c) $\sqrt{\frac{\pi}{16}}$ (d) $\sqrt{\frac{\pi}{13}}$

10. $\lim_{x\to\infty}\left(x^3\int_{-1/x}^{1/x}\frac{\ln(1+t^2)}{1+e^t}\,dt\right)$ is equal to

(a) $\frac{1}{3}$ (b) $\frac{2}{3}$ (c) 1 (d) 0

11. The value of $\sqrt{\pi\left(\int_0^{2008} x\,|\sin \pi x|\,dx\right)}$ is equal to

(a) $\sqrt{2008}$ (b) $\pi\sqrt{2008}$ (c) 1004 (d) 2008

12. If $\int_{-1/\sqrt{3}}^{1/\sqrt{3}}\frac{x^4}{1-x^4}\cos^{-1}\frac{2x}{1+x^2}\,dx = k\int_0^{1/\sqrt{3}}\frac{x^4}{1-x^4}$, then '$k$' is equal to

(a) π (b) 2π (c) 2 (d) 1

13. $\lim_{\lambda\to 0}\left(\int_0^1 (1+x)^{\lambda}\,dx\right)^{1/\lambda}$ is equal to

(a) 2 ln 2 (b) $\frac{4}{e}$ (c) $\ln\frac{4}{e}$ (d) 4

14. If $f(x)$ is continuous function such that $f(x)>0, \forall\ x\geq 0$ and $(f(x))^{2014}=1+\int_0^x f(t)\,dt$, then the values of $(f(2014))^{2013}$ is,

(a) 2013 (b) 2014 (c) 2015 (d) 2016

15. The value of constant $a>0$ such that $\int_0^a [\tan^{-1}\sqrt{x}]\,dx=\int_0^a [\cot^{-1}\sqrt{x}]\,dx$, where $[\cdot]$ denotes GIF is ....

(a) $\frac{2(3+\cos 4)}{1-\cos 4}$ (b) $\frac{(3-\cos 4)}{1+\cos 4}$
(c) $\frac{2(3+\cos 4)}{1+\cos 4}$ (d) $\frac{(3+\cos 4)}{1-\cos 4}$

16. Let $f: R\to[4,\infty)$ be an onto quadratic function, whose leading coefficient is 1. Such that $f'(x)+f'(2-x)=0$. Then, the value of $\int_1^3\frac{dx}{f(x)}$ is equal to

(a) $\frac{1}{4}$ (b) $\frac{1}{8}$ (c) $\frac{\pi}{4}$ (d) $\frac{\pi}{8}$

17. The value of $\lim_{n\to\infty}\frac{\pi}{n}\left(\frac{1}{\frac{\sin\pi(n+1)}{4n}}+\frac{1}{\frac{\sin\pi(n+2)}{4n}}+\ldots+\frac{1}{\frac{\sin\pi(n+n)}{4n}}\right)$ is equal to

(a) $4\ln(\sqrt{2}+1)$ (b) $2\ln(\sqrt{2}+1)$
(c) $2\ln(\sqrt{2}-1)$ (d) $4\ln(\sqrt{2}-1)$

18. If $f(x)=x^5+5x-1$, then $\int_5^{41}\frac{dx}{(f^{-1}(x))^5+5\cdot f^{-1}(x)}$ equals

(a) 0 (b) ln 2
(c) ln 7 (d) $\ln\left(\frac{41}{5}\right)$

19. The value of $\int_{-10}^{0}\frac{\left|\frac{2[x]}{2x-[x]}\right|}{\frac{2[x]}{2x-[x]}}\,dx$, where $[\cdot]$ denotes the greatest integer function is

(a) 10 (b) −10 (c) 9 (d) 8

20. If $\int_0^{\pi/2}\sin^{10}x\cos^{10}x\,dx=+2^{-n}\int_0^{\pi/2}(\sin^{10}x+\cos^{10}x)\,dx$, $(n\in N)$, then the value of n is equal to

(a) 7 (b) 9 (c) 10 (d) 11

More than One Correct Option Type Questions

21. Which of the following definite integral(s) vanishes?

(a) $\int_0^{\pi/2}\ln(\cot x)\,dx$ (b) $\int_0^{2\pi}\sin^3 x\,dx$
(c) $\int_{1/e}^{e}\frac{dx}{x(\ln x)^{1/3}}$ (d) $\int_0^{\pi}\sqrt{\frac{1+\cos 2x}{2}}\,dx$

22. The equation $10x^4-3x^2-1=0$ has

(a) atleast one root in $(-1, 0)$.
(b) atleast one root in $(0, 1)$.
(c) atleast two roots in $(-1, 1)$.
(d) no root in $(-1, 1)$.

23. Suppose $I_1=\int_0^{\pi/2}\cos(\pi\sin^2 x)\,dx$; $I_2=\int_0^{\pi/2}\cos(2\pi\sin^2 x)\,dx$ and $I_3=\int_0^{\pi/2}\cos(\pi\sin x)\,dx$, then

(a) $I_1=0$ (b) $I_2+I_3=0$
(c) $I_1+I_2+I_3=0$ (d) $I_2=I_3$

24. Let $f(x)=\int_{-1}^{1}(1-|t|)\cos(xt)\,dt$, then which of the following holds true?

(a) $f(0)$ is not defined.
(b) $\lim_{x\to 0} f(x)$ exists and is equal to 2.
(c) $\lim_{x\to 0} f(x)$ exists and is equal to 1.
(d) $f(x)$ is continuous at $x=0$.

25. The function f is continuous and has the property $f(f(x)) = 1 - x$ for all $x \in [0, 1]$ and $J = \int_0^1 f(x)\,dx$, then

(a) $f\left(\frac{1}{4}\right) + f\left(\frac{3}{4}\right) = 1$

(b) the value of J equals to 1/2

(c) $f\left(\frac{1}{3}\right) \cdot f\left(\frac{2}{3}\right) = 1$

(d) $\int_0^{\pi/2} \frac{\sin x\,dx}{(\sin x + \cos x)^3}$ has the same value as J

26. Let $f(x)$ is a real valued function defined by $f(x) = x^2 + x^2 \int_{-1}^{1} tf(t)\,dt + x^3 \int_{-1}^{1} f(t)\,dt$, then which of the following hold(s) good?

(a) $\int_{-1}^{1} t f(t)\,dt = \frac{10}{11}$ (b) $f(1) + f(-1) = \frac{30}{11}$

(c) $\int_{-1}^{1} t f(t)\,dt > \int_{-1}^{1} f(t)\,dt$ (d) $f(1) - f(-1) = \frac{20}{11}$

27. If $f(x)$ be a periodic function with period T, so that $f(x + 13) + f(x + 630) = 0$ and $\sum_{P=1}^{777} \int_P^{P+T} f(x)\,dx = \lambda \int_0^T f(x)\,dx$, then

(a) $T = 1234$ (b) $\lambda + T = 2011$

(c) λ, T both are prime (d) $\lambda + T = 2012$

28. Consider the integral $I_1 = \int_1^e (1 + x)(x + \ln x)^{100}\,dx$, $I_2 = \int_{\sin^{-1}\frac{1}{e}}^{\frac{\pi}{2}} (1 + e\sin x + \ln \sin x)^{101} \cos x\,dx$. If $I_1 + \frac{e}{101} I_2$ is $\frac{e(1 + e)^{101} - k}{101}$, then k is greater than or equal to

(a) 0 (b) 1

(c) 2 (d) -1

29. If $\int_0^1 \left(\sum_{k=1}^{2014} \frac{x^2}{x^3 + k^3}\right)\left(\prod_{k=1}^{2014} (x^3 + k^3)\right) dx = \frac{1}{\lambda}\left(\prod_{k=1}^{2014} (1 + k^3) - \mu^3\right)$, then,

(a) $\lambda = \frac{1}{3}$ (b) $\lambda = 3$

(c) $\mu = 2014$ (d) $\mu = 2014!$

30. If f is a differentiable function such that $f(x + y) = f(x) \cdot f(y), \forall\ x, y \in R$, $f(0) \neq 0$ and $f'(0) = 1$, then

(a) $\int_{-1}^{1} \frac{(\ln f(x))^2}{1 + (f(x))^2}\,dx = \frac{1}{3}$

(b) $\int_{-\pi/2}^{\pi/2} \frac{\cos(\ln f(x))}{1 + f(x)}\,dx = 1$

(c) $\int_{-2015}^{2015} \ln(\ln f(x) + \sqrt{1 + (\ln f(x))^2})\,dx = 0$

(d) $\int_0^2 (f(x) - \ln f(x))\,dx = e^2 - 1$

31. If $f(\theta) = |||3\cos\theta - \sin\theta| + 2\cos\theta| + \cos\theta|$, where $\theta \in \left(\frac{\pi}{2}, \pi\right)$, then

(a) $\int_{\frac{\pi}{2}}^{\pi} f(\theta)\,d\theta = 1$ (b) $f'\left(\frac{5\pi}{6}\right) = -\frac{\sqrt{3}}{2}$

(c) $\int_{\frac{\pi}{2}}^{\pi} f^2(\theta)\,d\theta = \frac{\pi}{4}$ (d) $f'\left(\frac{2\pi}{3}\right) = \frac{-1}{2}$

Passage Based Questions

Passage I

(Q. Nos. 32 and 33)

- We are given the curves $y = \int_{-\infty}^{x} f(t)dt$ through the point $\left(0, \frac{1}{2}\right)$ any $y = f(x)$, where $f(x) > 0$ and $f(x)$ is differentiable, $\forall\ x \in R$ through $(0, 1)$. Tangents drawn to both the curves at the points with equal abscissae intersect on the same point on the X-axis.

32. The number of solutions $f(x) = 2ex$ is equal to

(a) 0 (b) 1 (c) 2 (d) None of these

33. $\lim_{x \to \infty} (f(x))^{f(-x)}$ is

(a) 3 (b) 6 (c) 1 (d) None of these

Passage II

(Q. Nos. 34 and 35)

- Suppose $f(x)$ and $g(x)$ are two continuous functions defined for $0 \le x \le 1$. Given, $f(x) = \int_0^1 e^{x+t} \cdot f(t)\,dt$ and $g(x) = \int_0^1 e^{x+t} \cdot g(t)\,dt + x$.

34. The value of $f(1)$ equals

(a) 0 (b) 1 (c) e^{-1} (d) e

35. The value of $g(0) - f(0)$ equals

(a) $\frac{2}{3 - e^2}$ (b) $\frac{3}{e^2 - 2}$ (c) $\frac{1}{e^2 - 1}$ (d) 0

Passage III

(Q. Nos. 36 and 37)

- $f(x) = \int_0^x (4t^4 - at^3)\,dt$ and $g(x)$ is quadratic satisfying $g(0) + 6 = g'(0) - c = g''(c) + 2b = 0$. $y = h(x)$ and $y = g(x)$ intersect in 4 distinct points with abscissae x_i; $i = 1, 2, 3, 4$ such that $\sum \frac{i}{x_i} = 8$, $a, b, c \in R^+$ and $h(x) = f'(x)$.

36. Abscissae of point of intersection are in

(a) AP (b) GP

(c) HP (d) None of these

37. 'a' is equal to

(a) 6 (b) 8 (c) 20 (d) 12

Passage IV

(Q. Nos. 38 and 39)

- Consider $f:(0, \infty) \rightarrow \left(-\frac{\pi}{2}, \frac{\pi}{2}\right)$ defined as

$f(x)=\tan^{-1}\left(\frac{\log_e x}{(\log_e x)^2+1}\right)$.

38. The about function can be classified as
(a) Injective but nor surjective
(b) Surjective but not bijective
(c) Neither injective nor surjective
(d) Both injective and surjective

39. The value of $\int_0^{\infty}[f(x)]\,dx$ is equal to (where, [·] denotes the greatest integer function)
(a) $-\frac{\pi}{2}$
(b) $\frac{\pi}{2}$
(c) -1
(d) 1

Stem Based Questions

Stem I

(Q. Nos. 40 to 41)

- Let $P=\int_0^1\sqrt{\frac{x}{1-x}}\cdot\ln\left(\frac{x}{1-x}\right)dx$, $Q=\pi\ln\left(\frac{\sqrt{\alpha+1}+1}{2}\right)$ and

$R=\int_0^8 e^{\frac{Q}{P}}\,d\alpha$

40. The value of $[P]$ is equal to ....
(where [·] denores GIF)

41. The value of $3R$ is equal to ....

Stem II

(Q. Nos. 42 to 43)

- Suppose $\lim_{x\to 0}\frac{\int_0^x \frac{t^2 dt}{(a+t^r)^{1/p}}}{bx-\sin x}=l$, where $p\in N$, $p\geq 2$, $a>0$, $r>0$ and $b\neq 0$.

42. If $p=3$ and $l=1$, then the value of 'a' is equal to ....

43. If $p=2$ and $a=9$ and l exists, then the value of $3l$ is equal to ....

Single Integer Type Questions

44. If $f(x)=\sum_{n=1}\frac{\sin nx}{4^n}$ and $\int_0^{\pi} f(x)\,dx=\log\left(\frac{m}{n}\right)$, then the value of $(m+n)$ is ....

45. The value of $I=\int_{-\pi/2}^{\pi/2}\frac{\cos x\,dx}{1+2[\sin^{-1}(\sin x)]}$ (where, [·] denotes greatest integer function) is ....

46. If $f(n)=\frac{1}{\pi}\int_0^{\pi/2}\frac{\sin^2 n\theta}{\sin^2\theta}\,d\theta\ (n\in N)$, then the value of $\frac{f(15)+f(13)}{f(15)-f(a)}$ ....

47. Let $f(x)=\int_{-2}^{h(x)} e^{(1+t)^2}\,dt$ and $g(x)=f(h(x))$, where $h(x)$ is defined for all $x\in h$. If $g'(2)=e^4$ and $h'(2)=1$. Then, absolute value of sum for all possible value of $h(2)$, is ......

48. If $=\int_0^{\pi/2}\sin x\cdot\log(\sin x)dx=\log\left(\frac{K}{e}\right)$. Then, the value of K is ......

Numerical Value Type Questions

49. Let m, n be the distinct positive integers. Number of real values of $\alpha\in(-1,1)$ for which the integral $\int_{-\pi}^{\pi}\sin((m+\alpha)x)\sin((n+\alpha)x)\,dx$ vanishes is ....

50. Given that $\lim_{n\to\infty}\int_0^{\infty}\cos\frac{x}{2}\cos\frac{x}{4}\cos\frac{x}{8}\ldots\cos\frac{x}{2^{n-1}}\,dx=\frac{\pi}{2}$, then the value of $\int_0^{\infty}\frac{\sin^3 x}{x}\,dx=\lambda\pi$, then λ is equal to ...

51. Consider, $p(x)=x^3+ax^2+9x+b$, $a, b\in R$. If $p(2+x)+p(2-x)=2p(2)\ \forall\ x\in R$ and $p(x)+p(x+3)+p(4-x)+p(1-x)=20\ \forall\ x\in R$, then the value of $\int_{-a}^{a}p(x)\,dx$ is ....

52. If value of definite integral $\int_0^{\ln 2}\frac{(x-\ln 2)e^{x+\ln 2}}{e^{\ln(1+e^x)^2}\,dx}$ can be expressed in the form $\ln\left(\frac{a}{b}\right)$, where $a, b\in N$ and are relatively prime, then the value of $(a+b)$ is.........

53. If the value of definite integral $\int_{1/3}^{1/2}\left\{x\left[\frac{2}{x}\right]\right\}dx=\frac{m}{n}$, where m and n are coprime, then the absolute value of $(m-n)$ is ....
(where, [·] and {·} denotes GIF and FPF, respectively)

54. Let $F(n)=\int\frac{x^n}{e^x}\,dx$, then the value of definite integral $\int_2^5\left(e^{\int\frac{F(1)}{F(2)}dx}\right)^2 dx$ is .... where $F(1)$ and $F(2)$ contains no constant term. Also, $\int\frac{F(1)}{F(2)}\,dx$ contains no constant term.

55. If $\int_0^x \ln(\sin\theta)d\theta + \int_{-x}^{x} \ln\left(\cos\frac{\theta}{2} + \sin\frac{\theta}{2}\right) d\theta$
$+ \int_{-x}^{x} \ln(\cos\theta + \sin\theta)\, d\theta + \int_{-x}^{x} \ln(\cos 2\theta + \sin 2\theta)\, d\theta$
$+ 3x \ln 2 = 0$, then $\int_0^x \ln(\sin 8\theta)\, d\theta$ is equal to ....

56. If $f(x) = \begin{cases} 1 - |x|, & |x| \le 1 \\ 0, & |x| > 1 \end{cases}$ and
$g(x) = f(x-1) + f(x+1)$, then the value of $\int_{-3}^{5} g(x)\, dx$ is equal to ....

Matching Type Questions

57. Let $\lim_{T\to\infty} \frac{1}{T}\int_0^T (\sin x + \sin ax)^2\, dx = L$, then

Column I		Column II
(A) For $a = 0$, the value of L is	(p)	0
(B) For $a = 1$, the value of L is	(q)	1/2
(C) For $a = -1$, the value of L is	(r)	1
(D) For $a \in R - \{-1, 0, 1\}$, the value of L is	(s)	2

58. Match the following.

Column I		Column II
(A) If $f(x) = \int_0^{g(x)} \frac{dt}{\sqrt{1+t^3}}$, where $g(x) = \int_0^{\cos x} (1 + \sin t^2)\, dt$, then value of $f'\left(\frac{\pi}{2}\right)$ is	(p)	−2
(B) If $f(x)$ is a non-zero differentiable function such that $\int_0^x f(t)\, dt = \{f(x)\}^2$, $\forall x \in R$, then $f(2)$ is equal to	(q)	2
(C) If $\int_a^b (2 + x - x^2)\, dx$ is maximum, then $a + b$ is equal to	(r)	1
(D) If $\lim_{x\to 0}\left(\frac{\sin 2x}{x^3} + a + \frac{b}{x^2}\right) = 0$, then $3a + b$ has the value	(s)	−1

Previous Year Questions

59. Consider the equation $\int_1^e \frac{(\log_e x)^{1/2}}{x[a - (\log_e x)^{3/2}]^2}\, dx = 1$,
$a \in (-\infty, 0) \cup (1, \infty)$.
Which of the following statements is/are TRUE?
[More Than One Correct, 2022 Adv.]
(a) No a satisfies the above equation
(b) An integer a satisfies the above equation
(c) An irrational number a satisfies the above equation
(d) More than one a satisfy the above equation

60. The greatest integer less than or equal to
$\int_1^2 \log_2(x^3 + 1)dx + \int_1^{\log_2 9} (2^x - 1)^{\frac{1}{3}}\, dx$ is ....
[Numerical Value Type, 2022 Adv.]

61. Which of the following inequalities is/are TRUE?
[More Than One Correct, 2020 Adv.]
(a) $\int_0^1 x\cos x\, dx \ge \frac{3}{8}$
(b) $\int_0^1 x\sin x\, dx \ge \frac{3}{10}$
(c) $\int_0^1 x^2 \cos x\, dx \ge \frac{1}{2}$
(d) $\int_0^1 x^2 \sin x\, dx \ge \frac{2}{9}$

62. Let $f: R \to R$ be a differentiable function such that its derivative f' is continuous and $f(\pi) = -6$.
If $F: [0, \pi] \to R$ is defined by $F(x) = \int_0^x f(t)dt$, and if $\int_0^{\pi} (f'(x) + F(x))\cos x\, dx = 2$, then the value of $f(0)$ is ....
[Numerical Value Type, 2020 Adv.]

63. The value of the integral
$\int_0^{\pi/2} \frac{3\sqrt{\cos\theta}}{(\sqrt{\cos\theta} + \sqrt{\sin\theta})^5}\, d\theta$ equals ....
[Numerical Value Type, 2019 Adv.]

64. If $I = \frac{2}{\pi}\int_{-\pi/4}^{\pi/4} \frac{dx}{(1 + e^{\sin x})(2 - \cos 2x)}$, then $27I^2$ equals ....
[Numerical Value Type, 2019 Adv.]

EXERCISE 3

Challenging Problems

1. Find the error in steps to evaluate the following integral.

$$\int_0^{\pi} \frac{dx}{1+2\sin^2 x} = \int_0^{\pi} \frac{\sec^2 x\, dx}{\sec^2 x + 2\tan^2 x} = \int_0^{\pi} \frac{\sec^2 x\, dx}{1+3\tan^2 x}$$
$$= \frac{1}{\sqrt{3}} [\tan^{-1}(\sqrt{3}\tan x)]_0^{\pi} = 0$$

2. Evaluate $\int_{\alpha}^{\beta} \sqrt{\frac{x-\alpha}{\beta - x}}\, dx.$

3. Evaluate $\int_{\sqrt{(3a^2+b^2)/4}}^{\sqrt{(a^2+b^2)/2}} \frac{x}{\sqrt{(x^2-a^2)(b^2-x^2)}}\, dx.$

4. Evaluate $\int_0^{\pi/4} \frac{e^{\sec x}\left[\sin\left(x+\frac{\pi}{4}\right)\right]}{\cos x(1-\sin x)}\, dx.$

5. Evaluate $\int_0^{\pi} \frac{x^2 \cos x}{(1+\sin x)^2}\, dx.$

6. Compute the following integrals.

(i) $\int_0^{\infty} f(x^n + x^{-n}) \ln x \frac{dx}{x} = 0$

(ii) $\int_0^{\infty} f(x^n + x^{-n}) \ln x \frac{dx}{1+x^2} = 0$

7. Find a function $g : R \to R$, continuous in $[0, \infty)$ and positive in $(0, \infty)$ satisfying $g(0) = 1$ and $\frac{1}{2}\int_0^x g^2(t)\, dt = \frac{1}{x}\left(\int_0^x g(t)\, dt\right)^2.$

8. Prove that $\int_0^x e^{xt} \cdot e^{-t^2}\, dt = e^{x^2/4} \int_0^x e^{-t^2/4}\, dt.$

9. If $|a| < 1$, show that

$$\int_0^{\pi} \frac{\log(1+a\cos x)}{\cos x}\, dx = \pi \sin^{-1} a.$$

10. Evaluate $\int_0^{\pi/2} \operatorname{cosec}\theta \tan^{-1}(c\sin\theta)\, d\theta.$

11. If $f(x) = x + \int_0^1 (xy^2 + x^2 y)(f(y))\, dy$, find $f(x)$.

12. Evaluate $\int_0^{3\pi/2} (\log|\sin x|)(\cos(2nx))\, dx, n \in N.$

13. Evaluate $\int_0^1 (tx + 1 - x)^n\, dx, n \in N$ and t is independent of x. Hence, show

$$\int_0^1 x^k (1-x)^{n-k}\, dx = \frac{1}{{}^nC_k(n+1)}.$$

14. Evaluate $\int_0^{\infty} \frac{\ln x\, dx}{x^2 + 2x + 4}.$

Answer Key

Exercise 1

1. (a)	2. (a)	3. (a)	4. (a)	5. (a)	6. (c)	7. (c)	8. (d)	9. (a)	10. (c)
11. (b)	12. (a)	13. (c)	14. (a)	15. (a)	16. (b)	17. (a)	18. (b)	19. (a)	20. (a)
21. (c)	22. (a)	23. (2)	24. (3)	25. (9)	26. (2)	27. (3)	28. (7)	29. (1)	30. (2)
31. (0)	32. (2)	33. (5051)	34. (2)	35. (d)	36. (c)	37. (c)	38. (c)	39. (a)	40. (c)
41. (b)	42. (8)	43. (176)	44. (5)	45. (155)	46. (6)	47. (2)	48. (b)	49. (c)	50. (a)
51. (a)	52. (d)	53. (d)	54. (b)	55. (c)	56. (b)	57. (b)	58. (b)	59. (d)	60. (b)
61. (b)	62. (d)	63. (a)	64. (a)	65. (0)	66. (575)	67. (32)	68. (6)	69. (14)	70. (0)
71. (63)	72. (12)	73. (20)	74. (2)	75. (22)	76. (27)	77. (c)	78. (b)	79. (d)	80. (d)
81. (c)	82. (c)	83. (c)	84. (104)	85. (8)	86. (3)	87. (6)	88. (6)	89. (b)	90. (c)
91. (19)	92. (c)	93. (1)							

Exercise 2

1. (c)	2. (a)	3. (a)	4. (d)	5. (d)	6. (c)	7. (d)	8. (c)	9. (a)	10. (a)
11. (d)	12. (a)	13. (b)	14. (b)	15. (a)	16. (d)	17. (a)	18. (c)	19. (c)	20. (d)
21. (a,b,c)	22. (a,b,c)	23. (a,b,c)	24. (c,d)	25. (a,b,d)	26. (b,d)	27. (a,b)	28. (a,b,d)	29. (b,d)	30. (a,b,c)
31. (a,b,c,d)	32. (b)	33. (c)	34. (a)	35. (a)	36. (a)	37. (c)	38. (c)	39. (c)	40. (3)
41. (38)	42. (8)	43. (2)	44. (8)	45. (0)	46. (3)	47. (2)	48. (2)	49. (3)	50. (0.25)
51. (828)	52. (17)	53. (389)	54. (66)	55. (0)	56. (2)	57. (A) → (q), (B) → (s), (C) → (p), (D) → (r)			
58. (A) → (s), (B) → (r), (C) → (r), (D) → (q)				59. (c,d)	60. (5)	61. (a,b,d)	62. (4)	63. (0.5)	64. (4)

Solutions

Exercise 1 - JEE Main Pattern

1. Let $I = \int_0^4 \frac{(y^2 - 4y + 5)\sin(y-2)dy}{(2y^2 - 8y + 1)}$

Put $y - 2 = z \Rightarrow dy = dz$

$\therefore \quad I = \int_{-2}^{2} \frac{(z^2+1)\sin z}{(2z^2-7)} dz$

$\Rightarrow \quad I = 0$, as $\int_{-a}^{a} f(x)\,dx = 0$, when $f(-x) = -f(x)$

and $\quad f(z) = \frac{(z^2+1)\sin z}{(2z^2-7)}$ is an odd function.

2. Here, $\int_{\pi/2}^{x} \sqrt{(3 - 2\sin^2 t)}\,dt + \int_0^y \cos t\,dt = 0$

Differentiating both the sides, we get

$$(\sqrt{3 - 2\sin^2 x})\cdot 1 + (\cos y)\left(\frac{dy}{dx}\right) = 0$$

$\Rightarrow \quad \frac{dy}{dx} = \frac{-\sqrt{3 - 2\sin^2 x}}{\cos y}$

$\therefore \quad \left(\frac{dy}{dx}\right)_{(\pi,\pi)} = \frac{-\sqrt{3}}{-1} = \sqrt{3}$

3. Put $x = \tan\theta$

$\therefore \quad I = \int_0^{\pi/2} \frac{d\theta}{1 + (\tan\theta)^a} = \int_0^{\pi/2} \frac{(\cos\theta)^a}{(\sin\theta)^a + (\cos\theta)^a} d\theta \Rightarrow I = \frac{\pi}{4}$

4. $f'(x) = e^{g(x)} \cdot g'(x)$ and $g'(x) = \frac{x}{1+x^4}$

$\therefore \quad f'(x) = e^{g(x)} \cdot \frac{x}{1+x^4}, \quad [\because e^{g(2)} = e^0 = 1]$

Hence, $\quad f'(2) = e^{g(2)} \cdot g'(2) = e^0 \cdot \frac{2}{17} = \frac{2}{17}$

5. $\lim_{t\to 0} \ln\left(\frac{1}{t}\int_0^t (1 + a\sin bx)^{c/x}\,dx\right)$

$= \ln \lim_{t\to 0} \frac{\int_0^t (1 + a\sin b\,x)^{c/x}\,dx}{t} \quad \left[\because \frac{0}{0}\text{ form}\right]$

$= \ln \lim_{t\to 0} \frac{(1 + a\sin bt)^{c/t}}{1} \quad [\because 1^\infty \text{ form}]$

$= \ln e^{\lim_{t\to 0} \frac{a\sin bt}{t/c}} = \ln e^{abc} = abc$

6. Given, $f(x) = \int_{-1}^{x} e^{t^2}\,dt$; $h(x) = f(1 + g(x))$; $g(x) < 0$ for $x > 0$

Now, $\quad h(x) = \int_{-1}^{1+g(x)} e^{t^2}\,dt$

On differentiating, we get $\; h'(x) = e^{(1+g(x))^2} \cdot g'(x)$

Now, $\quad h'(1) = e \quad$ [given]

$\therefore \quad e^{(1+g(1))^2} \cdot g'(1) = e$

$\Rightarrow \quad (1 + g(1))^2 = 1$

$\Rightarrow \quad 1 + g(1) = \pm 1$

$\Rightarrow \quad g(1) = 0$ (not possible)

or $\quad g(1) = -2$

7. Clearly, f is an even function, hence

$I_1 = \int_0^\pi f[\cos(\pi - x)]\,dx = \int_0^\pi f(-\cos x)\,dx$

$= \int_0^\pi f(\cos x)\,dx$

$\therefore \quad I_1 = 2\int_0^{\pi/2} f(\cos x)\,dx = 2\int_0^{\pi/2} f(\sin x)\,dx = 2I_2$

$\Rightarrow \quad \frac{I_1}{I_2} = 2$

Alternate Solution

Let $u = \cos x \Rightarrow du = -\sin x\,dx$

$\therefore \quad I_1 = \int_{-1}^{1} \frac{f(u)}{\sqrt{1-u^2}} du$

$\Rightarrow \quad I_1 = 2\int_0^1 \frac{f(u)}{\sqrt{1-u^2}} du \quad$ ...(i)

Similarly, with $\sin x = t$,

$I_2 = \int_0^1 \frac{f(t)}{\sqrt{1-t^2}} dt \quad$ ...(ii)

From Eqs. (i) and (ii), $\quad \frac{I_1}{I_2} = 2$

8. Given, $I_1 = \int_{1-k}^{k} x f(x(1-x))\,dx$

and $\quad I_2 = \int_{1-k}^{k} f(x(1-x))\,dx$

Using King's property $\; I_1 = \int_{1-k}^{k} (1-x) f(x(1-x))\,dx$

$2I_1 = \int_{1-k}^{k} f(x(1-x))\,dx = I_2$

$\therefore \quad \frac{I_2}{I_1} = 2$

9. Here, $\quad f'(x) = (f(x))^2 > 0$; $\frac{d}{dx} f(g(x))|_{x=a}$

$= f'(g(x)) \lim_{x\to a} \frac{g(x) - g(a)}{x - a}$

It implies that $g(x)$ must be differentiable at $x = a$.

10. $\quad T_n = \frac{n}{n^2 + k^2x^2} = \frac{1}{n[1 + (k/n)^2 x^2]}$;

$$S = \frac{1}{n}\sum_{k=1}^{n} \frac{1}{1 + \underbrace{(k/n)^2}_{t} x^2} = \int_0^1 \frac{dt}{1 + t^2x^2}$$

$$= \frac{1}{x^2}\int_0^1 \frac{dt}{t^2 + (1/x^2)} = \left[\frac{1}{x}\tan^{-1}(tx)\right]_0^1 = \frac{\tan^{-1}(x)}{x}$$

11. $$\left[\frac{t^2}{2} - \log_2 a \cdot t\right]_0^2 = 2 - \log_2 (a^2) \qquad [\because a > 0]$$

$$\Rightarrow \quad (2 - 2\log_2 a) = 2 - 2\log_2 a$$

$$\Rightarrow \quad \log_2 4 - \log_2 a^2 = \log_2\left(\frac{4}{a^2}\right), (a \in R^+)$$

12. Put $\ln x = t$ or $x = e^t \Rightarrow dx = e^t\, dt$

$$\therefore \quad I = \int_{-\infty}^{\infty} f(e^t + e^{-t}) \frac{t}{e^t} e^t\, dt = \int_{-\infty}^{\infty} f(e^t + e^{-t})\, t\, dt = 0$$

[as the function is odd]

13. Given, $\displaystyle\int_0^{\infty} \frac{\ln t\, dt}{x^2 + t^2} = \frac{\pi \ln 2}{4}$

Let $t = x\tan\theta \Rightarrow dt = x \cdot \sec^2\theta\, d\theta$

Also, $x^2 + t^2 = x^2 + x^2\tan^2\theta = x^2\sec^2\theta$

$$\Rightarrow \quad \int_0^{\pi/2} \frac{\ln(x\tan\theta)\cdot x\sec^2\theta\, d\theta}{x^2\sec^2\theta} = \frac{\pi}{4}\ln(2)$$

$$\Rightarrow \quad \int_0^{\pi/2} \ln(x\tan\theta)\, d\theta = \frac{\pi}{4} x\ln(2) \qquad \text{...(i)}$$

$$\Rightarrow \quad \int_0^{\pi/2} \ln\left(x\tan\left(\frac{\pi}{2} - \theta\right)\right) d\theta = \frac{\pi}{4} x\ln(2)$$

$$\Rightarrow \quad \int_0^{\pi/2} \ln(x\cot\theta)\, d\theta = \frac{\pi}{4} x\ln(2) \qquad \text{...(ii)}$$

On adding Eqs. (i) and (ii), we get

$$\int_0^{\pi/2} [\ln(x\tan\theta) + \ln(x\cot\theta)]\, d\theta = 2 \times \frac{\pi}{4} x\ln(2)$$

$$\Rightarrow \quad \int_0^{\pi/2} \ln(x^2)\, d\theta = \frac{\pi}{2} x\ln(2)$$

$$\Rightarrow \quad \ln(x^2)\cdot\frac{\pi}{2} = \frac{\pi}{2} x\ln(2)$$

$$\Rightarrow \quad 2\ln(x) = x\ln(2) \Rightarrow x^2 = 2^x$$

On comparing $x = 2$ and if $x = 4$, $x^2 = 2^x$

So, number of solutions = 2

14. Put $\dfrac{x\pi}{n} = t$

$$\therefore \int_0^{\frac{16n^2}{\pi}} \cos\frac{\pi}{2}\left[\frac{\pi x}{n}\right] dx = \frac{n}{\pi}\int_0^{16n} \cos\frac{\pi}{2}[t]\, dt = 0$$

15. Let $x + \sqrt{12x - 36} = (x-3) + 3 + 2\sqrt{3}\sqrt{x-3} = |\sqrt{x-3} + \sqrt{3}|^2$

$x - \sqrt{12x-36} = (x-3) + \sqrt{3} - 2\sqrt{3}\sqrt{x-3} = |\sqrt{3} - \sqrt{x-3}|^2$

$$\therefore \quad \int_3^6 \left(\sqrt{x + \sqrt{12x-36}} + \sqrt{x - \sqrt{12x-36}}\right) dx$$

$$= \int_3^6 ((\sqrt{x-3} + \sqrt{3}) + (\sqrt{3} - \sqrt{x-3}))\, dx = 6\sqrt{3}$$

16. $$\mathcal{J}_n - \mathcal{J}_{n-1} = \int_0^{\pi/2} \frac{\sin^2 nx - \sin^2 (n-1)x}{\sin^2 x} dx$$

$$= \int_0^{\pi/2} \frac{\sin(2n-1)x \cdot \sin x}{\sin^2 x} dx = I_n$$

i.e. $\mathcal{J}_n - \mathcal{J}_{n-1} = I_n \Rightarrow \mathcal{J}_{n+1} - \mathcal{J}_n = I_{n+1}$

17. Let $\log_e x = t$, then $\dfrac{dx}{x} = dt$

$$\therefore I = \int_1^{2010} \left(1 + \frac{1-t}{t(t - \log_e t)}\right) dt = 2009 + \int_1^{2010} \frac{\frac{1}{t} - 1}{t - \log_e t} dt$$

$$= 2009 - [\log_e (t - \log_e t)]_1^{2010}$$

$$= 2009 - [\log_e (2010 - \log_e 2010)]$$

18. $$\int_{-1}^{1} \{x^2 + x - 3\}\, dx = \int_{-1}^{1} \{x^2 + x\}\, dx$$

$$= \int_{-1}^{1} (x^2 + x - [x^2 + x])\, dx$$

$$= \left(\frac{x^3}{3} + \frac{x^2}{2}\right)_{-1}^{1} - \int_{-1}^{0} [x^2 + x]\, dx - \int_0^{\frac{\sqrt{5}-1}{2}} [x^2 + x]\, dx - \int_{\frac{\sqrt{5}-1}{2}}^{1} [x^2 + x]\, dx$$

$$= \frac{2}{3} + 1 - 0 - \left(1 - \frac{\sqrt{5}-1}{2}\right) = \frac{1 + 3\sqrt{5}}{6}$$

19. $$f(x) = x^2 + \int_0^x e^{-t} f(x-t)\, dt$$

$$= x^2 + \int_0^x e^{-(x-t)} f(t)\, dt = x^2 + e^{-x}\int_0^x e^t f(t)\, dt$$

$$f'(x) = 2x + e^{-x}(e^x f(x) - 0) - e^{-x}\int_0^x e^t f(t)\, dt$$

$$= 2x + f(x) - (f(x) - x^2) = x^2 + 2x$$

$$f(x) = \frac{x^3}{3} + x^2 + k$$

$$= \frac{x^3}{3} + x^2 \qquad [\because f(0) = 0]$$

$\therefore f(1) + f(2) + \ldots + f(9)$

$$= \frac{1}{3}(1^3 + 2^3 + \ldots + 9^3) + (1^2 + 2^2 + \ldots + 9^2)$$

$$= \frac{1}{3}\left(\frac{81 \times 100}{4}\right) + \frac{9 \times 10 \times 19}{6} = 960$$

20. Period of $\tan x$ is π, Period of $\sin x$ is 2π } LCM is 2π

Required integration simplifies to

$$\int_0^{\pi/4} \sqrt{[\cos x + \{[\tan x] + \{\sin x\}\}]}\, dx$$

$$0 < x < \frac{\pi}{4}$$

$$\Rightarrow \quad [\tan x] = 0, \{\sin x\} = \sin x$$

$$= \int_0^{\pi/4} \sqrt{[\cos x + \sin x]}\, dx$$

$$= \int_0^{\pi/4} \sqrt{1}\, dx = \frac{\pi}{4}$$

21. $$\int_0^{\pi/3} [\sqrt{3}\tan x]\, dx = \int_0^{\pi/6} [\sqrt{3}\tan x]\, dx + \int_{\pi/6}^{\tan^{-1}\frac{2}{\sqrt{3}}} [\sqrt{3}\tan x]\, dx + \int_{\tan^{-1}\frac{2}{\sqrt{3}}}^{\pi/3} [\sqrt{3}\tan x]\, dx$$

$$= \frac{\pi}{2} - \tan^{-1}\frac{2}{\sqrt{3}} = \sin^{-1}\left(\sqrt{\frac{3}{7}}\right)$$

$$\Rightarrow \quad k = \frac{3}{7}$$

$$\therefore \quad \int_0^{2k} [\tan x]\, dx = \int_0^{6/7} [\tan x]\, dx$$

$$= \int_0^{\pi/4} [\tan x]\, dx + \int_{\pi/4}^{6/7} [\tan x]\, dx$$

$$= \frac{6}{7} - \frac{\pi}{4}$$

22. $g(x) = [\cos(\cos x)] + [\sin(\sin x)] = \begin{cases} -1, & -\pi < x < 0 \\ 0, & 0 < x < \pi \end{cases}$

$$\int_{-\pi}^{\pi} f(g(x))\,dx = \int_{-\pi}^{0} f(g(x))\,dx + \int_{0}^{\pi} f(g(x))\,dx$$

$$= \int_{-\pi}^{0} \cos^{-1}(-1)\,dx + \int_{0}^{\pi} \cos^{-1}(0)\,dx$$

$$= \pi^2 + \frac{\pi^2}{2} = \frac{3\pi^2}{2}$$

23. Let $\quad I = \int_{\pi/4}^{3\pi/4} \frac{dx}{1+\cos x}$

$$= \int_{\pi/4}^{3\pi/4} \frac{1-\cos x}{1-\cos^2 x}\,dx = \int_{\pi/4}^{3\pi/4} \frac{1-\cos x}{\sin^2 x}\,dx$$

$$= \int_{\pi/4}^{3\pi/4} \operatorname{cosec}^2 x - \operatorname{cosec} x \cot x)dx$$

$$= [-\cot x + \operatorname{cosec} x]_{\pi/4}^{3\pi/4}$$

$$= [(1+\sqrt{2}) - (-1+\sqrt{2})] = 2$$

24. Since, $\int_{\sin x}^{1} t^2 f(t)\,dt = 1 - \sin x,$

thus to find $f(x)$.

On differentiating both sides using Newton Leibnitz formula

i.e. $\quad \frac{d}{dx}\int_{\sin x}^{1} t^2 f(t)\,dt = \frac{d}{dx}(1-\sin x)$

$\Rightarrow \{1^2 f(1)\}\cdot(0) - (\sin^2 x)\cdot f(\sin x)\cdot\cos x = -\cos x$

$\Rightarrow \qquad f(\sin x) = \frac{1}{\sin^2 x}$

For $f\left(\frac{1}{\sqrt{3}}\right)$ is obtained when

$$\sin x = 1/\sqrt{3}$$

i.e. $\quad f\left(\frac{1}{\sqrt{3}}\right) = (\sqrt{3})^2 = 3$

25. Here, $\alpha = \int_0^1 e^{(9x + 3\tan^{-1} x)}\left(\frac{12+9x^2}{1+x^2}\right)dx$

Let $\quad 9x + 3\tan^{-1} x = t$

$\Rightarrow \quad \left(9 + \frac{3}{1+x^2}\right)dx = dt$

$\therefore \quad \alpha = \int_0^{9+3\pi/4} e^t\,dt = [e^t]_0^{9+3\pi/4} = e^{9+3\pi/4} - 1$

$\Rightarrow \log_e|1+\alpha| = 9 + \frac{3\pi}{4} \Rightarrow \log_e|\alpha+1| - \frac{3\pi}{4} = 9$

26. Given, $I = \int_0^1 \underset{\text{I}}{4x^3} \underset{\text{II}}{\frac{d^2}{dx^2}(1-x^2)^5}\,dx$

$$= \left[4x^3 \frac{d}{dx}(1-x^2)^5\right]_0^1 - \int_0^1 12x^2 \frac{d}{dx}(1-x^2)^5\,dx$$

$$= [4x^3 \times 5(1-x^2)^4\,(-2x)]_0^1$$

$$-12\left[[x^2(1-x^2)^5]_0^1 - \int_0^1 2x(1-x^2)^5\,dx\right]$$

$$= 0 - 0 - 12(0-0) + 12\int_0^1 2x(1-x^2)^5\,dx$$

$$= 12 \times \left[-\frac{(1-x^2)^6}{6}\right]_0^1 = 12\left[0 + \frac{1}{6}\right] = 2$$

27. $f(x) = \begin{vmatrix} \sin x + \sin 2x + \sin 3x & \sin 2x & \sin 3x \\ 3 + 4\sin x & 3 & 4\sin x \\ 1 + \sin x & \sin x & 1 \end{vmatrix}$

On applying $C_1 \to C_1 - (C_2 + C_3)$,

$$\begin{vmatrix} \sin x & \sin 2x & \sin 3x \\ 0 & 3 & 4\sin x \\ 0 & \sin x & 1 \end{vmatrix}$$

$$= \sin x(3 - 4\sin^2 x)$$

$$= 3\sin x - 4\sin^3 x$$

$$f(x) = \sin 3x$$

Now, $\int_0^{\pi/2} \sin 3x\,dx = \left[-\frac{\cos 3x}{3}\right]_0^{\pi/2}$

$$= 0 + \frac{1}{3} = \frac{1}{3}$$

So, $K = 3$

28. We have,

$$\int_0^{1.5} x[x^2]\,dx = \int_0^1 x[x^2]\,dx + \int_1^{\sqrt{2}} x[x^2]\,dx + \int_{\sqrt{2}}^{1.5} x[x^2]\,dx$$

$$= \int_0^1 (0 \times x)\,dx + \int_1^{\sqrt{2}} 1\,(x)\,dx + \int_{\sqrt{2}}^{1.5} 2x\,dx$$

$$= \left[\frac{x^2}{2}\right]_1^{\sqrt{2}} + [x^2]_{\sqrt{2}}^{1.5}$$

$$= \left(1 - \frac{1}{2}\right) + \left(\frac{9}{4} - 2\right)$$

$$= \frac{1}{2} + \frac{1}{4} = \frac{3}{4}$$

Hence, $p + q = 3 + 4 = 7$

29. We have,

$$L = \lim_{n\to\infty} \frac{2}{n}\left(f\left(\frac{1}{n}\right) + f\left(\frac{2}{n}\right) + \ldots + f(1)\right)$$

$$L = 2\lim_{n\to\infty} \frac{1}{n}\sum_{r=1}^{n} \log_2\left(1 + \tan\frac{\pi r}{4n}\right)$$

$$L = \frac{2}{\ln 2}\int_0^1 \ln\left(1 + \tan\frac{\pi x}{4}\right)dx \qquad \ldots\text{(i)}$$

$$L = \frac{2}{\ln 2}\int_0^1 \ln\left(1 + \tan\frac{\pi}{4}(1-x)\right)dx$$

$$= \frac{2}{\ln 2}\int_0^1 \ln\left(1 + \tan\left(\frac{\pi}{4} - \frac{\pi}{4}x\right)\right)dx$$

$$= \frac{2}{\ln 2}\int_0^1 \ln\left(1 + \frac{1 - \tan\frac{\pi}{4}x}{1 + \tan\frac{\pi}{4}x}\right)dx$$

$$L = \frac{2}{\ln 2}\int_0^1 \ln\left(\frac{2}{1 + \tan\frac{\pi}{4}x}\right)dx$$

$$= \frac{2}{\ln 2}\int_0^1 \left[\ln 2 - \ln\left(1 + \tan\frac{\pi x}{4}\right)\right]dx \qquad \ldots\text{(ii)}$$

Adding Eqs. (i) and (ii), we get

$$2L = \frac{2}{\ln 2}\int_0^1 \ln 2\, dx \Rightarrow 2L = \frac{2}{\ln 2}\cdot \ln 2 \Rightarrow L = 1$$

30. $f^2(x) = \int_0^x f(t)\frac{\cos t}{2+\sin t}\, dt$

Differentiating w.r.t. x using Leibnitz rule,

$$2f(x)\cdot f'(x) = f(x)\frac{\cos x}{2+\sin x}$$

$$2f'(x) = \frac{\cos x}{2+\sin x}$$

$$\Rightarrow \quad 2\int f'(x)\, dx = \int \frac{\cos x}{2+\sin x}\, dx$$

$$2f(x) = \log(2+\sin x) + \log c$$

Put $x = 0$, then

$$2f(0) = \log 2 + \log c \qquad [\because f(0) = 0]$$

$$\Rightarrow \quad \log c = -\log 2$$

$$\therefore \quad 2f(x) = \log(2+\sin x) - \log 2$$

$$2f(x) = \log\left(\frac{2+\sin x}{2}\right) \Rightarrow f(x) = \frac{1}{2}\log\left(\frac{2+\sin x}{2}\right)$$

Hence, $K = 2$

31. Given, $x\int_0^x (1-t)\sin f(t)\, dt = 2\int_0^x t\sin(f(t))\, dt$

Differentiating w.r.t. 'x', we get

$$\int_0^x (1-t)\sin[f(t)]\, dt + x(1-x)\sin[f(x)] = 2x\sin(f(x))$$

$$\Rightarrow \quad \int_0^x (1-t)\sin(f(t))\, dt = x^2\sin(f(x)) + x\sin f(x)$$

Again, differentiating, w.r.t. 'x', we get

$$(1-x)\sin(f(x)) = 2x\sin(f(x)) + x^2\cos(f(x))f'(x) + \sin(f(x)) + x\cos(f(x))f'(x)$$

$$\Rightarrow \quad -3x\sin(f(x)) = (x+x^2)\cos(f(x))\cdot f'(x)$$

$$\Rightarrow \quad \frac{-3x}{x(1+x)} = \cot(f(x))\cdot f'(x)$$

$$\Rightarrow f'(x)\cot(f(x)) + \frac{3}{1+x} = 0$$

32. We have, $f(x) = \int_1^x \sqrt{2-t^2}\, dt$

By Leibnitz rule,

$$f'(x) = \sqrt{2-x^2}$$

Now, $x^2 - f'(x) = 0 \Rightarrow x^4 = 2 - x^2$

$$\Rightarrow \quad x^4 + x^2 - 2 = 0 \Rightarrow (x^2+2)(x^2-1) = 0$$

$\therefore$ $x = \pm 1$ are the real value of x.

Therefore, the number of real roots of the equation $x^2 - f'(x) = 0$ is 2.

33. Let $I_n = \int_0^1 (1-x^{50})^n\, dx$

Integrating by parts, we get

$$I_n = (1-x^{50})^n\cdot x|_0^1 + \int_0^1 x\cdot 50n\cdot(1-x^{50})^{n-1}\cdot x^{49}\cdot dx$$

$$= 0 + 50n\int_0^1 x^{50}\cdot(1-x^{50})^{n-1}\cdot dx$$

$$= -50n\int_0^1 ((1-x^{50})-1)\cdot(1-x^{50})^{n-1}\cdot dx$$

$$= -50n\left[\int_0^1 (1-x^{50})^n\cdot dx - \int_0^1 (1-x^{50})^{n-1}\cdot dx\right]$$

$$= -50n(I_n - I_{n-1})$$

$$= -50n\, I_n + 50n\, I_{n-1}$$

$$\Rightarrow \quad I_n = -50n\, I_n + 50nI_{n-1}$$

$$\Rightarrow (1+50n)I_n = 50nI_{n-1}$$

$$\Rightarrow \quad \frac{I_n}{I_{n-1}} = \frac{50n}{(1+50n)}$$

Putting $n = 101$, then we get

$$\frac{I_{101}}{I_{100}} = \frac{50\times 101}{(1+50\times 101)} = \frac{5050}{5051}$$

So, $5050 \times \frac{I_{100}}{I_{101}} = 5051$

34. Let $I = \int_0^1 \cot^{-1}(1+x^2-x)\, dx$

$$\Rightarrow \quad I = \int_0^1 \cot^{-1}(1-x(1-x))\, dx$$

$$\Rightarrow \quad I = \int_0^1 \tan^{-1}\left(\frac{1}{1-x(1-x)}\right) dx$$

$$= \int_0^1 \tan^{-1}\left(\frac{x+(1-x)}{1-x(1-x)}\right) dx$$

$$\Rightarrow \quad I = \int_0^1 (\tan^{-1}x + \tan^{-1}(1-x))\, dx$$

$$\Rightarrow \quad I = \int_0^1 \tan^{-1}x\, dx + \int_0^1 \tan^{-1}(1-x)\, dx$$

$$= \int_0^1 \tan^{-1}x\, dx + \int_0^1 \tan^{-1}(1-(1-x))\, dx$$

$$\left[\because \int_0^a f(x)\, dx = \int_0^a f(a-x)\, dx\right]$$

$$= \int_0^1 \tan^{-1}x\, dx + \int_0^1 \tan^{-1}x\, dx$$

$$= 2\int_0^1 \tan^{-1}x\, dx$$

$$= 2\left[x\tan^{-1}x - \frac{1}{2}\log|1+x^2|\right]_0^1 = 2\left(\frac{\pi}{4} - \frac{1}{2}\log 2\right)$$

$$\Rightarrow \quad I = 2\left(\frac{\pi}{4} - \log\sqrt{2}\right)$$

Comparing with $K\left(\frac{\pi}{4} - \log\sqrt{2}\right)$, we get

$$K = 2$$

35. **Decoding the Question**

King Property of integration is

$$\int_a^b f(x)dx = \int_a^b f(a+b-x)dx$$

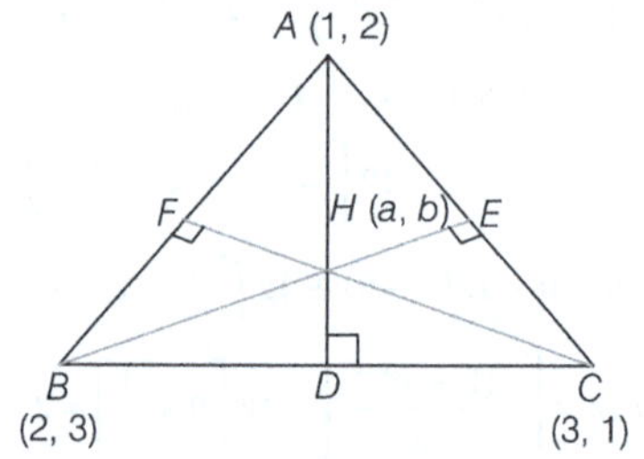

Slope of $AB = m_{AB} = \frac{3-2}{2-1} = 1$

$\therefore$ Slope of $CF = -1$

Now, equation of CF is

$$y - 1 = -1(x-3)$$

$$\Rightarrow \quad x + y = 4 \quad \text{...(i)}$$

i.e. orthocentre lies on Eq. (i).

i.e. (a, b) lies on Eq. (i).

So, $a + b = 4$

Given, $I_1 = \int_a^b x \sin(4x - x^2)dx$

$$\Rightarrow \quad I_1 = \int_a^b x\sin\{x(4-x)\}dx \quad \text{...(ii)}$$

$$\Rightarrow \quad I_1 = \int_a^b (a+b-x)\sin\{(a+b-x)[4-(a+b-x)]\}dx$$

[using king's property]

$$\Rightarrow \quad I_1 = \int_a^b (4-x)\sin\{(4-x)x\}dx \quad \text{...(iii)}$$

On adding Eqs. (ii) and (iii), we get

$$2I_1 = \int_a^b 4\sin\{x(4-x)\}\,dx$$

$$\Rightarrow \quad 2I_1 = 4I_2 \quad \left[\text{given, } I_2 = \int_a^b \sin(4x - x^2)dx\right]$$

$$\Rightarrow \quad \frac{I_1}{I_2} = 2$$

$$\Rightarrow \quad 36\left(\frac{I_1}{I_2}\right) = 36 \times 2 = 72$$

36. Let $I = \int_0^\pi \frac{1}{1 - 2a\cos x + a^2}dx$ ...(i)

$0 < a < 1$

$$\Rightarrow \quad I = \int_0^\pi \frac{1}{1 - 2a\cos(\pi - x) + a^2}dx$$

$$\Rightarrow \quad I = \int_0^\pi \frac{1}{1 + 2a\cos x + a^2}dx \quad \text{...(ii)}$$

On adding Eqs. (i) and (ii), we get

$$2I = \int_0^\pi \left[\frac{1}{(1+a^2) - 2a\cos x} + \frac{1}{(1+a^2) + 2a\cos x}\right]dx$$

$$\Rightarrow \quad 2I = 2\int_0^{\pi/2} \frac{2(1+a^2)}{(1+a^2)^2 - 4a^2\cos^2 x}dx$$

$$\Rightarrow \quad I = \int_0^{\pi/2} \frac{2(1+a^2)\cdot\sec^2 x}{(1+a^2)^2\sec^2 x - 4a^2}dx$$

$$= \int_0^{\pi/2} \frac{2\cdot(1+a^2)\cdot\sec^2 x}{(1+a^2)^2\tan^2 x + (1-a^2)^2}dx$$

$[\because \sec^2 x = 1 + \tan^2 x]$

$$I = \int_0^{\pi/2} \frac{\dfrac{2\cdot\sec^2 x}{1+a^2}}{\tan^2 x + \left(\dfrac{1-a^2}{1+a^2}\right)^2}dx$$

$$= \frac{2}{1-a^2}\left[\frac{\pi}{2} - 0\right] = \frac{\pi}{1-a^2}$$

37. Let $I = \int_{-\pi/2}^{\pi/2}\left(\frac{x^2\cos x}{1+\pi^x} + \frac{1+\sin^2 x}{1+e^{\sin x^{2023}}}\right)dx$

$$= \int_0^{\pi/2}\left[\left(\frac{x^2\cos x}{1+\pi^x} + \frac{1+\sin^2 x}{1+e^{(\sin x^{2023})}}\right) + \left(\frac{x^2\cos x}{1+\pi^{-x}} + \frac{1+\sin^2 x}{1+e^{-(\sin x^{2023})}}\right)\right]dx$$

$$= \int_0^{\pi/2}(x^2\cos x + 1 + \sin^2 x)dx$$

$$= \int_0^{\pi/2} x^2\cos x\,dx + \int_0^{\pi/2}(1+\sin^2 x)\,dx$$

Now, let $I_1 = \int_0^{\pi/2}(1+\sin^2 x)\,dx$

$$= \int_0^{\pi/2} 1\,dx + \int_0^{\pi/2}\left(\frac{1-\cos 2x}{2}\right)dx$$

$$= \frac{\pi}{2} + \frac{1}{2}\left(\frac{\pi}{2} + 0\right)$$

$$\Rightarrow \quad I_1 = \frac{\pi}{2} + \frac{\pi}{4} = \frac{3\pi}{4}$$

and $I_2 = \int_0^{\pi/2} x^2\cos x dx$

$$= [(x^2\sin x) - \int 2x\int\cos x\,dx]_0^{\pi/2}$$

$$= [x^2(\sin x) - 2\int x\sin x dx]_0^{\pi/2}$$

$$= [x^2\sin x - 2(-x\cos x + \sin x dx)]_0^{\pi/2}$$

$$= \frac{\pi^2}{4} - 2$$

$$\therefore \quad I = \frac{3\pi}{4} + \frac{\pi^2}{4} - 2 = \frac{\pi}{4}(\pi + a) - 2 \quad \text{[given]}$$

$$\therefore \quad a = 3$$

38. Given, $f: R \to R$, $f(x) = \frac{x}{(1+x^4)^{1/4}}$ and $g(x) = f(f(f(f(x))))$

Now, $fof(x) = \frac{f}{(1+f^4)^{1/4}} = \frac{\dfrac{x}{(1+x^4)^{1/4}}}{\left[1 + \left(\dfrac{x}{(1+x^4)^{1/4}}\right)^4\right]^{1/4}}$

$$= \frac{\dfrac{x}{(1+x^4)^{1/4}}}{\left[1 + \dfrac{x^4}{(1+x^4)}\right]^{1/4}} = \frac{x}{(1+2x^4)^{1/4}}$$

Similarly, $fofof = \frac{x}{(1+3x^4)^{1/4}}$

and $fofofof = \frac{x}{(1+4x^4)^{1/4}} = g(x)$

Now, according to the question,

$$18\int_0^{\sqrt{2\sqrt{5}}} x^2 \cdot g(x)dx$$

$$= 18\int_0^{\sqrt{2\sqrt{5}}} x^2 \cdot \frac{x}{(1+4x^4)^{1/4}}dx$$

$$= 18\int_0^{\sqrt{2\sqrt{5}}} \frac{x^3}{(1+4x^4)^{1/4}}dx$$

Let $1 + 4x^4 = t^4$

$\Rightarrow 16x^3dx = 4t^3dt$

$\Rightarrow \quad x^3dx = \frac{1}{4}t^3dt$

When $x = 0, t = 1$

and $x = \sqrt{2\sqrt{5}}, t = 3$

$$= 18\int_1^3 \frac{t^3}{4} \cdot \frac{dt}{t}$$

$$= \frac{18}{4}\int_1^3 t^2dt$$

$$= \frac{9}{2} \times \left[\frac{t^3}{3}\right]_1^3 = \frac{3}{2}(27-1)$$

$$= \frac{3}{2} \times 26 = 3 \times 13 = 39$$

39. Let $f, g : (0, \infty) \to R$

$$f(x) = \int_{-x}^{x} (|t| - t^2)\, e^{-t^2}dt$$

Differentiating w.r.t. x both side, we get

$$f'(x) = (|x| - x^2)\, e^{-x^2} - (|x| - x^2)\, e^{-x^2}(-1)$$

$$f'(x) = 2(|x| - x^2)\, e^{-x^2}$$

$$f'(x) = 2\,|x|\, e^{-x^2} - 2x^2e^{-x^2} \quad \text{...(i)}$$

$g : (0, \infty) \to R$

$$\Rightarrow \quad g(x) = \int_0^{x^2} t^{1/2}e^{-t}dt$$

$$\Rightarrow g'(x) = (xe^{-x^2})\, 2x - 0$$

$$\Rightarrow g'(x) = 2x^2e^{-x^2} \quad \text{...(ii)}$$

On adding Eqs. (i) and (ii), we get

$$f'(x) + g'(x) = 2xe^{-x^2}$$

Integrating both sides w.r.t. x,

$$f(x) + g(x) = \int_0^{\sqrt{\log_e 9}} 2xe^{-x^2}dx$$

Put $x^2 = t$

$2x\, dx = dt$

$$f(x) + g(x) = \int_0^{\log_e 9} e^{-t}dt = [-e^{-t}]_0^{\log_e 9}$$

$$f(x) + g(x) = -[e^{-\log_e 9} - e^0]$$

$$= 1 - \frac{1}{9} = \frac{8}{9}$$

$$\Rightarrow \quad 9(f(x) + g(x)) = 8$$

$$\Rightarrow \quad 9(f(\sqrt{\log_e 9}) + g(\sqrt{\log_e 9})) = 8$$

40. We have, $\quad I = \int_0^{\frac{\pi}{3}} \cos^4 x\,dx = a\pi + b\sqrt{3}$

$$= \int_0^{\frac{\pi}{3}} [\cos^2 x]^2 dx = \int_0^{\frac{\pi}{3}} \left[\frac{\cos 2x + 1}{2}\right]^2 dx$$

$$= \frac{1}{4}\int_0^{\frac{\pi}{3}} (1 + \cos^2 2x + 2\cos 2x)dx$$

$$= \frac{1}{4}\left[\frac{\pi}{3} + \int_0^{\frac{\pi}{3}} \cos^2 2x\,dx + [\sin 2x]_0^{\frac{\pi}{3}}\right]$$

$$= \frac{1}{4}\left[\frac{\pi}{3} + \int_0^{\frac{\pi}{3}}\left[\frac{1+\cos 4x}{2}\right]dx + \frac{\sqrt{3}}{2}\right]$$

$$= \frac{1}{4}\left[\frac{\pi}{3} + \frac{1}{2}\left(\frac{\pi}{3} + \frac{1}{4}(\sin 4x)_0^{\frac{\pi}{3}}\right) + \frac{\sqrt{3}}{2}\right]$$

$$= \frac{1}{4}\left[\frac{\pi}{3} + \frac{\pi}{6} + \frac{1}{8}\sin\frac{4\pi}{3} + \frac{\sqrt{3}}{2}\right]$$

$$= \frac{1}{4}\left[\frac{\pi}{2} + \frac{1}{8}\left(\frac{-\sqrt{3}}{2}\right) + \frac{\sqrt{3}}{2}\right] = \frac{\pi}{8} + \frac{7\sqrt{3}}{64}$$

$\therefore \quad a = \frac{1}{8}, b = \frac{7}{64}$

Now, $9a + 8b = \frac{9}{8} + \frac{7}{8} = 2$

41. $$I = \int_0^1 (2x^3 - 3x^2 - x + 1)^{\frac{1}{3}}dx \quad \text{...(i)}$$

$$= \int_0^1 [2(1-x)^3 - 3(1-x)^2 - (1-x) + 1]^{\frac{1}{3}}\,dx$$

$$= \int_0^1 [2(1 - x^3 + 3x^2 - 3x) - 3(1 + x^2 - 2x) - 1 + x + 1]^{\frac{1}{3}}\,dx$$

$$= \int_0^1 [2 - 2x^3 + 6x^2 - 6x - 3 - 3x^2 + 6x + x]^{\frac{1}{3}}\,dx$$

$$= \int_0^1 [-2x^3 + 3x^2 + x - 1]^{\frac{1}{3}}\,dx$$

$$= -\int_0^1 (2x^3 - 3x^2 - x + 1)^{\frac{1}{3}}dx = -I \quad \text{[from Eq. (i)]}$$

$\Rightarrow 2I = 0$

$\therefore \quad I = 0$

42. $$I = \int_{-\frac{\pi}{2}}^{\frac{\pi}{2}} \frac{8\sqrt{2}\cos x \cdot dx}{(1 + e^{\sin x})(1 + \sin^4 x)} \quad \text{...(i)}$$

$$= \alpha\pi + \beta\log_e(3 + 2\sqrt{2})$$

$$\Rightarrow \quad I = \int_{-\frac{\pi}{2}}^{\frac{\pi}{2}} \frac{8\sqrt{2}\cos x \cdot dx}{(1 + e^{-\sin x})(1 + \sin^4 x)} \quad \text{...(ii)}$$

On adding Eqs. (i) and (ii), we get

$$2I = \int_{-\frac{\pi}{2}}^{\frac{\pi}{2}} \frac{8\sqrt{2}\cos x(1 + e^{\sin x})}{(1 + e^{\sin x})(1 + \sin^4 x)}dx$$

$$\Rightarrow \quad 2I = 2\int_0^{\frac{\pi}{2}} \frac{8\sqrt{2}\cos x}{(1 + \sin^4 x)}dx$$

Put $\sin x = t$

$\therefore \cos x\, dx = dt$

$$\Rightarrow \quad I = 8\sqrt{2}\int_0^1 \frac{dt}{1+t^4} \Rightarrow I = 4\sqrt{2}\int_0^1 \frac{2}{1+t^4}dt$$

$$\Rightarrow \quad I = 4\sqrt{2}\int_0^1 \frac{(1+t^2)-(t^2-1)}{t^2\left(\frac{1}{t^2}+t^2\right)}\cdot dt$$

$$\Rightarrow \quad I = 4\sqrt{2}\left[\int_0^1 \frac{\left(\frac{1}{t^2}+1\right)}{\left(t-\frac{1}{t}\right)^2+2}dt - \int_0^1 \frac{\left(1-\frac{1}{t^2}\right)}{\left(t+\frac{1}{t}\right)^2-2}dt\right]$$

Put $t - \frac{1}{t} = z$, put $t + \frac{1}{t} = s$

$$\left(1+\frac{1}{t^2}\right)dt = dz; \left(1-\frac{1}{t^2}\right)dt = ds$$

$$I = 4\sqrt{2}\left[\int_{-\infty}^0 \frac{dz}{z^2+(\sqrt{2})^2} - \int_{\infty}^2 \frac{ds}{s^2-(\sqrt{2})^2}\right]$$

$$I = 4\sqrt{2}\left[\left(\frac{1}{\sqrt{2}}\tan^{-1}\frac{z}{\sqrt{2}}\right)_{-\infty}^0 - \left(\frac{1}{2\sqrt{2}}\log_e\left|\frac{s-\sqrt{2}}{s+\sqrt{2}}\right|\right)_{\infty}^2\right]$$

$$I = 2\pi + 2\ln(3+2\sqrt{2})$$

$$\alpha = 2, \beta = 2$$

Hence, $\alpha^2+\beta^2 = 4+4 = 8$

43. $I = \int_0^{\frac{\pi}{2}} \sin 2x \cos^{\frac{11}{2}} x\left(1+\cos^{\frac{5}{2}} x\right)^{\frac{1}{2}} dx$

Let $\cos x = t^2$ ($x=\frac{\pi}{2} \rightarrow t=0$; $x=0 \rightarrow t=1$)

$-\sin x\, dx = 2t\, dt$

$$I = \int_1^0 2t^2\cdot t^{11}\cdot(1+t^5)^{\frac{1}{2}}(-2t)dt = \int_0^1 4t^{14}\sqrt{1+t^5}\,dt$$

Let $1+t^5 = u^2$ ($t=1 \rightarrow u=\sqrt{2}$; $t=0 \rightarrow u=1$)

$\Rightarrow 1+t^5 = u^2 \Rightarrow 5t^4 dt = 2u\, du$

$$\Rightarrow \quad t^4 dt = \frac{2u}{5}du$$

$$\Rightarrow \quad I = 4\int_1^{\sqrt{2}} (u^2-1)^2\cdot u\cdot\frac{2u}{5}du$$

$$= \frac{8}{5}\int_1^{\sqrt{2}}(u^6-2u^4+u^2)du = \frac{8}{5}\left(\frac{u^7}{7}-\frac{2u^5}{5}+\frac{u^3}{3}\right)_1^{\sqrt{2}}$$

$$= \frac{8}{5}\left[\left(\frac{8\sqrt{2}}{7}-\frac{8\sqrt{2}}{5}+\frac{2\sqrt{2}}{3}\right)-\left(\frac{1}{7}-\frac{2}{5}+\frac{1}{3}\right)\right]$$

$$= \frac{8}{5}\left(\frac{22\sqrt{2}}{105}-\frac{8}{105}\right)$$

Now, according to the equation,

$$525I = 525\times\frac{8}{5}\left(\frac{22\sqrt{2}}{105}-\frac{8}{105}\right) = 176\sqrt{2}-64$$

$$n = 176$$

44. $f(x) = \dfrac{4^x}{4^x+2}$

$$f(1-x) = \frac{4^{1-x}}{4^{1-x}+2} = \frac{\frac{4}{4^x}}{\frac{4}{4^x}+2} = \frac{4}{4+2\cdot 4^x} = \frac{2}{4^x+2}$$

$\Rightarrow f(x)+f(1-x) = 1$

$$M = \int_{f(a)}^{f(1-a)} x\sin^4(x(1-x))\,dx$$

$$= \int_{f(a)}^{f(1-a)} (1-x)\sin^4(1-x)\cdot x\,dx$$

$$= \int_{f(a)}^{f(1-a)} \sin^4[(1-x)x]\,dx - \int_{f(a)}^{f(1-a)} x\sin^4[(1-x)x]\,dx$$

$\Rightarrow \quad M = N - M \Rightarrow 2M = N$

$\Rightarrow \quad \alpha = 2, \beta = 1$

$\therefore \alpha^2+\beta^2 = 5$

45. We have, $I = 9\int_0^9\left[\sqrt{\frac{10x}{x+1}}\right]dx$

Let $f(x) = \sqrt{\dfrac{10x}{x+1}}$

If $\dfrac{10x}{x+1} = 1 \Rightarrow x = 1/9$

If $\dfrac{10x}{x+1} = 4 \Rightarrow x = 2/3$

If $\dfrac{10x}{x+1} = 9 \Rightarrow x = 9$

$$\therefore \quad f(x) = \begin{cases} 0, & 0 \le x < 1/9 \\ 1, & 1/9 \le x < 2/3 \\ 2, & 2/3 \le x < 9 \end{cases}$$

$$\therefore \quad I = 9\left[\int_0^{1/9} 0dx + \int_{1/9}^{2/3} dx + \int_{2/3}^{9} 2dx\right]$$

$$= 9\left[\frac{2}{3}-\frac{1}{9}+18-\frac{4}{3}\right] = 9[18-7/9] = 155$$

46. $\int_{\pi/6}^{\pi/3}\sqrt{1-\sin 2x}\,dx = \alpha+\beta\sqrt{2}+\gamma\sqrt{3}$

Let $I = \int_{\pi/6}^{\pi/3}\sqrt{1-\sin 2x}\,dx$

$$= \int_{\pi/6}^{\pi/3}\sqrt{(\sin x-\cos x)^2}\,dx$$

$$= \int_{\pi/6}^{\pi/3}|\sin x-\cos x|\,dx$$

$$= \int_{\pi/6}^{\pi/4}(\cos x-\sin x)\,dx + \int_{\pi/4}^{\pi/3}(\sin x-\cos x)\,dx$$

$$= [\sin x + \cos x]_{\frac{\pi}{6}}^{\frac{\pi}{4}} - [\cos x + \sin x]_{\frac{\pi}{4}}^{\frac{\pi}{3}}$$

$$= \left(\sqrt{2} - \frac{1}{2} - \frac{\sqrt{3}}{2}\right) - \left(\frac{1}{2} + \frac{\sqrt{3}}{2} - \sqrt{2}\right) = 2\sqrt{2} - 1 - \sqrt{3}$$

$\alpha = -1, \beta = 2$ and $\gamma = -1$

$3\alpha + 4\beta - \gamma = -3 + 8 + 1 = 6$

47. Given, $f(x) = \int_0^x g(t) \log_e \left(\frac{1-t}{1+t}\right) dt$

$\Rightarrow \quad f'(x) = g(x) \log_e \left(\frac{1-x}{1+x}\right)$

Since, $g(x)$ and $\log_e\left(\frac{1-x}{1+x}\right)$ both are odd.

So, $f'(x)$ is an even function.

Hence, $f(x)$ is an odd function.

So, $f(x) + f(-x) = 0$

Now, $I = \int_{-\frac{\pi}{2}}^{\frac{\pi}{2}} \left(f(x) + \frac{x^2 \cos x}{1+e^x}\right) dx \quad$ ...(i)

$I = \int_{-\pi/2}^{\pi/2} \left\{f(-x) + \frac{x^2 \cos x}{1+e^{-x}}\right\} dx \quad$ ...(ii)

On adding Eqs. (i) and (ii), we get

$$2I = \int_{-\pi/2}^{\pi/2} x^2 \cos x\, dx = 2\int_0^{\pi/2} x^2 \cos x\, dx$$

$$I = x^2 \sin x \Big|_0^{\pi/2} - \int_0^{\pi/2} 2x \sin x\, dx$$

$$= \frac{\pi^2}{4} - 2\left\{[-x\cos x]_0^{\pi/2} - \int_0^{\pi/2} (-\cos x)\, dx\right\} = \frac{\pi^2}{4} - 2$$

Given that, $\frac{\pi^2}{\alpha^2} - \alpha = \frac{\pi^2}{4} - 2$

$\Rightarrow \quad \alpha = 2$

48. We have, $I = \int_0^1 \left(\frac{dx}{(5+2x-2x^2)(1+e^{(2-4x)})}\right) \quad$ ...(i)

$$= \int_0^1 \frac{dx}{\{5 + 2(1-x) - 2(1-x)^2\}(1+e^{2-4(1-x)})}$$

$I = \int_0^1 \frac{dx}{(5+2x-2x^2)(1+e^{4x-2})} \quad$ ...(ii)

On adding Eqs. (i) and (ii), we get

$$2I = \int_0^1 \frac{dx}{(5+2x-2x^2)}\left\{\frac{1}{(1+e^{2-4x})} + \frac{1}{(1+e^{4x-2})}\right\}$$

$= \int_0^1 \frac{dx}{(5+2x-2x^2)} \quad \left[\because \left\{\frac{1}{e^{2-4x}} + \frac{1}{e^{4x-2}}\right\} = 1\right]$

$\Rightarrow \quad I = \frac{1}{2}\int_0^1 \frac{dx}{(5+2x-2x^2)} \Rightarrow I = \frac{1}{2}\int_0^1 \frac{dx}{-2\left(x^2 - x - \frac{5}{2}\right)}$

$$= -\frac{1}{4}\int_0^1 \frac{dx}{\left[\left(x-\frac{1}{2}\right)^2 - \left(\frac{\sqrt{11}}{2}\right)^2\right]}$$

$$= \left(\frac{-1}{4} \times \frac{1}{2\times\frac{\sqrt{11}}{2}} \log\left|\frac{\left(x-\frac{1}{2}\right) - \left(\frac{\sqrt{11}}{2}\right)}{\left(x-\frac{1}{2}\right) + \left(\frac{\sqrt{11}}{2}\right)}\right|\right)_0^1$$

$$= \frac{2}{4} \times \frac{1}{\sqrt{11}} \log\left|\frac{\sqrt{11}+1}{\sqrt{11}-1}\right|$$

$$= \frac{1}{\sqrt{11}} \log\left(\frac{1+\sqrt{11}}{\sqrt{10}}\right) = \frac{1}{\alpha}\log_e\left(\frac{\alpha+1}{\beta}\right)$$

$\Rightarrow \quad \alpha = \sqrt{11}$ and $\beta = \sqrt{10}$

$\Rightarrow \quad \alpha^4 - \beta^4 = (\sqrt{11})^4 - (\sqrt{10})^4$

$= (11)^{4/2} - (10)^{4/2} = 121 - 100 = 21$

49. Let $I = \int_0^\infty \frac{6}{e^{3x} + 6e^{2x} + 11e^x + 6} dx$

$$= \int_0^\infty \frac{6}{(e^x+1)(e^x+2)(e^x+3)} dx$$

$$= 6\int_0^\infty \left[\frac{1}{2}\cdot\frac{1}{e^x+1} + \frac{(-1)}{e^x+2} + \frac{1/2}{e^x+3}\right] dx$$

[using partial decomposition]

$$= 3\int_0^\infty \frac{1}{e^x+1} dx - 6\int_0^\infty \frac{dx}{e^x+2} + 3\int_0^\infty \frac{dx}{e^x+3}$$

$$= 3\int_0^\infty \frac{e^{-x}\, dx}{e^{-x}+1} - 6\int_0^\infty \frac{e^{-x}\, dx}{1+2e^{-x}} + 3\int_0^\infty \frac{e^{-x}\, dx}{1+3e^{-x}}$$

$$= -3\,[\ln(1+e^{-x})]_0^\infty + 6\cdot\frac{1}{2}[\ln(1+2e^{-x})]_0^\infty + 3\left(\frac{-1}{3}\right)[\ln(1+3e^{-x})]_0^\infty$$

$= 3\ln 2 - 3\ln 3 + \ln 4$

$= 3\ln\frac{2}{3} + \ln 4 = \ln\frac{8}{27} + \ln 4 = \ln\frac{32}{27}$

50. Let $I = \frac{e^{-\frac{\pi}{4}} + \int_0^{\pi/4} e^{-x} \tan^{50} x\, dx}{\int_0^{\pi/4} e^{-x}(\tan^{49} x + \tan^{51} x)\, dx}$

Now, $\int_0^{\pi/4} e^{-x} \tan^{50} x\, dx$

$$= [-e^{-x}\tan^{50} x]_0^{\pi/4} + \int_0^{\pi/4} e^{-x}(50)\tan^{49} x \sec^2 x\, dx$$

$$= -e^{\frac{-\pi}{4}}(1)^{50} + 0 + 50\int_0^{\pi/4} e^{-x}\tan^{49} x(\tan^2 x + 1)\, dx$$

$= -e^{\frac{-\pi}{4}} + 50\int_0^{\pi/4} e^{-x}[\tan^{49} x + \tan^{51} x]\, dx \quad$ ...(i)

Now, $I = \frac{e^{-\frac{\pi}{4}} + \int_0^{\pi/4} e^{-x}\tan^{50} x dx}{\int_0^{\pi/4} e^{-x}(\tan^{49} x + \tan^{51} x)\, dx}$

Using Eq. (i), we get

$$I = \frac{50\int_0^{\pi/4} e^{-x}(\tan^{49} x + \tan^{51} x)\, dx}{\int_0^{\pi/4} e^{-x}(\tan^{49} x + \tan^{51} x)\, dx}$$

$\therefore \quad I = 50$

51. Given, $f:[0,2]\rightarrow R$

$$f(x)=\begin{cases} e^{\min\{x^2,\, x-[x]\}}, & x\in[0,1)\\ e^{[x-\log_e x]}, & x\in[1,2]\end{cases}$$

where $[x]=$ GIF

Now, $\int_0^2 xf(x)dx=\int_0^1 xf(x)dx+\int_1^2 x\, f(x)dx$

$$=\int_0^1 xe^{\min\{x^2,\, x-[x]\}}dx+\int_1^2 e^{[x-\log_e x]}\,dx$$

$$\Rightarrow \int_0^2 x\, f(x)dx=\int_0^1 x\, e^{x^2}dx+\int_1^2 xe^1\, dx$$

$$\left[\begin{array}{l}\because x^2<\{x\} \text{ when, } x\in[0,1)\\ \text{and } x-\log_e x\in[1,2), \text{ when } x\in[1,2]\end{array}\right.$$

$$\Rightarrow \int_0^2 xf(x)dx=\frac{1}{2}\int_0^1(2x)\cdot e^{x^2}dx+e\int_1^2 x\,dx$$

$$=\frac{1}{2}e^{x^2}\Big|_0^1+e^2\frac{x^2}{2}\Big|_1^2$$

$$=\frac{1}{2}(e^1-1)+\frac{e}{2}(4-1)$$

$$=\frac{e-1}{2}+\frac{3e}{2}=\frac{4e-1}{2}=2e-\frac{1}{2}$$

Hence, $\int_0^1 xf(x)\,dx=2e-\frac{1}{2}$

52. Given, $f:R\rightarrow R$

and $\int_0^{\pi/2} f(\sin 2x)\sin x\,dx+\alpha\int_0^{\pi/4} f(\cos 2x)\cdot\cos x\,dx=0$

Let $I_1=\int_0^{\pi/2} f(\sin 2x)\cdot\sin x\,dx$ ...(i)

and $I_2=\int_0^{\pi/4} f(\cos 2x)\cdot\cos dx$

Now, use $x\rightarrow\frac{\pi}{2}-x$ in I_1

$$\Rightarrow I_1=\int_0^{\pi/2} f\left(\sin\left(2\left(\frac{\pi}{2}-x\right)\right)\right)\cdot\sin\left(\frac{\pi}{2}-x\right)dx$$

$$I_1=\int_0^{\pi/2} f(\sin 2x)\cdot\cos x\,dx \quad \text{...(ii)}$$

On adding Eqs. (i) and (ii), we get

$$2I_1=\int_0^{\pi/2} f(\sin 2x)(\sin x+\cos x)dx$$

$$\Rightarrow 2I_1=2\int_0^{\pi/4} f(\sin 2x)\cdot(\sin x+\cos x)dx$$

[if $f(2a-x)=f(x)\Rightarrow\int_0^{2a} f(2a-x)dx=2\int_0^{a} f(2a-x)\,dx$]

$$\Rightarrow I_1=\int_0^{\pi/4} f(\sin 2x)\cdot(\sin x+\cos x)dx \quad \text{...(iii)}$$

Now, $I_2=\int_0^{\pi/4} f(\cos 2x)\cdot\cos x\,dx$

Use $x\rightarrow\frac{\pi}{4}-x$

$$I_2=\int_0^{\pi/4} f(\sin 2x)\cdot\left(\frac{\sin x+\cos x}{\sqrt{2}}\right)dx$$

$$\Rightarrow I_2=\frac{1}{\sqrt{2}}\int_0^{\pi/4} f(\sin 2x)\cdot(\sin x+\cos x)dx$$

$$\Rightarrow I_2=\frac{1}{\sqrt{2}}I_1 \quad \text{[use Eq. (iii)]}$$

$$\Rightarrow \sqrt{2}I_2=I_1$$

$$\Rightarrow I_1=\sqrt{2}I_2 \quad [\because I_1=-\alpha I_2]$$

$$\Rightarrow \alpha=-\sqrt{2}$$

Hence, the value of α is $-\sqrt{2}$.

53. Let $I=\int_{-\log_e 2}^{\log_e 2} e^x(\log_e(e^x+\sqrt{1+e^{2x}}))dx$

Let $e^x=t\Rightarrow e^x dx=dt$

When $x\rightarrow-\log_e 2$, then $t\rightarrow\frac{1}{2}$

When $x\rightarrow\log_e 2$, then $t\rightarrow 2$

$$I=\int_{1/2}^{2}\log_e(t+\sqrt{1+t^2})dt \quad \text{...(i)}$$

Applying integration by part method,

$$I=[t\log_e(t+\sqrt{1+t^2})]_{1/2}^{2}-\int_{1/2}^{2}\frac{t}{t+\sqrt{1+t^2}}\left(1+\frac{2t}{2\sqrt{1+t^2}}\right)dt$$

$$=2\log_e(2+\sqrt{5})-\frac{1}{2}\log_e\left(\frac{1+\sqrt{5}}{2}\right)-\int_{1/2}^{2}\frac{t}{\sqrt{1+t^2}}dt$$

$$=\log_e\left(\frac{(2+\sqrt{5})^2}{\left(\frac{1+\sqrt{5}}{2}\right)^{1/2}}\right)-\frac{1}{2}\int_{1/2}^{2}\frac{2t}{\sqrt{1+t^2}}dt \quad \text{...(ii)}$$

Let $I_1=\int_{1/2}^{2}\frac{2t}{\sqrt{1+t^2}}dt$

Let $1+t^2=\omega\Rightarrow 2tdt=d\omega$

When $t\rightarrow\frac{1}{2}$, then $\omega=\frac{5}{4}$

When $t\rightarrow 2$, then $\omega=5$

$$I_1=\int_{5/4}^{5}\frac{1}{\sqrt{\omega}}d\omega=[2\sqrt{\omega}]_{5/4}^{5}=2\left[\sqrt{5}-\frac{\sqrt{5}}{2}\right]=\sqrt{5}$$

Substitute value of I_1 in Eq. (ii), we get

$$I=\log_e\left(\frac{\sqrt{2}(2+\sqrt{5})^2}{\sqrt{1+\sqrt{5}}}\right)-\frac{\sqrt{5}}{2}$$

54. We have, $\int_0^{t^2}(f(x)+x^2)\,dx=\frac{4}{3}t^3,\ \forall\, t>0$

Differentiate using Leibnitz rule, we get

$$(f(t^2)+t^4)\times 2t=4t^2$$

$$f(t^2)+t^4=2t \Rightarrow f(t^2)=2t-t^4$$

Substitute $\frac{\pi}{2}$ for t, we get

$$f\left(\frac{\pi^2}{4}\right)=2\left(\frac{\pi}{2}\right)-\frac{\pi^4}{16}=\pi\left(1-\frac{\pi^3}{16}\right)$$

55. (c) Let $I=\int_0^{\pi} f(x)\sin x\,dx$ ...(i)

$$=\int_0^{\pi} f(\pi-x)\sin(\pi-x)\,dx$$

$$=\int_0^{\pi} f(\pi-x)\sin x\,dx \quad \text{...(ii)}$$

On adding Eqs. (i) and (ii), we get

$$2I=\int_0^{\pi}[f(x)+f(\pi-x)]\sin x\,dx$$

$$\Rightarrow \quad 2I=\int_0^{\pi}\pi^2\sin x\,dx=\pi^2\int_0^{\pi}\sin x\,dx$$

$$=\pi^2(-\cos x)_0^{\pi}=-\pi^2(-1-1)=2\pi^2$$

$$\Rightarrow \quad I=\pi^2$$

56. Let $I=\int_0^{\alpha}\frac{t^{50}}{1-t}\,dt=-\int_0^{\alpha}\frac{-t^{50}}{1-t}\,dt$

$$=-\int_0^{\alpha}\frac{1-t^{50}}{1-t}\,dt+\int_0^{\alpha}\frac{1}{1-t}\,dt$$

$$=-\int_0^{\alpha}(1+t+t^2+\ldots+t^{49})\,dt-[\log(1-t)]_0^{\alpha}$$

$$=-\left[t+\frac{t^2}{2}+\frac{t^3}{3}+\ldots+\frac{t^{50}}{50}\right]_0^{\alpha}-[\log(1-\alpha)-\log 1]$$

$$=-\left[\alpha+\frac{\alpha^2}{2}+\frac{\alpha^3}{3}+\ldots+\frac{\alpha^{50}}{50}\right]-\log(1-\alpha)$$

$$=-P_{50}(\alpha)-\beta=-(\beta+P_{50}(\alpha))$$

57. We have, $f(x)+\int_3^{x}\frac{f(t)}{t}\,dt=\sqrt{x+1},\ x\ge 3$

$$\Rightarrow \quad f'(x)+\frac{f(x)}{x}=\frac{1}{2\sqrt{x+1}}$$

Let $f(x)=y$,

Then, $\frac{dy}{dx}+\frac{y}{x}=\frac{1}{2\sqrt{x+1}}$

Which is a linear differential equation.

Now, IF $=e^{\int\frac{1}{x}dx}=e^{\log x}=x$

$\therefore$ Solution is given by

$$y\cdot x=\int x\cdot\frac{1}{2\sqrt{x+1}}\,dx+C$$

$$xy=\frac{1}{2}\int\frac{x+1-1}{\sqrt{x+1}}\,dx+C$$

$$xy=\frac{(x+1)^{3/2}}{3}-\sqrt{x+1}+C \quad \text{...(i)}$$

Again, $f(x)+\int_3^{x}\frac{f(t)}{t}\,dt=\sqrt{x+1}$

Put $x=3$, we have

$$f(3)+\int_3^{3}\frac{f(t)}{t}\,dt=\sqrt{3+1}\Rightarrow f(3)+0=2\Rightarrow f(3)=2$$

Putting $x=3$, $f(3)=y=2$ in Eq. (i), we get

$$6=\frac{8}{3}-2+C \Rightarrow C=\frac{16}{3}$$

$$\therefore \quad f(x)=\frac{1}{x}\left[\frac{(x+1)^{3/2}}{3}-\sqrt{x+1}+\frac{16}{3}\right]$$

Now, $12f(8)=\frac{12}{8}\left(\frac{(8+1)^{3/2}}{3}-\sqrt{8+1}+\frac{16}{3}\right)$

$$=\frac{3}{2}\left(9-3+\frac{16}{3}\right)=\frac{3}{2}\times\frac{34}{3}=17$$

58. Let $I=\int_0^{\alpha}\frac{x}{\sqrt{x+\alpha}-\sqrt{x}}\,dx$

$$=\int_0^{\alpha}\frac{x[\sqrt{x+\alpha}+\sqrt{x}]}{\alpha}\,dx$$

$$=\frac{1}{\alpha}\int_0^{\alpha}x\sqrt{x+\alpha}\,dx+\frac{1}{\alpha}\int_0^{\alpha}x^{3/2}dx$$

$$=\frac{1}{\alpha}\int_0^{\alpha}(x+\alpha-\alpha)\sqrt{x+\alpha}\,dx+\frac{1}{\alpha}\int_0^{\alpha}x^{3/2}dx$$

$$=\frac{1}{\alpha}\left[\int_0^{\alpha}(x+\alpha)^{3/2}dx\right]-\int_0^{\alpha}\sqrt{x+\alpha}\,dx+\frac{1}{\alpha}\int_0^{\alpha}x^{3/2}dx$$

$$=\left[\frac{2(x+\alpha)^{5/2}}{5\alpha}\right]_0^{\alpha}-\left[\frac{2}{3}(x+\alpha)^{3/2}\right]_0^{\alpha}+\left[\frac{2x^{5/2}}{5\alpha}\right]_0^{\alpha}$$

$$=\left[\frac{8\sqrt{2}\alpha^{5/2}}{5\alpha}-\frac{2\alpha^{5/2}}{5\alpha}\right]-\left[\frac{2\times 2\sqrt{2}\alpha^{3/2}}{3}-\frac{2\alpha^{3/2}}{3}\right]+\frac{2\alpha^{3/2}}{5}$$

$$=\frac{(24\sqrt{2}-6-20\sqrt{2}+10+6)\,\alpha^{3/2}}{15}=\left(\frac{4\sqrt{2}+10}{15}\right)\alpha^{3/2}$$

But, it is given, $I=\frac{16+20\sqrt{2}}{15}$

$$\therefore \quad \frac{4\sqrt{2}+10}{15}\alpha^{3/2}=\frac{16+20\sqrt{2}}{15}$$

$$\Rightarrow \quad \alpha^{3/2}=\frac{2\sqrt{2}\,[10+4\sqrt{2}]}{10+4\sqrt{2}}$$

$$\Rightarrow \quad \alpha^{3/2}=2\sqrt{2}\Rightarrow\alpha=2$$

59. Let $I=\frac{3(e-1)}{e}\int_1^{2}x^2 e^{[x]+[x^3]}\,dx$,

Since, integration limit is from 1 to 2.

So, $[x]=1$, when $1<x<2$

So, $\int_1^{2}x^2e^{1+[x^3]}\,dx=\int_1^{2}x^2e\,e^{[x^3]}dx$

$$=e\int_1^{2}x^2e^{[x^3]}\,dx$$

$$=e\int_1^{8}\frac{1}{3}e^{[t]}\,dt, \text{ where } t=x^3$$

x	1	2
t	1	8

$$=\frac{e}{3}\left[\int_1^{2}e^{[t]}\,dt+\int_2^{3}e^{[t]}dt+\int_3^{4}e^{[t]}dt+\ldots+\int_7^{8}e^{[t]}dx\right]$$

$$= \frac{e}{3}\left[\int_1^2 e\,dt + \int_2^3 e^2 dt + \int_3^4 e^3 dt + \ldots + \int_7^8 e^7 dt\right]$$

$$= \frac{e^2}{3}(1 + e + e^2 + \ldots + e^6) = \frac{e^2}{3}\left[\frac{e^7 - 1}{e - 1}\right]$$

$$\left[\because S_n = \frac{a(r^n - 1)}{r - 1}, r > 1 \quad \text{Here, } a = 1, r = e, n = 7\right]$$

$$\therefore \quad 1 = \frac{3(e-1)}{e} \times \frac{e^2}{3} \times \left(\frac{e^7 - 1}{e - 1}\right) = e(e^7 - 1) = e^8 - e$$

60. Let $I = \int_{1/2}^{2} \frac{\tan^{-1} x}{x} dx$ ...(i)

Put $x = \frac{1}{t}$, then $dx = \frac{-1}{t^2} dt$

$$\therefore \quad I = \int_2^{1/2} \frac{\tan^{-1}\left(\frac{1}{t}\right)}{\left(\frac{1}{t}\right)}\left(-\frac{1}{t^2}\right)dt = \int_{1/2}^{2} \frac{\tan^{-1}\left(\frac{1}{t}\right)}{t} dt = \int_{1/2}^{2} \frac{\cot^{-1} t}{t} dt \quad \text{...(ii)}$$

Replace t by x,

$$I = \int_{1/2}^{2} \frac{\cot^{-1} x}{x} dx$$

On adding Eqs. (i) and (ii), we get

$$2I = \int_{1/2}^{2} \frac{\tan^{-1} x + \cot^{-1} x}{x} dx = \int_{1/2}^{2} \frac{\left(\frac{\pi}{2}\right)}{x} dx$$

$$\Rightarrow \quad 2I = \frac{\pi}{2}[\log x]_{\frac{1}{2}}^{2} = \frac{\pi}{2}(\log 2 + \log 2)$$

$$\Rightarrow \quad I = \frac{\pi}{2} \log_e 2$$

61. Let $I = \int_1^2 \frac{t^4 + 1}{t^6 + 1} dt = \int_1^2 \frac{t^4 + 1}{(t^2)^3 + 1^3} dt$

$$= \int_1^2 \frac{t^4 + 1}{(t^2 + 1)(t^4 - t^2 + 1)} dt$$

$$= \int_1^2 \frac{dt}{t^2 + 1} + \int_1^2 \frac{t^2 dt}{(t^2 + 1)(t^4 - t^2 + 1)}$$

$$= \int_1^2 \frac{dt}{t^2 + 1} + \frac{1}{3}\int_1^2 \frac{3t^2 dt}{(t^3)^2 + 1}$$

Let $t^3 = u \Rightarrow 3t^2 dt = du$

When, $t = 1 \Rightarrow u = 1$

$t = 2 \Rightarrow u = 8$

$$\therefore \quad I = \int_1^2 \frac{dt}{t^2 + 1} + \frac{1}{3}\int_1^8 \frac{du}{u^2 + 1}$$

$$= [\tan^{-1} t]_1^2 + \frac{1}{3}[\tan^{-1} u]_1^8$$

$$= \tan^{-1} 2 - \frac{\pi}{4} + \frac{1}{3}\tan^{-1} 8 - \frac{\pi}{12}$$

$$= \tan^{-1} 2 + \frac{1}{3}\tan^{-1} 8 - \frac{\pi}{3}$$

62. $f(\alpha) = \int_1^{\alpha} \frac{\log_{10} t}{1 + t} dt, \alpha > 0$

$$f(\alpha) = \int_1^{\alpha} \frac{\log_e t}{\log_e 10\,(1 + t)} dt$$

$$f(e^3) = \int_1^{e^3} \frac{\log_e t\,dt}{\log_e 10\,(1 + t)} \quad \text{...(i)}$$

Put $t = \frac{1}{x} \Rightarrow x = \frac{1}{t} \Rightarrow dt = \frac{-1}{x^2} dx$

$$f(\alpha) = \int_1^{1/\alpha} \frac{-\ln x}{\ln 10\left(1 + \frac{1}{x}\right)}\left(\frac{-1}{x^2}\right)dx = \frac{1}{\ln 10}\int_1^{\frac{1}{\alpha}} \frac{\ln x}{x(x+1)} dx$$

$$f(e^{-3}) = \frac{1}{\ln 10}\int_1^{e^3} \frac{\ln t}{t(t+1)} dt \quad \text{...(ii) [replace } x \text{ by } t]$$

$$\therefore \quad f(e^3) + f(e^{-3}) = \frac{1}{\ln 10}\int_1^{e^3} \frac{\ln t}{1 + t}\left(1 + \frac{1}{t}\right) dt$$

$$= \frac{1}{\ln 10}\int_1^{e^3} \frac{\ln t}{t} dt = \frac{1}{\ln 10}\left[\frac{(\ln t)^2}{2}\right]_1^{e^3}$$

$$= \frac{1}{2\ln 10}(9 - 0) = \frac{9}{2\ln 10}$$

63. $f(x) = \int_0^2 e^{|x - t|} dt$

$$|x - t| = \begin{cases} x - t & : \ 0 < t < x \\ t - x & : \ x < t < 2 \end{cases}$$

$$f(x) = \int_0^x e^{x-t}\,dt + \int_x^2 e^{t-x}\,dt = [-e^{x-t}]_0^x + [e^{t-x}]_x^2$$

$$f(x) = -1 + e^x + \frac{e^2}{e^x} - 1 = e^x + \frac{e^2}{e^x} - 2$$

Now, we know that AM $\geq$ GM

$$\frac{e^x + \frac{e^2}{e^x}}{2} \geq \sqrt{e^x \cdot \frac{e^2}{e^x}}$$

$$\Rightarrow \quad e^x + \frac{e^2}{e^x} \geq 2e$$

$$\Rightarrow \quad \left(e^x + \frac{e^2}{e^x}\right)_{\min} = 2e$$

$$\Rightarrow \quad [(f(x)]_{\min} = 2e - 2 = 2(e - 1)$$

64. Let $I = 16\int_1^2 \frac{dx}{x^3(x^2 + 2)^2}$

$$I = 16\int_1^2 \frac{dx}{x^3 \cdot x^4\left(1 + \frac{2}{x^2}\right)^2}$$

Now, put $1 + \frac{2}{x^2} = t$

$$\Rightarrow \quad (-2)(2)\,x^{-3}\,dx = dt$$

$$\Rightarrow \quad \frac{dx}{x^3} = -\frac{dt}{4}$$

$$\Rightarrow \quad 1 + \frac{2}{x^2} = t \Rightarrow \frac{1}{x^2} = \left(\frac{t-1}{2}\right)$$

Now,

x	1	2
t	3	3/2

So, $I = 16\int_3^{3/2}\left(\frac{t-1}{2}\right)^2\left(\frac{1}{t^2}\right)\left(\frac{-dt}{4}\right)$

$$I = -\int_3^{3/2}\left(\frac{t-1}{t}\right)^2 dt$$

$$I = \int_{3/2}^{3}\left(1+\frac{1}{t^2}-\frac{2}{t}\right)dt$$

$$I = \left[t + \frac{t^{-2+1}}{(-2+1)} - 2\ln t\right]_{3/2}^{3}$$

$$I = \frac{8}{3} - 2\ln 3 - \left(\frac{3}{2}\right) + \frac{2}{3} + 2\,[\ln 3 - \ln 2]$$

$$I = \frac{11}{6} - 2\ln 2 = \frac{11}{6} - \ln 4$$

65. Given $f(x) = \int_0^{x\tan^{-1}x}\frac{e^{(t-\cos t)}}{1+t^{2023}}dt$ ...(i)

On differentiating Eq. (i), we get

$$f'(x) = \frac{e^{x\tan^{-1}x - \cos(x\tan^{-1}x)}}{1+(x\tan^{-1}x)^{2023}}\left(\frac{x}{1+x^2} + \tan^{-1}x\right) \quad \text{...(i)}$$

Also, for $x < 0$, $\tan^{-1}x \in \left(-\frac{\pi}{2}, 0\right)$ ...(ii)

for $x \geq 0$, $\tan^{-1}x \in \left[0, \frac{\pi}{2}\right]$ ...(iii)

From Eqs. (ii) and (iii), $x\tan^{-1}x \geq 0, \forall x \in R$

So, $\frac{e^{x\tan^{-1}x - \cos(x\tan^{-1}x)}}{1+(x\tan^{-1}x)^{2023}} > 0, \forall x \in R$ ...(iv)

$$\left.\begin{array}{l} \text{for } x<0, \frac{x}{1+x^2} + \tan^{-1}x < 0 \\ \text{Now, for } x>0, \frac{x}{1+x^2} + \tan^{-1}x > 0 \\ \text{for } x=0, \frac{x}{1+x^2} + \tan^{-1}x = 0 \end{array}\right\} \quad \text{...(v)}$$

From Eqs. (iv) and (v), we can easily say that $f(x)$ has minima at $x = 0$.

So, minimum value of

$$f(x) = f_{\min} = f(0) = \int_0^0 \frac{e^{(t-\cos t)}}{1+t^{2023}}dt = 0$$

66. Let $f(x) = |100x^2 - 1|$

$\Rightarrow f(-x) = |100(-x)^2 - 1| = |100x^2 - 1| = f(x)$

i.e. $f(x)$ is even function.

$\therefore I = \int_{-0.15}^{0.15} f(x)\,dx = 2\int_0^{0.15} f(x)dx$ ...(i)

Now, $|100x^2 - 1| = \begin{cases} 100x^2 - 1, & 100x^2 - 1 \geq 0 \\ 1 - 100x^2, & 100x^2 - 1 < 0 \end{cases}$

$$= \begin{cases} 100x^2 - 1, & x \in R - (-0.1, 0.1) \\ 1 - 100x^2, & x \in (-0.1, 0.1) \end{cases}$$

$\therefore$ $I = 2\left[\int_0^{0.1}(1-100x^2)dx + \int_{0.1}^{0.15}(100x^2 - 1)dx\right]$

$$= 2\left[\left(x - \frac{100x^3}{3}\right)_0^{0.1} + \left(\frac{100x^3}{3} - x\right)_{0.1}^{0.15}\right]$$

$$= 2\left(0.1 - \frac{100\times 0.001}{3} + \frac{100\times 0.003375}{3} - 0.15 - \frac{100\times 0.001}{3} + 0.1\right)$$

$$= \frac{23}{120} = \frac{k}{3000} \quad \text{[given]}$$

$\Rightarrow$ $k = 575$

67. We have, $\alpha(m,n) = \int_0^2 t^m(1+3t)^n\,dt$

Also, $11\alpha(10,6) + 18\alpha(11,5) = p(14)^6$

$\Rightarrow 11\int_0^2 t^{10}(1+3t)^6 dt + 18\int_0^2 t^{11}(1+3t)^5 dt = p(14)^6$

Using integration by part for expression $t^{10}(1+3t)^6$

$$\Rightarrow 11\left[\left[(1+3t)^6\times\frac{t^{11}}{11}\right]_0^2 - \int_0^2 6(1+3t)^5\times 3\times\frac{t^{11}}{11}dt\right]$$

$$+18\int_0^2 t^{11}(1+3t)^5 dt = P(14)^6$$

$\Rightarrow 7^6\times 2^{11} - 18\int_0^2 t^{11}(1+3t)^5 dt + 18\int_0^2 t^{11}(1+3t)^5 dt = p(14)^6$

$\Rightarrow$ $7^6\times 2^{11} = p(14)^6$

$\Rightarrow$ $(7\times 2)^6\times 2^5 = p(14)^6$

$\Rightarrow$ $p = 2^5 = 32$

68. $\int_0^{2.4}[x^2]\,dx$

$$= \int_0^1[x^2]dx + \int_1^{\sqrt{2}}[x^2]dx + \int_{\sqrt{2}}^{\sqrt{3}}[x^2]\,dx + \int_{\sqrt{3}}^{2}[x^2]\,dx + \int_2^{\sqrt{5}}[x^2]\,dx + \int_{\sqrt{5}}^{2.4}[x^2]\,dx$$

$$= \int_0^1 0dx + \int_1^{\sqrt{2}} 1\,dx + \int_{\sqrt{2}}^{\sqrt{3}} 2dx + \int_{\sqrt{3}}^{2} 3dx + \int_2^{\sqrt{5}} 4dx + \int_{\sqrt{5}}^{2.4} 5dx$$

$$= (\sqrt{2}-1) + 2(\sqrt{3}-\sqrt{2}) + 3(2-\sqrt{3}) + 4(\sqrt{5}-2) + 5(2.4-\sqrt{5})$$

$$= 9 - \sqrt{2} - \sqrt{3} - \sqrt{5}$$

$\Rightarrow \alpha = 9, \beta = -1, \gamma = -1, \delta = -1$

$\therefore \alpha + \beta + \gamma + \delta = 6$

69. Let $I = \frac{2}{\pi}\int_{\pi/6}^{5\pi/6}(8[\operatorname{cosec} x] - 5[\cot x])dx$

For $x \in \left(\frac{\pi}{6}, \frac{5\pi}{6}\right)$, $\operatorname{cosec} x \in [1, 2) \Rightarrow [\operatorname{cosec} x] = 1$

For $x \in \left(\frac{\pi}{6}, \frac{\pi}{4}\right)$, $[\cot x] = 1$

For $x \in \left(\frac{\pi}{4}, \frac{\pi}{2}\right)$, $[\cot x] = 0$

For $x \in \left(\frac{\pi}{2}, \frac{3\pi}{4}\right)$, $[\cot x] = -1$

For $x \in \left(\frac{3\pi}{4}, \frac{5\pi}{6}\right)$, $[\cot x] = -2$

$$\therefore I = \frac{2}{\pi}\int_{\pi/6}^{\pi/4} 8(1)dx - \int_{\pi/6}^{\pi/2} 5(1)dx - \int_{\pi/4}^{3\pi/4} 5(0)dx - \int_{\pi/2}^{5\pi/6} 5(-1)dx - \int_{3\pi/4}^{5\pi/6} 5(-2)dx$$

$$= \frac{2}{\pi} \times 7\pi = 14$$

70. We have, $f(x) = \dfrac{x}{(1+x^n)^{1/n}}$

$$\therefore \quad f(f(x)) = \frac{f(x)}{(1+(f(x))^n)^{1/n}} = \frac{\dfrac{x}{(1+x^n)^{1/n}}}{\left(1+\dfrac{x^n}{1+x^n}\right)^{1/n}} = \frac{x}{(1+2x^n)^{1/n}}$$

$$\Rightarrow f(f(f(x))) = \frac{x}{(1+3x^n)^{1/n}}$$

Similarly, $f^n(x) = \dfrac{x}{(1+nx^n)^{1/n}}$

Now, $\lim\limits_{n\to\infty}\int_0^1 x^{n-2}(f^n(x))dx$

$$\lim_{n\to\infty}\int_0^1 x^{n-2}\frac{x}{(1+nx^n)^{1/n}}dx = \lim_{n\to\infty}\int_0^1 \frac{x^{n-1}}{(1+nx^n)^{1/n}}dx$$

Let $1+nx^n = t \Rightarrow n^2x^{n-1}dx = dt$

When $x=0$, then $t=1$

When $x=1$, then $t=1+n$

$$\therefore \lim_{n\to\infty}\int_1^{1+n}\frac{dt}{n^2(t)^{1/n}} = \lim_{n\to\infty}\frac{1}{n^2}\int_1^{1+n}\frac{dt}{(t)^{1/n}}$$

$$= \lim_{n\to\infty}\frac{1}{n(n-1)}[(1+n)^{1-\frac{1}{n}}-1]$$

On putting $n = \dfrac{1}{h}$, when $n\to\infty$, then $h\to 0$

$$\therefore \quad \lim_{h\to 0}\frac{1}{\frac{1}{h}\left(\frac{1}{h}-1\right)}\left[\left(1+\frac{1}{h}\right)^{1-h}-1\right]$$

$$= \lim_{h\to 0}\frac{1}{\frac{1}{h}\left(\frac{1}{h}-1\right)}\left[1+(1-h)\left(1+\frac{1}{h}\right)+\ldots-1\right]$$

$$= \lim_{h\to 0}\frac{h^2}{1-h}\left[(1-h)\left(1+\frac{1}{h}\right)+\ldots\right]$$

$$= \lim_{h\to 0} h[h+1+\ldots.] = 0$$

71. Let $I = \int_0^1[(x^{21}+x^{14}+x^7)(2x^{14}+3x^7+6)^{1/7}]dx$

$$= \int_0^1[(x^{20}+x^{13}+x^6)x\,(2x^{14}+3x^7+6)^{1/7}]dx$$

$$= \int_0^1[(x^{20}+x^{13}+x^6)(2x^{21}+3x^{14}+6x^7)^{1/7}]dx$$

Put $2x^{21}+3x^{14}+6x^7 = t$

$\Rightarrow (42x^{20}+42x^{13}+42x^6)dx = dt$

$\Rightarrow \quad (x^{20}+x^{13}+x^6)\,dx = \dfrac{1}{42}dt$

Also, when $x=0 \Rightarrow t=0$

and when $x=1 \Rightarrow t = 2+3+6 = 11$

$$\therefore \quad I = \frac{1}{42}\int_0^{11} t^{\frac{1}{7}}dt = \frac{1}{42}\left[\frac{t^{\frac{1}{7}+1}}{\frac{1}{7}+1}\right]_0^{11} = \frac{7}{42\times 8}[11^{8/7}] = \frac{1}{48}(11)^{8/7}$$

$\therefore \quad l = 48, m = 8, n = 7$

So, $l + m + n = 48 + 8 + 7 = 63$

72. Let $L = \lim\limits_{x\to 0}\dfrac{48}{x^4}\displaystyle\int_0^x \frac{t^3}{t^6+1}dt$

$$= \lim_{x\to 0} 48\,\frac{\int_0^x \frac{t^3}{t^6+1}dt}{x^4} \qquad \left[\frac{0}{0}\text{ form}\right]$$

On applying L'Hopital rule, we get

$$L = 48\lim_{x\to 0}\frac{\frac{x^3}{x^6+1}}{4x^3} = 48\times\lim_{x\to 0}\frac{x^3}{x^6+1}\times\frac{1}{4x^3} = 48\times\frac{1}{4}\times\frac{1}{1} = 12$$

73. Let $I = \displaystyle\int_{1/3}^{3}|\log_e x|\,dx$

$$\therefore \quad |\log_e x| = \begin{cases}-\log_e x, & x\in(0,1)\\ \log_e x, & x>1\end{cases}$$

$$= \int_{1/3}^{1}|\log_e x|\,dx + \int_1^3|\log_e x|\,dx$$

$$= -\int_{1/3}^{1}\log_e x\,dx + \int_1^3 \log_e x\,dx$$

$$= \frac{2}{3} - \frac{1}{3}\ln 3 + 3\ln 3 - 2$$

$$= \frac{8}{3}\ln 3 - \frac{4}{3} = \frac{4}{3}(2\ln 3 - \ln e)$$

$$= \frac{4}{3}\ln\left(\frac{3^2}{e}\right) = \frac{m}{n}\log_e\left(\frac{n^2}{e}\right)$$

$\therefore m = 4, n = 3$

$\therefore m^2 + n^2 - 5 = 20$

74. Let $I = \dfrac{8}{\pi}\displaystyle\int_0^{\pi/2}\frac{(\cos x)^{2023}}{(\sin x)^{2023}+(\cos x)^{2023}}dx$ ...(i)

As we know that

$$\int_0^a f(x)\,dx = \int_0^a f(a-x)dx$$

So, $$I = \frac{8}{\pi}\int_0^{\pi/2}\frac{\left[\cos\left(\frac{\pi}{2}-x\right)\right]^{2023}}{\left[\sin\left(\frac{\pi}{2}-x\right)\right]^{2023}+\left[\cos\left(\frac{\pi}{2}-x\right)\right]^{2023}}dx$$

$$\Rightarrow \quad I = \frac{8}{\pi}\int_0^{\pi/2}\frac{(\sin x)^{2023}}{(\cos x)^{2023}+(\sin x)^{2023}}dx \qquad \text{...(ii)}$$

On adding Eqs. (i) and (ii), we get

$$2I = \frac{8}{\pi}\left[\int_0^{\pi/2}\frac{(\cos x)^{2023}+(\sin x)^{2023}}{(\sin x)^{2023}+(\cos x)^{2023}}dx\right]$$

$$\Rightarrow \quad 2I = \frac{8}{\pi}\int_0^{\pi/2} 1 \cdot dx \Rightarrow I = \frac{4}{\pi}[x]_0^{\frac{\pi}{2}}$$

$$\Rightarrow \quad I = \frac{4}{\pi}\left[\frac{\pi}{2} - 0\right] \Rightarrow I = 2$$

75. Let $I = \int_0^3 |x^2 - 3x + 2|\, dx$

Put $x^2 - 3x + 2 = 0 \Rightarrow (x-1)(x-2) = 0 \Rightarrow x = 1, 2$

So, limits of integration breaks at $x = 1, 2$.

i.e. $I = \int_0^1 |x^2 - 3x + 2|dx + \int_1^2 |x^2 - 3x + 2|dx + \int_2^3 |x^2 - 3x + 2|dx$

$$\Rightarrow I = \left(\frac{x^3}{3} - \frac{3x^2}{2} + 2x\right)_0^1 - \left(\frac{x^3}{3} - \frac{3x^2}{2} + 2x\right)_1^2 + \left(\frac{x^3}{3} - \frac{3x^2}{2} + 2x\right)_2^3$$

$$\Rightarrow I = \frac{5}{6} - \left(\frac{2}{3} - \frac{5}{6}\right) + \left(\frac{3}{2} - \frac{2}{3}\right) = \frac{11}{6}$$

$$\therefore \quad 12I = 12 \times \frac{11}{6} = 22$$

76. Given, $x \in \left[0, \frac{\pi}{2}\right]$

and $f(x) + \int_0^x f(t)\sqrt{1 - (\ln f(t))^2}\, dt = e$ ... (i)

On differentiating on both sides, we get

$$f'(x) + f(x)\sqrt{1 - (\ln f(x))^2} = 0$$

$$\Rightarrow \quad f'(x) = -f(x)\sqrt{1 - (\ln f(x))^2}$$

$$\frac{-f'(x)}{f(x)\sqrt{1 - (\ln f(x))^2}} = 1$$

On integrating both sides, we get

$$-\int \frac{f'(x)}{f(x)\sqrt{1 - (\ln f(x))^2}}\, dx = \int 1\, dx$$

Let $\ln f(x) = t$

$$\therefore \quad \frac{1}{f(x)} \cdot f'(x)\, dx = dt$$

$$\therefore \quad -\int \frac{dt}{\sqrt{1 - t^2}} = \int 1 \cdot dx$$

$$\Rightarrow \quad \cos^{-1} t = x + c$$

$$\Rightarrow \quad \cos^{-1}(\ln f(x)) = x + c$$

$$\Rightarrow \quad \cos^{-1}(\ln f(0)) = 0 + c$$

$$\Rightarrow \quad \cos^{-1}(\ln e) = c = \cos^{-1}(1) = c \Rightarrow c = 0$$

$$\therefore \quad \cos^{-1}(\ln f(x)) = x$$

$\because$ From Eq. (i),

$$f(0) + \int_0^x f(t)\sqrt{1 - (\ln f(x))^2}\, dt = e$$

$$f(0) = e$$

$$\therefore \left(6 \ln f\left(\frac{\pi}{6}\right)\right)^2 = \left(6\cos\left(\frac{\pi}{6}\right)\right)^2 = \left(6 \times \frac{\sqrt{3}}{2}\right)^2 = (3\sqrt{3})^2 = 27$$

77. $I = \int_{\pi/4}^{\pi/3} \left(\frac{8\sin x - \sin 2x}{x}\right) dx$

Consider $f(x) = 8\sin x - \sin 2x \Rightarrow f(0) = 0$

Now, $f'(x) = 8\cos x - 2\cos 2x$

$$f''(x) = -8\sin x + 4\sin 2x$$

$$= -8\sin x(1 - \cos x) < 0, \forall\, x \in (0, \pi)$$

$$\therefore \quad f'\left(\frac{\pi}{3}\right) < f'(x) < f'\left(\frac{\pi}{4}\right) \Rightarrow 5 < f'(x) < 4\sqrt{2}$$

$$\therefore \quad \int_0^x 5\,dx < \int_0^x f'(x)dx < \int_0^x 4\sqrt{2}dx$$

$$\Rightarrow \quad 5x < f(x) - f(0) < 4\sqrt{2}x$$

$$\Rightarrow \quad 5 < \frac{f(x)}{x} < 4\sqrt{2} \qquad [\because f(0) = 0]$$

$$\Rightarrow \quad \int_{\pi/4}^{\pi/3} 5\,dx < \int_{\pi/4}^{\pi/3} \frac{f(x)}{x}\,dx < \int_{\pi/4}^{\pi/3} 4\sqrt{2}dx$$

$$\therefore \quad \frac{5\pi}{12} < I < \frac{\sqrt{2}\pi}{3}$$

78. Take first modulus part of the given integral.

$$\int_0^2 |2x^2 - 3x|dx$$

Let $2x^2 - 3x = 0 \Rightarrow x = 0,\ x = 3/2$

$$= \int_0^{3/2} (3x - 2x^2)dx + \int_{3/2}^2 (2x^2 - 3x)dx = \frac{19}{12}$$

Now, take greatest integer function integral.

$$\text{Let } x - \frac{1}{2} = p \Rightarrow \int_{-\frac{1}{2}}^{\frac{3}{2}} [p]dx = \int_0^2 \left[x - \frac{1}{2}\right]dx$$

$$= \int_{-\frac{1}{2}}^{\frac{3}{2}} [p]dx = \int_{-\frac{1}{2}}^{0} (-1) \cdot dx + \int_0^1 (0)dx + \int_1^{\frac{3}{2}} (1) \cdot dx = 0$$

$$\int_0^2 |2x^2 - 3x|dx + \left[x - \frac{1}{2}\right]dx = \frac{19}{12} + 0 = \frac{19}{12}$$

79. Given integral is

$$I = \int_0^{20\pi} (|\sin x| + |\cos x|)^2\, dx;$$

$$I = 40\int_0^{\pi/2} (\sin x + \cos x)^2\, dx \qquad \text{[Jack property]}$$

$$\Rightarrow \quad I = 40\int_0^{\pi/2} (1 + \sin 2x)dx = 40\left[x - \frac{1}{2}\cos 2x\right]_0^{\pi/2}$$

$$\Rightarrow \quad I = 20(\pi + 2)$$

80. $I = \int_0^5 \cos\left(\pi x - \pi\left[\frac{x}{2}\right]\right)dx$

$$\left[\frac{x}{2}\right] = \begin{cases} 0, & 0 \le x < 2 \\ 1, & 2 \le x < 4 \\ 2, & 4 \le x \le 5 \end{cases}$$

Thus, $I = \int_0^2 \cos(\pi x)dx + \int_2^4 \cos(\pi x - \pi)dx + \int_4^5 \cos(\pi x - 2\pi)\, dx$

$$\Rightarrow \quad I = \left[\frac{\sin \pi x}{\pi}\right]_0^2 + \left[\frac{\sin(\pi x - \pi)}{\pi}\right]_2^4 + \left[\frac{\sin(\pi x - 2\pi)}{\pi}\right]_4^5$$

$$\Rightarrow \quad I = 0$$

81. $\int_0^2 (\sqrt{2x}dx - \int_0^2 (\sqrt{1-(x-1)^2})dx$

$$= \int_0^2 \left(1-\frac{y^2}{2}\right)dy - \int_0^1 \sqrt{1-y^2}dy + 1 + I$$

$$\Rightarrow \frac{8}{3} - 2\int_0^1 \sqrt{1-y^2}dy = \frac{2}{3} + 1 - \int_0^1 \sqrt{1-y^2}dy + I$$

$$\Rightarrow \quad I = 1 - \int_0^1 \sqrt{1-y^2}\, dy$$

$$\Rightarrow \quad I = \int_0^1 (1-\sqrt{1-y^2})dy$$

82. Given integral is $\int_0^1 [-8x^2 + 6x - 1]dx$, Take $f(x) = 0$,

When $f(x) = -8x^2 + 6x - 1$.

Then, $x = \frac{1}{4}, \frac{1}{2}$

Put $x = 1$ in $f(x)$ then $y = -3$

Now, find the values of x for the values of $y = -1$ and -2

$$= \int_0^{1/4} (-1)dx + \int_{1/4}^{1/2} 0dx + \int_{1/2}^{3/4} (-1)dx + \int_{3/4}^{\frac{3+\sqrt{17}}{8}} (-2)dx + \int_{\frac{3+\sqrt{17}}{8}}^{1} (-3)dx$$

$$= -[x]_0^{1/4} + 0 - [x]_{1/2}^{3/4} + (-2)[x]_{3/4}^{\frac{3+\sqrt{17}}{8}} + (-3)[x]_{\frac{3+\sqrt{17}}{8}}^{1}$$

Apply the limit,

$$-\left(\frac{1}{4}-0\right) - \left(\frac{3}{4}-\frac{1}{2}\right) - 2\left(\frac{3+\sqrt{17}}{8}-\frac{3}{4}\right) - 3\left(1-\frac{3+\sqrt{17}}{8}\right)$$

$$= -\frac{1}{4} - \frac{1}{4} + \frac{-6-2\sqrt{17}}{8} + \frac{3}{2} - 3 + \frac{9+3\sqrt{17}}{8}$$

$$= \frac{\sqrt{17}-13}{8}$$

83. Let $I = \int_0^\pi \frac{e^{\cos x} \sin x}{(1+\cos^2 x)(e^{\cos x} + e^{-\cos x})} dx$ ...(i)

Using the property, $\int_0^a f(x)\, dx = \int_0^a f(a-x)\, dx$

$$I = \int_0^\pi \frac{e^{\cos(\pi - x)} \sin(\pi - x)}{(1+\cos^2(\pi - x))\, [e^{\cos(\pi - x)} + e^{-\cos(\pi - x)}]} dx$$

$$I = \int_0^\pi \frac{e^{-\cos x} \sin x}{(1+\cos^2 x)(e^{-\cos x} + e^{\cos x})} dx \quad ...(ii)$$

Adding Eqs. (i) and (ii), we get

$$2I = \int_0^\pi \frac{\sin x(e^{\cos x} + e^{-\cos x})}{(1+\cos^2 x)(e^{\cos x} + e^{-\cos x})} dx = \int_0^\pi \frac{\sin x}{(1+\cos^2 x)} dx$$

Let $\cos x = t \Rightarrow -\sin x\, dx = dt$ or $\sin x\, dx = -dt$

When $x \to 0$ then $t \to 1$ and $x \to \pi$ then $t \to -1$

$$\Rightarrow 2I = -\int_1^{-1} \frac{1}{1+t^2} dt \Rightarrow 2I = [\tan^{-1} t]_{-1}^{1}$$

$$\Rightarrow 2I = \tan^{-1}(1) - [\tan^{-1}(-1)]$$

$$= \frac{\pi}{4} - \left(\frac{-\pi}{4}\right) \Rightarrow I = \pi/4$$

84. Let $I = 60\int_0^{\frac{\pi}{2}} \frac{\sin 6x}{\sin x} dx$

$$= 60 \times 2\int_0^{\pi/2} \frac{\sin 3x \cos 3x}{\sin x}$$

$$= 120\int_0^{\frac{\pi}{2}} \frac{(3\sin x - 4\sin^3 x)(4\cos^3 x - 3\cos x)dx}{\sin x}$$

$$= 120\int_0^{\frac{\pi}{2}} (3 - 4\sin^2 x)(4\cos^2 x - 3)\cos x\, dx$$

$$= 120\int_0^{\frac{\pi}{2}} (3 - 4\sin^2 x)(4(1-\sin^2 x) - 3)\cos x\, dx$$

$$= 120\int_0^{\frac{\pi}{2}} (3 - 4\sin^2 x)(1 - 4\sin^2 x)\cos x\, dx$$

Let $\sin x = t$, then $\cos x\, dx = dt$

When, $x \to 0$, then $t \to 0$

When, $x \to \frac{\pi}{2}$, then $t \to 1$

$$= 120\int_0^1 (3-4t^2)(1-4t^2)dt = 120\int_0^1 (3 - 16t^2 + 16t^4)\, dt$$

$$= 120\left[3t - \frac{16t^3}{3} + \frac{16t^5}{5}\right]_0^1 = 120\left[3 - \frac{16}{3} + \frac{16}{5}\right]$$

$$= 120\left[\frac{45-80+48}{15}\right] = 8 \times 13 = 104$$

85. Given integral is

$$f(x) + \int_0^x (x-t)f'(t)\, dt = (e^{2x} + e^{-2x})\cos 2x + \frac{2x}{a} \quad ...(ii)$$

Here, $\quad f(0) = 2$ ...(ii)

Differentiate Eq. (i) w.r.t. x, we get

$$f'(x) + \int_0^x f'(t)dt + xf'(x) - xf'(x)$$
$$= 2(e^{2x} - e^{-2x})\cos 2x - 2(e^{2x} + e^{-2x})\sin 2x + \frac{2}{a}$$

$$\Rightarrow f'(x) + f(x) - f(0)$$
$$= 2(e^{2x} - e^{-2x})\cos 2x - 2(e^{2x} + e^{-2x})\sin 2x + \frac{2}{a}$$

Replace x by 0 we get.

$$\Rightarrow \quad 4 = \frac{2}{a} \Rightarrow a = \frac{1}{2} \quad [\because f'(0) = 4]$$

Therefore, $(2a+1)^5 a^2 = 2^5\left(\frac{1}{2}\right)^2 = 8$

86. Let $I = \frac{24}{\pi}\int_0^{\sqrt{2}} \frac{(2-x^2)}{(x^2+2)\sqrt{4+x^4}} dx$

$$= \frac{24}{\pi}\int_0^{\sqrt{2}} \frac{x^2\left(\frac{2}{x^2}-1\right)}{x\left(x+\frac{2}{x}\right) \times x\sqrt{\frac{4}{x^2}+x^2}}$$

$$= \frac{24}{\pi}\int_0^{\sqrt{2}} \frac{\left(\frac{2}{x^2}-1\right)}{\left(x+\frac{2}{x}\right)\sqrt{\left(x+\frac{2}{x}\right)^2 - 4}} dx$$

Let $x+\frac{2}{x}=p \Rightarrow dp=\left(1-\frac{2}{x^2}\right)dx$

$$I=-\frac{24}{\pi}\int_0^{\sqrt{2}}\frac{dt}{p\sqrt{p^2-4}}$$

$$\therefore \quad I=-\frac{24}{\pi}\times\frac{1}{2}\sec^{-1}\left(\frac{x+\frac{2}{x}}{2}\right)\Bigg|_0^{\sqrt{2}}$$

$$=-\frac{12}{\pi}\left[\sec^{-1}\left(\frac{2\sqrt{2}}{2}\right)-\sec^{-1}(\infty)\right]$$

$$=-\frac{12}{\pi}\left[\frac{\pi}{4}-\frac{\pi}{2}\right]=-\frac{12}{\pi}\left[-\frac{\pi}{4}\right]=3$$

87. We will use King's rule,

$$\int_0^a f(x)\,dx=\int_0^a f(a-x)\,dx$$

Let $I=\frac{48}{\pi^4}\int_0^{\pi}\left(\frac{3\pi x^2}{2}-x^3\right)\frac{\sin x}{1+\cos^2 x}dx$ ...(i)

$$I=\frac{48}{\pi^4}\int_0^{\pi}\left\{\frac{3\pi}{2}(\pi-x)^2-(\pi-x)^3\right\}\frac{\sin(\pi-x)}{1+\cos^2(\pi-x)}dx$$

$$=\frac{48}{\pi^4}\int_0^{\pi}\left\{\frac{3\pi}{2}(\pi-x)^2-(\pi-x)^3\right\}\frac{\sin x}{1+\cos^2 x}dx \quad \text{...(ii)}$$

On adding Eqs. (i) and (ii),

$$2I=\frac{48}{\pi^4}\int_0^{\pi}\frac{\sin x}{1+\cos^2 x}\left[\frac{3\pi x^2}{2}-x^3+\frac{3\pi^3}{2}+\frac{3\pi x^2}{2}-3\pi^2 x-(\pi^3-x^3-3\pi^2 x+3\pi x^2)\right]dx$$

$$\Rightarrow \quad 2I=\frac{48}{\pi^4}\int_0^{\pi}\frac{\sin x}{1+\cos^2 x}\times\frac{\pi^3}{2}dx$$

$$\Rightarrow \quad 2I=\frac{24}{\pi}\int_0^{\pi}\frac{\sin x}{1+\cos^2 x}dx \Rightarrow I=\frac{12}{\pi}\int_0^{\pi}\frac{\sin x}{1+\cos^2 x}dx$$

$$\Rightarrow \quad I=-\frac{12}{\pi}[\tan^{-1}(\cos x)]_0^{\pi} \Rightarrow I=-\frac{12}{\pi}\left[-\frac{\pi}{4}-\frac{\pi}{4}\right]$$

$$\therefore \quad I=\frac{12}{2}=6$$

88. As given integral, do partial fraction using,

$$\frac{1}{(x^2-4)(x^2-1)}=\frac{A}{(x^2-4)}-\frac{B}{(x^2-1)}$$

$$1=A(x^2-1)-B(x^2-4)$$

So, $A=B=\frac{1}{3}$

$$\frac{12}{3}\left[\int_3^b\left(\frac{1}{x^2-4}-\frac{1}{x^2-1}\right)dx\right]=\log\frac{49}{40}$$

$$\frac{12}{3}\left[\frac{1}{4}\log\left|\frac{x-2}{x+2}\right|-\frac{1}{2}\log\left|\frac{x-1}{x+1}\right|\right]_3^b=\log\frac{49}{40}$$

$$\frac{(b-2)(b+1)^2}{(b+2)(b-1)^2}=\frac{49}{40}$$

Use try and error method, when put $b=6$ then LHS = RHS
Therefore, $b=6$

89. Let $I=\int_{-1}^{1}\log(x+\sqrt{x^2+1})dx$

Let $f(x)=\log(x+\sqrt{x^2+1})$

Now, $f(-x)=\log(-x+\sqrt{x^2+1})$

$$=\log\left((\sqrt{x^2+1}-x)\times\left(\frac{\sqrt{x^2+1}+x}{\sqrt{x^2+1}+x}\right)\right)$$

$$=\log\left(\frac{x^2+1-x^2}{\sqrt{x^2+1}+x}\right)=\log\left(\frac{1}{x+\sqrt{x^2+1}}\right)$$

$$=\log 1-\log(x+\sqrt{x^2+1})$$

$$=-\log(x+\sqrt{x^2+1})$$

$$\Rightarrow \quad f(-x)=-f(x)$$

$\because$ $\log(x+\sqrt{x^2+1})$ is an odd function,

$$\therefore \int_{-1}^{1}\log(x+\sqrt{x^2+1})dx=0$$

90. Let $I=\int_{\frac{\pi}{24}}^{\frac{5\pi}{24}}\frac{dx}{1+\sqrt[3]{\tan 2x}}$

$$\because \int_a^b f(x)dx=\int_a^b f(a+b-x)dx \Rightarrow \int_{\frac{\pi}{24}}^{\frac{5\pi}{24}}\frac{dx}{1+\left[\tan 2\left(\frac{\pi}{4}-x\right)\right]^{\frac{1}{3}}}$$

$$I=\int_{\frac{\pi}{24}}^{\frac{5\pi}{24}}\frac{dx}{1+\sqrt[3]{\cot 2x}}=\int_{\frac{\pi}{24}}^{\frac{5\pi}{24}}\frac{\sqrt[3]{\tan 2x}}{1+\sqrt[3]{\tan 2x}}$$

On adding Eqs. (i) and (ii), we get

$$\Rightarrow \quad 2I=\int_{\frac{\pi}{24}}^{\frac{5\pi}{24}}\frac{1+\sqrt[3]{\tan 2x}}{1+\sqrt[3]{\tan 2x}}dx$$

$$\Rightarrow \quad 2I=\int_{\frac{\pi}{24}}^{\frac{5\pi}{24}}1\,dx=[x]_{\frac{\pi}{24}}^{\frac{5\pi}{24}}$$

$$\Rightarrow \quad 2I=\frac{4\pi}{24}$$

$$\therefore \quad I=\frac{\pi}{12}$$

91. $\int_{-2}^{2}|3x^2-3x-6|dx=I$ (say)

$$I=3\int_{-2}^{2}|x^2-x-2|dx$$

$$=3\left[\int_{-2}^{-1}(x^2-x-2)dx+\int_{-1}^{2}(-x^2+x+2)dx\right]$$

$$=3\left[\left(\frac{x^3}{3}-\frac{x^2}{2}-2x\right)_{-2}^{-1}-\left(\frac{x^3}{3}-\frac{x^2}{2}-2x\right)_{-1}^{2}\right]=19$$

92. Given integral $\int_{-\pi}^{\pi} |\pi - |x|| \, dx$

$$= 2\int_0^{\pi} |\pi - |x|| \, dx = 2\int_0^{\pi} |\pi - x| \, dx$$

$$= 2\int_0^{\pi} (\pi - x) dx \qquad [\because x \in (0, \pi)]$$

$$= 2\left[\pi x - \frac{x^2}{2}\right]_0^{\pi} = 2\left[\pi^2 - \frac{\pi^2}{2}\right]$$

$$= 2\left(\frac{\pi^2}{2}\right) = \pi^2$$

93. The integral, $I = \int_1^2 |2x - [3x]| \, dx$

$$= \int_1^{4/3} |2x - 3| \, dx + \int_{4/3}^{5/3} |2x - 4| dx + \int_{5/3}^{2} |2x - 5| dx$$

$$= \int_1^{4/3} (3 - 2x) dx + \int_{4/3}^{5/3} (4 - 2x) \, dx + \int_{5/3}^{2} (5 - 2x) \, dx$$

$$= [3x - x^2]_1^{4/3} + [4x - x^2]_{4/3}^{5/3} + [5x - x^2]_{5/3}^{2}$$

$$= \left(4 - \frac{16}{9} - 3 + 1\right) + \left(\frac{20}{3} - \frac{25}{9} - \frac{16}{3} + \frac{16}{9}\right) + \left(10 - 4 - \frac{25}{3} + \frac{25}{9}\right)$$

$$= (2 + 6) + \left(\frac{20}{3} - \frac{16}{3} - \frac{25}{3}\right) + \left(-\frac{16}{9} - \frac{25}{9} + \frac{16}{9} + \frac{25}{9}\right)$$

$$= 8 - \frac{21}{3} = 8 - 7 = 1$$

Exercise 2 - JEE Advanced Pattern

1. Hence, $f(x) = x^2 + ax - b$

The solution of $f(x) =$ minimum $f(x)$ is $x = \frac{-a}{2}$.

Given, $f(x)_{\text{minimum}}$ is at $x = 0$.

$\Rightarrow \quad \frac{-a}{2} = 0$ or $a = 0$

$\therefore \quad f(x) = x^2 - b = 0$ has roots α and β.

$\Rightarrow \quad \alpha = \sqrt{b}$ and $\beta = -\sqrt{b}$

$\Rightarrow \quad \int_{\alpha}^{\beta} x^3 dx = \int_{\sqrt{b}}^{-\sqrt{b}} x^3 dx = 0$

$$\left[\int_{-a}^{a} f(x)dx = 0, \text{ when } f(-x) = f(x)\right]$$

2. Here, $-4 \le x \le 4 \Rightarrow 0 \le \frac{x^2}{17} < 1$

$\therefore \left[\frac{x^2}{17}\right] = 0$ and $\sin^{-1}(\sin x)$ is an odd function.

Let, $I = \int_{-4}^{4} \frac{\sin^{-1}(\sin x)}{(1 + x^2) \times 1} dx + \int_{-4}^{4} \frac{\cos^{-1}(\cos x)}{(1 + x^2) \times 1} dx$

$$= 0 + 2\int_0^4 \frac{\cos^{-1}(\cos x)}{(1 + x^2)} dx$$

$$I = 2\left[\int_0^{\pi} \frac{x}{1 + x^2} dx + \int_{\pi}^{4} \frac{\pi - x}{(1 + x^2)} dx\right]$$

$$= \log(1 + \pi^2) + 2\pi(\tan^{-1} x)_{\pi}^{4} - [\log(1 + 16) - \log(1 + \pi^2)]$$

$$= \log(1 + \pi^2) + 2\pi(\tan^{-1} 4 - \tan^{-1} \pi) - \log \frac{17}{1 + \pi^2}$$

$$= \log \frac{(1 + \pi^2) \cdot (1 + \pi^2)}{17} + 2\pi \tan^{-1}\left[\tan^{-1}\left(\frac{4 - \pi}{1 + 4\pi}\right)\right]$$

$$= \log\left(\frac{(1 + \pi^2)^2}{17}\right) + 2\pi \tan^{-1}\left(\frac{4 - \pi}{1 + 4\pi}\right)$$

On comparing with $\log\left(\frac{(1 + \pi^2)^2}{a}\right) + b\pi \tan^{-1}\left(\frac{c - \pi}{1 + c\pi}\right)$, we get

$$a = 17, b = 2 \text{ and } c = 4$$

$\therefore \quad a - (2b + c) = 17 - 8 = 9$ and $\frac{a - 5}{c} = 3$

Thus, the number of ways to distribute 9 distinct bijective into 3 persons equally is $\frac{9!}{(3!)^3}$.

3. $I = \int_0^{3\pi/4} (\sin x + \cos x) \, dx + \int_0^{3\pi/4} \underset{\text{I}}{x} \underset{\text{II}}{(\sin x - \cos x)} \, dx$

$$= \int_0^{3\pi/4} (\sin x + \cos x) \, dx + [x(-\cos x - \sin x)]_0^{3\pi/4} + \int_0^{3\pi/4} (\sin x + \cos x) \, dx$$

$$= 2\int_0^{3\pi/4} (\sin x + \cos x) \, dx + 0 = 2[-\cos x + \sin x]_0^{3\pi/4}$$

$$= 2\left[+\frac{1}{\sqrt{2}} + \frac{1}{\sqrt{2}} + 1\right] = 2(\sqrt{2} + 1)$$

$$= 2 \tan \frac{3\pi}{8}$$

4. We have, $C_n = \int_{\frac{1}{n+1}}^{\frac{1}{n}} \frac{\tan^{-1}(nx)}{\sin^{-1}(nx)} dx$

$$C_n = \frac{1}{n} \int_{\frac{n}{n+1}}^{1} \frac{\tan^{-1}(t)}{\sin^{-1}(t)} dt \qquad [\text{put } nx = t]$$

Now, $L = \lim_{n \to \infty} n^2 \cdot C_n = \lim_{n \to \infty} n \int_{\frac{n}{n+1}}^{1} \frac{\tan^{-1} t}{\sin^{-1} t} dt \, (\infty \times 0)$

$$L = \frac{\int_{\frac{n}{n+1}}^{1} \frac{\tan^{-1} t}{\sin^{-1} t} dt}{\frac{1}{n}} \qquad \left[\frac{0}{0} \text{ form}\right]$$

Applying Leibnitz rule,

$$L = \lim_{n \to \infty} \frac{0 - \frac{\tan^{-1} \frac{n}{n+1}}{\sin^{-1} \frac{n}{n+1}} \left(\frac{1}{(n+1)^2}\right)}{-\frac{1}{n^2}} = \frac{\pi}{4} \cdot \frac{2}{\pi} = \frac{1}{2}$$

5. $\int_{-3}^{3} \frac{t^2 \sin 2t}{t^2 + 1} dt = 0$ as the integrand is an odd function.

Also, $\int_0^1 \frac{dt}{t^2 + 2t \cos \alpha + 1}$

$$= \frac{1}{\sin \alpha} \tan^{-1} \frac{t + \cos \alpha}{\sin \alpha} \Bigg|_0^1 = \frac{\alpha}{2 \sin \alpha}$$

Thus, the given equation reduces to

$$x^2 \cdot \frac{\alpha}{2 \sin \alpha} - 2 = 0 \Rightarrow x = \pm 2\sqrt{\frac{\sin \alpha}{\alpha}}$$

6. $T_r = \dfrac{1}{\sqrt{\dfrac{r}{n}}\cdot n\left(3\sqrt{\dfrac{r}{n}}+4\right)^2}$

$$S = \frac{1}{n}\sum_{1}^{4n}\frac{1}{\left(3\sqrt{\dfrac{r}{n}}+4\right)^2\cdot\sqrt{\dfrac{r}{n}}} = \int_0^4 \frac{dx}{\sqrt{x}\,(3\sqrt{x}+4)^2}$$

Put $3\sqrt{x}+4 = t \Rightarrow \dfrac{3}{2}\cdot\dfrac{1}{\sqrt{x}}\,dx = dt$

$$= \frac{2}{3}\int_4^{10}\frac{dt}{t^2} = \frac{2}{3}\left[\frac{1}{t}\right]_{10}^4 = \frac{2}{3}\left[\frac{1}{4}-\frac{1}{10}\right] = \frac{2}{3}\cdot\frac{6}{40} = \frac{1}{10}$$

7. Given, $f'(x) = f(x) \Rightarrow f(x) = Ce^x$

Since, $f(0) = 1 \quad \therefore \quad 1 = f(0) = C$

$\therefore f(x) = e^x$ and hence $g(x) = x^2 - e^x$

Thus, $\int_0^1 f(x)\,g(x)\,dx = \int_0^1 (x^2e^x - e^{2x})\,dx$

$$= [x^2e^x]_0^1 - 2\int_0^1 xe^x\,dx - \left[\frac{e^{2x}}{2}\right]_0^1$$

$$= (e-0) - 2\,[(xe^x)_0^1 - (e^x)_0^1\,] - \frac{1}{2}(e^2-1)$$

$$= (e-0) - 2\,[(e-0)-(e-1)] - \frac{1}{2}(e^2-1)$$

$$= e - \frac{1}{2}e^2 - \frac{3}{2}$$

8. Here, $f'(x) = \dfrac{1}{\sqrt{1+g^2(x)}}\,g'(x);$

Now, $f'\left(\dfrac{\pi}{2}\right) = \dfrac{g'(\pi/2)}{\sqrt{1+g^2(\pi/2)}};$

$$g\left(\frac{\pi}{2}\right) = 0 = g'\left(\frac{\pi}{2}\right)$$

But $g'(x) = [1+\sin(\cos^2 x)](-\sin x)$

$$g'\left(\frac{\pi}{2}\right) = 1(-1) = -1$$

Hence, $f'\left(\dfrac{\pi}{2}\right) = -1$ as $h'(0^+) = -1$

9. $I(a) = \int_0^{\pi}\left(\dfrac{x^2}{a^2} + a^2\sin^2 x + 2x\sin x\right)dx \quad \left[\because \int_0^{\pi} x\sin x\,dx = \pi\right]$

$$\therefore \quad I(a) = \frac{\pi^3}{3a^2} + \frac{\pi a^2}{2} + 2\pi$$

$$= \pi\left[\frac{\pi^2}{3a^2} + \frac{a^2}{2}\right] + 2\pi$$

$$= \pi\left[\left(\frac{\pi}{\sqrt{3}a} - \frac{a}{\sqrt{2}}\right)^2 + \frac{2\pi}{\sqrt{6}}\right] + 2\pi$$

$I(a)$ is minimum when $\dfrac{\pi}{\sqrt{3}a} = \dfrac{a}{\sqrt{2}} \Rightarrow a^2 = \pi\sqrt{\dfrac{2}{3}}$

$$\Rightarrow \quad a = \sqrt{\pi\sqrt{\frac{2}{3}}}$$

Also, $[I(a)]_{\min} = 2\pi + \pi^2\sqrt{\dfrac{2}{3}}$

10. Consider $I = \int_{-1/x}^{1/x}\dfrac{\ln(1+t^2)}{1+e^t}\,dt$ ...(i)

$$\Rightarrow \quad I = \int_{-1/x}^{1/x}\frac{\ln(1+t^2)}{1+e^{-t}}\,dt$$

$I = \int_{-1/x}^{1/x}\dfrac{\ln(1+t^2)\,e^t}{1+e^t}\,dt$ ...(ii)

On adding Eqs. (i) and (ii), we get

$$2I = \int_{-1/x}^{1/x}\ln(1+t^2)\,dt = 2\int_0^{1/x}\ln(1+t^2)\,dt$$

$$\Rightarrow \quad I = \int_0^{1/x}\ln(1+t^2)\,dt$$

Hence, $l = \lim_{x\to\infty} x^3\int_0^{1/x}\ln(1+t^2)\,dt$

$= \lim_{x\to\infty}\dfrac{\int_0^{1/x}\ln(1+t^2)\,dt}{x^{-3}}$ $\quad\left[\dfrac{0}{0}\text{ form}\right]$

Using L' Hospital's rule,

$$l = \lim_{x\to 0}\frac{x^4\ln\left(1+\dfrac{1}{x^2}\right)\cdot\left(-\dfrac{1}{x^2}\right)}{-3}$$

$$= \frac{1}{3}\lim_{x\to\infty} x^2\ln\left(1+\frac{1}{x^2}\right)$$

$= \dfrac{1}{3}\lim_{x\to\infty}\ln\left(1+\dfrac{1}{x^2}\right)^{x^2}$ $\quad(1^{\infty}$ form)

$$= \lim_{x\to\infty}\frac{1}{3}\,x^2\left(1+\frac{1}{x^2}-1\right) = \frac{1}{3}$$

11. Put $\pi x = t \Rightarrow dx = \dfrac{dt}{\pi}$

$\therefore \quad I = \dfrac{1}{\pi}\cdot\dfrac{\pi}{\pi}\int_0^{2008\pi} t\,|\sin t|\,dt = \dfrac{1}{\pi}\int_0^{2008\pi} t\,|\sin t|\,dt$ ...(i)

$\Rightarrow \quad I = \dfrac{1}{\pi}\int_0^{2008\pi}(2008\pi - t)\,|\sin t|\,dt$ ...(ii)

On adding Eqs. (i) and (ii), we get

$$2I = \frac{2008\pi}{\pi}\int_0^{2008\pi}|\sin t|\,dt = (2008)^2\cdot\int_0^{\pi}|\sin t|\,dt$$

$$\Rightarrow \quad I = (2008)^2$$

$$\Rightarrow \quad \sqrt{I} = 2008$$

12. Let $I = \int_{-1/\sqrt{3}}^{1/\sqrt{3}}\dfrac{x^4}{1-x^4}\cos^{-1}\dfrac{2x}{1+x^2}\,dx$ ...(i)

$\Rightarrow I = \int_{-1/\sqrt{3}}^{1/\sqrt{3}}\dfrac{x^4}{1-x^4}\cos^{-1}\left(\dfrac{-2x}{1-x^4}\right)dx$ [using King's property]

$\Rightarrow \quad I = \int_{-1/\sqrt{3}}^{1/\sqrt{3}}\dfrac{x^4}{1-x^4}\left(\pi - \cos^{-1}\dfrac{2x}{1-x^4}\right)dx$ ...(ii)

On adding Eqs. (i) and (ii), we get

$$\therefore \quad 2I = \pi\int_{-1/\sqrt{3}}^{1/\sqrt{3}}\frac{x^4}{1-x^4}\,dx$$

$$\Rightarrow \quad 2I = 2\pi\int_0^{1/\sqrt{3}}\frac{x^4}{1-x^4}\,dx$$

$$\therefore \quad k = \pi$$

13. $\lim_{\lambda\to 0}\left(\int_0^1 (1+x)^\lambda\,dx\right)^{1/\lambda} = \lim_{\lambda\to 0}\left(\left|\frac{(1+x)^{\lambda+1}}{\lambda+1}\right|_0^1\right)^{1/\lambda}$

$= \lim_{\lambda\to 0}\left(\frac{2^{\lambda+1}-1}{\lambda+1}\right)^{1/\lambda}$ $[1^\infty \text{ form}]$

$= e^{\lim_{\lambda\to 0}\frac{1}{\lambda}\left(\frac{2^{\lambda+1}-1-\lambda-1}{\lambda+1}\right)} = e^{\lim_{\lambda\to 0}\left(\frac{2^{\lambda+1}-2-\lambda}{\lambda(\lambda+1)}\right)}$

$= e^{\lim_{\lambda\to 0}\left(\frac{2(2^\lambda-1)}{\lambda}-1\right)} = e^{2\ln 2-1} = e^{\ln\left(\frac{4}{e}\right)} = \frac{4}{e}$

14. $(f(x))^{2014} = 1 + \int_0^x f(t)dt$

On putting $x = 0$, we get

$f(0) = 1$

Using Liebnitz's rule,

$2014\,(f(x))^{2013}\ f'(x) = f(x)$

$2014(f(x))^{2012}\ f'(x) = 1$

Let $y = f(x)$

$\Rightarrow \quad 2014\int y^{2012}dy = \int dx$

$\Rightarrow \quad \frac{2014y^{2013}}{2013} = x + C$

$(f(x))^{2013} = \frac{2013}{2014}(x+C)$

$f(0) = 1 = \frac{2013}{2014}(C) \Rightarrow C = \frac{2014}{2013}$

$(f(2014))^{2013} = \frac{2013}{2014}(2014 + C)$

$= 2013 + \frac{2013}{2014}C = 2014$

15. The given integral can be equal only, if $a > \tan^2 1$

$\int_0^a [\tan^{-1}\sqrt{x}]dx = \int_0^{\tan^2 1}[\tan^{-1}\sqrt{x}]\,dx + \int_{\tan^2 1}^a [\tan^{-1}\sqrt{x}]\,dx$

$= 0 + 1\cdot\int_{\tan^2 1}^a dx = a - \tan^2 1$

$\int_0^a [\cot^{-1}\sqrt{x}]\,dx = \int_0^{\cot^2 1}[\cot^{-1}\sqrt{x}]\,dx + \int_{\cot^2 1}^a [\cot^{-1}\sqrt{x}]\,dx$

$= \int_0^{\cot^2 1} 1\,dx + 0$

$= 1\,(\cot^2 1 - 0)$

$\Rightarrow \quad a = \tan^2 1 + \cot^2 1$

$= \frac{\sin^2 1}{\cos^2 1} + \frac{\cos^2 1}{\sin^2 1} = \frac{1-\cos 2}{1+\cos 2} + \frac{1+\cos 2}{1-\cos 2}$

$= \frac{(1-\cos 2)^2 + (1+\cos 2)^2}{\sin^2 2} = \frac{2\,(1+\cos^2 2)}{\sin^2 2}$

$= \frac{2\,(2+2\cos^2 2)}{2\sin^2 2} = \frac{2(3+\cos 4)}{(1-\cos 4)}$

16. $f'(x) + f'(2-x) = 0$

On integrating, we get

$f(x) - f(2-x) = \lambda$

On putting $x = 1$, we get

$\lambda = 0$

$\therefore f(x) = f(2-x)$ or $f(1+x) = f(1-x)$,

Therefore, $f(x)$ is symmetrical about line $x = 1$.

$\therefore \quad f(1) = 4$

$\therefore \quad y = f(x) = (x-1)^2 + 4$

$\int_1^3 \frac{dx}{(x-1)^2+4} = \left[\frac{1}{2}\tan^{-1}\left(\frac{x-1}{2}\right)\right]_1^3$

$= \frac{1}{2}[\tan^{-1}1 - \tan^{-1}0] = \frac{\pi}{8}$

17. Let

$$S = \lim_{n\to\infty}\frac{\pi}{n}\left(\frac{1}{\sin\frac{\pi(n+1)}{4n}} + \frac{1}{\sin\frac{\pi(n+2)}{4n}} + \frac{1}{\sin\frac{\pi(n+3)}{4n}} + \dots + \frac{1}{\sin\frac{\pi(n+n)}{4n}}\right)$$

$\Rightarrow S = \lim_{n\to\infty}\frac{\pi}{n}\sum_{r=1}^{n}\frac{1}{\sin\frac{(n+r)\pi}{4n}}$

$= \pi\lim_{n\to\infty}\frac{1}{n}\sum_{r=1}^{n}\frac{1}{\sin\left(\frac{\pi}{4}+\frac{\pi r}{4n}\right)} = \pi\int_0^1 \frac{dx}{\sin\left(\frac{(1+x)\pi}{4}\right)}$

$S = \pi\int_0^1 \operatorname{cosec}\left(\frac{(x+1)\pi}{4}\right)dx$

$= \pi\times\frac{4}{\pi}\left[\ln\left(\tan\frac{(x+1)}{8}\right)\right]_0^1 = 4\,[0 - \ln(\sqrt{2}-1)]$

Hence, $S = 4\ln(\sqrt{2}+1)$

18. $f(x) = x^5 + 5x - 1$

$f(1) = 5 \Rightarrow f^{-1}(5) = 1$

$f(2) = 41 \Rightarrow f^{-1}(41) = 2$

On putting $f^{-1}(x) = t$

$\therefore \quad I = \int_1^2 \frac{f'(t)}{t^5+5t}\,dt = \int_1^2 \frac{5t^4+5}{t^5+5t}\,dt$

$= \ln(t^5+5t)]_1^2$

$= \ln 42 - \ln 6$

$= \ln 7$

19. $\int_{-(n+1)}^{-n} \frac{\left|\frac{2[x]}{2x-[x]}\right|}{\frac{2[x]}{2x-[x]}}\,dx$

$= \int_{-(n+1)}^{-n} \frac{\left|\frac{-2(n+1)}{2x+(n+1)}\right|}{\frac{-2(n+1)}{2x+(n+1)}}\,dx$

$= -\int_{-(n+1)}^{-n}\frac{2x+n+1}{|2x+n+1|}\,dx$

$= -\frac{1}{2}[|2x+n+1|]_{-(n+1)}^{-n}$ $\left[\because \int\frac{x}{|x|}\,dx = |x| + C\right]$

$= -\frac{1}{2}[|1-n| - |1+n|]$

$$= \begin{cases} 0, \text{ if } n = 0 \\ -\dfrac{1}{2}(n-1-n-1), \text{ if } n \geq 1 \end{cases}$$

$$= \begin{cases} 0, & \text{if } n = 0 \\ 1, & \text{if } n \geq 1 \end{cases}$$

$$\therefore \int_{-10}^{0} f(x)\,dx = \int_{-10}^{-9} f(x)\,dx + \int_{-9}^{-8} f(x)\,dx + \ldots + \int_{-1}^{0} f(x)\,dx$$

$$= 1 + 1 + \ldots + 1 + 0 = 9$$

20. $I = 2^{-10} \int_0^{\pi/2} (\sin 2x)^{10}\, dx$

On putting $2x = t \Rightarrow dx = \dfrac{dt}{2}$

$$I = \frac{2^{-10}}{2} \int_0^{\pi} (\sin t)^{10}\, dt$$

$$= 2^{-10} \int_0^{\pi/2} (\sin t)^{10}\, dt$$

$$I = 2^{-10} \int_0^{\pi/2} (\cos t)^{10}\, dt$$

$$2I = 2^{-10} \int_0^{\pi/2} ((\sin x)^{10} + (\cos x)^{10})\, dx$$

$$I = 2^{-11} \int_0^{\pi/2} ((\sin x)^{10} + (\cos x)^{10})\, dx$$

$\Rightarrow \quad n = 11$

21. (a) $I = \int_0^{\pi/2} \ln(\cot x)\, dx \Rightarrow I = \int_0^{\pi/2} \ln(\tan x)\, dx$

$$I = -\int_0^{\pi/2} \ln(\cot x)\, dx \Rightarrow I = -I \Rightarrow I = 0$$

(b) $I = \int_0^{2\pi} \sin^3 x\, dx = -\int_0^{2\pi} \sin^3 x\, dx \Rightarrow I = 0$

(c) At $x = \dfrac{1}{t}$, $I = \displaystyle\int_e^{1/e} \frac{-(1/t^2)\,dt}{-1/t(\ln t)^{1/3}} = -\int_{1/e}^{e} \frac{dt}{t(\ln t)^{1/3}}$

$$I = -1 \text{ or } I = 0$$

(d) $\sqrt{\dfrac{1+\cos 2x}{2}} > 0 \Rightarrow \displaystyle\int_0^{\pi} \sqrt{\frac{1+\cos 2x}{2}}\, dx > 0$

22.

> **Decoding the Question**
> There will be atleast one root in (α, β) if $f(\alpha) \cdot f(\beta) < 0$
> Now, in the problem, $f(-1) \cdot f(0) = -6 < 0$ and
> $f(0) + f(1) = -6 < 0$

$$I = \int_0^1 (10x^4 - 3x^2 - 1)\, dx = [2x^5 - x^3 - x]_0^1 = 0$$

Since, $f(x)$ is even, hence must have a root in $(-1, 0)$.

23. We have, $I_1 = \int_0^{\pi/2} \cos(\pi \sin^2 x)\, dx$

$$I_1 = \int_0^{\pi/2} \cos(\pi \cos^2 x)\, dx$$

On adding, $2I_1 = \int_0^{\pi/2} \cos(\pi \sin^2 x) + \cos(\pi \cos^2 x)\, dx$

$$= \int_0^{\pi/2} 2\cos\left(\frac{\pi}{2}\right) \cdot \cos\left(\frac{\pi}{2} \cos 2x\right) dx = 0$$

$\Rightarrow \quad I_1 = 0 \quad \ldots$(i)

Now, $\quad I_2 = \int_0^{\pi/2} \cos\{\pi(1 - \cos 2x)\}\, dx$

$$= -\int_0^{\pi/2} \cos(\pi \cos 2x)\, dx$$

$$= -\frac{1}{2} \int_0^{\pi} \cos(\pi \cos t)\, dt \quad [\text{put } 2x = t]$$

$$= -\frac{2}{2} \int_0^{\pi/2} \cos(\pi \cos t)\, dt = I_3$$

$\Rightarrow \quad I_2 + I_3 = 0$

$$I_3 = -\int_0^{\pi/2} \cos(\pi \sin t)\, dt$$

$\therefore \quad I_2 + I_3 = 0 \quad \ldots$(ii)

Hence, $\quad I_1 + I_2 + I_3 = 0$

24. $f(x) = 2\int_0^1 \underbrace{(1-t)}_{\text{I}} \underbrace{\cos(xt)}_{\text{II}}\, dt$

$$= 2\left[(1-t)\frac{\sin xt}{x}\Bigg|_0^t + \frac{1}{x}\int_0^1 \sin xt\, dt\right] = 2\left[\left|0 - \frac{1}{x^2}\cos xt\right|_0^1\right]$$

$f(x) = 2\left[\dfrac{1 - \cos x}{x^2}\right] \qquad (x \neq 0)$

If $x = 0$, then $f(x) = \int_{-1}^{1} (1 - |t|)\, dt = 2\int_0^1 (1-t)\, dt = 1$

$\therefore$ Option (c) is correct.

Hence, $f(x) = \begin{cases} 2\left(\dfrac{1-\cos x}{x^2}\right), & \text{if } x \neq 0 \\ 1, & \text{if } x = 0 \end{cases}$

$\therefore$ f is continuous at $x = 0$.

$\therefore$ Option (d) is correct.

25. Given, $f(f(x)) = -x + 1$

Replacing x by $f(x)$, we get

$$f(f(f(x))) = -f(x) + 1$$

$$f(1-x) = -f(x) + 1$$

$$f(x) + f(1-x) = 1 \quad \ldots\text{(i)}$$

Now, $\mathcal{J} = \int_0^1 f(x)\, dx = \int_0^1 f(1-x)\, dx$ (using King's property)

$\Rightarrow \quad 2\mathcal{J} = \int_0^1 (f(x) + f(1-x))\, dx$

$\Rightarrow \quad 2\mathcal{J} = \int_0^1 dx = 1 \Rightarrow \mathcal{J} = \dfrac{1}{2}$

Put $x = \dfrac{1}{4}$ in Eq. (i),

$$f\left(\frac{1}{4}\right) + f\left(1 - \frac{1}{4}\right) = 1 \Rightarrow f\left(\frac{1}{4}\right) + f\left(\frac{3}{4}\right) = 1$$

Now, $I = \displaystyle\int_0^{\pi/2} \frac{\sin x}{(\sin x + \cos x)^3}\, dx$

$$I = \int_0^{\pi/2} \frac{\sin\left(\frac{\pi}{2} - x\right)}{\left(\sin\left(\frac{\pi}{2} - x\right) + \cos\left(\frac{\pi}{2} - x\right)\right)^3}\, dx$$

$$\Rightarrow \quad I = \int_0^{\pi/2} \frac{\cos x}{(\cos x + \sin x)^3}\, dx$$

$$\therefore \; 2I = \int_0^{\pi/2} \frac{1}{(\sin x + \cos x)^2}\, dx = \frac{1}{2}\int_0^{\pi/2} \frac{dx}{\left(\frac{1}{\sqrt{2}}\sin x + \frac{1}{\sqrt{2}}\cos x\right)^2}$$

$$= \frac{1}{2}\int_0^{\pi/2} \frac{dx}{\sin^2\left(\frac{\pi}{4} + x\right)}$$

$$= \frac{1}{2}\int_0^{\pi/2} \text{cosec}^2\left(\frac{\pi}{4}+x\right)dx = -\frac{1}{2}\left[\cot\left(\frac{\pi}{4}+x\right)\right]_0^{\pi/2}$$

$$= -\frac{1}{2}[-1-1] = 1$$

$$\Rightarrow \quad I = \frac{1}{2}$$

26. We have, $f(x) = x^2 + ax^2 + bx^3$

where, $\quad a = \int_{-1}^{1} t\,f(t)\,dt$ and $b = \int_{-1}^{1} f(t)\,dt$

Now, $\quad a = \int_{-1}^{1} t\,[(a+1)\,t^2 + bt^3]\,dt$

$$\Rightarrow \quad a = 2b\int_0^1 t^4 dt = \frac{2b}{5} \quad \text{...(i)}$$

Again, $\quad b = \int_{-1}^{1} f(t)\,dt = \int_{-1}^{1} ((a+1)\,t^2 + bt^3)\,dt$

$$\Rightarrow \quad b = 2\int_0^1 (a+1)\,t^2\,dt$$

$$\Rightarrow \quad b = \frac{2(a+1)}{3} \quad \text{...(ii)}$$

From Eqs. (i) and (ii), $\frac{5a}{2} = \frac{2(a+1)}{3}$

$$\Rightarrow \quad \left(\frac{5}{2}-\frac{2}{3}\right)a = \frac{2}{3} \Rightarrow \frac{11}{6}a = \frac{2}{3}$$

$$\Rightarrow \quad a = \frac{4}{11} \text{ and } b = \frac{10}{11}$$

Hence, $\quad \int_{-1}^{1} t\,f(t)\,dt = \frac{4}{11}$ and $\int_{-1}^{1} f(t)\,dt = \frac{10}{11}$

$\therefore$

$$f(x) = (a+1)\,x^2 + bx^3$$

$$f(1) = (a+1) + b$$

$$f(-1) = (a+1) - b$$

$$\Rightarrow \quad f(1) + f(-1) = 2(a+1) = \frac{30}{11}$$

and $\quad f(1) - f(-1) = 2b = \frac{20}{11}$

27. $f(x+13) + f(x+630) = 0 \quad \text{...(i)}$

On putting $x = x + 617$

$$\Rightarrow \quad f(x+630) + f(x+1247) = 0 \quad \text{...(ii)}$$

$$\Rightarrow \quad f(x+1247) - f(x+13) = 0$$

$$\Rightarrow \quad f(x+1247) = f(x+13)$$

Replace $x = x - 13 \Rightarrow f(x+1234) = f(x)$

$f(x)$ is periodic with period $T = 1234$

$$\sum_{P=1}^{777}\int_P^{P+T} f(x)\,dx = \sum_{P=1}^{777}\int_0^T f(x)\,dx = 777\int_0^T f(x)\,dx$$

$$\Rightarrow \quad \lambda = 777$$

$$\Rightarrow \quad \lambda + T = 777 + 1234 \Rightarrow \lambda + T = 2011$$

28. $I_1 = \int_1^e x\left(\frac{1+x}{x}\right)(x + \ln x)^{100}\,dx$

$$\because \quad \frac{d}{dx}(x + \ln x) = 1 + \frac{1}{x} = \frac{1+x}{x}$$

$$I_1 = \left[\frac{x\,(x+\ln x)^{101}}{101}\right]_1^e - \int_1^e \frac{(x+\ln x)^{101}}{101}$$

$$\Rightarrow \quad I_1 = \frac{e\,(e+1)^{101} - 1}{101} - \frac{1}{101}\int_1^e (x + \ln x)^{101}\,dx$$

$$I_2 = \frac{1}{e}\int_1^e (t + \ln t)^{101}\,dt$$

Taking $e \sin x = t$

$$\Rightarrow \quad I_1 + \frac{eI_2}{101} = \frac{e\,(e+1)^{101} - 1}{101}$$

Hence, k is 1.

29. Let $\quad A = (x^3 + 1^3)(x^3 + 2^3)\ldots(x^3 + 2014)^3$

$$\therefore \quad \text{LHS} = \frac{1}{3}\int_0^1 dA = \frac{1}{\lambda}\left(\prod_{k=1}^{2014}(1 + k^3) - \mu^3\right)$$

$$\therefore \quad \lambda = 3, \mu = 2014!$$

30. $f(x+y) = f(x)\cdot f(y),\ \forall\ x, y \in R$

$$f(0) \neq 0,\ f'(0) = 1$$

$$f(x) = a^{kx}$$

$$f'(x) = a^{kx}\ \ln a^k$$

$$\Rightarrow f'(0) = 1 \Rightarrow \ln a^k = 1 \Rightarrow a^k = e$$

$$f(x) = e^x$$

(a) $\int_{-1}^{1}\frac{(\ln e^x)^2}{1+(e^x)^2}\,dx = \int_{-1}^{1}\frac{x^2}{1+e^{2x}}\,dx$

$$= \int_0^1 \frac{x^2}{1+e^{2x}} + \frac{x^2}{1+\frac{1}{e^{2x}}}\,dx$$

$$= \int_0^1 x^2\,dx = \frac{1}{3}$$

(b) $\int_{-\frac{\pi}{2}}^{\frac{\pi}{2}}\frac{\cos \ln e^x}{1+e^x}\,dx = \int_{-\frac{\pi}{2}}^{\frac{\pi}{2}}\cos x\left(\frac{1}{e^x+1} + \frac{e^x}{e^x+1}\right)dx$

$$= \sin x\,\Big|_0^{\frac{\pi}{2}} = 1 - 0 = 1$$

(c) $\int_{-2015}^{2015}\ln\left(\ln e^x + \sqrt{1+(\ln e^x)^2}\right)dx$

$$= \int_{-2015}^{2015}\ln\left(x + \sqrt{1+x^2}\right)dx = 0$$

[$\because$ odd function]

(d) $\int_0^2 (e^x - x)\,dx = e^x - \frac{x^2}{2}\Big|_0^2 = e^2 - 3$

31.

> **Decoding the Question**
>
> Let $a - b < 0$, then $|a - b|$ will open as $(b - a)$, because output of modulus is always positive value.

$$f(\theta) = |||\,3\cos\theta - \sin\theta\,| + 2\cos\theta\,| + \cos\theta\,|$$

$$f(\theta) = ||\,\sin\theta - 3\cos\theta + 2\cos\theta\,| + \cos\theta\,|$$

$$= ||\,\sin\theta - \cos\theta\,| + \cos\theta\,|$$

$$= |\,\sin\theta - \cos\theta + \cos\theta\,| = |\,\sin\theta\,| = \sin\theta$$

(a) $\int_{\frac{\pi}{2}}^{\pi}\sin\theta\,d\theta = -(\cos\theta)_{\frac{\pi}{2}}^{\pi} = -(-1-0) = 1$

(b) $f(\theta) = \sin\theta$

$$f'(\theta) = \cos\theta$$

$$\Rightarrow f'\left(\frac{5\pi}{6}\right) = \frac{-\sqrt{3}}{2}$$

(c) $I = \int_{\frac{\pi}{2}}^{\pi} \sin^2\theta \, d\theta$ ...(i)

Applying property, $\int_a^b f(x)dx = \int_a^b f(a+b-x)dx$

$$I = \int_{\frac{\pi}{2}}^{\pi} \cos^2\theta \, d\theta \quad ...(ii)$$

On adding Eqs. (i) and (ii), we get

$$2I = \int_{\frac{\pi}{2}}^{\pi} I \cdot d\theta = \frac{\pi}{2} \Rightarrow I = \frac{\pi}{4}$$

(d) $f'(\theta) = \cos\theta$

$$f'\left(\frac{2\pi}{3}\right) = \frac{-1}{2}$$

Solutions (Q.Nos. 32-33)

We have the equations of the tangents to the curve $y = \int_{-\infty}^{x} f(t)dt$ and $y = f(x)$ at arbitrary points on them are

$$Y - \int_{-x}^{x} f(t)\,dt = f(x)(X - x) \quad ...(i)$$

and $\quad Y - f(x) = f'(x)(X - x)$ ...(ii)

As Eqs. (i) and (ii) intersect at the same point on the X-axis

Putting $Y = 0$ and equating x-coordinates, we have

$$x - \frac{f(x)}{f'(x} = x - \frac{\int_{-\infty}^{x} f(t)\,dt}{f(x)}$$

$$\Rightarrow \frac{f(x)}{\int_{-\infty}^{x} f(t)\,dt} = \frac{f'(x)}{f(x)} \Rightarrow \int_{-\infty}^{x} f(t)\,dt = cf(x) \quad ...(iii)$$

As, $f(0) = 1 \Rightarrow \int_{-\infty}^{0} f(t)\,dt = c \times 1 \Rightarrow c = \frac{1}{2}$

$\Rightarrow \int_{-\infty}^{x} f(t)\,dt = \frac{1}{2} f(x)$; differentiating both the sides and integrating and using boundary conditions, we get $f(x) = e^{2x}$; $y = 2ex$ is tangent to $y = e^{2x}$.

$\therefore$ Number of solutions = 1.

Clearly, $f(x)$ is increasing for all x.

$$\therefore \quad \lim_{x \to \infty} (e^{2x})^{e^{-2x}} = 1 \quad [\infty^0 \text{ form}]$$

Solutions (Q.Nos. 34-35)

34. Here, $f(x) = e^x \underbrace{\int_0^1 e^t \cdot f(t)\,dt}_{A \text{ (say)}}$

$$f(x) = Ae^x \quad ...(i)$$

$$\Rightarrow \quad f(t) = Ae^t$$

where, $A = \int_0^1 e^t \cdot f(t)\,dt \Rightarrow A = \int_0^1 e^t \cdot Ae^t\,dt; A = A\int_0^1 e^{2t}\,dt$

Now, $A\left[\int_0^1 e^{2t}dt - 1\right] = 0 \Rightarrow A = 0$, as $\int_0^1 e^{2t}\,dt \neq 0$

Hence, $\quad f(x) = 0 \Rightarrow f(1) = 0$

35. Again, $\quad g(x) = e^x \int_0^1 e^t\, g(t)\,dt + x$

$$\Rightarrow \quad g(x) = Be^x + x \quad ...(ii)$$

$$\Rightarrow \quad g(t) = Be^t + t$$

where, $\quad B = \int_0^1 e^t\, g(t)\,dt \Rightarrow B = \int_0^1 e^t(Be^t + t)\,dt$

$$\Rightarrow \quad B = B\int_0^1 e^{2t}\,dt + \int_0^1 e^t \cdot t\,dt$$

But $\quad \int_0^1 e^{2t}\,dt = \frac{1}{2}(e^2 - 1)$ and $\int_0^1 te^t\,dt = 1$

$$\therefore \quad B = \frac{B}{2}(e^2 - 1) + 1 \Rightarrow 2B = B(e^2 - 1) + 2$$

$$\Rightarrow \quad 3B = Be^2 + 2 \Rightarrow B = \frac{2}{3 - e^2}$$

From Eq. (ii), $\quad g(x) = \left(\frac{2}{3 - e^2}\right)e^x + x$

$$\Rightarrow \quad g(0) = \frac{2}{3 - e^2}$$

Also, $\quad f(0) = 0$

$$\therefore \quad g(0) - f(0) = \frac{2}{3 - e^2} - 0 = \frac{2}{3 - e^2}$$

Solutions (Q.Nos. 36-37)

We have, $g(x) = g(0) + xg'(0) + \frac{x^2}{2}g''(0) = -bx^2 + cx - 6$

$h(x) = g(x) = 4x^4 - ax^3 + bx^2 - cx + 6 = 0$ has 4 distinct real roots. Using Descarte's rule of signs.

Given, biquadratic equation has 4 distinct positive roots.

Let the roots be x_1, x_2, x_3 and x_4.

Now, $$\frac{\frac{1}{x_1} + \frac{2}{x_2} + \frac{3}{x_3} + \frac{4}{x_4}}{4} \geq \sqrt[4]{\frac{24}{x_1 x_2 x_3 x_4}}$$

$$\Rightarrow \quad 2 \geq 2 \Rightarrow \frac{1}{x_1} = \frac{2}{x_2} = \frac{3}{x_3} = \frac{4}{x_4} = k$$

$$\Rightarrow \quad \frac{1}{x_1} \cdot \frac{2}{x_2} \cdot \frac{3}{x_3} \cdot \frac{4}{x_4} = k^4$$

$$\Rightarrow \quad \frac{24}{3/2} = k^4$$

$$\Rightarrow \quad k = 2$$

$\therefore$ Roots are $\frac{1}{2}, 1, \frac{3}{2}$ and 2.

Abscissae of point of intersection are in AP.

Also, $a = 20$

Solutions (Q.Nos. 38-39)

38. Here, $f(x) = \tan^{-1}\left(\frac{\log_e x}{(\log_e x)^2 + 1}\right), 0 < x < \infty$

attains minimum at $x = \frac{1}{e}$ and maximum at $x = e$.

Also, $f(x)$ has $y = 0$ as asymptotes.

$\therefore \quad f(x)$ can be shown as

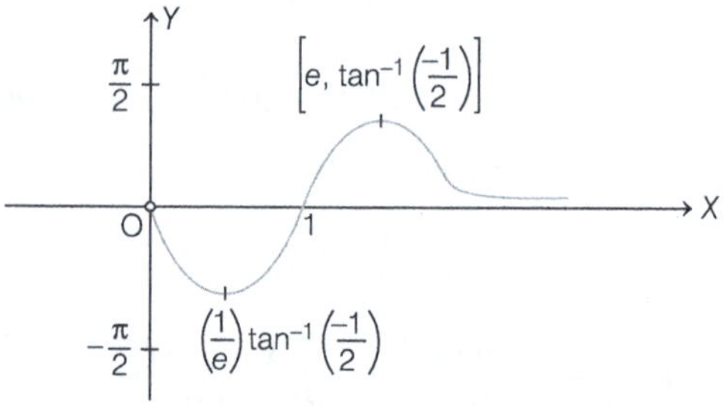

Clearly, $f(x)$ is neither injective nor subjective, also graph for $[f(x)]$ can be shown, as

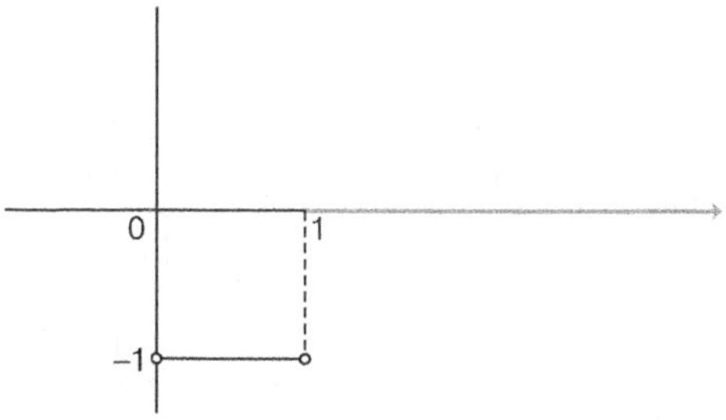

39. $\int_0^{\infty}[f(x)]dx = \int_0^1 -1\cdot dx + \int_1^{\infty} 0\cdot dx = [-x]_0^1 = -1$

40. $P = \int_0^1 \sqrt{\dfrac{x}{1-x}}\ln\left(\dfrac{x}{1-x}\right)dx$

On putting $\dfrac{x}{1-x} = t^2 \Rightarrow x = t^2 - t^2x$

$$\Rightarrow \quad x = \frac{t^2}{1+t^2} = 1 - \frac{1}{1+t^2}$$

$$dx = \frac{2t}{(1+t^2)^2}$$

$$P = \int_0^{\infty} t\,(2\ln t)\frac{2t}{(1+t^2)^2}dt$$

$$= 2\int_0^{\infty}\underset{\text{I}}{(t\ln t)}\cdot\underset{\text{II}}{\frac{2t}{(1+t^2)^2}}dt$$

$$= 2\left[(t\ln t) - \left(\frac{1}{1+t^2}\right)\right]_0^{\infty} + 2\left[\int_0^{\infty}\frac{(1+\ln t)}{1+t^2}dt\right]$$

$$= 2[0] + 2\left[\int_0^{\infty}\frac{1}{1+t^2}dt + \int_0^{\infty}\frac{\ln t}{1+t^2}\right]$$

$$= 2[\tan^{-1}t]_0^{\infty} + 0 = 2\left(\frac{\pi}{2} - 0\right) = \pi$$

$\therefore \quad [P] = 3$

41. $R = \int_0^8 e^{\frac{Q}{P}}d\alpha = \int_0^8 e^{\frac{\pi\ln\left(\frac{\sqrt{\alpha+1}+1}{2}\right)}{\pi}}d\alpha$

$$= \int_0^8 \frac{\sqrt{\alpha+1}+1}{2}d\alpha = \frac{1}{2}\left[\frac{(\alpha+1)^{\frac{3}{2}}}{\frac{3}{2}} + \frac{\alpha}{2}\right]_0^8$$

$R = \dfrac{38}{3}$

$\therefore 3R = 38$

42. Given, $l = \lim\limits_{x\to 0}\dfrac{\int_0^x \frac{t^2dt}{(a+t^r)^{1/p}}}{bx - \sin x} = \lim\limits_{x\to 0}\dfrac{\frac{x^2}{(a+x^r)^{1/p}}}{b-\cos x}$

Using L'Hospital's rule,

$$l = \lim_{x\to 0}\frac{x^2}{(a+x^r)^{1/p}}\cdot\frac{x^2}{(1-\cos x)}\cdot\frac{1}{x^2}$$

$$= 2\lim_{x\to 0}\frac{1}{(a+x^r)^{1/p}} = \frac{2}{a^{1/p}}$$

If $p = 3$ and $l = 1$, then $1 = \dfrac{2}{a^{1/3}} \Rightarrow a = 8$

43. If, $p = 2$ and $a = 9$, then $l = \dfrac{2}{9^{1/2}} = \dfrac{2}{3}$

$$\Rightarrow \quad 3l = 2$$

44. Let $B = \sum\limits_{n=1}\dfrac{\sin nx}{4^n} = \dfrac{\sin x}{4} + \dfrac{\sin 2x}{4^2} + \ldots$

and $A = 1 + \cos\dfrac{x}{4} + \cos\dfrac{2x}{4^2} + \ldots$

$\therefore A + iB = 1 + \dfrac{e^{ix}}{4} + \dfrac{e^{i2x}}{4^2} + \ldots = \dfrac{1}{1-\dfrac{e^{ix}}{4}}$

Thus, B imaginary part of $\dfrac{1}{1-\dfrac{e^{ix}}{4}} = \dfrac{4}{4-\cos x - i\sin x}$

$$\therefore \quad B = \frac{4\sin x}{17 - \theta\cos x} \Rightarrow f(x) = \frac{4\sin x}{17-\theta\cos x}$$

and $\int_0^{\pi} f(x)dx = \int_0^{\pi}\dfrac{4\sin x}{17-\theta\cos x} = \dfrac{1}{2}\log\left(\dfrac{25}{9}\right)$

$$= \log\left(\frac{5}{3}\right) = \log\left(\frac{m}{n}\right)$$

$\therefore \quad m + n = 8$

45. Here, $I = \int_{-\pi/2}^{\pi/2}\dfrac{\cos x dx}{1 + 2[\sin^{-1}(\sin x)]}$

$$= \int_{-\pi/2}^{-1}\frac{\cos x}{-3}dx + \int_{-1}^{0}\frac{\cos x dx}{-1} + \int_0^1 \cos x dx + \int_1^{\pi/2}\frac{\cos x}{3}dx$$

$$= \frac{1}{3}\int_{-1}^{-\pi/2}\cos x dx + \int_0^{-1}\cos x dx + \int_0^1 \cos x dx + \frac{1}{3}\int_1^{\pi/2}\cos x dx$$

$$= \frac{1}{3}\int_0^{\pi/2}\cos t(-dt) + \int_0^1 \cos(t)\cdot(-dt)$$

$$+ \int_0^1 \cos x dx + \frac{1}{3}\int_1^{\pi/2}\cos x dx$$

$$= 0$$

46. Here, $f(n+1) - f(n) = \dfrac{1}{\pi}\int_0^{\pi/2}\dfrac{\sin^2(n+1)\theta - \sin^2 n\theta}{\sin^2\theta}d\theta$

$$= \frac{1}{\pi}\int_0^{\pi/2}\frac{\sin(2n+1)\theta\cdot\sin\theta}{\sin^2\theta}d\theta$$

$$= \frac{1}{\pi}\int_0^{\pi/2}\frac{\sin(2n+1)\theta}{\sin^2\theta}d\theta$$

$$= \frac{1}{\pi}\left(\int_0^{\pi/2}\frac{\sin 2n\theta\cdot\cos\theta}{\sin\theta}d\theta + \int_0^{\pi/2}\cos 2n\theta d\theta\right)$$

Using, $\cos\theta + \cos 3\theta + \cos 5\theta + \ldots + \cos(2n-1)\theta$

$$= \frac{\sin\frac{n\cdot(2\theta)}{2}}{\sin\left(\frac{2\theta}{2}\right)}\cdot\cos(\theta + (n-1)\theta)$$

i.e. $\cos\theta + \cos 3\theta + \cos 5\theta + \ldots + \cos(2n-1)\theta = \dfrac{1}{2}\left(\dfrac{\sin 2n\theta}{\sin\theta}\right)$

$\therefore f(n+1) - f(n) = \dfrac{1}{\pi}$

$$\left[2\int_0^{\pi/2}\cos\theta + \cos 3\theta + \ldots + \cos(2n-1)\theta\cdot\cos\theta d\theta + 0\right]$$

$$= \frac{1}{\pi}\int_0^{\pi/2}\{(2\cos\theta\cos\theta) + (2\cos 3\theta\cos\theta)$$

$$+ \ldots (2\cos(2n-1)\cdot\cos\theta)\}d\theta$$

$$= \frac{1}{\pi}\int_0^{\pi/2} 1\cdot d\theta, \text{ as } \int_0^{\pi/2}\cos 2n\theta\, d\theta = 0$$

$\therefore \quad f(n+1) - f(n) = \dfrac{1}{2}$

If $\quad n = 1,\ f(2) - f(1) = \dfrac{1}{2}\ \left(\text{as } f(1) = \dfrac{1}{2}\right) \Rightarrow f(2) = \dfrac{2}{2}$

If $\quad n = 2,\ f(3) - f(2) = \dfrac{1}{2} \Rightarrow f(3) = \dfrac{3}{2}$ and so on.

$\therefore \quad f(n) = \dfrac{n}{2}$

Hence, $\dfrac{f(15) + f(3)}{f(15) - f(9)} = \dfrac{\frac{15}{2} + \frac{3}{2}}{\frac{15}{2} - \frac{9}{2}} = 3$

47. Here, $g(x) = \int_{-2}^{h(x)} e^{(1+t)^2} dt$

$\Rightarrow \quad g'(x) = h'(x) \cdot e^{(1+h(x))^2}$

$\Rightarrow \quad g'(2) = h'(2) \cdot e^{(1+h(2))^2}$

$\Rightarrow e^4 = 1 \cdot e^{(1+h(2))^2}$, given $g'(2) = e^4$ and $h'(2) = 1$

$\therefore \quad (1 + h(2))^2 = 4 \Rightarrow 1 + h(2) = 2, -2$

$\therefore \quad h(2) = -3, 1$

$\therefore$ Absolute sum for all possible values of $h(2) = |-3 + 1| = 2$

48. Let $I = \int_0^{\pi/2} \sin x \cdot \log(\sin x) dx = \dfrac{1}{2}\int_0^{\pi/2} \sin x \cdot \log(\sin^2 x) dx$

$= \dfrac{1}{2}\int_0^{\pi/2} \sin x \cdot \log(1 - \cos^2 x) dx$

Put $\cos x = t \Rightarrow -\sin x\, dx = dt$

$\therefore \quad I = \dfrac{1}{2}\int_0^1 \log(1 - t^2) dt$

$= \dfrac{1}{2}\int_0^1 \left(-t^2 - \dfrac{(-t^2)^2}{2} + \dfrac{(-t^2)^3}{2} \ldots\right) dt$

$= \dfrac{1}{2}\left[\dfrac{-t^3}{3} - \dfrac{t^5}{10} + \dfrac{t^7}{21} \ldots\right]_0^1 = \dfrac{1}{2}\left[\dfrac{-1}{3} - \dfrac{1}{10} + \dfrac{1}{21} \ldots\right]$

$= -\dfrac{1}{2}\left[\dfrac{1}{3} + \dfrac{1}{10} + \dfrac{1}{21} + \ldots\right] = -\left[\dfrac{1}{2 \times 3} + \dfrac{1}{20} + \dfrac{1}{42} + \ldots\right]$

$= -\left[\left(\dfrac{1}{2} - \dfrac{1}{3}\right) + \left(\dfrac{1}{4} - \dfrac{1}{5}\right) + \left(\dfrac{1}{6} - \dfrac{1}{7}\right) + \ldots\right]$

$= \log_e 2 - 1 = \log_e\left(\dfrac{2}{e}\right)$

$\therefore \quad K = 2$

49. Let us consider that

$$2\int_0^{\pi} \sin(m + \alpha)x \cdot \sin(n + \alpha)x\, dx = 0$$

$\Rightarrow \int_0^{\pi} (\cos(m - n)x - \cos(m + n + 2\alpha)x)\, dx = 0$

$\Rightarrow \dfrac{\sin(m - n)x}{m - n}\Bigg|_0^{\pi} - \dfrac{\sin(m + n + 2\alpha)x}{m + n + 2\alpha}\Bigg|_0^{\pi} = 0$

$\Rightarrow \quad \sin(m + n + 2\alpha)\pi = 0$

$\Rightarrow 2\alpha$ must be an integer.

But $\alpha \in (-1, 1) \Rightarrow \alpha = -\dfrac{1}{2}, 0, \dfrac{1}{2}$

Hence, there are three values of α.

50. $\lim\limits_{n\to\infty} \int_0^{\infty} \dfrac{\cos\dfrac{x}{2} \cos\dfrac{x}{2^2} \cos\dfrac{x}{2^3} \ldots \cos\dfrac{x}{2^{n-1}}\left(2\sin\dfrac{x}{2^{n-1}}\right)}{2\sin\dfrac{x}{2^{n-1}}} dx = \dfrac{\pi}{2}$

$\Rightarrow \quad \lim\limits_{n\to\infty}\int_0^{\infty} \dfrac{\sin x}{2^{n-1}\sin\dfrac{x}{2^{n-1}}} dx = \lim\limits_{n\to\infty}\int_0^{\infty} \dfrac{\sin x\left(\dfrac{x}{2^{n-1}}\right)}{x\left(\sin\dfrac{x}{2^{n-1}}\right)} dx = \dfrac{\pi}{2}$

$\Rightarrow \quad \int_0^{\infty} \dfrac{\sin x}{x} dx = \dfrac{\pi}{2}$

$\Rightarrow \int_0^{\infty} \dfrac{\sin^3 x}{x} dx = \int_0^{\infty} \dfrac{3\sin x - \sin 3x}{4x} dx$

$[\because \sin 3x = 3\sin x - 4\sin^3 x]$

$= \dfrac{3}{4}\int_0^{\infty} \dfrac{\sin x}{x} dx - \int_0^{\infty} \dfrac{\sin 3x}{3x}\left(\dfrac{1}{4}\right) d(3x)$

$= \dfrac{3}{4}\left(\dfrac{\pi}{2}\right) - \dfrac{1}{4}\left(\dfrac{\pi}{2}\right) = \dfrac{1}{2} \cdot \dfrac{\pi}{2} = \dfrac{\pi}{4}$

$\therefore \quad \lambda = \dfrac{1}{4} = 0.25$

51. Given, $p(2 + x) + p(2 - x) = 2p(2)$ ...(i)

$x \to x - 2$ in Eq. (i)

$\Rightarrow \quad p(x) + p(4 - x) = 2p(2)$ ...(ii)

$x \to x + 1$ in Eq. (i)

$\Rightarrow \quad p(x + 3) + p(1 - x) = 2p(2)$ ...(iii)

On adding in Eqs. (ii) and (iii), we get

$$20 = 4p(2) \Rightarrow p(2) = 5$$

Now, differentiate Eq. (i) w.r.t. x, we get

$$p'(2 + x) - p'(2 - x) = 0$$

$\Rightarrow \quad p'(2 + x) = p'(2 - x)$

$\therefore p'(x)$ is symmetric about $x = 2$

$p'(x) = 3x^2 + 2\alpha + 9$

$\Rightarrow \quad \dfrac{-2a}{6} = 2 \Rightarrow \alpha = -6$

$p(2) = 8 + 4a + 18 + b = 5$

$\Rightarrow \quad 8 - 24 + 18 + b = 5 \Rightarrow b = 3$

$\therefore \quad p(x) = x^3 - 6x^2 + 9x + 3$

$I = \int_{+6}^{-6} (x^3 - 6x^2 + 9x + 3)\, dx$

$= \int_{-6}^{6} (6x^2 - 3) dx = \int_0^6 (6x^2 - 3)\, dx = 828$

52. Let $I = 2\int_0^{\ln 2} \dfrac{(x - \ln 2)\, e^x}{(1 + e^x)^2} dx = 2\int_0^{\ln 2} \underbrace{(x - \ln 2)}_{\text{I}} \underbrace{\dfrac{e^x}{(1 + e^x)^2}}_{\substack{\text{II} \\ \text{(IBP)}}} dx$

On integrating by parts, we get

$I = 2\left[\dfrac{-(x - \ln 2)}{1 + e^x}\Bigg|_0^{\ln} + \int_0^{\ln 2} \dfrac{dx}{1 + e^x}\right]$

$= 2\left[\dfrac{x - \ln 2}{1 + e^x}\right]_{\ln 2}^{0} + \int_0^{\ln 2} \dfrac{e^x\, dx}{e^x(1 + e^x)}$

$= 2\left[\left(-\dfrac{\ln 2}{2}\right) + \int_1^2 \dfrac{dt}{t(t + 1)}\right]$

$$= -\ln 2 + 2\left[\ln\frac{t}{t+1}\right]_1^2 = -\ln 2 + 2\left[\ln\frac{2}{3} + \ln 2\right]_1^2$$

$$= -\ln 2 + 2\left[\ln\frac{4}{3}\right] = \ln\frac{16}{9} - \ln 2 = \ln\left(\frac{8}{9}\right)$$

$\Rightarrow \quad a + b = 17$

53. As, $\frac{1}{3} < x < \frac{1}{2} \Rightarrow 2 < \frac{1}{x} < 3 \Rightarrow 4 < \frac{2}{x} < 6$

$\Rightarrow \left[\frac{2}{x}\right] = 4$ or 5

Case I

$$4 < \frac{2}{x} < 5 \Rightarrow 2 < \frac{1}{x} < \frac{5}{2}$$

$$\Rightarrow \quad \left[\frac{2}{x}\right] = 4 \Rightarrow \frac{2}{5} < x < \frac{1}{2} \Rightarrow \frac{8}{5} < 4x < 2$$

Case II

$$5 < \frac{2}{x} < 6 \Rightarrow \frac{5}{2} < \frac{1}{x} < 3$$

$$\Rightarrow \quad \left[\frac{2}{x}\right] = 5$$

$$\Rightarrow \quad \frac{1}{3} < x < \frac{2}{5} \Rightarrow \frac{5}{3} < 5x < 2$$

Now, $I = \int_{1/3}^{2/5} \{5x\}\, dx + \int_{2/5}^{1/2} \{4x\}\, dx$

$\{5x\} = 5x - [5x]$

$\Rightarrow \{5x\} = 5x - 1 \Rightarrow \{4x\} = 4x - 1$

$$\therefore \quad I = \int_{1/3}^{2/5} (5x - 1)dx + \int_{2/5}^{1/2} (4x - 1)\, dx$$

$$I = \left[\left(\frac{5x^2}{2} - x\right)\right]_{1/3}^{2/5} + [(2x^2 - x)]_{2/5}^{1/2}$$

$$I = \frac{5}{2}\left[\frac{4}{25} - \frac{1}{9}\right] - \left(\frac{2}{5} - \frac{1}{3}\right) + 2\left(\frac{1}{4} - \frac{4}{25}\right) - \left(\frac{1}{2} - \frac{2}{5}\right)$$

$$I = \frac{61}{450} = \frac{m}{n} = |m - n| = 389$$

54. $F(1) = \int xe^{-x}\, dx = -e^{-x}\, x - e^{-x}\,(x + 1)$

$F(2) = \int e^{-x}\, x^2 dx = -e^{-x}\,(x^2 + 2x + 2)$

$$\therefore \quad \frac{F(1)}{F(2)} = \frac{(x + 1)}{(x + 1)^2 + 1}$$

$$\Rightarrow \quad \int \frac{F(1)}{F(2)}\, dx = \int \frac{(x + 1)}{(x + 1)^2 + 1}\, dx$$

$$(x + 1)^2 + 1 = t \Rightarrow (x + 1)\, dx = \frac{1}{2}\, dt$$

$$= \frac{1}{2}\int \frac{dt}{t} = \frac{1}{2}\ln(t) = \ln\sqrt{t}$$

$$\therefore \left(e^{\int \frac{F(1)}{F(2)} dx}\right)^2 = (\sqrt{t})^2 = t = (x + 1)^2 + 1$$

Hence, $\int_2^5 \left[((x + 1)^2 + 1)\, dx = \frac{(x + 1)^3}{3} + x\right]_2^5$

$= (72 + 5) - (9 + 2)$

$= 77 - 11 = 66$

55. $\int_{-x}^{x} \ln\left(\cos\frac{\theta}{2} + \sin\frac{\theta}{2}\right) d\theta$

$$= \int_0^x \left(\ln\left(\cos\frac{\theta}{2} + \sin\frac{\theta}{2}\right) + \left(\ln\left(\cos\frac{\theta}{2} - \sin\frac{\theta}{2}\right)\right)\right) d\theta$$

$$= \int_0^x \ln\cos\theta\, d\theta$$

So, the given definite integral

$$= \int_0^x (\ln\sin\theta + \ln\cos\theta + \ln\cos 2\theta + \ln\cos 4\theta)\, d\theta + 3x\ln 2 = 0$$

$$\Rightarrow \int_0^x \ln\sin 8\theta - 3x\ln 2 + 3x\ln 2 = 0$$

$$\Rightarrow \quad \int_0^x \ln\sin 8\theta\, d\theta = 0$$

56. Graph of $y = f(x)$

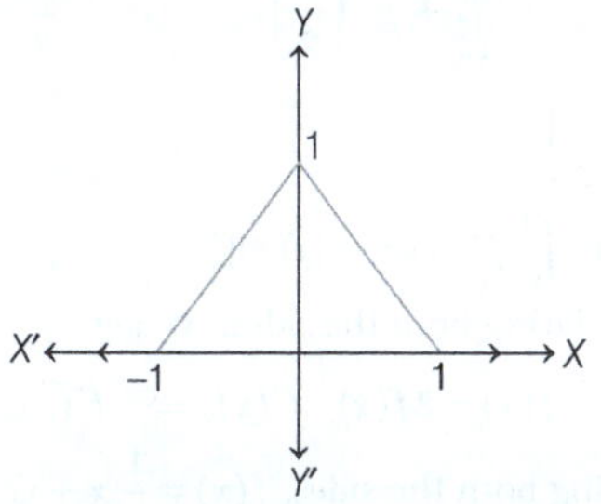

$$\int_{-3}^{5} g(x)\, dx = \int_{-3}^{5} f(x - 1)\, dx + \int_{-3}^{5} f(x + 1)\, dx$$

$$= \int_{-4}^{4} f(x)\, dx + \int_{-2}^{6} f(x)\, dx$$

$$= 2\int_{-1}^{1} (1 - |x|)\, dx$$

[$\because$ in the remaining interval $f(x) = 0$]

$= 2$

57. (A) For $a = 0$, $I = \int_0^T \sin^2 x\, dx$

$$= \int_0^T \frac{1 - \cos 2x}{2}\, dx$$

$$= \left[\frac{x}{2} - \frac{1}{4}\sin 2x\right]_0^T$$

$$= \frac{T}{2} - \frac{1}{4}\sin 2T$$

$$\therefore \quad L = \frac{1}{2} - \lim_{T\to\infty} \frac{1}{4}\frac{\sin 2T}{T} = \frac{1}{2}$$

(B) For $a = 1$, $\int_0^T 4\sin^2 x\, dx \Rightarrow L = 2$

(C) For $a = -1$, $\int_0^T 0\, dx = 0 \Rightarrow L = 0$

(D) For $a \neq 0, -1, 1$,

$$I = \int_0^T (\sin^2 x + \sin^2 ax + 2\sin x \cdot \sin ax)\, dx$$

$$= \int_0^T \left(\frac{1 - \cos 2x}{2} + \frac{1 - \cos 2ax}{2} + \cos(a - 1)x - \cos(a + 1)x\right) dx$$

$$= \left[x - \frac{1}{4}\sin 2x - \frac{1}{4a}\sin 2ax + \frac{\sin(a - 1)x}{a - 1} - \frac{\sin(a + 1)x}{a + 1}\right]_0^T$$

$$\therefore L = \lim_{T\to\infty} \frac{T}{T} - \lim_{T\to\infty} \frac{1}{T}$$

$$\left[\frac{1}{4}\sin 2x - \frac{1}{4a}\sin 2ax + \frac{\sin(a-1)x}{a-1} - \frac{\sin(a+1)x}{a+1}\right]_0^T$$

$$\Rightarrow L = 1$$

58. (A) We have, $f'(x) = \dfrac{g'(x)}{\sqrt{1+g^3(x)}}$

and $g'(x) = (1+\sin(\cos^2 x))(-\sin x)$

Hence, $f'(x) = \dfrac{(1+\sin(\cos^2 x))(-\sin x)}{\sqrt{1+g^3(x)}}$

$$f'\left(\frac{\pi}{2}\right) = \frac{1+0}{\sqrt{1+g^3\left(\frac{\pi}{2}\right)}} = -1, \; g\left(\frac{\pi}{2}\right) = 0$$

$$\therefore \quad f'\left(\frac{\pi}{2}\right) = -1$$

(B) We have, $\int_0^x f(x)\,dx = \{f(x)\}^2$

Differentiating both the sides, we get

$$f(x) = 2f(x)\cdot f'(x) \Rightarrow f'(x) = \frac{1}{2}$$

Integrating both the sides, $f(x) = \dfrac{1}{2}x + C$

where, $f(0) = 0 \Rightarrow C = 0$

$$\Rightarrow \quad f(x) = \frac{x}{2} \Rightarrow f(2) = 1$$

(C) Maximum when $a = -1, b = 2 \Rightarrow a + b = 1$

(D) If $\displaystyle\lim_{x\to 0} \frac{\sin 2x}{x^3} + a + \frac{b}{x^2} = 0$, then

$$\lim_{x\to 0} \frac{\sin 2x + ax^3 + bx}{x^3} = 0$$

For limit to exist $2 + b = 0 \Rightarrow b = -2$

$$\therefore \quad \lim_{x\to 0} \frac{\sin 2x + ax^3 - 2x}{x^3} = 0$$

Using left hand rule and solving, we get

$$a = \frac{4}{3}$$

$$\therefore \quad 3a + b = 2$$

59. Let $I = \displaystyle\int_1^e \frac{(\ln x)^{1/2}}{x[a-(\ln x)^{3/2}]^2}\,dx$

Let $a - (\ln x)^{3/2} = z$

$$\Rightarrow -\frac{3}{2}(\ln x)^{1/2}\cdot\frac{1}{x}\,dx = dz$$

$$\Rightarrow \quad \frac{(\ln x)^{1/2}\,dx}{x} = -\frac{2}{3}\,dz$$

x	1	e
z	a	$a-1$

$$\therefore I = \int_a^{a-1} \frac{\left(-\frac{2}{3}\right)dz}{z^2} = -\frac{2}{3}\left(\frac{z^{-2+1}}{-2+1}\right)_a^{a-1}$$

$$= \frac{-2}{3}\left[\frac{z^{-1}}{-1}\right]_a^{a-1}$$

$$= \frac{2}{3}\left(\frac{1}{a-1} - \frac{1}{a}\right)$$

$$= \frac{2}{3}\left(\frac{a-a+1}{a^2-a}\right) = \frac{2}{3}\frac{1}{a(a-1)}$$

Given, $I = 1$

$$\Rightarrow \quad \frac{2}{3}\frac{1}{a(a-1)} = 1$$

$$\Rightarrow \quad 3a^2 - 3a - 2 = 0$$

$$\Rightarrow \quad a = \frac{3 \pm \sqrt{9 - 4\cdot(3)\cdot(-2)}}{6} = \frac{3\pm\sqrt{9+24}}{6}$$

$$\Rightarrow \quad a = \frac{3\pm\sqrt{33}}{6}$$

60. $\displaystyle\int_1^2 \log_2(x^3+1)\,dx + \int_1^{\log_2 9} (2^x - 1)^{1/3}\,dx$

Let $f(x) = y = \log_2(x^3+1)$

$\Rightarrow x^3 + 1 = 2^y \Rightarrow x = (2^y - 1)^{1/3}$

$\Rightarrow f^{-1}(x) = (2^x - 1)^{1/3}$

[using $\displaystyle\int_a^b f(x)\,dx + \int_{f(a)}^{f(b)} f^{-1}(x)\,dx = bf(b) - af(a)$]

So, $\displaystyle\int_1^2 \log_2(x^3+1)\,dx + \int_1^{\log_2 9}(2^x-1)^{1/3}\,dx$

$$= 2\log_2 9 - 1\times 1 = 4\log_2 3 - 1$$

$\therefore [4\log_2 3 - 1] = 5$

61.

> **Decoding the Question**
>
> In this type of problems where inequality or other problems where limits are unsolved, use of series is very useful. Some important series are
>
> $\sin x = x - \dfrac{x^3}{3!} + \dfrac{x^5}{5!} - \dfrac{x^7}{7!}\ldots$, $\cos x = 1 - \dfrac{x^2}{2!} + \dfrac{x^4}{4!} - \dfrac{x^6}{6!}\ldots$
>
> $\log(1+x) = x - \dfrac{x^2}{2} + \dfrac{x^3}{3} - \dfrac{x^4}{4}\ldots$, $\tan x \in (-1, 1]$,
>
> $a^x = 1 + \dfrac{x\ln a}{1!} + \dfrac{x^2\ln^2 a}{2!} + \dfrac{x^3\ln^3 a}{3!}\ldots$, $\tan a > 0$

$$\because \quad \cos x = 1 - \frac{x^2}{2!} + \frac{x^4}{4!} - \frac{x^6}{6!} + \ldots$$

$$\text{and } \sin x = x - \frac{x^3}{3!} + \frac{x^5}{5!} - \frac{x^7}{7!} + \ldots$$

$$\therefore \int_0^1 x\cos x\,dx \ge \int_0^1 \left(x - \frac{x^3}{2!}\right)dx = \left[\frac{x^2}{2} - \frac{x^4}{8}\right]_0^1 = \frac{1}{2} - \frac{1}{8} = \frac{3}{8}$$

$$\Rightarrow \int_0^1 x\cos x\,dx \ge \frac{3}{8}$$

and, $\displaystyle\int_0^1 x\sin dx \ge \int_0^1 \left(x^2 - \frac{x^4}{6}\right)dx$

$$= \left[\frac{x^3}{3} - \frac{x^5}{30}\right]_0^1 = \frac{1}{3} - \frac{1}{30} = \frac{9}{30} = \frac{3}{10}$$

$$\Rightarrow \int_0^1 x\sin x\,dx \ge \frac{3}{10}$$

and, $\int_0^1 x^2 \cos x\, dx \geq \int_0^1 \left(x^2 - \frac{x^4}{2}\right) dx = \left[\frac{x^3}{3} - \frac{x^5}{10}\right]_0^1 = \frac{1}{3} - \frac{1}{10} = \frac{7}{30}$

$\therefore \int_0^1 x^2 \cos x\, dx \geq \frac{7}{30}$

and, $\int_0^1 x^2 \sin x\, dx \geq \int_0^1 \left(x^3 - \frac{x^5}{6}\right) dx$

$$= \left[\frac{x^4}{3} - \frac{x^6}{10}\right]_0^1 = \frac{1}{4} - \frac{1}{36} = \frac{8}{36} = \frac{2}{9}$$

$\therefore \int_0^1 x^2 \sin x\, dx \geq \frac{2}{9}$

Thus, options *a*, *b* and *d* are correct.

62. It is given that, for functions

$f : R \to R$ and $F : [0, \pi] \to R$,

$$F(x) = \int_0^x f(t) dt,$$

where $f(\pi) = -6$

$$F'(x) = f(x) \Rightarrow F'(\pi) = f(\pi) = -6 \quad \text{...(i)}$$

Now, $\int_0^\pi (f'(x) + F(x)) \cos x\, dx$

$$= \int_0^\pi f'(x) \cos x dx + \int_0^\pi F(x) \cos x dx$$

$$= [\cos x\, f(x)]_0^\pi + \int_0^\pi f(x) \sin x\, dx + \int_0^\pi F(x) \cos x\, dx$$

[by integration by parts]

$$= (-1)(-6) - f(0) + [(\sin x) F(x)]_0^\pi - \int_0^\pi F(x) \cos x\, dx + \int_0^\pi F(x) \cos x\, dx$$

$$= 6 - f(0) = 2 \quad \text{[given]}$$

$\Rightarrow f(0) = 4$

63. The given integral

$$I = \int_0^{\pi/2} \frac{3\sqrt{\cos\theta}}{(\sqrt{\cos\theta} + \sqrt{\sin\theta})^5} d\theta \quad \text{... (i)}$$

$$\Rightarrow I = \int_0^{\pi/2} \frac{3\sqrt{\sin\theta}}{(\sqrt{\sin\theta} + \sqrt{\cos\theta})^5} d\theta \quad \text{...(ii)}$$

[using the property $\int_0^a f(x)\, dx = \int_0^a f(a - x)\, dx$]

Now, on adding integrals (i) and (ii), we get

$$2I = \int_0^{\pi/2} \frac{3}{(\sqrt{\sin\theta} + \sqrt{\cos\theta})^4} d\theta = \int_0^{\pi/2} \frac{3\sec^2\theta}{(1 + \sqrt{\tan\theta})^4} d\theta$$

Now, let $\tan\theta = t^2 \Rightarrow \sec^2\theta\, d\theta = 2t\, dt$

and at $\theta = \frac{\pi}{2}, t \to \infty$ and at $\theta = 0, t \to 0$

$$\text{So, } 2I = \int_0^\infty \frac{6t\, dt}{(1+t)^4} = 6\int_0^\infty \frac{t + 1 - 1}{(t+1)^4} dt$$

$$\Rightarrow \quad I = 3\left[\int_0^\infty \frac{dt}{(t+1)^3} - \int_0^\infty \frac{dt}{(t+1)^4}\right]$$

$$\Rightarrow \quad I = 3\left[-\frac{1}{2(t+1)^2} + \frac{1}{3}\frac{1}{(t+1)^3}\right]_0^\infty$$

$$\Rightarrow \quad I = 3\left(\frac{1}{2} - \frac{1}{3}\right) = 3\left(\frac{1}{6}\right) = \frac{1}{2} \Rightarrow I = 0.5$$

64. Given, $I = \frac{2}{\pi}\int_{-\pi/4}^{\pi/4} \frac{dx}{(1 + e^{\sin x})(2 - \cos 2x)}$ ...(i)

On applying property $\int_a^b f(x) dx = \int_a^b f(a + b - x)\, dx$, we get

$$I = \frac{2}{\pi}\int_{-\pi/4}^{\pi/4} \frac{e^{\sin x} dx}{(1 + e^{\sin x})(2 - \cos 2x)} \quad \text{...(ii)}$$

On adding integrals (i) and (ii), we get

$$2I = \frac{2}{\pi}\int_{-\pi/4}^{\pi/4} \frac{dx}{2 - \cos 2x}$$

$$\Rightarrow \quad I = \frac{1}{\pi}\int_{-\pi/4}^{\pi/4} \frac{dx}{2 - \frac{1 - \tan^2 x}{1 + \tan^2 x}} \quad \left[\text{as } \cos 2x = \frac{1 - \tan^2 x}{1 + \tan^2 x}\right]$$

$$= \frac{2}{\pi}\int_0^{\pi/4} \frac{\sec^2 x}{1 + 3\tan^2 x} dx$$

$$\left[\because \frac{\sec^2 x}{1 + 3\tan^2 x} \text{ is even function}\right]$$

Let $\sqrt{3}\tan x = t$

$\Rightarrow \sqrt{3}\sec^2 x\, dx = dt$, and at $x = 0, t = 0$ and at $x = \sqrt{3}, t = \sqrt{3}$

So, $$I = \frac{2}{\pi}\int_0^{\sqrt{3}} \frac{1}{\sqrt{3}} \frac{dt}{1 + t^2}$$

$$= \frac{2}{\sqrt{3}\pi}[\tan^{-1} t]_0^{\sqrt{3}} = \frac{2}{\sqrt{3}\pi}\left(\frac{\pi}{3}\right) = \frac{2}{3\sqrt{3}}$$

$$\Rightarrow \quad 27I^2 = 4$$

Exercise 3 - Challenging Problems

1. Here, the Newton-Leibnitz's formula for evaluating the definite integrals is not applicable because the anti-derivative,

$$f(x) = \frac{1}{\sqrt{3}}[\tan^{-1}(\sqrt{3}\tan x)]$$

has a discontinuity at the point $x = \frac{\pi}{2}$ which lies in the interval $[0, \pi]$.

$$\text{LHL} = \lim_{h \to 0} \frac{1}{\sqrt{3}} \tan^{-1} \sqrt{3}\left[\tan\left(\frac{\pi}{2} - h\right)\right] \text{ at } x = \frac{\pi}{2}$$

$$= \lim_{h \to 0} \frac{1}{\sqrt{3}} \tan^{-1}(\sqrt{3}\cot h)$$

$$= \lim_{h \to 0} \frac{1}{\sqrt{3}} \tan^{-1}(\infty) = \frac{\pi}{2\sqrt{3}} \quad \text{...(i)}$$

Also, $$\text{RHL} = \lim_{h \to 0} \frac{1}{\sqrt{3}} \tan^{-1} \sqrt{3}\left[\tan\left(\frac{\pi}{2} + h\right)\right] \text{ at } x = \frac{\pi}{2}$$

$$= \lim_{h \to 0} \frac{1}{\sqrt{3}} \tan^{-1}(-\sqrt{3}\cot h)$$

$$= \lim_{h \to 0} \frac{1}{\sqrt{3}} \tan^{-1}(-\infty) = -\frac{\pi}{2\sqrt{3}} \quad \text{...(ii)}$$

From Eqs. (i) and (ii), LHL $\neq$ RHL at $x = \pi / 2$

$\Rightarrow$ Anti-derivative $f(x)$ is discontinuous at $x = \pi / 2$.

So, the correct solution for above integral;

$$I = \int_0^\pi \frac{dx}{1 + 2\sin^2 x} = \int_0^\pi \frac{\sec^2 x\, dx}{1 + 3\tan^2 x} \quad \text{...(iii)}$$

Using, $\int_0^{2a} f(x)\,dx = \begin{cases} 0, & f(2a-x) = -f(x) \\ 2\int_0^a f(x)\,dx, & f(2a-x) = f(x) \end{cases}$

We know, if $f(x) = \dfrac{\sec^2 x}{1+3\tan^2 x}$ $f(\pi - x) = f(x)$

$\therefore$ Eq. (iii) reduces to $I = 2\int_0^{\pi/2} \dfrac{\sec^2 x\,dx}{1+3\tan^2 x}$

$$= 2\cdot\frac{1}{\sqrt{3}}\int_0^{\infty}\frac{dt}{1+t^2}$$

[put $\sqrt{3}\tan x = t \Rightarrow \sqrt{3}\sec^2 x\,dx = dt$]

$$= \frac{2}{\sqrt{3}}[\tan^{-1}(t)]_0^{\infty}$$

$$= \frac{2}{\sqrt{3}}(\tan^{-1}\infty - \tan^{-1} 0)$$

$$= \frac{2}{\sqrt{3}}\left(\frac{\pi}{2} - 0\right) = \frac{\pi}{\sqrt{3}}$$

$\therefore$ $\int_0^{\pi} \dfrac{dx}{1+2\sin^2 x} = \dfrac{\pi}{\sqrt{3}}$

2. Let $I = \int_{\alpha}^{\beta} \sqrt{\dfrac{x-\alpha}{\beta - x}}\,dx$ ...(i)

Put $x = \alpha\cos^2 t + \beta \sin^2 t$

$\therefore$ $x - \alpha = \alpha\cos^2 t + \beta\sin^2 t - \alpha = \beta\,[\sin^2(t) + \alpha(\cos^2 t - 1)]$

$= \beta\sin^2 t - \alpha\sin^2 t$

$\Rightarrow$ $(x-\alpha) = (\beta - \alpha)\sin^2 t$

Similarly, $\beta - x = (\beta - \alpha)\cos^2 t$

$\therefore$ $dx = 2(\beta - \alpha)\sin t\cos t\,dt$

where, $x = \alpha \Rightarrow \sin^2 t = 0 \Rightarrow t = 0$ [$\because \alpha < \beta$]

and $x = \beta \Rightarrow \cos^2 t = 0 \Rightarrow t = \pi/2$

$\therefore$ Eq. (i) reduces to

$$I = \int_0^{\pi/2}\sqrt{\frac{(\beta-\alpha)\sin^2 t}{(\beta-\alpha)\cos^2 t}}\cdot 2(\beta-\alpha)\sin t\cos t\,dt$$

$$= \int_0^{\pi/2}\frac{\sin t}{\cos t}\cdot 2(\beta-\alpha)\sin t\cos t\,dt$$

$$\left[\because \sqrt{\frac{\sin^2 t}{\cos^2 t}} = +\frac{\sin t}{\cos t} \text{ as } t \in [0, \pi/2]\right]$$

$$= (\beta-\alpha)\int_0^{\pi/2} 2\sin^2 t\,dt$$

$$= (\beta-\alpha)\int_0^{\pi/2}(1-\cos 2t)\,dt$$

$$= (\beta-\alpha)\left(t - \frac{\sin 2t}{2}\right)_0^{\pi/2}$$

$$= (\beta-\alpha)\left[\left(\frac{\pi}{2} - \frac{1}{2}\sin\pi\right) - \left(0 - \frac{1}{2}\sin 0\right)\right]$$

$$= (\beta-\alpha)\left[\frac{\pi}{2}\right]$$

$\therefore$ $I = \dfrac{\pi}{2}(\beta - \alpha)$

Alternate Solution

Let $I = \int_{\alpha}^{\beta}\sqrt{\dfrac{x-\alpha}{\beta-x}}\,dx$ $\left[\begin{array}{l}\text{put } \sqrt{\beta - x} = t \\ \text{or } \quad \beta - x = t^2 \\ \Rightarrow -dx = 2t\,dt\end{array}\right]$

When $x = \alpha$, then $\beta - \alpha = t^2 \Rightarrow \sqrt{\beta-\alpha} = t$

When $x = \beta$, then $0 = t^2 \Rightarrow 0 = t$

$\therefore$ $I = \int_{\sqrt{\beta-\alpha}}^{0}\dfrac{\sqrt{(\beta - t^2) - \alpha}}{t}(-2t)\,dt$

$$= -2\int_{\sqrt{\beta-\alpha}}^{0}\sqrt{(\beta-\alpha) - t^2}\,dt$$

$$= 2\int_0^{\sqrt{\beta-\alpha}}\sqrt{(\sqrt{\beta-\alpha})^2 - t^2}\,dt$$

$$= 2\left\{\frac{t}{2}\sqrt{(\beta-\alpha)-t^2} + \frac{(\beta-\alpha)}{2}\sin^{-1}\left(\frac{t}{\sqrt{\beta-\alpha}}\right)\right\}_0^{\sqrt{\beta-\alpha}}$$

$$= 2\left[\left\{0 + \frac{(\beta-\alpha)}{2}\sin^{-1}(1)\right\} - \left\{0 + \frac{(\beta-\alpha)}{2}\sin^{-1}(0)\right\}\right]$$

$$= \frac{2(\beta-\alpha)}{2}\cdot\frac{\pi}{2}$$

$$= \frac{\pi}{2}(\beta-\alpha)$$

3. Let $I = \int_{\sqrt{(3a^2+b^2)/4}}^{\sqrt{(a^2+b^2)/2}} \dfrac{x}{\sqrt{(x^2-a^2)(b^2-x^2)}}\,dx$ ...(i)

Put $x^2 = a^2\cos^2 t + b^2\sin^2 t$

$\Rightarrow$ $2x\,dx = [2a^2\cos t(-\sin t) + 2b^2\sin t(\cos t)]\,dt$

$\Rightarrow$ $x\,dx = \dfrac{1}{2}(b^2 - a^2)\sin 2t\,dt$

For $x^2 = \dfrac{a^2+b^2}{2} = a^2\cos^2 t + b^2\sin^2 t,$

$a^2 + b^2 = 2(1 - \sin^2 t)\,a^2 + 2b^2\sin^2 t$

or $(a^2+b^2) = 2a^2 + 2(b^2 - a^2)\sin^2 t$

$\Rightarrow \sin^2 t = \dfrac{1}{2} \Rightarrow \cos 2t = 0 \Rightarrow t = \dfrac{\pi}{4}$

For $x^2 = \dfrac{3a^2+b^2}{4} = a^2\cos^2 t + b^2\sin^2 t,$

$3a^2 + b^2 = 4a^2 + 4(b^2 - a^2)\sin^2 t$

$\Rightarrow \sin^2 t = \dfrac{1}{4} \Rightarrow \cos 2t = \dfrac{1}{2} \Rightarrow t = \dfrac{\pi}{6}$

$\therefore$ Eq. (i) reduces to

$$I = \int_{\pi/6}^{\pi/4}\frac{1}{2}\cdot\frac{(b^2-a^2)\sin 2t}{\sqrt{(b^2-a^2)\sin^2 t\,(b^2-a^2)\cos^2 t}}\,dt$$

$$= \int_{\pi/6}^{\pi/4} dt = (t)_{\pi/6}^{\pi/4} = \left(\frac{\pi}{4} - \frac{\pi}{6}\right) = \frac{\pi}{12}$$

4. Let $I = \int_0^{\pi/4}\dfrac{e^{\sec x}\left[\sin\left(x + \dfrac{\pi}{4}\right)\right]}{\cos x(1 - \sin x)}\,dx$

$$= \frac{1}{\sqrt{2}}\int_0^{\pi/4}\frac{e^{\sec x}(\sin x + \cos x)(1+\sin x)}{\cos x(1-\sin^2 x)}\,dx$$

$$= \frac{1}{\sqrt{2}}\int_0^{\pi/4}\frac{e^{\sec x}(\sin x + \cos x)(1+\sin x)}{\cos^2 x\cdot\cos x}\,dx$$

$$= \frac{1}{\sqrt{2}} \int_0^{\pi/4} e^{\sec x} \cdot (\sec x \tan x + \sec x)(\sec x + \tan x)\, dx$$

$$= \frac{1}{\sqrt{2}} \int_0^{\pi/4} e^{\sec x} \cdot [\sec x \tan x (\sec x + \tan x) + \sec^2 x + \sec x \tan x]\, dx$$

$$= \frac{1}{\sqrt{2}} \int_0^{\pi/4} e^{\sec x} \cdot [\sec x \tan x (\sec x + \tan x + 1) + \sec^2 x]\, dx$$

$$= \frac{1}{\sqrt{2}} \int_0^{\pi/4} e^{\sec x} \cdot \sec x \tan x (\sec x + \tan x + 1) + \frac{1}{\sqrt{2}} \int_0^{\pi/4} e^{\sec x} \cdot \sec^2 x\, dx$$

Applying integration by parts,

$$I = \frac{1}{\sqrt{2}} \{(\sec x + \tan x + 1)\, e^{\sec x}\}_0^{\pi/4} - \frac{1}{\sqrt{2}} \int_0^{\pi/4} (\sec x \tan x + \sec^2 x) \cdot e^{\sec x} dx + \frac{1}{\sqrt{2}} \int_0^{\pi/4} e^{\sec x} \cdot \sec^2 x\, dx$$

$$= \frac{1}{\sqrt{2}} \{(\sqrt{2} + 1 + 1)\, e^{\sqrt{2}} - (1 + 1)\, e\} - \frac{1}{\sqrt{2}} [e^{\sec x}]_0^{\pi/4}$$

$$= \frac{1}{\sqrt{2}} (\sqrt{2} + 2)\, e^{\sqrt{2}} - \sqrt{2} e - \frac{1}{\sqrt{2}} (e^{\sqrt{2}} - e)$$

$$= \frac{1}{\sqrt{2}} (1 + \sqrt{2})\, e^{\sqrt{2}} - \frac{e}{\sqrt{2}}$$

5. Let $I = \int_0^{\pi} \frac{x^2 \cos x}{(1 + \sin x)^2} dx = \int_0^{\pi} x^2 \{(1 + \sin x)^{-2} \cos x\}\, dx$

Applying integration by parts,

$$I = \left(x^2 \frac{(1 + \sin x)^{-1}}{-1} \right)_0^{\pi} - \int_0^{\pi} 2x \cdot \frac{(1 + \sin x)^{-1}}{-1} dx$$

$$= (-\pi^2 + 0) + 2 \int_0^{\pi} \frac{x}{1 + \sin x} dx \quad \text{...(i)}$$

$$\left[\text{using, } \int_0^a f(x)\, dx = \int_0^a f(a - x)\, dx\right]$$

$$I = -\pi^2 + 2 \int_0^{\pi} \frac{(\pi - x)}{1 + \sin x} dx \quad \text{...(ii)}$$

Adding Eqs. (i) and (ii), we get

$$2I = -2\pi^2 + 2 \int_0^{\pi} \frac{\pi}{1 + \sin x} dx$$

$$= -2\pi^2 + 2\pi \int_0^{\pi} \frac{1 - \sin x}{\cos^2 x} dx$$

$$= -2\pi^2 + 2\pi [\tan x - \sec x]_0^{\pi}$$

$$= -2\pi^2 + 2\pi [0 - (-1 - 1)]$$

$$= -2\pi^2 + 4\pi$$

$$\therefore \quad I = -\pi^2 + 2\pi$$

6. (i) Let $t = \ln x \Rightarrow x = e^t$

$$dx = e^t\, dt \quad \text{or} \quad \frac{dx}{x} = dt$$

Also, $x = 0 \Rightarrow t = -\infty$ and $x = \infty \Rightarrow t = \infty$

$$\therefore \int_0^{\infty} f(x^n + x^{-n}) \ln x \frac{dx}{x} = \int_{-\infty}^{\infty} f(e^{nt} + e^{-nt}) \cdot t\, dt = 0$$

[$\because$ integrand is an odd function of t]

(ii) $\int_0^{\infty} f(x^n + x^{-n}) \ln x \cdot \frac{dx}{1 + x^2}$

$$= \int_{-\infty}^{\infty} f(e^{nt} + e^{-nt}) \cdot t \cdot \frac{e^t}{1 + e^{2t}} \cdot dt$$

Now, if $h(t) = f(e^{nt} + e^{-nt}) \cdot \frac{t\, e^t}{1 + e^{2t}}$

Then, $h(-t) = f(e^{-nt} + e^{nt}) \cdot (-t) \cdot \frac{1}{e^t + e^{-t}}$

$$\left[\because \frac{e^t}{1 + e^{2t}} = \frac{1}{e^{-t} + e^t}\right]$$

$$h(-t) = -h(t)$$

Thus, integrand is an odd function and hence

$$\int_0^{\infty} f(x^n + x^{-n}) \ln x \cdot \frac{dx}{1 + x^2} = 0$$

7. Let $f(x) = \int_0^x g(t)\, dt$

$$\Rightarrow \quad f'(x) = g(x)$$

$$\Rightarrow \frac{1}{2} \int_0^x (f'(t))^2\, dt = \frac{1}{2} \int_0^x g^2(t)\, dt \quad \text{...(i)}$$

$$\Rightarrow \frac{1}{2} \left[\int_0^x g(t) \right]^2 = \frac{1}{2} (f(x))^2$$

$$\Rightarrow \frac{1}{2} \frac{\left[\int_0^x g(t) \right]^2}{x} = \frac{1}{2} \frac{(f(x))^2}{x}$$

$$\Rightarrow \frac{1}{2} \cdot \frac{1}{2} \left[\int_0^x g^2(t) \right] dt = \frac{1}{2} \frac{(f(x))^2}{x}$$

$$\Rightarrow \frac{1}{2} \int_0^x (f'(t))^2\, dt = \frac{1}{2} \frac{(f(x))^2}{x} \quad \text{[using Eq. (i)]}$$

Differentiating both the sides w.r.t. x, we get

$$\frac{1}{2} [f'(x)]^2 = \frac{x\, 2\, f(x)\, f'(x) - (f(x))^2}{x^2}$$

$$\Rightarrow \frac{1}{2} [g(x)]^2\, x^2 = 2x\, f(x)\, (g(x)) - (f(x))^2$$

$$\Rightarrow \left(\frac{x\, g(x)}{f(x)} \right)^2 = 4 \left(\frac{x\, g(x)}{f(x)} \right) - 2$$

$$\Rightarrow \quad t^2 - 4t + 2 = 0, \text{ where } t = \frac{x\, g(x)}{f(x)}$$

$$\Rightarrow \quad t = \frac{4 \pm \sqrt{8}}{2} = 2 \pm \sqrt{2}$$

or $$\frac{x\, f'(x)}{f(x)} = 2 \pm \sqrt{2}$$

$\Rightarrow \ln f(x) = 2 \pm \sqrt{2} \ln x + \text{constant}$

$\Rightarrow \quad f(x) = cx^{2 + \sqrt{2}}$ or $cx^{2 - \sqrt{2}}$

$\Rightarrow \quad g(x) = f'(x) = c_1\, x^{1 + \sqrt{2}}$ or $c_2\, x^{1 - \sqrt{2}}$

where, c_1 and c_2 are constants of integration.

But g is continuous on $[0, \infty)$, then $c_2\, x^{1 - \sqrt{2}}$ is ruled out.

Hence, $g(x) = c_1\, x^{1 + \sqrt{2}}$

Also, $g(0) = c^1 = 1 \Rightarrow g(x) = x^{1 + \sqrt{2}}$

8. Let $I = \int_0^x e^{xt} \cdot e^{-t^2}\, dt$. Put $t = \dfrac{x+z}{2} \Rightarrow dt = \dfrac{1}{2} dz$

$$\therefore \quad I = \int_0^x e^{tx} \cdot e^{-t^2}\, dt = \frac{1}{2}\int_{-x}^{x} e^{\left(\frac{x+z}{2}\right)x} \cdot e^{-\left(\frac{x+z}{2}\right)^2} dz$$

$$= \frac{1}{2}\int_{-x}^{x} e^{\left(\frac{x+z}{2}\right)\left(x - \frac{x+z}{2}\right)} dz = \frac{1}{2}\int_{-x}^{x} e^{\left(\frac{x+z}{2}\right)\left(\frac{x-z}{2}\right)} dz$$

$$= \frac{1}{2}\int_{-x}^{x} e^{\frac{x^2}{4} - \frac{z^2}{4}} dz = \frac{1}{2} e^{x^2/4} \cdot \int_{-x}^{x} e^{-z^2/4} dz$$

$$= \frac{1}{2} e^{x^2/4} \int_{-x}^{x} e^{-t^2/4} dt = \frac{1}{2} e^{x^2/4} \cdot 2\int_0^x e^{-t^2/4} dt$$

$$\left[\text{using, } \int_{-a}^{a} f(x)\, dx = 2\int_0^a f(x)\, dx, \text{ when } f(-x) = f(x)\right]$$

$$= e^{x^2/4} \int_0^x e^{-t^2/4} dt$$

$$\Rightarrow \quad \int_0^x e^{xt} \cdot x^{-t^2}\, dt = e^{x^2/4} \int_0^x e^{-t^2/4} dt$$

9. Given, $|a| < 1$

Let $f(a) = \displaystyle\int_0^\pi \frac{\log(1 + a\cos x)}{\cos x} dx$

$$\therefore \quad f'(a) = \int_0^\pi \frac{\cos x}{\cos x \cdot (1 + a\cos x)} dx$$

$$= \int_0^\pi \frac{dx}{1 + a\cos x}$$

[differentiating w.r.t. 'a' using Leibnitz rule]

$$\left[\text{put } \tan\frac{x}{2} = t \Rightarrow \frac{dx}{dt} = \frac{2}{1+t^2}, \text{ when } x = 0, t = 0 \text{ and when } x = \pi, t \to \infty\right]$$

$$\Rightarrow f'(a) = \int_0^\infty \frac{\frac{2dt}{1+t^2}}{1 + a\left(\frac{1-t^2}{1+t^2}\right)}$$

$$= \int_0^\infty \frac{2dt}{(1+t^2) + a(1-t^2)}$$

$$= \int_0^\infty \frac{2dt}{(1-a)t^2 + (1+a)}$$

$$= \frac{2}{1-a}\int_0^\infty \frac{dt}{t^2 + \left(\sqrt{\frac{1+a}{1-a}}\right)^2}$$

$$= \frac{2}{1-a} \cdot \frac{1}{\sqrt{(1+a)/(1-a)}} \cdot \left(\tan^{-1} t\sqrt{\frac{1-a}{1+a}}\right)_0^\infty$$

$$= \frac{2}{\sqrt{1-a^2}} \cdot \frac{\pi}{2} = \frac{\pi}{\sqrt{1-a^2}}$$

[integrating both the sides w.r.t. 'a']

$$\Rightarrow \quad f(a) = \pi\sin^{-1} a + c$$

But $f(0) = \displaystyle\int_0^\pi \frac{\log(1 + 0\cos x)\, dx}{\cos x} = 0$

$$\Rightarrow \quad c = 0$$

$$\therefore \quad f(a) = \pi\sin^{-1} a$$

10. Let $\quad f(c) = \displaystyle\int_0^{\pi/2} \operatorname{cosec}\theta \cdot \tan^{-1}(c\sin\theta)\, d\theta$

$$\therefore \quad f'(c) = \int_0^{\pi/2} \operatorname{cosec}\theta \cdot \frac{(\sin\theta)}{1 + c^2\sin^2\theta} d\theta + 0 - 0$$

$$= \int_0^{\pi/2} \frac{d\theta}{1 + c^2\sin^2\theta}$$

$$= \int_0^{\pi/2} \frac{\operatorname{cosec}^2\theta\, d\theta}{c^2 + \operatorname{cosec}^2\theta}$$

$$= \int_0^{\pi/2} \frac{\operatorname{cosec}^2\theta\, d\theta}{(c^2+1) + \cot^2\theta}$$

$$= -\frac{1}{\sqrt{c^2+1}}\left(\tan^{-1}\frac{\cot\theta}{\sqrt{c^2+1}}\right)_0^{\pi/2}$$

$$f'(c) = \frac{\pi}{2\sqrt{c^2+1}}$$

Integrating both the sides, we get

$$f(c) = \int \frac{\pi\, dc}{2\sqrt{c^2+1}} = \frac{\pi}{2}\log(c + \sqrt{c^2+1}) + A$$

where, $f(0) = A$

But $\quad f(0) = \displaystyle\int_0^{\pi/2} \operatorname{cosec}\theta \tan^{-1}(0)\, d\theta = 0$

$$\Rightarrow \quad f(c) = \frac{\pi}{2}\log(c + \sqrt{c^2+1})$$

11. Given, $f(x) = x + x\displaystyle\int_0^1 y^2 f(y)\, dy + x^2 \int_0^1 y\, f(y)\, dy$

$$= x\left(1 + \int_0^1 y^2 f(y)\, dy\right) + x^2\left(\int_0^1 y\, f(y)\, dy\right)$$

$\Rightarrow$ $f(x)$ is a quadratic expression.

$\Rightarrow \quad f(x) = ax + bx^2 \quad$ or $\quad f(y) = ay + by^2 \qquad$ ...(i)

where, $\quad a = 1 + \displaystyle\int_0^1 y^2 f(y)\, dy = 1 + \int_0^1 y^2(ay + by^2)\, dy$

$$= 1 + \left(\frac{ay^4}{4} + \frac{by^5}{5}\right)_0^1 \quad a = 1 + \left(\frac{a}{4} + \frac{b}{5}\right)$$

$$\Rightarrow \quad 20a = 20 + 5a + 4b$$

or $\quad 15a - 4b = 20 \qquad$ ...(ii)

and $\quad b = \displaystyle\int_0^1 y\, f(y)\, dy = \int_0^1 y(ay + by^2)\, dy$

$$= \left(\frac{ay^3}{3} + \frac{by^4}{4}\right)_0^1$$

$$\Rightarrow \quad b = \frac{a}{3} + \frac{b}{4}$$

$$\Rightarrow \quad 12b = 4a + 3b$$

or $\quad 9b - 4a = 0 \qquad$ ...(iii)

From Eqs. (ii) and (iii), we get

$$a = \frac{180}{119}$$

and $\quad b = \dfrac{80}{119}$

$\therefore$ Eq. (i) reduces to

$$f(x) = \frac{80x^2 + 180x}{119}$$

12. Let $I(n) = \int_0^{3\pi/2} \underset{\text{I}}{(\log|\sin x|)} \underset{\text{II}}{(\cos 2nx)}\, dx$

$$I(n) = \left(\log|\sin x| \cdot \frac{\sin 2nx}{2n} \right)_0^{3\pi/2} - \int_0^{3\pi/2} \cot x \cdot \frac{\sin 2nx}{2n}\, dx$$

[using integration by parts]

$$I(n) = 0 - \frac{1}{2n} \int_0^{3\pi/2} \frac{\sin 2nx \cdot \cos x}{\sin x}\, dx = 0 - \frac{1}{2} I_1(n) \quad \text{...(i)}$$

Let $I_1(n) = \int_0^{3\pi/2} \frac{\sin(2nx)\cos x}{\sin x}\, dx$

$$I_1(n+1) = \int_0^{3\pi/2} \frac{\sin(2n+2)x \cdot \cos x}{\sin x}\, dx$$

$$\therefore\ I_1(n+1) - I_1(n) = \int_0^{3\pi/2} \frac{(\sin(2n+2)x - \sin 2nx) \cdot \cos x}{\sin x}\, dx$$

$$= \int_0^{3\pi/2} \frac{2\cos(2n+1)x \cdot \sin x \cdot \cos x}{\sin x}\, dx$$

$$= \int_0^{3\pi/2} (\cos(2n+2)x + \cos 2nx)\, dx$$

$$= \left(\frac{\sin(2n+2)x}{(2n+2)} + \frac{\sin(2n)x}{2n} \right)_0^{3\pi/2}$$

$$= 0 + 0$$

$$\Rightarrow \quad I_1(n+1) = I_1(n) = \ldots = I_1(1)$$

$$\therefore \quad I_1(1) = \int_0^{3\pi/2} \frac{\sin 2x \cdot \cos x}{\sin x}\, dx$$

$$= \int_0^{3\pi/2} \frac{2\sin x\cos x \cdot \cos x}{\sin x}\, dx$$

$$= \int_0^{3\pi/2} 2\cos^2 x\, dx$$

$$= \int_0^{3\pi/2} (1 + \cos 2x)\, dx$$

$$= \left(x + \frac{\sin 2x}{2} \right)_0^{3\pi/2}$$

$$\Rightarrow \quad I_1(1) = \frac{3\pi}{2} = I_1(n)$$

$$\Rightarrow \quad I(n) = -\frac{1}{2n} I_1(n) \quad \text{[using Eq. (i)]}$$

$$\therefore \quad I(n) = -\frac{3\pi}{4n}$$

13. Here, $I = \int_0^1 (tx + 1 - x)^n\, dx = \int_0^1 ((t-1)x + 1)^n\, dx$

$$= \left\{ \frac{((t-1)x+1)^{n+1}}{(n+1)(t-1)} \right\}_0^1$$

$$= \frac{1}{n+1} \{t^n + t^{n-1} + t^{n-2} + \ldots + t + 1\} \quad \text{...(i)}$$

Again, $I = \int_0^1 (tx + 1 - x)^n\, dx = \int_0^1 \{(1-x) + tx\}^n\, dx$

$$= \int_0^1 \{{}^nC_0 (1-x)^n + {}^nC_1 (1-x)^{n-1}(tx) + {}^nC_2 (1-x)^{n-2} (tx)^2 + \ldots + {}^nC_r (1-x)^{n-r}(tx)^r + \ldots + {}^nC_n (tx)^n\}\, dx$$

$$= \int_0^1 \left\{ \sum_{r=0}^{n} {}^nC_r (1-x)^{n-r} (tx)^r \right\} dx$$

$$= \sum_{r=0}^{n} {}^nC_r\, t^r \int_0^1 \{(1-x)^{n-r} x^r\}\, dx \quad \text{...(ii)}$$

From Eqs. (i) and (ii),

$$\sum_{r=0}^{n} {}^nC_r t^r \int_0^1 (1-x)^{n-r} x^r dx = \frac{1}{n+1} \{t^n + t^{n-1} + t^{n-2} + \ldots + t + 1\}$$

Equating coefficient of t^k on both the sides, we get

$${}^nC_k \int_0^1 (1-x)^{n-k} x^k\, dx = \frac{1}{n+1}$$

$$\Rightarrow \quad \int_0^1 (1-x)^{n-k} x^k\, dx = \frac{1}{{}^nC_k (n+1)}$$

14. **Decoding the Question**

For $a > 0$, $I = \int_0^\infty \frac{\ln x\, dx}{ax^2 + bx + a} = 0$

[**Hint** By putting $x = 1/t$, we get $I = -I$, so $I = 0$]

$I = \int_0^\infty \frac{\ln x\, dx}{x^2 + 2x + 4}$ (put $x = 2t \Rightarrow dx = 2dt$ to make coefficient of x^2 and constant term same)

$$= 2\int_0^\infty \frac{\ln 2 + \ln t}{4(t^2 + t + 1)} dt = \frac{\ln 2}{2} \underbrace{\int_0^\infty \frac{dt}{t^2 + t + 1}}_{I_1} + \frac{1}{2} \underbrace{\int_0^\infty \frac{\ln t\, dt}{t^2 + t + 1}}_{I_2 = \text{zero}}$$

$$I_2 = \int_0^\infty \frac{\ln t\, dt}{t^2 + t + 1} \quad \left(\text{put } t = \frac{1}{y} \Rightarrow dt = -\frac{1}{y^2} dy \right)$$

$$I_2 = \int_\infty^0 \frac{\ln y \cdot (+1)}{\left(\frac{1}{y^2} + \frac{1}{y} + 1 \right) y^2} dy$$

$$I_2 = \int_\infty^0 \frac{\ln y\, dy}{y^2 + y + 1} = -\int_\infty^0 \frac{\ln y\, dy}{y^2 + y + 1} = -I_2$$

$$\text{Now, } I_1 = \int_0^\infty \frac{dt}{\left(t + \frac{1}{2}\right)^2 + \left(\frac{\sqrt{3}}{2}\right)^2} = \left[\frac{2}{\sqrt{3}} \tan^{-1} \frac{[t + (1/2)]^2}{\sqrt{3}} \right]_0^\infty$$

$$= \frac{2}{\sqrt{3}} \left[\frac{\pi}{2} - \frac{\pi}{6} \right] = \frac{2\pi}{3\sqrt{3}}$$

$$\therefore \quad I = \frac{\ln 2}{2} \cdot \frac{2\pi}{3\sqrt{3}} = \frac{\pi \ln 2}{3\sqrt{3}}$$

> Why do children dread Mathematics? Because of the wrong approach. Because it is looked at as a subject.
>
> **-Shakuntla Devi**

3

Area of Bounded Regions

Learning Milestones

Milestone 1 Sketching of Some Common Curves and Asymptotes

- Sketching of Some Common Curves
- Some More Curves Which Occur Frequently in Mathematics in Standard Forms
- Curve Sketching
- Asymptotes
- Area of the Cartesian Curve

Milestone 2 Area Bounded by Two or More Curves

- Area Bounded by Two or More Curves
- Area Bounded by Inverse of Given Function Without Getting Inverse Function

Practice Milestones

Practice Milestone 1- JEE Main Pattern

Practice Milestone 2 - JEE Advanced Pattern

Practice Milestone 3 - Challenging Problems

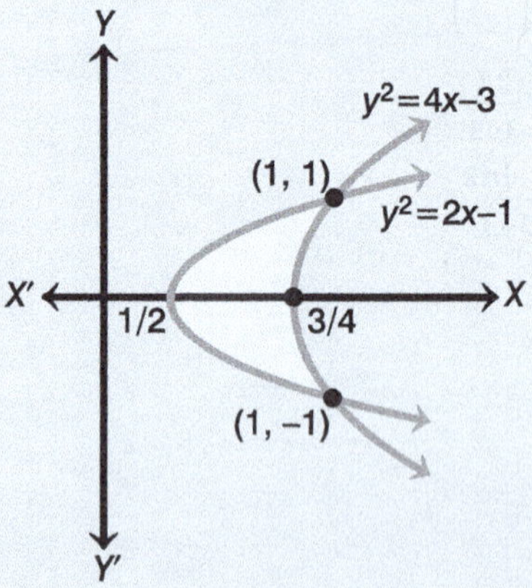

Milestone 1 Sketching of Some Common Curves and Asymptotes

• Sketching of Some Common Curves • Some More Curves Which Occur Frequently in Mathematics in Standard Forms • Curve Sketching • Asymptotes • Area of the Cartesian Curve

3.1 Sketching of Some Common Curves

For finding the area of a given region, we require the knowledge of some standard curves.

(i) Straight Line

Every first degree equation in x, y represents a straight line. So, the general equation of a line is $ax + by + c = 0$.

To draw a straight line find the points, where it meets with the coordinate axes by putting $y = 0$ and $x = 0$ respectively in its equation.

By joining these two points we get the sketch of the line. Sometimes the equation of a line is given in the form $y = mx$.

This equation represents a line passing through the origin and inclined at an angle $\tan^{-1} m$ with the positive direction of X-axis. The equation of the form $x = a$ and $y = b$ represents straight lines parallel to Y-axis and X-axis, respectively.

Region Represented by a Linear Inequality

To find the region represented by linear inequality $ax + by \le c$ and $ax + by \ge c$, we proceed as follows

(i) Convert the inequality into equality to obtain a linear equation in x, y.

(ii) Draw the straight line represented by it.

(iii) The straight line obtained in (ii) divides the XY-plane in two parts.

To determine the region represented by the inequality choose some convenient points; e.g. origin or some points on the coordinate axes.

If the coordinates of a point satisfy the inequality, then region containing the points is the required region, otherwise the region not containing the point is required region.

Example 1. Mark the region represented by $3x + 4y \le 12$.

Sol. Converting the inequality into equation, we get $3x + 4y = 12$.

This line meets the coordinate axes at (4, 0) and (0, 3), respectively. Join these points to obtain straight line represented by $3x + 4y = 12$.

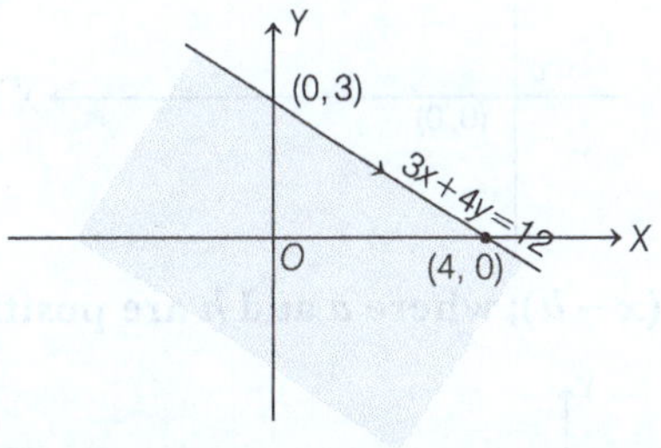

This straight line divides the plane in two parts. One part contains the origin and the other does not contains the origin. Clearly, (0, 0) satisfy the inequality $3x + 4y < 12$. So, the region represented by $3x + 4y < 12$ is region containing the origin as shown in the figure.

(ii) Circle

The general equation of a circle is

$$x^2 + y^2 + 2gx + 2fy + c = 0$$

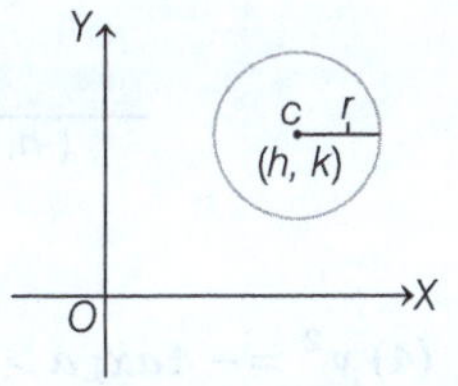

∴ The second degree equation in x, y such that coefficient of x^2 = coefficient of y^2 and there is no term containing xy; it always represents a circle. To draw a sketch of a circle, we write the equation instandard form $(x - h)^2 + (y - k)^2 = r^2$, whose centre is (h, k) and radius is r.

JEE Focus Points

- The inequality $(x - a)^2 + (y - b)^2 < r^2$ represents the interior of a circle.
- The inequality $(x - a)^2 + (y - b)^2 > r^2$ represents the exterior of a circle (i.e. region lying outside the circle).

(iii) Parabola

It is the locus of points such that its distance from a fixed point is equal to its distance from a fixed straight line.

Taking the fixed straight line $x = -a, a > 0$ and fixed point $(a, 0)$, we get the equation of parabola $y^2 = 4ax$.

Steps to Sketch the Curve

(i) It passes through (0, 0).

(ii) It is symmetrical about axis of X.

(iii) No part of the curve lies on the negative side of axis of X.

(iv) Curve turns at (0, 0) which is called the vertex of the curve.

(v) The curve extends to infinity. It is not a closed curve.

(1) $y^2 = 4ax$ (Standard equation of parabola)

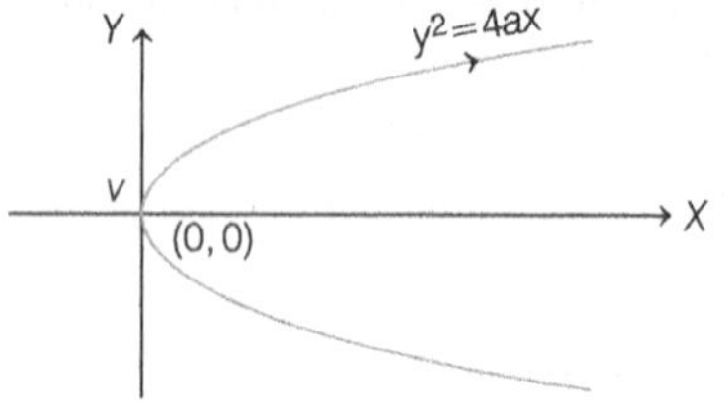

(2) $y^2 = 4a(x - h)$; where a and h are positive.

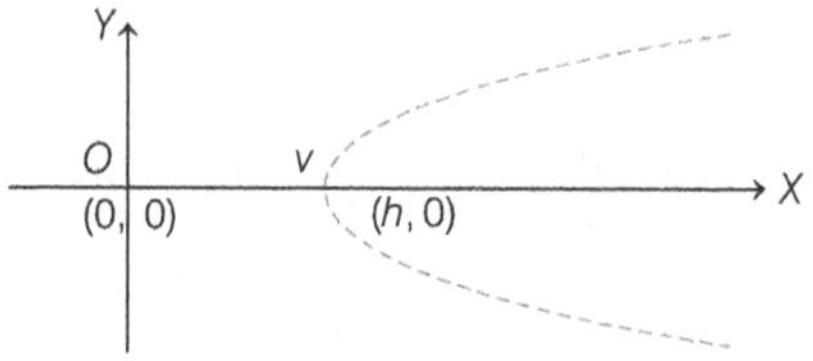

(3) $y^2 = 4a(x + h)$; where a and h are positive.

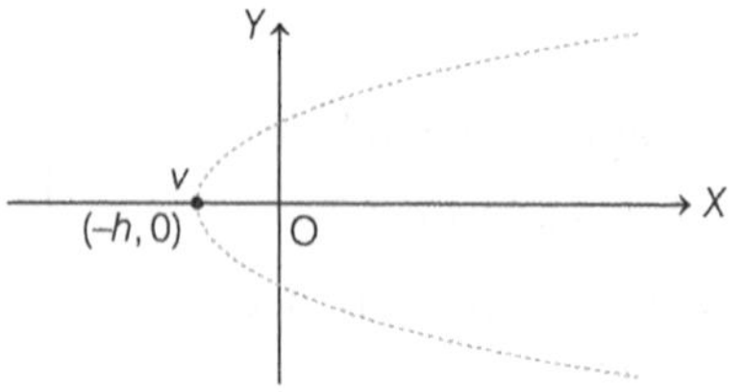

(4) $y^2 = -4ax$; $a > 0$

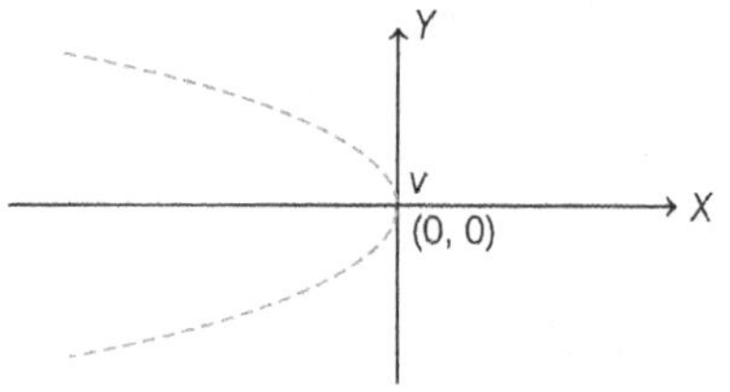

(5) $y^2 = -4a(x - h)$; $a, h > 0$

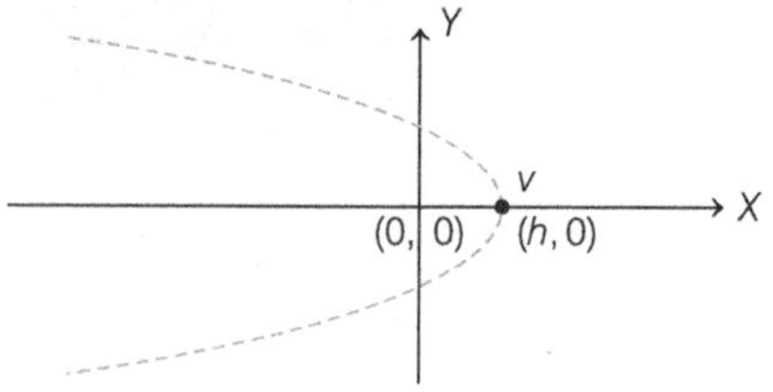

(6) $y^2 = -4a(x + h)$; $a, h > 0$

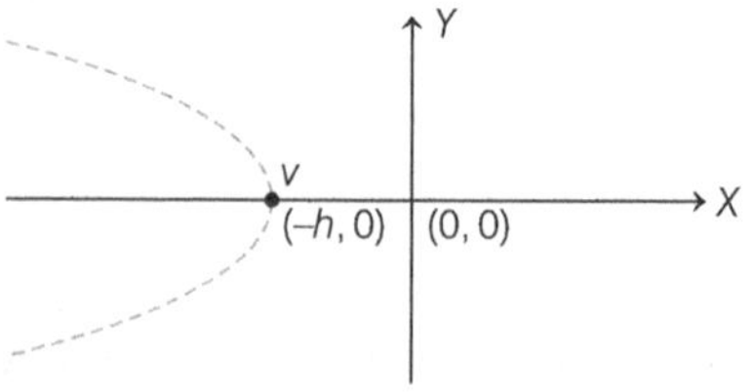

(7) $x^2 = 4ay$; $a > 0$

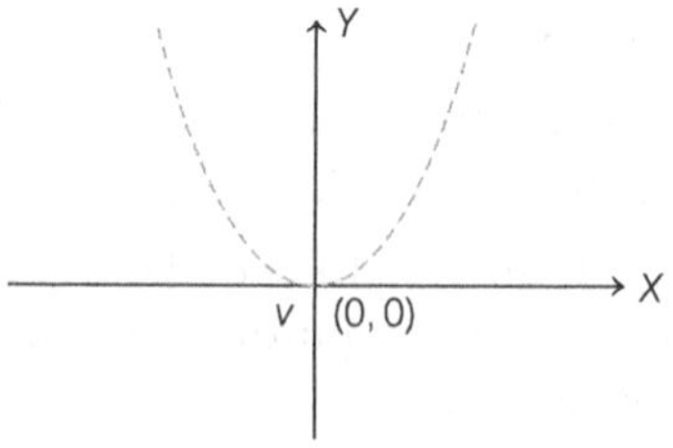

(8) $x^2 = 4a(y + k)$; $a > 0, k > 0$

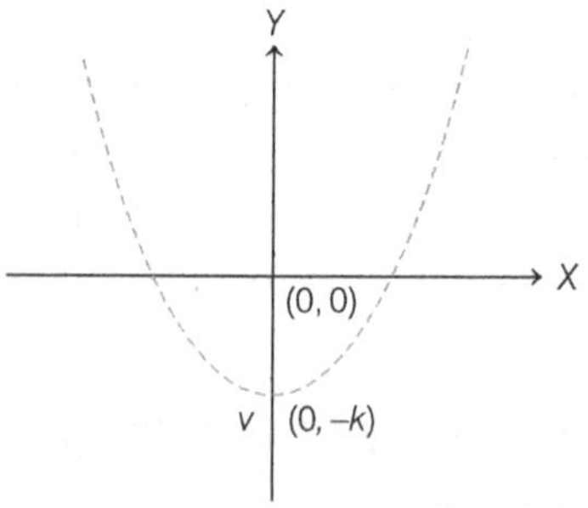

(9) $x^2 = 4a(y - k)$; $a, k > 0$

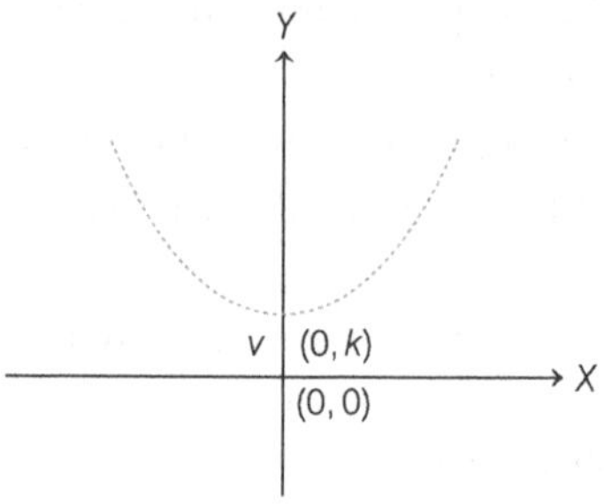

(10) $x^2 = -4ay; a > 0$

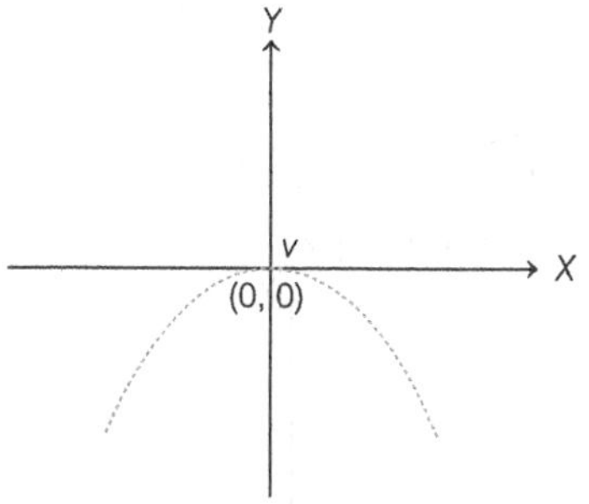

(11) $x^2 = -4a(y + k); a, k > 0$

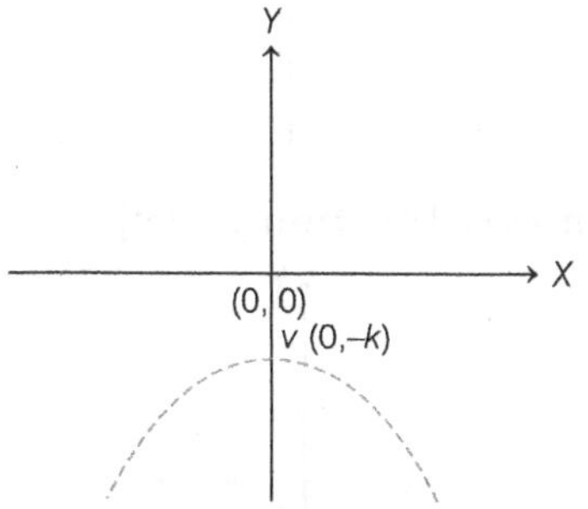

(12) $x^2 = -4a(y - k); a, k > 0$

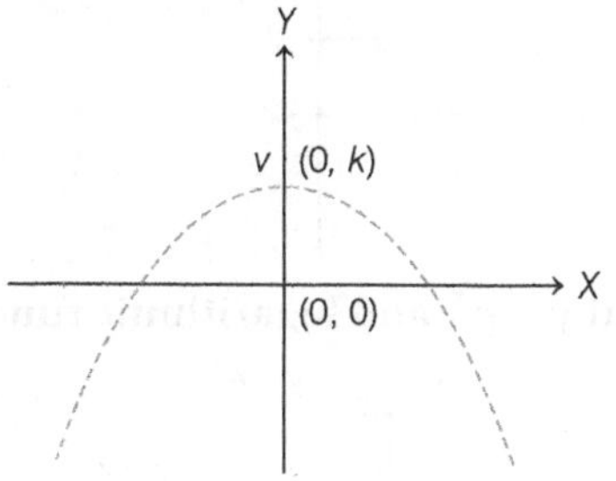

(iv) Ellipse

An ellipse is the locus of a moving point such that the ratio of its distance from a fixed point to its distance from a fixed line is a constant less than unity.

(1) $\frac{x^2}{a^2} + \frac{y^2}{b^2} = 1; a > 0, b > 0$

(Standard equation of the ellipse)

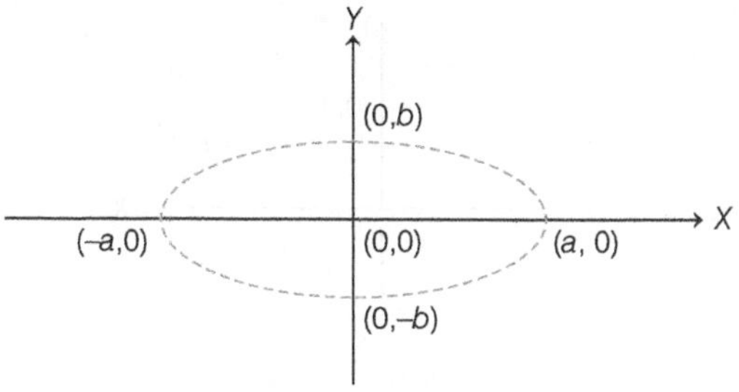

(2) $\frac{x^2}{a^2} + \frac{y^2}{b^2} = 1; b > a > 0$ **(Vertical ellipse)**

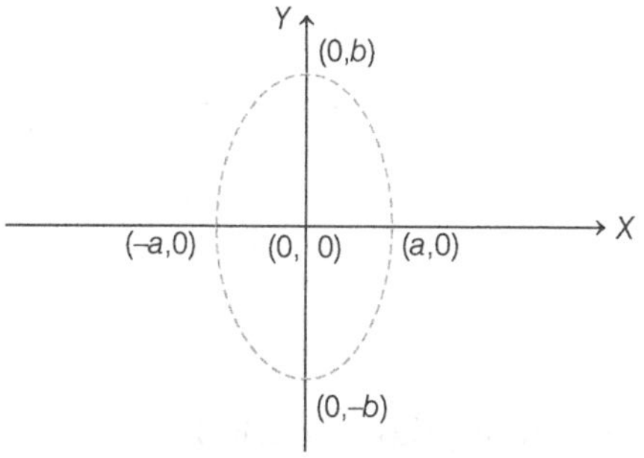

(3) $\frac{(x-h)^2}{a^2} + \frac{(y-k)^2}{b^2} = 1; a > 0, b > 0$ **and** $a > b$

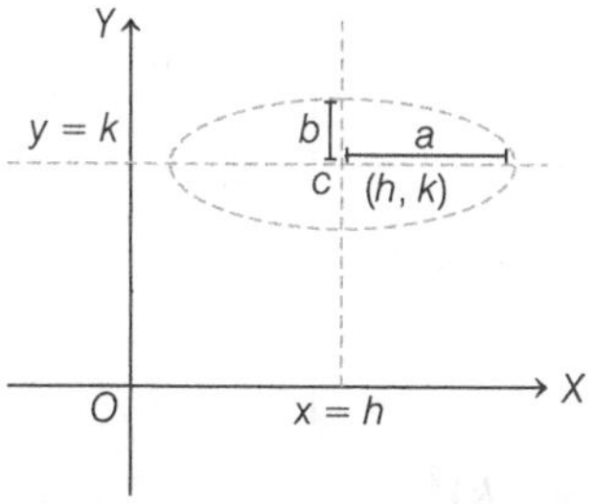

(4) $\frac{(x-h)^2}{a^2} + \frac{(y-k)^2}{b^2} = 1$, **where** $a < b$

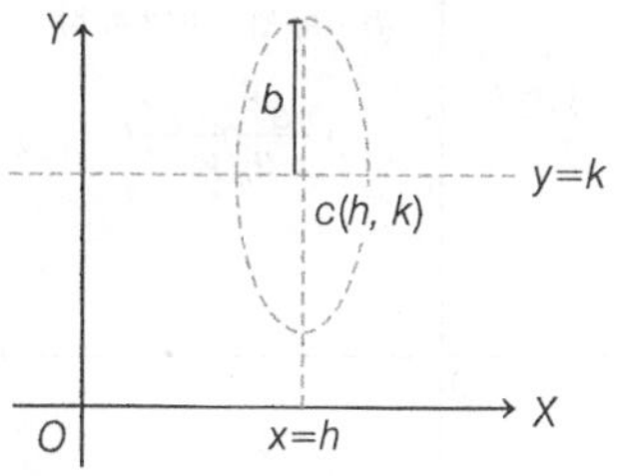

(v) Hyperbola

A hyperbola is the locus of a moving point such that the **difference** of its distances from two fixed points is always constant. The two fixed point are called the foci of the hyperbola.

(1) $\frac{x^2}{a^2} - \frac{y^2}{b^2} = 1$ **(Standard equation of hyperbola)**

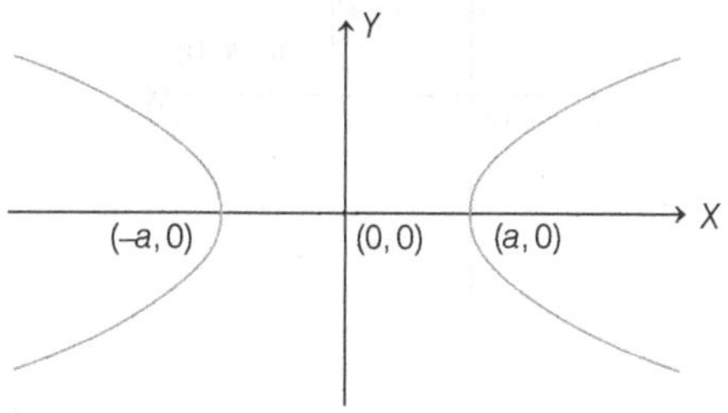

(2) $\dfrac{y^2}{b^2} - \dfrac{x^2}{a^2} = 1$ **(Conjugate hyperbola)**

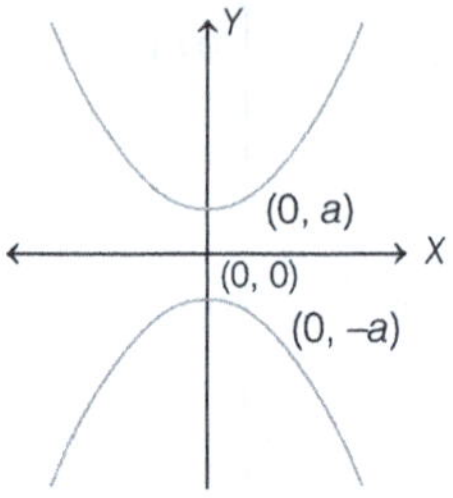

(3) $xy = c^2$ **(Rectangular hyperbola)**

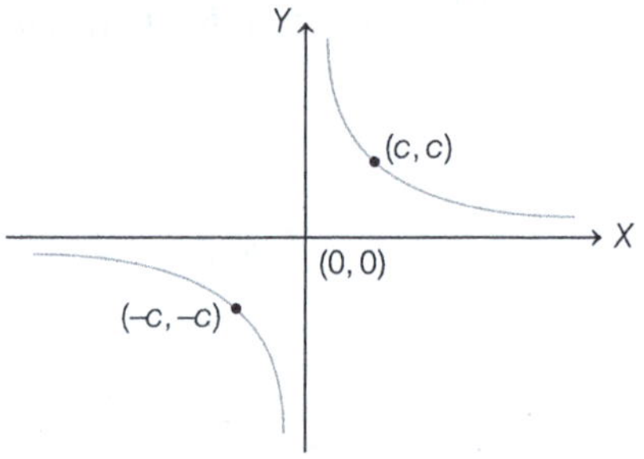

(4) $\dfrac{(x-h)^2}{a^2} - \dfrac{(y-k)^2}{b^2} = 1;\ a > b > 0$

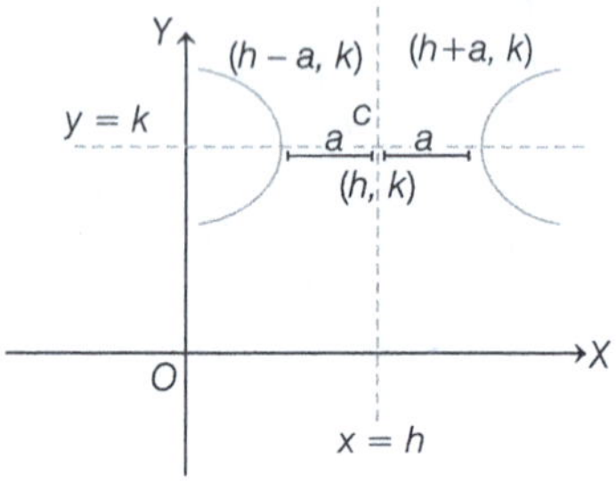

(5) $\dfrac{(x-h)^2}{a^2} - \dfrac{(y-k)^2}{b^2} = -1$

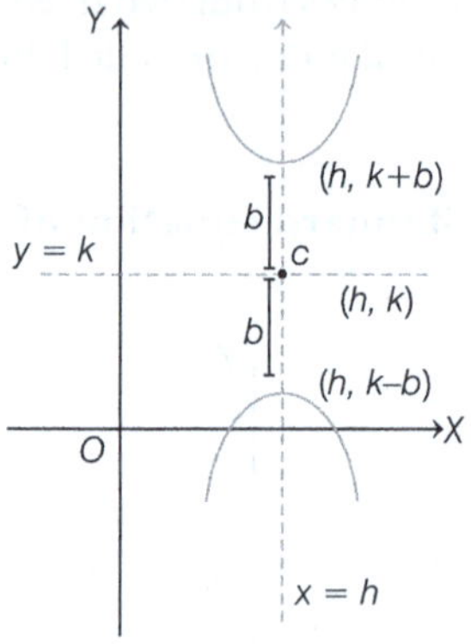

3.2 Some More Curves Which Occur Frequently in Mathematics in Standard Forms

1. Modulus function, $y = |x|$

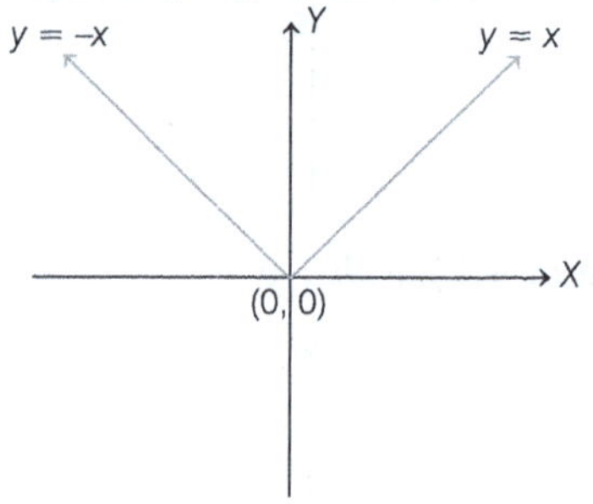

2. Greatest integer function $y = [x]$

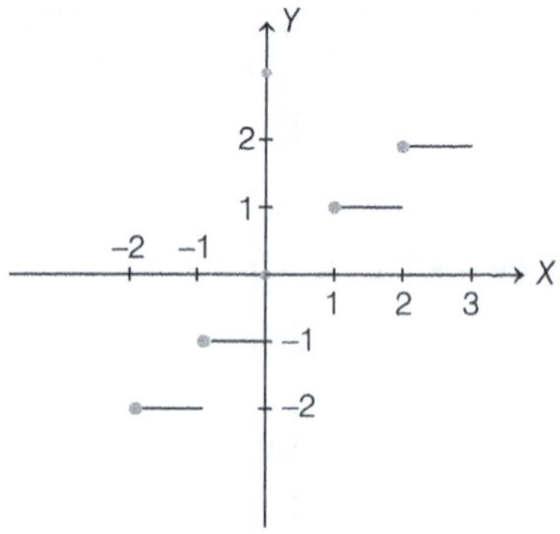

3. Exponential $y = e^x$ and logarithmic function $y = \ln x$

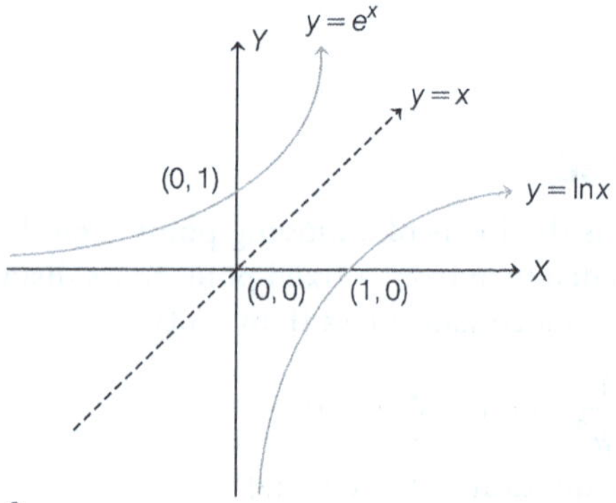

4. $y = e^{-x^2}$

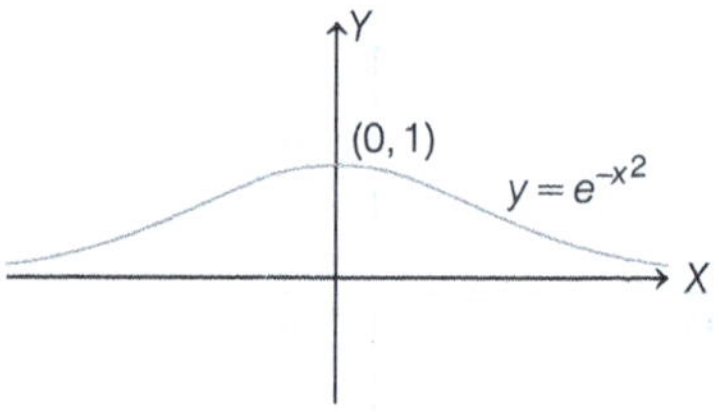

5. $y = \dfrac{1}{x^a}, a > 0$

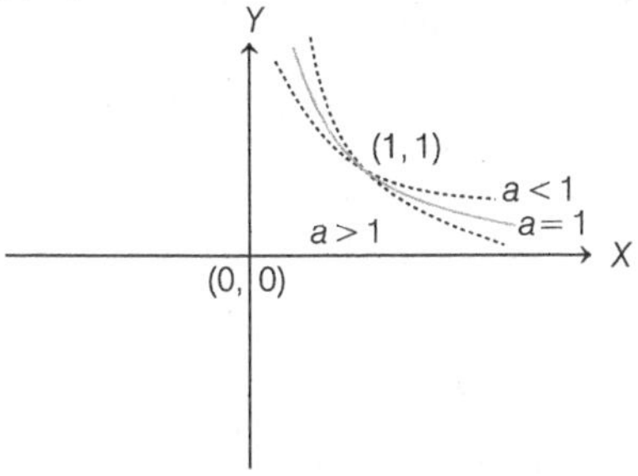

6. $y = \dfrac{1}{1 + x^2}$

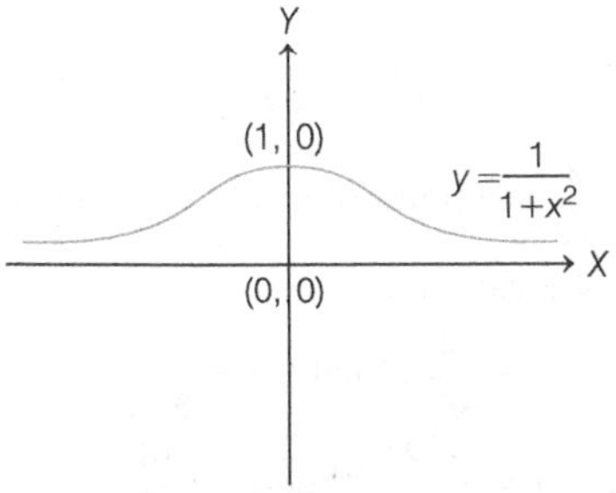

7. The Astroid

Its cartesian equation is $x^{2/3} + y^{2/3} = a^{2/3}$

Its parametric equation is $x = a\cos^3 t, y = a\sin^3 t$

and it could be plotted as

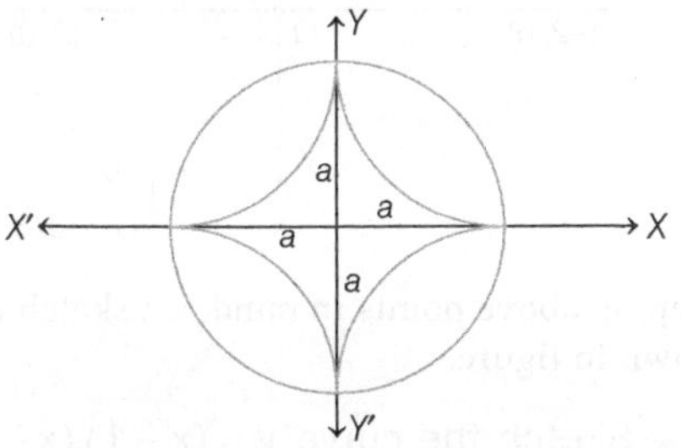

3.3 Curve Sketching

For the evaluation of area of bounded regions it is very essential to know the rough sketch of the curves. The following points are very useful to draw a rough sketch of a curve.

(i) Symmetry

- **Symmetry about X-axis** If all powers of y in the equation of the given curve are even, then it is symmetric about X-axis, i.e. the shape of the curve above X-axis is exactly identical to its shape below X-axis.

  e.g. $y^2 = 4ax$ is symmetric about X-axis.

- **Symmetry about Y-axis** If all powers of x in the equation of the given curve are even, then it is symmetric about Y-axis.

  e.g. $x^2 = 4ay$ is symmetric about Y-axis.

- **Symmetry in opposite quadrants** If by putting $-x$ for x and $-y$ for y, the equation of curve remains same, then it is symmetric in opposite quadrants.

  e.g. $xy = c^2$, $x^2 + y^2 = a^2$ are symmetric in opposite quadrants.

- **Symmetric about the line $y = x$** If the equation of a given curve remains unaltered by interchanging x and y, then it is symmetric about the line $y = x$ which passes through the origin and makes an angle of 45° with positive direction of X-axis.

(ii) Origin and Tangents at the Origin

See whether the curve passes through origin or not. If the point (0, 0) satisfies the equation of the curve, then it passes through the origin and in such a case to find the equations of the tangents at the origin, equate the lowest degree term to zero. e.g. $y^2 = 4ax$ passes through the origin. The lowest degree term in this equation is $4ax$. Equating $4ax$ to zero, we get $x = 0$.

So, $x = 0$ i.e. Y-axis is tangent at the origin to $y^2 = 4ax$.

(iii) Points of Intersection of Curve with the Coordinate Axes

By putting $y = 0$ in the equation of the given curve, find points where the curve crosses the X-axis. Similarly, by putting $x = 0$ in the equation of the given curve we can find points where the curve crosses the Y-axis.

e.g. To find the points where the curve $xy^2 = 4a^2(2a - x)$ meets X-axis, we put $y = 0$ in the equation which gives $4a^2(2a - x) = 0$ or $x = 2a$. So, the curve $xy^2 = 4a^2(2a - x)$, meets X-axis at $(2a, 0)$. This curve does not intersect Y-axis, because by putting $x = 0$ in the equation of the given curve get an absurd result.

(iv) Regions where the Curve Does Not Exist

Determine the regions in which the curve does not exist. For this, find the value of y in terms of x from the equation of the curve and find the value of x for which y is imaginary. Similarly, find the value of x in terms of y and determine the values of y for which x is imaginary. The curve does not exist for these values of x and y.

e.g. The values of y obtained from $y^2 = 4ax$ are imaginary for negative values of x. So, the curve does not exist on the left side of Y-axis. Similarly, the curve $a^2y^2 = x^2(a-x)$ does not exist for $x > a$ as the values of y are imaginary for $x > a$.

(v) Special Points

Find the points at which $\frac{dy}{dx} = 0$. At these points the tangent to the curve is parallel to X-axis.

Find the points at which $\frac{dx}{dy} = 0$. At these points the tangents to the curve is parallel to Y-axis.

(vi) Sign of dy/dx and Points of Maxima and Minima

Find the interval in which $\frac{dy}{dx} > 0$. In this interval, the function is monotonically increasing, find the interval in which $\frac{dy}{dx} < 0$. In this interval, the function is monotonically decreasing.

Put $\frac{dy}{dx} = 0$ and check the sign of $\frac{d^2y}{dx^2}$ at the points so obtained to find the points of maxima and minima.

Keeping the above facts in mind and plotting some points on the curve one can easily have a rough sketch of the curve. Following examples will clear the procedure.

Example 2. Sketch the curve $y = x^3 - 4x$.

Sol. We note the following points about the curve

(i) The equation of the curve remains same, if x is replaced by $(-x)$ and y by $(-y)$, so it is symmetric in opposite quadrants.
Consequently, the curve in the first quadrant is identical to the curve in third quadrant and the curve in second quadrant is similar to the curve in fourth quadrant.

(ii) The curve passes through the origin. Equating the lowest degree term $y + 4x$ to zero, we get $y + 4x = 0$ or $y = -4x$. So, $y = -4x$ is tangent to the curve at the origin.

(iii) Putting $y = 0$ in the equation of the curve, we obtain $x^3 - 4x = 0 \Rightarrow x = 0, \pm 2$. So, the curve meets X-axis at $(0, 0)$, $(2, 0)$, $(-2, 0)$.
Putting $x = 0$ in the equation of the curve, we get $y = 0$. So, the curve meets Y-axis at $(0, 0)$ only.

(iv) $y = x^3 - 4x \Rightarrow \frac{dy}{dx} = 3x^2 - 4$

Now, $\frac{dy}{dx} > 0 \Rightarrow 3x^2 - 4 > 0$

$\Rightarrow \left(x - \frac{2}{\sqrt{3}}\right)\left(x + \frac{2}{\sqrt{3}}\right) > 0$

$\Rightarrow x < -\frac{2}{\sqrt{3}}$ or $x > \frac{2}{\sqrt{3}}$ (using number line rule)

and $\frac{dy}{dx} < 0 \Rightarrow -\frac{2}{\sqrt{3}} < x < \frac{2}{\sqrt{3}}$

So, the curve is decreasing in the interval $\left(\frac{-2}{\sqrt{3}}, \frac{2}{\sqrt{3}}\right)$ and increasing for $x > \frac{2}{\sqrt{3}}$ or $x < -\frac{2}{\sqrt{3}}$.

$x = -\frac{2}{\sqrt{3}}$ is a point of local maximum and $x = \frac{2}{\sqrt{3}}$ is point of local minimum.

When $x = \frac{2}{\sqrt{3}}$, then $y = -\frac{16}{3\sqrt{3}}$

When $x = -\frac{2}{\sqrt{3}}$, then $y = \frac{16}{3\sqrt{3}}$

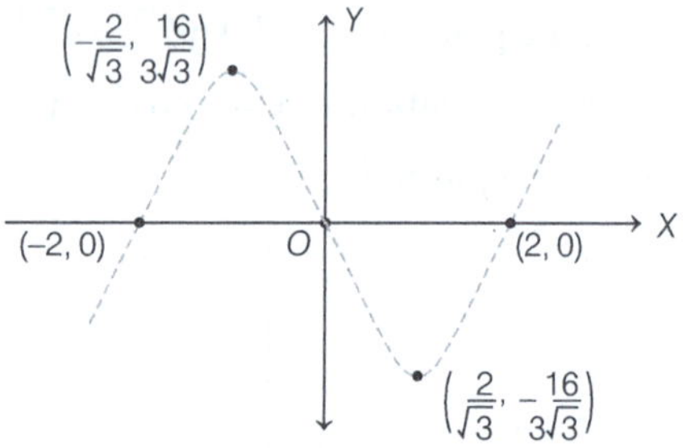

Keeping above points in mind, we sketch the curve as shown in figure.

Example 3. Sketch the curve $y = (x-1)(x-2)(x-3)$.

Sol. We note the following points about the given curve

(i) The curve does not have any type of symmetry about the coordinate axes and also in opposite quadrants.

(ii) The curve does not pass through the origin.

(iii) Putting $y = 0$ in the equation of the curve, we get $(x-1)(x-2)(x-3) = 0 \Rightarrow x = 1, 2, 3$. So, the curve meets X-axis at $(1, 0)$, $(2, 0)$ and $(3, 0)$.

Putting $x = 0$ in the equation of the curve, we get $y = -6$. So, the curve crosses Y-axis at $(0, -6)$.

We observe that

$x < 1 \Rightarrow y < 0$

$1 < x < 2 \Rightarrow y > 0$

$2 < x < 3 \Rightarrow y < 0$

and $x > 3 \Rightarrow y > 0$

Clearly, y decreases as x decreases for all $x < 1$ and y increases as x increases for $x > 3$.

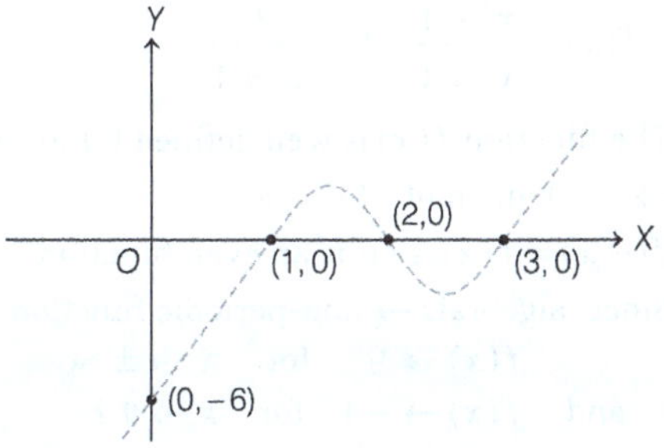

Keeping all the above points in mind, we sketch the curve as shown in figure.

Example 4. Sketch the curve $y = \sin 2x$.

Sol. We note the following points about the curve

(i) The equation of the curve remains unchanged, if x is replaced by $(-x)$ and y by $(-y)$, so it is symmetric in opposite quadrants. Consequently, the shape of the curve is similar in opposite quadrants.

(ii) The curve passes through origin.

(iii) Putting $x = 0$ in the equation of the curve, we get $y = 0$. So, the curve crosses the Y-axis at $(0, 0)$ only.

Putting $y = 0$ in the equation of the curve, we get

$$\sin 2x = 0 \Rightarrow 2x = n\pi,\ n \in Z \Rightarrow x = \frac{n\pi}{2},\ n \in Z$$

So, the curve cuts the X-axis at the points

$$\ldots, (-\pi, 0), (-\pi/2, 0), (0, 0), (\pi/2, 0), (\pi, 0), \ldots$$

(iv) $y = \sin 2x \Rightarrow \dfrac{dy}{dx} = 2\cos 2x$ and $\dfrac{d^2y}{dx^2} = -4\sin 2x$

Now, $\dfrac{dy}{dx} = 0 \Rightarrow \cos 2x = 0$

$$\Rightarrow \quad 2x = \pm\frac{\pi}{2}, \pm\frac{3\pi}{2}, \ldots$$

$$\Rightarrow \quad x = \pm\frac{\pi}{4}, \pm\frac{3\pi}{4}, \ldots$$

Clearly, $\dfrac{d^2y}{dx^2} < 0$ at $x = \dfrac{\pi}{4}, \dfrac{5\pi}{4}, \ldots$

and at $x = -\dfrac{3\pi}{4}, -\dfrac{7\pi}{4}, \ldots$

and $\dfrac{d^2y}{dx^2} > 0$ at $x = \dfrac{3\pi}{4}, \dfrac{7\pi}{4}, \ldots$

and at $x = -\dfrac{\pi}{4}, -\dfrac{5\pi}{4}, \ldots$

So, the points $x = \dfrac{\pi}{4}, \dfrac{5\pi}{4}, \dfrac{7\pi}{4}, \ldots$

and $x = -\dfrac{3\pi}{4}, -\dfrac{7\pi}{4}, \ldots$ are points of local maximum and local maximum values at these points are 1.

Similarly, $x = -\dfrac{\pi}{4}, -\dfrac{5\pi}{4}, \ldots$ and $x = \dfrac{3\pi}{4}, \dfrac{7\pi}{4}, \ldots$ are points of local minimum and local minimum value at these points is (-1).

(v) $\sin 2(x + \pi) = \sin 2x$ for all x. So, the periodicity of the function is π. This means that the pattern of the curve repeats at intervals of length π.

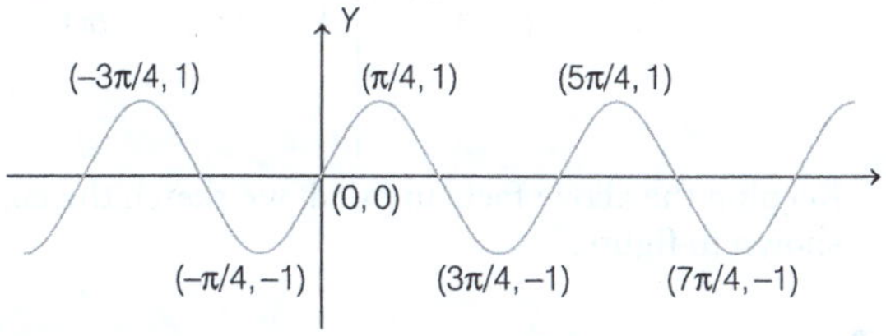

Thus, keeping in mind, we sketch the curve as shown in figure.

Example 5. Sketch the curve $y = \sin^2 x$.

Sol. We note the following points about the curve

(i) The equation of the curve remains same, if x is replaced by $(-x)$. So, the curve is symmetric about Y-axis, i.e. the curve on the left side of Y-axis is identical to the curve on its right side.

(ii) The curve meets the coordinate axes at the same points, where $y = \sin x$ meets them.

(iii) $y = \sin^2 x \Rightarrow \dfrac{dy}{dx} = \sin 2x$ and $\dfrac{d^2y}{dx^2} = 2\cos 2x$

Now, $\dfrac{dy}{dx} = 0 \Rightarrow \sin 2x = 0 \Rightarrow 2x = n\pi,\ n \in Z$

$$\Rightarrow x = \frac{n\pi}{2},\ n \in Z \Rightarrow x = \pm\pi/2, \pm\pi, \pm 3\pi/2, \pm 2\pi, \ldots$$

Clearly, $\dfrac{d^2y}{dx^2} < 0$ at $x = \pm\pi/2, \pm 3\pi/2, \pm 5\pi/2, \ldots$

and $\dfrac{d^2y}{dx^2} > 0$ at $x = \pm\pi, \pm 2\pi, \pm 3\pi \ldots$

So, $x = \pm\pi/2, \pm 3\pi/2, \pm 5\pi/2, \ldots$ are the points of local maximum and local maximum value at these points is 1.

Points $x = \pm\pi, \pm 2\pi, \pm 3\pi, \ldots$ are points of local minimum and the local minimum value at these points is 0.

(iv) $y = \sin^2 x \Rightarrow \dfrac{dy}{dx} = \sin 2x$

Clearly, $\dfrac{dy}{dx} > 0$ when $0 < x < \dfrac{\pi}{2}$

and $\dfrac{dy}{dx} < 0$ when $\dfrac{\pi}{2} < x < \pi$.

So, the given curve is increasing in the interval $[0, \pi/2]$ and decreasing in $[\pi/2, \pi]$.

(v) $\sin^2(\pi + x) = \sin^2 x$ for all x. So, the periodicity of the function is π. This means that the shape of the curve repeats at the interval of length π.

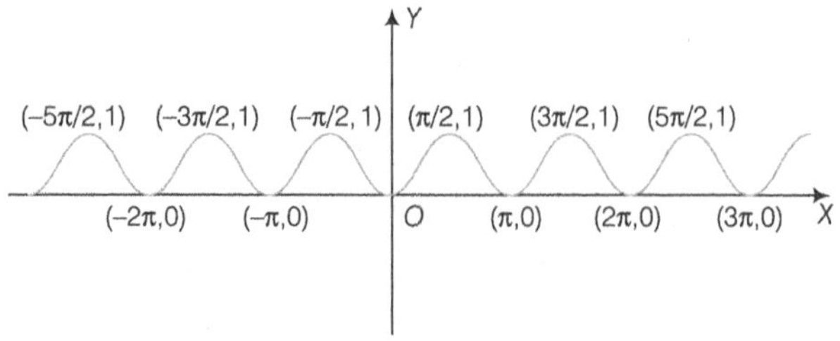

Keeping the above facts in mind, we sketch the curve as shown in figure.

3.4 Asymptotes

The straight line AB is called the asymptote of curve $y = f(x)$, if the distance MK from M a point on the curve $y = f(x)$ to the straight line AB tends to zero as M recedes infinity.

In other words, the straight line AB meets the curve $y = f(x)$ at infinity (K is a point on AB). Thus,

(i) If $f(x) \to \pm\infty$ for $x \to a$, then the straight line $x = a$ is the asymptote of the curve $y = f(x)$.

(ii) If in the right hand member of the equation of the curve $y = f(x)$ it is possible to single out a linear part so that the remaining part tends to zero as $x \to \pm\infty$, i.e. if $y = f(x) = Kx + b + g(x)$ and $g(x) \to 0$ for $x \to \pm\infty$, then the straight line $y = Kx + b$ is the asymptote of the curve.

(iii) If there exist finite limits $\lim\limits_{x \to \pm\infty} \dfrac{f(x)}{x} = K$ and $\lim\limits_{x \to \pm\infty} [f(x) - Kx] = b$, then the straight line $y = Kx + b$ is the asymptote of the curve.

Methods to Sketch Curves

While constructing the graphs of functions, it is expedient to follow the procedure given below:

(i) Find the domain of definition of the function.
(ii) Determine the odd-even nature of the function.
(iii) Find the period of the function if its periodic.
(iv) Find the asymptotes of the function.
(v) Check the behaviour of the function for $x \to 0\pm$
(vi) Find the values of x, if possible for which $f(x) \to 0$.
(vii) The interval of increase and decrease of the function in its range. Hence, determine the greatest and the least values of the function if any.

Example 6. Construct the graph for $f(x) = \dfrac{x^2 - 1}{x^2 + 1}$.

Sol. Here, $f(x) = \dfrac{x^2 - 1}{x^2 + 1} = 1 - \dfrac{2}{x^2 + 1}$

(i) The function $f(x)$ is well defined for all real x.
$\Rightarrow$ Domain of $f(x) \in R$.

(ii) $f(-x) = f(x)$, so it is an even function.

(iii) Since, algebraic $\to$ non-periodic function.
$$f(x) \to 1 \quad \text{for} \quad x \to \pm\infty$$
$$\text{and} \quad f(x) \to -1 \quad \text{for} \quad x \to 0\pm$$
It may be observed that $f(x) < 1$ for any $x \in R$ and consequently its graph lies below the line $y = 1$ which is asymptote to the graph of the given function.

Again, $\dfrac{2}{x^2 + 1}$ decreases for $(0, \infty)$ and increases for $(-\infty, 0)$, thus $f(x)$ increases for $(0, \infty)$ and decreases for $(-\infty, 0)$ in its range.

(iv) The greatest value $\to 1$ for $x \to \pm\infty$ and the least value is -1 for $x = 0$.

Thus, its graph is as shown in figure

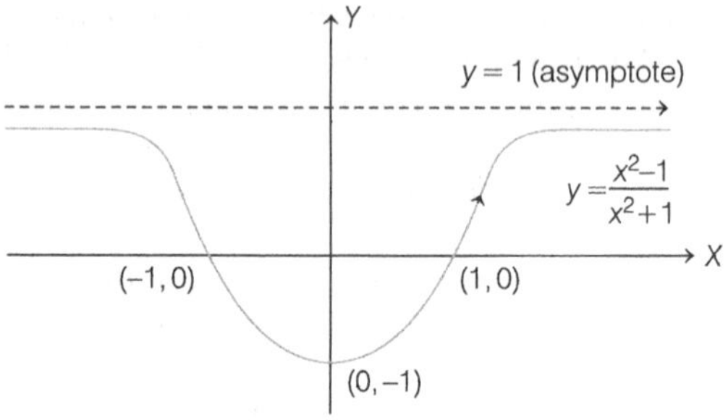

Example 7. Construct the graph for $f(x) = x + \dfrac{1}{x}$.

Sol. The function is defined for all x except for $x = 0$.
It is an odd function for $x \neq 0$.
It is not a periodic function.
For $x \to 0+$, $f(x) \to +\infty$; for $x \to 0-$, $f(x) \to -\infty$
For $x \to -\infty$, $f(x) \to -\infty$; for $x \to \infty$, $f(x) \to \infty$
$$\therefore \quad \lim_{x \to \pm\infty} (f(x) - x) = 0$$
$\therefore$ The straight lines $x = 0$ and $y = x$ are the asymptotes of the graph of the given function.
Now, consider $f(x_2) - f(x_1)$ (for $x_2 > x_1$)
$$= (x_2 - x_1) + \frac{1}{x_2} - \frac{1}{x_1}$$
$$= (x_2 - x_1)\left[1 - \frac{1}{x_1 x_2}\right] < 0 \text{ for}$$
$x_1 x_2 \in (0, 1]$
and it is > 0 for $x_1 x_2 \in [1, \infty)$.
Thus, $f(x)$ increases for $x \in [1, \infty)$ and decreases for $x \in (0, 1]$.

Thus, the least value of the function is at $x = 1$ which is $f(1) = 2$. Thus, its graph can be drawn as

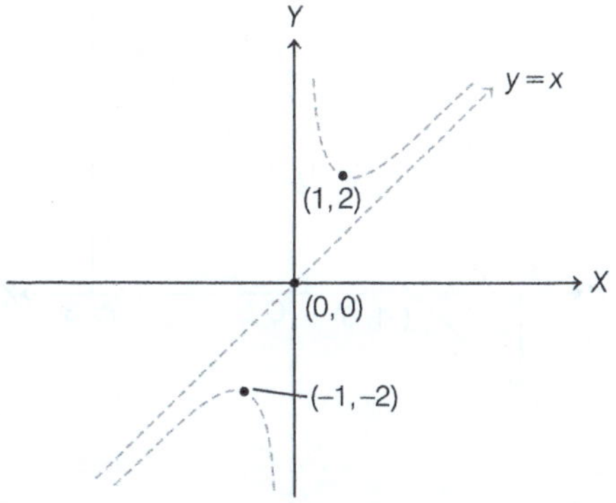

Example 8. Construct the graph for $f(x) = \dfrac{1}{1+e^{1/x}}$.

Sol. The function is defined for all x except for $x = 0$. It is neither even nor an odd function. It is not a periodic function.

For $x \to 0+$ $\quad f(x) \to 0$;

For $x \to 0-$, $\quad f(x) \to 1$

For $x \to \infty$ $\quad f(x) \to \frac{1}{2}$;

For $x \to -\infty$, $\quad f(x) \to \frac{1}{2}$

$$\therefore \quad \lim_{x \to \pm\infty} f(x) = \frac{1}{2}$$

$\therefore$ The straight line $y = \frac{1}{2}$ is asymptote of the graph of the given function.

As x increases from $(0, \infty)$, $\frac{1}{x}$ decreases from $(0, \infty)$ and $e^{1/x}$ decreases from $(0, \infty)$.

Thus, $(1 + e^{1/x})$ decreases from $(2, \infty)$.

$\therefore$ $f(x)$ increases from $\left(0, \frac{1}{2}\right)$ for $x \in (0, \infty)$.

Similarly, $f(x)$ increases from $(1/2, 1)$ for $x \to (-\infty, 0)$.
i.e. $f(x)$ is an increasing function except for $x = 0$.
Thus, its graph can be drawn as shown in figure

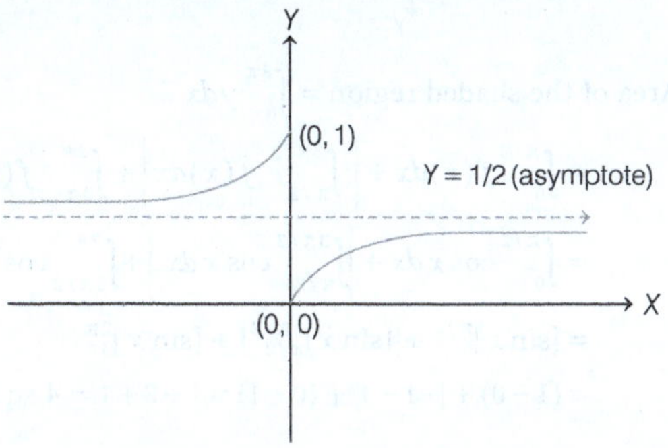

3.5 Area of the Cartesian Curve

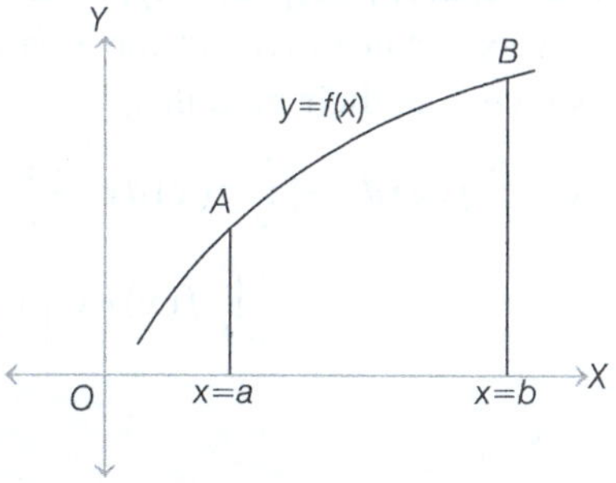

If $f(x)$ is a single value and continuous function of x in the interval $[a, b]$.

Let $f(x) \geq 0$ for every x in $[a, b]$.

Then, the area bounded by the curve $y = f(x)$, the axis and the ordinate $x = a$ and $x = b$, $a < b$ is represented by

$$\int_a^b y\,dx = \int_a^b f(x)\,dx$$

Area of the Region Bounded by a Single Curve and the Coordinate Axis

(i) The area bounded by the curve $y = f(x)$, X-axis and the straight line $x = a$ and $x = b\,(a < b)$ is given by

$$A = \int_a^b y\,dx = \int_a^b f(x)\,dx$$

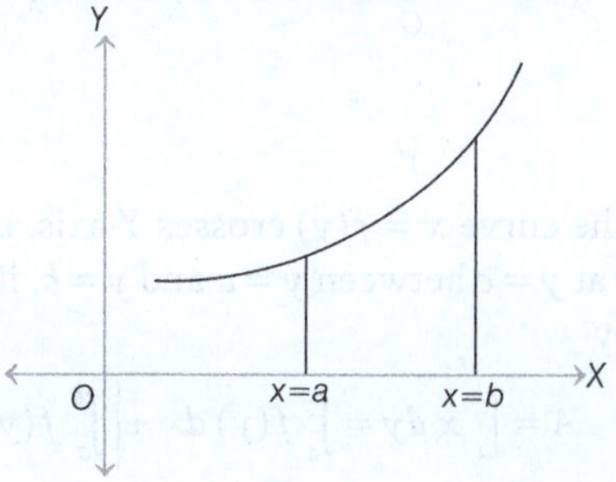

(ii) If $f(x) \leq 0$ for all in $[a, b]$, the area bounded by the curve $y = f(x)$, X-axis and the straight line $x = a$ and $x = b$, $(a < b)$ is

$$A = \int_a^b (-y)\,dx = \left|\int_a^b f(x)\,dx\right|$$

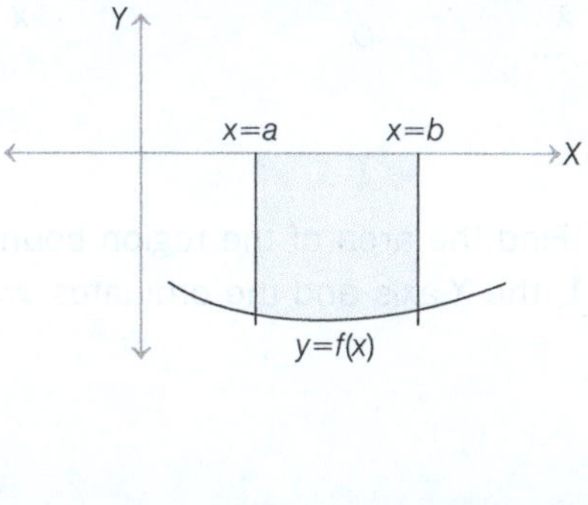

(iii) If the graph of $f(x)$ crosses X-axis between $x = a$ and $x = b$ and $x = c, d, e, f$ respectively, its area (which lie below the X-axis is negative but the area is taken positive, so we take their modulus)

$$A = \int_a^b y dx = \int_a^c f(x)\,dx + \left|\int_c^d f(x)\,dx\right| + \int_d^e f(x)\,dx + \left|\int_e^f f(x)\,dx\right| + \int_f^b f(x)\,dx$$

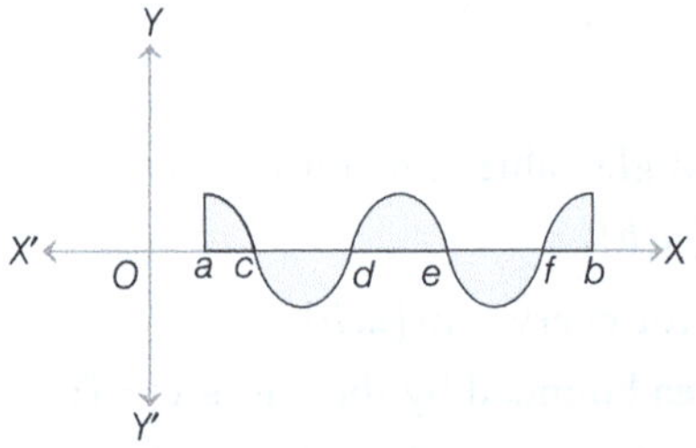

(iv) The area enclosed by the curve $x = f(x)$, Y-axis and the abscissae $y = c$ and $y = d$, $(c < d)$ is given by

$$A = \int_c^d x\,dy = \int_c^d f(y)\,dy$$

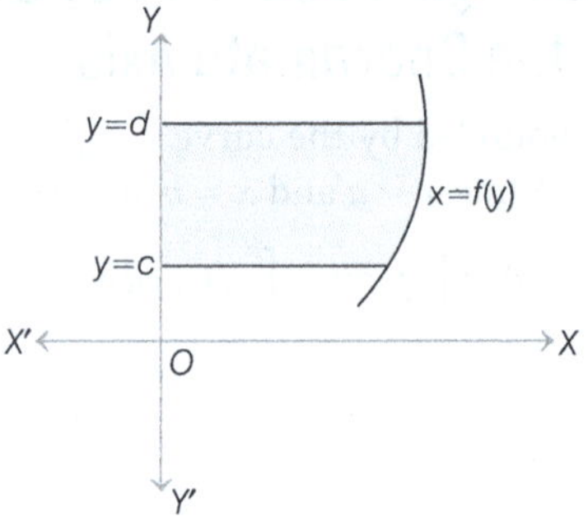

(v) When the curve $x = f(y)$ crosses Y-axis, i.e. changes its sign at $y = c$ between $y = a$ and $y = b$, its area is given by

$$A = \int_a^b x\,dy = \int_a^c f(y)\,dx + \left|\int_c^b f(y)\,dy\right|$$

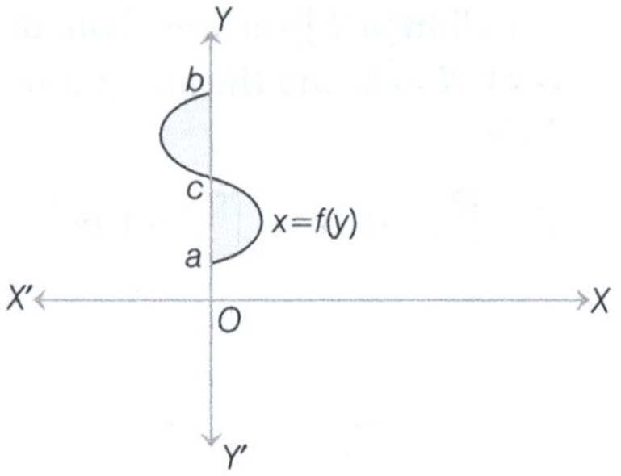

Example 9. Find the area of the region bounded by the line $y - x = 1$, the X-axis and the ordinates $x = -2$ and $x = 3$.

Sol. Given curve $y - x = 1 \Rightarrow y = 1 + x$

The graph of curve are

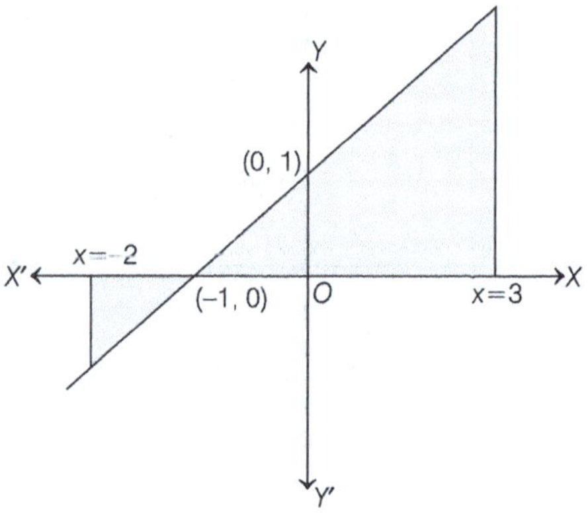

Area of the shaded region $= \int_{-2}^{3} y\,dx$

$$= \left|\int_{-2}^{-1} f(x)dx\right| + \int_{-1}^{3} f(x)dx$$

$$= \left|\int_{-2}^{-1} (x+1)dx\right| + \int_{-1}^{3} (x+1)dx$$

$$= \left|\left(\frac{x^2}{2} + x\right)_{-2}^{-1}\right| + \left(\frac{x^2}{2} + x\right)_{-1}^{3}$$

$$= \left|\left(\frac{1-4}{2}\right) + (-1+2)\right| + \left(\frac{9-1}{2} + 3 + 1\right)$$

$$= \left|-\frac{3}{2} + 1\right| + \left(\frac{8}{2} + 4\right) = \frac{1}{2} + 8 = \frac{17}{2} \text{ sq unit}$$

Example 10. Find the area bounded by the curve $y = \cos x$, X-axis and the ordinates $x = 0$ and $x = 2\pi$.

Sol. The graph of curve $y = \cos x$ are

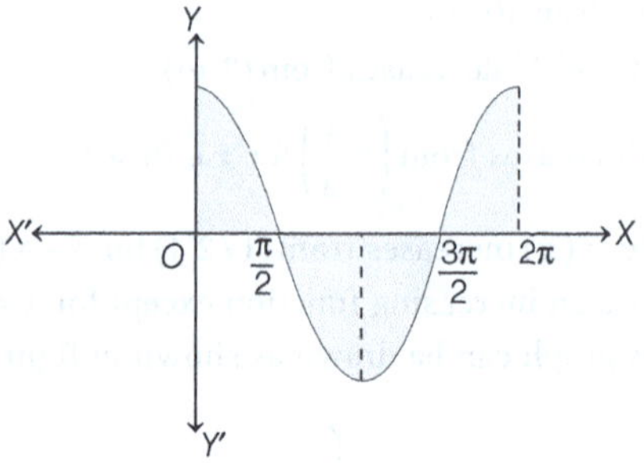

Area of the shaded region $= \int_0^{2\pi} y\,dx$

$$= \int_0^{\pi/2} f(x)dx + \left|\int_{\pi/2}^{3\pi/2} f(x)dx\right| + \int_{3\pi/2}^{2\pi} f(x)dx$$

$$= \int_0^{\pi/2} \cos x\,dx + \left|\int_{\pi/2}^{3\pi/2} \cos x\,dx\right| + \int_{3\pi/2}^{2\pi} \cos x\,dx$$

$$= [\sin x]_0^{\pi/2} + |[\sin x]_{\pi/2}^{3\pi/2}| + [\sin x]_{3\pi/2}^{2\pi}$$

$$= (1-0) + |-1-1| + (0+1) = 1 + 2 + 1 = 4 \text{ sq unit}$$

Example 11. Find the area enclosed by $y = x(x-1)(x-2)$ and X-axis.

Sol. The given curve is $y = x(x-1)(x-2)$. It passes through $(0, 0)$, $(1, 0)$ and $(2, 0)$.

The graph of the curve is as below

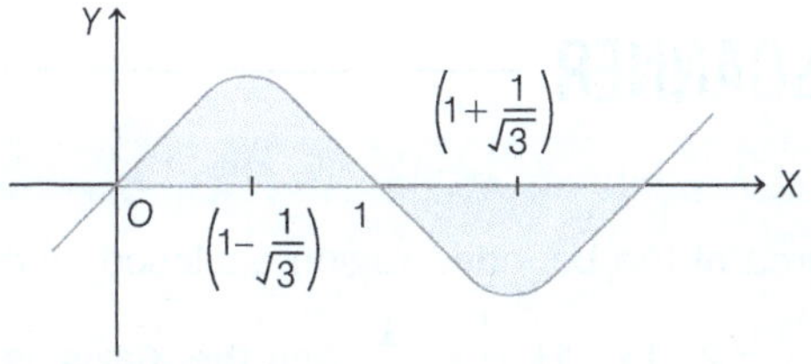

Hence, required area

$$= \int_0^1 x(x-1)(x-2)\,dx + \left|\int_1^2 x(x-1)(x-2)\,dx\right|$$

$$= \int_0^1 (x^3 - 3x^2 + 2x)\,dx + \left|\int_1^2 (x^3 - 3x^2 + 2x)\,dx\right|$$

$$= \left(\frac{x^4}{4} - x^3 + x^2\right)_0^1 + \left|\left(\frac{x^4}{4} - x^3 + x^2\right)_1^2\right|$$

$$= \left(\frac{1}{4} - 1 + 1\right) + \left|(4 - 8 + 4) - \left(\frac{1}{4} - 1 + 1\right)\right|$$

$$= \frac{1}{4} + \frac{1}{4} = \frac{1}{2} \text{ sq unit}$$

Example 12. Let $g(x) = \cos x^2$, $f(x) = \sqrt{x}$ and α, β $(\alpha < \beta)$ be the roots of the quadratic equation $18x^2 - 9\pi x + \pi^2 = 0$. Then, the area (in sq units) bounded by the curve $y = gof(x)$ and the lines $x = \alpha$, $x = \beta$ and $y = 0$, is

(a) $\frac{1}{2}(\sqrt{3} + 1)$ (b) $\frac{1}{2}(\sqrt{3} - \sqrt{2})$

(a) $\frac{1}{2}(\sqrt{2} + 1)$ (d) $\frac{1}{2}(\sqrt{3} - 1)$

Sol. (d) Given, $18x^2 - 9\pi x + \pi^2 = 0$

$\Rightarrow \quad (3x - \pi)(6x - \pi) = 0$

$\Rightarrow \quad x = \frac{\pi}{6}, \frac{\pi}{3} \Rightarrow \alpha = \frac{\pi}{6}, \beta = \frac{\pi}{3}$

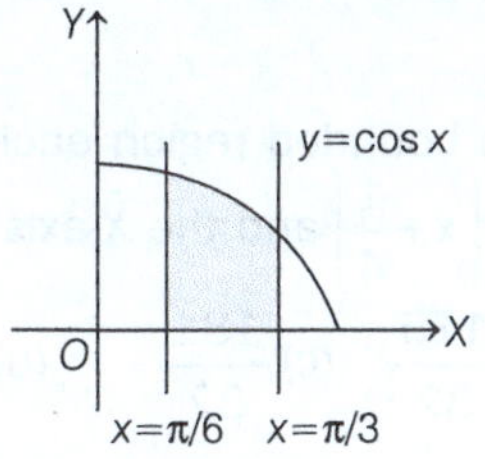

Also, $gof(x) = g(\sqrt{x}) = \cos x$

Required area $= \int_{\pi/6}^{\pi/3} \cos x\,dx = \frac{\sqrt{3} - 1}{2}$

Example 13. Find the area bounded by region $1 \le |x + 2| + |y - 1| \le 2$.

Sol. Given, $1 \le |x + 2| + |y - 1| \le 2$

Let $x + 2 = x'$ and $y - 1 = y'$

$\Rightarrow \quad 1 \le |x'| + |y'| \le 2$

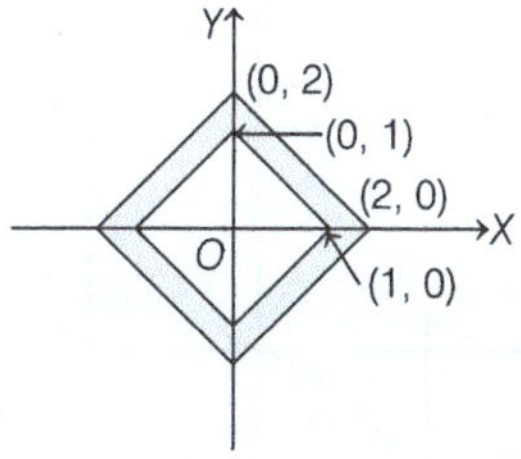

Required area is area enclosed between curves $|x'| + |y'| = 1$ and $|x'| + |y'| = 2$, which is shown as shaded region in figure.

$$\text{Required area} = 4\left[\frac{1}{2} \times 2 \times 2 - \frac{1}{2} \times 1 \times 1\right]$$

$$= 4\left(\frac{3}{2}\right)$$

$$= 6 \text{ sq units}$$

Example 14. Find the area bounded by curve $[x] + [y] = 4$ in Ist quadrant (where $[\cdot]$ denotes GIF).

Sol. If $0 \le x < 1$, $[x] = 0$

$\Rightarrow \quad [y] = 4$ and $4 \le y < 5$

If $1 \le x < 2$, $[x] = 1$

$\Rightarrow \quad [y] = 3$

$\Rightarrow \quad 3 \le y < 4$

If $2 \le x < 3$, $[x] = 2$

$\Rightarrow \quad [y] = 2$

$\Rightarrow \quad 2 \le y < 3$

If $3 \le x < 4$, $[x] = 3$

$\Rightarrow \quad [y] = 1$

$\Rightarrow \quad 1 \le y < 2$

If $4 \le x < 5$, $[x] = 4$

$\Rightarrow \quad [y] = 0$

$\Rightarrow \quad 0 \le y < 1$

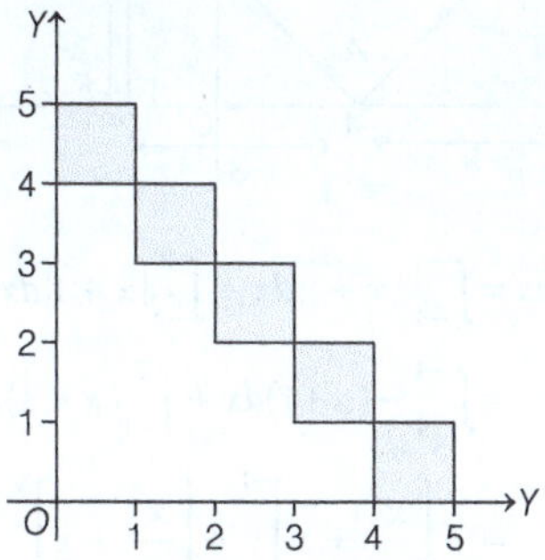

Required area $= 5 \times 1 = 5$ sq units

Example 15. Find the area bounded by the curve $y = \sin^{-1} x$ and the lines $x = 0, |y| = \frac{\pi}{2}$.

Sol. The graph of $y = \sin^{-1} x$ are

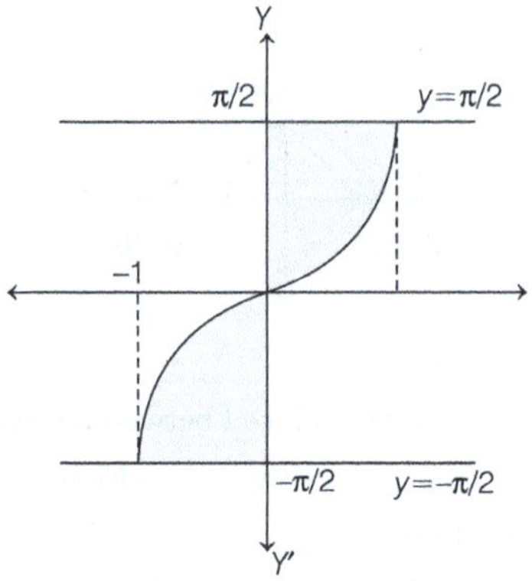

The area of shaded region,

$$A = \int_{-\pi/2}^{\pi/2} f(y)dy$$
$$= \left|\int_{-\pi/2}^{0} f(y)dy\right| + \int_{0}^{\pi/2} f(y)dy$$
$$= \left|\int_{-\pi/2}^{0} \sin y\, dy\right| + \int_{0}^{\pi/2} \sin y\, dy$$
$$= \left|[-\cos y]_{-\pi/2}^{0}\right| + [-\cos y]_{0}^{\pi/2}$$
$$= |-1+0| + [-0+1]$$
$$= 1 + 1 = 2 \text{ sq unit}$$

Example 16. Sketch the graph $y = |x+1|$. Evaluate $\int_{-4}^{2} |x+1|\, dx$. What does the value of this integral represents on the graph.

Sol. Here, $y = |x+1| = \begin{cases} (x+1), & \text{if } x \geq -1 \\ -(x+1), & \text{if } x < -1 \end{cases}$

which can be shown as

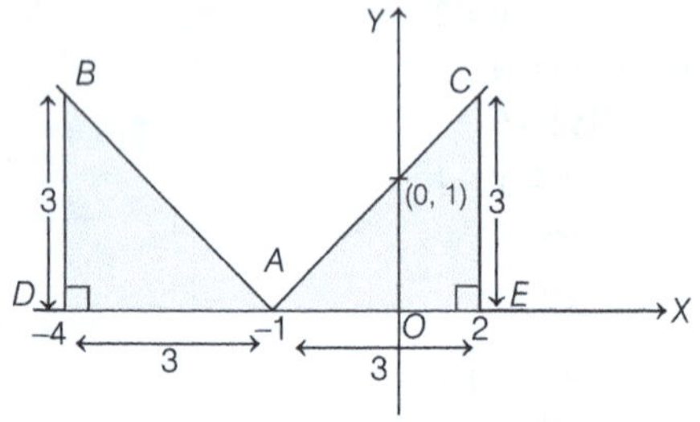

$$\therefore \int_{-4}^{2} |x+1| dx = \int_{-4}^{-1} |x+1| dx + \int_{-1}^{2} |x+1| dx$$
$$= \int_{-4}^{-1} -(x+1)dx + \int_{-1}^{2} (x+1)dx$$
$$= -\left[\frac{x^2}{2} + x\right]_{-4}^{-1} + \left[\frac{x^2}{2} + x\right]_{-1}^{2} = 9$$

Representation of the value 9 of integral on graph.

i.e. $\frac{1}{2}(3)(3) + \frac{1}{3}(3)(3) = \frac{9}{2} + \frac{9}{2}$
$= 9$

[$\because$ Area of triangle $= \frac{1}{2} \times$ Base $\times$ Height]

JEE SCANNER

Example Similar to PYQ Asked in JEE Main 2022

The area of the bounded region enclosed by the curve $y = 2 - |x-1| - \left|x + \frac{1}{2}\right|$ and the X-axis, is

(a) $\frac{9}{4}$ (b) $\frac{45}{16}$ (c) $\frac{3}{2}$ (d) $\frac{63}{16}$

Sol. (c) $y = \begin{cases} 2 + (x-1) + \left(x + \frac{1}{2}\right), & x < -\frac{1}{2} \\ 2 + (x-1) - \left(x + \frac{1}{2}\right), & -\frac{1}{2} \leq x < 1 \\ 2 - (x-1) - \left(x + \frac{1}{2}\right), & x \geq 1 \end{cases}$

$= \begin{cases} \frac{3}{2} + 2x, & x < -\frac{1}{2} \\ \frac{1}{2}, & -\frac{1}{2} \leq x < 1 \\ \frac{5}{2} - 2x, & x \geq 1 \end{cases}$

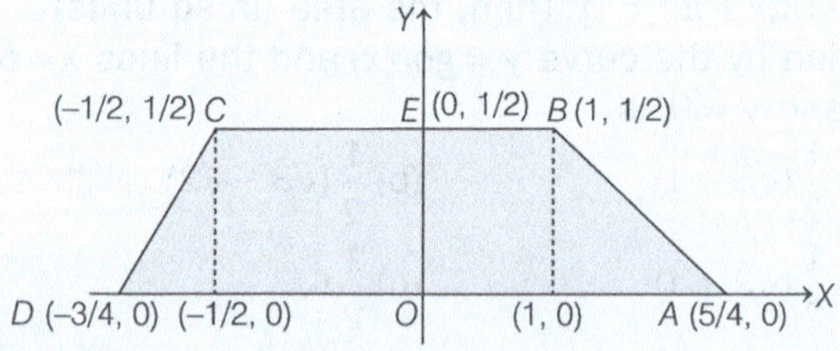

$\therefore$ Required area $= \frac{1}{2}(AD + BC) \cdot OE$

$= \frac{1}{2}\left(2 + \frac{3}{2}\right) \times \frac{1}{2} = \frac{3}{2}$ sq units

Skill Builder

The area of the bounded region enclosed by the curve $y = 4 - |x-2| - \left|x + \frac{1}{4}\right|$ and the X-axis is

(a) $\frac{45}{8}$ (b) $\frac{175}{32}$ (c) $\frac{181}{32}$ (d) $\frac{89}{16}$

For Sol.

■ **For more practice** See Q.13 of Milestone Practice 3.1.

Example 17. Find the area of the ellipse $\frac{x^2}{a^2}+\frac{y^2}{b^2}=1.$

Sol. Using the symmetry of the figure; required area is given by

$$A = 4\,(\text{area } OABO)$$

$$= 4\int_0^a y\,dx, \text{ where } \frac{x^2}{a^2}+\frac{y^2}{b^2}=1$$

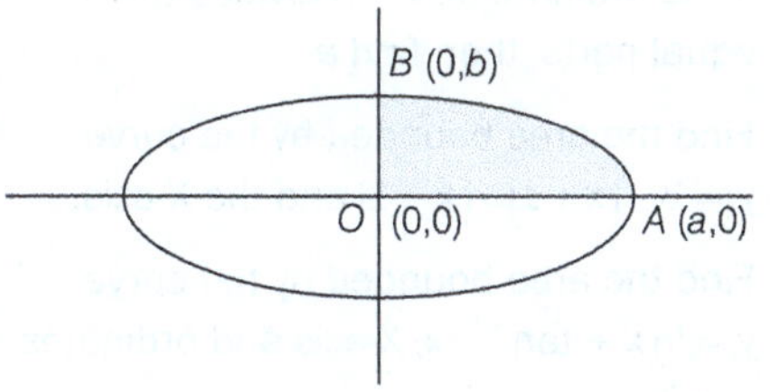

$$\therefore \quad \frac{y^2}{b^2} = 1 - \frac{x^2}{a^2}$$

$$\Rightarrow \quad y^2 = \frac{b^2}{a^2}(a^2 - x^2) \Rightarrow y = \pm\frac{b}{a}\sqrt{a^2 - x^2}$$

In the first quadrant,

$$y = \frac{b}{a}\sqrt{a^2 - x^2}$$

$$A = 4\int_0^a \frac{b}{a}\sqrt{a^2 - x^2}\,dx = 4\frac{b}{a}\int_0^a \sqrt{a^2 - x^2}\,dx$$

$$= 4\frac{b}{a}\left\{\frac{x}{2}\sqrt{a^2 - x^2} + \frac{a^2}{2}\sin^{-1}\frac{x}{a}\right\}_0^a$$

$$= 4\frac{b}{a}\left[\left\{0+\frac{a^2}{2}\sin^{-1}\frac{a}{a}\right\} - \{0+0\}\right]$$

$$= \frac{4b}{a}\cdot\frac{a^2}{2}\sin^{-1}(1) = 2ab\left(\frac{\pi}{2}\right)$$

$$A = \pi ab \text{ sq units}$$

Example 18. Find the area bounded by the hyperbola $x^2 - y^2 = a^2$ between the straight lines $x = a$ and $x = 2a$.

Sol. We use the symmetry of figure.

Required area, $A = 2\int_a^{2a} y\,dx,$

where $x^2 - y^2 = a^2$

i.e. $\quad x^2 - a^2 = y^2$

$$\therefore \quad y = \pm\sqrt{x^2 - a^2}$$

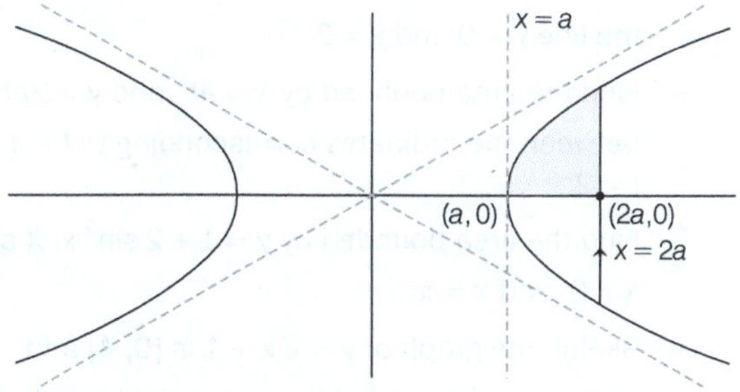

In the first quadrant; $y = +\sqrt{x^2 - a^2}$

$$\therefore\ A = 2\int_a^{2a}\sqrt{x^2 - a^2}\,dx$$

$$= 2\left[\frac{x}{2}\sqrt{x^2 - a^2} - \frac{a^2}{2}\log(x + \sqrt{x^2 - a^2})\right]_a^{2a}$$

$$= 2\left[\left\{a\sqrt{4a^2 - a^2} - \frac{a^2}{2}\log(2a + \sqrt{4a^2 - a^2})\right\} - \left\{0 - \frac{a^2}{2}\log a\right\}\right]$$

$$= 2\left[a\sqrt{3a^2} - \frac{a^2}{2}\log(2a + a\sqrt{3}) + \frac{a^2}{2}\log a\right]$$

$$= 2\left[a^2\sqrt{3} - \frac{a^2}{2}\log\left(\frac{2a + a\sqrt{3}}{a}\right)\right]$$

$$= 2a^2\sqrt{3} - a^2\log(2 + \sqrt{3}) \text{ sq units}$$

Milestone Practice 3.1

1. Find the area under the curve $y=(x^2+2)^2+2x$ between the ordinates $x=0$ and $x=2$.
2. Find the area bounded by the curve $y^2=2y-x$ and the Y-axis.
3. Find the area bounded by the curve $y=4-x^2$ and the line $y=0$ and $y=3$.
4. Find the area bounded by $x=at^2$ and $y=2at$ between the ordinates corresponding to $t=1$ and $t=2$.
5. Find the area bounded by $y=1+2\sin^2 x$, X-axis, $x=0$ and $x=\pi$.
6. Sketch the graph of $y=\sqrt{x}+1$ in [0, 4] and determine the area of the region enclosed by the curve, the axis of X and the lines $x=0$, $x=4$.
7. Find the area of the region bounded by the curve $xy-3x-2y-10=0$, X-axis and the lines $x=3$, $x=4$.
8. Find the area bounded by curve $y=\cos^{-1}(\cos x)$ and line $y=3$ from ordinates $x=\pi$ to $x=3\pi$.
9. Find the area enclosed by region $|x-3|+|y+2|\le 5$.
10. Find the area bounded by curve $x=y^2-y^3$ and Y-axis.
11. Let $f(x)$ be a continuous function such that $f(x)\ge 0$ and the area bounded by the curve $y=f(x)$, the X-axis and the ordinates $x=0$ and $x=a$ is $\left(\frac{a^2}{2}+\frac{a}{2}\sin a+\frac{\pi}{2}\cos a\right)$ sq units. Then, find $f(\pi)+f(-\pi)+f\left(\frac{\pi}{2}\right)$.
12. Find the area of bounded by the X-axis part of the curve $y=1+\frac{8}{x^2}$ and the ordinates $x=2$ and $x=4$. If the ordinate at $x=a$ divides the area into two equal parts, then find a.
13. Find the area bounded by the curve $y=3-|x+1|-|x-1|$ and the X-axis.
14. Find the area bounded by the curve $y=\ln x+\tan^{-1}x$, X-axis and ordinates $x=1$ and $x=2$.
15. Find the area bounded by the curve $y=\big||x|\ln|x|\big|$ and X-axis.
16. Let $f:[0,\infty)\to R$ be a continuous and strictly increasing function such that $f^3(x)=\int_0^x tf^2(t)\,dt$, $\forall\ x\ge 0$. The area enclosed by $y=f(x)$, then find X-axis and the ordinates $x=3$.
17. The figure shows two regions in the first quadrant.

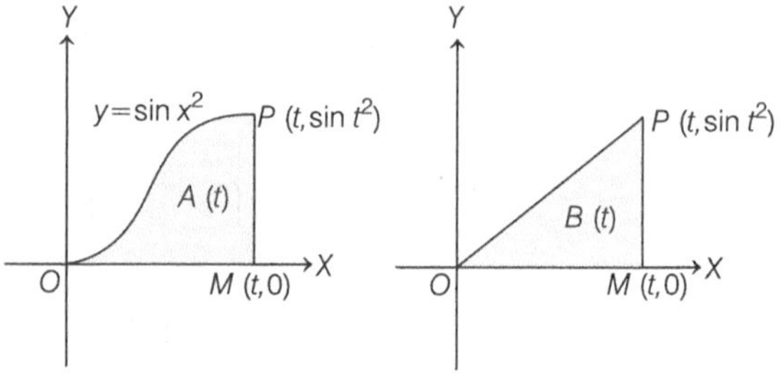

$A(t)$ is the area under the curve $y=\sin x^2$ from 0 to t and $B(t)$ is the area of the triangle with vertices O, P and $M(t,0)$. Find the value of $\lim_{t\to 0}\frac{3A(t)}{B(t)}$.

Answer Key

1. $\frac{436}{15}$ sq units
2. $\frac{4}{3}$ sq units
3. $\frac{28}{3}$ sq units
4. $\frac{56}{3}a^2$ sq unit
5. 2π sq units
6. $\frac{28}{3}$ sq units
7. $(3+16\ln 2)$ sq units
8. $(\pi-3)^2$ sq unit
9. 10 sq units
10. $\frac{1}{12}$ sq units
11. $\frac{1}{2}$
12. Area = 4 sq units, $a=2\sqrt{2}$
13. $\frac{5}{2}$ sq units
14. $\frac{5}{2}\ln 2+2\tan^{-1}2-\frac{1}{2}\ln 5-\frac{\pi}{4}-1$
15. $\frac{1}{2}$ sq units
16. $\frac{3}{2}$
17. 2

For Detailed Solution

Milestone 2 Area Bounded by Two or More Curves

3.6 Area Bounded by Two or More Curves

Area bounded by the curves $y = f(x)$, $y = g(x)$ and the lines $x = a$ and $x = b$.

Let the curves $y = f(x)$ and $y = g(x)$ be represented by AB and CD, respectively. We assume that the two curves do not intersect each other in the interval $[a, b]$.

Thus, shaded area = Area of curvilinear trapezoid $APQB$

− Area of curvilinear trapezoid $CPQD$

$$= \int_a^b f(x)\,dx - \int_a^b g(x)\,dx = \int_a^b \{ f(x) - g(x)\}\,dx$$

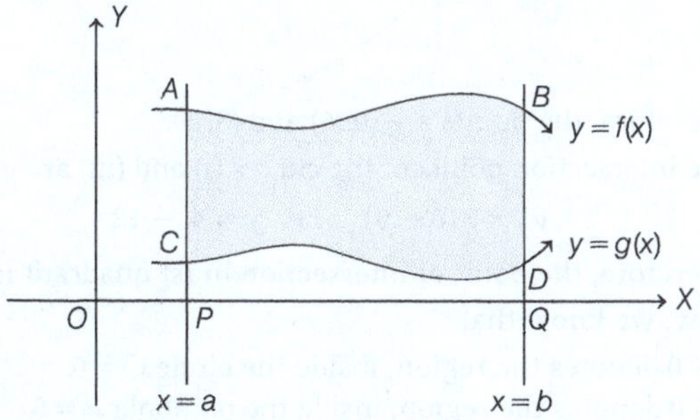

Now, consider the case when $f(x)$ and $g(x)$ intersect each other in the interval $[a, b]$.

First of all we should find the intersection point of $y = f(x)$ and $y = g(x)$.

For that we solve $f(x) = g(x)$. Let the root is $x = c$. (We consider only one intersection point to illustrate the phenomenon).

Thus, required (shaded) area

$$= \int_a^c \{f(x) - g(x)\}dx + \int_c^b \{g(x) - f(x)\}\,dx$$

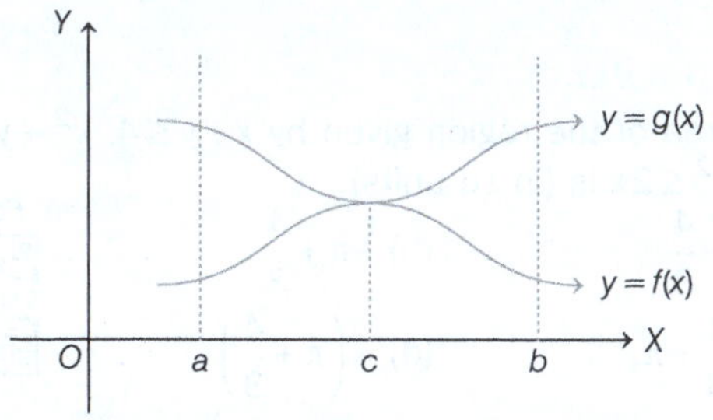

If confusion arises in such case evaluate $\int_a^b |\, f(x) - g(x)\,|\,dx$ which gives the required area.

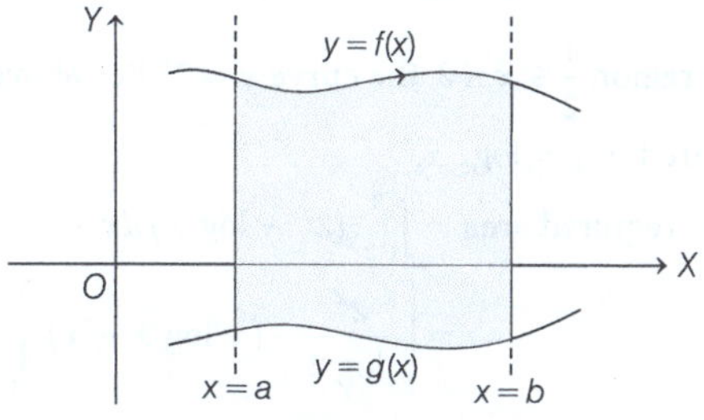

Fig. (i)

Area between two curves $y = f(x)$, $y = g(x)$ and the lines $x = a$ and $x = b$ is always given by $\int_a^b \{f(x) - g(x)\}\,dx$ provided $f(x) > g(x)$ in $[a, b]$; the position of the graph is immaterial. As shown in Fig. (i), (ii) and (iii).

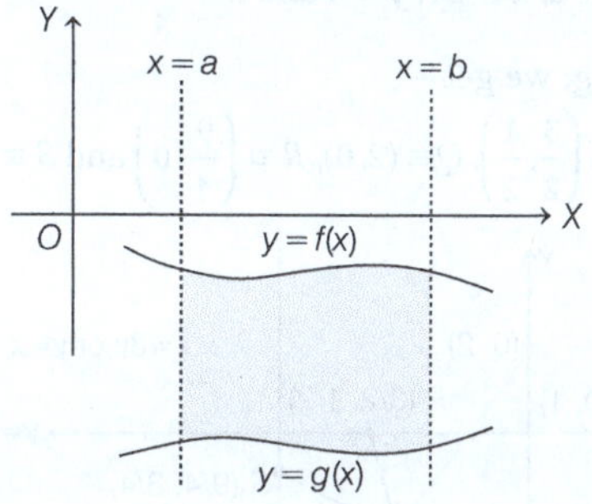

Fig. (ii)

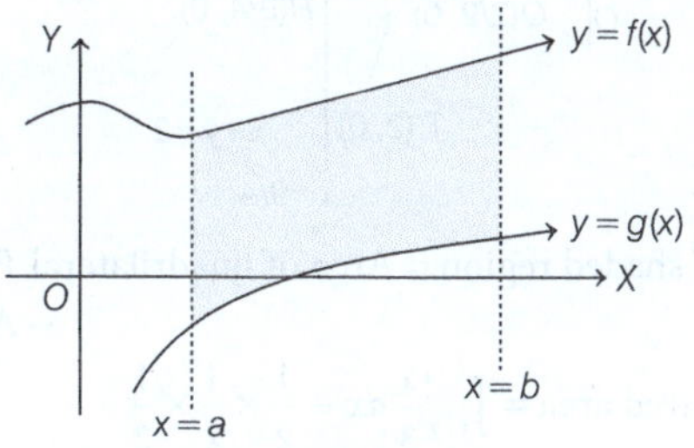

Fig. (iii)

Example 19. Sketch the curves and identify the region bounded by $x = 1/2$, $x = 2$, $y = \log_e x$ and $y = 2^x$. Find the area of this region.

Sol. The required area is the shaded portion in the following figure.

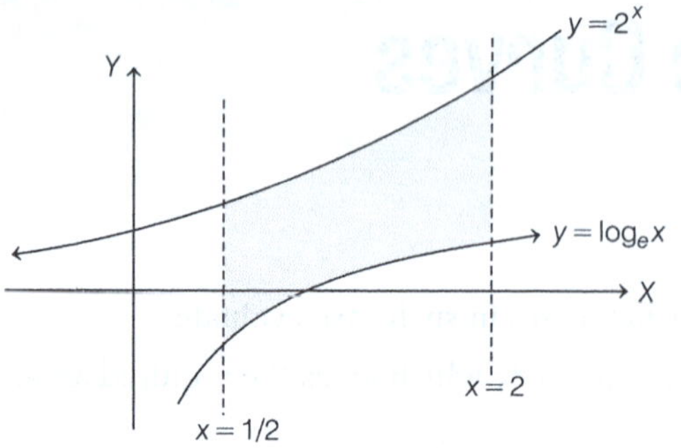

In the region $\frac{1}{2} \le x \le 2$; the curve $y = 2^x$ lies above as compared to $y = \log_e x$.

Hence, required area $= \int_{1/2}^{2} (2^x - \log x)\, dx$

$$= \left[\frac{2^x}{\log 2} - (x \log x - x) \right]_{1/2}^{2}$$

$$= \left(\frac{4 - \sqrt{2}}{\log 2} - \frac{5}{2} \log 2 + \frac{3}{2} \right) \text{sq units}$$

Example 20. Find the area of the region $\{(x, y) : 0 \le x \le \frac{9}{4},\ 0 \le y \le 1,\ x \ge 3y,\ x + y \ge 2\}$.

Sol. Let $x + y = 2$, $x = 3y$, $y = 1$ and $x = \frac{9}{4}$

On solving, we get

$$P \equiv \left(\frac{3}{2}, \frac{1}{2} \right), Q \equiv (2, 0), R \equiv \left(\frac{9}{4}, 0 \right) \text{ and } S \equiv \left(\frac{9}{4}, \frac{3}{4} \right)$$

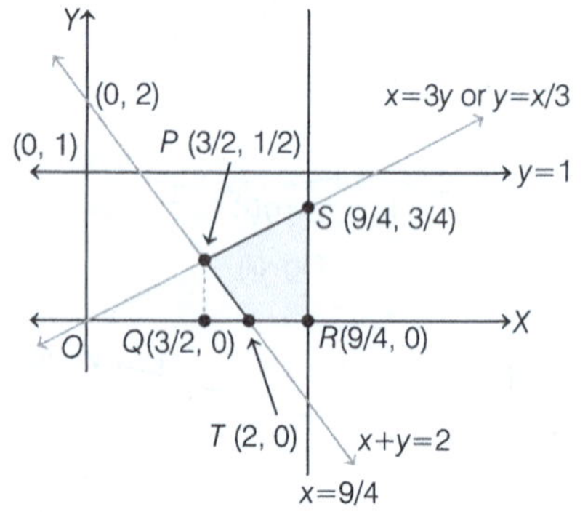

Area of shaded region = Area of quadrilateral $PQRS$ − Area of ΔPQT

$$\therefore \text{ Required area} = \int_{3/2}^{9/4} \frac{x}{3} dx - \frac{1}{2} \times \frac{1}{2} \times \frac{1}{2}$$

$$= \frac{1}{6} [x^2]_{3/2}^{9/4} - \frac{1}{8} = \frac{1}{6} \times \frac{45}{16} - \frac{1}{8}$$

$$= \frac{11}{32} \text{ sq units}$$

JEE SCANNER

Example Similar to PYQ Asked in JEE Main 2021

The area of the region given by $x + y \le 6$, $x^2 + y^2 \le 6y$ and $y^2 \le 8x$ is (in sq unit)

(a) $\left(\frac{9\pi}{4} - \frac{1}{3} \right)$ (b) $\left(\frac{9\pi}{4} + \frac{1}{6} \right)$ (c) $\left(\frac{9\pi}{4} - \frac{1}{6} \right)$ (d) $\frac{9\pi}{8} - \frac{1}{6}$

Sol. Let us consider the curves

$$P \equiv y^2 - 8x = 0 \quad \text{...(i)}$$

$$C \equiv x^2 + y^2 = 6y$$

i.e. $$x^2 + (y - 3)^2 - 9 = 0 \quad \text{...(ii)}$$

and $$S \equiv x + y - 6 = 0 \quad \text{...(iii)}$$

The intersection points of the curves (ii) and (iii) are given by

$$(6 - y)^2 + y^2 - 6y = 0 \text{ i.e. } y = 3, 6$$

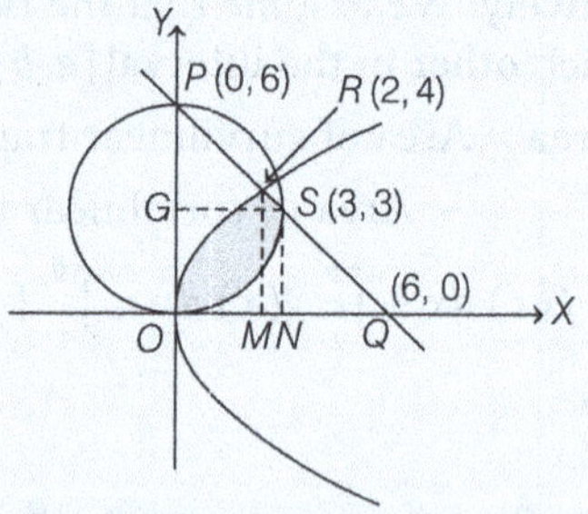

Therefore, the points are (0, 6) and (3, 3).

The intersection points of the curves (i) and (iii) are given by

$$y^2 = 8(6 - y), \quad \text{i.e. } y = 4, -12$$

Therefore, the point of intersection in Ist quadrant is (2, 4).

Now, we know that

$C \le 0$ denotes the region, inside the circle $C = 0$.

$P \le 0$ denotes the region, inside the parabola $P = 0$.

$S \le 0$ denotes the region, which is negative side of the line $S = 0$.

$\therefore$ Required area

= Area of curvilinear $OMRO$

+ Area of trapezium $MNSR$ − Area of curvilinear $ONSO$

$= \int_0^2 \sqrt{8x}\, dx + \frac{1}{2}(MR + NS) \cdot MN$

− (Area of square $ONSG$ − Area of sector $OSGO$)

$= \int_0^2 \sqrt{8x}\, dx + \frac{1}{2}(4 + 3) \cdot 1 - \left(3^2 - \frac{\pi \cdot 3^2}{4} \right)$

$= \left(\frac{9\pi}{4} - \frac{1}{6} \right)$ sq units

Skill Builder

The area of the region given by $x + y \le 4$, $x^2 + y^2 \le 4y$ and $y^2 \le 2x$ is (in sq units)

(a) $\pi + \frac{4}{3}$ (b) $-\pi + \frac{4}{3}$

(c) $-\frac{4}{3} + \pi$ (d) $-\left(\pi + \frac{4}{3} \right)$

For Sol.

■ **For more practice** See Q.5 of Milestone Practice 3.2.

Example 21. Find the area of the region $\{(x, y): 0 \le y \le x^2 + 1, 0 \le y \le x + 1, 0 \le x \le 2\}$.

Sol. Let $R = \{(x, y): 0 \le y \le x^2 + 1, 0 \le y \le x + 1, 0 \le x \le 2\}$

$$= \{(x, y): 0 \le y \le x^2 + 1\} \cap \{(x, y): 0 \le y \le x + 1\} \cap \{(x, y): 0 \le x \le 2\}$$

$$= R_1 \cap R_2 \cap R_3$$

where, $R_1 = \{(x, y): 0 \le y \le x^2 + 1\}$

$R_2 = \{(x, y): 0 \le y \le x + 1\}$

and $R_3 = \{(x, y): 0 \le x \le 2\}$

Thus, the sketch of R_1, R_2 and R_3 are

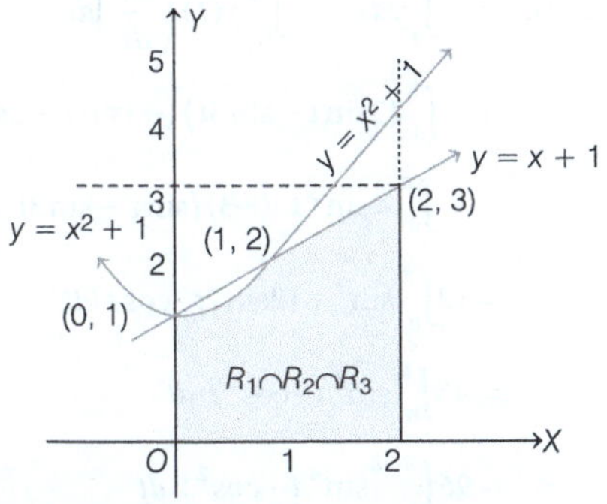

From the above figure,

$$\text{Required area} = \int_0^1 (x^2 + 1)\, dx + \int_1^2 (x + 1)\, dx$$

$$= \left(\frac{x^3}{3} + x\right)_0^1 + \left(\frac{x^2}{2} + x\right)_1^2 = \left(\frac{1}{3} + 1\right) + \left(\frac{4}{2} + 2 - \frac{1}{2} - 1\right)$$

$$= \frac{4}{3} + \frac{5}{2} = \frac{23}{6} \text{ sq units}$$

Example 22. If for some $\alpha > 0$, the area of the region $\{(x, y): |x + \alpha| \le y \le 2 - |x|\}$ is equal to $\frac{3}{2}$, then find the area of the region $\{(x, y): 0 \le y \le x + 2\alpha, |x| \le 1\}$.

Sol.

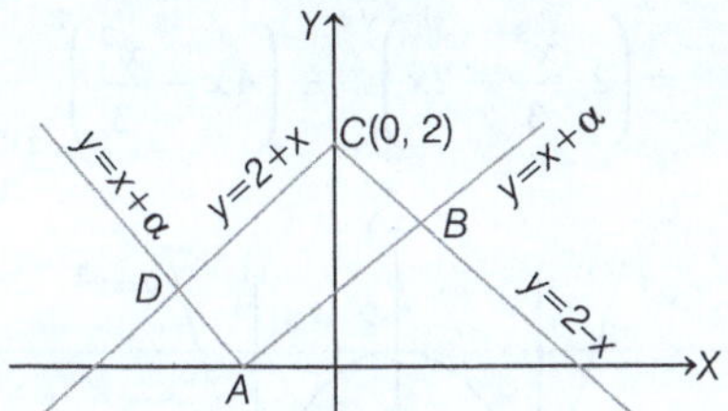

On solving $y = |x + \alpha|$ and $y = 2 - |x|$, we get

$$D \equiv \left(-\frac{(\alpha + 2)}{2}, \frac{2 - \alpha}{2}\right) \text{ and } B \equiv \left(\frac{2 - \alpha}{2}, \frac{2 + \alpha}{2}\right)$$

$$\therefore\ AD = \frac{2 - \alpha}{\sqrt{2}} \text{ and } AB = \frac{2 + \alpha}{\sqrt{2}}$$

$$\text{Area of } ABCD = \frac{2 - \alpha}{\sqrt{2}} \times \frac{2 + \alpha}{\sqrt{2}} = \frac{3}{2} \quad \text{[given]}$$

$$\Rightarrow\quad 4 - \alpha^2 = 3 \Rightarrow \alpha = 1 \quad [\because \alpha > 0]$$

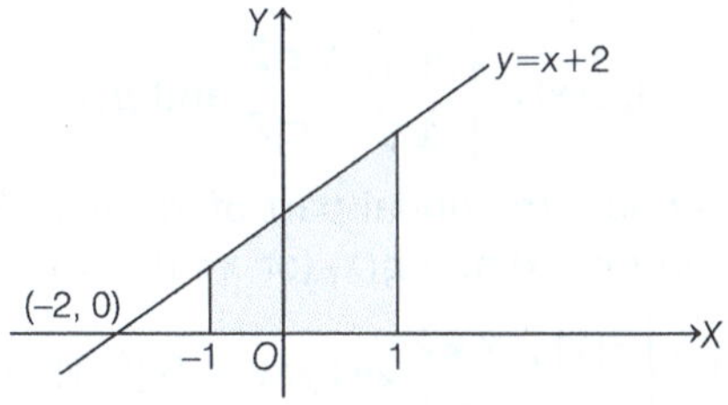

$$\text{Required area} = \int_{-1}^{1} (x + 2)dx = \left[\frac{x^2}{2} + 2x\right]_{-1}^{1} = 4 \text{ sq units}$$

JEE SCANNER

Example Similar to PYQ Asked in JEE Main 2023

The area common to the region determined by $y \ge \sqrt{x}$ and $x^2 + y^2 < 2$ has the value

(a) π sq units
(b) $(2\pi - 1)$ sq units
(c) $\left(\frac{\pi}{4} - \frac{1}{6}\right)$ sq units
(d) None of these

Sol. (c) The region formed by $y \ge \sqrt{x}$ is the outer region of the parabola $y^2 = x$, when $y \ge 0$ and $x \ge 0$ and $x^2 + y^2 < 2$ is the region inner to circle $x^2 + y^2 = 2$ shown as in figure.

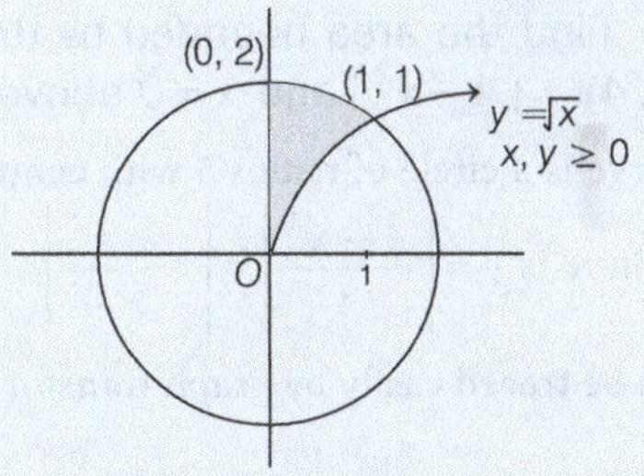

Now, to find the point of intersection put $y^2 = x$ in $x^2 + y^2 = 2$.

$$\Rightarrow\quad x^2 + x - 2 = 0 \Rightarrow (x + 2)(x - 1) = 0$$

$$\Rightarrow\quad x = 1, \text{ as } x \ge 0$$

$$\therefore\ \text{Required area} = \int_0^1 (\sqrt{2 - x^2} - \sqrt{x})\, dx$$

$$= \left[\frac{x\sqrt{2 - x^2}}{2} + \sin^{-1}\frac{x}{\sqrt{2}} - \frac{2}{3}x^{3/2}\right]_0^1$$

$$= \frac{1}{2} + \frac{\pi}{4} - \frac{2}{3} = \left(\frac{\pi}{4} - \frac{1}{6}\right) \text{ sq units}$$

Skill Builder

The area common to the region determined by $y > 2\sqrt{x}$ and $x^2 + y^2 < 5$ has the value

(a) $\frac{1}{3}$
(b) $\frac{5}{2}\sin^{-1}\left(\frac{1}{\sqrt{5}}\right) + \frac{1}{3}$
(c) $\frac{5}{2}\sin^{-1}\left(\frac{1}{\sqrt{5}}\right) - \frac{1}{3}$
(d) None of these

For Sol.

■ **For more practice** See Q.9 of Milestone Practice 3.2.

Example 23. If $f(x)=\begin{cases}\sqrt{\{x\}}, & x\notin Z\\ 1, & x\in Z\end{cases}$ and $g(x)=\{x\}^2$ (where, {} denotes fractional part of x), then find the area bounded by $f(x)$ and $g(x)$ for $x\in[0,10]$.

Sol. As, $f(x)=\begin{cases}\sqrt{\{x\}}, & x\notin Z\\ 1, & x\in Z\end{cases}$ and $g(x)=\{x\}^2$, where both $f(x)$ and $g(x)$ are periodic with period '1' shown as

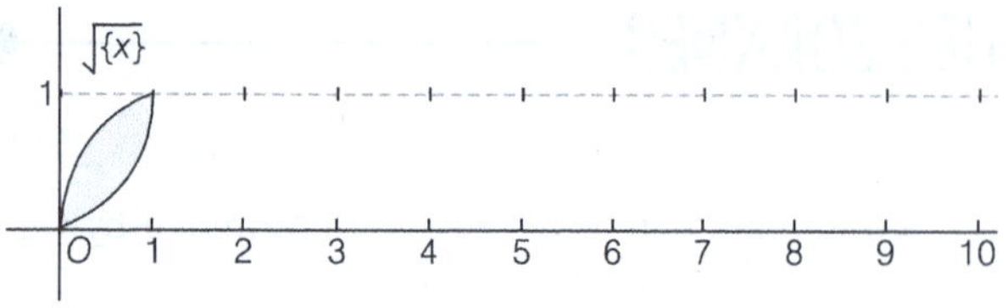

Thus, required area

$$=10\int_0^1[\sqrt{\{x\}}-\{x\}^2]\,dx=10\int_0^1[(x)^{1/2}-x^2]\,dx$$

$$=10\left[\frac{x^{3/2}}{3/2}-\frac{x^3}{3}\right]_0^1=10\left(\frac{2}{3}-\frac{1}{3}\right)=\frac{10}{3}\text{ sq units}$$

Example 24. Find the area bounded by the curves $x^2+y^2=25$, $4y=|4-x^2|$ and $x=0$ above the X-axis.

Sol. The 1st curve is a circle of radius 5 with centre at (0, 0).

The 2nd curve is $y=\left|\frac{4-x^2}{4}\right|=\left|1-\frac{x^2}{4}\right|$

which can be traced easily by graph transformation.

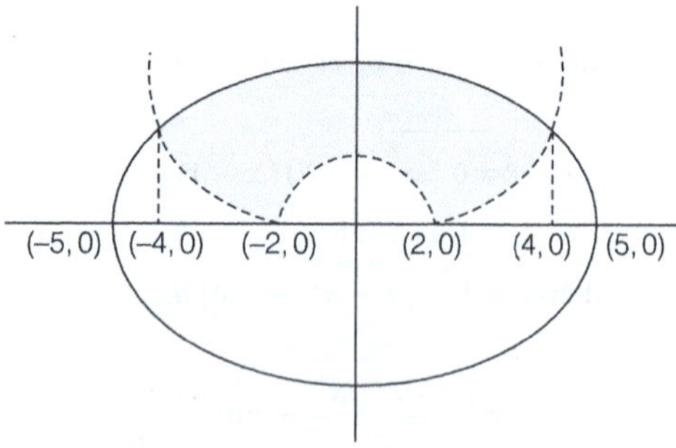

When the two curves intersect each other, then

$$x^2+\left(1-\frac{x^2}{4}\right)^2=25\Rightarrow x=\pm 4$$

Hence, the required area $=2\int_0^4\left(\sqrt{25-x^2}-\left|1-\frac{x^2}{4}\right|\right)dx$

$$=2\left[\int_0^4\sqrt{25-x^2}\,dx-\int_0^2\left(1-\frac{x^2}{4}\right)dx+\int_2^4\left(1-\frac{x^2}{4}\right)dx\right]$$

$$=2\left[\left(\frac{x}{2}\sqrt{25-x^2}+\frac{25}{2}\sin^{-1}\frac{x}{5}\right)_0^4-\left(x-\frac{x^3}{12}\right)_0^2+\left(x-\frac{x^3}{12}\right)_2^4\right]$$

$$=2\left[\left(6+\frac{25}{2}\sin^{-1}\frac{4}{5}\right)-\left(2-\frac{8}{12}\right)+\left(4-\frac{64}{12}-2+\frac{8}{12}\right)\right]$$

$$=2\left[6+\frac{25}{2}\sin^{-1}\left(\frac{4}{5}\right)-\frac{4}{3}-\frac{8}{3}\right]=\left\{25\sin^{-1}\left(\frac{4}{5}\right)+4\right\}$$

Example 25. Find the area enclosed by curve $x=3\cos t+\cos 3t$ and $y=3\sin t-\sin 3t$, where $0\le t\le\pi$.

Sol. Given, $y=f(x)$ is non-negative on the interval $a\le x\le b$, where x is decreasing as t increases.

Required area $=-\int_a^b y\,dx=-\int_{t_1}^{t_2}y(t)\left(\frac{dx}{dt}\right)dt$

$$=-\int_0^{\pi}(3\sin t-\sin 3t)(-3\sin t-3\sin 3t)\,dt$$

$$=-\int_0^{\pi}4\sin^3 t\cdot(-3)(\sin t+\sin 3t)\,dt$$

$$=12\int_0^{\pi}\sin^3 t\,(2\sin 2t\cdot\cos t)\,dt$$

$$=48\int_0^{\pi}\sin^4 t\cdot\cos^2 t\,dt$$

$$=96\int_0^{\pi/2}\sin^4 t\cdot\cos^2 t\,dt$$

$$=96\left(\frac{3\times1\times1}{6\times4\times2}\cdot\frac{\pi}{2}\right)=3\pi\text{ sq units}$$

[using wallis formula]

Example 26. Find the area of the region bounded by the curves $y=x^2$, $y=|2-x^2|$ and $y=2$, which lies to the right of the line $x=1$.

Sol. The region bounded by given curves on the right side of $x=1$ is shown as

Required area $=\int_1^{\sqrt2}\{x^2-(2-x^2)\}\,dx+\int_{\sqrt2}^2\{4-x^2\}\,dx$

$$=\int_1^{\sqrt2}(2x^2-2)\,dx+\int_{\sqrt2}^2(4-x^2)\,dx$$

$$=\left(2\cdot\frac{x^3}{3}-2x\right)_1^{\sqrt2}+\left(4x-\frac{x^3}{3}\right)_{\sqrt2}^2$$

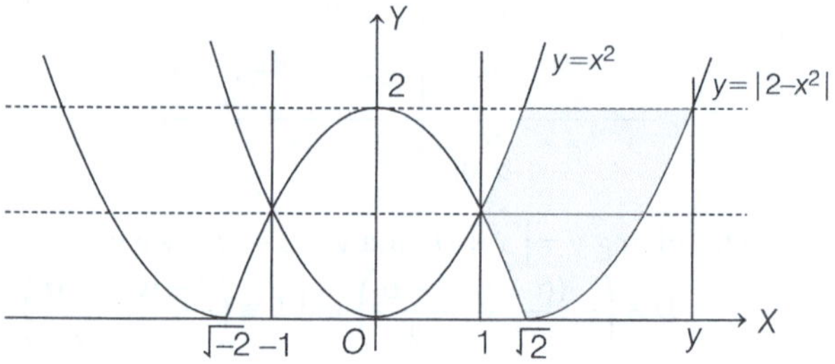

$$=\left(\frac{4\sqrt2}{3}-2\sqrt2\right)-\left(\frac{2}{3}-2\right)+\left(8-\frac{8}{3}\right)-\left(4\sqrt2-\frac{2\sqrt2}{3}\right)$$

$$=\left(-4\sqrt2+\frac{20}{3}\right)=\left(\frac{20-12\sqrt2}{3}\right)\text{ sq units}$$

Example 27. The area enclosed by the curve $|y| = \sin 2x$, when $x \in [0, 2\pi]$ is

(a) 1 sq unit (b) 2 sq units
(c) 3 sq units (d) 4 sq units

Sol. (d) As, we know $y = \sin 2x$ could be plotted as

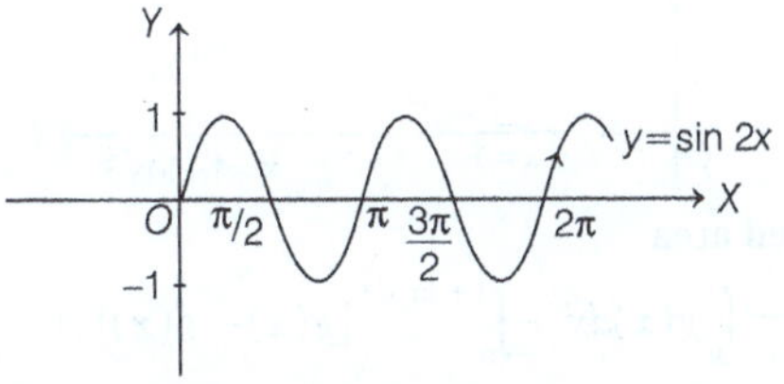

Thus, $|y| = \sin 2x$ is whenever positive, y can have both positive and negative values, i.e. the curve is symmetric about the axes.

$\sin 2x$ is positive only in $0 \le x \le \dfrac{\pi}{2}$ and $\pi \le x \le \dfrac{3\pi}{2}$.

Thus, the curve consists of two loops one in $\left[0, \dfrac{\pi}{2}\right]$ and another in $\left[\pi, \dfrac{3\pi}{2}\right]$.

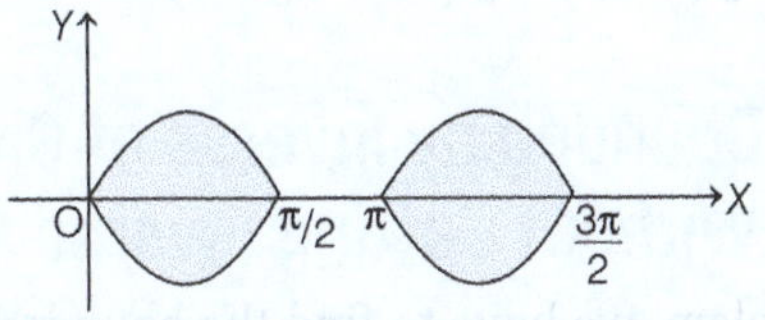

Thus, the required area $= 4\displaystyle\int_0^{\pi/2} (\sin 2x)\, dx$

$$= 4\left(-\frac{\cos 2x}{2}\right)_0^{\pi/2}$$

$$= -2(\cos \pi - \cos 0)$$

$$= -2(-1-1)$$

$$= 4 \text{ sq units}$$

Example 28. Let $f(x) = \max\left\{\sin x, \cos x, \dfrac{1}{2}\right\}$, then determine the area of region bounded by the curves $y = f(x)$, X-axis, Y-axis and $x = 2\pi$.

Sol. We have, $f(x) = \max\left\{\sin x, \cos x, \dfrac{1}{2}\right\}$. Graphically, $f(x)$ could be drawn as

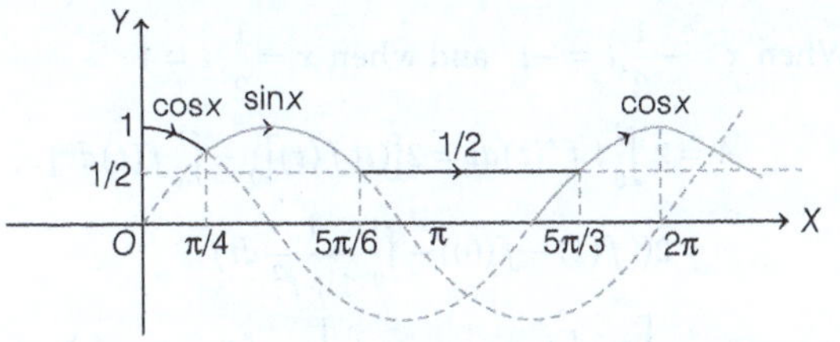

Here, the graph is plotted between 0 to 2π and between the points of intersection the maximum portion is included, thus the shaded part is required area

	Interval	Value of $f(x)$
i.e. for	$0 \le x < \pi/4$	$\cos x$
for	$\pi/4 \le x < 5\pi/6$	$\sin x$
for	$5\pi/6 \le x < 5\pi/3$	$1/2$
for	$5\pi/3 \le x < 2\pi$	$\cos x$

Hence, required area

$$I = \int_0^{\pi/4} \cos x\, dx + \int_{\pi/4}^{5\pi/6} \sin x\, dx + \int_{5\pi/6}^{5\pi/3} \frac{1}{2}\, dx + \int_{5\pi/3}^{2\pi} \cos x\, dx$$

$$= (\sin x)_0^{\pi/4} - (\cos x)_{\pi/4}^{5\pi/6} + \frac{1}{2}(x)_{5\pi/6}^{5\pi/3} + (\sin x)_{5\pi/3}^{2\pi}$$

$$= \left(\frac{1}{\sqrt{2}} - 0\right) - \left(-\frac{\sqrt{3}}{2} - \frac{1}{\sqrt{2}}\right) + \frac{1}{2}\left(\frac{5\pi}{3} - \frac{5\pi}{6}\right) + \left(0 + \frac{\sqrt{3}}{2}\right)$$

$$= \left(\frac{5\pi}{12} + \sqrt{2} + \sqrt{3}\right) \text{ sq units}$$

Example 29. Find the area of the region enclosed by the curve $5x^2 + 6xy + 2y^2 + 7x + 6y + 6 = 0$.

Sol. Comparing $ax^2 + 2hxy + by^2 + 2gx + 2fy + c = 0$, we get

$a = 5, b = 2, h = 3, g = 7/2, f = 3$ and $c = 6$

$$\Rightarrow \quad h^2 - ab = -1 < 0$$

So, the above equation represents an ellipse.

$$\therefore \quad 2y^2 + 6(1+x)y + (5x^2 + 7x + 6) = 0$$

$$\Rightarrow \quad y = \frac{-3(1+x) \pm \sqrt{(3-x)(x-1)}}{2}$$

Clearly, the values of y are real for all $x \in [1, 3]$. Thus, the graph is as shown below.

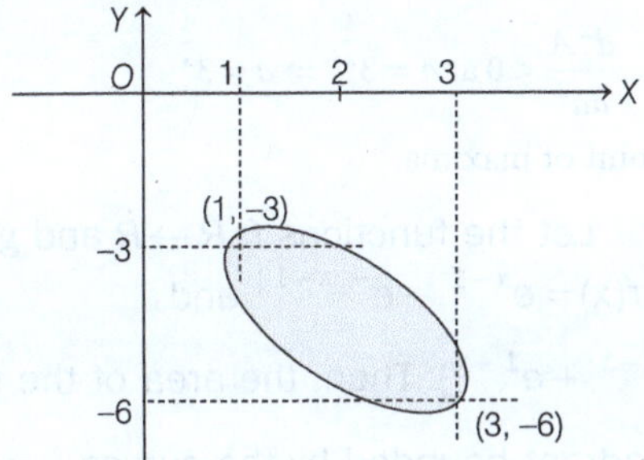

Thus, the required area

$$= \left| \int_1^3 \left(\frac{-3(1+x) - \sqrt{(3-x)(x-1)}}{2} \right) - \left(\frac{-3(1+x) + \sqrt{(3-x)(x-1)}}{2} \right) dx \right|$$

$$= \left| -\int_1^3 \sqrt{(3-x)(x-1)}\, dx \right| = \left| \int_1^3 \sqrt{1^2 - (x-2)^2}\, dx \right|$$

$$= \left| -\left\{ \frac{1}{2}(x-2)\sqrt{-x^2 + 4x - 3} + \frac{1}{2}\sin^{-1}\left(\frac{x-2}{1}\right) \right\}_1^3 \right|$$

$$= \frac{\pi}{2} \text{ sq units}$$

Example 30. Find the value(s) of the parameter a ($a>0$) for each of which the area of the figure bounded by the straight line, $y=\dfrac{a^2-ax}{1+a^4}$ and the parabola $y=\dfrac{x^2+2ax+3a^2}{1+a^4}$ is the greatest.

Sol. Given curves, $y=\dfrac{a^2-ax}{1+a^4}$, $y=\dfrac{x^2+2ax+3a^2}{1+a^4}$

Solving them to get point of intersection.

$$\Rightarrow \quad a^2-ax=x^2+2ax+3a^2$$

$$\Rightarrow \quad x^2+3ax+2a^2=0 \Rightarrow (x+2a)(x+a)=0$$

$$\Rightarrow \quad x=-a,-2a$$

$$\text{Required area}=\left|\int_{-2a}^{-a}\left(\frac{x^2+2ax+3a^2}{1+a^4}-\frac{a^2-ax}{1+a^4}\right)dx\right|$$

$$=\left|\int_{-2a}^{-a}\frac{(x^2+3ax+2a^2)}{1+a^4}\,dx\right|$$

$$=\left|\frac{1}{1+a^4}\left[\frac{x^3}{3}+\frac{3ax^2}{2}+2a^2x\right]_{-2a}^{-a}\right|$$

$$=\frac{a^3}{6(a^4+1)}=A \text{ (say)}$$

For greatest area, $\dfrac{dA}{da}=0 \Rightarrow \dfrac{(a^4+1)3a^2-4a^3(a^3)}{6(a^4+1)^2}=0$

$$\Rightarrow \quad 3a^6+3a^2-4a^6=0 \Rightarrow a^4=3 \Rightarrow a=3^{\frac{1}{4}}$$

$$\frac{d^2A}{da^2}<0 \text{ at } a=3^{\frac{1}{4}} \Rightarrow a=3^{\frac{1}{4}}$$

is the point of maxima.

Example 31. Let the functions $f:R\to R$ and $g:R\to R$ be defined by $f(x)=e^{x-1}-e^{-|x-1|}$ and $g(x)=\dfrac{1}{2}(e^{x-1}+e^{1-x})$. Then, the area of the region in the first quadrant bounded by the curves $y=f(x)$, $y=g(x)$ and $x=0$ is

(a) $(2-\sqrt{3})+\dfrac{1}{2}(e-e^{-1})$ (b) $(2+\sqrt{3})+\dfrac{1}{2}(e-e^{-1})$

(c) $(2-\sqrt{3})+\dfrac{1}{2}(e+e^{-1})$ (d) $(2+\sqrt{3})+\dfrac{1}{2}(e+e^{-1})$

Sol. (a) $f(x)=e^{x-1}-e^{-|x-1|}$

$$\therefore f(x)=\begin{cases}0, & x\le 1\\ e^{x-1}-e^{1-x}, & x>1\end{cases} \text{ and } g(x)=\frac{1}{2}(e^{x-1}+e^{1-x})$$

If $f(x)=g(x)$

$$\Rightarrow e^{x-1}-e^{-(x-1)}=\frac{e^{x-1}+e^{1-x}}{2} \Rightarrow e^{2(x-1)}=3$$

$$\Rightarrow \quad x=\frac{1}{2}\ln 3+1=1+\ln\sqrt{3}$$

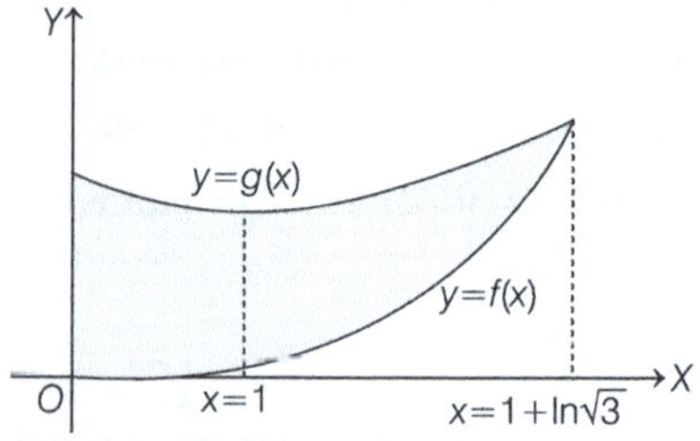

Required area

$$=\int_0^1 g(x)dx+\int_a^{1+\ln\sqrt{3}}[g(x)-f(x)]dx$$

$$=\int_0^1\frac{1}{2}(e^{x-1}+e^{1-x})dx$$

$$+\int_1^{1+\ln\sqrt{3}}\left(\frac{1}{2}(e^{x-1}+e^{1-x})-(e^{x-1}-e^{1-x})\right)dx$$

$$=\frac{1}{2}[e^{x-1}-e^{1-x}]_0^1+\left[-\frac{1}{2}e^{x-1}-\frac{3}{2}e^{1-x}\right]_1^{1+\ln\sqrt{3}}$$

$$=\frac{1}{2}\left(e-\frac{1}{e}\right)-\frac{1}{2}\left(\sqrt{3}+\frac{3}{\sqrt{3}}-4\right)=(2-\sqrt{3})+\frac{1}{2}\left(e-\frac{1}{e}\right)$$

3.7 Area Bounded by Inverse of Given Function Without Getting Inverse Function

In some problem, we have to find the bounded area which involves inverse function of the given function and other curves, but when if the inverse function cannot be determined, in this case we find the area using substitution method using and integration by parts.

Example 32. If $f:[-1,1]\to\left[-\dfrac{1}{2},\dfrac{1}{2}\right]$, $f(x)=\dfrac{x}{1+x^2}$, then find the area bounded by $y=g(x)$, X-axis $x=-\dfrac{1}{2}$ and $x=\dfrac{1}{2}$, where $g(x)$ is the inverse of $f(x)$.

Sol. Required area $A=\displaystyle\int_{-1/2}^{1/2}g(x)dx$

$$A=\int_{-1/2}^{1/2}f^{-1}(x)dx$$

Put $f^{-1}(x)=t \Rightarrow x=f(t) \Rightarrow dx=f'(t)dt$

When $x=-\dfrac{1}{2}, t=-1$ and when $x=\dfrac{1}{2}, t=1$

$$\because \quad A=2\int_0^1 tf'(t)dt=2[(t(f(t)]_0^1-\int_0^1 f(t)dt]$$

$$=2((f(1)-f(0))-\int_0^1\frac{t}{1+t^2}dt)$$

$$=2\left[\frac{1}{2}-\left[\frac{1}{2}\log(1+t^2)\right]_0^1\right]=2\left(\frac{1}{2}-\frac{1}{2}\log 2\right)$$

$$=(1-\log 2) \text{ sq units}$$

Milestone Practice 3.2

1. The area of the region bounded by $y^2 = 2x + 1$ and $x - y - 1 = 0$ is
(a) 2/3 (b) 4/3 (c) 8/3 (d) 16/3

2. Area of the region bounded by the curves $y = 2^x, y = 2x - x^2, x = 0$ and $x = 2$ is given by
(a) $\frac{3}{\log 2} - \frac{4}{3}$ (b) $\frac{3}{\log 2} + \frac{4}{3}$
(c) $3 \log 2 - \frac{4}{3}$ (d) None of these

3. The area of the figure bounded by the cuves $y = e^x, y = e^{-x}$ and the straight line $x = 1$ is
(a) $e + \frac{1}{e}$ (b) $e - \frac{1}{e}$
(c) $e + \frac{1}{e} - 2$ (d) None of these

4. The curve $y = ax^2 + bx + c$ passes through the point (1, 2) and its tangent at origin is the line $y = x$. The area bounded by the curve, the ordinate of the curve at minima and the tangent line is
(a) $\frac{1}{24}$ (b) $\frac{1}{12}$ (c) $\frac{1}{8}$ (d) $\frac{1}{6}$

5. The area of the region given by $x + y \le 8$, $x^2 + y^2 \le 8y$ and $y^2 \le 4x$ is (in sq units)
(a) -4π (b) $-4\pi + \frac{16}{3}$
(c) $-4\pi + \frac{64}{3}$ (d) $4\pi - \frac{16}{3}$

6. The area bounded by the curves $y = xe^x, y = xe^{-x}$ and the line $x = 1$ is
(a) $\frac{2}{e}$ (b) $1 - \frac{2}{e}$ (c) $\frac{1}{e}$ (d) $1 - \frac{1}{e}$

7. The area bounded by the inverse function of $y = f(x) = x^3 + 1$ between ordinates $x = -7$ and $x = 2$ and X-axis is
(a) $\frac{51}{4}$ (b) $\frac{43}{4}$ (c) $\frac{45}{4}$ (d) $\frac{67}{4}$

8. The area bounded by the curves $y = x^2 + 2$ and $y = 2|x| - \cos \pi x$ is
(a) $\frac{2}{3}$ (b) $\frac{8}{3}$ (c) $\frac{4}{3}$ (d) $\frac{1}{3}$

9. The area common to the region determined by $x, y \ge 0, y \ge \sqrt{3x}$ and $x^2 + y^2 \le 4$ is
(a) $\left(\frac{\pi}{6} + \frac{\sqrt{3}}{6}\right)$ sq units (b) $\left(\frac{\pi}{3} - \frac{\sqrt{3}}{6}\right)$ sq units
(c) $\left(\frac{\pi}{3} + \frac{\sqrt{3}}{6}\right)$ sq units (d) $\left(\frac{\pi}{6} - \frac{\sqrt{3}}{6}\right)$ sq units

10. A point P moves inside a triangle formed by $A(0, 0)$, $B(1, \sqrt{3}), C(2, 0)$ such that $\min\{PA, PB, PC\} = 1$, then the area bounded by the curve traced by P, is
(a) $3\sqrt{3} - \frac{3\pi}{2}$ (b) $\sqrt{3} + \frac{\pi}{2}$
(c) $\sqrt{3} - \frac{\pi}{2}$ (d) $3\sqrt{3} + \frac{3\pi}{2}$

11. The graph of $y^2 + 2xy + 40|x| = 400$ divides the plane into regions. The area of the bounded region is
(a) 400 (b) 800
(c) 600 (c) None of these

12. The area of the region defined by $||x| - |y|| \le 1$ and $x^2 + y^2 \le 1$ in the XY- plane is
(a) 0 (b) 2 (c) 3 (d) 1

13. If the area bounded by $f(x) = \frac{x^3}{3} - x^2 + a$ and the straight lines $x = 0$, $x = 2$ and the X-axis is minimum, then the value of a is
(a) $\frac{1}{3}$ (b) $\frac{2}{3}$ (c) $\frac{4}{3}$ (d) $\frac{5}{3}$

14. The area of the region enclosed by the curve $|y| = -(1 - |x|)^2 + 5$, is
(a) $\frac{8}{3}(7 + 5\sqrt{5})$ sq units (b) $\frac{2}{3}(7 + 5\sqrt{5})$ sq units
(c) $\frac{2}{3}(5\sqrt{5} - 7)$ sq units (d) None of these

15. The area bounded by the curve $f(x) = ||\tan x + \cot x| - |\tan x - \cot x||$ between the lines $x = 0$, $x = \frac{\pi}{2}$ and the X-axis is
(a) $\log 3$ (b) $\log \sqrt{2}$
(c) $2\log 2$ (d) $\sqrt{2} \log 2$

16. The area bounded by the curve $x = a \cos^3 t$ and $y = a \sin^3 t$ is
(a) $\frac{3\pi a^2}{8}$ (b) $3\pi a^2$ (c) $\frac{3\pi a}{8}$ (d) $3\pi a$

Answer Key

1. (d)	2. (a)	3. (c)	4. (a)	5. (d)	6. (a)
7. (a)	8. (b)	9. (b)	10. (c)	11. (b)	12. (b)
13. (b)	14. (a)	15. (c)	16. (a)		

For Detailed Solution

JEE Pattern EXAMPLES

Single Option Correct Type Questions

Example 1 *If A denotes the area bounded by* $f(x) = \left|\dfrac{\sin x + \cos x}{x}\right|$, *X-axis,* $x = \pi$ *and* $x = 3\pi$, *then*

(a) $1 < A < 2$ (b) $0 < A < 2$
(c) $2 < A < 3$ (d) None of these

Sol. (b) $\dfrac{2\sqrt{2}}{2\pi} < \displaystyle\int_{\pi}^{2\pi} \dfrac{|\sin x + \cos x|}{x}\,dx < \dfrac{2\sqrt{2}}{\pi}$

$$\left[\because \pi < x < 2\pi \Rightarrow \frac{1}{2\pi} < \frac{1}{x} < \frac{1}{\pi}\right] \quad \text{...(i)}$$

$$\frac{2\sqrt{2}}{3\pi} < \int_{2\pi}^{3\pi} \frac{|\sin x + \cos x|}{x}\,dx < \frac{2\sqrt{2}}{2\pi} \quad \text{...(ii)}$$

On adding Eqs. (i) and (ii), we get

$$\frac{5\sqrt{2}}{3\pi} < A < \frac{3\sqrt{2}}{\pi} \Rightarrow 0.75 < A < 1.3$$

Example 2 *The area of the region included between the regions satisfying* $\min(|x|, |y|) \ge 1$ *and* $x^2 + y^2 \le 5$ *is*

(a) $\dfrac{5}{2}\left(\sin^{-1}\dfrac{2}{\sqrt{5}} - \sin^{-1}\dfrac{1}{\sqrt{5}}\right) - 4$

(b) $10\left(\sin^{-1}\dfrac{2}{\sqrt{5}} - \sin^{-1}\dfrac{1}{\sqrt{5}}\right) - 4$

(c) $\dfrac{2}{5}\left(\sin^{-1}\dfrac{2}{\sqrt{5}} - \sin^{-1}\dfrac{1}{\sqrt{5}}\right) - 4$

(d) $15\left(\sin^{-1}\dfrac{2}{\sqrt{5}} - \sin^{-1}\dfrac{1}{\sqrt{5}}\right) - 4$

Sol. (b) Shaded region depicts $\min(|x|, |y|) \ge 1$

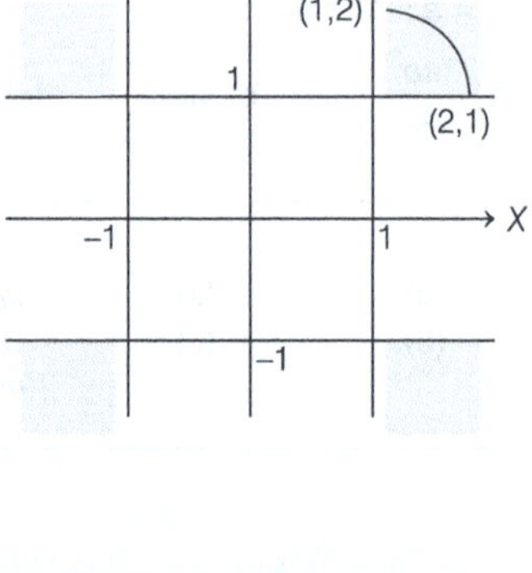

$$\text{Required area} = 4\int_1^2 (\sqrt{5 - x^2} - 1)\,dx$$

$$= 10\left(\sin^{-1}\frac{2}{\sqrt{5}} - \sin^{-1}\frac{1}{\sqrt{5}}\right) - 4$$

JEE SCANNER

Example 3 Similar to PYQ Asked in JEE Main 2024

The area bounded by the curve $x^2 = ky, k > 0$ *and the line* $y = 3$ *is 12 sq units, then the value of k is*

(a) 4 (b) 5 (c) 3 (d) 6

Sol. (c) Bounded area $= 2\displaystyle\int_0^3 x\,dy$

$$= 2\int_0^3 \sqrt{k}\sqrt{y}\,dy$$

$$= 2\sqrt{k} \cdot \frac{2}{3}[y^{3/2}]_0^3$$

$$= \frac{4}{3} \cdot \sqrt{k} \times 3\sqrt{3} \text{ sq units}$$

$$= 12 \text{ sq units} \quad \text{[given]}$$

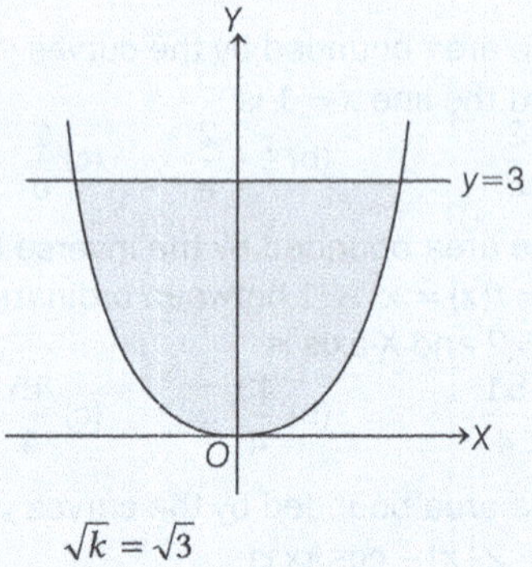

$\Rightarrow \quad \sqrt{k} = \sqrt{3}$

$\therefore \quad k = 3$

Skill Builder

The area bounded by the parabolas $y = 4x^2$, $y = \dfrac{x^2}{9}$ and the line $y = 2$ is

(a) $\dfrac{20\sqrt{2}}{3}$ sq units (b) $\dfrac{10\sqrt{2}}{3}$ sq units

(c) $\dfrac{20}{3}$ sq units (d) $\dfrac{10}{3}$ sq units

For Sol.

Example 4 *If $f(x) \geq 0, \forall x \in (0, 2)$ and $y = f(x)$ makes positive intercepts of 2 and 1 unit on X and Y-axes, respectively and encloses an area of 3/4 unit with axes, then $\int_0^2 xf'(x)\,dx$ is*

(a) $\frac{3}{4}$ (b) 1

(c) $\frac{5}{4}$ (d) $-\frac{3}{4}$

Sol. (d) $I = xf(x)|_0^2 - \int_0^2 f(x)\,dx = 0 - \frac{3}{4} = -\frac{3}{4}$

Example 5 *The area of the region between the curves $y = \sqrt{\frac{1+\sin x}{\cos x}}$ and $y = \sqrt{\frac{1-\sin x}{\cos x}}$ and bounded by the lines $x = 0$ and $x = \frac{\pi}{4}$ is*

(a) $\int_0^{\sqrt{2}-1} \frac{t}{(1+t^2)\sqrt{1-t^2}}\,dt$ (b) $\int_0^{\sqrt{2}-1} \frac{4t}{(1+t^2)\sqrt{1-t^2}}\,dt$

(c) $\int_0^{\sqrt{2}+1} \frac{4t}{(1+t^2)\sqrt{1-t^2}}\,dt$ (d) $\int_0^{\sqrt{2}+1} \frac{t}{(1+t^2)\sqrt{1-t^2}}\,dt$

Sol. (b) Required area $= \int_0^{\pi/4} \left(\sqrt{\frac{1+\sin x}{\cos x}} - \sqrt{\frac{1-\sin x}{\cos x}} \right) dx$

$$\left[\because \frac{1+\sin x}{\cos x} > \frac{1-\sin x}{\cos x} > 0 \right]$$

$$= \int_0^{\pi/4} \left(\sqrt{\frac{1 + \frac{2\tan\frac{x}{2}}{1+\tan^2\frac{x}{2}}}{\frac{1-\tan^2\frac{x}{2}}{1+\tan^2\frac{x}{2}}}} - \sqrt{\frac{1 - \frac{2\tan\frac{x}{2}}{1+\tan^2\frac{x}{2}}}{\frac{1-\tan^2\frac{x}{2}}{1+\tan^2\frac{x}{2}}}} \right) dx$$

$$= \int_0^{\pi/4} \left(\sqrt{\frac{\left(1+\tan\frac{x}{2}\right)^2}{1-\tan^2\frac{x}{2}}} - \sqrt{\frac{\left(1-\tan\frac{x}{2}\right)^2}{1-\tan^2\frac{x}{2}}} \right) dx$$

$$= \int_0^{\pi/4} \frac{1+\tan\frac{x}{2} - 1 + \tan\frac{x}{2}}{\sqrt{1-\tan^2\frac{x}{2}}}\,dx$$

$$= \int_0^{\pi/4} \frac{2\tan\frac{x}{2}}{\sqrt{1-\tan^2\frac{x}{2}}}\,dx$$

Put $\tan\frac{x}{2} = t$

$\therefore$ Area $= \int_0^{\sqrt{2}-1} \frac{4t}{(1+t^2)\sqrt{1-t^2}}\,dt$

Example 6 *Suppose $y = f(x)$ and $y = g(x)$ are two functions whose graphs intersect at three points $(0, 4)$, $(2, 2)$ and $(4, 0)$ with $f(x) > g(x)$ for $0 < x < 2$ and $f(x) < g(x)$ for $2 < x < 4$. If $\int_0^4 [f(x) - g(x)]dx = 10$ and $\int_2^4 [g(x) - f(x)]dx = 5$, then the area between two curves for $0 < x < 2$, is*

(a) 5 (b) 10 (c) 15 (d) 20

Sol. (c)

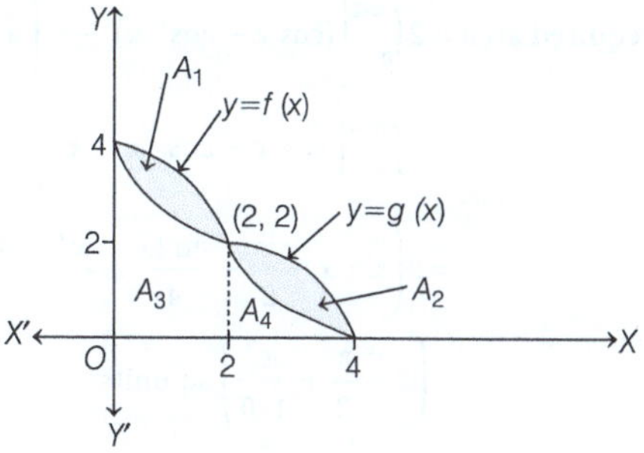

Given, $\int_0^4 f(x)dx - \int_0^4 g(x)dx = 10$

$(A_1 + A_3 + A_4) - (A_2 + A_3 + A_4) = 10$

$A_1 - A_2 = 10$ ...(i)

Again, $\int_2^4 g(x)dx - \int_2^4 f(x)dx = 5$

$\Rightarrow$ $(A_2 + A_4) - A_4 = 5 \Rightarrow A_2 = 5$ ...(ii)

On adding Eqs. (i) and (ii), we get

$A_1 = 15$

Example 7 *Area bounded by $y = e^{-x}$ and $y = e^x$ and the directrix of the conic $y^2 - 4x - 4y + 12 = 0$ is*

(a) $\frac{1}{2}\sum_{r=1}^{\infty} \frac{1}{(20)!}$ (b) $\sum_{r=0}^{\infty} \frac{1}{(2r)!}$

(c) $\sum_{r=1}^{\infty} \frac{1}{(2r)!}$ (d) $2\sum_{r=1}^{\infty} \frac{1}{(2r)!}$

Sol. (d) Given, conic is $(y-2)^2 = 4(x-2)$

$\therefore$ Directrix $= x - 2 + 1 = 0 \Rightarrow x = 1$

$\therefore$ Required area $= \int_0^1 (e^x - e^{-x})dx = e + \frac{1}{e} - 2 = 2\sum_{r=1}^{\infty} \frac{1}{(2r)!}$

Example 8 *If the total area bounded by the curves $y = \cos x - \cos^2 x$ and $y = x^2\left(x^2 - \frac{\pi^2}{4}\right)$ is $\left(k - \frac{\pi}{2} + \frac{\pi^m}{n}\right)$, then $\frac{n}{m+k+3}$ equals*

(a) 9 (b) 10

(c) 8 (d) 12

Sol. (d) Here, $y = \cos x - \cos^2 x$ and $y = x^2\left(x^2 - \frac{\pi^2}{4}\right)$ both curves meet at $2 = 0, \pm \frac{\pi}{2}$.

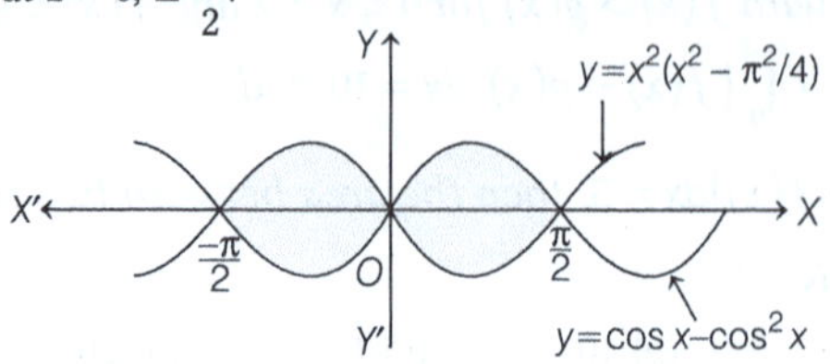

Thus, required area $= 2\int_0^{\pi/2}\left[(\cos x - \cos^2 x) - x^2\left(x^2 - \frac{\pi^2}{4}\right)\right]dx$

$$= 2\int_0^{\pi/2}\left(\cos x - \cos^2 x - x^4 + \frac{\pi^2}{4}x^2\right)dx$$

$$= 2\left(\sin x - \frac{x}{2} - \frac{\sin 2x}{4} - \frac{x^5}{5} + \frac{\pi^2 x^3}{12}\right)_0^{\pi/2}$$

$$= \left(2 - \frac{\pi}{2} + \frac{\pi^5}{120}\right) \text{ sq units}$$

Here, $k = 2$, $m = 5$ and $n = 120$

$$\therefore \quad \frac{n}{m + k + 3} = 12$$

Example 9 *Area bounded by* $y = \left[\sin^2 \frac{x}{2} + \sqrt{\cos \frac{x}{2}}\right]$ *and* $y = \left|\sin x - \frac{1}{2}\right|$, $x = 0$, $x = \pi$ *(where* [·] *represents the greatest integer function) is*

(a) $\frac{1}{6}[7\pi + 12(1 - \sqrt{3})]$ (b) $7\pi + 12(1 + \sqrt{3})$

(c) $\frac{\pi}{2} + 1 - \sqrt{3}$ (d) $\frac{\pi}{2} + 1 + \sqrt{3}$

Sol. (a)

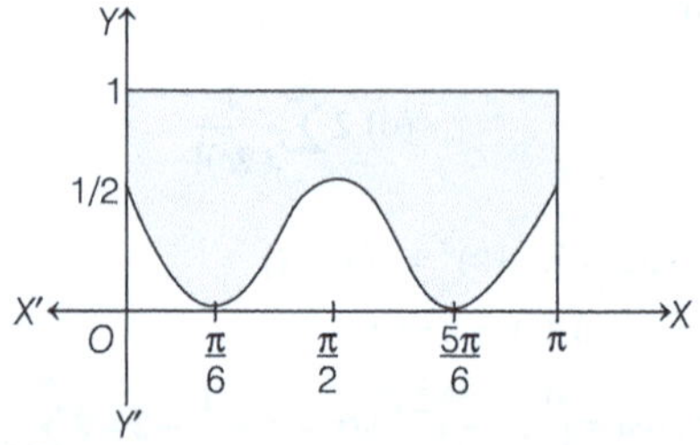

$$1 \le \sin^2 \frac{x}{2} + \sqrt{\cos \frac{x}{2}} < 2 \Rightarrow \left[\sin^2 \frac{x}{2} + \sqrt{\cos \frac{x}{2}}\right] = 1$$

$\therefore$ Required area

$$= \pi - 2\left[\int_0^{\pi/6}\left(\frac{1}{2} - \sin x\right)dx + \int_{\pi/6}^{\pi/2}\left(\sin x - \frac{1}{2}\right)dx\right]$$

$$= \pi - 2\left[\left(\frac{x}{2} + \cos x\right)_0^{\pi/6} + \left(-\cos x - \frac{x}{2}\right)_{\pi/6}^{\pi/2}\right]$$

$$= \frac{7\pi}{6} + 2(1 - \sqrt{3})$$

JEE SCANNER

Example 10 Similar to PYQ Asked in JEE Main 2024

The parabolas $y^2 = x$ *and* $x^2 = 8y$ *divide the rectangular region bounded by the lines* $x = 4, y = 2$ *and the coordinate axes. If* A_1, A_2, A_3 *are the areas of these parts numbered from top to bottom respectively, then*

(a) $A_1 : A_2 = 1:1$ (b) $A_2 : A_3 - 1:2$

(c) $A_1 : A_3 = 2:1$ (d) $A_1 : (A_1 + A_2) = 1:3$

Sol. (a) $y^2 = x$ and $x^2 = 8y$ meet at $O(0, 0)$ and $A(4, 2)$.

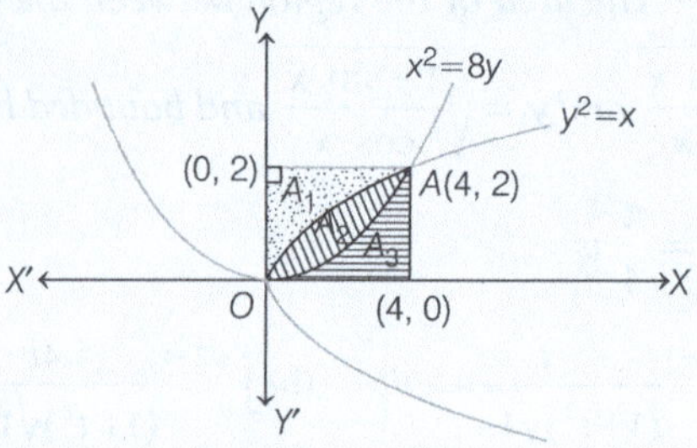

Now, $A_3 = \int_0^4 \frac{x^2}{8} dx$

$$= \frac{1}{8}\left[\frac{x^3}{3}\right]_0^4$$

$$= \left(\frac{8}{3}\right) \text{ sq units}$$

$$A_2 = \int_0^4 \sqrt{x}\, dx - A_3$$

$$= \frac{2}{3}[x^{3/2}]_0^4 - \frac{8}{3} = \frac{16}{3} - \frac{8}{3}$$

$$= \left(\frac{8}{3}\right) \text{ sq units}$$

and $A_1 = 4 \times 2 - (A_2 + A_3)$

$$= 8 - \left(\frac{8}{3} + \frac{8}{3}\right) = 8 - \frac{16}{3} = \left(\frac{8}{3}\right) \text{ sq units}$$

Hence, $A_1 : A_2 = 1 : 1$

Skill Builder

Consider the curves $C_1 : y^2 = 4[\sqrt{y}]x$ and $C_2 : x^2 = 4[\sqrt{x}]y$, where [·] denotes the greatest integer function, find the area of the region enclosed by these two curves within the square formed by the lines, $x = 1, y = 1, x = 4, y = 4$.

(a) $\frac{11}{3}$ sq units (b) $\frac{22}{3}$ sq units

(c) $\frac{7}{3}$ sq units (d) $\frac{11}{7}$ sq units

For Sol.

Example 11 *The following figure shows the graph of a continuous function $y = f(x)$ on the interval $[1, 3]$. The points A, B, C have coordinates (1, 1), (3, 2), (2, 3) respectively, and the lines L_1 and L_2 are parallel with L_1 being tangent to the curve at C. If the area under the graph of $y = f(x)$ from $x = 1$ to $x = 3$ is 4 sq units, then the area of the shaded region is*

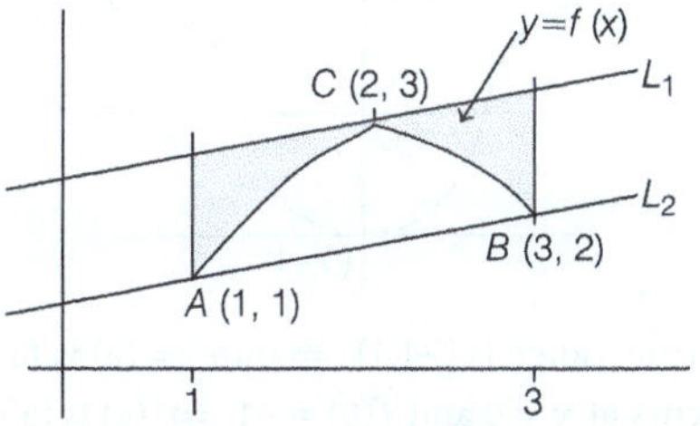

(a) 1 (b) 2 (c) 3 (d) 4

Sol. (b) Equation of $L_2 : y - 1 = \frac{2-1}{3-1}(x-1)$

or $2y - 2 = x - 1 \Rightarrow 2y - x = 1$

$\Rightarrow$ Slope of $L_2 = \frac{1}{2}$

Equation of $L_1 : y - 3 = \frac{1}{2}(x-2)$ or $2y - x = 4$

$\therefore \quad D\left(1, \frac{5}{2}\right)$ and $E\left(3, \frac{7}{2}\right)$

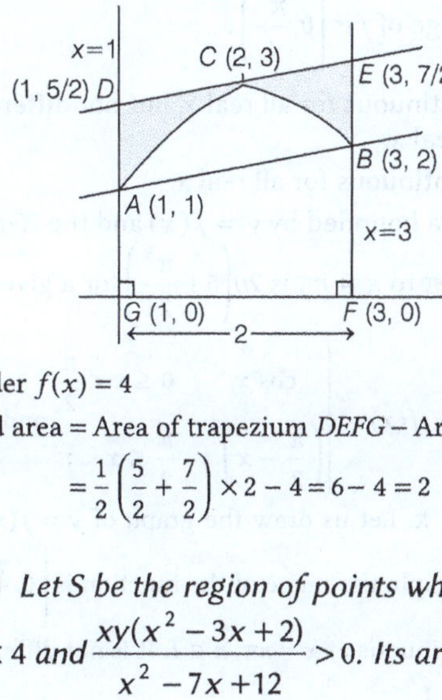

Area under $f(x) = 4$

$\therefore$ Shaded area = Area of trapezium $DEFG$ – Area under $f(x)$

$$= \frac{1}{2}\left(\frac{5}{2} + \frac{7}{2}\right) \times 2 - 4 = 6 - 4 = 2$$

Example 12 *Let S be the region of points which satisfies $y^2 < 16x, x < 4$ and $\frac{xy(x^2 - 3x + 2)}{x^2 - 7x + 12} > 0$. Its area is*

(a) $\frac{8}{3}$ (b) $\frac{64}{3}$ (c) $\frac{32}{3}$ (d) None of these

Sol. (b) $\frac{xy(x^2 - 3x + 2)}{(x^2 - 7x + 12)} > 0 \Rightarrow \frac{xy(x-1)(x-2)}{(x-3)(x-4)} > 0$

$$\Rightarrow \begin{cases} y > 0, & \text{if } \frac{x(x-1)(x-2)}{(x-3)(x-4)} > 0 \\ y < 0, & \text{if } \frac{x(x-1)(x-2)}{(x-3)(x-4)} < 0 \end{cases}$$

$$\Rightarrow \begin{cases} y > 0, & \text{if } x \in (0, 1) \cup (2, 3) \cup (4, \infty) \\ y < 0, & \text{if } x \in (-\infty, 0) \cup (1, 2) \cup (3, 4) \end{cases}$$

$y^2 < 16x$ is interior of the parabola $y^2 = 16x$

Region is as shown in the following figure.

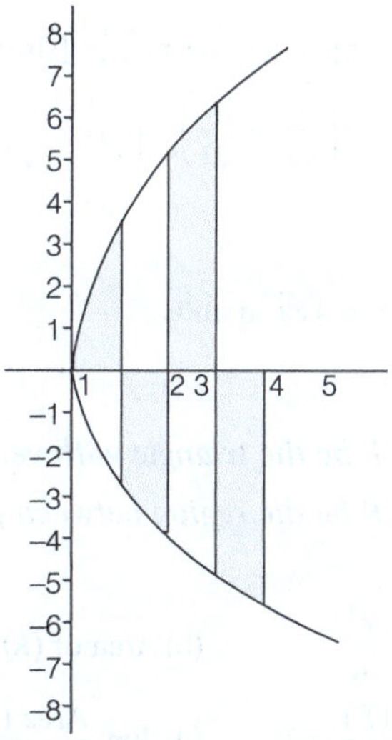

From the figure, required area

= Half of the area of the region bounded by $y^2 = 16x$ and $x = 4$

$$= \frac{1}{2}\left(2\int_0^4 4\sqrt{x}\,dx\right) = \frac{64}{3}$$

Example 13 *Area bounded by the curves $y = x - \sin x$, $y = x + \cos x$, for $x \in \left(-\frac{\pi}{4}, \frac{7\pi}{4}\right)$ is*

(a) $2\sqrt{2}$ (b) 1 (c) $4\sqrt{2}$ (d) 0

Sol. (c) We have, $y = f(x) = x + \cos x$, $y = g(x) = x - \sin x$

On solving these curves, we get

$$x - \sin x = x + \cos x \Rightarrow -\sin x = \cos x$$

$\therefore \quad \tan x = -1$

$\therefore \quad x = n\pi - \frac{\pi}{4}, n \in I$

Also, $f'(x) = 1 - \sin x \geq 0$

and $g'(x) = 1 - \cos x \geq 0$

Thus, both $f(x)$ and $g(x)$ are increasing function. Graph of function are as shown in the following figure.

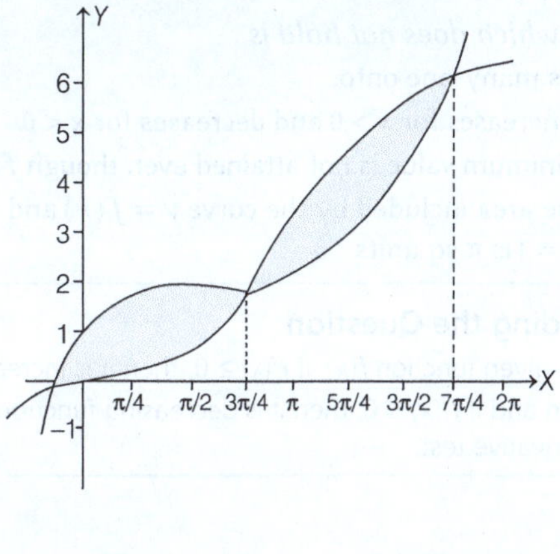

$\therefore$ Required area $= \int_{-\pi/4}^{3\pi/4} [(x + \cos x) - (x - \sin x)]dx$

$$+ \int_{3\pi/4}^{7\pi/4} [(x - \sin x) - (x + \cos x)]dx$$

$$= \int_{-\pi/4}^{3\pi/4} (\cos x + \sin x)dx - \int_{3\pi/4}^{7\pi/4} (\cos x + \sin x)dx$$

$$= [\sin x - \cos x]_{-\pi/4}^{3\pi/4} - [\sin x - \cos x]_{3\pi/4}^{7\pi/4}$$

$$= \left(\frac{1}{\sqrt{2}} + \frac{1}{\sqrt{2}}\right) - \left(\frac{-1}{\sqrt{2}} - \frac{1}{\sqrt{2}}\right) - \left(-\frac{1}{\sqrt{2}} - \frac{1}{\sqrt{2}}\right) + \left(\frac{1}{\sqrt{2}} + \frac{1}{\sqrt{2}}\right)$$

$= 4\sqrt{2}$ sq units

More than One Correct Option Type Questions

Example 14 *Let T be the triangle with vertices $(0, 0)$, $(0, c^2)$ and (c, c^2) and let R be the region between $y = cx$ and $y = x^2$, where $c > 0$, then*

(a) Area $(R) = \dfrac{c^3}{6}$ (b) Area of $(R) = \dfrac{c^3}{3}$

(c) $\lim_{c \to 0^+} \dfrac{\text{Area }(T)}{\text{Area }(R)} = 3$ (d) $\lim_{c \to 0^+} \dfrac{\text{Area }(T)}{\text{Area }(R)} = \dfrac{3}{2}$

Sol. (a, c) Area $(T) = \dfrac{c \cdot c^2}{2} = \dfrac{c^3}{2}$

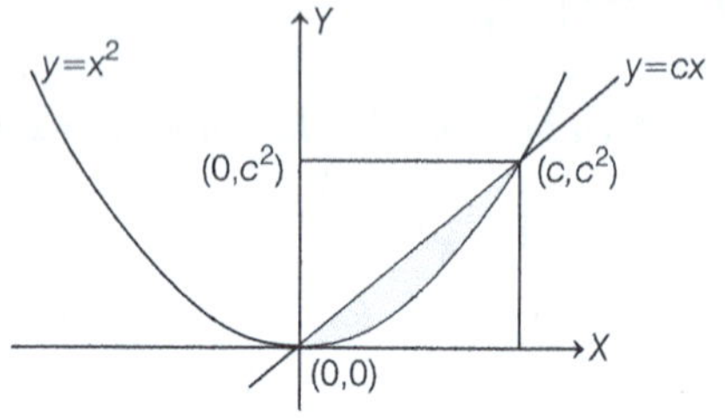

$$\text{Area }(R) = \frac{c^3}{2} - \int_0^c x^2\, dx = \frac{c^3}{2} - \frac{c^3}{3} = \frac{c^3}{6}$$

$$\therefore \quad \lim_{c \to 0^+} \frac{\text{Area}(T)}{\text{Area }(R)} = \lim_{c \to 0^+} \frac{c^3}{2} \cdot \frac{6}{c^3} = 3$$

Example 15 *Suppose f is defined from $R \to [-1, 1]$ as $f(x) = \dfrac{x^2 - 1}{x^2 + 1}$, where R is the set of real number. Then, the statement which does not hold is*

(a) f is many-one onto.

(b) f increases for $x > 0$ and decreases for $x < 0$.

(c) minimum value is not attained even though f is bounded.

(d) the area included by the curve $y = f(x)$ and the line $y = 1$ is π sq units.

> **Decoding the Question**
> For the given function $f(x)$, if $f'(x) \geq 0$, then it is increasing function and if $f'(x) \leq 0$, then it is decreasing function, which is first derivative test.

Sol. (a, c, d) $y = f(x) = \dfrac{x^2 - 1}{x^2 + 1} = 1 - \dfrac{2}{x^2 + 1}$

$f'(x) = \dfrac{4x}{(x^2 + 1)^2}$ $x > 0$, f is increasing and $x < 0$, f is decreasing.

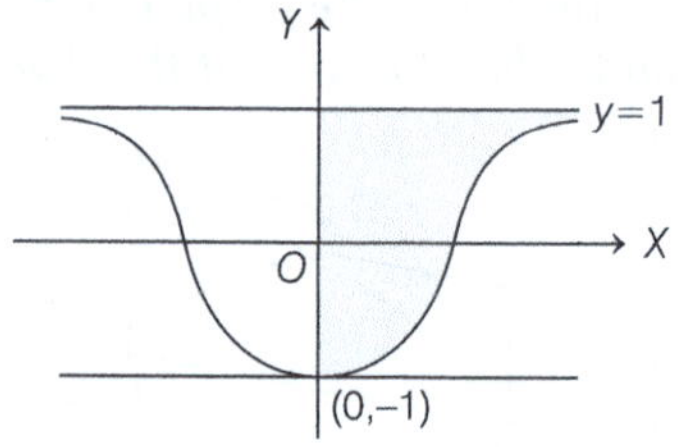

$\Rightarrow$ (b) is true; range is $[-1, 1)$ $\Rightarrow$ into $\Rightarrow$ (a) is false; minimum value occurs at $x = 0$ and $f(0) = -1$ $\Rightarrow$ (c) is false.

$$A = 2\int_0^{\infty} \left(1 - \frac{x^2 - 1}{x^2 + 1}\right) dx = 4\int_0^{\infty} \frac{dx}{x^2 + 1}$$

$$= [4 \cdot \tan^{-1} x]_0^{\infty} = 4 \cdot \frac{\pi}{2} = 2\pi \Rightarrow \text{(d) is false.}$$

Example 16 *Consider $f(x) = \begin{cases} \cos x, & 0 \leq x < \dfrac{\pi}{2} \\ \left(\dfrac{\pi}{2} - x\right)^2, & \dfrac{\pi}{2} \leq x < \pi \end{cases}$ such that f is periodic with period π, then*

(a) the range of f is $\left[0, \dfrac{\pi^2}{4}\right)$.

(b) f is continuous for all real x, but not differentiable for some real x.

(c) f is continuous for all real x.

(d) the area bounded by $y = f(x)$ and the X-axis from $x = -n\pi$ to $x = n\pi$ is $2n\left(1 + \dfrac{\pi^3}{24}\right)$ for a given $n \in N$.

Sol. (a, d) Given, $f(x) = \begin{cases} \cos x, & 0 \leq x < \dfrac{\pi}{2} \\ \left(\dfrac{\pi}{2} - x\right)^2, & \dfrac{\pi}{2} \leq x < \pi \end{cases}$ and f is periodic with period π. Let us draw the graph of $y = f(x)$.

From the graph, the range of the function is $\left[0, \dfrac{\pi^2}{4}\right)$.

It is discontinuous at $x = n\pi$, $n \in I$. It is not differentiable at $x = \dfrac{n\pi}{2}$, $n \in I$.

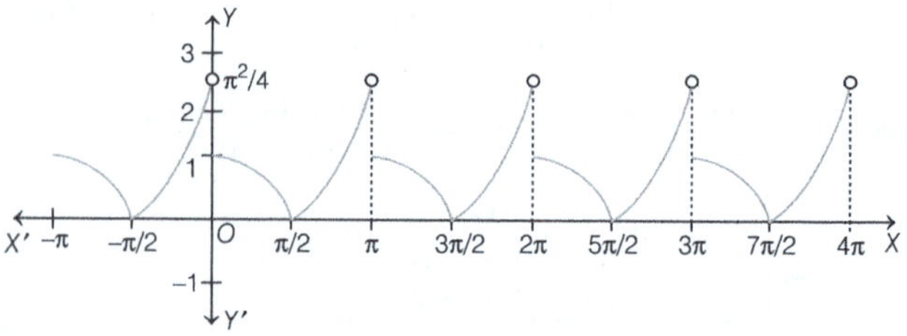

Area bounded by $y = f(x)$ and the X-axis from $-n\pi$ to $n\pi$ for $n \in N$

$$= 2n \int_0^{\pi} f(x)\,dx = 2n\left[\int_0^{\pi/2} \cos x\,dx + \int_{\pi/2}^{\pi}\left(\frac{\pi}{2} - x\right)^2 dx\right]$$

$$= 2n\left(1 + \frac{\pi^3}{24}\right)$$

Example 17 *Consider the functions $f(x)$ and $g(x)$, both defined from $R \to R$ and are defined as $f(x) = 2x - x^2$ and $g(x) = x^n$, where $n \in N$. If the area between $f(x)$ and $g(x)$ is 1/2, then n is a divisor of*

(a) 12 (b) 15 (c) 20 (d) 30

Sol. (b, c, d) Solving $f(x) = 2x - x^2$ and $g(x) = x^n$, we have

$$2x - x^2 = x^n \Rightarrow x = 0 \text{ and } x = 1$$

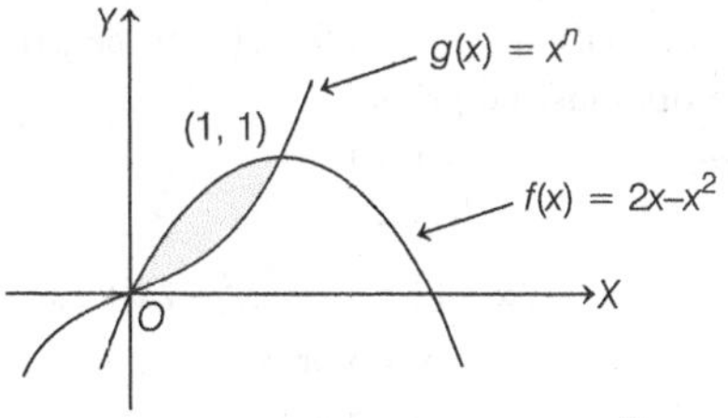

$$A = \int_0^1 (2x - x^2 - x^n)\,dx = \left[x^2 - \frac{x^3}{3} - \frac{x^{n+1}}{n+1}\right]_0^1$$

$$= 1 - \frac{1}{3} - \frac{1}{n+1} = \frac{2}{3} - \frac{1}{n+1}$$

Since, $\frac{2}{3} - \frac{1}{n+1} = \frac{1}{2}$

$\Rightarrow \frac{2}{3} - \frac{1}{2} = \frac{1}{n+1}$

$\Rightarrow \frac{4-3}{6} = \frac{1}{n+1}$

$\Rightarrow n + 1 = 6$

$\Rightarrow n = 5$

Thus, n is a divisor of 15, 20, 30.

Example 18 *Area of the region bounded by the curve $y = e^x$ and lines $x = 0$ and $y = e$ is*

(a) $e - 1$ (b) $\int_1^e \ln(e + 1 - y)\,dy$

(c) $e - \int_0^1 e^x\,dx$ (d) $\int_1^e \ln y\,dy$

Sol. (b, c, d) Shaded area $= e - \left(\int_0^1 e^x\,dx\right) = 1$

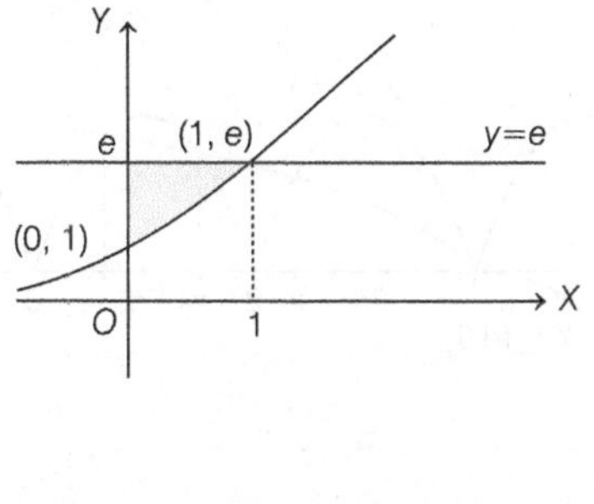

Also, $\int_1^e \ln(e + 1 - y)\,dy$

Put $e + 1 - y = t \Rightarrow -dy = dt$

$$= \int_e^1 \ln t(-dt) = \int_1^e \ln t\,dt$$

$$= \int_1^e \ln y\,dy = 1$$

Example 19 *Let $y = f(x)$, $y = g(x)$ be two curve defined by $x = f^2(x) - 1$ and $x = |g(x)|\sqrt{1 - g^2(x)}$.*

(a) Area bounded by $y = f(x)$ and Y-axis is $\frac{4}{3}$ sq units.

(b) Area bounded by $y = f(x)$ and Y-axis is $\frac{2}{3}$ sq units.

(c) Area bounded by $y = g(x)$ with positive Y-axis is $\frac{1}{3}$ sq units.

(d) Area bounded by $y = g(x)$ with positive Y-axis is $\frac{1}{6}$ sq units.

Sol. (a, c) Area $= \Delta_1 = 2\left|\int_0^1 x\,dy\right| = 2\left|\int_0^1 (y^2 - 1)\,dy\right|$

$$= 2\left|\left[\frac{y^3}{3} - y\right]_0^1\right|$$

$$= 2\left|\left(\frac{1}{3} - 1\right)\right|$$

$$= \frac{4}{3} \text{ sq units}$$

Area $= \Delta_2 = \left|\int_0^1 x \cdot dy\right| = \left|\int_0^1 y \cdot \sqrt{1 - y^2}\,dy\right|$ $[\because y > 0]$

Put $y = \sin\theta$, then $dy = \cos\theta\,d\theta$

$$\text{Area} = \left|\int_0^{\pi/2} \cos^2\theta \sin\theta\,d\theta\right| = \left[\frac{\cos^3\theta}{3}\right]_0^{\pi/2} = \frac{1}{3} \text{ sq units}$$

Example 20 *Let $f(x) = \min\left\{x^2, \frac{1}{1 + 2x^2}\right\}$*

(a) The number of points for which $f(x)$ is not differentiable is 2.

(b) The number of points for which $f(x)$ is not differentiable is 3.

(c) The area bounded by $f(x)$ and X-axis is $\frac{1}{\sqrt{2}}\left(\frac{1}{3} + \frac{\pi}{4}\right)$.

(d) The area bounded by $f(x)$ and X-axis is $\frac{1}{\sqrt{2}}\left(\frac{1}{3} + \frac{\pi}{2}\right)$.

Decoding the Question

We know that $f(x)$ is differentiable at a, if its derivative $f'(a)$ exists at every point in its domain.

Sol. (a, d) The curve $y = x^2$, $y = \dfrac{1}{1+2x^2}$ intersect at $x = \pm \dfrac{1}{\sqrt{2}}$

$$\therefore f(x) = \begin{cases} \dfrac{1}{1+2x^2}, & \text{for } x \le \dfrac{-1}{\sqrt{2}} \\ x^2, & \text{for } \dfrac{-1}{\sqrt{2}} < x < \dfrac{1}{\sqrt{2}} \\ \dfrac{1}{1+2x^2}, & \text{for } x \ge \dfrac{1}{\sqrt{2}} \end{cases}$$

f is not differentiable at two points, $x = \pm \dfrac{1}{\sqrt{2}}$

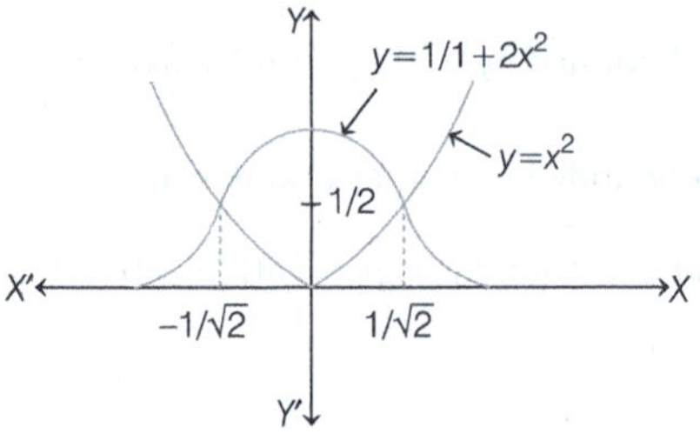

$$A = 2\left[\int_0^{1/\sqrt{2}} x^2 dx + \int_{1/\sqrt{2}}^{\infty} \frac{1}{1+2x^2} dx\right]$$

$$= 2\left[\frac{1}{6\sqrt{2}} + \frac{1}{\sqrt{2}} (\tan^{-1}(\sqrt{2}x))_{1/\sqrt{2}}^{\infty}\right]$$

$$= 2\left[\frac{1}{6\sqrt{2}} + \frac{1}{\sqrt{2}}\left(\frac{\pi}{2} - \frac{\pi}{4}\right)\right]$$

$$= \frac{1}{3\sqrt{2}} + \frac{\pi}{2\sqrt{2}} = \frac{1}{\sqrt{2}}\left(\frac{1}{3} + \frac{\pi}{2}\right)$$

Example 21 *Let A_r be the area of the region bounded by the curve $(6y^2 r - x) = 1$, $(6\pi^2 y - x) = 0$. Then,*

(a) $\sqrt{A_1} \cdot \sqrt{A_2} \cdot \sqrt{A_3}, \ldots$ are in GP.

(b) $\sqrt{A_1} \cdot \sqrt{A_2} \cdot \sqrt{A_3}, \ldots$ are in HP.

(c) $\lim_{n \to \infty} [\sqrt{A_1}\sqrt{A_2}\sqrt{A_3} + \sqrt{A_2}\sqrt{A_3}\sqrt{A_4} + \ldots n \text{ terms}] = \dfrac{1}{4}\left(\dfrac{e}{\pi}\right)^9$

(d) $\lim_{n \to \infty} [e^{\frac{-1}{\sqrt{A_1}}} + e^{\frac{-1}{\sqrt{A_2}}} + e^{\frac{-1}{\sqrt{A_3}}} + \ldots n \text{ terms}] = (e^{\pi^3/e^3} - 1)^{-1}$

Sol. (b, c, d) In section point $P \cdot \left(\dfrac{6\pi^4}{r}, \dfrac{\pi^2}{r}\right)$

$$A_r = \int_0^{\pi^2/r} (6\pi^2 y - 6y^2 r) dy = \frac{\pi^6}{r^2}$$

(b) $\sqrt{A_r} = \dfrac{\pi^3}{r} \Rightarrow \sqrt{A_1} \cdot \sqrt{A_2}, \ldots$ are in HP.

(c) $\sqrt{A_r A_{r+1} A_{r+2}} = \dfrac{\pi^9}{2} \dfrac{2}{r(r+1)(r+2)}$

$$= \left(\frac{1}{2}\right)\left(\frac{\pi^9}{2}\right)\left(\frac{1}{r(r+1)} - \frac{1}{(r+1)(r+2)}\right)$$

$$\therefore \lim_{n \to \infty} \sum_{r=1}^{n} \sqrt{A_r A_{r+1} A_{r+2}} = \frac{\pi^9}{4}$$

(d) $e^{\frac{-1}{\sqrt{A_r}}} = e^{-(\pi/e)^{3/r}} = (e^{\pi^3/e^3})^{-r}$

$$\therefore \lim_{n \to \infty} \sum_{r=1}^{n} (e^{\pi^3/e^3})^{-r} = (e^{\pi^3/e^3} - 1)^{-1}$$

Passage Based Questions

Passage I

(Ex. Nos. 22 to 23)

Consider the function $f(x) = x^3 - 8x^2 + 20x - 13$.

Example 22 *Number of positive integers x for which $f(x)$ is a prime number, is*

(a) 1 (b) 2 (c) 3 (d) 4

Sol. (c) $f(x) = (x-1)(x^2 - 7x + 13)$ for $f(x)$ to be prime atleast one of the factors must be prime.

Therefore, $x - 1 = 1$

$\Rightarrow$ $x = 2$

or $x^2 - 7x + 13 = 1 \Rightarrow x^2 - 7x + 12 = 0$

$\Rightarrow$ $x = 3$ or 4

$\Rightarrow$ $x = 2, 3, 4$

Example 23 *Area enclosed by $y = f(x)$ and the coordinate axes is*

(a) 65/12 (b) 13/12

(c) 71/12 (d) None of these

Sol. (a) $A = \left|\int_0^1 f(x)\,dx\right| = \left|\int_0^1 (x^3 - 8x^2 + 20x - 13)\,dx\right| = \dfrac{65}{12}$

Passage II

(Ex. Nos. 24 to 25)

Let $h(x) = f(x) - g(x)$, where $f(x) = \sin^4 \pi x$ and $g(x) = \ln x$. Let $x_0, x_1, x_2, \ldots, x_{n+1}$ be the roots of $f(x) = g(x)$ in increasing order.

Example 24 *The absolute area enclosed by $y = f(x)$ and $y = g(x)$ is given by*

(a) $\sum_{r=0}^{n} \int_{x_r}^{x_{r+1}} (-1)^r h(x)\,dx$ (b) $\sum_{r=0}^{n} \int_{x_r}^{x_{r+1}} (-1)^{r+1} h(x)\,dx$

(c) $2\sum_{r=0}^{n} \int_{x_r}^{x_{r+1}} (-1)^r h(x)\,dx$ (d) $\dfrac{1}{2}\sum_{r=0}^{n} \int_{x_r}^{x_{r+1}} (-1)^{r+1} h(x)\,dx$

Sol. (a)

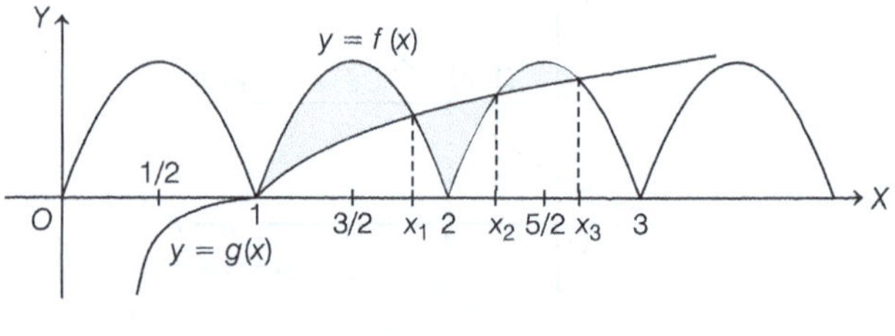

Example 25 *The whole area bounded by $y = f(x)$, $y = g(x)$ and $x = 0$ is*

(a) $\frac{11}{8}$ (b) $\frac{8}{3}$ (c) 2 (d) $\frac{13}{3}$

Sol. (a) Required area $= \int_0^1 \sin^4 \pi x\, dx - \int_0^1 \ln x\, dx = \frac{11}{8}$

Passage III

(Ex. Nos. 26 to 27)

Consider the function defined implicitly by the equation $y^3 - 3y + x = 0$ on various intervals in the real line. If $x \in (-\infty, -2) \cup (2, \infty)$, the equation implicitly defines a unique real-valued differentiable function $y = f(x)$. If $x \in (-2, 2)$, the equation implicitly defines a unique real-valued differentiable function $y = g(x)$ satisfying $g(0) = 0$.

Example 26 *If $f(-10\sqrt{2}) = 2\sqrt{2}$, then $f''(-10\sqrt{2})$ is equal to*

(a) $\frac{4\sqrt{2}}{7^3 3^2}$ (b) $-\frac{4\sqrt{2}}{7^3 3^2}$ (c) $\frac{4\sqrt{2}}{7^3 3}$ (d) $-\frac{4\sqrt{2}}{7^3 3}$

Sol. (b) $\because$ $y^3 - 3y + x = 0$

On differentiating, we get

$$3y^2 y' - 3y' + 1 = 0 \Rightarrow y' = \frac{1}{3(1 - y^2)} \quad \text{...(i)}$$

$$\Rightarrow \quad y'(-10\sqrt{2}) = \frac{1}{3\{1 - (2\sqrt{2})^2\}}$$

$$\Rightarrow \quad y'(-10\sqrt{2}) = \frac{1}{3\{1 - (2\sqrt{2})^2\}} = \frac{1}{3\,(1 - 8)} = -\frac{1}{21}$$

Again, on differentiating Eq. (i), we get

$$y'' = \frac{6yy'^2}{3(1 - y^2)} \Rightarrow y''(-10\sqrt{2}) = \frac{6 \cdot 2\sqrt{2} \cdot \left(\frac{1}{21}\right)^2}{3(1 - 8)} = -\frac{4\sqrt{2}}{7^3 \cdot 3^2}$$

Example 27 *The area of the region bounded by the curve $y = f(x)$, the X-axis and the line $x = a$ and $x = b$, where $-\infty < a < b < -2$ is*

(a) $\int_a^b \frac{x}{3[\{f(x)\}^2 - 1]} dx + bf(b) - af(a)$

(b) $-\int_a^b \frac{x}{3[\{f(x)\}^2 - 1]} dx - bf(b) + af(a)$

(c) $\int_a^b \frac{x}{3[\{f(x)\}^2 - 1]} dx - bf(b) + af(a)$

(d) $-\int_a^b \frac{x}{3[\{f(x)\}^2 - 1]} dx - bf(b) + af(a)$

Sol. (a) Required area $= \int_a^b f(x)\, dx = [xf(x)]_a^b - \int_a^b xf'(x)\, dx$

$$= bf(b) - af(a) + \int_a^b \frac{x}{3[\{f(x)\}^2 - 1]} dx$$

Stem Based Questions

Stem I

(Ex. Nos. 28 and 29)

Let $f(x) = \min\{x - [x], -x - [x]\}, -2 \le x \le 2$ (where $[\cdot]$ denotes greatest integer function). The number of solution of the equation $x^2 + 2f(x) = 1$ is n and the area bounded by $y = f(x)$ and $y = 1 - x^2$ is $\frac{a}{b}$.

Example 28 *The value of n is ... .*

Example 29 *The value of $a + b$ is ... .*

Sol. (28 and 29)

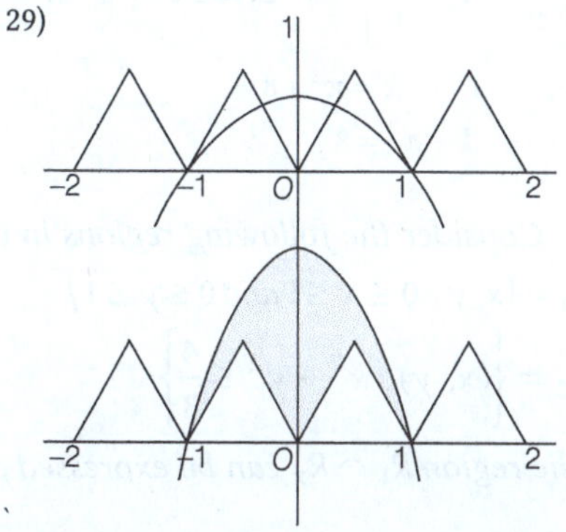

From graph, there are 4 solutions.

$\therefore$ $n = 4$

$2f(x) = 1 - x^2$

Now, Area $= 2 \times \int_0^1 (1 - x^2) dx - 2 \times \left(\frac{1}{2} \times 1 \times \frac{1}{2}\right)$

$= 2\left(1 - \frac{1}{3}\right) - \frac{1}{2} = \frac{4}{3} - \frac{1}{2} = \frac{5}{6}$

$\Rightarrow$ $a + b = 11$

Ans. 28. (4) **29.** (11)

Single Integer Answer Type Questions

Example 30 *If the area bounded by the curves $y = \sin^{-1}|\sin x| + \cos^{-1}(\cos x)$ and $y = \cos x + \pi$ and the line $\alpha = 0$ and $x = 4\pi$ is k, then $k - \pi^2$ equals to ....*

Sol. (8) Let $f(x) = \sin^{-1}|\sin x| + \cos^{-1}(\cos x)$

$\Rightarrow$ $f(x) = \sin^{-1}(\sin x) + \cos^{-1}(\cos x)$ (for $0 \le x \le \pi$)

$$\Rightarrow \quad f(x) = \begin{cases} 2x, & 0 \le x \le \frac{\pi}{2} \\ \pi, & \frac{\pi}{2} < x < \frac{3\pi}{2} \\ 4\pi - 2x, & \frac{3\pi}{2} < x \le 2\pi \end{cases}$$

$\Rightarrow$ The area bounded is shown in figure.

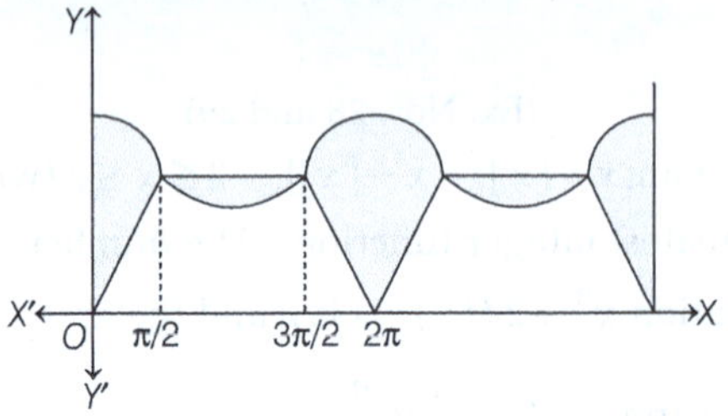

$$\Rightarrow A = 4\int_0^{\pi/2}(\pi + \cos x - 2x)dx + 2\int_{\pi/2}^{3\pi/2}[\pi - (\pi + \cos x)]dx$$

$$= 4[\pi x + \sin x - x^2]_0^{\pi/2} - 2[\sin x]_{\pi/2}^{3\pi/2}$$

$$= 4\left[\frac{\pi^2}{2} + 1 - \frac{\pi^2}{4}\right] - 2[-2] \Rightarrow 2\pi^2 + 4 - \pi^2 + 4 = (\pi^2 + 8)$$

Therefore, $k = \pi^2 + 8$

$\therefore$ $k - \pi^2 = 8$

Example 31 *Consider the following regions in the plane*

$$R_1 = \{x, y : 0 \le x \le 1 \text{ and } 0 \le y \le 1\}$$

$$R_2 = \left\{(x, y) : x^2 + y^2 \le \frac{4}{3}\right\}$$

The area of the region $R_1 \cap R_2$ can be expressed as $\dfrac{a\sqrt{3} + b\pi}{9}$, where a and b are integers. Then, the value of $a + b$ is ....

Sol. (4)

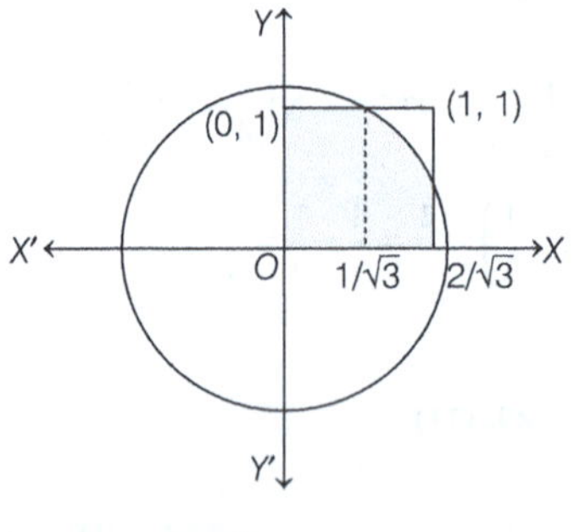

Required area, $A = \dfrac{1}{\sqrt{3}} \times 1 + A_1$, where $A_1 = \displaystyle\int_{\frac{1}{\sqrt{3}}}^{1} \sqrt{\left(\frac{4}{3}\right) - x^2}\,dx$

On putting $x = \dfrac{2}{\sqrt{3}}\sin\theta$,

$$= \int_{\pi/6}^{\pi/3} \frac{2}{\sqrt{3}}\cos\theta \cdot \frac{2}{\sqrt{3}}\cos\theta\, d\theta = \frac{2}{3}\int_{\pi/6}^{\pi/3}(\cos 2\theta + 1)d\theta$$

$$= \frac{2}{3}\left[\frac{1}{2}\sin 2\theta + \theta\right]_{\pi/6}^{\pi/3} = \frac{2}{3}\left[\frac{1}{2}\cdot\frac{\sqrt{3}}{2} + \frac{\pi}{3} - \frac{1}{2}\cdot\frac{\sqrt{3}}{2} - \frac{\pi}{6}\right]$$

$$= \frac{2}{3}\cdot\frac{\pi}{6} = \frac{\pi}{9}$$

$$\therefore \quad A = \frac{1}{\sqrt{3}} + \frac{\pi}{9} \Rightarrow \frac{3\sqrt{3} + \pi}{9} = \frac{a\sqrt{3} + b\pi}{9}$$

Hence, $a = 3$, $b = 1$ and $a + b = 4$

JEE SCANNER

Example 32 Similar to PYQ Asked in JEE Main 2024

The area enclosed by circle $x^2 + y^2 = 4$, parabola $y = x^2 + x + 1$, the curve $y = \left[\sin^2\dfrac{x}{4} + \cos\dfrac{x}{4}\right]$ and X-axis is k, then value of [k] is ......
(where [·] is the greatest integer function)

Sol. (3) $y = \left[\sin^2\dfrac{x}{4} + \cos\dfrac{x}{4}\right]$

$\because$ $1 < \sin^2\dfrac{x}{4} + \cos\dfrac{x}{4} < 2$ for $x \in [-2, 2]$

$\therefore$ $y = \left[\sin^2\dfrac{x}{4} + \cos\dfrac{x}{4}\right] = 1$

Now, we have to find out the area enclosed by the circle $x^2 + y^2 = 4$, parabola $\left(y - \dfrac{3}{4}\right) = \left(x + \dfrac{1}{2}\right)^2$, line $y = 1$ and X-axis.

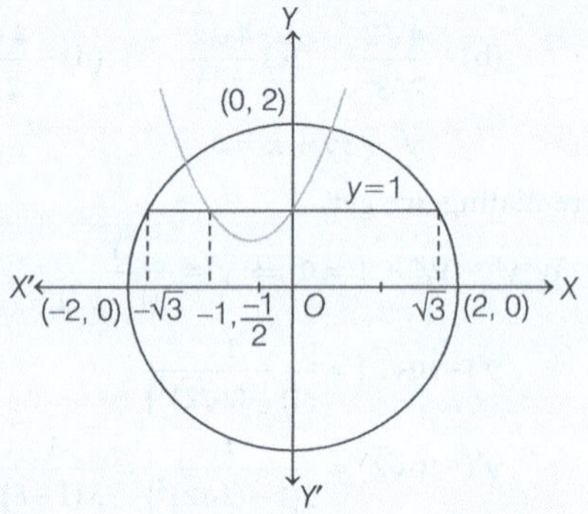

Hence, the required area

$$= \sqrt{3} \times 1 + (\sqrt{3} - 1) \times 1 + \int_{-1}^{0}(x^2 + x + 1)dx + 2\int_{\sqrt{3}}^{2}\sqrt{(4 - x^2)}\,dx$$

$$= (2\sqrt{3} - 1) + \left[\frac{x^3}{3} + \frac{x^2}{2} + x\right]_{-1}^{0} + 2\left[\frac{x}{2}\sqrt{(4 - x^2)} + 2\sin^{-1}\left(\frac{x}{2}\right)\right]_{\sqrt{3}}^{2}$$

$$= (2\sqrt{3} - 1) + \left[0 - \left(-\frac{1}{3} + \frac{1}{2} - 1\right)\right] + 2\left[(0 + \pi) - \left(\frac{\sqrt{3}}{2} + \frac{2\pi}{3}\right)\right]$$

$$= (2\sqrt{3} - 1) + \frac{5}{6} + \frac{2\pi}{3} - \sqrt{3}$$

$$= \left(\frac{2\pi}{3} + \sqrt{3} - \frac{1}{6}\right) = \left(\frac{2 \times 3.14}{3} + 1.732 - \frac{1}{6}\right)$$

$$= 2.093 + 1.732 - 0.166 = 3.65 = 3.7$$

$\therefore$ $[3.7] = 3$

Skill Builder

For Sol.

The area enclosed between the circle $x^2 + y^2 - 2x + 4y - 11 = 0$ and the parabola $y = -x^2 + 2x + 1 - 2\sqrt{3}$ is k, then the value of [k] is (where [·] is the greatest integer function) ......

Example 33 *For each positive integers $x > 1$, A_n represents the area of region restricted to the following two inequalities $\frac{x^2}{n^2} + y^2 \le 1$ and $x^2 + \frac{y^2}{n^2} \le 1$. Then, $\lim\limits_{n\to\infty} A_n$ is equal to ......*

Sol. (4)

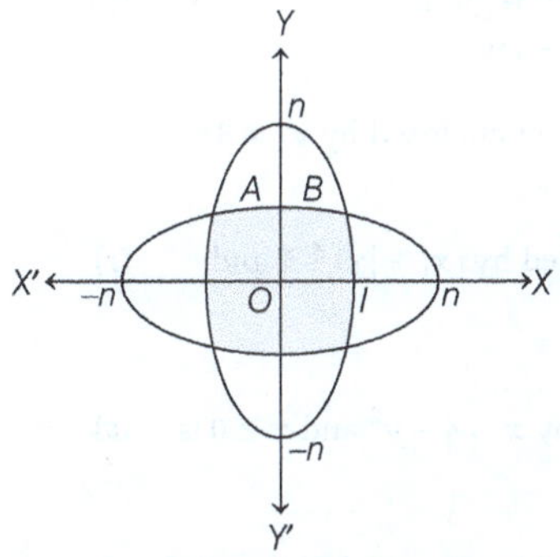

The intersecting points of the ellipse are

$$(x, y) = \left(\frac{n}{\sqrt{n^2+1}}, \frac{n}{\sqrt{n^2+1}}\right), \left(\frac{n}{\sqrt{n^2+1}}, \frac{-n}{\sqrt{n^2+1}}\right),$$
$$\left(\frac{-n}{\sqrt{n^2+1}}, \frac{n}{\sqrt{n^2+1}}\right), \left(\frac{-n}{\sqrt{n^2+1}}, \frac{-n}{\sqrt{n^2+1}}\right)$$

Notice that the region is symmetric with respect to X-axis, Y-axis, $y = x$ and $y = -x$.

Hence, $A_n = 8 \cdot B_n$,

where B_n = Area between the Y-axis, $y = x$ and $y = \frac{\sqrt{n^2 - x^2}}{n}$.

As, $n \to \infty$, $\lim\limits_{n\to\infty} \frac{n}{n^2+1} = 1$ and B_n approaches the area of ΔAOB,

where $O = (0, 0)$, $A = (1, 0)$ and $B = (1, 1)$.

$$\therefore \lim_{n\to\infty} A_n = 8 \cdot \left(\frac{1}{2} \cdot 1 \cdot 1\right) = 4$$

Example 34 *Let R be real numbers and $f : R \to R$ such that $\forall\, x, y \in R, |f(x) - f(y)| \le |x - y|^{100}$ and $f(100) = 1$, then the area bounded by curve $y = \min.\{f(x), x^2, e^{2-x}\}$, X-axis, Y-axis and line $x = 4$ is .... (given, $e = 2.718$)*

Sol. (2) We have, $\quad |f(x) - f(y)| \le |x - y|^{100}$

$$\Rightarrow \quad \left|\frac{f(x) - f(y)}{x - y}\right| \le |x - y|^{99}$$

Now, $\left|\lim\limits_{y\to x} \frac{f(x) - f(y)}{x - y}\right| \le \lim\limits_{y\to x} |x - y|^{99}$

$$\Rightarrow \quad |f'(x)| \le 0$$

i.e. $\quad f'(x) = 0$

$\Rightarrow \quad f(x) = c \quad$ (constant)

Given, $f(100) = 1 \Rightarrow c = 1$

$\therefore \quad f(x) = 1$

Now, $y = \min\{f(x), x^2, e^{2-x}\}$

$= \min\{1, x^2, e^{2-x}\}$

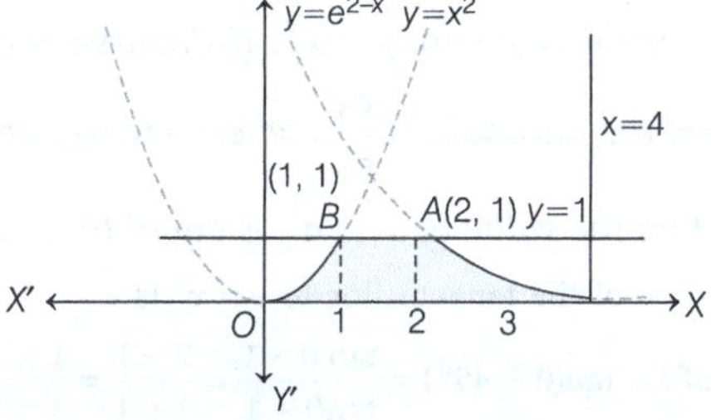

$$\therefore \text{The required area} = \int_0^1 x^2\,dx + (2-1)\times 1 + \int_2^4 e^{2-x}\,dx$$

$$= \left[\frac{x^3}{3}\right]_0^1 + 1 + e^2\left[\frac{e^{-x}}{-1}\right]_2^4$$

$$= \frac{1}{3} + 1 + e^2(-e^{-4} + e^{-2})$$

$$= \frac{4}{3} + 1 - e^{-2}$$

$$= \left(\frac{7}{3} - \frac{1}{e^2}\right) = \frac{7}{3} - \frac{1}{(2.718)^2}$$

$$= 2.333 - 0.135$$

$$= 2.19$$

$$\approx 2 \text{ sq units}$$

Numerical Value Type Questions

Example 35 *If the area enclosed by the curves $f(x) = \cos^{-1}(\cos x)$ and $g(x) = \sin^{-1}(\cos x)$ in $x \in \left[\frac{9\pi}{4}, \frac{15\pi}{4}\right]$ is $\frac{a\pi^2}{b}$. (where a and b are co-prime), then $(a + b)$ is ....*

Sol. (17) We have, $g(x) = \sin^{-1}(\cos x) = \frac{\pi}{2} - \cos^{-1}(\cos x)$

Both the curve bound the regions of some area in $\left[\frac{\pi}{4}, \frac{7\pi}{4}\right], \left[\frac{9\pi}{4}, \frac{15\pi}{4}\right]$ and so on.

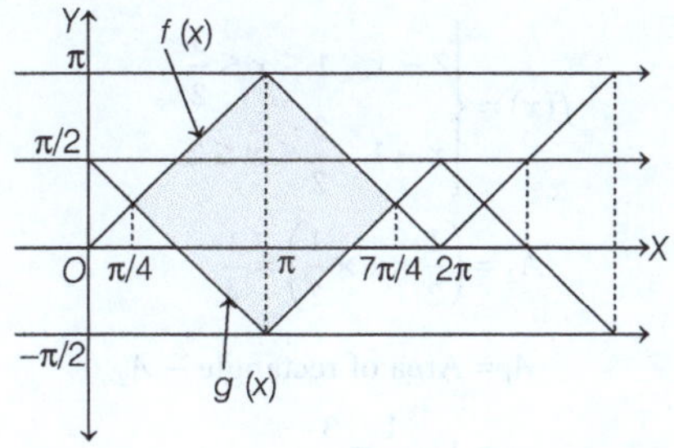

$\therefore$ Required area = Area of shaded square $= \frac{9\pi^2}{8} = \frac{a\pi^2}{b}$

$\therefore \; a = 9$ and $b = 8$

Hence, $a + b = 17$

Example 36 *Let l be the line obtained by rotating the tangent line, drawn to the parabola $y = x^2$ at the point $A(1, 1)$ about an angle of 45° in clockwise sense. Let B be the other intersection of the line with $y = x^2$. If the area enclosed by the line l and the parabola is $\frac{a_1}{a_2}$, where (a_1, a_2) are coprimes, then the value of $a_1 + a_2$ is equal to ....*

Sol. (287) Slope of the tangent line to $y = x^2$ is 2.

$$\text{Slope of } l = \tan(\theta - 45°) = \frac{\tan\theta - 1}{\tan\theta + 1} = \frac{2-1}{2+1} = \frac{1}{3}$$

Equation of $l : y = \frac{1}{3}(x-1) + 1$ and point of intersection of l with $y = x^2$ is $x = \frac{-2}{3}$ and $x = 1$.

$$\therefore \text{ Required area} = \int_{-2/3}^{1}\left(\frac{x+2}{3} - x^2\right)dx = \frac{125}{162}$$

$$\Rightarrow \quad a_1 + a_2 = 287$$

Example 37 *If $f(x) = \max\left(\frac{1}{\pi}\cos^{-1}(\cos \pi x)\cdot\{x\}\right)$ and $g(x) = \min\left(\frac{1}{\pi}\cos^{-1}(\cos \pi x)\cdot\{x\}\right)$ (where {} represent fraction part of x) and A denotes, area of the region bounded by $y = f(x)$, X-axis and the lines $x = 1$, $x = 2$, A_2 denotes area of the region bounded by $y = g(x)$, X-axis and the lines $x = 1$, $x = 2$, then the value of $A_1 \cdot A_2$ is ....*

Sol. (0.1875)

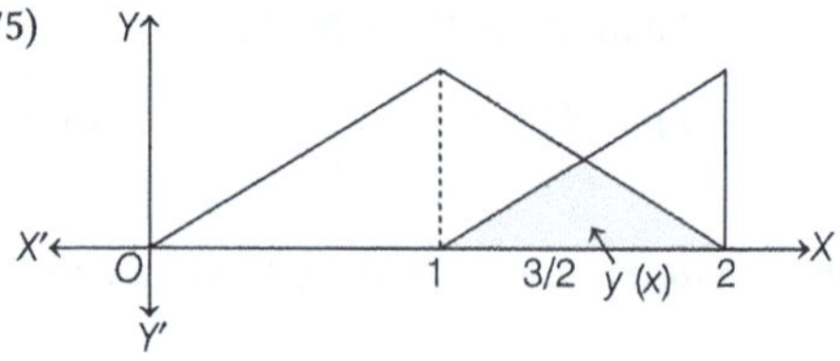

$$\cos^{-1}(\cos \pi x) = \begin{cases} \pi x, & 0 \le \pi x \le \pi \Rightarrow 0 \le x \le 1 \\ 2\pi - \pi x, & \pi \le \pi x \le 2\pi \Rightarrow 1 \le x \le 2 \end{cases}$$

$$\therefore \quad \frac{1}{\pi}\cos^{-1}(\cos \pi x) = \begin{cases} x, & 0 \le x \le 1 \\ 2 - x, & 1 \le x \le 2 \end{cases}$$

$$\therefore \quad f(x) = \begin{cases} 2 - x, & 1 \le x \le \frac{3}{2} \\ x - 1, & \frac{3}{2} \le x \le 2 \end{cases}$$

$$A_2 = \left(\frac{1}{2} \times 1 \times \frac{1}{2}\right) = \frac{1}{4}$$

$$\therefore \quad A_1 = \text{Area of rectangle} - A_2$$

$$= 1 - \frac{1}{4} = \frac{3}{4}$$

$$\therefore \quad A_1 \cdot A_2 = \frac{3}{4} \times \frac{1}{4} = \frac{3}{16} = 0.1875$$

Matching Type Questions

Example 38 *Match the following.*

	Column I		Column II
(A)	Area bounded by region $0 \le y \le 4x - x^2 - 3$ is	(p)	$\frac{32}{3}$
(B)	Area of the region enclosed by $y^2 = 8x$ and $y = 2x$ is	(q)	$\frac{1}{2}$
(C)	The area bounded by $\|x\| + \|y\| \le 1$ and $\|x\| \ge \frac{1}{2}$ is	(r)	$\frac{8}{3}$
(D)	Area bounded by $x \le 4 - y^2$ and $x \ge 0$ is	(s)	$\frac{4}{3}$

Sol. (A) → (s); (B) → (s); (C) → (q); (D) → (p)

(A) $0 \le y \le 4x - x^2 - 3$

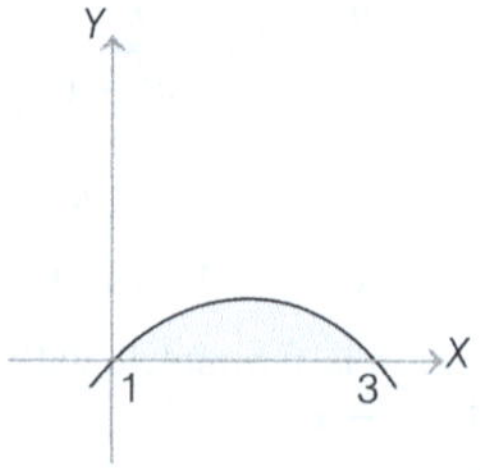

At $y = 0$, $x^2 - 4x + 3 = 0 \Rightarrow x = 1, x = 3$

$$A = \int_1^3 (4x - x^2 - 3)\,dx = \frac{4}{3}$$

(B) $8x = 4x^2$

intersection point (0, 0), (2, 4)

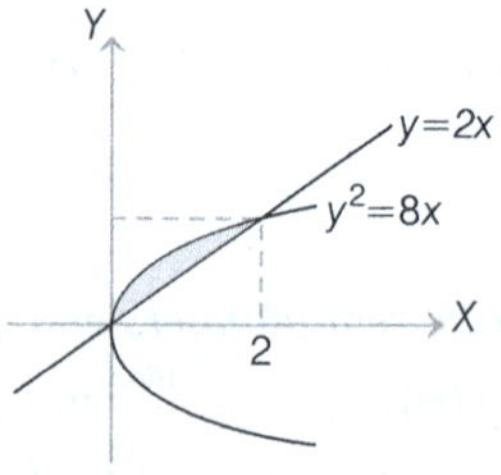

$$A = \int_0^4 \left(\frac{y}{2} - \frac{y^2}{8}\right)dy = \left(\frac{y^2}{4} - \frac{y^3}{24}\right)_0^4 = 4 - \frac{8}{3} = \frac{4}{3}$$

(C)

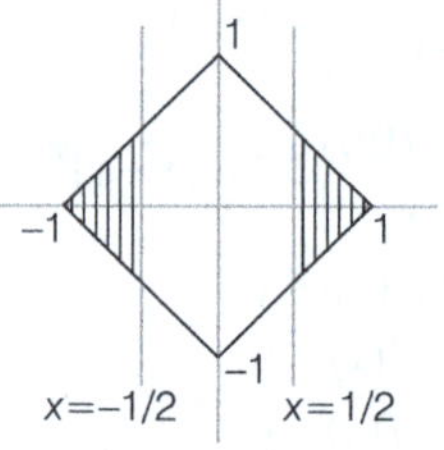

$$\text{Required area} = 4\left(\frac{1}{2} \times \frac{1}{2} \times \frac{1}{2}\right) = \frac{1}{2}$$

(D)

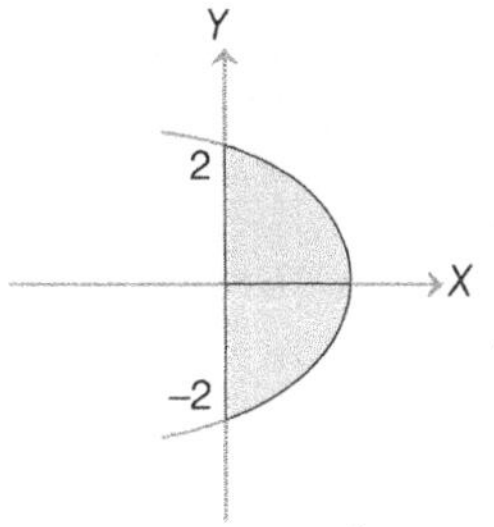

$$A = \int_{-2}^{2} (4 - y^2)\,dy = \left(4y - \frac{y^3}{3}\right)_{-2}^{2} = \frac{32}{3}$$

Example 39 *Match the following.*

	Column I		Column II
(A)	Area bounded by $-4y^2 = x$ and $x - 1 = -5y^2$ is	(p)	9
(B)	The area bounded by curve $[x] + [y] = 2023$ in Ist quadrant, where $[\cdot]$ is GIF, is	(q)	1
(C)	The region inclused between curve $x^2 + y^2 = 9$ and $\sqrt{\lvert x\rvert} + \sqrt{\lvert y\rvert} = \sqrt{3}$ is $k\pi - 6$, then k is equal to	(r)	$\frac{4}{3}$
(D)	The value of $a (a > 0)$ for which the area bounded by curves $y = \frac{x}{6} + \frac{1}{x^2}$, $y = 0$, $x = a$ and $x = 2a$ is least	(s)	2024

Sol. (A) → (r); (B) → (s); (C) → (p); (D) → (q)

(A) The points of intersection of $-4y^2 = x$ and $x - 1 = -5y^2$ are $(-4, -1)$ and $(-4, 1)$.

Hence, area $= 2\left[\int_0^1 (1 - 5y^2)\,dy - \int_0^1 -4y^2\,dy\right] = \frac{4}{3}$

(B)

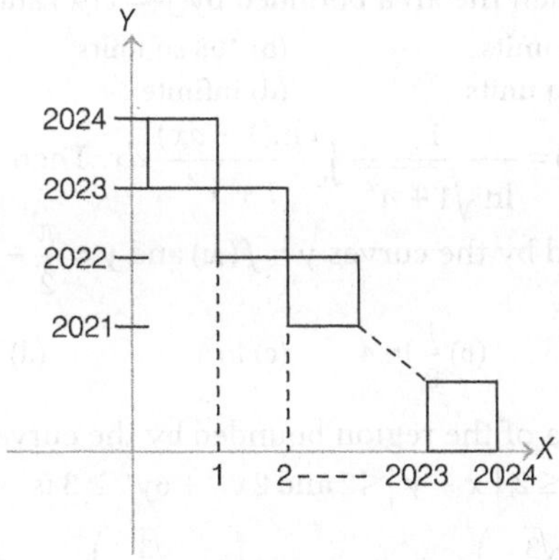

Area of figure $= 2024 \times 1 = 2024$

(C) Let $y_1 = (\sqrt{3} - \sqrt{x})^2 = 3 + x - 2\sqrt{3}\sqrt{x}$

and $y_2 = \sqrt{9 - x^2}$

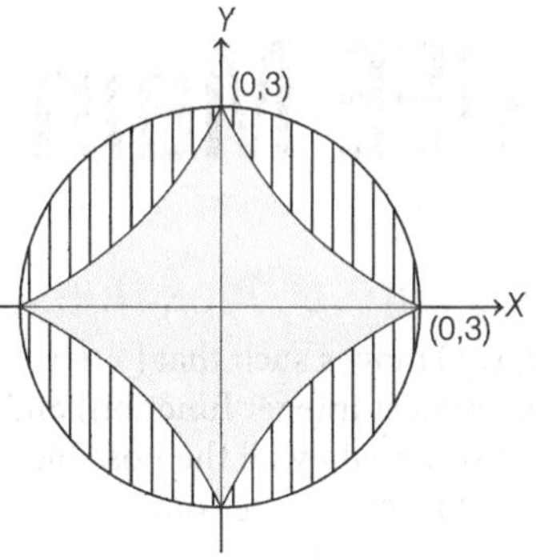

∴ Required area

$$= 4\left[\int_0^3 \sqrt{9 - x^2}\,dx - \int_0^3 (3 + x - 2\sqrt{3}\sqrt{x})\,dx\right]$$

$$= 4\left[\frac{x}{2}\sqrt{9 - x^2} + \frac{9}{2}\sin^{-1}\frac{x}{3} - 3x - \frac{x^2}{2} + 2\sqrt{3} \times \frac{2}{3}x^{3/2}\right]_0^3$$

$$= 4\left[\frac{3}{2}\sqrt{9 - 9} + \frac{9}{2}\sin^{-1}\left(\frac{3}{3}\right) - 9 - \frac{9}{2} + \frac{4\sqrt{3}}{3}3^{3/2}\right]$$

$$= 4\left(\frac{9\pi}{4} - \frac{3}{2}\right)$$

$$= 9\pi - 6$$

∴ $k = 9$

(D) $f(x) = \int_a^{2a} \left(\frac{x}{6} + \frac{1}{x^2}\right) dx$

$$= \left(\frac{x^2}{12} - \frac{1}{x}\right)\Bigg|_a^{2a}$$

$$= \frac{4a^2}{12} - \frac{1}{2a} - \frac{a^2}{12} + \frac{1}{a}$$

$$= \frac{a^2}{4} + \frac{1}{2a}$$

Let $f'(a) = \frac{2a}{4} - \frac{1}{2a^2}$

$\Rightarrow f'(1) = 0$

$\Rightarrow \quad a = 1$ is a point of minima.

EXERCISE 1

JEE Main Pattern

Single Option Correct Type Questions

1. A point $P(x, y)$ moves such that $[x + y + 1] = [x]$. (where $[\cdot]$ denotes greatest integer function) and $x \in (0, 2)$, then the area represented by all the possible positions of P, is
(a) $\sqrt{2}$ (b) $2\sqrt{2}$ (c) $4\sqrt{2}$ (d) 2

2. If $f : [-1, 1] \to \left[-\frac{1}{2}, \frac{1}{2}\right]$, $f(x) = \frac{x}{1 + x^2}$. The area bounded by $y = f^{-1}(x)$, X-axis, $x = \frac{1}{2}$, $x = -\frac{1}{2}$ is
(a) $\frac{1}{2}\log e$ (b) $\log\left(\frac{e}{2}\right)$ (c) $\frac{1}{2}\log\frac{e}{3}$ (d) $\frac{1}{2}\log\left(\frac{e}{2}\right)$

3. If the area bounded by the curve $y = x^2 + 1$, $y = x$ and the pair of lines $x^2 + y^2 + 2xy - 4x - 4y + 3 = 0$ is K units, then the area of the region bounded by the curve $y = x^2 + 1$, $y = \sqrt{x - 1}$ and the pair of lines $(x + y - 1)(x + y - 3) = 0$, is
(a) K (b) $2K$
(c) $\frac{K}{2}$ (d) None of these

4. The area bounded by the curves $y = -\sqrt{-x}$ and $x = -\sqrt{-y}$ where $x, y \le 0$ is
(a) cannot be determined
(b) 1/3
(c) 2/3
(d) same as that of the figure bounded by the curves $y = \sqrt{-x}$; $x \le 0$ and $x = \sqrt{-y}$; $y \le 0$

5. $y = f(x)$ is a function which satisfies
(i) $f(0) = 0$ (ii) $f''(x) = f'(x)$ and (iii) $f'(0) = 1$
Then, the area bounded by the graph of $y = f(x)$, the lines $x = 0$, $x - 1 = 0$ and $y + 1 = 0$, is
(a) e (b) $e - 2$ (c) $e - 1$ (d) $e + 1$

6. The area bounded by the curve $y = xe^{-x}$; $xy = 0$ and $x = c$ where c is the x-coordinate of the curve's inflection point, is
(a) $1 - 3e^{-2}$ (b) $1 - 2e^{-2}$ (c) $1 - e^{-2}$ (d) 1

7. If $(a, 0)$; $a > 0$ is the point where the curve $y = \sin 2x - \sqrt{3}\sin x$ cuts the X-axis first, A is the area bounded by this part of the curve, the origin and the positive X-axis, then
(a) $4A + 8\cos a = 7$ (b) $4A + 8\sin a = 7$
(c) $4A - 8\sin a = 7$ (d) $4A - 8\cos a = 7$

8. Let $S = \left\{(x, y) : \frac{y(3x - 1)}{x(3x - 2)} < 0\right\}$,
$S' = \{(x, y) \in A \times B : -1 \le A \le 1, -1 \le B \le 1\}$,
then the area of the region enclosed by all points in $S \cap S'$ is
(a) 1 (b) 2 (c) 3 (d) 4

9. The area of the region bounded between the curves $y = e||x|\ln|x||$, $x^2 + y^2 - 2(|x| + |y|) + 1 \ge 0$ and X-axis where $|x| \le 1$, if α is the x-coordinate of the point of intersection of curves in 1st quadrant, is
(a) $4\left[\int_0^\alpha ex\ln x\,dx + \int_\alpha^1 (1 - \sqrt{1 - (x - 1)^2})\,dx\right]$
(b) $4\left[\int_0^\alpha ex\ln x\,dx + \int_1^\alpha (1 - \sqrt{1 - (x - 1)^2})\,dx\right]$
(c) $4\left[-\int_0^\alpha ex\ln x\,dx + \int_\alpha^1 (1 - \sqrt{1 - (x - 1)^2})\,dx\right]$
(d) $2\left[\int_0^\alpha ex\ln x\,dx + \int_1^\alpha (1 - \sqrt{1 - (x - 1)^2})\,dx\right]$

10. Let $P(x) = x^3 - 3b^2x + 16$. If $P(|x|)$ has exactly two real roots, then the area bounded by $y = P(x)$ and X-axis is
(a) 81 sq units (b) 108 sq units
(c) 168 sq units (d) infinite

11. Let $f(a) = \frac{1}{\ln\sqrt{1 + a^2}} \int_0^a \frac{\ln(1 + ax)}{1 + x^2}\,dx$. Then, area bounded by the curves $y = f(x)$ and $y = \frac{\pi}{2} - f(x)$ and the Y-axis is
(a) $\ln 2$ (b) $\frac{1}{2}\ln 4$ (c) $\ln 5$ (d) $\ln 3$

12. The area of the region bounded by the curves $|x + y| \le 2$, $|x - y| \le 2$ and $2x^2 + 6y^2 \ge 3$ is
(a) $\left(8 + \frac{\sqrt{3}}{2}\pi\right)$ sq units (b) $\left(8 - \frac{\sqrt{3}}{2}\pi\right)$ sq units
(c) $\left(4 - \frac{3\sqrt{3}}{2}\pi\right)$ sq units (d) $\left(8 - \frac{3\sqrt{3}}{2}\pi\right)$ sq units

13. Let $f : [0, \infty] \to R$ be a continuous and strictly increasing function such that $f^3(x) = \int_0^x t f^2(t)\,dt$, $\forall\ x > 0$. The area enclosed by $y = f(x)$, the X-axis and the ordinate at $x = 3$, is
(a) 1 (b) $\frac{3}{2}$ (c) 2 (d) 3

14. Area of the region in which point $P(x, y), (x>0)$ lies: such that $y \le \sqrt{16-x^2}$ and $\left|\tan^{-1}\left(\frac{y}{x}\right)\right| \le \frac{\pi}{3}$ is

(a) $\left(\frac{16}{3}\pi\right)$ (b) $\left(\frac{8\pi}{3}+8\sqrt{3}\right)$

(c) $(4\sqrt{3}-\pi)$ (d) $(\sqrt{3}-\pi)$

15. In the shown figure, half a period of $\sin x$ from 0 to π is not split into two regions (light and dark shaded) of equal area by a line through the origin. If the line and the sine function intersect at a point whose x-coordinate is k, then k satisfies the equation

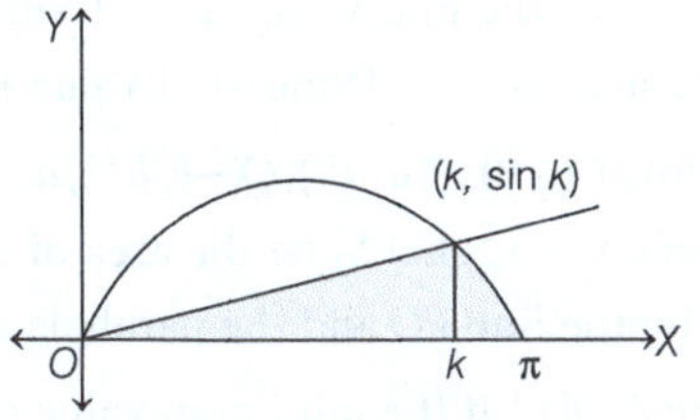

(a) $k \cos k + 2 \sin k = 0$ (b) $k \sin k + 2 \cos k = 0$
(c) $k \cos k - 2 \cos k = 0$ (d) $k \cos k - 2 \sin k = 0$

16. Let A_n be the area of region bounded by a curve $y = x^3(1-x^2)^n, 0 \le x \le 1$ and the X-axis, then the value of $\sum_{n=1}^{\infty} A_n$ is equal to

(a) $\frac{1}{5}$ (b) $\frac{1}{2}$ (c) $\frac{1}{4}$ (d) $\frac{1}{6}$

17. The area of bounded by the curve $4|x-2017^{2017}|+5|y-2017^{2017}| \le 20$, is

(a) 60 (b) 50 (c) 40 (d) 30

18. $f(x)$ is an increasing function such that $f''(x) > 0, \forall x \in R; f(0) = 0$: If $f(1) = 1$, $\int_0^1 f^{-1}(x)dx = k$, then area bounded by $f(x)$ and $f^{-1}(x)$ can be

(a) $2k-2$ (b) $2k-1$ (c) $1-2k$ (d) k

19. Area of the region enclosed between the curves $x = y^2 - 1$ and $x = |y|\sqrt{1-y^2}$ is

(a) 1 (b) 4/3 (c) 2/3 (d) 2

20. Area bounded by $y = f^{-1}(x)$ and tangent and normal drawn to it at the points with abscissae π and 2π, where $f(x) = \sin x - x$ is

(a) $\frac{\pi^2}{2}-1$ (b) $\frac{\pi^2}{2}-2$ (c) $\frac{\pi^2}{2}-4$ (d) $\frac{\pi^2}{2}$

21. The area bounded by the curves $y = \sqrt{5-x^2}$ and $y = |x-1|$ is

(a) $\frac{5\pi}{4}-2$ sq units (b) $\frac{5\pi-2}{4}$ sq units

(c) $\frac{5\pi-2}{2}$ sq units (d) $\frac{\pi}{2}-5$ sq units

22. The area (in sq units) of the region $\{(x, y) : x \ge 0, x + y \le 3, x^2 \le 4y$ and $y \le 1 + \sqrt{x}\}$ is

(a) $\frac{59}{12}$ (b) $\frac{3}{2}$ (c) $\frac{7}{3}$ (d) $\frac{5}{2}$

23. Let f be a differentiable function satisfying the condition $f\left(\frac{x}{y}\right) = \frac{f(x)}{f(y)}, y \ne 0, f(y) \ne 0 \, \forall \, x, y \in R$ and $f'(1) = 2$. If the smaller area enclosed by $y = f(x)$ and $x^2 + y^2 = 2$ is A, then the value of A is

(a) $\left(\frac{1}{6}+\frac{\pi}{3}\right)$ sq units (b) $\left(\frac{1}{6}-\frac{\pi}{3}\right)$ sq units

(c) $\left(\frac{1}{3}-\frac{\pi}{2}\right)$ sq units (d) $\left(\frac{1}{3}+\frac{\pi}{2}\right)$ sq units

Numerical Value Type Questions

24. The area enclosed between the curve $y = \ln(x+e)$, $x = \ln\left(\frac{1}{y}\right)$ and X-axis is ......

25. Let T be the tangent to the ellipse $E : x^2 + 4y^2 = 5$ at the point $P(1, 1)$. If the area of the region bounded by the tangent T, ellipse E and line $x = 1$ and $x = \sqrt{5}$ is $\alpha\sqrt{5} + \beta + \gamma \cos^{-1}\left(\frac{1}{\sqrt{5}}\right)$, then $4|\alpha + \beta + \gamma|$ is equal to ......

26. Let a and b respectively be the points of local maxima and local minima of the function $f(x) = 2x^3 - 3x^2 - 12x$. If A is the total area of the region bounded by $y = f(x)$, the X-axis and the lines $x = a$ and $x = b$, then $4A$ is equal to ......

27. The set of point (x, y) in the plane satisfying $x^{2/5} + |y| = 1$ form a curve enclosing a region of area $\frac{p}{q}$ sq units, when p and q are relatively prime positive integers, then $p - q$ is ......

28. The area of the region bounded by the X-axis and the curves defined by

$$\begin{cases} y = \tan x, & -\frac{\pi}{3} \le x \le \frac{\pi}{3} \\ y = \cot x, & \frac{\pi}{6} \le x \le \frac{\pi}{2} \end{cases}$$

is $\log k$, then the value of k is ......

29. If the line $y = mx$ bisects the area enclosed by the lines $x = 0, y = 0, x = \frac{3}{2}$ and the curve $y = 1 + 4x - x^2$, then $12m$ is equal to ......

30. The area of region bounded by the parabola $(y-2)^2 = (x-1)$, the tangent to it at the point, whose ordinate is 3 and the X-axis, is ......

31. The area of the region $A = \{(x, y): 0 \le y \le x|x| + 1$ and $-1 \le x \le 1\}$ is ......

32. The area bounded by the curves $y = \ln|x|$ and $y = 1 - |x|$ is ......

33. Consider $f(x) = x^2 - 3x + 2$. The area bounded by $|y| = |f(|x|)|, x \ge 1$ is A, then find the value of $3A + 2$.

34. The value of $c + 2$ for which the area of the figure bounded by the curve $y = 8x^2 - x^5$; the straight lines $x = 1$ and $x = c$ and X-axis is equal to $\frac{16}{3}$, is ....

35. The area bounded by $y = 2 - |2 - x|$; $y = \frac{3}{|x|}$ is $\frac{k - 3\ln 3}{2}$, then k is equal to ....

36. The area of region bounded by $x = -1$, $x = 2$, $y = x^2 + 1$ and $y = 2x - 2$ is ......

Previous Years Questions

37. The area (in sq units) of the region bounded by the parabola $y^2 = 4(x - 2)$ and the line $y = 2x - 8$, is **[Single Correct Type, 2024 Main]**

(a) 6 (b) 9 (c) 7 (d) 8

38. The area of the region $\left\{(x, y): y^2 \le 4x, x < 4, \frac{xy(x-1)(x-2)}{(x-3)(x-4)} > 0, x \ne 3\right\}$ is **[Single Correct Type, 2024 Main]**

(a) $\frac{32}{3}$ (b) $\frac{8}{3}$ (c) $\frac{64}{3}$ (d) $\frac{16}{3}$

39. The area of the region enclosed by the parabolas $y = 4x - x^2$ and $3y = (x - 4)^2$ is equal to **[Single Correct Type, 2024 Main]**

(a) $\frac{14}{3}$ (b) 6 (c) 4 (d) $\frac{32}{9}$

40. The area enclosed by the curves $xy + 4y = 16$ and $x + y = 6$ is equal to **[Single Correct Type, 2024 Main]**

(a) $30 - 32\log_e 2$ (b) $32 - 30\log_e 2$
(c) $30 - 28\log_e 2$ (d) $28 - 30\log_e 2$

41. Let the area of the region $\{(x, y): x - 2y + 4 \ge 0, x + 2y^2 \ge 0, x + 4y^2 \le 8, y \ge 0\}$ be $\frac{m}{n}$, where m and n are coprime numbers. Then, $m + n$ is equal to .... **[Numerical Value Type, 2024 Main]**

42. If the area of the region $\{(x, y): 0 \le y \le \min\{2x, 6x - x^2\}$ is A, then $12A$ is equal to .... **[Numerical Value Type, 2024 Main]**

43. The area (in sq units) of the part of the circle $x^2 + y^2 = 169$ which is below the line $5x - y = 13$ is $\frac{\pi\alpha}{2\beta} - \frac{65}{2} + \frac{\alpha}{\beta}\sin^{-1}\left(\frac{12}{13}\right)$, where α, β are coprime numbers. Then, $\alpha + \beta$ is equal to .... **[Numerical Value Type, 2024 Main]**

44. Let the area of the region $\{(x, y): 0 \le x \le 3, 0 \le y \le \min\{x^2 + 2, 2x + 2\}\}$ be A. Then, $12A$ is equal to .... **[Numerical Value Type, 2024 Main]**

45. The area of the region enclosed by the parabola $(y - 2)^2 = x - 1$, the line $x - 2y + 4 = 0$ and the positive coordinate axes is .... . **[Numerical Value Type, 2024 Main]**

46. Three points $O(0, 0)$, $P(a, a^2)$, $Q(-b, b^2)$, $a > 0, b > 0$, are on the parabola $y = x^2$. Let S_1 be the area of the region bounded by the line PQ and the parabola and S_2 be the area of the ΔOPQ. If the minimum value of $\frac{S_1}{S_2}$ is $\frac{m}{n}$, $gcd(m, n) = 1$, then $m + n$ is equal to .... **[Numerical Value Type, 2024 Main]**

47. The area bounded by the curves $y = |x - 1| + |x - 2|$ and $y = 3$ is equal to **[Single Correct Type, 2023 Main]**

(a) 4 (b) 5 (c) 6 (d) 3

48. Let A be the area bounded by the curve $y = x|x - 3|$, the X-axis and the ordinates $x = -1$ and $x = 2$. Then, $12A$ is equal to .... **[Numerical Value Type, 2023 Main]**

49. Let α be the area of the larger region bounded by the curve $y^2 = 8x$ and the lines $y = x$ and $x = 2$, which lies in the first quadrant. Then, the value of 3α is equal to .... **[Numerical Value Type, 2023 Main]**

50. The area of the region $\{(x, y): x^2 \le y \le |x^2 - 4|\}$ and $y \ge 1$ is **[Single Correct Type, 2023 Main]**

(a) $\frac{3}{4}(4\sqrt{2} - 1)$ (b) $\frac{3}{4}(4\sqrt{2} + 1)$
(c) $\frac{4}{3}(4\sqrt{2} - 1)$ (d) $\frac{4}{3}(4\sqrt{2} + 1)$

51. The area of the region enclosed by the curve $f(x) = \max\{\sin x, \cos x\}, -\pi \le x \le \pi$ and the X-axis is **[Single Correct Type, 2023 Main]**

(a) $2\sqrt{2}(\sqrt{2} + 1)$ (b) $4(\sqrt{2})$
(c) 4 (d) $2(\sqrt{2} + 1)$

52. The area of the region enclosed by the curve $y = x^3$ and its tangent at the point $(-1, -1)$ is **[Single Correct Type, 2023 Main]**

(a) $\frac{23}{4}$ (b) $\frac{19}{4}$ (c) $\frac{31}{4}$ (d) $\frac{27}{4}$

53. Area of the region $\{(x, y) : x^2 + (y-2)^2 \le 4, x^2 \ge 2y\}$ is **[Single Correct Type, 2023 Main]**

(a) $\pi - \frac{8}{3}$ (b) $2\pi + \frac{16}{3}$ (c) $2\pi - \frac{16}{3}$ (d) $\pi + \frac{8}{3}$

54. The area of the region $\{(x, y): x^2 \le y \le 8 - x^2, y \le 7\}$ is **[Single Correct Type, 2023 Main]**

(a) 21 (b) 20
(c) 18 (d) 24

55. The area of the region given by $\{(x, y) : xy \le 8, 1 \le y \le x^2\}$ is **[Single Correct Type, 2023 Main]**

(a) $16\log_e 2 + \frac{7}{3}$ (b) $16\log_e 2 - \frac{14}{3}$
(c) $8\log_e 2 + \frac{7}{6}$ (d) $8\log_e 2 - \frac{13}{3}$

56. Let q be the maximum integral value of p in [0, 10] for which the roots of the equation $x^2 - px + \frac{5}{4}p = 0$ are rational. Then, the area of the region $\{(x, y) : 0 \le y \le (x-q)^2, 0 \le x \le q\}$ is **[Single Correct Type, 2023 Main]**

(a) 125 / 3 (b) 243 (c) 25 (d) 164

57. Let Δ be the area of the region $\{(x, y) \in R^2 : x^2 + y^2 \le 21, y^2 \le 4x, x \ge 1\}$. Then, $\frac{1}{2}\left(\Delta - 21\sin^{-1}\frac{2}{\sqrt{7}}\right)$ is equal to **[Single Correct Type, 2023 Main]**

(a) $2\sqrt{3} - \frac{2}{3}$ (b) $\sqrt{3} - \frac{2}{3}$
(c) $\sqrt{3} - \frac{4}{3}$ (d) $2\sqrt{3} - \frac{1}{3}$

58. The area of the region
$A = \left\{(x, y) : |\cos x - \sin x| \le y \le \sin x, 0 \le x \le \frac{\pi}{2}\right\}$ is

[Single Correct Type, 2023 Main]

(a) $\sqrt{5} + 2\sqrt{2} - 4.5$ (b) $\frac{3}{\sqrt{5}} - \frac{3}{\sqrt{2}} + 1$
(c) $1 - \frac{3}{\sqrt{2}} + \frac{4}{\sqrt{5}}$ (d) $\sqrt{5} - 2\sqrt{2} + 1$

59. Let $A = \{(x, y) \in R^2 : y \ge 0, 2x \le y \le \sqrt{4 - (x-1)^2}\}$ and $B = \{(x, y) \in R \times R : 0 \le y \le \min\{2x, \sqrt{4-(x-1)^2}\}\}$. Then, the ratio of the area of A to the area of B is **[Single Correct Type, 2023 Main]**

(a) $\frac{\pi}{\pi - 1}$ (b) $\frac{\pi + 1}{\pi - 1}$ (c) $\frac{\pi - 1}{\pi + 1}$ (d) $\frac{\pi}{\pi + 1}$

60. The area enclosed by the curves $y^2 + 4x = 4$ and $y - 2x = 2$ is **[Single Correct Type, 2023 Main]**

(a) $\frac{25}{3}$ (b) $\frac{23}{3}$ (c) 9 (d) $\frac{22}{3}$

61. If the area bounded by the curve $2y^2 = 3x$, lines $x + y = 3$, $y = 0$ and outside the circle $(x-3)^2 + y^2 = 2$ is A, then $4(\pi + 4A)$ is equal to .... **[Numerical Value Type, 2023 Main]**

62. If A is the area in the first quadrant enclosed by the curve $C : 2x^2 - y + 1 = 0$, the tangent to C at the point (1, 3) and the line $x + y = 1$, then the value of $60A$ is .... **[Numerical Value Type, 2023 Main]**

63. If the area of the region $\{(x, y) : |x^2 - 2| \le y \le x\}$ is A, then $6A + 16\sqrt{2}$ is equal to .... **[Numerical Value Type, 2023 Main]**

64. Let $y = p(x)$ be the parabola passing through the points (– 1, 0), (0, 1) and (1, 0). If the area of the region $\{(x, y) : (x+1)^2 + (y-1)^2 \le 1, y \le p(x)\}$ is A, then $12(\pi - 4A)$ is equal to .... **[Numerical Value Type, 2023 Main]**

65. Let the area enclosed by the lines $x + y = 2$, $y = 0$, $x = 0$ and the curve $f(x) = \min\left\{x^2 + \frac{3}{4}, 1 + [x]\right\}$, where $[x]$ denotes the greatest integer $\le x$, be A. Then, the value of $12A$ is .... **[Numerical Value Type, 2023 Main]**

66. If the area of the region $S = \{(x, y) : 2y - y^2 \le x^2 \le 2y, x \ge y\}$ is equal to $\frac{n+2}{n+1} - \frac{\pi}{n-1}$, then the natural number n is equal to .... **[Numerical Value Type, 2023 Main]**

67. Let for $x \in R$, $f(x) = \frac{x + |x|}{2}$ and $g(x) = \begin{cases} x, & x < 0 \\ x^2, & x \ge 0 \end{cases}$, then area bounded by the curve $y = (fog)(x)$ and the lines $y = 0$, $2y - x = 15$ is equal to .... **[Numerical Value Type, 2023 Main]**

68. Let the area of the region $\{(x, y) : |2x - 1| \le y \le |x^2 - x|, 0 \le x \le 1\}$ be A. Then, $(6A + 11)^2$ is equal to .... **[Numerical Value Type, 2023 Main]**

69. If the area enclosed by the parabolas $P_1 : 2y = 5x^2$ and $P_2 : x^2 - y + 6 = 0$ is equal to the area enclosed by P_1 and $y = \alpha x$, $\alpha > 0$, then α^3 is equal to .... **[Numerical Value Type, 2023 Main]**

70. The odd natural number a, such that the area of the region bounded by $y = 1$, $y = 3$, $x = 0$, $x = y^a$ is $\frac{364}{3}$, is equal to **[Single Correct Type, 2022 Main]**

(a) 3 (b) 5
(c) 7 (d) 9

71. The area bounded by the curve $y = |x^2 - 9|$ and the line $y = 3$ is **[Single Correct Type, 2022 Main]**
(a) $4(2\sqrt{3} + \sqrt{6} - 4)$ (b) $4(4\sqrt{3} + \sqrt{6} - 4)$
(c) $8(4\sqrt{3} + 3\sqrt{6} - 9)$ (d) $8(4\sqrt{3} + 2\sqrt{6} - 9)$

72. Let $f(x) = \max\{|x+1|, |x+2|, \ldots, |x+5|\}$. Then, $\int_{-6}^{0} f(x)\,dx$ is equal to ....
[Numerical Value Type, 2022 Main]

73. The area of the region $\{(x, y) : |x - 1| \le y \le \sqrt{5 - x^2}\}$ is equal to **[Single Correct Type, 2022 Main]**
(a) $\frac{5}{2}\sin^{-1}\left(\frac{3}{5}\right) - \frac{1}{2}$ (b) $\frac{5\pi}{4} - \frac{3}{2}$
(c) $\frac{3\pi}{4} + \frac{3}{2}$ (d) $\frac{5\pi}{4} - \frac{1}{2}$

74. The area of the region enclosed by $y \le 4x^2$, $x^2 \le 9y$ and $y \le 4$, is equal to **[Single Correct Type, 2022 Main]**
(a) $\frac{40}{3}$ (b) $\frac{56}{3}$ (c) $\frac{112}{3}$ (d) $\frac{80}{3}$

75. The area of the smaller region enclosed by the curves $y^2 = 8x + 4$ and $x^2 + y^2 + 4\sqrt{3}x - 4 = 0$ is equal to
[Single Correct Type, 2022 Main]
(a) $\frac{1}{3}(2 - 12\sqrt{3} + 8\pi)$ (b) $\frac{1}{3}(2 - 12\sqrt{3} + 6\pi)$
(c) $\frac{1}{3}(4 - 12\sqrt{3} + 8\pi)$ (d) $\frac{1}{3}(4 - 12\sqrt{3} + 6\pi)$

76. The area of the region given by $A = \{(x, y);\ x^2 \le y \le \min\{x + 2, 4 - 3x\}\}$ is
[Single Correct Type, 2022 Main]
(a) 31/8 (b) 17/6 (c) 19/6 (d) 27/8

77. The area enclosed by $y^2 = 8x$ and $y = \sqrt{2}x$ that lies outside the triangle formed by $y = \sqrt{2}x$, $x = 1$, $y = 2\sqrt{2}$, is equal to **[Single Correct Type, 2022 Main]**
(a) $\frac{16\sqrt{2}}{6}$ (b) $\frac{11\sqrt{2}}{6}$ (c) $\frac{13\sqrt{2}}{6}$ (d) $\frac{5\sqrt{2}}{6}$

78. The area of the region enclosed between the parabolas $y^2 = 2x - 1$ and $y^2 = 4x - 3$ is
[Single Correct Type, 2022 Main]
(a) 1/3 (b) 1/6 (c) 2/3 (d) 3/4

79. Area $\left\{(x, y) : x^2 + y^2 \le a^2 \text{ and } \frac{x^2}{a^2} + \frac{y^2}{b^2} \ge 1\right\} = 30\pi$ and
Area $\left\{(x, y) : x^2 + y^2 \ge b^2 \text{ and } \frac{x^2}{a^2} + \frac{y^2}{b^2} \le 1\right\} = 18\pi$.
Then, the value of $(a - b)^2$ is equal to ....
[Numerical Value Type, 2022 Main]

80. Let the area enclosed by the X-axis and the tangent and normal drawn to the curve $4x^3 - 3xy^2 + 6x^2 - 5xy - 8y^2 + 9x + 14 = 0$ at the point $(-2, 3)$ be A. Then, $8A$ is equal to ....
[Numerical Value Type, 2022 Main]

81. The area, enclosed by the curves $y = \sin x + \cos x$ and $y = |\cos x - \sin x|$ and the lines $x = 0$, $x = \pi/2$, is
[Single Correct Type, 2021 Main]
(a) $2\sqrt{2}(\sqrt{2} + 1)$ sq units (b) $2\sqrt{2}(\sqrt{2} - 1)$ sq units
(c) $3\sqrt{2}(\sqrt{2} + 1)$ sq units (d) $2(2\sqrt{2} - 1)$ sq units

82. The area of the region bounded by $y - x = 2$ and $x^2 = y$ is equal to **[Single Correct Type, 2021 Main]**
(a) 16/3 (b) 2/3
(c) 9/2 (d) 4/3

83. The area of the region $S = \{(x, y) : 3x^2 \le 4y \le 6x + 24\}$ is .... **[Numerical Value Type, 2021 Main]**

84. The area (in sq. units) of the largest rectangle $ABCD$ whose vertices A and B lie on the X-axis and vertices C and D lie on the parabola, $y = x^2 - 1$ below the X-axis, is
[Single Correct Type, 2020 Main]
(a) $\frac{4}{3\sqrt{3}}$ (b) $\frac{2}{3\sqrt{3}}$
(c) $\frac{1}{3\sqrt{3}}$ (d) $\frac{4}{3}$

85. The area (in sq. units) of the region $A = \{(x, y) : (x - 1)[x] \le y \le 2\sqrt{x}, 0 \le x \le 2\}$, where $[t]$ denotes the greatest integer function, is
[Single Correct Type, 2020 Main]
(a) $\frac{8}{3}\sqrt{2} - \frac{1}{2}$ (b) $\frac{4}{3}\sqrt{2} + 1$
(c) $\frac{8}{3}\sqrt{2} - 1$ (d) $\frac{4}{3}\sqrt{2} - \frac{1}{2}$

EXERCISE 2

JEE Advanced Pattern

Single Option Correct Type Questions

1. Let 'a' be a positive constant number. Consider two curves $C_1: y = e^x$, $C_2: y = e^{a-x}$. Let S be the area of the part surrounding by C_1, C_2 and the Y-axis, then $\lim_{a \to 0} \frac{S}{a^2}$ equals

(a) 4 (b) 1/2 (c) 0 (d) 1/4

2. 3 points $O(0,0)$, $P(a, a^2)$, $Q(-b, b^2)(a > 0, b > 0)$ are on the parabola $y = x^2$. Let S_1 be the area bounded by the line PQ and the parabola and let S_2 be the area of the ΔOPQ, the minimum value of S_1/S_2 is

(a) 4/3 (b) 5/3 (c) 2 (d) 7/3

3. Area enclosed by the graph of the function $y = (\ln^2 x) - 1$ lying in the 4th quadrant is

(a) $\frac{2}{e}$ (b) $\frac{4}{e}$ (c) $2\left(e + \frac{1}{e}\right)$ (d) $4\left(e - \frac{1}{e}\right)$

4. Suppose $g(x) = 2x + 1$ and $h(x) = 4x^2 + 4x + 5$ and $h(x) = (fog)(x)$. The area enclosed by the graph of the function $y = f(x)$ and the pair of tangents drawn to it from the origin, is

(a) 8/3 (b) 16/3
(c) 32/3 (d) None of these

5. A function $y = f(x)$ satisfies the differential equation $\frac{dy}{dx} - y = \cos x - \sin x$, with initial condition that y is bounded when $x \to \infty$. The area enclosed by $y = f(x)$, $y = \cos x$ and the Y-axis in the 1st quadrant

(a) $\sqrt{2} - 1$ (b) $\sqrt{2}$ (c) 1 (d) $1/\sqrt{2}$

6. If the area bounded between X-axis and the graph of $y = 6x - 3x^2$ between the ordinates $x = 1$ and $x = a$ is 19 sq units, then a can take the value

(a) 4 or -2
(b) two values are in $(2,3)$ and one in $(-1,0)$
(c) two values one in $(3,4)$ and one in $(-2,-1)$
(d) None of the above

7. If $f(x) = x - 1$ and $g(x) = |f(|x|) - 2|$, then the area bounded by $y = g(x)$ and the curve $x^2 - 4y + 8 = 0$ is equal to

(a) $\frac{4}{3}(4\sqrt{2} - 5)$ (b) $\frac{4}{3}(4\sqrt{2} - 3)$
(c) $\frac{8}{3}(4\sqrt{2} - 3)$ (d) $\frac{8}{3}(4\sqrt{2} - 5)$

8. A point P lying inside the curve $y = \sqrt{2ax - x^2}$ is moving such that its shortest distance from the curve at any position is greater than its distance from X-axis. The point P enclose a region whose area is equal to

(a) $\frac{\pi a^2}{2}$ (b) $\frac{a^2}{3}$ (c) $\frac{2a^2}{3}$ (d) $\left(\frac{3\pi - 4}{6}\right)a^2$

9. The area of the region $\{(x, y) : x^2 + y^2 \le 5, \, ||x| - |y|| \ge 1\}$ is ... (in sq units)

(a) $4\left(\pi - \tan^{-1}\left(\frac{24}{7}\right)\right) - 4$ (b) $5\left(\pi - \tan^{-1}\left(\frac{24}{7}\right)\right) - 4$
(c) $3\left(\pi - \tan^{-1}\left(\frac{24}{7}\right)\right) - 4$ (d) $2\left(\pi - \tan^{-1}\left(\frac{24}{7}\right)\right) - 1$

10. Area remains invariant under translation of coordinate axes. Using it find the area of the region described by the inequality $|3x - 18| + |2y + 7| \le 3$.

(a) 3 (b) 2
(c) 4 (d) None of these

11. Let $f : [0, \infty) \to R$ be a continuous and strictly increasing function such that $f^3(x) = \int_0^x t f^2(t)\, dt, \forall x > 0$. The area enclosed by $y = f(x)$, the X-axis and the ordinate at $x = 3$ is

(a) $\frac{1}{2}$ sq unit (b) 1 sq unit
(c) 2 sq units (d) $\frac{3}{2}$ sq units

12. The smaller area enclosed by $y = f(x)$, when $f(x)$ is polynomial of least degree satisfying $\lim_{x \to 0}\left[1 + \frac{f(x)}{x^3}\right]^{1/x} = e$ and the circle $x^2 + y^2 = 2$ above the X-axis, is

(a) $\frac{\pi}{2}$ sq units (b) $\frac{3}{5}$ sq unit
(c) $\frac{\pi}{2} - \frac{3}{5}$ sq units (d) $\frac{\pi}{2} + \frac{3}{5}$ sq units

More than One Correct Option Type Questions

13. The triangle formed by the normal to the curve $f(x) = x^2 - ax + 2a$ at the point (2, 4) and the coordinate axes lies in second quadrant, if its area is 2 sq units, then a can be

(a) 2 (b) 17/4 (c) 5 (d) 19/4

14. If A_i is the area bounded by $|x - a_i| + |y| = b_i$, $i \in N$, where $a_{i+1} = a_i + \frac{3}{2}b_i$ and $b_{i+1} = \frac{b_i}{2}$, $a_1 = 0$, $b_1 = 32$, then

(a) $A_3 = 128$ (b) $A_3 = 256$

(c) $\lim_{n\to\infty} \sum_{i=1}^{n} A_i = \frac{8}{3}(32)^2$ (d) $\lim_{n\to\infty} \sum_{i=1}^{n} A_i = \frac{4}{3}(16)^2$

15. Let $f(x)$ be a polynomial of degree 4 satisfying

$$\left(\int_1^x A(t)\,B(t)dt\right)\cdot\left(\int_1^x C(t)\,D(t)dt\right) - \left(\int_1^x A(t)\,C(t)dt\right)\cdot\left(\int_1^x B(t)D(t)dt\right) = f(x), \forall\, x \in R,$$

where $A(x)$, $B(x)$, $C(x)$, $D(x)$ are non-constant continuous and differentiable functions. It is given that the leading coefficient of $f(x)$ is 1, then

(a) area included between the line $y = x - 1$ and $y = f(x)$ is $\frac{3}{10}$.

(b) area included between the line $y = x - 1$ and $y = f(x)$ is $\frac{3}{8}$.

(c) area of the smaller region intercepted between the curves $y = f(x)$ and $x^2 + y^2 = 1$, is $\frac{\pi}{4} - \frac{1}{5}$.

(d) area of the smaller region intercepted between the curves $y = f(x)$ and $x^2 + y^2 = 1$, is $\frac{\pi}{4} + \frac{1}{5}$.

16. Area bounded by $y = \sec^{-1} x$, $y = \cot^{-1} x$ and line $x = 1$ is given by

(a) $\int_1^{\sqrt{\frac{1+\sqrt{5}}{2}}} (\cot^{-1} x - \sec^{-1} x)dx$

(b) $\int_0^{\alpha} \sec y\, dy + \int_0^{\pi/4}\left(\cot y\, dy - \frac{\pi}{4}\right)$, where $\sin\alpha = \cos^2\alpha$

(c) $\int_0^{\alpha} \sec y\, dy + \int_{\alpha}^{\pi/4} \cot y\, dy - \frac{\pi}{4}$, where $\sin\alpha = \cos^2\alpha$

(d) $\int_1^{\frac{1+\sqrt{5}}{2}} (\cot^{-1} x - \sec^{-1} x)dx$

17. Let A_r be the area of the region bounded between the curves $y^2 = (e^{-kr})x$ (where $k > 0$, $r \in N$) and the line $y = mx$ (where $m \neq 0$), k and m are some constants. Then, which of the following is (are) correct?

(a) $A_1, A_2, A_3, \ldots$ are in GP with common ratio equals e^{-2k}.

(b) $A_1, A_2, A_3, \ldots$ are in GP with common ratio equals e^{-k}.

(c) If $\lim_{n\to\infty} \sum_{i=1}^{n} A_i = \frac{1}{48(e^{2k} - 1)}$, then m equals 2.

(d) If $\lim_{n\to\infty} \sum_{i\to\infty}^{n} A_i = \frac{1}{48(e^{2k} - 1)}$, then m equals 3.

18. If the area bounded by $y = (\sin x)^{\operatorname{cosec} x}$, $y = (\operatorname{cosec} x)^{\sin x}$, $y = (\sin x)^{\sin x}$ and $y = (\operatorname{cosec} x)^{\operatorname{cosec} x}$ between the coordinates $x = 0$, $x = \frac{\pi}{2}$ denoted by A_1, A_2, A_3 and A_4, then

(a) A_4 is the greatest (b) A_1 is the least

(c) $A_2 > A_3$ (d) $A_2 < A_3$

19. The area of the region bounded by the curve $y = e^{x^2}$ and the line $y = e$ is

(a) $2\int_1^e \sqrt{\log_e y}\, dy$ (b) $2e - \int_{-1}^{1} e^{x^2} dx$

(c) $\int_{-1}^{1} (e - e^{x^2})dx$ (d) $2\int_0^1 \sqrt{x}\, e^{x^2} dx$

20. If the line $x = \alpha$ divides the area of the region $R = \{(x, y) \in R^2 : x^3 \le y \le x, 0 \le x \le 1\}$ into two equal parts, then

(a) $0 < \alpha \le \frac{1}{2}$ (b) $\frac{1}{2} < \alpha < 1$

(c) $2\alpha^4 - 4\alpha^2 + 1 = 0$ (d) $\alpha^4 + 4\alpha^2 - 1 = 0$

21. Which of the following have the same bounded area?

(a) $f(x) = \sin x$ and $g(x) = \sin^2 x$, where $0 \le x \le 10\pi$

(b) $f(x) = \sin x$ and $g(x) = |\sin x|$, where $0 \le x \le 20\pi$

(c) $f(x) = |\sin x|$ and $g(x) = \sin^3 x$, where $0 \le x \le 10\pi$

(d) $f(x) = \sin x$ and $g(x) = \sin^4 x$, where $0 \le x \le 10\pi$

22. For what values of m, the area of the region bounded by the curves $y = x - x^2$ and the line $y = mx$ equals $\frac{9}{2}$?

(a) −4 (b) −2

(c) 2 (d) 4

Passage Based Questions

Passage I

(Q. Nos. 23 and 24)

- Let $f(x) = \frac{ax^2 + bx + c}{x^2 + 1}$ such that $y = -2$ is an asymptote of the curve $y = f(x)$. The curve $y = f(x)$ is symmetric about Y-axis and its maximum values is 4. Let $h(x) = f(x) - g(x)$, where $f(x) = \sin^4 \pi x$ and $g(x) = \log_e x$. Let $x_0, x_1, x_2, \ldots x_{n+1}$ be the roots of $f(x) = g(x)$ in increasing order.

23. Then, the absolute area enclosed by $y = f(x)$ and $y = g(x)$ is given by

(a) $\sum_{r=0}^{n} \int_{x_r}^{x_{r+1}} (-1)^r \cdot h(x)dx$ (b) $\sum_{r=0}^{n} \int_{x_r}^{x_{r+1}} (-1)^{r+1} \cdot h(x)dx$

(c) $2\sum_{r=0}^{n} \int_{x_r}^{x_{r+1}} (-1)^r \cdot h(x)dx$ (d) $\frac{1}{2} \cdot \sum_{r=0}^{n} \int_{x_r}^{x_{r+1}} (-1)^{r+1} h(x)dx$

24. The whole area bounded by $y = f(x), y = g(x)\ x = 0$ is

(a) 11/8 (b) 8/3 (c) 2 (d) 13/3

Passage II

(Q. Nos. 25 and 26)

- Let $f(x) = x^2 - 3x + 2$ be a function, $\forall\ x \in R$.

25. The area bounded by the curve $f(|x|)$ and X-axis is

(a) 2 sq units (b) $\frac{5}{2}$ sq units

(c) $\frac{3}{5}$ sq units (d) $\frac{5}{3}$ sq units

26. The area bounded by the curve $|f(|x|)|$ between $1 \le |x| \le 2$, and the X-axis is

(a) $\frac{1}{5}$ sq unit (b) $\frac{1}{4}$ sq unit

(c) $\frac{1}{3}$ sq unit (d) $\frac{1}{2}$ sq unit

Passage III

(Q. Nos. 27 and 28)

- Computing areas with parametrically represented boundaries :

If the boundary of a figure is represented by parametric equations i.e. $x = x(t), y = y(t)$, then the area of the figure is evaluated by one of the three formulae

$$S = -\int_{\alpha}^{\beta} y(t) \cdot x'(t)\, dt,\ S = \int_{\alpha}^{\beta} x(t) \cdot y'(t)\, dt$$

$$S = \frac{1}{2}\int_{\alpha}^{\beta} (xy' - yx')\, dt$$

where, α and β are the values of the parameter 't' corresponding, respectively to the beginning and the end of the traversal of the curve corresponding to increasing 't'.

27. The area enclosed by the asteroid $\left(\frac{x}{a}\right)^{2/3} + \left(\frac{y}{a}\right)^{2/3} = 1$ is

(a) $\frac{3}{4}a^2\pi$ (b) $\frac{3}{18}\pi a^2$ (c) $\frac{3}{8}\pi a^2$ (d) $\frac{3}{4}a\pi$

28. The area of the region bounded by an arc of the cycloid $x = a(t - \sin t), y = a(1 - \cos t)$ and the X-axis is

(a) $6\pi a^2$ (b) $3\pi a^2$

(c) $4\pi a^2$ (d) None of these

Passage IV

(Q. Nos. 29 and 30)

- Consider the area $S_0, S_1, S_2 \ldots$ bounded by the X-axis and halfwaves of the curve $y = e^{-x} \sin x$, where $x \ge 0$.

29. The value of S_0 is

(a) $\frac{1}{2}(1 + e^{\pi})$ sq units (b) $\frac{1}{2}(1 + e^{-\pi})$ sq units

(c) $\frac{1}{2}(1 - e^{-\pi})$ sq units (d) $\frac{1}{2}(e^{\pi} - 1)$ sq units

30. $\sum_{n=0}^{\infty} S_n$ is equal to

(a) $\frac{1 + e^n}{1 - e^{-n}}$ (b) $\frac{\frac{1}{2}(1 + e^{\pi})}{1 - e^{-\pi}}$

(c) $\frac{1}{2(1 - e^{-\pi})}$ (d) None of these

Stem Based Questions

Stem I

(Q. Nos. 31 and 32)

- Let $f(x)$ be a continuous and positive function in $[0, 5]$ and the area bounded by the graph of $y = f(x)$ and X-axis for $0 \le x \le 5$ is 8. $A(c)$ denotes the area between the graph of $y = f(x)$ and X-axis for $0 \le x \le c$ and $B(c)$ denotes the area between the graph of $y = f(x)$ and X-axis for $C \le x \le 5$. Also, $R(c) = \frac{A(c)}{B(c)}$, $R(3) = 1$ and $\frac{dR}{dc}$ is equal to 7 at $c = 3$.

31. The value of $A(3)$ is equal to ....

32. The value of $A'(c) + B'(c)$ at $c = 10$, is ....

Stem II

(Q. Nos. 33 and 34)

- Suppose that $f(\alpha)$ denotes the area of the region bounded by

$$x = 0,\ x = 2,\ y^2 = 4x$$

and $y = |\alpha x - 1| + |\alpha x - 2| + \alpha x$,

where $\alpha \in [0, 1]$.

33. The value of $f(\alpha) + \frac{8\sqrt{2}}{3}$, when $\alpha = 0$, is ....

34. The value of $f(\alpha) + \frac{8\sqrt{2}}{3}$, when $\alpha = 1$, is ....

Single Integer Type Questions

35. A point P moves in XY-plane in such a way that $[|x|] + [|y|] = 1$, where $[\cdot]$ denotes the greatest integer function. Area of the region representing all possible of the point P is equal to ....

36. Let $f:[0,1]\to\left[0,\frac{1}{2}\right]$ be a function such that $f(x)$ is a polynomial of 2nd degree, satisfy the following condition
(a) $f(0)=0$
(b) has a maximum value of $\frac{1}{2}$ at $x=1$.
If A is the area bounded by $y=f(x); y=f^{-1}(x)$ and the line $2x+2y-3=0$ in 1st quadrant, then the value of $24A$ is equal to ....

37. Let $f(x)=\min\left\{\sin^{-1}x, \cos^{-1}x, \frac{\pi}{6}\right\}, x\in[0,1]$. If area bounded by $y=f(x)$ and X-axis, between the lines $x=0$ and $x=1$ is $\frac{a-X}{b(\sqrt{3}+1)}$. Then, $(a-b)$ is ....

38. If A be the area of the region bounded by $y=2011^x\log 2011$, $y=2011^{-x}\log 2011$ and $x=1$, then $[A+2]\{A\}=?$ (where $[x]$ denotes integral part and $\{x\}$ denotes fractional part of x).

39. Let S_k be the area bounded by the curve $y=x^2(1-x)^k$ and the lines $x=0$, $y=0$ and $x=1$. If $\lim_{n\to\infty}\sum_{k=1}^{n}S_k$ equals $\frac{p}{q}$, where $p, q\in N$, then find the least value of $(p+q)$.

40. Let $f(x)=\cos^{-1}\left(\frac{2x}{1+x^2}\right), g(x)=\cot^{-1}\left(\frac{2x}{x^2-1}\right)$, where $x\in(-1,1)$. If the area bounded by the curves $y=f(x)+g(x)$ and $y=\pi x^2$ is A, then find the value of $[A]$.

41. Let S_1 and S_2 be the set of points in XY-plane (where $x\ge 0$ and $y\in R$) defined as
$$S_1=\{(x,y):|x+|x||+|y+|y||<2\}$$
and $S_2=\{(x,y):|x-|x||+|y-|y||\le 2\}$.
If the area of intersection of S_1 and S_2 is A, then find the value of $2A$.

42. Let $f(x)=1+\cos x$ and $g(x)=\frac{a}{bx^2+cx+1}$. If $f(0)=g(0), f'(0)=g'(0)\cdot f'(0)$ and the area bounded by the graph of $g(x)$ and X-axis is $k\pi$, then find the value of k.

43. If C is a constant such that the line joining the points $(0,3), (5,-2)$ is a tangent to $y=\frac{c}{x+1}$, then the area of the region bounded by the curve and X-axis and $x=1$, $x=2$ is $\lambda\left\{1-\frac{1}{2\cdot 2}+\frac{1}{2^2\cdot 3}+\frac{1}{2^3\cdot 4}+\dots\infty\right\}$, then find the value of λ.

Numerical Value Type Questions

44. If the area bounded by the curve $f(x)=\cos^{-1}\left(\sin\left(\left\{\frac{\pi}{2}\right\}-[\sin x]\right)\right)$ and X-axis from $x=0$ to $x=2\pi$ is k, then find the value of k, where $[\cdot]$ is GIF and $\{\cdot\}$ is *FPF*.

45. The minimum area bounded by the function $y=f(x)$ and $y=\alpha x+9\ (\alpha\in R)$, where f satisfies the relation $f(x+y)=f(x)+f(y)+y\sqrt{f(x)}, \forall\ x, y\in R$ and $f'(0)=0$ is $9A$. Find the value of A.

46. If area bounded by the curve $y=\left[\frac{|x|}{\sqrt{2011}}\right]$ and $x^2+y=2011$ be expressed as $2\lambda(2011)^{\frac{1}{\lambda}}$, then $\frac{1}{\lambda}$ is where $[\cdot]$ denotes GIF.

Matching Type Questions

47. Match the statements of Column I with values of Column II.

	Column I		Column II
(A)	The area bounded by the curve $y=x+\sin x$ and its inverse function between the ordinates $x=0$ to $x=2\pi$ is $4s$. Then, the value of s is	(p)	2
(B)	The area bounded by $y=xe^{\lvert x\rvert}$ and lies $\lvert x\rvert=1, y=0$ is	(q)	1
(C)	The area bounded by the curves $y^2=x^3$ and $\lvert y\rvert=2x$ is	(r)	$\frac{16}{5}$
(D)	The smaller are included between the curves $\sqrt{\lvert x\rvert}+\sqrt{\lvert y\rvert}=1$ and $\lvert x\rvert+\lvert y\rvert=1$ is	(s)	$\frac{1}{3}$

48. Match the following :

	Column I		Column II
(A)	Area enclosed by $y=\lvert x\rvert$, $\lvert x\rvert=1$ and $y=0$ is	(p)	2
(B)	Area enclosed by the curve $y=\sin x$, $x=0$, $x=\pi$ and $y=0$ is	(q)	4
(C)	If the area of the region bounded by $x^2\le y$ and $y\le x+2$ is $\frac{k}{4}$, then k is equal to	(r)	27
(D)	Area of the quadrilateral formed by tangents at the ends of latusrectum of ellipse of ellipse $\frac{x^2}{9}+\frac{y^2}{5}=1$ is	(s)	18

49. Match the following :

	Column I		Column II
(A)	Area of region formed by points (x, y) satisfying $[x]^2 = [y]^2$ for $0 \le x \le 4$ is equal to (where [.] denotes greatest integer function)	(p)	48
(B)	The area of region formed by points (x, y) satisfying $x + y \le 6$, $x^2 + y^2 \le 6y$ and $y^2 \le 8x$ is $\frac{k\pi - 2}{12}$, then k is equal to	(q)	27
(C)	The area in the first quadrant bounded by curve $y = \sin x$ and the line $\frac{2y-1}{\sqrt{2}-1} = \frac{2}{\pi}(6x - \pi)$ is $\left[\frac{\sqrt{3}-\sqrt{2}}{2} - \frac{(\sqrt{2}+1)\pi}{k}\right]$, then k is equal to	(r)	7
(D)	If the area bounded by the graph of $y = xe^{-ax}$, $(a > 0)$ and the abscissa axis is $\frac{1}{9}$, then the value of 'a' is equal to	(s)	3

Previous Year Questions

50. Let $n \ge 2$ be a natural number and $f : [0, 1] \to R$ be the function defined by

$$f(x) = \begin{cases} n(1-2nx) & \text{if } 0 \le x \le \frac{1}{2n} \\ 2n(2nx-1) & \text{if } \frac{1}{2n} \le x \le \frac{3}{4n} \\ 4n(1-nx) & \text{if } \frac{3}{4n} \le x \le \frac{1}{n} \\ \frac{n}{n-1}(nx-1) & \text{if } \frac{1}{n} \le x \le 1 \end{cases}$$

If n is such that the area of the region bounded by the curves $x = 0$, $x = 1$, $y = 0$ and $y = f(x)$ is 4, then the maximum value of the function f is .... .

[Numerical Value Type, 2023 Adv.]

51. Consider the functions $f, g : R \to R$ defined by

$$f(x) = x^2 + \frac{5}{12} \text{ and } g(x) = \begin{cases} 2\left(1 - \frac{4|x|}{3}\right), & |x| \le \frac{3}{4}, \\ 0, & |x| > \frac{3}{4} \end{cases}$$

If α is the area of the region $\{(x, y) \in R \times R : |x| \le \frac{3}{4}, 0 \le y \le \min\{f(x), g(x)\}\}$, then the value of 9α is ......

[Numerical Value Type, 2022 Adv.]

52. The area of the region $\left\{(x, y) : 0 \le x \le \frac{9}{4}, 0 \le y \le 1, x \ge 3y, x + y \ge 2\right\}$ is

[Single Correct Type, 2021 Adv.]

(a) $\frac{11}{32}$ (b) $\frac{35}{96}$ (c) $\frac{37}{96}$ (d) $\frac{13}{32}$

53. Let the functions $f : R \to R$ and $g : R \to R$ be defined by

$$f(x) = e^{x-1} - e^{-|x-1|} \text{ and } g(x) = \frac{1}{2}(e^{x-1} + e^{1-x}).$$

Then, the area of the region in the first quadrant bounded by the curves $y = f(x)$, $y = g(x)$ and $x = 0$ is

[Single Correct Type, 2020 Adv.]

(a) $(2 - \sqrt{3}) + \frac{1}{2}(e - e^{-1})$ (b) $(2 + \sqrt{3}) + \frac{1}{2}(e - e^{-1})$

(c) $(2 - \sqrt{3}) + \frac{1}{2}(e + e^{-1})$ (d) $(2 + \sqrt{3}) + \frac{1}{2}(e + e^{-1})$

EXERCISE 3

Challenging Problems

1. A curve $y = f(x)$ passes through the point $P(1, 1)$, the normal to the curve at P is $a(y - 1) + (x - 1) = 0$. If the slope of the tangent at any point on the curve is proportional to the ordinate of that point, determine the equation of the curve. Also, obtain the area bounded by the Y-axis, the curve and the normal to the curve at P.

2. Find all the possible values of $b > 0$, so that the area of the bounded region enclosed between the parabolas $y = x - bx^2$ and $y = \frac{x^2}{b}$ is maximum.

3. Let C_1 and C_2 be the graphs of the function $y = x^2$ and $y = 2x$, $0 \le x \le 1$, respectively. Let C_3 be the graph of a function $y = f(x)$; $0 \le x \le 1$, $f(0) = 0$. For a point P on C_1, let the lines through P parallel to the axes, meets C_2 and C_3 at Q and R respectively. If for every position of P on (C_1), the areas of the shaded region OPQ and ORP are equal, determine the function $f(x)$.

4. Find the area of the region bounded by the curves $y = ex \log x$ and $y = \frac{\log x}{ex}$.

5. Let A_n be the area bounded by the curve $y=(\tan x)^n$ and the lines $x=0$, $y=0$ and $x=\frac{\pi}{4}$. Prove that for $n>2$; $A_n+A_{n-2}=\frac{1}{n-1}$ and deduce that $\frac{1}{2n+2}<A_n<\frac{1}{2n-2}$.

6. Consider a square with vertices at (1, 1) (−1, 1), (−1, −1) and (1, −1). Let S be the region consisting of all points inside the square which are nearer to the origin than to any edge. Sketch the region S and find its area.

7. Prove that the areas $S_0, S_1, S_2, \ldots$ bounded by the X-axis and half-waves of the curve $y=e^{-\alpha x}\sin\beta x$, $x\,|\,0$. form a geometric progression with the common ratio $g=e^{-\pi\alpha/\beta}$.

8. Let $b\neq 0$ and for $j=0,1,2,\ldots,n$. Let S_j be the area of the region bounded by Y-axis and the curve $x\cdot e^{ay}=\sin by$, $\frac{j\pi}{b}\le y\le\frac{(j+1)\pi}{b}$. Show that $S_0, S_1, S_2, \ldots, S_n$ are in geometric progression. Also, find their sum for $a=-1$ and $b=\pi$.

9. For any real t, $x=2+\frac{e^t+e^{-t}}{2}$, $y=2+\frac{e^t-e^{-t}}{2}$ is a point on the hyperbola $x^2-y^2-4x+4y-1=0$. Find the area bounded by the hyperbola and the lines joining the centre to the points corresponding to t_1 and $-t_1$.

10. Find the area enclosed by circle $x^2+y^2=4$, parabola $y=x^2+x+1$, the curve $y=\left[\sin^2\frac{x}{4}+\cos\frac{x}{4}\right]$ and X-axis (where, [·] is the greatest integer function).

11. Let $f(x)=\begin{cases}-2, & -3\le x\le 0\\ x-2, & 0<x\le 3\end{cases}$, where $g(x)=\min\{f(|x|)+|f(x)|, f(|x|)-|f(x)|\}$. Find the area bounded by the curve $g(x)$ and the X-axis between the ordinates at $x=3$ and $x=-3$.

12. Find the area of region enclosed by the curve $\frac{(x-y)^2}{a^2}+\frac{(x+y)^2}{b^2}=2\,(a>b)$, the line $y=x$ and the positive X-axis.

13. Find the area of the region which contains all the points satisfying condition $|x-2y|+|x+2y|\le 8$ and $xy\ge 2$.

14. Find the area of the region bounded by $y=f(x)$, $y=|g(x)|$ and the lines $x=0$, $x=2$, where f, g are continuous functions satisfying

$$f(x+y)=f(x)+f(y)-8xy,\ \forall\ x,y\in R$$

and $$g(x+y)=g(x)+g(y)+3xy(x+y),\ \forall\ x,y\in R$$

Also, $f'(0)=8$ and $g'(0)=-4$.

Answer Key

Exercise 1

1. (d)	2. (b)	3. (b)	4. (b)	5. (c)	6. (a)	7. (a)	8. (b)	9. (d)	10. (b)
11. (a)	12. (b)	13. (b)	14. (b)	15. (b)	16. (c)	17. (c)	18. (b)	19. (d)	20. (b)
21. (b)	22. (d)	23. (d)	24. (2)	25. (5)	26. (114)	27. (1)	28. (4)	29. (26)	30. (9)
31. (2)	32. (3)	33. (7)	34. (1)	35. (4)	36. (9)	37. (b)	38. (a)	39. (b)	40. (a)
41. (119)	42. (304)	43. (171)	44. (164)	45. (5)	46. (7)	47. (a)	48. (62)	49. (22)	50. (c)
51. (c)	52. (d)	53. (b)	54. (b)	55. (b)	56. (b)	57. (c)	58. (d)	59. (c)	60. (c)
61. (42)	62. (16)	63. (27)	64. (16)	65. (17)	66. (5)	67. (72)	68. (125)	69. (600)	70. (b)
71. (d)	72. (21)	73. (d)	74. (d)	75. (c)	76. (b)	77. (c)	78. (a)	79. (12)	80. (170)
81. (b)	82. (c)	83. (27)	84. (a)	85. (a)					

Exercise 2

1. (d)	2. (a)	3. (b)	4. (b)	5. (a)	6. (c)	7. (a)	8. (c)	9. (b)	10. (a)
11. (d)	12. (d)	13. (b,c)	14. (a,c)	15. (a,c)	16. (a,c)	17. (a,c)	18. (a,b,c)	19. (a,b,c)	20. (b,c)
21. (a,c,d)	22. (b,d)	23. (a)	24. (a)	25. (a)	26. (c)	27. (c)	28. (b)	29. (b)	30. (b)
31. (4)	32. (0)	33. (6)	34. (5)	35. (8)	36. (5)	37. (3)	38. (1)	39. (7)	40. (4)
41. (3)	42. (4)	43. (2)	44. (3.14)	45. (72)	46. (1.5)	47. (A) → p, (B) → p, (C) → r, (D) → s			
48. (A) → p, (B) → p, (C) → s, (D) → r		49. (A) → r, (B) → q, (C) → p, (D) → s				50. (8)	51. (6)	52. (a)	53. (a)

Solutions

Exercise 1 - JEE Main Pattern

1. Here, $[x + y] = [x] - 1$

when $x \in [0, 1) \Rightarrow [x + y] = -1$

$$-1 \le x + y < 0 \quad \text{...(i)}$$

when $\quad x \in [1, 2)$

$\Rightarrow \quad [x + y] = 0$

$\therefore \quad 0 \le x + y < 1 \quad$ ...(ii)

which can be shown, as

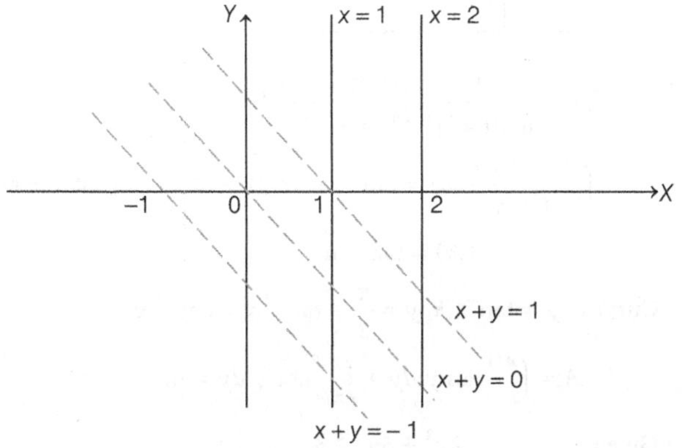

$\therefore$ Required area = 2

2. Required area $= 2\int_0^{1/2} f^{-1}(x)\, dx$

Let $\quad f^{-1}(x) = t \Rightarrow x = f(t) \Rightarrow dx = f'(t)dt$

$$\therefore \quad A = 2\int_0^1 t \cdot f'(t)dt$$

$$= 2\left[(t \cdot f(t))_0^1 - \int_0^1 1 \cdot f(t)dt\right]$$

$$= 2\left[f(1) - \int_0^1 \frac{t}{1+t^2}\, dt\right]$$

$$= 2\left[f(1) - \frac{1}{2}\left(\log_e(1+t^2)\right)_0^1\right]$$

$$= 2\left[f(1) - \frac{1}{2}\log_e 2\right]$$

$$= 2\left[\frac{1}{2} - \frac{1}{2}\log_e 2\right]$$

$$= 1 - \log_e 2$$

$$= \log\left(\frac{e}{2}\right)$$

3. Here, $y = x^2 + 1$ and $y = \sqrt{x-1}$ are inverse of each other.

The shaded area is given K units.

$\Rightarrow$ Area of the region bounded by $y = x^2 + 1, y = \sqrt{x-1}$ and $(x + y - 1)(x + y - 3) = 0$, is $2K$ units.

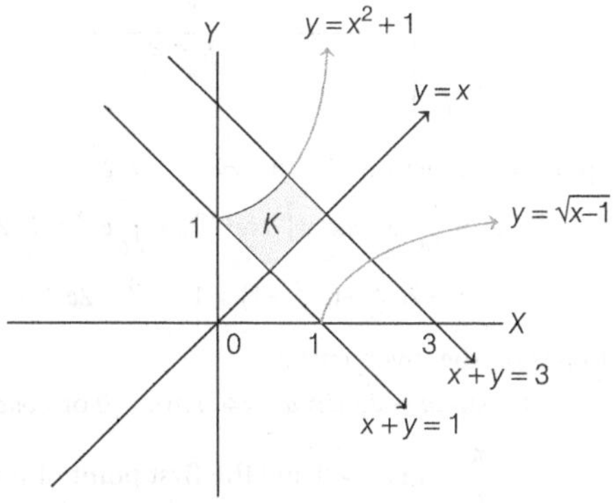

4. $y = -\sqrt{-x} \quad \Rightarrow y^2 = -x$, where x and y both negative

$x = -\sqrt{-y} \quad \Rightarrow x^2 = -y$, where x and y both negative

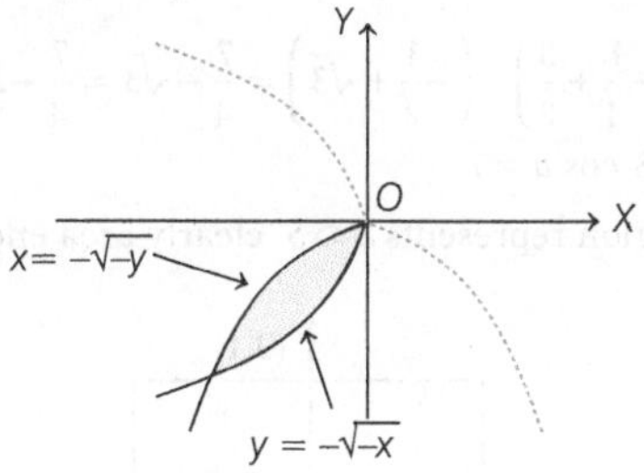

Since, $\quad A = \dfrac{16ab}{3}$

where, $\quad a = b = \dfrac{1}{4}$

$\therefore \quad A = \dfrac{1}{3}$

5. $\dfrac{f''(x)}{f'(x)} = 1.$

Integrating, $\ln(f'(x)) = x + C, \;\; f'(0) = 1 \Rightarrow C = 0$

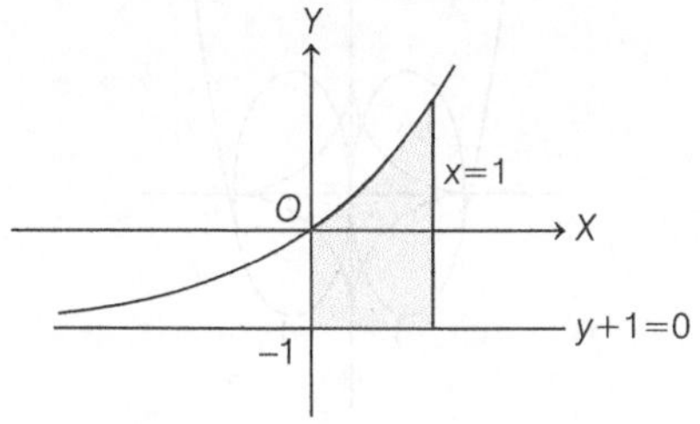

$f'(x) = e^x \Rightarrow f(x) = e^x + k, f(0) = 0 \Rightarrow k = -1$

$f(x) = e^x - 1$

Area $= \int_0^1 (e^x - 1 + 1)\, dx = [e^x]_0^1 = e - 1$

6. **Decoding the Question**
Use here, for point of inflection, $f''(x) = 0$

$y = xe^{-x}$

$y' = e^{-x} - xe^{-x} = (1-x)e^{-x}$ increasing for $x < 1$

$y'' = -e^{x} - [e^{-x} - xe^{-x}] = e^{-x}[-1-1+x] = (x-2)e^{-x}$

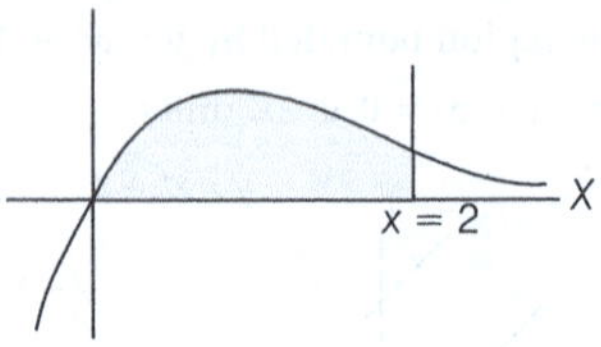

For point of inflection $y'' = 0 \Rightarrow x = 2$

$$A = \int_0^2 xe^{-x}dx = [-xe^{-x}]_0^2 + \int_0^2 e^{-x} = (-2e^{-2}) - (e^{-x})_0^2$$

$$= -2e^{-2} - (e^{-2} - 1) = 1 - e^{-2} - 2e^{-2} = 1 - 3e^{-2}$$

7. $(a, 0)$ lies on the given curve

$\therefore \quad 0 = \sin 2a - \sqrt{3}\sin a \Rightarrow \sin a = 0$ or $\cos a = \sqrt{3}/2$

$\Rightarrow \quad a = \dfrac{\pi}{6}$ (as $a > 0$ and the first point of intersection with positive X-axis)

and $A = \displaystyle\int_0^{\pi/6} (\sin 2x - \sqrt{3}\sin x)\,dx = \left(-\frac{\cos 2x}{2} + \sqrt{3}\cos x\right)_0^{\pi/6}$

$$= \left(-\frac{1}{4} + \frac{3}{2}\right) - \left(-\frac{1}{2} + \sqrt{3}\right) = \frac{7}{4} - \sqrt{3} = \frac{7}{4} - 2\cos a$$

$\Rightarrow \quad 4A + 8\cos a = 7$

8. Shaded region represents $S \cap S'$ clearly area enclosed is 2 sq units.

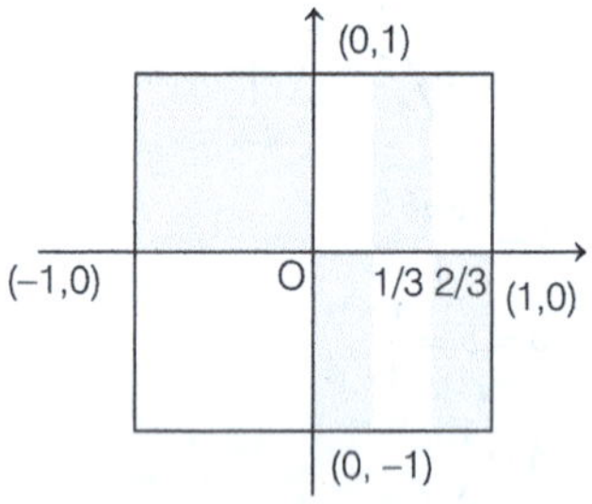

9. Required area is $2\left[\int_0^{\alpha} ex \ln x\, dx + \int_1^{\alpha} (1 - \sqrt{1-(x-1)^2})\, dx\right]$

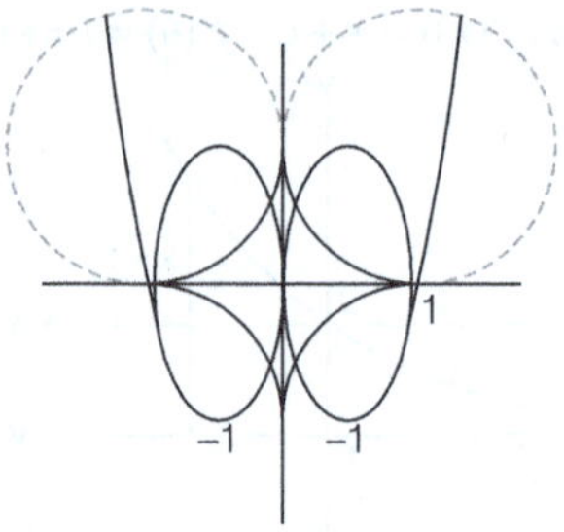

10. $P(|x|)$ has two roots only when $P(|b|) = 0$

$\Rightarrow \quad b^2 = 4 \Rightarrow |b| = 2$

$P(x) = x^3 - 12x + 16$

$\therefore$ The roots of $P(x)$ are $-4, 2$.

$$\int_{-4}^{2} P(x)dx = \int_{-4}^{2} (x^3 - 12x + 16)dx$$

$$= \frac{1}{4}(2^4 - 4^4) - \frac{12}{2}(2^2 - 4^2) + 16(6)$$

$$= -60 + 72 + 96 = 108$$

11.

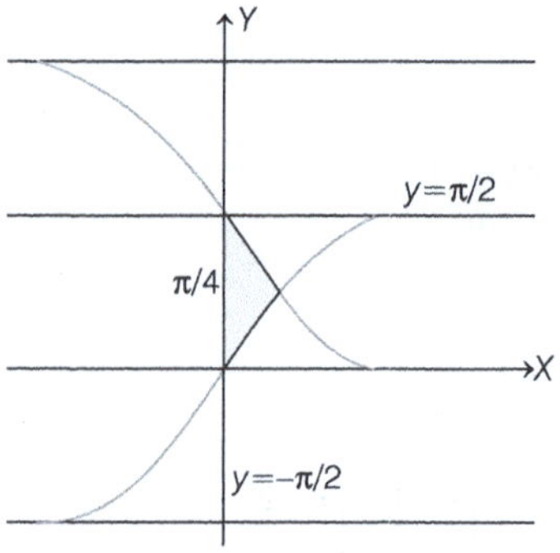

$$f(a) = \frac{1}{\ln\sqrt{1+a^2}} \int_0^a \frac{\ln(1+ax)}{1+x^2}dx$$

$$\int_0^a \frac{\ln(1+ax)}{1+x^2}dx = \tan^{-1} a \cdot \ln\sqrt{1+a^2} \qquad [\text{put } x = \tan\theta]$$

$\therefore \quad f(a) = \tan^{-1} a$

Curves, $y = \tan^{-1} x$, $y = \dfrac{\pi}{2} - \tan^{-1} x = \cot^{-1} x$

$$A = \int_0^{\pi/4} \tan y\, dy + \int_{\pi/4}^{\pi/2} \cot y\, dy = \ln 2$$

12. Given, $\quad 2x^2 + 6y^2 \ge 3 \qquad$ ...(i)

Area of ellipse $= \pi \times \dfrac{\sqrt{3}}{\sqrt{2}} \times \dfrac{1}{\sqrt{2}} = \dfrac{\pi\sqrt{3}}{2}$

$|x + y| \le 2 \Rightarrow -2 \le (x+y) \le 2 \qquad$ ...(ii)

$|x - y| \le 2 \Rightarrow -2 \le (x-y) \le 2 \qquad$ ...(iii)

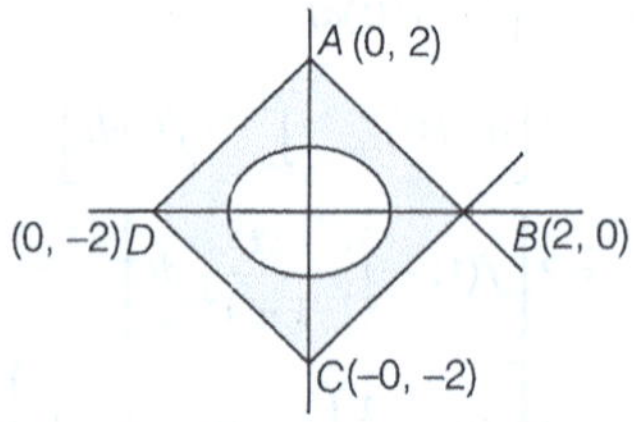

Area of $ABCD = (2\sqrt{2})^2 = 8$

$\therefore$ Required area $= \left(8 - \dfrac{\pi\sqrt{3}}{2}\right)$ sq units

13. We have, $f^3(x) = \displaystyle\int_0^x tf^2(t)dt$

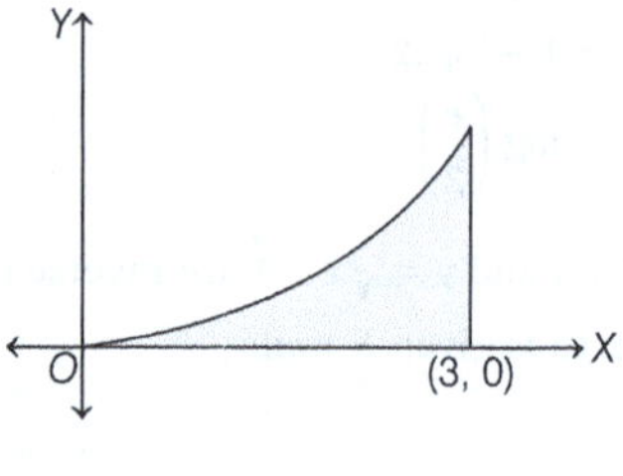

On differentiating w.r.t. x, we get

$\Rightarrow \quad 3f^2(x)\,f'(x) = xf^2(x) \Rightarrow f^2(x)\,[3f'(x) - x] = 0$

As, $f(x) \neq 0 \Rightarrow f'(x) = \dfrac{x}{3}$; $f(x) = \dfrac{x^2}{6} + C$

$$A = \frac{1}{6}\int_0^3 x^2 dx = \left[\frac{x^3}{18}\right]_0^3 = \frac{3}{2}$$

14. Required area is the area of shaded region $(APOQ)$

$= \text{Area of } \Delta OAQ + \text{Area of sector } (OAP)$

$$= \frac{1}{2} \times 4 \times 4\sqrt{3} + \frac{\pi(4 \times 4)}{6} = \left(\frac{8\pi}{3} + 8\sqrt{3}\right)$$

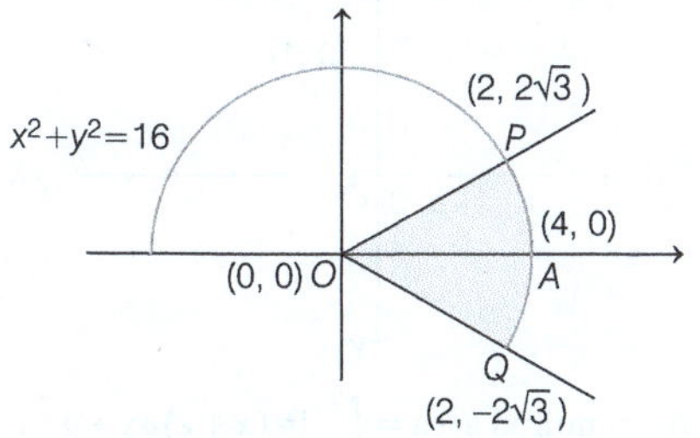

15. Clearly, we have

$$\frac{k \sin k}{2} + \int_k^{\pi} \sin x dx = 1 \qquad \left[\text{using } \int_0^{\pi} \sin x dx = 2\right]$$

$\Rightarrow \quad \dfrac{k \sin k}{2} - \cos x\Big|_k^{\pi} = 1$

$\Rightarrow \quad k \sin k + 2\,[1 + \cos k] = 2$

So, $\quad k \sin k + 2 \cos k = 0$

16.

> **Decoding the Question**
> Here, use king property, which is
> $\int_a^b f(x)\,dx = \int_a^b f(a + b - x)\,dx$

Let $A_n = \int_0^1 x^3 (1 - x^2)^n dx$

Put $x^2 = t \Rightarrow xdx = \dfrac{1}{2}dt$

$\therefore \quad A_n = \dfrac{1}{2}\int_0^1 t(1-t)^n dt = \dfrac{1}{2}\int_0^1 t^n (1-t) dt \qquad$ [using king property]

$\Rightarrow A_n = \dfrac{1}{2}\left(\dfrac{1}{n+1} - \dfrac{1}{n+2}\right) \Rightarrow \sum_{n=1}^{\infty} A_n = \dfrac{1}{4}$

17. Area of bounded region by $4\,|x - 2017^{2017}| + 5\,|y - 2017^{2017}| \leq 20$, is same as area of the region bounded by $4|x| + 5\,|y| \leq 20$.

$\Rightarrow \quad 4 \times \dfrac{1}{2} \times 4 \times 5 = 40$

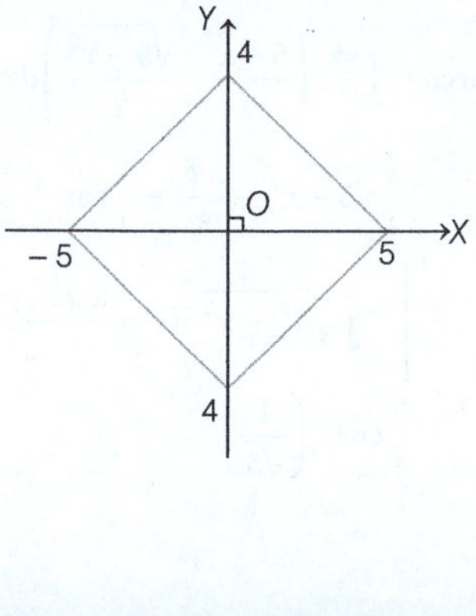

18. Clearly, required area $= 2\int_0^1 (f^{-1}(x) - x)dx$

$= 2k - 1$ sq units

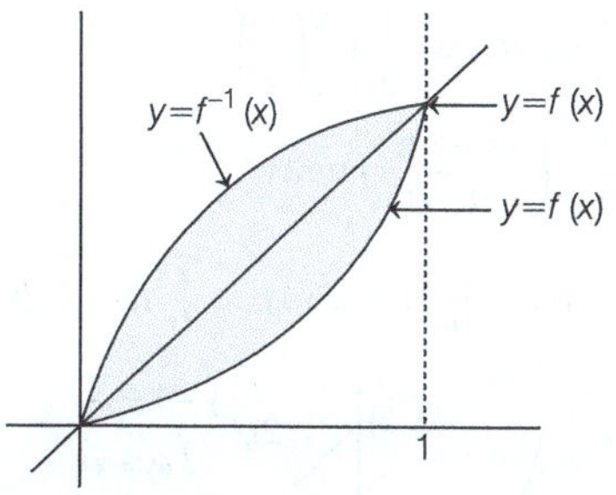

19. $A = 2\int_0^1 [y\sqrt{1-y^2} - (y^2 - 1)]\,dy = 2$

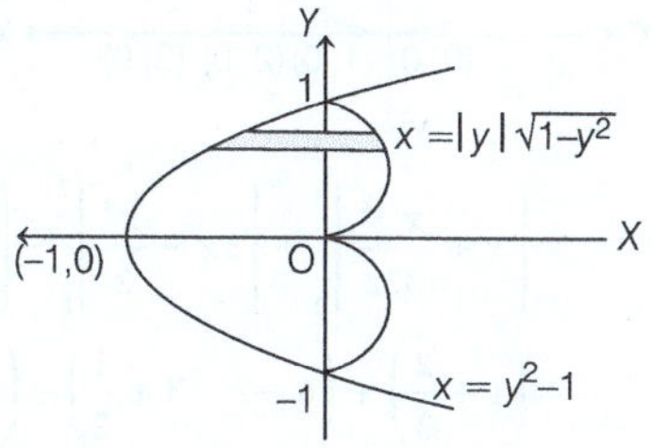

20. Required area, $A = \int_{\pi}^{2\pi} ((\sin x - x) + 2\pi)\,dx$

$$= \frac{\pi^2}{2} - 2 \text{ sq units}$$

21. The graph of $y = |x - 1|$ and $y = \sqrt{5 - x^2}$ are shown

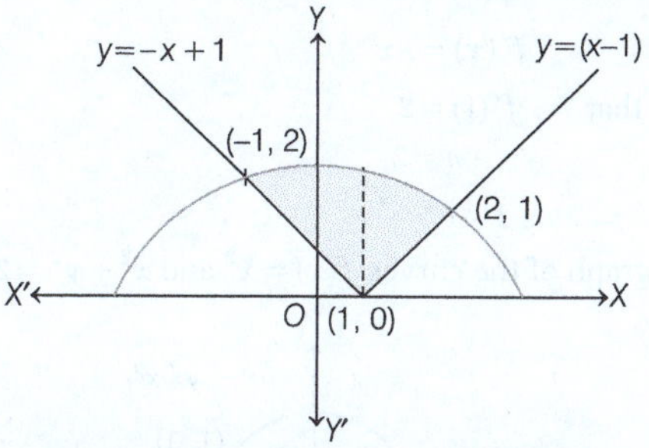

Let A be the area bounded by the given curves, then

$$A = \int_{-1}^{1} [\sqrt{5-x^2} - (-x+1)]dx + \int_1^2 [\sqrt{5-x^2} - (x-1)]dx$$

$$A = \int_{-1}^{1} \sqrt{5-x^2}\,dx + \int_1^2 \sqrt{5-x^2}\,dx + \int_{-1}^{1}(x-1)dx + \int_1^2 (-x+1)dx$$

$$= \int_{-1}^{2} \sqrt{5-x^2}\,dx + \left[\frac{x^2}{2} - x\right]_{-1}^{1} + \left[-\frac{x^2}{2} + x\right]_1^2$$

$$= \left[\frac{x}{2}\sqrt{5-x^2} + \frac{5}{2}\sin^{-1}\left(\frac{x}{\sqrt{5}}\right)\right]_{-1}^{2} + \left[\left(\frac{1}{2} - 1\right) - \left(\frac{1}{2} + 1\right)\right] + \left[(-2+2) - \left(-\frac{1}{2} + 1\right)\right]$$

$$= 1 + \frac{5}{2}\sin^{-1}\frac{2}{\sqrt{5}} + 1 + \frac{5}{2}\sin^{-1}\frac{1}{\sqrt{5}} - \frac{5}{2}$$

$$= -\frac{1}{2} + \frac{5}{2}\left[\sin^{-1}\left(\frac{2}{\sqrt{5}}\sqrt{1-\frac{1}{5}} + \frac{1}{\sqrt{5}}\sqrt{1-\frac{4}{5}}\right)\right]$$

$$= -\frac{1}{2} + \frac{5}{2}\sin^{-1}(1) = -\frac{1}{2} + \frac{5}{2}\left(\frac{\pi}{2}\right)$$

$$= \frac{5\pi}{4} - \frac{1}{2} = \left(\frac{5\pi - 2}{4}\right) \text{ sq units}$$

22. $\therefore$ Required area $= \int_0^1 (1+\sqrt{x})dx + \int_1^2 (3-x)dx - \int_0^2 \frac{x^2}{4}dx$

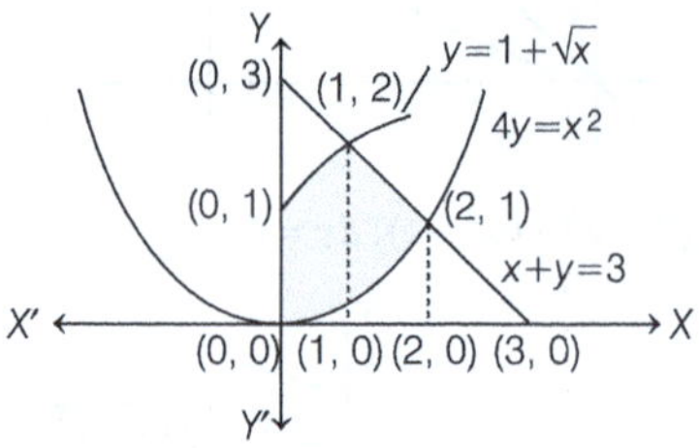

$$= \left[x + \frac{x^{3/2}}{3/2}\right]_0^1 + \left[3x - \frac{x^2}{2}\right]_1^2 - \left[\frac{x^3}{12}\right]_0^2$$

$$= \left(1 + \frac{2}{3}\right) + \left(6 - 2 - 3 + \frac{1}{2}\right) - \left(\frac{8}{12}\right)$$

$$= \frac{5}{3} + \frac{3}{2} - \frac{2}{3} = \frac{5}{2} \text{ sq units}$$

23. We have, $f\left(\frac{x}{y}\right) = \frac{f(x)}{f(y)}$

Let $f(x) = x^n$

$f'(x) = nx^{n-1}$

Given that $f'(1) = 2$

$\Rightarrow$ $n = 2$

So, $f(x) = x^2$

Now, graph of the curves $f(x) = x^2$ and $x^2 + y^2 = 2$ is

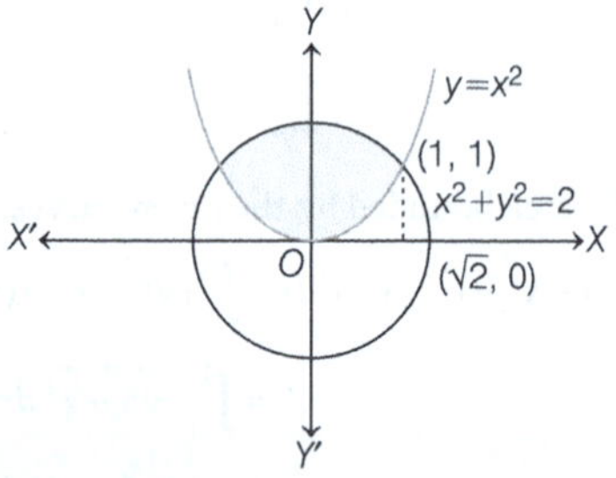

For intersection of $y = x^2$ and $x^2 + y^2 = 2$,

$$x^2 + x^4 = 2$$

On putting $x^2 = t$,

$$t^2 + t = 2$$

$\Rightarrow$ $t^2 + t - 2 = 0 \Rightarrow (t-1)(t+2) = 0$

$\Rightarrow$ $(x^2 - 1)(x^2 + 2) = 0 \Rightarrow x = \pm 1$

Now, required area

$$A = 2\int_0^1 [\sqrt{2 - x^2} - x^2]dx$$

$$= 2\left[\frac{x}{2}\sqrt{2 - x^2} + \frac{2}{2}\sin^{-1}\left(\frac{x}{\sqrt{2}}\right) - \frac{x^3}{3}\right]_0^1$$

$$= 2\left[\frac{1}{2} + \frac{\pi}{4} - \frac{1}{3}\right] = 2\left(\frac{1}{6} + \frac{\pi}{4}\right)$$

$$\therefore A = \left(\frac{1}{3} + \frac{\pi}{2}\right) \text{ sq units}$$

24. The given curve are $y = \ln(x + e)$ and $x = \ln\left(\frac{1}{y}\right)$

$\Rightarrow$ $\frac{1}{y} = e^x \Rightarrow y = e^{-x}$

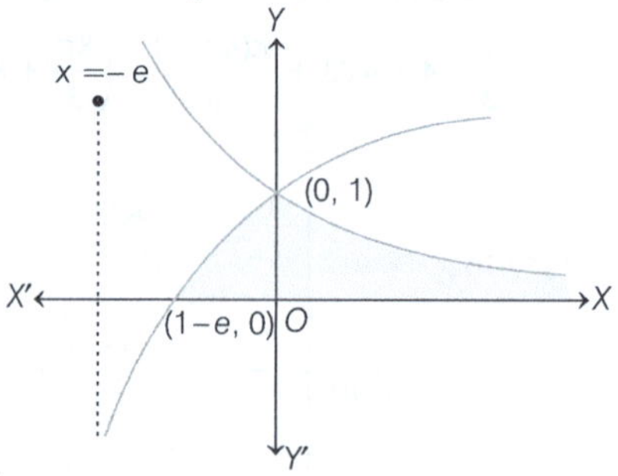

Hence, the required area $= \int_{1-e}^{0} \ln(x+e)dx + \int_0^\infty e^{-x}dx$

$$= \int_1^e \ln t\, dt + \int_0^\infty e^{-x}dx$$

[$\because$ putting $x + e = t$]

$$= [t\ln t - t]_1^e - [e^{-x}]_0^\infty$$

$$= (e - e) - (0 - 1) - [0 - 1] = 1 + 1 = 2$$

25. Given, ellipse $E : x^2 + 4y^2 = 5$

Differentiating w.r.t. x, we get

$$2x + 8y\frac{dy}{dx} = 0 \Rightarrow \frac{dy}{dx} = -\frac{2x}{8y} \Rightarrow \frac{dy}{dx} = \frac{-x}{4y}$$

At (1, 1), $\frac{dy}{dx} = -\frac{1}{4}$

Equation of tangent at (1, 1) is

$$y - 1 = -\frac{1}{4}(x - 1) \Rightarrow x + 4y = 5$$

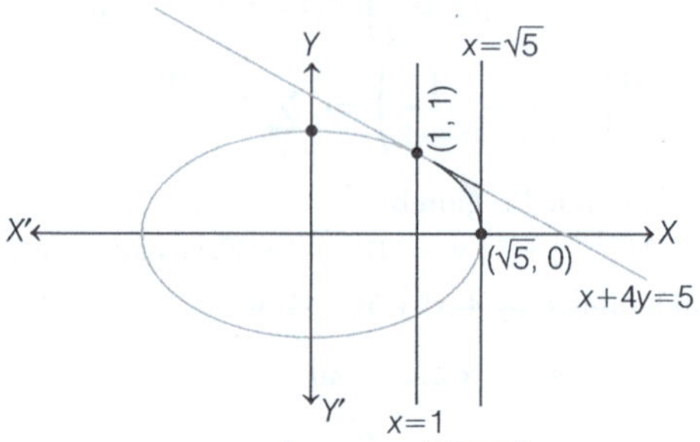

$\therefore$ Required area $= \int_1^{\sqrt{5}} \left(\frac{5 - x}{4} - \frac{\sqrt{5 - x^2}}{2}\right)dx$

$$= \left[\frac{5x}{4} - \frac{x^2}{8} - \frac{x}{4}\sqrt{5 - x^2} - \frac{5\pi}{8} + \frac{5}{4}\cos^{-1}\frac{x}{\sqrt{5}}\right]_1^{\sqrt{5}}$$

$$\left[\because \int \sqrt{a^2 - x^2}\, dx = \frac{x\sqrt{a^2 - x^2}}{2} + \frac{a^2}{2}\sin^{-1}\left(\frac{x}{a}\right)\right]$$

$$= \frac{5}{4}\sqrt{5} - \frac{5}{4} - \frac{5}{4}\cos^{-1}\left(\frac{1}{\sqrt{5}}\right)$$

By comparing, $\alpha = \frac{5}{4}$, $\beta = -\frac{5}{4}$ and $\gamma = -\frac{5}{4}$

$$\therefore \quad 4|\alpha+\beta+\gamma| = 4\left|\frac{5}{4}-\frac{5}{4}-\frac{5}{4}\right|$$

$$= 4\left|-\frac{5}{4}\right| = 5$$

26. We have, $f(x) = 2x^3 - 3x^2 - 12x$

$$f'(x) = 6x^2 - 6x - 12 = 6(x-2)(x+1)$$

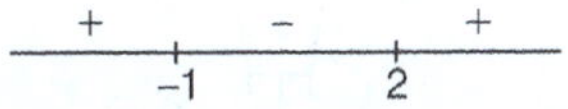

Hence, $x = -1$ is the point of local maxima and $x = 2$ is the point of local minima.

Graph of $f(x)$ is

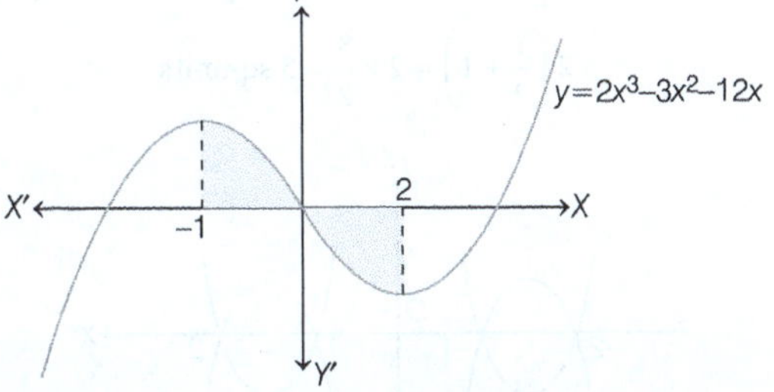

$$\text{Area, } A = \int_{-1}^{0} (2x^3 - 3x^2 - 12x)dx + \left|\int_0^2 (2x^3 - 3x^2 - 12x)dx\right|$$

$$= \left[\frac{x^4}{2} - x^3 - 6x^2\right]_{-1}^{0} + \left|\left[\frac{x^4}{2} - x^3 - 6x^2\right]_0^2\right|$$

$$= \frac{9}{2} + |-24| = \frac{9}{2} + 24 = \frac{57}{2}$$

Hence, $4A = 4 \times \frac{57}{2} = 114$

27. We have, $x^{2/5} + |y| = 1$

Then, curves are

$$x^{2/5} + y = 1 \text{ and } x^{2/5} - y = 1$$

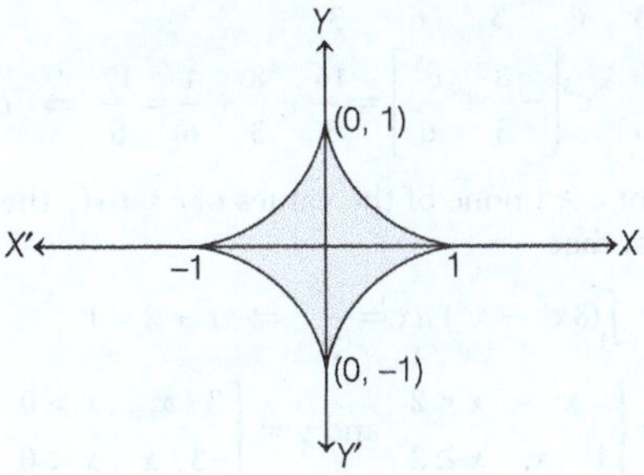

$$\therefore \text{ Required area} = 4\int_0^1 (1 - x^{2/5})dx = 4\left[x - \frac{5}{7}x^{7/5}\right]_0^1$$

$$= 4\left[1 - \frac{5}{7}\right]$$

$$= 4\left(\frac{2}{7}\right) = \frac{8}{7}$$

Hence, $p - q = 8 - 7 = 1$

28. Given, curves are

$$\begin{cases} y = \tan x, & -\frac{\pi}{3} \le x \le \frac{\pi}{3} \\ y = \cot x, & \frac{\pi}{6} \le x \le \frac{\pi}{2} \end{cases}$$

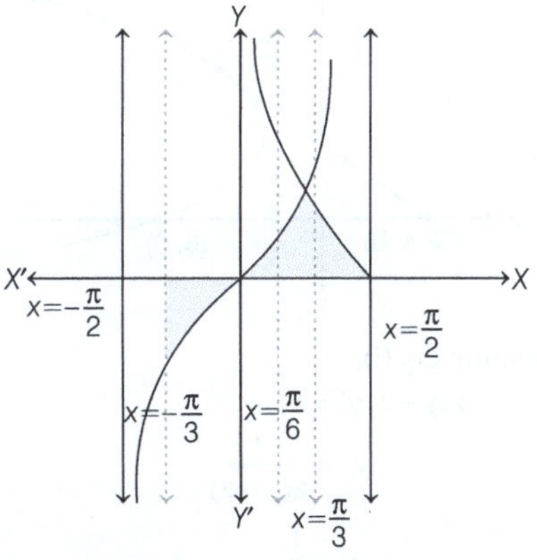

Hence, the required area

$$= \left|\int_{-\pi/3}^{0} \tan x\,dx\right| + \int_0^{\pi/4} \tan x\,dx + \int_{\pi/4}^{\pi/2} \cot x\,dx$$

$$= |[\log\sec x]_{-\pi/3}^{0}| + [\log\sec x]_0^{\pi/4} + [\log(\sin x)]_{\pi/4}^{\pi/2}$$

$$= \log(2) + \log(\sqrt{2}) - \log\left(\frac{1}{\sqrt{2}}\right)$$

$$= \log 2 + 2\log(\sqrt{2})$$

$$= \log 2 + \log 2$$

$$= (\log 4) \text{ sq units}$$

$$\Rightarrow \quad k = 4$$

29. Graph of given curves

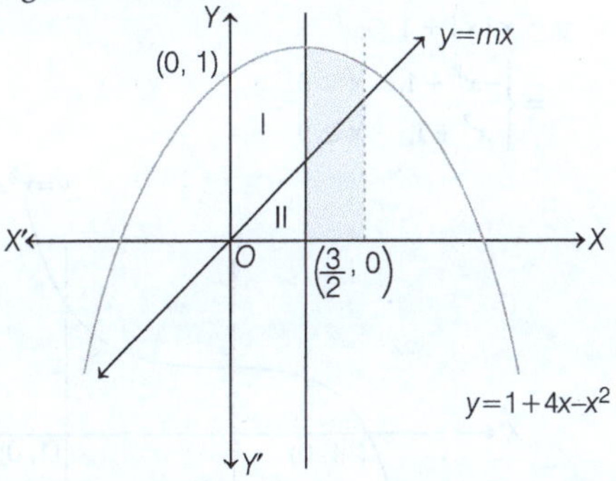

According to question,

$$\frac{1}{2}\int_0^{3/2} (1 + 4x - x^2)dx = \int_0^{3/2} mx\,dx$$

$$\Rightarrow \quad \frac{1}{2}\left[\left(x + 2x^2 - \frac{x^3}{3}\right)\right]_0^{3/2} = \frac{m}{2}[x^2]_0^{3/2}$$

$$\Rightarrow \quad \frac{3}{2} + \frac{9}{2} - \frac{9}{8} = \frac{9}{4}m$$

$$\Rightarrow \quad \frac{48-9}{8} = \frac{9}{4}m \Rightarrow m = \frac{39}{18} = \frac{13}{6}$$

Hence, $12m = 12 \times \frac{13}{6} = 26$

30. We have, $(y-2)^2 = (x-1)$ ...(i)

When $y = 3 \Rightarrow x = 2$

Then, point of contact is (2, 3)

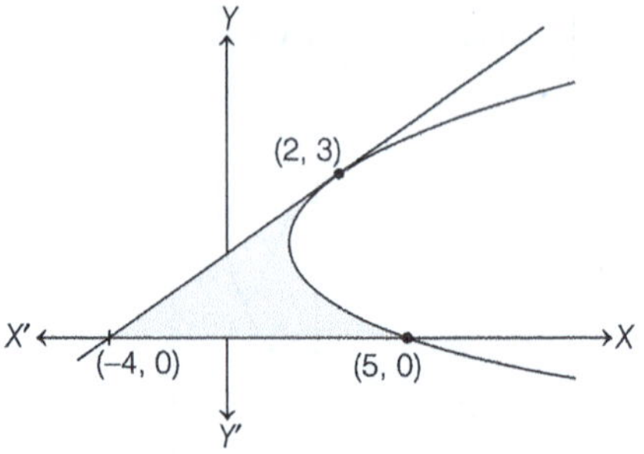

Differentiating Eq. (i),

$$2(y-2)y' = 1$$

$$\Rightarrow \quad y' = \frac{1}{2(y-2)}$$

At (2, 3), $\quad y' = \frac{1}{2}$

Equation of tangent is

$$(y-3) = \frac{1}{2}(x-2)$$

$$\Rightarrow \quad x - 2y + 4 = 0$$

Now, area of required region

$$= \int_0^3 [((y-2)^2+1)-(2y-4)]dy$$

$$= \int_0^3 (y^2-6y+9)dy = \left[\frac{y^3}{3} - 3y^2 + 9y\right]_0^3$$

$$= 9 - 27 + 27 = 9 \text{ sq units}$$

31. Let $\quad y = x|x| + 1$

$$= \begin{cases} -x^2+1, & x < 0 \\ x^2+1, & x \ge 0 \end{cases}$$

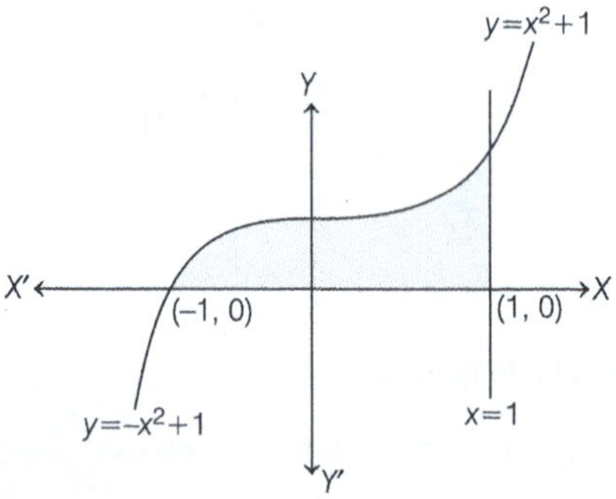

$$\therefore \text{ Required area} = \int_{-1}^0 (-x^2+1)dx + \int_0^1 (x^2+1)dx$$

$$= \left[-\frac{x^3}{3} + x\right]_{-1}^0 + \left[\frac{x^3}{3} + x\right]_0^1$$

$$= 0 - \left(\frac{1}{3} + (-1)\right) + \left(\frac{1}{3} + 1\right)$$

$$= -\frac{1}{3} + 1 + \frac{1}{3} + 1 = 2 \text{ sq units}$$

32. Given, curves are $y = \ln|x|$ and $y = 1 - |x|$

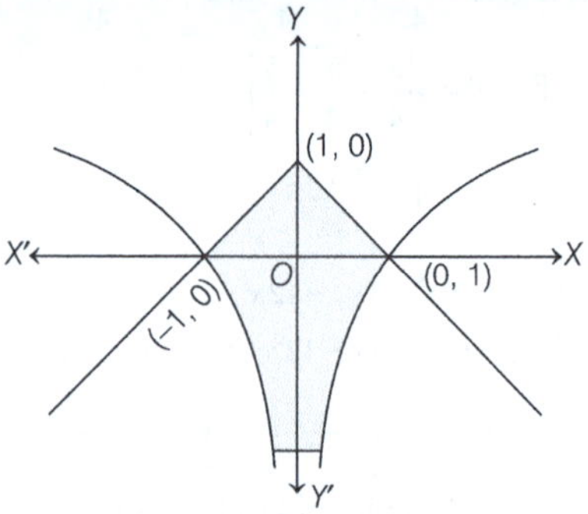

Hence, the required area

$$= 2\left[\frac{1}{2} \times 1 \times 1 + \int_{-\infty}^0 e^y dy\right]$$

$$= 2\left(\frac{1}{2} + 1\right) = 2 \times \frac{3}{2} = 3 \text{ sq units}$$

33.

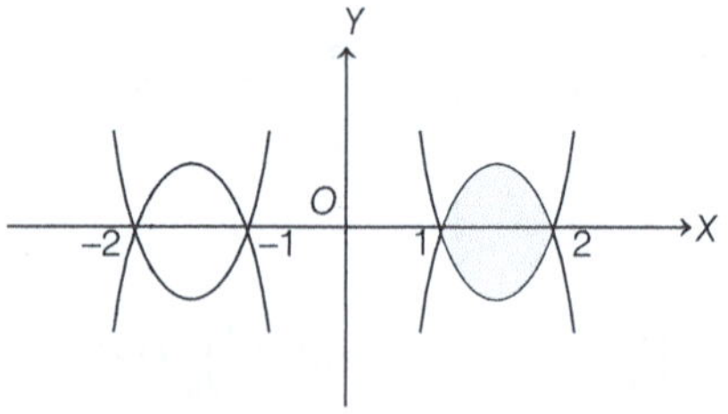

Area is given by $A = 2\int_0^1 (x^2 - 3x + 2)\, dx = \frac{5}{3}$

$$\Rightarrow \quad 3A + 2 = 3 \cdot \frac{5}{3} + 2 = 7$$

34.

> **Decoding the Question**
> On solving this question, we use two conditions, first $c < 1$ and second $c \ge 1$.

For $c < 1$; $\int_c^1 (8x^2 - x^5)\, dx = \frac{16}{3}$

$$\Rightarrow \quad \frac{8}{3} - \frac{1}{6} - \frac{8c^3}{3} - \frac{c^6}{6} = \frac{16}{3}$$

$$\Rightarrow \quad c^3\left[-\frac{8}{3} + \frac{c^3}{6}\right] = \frac{16}{3} - \frac{8}{3} + \frac{1}{6} = \frac{17}{6} \Rightarrow c = -1$$

Again, for $c \ge 1$ none of the values of c satisfy the required condition that

$$\int_1^c (8x^2 - x^5)\, dx = \frac{16}{3} \Rightarrow c + 2 = 1$$

35. $$y = \begin{cases} x; & x < 2 \\ 4 - x; & x \ge 2 \end{cases} \text{ and } y = \begin{cases} 3/x; & x > 0 \\ -3/x & x < 0 \end{cases}$$

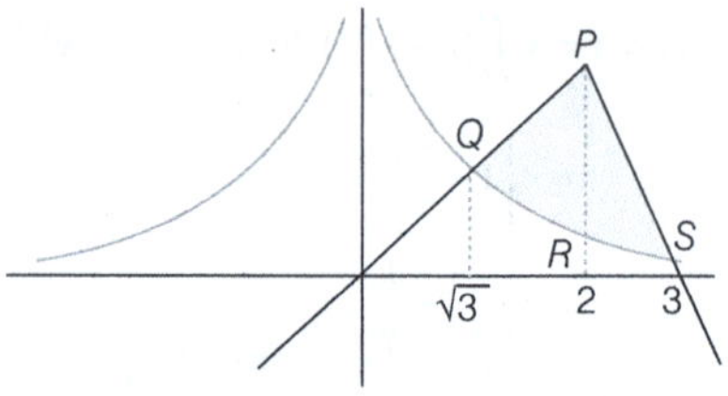

Required area = $PQRSP$

$= \text{Area } PQRP + \text{Area } PRSP$

$$= \left|\int_{\sqrt{3}}^{2}\left(x - \frac{3}{x}\right)dx\right| + \left|\int_{2}^{3}\left((4-x) - \frac{3}{x}\right)dx\right|$$

$$= \frac{4 - 3\ln 3}{2} \text{ sq units}$$

$\therefore \quad k = 4$

36. The shaded region for given equations is

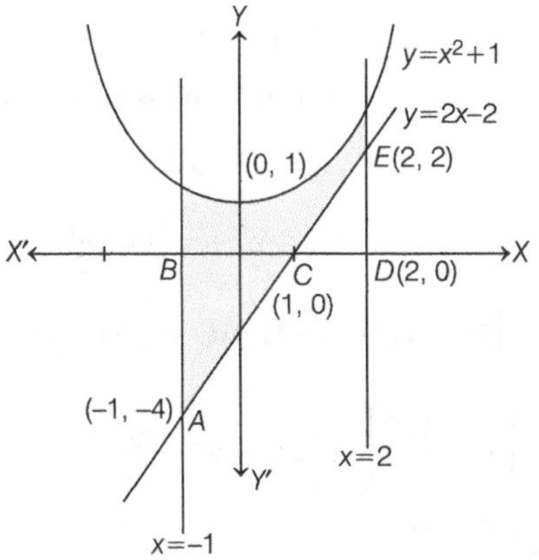

Area, $A_1 = \text{ar}(\Delta ABC) = \frac{1}{2}(2)(4) = 4$ sq units

Area, $A_2 = \text{ar}(CDE)$

$$A_2 = \frac{1}{2} \times 1 \times 2 = 1 \text{ sq unit}$$

and area of region between parabola and X-axis

$$A_3 = \int_{-1}^{2}(x^2+1)dx = \left[\frac{x^3}{3} + x\right]_{-1}^{2}$$

$$= \left(\frac{8}{3}+2\right) - \left(\frac{-1}{3} - 1\right) = 6$$

$\therefore$ Required area $= 6 + 4 - 1 = 9$ sq units

37. Given, curve $y^2 = 4(x-2)$ and line $y = 2x - 8$

Firstly, we draw the graph

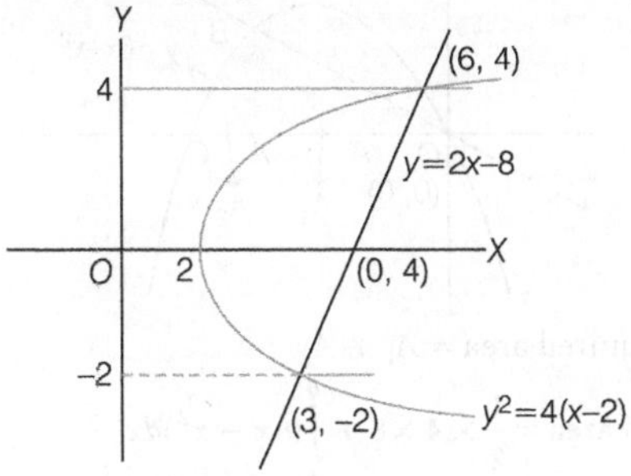

$\therefore$ Required area $= \int_{-2}^{4} x_l dy - \int_{-2}^{4} x_P dy$

$$= \int_{-2}^{4}\left[\left(\frac{(y+8)}{2}\right) - \left(\frac{y^2}{4} + 2\right)\right]dy$$

$$= \left[\frac{1}{2}\left(\frac{y^2}{2} + 8y\right) - \left(\frac{y^3}{12} + 2y\right)\right]_{-2}^{4}$$

$$= \left[\frac{y^2}{4} - \frac{y^3}{12} + 2y\right]_{-2}^{4}$$

$$= \left[\left(4 - \frac{16}{3} + 8\right) - \left(1 + \frac{2}{3} - 4\right)\right]$$

$= 9$ sq units

38.

> **Decoding the Question**
>
> For solving such question, we use two cases, first case $y > 0$ and second case $y < 0$.

Region $y^2 \le 4x,\ x < 4$

$$\frac{xy(x-1)(x-2)}{(x-3)(x-4)} > 0$$

Case I $y > 0$

The inequality becomes,

$$\frac{x(x-1)(x-2)}{(x-3)(x-4)} > 0$$

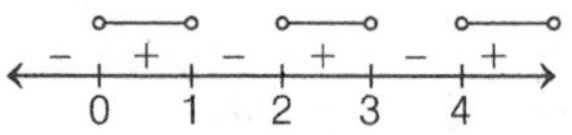

$x \in (0, 1) \cup (2, 3)$

Case II $y < 0$

$$\Rightarrow \quad \frac{x(x-1)(x-2)}{(x-3)(x-4)} < 0$$

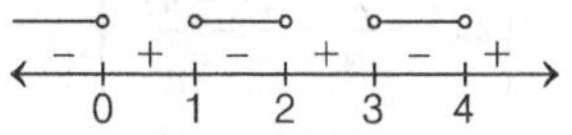

$x \in (1, 2) \cup (3, 4)$

Graph

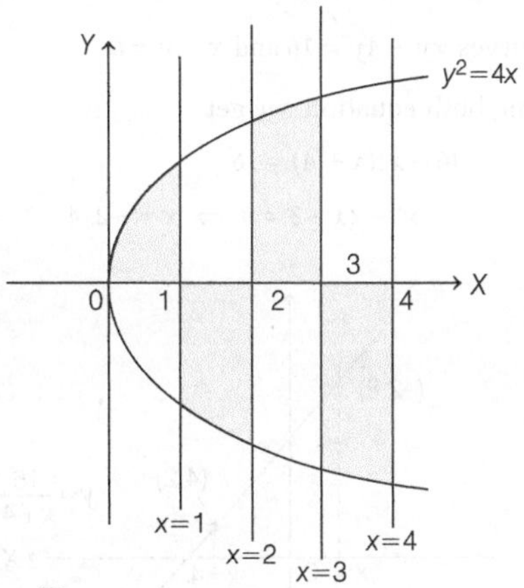

$y = 2\sqrt{x}\, dx$

$\therefore \text{Area} = \int_0^4 2\sqrt{x}$ [due to symmetry]

$$= 2\frac{x^{3/2}}{3/2} = \frac{4}{3}(4)^{3/2} = \frac{32}{3}$$

39. The given curve are

$C_1 : y = 4x - x^2$

So, $\quad C_1 : y = 4 - (x-2)^2$

$C_2 : (x-4)^2 = 3y$

$C_1 : y = -(x^2 - 4x)$

$C_1 : y = -(x^2 - 4x + 4 - 4)$

$C_1 : y = 4 - (x-2)^2$

$C_1 : (x-2)^2 = -(y-4)$

Solving two curves

$$3(4x - x^2) = (x-4)^2 \Rightarrow 4x^2 - 20x + 16 = 0$$

$$\Rightarrow \quad x^2 - 5x + 4 = 0 \Rightarrow x = 1, 4$$

Both curves intersect at (1, 3) and (4, 0).

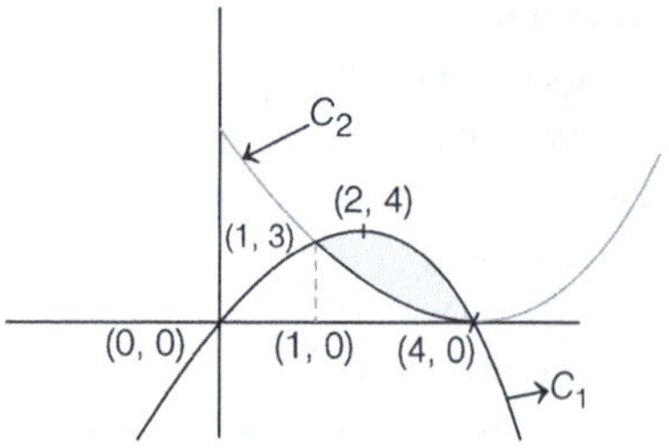

$$\therefore \text{ Shaded area} = \int_1^4 (y_{C_1} - y_{C_2})\, dx$$

$$= \int_1^4 \left((4x - x^2) - \frac{(x-4)^2}{3} \right) dx$$

$$= \left[2x^2 - \frac{x^3}{3} - \frac{(x-4)^3}{9} \right]_1^4$$

$$= \left(32 - \frac{64}{3} - 0 \right) - \left(2 - \frac{1}{3} + 3 \right) = 6 \text{ units}$$

40. Given, curves $xy + 4y = 16$ and $x + y = 6$

On solving both equation, we get

$$(6 - x)(x + 4) = 16$$

$$\Rightarrow \quad x^2 - 2x - 8 = 0 \Rightarrow x = -2, 4$$

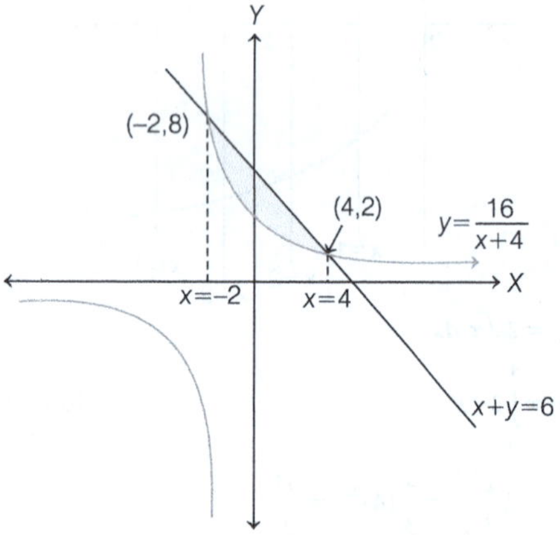

$$\therefore \text{ Required area} = \int_{-2}^{4} \left[(6 - x) - \left(\frac{16}{x+4} \right) \right] dx$$

$$= \left[6x - \frac{x^2}{2} - 16 \log_e (x+4) \right]_{-2}^{4} = 30 - 32 \log_e 2$$

41. To drawn the region, we consider equations as

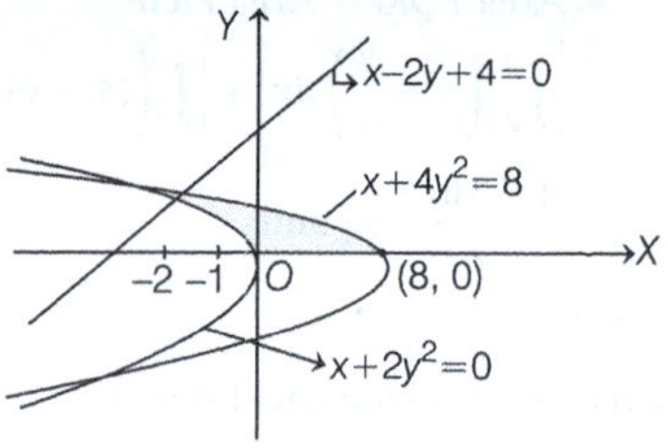

$$x - 2y + 4 = 0 \quad \text{...(i)}$$

and $$x + 2y^2 = 0 \Rightarrow y^2 = -\frac{1}{2}x \quad \text{...(ii)}$$

and $$x + 4y^2 = 8$$

$$\Rightarrow \quad y^2 = -\frac{1}{4}(x - 8) \quad \text{...(iii)}$$

$$\text{Area, } A = \int_0^1 [(8 - 4y^2) - (-2y^2)] dy + \int_1^{3/2} [(8 - 4y^2) - (2y - 4)] dy$$

$$= \left[8y - \frac{2y^3}{3} \right]_0^1 + \left[12y - y^2 - \frac{4y^3}{3} \right]_1^{3/2}$$

$$= \frac{107}{12} = \frac{m}{n}$$

Hence, $m + n = 107 + 12 = 119$

42. Given, curves $\quad y = 2x \quad$ ...(i)

and $\quad y = 6x - x^2 \quad$ ...(ii)

On solving Eqs. (i) and (ii), we get

$$2x = 6x - x^2$$

$$\Rightarrow \quad x^2 - 4x = 0$$

$$\Rightarrow \quad x(x-4) = 0 \Rightarrow x = 0, 4$$

$$\therefore \quad y = 0, 8$$

$$\therefore \quad (x, y) \equiv (0, 0) \text{ or } (4, 8)$$

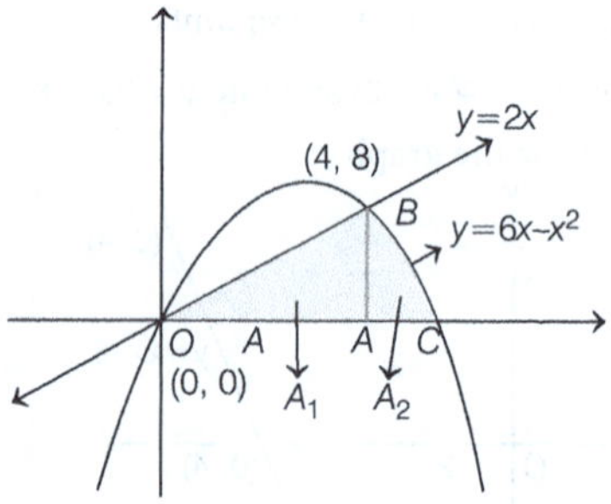

Now, required area $= A_1 + A_2$

$$\text{Required area} = \frac{1}{2} \times 4 \times 8 + \int_4^6 (6x - x^2) dx$$

$$\Rightarrow \quad A = 16 + \left[3x^2 - \frac{x^3}{3} \right]_4^6$$

$$\Rightarrow \quad A = 16 + \left(\frac{28}{3} \right)$$

$$\therefore \quad 12A = (12 \times 16 + 28 \times 4)$$

$$= 304 \text{ sq units}$$

43. Given equation of circle, $x^2 + y^2 = 169$

Centre = (0, 0) and Radius = 13

$\therefore$ Intersecting point of circle and line is (5, 12)

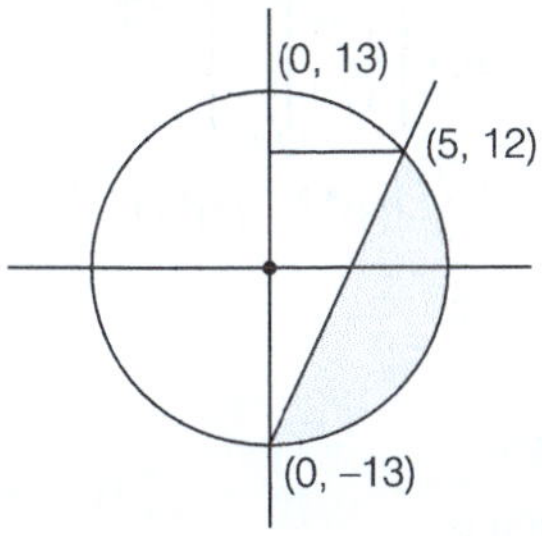

$\therefore$ Required area

$$= \frac{\pi(13)^2}{2} - \left[\frac{1}{2} \times 25 \times 5 + \int_{12}^{13} \sqrt{(169 - y^2)}\, dy\right]$$

$$= \frac{169\pi}{2} - \left[\frac{125}{2} + \left\{\frac{y}{2}\sqrt{169 - y^2} + \frac{169}{2}\sin^{-1}\left(\frac{y}{13}\right)\right\}_{12}^{13}\right]$$

$$= \frac{169\pi}{2} - \frac{125}{2} - \left[\frac{169}{2} \times \frac{\pi}{2} - 6 \times 5 - \frac{169}{2}\sin^{-1}\frac{12}{13}\right]$$

$$= \frac{169\pi}{4} - \frac{65}{2} + \frac{169}{2}\sin^{-1}\frac{12}{13}$$

$\therefore \alpha = 169, \beta = 2$

$\therefore \alpha + \beta = 171$

44. Region $= \{(x, y) : 0 \le x \le 3, 0 \le y \le \min(x^2 + 2, 2x + 2)\}$

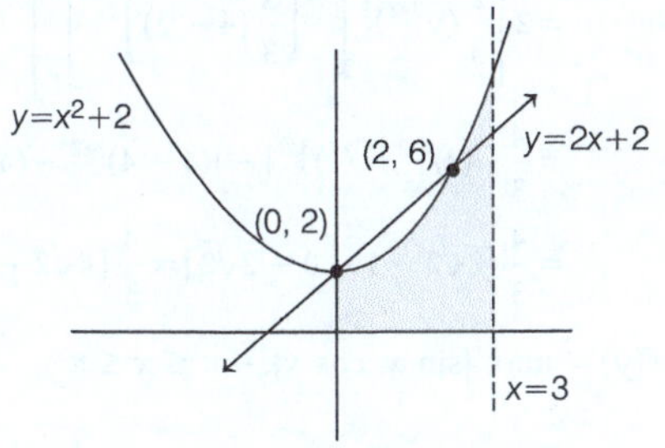

$$A = \int_0^2 x^2 + 2 + \int_2^3 2x + 2$$

$$= \left[\frac{x^3}{3} + 2x\right]_0^2 + [x^2 + 2x]_2^3$$

$$= \frac{8}{3} + 4 + [9 + 6 - 4 - 4]$$

$$= \frac{8}{3} + 4 + 7 = 11 + \frac{8}{3}$$

$\therefore\ 12A = 12 \times 11 + 32 = 132 + 32 = 164$

45. Parabola $(y - 2)^2 = x - 1$

Line $\quad x - 2y + 4 = 0 \quad$ ...(i)

$\Rightarrow \quad x = 2(y - 2)$

Let $\quad y - 2 = Y$

$\Rightarrow \quad Y^2 = x - 1$ and $x = 2Y$

Solving $\quad Y^2 = 2Y - 1 \Rightarrow (Y - 1)^2 = 0$

$\Rightarrow \quad Y = 1 \Rightarrow y - 2 = 1 \Rightarrow y = 3$

and $\quad x = 2 \quad$ [from Eq (i)]

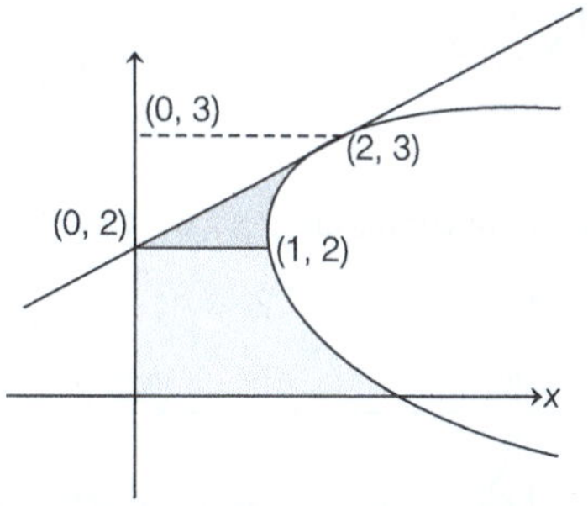

Enclosed area w.r.t. X-axis

$$= \int_0^3 x\, dy - \text{Area of triangle} = \int_0^3 [(y - 2)^2 + 1] - \frac{1}{2} \times 1 \times 2$$

$$= \left[\frac{(y - 2)^3}{3} + y\right]_0^3 - 1 = \frac{1}{3} + 3 - \left(-\frac{8}{3}\right) - 1 = 6 - 1 = 5$$

46. We have, $y = x^2$

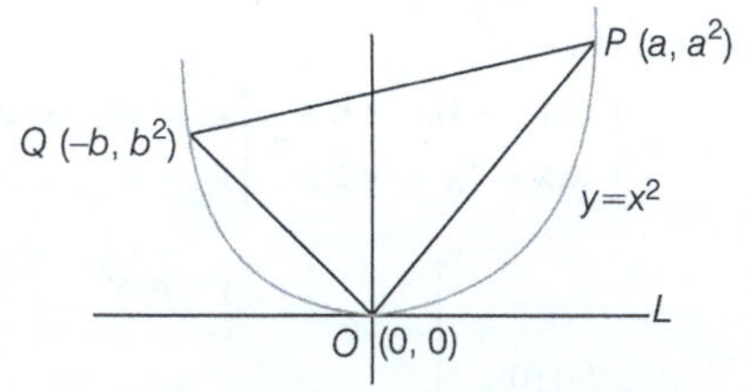

$$PQ, (y - b^2) = \frac{a^2 - b^2}{a + b}(x + b)$$

$$PQ, (a - b)x - y + ab = 0$$

Now, $\quad S_1 = \int_{-b}^{a} [(a - b)x + ab] - [x^2]dx$

$$S_1 = \left[(a - b)\frac{x^2}{2} + abx - \frac{x^3}{3}\right]_{-b}^{a}$$

$$S_1 = (a - b)\frac{(a^2 - b^2)}{2} + ab(a + b) - \frac{1}{3}[a^3 + b^3]$$

$$S_1 = \frac{(a + b)}{6}[a^2 + b^2 + 2ab]$$

$$\Rightarrow \quad S_1 = \frac{(a + b)^3}{6}$$

$$\text{Area of } \Delta OPQ = S_2 = \frac{1}{2}\begin{vmatrix} 0 & 0 & 1 \\ a & a^2 & 1 \\ -b & b^2 & 1 \end{vmatrix} = \frac{1}{2}[ab(a + b)]$$

$$\text{Now, } \frac{S_1}{S_2} = \frac{\frac{(a + b)^3}{6}}{\frac{ab}{2}(a + b)} \Rightarrow \frac{1}{3ab}(a + b)^2 = \frac{1}{3}\left[\frac{a}{b} + \frac{b}{a} + 2\right]$$

as, $a, b > 0$

So, using AM, GM

$$\frac{\frac{a}{b} + \frac{b}{a}}{2} \ge \left(\frac{a}{b} \times \frac{b}{a}\right)^{\frac{1}{2}} \Rightarrow \frac{a}{b} + \frac{b}{a} \ge 2$$

Minimum $\left(\dfrac{S_1}{S_2}\right) = \dfrac{4}{3}$

$\therefore \quad m = 4, n = 3$

So, $\quad m + n = 7$

47. Given equation of curves are $y = |x - 1| + |x - 2|$ and $y = 3$

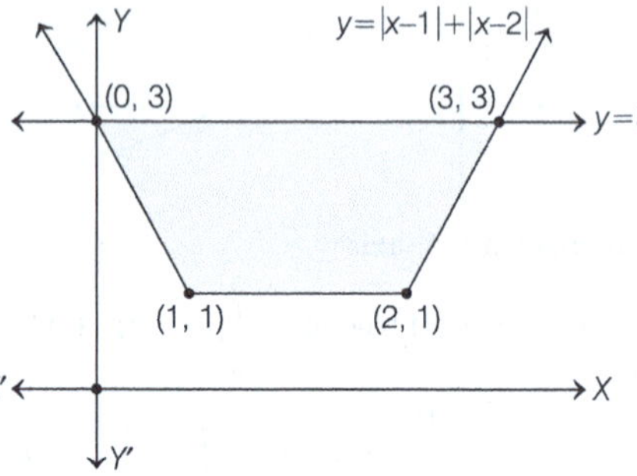

Now, the required area = Area of trapezium

$$= \frac{1}{2}(1 + 3) \times 2 = 4$$

48. We have, $y = x|x - 3|$

$$= \begin{cases} -x(x-3), & x < 3 \\ x(x-3), & x \ge 3 \end{cases} = \begin{cases} 3x - x^2, & x < 3 \\ x^2 - 3x, & x \ge 3 \end{cases}$$

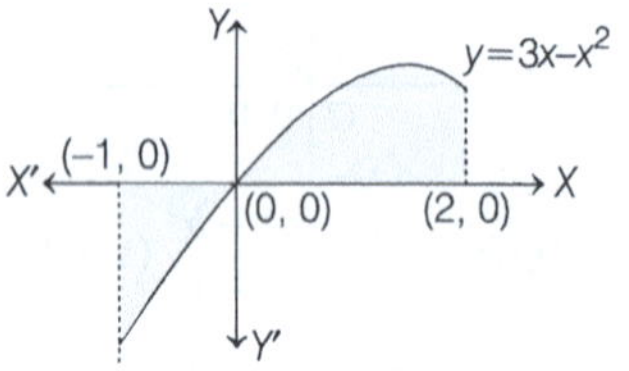

$\therefore$ Required area, $A = \int_{-1}^{0} -(3x - x^2)dx + \int_0^2 (3x - x^2)\, dx$

$$= -\left[\frac{3x^2}{2} - \frac{x^3}{3}\right]_{-1}^{0} + \left[\frac{3x^2}{2} - \frac{x^3}{3}\right]_0^2$$

$$= -\left[0 - \left(\frac{3}{2} + \frac{1}{3}\right)\right] + \left[\left(6 - \frac{8}{3}\right) - 0\right]$$

$$= \frac{3}{2} + \frac{1}{3} + 6 - \frac{8}{3} = \frac{9 + 2 + 36 - 16}{6} = \frac{31}{6}$$

$\therefore \qquad 12A = 12 \times \dfrac{31}{6} = 62$

49. Given equation of curves are

$$y^2 = 8x \qquad \text{...(i)}$$

$$y = x \qquad \text{...(ii)}$$

and $$x = 2 \qquad \text{...(iii)}$$

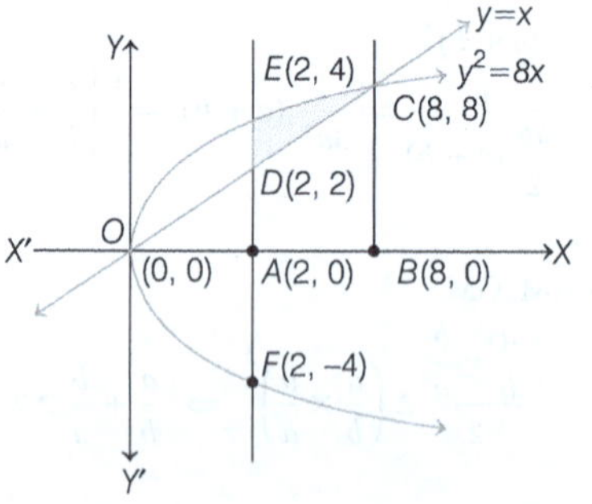

Hence, area of shaded portion is

$$\int_2^8 (\sqrt{8x} - x)\,dx = \int_2^8 2\sqrt{2}\,\sqrt{x}\,dx - \int_2^8 x\,dx$$

$$= 2\sqrt{2}\left[\frac{x^{3/2}}{3/2}\right]_2^8 - \left[\frac{x^2}{2}\right]_2^8$$

$$= \frac{4\sqrt{2}}{3}[(8)^{3/2} - (2)^{3/2}] - \frac{1}{2}[(8)^2 - (2)^2]$$

$$= \frac{22}{3} = \alpha \qquad \text{[given]}$$

Hence, $3\alpha = 22$

50. The given region is

$\{(x, y), x^2 \le y \le |x^2 - 4|, y \ge 1\}$

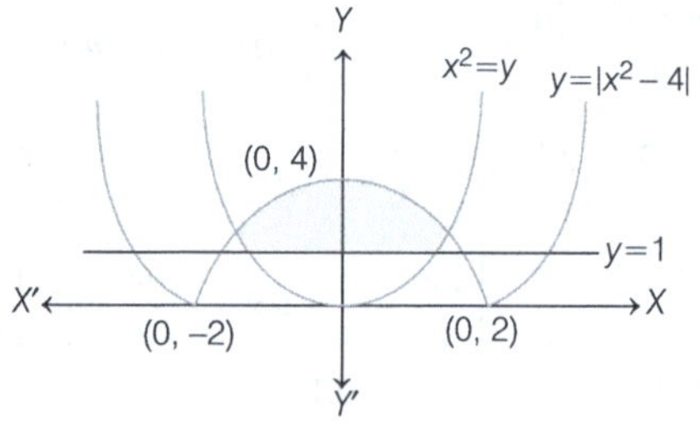

Then, area of required shaded region is

$$2\left[\int_1^2 \sqrt{y}dy + \int_2^4 \sqrt{4 - y}dy\right]$$

$$= 2\left[\frac{2}{3}(y^{3/2})_1^2 \left[-\left(\frac{2}{3}(4 - y)\right)^{3/2}\right]_2^4\right]$$

$$= \frac{4}{3}[\{(2)^{3/2} - (1)^{3/2}\} - \{(4 - 4)^{3/2} - (4 - 2)^{3/2}\}]$$

$$= \frac{4}{3}[2\sqrt{2} - 1 - 0 + 2\sqrt{2}] = \frac{4}{3}[4\sqrt{2} - 1]$$

51. Given, $f(y) = \max\{\sin x, \cos x\}, -\pi \le x \le \pi$

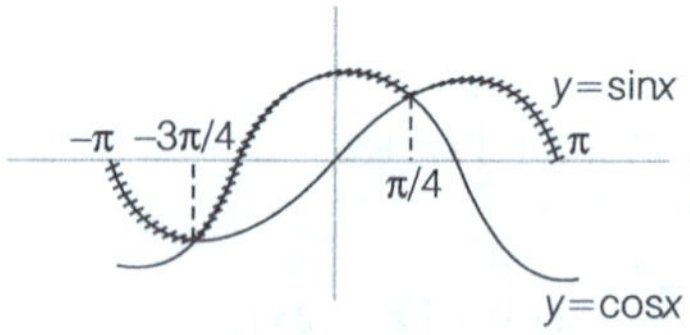

Thus, required area of the region enclosed by the curve $f(x)$, $-\pi \le x \le \pi$, and the X-axis is

$$\int_{-\pi}^{-3\pi/4} (-\sin x)\,dx + \int_{-3\pi/4}^{-\pi/2} (-\cos x)\,dx$$

$$+ \int_{-\pi/2}^{\pi/4} (\cos x)\,dx + \int_{\pi/4}^{\pi} \sin x\,dx$$

$$= (\cos x)_{-\pi}^{-3\pi/4} - (\sin x)_{-3\pi/4}^{-\pi/2} + (\sin x)_{-\pi/2}^{\pi/4} - (\cos x)_{\pi/4}^{\pi}$$

$$= \left(-\frac{1}{\sqrt{2}} + 1\right) - \left(-1 + \frac{1}{\sqrt{2}}\right) + \left(\frac{1}{\sqrt{2}} + 1\right) - \left(-1 - \frac{1}{\sqrt{2}}\right)$$

$$= -\frac{1}{\sqrt{2}} + 1 + 1 - \frac{1}{\sqrt{2}} + \frac{1}{\sqrt{2}} + 1 + 1 + \frac{1}{\sqrt{2}}$$

$$= 4$$

52. Given region is, $y = x^3 \Rightarrow \dfrac{dy}{dx} = 3x^2$

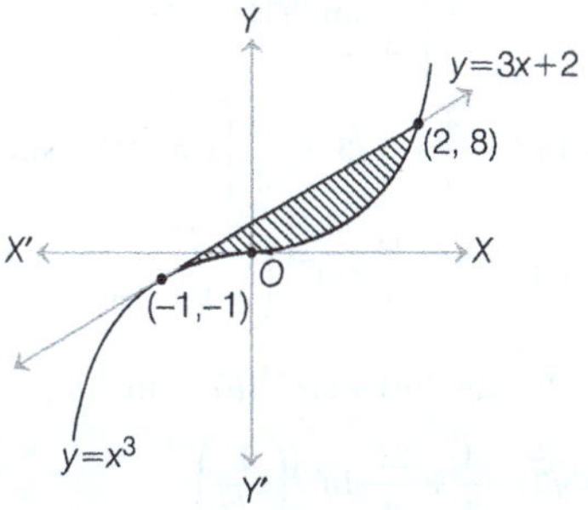

Slope of tangent at $(-1, -1) = 3(-1)^2 = 3$

So, equation of tangent : $y + 1 = 3(x + 1)$

$\Rightarrow \quad 3x + 2 = y$

Solving with $y = x^3$,

$$3x + 2 = x^3 \Rightarrow x^3 - 3x - 2 = 0$$

$$\Rightarrow \quad (x+1)(x^2 - x - 2) = 0$$

$$\Rightarrow \quad (x+1)^2(x-2) = 0 \Rightarrow x = -1, 2$$

$$\text{Required area} = \int_{-1}^{2} (3x + 2 - x^3)\,dx = \left[\frac{3x^2}{2} + 2x - \frac{x^4}{4}\right]_{-1}^{2}$$

$$= \left[\frac{3 \cdot 2^2}{2} + 2 \cdot 2 - \frac{2^4}{4}\right] - \left(\frac{3 \cdot (-1)^2}{2} + 2(-1) - \frac{(-1)^4}{4}\right)$$

$$= \frac{27}{4} \text{ sq units}$$

53. We have, $x^2 + (y-2)^2 \le 2^2$ and $x^2 \ge 2y$

Solving the given equation of parabola and circle, we get

$$2y + (y-2)^2 = 4$$

$$y = 0 \text{ or } 2$$

If $y = 0$, then $x = 0$

and if $y = 2$, then $x = \pm 2$

The intersecting point of circle and parabola are $(0, 0), (-2, 2), (2, 2)$.

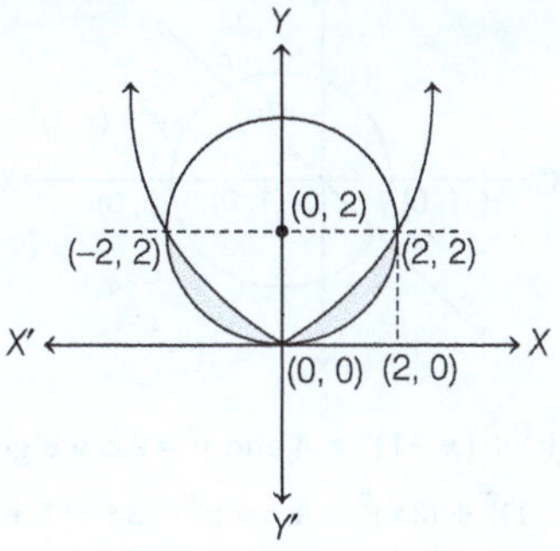

Area of the shaded region

$$= 2\int_0^2 \left[\frac{x^2}{2} - (\sqrt{4 - x^2} + 2)\right] dx$$

$$= 2\left|\left[\frac{x^3}{6} - \frac{x}{2}\sqrt{4 - x^2} - 2\sin^{-1}\left(\frac{x}{2}\right) - 2x\right]_0^2\right|$$

$$= 2\left|\left[\frac{8}{6} - 2 \times \frac{\pi}{2} - 4\right]\right|$$

$$= 2\left|\left[\frac{4}{3} - \pi - 4\right]\right| = 2\pi + \frac{16}{3} \text{ sq units}$$

54. Given region is

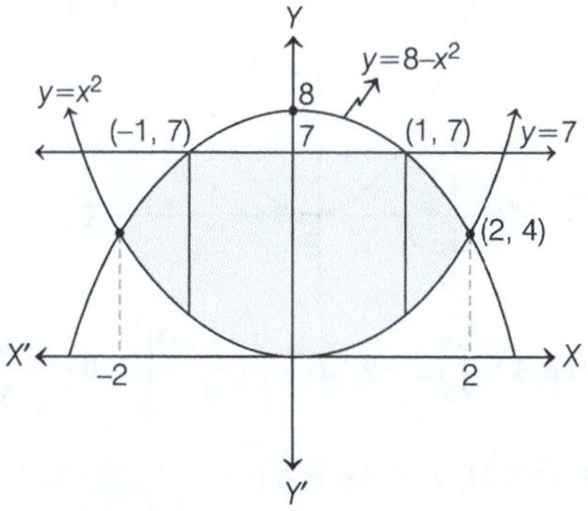

$$\text{Required area} = 2\int_0^1 (7 - x^2)\,dx + 2\int_1^2 (8 - x^2 - x^2)\,dx$$

$$= 2\left[7x - \frac{x^3}{3}\right]_0^1 + 2\left[8x - \frac{2x^3}{3}\right]_1^2 = 2\left(\frac{20}{3}\right) + 2\left(\frac{10}{3}\right)$$

$$\Rightarrow \quad \frac{40}{3} + \frac{20}{3} = \frac{60}{3} = 20$$

55. We have, $xy \le 8, 1 \le y \le x^2$

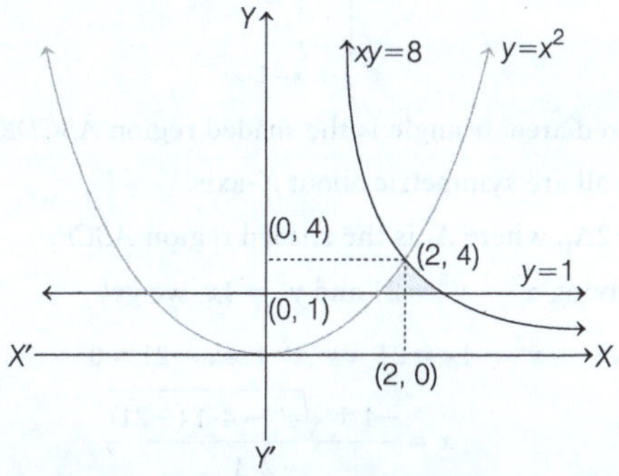

$$\therefore \text{ Required area} = \int_1^4 \left(\frac{8}{y} - \sqrt{y}\right) dy = \left[8\log y - \frac{2}{3}y^{3/2}\right]_1^4$$

$$= \left[8\log 4 - \frac{2}{3}(4)^{3/2}\right] - \left[8\log 1 - \frac{2}{3}\right]$$

$$= 16\log 2 - \frac{14}{3}$$

56. Given that q is the maximum integral value of p in $[0, 10]$ for which the roots of the equation $x^2 - px + \frac{5}{4}p = 0$ are rational.

Now, $D = (-p)^2 - 4 \times 1 \times \frac{5}{4}p = p^2 - 5p = p(p-5)$

In $\quad p \in [0, 10]$;

Let $\quad p = 10$

$D = 10 \times (10 - 5) = 50$ [reject]

[$\because$ D is not a perfect square]

Let $\quad p = 9$

$D = 9 \times (9 - 5) = 36$ [select]

[D is a perfect square]

So, $\quad q = 9$

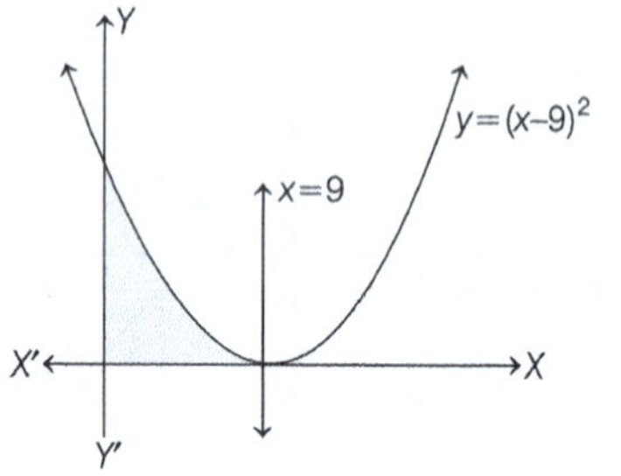

Now, Area $A = \int_0^9 (x-9)^2 dx = \left|\dfrac{(x-9)^3}{3}\right|_0^9 = 0 - \dfrac{(-9)^3}{3} = 243 \text{ unit}^2$

57. For $x^2 + y^2 \le 21, y^2 \le 4x, x \ge 1$

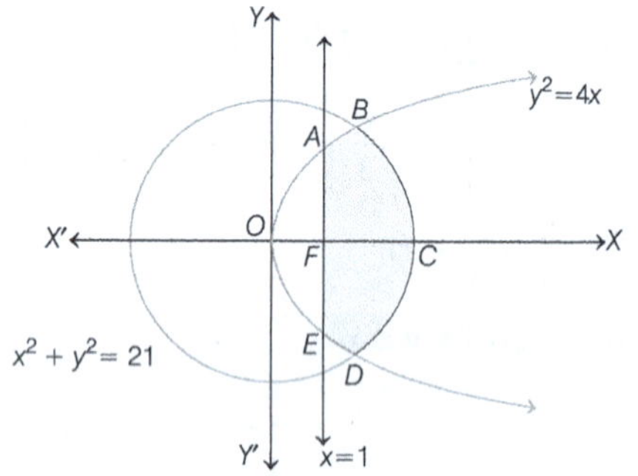

Required area, triangle is the shaded region $ABCDEFA$.

Since, all are symmetric about X-axis.

$\therefore \Delta = 2\Delta_1$, where Δ_1 is the shaded region $ABCF$.

On solving $x^2 + y^2 = 21$ and $y^2 = 4x$, we get

$$x^2 + 4x = 21 \Rightarrow x^2 + 4x - 21 = 0$$

$$\Rightarrow \quad x = \frac{-4 \pm \sqrt{4^2 - 4 \cdot 1(-21)}}{2 \cdot 1}$$

$$= \frac{-4 \pm 10}{2} = 3, -7$$

For B, we get $B(3, \sqrt{4 \cdot 3})$ i.e. $B(3, 2\sqrt{3})$

Also, putting $y = 0$ in $x^2 + y^2 = 21$, we get

$$x = \pm\sqrt{21}$$

$\therefore C(\sqrt{21}, 0)$

Now, $\Delta_1 = \int_1^3 2\sqrt{x}\, dx + \int_3^{\sqrt{21}} \sqrt{21 - x^2}\, dx$

$$= \frac{2 \cdot 2}{3}(x^{3/2})_1^3 + \left[\frac{x\sqrt{21 - x^2}}{2} + \frac{21}{2}\sin^{-1}\left(\frac{x}{\sqrt{21}}\right)\right]_3^{\sqrt{21}}$$

$$\left[\because \int x^n dx = \frac{x^{n+1}}{n+1} + c, n \ne -1 \text{ and} \right.$$

$$\left. \int \sqrt{a^2 - x^2}\, dx = \frac{x\sqrt{a^2 - x^2}}{2} + \frac{a^2}{2}\sin^{-1}\left(\frac{x}{a}\right) + C\right]$$

$$\Rightarrow \quad \Delta_1 = \frac{4}{3}(3\sqrt{3} - 1) + \left[\frac{21}{2}\sin^{-1}(1) - \frac{3\sqrt{21 - 3^2}}{2} - \frac{21}{2}\sin^{-1}\left(\frac{3}{\sqrt{21}}\right)\right]$$

$$= 4\sqrt{3} - \frac{4}{3} - 3\sqrt{3} + \frac{21}{2}\left[\sin^{-1}(1) - \sin^{-1}\left(\frac{3}{\sqrt{21}}\right)\right]$$

$$= \sqrt{3} - \frac{4}{3} + \frac{21}{2}\sin^{-1}\left(1 \cdot \sqrt{1 - \frac{9}{21}} - \frac{3}{\sqrt{21}} \cdot \sqrt{1 - 1^2}\right)$$

$$[\because \sin^{-1}(a) - \sin^{-1}(b) = \sin^{-1}(a\sqrt{1 - b^2} - b\sqrt{1 - a^2})]$$

$$= \sqrt{3} - \frac{4}{3} + \frac{21}{2}\sin^{-1}\left(\frac{2}{\sqrt{7}}\right)$$

$$\therefore \quad \Delta = 2\Delta_1 = 2\sqrt{3} - \frac{8}{3} + 21\sin^{-1}\left(\frac{2}{\sqrt{7}}\right)$$

Thus, $\dfrac{1}{2}\left[\Delta - 21\sin^{-1}\left(\dfrac{2}{\sqrt{7}}\right)\right] = \sqrt{3} - \dfrac{4}{3}$

58.

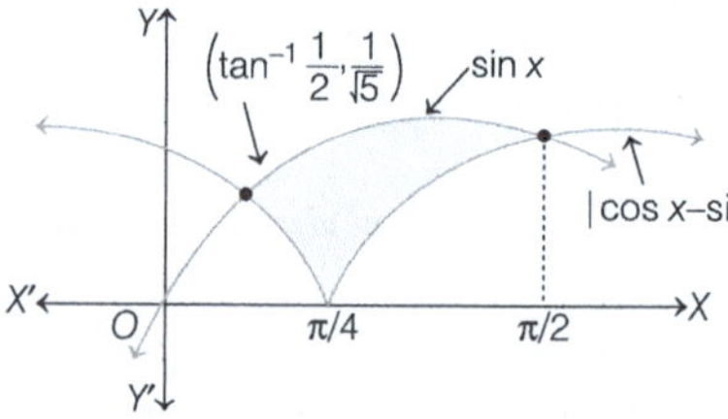

$\therefore \cos x - \sin x = \sin x, \cos x - \sin x = -\sin x$

$\Rightarrow \quad \cos x = 2\sin x, \cos x = 0 \Rightarrow \tan x = \dfrac{1}{2}, x = \dfrac{\pi}{2}$

$$\therefore \int_{\tan^{-1} 1/2}^{\pi/4} (\sin x - \cos x + \sin x)\, dx + \int_{\pi/4}^{\pi/2} (\sin x + \cos x - \sin x)\, dx$$

$$= \int_{\tan^{-1} 1/2}^{\pi/4} (2\sin x - \cos x)\, dx + \int_{\pi/4}^{\pi/2} \cos x\, dx$$

$$= -2\cos x - \sin x\Big|_{\tan^{-1}\frac{1}{2}}^{\pi/4} + \sin x\Big|_{\pi/4}^{\pi/2}$$

$$= \sqrt{5} - 2\sqrt{2} + 1$$

59. We have, $A = \{(x, y) \in R^2 : y \ge 0, 2x \le y \le \sqrt{4 - (x-1)^2}\}$

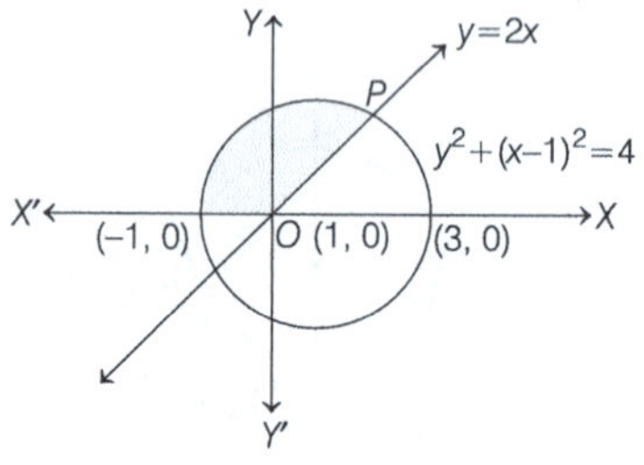

On solving $y^2 + (x-1)^2 = 4$ and $y = 2x$, we get

$$(x-1)^2 + (2x)^2 = 4 \Rightarrow x^2 - 2x + 1 + 4x^2 = 4$$

$$\Rightarrow \quad 5x^2 - 2x - 3 = 0$$

$$\Rightarrow \quad x = \frac{2 \pm \sqrt{(-2)^2 - 4 \cdot 5(-3)}}{2 \cdot 5}$$

$$= \frac{2 \pm \sqrt{4 + 60}}{2 \cdot 5} = \frac{2 \pm 8}{10} = 1, -\frac{3}{5}$$

For P, $x = 1$;

$\therefore\ y = 2$ i.e $P(1, 2)$

A is the shaded region

$$= \left|\int_{-1}^{1} \sqrt{4-(x-1)^2}\,dx - \int_{0}^{1} (2x)\,dx\right|$$

$$= \left|\left(\frac{(x-1)\sqrt{4-(x-1)^2} + 4\sin^{-1}\left(\frac{x-1}{2}\right)}{2}\right)\right|_{-1}^{1} - [x^2]_0^1$$

$$\left[\because \int \sqrt{a^2-x^2}\,dx = \frac{x\sqrt{a^2-x^2} + a^2\sin^{-1}\left(\frac{x}{a}\right)}{2} + c\right]$$

$$= \left|0 - \left(\frac{(-2)\sqrt{4-(-2)^2} + 4\sin^{-1}\left(\frac{-2}{2}\right)}{2}\right) - (1^2 - 0^2)\right|$$

$= (\pi - 1)$ sq units

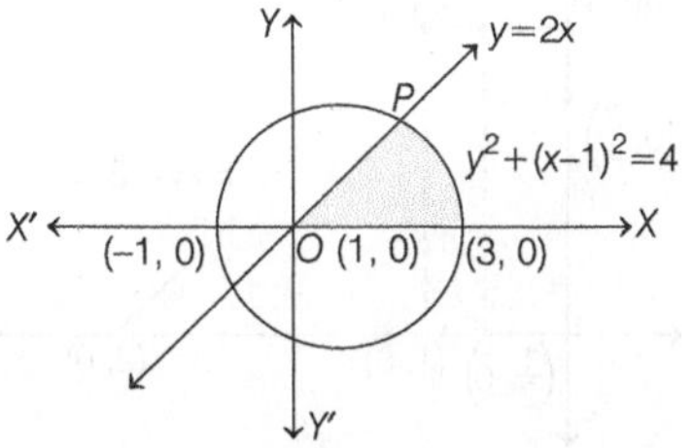

B is the shaded region = Area of semi-circle − A

$$= \left[\frac{\pi(4)}{2} - (\pi - 1)\right] \text{ sq units}$$

$= (\pi + 1)$ sq units

So, required ratio $= \dfrac{\pi - 1}{\pi + 1}$

60. Given equation of curves are

$$y^2 + 4x = 4 \quad \text{...(i)}$$

and $\quad y - 2x = 2 \quad$ ...(ii)

$\Rightarrow \quad y = 2x - 2$

On putting in Eq. (i), we get

$$(2x + 2)^2 + 4x = 4$$

$\Rightarrow \quad 4x^2 + 4 + 8x + 4x = 4 \Rightarrow 4x^2 + 12x = 0$

$\Rightarrow \quad 4x(x + 3) = 0 \Rightarrow x = 0, -3$

From Eq. (ii),

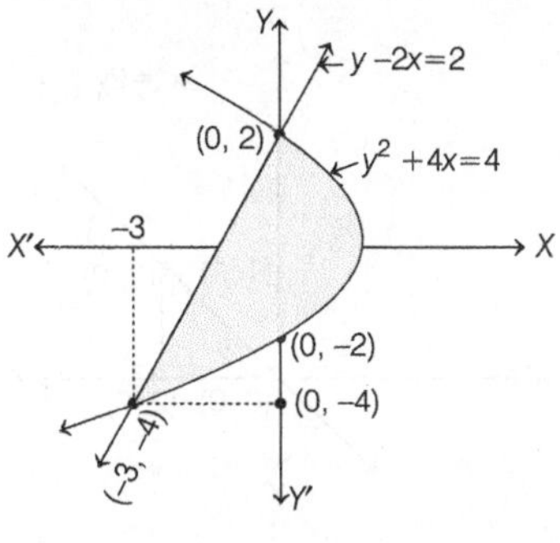

When $x = 0, y = 2$

When $x = -3, y = -4$

So, points of intersection of Eqs. (i) and (ii) are (0, 2) and (− 3, − 4).

$$\text{Now, required area} = \int_{y=-4}^{y=2} (x_p - x_l)\,dy$$

$$= \int_{-4}^{2} \left(\frac{4-y^2}{4} - \frac{y-2}{2}\right) dy$$

$$= \int_{-4}^{2} \left(2 - \frac{y^2}{4} - \frac{y}{2}\right) dy = \left[2y - \frac{y^3}{12} - \frac{y^2}{4}\right]_{-4}^{2}$$

$$= \left(4 - \frac{8}{12} - 1\right) - \left(-8 + \frac{16}{3} - 4\right)$$

$$= \left(3 - \frac{2}{3}\right) + 12 - \frac{16}{3} = 9 \text{ sq units}$$

61.

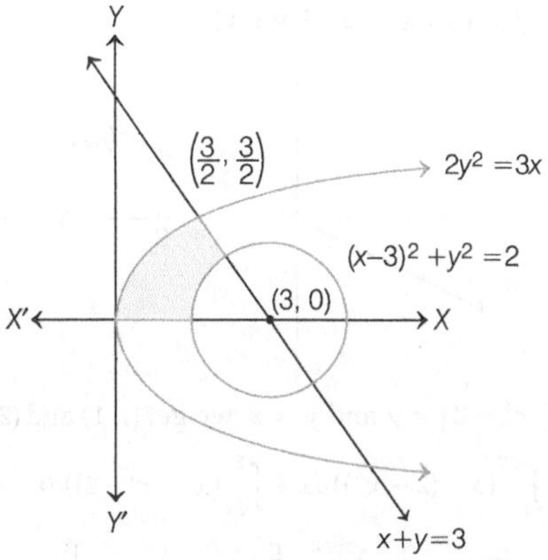

$$A = \text{Required area} = \int_0^{3/2} \left[(3 - y) - \left(\frac{2y^2}{3}\right)\right] dy - \pi\,[\sqrt{2}]^2 \cdot \frac{1}{8}$$

$$= \left[\left(3y - \frac{y^2}{2} - \frac{2}{9}y^3\right)\right]_0^{3/2} - \frac{\pi}{4}$$

$$= 3 \times \frac{3}{2} - \frac{9}{8} - \frac{2}{9} \times \frac{27}{8} - \frac{\pi}{4} = \frac{36 - 9 - 6}{8} - \frac{\pi}{4} = \frac{21}{8} - \frac{\pi}{4}$$

$$\text{So, } 4(\pi + 4A) = 4\left(\pi + 4\left(\frac{21}{8} - \frac{\pi}{4}\right)\right) = 42$$

62. Given, $c = 2x^2 - y + 1 = 0 \Rightarrow y = 3x + 1$

Tangent to c at point (1, 3) and line $x + y = 1$

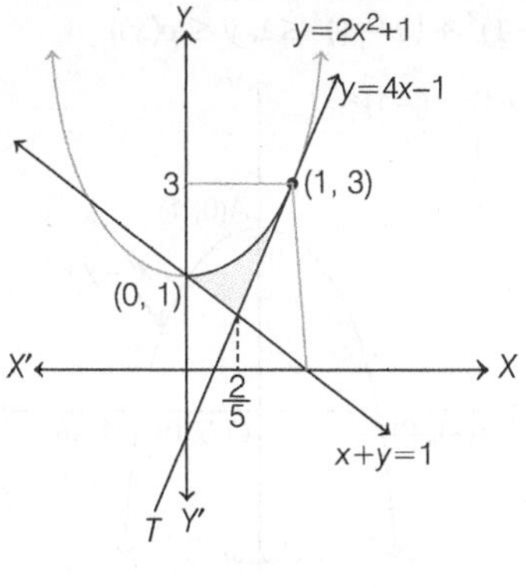

Tangent $= dy/dx = 4x$

$y - 3 = 4(x-1) \Rightarrow y = 4x - 1$

Hence, shaded area $= A$

$$A = \int_0^{2/5}[(2x^2+1)-(1-x)]dx + \int_{2/5}^{1}[(2x^2+1)-(4x-1)]dx$$

$$= \int_0^{2/5}(2x^2+x)dx + \int_{2/5}^{1}(2x^2-4x+2)dx$$

$$= \left(\frac{2}{3}x^3 + \frac{x^2}{2}\right)\Bigg|_0^{2/5} + \left(\frac{2}{3}x^3 - 2x^2 + 2x\right)\Bigg|_{2/5}^{1}$$

$$= \frac{16}{3\times 5^3} + \frac{2}{5^2} + \frac{2}{3} - 2 + 2 - \frac{16}{3\times 5^3} + \frac{8}{5^2} - \frac{4}{5}$$

$$= \frac{10}{25} + \frac{2}{3} - \frac{4}{5} = \frac{2}{5} + \frac{2}{3} - \frac{4}{5} = \frac{2}{3} - \frac{2}{5}$$

$$\Rightarrow A = \frac{4}{15} \Rightarrow 60A = 60 \times \frac{4}{15} = 16$$

63. We have, $\{(x, y) : |x^2 - 2| \le y \le x\}$

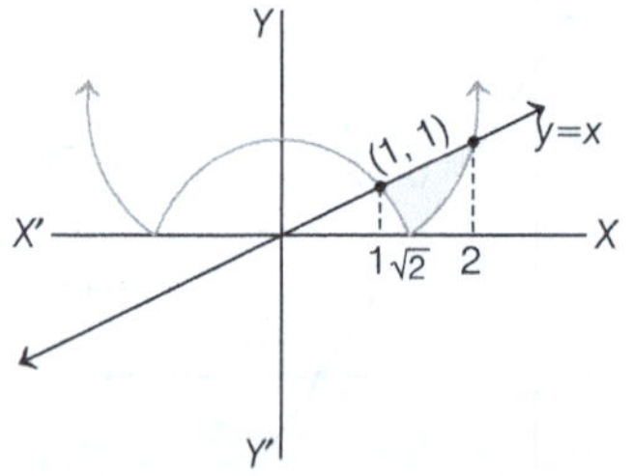

Solving $|x^2 - 2| = y$ and $y = x$, we get (1, 1) and (2, 2)

$$A = \int_1^{\sqrt{2}}(x-(2-x^2))dx + \int_{\sqrt{2}}^{2}(x-(x^2-2))dx$$

$$= \left[\frac{x^2}{2} - 2x + \frac{x^3}{3}\right]_1^{\sqrt{2}} + \left[\frac{x^2}{2} - \frac{x^3}{3} + 2x\right]_{\sqrt{2}}^{2}$$

$$= \left(1 - 2\sqrt{2} + \frac{2\sqrt{2}}{3}\right) - \left(\frac{1}{2} - 2 + \frac{1}{3}\right) + \left(2 - \frac{8}{3} + 4\right) - \left(1 - \frac{2\sqrt{2}}{3} + 2\sqrt{2}\right)$$

$$= \frac{-8\sqrt{2}}{3} + \frac{9}{2} = \frac{-16\sqrt{2}+27}{6}$$

$$\Rightarrow 6A = -16\sqrt{2} + 27 \Rightarrow 6A + 16\sqrt{2} = 27$$

64. Let $y = p(x)$ be the parabola passing through the points $(-1, 0)$ $(0, 1)$ $(1, 0)$.

Now, to find the area of the region

$\{(x, y), (x+1)^2 + (y-1)^2 \le 1, y \le p(x)\}$

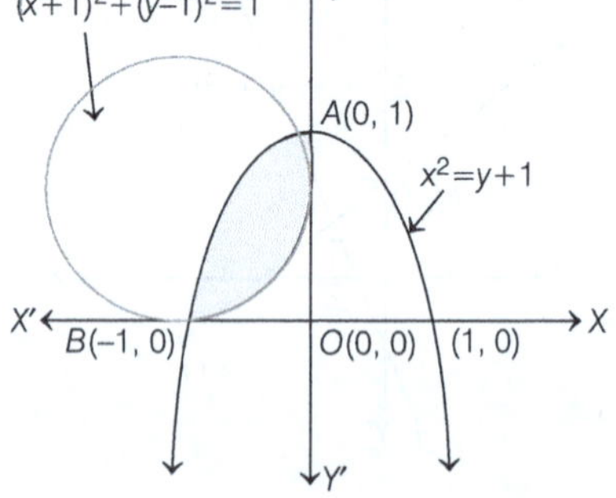

The area of shaded region is

$$A = \int_{-1}^{0}\{(1-x^2) - (1 - \sqrt{1-(x+1)^2}\}dx$$

$$= \int_{-1}^{0}\{-x^2\sqrt{1-(x+1)^2}\}dx$$

$$= \int_{-1}^{0}(-x^2)dx + \int_{-1}^{0}\sqrt{1-(x+1)^2}dx$$

$$= -\left(\frac{x^3}{3}\right)_{-1}^{0} + \left[\frac{\sqrt{1-(x+1)^2}}{2} + \frac{1}{2}\sin^{-1}(x+1)\right]_{-1}^{0}$$

$$= -\frac{1}{3} + \left[\frac{1}{2} + \frac{\pi}{4} - \frac{1}{2}\right] = \frac{\pi}{4} - 1/3$$

Now, $12(\pi - 4A) = 12\left(\pi - 4\left(\frac{\pi}{4} - \frac{1}{3}\right)\right) = 16$

65.

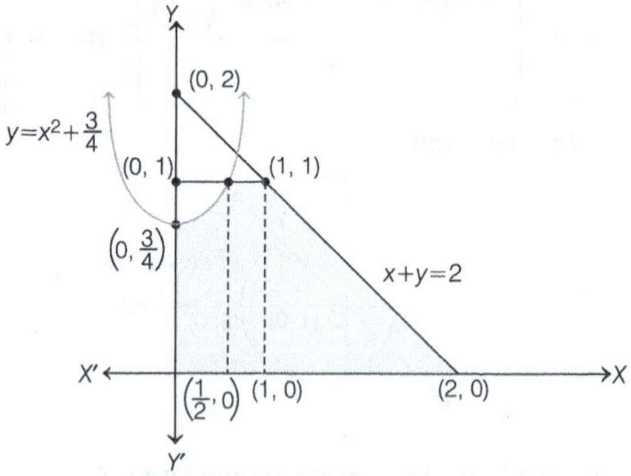

When $0 \le x < 1$, then $1 + [x] = 1 + 0 = 1$

$$A = \int_0^{1/2}\left(x^2 + \frac{3}{4}\right)dx + \left(\frac{1}{2}\times 1\right) + \left(\frac{1}{2}\times 1 \times 1\right)$$

$$= \left[\frac{x^3}{3}\right]_0^{1/2} + \frac{3}{4}[x]_0^{1/2} + 1 = \frac{1}{3}\cdot\frac{1}{8} + \frac{3}{4}\times\frac{1}{2} + 1$$

$$= \frac{1}{24} + \frac{3}{8} + 1 = \frac{1+9+24}{24} = \frac{34}{24} = \frac{17}{12}$$

$\therefore$ $12A = 17$

66. Given region, $S = \{(x, y) : 2y - y^2 \le x^2 \le 2y, x \ge y\}$

Here, we have three curves

$$2y - y^2 = x^2 \quad \text{...(i)}$$

$$x^2 = 2y \quad \text{...(ii)}$$

and $$x = y \quad \text{...(iii)}$$

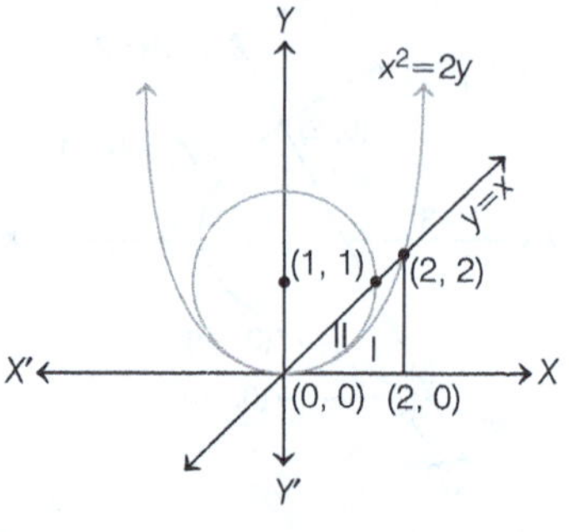

From Eq. (i), $x^2 + y^2 - 2y = 0$

$\Rightarrow \quad x^2 + (y-1)^2 = 1$

is a circle with centre (0, 1) and radius is 1.

Intersection points of Eqs. (i) and (iii) are

$$2x - x^2 = x^2$$

$$\Rightarrow \quad 2x^2 = 2x \Rightarrow x(x-1) = 0$$

$$\Rightarrow \quad x = 0, 1$$

When $x = 0$, then $y = 0$

and when $x = 1$, then $y = 1$

$\therefore$ Required points are (0, 0) and (1, 1).

Also, intersection points of Eqs. (ii) and (iii),

$$x^2 = 2x \Rightarrow x(x-2) = 0$$

$$\Rightarrow \quad x = 0, 2$$

When $x = 0$, then $y = 0$

and when $x = 2$, then $y = 2$

$\therefore$ Required points are (0, 0) and (2, 2).

$\therefore$ Required area = Area of triangle − Area of part I − Area of part II

$$= \frac{1}{2} \times 2 \times 2 - \int_0^2 \frac{x^2}{2} dx - \left(\frac{\pi}{4} - \frac{1}{2}\right)$$

$$= 2 - \frac{1}{2}\left(\frac{x^3}{3}\right)_0^2 - \frac{\pi}{4} + \frac{1}{2}$$

$$= 2 - \frac{1}{2} \times \frac{8}{3} - \frac{\pi}{4} + \frac{1}{2}$$

$$= \frac{7}{6} - \frac{\pi}{4}$$

$$= \frac{5+2}{5+1} - \frac{\pi}{5-1}$$

$\therefore \quad n = 5$

67. We have, $f(x) = \dfrac{x + |x|}{2} = \begin{cases} x, & x \ge 0 \\ 0, & x < 0 \end{cases}$

and $\quad g(x) = \begin{cases} x, & x < 0 \\ x^2, & x \ge 0 \end{cases}$

$\therefore \quad fog(x) = f(g(x))$

$$= \begin{cases} g(x), & g(x) \ge 0 \\ 0, & g(x) < 0 \end{cases}$$

$$= \begin{cases} x^2, & x \ge 0 \\ 0, & x < 0 \end{cases}$$

Also, equation of line is $2y - x = 15$

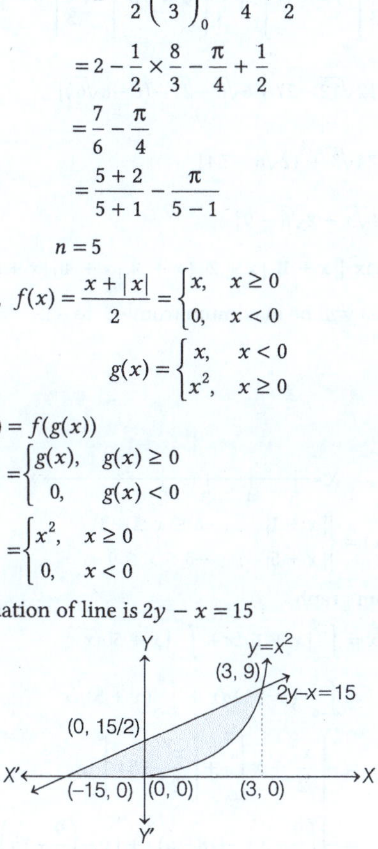

Intersecting points of $y = x^2$ and $2y - x = 15$ is (3, 9).

$$\therefore \text{Required area} = \int_0^3 \left(\frac{x+15}{2} - x^2\right) dx + \int_{-15}^0 \frac{x+15}{2} dx$$

$$= \left[\frac{x^2}{4} + \frac{15}{2}x - \frac{x^3}{3}\right]_0^3 + \left[\frac{x^2}{4} + \frac{15}{2}x\right]_{-15}^0$$

$$= \left(\frac{9}{4} + \frac{45}{2} - 9\right) + \left(-\frac{225}{4} + \frac{225}{2}\right) = 72$$

68. We have, $|2x-1| \le y \le |x^2 - x|$, $0 \le x \le 1$

$\therefore \quad y \ge |2x-1|$ and $y \le |x^2 - x|$, $0 \le x \le 1$

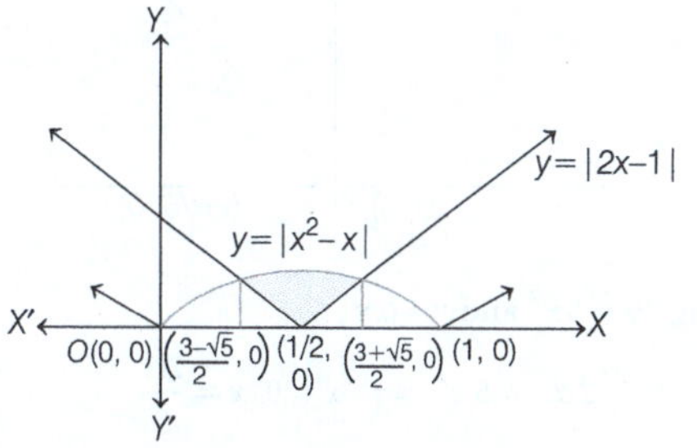

Now, $y = x^2 - x$

$$\Rightarrow 2x - 1 = x^2 - x \Rightarrow x^2 - 3x + 1 = 0$$

$$\Rightarrow \quad x = \frac{3 \pm \sqrt{9-4}}{2} = \frac{3 \pm \sqrt{5}}{2}$$

So, both curve intersect at $x = \dfrac{3+\sqrt{5}}{2}$ and $x = \dfrac{3-\sqrt{5}}{2}$.

$$\therefore \text{ Required area, } A = 2\int_{\frac{3-\sqrt{5}}{2}}^{1/2} [(x - x^2) - (1 - 2x)]\, dx$$

$$= 2\int_{\frac{3-\sqrt{5}}{2}}^{1/2} (-x^2 + 3x - 1) dx$$

$$= 2\left[-\frac{x^3}{3} + \frac{3}{2}x^2 - x\right]_{\frac{3-\sqrt{5}}{2}}^{\frac{1}{2}} = \frac{5\sqrt{5} - 11}{6}$$

$$\therefore \quad 6A + 11 = 5\sqrt{5} \Rightarrow (6A + 11)^2 = 125$$

69. Parabola $P_1 : 2y = 5x^2$, Vertex : (0, 0)

Parabola $P_2 : x^2 - y + 6 = 0 \Rightarrow x^2 = (y - 6)$, Vertex (0, 6)

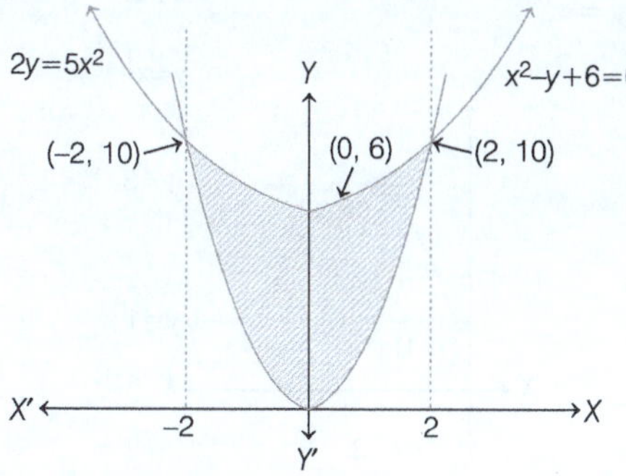

For their intersection, $x^2 - \dfrac{5}{2}x^2 + 6 = 0$

$$\frac{-3x^2}{2} + 6 = 0$$

$$x = \pm 2$$

$$\text{Area} = 2\int_0^2 (x^2+6) - \frac{5x^2}{2}\,dx$$

$$= 2\int_0^2 \left(\frac{-3x^2}{2}+6\right)dx = 2\left[-\frac{x^3}{2}+6x\right]_0^2$$

$$= 2[-4+12] = 16 \qquad \text{...(i)}$$

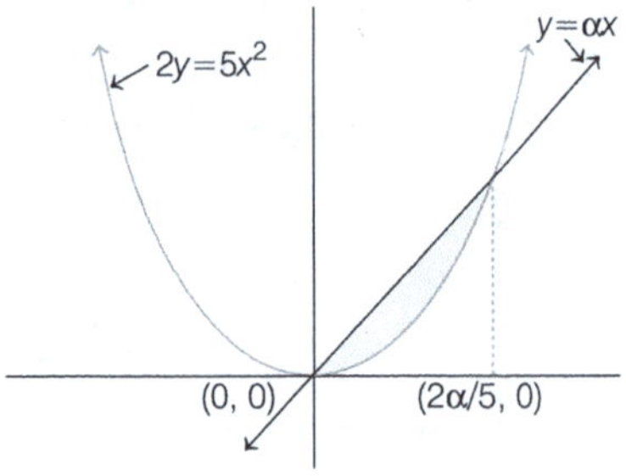

Solving $2y = 5x^2$ and $y = \alpha x$,

$$2\alpha x = 5x^2 \Rightarrow x = 0,\ x = \frac{2\alpha}{5}$$

$$A = \int_0^{2\alpha/5} \alpha x - \frac{5}{2}x^2\,dx$$

$$= \left[\frac{\alpha x^2}{2} - \frac{5x^3}{6}\right]_0^{2\alpha/5}$$

$$= \left[\frac{\alpha}{2}\cdot\frac{4\alpha^2}{25} - \frac{5}{6}\cdot\frac{8\alpha^3}{125}\right] \qquad \text{...(ii)}$$

Given that area by Eqs. (i) and (ii) are same.

So, $\alpha^3\left[\frac{4}{50} - \frac{40}{750}\right] = 16$

$$\alpha^3 \times \frac{20}{750} = 16$$

$$\Rightarrow \qquad \alpha^3 = 600$$

70. Given curves are $y = 3$, $y = 1$, $x = 0$ and $x = y^a$ and area of region is $\frac{364}{3}$ sq units.

Take $y^a = x$

$$\Rightarrow \quad y = x^{1/a}$$

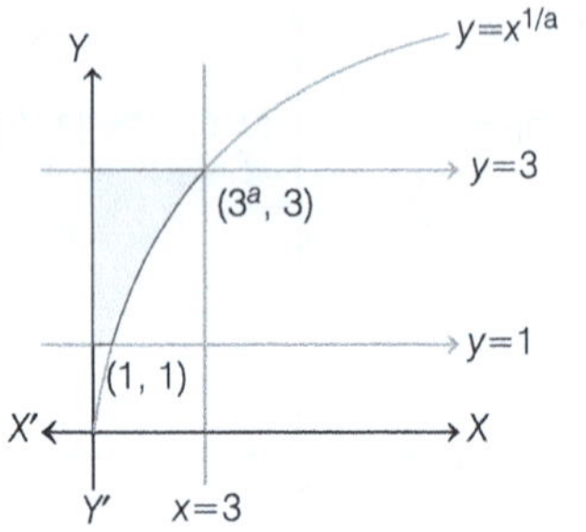

Required area $\int_0^3 x\,dy = \int_1^3 y^a\,dy = \left[\frac{y^{a+1}}{a+1}\right]_1^3$

$$\Rightarrow \quad \frac{3^{a+1}-1}{a+1} = \frac{364}{3} \qquad \text{[given]}$$

[take a only odd number]

Put $a = 5$, then

$$(3^6-1)/6 = 364/3$$

$$3^6 = 729 = 3^6$$

Therefore, LHS = RHS

Thus, $a = 5$ is the correct value.

71.

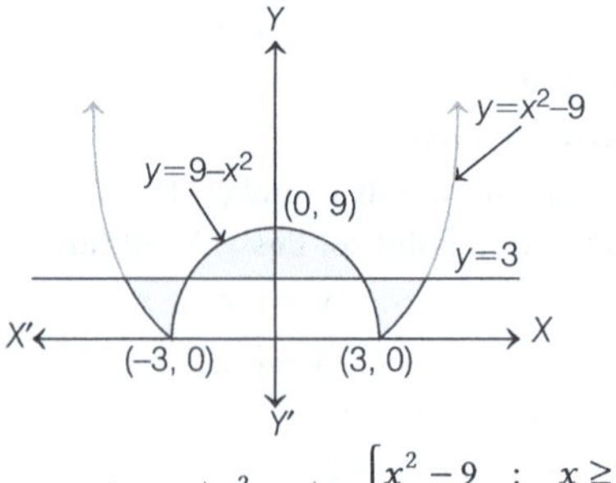

The given curve is $y = |x^2-9| = \begin{cases} x^2-9 & ; \quad x \ge 3 \\ 9-x^2 & ; \quad x < 3 \end{cases}$

and the line is $y = 3$

Thus, area of shaded region

$$= 2\int_0^3 (\sqrt{9+y} - \sqrt{9-y})dy + 2\int_3^9 (\sqrt{9-y})\,dy$$

$$= 2\left[\frac{2}{3}\left[(9+y)^{\frac{3}{2}}\right]_0^3 + \frac{2}{3}\left[(9-y)^{\frac{3}{2}}\right]_0^3 - \frac{2}{3}\left[(9-y)^{\frac{3}{2}}\right]_3^9\right]$$

$$= \frac{4}{3}[12\sqrt{12} - 27 + 6\sqrt{6} - 27 - (0 - 6\sqrt{6})]$$

$$= \frac{4}{3}[24\sqrt{3} + 12\sqrt{6} - 54]$$

$$= 8[4\sqrt{3} + 2\sqrt{6} - 9]$$

72. $f(x) = \max\{|x+1|, |x+2|, |x+3|, |x+4|, |x+5|\}$

Since, area will be maximum from –5 to –1.

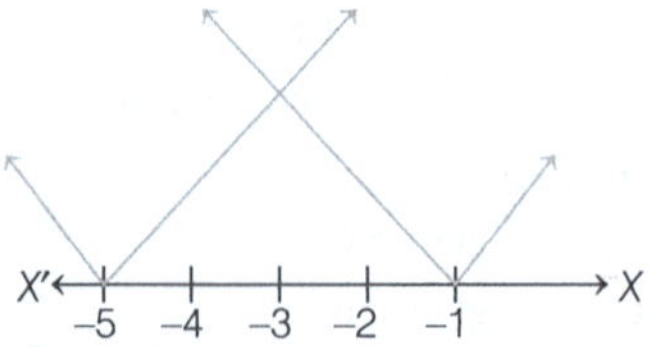

Now, $f(x) = \begin{cases} |x+1| & , \quad -6 \le x \le -3 \\ |x+5| & , \quad -3 \le x \le 0 \end{cases}$

Thus, from graph,

$$\int_{-6}^0 f(x)dx = \int_{-6}^{-3} |x+1|dx + \int_{-3}^0 |x+5|dx$$

$$= \int_{-6}^{-3} -(x+1)dx + \int_{-3}^0 (x+5)dx$$

$$= -\left[\frac{x^2}{2}+x\right]_{-6}^{-3} + \left[\frac{x^2}{2}+5x\right]_{-3}^0$$

$$= -\left[\left(\frac{9}{2}-3\right) - (18-6)\right] + \left[0 - \left(\frac{9}{2}-15\right)\right]$$

$$= -\left[\frac{3}{2} - 12\right] + \frac{21}{2} = \frac{21}{2} + \frac{21}{2} = 21$$

73.

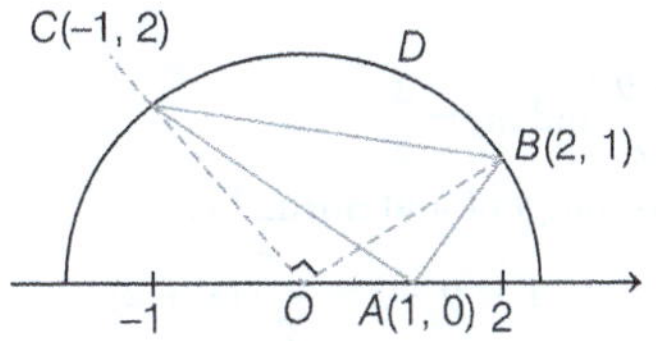

We are given that the condition, $|x-1| < y < \sqrt{5-x^2}$

Let $|x-1| = \sqrt{5-x^2}$

$\Rightarrow (x-1)^2 = 5-x^2 \Rightarrow x^2 - x - 2 = 0 \Rightarrow x = 2, -1$

$\therefore$ Required area = Area of ΔABC + Area of region BCD

$$= \frac{1}{2}\begin{vmatrix} 1 & 0 & 1 \\ 2 & 1 & 1 \\ -1 & 2 & 1 \end{vmatrix} + \frac{\pi}{4}(\sqrt{5})^2 - \frac{1}{2}(\sqrt{5})^2$$

$$= \frac{5\pi}{4} - \frac{1}{2} \text{ sq units}$$

74. Now, draw the required region,

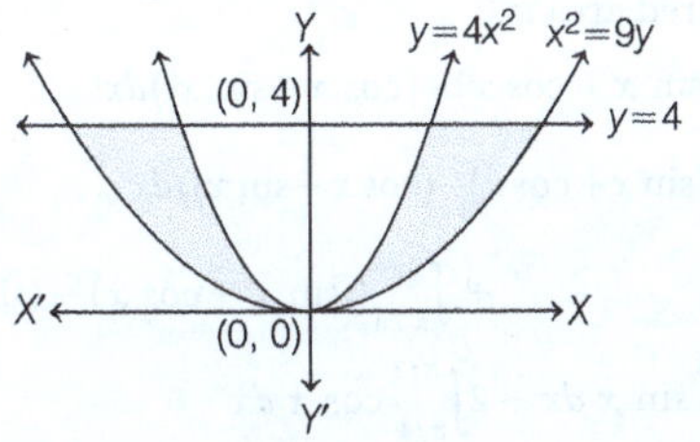

The area of required region $= 2 \cdot \int_0^4 \left(3\sqrt{y} - \frac{\sqrt{y}}{2}\right) dy$

$$= 2 \cdot \int_0^4 \frac{5}{2}\sqrt{y}\,dy = \frac{80}{3} \text{ sq units}$$

75. $y^2 = 8x + 4,\ x^2 + y^2 + 4\sqrt{3}x - 4 = 0$

$\therefore$ Curves are $x = \frac{y^2-4}{8}$ and $(x + 2\sqrt{3})^2 + y^2 = 16$

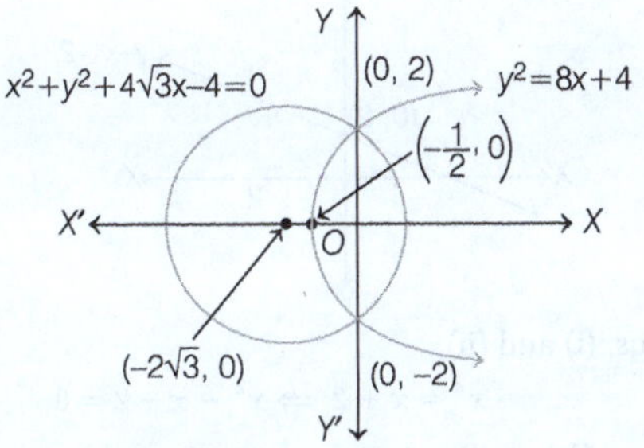

For point of intersection, put $y^2 = 8x + 4$ in the second equation

$$x^2 + 8x + 4 + 4\sqrt{3}x - 4 = 0$$

$\Rightarrow \quad x = 0$ or $x = -8 - 4\sqrt{3}$ [rejected]

$\Rightarrow \quad y = 2$ or $y = -2$

Take the area about Y-axis,

$$A = 2\int_0^2 (\sqrt{16-y^2} - 2\sqrt{3})dy - \int_0^2 \left(\frac{y^2-4}{8}\right)dy$$

$$= 2\left[\frac{y}{2}\sqrt{16-y^2} + \frac{16}{2}\sin^{-1}\left(\frac{y}{4}\right) - 2\sqrt{3}y - \frac{y^3}{24} + \frac{y}{2}\right]_0^2$$

$$= \frac{1}{3}[8\pi + 4 - 12\sqrt{3}] \text{ sq units}$$

76. Given that, $A = \{(x, y);\ x^2 \le y \le \min\{x+2, 4-3x\}\}$

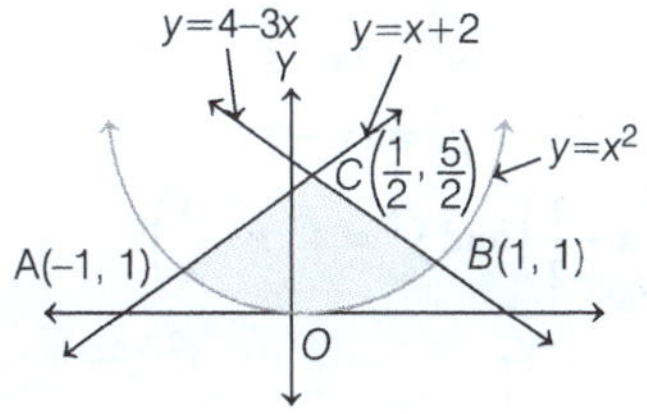

Thus, the point of intersection of $y = x^2$ and $y = 4 - 3x$ is $B(1, 1)$ and the point of intersection of $y = x + 2$ and $y = x^2$ is $A(-1, 1)$ and also the point of intersection of $y = x + 2$ and $y = 4 - 3x$ is $C\left(\frac{1}{2}, \frac{5}{2}\right)$.

So, the required region $ACBA$ is

$$\int_{-1}^{1/2} (x + 2 - x^2)\,dx + \int_{1/2}^{1} (4 - 3x - x^2)\,dx$$

$$= \left[\frac{x^2}{2} + 2x - \frac{x^3}{3}\right]_{-1}^{1/2} + \left[4x - \frac{3x^2}{2} - \frac{x^3}{3}\right]_{1/2}^{1}$$

$$= \left[\frac{1}{2}\left(\frac{1}{4}\right) + 2\left(\frac{1}{2}\right) - \frac{1}{3}\left(\frac{1}{2}\right)^3\right] - \left[\frac{(-1)^2}{2} + 2(-1) - \frac{(-1)^3}{3}\right]$$

$$+ \left[4(1) - \frac{3}{2}(1)^2 - \frac{(1)^3}{3}\right] - \left[4\left(\frac{1}{2}\right) - \frac{3\left(\frac{1}{2}\right)^2}{2} - \frac{\left(\frac{1}{2}\right)^3}{3}\right]$$

$$= \left(\frac{1}{8} + 1 - \frac{1}{24}\right) - \left(\frac{1}{2} - 2 + \frac{1}{3}\right) + \left(4 - \frac{3}{2} - \frac{1}{3}\right) - \left(2 - \frac{3}{8} - \frac{1}{24}\right)$$

$$= \frac{17}{6} \text{ sq units}$$

77. Given, $y^2 = 8x$ and $y = \sqrt{2}x$

Lines for triangle, $y = \sqrt{2}x,\ x = 1,\ y = 2\sqrt{2}$

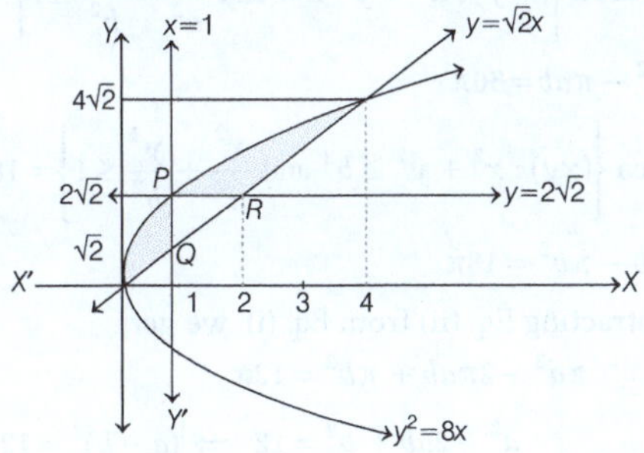

Required area $= \int_0^4 (y_{\text{curve}} - y_{\text{line}})\,dx$ − Area of ΔPQR

$$= \int_0^4 (\sqrt{8x} - \sqrt{2}x)dx - \frac{1}{2} \times \sqrt{2} \times 1$$

$$= \sqrt{2}\left[\frac{2x^{3/2}}{3/2} - \frac{x^2}{2}\right]_0^4 - \frac{\sqrt{2}}{2}$$

$$= 2\sqrt{2}\left(\frac{16}{3}-\frac{0}{3}\right)-\sqrt{2}\left(\frac{16}{2}-\frac{0}{2}\right)-\frac{\sqrt{2}}{2}$$

$$= \frac{32\sqrt{2}}{3}-8\sqrt{2}-\frac{\sqrt{2}}{2}$$

$$= \frac{64\sqrt{2}-48\sqrt{2}-3\sqrt{2}}{6}=\frac{13\sqrt{2}}{6} \text{ sq units}$$

78. Given, $y^2 = 2x - 1$ ... (i)

and $y^2 = 4x - 3$ ... (ii)

$$\Rightarrow y^2 = 2\left(x-\frac{1}{2}\right) \text{ and } y^2 = 4\left(x-\frac{3}{4}\right)$$

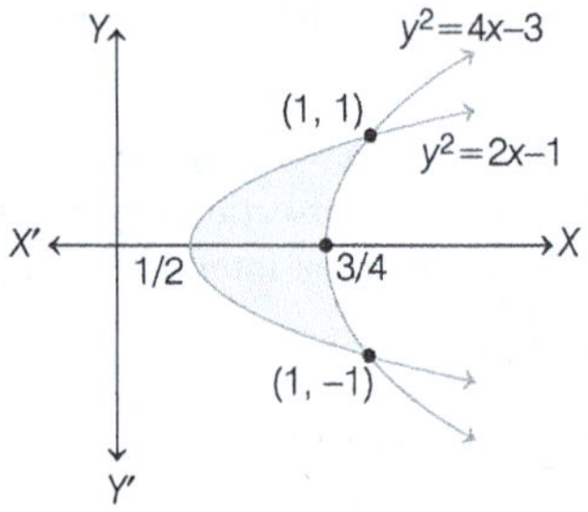

On comparing both the equations, we get

$$2x-1 = 4x-3 \Rightarrow 2x = 2 \Rightarrow x = 1$$

$$\Rightarrow \quad y^2 = 2\times 1 - 1$$

$$\Rightarrow \quad y^2 = 1 \Rightarrow y = \pm 1$$

The two intersection point of the parabolas are (1, 1) and (1, −1).

$$\text{Area of the shaded region} = 2\int_0^1\left(\frac{y^2+3}{4}-\frac{y^2+1}{2}\right)dy$$

$$= 2\int_0^1 \frac{y^2+3-2y^2-2}{4}\,dy$$

$$= \frac{1}{2}\int_0^1 (1-y^2)\,dy = \frac{1}{2}\left[y-\frac{y^3}{3}\right]_0^1$$

$$= \frac{1}{2}\left[1-\frac{1}{3}\right] = \frac{1}{2}\times\frac{2}{3} = \frac{1}{3} \text{ sq units}$$

79. Given, area $\left\{(x, y) : x^2 + y^2 \le a \text{ and } \frac{x^2}{a^2}+\frac{y^2}{b^2} \ge 1\right\} = 30\pi$

So, $\pi a^2 - \pi ab = 30\pi$ ...(i)

and area $\left\{(xy) : x^2 + y^2 \ge b^2 \text{ and } \frac{x^2}{a^2}+\frac{y^2}{b^2} \le 1\right\} = 18\pi$

So, $\pi ab - \pi b^2 = 18\pi$ ...(ii)

On subtracting Eq. (ii) from Eq. (i), we get

$$\pi a^2 - 2\pi ab + \pi b^2 = 12\pi$$

$$\Rightarrow \quad a^2 - 2ab + b^2 = 12 \Rightarrow (a-b)^2 = 12$$

80. Given curve is $4x^3 - 3xy^2 + 6x^2 - 5xy - 8y^2 + 9x + 14 = 0$

Differentiating on both sides,

$$12x^2 - 3y^2 - 6xyy' + 12x - 5y - 5xy' - 16yy' + 9 = 0$$

Satisfy the point (− 2, 3),

$$\Rightarrow \quad 48 - 27 + 36y' - 24 - 15 + 10y' - 48y' + 9 = 0$$

$$\Rightarrow \quad 2y' = -9$$

So, $m_1 = \frac{-9}{2}$ and $m_2 = \frac{2}{9}$

Equation of tangent and normal is

$$T \equiv y - 3 = \frac{-9}{2}(x+2) \quad [T = \text{tangent}]$$

Put $y = 0 \Rightarrow x = \frac{-4}{3}$

$$N \equiv y - 3 = \frac{2}{9}(x+2) \quad [N = \text{Normal}]$$

Putting $y = 0 \Rightarrow x = \frac{-31}{2}$

Therefore, required area $= \left(\frac{1}{2}\times \text{Base}\times\text{Height}\right)$

$$A = \frac{1}{2}\times\left(\frac{(-4)}{3}+\frac{31}{2}\right)(3)$$

$$= \frac{1}{2}\left(\frac{85}{6}\right)\cdot 3 = \frac{85}{4}$$

$\therefore \quad 8A = 170$

81. The required area is

$$A = \int_0^{\pi/2}((\sin x + \cos x) - |\cos x - \sin x|)\,dx$$

$$A = \int_0^{\pi/4}((\sin x + \cos x) - (\cos x - \sin x))\,dx$$

$$+ \int_{\pi/4}^{\pi/2}((\sin x + \cos x) - (\sin x - \cos x))\,dx$$

$$A = 2\int_0^{\pi/4}\sin x\,dx + 2\int_{\pi/4}^{\pi/2}\cos x\,dx$$

$$A = -2\left(\frac{1}{\sqrt{2}}-1\right)+2\left(1-\frac{1}{\sqrt{2}}\right)$$

$$A = 4 - 2\sqrt{2} = 2\sqrt{2}(\sqrt{2}-1) \text{ sq units}$$

82. The given equations are

$y - x = 2$ ...(i)

and $x^2 = y$ ...(ii)

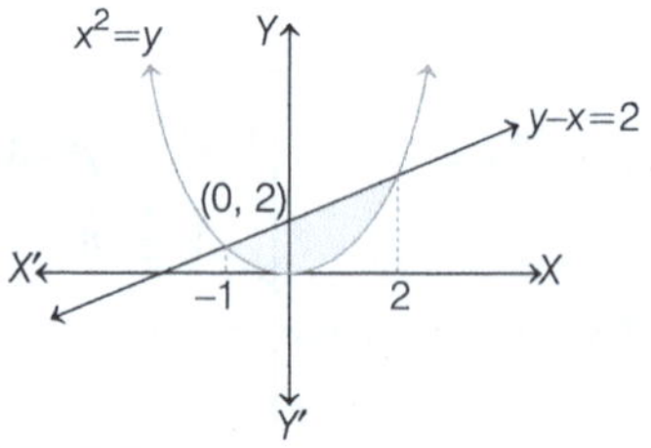

From Eqs. (i) and (ii),

$$x^2 = x + 2 \Rightarrow x^2 - x - 2 = 0$$

$$\Rightarrow \quad (x+1)(x-2) = 0 \Rightarrow x = -1, 2$$

$$\text{Area of shaded region} = \int_{-1}^{2}[(x+2)-x^2]\,dx$$

$$= \left[\frac{x^2}{2}+2x-\frac{x^3}{3}\right]_{-1}^{2}$$

$$= \left(2+4-\frac{8}{3}\right)-\left(\frac{1}{2}-2+\frac{1}{3}\right)$$

$$= \frac{9}{2} \text{ sq units}$$

83.

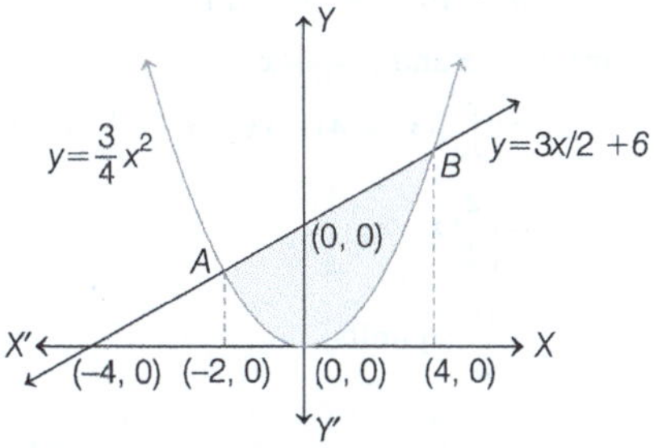

We have, $y=\left(\frac{3}{4}\right)x^2$ and $y=\left(\frac{3x}{2}\right)+6$

$\Rightarrow \quad \frac{3x^2}{4}=\frac{3x}{2}+6 \Rightarrow 3x^2=6x+24$

$\Rightarrow x^2-2x-8=0 \Rightarrow (x-4)(x+2)=0$

$\Rightarrow \quad x=-2, 4 \Rightarrow y=3, 12$

$A(-2, 3)$ and $B(4, 12)$

$\therefore$ Required area $=\int_{-2}^{4}\left[\left(\frac{3x}{2}+6\right)-\left(\frac{3x^2}{4}\right)\right]dx$

$$=\left[\frac{3x^2}{4}+6x-\frac{x^3}{4}\right]_{-2}^{4}$$

$$=[(12+24-16)-(3-12+2)]$$

$$=(20+7)=27 \text{ sq units}$$

84. Equation of given parabola $y=x^2-1$

According to symmetry.

Let the coordinate of $A(-a, 0)$, $B(a, 0)$ $C(a, a^2-1)$ and $D(-a, a^2-1)$.

$\therefore$ Area of rectangle $P(a)=2a(a^2-1)$

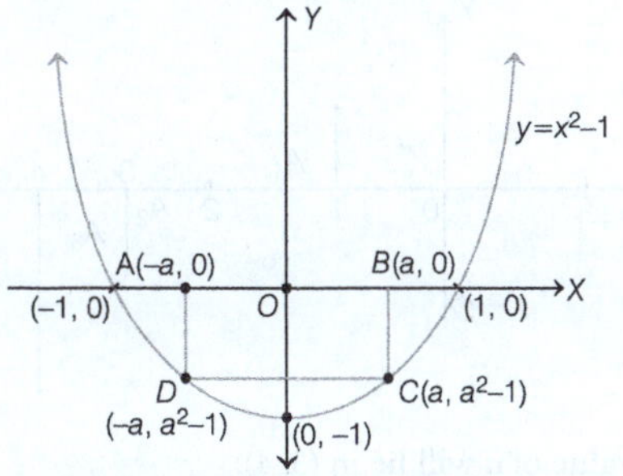

Now, for maxima $P'(a)=0$

$\Rightarrow \quad 2(a^2-1)+4a^2=0$

$\Rightarrow \quad 3a^2=1 \Rightarrow a=1/\sqrt{3}$ units

$\therefore$ Area of largest rectangle is

$$\left|\frac{2}{\sqrt{3}}\left(\frac{1}{3}-1\right)\right|=\frac{4}{3\sqrt{3}} \text{ sq units}$$

85. As we know that

$$y=(x-1)[x]=\begin{cases} 0, & 0\le x<1 \\ x-1, & 1\le x<2 \\ 2(x-1), & x=2 \end{cases}$$

Now, on drawing the graph of given region with the help of equation of curves $y=(x-1)[x]$ and $y=2\sqrt{x}$

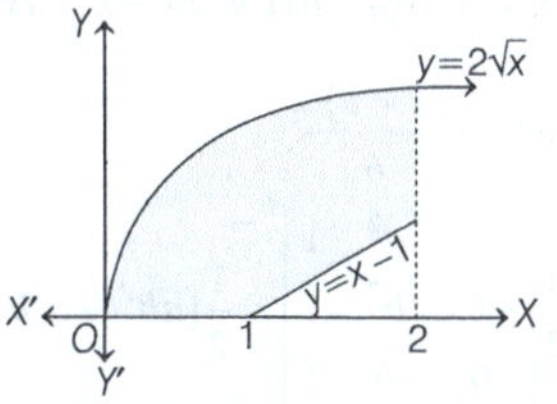

$\therefore$ Area of given region $=\int_0^1 2\sqrt{x}\,dx+\int_1^2(2\sqrt{x}-x+1)dx$

$$=\left[\frac{4}{3}x^{3/2}\right]_0^1+\left[\frac{4}{3}x^{3/2}-\frac{x^2}{2}+x\right]_1^2$$

$$=\frac{4}{3}+\left[\frac{8\sqrt{2}}{3}-2+2-\frac{4}{3}+\frac{1}{2}-1\right]$$

$$=\frac{8\sqrt{2}}{3}-\frac{1}{2} \text{ sq units}$$

Exercise 2 - JEE Advanced Pattern

1. Solving, $e^x=e^{a-x}$, we get

$$e^{2x}=e^a \Rightarrow x=\frac{a}{2}$$

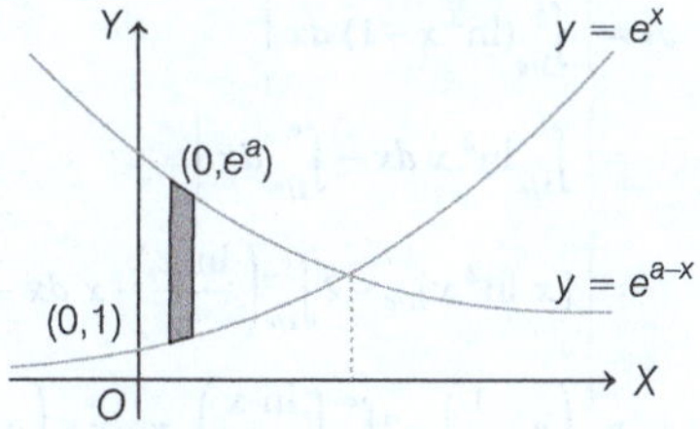

$$S=\int_0^{a/2}(e^a\cdot e^{-x}-e^x)\,dx=[-(e^a\cdot e^{-x}+e^x)]_0^{a/2}$$

$$=(e^a+1)-(e^{a/2}+e^{a/2})$$

$$=e^a-2e^{a/2}+1=(e^{a/2}-1)^2$$

$\therefore \quad \frac{S}{a^2}=\left(\frac{e^{a/2}-1}{a}\right)^2=\frac{1}{4}\left(\frac{e^{a/2}-1}{a/2}\right)^2$

$\therefore \quad \lim_{a\to 0}\frac{S}{a^2}=\frac{1}{4}$

2. $m_{PQ}=\frac{a^2-b^2}{a+b}=a-b$ equation of PQ

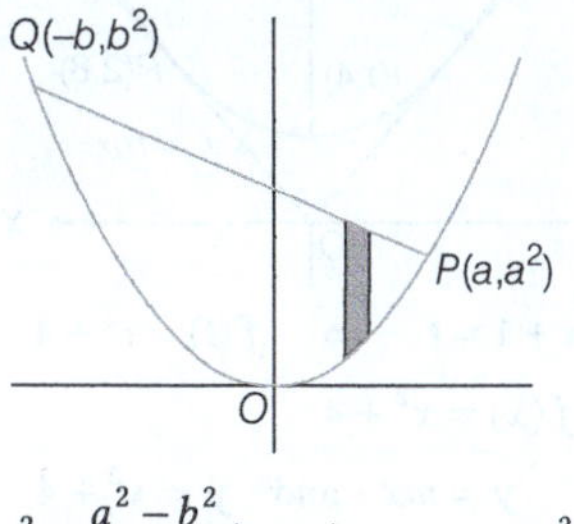

$y-a^2=\frac{a^2-b^2}{a+b}(x-a)$ or $y-a^2=(a-b)(x-a)$

$$y = a^2 + x(a-b) - a^2 + ab$$
$$y = (a-b)x + ab$$
$$\therefore \quad S_1 = \int_{-b}^{a} ((a-b)x + ab - x^2)\, dx$$

which simplifies to $\dfrac{(a+b)^3}{6}$. ...(i)

Also, $S_2 = \dfrac{1}{2}\begin{vmatrix} a & a^2 & 1 \\ -b & b^2 & 1 \\ 0 & 0 & 1 \end{vmatrix} = \dfrac{1}{2}[ab^2 + a^2 b] = \dfrac{1}{2}ab\,(a+b)$ ...(ii)

$$\therefore \quad \frac{S_1}{S_2} = \frac{(a+b)^3}{6} \cdot \frac{2}{ab\,(a+b)} = \frac{(a+b)^2}{3ab} = \frac{1}{3}\left[\frac{a}{b} + \frac{b}{a} + 2\right]$$
$$\therefore \quad \left.\frac{S_1}{S_2}\right|_{\min} = \frac{4}{3}$$

3. $y = (\ln^2 x) - 1 \Rightarrow y' = \dfrac{2\ln x}{x} = 0 \Rightarrow x = 1$

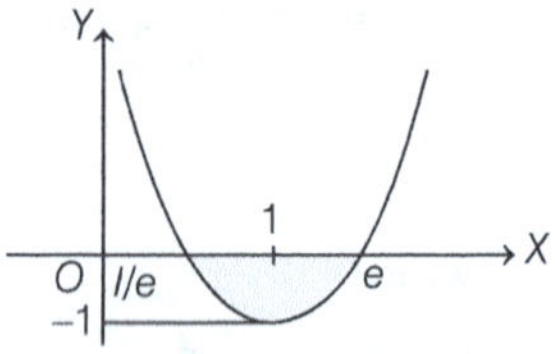

$x > 1$, y increasing and $0 < x < 1$, y is decreasing

$$A = \left| \int_{1/e}^{e} (\ln^2 x - 1)\, dx \right|$$
$$= \left| \int_{1/e}^{e} \ln^2 x\, dx - \int_{1/e}^{e} dx \right|$$
$$= \left| [x \ln^2 x]_{1/e}^{e} - 2\int_{1/e}^{e} \left(\frac{\ln x}{x}\right) \cdot x\, dx - \left(e - \frac{1}{e}\right) \right|$$
$$= \left| \left(e - \frac{1}{e}\right) - 2\int_{1/e}^{e} \left(\frac{\ln x}{x}\right) \cdot x\, dx - \left(e - \frac{1}{e}\right) \right|$$
$$= \left| -2\left[[x \ln x]_{1/e}^{e} - \int_{1/e}^{e} dx \right] \right|$$
$$= \left| -2\left[\left(e + \frac{1}{e}\right) - \left(e - \frac{1}{e}\right) \right] \right| = \left|\frac{4}{e}\right| = \frac{4}{e}$$

4. Given, $g(x) = 2x + 1$; $h(x) = (2x+1)^2 + 4$

Now, $\quad h(x) = f[g(x)]$
$$(2x+1)^2 + 4 = f(2x+1)$$

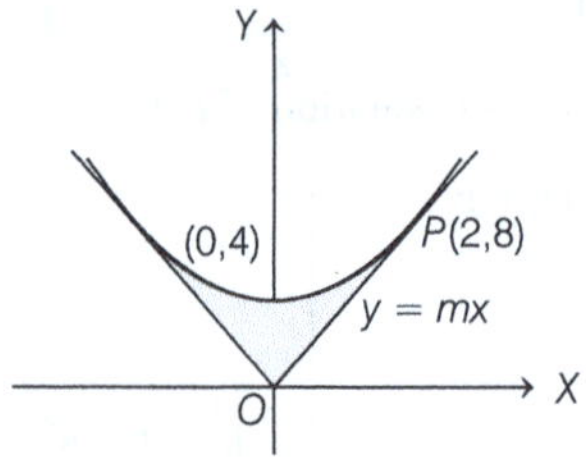

Let $\quad 2x + 1 = t \Rightarrow f(t) = t^2 + 4$

$\therefore \quad f(x) = x^2 + 4$ ...(i)

Solving, $\quad y = mx$ and $y = x^2 + 4$
$$x^2 - mx + 4 = 0$$

Put $D = 0$; $\quad m^2 = 16 \Rightarrow m = \pm 4$

Tangents are $y = 4x$ and $y = -4x$

$$A = 2\int_0^2 [(x^2 + 4) - 4x]\, dx = 2\int_0^2 (x-2)^2 dx$$
$$= \left[\frac{2}{3}(x-2)^3\right]_0^2$$
$$= \frac{16}{3} \text{ sq units}$$

5. $\text{IF} = e^{-x}$

$\therefore \; ye^{-x} = \int e^{-x}(\cos x - \sin x)\, dx.$

Put $-x = t = -\int e^{t}(\cos t + \sin t)\, dt$
$$= -e^{t} \sin t + C$$
$$ye^{-x} = e^{-x} \sin x + C$$

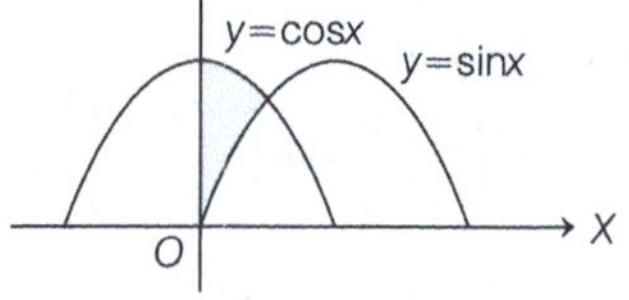

Since, y is bounded when $x \to \infty \Rightarrow C = 0$

$\therefore \quad y = \sin x$

$$\text{Area} = \int_0^{\pi/4} (\cos x - \sin x)\, dx = \sqrt{2} - 1$$

6. $I = \int (6x - 3x^2)\, dx = \dfrac{6x^2}{2} - \dfrac{3x^3}{3} = 3x^2 - x^3 = x^2(3 - x)$

$A_1 = I(2) - I(1) = 4 - 2 = 2$ units

$A_2 = I(2) - I(3) = 4 - 0 = 4$ units

$A_3 = I(3) - I(4) = 0 - (-16) = 16$ units

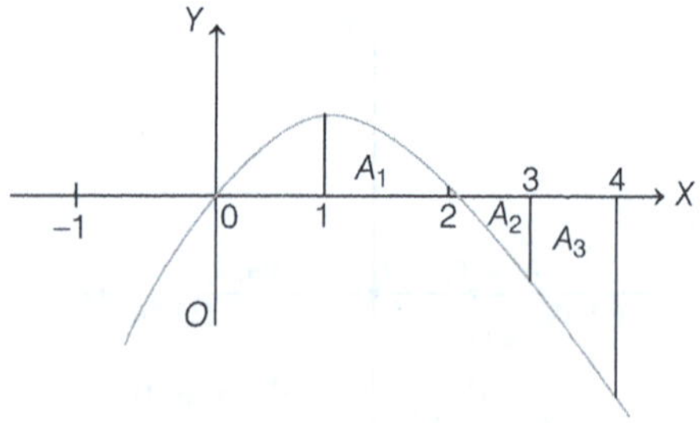

$\Rightarrow$ One value of a will lie in (3, 4).

Using symmetry, other will lie in (–2, –1).

7. $g(x) = |f(|x|) - 2| = ||x| - 1 - 2| = ||x| - 3|$

$$= \begin{cases} (|x| - 3), & x < -3 \\ -(|x| - 3), & -3 \le x < 3 \\ |x| - 3 & x \ge 3 \end{cases} = \begin{cases} -x - 3, & x < -3 \\ -(-x - 3), & -3 \le x < 0 \\ -(x - 3), & 0 \le x < 3 \\ x - 3, & x \ge 3 \end{cases}$$

$$= \begin{cases} -x - 3, & x < -3 \\ x + 3, & -3 \le x < 0 \\ -x + 3, & 0 \le x < 3 \\ x - 3, & x \ge 3 \end{cases}$$

Now, $x^2 - 4y + 8 = 0$

$\Rightarrow$ $x^2 = 4(y - 2)$

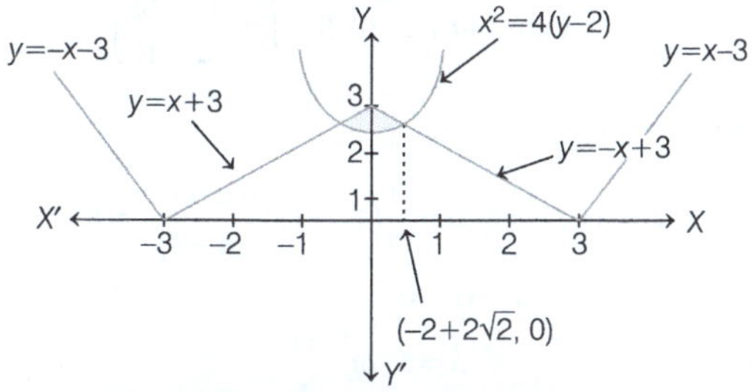

For point of intersection,

$$x^2 - 4(-x + 3) + 8 = 0$$

$$\Rightarrow \quad x^2 + 4x - 4 = 0$$

$$\Rightarrow \quad x = \frac{-4 \pm \sqrt{16 + 16}}{2} = -2 \pm 2\sqrt{2}$$

$\therefore$ Point of intersection is at $x = -2 + 2\sqrt{2}$

$$\therefore \text{ Required area} = 2\int_0^{-2+2\sqrt{2}} \left[(-x + 3) - \left(\frac{x^2 + 8}{4}\right)\right] dx$$

$$= \frac{2}{4}\int_0^{-2+2\sqrt{2}} (4 - 4x - x^2)\, dx = \frac{1}{2}\left[4x - 2x^2 - \frac{x^3}{3}\right]_0^{-2+2\sqrt{2}}$$

$$= \frac{1}{6}\,[12x - 6x^2 - x^3]_0^{-2+2\sqrt{2}}$$

$$= \frac{1}{6}[12(-2 + 2\sqrt{2}) - 6(-2 + 2\sqrt{2})^2 - (-2 + 2\sqrt{2})^3]$$

$$= \frac{1}{6}\,[-24 + 24\sqrt{2} - 6(4 + 8 - 8\sqrt{2}) - (-8 + 16\sqrt{2}) + 24\sqrt{2} - 48]$$

$$= \frac{1}{6}\,[-24 + 24\sqrt{2} - 72 + 48\sqrt{2} + 56 - 40\sqrt{2}]$$

$$= \frac{1}{6}\,[32\sqrt{2} - 40] = \frac{8}{6}\,(4\sqrt{2} - 5)$$

$$= \frac{4}{3}(4\sqrt{2} - 5)$$

8. $y = \sqrt{2ax - x^2} \Rightarrow (x - a)^2 + y^2 = a^2$

Let $P(h,k)$ be a point, then $BP > PN$

For the bounded condition $BP = PN = k$

Now, $AP = a - k = \sqrt{(h - a)^2 + k^2} \Rightarrow k = h - \dfrac{h^2}{2a}$

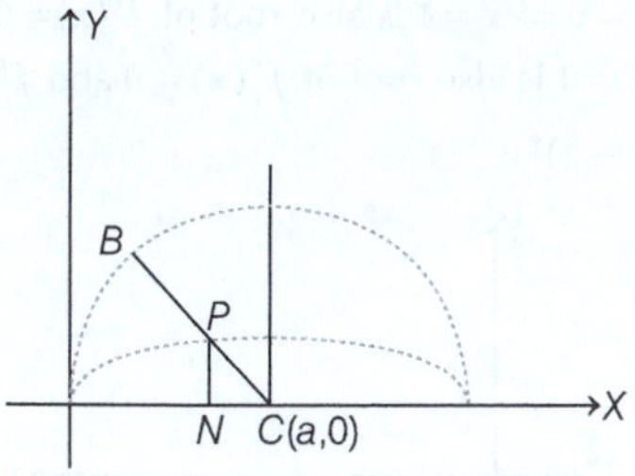

$\therefore$ Boundary of the region is $y = x - \dfrac{x^2}{2a}$

$$\text{Required area} = 2\int_0^a \left(x - \frac{x^2}{2a}\right) dx = \frac{2a^2}{3}$$

9. If $y = x - 1 \Rightarrow x^2 + (x - 1)^2 = 5 \Rightarrow x = 2\,(x \neq -1)$

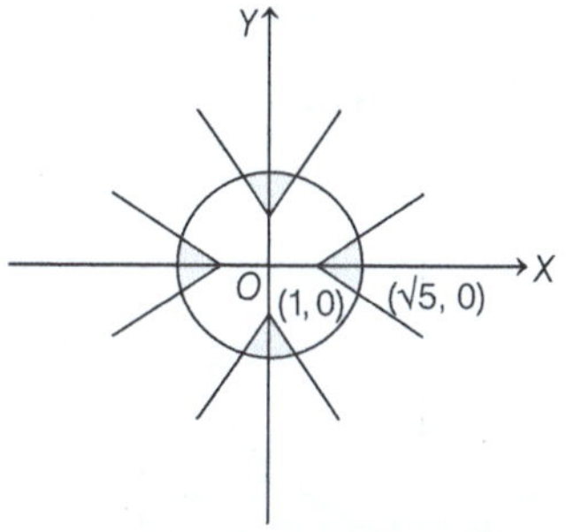

$$\therefore \text{ Required area} = 8\left(\frac{1}{2}\cdot 1\cdot 1 + \int_2^{\sqrt{5}} \sqrt{5 - x^2}\,dx\right)$$

$$= 4 + 8\left[\frac{x}{2}\sqrt{5 - x^2} + \frac{5}{2}\sin^{-1}\left(\frac{x}{\sqrt{5}}\right)\right]_2^{\sqrt{5}}$$

$$= 10\pi - 20\sin^{-1}\left(\frac{2}{\sqrt{5}}\right) - 4 = 20\cos^{-1}\left(\frac{2}{\sqrt{5}}\right) - 4$$

$$= 20\tan^{-1}\left(\frac{1}{2}\right) - 4 = 5\left(\pi - \tan^{-1}\left(\frac{24}{7}\right) - 4\right)$$

$$\left[\because 4\tan^{-1}\left(\frac{1}{2}\right) = \pi - \tan^{-1}\left(\frac{24}{7}\right)\right]$$

10. $|3x - 18| + |2y + 7| \le 3$

$$\Rightarrow \frac{3|x - 6|}{3} + \frac{2\left|y + \frac{7}{2}\right|}{3} \le 1 \Rightarrow |x - 6| + \frac{\left|y + \frac{7}{2}\right|}{\frac{3}{2}} \le 1$$

Area remains invariant under translation of coordinate axes.

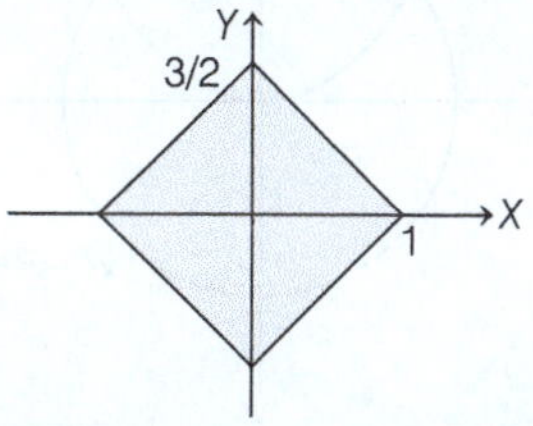

Let $x - 6 = x'$ and let $y + \dfrac{7}{2} = y' \Rightarrow |x'| + \dfrac{|y'|}{\frac{3}{2}} \le 1$

$$\text{Required shaded area} = 4\left[\frac{1}{2}(1)\left(\frac{3}{2}\right)\right] = 3$$

11. We have, $f^3(x) = \int_0^x t\, f^2(t)\,dt$

On differentiating w.r.t. x, we get

$$3f^2(x)f'(x) = xf^2(x)$$

$$\Rightarrow \quad f^2(x)[3f'(x) - x] = 0$$

As, $\quad f(x) \neq 0$

$$\Rightarrow \quad f'(x) = \frac{x}{3}$$

$$\Rightarrow \quad f(x) = \frac{x^2}{6} + C$$

But $f(0) = 0$

$\Rightarrow C = 0$

$\Rightarrow f(x) = \frac{x^2}{6}$

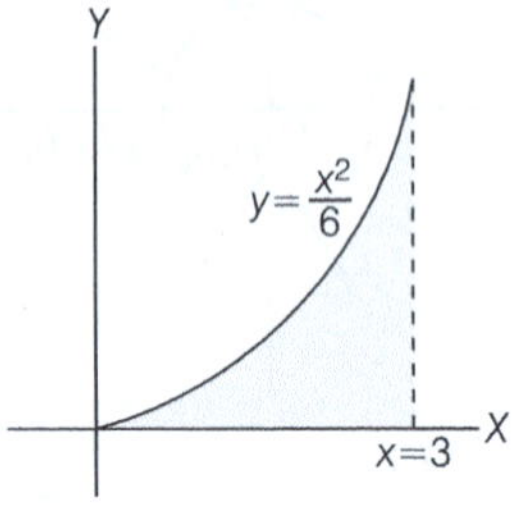

$\therefore$ Area, $A = \frac{1}{6}\int_0^3 x^2 dx = \left[\frac{x^3}{18}\right]_0^3 = \frac{3}{2}$ sq units

12. We have, $\lim_{x \to 0}\left[1 + \frac{f(x)}{x^3}\right]^{1/x}$ exists.

So, $\lim_{x \to 0} \frac{f(x)}{x^3} = 0$

It means $f(x) = a_4x^4 + a_5x^5 + \ldots + a_nx^n, a_n \neq 0, \ n \geq 4$

$f(x)$ is of least degree $f(x) = a_4x^4$

$$\lim_{x \to 0}\left[1 + \frac{f(x)}{x^3}\right]^{1/x} = e, a_4 = 1, f(x) = x^4$$

The graph of $y = x^4$ and $x^2 + y^2 = 2$

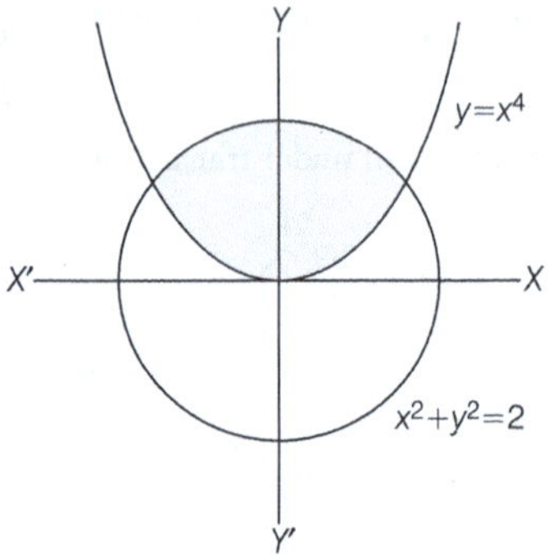

$\therefore$ Area $= 2\int_0^1 (\sqrt{2 - x^2} - x^4)dx$

$$\text{Area} = 2\left[\frac{x\sqrt{2-x^2}}{2} + \frac{2}{2}\sin^{-1}\left(\frac{x}{\sqrt{2}}\right) - \frac{x^5}{5}\right]_0^1$$

$$= 2\left[\left(\frac{1}{2} + \frac{\pi}{4} - \frac{1}{5}\right) - 0\right]$$

$$= 1 + \frac{\pi}{2} - \frac{2}{5}$$

$$= \left(\frac{\pi}{2} + \frac{3}{5}\right) \text{ sq units}$$

13. $f'(x) = 2x - a.$

At (2, 4), $f'(x) = 4 - a$

Equation of normal at (2, 4) is $(y - 4) = -\frac{1}{(4-a)}(x - 2)$

Let point of intersection with X and Y-axes be A and B respectively, then

$$A \equiv (-4a + 18, 0) \ B \equiv \left(0, \frac{4a - 18}{a - 4}\right)$$

Since, $a > \frac{9}{2}$ as

$\therefore$ Area of triangle $= \frac{1}{2}(4a - 18)\frac{(4a-18)}{(a-4)} = 2$

$\Rightarrow (4a - 17)(a - 5) = 0$

$\Rightarrow a = 5$ or $\frac{17}{4}$

14. $a_1 = 0, b_1 = 32, a_2 = a_1 + \frac{3}{2}b_1 = 48, b_2 = \frac{b_1}{2} = 16$

$a_3 = 48 + \frac{3}{2}16 = 72, b_3 = \frac{16}{2} = 8$

So, the three loops from $i = 1$ to $i = 3$ are alike.

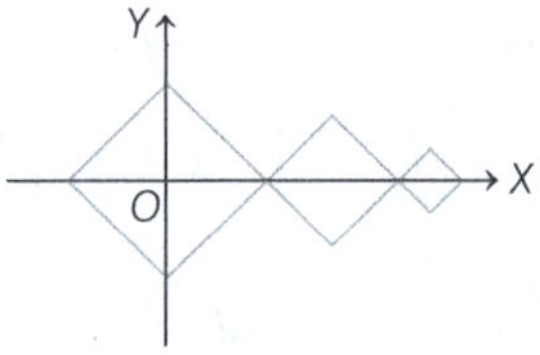

Now, area of ith loop (square) $= \frac{1}{2}(\text{diagonal})^2 = \frac{1}{2}(2b_i)^2 = 2(b_i)^2$

$$A_3 = 2(b_3)^2 = 2 \times 8^2 = 128$$

So, $\frac{2(b_{i+1})^2}{2(b_i)^2} = \frac{1}{4}$

So, the areas form a GP series.

So, the sum of the GP upto infinite terms

$$= A_1 \frac{1}{1-r} = 2(32)^2 \times \frac{1}{1 - \frac{1}{4}}$$

$$= 2 \times (32)^2 \times \frac{4}{3} = \frac{8}{3}(32)^2 \text{ sq units}$$

15. Clearly, $x = 1$ is a root of $f(x) = 0$

and $f'(x) = A(x)\,B(x) \cdot \int_1^x C(t)D(t)dt + C(x)\,D(x)\int_1^x A(t)B(t)dt$

$$-A(x)\,C(x)\int_1^x B(t)\,D(t)dt - B(x)\,D(x) \cdot \int_1^x A(t)\,C(t)dt$$

Now, $f'(1) = 0 \Rightarrow x = 1$ is also root of $f'(x) = 0$

Similarly, $x = 1$ is also root of $f''(x) = 0$ and $f'''(x) = 0$

$\therefore f(x) = (x - 1)^4$

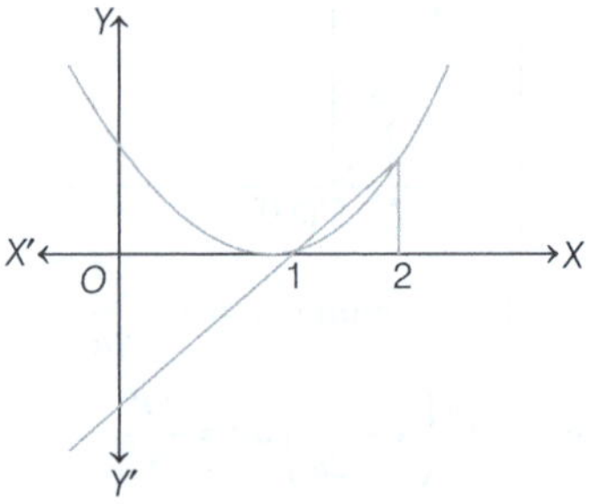

Required area $= \frac{1}{2} - \int_1^2 (x-1)^4\,dx = \frac{3}{10}$

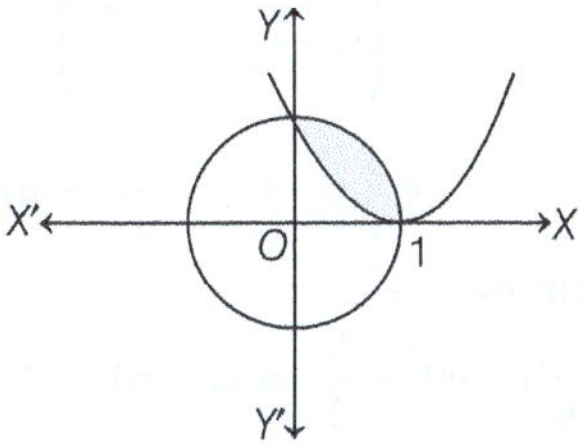

Required area $= \frac{\pi}{4} - \int_0^1 (x-1)^4\,dx = \frac{\pi}{4} - \frac{1}{5}$

16. $\sec^{-1} x = \cot^{-1} x \Rightarrow x = \sec(\cot^{-1} x) = \frac{\sqrt{1+\sqrt{x^2}}}{x}$

$\Rightarrow \quad x^4 - x^2 - 1 = 0 \Rightarrow x^2 = \frac{1+\sqrt{5}}{2}$

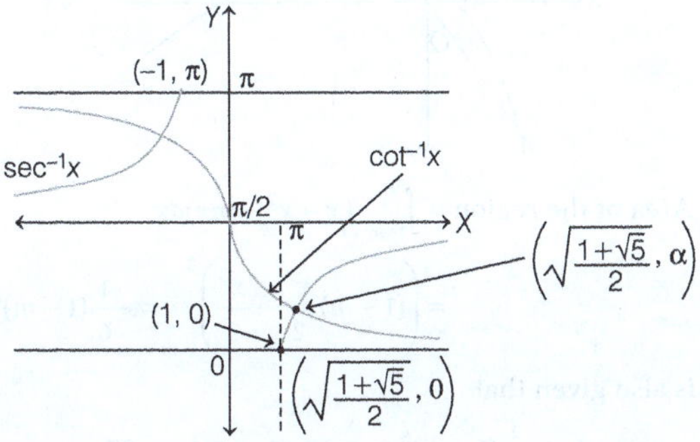

Required area $= \int_1^{\sqrt{\frac{1+\sqrt{5}}{2}}} (\cot^{-1} x - \sec^{-1} x)\,dx$

or $\int_0^{\alpha} (\sec y)dy + \int_{\alpha}^{\pi/4} \cot y\, dy - \frac{\pi}{4}$

where, $\sec^{-1} x = \alpha = \cot^{-1} x$

$\Rightarrow \quad x = \sec\alpha = \cot\alpha \Rightarrow \cos^2\alpha = \sin\alpha$

17.

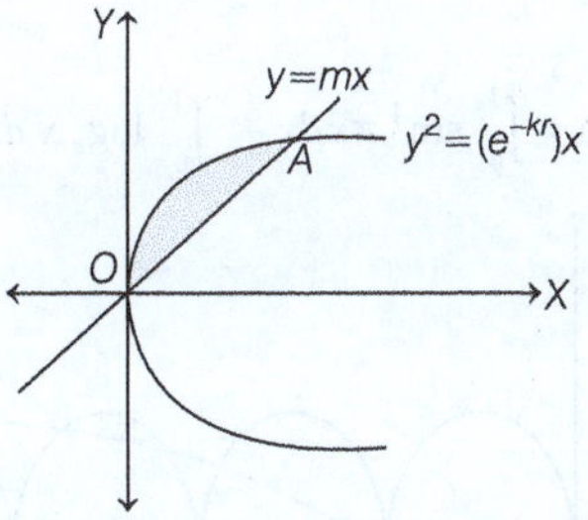

Solving the two equations,

$$m^2x^2 = (e^{-kr})x;\ x_1 = 0,\ x_2 = \frac{e^{-2kr}}{6m^3}$$

So, $\quad A_r = \int_{x_1}^{x_2} \left(e^{\frac{-kr}{2}} \sqrt{x} - mx \right) dx = \frac{e^{-2kr}}{6m^3}$

Now, $\frac{A_{r+1}}{A_r} = \frac{e^{-2k(r+1)}}{e^{-2kr}} = e^{-2k} = \text{constant}$

So, the sequence, $A_1, A_2, A_3, \ldots$ is in GP.

$$\lim_{n\to\infty} \sum_{i=1}^{n} A_i = \frac{e^{-2k}}{6m^3} \times \frac{e^{2k}}{e^{2k-1}} = \frac{1}{6m^3(e^{2k-1})}$$

18. For $x \in \left(0, \frac{\pi}{2}\right)$

$$0 < \sin x < 1 < \operatorname{cosec} x < \infty$$

So, $\sin x^{\operatorname{cosec} x} < \sin x^{\sin x} < \operatorname{cosec} x^{\sin x} < \operatorname{cosec} x^{\operatorname{cosec} x}$

$$A_1 < A_3 < A_2 < A_4$$

19. Given, $\quad y = e^{x^2}$ and $y = e$

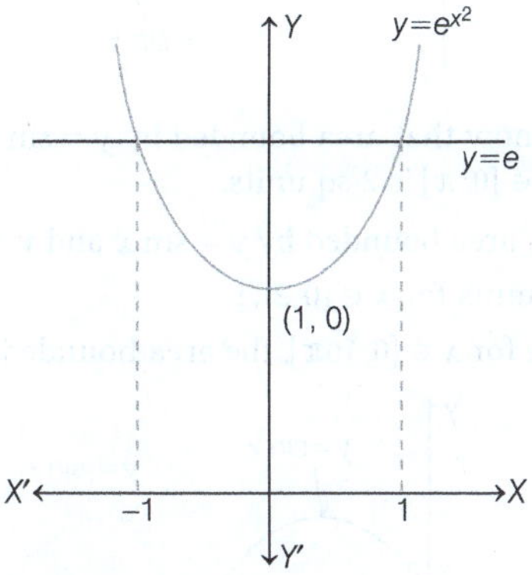

Area, $\quad A = \int_{-1}^{1} (e - e^{x^2})dx = 2e - \int_{-1}^{1} e^{x^2}dx$

$$y = e^{x^2}$$

$\therefore \quad \log_e y = x^2 \Rightarrow x = \pm\sqrt{\log_e y}$

$\therefore$ Area, $A = 2\int_1^e \sqrt{\log_e y}\, dy$

Now, put $\log_e y = t$

$\therefore \quad y = e^t$

$\therefore \quad dy = e^t dt$

So, area, $A = 2\int_0^1 \sqrt{t}\, e^t dt$

20. It is given that $x = \alpha$ divides the shaded region into two equal parts.

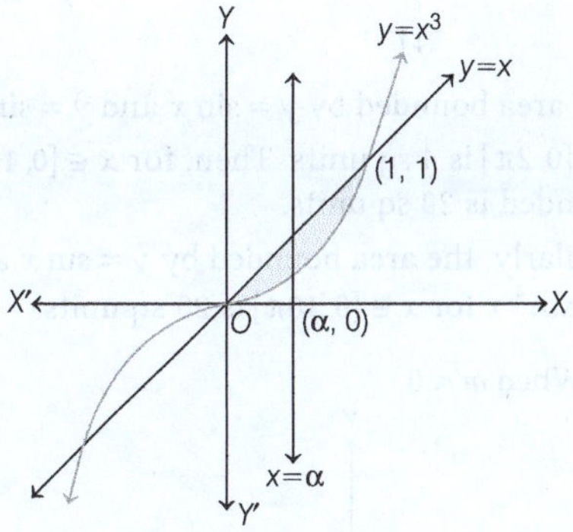

$\therefore \quad 2\int_0^{\alpha} (x - x^3)dx = \int_0^1 (x - x^3)dx \Rightarrow 2\left[\frac{x^2}{2} - \frac{x^4}{4}\right]_0^{\alpha} = \left[\frac{x^2}{2} - \frac{x^4}{4}\right]_0^1$

$\Rightarrow \quad \alpha^2 - \frac{\alpha^4}{2} = \frac{1}{4} \Rightarrow 2\alpha^4 - 4\alpha^2 + 1 = 0$

Let $f(\alpha) = 2\alpha^4 - 4\alpha^2 + 1.$

Then, $f(1) = -1 < 0$

and $f\left(\frac{1}{2}\right) = \frac{1}{8} > 0 \Rightarrow \frac{1}{2} < \alpha < 1$

21. (a)

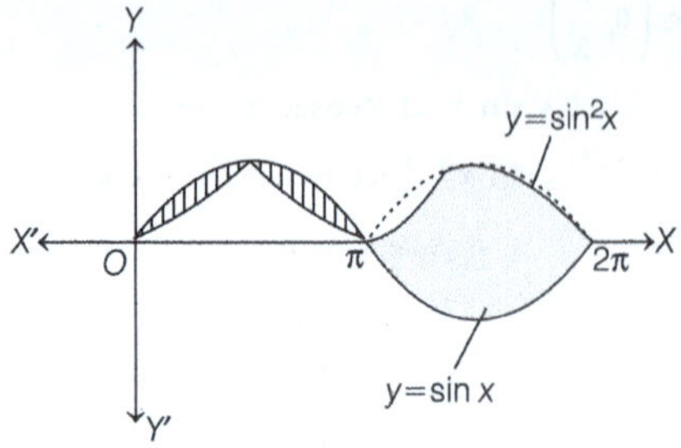

We know that area bounded by $y = \sin x$ and X-axis for $x \in [0, \pi]$ is 2 sq units.

Then, area bounded by $y = \sin x$ and $y = \sin^2 x$ is 4 sq. units for $x \in [0, 2\pi]$.

Then, for $x \in [0, 10\pi]$, the area bounded is 20 sq units.

(b)

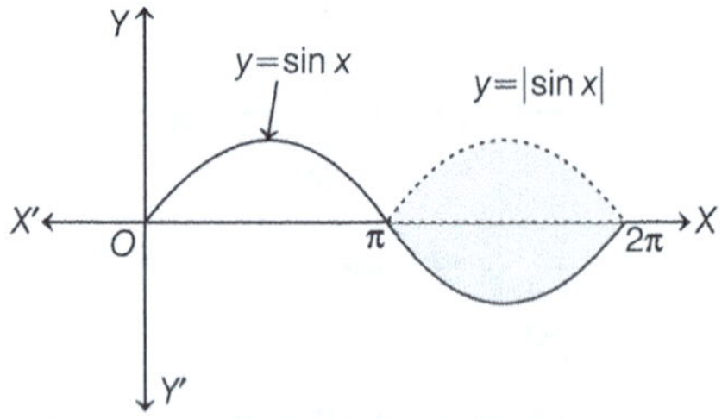

The area bounded by $y = |\sin x|$ and $y = |\sin x|$ for $x \in [0, 2\pi]$ is 4 sq units.

Then, for $x \in [0, 20\pi]$, the area bounded is 40 sq units.

(c)

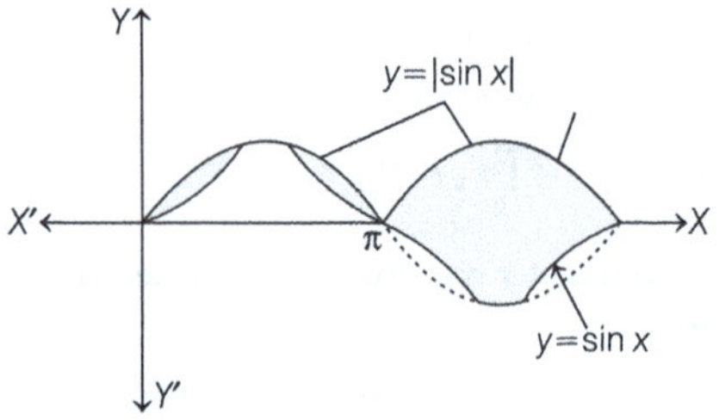

The area bounded by $y = \sin x$ and $y = \sin^3 x$ for $x \in [0, 2\pi]$ is 4 sq units. Then, for $x \in [0, 10\pi]$, the area bounded is 20 sq units.

(d) Similarly, the area bounded by $y = \sin x$ and $y = \sin^4 x$ for $x \in [0, 10\pi]$ is 20 sq units.

22. **Case I** When $m < 0$

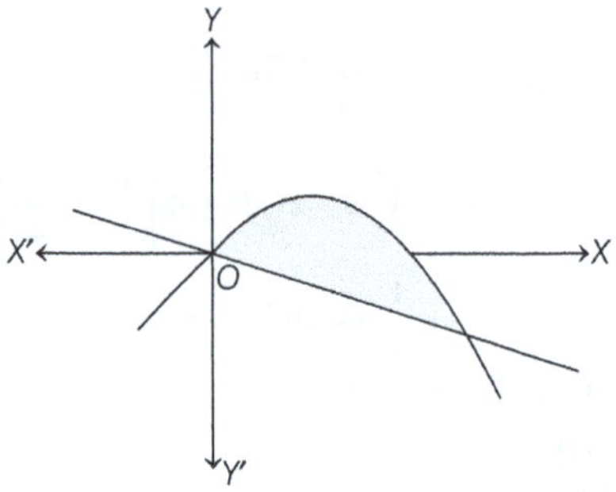

$\therefore$ Area of the region $= \int_0^{1-m} [(x - x^2) - mx]dx$

$$= \left((1-m)\frac{x^2}{2} - \frac{x^3}{3}\right)_0^{1-m}$$

$$= \frac{1}{2}(1-m)^3 - \frac{1}{3}(1-m)^3 = \frac{1}{6}(1-m)^3$$

Also, it is given that

$$\frac{1}{6}(1-m)^3 = \frac{9}{2} \Rightarrow (1-m)^3 = 27$$

$$\Rightarrow \quad (1-m) = 3 \Rightarrow m = -2$$

Case II When $m > 0$

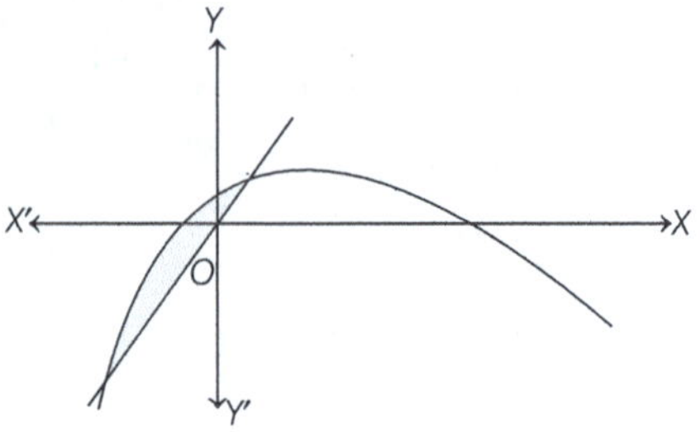

$\therefore$ Area of the region $= \int_{1-m}^{0} (x - x^2 - mx)dx$

$$= \left((1-m)\frac{x^2}{2} - \frac{x^3}{3}\right)_{1-m}^{0} = -\frac{1}{6}(1-m)^3$$

It is also given that

$$-\frac{1}{6}(1-m)^3 = \frac{9}{2} \Rightarrow (1-m)^3 = -27$$

$$\Rightarrow \quad 1 - m = -3 \Rightarrow m = 4$$

23. Since, absolute area

$$= \int_{x_0}^{x_1} h(x)\,dx + \int_{x_1}^{x_2} -h(x)\,dx + \int_{x_2}^{x_3} h(x)\,dx$$

$$= \sum_{r=0}^{n} \int_{x_r}^{x_{r+1}} (-1)^r \cdot h(x)\,dx$$

24. Required area $= \int_0^1 \sin^4 \pi x\,dx - \int_0^1 \log_e x\,dx = \frac{11}{8}$

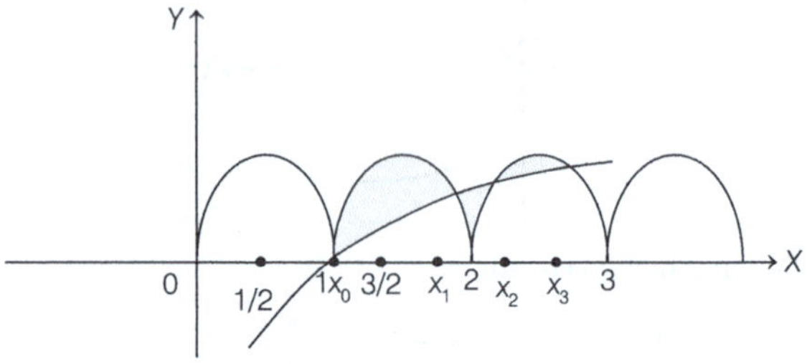

25. The graph of $f(|x|)$ is,

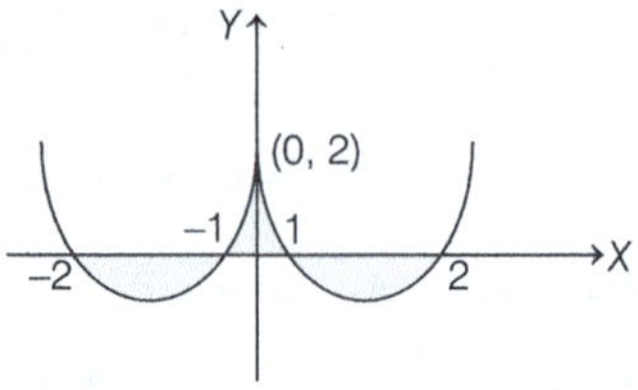

$\therefore$ Required area $= 2\int_0^1 f(x)dx + 2\left|\int_1^2 f(x)dx\right|$

$$= 2\int_0^1 (x^2 - 3x + 2)dx + 2\left|\int_1^2 (x^2 - 3x + 2)\right|dx$$

$$= 2\left[\frac{x^3}{3} - \frac{3x^2}{2} + 2x\right]_0^1 + 2\left[\frac{x^3}{3} - \frac{3x^2}{2} + 2x\right]_1^2$$

$$= 2\left[\frac{1}{3} - \frac{3}{2} + 2 - 0\right] + 2\left[\frac{8}{3} - 6 + 4 + \frac{3}{2} - \frac{1}{3} - 2\right]$$

$$= 2 \times \frac{5}{6} + 2 \times \frac{1}{6} = \frac{5}{3} + \frac{1}{3} = \frac{6}{3}$$

$= 2$ sq units

26. The graph of $|f(|x|)|$ is

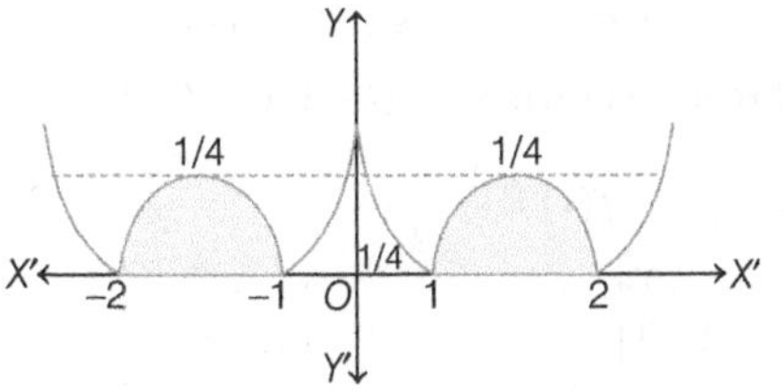

$\because 1 \le |x| \le 2$

$\because x \in [-2, -1] \cup [1, 2]$

$\because$ Required area $= 2\left|\int_1^2 f(x)\,dx\right| = 2\left|\int_1^2 (x^2 - 3x + 2)dx\right|$

$$= 2\left|\left\{\frac{x^3}{3} - \frac{3x^2}{2} + 2x\right\}_1^2\right|$$

$$= 2\left|\left\{\left(\frac{18}{3} - \frac{12}{2} + 4\right) - \left(\frac{1}{3} - \frac{3}{2} + 2\right)\right\}\right|$$

$$= 2\left|\frac{2}{3} - \frac{5}{6}\right| = \frac{1}{3} \text{ sq unit}$$

27. Clearly, $x = a\sin^3 t, y = a\cos^3 t, (0 \le t \le 2\pi)$

$$S = \int_0^{2\pi} a\sin^3 t \cdot a \cdot 3\cos^2 t(-\sin t)\,dt$$

$$= -3a^2 \times \int_0^{\pi/2} \sin^4 t\cos^2 t\,dt$$

$$= -3a^2 \times \frac{\Gamma\frac{5}{2}\Gamma\frac{3}{2}}{2\Gamma\frac{4+2+2}{2}} = -3a^2\frac{\frac{3}{2}\times\frac{1}{2}\sqrt{\pi}\times\frac{1}{2}\sqrt{\pi}}{2\times3\times2\times1}$$

$$= -\frac{3}{8}\pi a^2 = \frac{3}{8}\pi a^2 \qquad \text{[absolute value]}$$

28. $S = -\int_0^{2\pi} a(1 - \cos t)a(1 - \cos t)\,dt$

$$= -a^2\int_0^{2\pi} (1 - 2\cos t + \cos^2 t)\,dt$$

$$= -a^2\int_0^{2\pi}\left(1 - 2\cos t + \left(\frac{1 + \cos 2t}{2}\right)\right)dt$$

$$= -\frac{a^2}{2}\int_0^{2\pi} [3 - 4\cos t + \cos 2t]_0^{2\pi}$$

$$= -3\pi a^2 = 3\pi a^2 \qquad \text{[absolute value]}$$

29. Since, $-1 \le \sin x \le 1$, the curve $y = e^{-x}\sin x$ is bounded by the curves $y = e^{-x}$ and $y = e^{-x}$.

Also, the curve $y = e^{-x}\sin x$ intersects the positive semi-axis OX at the points, where $\sin x = 0$, where $x_n = n\pi$, $n \in Z$.

Also, $[y_n] = [y\text{-coordinate in the half-wave } S_n]$

$= (-1)^n e^{-x}\sin x$ and in S_n

$n\pi \le x \le (n+1)\pi$

$$\therefore \quad S_n = (-1)^n\int_{n\pi}^{(n+1)\pi} e^{-x}\sin x\,dx$$

$$= \frac{(-1)^{n+1}}{2}[e^{-x}(-\sin x + \cos x)]_{n\pi}^{(n+1)\pi}$$

$$= \frac{(-1)^{n+1}}{2}[e^{-(n+1)\pi}(-1)^{n+1} - e^{-n\pi}(-1)^n]$$

$$= \frac{e^{-n\pi}}{2}(1 + e^{-\pi})$$

$$\Rightarrow \quad \frac{S_{n+1}}{S_n} = e^{-\pi}$$

and $S_0 = \frac{1}{2}(1 + e^{-\pi})$ sq units

30. $$\sum_{n=0}^{\infty} S_n = \frac{\frac{1}{2}(1 + e^{\pi})}{1 - e^{-\pi}}$$

$$\because \sum_{k=0}^{n} S_k = S_0 + S_1 + S_2 + S_3 + \ldots + S_n$$

$$= \left(\frac{1 + e^{-\pi}}{2}\right) + e^{-\pi}\frac{(1 + e^{-\pi})}{2} + e^{-2\pi}\frac{(1 + e^{-\pi})}{2} + \ldots + \frac{e^{-n\pi}(1 + e^{-\pi})}{2}$$

$$\sum_{k=0}^{\infty} S_k = \lim_{n\to\infty}\left(\sum_{k=0}^{n} S_n\right) = \left(\frac{1 + e^{-\pi}}{2}\right)\cdot\frac{1}{1 - e^{-\pi}}$$

[common ratio $= e^{-\pi}$]

$$\therefore \quad \sum_{n=0}^{\infty} S_n = \frac{\frac{1}{2}(1 + e^{\pi})}{1 - e^{-\pi}}$$

Sol. (31-32)

Given, $A(c) = \int_0^c f(x)dx$

and $B(c) = \int_c^5 f(x)dx$

$\therefore \quad A'(c) = f(c)$ ...(i)

and $B'(c) = -f(c)$ ...(ii)

$\Rightarrow \quad A'(c) + B'(c) = 0$

Now, $A(3) + B(3) = \int_0^3 f(x)dx + \int_3^5 f(x)dx$

$\Rightarrow \quad A(3) + B(3) = \int_0^3 f(x)dx + \int_3^5 f(x)dx$

$\Rightarrow \quad A(3) + B(3) = \int_0^5 f(x)dx = 8$

Also, given $R(3) = 1 \Rightarrow A(3) = B(3)$

Hence, $A(3) = B(3) = 4$ [using Eq. (iii)]

Ans. 31. (4) **32.** (0)

33. When $\alpha = 0$, then $f(0)$ denotes that area of the shaded region bounded by $x = 0$, $y = 3$, $x = 2$ and $y^2 = 4x$

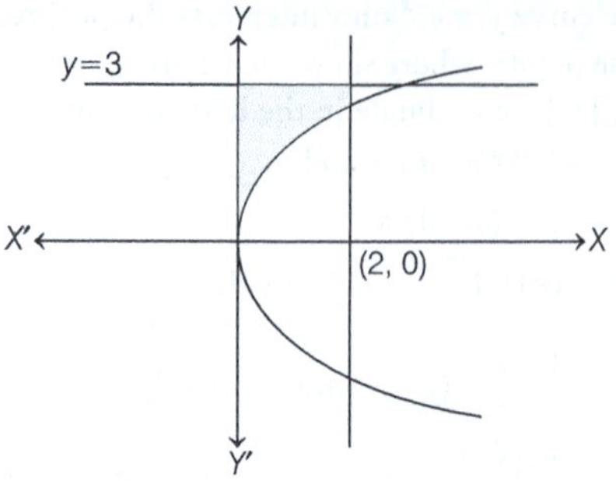

$$\therefore \quad f(0) = \int_0^2 (3-y)\,dx = \int_0^2 (3-2\sqrt{x})\,dx$$

$$= \left[3x - \frac{4x^{3/2}}{3}\right]_0^2 = 6 - \frac{8\sqrt{2}}{3}$$

So, $f(0) + \dfrac{8\sqrt{2}}{3} = 6$

34. When $\alpha = 1$, then $f(1)$ is the area of shaded region bounded by $x = 0$, $x = 2$, $y^2 = 4x$

and $\quad y = |x-1| + |x-2| + x$

$$y = \begin{cases} -x+3, & x < 1 \\ x+1, & 1 \le x < 2 \\ 3x-3, & x \ge 2 \end{cases}$$

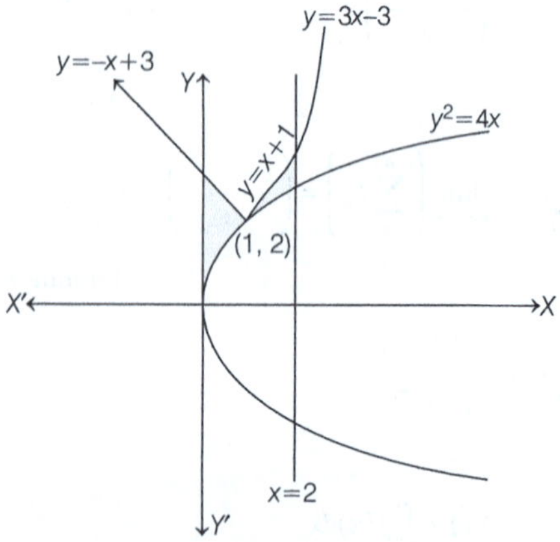

$$f(1) = \int_0^1 (-x+3-2\sqrt{x})\,dx + \int_1^2 (x+1-2\sqrt{x})\,dx$$

$$= \left[-\frac{x^2}{2} + 3x - \frac{4}{3}x^{3/2}\right]_0^1 + \left[\frac{x^2}{2} + x - \frac{4}{3}x^{3/2}\right]_1^2$$

$$= \left(-\frac{1}{2} + 3 - \frac{4}{3}\right) + \left(2 + 2 - \frac{8\sqrt{2}}{3} - \frac{1}{2} - 1 + \frac{4}{3}\right)$$

$$f(1) = 5 - \frac{8}{3}\sqrt{2} \Rightarrow f(1) + \frac{8}{3}\sqrt{2} = 5$$

35. If $[|x|] = 1$ and $[|y|] = 0$, then $1 \le |x| < 2, 0 \le |y| < 1$

$\Rightarrow \quad x \in (-2, -1] \cup [1, 2), y \in (-1, 1)$

If $\quad [|x|] = 0, [|y|] = 1$

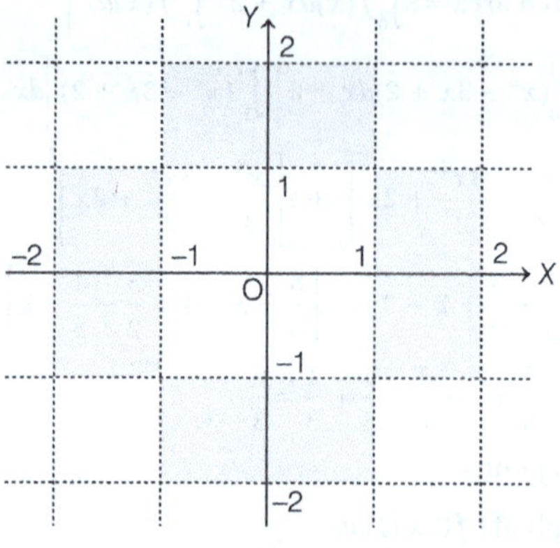

Then, $\quad x \in (-1, 1), y \in (-2, -1] \cup [1, 2]$

Area of required region $= 4(2-1)(1-(-1)) = 8$ sq units

36. Clearly, $\quad f(x) = \dfrac{2x - x^2}{2}$

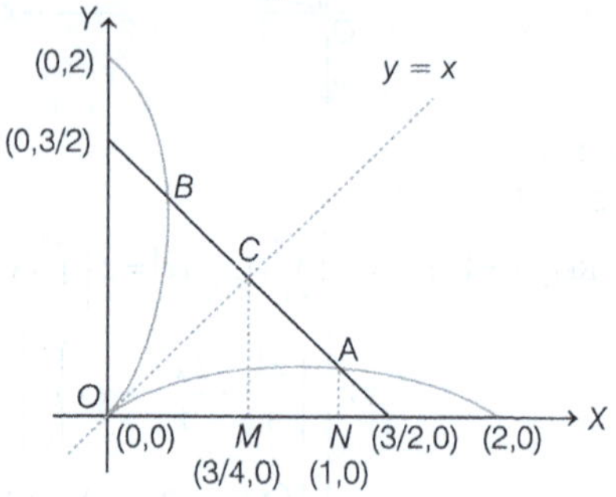

Since, $2x + 2y = 3$; passes through $A\left(1, \dfrac{1}{2}\right)$ and $B\left(\dfrac{1}{2}, 1\right)$

so bounded area A

= Area OAB = 2 [Area OCM + Area $CMNA$ − Area ONA]

$$= 2\left[\frac{1}{2} \times \frac{3}{4} \times \frac{3}{4} + \frac{1}{2}\left(\frac{3}{4} + \frac{1}{2}\right) \times \frac{1}{4} - \frac{1}{2}\int_0^1 (2x - x^2)\,dx\right] = \frac{5}{24}$$

$\Rightarrow \quad 24A = 5$

37. $f(x) = \min\left\{\sin^{-1} x, \cos^{-1}, x - \dfrac{\pi}{6}\right\}, x \in [0, 1]$

$$\therefore \text{Area} = \int_0^{1/2} \sin^{-1} x, dx + \frac{1}{2}\left(\frac{\sqrt{3}}{2} - \frac{1}{2}\right) + \int_{\sqrt{3}/2}^1 \cos^{-1} x\,dx$$

$$= (x\sin^{-1} x + \sqrt{1-x^2})_0^{1/2} + \frac{\sqrt{3}-1}{4} + (x\cos^{-1} x - \sqrt{1-x^2})_{\sqrt{3}/2}$$

$$= \frac{\pi}{2}(1 - \sqrt{3}) + \frac{\sqrt{3}-1}{2} + \frac{\sqrt{3}-1}{2}$$

$$= (\sqrt{3} - 1)\left(\frac{3}{4} - \frac{\pi}{12}\right)$$

$$= \frac{9 - \pi}{6(\sqrt{3}+1)} = \frac{a - \pi}{b(\sqrt{3}+1)}$$

$\therefore \quad a = 9, b = 6$

$\Rightarrow \quad a - b = 3$

38. $y = (2011)^x \log 2011 = k^x \log k$ [let $k = 2011$]

$y = (2011)^{-x} \log 2011 = \log^{\frac{k}{k^x}}$

$$\text{Area} = \int_0^1 k^x \log k - \int_0^1 k^{-x} \log k \, dx$$

$$= \log k \frac{\{k^x\}_0^1}{\log k} + \log k \frac{\{k^{-x}\}_0^1}{\log k}$$

$$= (k-1) + \left(\frac{1}{k-1}\right) = k + \frac{1}{k} - 2$$

$\Rightarrow \quad A = 2009 + \dfrac{1}{2011}$

$\Rightarrow \quad A + 2 = 2011 + \dfrac{1}{2011}$

$\Rightarrow \quad [A+2] = 2011; \{A\} = \dfrac{1}{2011}$

$\therefore \quad [A+2] = 2011$

$\therefore \quad [A+2]\{A\} = 1$

39. $S_k = \int_0^1 x^2(1-x)^k dx = \int_0^1 (1-x^2)x^k dx$

$$= \int_0^1 (x^k - 2x^{k+1} + x^{k+2}) dx$$

$$= \frac{1}{k+1} - \frac{2}{k+2} + \frac{1}{k+3}$$

Now, $\lim_{n \to \infty} \sum_{k=1}^{n} S_k = \sum_{k=1}^{\infty}\left(\frac{1}{k+1} - \frac{1}{k+2}\right) - \sum_{k=1}^{\infty}\left(\frac{1}{k+2} - \frac{1}{k+3}\right)$

$$= \frac{1}{2} - \frac{1}{3} = \frac{1}{6} = \frac{p}{q}$$

$\Rightarrow \quad (p+q) = 7$

40. $f(x) = \dfrac{\pi}{2} - \sin^{-1}\left(\dfrac{2x}{1+x^2}\right) = \dfrac{\pi}{2} - 2\tan^{-1} x$

$g(x) = \dfrac{\pi}{2} - \tan^{-1}\left(\dfrac{2x}{x^2-1}\right) = \dfrac{\pi}{2} + 2\tan^{-1} x$

$$y = f(x) + g(x) = \pi \Rightarrow y = \pi x^2$$

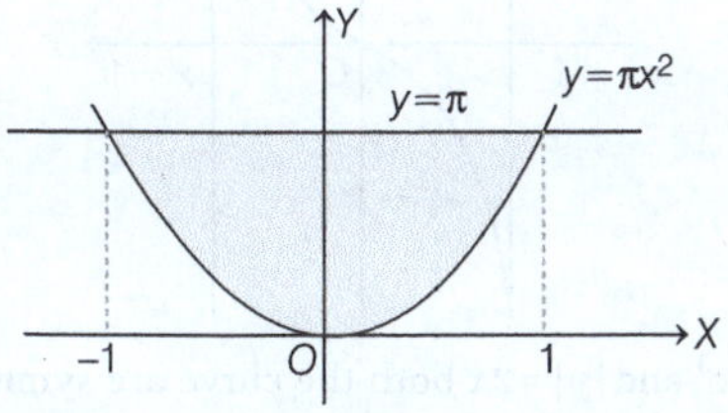

Required area $= 2\pi - 2\int_0^1 \pi x^2 dx$

$$A = 2\pi \cdot 2\pi \cdot \frac{1}{3} = \frac{4\pi}{3} = 4.19$$

$\therefore \quad [A] = 4$

41. **Case I** $x \ge 0$ and $y \ge 0$

$S_1 : 2x + 2y \le 2 \Rightarrow x + y \le 1$

and S_2 : True

$$A = \frac{1}{2} \times 1 \times 1 = \frac{1}{2}$$

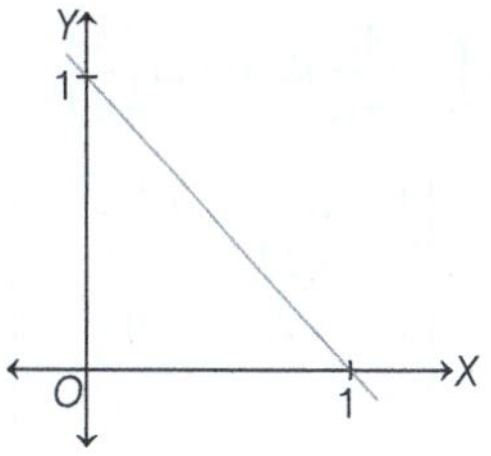

Case II $x \ge 0$ and $y \le 0$

$S_1 : 2x \le 2 \Rightarrow x \le 1$

$S_2 : -2y \le 2 \Rightarrow y \le -1$

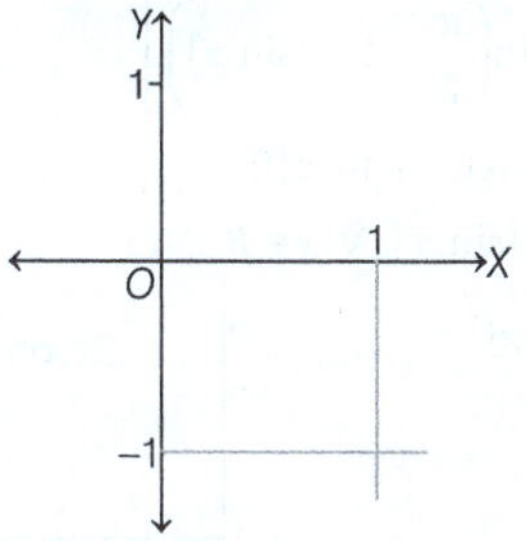

Area = 1

$\therefore \quad \text{Area} = \dfrac{1}{2} + 1 = \dfrac{3}{2} = A \Rightarrow 2A = 3$

42. $f(0) = g(0) \Rightarrow 2 = a$

$f'(0) = g'(0) \Rightarrow 0 = -a \cdot c$

$\therefore \quad c = 0$

$$f''(0) = g''(0) \Rightarrow b = \frac{1}{4}$$

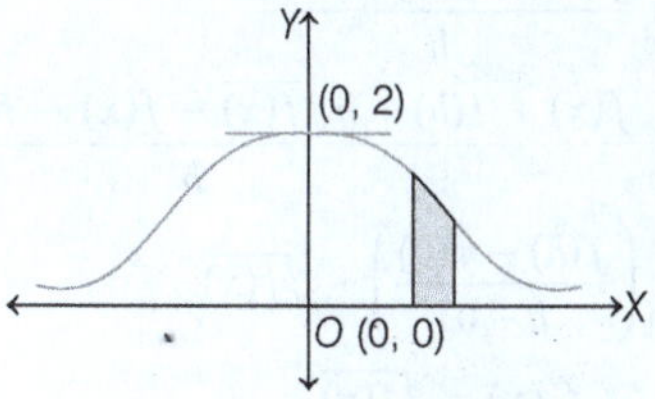

$\therefore \quad g(x) = \dfrac{2}{\dfrac{x^2}{4} + 1} = \dfrac{8}{x^2 + 4}$

$$A = 2\int_0^{\infty} \frac{8}{x^2+4} dx$$

$$= 16\left[\tan^{-1}\frac{x}{2}\right]_0^{\infty} = 8 \cdot \frac{\pi}{2} = 4\pi$$

$\therefore \quad k = 4$

43. Equation of line: $x + y = 3 \Rightarrow x + \dfrac{c}{x+1} = 3$

$\Rightarrow \quad x^2 + x + c = 3x + 3$

$\Rightarrow \quad x^2 + 2x + (c-3) = 0$

For tangency $D = 0 \Rightarrow 4 = 4(c-3) \Rightarrow c - 3 = 1$

$\Rightarrow \quad c = 4$

$$y = \frac{4}{x+1}$$

$$\text{Required area} = \int_1^2 \frac{4}{x+1}dx = 4\ln\left(\frac{3}{2}\right)$$

$$= 4\left\{\frac{\frac{1}{2}}{1} - \frac{\left(\frac{1}{2}\right)^2}{2} + \frac{\left(\frac{1}{2}\right)^3}{3} \dots\right\}$$

$$= 2\left\{1 - \frac{1}{2\cdot 2} - \frac{1}{2^2\cdot 3} + \dots \infty\right\}$$

Clearly, $\lambda = 2$

44. $f(x) = \cos^{-1}\left[\sin\left(\frac{\pi}{2} - 1 - [\sin x]\right)\right]$

$$= \cos^{-1}(\cos(1 + [\sin x]))$$

$\therefore \quad f(x) = 1 + [\sin x], \forall\, x \in R$

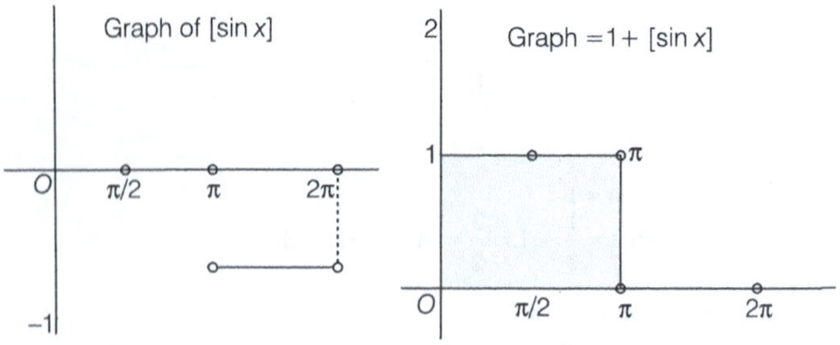

$\therefore$ Required area $= \pi$ sq units

Hence, $k = 3.14$

45. $f'(x) = \lim_{n\to 0} \frac{f(x+h) - f(x+0)}{h}$

$$= \lim_{n\to 0} \frac{f(x) + f(h) + h\sqrt{f(x)} - f(x) - f(0) - 0\sqrt{f(x)}}{h}$$

$$= \lim_{n\to 0} \left(\frac{f(h) - f(0)}{h - 0}\right) + \sqrt{f(x)}$$

$$f'(x) = \sqrt{f(x)}$$

$$\int \frac{f'(x)}{\sqrt{f(x)}}dx = \int dx$$

$$2\sqrt{f(x)} = x + C \Rightarrow f(x) = \frac{x^2}{4}$$

When, $a = 0$ area is minimum.

Required minimum area $= 2\int_2^9 2\sqrt{y}dy$

$$\Rightarrow \quad 4\left(\frac{y^{3/2}}{3/2}\right)_0^9 = 72 \text{ sq units}$$

46. $x^2 + y = 2011 \Rightarrow x^2 = -(y - 2011)$

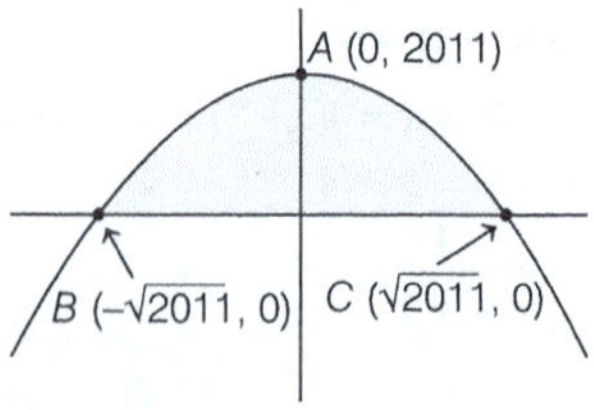

Parabola vertex $A(0, 2011)$

$$-\sqrt{2011} < x < \sqrt{2011}$$

$$\Rightarrow \quad |x| < \sqrt{2011} \Rightarrow 0 \le \frac{|x|}{\sqrt{2011}} < 1$$

$$\therefore \quad \left[\frac{|x|}{\sqrt{2011}}\right] = 0$$

First curve will be $y = 0$

$$\text{Required area} = \int_{-\sqrt{2011}}^{\sqrt{2011}} (2011 - x^2)dx = 2\left(\frac{2}{3}\right)(2011)^{3/2}$$

$$\lambda = \frac{2}{3} \Rightarrow \frac{1}{\lambda} = \frac{3}{2} = 1.5$$

47. (A) Required area = 4s

$$A = 4\left[\int_0^\pi (x + \sin x)\,dx - \int_0^\pi x\,dx\right]$$

$$A = 4\left[\frac{\pi^2}{2} - \cos\pi + \cos 0 - \frac{\pi^2}{2}\right] = 8 \text{ sq units}$$

$$A = 4s = 8 \Rightarrow s = 2$$

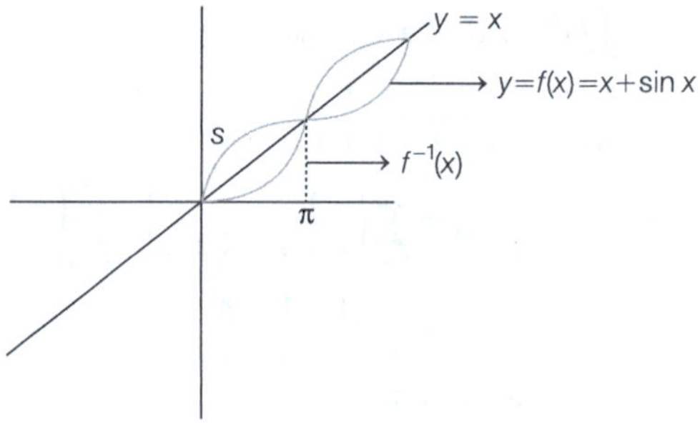

(B) Required area $= 2\int_0^1 xe^x\,dx = 2[xe^x - e^x]_0^1 = 2$

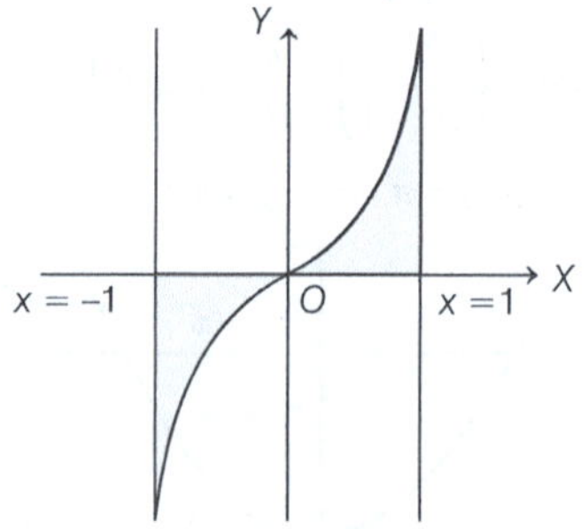

(C) $y^2 = x^3$ and $|y| = 2x$ both the curve are symmetric about Y-axis

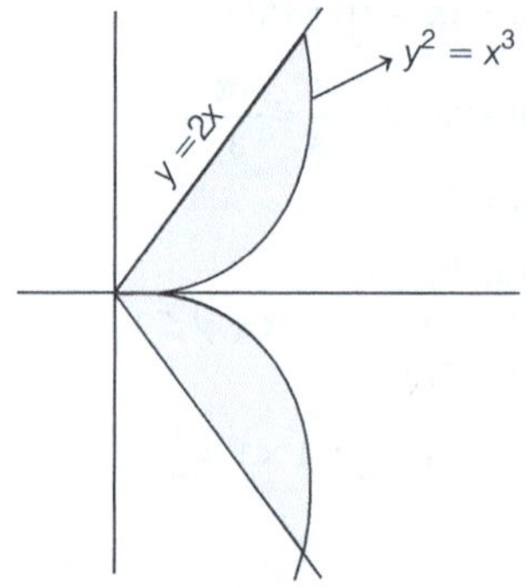

$$4x^2 = x^3 \Rightarrow x = 0, 4$$

$$\text{Required area} = 2\int_0^4 (2x - x^{3/2})\, dx = \frac{16}{5}$$

(D) $\sqrt{x} + \sqrt{|y|} = 1$

Above curve is symmetric about X-axis

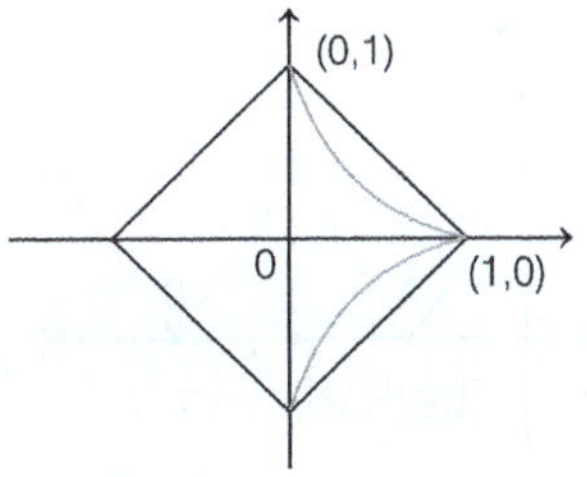

$$\sqrt{|y|} = 1 - \sqrt{x} \text{ and } \sqrt{x} = 1 - \sqrt{|y|}$$

$$\Rightarrow \text{ for } x > 0, y > 0, \sqrt{y} = 1 - \sqrt{x}$$

$$\frac{1}{2\sqrt{y}}\frac{dy}{dx} = -\frac{1}{2\sqrt{x}}$$

$$\frac{dy}{dx} = -\sqrt{\frac{x}{y}} \Rightarrow \frac{dy}{dx} < 0$$

Function is decreasing required area $= \int_0^1 (2\sqrt{x} - 2x) = \frac{1}{3}$.

48. (A) The area = 2 units

(B) Area enclosed $= \int_0^{\pi} \sin x \, dx = 2$

(C) The line $y = x + 2$ intersects $y = x^2$ at $x = -1$ and $x = 2$

The given region is shaded region area

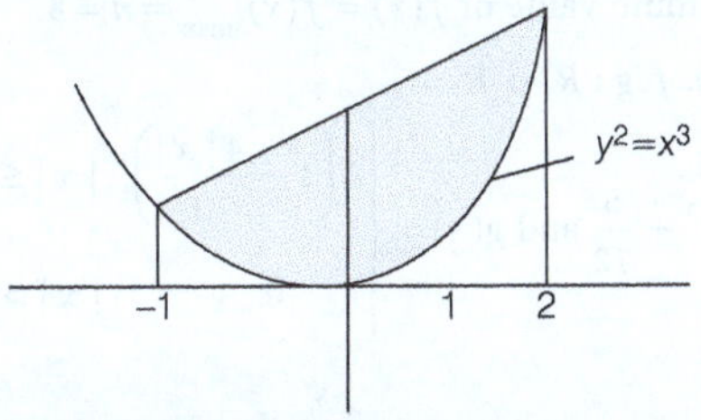

$$= \frac{15}{2} - \int_{-1}^{2} x^2 \, dx = \frac{9}{2} = \frac{k}{4}$$

$\therefore \; k = 18$

(D) Here, $a^2 = 9, b^2 = 5, b^2 = a^2(1 - e^2)$

$$\Rightarrow \quad e^2 = \frac{4}{9} = \frac{2}{3}$$

Equation of tangent at $\left(2, \frac{5}{3}\right)$ is $\frac{2x}{9} + \frac{y}{3} = 1$

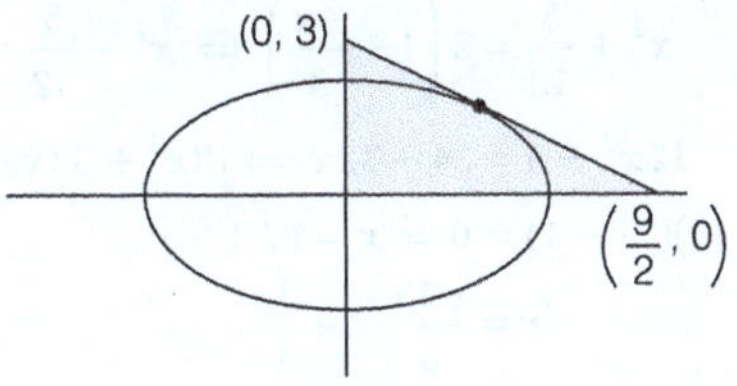

x-intercept $= \frac{9}{2}$, y-intercept $= 3$

$$\text{Area} = 4 \times \frac{9}{2} \times 3 \times \frac{1}{2} = 27 \text{ sq units}$$

49. (A) We have, $[x]^2 = [y]^2, 0 \le x \le 4$

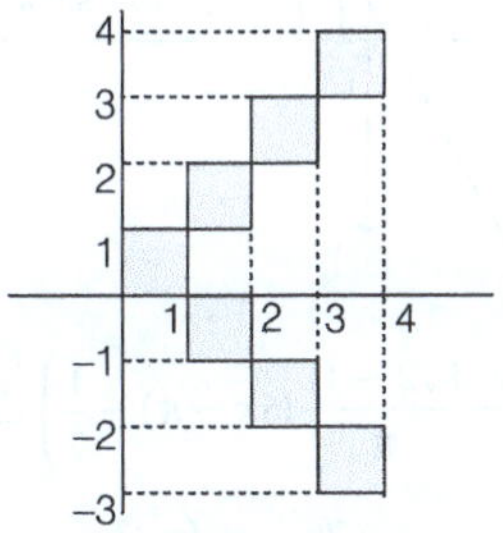

$$[y] = \pm [x]$$

$x \in [0, 1) \Rightarrow y \in [0, 1)$

$x \in [1, 2) \Rightarrow y \in [-1, 0) \cup [1, 2)$

$x \in [2, 3) \Rightarrow y \in [-2, -1) \cup [2, 3)$

$x \in [3, 4) \Rightarrow y \in [-3, -2) \cup [3, 4)$

$x = 4 \Rightarrow y \in [-4, -3) \cup [4, 5)$

Hence, the required area = 7 sq units

(B) We have, $x + y \le 6$, $x^2 + y^2 \le 6y$ and $y^2 \le 8x$

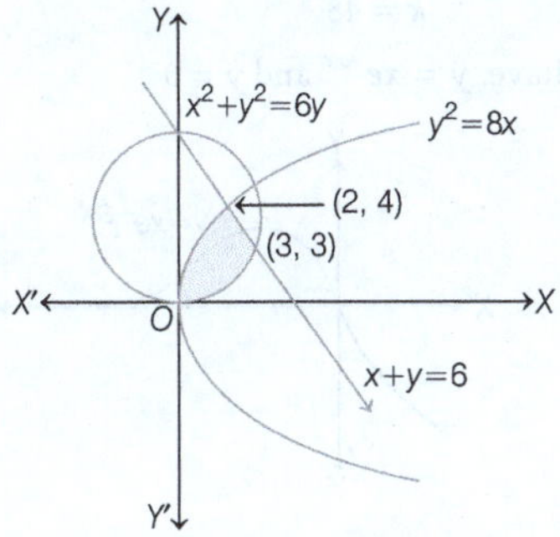

$\therefore$ Area of shaded region

$$\int_0^2 \sqrt{8x}\, dx + \int_2^3 (6 - x)\, dx - \int_0^3 (3 - \sqrt{9 - x^2})\, dx$$

$$= 2\sqrt{2} \times \frac{2}{3}[x^{3/2}]_0^2 + \left[6x - \frac{x^2}{2}\right]_2^3$$

$$- \left[3x - \frac{x}{2}\sqrt{9 - x^2} - \frac{9}{2}\sin^{-1}\frac{x}{3}\right]_0^3$$

$$= \frac{4\sqrt{2}}{3}[2^{3/2}] + \left(18 - \frac{9}{2}\right) - (12 - 2) - \left[9 - \frac{9}{2}\frac{\pi}{2}\right]$$

$$= \frac{16}{3} + \frac{27}{2} - 10 - 9 + \frac{9}{4}\pi$$

$$= \frac{9}{4}\pi - \frac{1}{6}$$

$$= \frac{27\pi - 2}{12}$$

$\therefore \; k = 27$

(C) We have, $y = \sin x$ and $\dfrac{2y-1}{\sqrt{2}-1} = \dfrac{2}{\pi}(6x - \pi)$

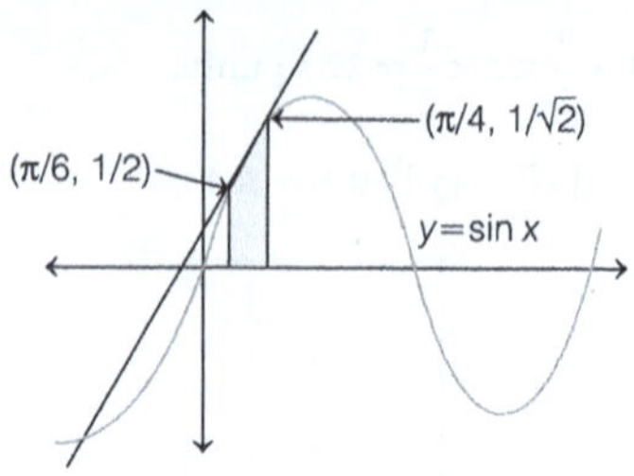

Area of region

$$\int_{\pi/6}^{\pi/4} \left(\sin x - \frac{(\sqrt{2}-1)}{\pi}(6x - \pi) - \frac{1}{2} \right) dx$$

$$= \left[-\cos x - \frac{(\sqrt{2}-1)}{\pi}\left(\frac{6x^2}{2} - \pi x \right) - \frac{1}{2}x \right]_{\pi/6}^{\pi/4}$$

$$= \left(-\cos\frac{\pi}{4} + \cos\frac{\pi}{6} \right) - \left(\frac{\sqrt{2}-1}{\pi} \right)$$

$$\left[\left(\frac{6\pi^2}{32} - \frac{\pi^2}{4} \right) - \left(\frac{6\pi^2}{72} - \frac{\pi^2}{6} \right) \right] - \frac{1}{2}\left(\frac{\pi}{4} - \frac{\pi}{6} \right)$$

$$= \frac{\sqrt{3}-\sqrt{2}}{2} - \frac{(\sqrt{2}+1)\pi}{48}$$

$\therefore \; k = 48$

(D) We have, $y = xe^{-ax}$ and $y = 0$

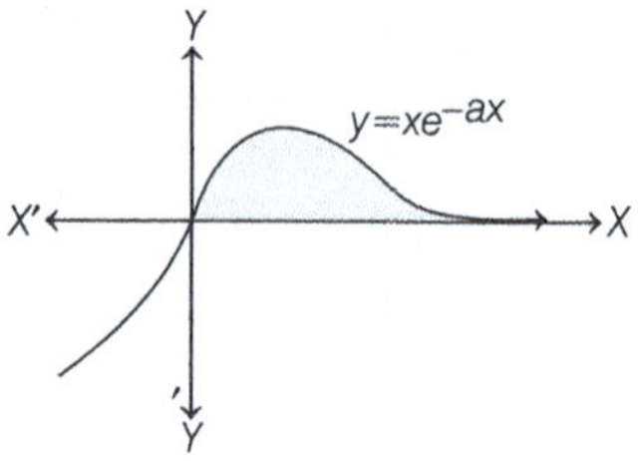

$\therefore$ Area of shaded region $= \displaystyle\int_0^\infty xe^{-ax}\, dx$

$$\Rightarrow \quad \frac{1}{9} = \left[\frac{-xe^{-ax}}{a} - \frac{e^{-ax}}{a^2} \right]_0^\infty \Rightarrow \frac{1}{9} = 0 + \frac{1}{a^2}$$

$$\Rightarrow \quad a^2 = 9$$

$$\Rightarrow \quad a = 3 \qquad [\because a > 0]$$

50. Given, $f(x) = \begin{cases} n(1-2nx), & 0 \le x < \dfrac{1}{2n} \\ 2n(2nx-1), & \dfrac{1}{2n} \le x < \dfrac{3}{4n} \\ 4n(1-nx), & \dfrac{3}{4n} \le x \le \dfrac{1}{n} \\ \dfrac{n}{n-1}(nx-1), & \dfrac{1}{n} \le x \le 1 \end{cases}$

where, $x \in [0, 1]$.

Now, we observe that, $f(x)$ is decreasing in $\left[0, \dfrac{1}{2n}\right]$ and in $\left[\dfrac{3}{4n}, \dfrac{1}{n}\right]$ but $f(x)$ is increasing in $\left[\dfrac{1}{2n}, \dfrac{3}{4n}\right]$ as well as in $\left[\dfrac{1}{n}, 1\right]$.

Let draw the graph of $f(x)$.

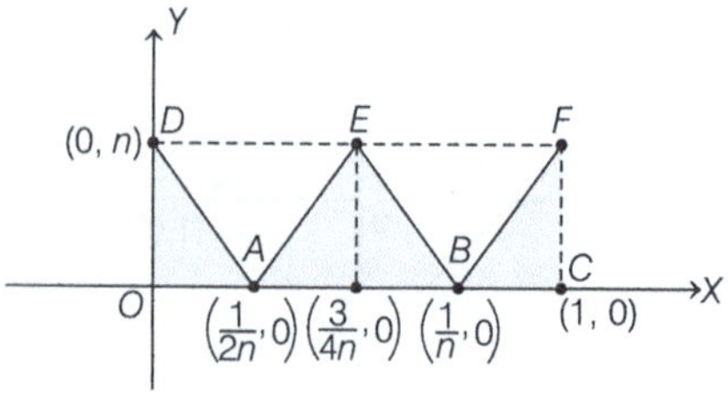

Given area of the region bounded by the curves $x = 0$, $x = 1$, $y = 0$ and $y = f(x)$ is 4.

$\Rightarrow ar(\Delta OAD) + ar(\Delta AEB) + ar(\Delta BEC) = 4$

$$\Rightarrow \frac{1}{2} \times \frac{1}{2n} \times n + \frac{1}{2} \times \left(\frac{1}{n} - \frac{1}{2n} \right) \times n + \frac{1}{2} \times \left(1 - \frac{1}{n} \right) \times n = 4$$

$$\Rightarrow \quad \frac{1}{4} + \frac{1}{2} \times \frac{1}{2n} \times n + \frac{1}{2} \times \frac{n-1}{n} \times n = 4$$

$$\Rightarrow \quad \frac{1}{4} + \frac{1}{4} + \frac{n-1}{2} = 4$$

$$\Rightarrow \quad \frac{n-1}{2} = 4 - \frac{1}{2} = \frac{7}{2}$$

$$\Rightarrow \quad n - 1 = 7$$

$$\Rightarrow \quad n = 8$$

Also, we observe that, from graph $f(x)$ can attain a maximum height $= n$.

So, maximum value of $f(x) = f(x)|_{max} = n = 8$

51. We have, $f, g : R \to R$

$$f(x) = x^2 + \frac{5}{12} \text{ and } g(x) = \begin{cases} 2\left(1 - \dfrac{4|x|}{3}\right), & |x| \le \dfrac{3}{4} \\ 0, & |x| > \dfrac{3}{4} \end{cases}$$

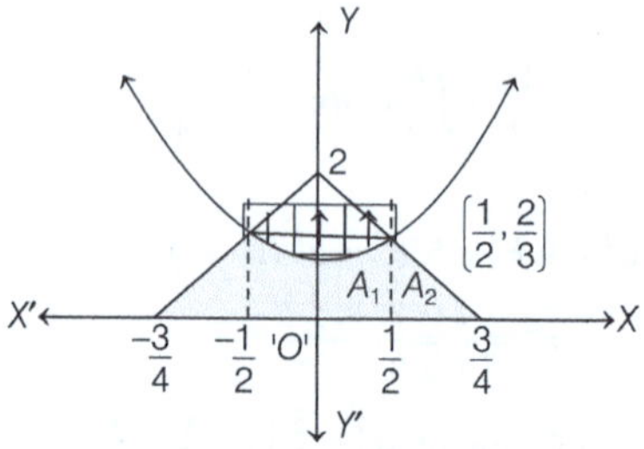

Finding intersection of f and g

$$x^2 + \frac{5}{12} = 2\left(1 - \frac{4x}{3}\right) \Rightarrow x^2 + \frac{5}{12} = \frac{6 - 8x}{3}$$

$$\Rightarrow \quad 12x^2 + 5 = 24 - 32x \Rightarrow 12x^2 + 32x - 19 = 0$$

$$\Rightarrow (6x + 19)(2x - 1) = 0 \Rightarrow x = 1/2,$$

and $\quad x = \dfrac{-19}{6} < -\dfrac{3}{4} \qquad$ [rejected]

The shaded region is symmetric about Y-axis.

Area of shaded region $= 2\,[A_1 + A_2]$

$$\alpha = 2\left[\int_0^{1/2}\left(x^2+\frac{5}{12}\right)dx + \int_{1/2}^{3/4} 2\left(1-\frac{4x}{3}\right)dx\right]$$

$$\Rightarrow \quad \alpha = 2\left[\frac{x^3}{3}+\frac{5}{12}x\right]_0^{1/2} + 4\left[x-\frac{4}{3}\cdot\frac{x^2}{2}\right]_{1/2}^{3/4}$$

$$\Rightarrow \quad \alpha = \frac{2}{3}\left[x^3+\frac{5}{4}x\right]_0^{1/2} + 4\left[x-\frac{2}{3}x^2\right]_{1/2}^{3/4}$$

$$\Rightarrow \quad \alpha = \frac{2}{3}\left[\frac{1}{8}+\frac{5}{8}-0-0\right] + 4\left[\left(\frac{3}{4}-\frac{3}{8}\right)-\left(\frac{1}{2}-\frac{1}{6}\right)\right]$$

$$\Rightarrow \quad \alpha = \frac{1}{2}+4\left[\frac{3}{8}-\frac{1}{3}\right] = \frac{1}{2}+\frac{1}{6} = \frac{2}{3}$$

$$\Rightarrow \quad 9\alpha = \frac{2}{3}\times 9 = 6$$

52. Method I

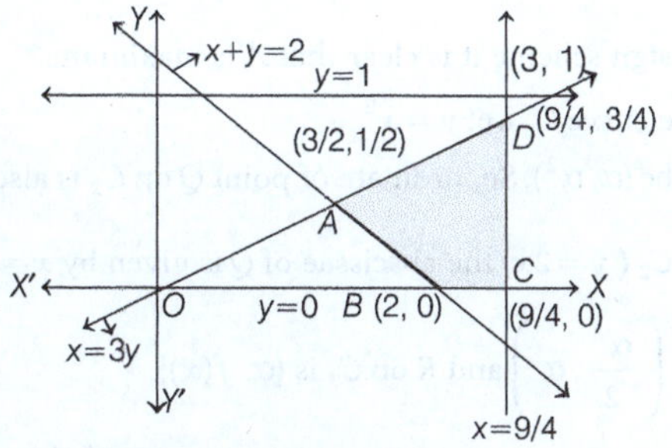

Required area = Shaded region

On solving $x + y = 2$ and $x = 3y$, we get

$$A \equiv \left(\frac{3}{2}, \frac{1}{2}\right)$$

On solving $y = 0$ and $x + y = 2$, we get

$$B \equiv (2, 0)$$

On solving $x = 9/4$ and $x = 3y$, we get

$$D \equiv (9/4, 3/4)$$

and $\quad C \equiv (9/4, 0) \rightarrow$ (obviously)

So, required area = shaded region

$$= \frac{1}{2}\begin{vmatrix} 3/2 & 1/2 & 1 \\ 2 & 0 & 1 \\ 9/4 & 3/4 & 1 \end{vmatrix} + \frac{1}{2}\times\left(\frac{9}{4}-2\right)\times 3/4$$

$$= \frac{1}{2}\times\left\{-2\left(\frac{1}{2}-\frac{3}{4}\right)-\left(\frac{9}{8}-\frac{9}{8}\right)\right\}+\frac{1}{2}\times\frac{1}{4}\times\frac{3}{4}$$

$$= \frac{1}{4}+\frac{3}{32}$$

$$= \frac{11}{32} \text{ sq unit}$$

Method II Required area = Area of ΔOCD – Area of ΔOBA

$$= \frac{1}{2}\times\left(\frac{9}{4}-0\right)\times\frac{3}{4}-\frac{1}{2}\times(2-0)\times\frac{1}{2}$$

$$= \frac{27}{32}-\frac{1}{2} = \frac{27}{32}-\frac{16}{32} = \frac{11}{32} \text{ sq unit}$$

53. The given functions $f: R \rightarrow R$ and $g: R \rightarrow R$ be defined by

$$f(x) = e^{x-1} - e^{-|x-1|} = \begin{cases} e^{x-1} - e^{1-x}, & x \geq 1 \\ 0, & x < 1 \end{cases}$$

and $\quad g(x) = \dfrac{1}{2}(e^{x-1} + e^{1-x})$

For point of intersection of curves $f(x)$ and $g(x)$ put $f(x) = g(x)$

for $x \geq 1$, $e^{x-1} - e^{1-x} = \dfrac{1}{2}(e^{x-1} + e^{1-x})$

$$\Rightarrow \quad e^{x-1} = 3e^{1-x} \Rightarrow e^{2x} = 3e^2$$

$$\Rightarrow \quad x = \frac{1}{2}\log_e^3 + 1$$

So, required area is

$$\int_0^{1/2\log_e^3+1} (g(x) - f(x))dx$$

$$= \int_0^{1/2\log_e^3+1} g(x)dx - \int_1^{1/2\log_e^3+1} f(x)dx$$

$$= \frac{1}{2}\int_0^{1/2\log_e^3+1}(e^{x-1}+e^{1-x})dx - \int_1^{1/2\log_e^3+1}(e^{x-1}-e^{1-x})dx$$

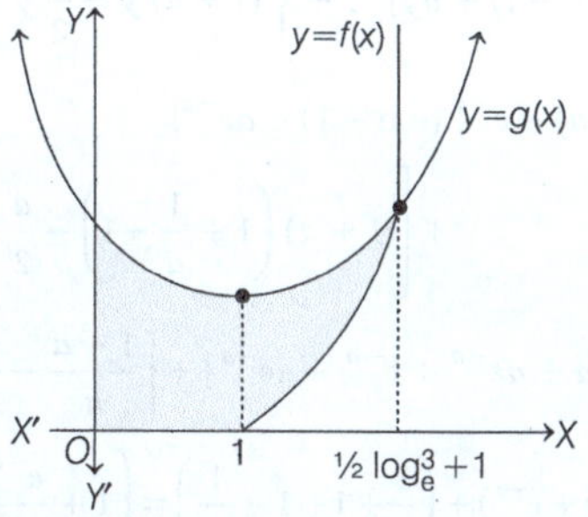

$$= \frac{1}{2}\left[e^{x-1}-e^{1-x}\right]_0^{\frac{1}{2}\log_e^3+1} - \left[e^{x-1}+e^{1-x}\right]_1^{\frac{1}{2}\log_e^3+1}$$

$$= \frac{1}{2}\left[\sqrt{3}-\frac{1}{\sqrt{3}}-e^{-1}+e\right]-\left[\sqrt{3}+\frac{1}{\sqrt{3}}-1-1\right]$$

$$= \frac{1}{\sqrt{3}}+\frac{1}{2}(e-e^{-1})-\frac{4}{\sqrt{3}}+2$$

$$= (2-\sqrt{3})+\frac{1}{2}(e-e^{-1}) \text{ sq units}$$

Exercise 3 - Challenging Problems

1. Here, slope of the normal at $P\,(x, y)$.

$\Rightarrow$ Slope of the line $a\,(y-1)+(x-1)=0$ is $-\dfrac{1}{a}$.

$\therefore$ Slope of the tangent at $P = a$,

$$\left(\frac{dy}{dx}\right)_P = a \qquad \text{...(i)}$$

It is given that the slope of the tangent at any point on the curve $y = f(x)$ is proportional to the ordinate of the point.

$$\therefore \quad \frac{dy}{dx} \propto y \Rightarrow \frac{dy}{dx} = \lambda y$$

$$\Rightarrow \quad \left(\frac{dy}{dx}\right)_{(1,1)} = \lambda \Rightarrow a = \lambda$$

$\therefore \quad \frac{dy}{dx} = ay \quad \Rightarrow \quad \frac{dy}{y} = a\,dx$

$\Rightarrow \quad \log y = ax + \log c$

$\Rightarrow \quad y = ce^{ax}$, which passes through $P(1, 1)$

$\therefore \quad c = e^{-a}$

$\Rightarrow$ Curve is $\quad y = e^{-a} e^{ax} \quad \Rightarrow \quad y = e^{a(x-1)}$

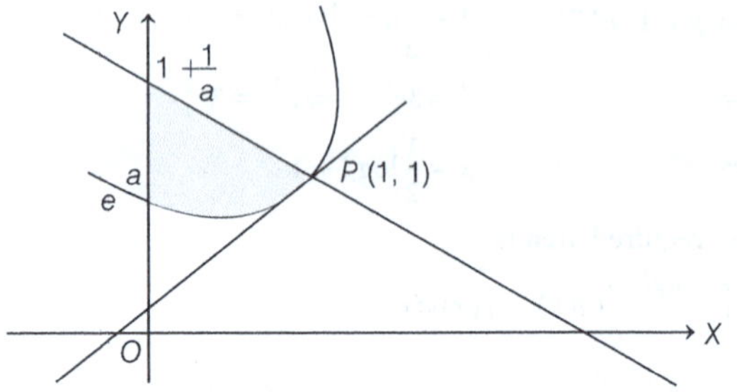

$\therefore$ Required area $= \frac{1}{a}\int_{e^{-a}}^{1} (\log y + a)\,dy + \int_{1}^{1+1/a} \{(1+a) - ay\}dy$

$= \frac{1}{a}\{y(\log y - 1) + ay\}_{e^{-a}}^{1} + \left\{(1+a)y - \frac{a}{2}y^2\right\}_{a}^{1+\frac{1}{a}}$

$= \frac{1}{a}\{(-1+a) - e^{-a}(-a-1) - ae^{-a}\}$

$+ \left[(1+a)\left(1 + \frac{1}{a} - 1\right) - \frac{a}{2}\left\{\left(1+\frac{1}{a}\right)^2 - 1^2\right\}\right]$

$= \frac{1}{a}[-1 + a + ae^{-a} + e^{-a} - ae^{-a}] + \left[\frac{1+a}{a} - \frac{a}{2}\left(2 + \frac{1}{a}\right)\frac{1}{a}\right]$

$= \frac{1}{a}(-1 + a + e^{-a}) + \left(\frac{1}{a} + 1 - 1 - \frac{1}{2a}\right) = \left(1 + \frac{e^{-a}}{a} - \frac{1}{2a}\right)$ sq units

2. **Decoding the Question**

For maximum or minimum value area, use $\frac{dA}{db} = 0$ and sign scheme for $\frac{dA}{db}$.

Eliminating y from $y = \frac{x^2}{b}$ and $y = x - bx^2$, we get

$$x^2 = bx - b^2x^2$$

$$\Rightarrow \quad x = 0, \frac{b}{1+b^2}$$

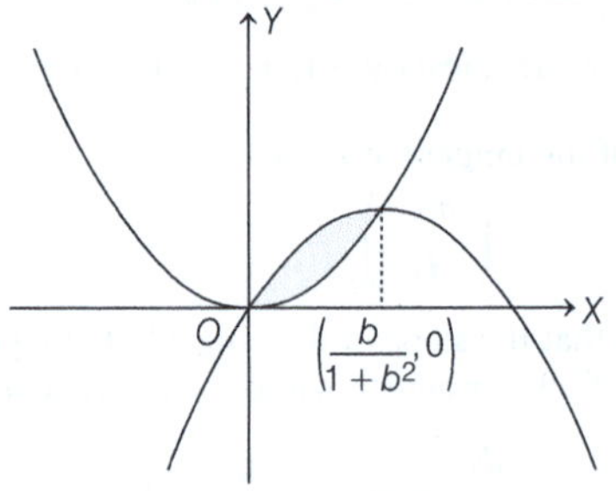

Thus, the area enclosed between the parabolas,

$$A = \int_0^{b/(1+b^2)} \left(x - bx^2 - \frac{x^2}{b}\right) dx$$

$$= \int_0^{b/1+b^2} \left\{x - x^2\left(\frac{1+b^2}{b}\right)\right\} dx$$

$$= \left(\frac{x^2}{2} - \frac{x^3}{3}\cdot\frac{1+b^2}{b}\right)_0^{b/1+b^2}$$

$$= \frac{1}{6}\cdot\frac{b^2}{(1+b^2)^2}$$

For maximum value of A, $\frac{dA}{db} = 0$

But $\frac{dA}{db} = \frac{1}{6}\cdot\frac{(1+b^2)^2\cdot 2b - b^2\cdot 2(1+b^2)\cdot 2b}{(1+b^2)^4} = \frac{1}{3}\cdot\frac{b(1-b^2)}{(1+b^2)^3}$

Hence, $\frac{dA}{db} = 0$ gives $b = -1, 0, 1$ since $b > 0$

Therefore, we consider only $b = 1$

Sign scheme for $\frac{dA}{db}$ around $b = 1$ is as below

$0 \longleftarrow + \quad 1 \quad - \longrightarrow \infty$

From sign scheme it is clear that A is maximum.

3. On the curve C_1 i.e. $y = x^2$.

Let P be (α, α^2). So, ordinate of point Q on C_2 is also α^2.

Now, C_2 ($y = 2x$) the abscissae of Q is given by $x = \frac{y}{2} = \frac{\alpha^2}{2}$.

$\therefore Q$ is $\left(\frac{\alpha^2}{2}, \alpha\right)$ and R on C_3 is $\{\alpha, f(x)\}$.

Now, area of $\Delta OPQ = \int_0^{\alpha^2} (x_1 - x_2)\,dy = \int_0^{\alpha^2} \left(\sqrt{y} - \frac{y}{2}\right) dy$

$$= \frac{2}{3}\alpha^3 - \frac{\alpha^4}{4} \quad \text{...(i)}$$

Again, area of $\Delta ORP = \int_0^{\alpha} (y_1 - y_2)dx = \int_0^{\alpha^2} \{x^2 - f(x)\}\,dx$ ...(ii)

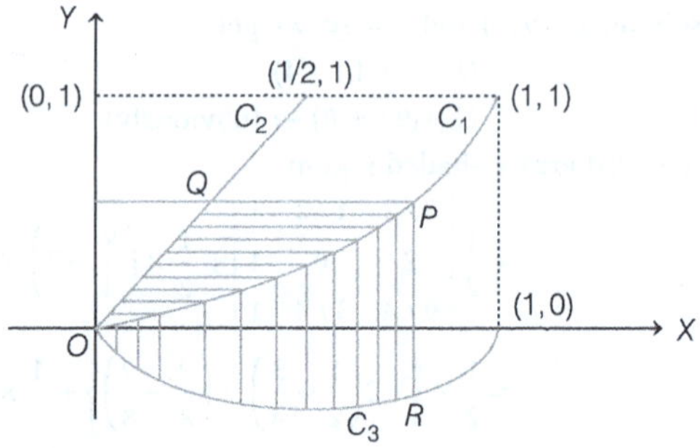

Thus, from Eqs. (i) and (ii), we get

$$\frac{2\alpha^3}{3} - \frac{\alpha^4}{4} = \int_0^{\alpha} \{x^2 - f(x)\}\,dx$$

Differentiating both the sides w.r.t. α, we get

$$2\alpha^2 - \alpha^3 = \alpha^2 - f(\alpha)$$

$$\Rightarrow \quad f(\alpha) = \alpha^3 - \alpha^2$$

$$\Rightarrow \quad f(x) = x^3 - x^2$$

4. Both the curves are defined for $x > 0$. Both are positive when $x > 1$ and negative when $0 < x < 1$.

We know that, $\lim_{x \to 0^+} \log x \to -\infty$

Therefore, $\lim_{x \to 0^+} \dfrac{\log x}{ex} \to -\infty$

Thus, Y-axis is asymptote of second curve.

and $\lim_{x \to 0^+} ex \log x$ $[(0)(-\infty)$ form$]$

$$= \lim_{x \to 0^+} \frac{e \log x}{1/x} \qquad \left[-\frac{\infty}{\infty} \text{ form}\right]$$

$$= \lim_{x \to 0^+} \frac{e(1/x)}{(-1/x^2)} = 0 \quad \text{[using L'Hospital's rule]}$$

Thus, the first curve starts from (0, 0) but does not include (0, 0). Now, the given curves intersect therefore

$$ex \log x = \frac{\log x}{ex}$$

i.e. $\quad (e^2x^2 - 1) \log x = 0$

i.e. $\quad x = 1, \dfrac{1}{e} \qquad [\because x > 0]$

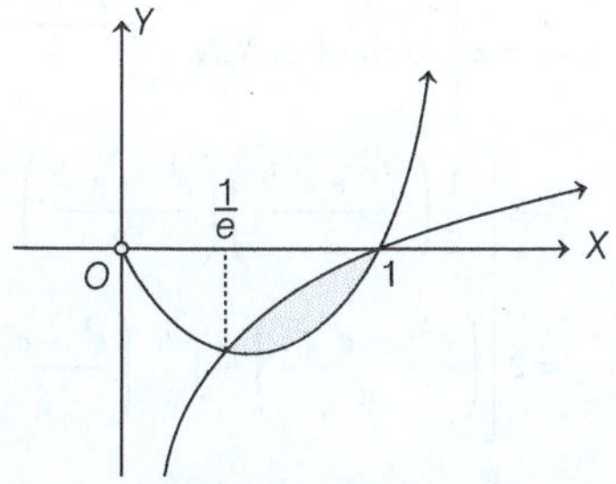

Therefore, using the above results figure could be drawn as

$$\therefore \text{ Required area} = \int_{1/e}^{1} \left(\frac{\log x}{ex} - ex \log x \right) dx$$

$$= \frac{1}{e}\left[\frac{(\log x)^2}{2}\right]_{1/e}^{1} - e\left[\frac{x^2}{4}(2\log x - 1)\right]_{1/e}^{1} = \frac{e^2 - 5}{4e}$$

5. First part We have, $A_n = \int_0^{\pi/4} (\tan x)^n \, dx$

Hence, $\quad A_{n-2} = \int_0^{\pi/4} (\tan x)^{n-2} \, dx$

$$\therefore \quad A_n + A_{n-2} = \int_0^{\pi/4} (\tan x)^{n-2} (\tan^2 x + 1) \, dx$$

$$= \int_0^{\pi/4} (\tan x)^{n-2} \cdot \sec^2 x \, dx$$

Let $\tan x = t$, so that $\sec^2 x \, dx = dt$

$$\therefore \quad A_n + A_{n-2} = \int_0^1 t^{n-2} \, dt = \left(\frac{t^{n-1}}{n-1}\right)_0^1 = \frac{1}{n-1} \qquad \text{...(i)}$$

Second part

Since, $\quad 0 \le x \le \pi/4 \;\therefore\; 0 \le \tan x \le 1$

$$\Rightarrow \quad \tan^{n+2} x < \tan^n x < \tan^{n-2} x$$

$$\Rightarrow \int_0^{\pi/4} \tan^{n+2} x \, dx < \int_0^{\pi/4} \tan^n x \, dx < \int_0^{\pi/4} \tan^{n-2} x \, dx$$

$$\Rightarrow A_{n+2} < A_n < A_{n-2} \Rightarrow A_n + A_{n+2} < 2A_n < A_n + A_{n-2}$$

$$\therefore \quad \frac{1}{n+1} < 2A_n < \frac{1}{n-1}$$

$$\Rightarrow \quad \frac{1}{2(n+1)} < A_n < \frac{1}{2(n-1)} \qquad \text{[using Eq. (i)]}$$

6. For the points lying in the ΔOAB the edge AB i.e. $x = 1$ is the closest edge. Therefore, if the distance of a point $P(x, y)$ (lying in the ΔOAB) from origin is less than that of its distance from the edge $x = 1$ it will fall in the region S.

$$\therefore \quad OP \le PQ$$

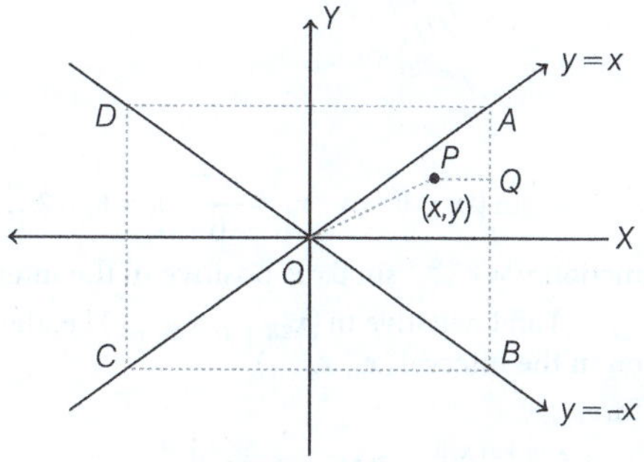

$$\Rightarrow \quad \sqrt{x^2 + y^2} \le 1 - x$$

$$\Rightarrow \quad x^2 + y^2 \le x^2 - 2x + 1 \Rightarrow y^2 \le 1 - 2x$$

Similarly, for points lying in the ΔOAD the side $y = 1$ is the closest side and therefore the region S is determined by

$$x^2 \le 1 - 2y$$

Since, the edges are symmetric about the origin. Hence, by the above inequality and by symmetry, the required area will be the shaded portion in the figure given below

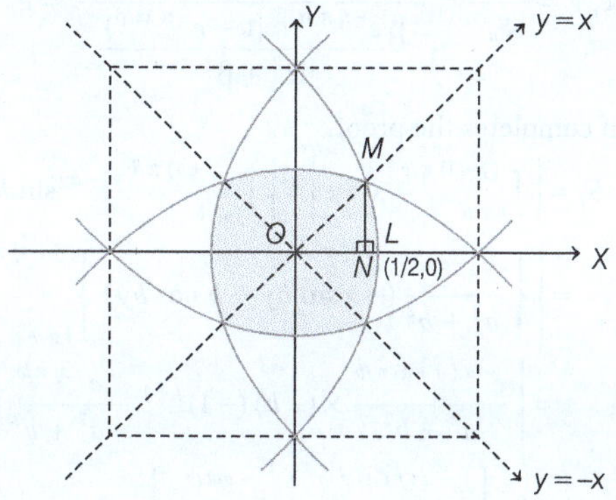

Now, when the curves $y^2 = 1 - 2x$ and $y = x$ intersect each other, then

$$x^2 = 1 - 2x \Rightarrow x^2 + 2x - 1 = 0$$

$$\Rightarrow \quad x = \sqrt{2} - 1, -\sqrt{2} - 1$$

Hence, the intersection points in the first quadrant is $(\sqrt{2} - 1, \sqrt{2} - 1)$.

$\therefore$ Required area $= 8$ [Area of curvilinear ΔOLM]

$$= 8\left[\frac{1}{2}(\sqrt{2}-1)(\sqrt{2}-1) + \int_{\sqrt{2}-1}^{1/2} \sqrt{1-2x} \, dx\right]$$

$$= 8\left[\frac{1}{2}(3 - 2\sqrt{2}) + \left(\frac{2(1-2x)^{3/2}}{3(-2)}\right)_{\sqrt{2}-1}^{1/2}\right]$$

$$= \frac{4}{3}(4\sqrt{2} - 5)$$

7. The curve $y = e^{-\alpha x} \sin \beta x$ intersects the positive X-axis at the points where $y = 0$.

$$\therefore \quad e^{-\alpha x} \sin \beta x = 0$$

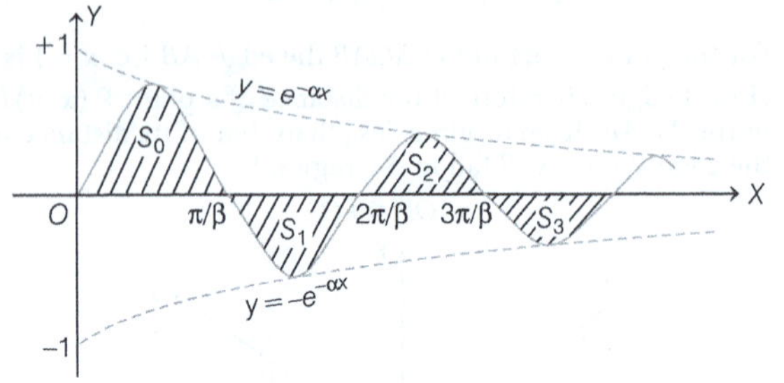

$$\Rightarrow \quad \sin \beta x = 0 \Rightarrow x_n = \frac{n\pi}{\beta}, n = 0, 1, 2, \dots$$

The function $y = e^{-\alpha x} \sin \beta x$ is positive in the interval (x_{2K}, x_{2K+1}) and negative in (x_{2K+1}, x_{2K+2}) i.e. the sign of the function in the interval (x_n, x_{n+1}).

Therefore,

$$S_n = \left| \int_{n\pi/\beta}^{(n+1)\pi/\beta} e^{-\alpha x} \sin \beta x \, dx \right|$$

$$= \left| \left\{ \frac{(-1)^{n+1} e^{-\alpha x}}{\alpha^2 + \beta^2} (\alpha \sin \beta x + \beta \cos \beta x) \right\}_{n\pi/\beta}^{(n+1)\pi/\beta} \right|$$

$$= \frac{\beta e^{-n\pi\alpha/\beta}}{(\alpha^2 + \beta^2)} \{1 + e^{-\pi\alpha/\beta}\}$$

Hence, $g = \dfrac{S_{n+1}}{S_n} = \dfrac{\dfrac{\beta e^{-(n+1)\pi\alpha/\beta} \{1 + e^{-\pi\alpha/\beta}\}}{(\alpha^2 + \beta^2)}}{\dfrac{\beta e^{-n\pi\alpha/\beta} \{1 + e^{-\pi\alpha/\beta}\}}{\alpha^2 + \beta^2}} = e^{-\pi\alpha/\beta}$

which completes the proof.

8. Here, $S_j = \left| \int_{j\pi/b}^{(j+1)\pi/b} x \, dy \right| = \left| \int_{j\pi/b}^{(j+1)\pi/b} e^{-ay} \sin by \, dy \right|$

$$= \left| \left\{ \frac{e^{-ay}}{a^2 + b^2} (-a \sin by - b \cos by) \right\}_{j\pi/b}^{(j+1)\pi/b} \right|$$

$$= \left| \frac{e^{-a(j+1)\pi/b}}{a^2 + b^2} \times (-b)(-1)^{j+1} - \frac{e^{-aj\pi/b}}{a^2 + b^2} (-b)(-1)^j \right|$$

$$= |b| \left\{ \frac{e^{-a(j+1)\pi/b}}{a^2 + b^2} + \frac{e^{-aj\pi/b}}{a^2 + b^2} \right\}$$

$$= |b| \frac{e^{-aj\pi/b}}{a^2 + b^2} \{e^{-a\pi/b} + 1\}; \{j = 0, 1, 2, \dots, n\}$$

Now, $\dfrac{S_{j+1}}{S_j} = |b| \dfrac{e^{-a(j+1)\pi/b}}{a^2 + b^2} \{e^{-a\pi/b} + 1\} \Big| \, |b| \dfrac{e^{-aj\pi/b}}{a^2 + b^2} \{e^{-a\pi/b} + 1\}$

$$= e^{-a\pi/b} \text{ for all } j = 0, 1, 2, \dots, n$$

Hence, $S_0, S_1, S_2, \dots, S_n$ are in GP with common ratio $e^{-a\pi/b}$.

For $a = -1$ and $b = \pi$, we have

$$S_j = \frac{e^j \pi (e + 1)}{\pi^2 + 1}; \; j = 0, 1, 2, \dots, n$$

$$\therefore \quad \sum_{j=0}^{n} S_j = \sum_{j=0}^{n} \frac{e^{j\pi} (e + 1)}{\pi^2 + 1} = \frac{(e + 1)\pi}{\pi + 1} \left\{ \frac{e^{n+1} - 1}{e - 1} \right\}$$

9. The points $x = 2 + \dfrac{e^t + e^{-t}}{2}$, $y = 2 + \dfrac{e^t - e^{-t}}{2}$ is on the curve

$$(x - 2)^2 - (y - 2)^2 = 1 \quad \text{or} \quad x^2 - y^2 - 4x + 4y - 1 = 0$$

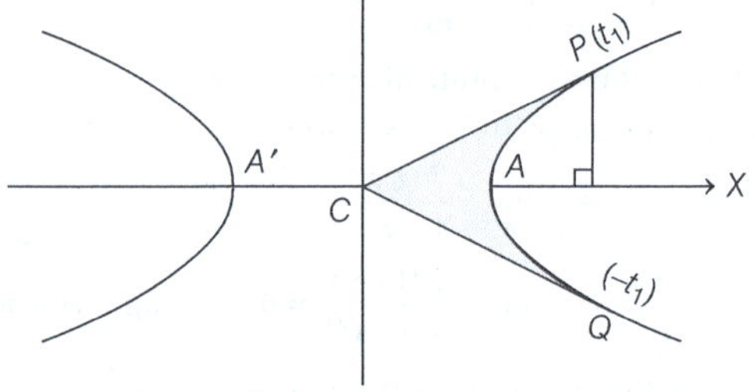

Put $(x - 2) = x$, $(y - 2) = y$

$$\therefore \quad x^2 - y^2 = 1 \text{ and } x = \frac{e^t + e^{-t}}{2}, y = \frac{e^t - e^{-t}}{2}$$

We have to find the area of the region bounded by the curve $x^2 - y^2 = 1$ and the lines joining the centre $x = 0$, $y = 0$ to the point (t_1) and $(-t_1)$.

$$\therefore \text{Required area} = 2 \left[\text{Area of } \Delta PCN - \int_1^{\frac{e^{t_1} + e^{-t_1}}{2}} y \, dx \right]$$

$$= 2 \left[\frac{1}{2} \left(\frac{e^{t_1} + e^{-t_1}}{2} \right) \left(\frac{e^{t_1} - e^{-t_1}}{2} \right) - \int_1^{t_1} y \frac{dx}{dt} dt \right]$$

$$= 2 \left[\left(\frac{e^{2t_1} - e^{-2t_1}}{8} \right) - \int_0^{t_1} \left(\frac{e^t - e^{-t}}{2} \right)^2 dt \right]$$

$$= \frac{e^{2t_1} - e^{-2t_1}}{4} - \frac{1}{2} \int_0^{t_1} (e^{2t} + e^{-2t} - 2) \, dt$$

$$= \frac{e^{2t_1} - e^{-2t_1}}{4} - \frac{1}{2} \left[\frac{e^{2t_1}}{2} - \frac{e^{-2t_1}}{2} - 2t_1 \right]_0^{t_1}$$

$$= \frac{e^{2t_1} - e^{-2t_1}}{4} - \frac{1}{2} \left[\frac{e^{2t_1}}{2} - \frac{e^{-2t_1}}{2} - 2t_1 \right] = t_1$$

10. $\because \quad y = \left[\sin^2 \dfrac{x}{4} + \cos \dfrac{x}{4} \right]$

$$\because \quad 1 < \sin^2 \frac{x}{4} + \cos \frac{x}{4} < 2$$

For $x \in (-2, 2]$

$$\therefore \quad y = \left[\sin^2 \frac{x}{4} + \cos \frac{x}{4} \right] = 1$$

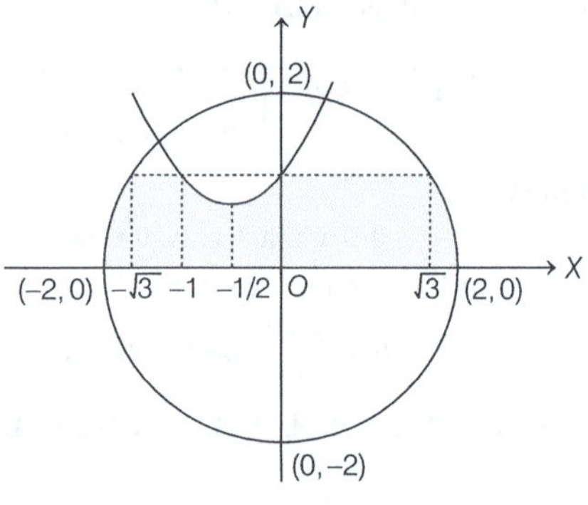

Now, we have to find out the area enclosed by the circle $x^2 + y^2 = 4$, parabola $\left(y - \frac{3}{4}\right) = \left(x + \frac{1}{2}\right)^2$, line $y = 1$ and X-axis. Required area is shaded area in the figure.

Hence, required area

$$= \sqrt{3} \times 1 + (\sqrt{3} - 1) \times 1 + \int_{-1}^{0} (x^2 + x + 1)\, dx + 2\int_{\sqrt{3}}^{2} (\sqrt{4 - x^2})\, dx$$

$$= (2\sqrt{3} - 1) + \left[\frac{x^3}{3} + \frac{x^2}{2} + x\right]_{-1}^{0} + 2\left[\frac{x}{2}\sqrt{4 - x^2} + 2\sin^{-1}\left(\frac{x}{2}\right)\right]_{\sqrt{3}}^{2}$$

$$= (2\sqrt{3} - 1) + \left[0 - \left(-\frac{1}{3} + \frac{1}{2} - 1\right)\right] + 2\left[(0 + \pi) - \left(\frac{\sqrt{3}}{2} + \frac{2\pi}{3}\right)\right]$$

$$= (2\sqrt{3} - 1) + \frac{5}{6} + \frac{2\pi}{3} - \sqrt{3}$$

$$= \left(\frac{2\pi}{3} + \sqrt{3} - \frac{1}{6}\right) \text{ sq units}$$

11. Here, $f(|x|) = \begin{cases} -x - 2, & -3 \le x \le 0 \\ x - 2, & 0 < x \le 3 \end{cases}$

$$|f(x)| = \begin{cases} 2, & -3 \le x \le 0 \\ -x + 2, & 0 < x \le 2 \\ x - 2, & 2 < x \le 3 \end{cases}$$

$$\therefore \quad f(|x|) - |f(x)| = \begin{cases} -x - 4, & -3 \le x \le 0 \\ 2x - 4, & 0 < x \le 2 \\ 0, & 2 < x \le 3 \end{cases}$$

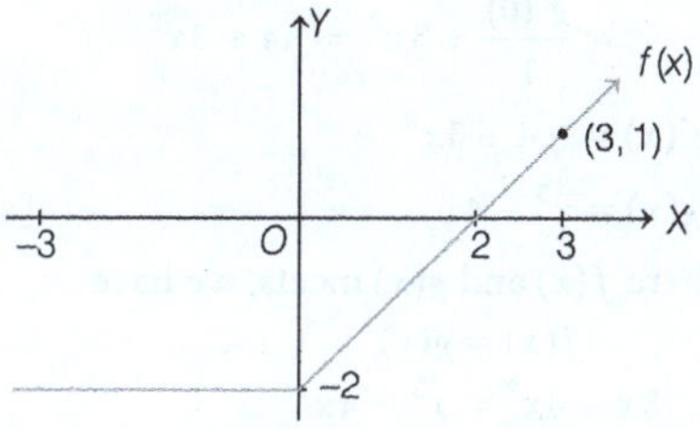

Graph of f (x)

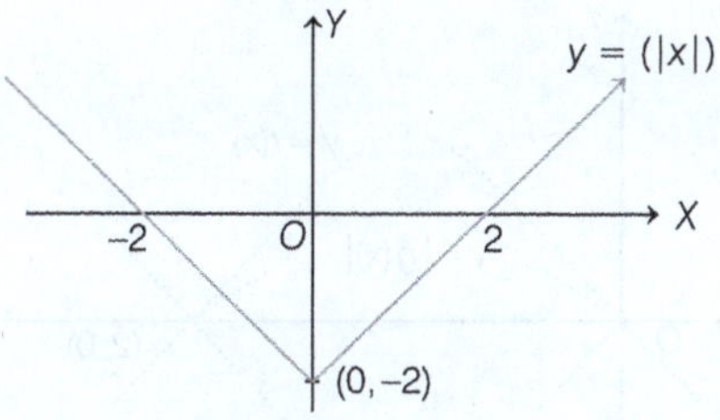

Graph of f (|x|)

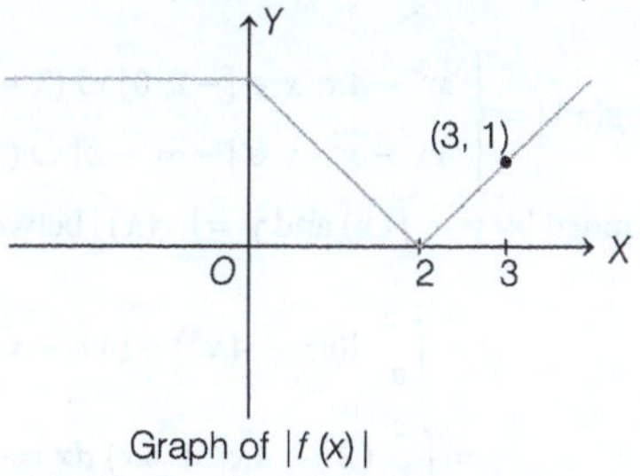

Graph of |f (x)|

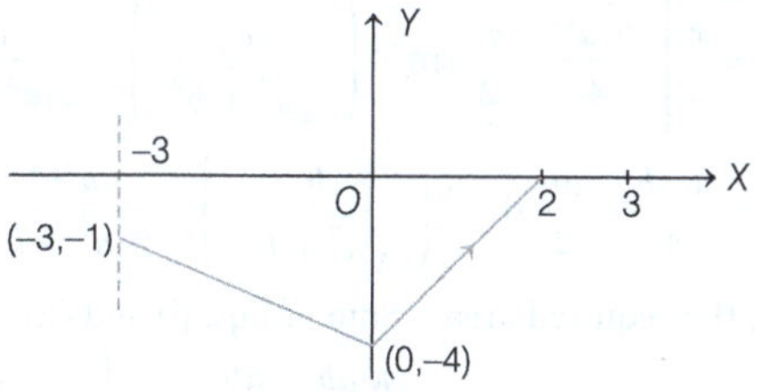

Graph of $g(x)$

Since, $|f(x)|$ is always positive.

$$g(x) = f(|x|) - |f(x)|$$

where the graphs could be drawn as shown in above figures.

From the graph, required area

$$= \frac{1}{2}(1 + 4) \times 3 + \left(\frac{1}{2} \times 2 \times 4\right) + 0 = \frac{23}{2} \text{ sq units}$$

12. The given curve $\frac{(x - y)^2}{a^2} + \frac{(x + y)^2}{b^2} = 2$ is an ellipse major and minor axes are $x - y = 0$ and $x + y = 0$, respectively. The required area is shown with shaded region.

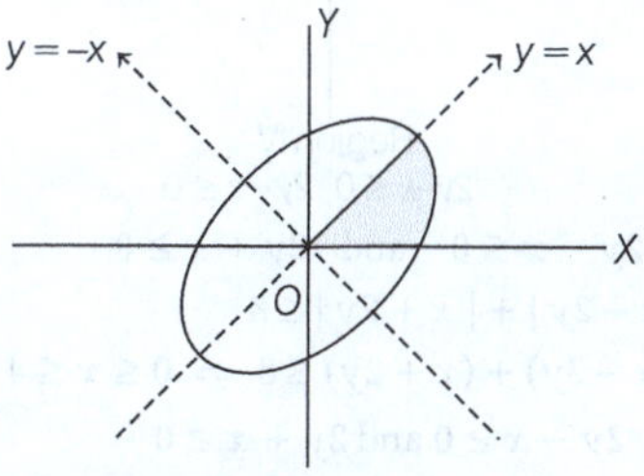

Instead of directly solving the problem we can solve equivalent problem with equivalent ellipse whose axes are $x = 0$ and $y = 0$.

The equivalent region is shown as $(OA'B'O)$ where the equation of ellipse is $\frac{x^2}{a^2} + \frac{y^2}{b^2} = 1$.

$\therefore$ Required area = Area $(\Delta OA'A'' + A'A''B')$

where, $\quad A' = \left(\frac{ab}{\sqrt{a^2 + b^2}}, \frac{ab}{\sqrt{a^2 + b^2}}\right)$

Area

$$\Delta OA'A'' = \frac{1}{2} \times \frac{ab}{\sqrt{a^2 + b^2}} \times \frac{ab}{\sqrt{a^2 + b^2}} = \frac{1}{2}\left(\frac{a^2 b^2}{a^2 + b^2}\right) \quad \text{...(i)}$$

$$\text{Area of } A'B'A'' = \int_{\frac{ab}{\sqrt{a^2 + b^2}}}^{a} b\sqrt{\left(1 - \frac{x^2}{a^2}\right)}\, dx$$

$$= \frac{b}{a} \cdot \int_{\frac{ab}{\sqrt{a^2 + b^2}}}^{a} \sqrt{a^2 - x^2}\, dx$$

$$= \frac{b}{a}\left[\frac{x}{2}\sqrt{a^2 - x^2} + \frac{a^2}{2}\sin^{-1}\frac{x}{a}\right]_{ab/\sqrt{a^2 + b^2}}^{a}$$

$$= \frac{b}{a}\left[0 + \frac{a^2}{2} \cdot \frac{\pi}{2} - \frac{ab}{2\sqrt{a^2 + b^2}} \cdot \sqrt{\left(a^2 - \frac{a^2 b^2}{a^2 + b^2}\right)} - \frac{a^2}{2}\sin^{-1}\frac{b}{\sqrt{a^2 + b^2}}\right]$$

$$=\frac{b}{a}\left[\frac{\pi a^2}{4}-\frac{a^2}{2}\sin^{-1}\left(\frac{b}{\sqrt{a^2+b^2}}\right)-\frac{a^3b}{2(a^2+b^2)}\right]$$

$$=\frac{\pi ab}{4}-\frac{ab}{2}\sin^{-1}\left(\frac{b}{\sqrt{a^2+b^2}}\right)-\frac{a^2b^2}{2(a^2+b^2)} \quad \text{...(ii)}$$

Hence, the required area = Sum of Eqs. (i) and (ii)

$$=\frac{\pi ab}{4}-\frac{ab}{2}\sin^{-1}\left(\frac{b}{\sqrt{a^2+b^2}}\right)$$

13. The line $y=\pm\frac{x}{2}$ divide the xy plane in four parts

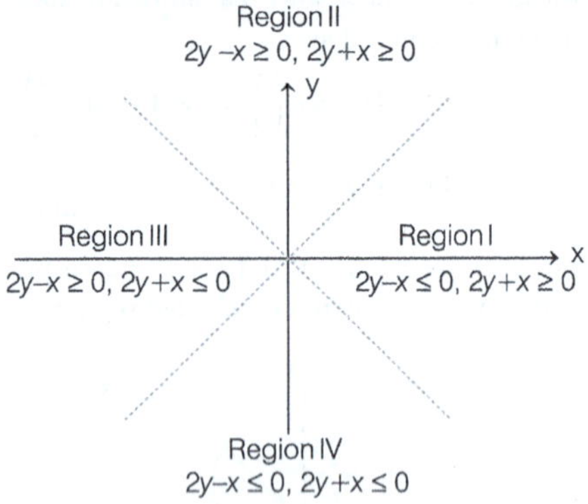

Region I $2y-x\le 0$ and $2y+x\ge 0$

So that, $|x-2y|+|x+2y|\le 8$

$\Rightarrow \quad (x-2y)+(x+2y)\le 8 \Rightarrow 0\le x\le 4$

Region II $2y-x\ge 0$ and $2y+x\ge 0$

So that, $\quad |x-2y|+|x+2y|\le 8$

$\Rightarrow \quad -(x-2y)+(x+2y)\le 8 \Rightarrow 0\le y\le 2$

Region III $2y+x\le 0,\ 2y-x\ge 0$

So that, $\quad |x-2y|+|x+2y|\le 8$

$\Rightarrow \quad -(x-2y)-(x+2y)\le 8 \Rightarrow -4\le x\le 0$

Region IV $2y+x\le 0,\ 2y-x\le 0$

So that, $\quad |x-2y|+|x+2y|\le 8 \Rightarrow -2\le y\le 0$

Here, all the points lie in the rectangle.

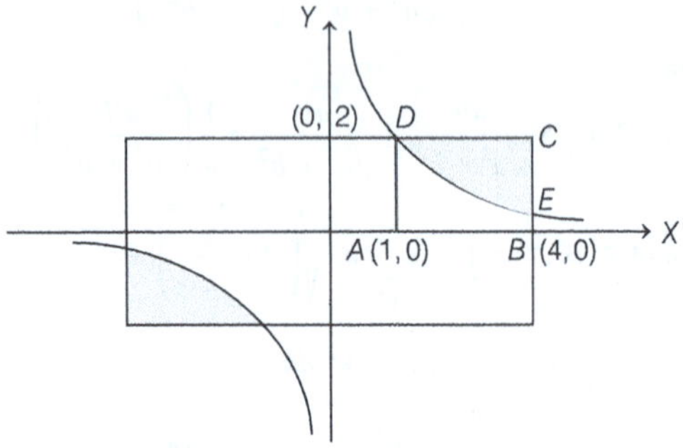

Also, the hyperbola $xy=2$ meets the sides of the rectangle at the points $(1, 2)$ and $(4, 1/2)$ in the 1st quadrant graphically.

Hence, required area

= 2 (Area of rectangle $ABCD$ – Area of $ABEDA$)

$$=2\left(3\times 2-\int_1^4 \frac{2}{x}\,dx\right)=2(6-2\log 4)\text{ sq units}$$

14. Here, $f(x+y)=f(x)+f(y)-8xy$

Replacing $x, y\to 0$, we get $f(0)=0$

Now, $f'(x)=\lim_{h\to 0}\frac{f(x+h)-f(x)}{h}=\lim_{y\to 0}\frac{f(x+y)-f(x)}{y}$

$$=\lim_{y\to 0}\frac{f(x)+f(y)-8xy-f(x)}{y}$$

$$=\lim_{y\to 0}\left\{\frac{f(y)}{y}-\frac{8xy}{y}\right\}$$

$$=\lim_{y\to 0}\left(\frac{f'(y)}{1}\right)-8x \quad \text{[using L'Hospital's rule]}$$

$$=f'(0)-8x=8-8x \quad \text{[given, } f'(0)=8]$$

$\Rightarrow \quad f'(x)=8-8x$

Integrating both the sides, we get

$$f(x)=8x-4x^2+c$$

As $\quad f(0)=0\Rightarrow c=0$

$\Rightarrow \quad f(x)=8x-4x^2 \quad \text{...(i)}$

Also, $\quad g(x+y)=g(x)+g(y)+3xy(x+y)$

Replacing $x, y\Rightarrow 0$, we get $g(0)=0$

Now, $\quad g'(x)=\lim_{y\to 0}\frac{g(x+y)-g(x)}{y}$

$$=\lim_{y\to 0}\frac{g(x)+g(y)+3x^2y+3xy^2-g(x)}{y}$$

$$=\lim_{y\to 0}\left[\frac{g(y)}{y}+\frac{y(3x^2+3xy)}{y}\right]$$

$$=\frac{g'(0)}{1}+3x^2=-4+3x^2$$

$\therefore \quad g'(x)=-4+3x^2$

$\Rightarrow \quad g(x)=x^3-4x \quad$ [as $g(0)=0$] ...(ii)

Points where $f(x)$ and $g(x)$ meets, we have

$$f(x)=g(x)$$

or $\quad 8x-4x^2=x^3-4x$

$\Rightarrow \quad x=0, 2, -6$

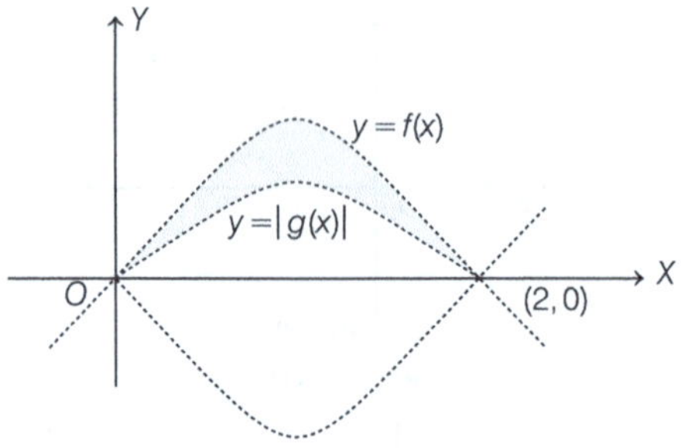

Now, $\quad |g(x)|=\begin{cases} x^3-4x, & x\in[-2, 0]\cup(2, \infty) \\ 4x-x^3, & x\in[-\infty, -2]\cup(0, 2)\end{cases}$

$\therefore$ Area bounded by $y=f(x)$ and $y=|g(x)|$ between $x=0$ to $x=2$

$$=\int_0^2 \{(8x-4x^2)-(4x-x^3)\}\,dx$$

$$=\int_0^2 (x^3-4x^2+4x)\,dx=\frac{4}{3}\text{ sq units}$$

4

"

If I were again beginning my studies, I would follow the advise of Plato and start with Mathematics.

-Galileo Galilei

Differential Equation

Learning Milestones

Milestone 1 Order, Degree and Formation of Differential Equation
- Order of Differential Equation
- Degree of Differential Equation
- Linear and Non-linear Differential Equation
- Formation of Differential Equation

Milestone 2 Solution of Differential Equation
- General and Particular Solution of Differential Equation
- Differential Equations of the First Order and First Degree
- Homogeneous Differential Equation

Milestone 3 Linear Differential Equation
- First Order Linear Differential Equations
- Bernoulli's Equation
- Orthogonal Trajectory

Milestone 4 Exact Differential Equations

Milestone 5 Application of First Order Differential Equations
- Growth and Decay Problems
- Geometrical Applications

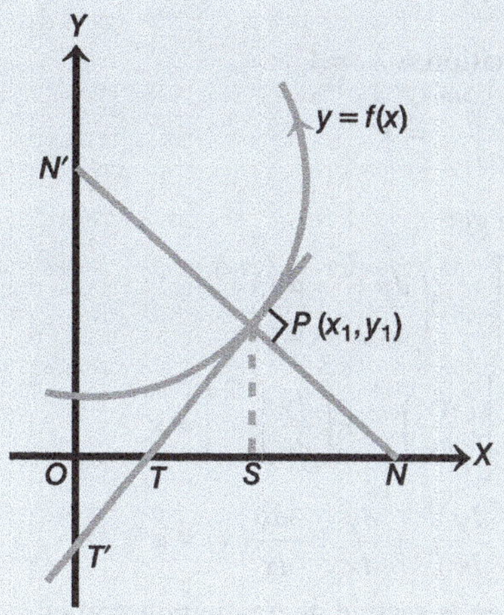

Practice Milestones

Practice Milestone 1- JEE Main Pattern

Practice Milestone 2 - JEE Advanced Pattern

Practice Milestone 3 - Challenging Problems

Milestone 1 Order, Degree and Formation of Differential Equation

- Order of Differential Equation • Degree of Differential Equation
- Linear and Non-linear Differential Equation • Formation of Differential Equation

Definition An equation that involves independent and dependent variables and the derivatives of the dependent variables is called a differential equation.

A differential equation is said to be ordinary if the differential coefficient have reference to a single independent variable only.

e.g. $$\frac{d^3y}{dx^3} - 2\frac{d^2y}{dx^2} + \frac{dy}{dx} + \sin x = 0$$

A differential equation is said to be partial if there are two or more independent variables

e.g. $$\frac{dy}{dx} + \frac{dx}{dy} + \frac{du}{dz} = 0$$

But in this chapter we shall confine ourselves to the study of the ordinary differential equation only.

4.1 Order of Differential Equation

The order of a differential equation is the order of the highest order derivatives appearing in the equation and it is an positive integer.

e.g. In the equation $\frac{d^2y}{dx^2} + \frac{dy}{dx} + y = \sin x$

The order of the highest order derivative is 2.

So, its order is 2.

4.2 Degree of a Differential Equation

The degree of a differential equation is the degree of the highest order derivatives when differential coefficient are made free from radical and fraction.

JEE Focus Points

- The degree is always natural number.
- The degree of differential equation may or may not exists.

Example 1. Find the order and degree (if defined) of the following differential equations :

(i) $y = 1 + \left(\frac{dy}{dx}\right) + \frac{1}{2!}\left(\frac{dy}{dx}\right)^2 + \frac{1}{3!}\left(\frac{dy}{dx}\right)^3 + \dots$

(ii) $\left(\frac{d^3y}{dx^3}\right)^{2/3} = \frac{dy}{dx} + 2$

(iii) $\frac{d^2y}{dx^2} = x \ln\left(\frac{dy}{dx}\right)$

Sol. (i) The given differential equation can be rewritten as

$$y = e^{dy/dx} \Rightarrow \frac{dy}{dx} = \ln y$$

Hence, its order is 1 and degree 1.

(ii) The given differential equation can be rewritten as

$$\left(\frac{d^3y}{dx^3}\right)^2 = \left(\frac{dy}{dx} + 2\right)^3.$$

Hence, its order is 3 and degree 2.

(iii) Its order is obviously 2.

Since, the given differential equation cannot be written as a polynomial in all the differential coefficients, the degree of the equation is not defined.

Example 2. Let λ_1 and λ_2 be order and degree of differential equation $\left(\frac{dy}{dx}\right)^{1/3} + \left(\frac{dy}{dx}\right)^{2/3} = x$, then find $|(\lambda_1 - \lambda_2)|$.

Sol. Order of differential equation $= \lambda_1 = 1$

$$\left(\frac{dy}{dx}\right)^{1/3} + \left(\frac{dy}{dx}\right)^{2/3} = x$$

On cubing both side, we get

$$\left[\left(\frac{dy}{dx}\right)^{1/3}\right]^3 + \left[\left(\frac{dy}{dx}\right)^{2/3}\right]^3 + 3\left(\frac{dy}{dx}\right)^{1/3}\left(\frac{dy}{dx}\right)^{2/3}$$

$$\left[\left(\frac{dy}{dx}\right)^{1/3} + \left(\frac{dy}{dx}\right)^{2/3}\right] = x^3$$

$$\Rightarrow \left(\frac{dy}{dx}\right)^2 + \frac{dy}{dx} + \frac{3dy}{dx}(x) = x^3$$

Now, differential equation is second degree in polynomial form of derivatives.

Hence, degree of differential equation $= \lambda_2 = 2$

Now, $|(\lambda_1 - \lambda_2)| = 1$

4.3 Linear and Non-linear Differential Equation

A differential equation is a linear differential equation if it is expressible in the form

$$a_0 \frac{d^n y}{dx^n} + a_1 \frac{d^{n-1} y}{dx^{n-1}} + a_2 \frac{d^{n-2} y}{dx^{n-2}} + \ldots + a_{n-1} \frac{dy}{dx} + a_n y = Q$$

where $a_0, a_1, a_2, \ldots, a_n$ and Q are either constants or functions of independent variable x.

Thus, if a differential equation when expressed in the form of a polynomial involves the derivatives and dependent variable in the first power and there are no product of these, and also the coefficient of the various terms are either constants or functions of the independent variable, then it is said to be linear differential equation. Otherwise, it is a non-linear differential equation.

It follows from the above definition that a differential equation will be non-linear differential equation if

(i) its degree is more than one.

(ii) any of the differential coefficient has exponent more than one.

(iii) exponent of the dependent variable is more than one.

(iv) Products containing dependent variable and its differential coefficient are present.

e.g. The differentiable equation $\left(\frac{d^3y}{dx^3}\right)^2 - 6\left(\frac{d^2y}{dx^2}\right) - 4y = 0$,

is a non-linear differential equation, because its degree is 2, more than one.

e.g. The differential equation, $\left(\frac{d^3y}{dx^3}\right) + 2\left(\frac{dy}{dx}\right)^2 + 9y = x$,

is non-linear differential equation, because differential coefficient $\frac{dy}{dx}$ has exponent 2.

e.g. The differential equation $(x^2 + y^2)\,dx - 2xydy = 0$ is a non-linear differential equation, because the exponent of dependent variable y is 2 and it involves the product of y and $\frac{dy}{dx}$.

e.g. Consider the differential equation

$$\left(\frac{d^2y}{dx^2}\right) - 5\left(\frac{dy}{dx}\right) + 6y = \sin x$$

This is a linear differential equation of order 2 and degree one.

4.4 Formation of Differential Equation

If an equation in independent and dependent variables involving some arbitrary constants is given, then a differential equation is obtained as follows :

(i) Differentiate the given equation w.r.t. the independent variable (say x) as many times as the number of arbitrary constants in it.

(ii) Eliminate the arbitrary constants.

(iii) The eliminant is the required differential equation.
i.e. If we have an equation $f(x, y, c_1, c_2, \ldots, c_n) = 0$

Containing n arbitrary constants $c_1, c_2, c_3, \ldots, c_n$, then by differentiating this n times, we shall get n-equations.

Now, among these n-equations and the given equation, in all $(n+1)$ equations, if the n arbitrary constants $c_1, c_2, c_3, \ldots, c_n$ are eliminated, we shall evidently get a differential equation of the nth order. For there being n differentiation, the resulting equation must contain a derivative of the nth order.

Algorithm for Formation of Differential Equations

Step I Write the given equation involving independent variable x (say), dependent variable y (say) and the arbitrary constant.

Step II Obtain the number of arbitrary constants in Step I. Let there be n arbitrary constants.

Step III Differentiate the relation in Step I, n times with respect to x.

Step IV Eliminate arbitrary constants with the help of n equations involving differential coefficients obtained in Step III and an equation in Step I.

The equation so obtained is the desired differential equation.

The following examples will illustrate the above procedure.

Example 3. Find the differential equation whose solution represents the family $xy = ae^x + be^{-x}$.

Sol. $$xy = ae^x + be^{-x} \quad \ldots\text{(i)}$$

Differentiating Eq. (i) w.r.t. x, we get

$$x\frac{dy}{dx} + y = ae^x - be^{-x} \quad \ldots\text{(ii)}$$

Differentiating Eq. (ii) w.r.t. x, we get

$$x\frac{d^2y}{dx^2} + \frac{dy}{dx} \cdot 1 + \frac{dy}{dx} = ae^x + be^{-x} \quad \ldots\text{(iii)}$$

Using Eqs. (i) and (iii), we get

$$x\frac{d^2y}{dx^2} + 2\frac{dy}{dx} = xy$$

which is the required differential equation.

Example 4. Find the differential equation whose solution represents the family $c(y+c)^2 = x^3$.

Sol. Differentiating $c(y+c)^2 = x^3$ w.r.t. x, we get

$$c[2(y+c)]\frac{dy}{dx} = 3x^2 \quad \text{...(i)}$$

But from Eq. (i), we have

$$\frac{2x^3}{(y+c)^2}(y+c)\frac{dy}{dx} = 3x^2 \Rightarrow \frac{2x^3}{y+c}\cdot\frac{dy}{dx} = 3x^2$$

i.e. $$\frac{2x}{y+c}\cdot\frac{dy}{dx} = 3 \Rightarrow \frac{2x}{3}\left[\frac{dy}{dx}\right] = y+c$$

$\therefore$ $$c = \frac{2x}{3}\left[\frac{dy}{dx}\right] - y$$

Substituting c in Eq. (i), we get

$$\left[\frac{2x}{3}\left(\frac{dy}{dx}\right) - y\right]\left[\frac{2x}{3}\frac{dy}{dx}\right]^2 = x^3$$

which is the required differential equation.

Example 5. The differential equation of all non-vertical lines in a plane is given by

(a) $\dfrac{d^2y}{dx^2} = 0$ (b) $\dfrac{d^2x}{dy^2} = 0$

(c) $\dfrac{d^2x}{dy^2} = 0$ and $\dfrac{d^2y}{dx^2} = 0$ (d) All of these

Sol. (a) The equation of the family of all non-vertical lines in a plane is given by $ax + by = 1$, where $b \neq 0$ and $a \in R$.

Differentiating both the sides w.r.t. x, we get

$$a + b\frac{dy}{dx} = 0 \quad (\text{as } b \neq 0 \text{ and } a \in R)$$

Again, differentiating both the sides w.r.t. x, we get

$$b\frac{d^2y}{dx^2} = 0 \quad (\text{as } b \neq 0 \text{ and } a \in R)$$

$$\Rightarrow \frac{d^2y}{dx^2} = 0 \quad (\text{as } b \neq 0)$$

$\therefore$ Differential equation of all non-vertical lines in a plane is

$$\frac{d^2y}{dx^2} = 0$$

Example 6. The differential equation of all straight lines which are at a constant distance p from the origin, is

(a) $(y + xy_1)^2 = p^2(1 + y_1^2)$ (b) $(y - xy_1^2) = p^2(1 + y_1)^2$

(c) $(y - xy_1)^2 = p^2(1 + y_1^2)$ (d) None of these

Sol. (c) As, we know $x\cos\alpha + y\sin\alpha = p$ ...(i)
Represents the family of straight lines which are at a constant distance p from origin.

Differentiating Eq. (i) w.r.t. x, we get

$$\cos\alpha + \sin\alpha\cdot\frac{dy}{dx} = 0 \Rightarrow \tan\alpha = -\frac{1}{y_1}$$

or $$\sin\alpha = \frac{1}{\sqrt{1+y_1^2}} \text{ and } \cos\alpha = -\frac{y_1}{\sqrt{1+y_1^2}} \quad \text{...(ii)}$$

From Eqs. (i) and (ii), we get

$$\frac{-xy_1}{\sqrt{1+y_1^2}} + \frac{y}{\sqrt{1+y_1^2}} = p \Rightarrow (y - xy_1)^2 = p^2(1 + y_1^2)$$

which is required differential equation.

Example 7. The differential equation of all circles in the first quadrant which touch the coordinate axes is

(a) $(x-y)^2(1+(y')^2) = (x+yy')^2$

(b) $(x+y)^2(1+(y')^2) = (x+y')^2$

(c) $(x-y)^2(1+y') = (x+yy')^2$

(d) None of the above

Sol. (a) Equation of circles touching coordinate axes is

$$(x-a)^2 + (y-a)^2 = a^2 \quad \text{...(i)}$$

Differentiating of Eq. (i) w.r.t. x, we get

$$2(x-a) + 2(y-a)y' = 0 \Rightarrow a = \frac{x + yy'}{1+y'}, \quad \text{...(ii)}$$

where $y' = \dfrac{dy}{dx}$

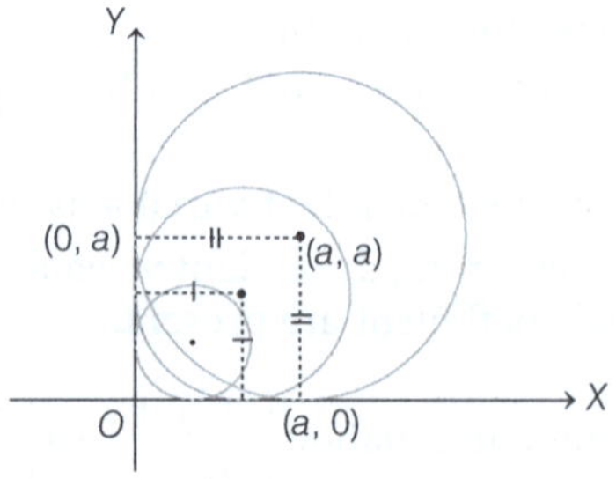

From Eqs. (i) and (ii), we get

$$\left(x - \frac{x+yy'}{1+y'}\right)^2 + \left(y - \frac{x+yy'}{1+y'}\right)^2 = \left(\frac{x+yy'}{1+y'}\right)^2$$

$$\Rightarrow \left(\frac{xy' - yy'}{1+y'}\right)^2 + \left(\frac{y-x}{1+y'}\right)^2 = \left(\frac{x+yy'}{1+y'}\right)^2$$

$$\Rightarrow (x-y)^2(y')^2 + (y-x)^2 = (x+yy')^2$$

$$\Rightarrow (x-y)^2(1+(y')^2) = (x+yy')^2$$

Example 8. The differential equation of all conics whose centre lies at origin, is given by

(a) $(3xy_2 + x^2y_3)(y - xy_1) = 3xy_2(y - xy_1 - x^2y_2)$

(b) $(3xy_1 + x^2y_2)(y_1 - xy_3) = 3xy_1(y - xy_2 - x^2y_3)$

(c) $(3xy_2 + x^2y_3)(y_1 - xy) = 3xy_1(y - xy_1 - x^2y_2)$

(d) None of the above

Sol. (a) Equation of all conics whose centre lies at origin, is

$$ax^2 + 2hxy + by^2 = 1 \quad \text{...(i)}$$

Differentiating Eq. (i) w.r.t. x, we get

$$2ax + 2hxy_1 + 2hy + 2byy_1 = 0$$

$$\Rightarrow ax + h(y + xy_1) + byy_1 = 0$$

Multiplying by x equation becomes,

$$ax^2 + h(xy + x^2y_1) + bxyy_1 = 0 \quad \text{...(ii)}$$

Subtracting Eqs. (i) and (ii), we get

$$h(xy - x^2y_1) + b(y^2 - xyy_1) = 1$$

$$\Rightarrow \quad (hx + by)\,y - xy_1(hx + by) = 1$$

$$\Rightarrow \quad (hx + by)(y - xy_1) = 1$$

$$\Rightarrow \quad hx + by = \frac{1}{y - xy_1} \quad \text{...(iii)}$$

Again, differentiating w.r.t. x, we get

$$h + by_1 = -\frac{(y_1 - xy_2 - y_1)}{(y - xy_1)^2} \text{ or } h + by_1 = \frac{xy_2}{(y - xy_1)^2} \quad \text{...(iv)}$$

From Eqs. (iii) and (iv), we get

$$b(y - xy_1) = \frac{y - xy_1 - x^2y_2}{(y - xy_1)^2}$$

$$\Rightarrow \quad b = \frac{y - xy_1 - x^2y_2}{(y - xy_1)^3} \quad \text{...(v)}$$

Again, differentiating both the sides w.r.t. x, we get

$$0 = \frac{y_1 - y_1 - 3xy_2 - x^2y_3}{(y - xy_1)^3} + \frac{3(y - xy_1 - x^2y_2)\,xy_2}{(y - xy_1)^4}$$

$$\Rightarrow \quad (3xy_2 + x^2y_3)(y - xy_1) = 3xy_2(y - xy_1 - x^2y_2)$$

Milestone Practice 4.1

1. The differential equation of all parabolas whose axis of symmetry is along X-axis is of order.
   (a) 2 (b) 3
   (c) 1 (d) None of these

2. The order and degree of the differential equation of all tangent lines to the parabola $x^2 = 4y$ is
   (a) 1, 2 (b) 2, 2 (c) 3, 1 (d) 4, 1

3. The degree of the differential equation $\frac{d^2y}{dx^2} + 3\left(\frac{dy}{dx}\right)^2 = x^2 \log\left(\frac{d^2y}{dx^2}\right)$ is
   (a) 1 (b) 2
   (c) 3 (d) Not defined

4. The degree of the differential equation satisfying the relation $\sqrt{1+x^2} + \sqrt{1+y^2} = \lambda(x\sqrt{1+y^2} - y\sqrt{1+x^2})$ is
   (a) 1 (b) 2 (c) 3 (d) 4

5. The degree of the differential equation $\left(\frac{d^2y}{dx^2}\right)^2 + \left(\frac{dy}{dx}\right)^2 = x\sin\left(\frac{d^2y}{dx^2}\right)$ is
   (a) 1 (b) 2
   (c) 3 (d) Not defined

6. The order of the differential equation whose general solution is given by $y = c_1\cos(2x + c_2) - (c_3 + c_4)a^{x+c_5} + c_6\sin(x - c_7)$ is (where, c_i, $i = 1, 2, \ldots, 7$ are arbitrary constant)
   (a) 3 (b) 4 (c) 5 (d) 6

7. The differential equation of all circles touching the Y-axis at origin, is
   (a) $y^2 - x^2 = 2xy\frac{dy}{dx}$ (b) $y^2 - x^2 = 2xy\frac{dx}{dy}$
   (c) $x^2 - y^2 = 2xy\frac{dy}{dx}$ (d) $x^2 - y^2 = 2xy\frac{dx}{dy}$

8. The differential equation of all parabolas having their axes of symmetry coincident with the axes of x, is
   (a) $yy_2 + y_1^2 = y + y_1$ (b) $yy_2 + y_1^2 = 0$
   (c) $yy_2 + y_1^2 = y_1$ (d) None of these

9. The differential equation of all conics whose axes coincide with the coordinate axes, is
   (a) $xyy_2 + xy_1^2 - yy_1 = 0$ (b) $yy_2 + y_1^2 - yy_1 = 0$
   (c) $xyy_2 + (x - y)\,y_1 = 0$ (d) None of these

10. The differential equation having $y = (\sin^{-1} x)^2 + A(\cos^{-1} x) + B$, where A and B are arbitrary constant, is
    (a) $(1 - x^2)\,y_2 - xy_1\,2$ (b) $(1 - x^2)\,y_2 + yy_1 = 0$
    (c) $(1 - x)\,y_2 + xy_1 = 0$ (d) None of these

11. The differential equation of circles passing through the points of intersection of unit circle with centre at the origin and the line bisecting the first quadrant, is
    (a) $y_1(x^2 + y^2 - 1) + (x + yy_1) = 0$
    (b) $(y_1 - 1)(x^2 + y^2 - 1) + (x + yy_1)\,2(x - y) = 0$
    (c) $(x^2 + y^2 - 1) + yy_2 = 0$
    (d) None of the above

12. The differential equation of all non-horizontal lines in a plane is given by
    (a) $\frac{d^2y}{dx^2} = 0$ (b) $\frac{d^2x}{dy^2} = 0$
    (c) $\frac{d^2y}{dx^2} = 0$ and $\frac{d^2x}{dy^2} = 0$ (d) All of these

13. The differential equations of all circles touching the X-axis at origin is
    (a) $(y^2 - x^2) = 2xy\left(\frac{dy}{dx}\right)$ (b) $(x^2 - y^2)\frac{dy}{dx} = 2xy$
    (c) $(x^2 - y^2) = 2xy\left(\frac{dy}{dx}\right)$ (d) None of these

Answer Key

1. (a)	2. (a)	3. (d)	4. (a)	5. (d)
6. (c)	7. (a)	8. (b)	9. (a)	10. (a)
11. (b)	12. (b)	13. (b)		

For Detailed Solution

Milestone 2 Solution of Differential Equation

• General and Particular Solution of Differential Equation • Differential Equations of the First Order and First Degree • Homogeneous Differential Equation

4.5 General and Particular Solution of a Differential Equation

The solution of the differential equation is a relation between the variables of the equation not containing the derivatives, but satisfying the given differential equation (i.e. from which the given differential equation can be derived).

Thus, the solution of $\frac{dy}{dx} = e^x$ could be obtained by simply integrating both the sides, i.e. $y = e^x + C$ and that of, $\frac{dy}{dx} = px + q$ is $y = p\frac{x^2}{2} + qx + C$, where C is arbitrary constant.

(i) **A general solution or an integral** of a differential equation is a relation between the variables (not involving the derivatives) which contains the same number of the arbitrary constants as the order of the differential equation.

e.g. a general solution of the differential equation $\frac{d^2x}{dt^2} = -4x$ is $x = A\cos 2t + B\sin 2t$, where A and B are the arbitrary constants.

(ii) **Particular solution or particular integral** is that solution of the differential equation obtained from the general solution by assigning particular values to the arbitrary constant in the general solution.

e.g. $x = 10\cot 2t + 5\sin 2t$ is a particular solution of differential equation $\frac{d^2x}{dt^2} = -4x$.

4.6 Differential Equations of the First Order and First Degree

In this section, we shall discuss the differential equations which are of first order and first degree only.

A differential equation of first order and first degree is of the form $\frac{dy}{dx} = f(x, y)$.

JEE SPIKE

All the differential equations, even of first order and first degree, cannot be solved. However, if they belong to any of the standard forms which we are going to discuss, in the subsequent articles they can be solved.

Equations in Which the Variables are Separable

The equation $\frac{dy}{dx} = f(x, y)$ is said to be in variables separable form, if we can express it in the form $f(x)\,dx = g(y)\,dy$.

By integrating this, solution of the equation is obtained which is, $\int f(x)\,dx = \int g(y)\,dy + C$

Example 9. Solve $\sec^2 x \tan y\, dx + \sec^2 y \tan x\, dy = 0$.

Sol. Dividing the given equation by $\tan x \tan y$, we get

$$\frac{\sec^2 x}{\tan x}dx + \frac{\sec^2 y}{\tan y}dy = 0$$

This is variable-separable type.

On integrating both sides, we get

$$\int \frac{\sec^2 x}{\tan x}dx + \int \frac{\sec^2 y}{\tan y}dy = C'$$

$$\ln|\tan x| + \ln|\tan y| = \ln C, \text{ where } C' = \ln C$$

or $\quad \ln|\tan x \cdot \tan y| = \ln C;\ (C > 0)$

$\Rightarrow \quad |\tan x \cdot \tan y| = C$

This is the general solution.

Example 10. Solve $\sqrt{1 + x^2 + y^2 + x^2y^2} + xy\frac{dy}{dx} = 0$.

Sol. The given differential equation can be written as

$$\sqrt{(1+y^2)(1+x^2)} = -xy\frac{dy}{dx}$$

$\Rightarrow$
$$-\frac{\sqrt{1+x^2}\,dx}{x} = \frac{y\,dy}{\sqrt{1+y^2}}$$

This is the variable-separable form.

$\therefore$ Integrating both the sides, we get

$$-\int \frac{\sqrt{1+x^2}}{x}\,dx = \int \frac{y}{\sqrt{1+y^2}}\,dy$$

$$\Rightarrow -\left[\sqrt{1+x^2} + \frac{1}{2}\log\left(\frac{\sqrt{1+x^2}-1}{\sqrt{1+x^2}+1}\right)\right] = \sqrt{1+y^2} + C$$

This is the general solution to the given differential equation.

Example 11. Solve $y - x\dfrac{dy}{dx} = a\left(y^2 + \dfrac{dy}{dx}\right)$.

Sol. Rewriting the given equation as

$$y - ay^2 = (x+a)\frac{dy}{dx}$$

$$\Rightarrow \quad \frac{dy}{y(1-ay)} = \frac{dx}{(x+a)}$$

This is the variable-separable form.

Integrating both the sides, we get

$$\int \frac{dy}{y(1-ay)} = \int \frac{dx}{(x+a)}$$

$$\Rightarrow \quad \int\left(\frac{1}{y} + \frac{a}{1-ay}\right)dy = \int \frac{dx}{x+a}$$

$$\Rightarrow \quad \ln y - \frac{a}{a}\ln(1-ay) + \ln C = \ln(a+x)$$

$$\Rightarrow \quad \ln\left(\frac{(a+x)(1-ay)}{y}\right) = \ln(C)$$

or $\quad Cy = (a+x)(1-ay)$ is the general solution.

Example 12. Solve $e^{dy/dx} = x+1$, given that when $x = 0, y = 3$.

Sol. This is an example of particular solution.

$$e^{(dy/dx)} = x+1$$

$$\therefore \quad \frac{dy}{dx} = \ln(x+1)$$

$$\therefore \quad \int dy = \int \ln(x+1)\,dx \qquad \text{(integration by parts)}$$

i.e. $\quad y = x\ln(x+1) - \displaystyle\int \frac{x}{x+1}\,dx$

i.e. $\quad y = x\ln(x+1) - x + \ln(x+1) + C$

This is the general solution.

To find the particular solution, put $x = 0$, $y = 3$ in the general equation.

$$\therefore \quad 3 = 0 - 0 + 0 + C$$

$$\therefore \quad C = 3$$

$\therefore$ The required particular solution is,

$$y = (x+1)\ln(x+1) - x + 3$$

JEE SCANNER

Example Similar to PYQ Asked in JEE Main 2024

If $\dfrac{dx}{dy} - \dfrac{2^{y-x}(2^x-1)}{2^y-1} = 0$, $x, y > 0$, $y(1) = 1$, *then* $y(2)$ *is equal to*

(a) $2 + \log_2 3$ (b) $1 + \log_2 3$

(c) $1 - \log_2 3$ (d) $\log_2 4$

Sol. (d) Given, $\dfrac{dx}{dy} - \dfrac{2^{y-x}(2^x-1)}{2^y-1} = 0$, $x, y > 0$,

$y(1) = 1$, $y(2) = ?$

Now, $\quad \dfrac{dx}{dy} = \dfrac{2^y(2^x-1)}{2^x(2^y-1)} \Rightarrow \displaystyle\int \frac{2^y}{2^y-1}\,dy = \int \frac{2^x}{2^x-1}\,dx$

$$\Rightarrow \quad \frac{1}{\ln 2}\int \frac{2^y \ln 2}{2^y - 1}\,dy = \frac{1}{\ln 2}\int \frac{2^x \ln 2}{2^x-1}\,dx$$

$$\Rightarrow \quad \frac{1}{\ln 2}\ln|2^y - 1| = \frac{1}{\ln 2}\ln|2^x - 1| + C$$

At $x = 1$ and $y = 1$

On putting these values in above equation relation, we get

$$C = 0$$

$$\ln|2^y - 1| - \ln|2^x - 1| = 0 \Rightarrow (2^x - 1) = 2^y - 1$$

$$\Rightarrow \quad 2^y - 1 = 2^x - 1 \Rightarrow 2^y = 2^x$$

At $x = 2$, $\quad 2^y = 4 \Rightarrow y = \log_2 4$

Skill Builder

If $\dfrac{dx}{dy} - \dfrac{4^{y-x}(4^x-1)}{4^y-1} = 0$, $x, y > 0$, $y(1) = 1$, then $y(3)$ is equal to

(a) $\log_2 64$ (b) $\log_4 64$

(c) $\log_4 64 - 1$ (d) $\log_4 64 + 1$

For Sol.

■ **For more practice** See Q.1 of Milestone Practice 4.2.

Example 13. Find the solution of the curve of the differential equation $(1+e^{-y})(1+x^2)\dfrac{dy}{dx} = x^2$ which passes through origin.

Sol. Given differential equation

$$(1+e^{-y})(1+x^2)\frac{dy}{dx} = x^2 \Rightarrow (1+e^{-y})dy = \frac{x^2}{1+x^2}dx$$

On integrating both sides, we get

$$\int(1+e^{-y})dy = \int \frac{x^2}{1+x^2}dx \Rightarrow y - e^{-y} = \int\left(\frac{x^2+1}{1+x^2} - \frac{1}{1+x^2}\right)dx$$

$$\Rightarrow \quad y - e^{-y} = x - \tan^{-1}x + C$$

Since, this is passes through origin

$$0 - e^{-0} = 0 - 0 + C \Rightarrow C = -1$$

$\therefore$ Equation of curve is $y - e^{-y} = x - \tan^{-1}x - 1$.

Differential Equations Reducible to the Separable Variable Type

Sometimes differential equation of the first order cannot be solved directly by variable separation but by some substitution we can reduce it to a differential equation with separable variable. "A differential equation of the form $\frac{dy}{dx} = f(ax + by + c)$ is solved by writing $ax + by + c = t$."

Example 14. Solve $\frac{dy}{dx} = \sin^2(x + 3y) + 5$.

Sol. Let $x + 3y = t$, so that $1 + \frac{3dy}{dx} = \frac{dt}{dx}$

The given differential equation becomes,

$$\frac{1}{3}\left(\frac{dt}{dx} - 1\right) = \sin^2(t) + 5 \Rightarrow \frac{dt}{dx} = 3\sin^2 t + 16$$

$$\Rightarrow \int \frac{dt}{3\sin^2 t + 16} = \int dx \Rightarrow \int \frac{\sec^2 t\, dt}{3\tan^2 t + 16\sec^2 t} = x + C$$

$$\Rightarrow \int \frac{\sec^2 t\, dt}{19\tan^2 t + 16} = x + C$$

$$\Rightarrow \int \frac{du}{19u^2 + 16} = x + C \quad [\text{put } \tan t = u \Rightarrow \sec^2 t\, dt = du]$$

$$\Rightarrow \frac{1}{19}\int \frac{du}{u^2 + \frac{16}{19}} = x + C$$

$$\Rightarrow \frac{1}{19}\frac{\sqrt{19}}{4}\tan^{-1}\left(\frac{\sqrt{19}u}{4}\right) = x + C$$

$$\Rightarrow \frac{1}{4\sqrt{19}}\left\{\tan^{-1}\left(\frac{\sqrt{19}}{4}\tan(x + 3y)\right)\right\} = x + C$$

Example 15. Solve $(x + y)^2 \frac{dy}{dx} = a^2$.

Sol.

$$(x + y)^2 \frac{dy}{dx} = a^2 \qquad \text{...(i)}$$

Put $x + y = t \Rightarrow 1 + \frac{dy}{dx} = \frac{dt}{dx}$ or $\frac{dy}{dx} = \left(\frac{dt}{dx} - 1\right)$

$\therefore$ Eq. (i) reduces to $t^2\left\{\frac{dt}{dx} - 1\right\} = a^2$

i.e. $t^2 \frac{dt}{dx} = a^2 + t^2$, separating the variable and integrating.

$$\int dx = \int \frac{t^2}{a^2 + t^2}\, dt = \int \left(1 - \frac{a^2}{a^2 + t^2}\right) dt$$

$$\therefore \quad x = t - a\tan^{-1}\left(\frac{t}{a}\right) + C$$

i.e. $$x = x + y - a\tan^{-1}\left(\frac{x + y}{a}\right) + C$$

i.e. $y = a\tan^{-1}\left(\frac{x + y}{a}\right) - C$ is the required general solution.

JEE SCANNER

Example Similar to PYQ Asked in JEE Main 2024

If the solution of the differential equation $(2x + 3y - 1)\,dx + (4x + 6y - 5)\,dy = 0$, $y(0) = 2$ is $\alpha x + \beta y + 9\ln(2x + 3y - \gamma) = 12$, then $3\alpha + 2\beta + \gamma$ is

(a) 14 (b) 15

(c) 28 (d) 10

Sol. (c) $(2x + 3y - 1)\,dx + (4x + 6y - 5)\,dy = 0$ ...(i)

Substitute $u = 2x + 3y - 1$

$$\therefore \quad \frac{du}{dx} = 2 + \frac{3dy}{dx} \text{ or } \frac{dy}{dx} = \frac{1}{3}\left(\frac{du}{dx} - 2\right)$$

$\therefore$ Eq. (i) reduces to

$$u + (2u - 3)\frac{1}{3}\left(\frac{du}{dx} - 2\right) = 0$$

i.e. $$u - \frac{2}{3}(2u - 3) + \frac{1}{3}(2u - 3)\frac{du}{dx} = 0$$

i.e. $$\frac{-u + 6}{3} + \frac{1}{3}(2u - 3)\frac{du}{dx} = 0$$

Writing this in the variable-separable form

$$\left(\frac{2u - 3}{u - 6}\right) du = dx$$

$$\therefore \quad \int dx = \int \frac{2u - 3}{u - 6}\, du$$

$$\therefore \quad x + C = \int \frac{2(u - 6) + 9}{(u - 6)}\, du$$

$$\therefore \quad x + C = 2u + 9\ln|u - 6|$$

$$\therefore \quad x + C = 2(2x + 3y - 1) + 9\ln|2x + 3y - 7|$$

$$3x + 6y - 2 + 9\ln|2x + 3y - 7| = C$$

Put $x = 0, y = 2$, we get

$$C = 10$$

$$\therefore \quad 3x + 6y + 9\ln(2x + 3y - 7) = 12$$

$$\because \quad \alpha = 3,\ \beta = 6,\ \gamma = 7$$

$$3\alpha + 2\beta + \gamma = 9 + 12 + 7$$

$$= 28$$

Skill Builder

If the solution of the differential equation $(3x + 4y - 5)\,dx + (6x + 8y - 10)\,dy = 0$, $y(1) = 5$ is $\frac{\alpha x + \beta}{\gamma \log 2}$. Then, the value of $4\alpha + 5\beta + \gamma\log(4)$ is

(a) 48

(b) 51

(c) 55

(d) 60

For Sol.

▪ **For more practice** See Q.4 of Milestone Practice 4.2.

4.7 Homogeneous Differential Equation

By definition, a homogeneouos function $f(x, y)$ of degree n satisfies the property

$$f(\lambda x, \lambda y) = \lambda^n f(x, y)$$

e.g. The functions

$$f_1(x, y) = x^3 + y^3$$
$$f_2(x, y) = x^2 + xy + y^2$$
$$f_3(x, y) = x^3 e^{x/y} + xy^2$$

are all homogeneous functions, of degrees three, two and three respectively (verify this assertion).

Observe that any homogeneous function $f(x, y)$ of degree n can be equivalently written as follows :

$$f(x, y) = x^n f\left(\frac{y}{x}\right) = y^n f\left(\frac{x}{y}\right)$$

e.g. $$f(x, y) = x^3 + y^3 = x^3\left(1 + \left(\frac{y}{x}\right)^3\right) = y^3\left(1 + \left(\frac{x}{y}\right)^3\right)$$

Having seen homogeneous functions we define homogeneous DEs as follows :

Any DE of the form $M(x, y)\, dx + N(x, y) dy = 0$ or $\frac{dy}{dx} = -\frac{M(x, y)}{N(x, y)}$ is called homogeneous if $M(x, y)$ and $N(x, y)$ are homogeneous functions of the same degree.

What is so special about homogeneous DEs? Well, it turns out that they are extremely simple to solve.

To see how, we express both $M(x, y)$ and $N(x, y)$ as, say $x^n M\left(\frac{y}{x}\right)$ and $x^n N\left(\frac{y}{x}\right)$. This can be done since $M(x, y)$ and $N(x, y)$ are both homogeneous function of degree n. Doing this reduces our DE to

$$\frac{dy}{dx} = -\frac{M(x, y)}{N(x, y)} = \frac{x^n M\left(\frac{y}{x}\right)}{x^n N\left(\frac{y}{x}\right)} = -\frac{M\left(\frac{y}{x}\right)}{N\left(\frac{y}{x}\right)} = P\left(\frac{y}{x}\right)$$

(The function $P(t)$ stands for $\frac{-M(t)}{N(t)}$)

Now, the simple substitution $y = vx$ reduces this DE to a VS form

$$y = vx \Rightarrow \frac{dy}{dx} = v + x\frac{dy}{dx}$$

Thus, $\frac{dy}{dx} = p\left(\frac{y}{x}\right)$ transforms to

$$v + x\frac{dv}{dx} = P(v) \Rightarrow \frac{dv}{P(v) - v} = \frac{dx}{x}$$

This can now be integraed directly since it is in variable separable form.

Alogorithm for Solving Homogeneous Differential Equation

Step I Put the differential equation in the form

$$\frac{dy}{dx} = \frac{\phi(x, y)}{\psi(x, y)}$$

Step II Put $y = vx$ and $\frac{dy}{dx} = v + x\frac{dv}{dx}$ in the equation in Step I and can out x from the right hand side. The equation reduces to the form $v + x\frac{dv}{dx} = f(v)$.

Step III Shift v on RHS and seperate the variables in v and x.

Step IV Integrate both sides to obtain the solution in terms of v and x.

Step V Replace v by $\frac{y}{x}$ in the solution obtained in Step IV to obtain the solution in terms of x and y.

Following examples illustrate the procedure.

Example 16. Solve $y\, dx + (2\sqrt{xy} - x)\, dy = 0$.

Sol. $$y\, dx + (2\sqrt{xy} - x)\, dy = 0 \quad \text{...(i)}$$

This is homogeneous type. Substitute $y = vx$

$$\therefore \quad \frac{dy}{dx} = v + \frac{x\, dv}{dx}$$

$\therefore$ Equation (i) reduces to

$$vx\, dx + (2\sqrt{x^2 v} - x)(v\, dx + x\, dv) = 0$$

i.e. $$x \cdot \{ v dx + (2\sqrt{v} - 1)\, v\, dx + x\, dv\, (2\sqrt{v} - 1)\} = 0$$

i.e. $$dx\, (2v^{3/2} - v + v) + x\, dv\, (2\sqrt{v} - 1) = 0$$

Separating the variables, $\frac{dx}{x} + \left(\frac{2\sqrt{v} - 1}{2v^{3/2}}\right) dv = 0$

Integrating both the sides, $\ln|x| + \ln|v| + \frac{1}{\sqrt{v}} = C$

or $\ln|xv| + \frac{1}{\sqrt{v}} = C$ or $\ln|y| + \sqrt{\frac{x}{y}} = C \quad \left[\because v = \frac{y}{x}\right]$

which is the general solution.

Example 17. Solve $(1 + 2\, e^{x/y})\, dx + 2\, e^{x/y}\, (1 - x/y)\, dy = 0$.

Sol. The appearance of x/y in the equation suggests the substitution $x = vy$ or $dx = v\, dy + y\, dv$.

$\therefore$ The given equation is

$$(1 + 2e^v)(v\, dy + y\, dv) + 2e^v (1 - v)\, dy = 0$$

i.e. $$y(1 + 2e^v)\, dv + (v + 2e^v)\, dy = 0$$

i.e. $$\frac{1 + 2e^v}{v + 2e^v}\, dv + \frac{dy}{y} = 0$$

Integrating, $\int \frac{1+2e^v}{v+2e^v}dv + \int \frac{dy}{y} = 0$

$$\log|v+2e^v| + \log|y| = \log|C|$$

$$\Rightarrow \quad (v+2e^v)y = C$$

$$\Rightarrow \quad \left(\frac{x}{y}+2e^{x/y}\right)y = C \qquad \left[\because v = \frac{x}{y}\right]$$

$$\Rightarrow \quad (x+2ye^{x/y}) = C,$$

which is required solution.

Example 18. Let $y = y(x)$ be the solution of the differential equation $(3y^2 - 5x^2)ydx + 2x(x^2 - y^2)dy = 0$ such that $y(1) = 1$, then $|(y(2))^3 - 12y(2)|$ is equal to

(a) $16\sqrt{2}$ (b) 32

(c) $32\sqrt{2}$ (d) 64

Sol. (c) We have, $(3y^2 - 5x^2)ydx + 2x(x^2 - y^2)dy = 0$

$$\Rightarrow \quad \frac{dy}{dx} = \frac{y(5x^2-3y^2)}{2x(x^2-y^2)} \qquad ...(i)$$

which is a homogeneous differential equation.

On putting $y = vx$ and $\frac{dy}{dx} = v + x\frac{dv}{dx}$ in Eq. (i), we get

$$v + x\frac{dv}{dx} = \frac{vx(5x^2-3v^2x^2)}{2x(x^2-v^2x^2)}$$

$$\Rightarrow \quad v + x\frac{dv}{dx} = \frac{v(5-3v^2)}{2(1-v^2)} \Rightarrow \frac{xdv}{dx} = \frac{3v-v^3}{2(1-v^2)}$$

$$\Rightarrow \quad \frac{2(1-v^2)}{3v-v^3}dv = \frac{dx}{x}$$

On integrating both the sides, we get

$$2\int \frac{(1-v^2)}{3v-v^3}dv = \int \frac{dx}{x}$$

$$\Rightarrow \quad \frac{2}{3}\int \frac{3-3v^2}{3v-v^3}dv = \int \frac{dx}{x}$$

$$\Rightarrow \quad \log|3v-v^3| = \log(Cx)^{3/2}$$

$$\Rightarrow \quad 3v - v^3 = C^{3/2}x^{3/2}$$

$$\Rightarrow \quad \frac{3y}{x} - \frac{y^3}{x^3} = C^{3/2}x^{3/2} \qquad [\because y = vx]$$

When $x = 1, y = 1$

$$\therefore \quad 3 - 1 = C^{3/2} \Rightarrow C^{3/2} = 2$$

$$\therefore \quad \frac{3y}{x} - \frac{y^3}{x^3} = 2x^{3/2}$$

$$\Rightarrow \quad 3x^2y - y^3 = 2x^{9/2}$$

Now, putting $x = 2$, we get

$$12y(2) - y^3(2) = 2 \times 2^{9/2}$$

$$\Rightarrow \quad -(y^3(2) - 12y(2)) = 2^{11/2}$$

$$\Rightarrow \quad |y^3(2) - 12y(2)| = 32\sqrt{2}$$

Example 19. The solution of the differential equation $\frac{dy}{dx} = -\left(\frac{x^2+3y^2}{3x^2+y^2}\right)$, $y(1) = 0$ is

(a) $\log_e|x+y| - \frac{2xy}{(x+y)^2} = 0$

(b) $\log_e|x+y| - \frac{xy}{(x+y)^2} = 0$

(c) $\log_e|x+y| + \frac{2xy}{(x+y)^2} = 0$

(d) $\log_e|x+y| + \frac{xy}{(x+y)^2} = 0$

Sol. (c) The given equation is,

$$\frac{dy}{dx} = -\left(\frac{x^2+3y^2}{3x^2+y^2}\right) \qquad ...(i)$$

On substituting $y = vx$,

$$\Rightarrow \quad \frac{dy}{dx} = v + x\frac{dv}{dx}$$

Then, $$v + x\frac{dv}{dx} = -\left(\frac{x^2+3v^2x^2}{3x^2+v^2x^2}\right)$$

$$\Rightarrow \quad v + x\frac{dv}{dx} = -\left[\frac{1+3v^2}{3+v^2}\right] \Rightarrow x\frac{dv}{dx} = \frac{-(1+3v^2)}{3+v^2} - v$$

$$\Rightarrow \quad x\frac{dv}{dx} = \frac{-(1+3v^2+3v+v^3)}{3+v^2}$$

On variable separable and integrating,

$$\int \frac{3+v^2}{(1+v)^3}dv = -\int \frac{1}{x}dx$$

We can write on using partial fraction,

$$\frac{3+v^2}{(1+v)^3} = \frac{1}{v+1} - \frac{2}{(v+1)^2} + \frac{4}{(v+1)^3}$$

$$\therefore \quad \int \left[\frac{1}{v+1} - \frac{2}{(v+1)^2} + \frac{4}{(v+1)^3}\right]dv = -\int \frac{1}{x}dx$$

$$\Rightarrow \quad \ln|v+1| + \frac{2}{(v+1)} - \frac{2}{(v+1)^2} = -\ln|x| + C$$

$$\Rightarrow \quad \ln\left|\frac{y}{x}+1\right| + \frac{2[y/x+1-1]}{(y/x+1)^2} = -\ln|x| + C$$

$$\Rightarrow \quad \ln\left|\frac{y+x}{x}\right| + \frac{2xy}{(x+y)^2} = -\ln|x| + C$$

or $$\ln|x+y| + \frac{2xy}{(x+y)^2} = C \qquad ...(ii)$$

Given $y(1) = 0$, put in Eq. (ii), we get $C = 0$

Hence, $\ln|x+y| + \frac{2xy}{(x+y)^2} = 0$

$$\Rightarrow \log_e|x+y| + \frac{2xy}{(x+y)^2} = 0$$

Reducible to Homogeneous Form

TYPE I

Many a times, the differntial equation specified may not be homogeneous but some suibtale manipulation might reduce it to a homogeneous form.

Generally, such equations involve a function of a rational expression whose numerator and denominator are linear functions of the variable, i.e. of the form

$$\frac{dy}{dx} = f\left(\frac{ax + by + c}{dx + cy + f}\right) \quad \ldots\text{(i)}$$

Note that the presence of the constant c and f causes this differential equation to be non-homogeneous.

To make it homogeneous, we use the substitutions

$$x \to X + h, \; y \to Y + k$$

and select h and k so that

$$\left.\begin{aligned} ah + bk + c = 0 \\ dh + ek + f = 0 \end{aligned}\right\} \quad \ldots\text{(ii)}$$

This can always be done $\left(\text{if } \frac{a}{b} \neq \frac{d}{e}\right)$.

The RHS of the differential equation in Eq. (i) now reduces to

$$= f\left(\frac{a(X + h) + b(Y + k) + c}{d(X + h) + e(Y + k + f)}\right)$$

$$= f\left(\frac{aX + bY}{dX + eY}\right) \quad \text{[using Eq. (ii)]}$$

This expression is clearly homogeneous. The LHS of Eq. (i) is $\frac{dy}{dx}$ which equals $\frac{dy}{dY} \cdot \frac{dY}{dX} \cdot \frac{dX}{dx}$.

Since, $\frac{dy}{dY} \cdot \frac{dx}{dX} = 1$, the LHS $\frac{dy}{dx}$ equals $\frac{dY}{dX}$.

Thus, our equation becomes

$$\frac{dY}{dX} = f\left(\frac{aX + bY}{dX + eY}\right) \quad \ldots\text{(iii)}$$

We have thus succeeded in transforming the non-homogeneous differential equation in Eq. (i) to the homogeneous differential equation in Eq. (iii). This can now be solved as described earlier.

Example 20. Solve the differential equation $\frac{dy}{dx} = \frac{x + 2y + 3}{2x + 3y + 4}$.

Sol. We substitute $x \to X + h$ and $y \to Y + k$ where h, k need to be determined

$$\frac{dy}{dx} = \frac{dY}{dX} = \frac{(X + h) + 2(Y + k) + 3}{2(X + h) + 3(Y + k) + 4}$$

$$\Rightarrow \quad \frac{dY}{dX} = \frac{(X + 2Y) + (h + 2k + 3)}{(2X + 3Y) + (2h + 3k + 4)} \quad \ldots\text{(i)}$$

h and k must be chosen so that

$$h + 2k + 3 = 0 \text{ and } 2h + 3k + 4 = 0$$

On solving, we get $h = 1, k = -2$

Eq. (i) reduces to $\frac{dY}{dX} = \frac{X + 2Y}{2X + 3Y}$ ...(ii)

which is a homogeneous equation.

Put $Y = vX \Rightarrow \frac{dY}{dX} = v + X\frac{dv}{dX}$

From Eq. (ii), $v + X\frac{dv}{dX} = \frac{1 + 2v}{2 + 3v} \Rightarrow \frac{2 + 3v}{1 - 3v^2}dv = \frac{dX}{X}$

On integrating, we get

$$\int \frac{2 + 3v}{1 - 3v^2}dv = \int \frac{dX}{X}$$

$$\Rightarrow \quad \frac{1}{\sqrt{3}}\log\left|\frac{1 + \sqrt{3}v}{1 - \sqrt{3}v}\right| - \frac{1}{2}\log|(1 - 3v^2)| = \log|x| + \log C$$

$$\Rightarrow \frac{1}{\sqrt{3}}\log\left|\frac{X + \sqrt{3}Y}{X - \sqrt{3}Y}\right| - \frac{1}{2}\log|(X^2 - 3Y^2)| = \log C$$

$$\Rightarrow \frac{1}{\sqrt{3}}\log\left|\frac{(x - 1) + \sqrt{3}(y + 2)}{(x - 1) - \sqrt{3}(y + 2)}\right| - \frac{1}{2}\log |(x^2 - 3y^2 - 2x - 12y - 11)| = \log C$$

[put $X = x - 1, Y = y + 2$]

which is the required solution of the given differential equation.

TYPE II

Suppose our differential equation is of the form $\frac{dy}{dx} = f\left(\frac{ax + by + c}{dx + ey + f}\right)$. We try to find h, k so that

$$ah + bk + c = 0, \quad dh + ek + f = 0$$

What if this system does not yield a solution? Recall that this will happen if $\frac{a}{b} = \frac{d}{e}$. How do we reduce the DE to a homogeneous one in such a case?

Let $\frac{a}{d} = \frac{b}{e} = \lambda$ (say). Thus, $\frac{ax + by + c}{dx + ey + f} = \frac{\lambda(dx + ey) + c}{dx + ey + f}$

This suggests the substitution $dx + ey = v$, which will give

$$d + e\frac{dy}{dx} = \frac{dv}{dx} \Rightarrow \frac{dy}{dx} = \frac{1}{e}\left(\frac{dv}{dx} - d\right)$$

Thus, our differential equation reduces to

$$\frac{1}{e}\left(\frac{dv}{dx} - d\right) = \frac{\lambda v + c}{v + f}$$

$$\Rightarrow \quad \frac{dv}{dx} = \frac{\lambda ev + ec}{v + f} + d = \frac{(\lambda e + d)v + (ec + df)}{v + f}$$

$$\Rightarrow \quad \frac{(v + f)}{(\lambda e + d)\,v + ec + df}dv = dx$$

which is in variable separable form and hence can be solved.

Example 21. Solve the differential equation $\dfrac{dy}{dx}=\dfrac{x+2y-1}{x+2y+1}$.

Sol. Note that h, k do not exist in this case which can reduce this differential equation to homogeneous form. Thus, we use the substitution

$$x+2y=v \Rightarrow 1+2\frac{dy}{dx}=\frac{dv}{dx}$$

Thus, our differential equation becomes

$$\frac{1}{2}\left(\frac{dv}{dx}-1\right)=\frac{v-1}{v+1} \Rightarrow \frac{dv}{dx}=\frac{2v-2}{v+1}+1=\frac{3v-1}{v+1}$$

$$\Rightarrow \quad \frac{v+1}{3v-1}\,dv=dx \Rightarrow \frac{1}{3}\left(1+\frac{4}{3v-1}\right)dv=dx$$

On integrating, we get

$$\frac{1}{3}\left(v+\frac{4}{3}\ln(3v-1)\right)=x+C_1$$

Substituting $v=x+2y$, we get

$$x+2y+\frac{4}{3}\ln(3x+6y-1)=3x+C_2$$

$$\Rightarrow \quad y-x+\frac{2}{3}\ln(3x+6y-1)=C$$

Example 22. The solution of the differential equation $\dfrac{dy}{dx}=\dfrac{\sin y+x}{\sin 2y-x\cos y}$ is

(a) $\sin^2 y=x\sin y+\dfrac{x^2}{2}+C$

(b) $\sin^2 y=x\sin y-\dfrac{x^2}{2}+C$

(c) $\sin^2 y=x+\sin y+\dfrac{x^2}{2}+C$

(d) $\sin^2 y=x-\sin y+\dfrac{x^2}{2}+C$

Sol. (a) Here, $\dfrac{dy}{dx}=\dfrac{\sin y+x}{\sin 2y-x\cos y} \Rightarrow \cos y\dfrac{dy}{dx}=\dfrac{\sin y+x}{2\sin y-x}$

Put $\sin y=t \Rightarrow \dfrac{dt}{dx}=\cos y\dfrac{dy}{dx} \Rightarrow \dfrac{dt}{dx}=\dfrac{t+x}{2t-x}$

Put $t=vx \Rightarrow \dfrac{dt}{dx}=v+x\dfrac{dv}{dx} \Rightarrow \dfrac{x\,dv}{dx}+v=\dfrac{vx+x}{2vx-x}=\dfrac{v+1}{2v-1}$

$$\therefore \quad x\frac{dv}{dx}=\frac{v+1}{2v-1}-v=\frac{v+1-2v^2+v}{2v-1}$$

or $$\frac{2v-1}{-2v^2+2v+1}\,dv=\frac{dx}{x}$$

On solving, we get

$$\frac{1}{2}\left(\frac{2v-1}{v^2-v-\frac{1}{2}}\right)dv=-\frac{dx}{x}$$

On integrating both sides, we get

$$\frac{1}{2}\log\left(v^2-v-\frac{1}{2}\right)=-\log(x)+\log(C)$$

$$\Rightarrow \log\left(v^2-v-\frac{1}{2}\right)^{1/2}+\log(x)=\log(C)$$

$$\Rightarrow \quad x\left(v^2-v-\frac{1}{2}\right)^{1/2}=C$$

$$\Rightarrow \quad x\left(\frac{t^2}{x^2}-\frac{t}{x}-\frac{1}{2}\right)^{1/2}=C \qquad \left[\because v=\frac{t}{x}\right]$$

$$\Rightarrow \quad x\left(\frac{\sin^2 y}{x^2}-\frac{\sin y}{x}-\frac{1}{2}\right)^{1/2}=C \qquad [\because t=\sin y]$$

$$\Rightarrow \quad \left(\sin^2 y-x\sin y-\frac{x^2}{2}\right)^{1/2}=C$$

$$\Rightarrow \quad \sin^2 y-x\sin y-\frac{x^2}{2}=C^2=C$$

$$\Rightarrow \quad \sin^2 y=x\sin y+\frac{x^2}{2}+C$$

Milestone Practice 4.2

1. If $\dfrac{dx}{dy}-\dfrac{e^{y-x}(e^x-1)}{e^y}=0,\ x, y>0,\ y(0)=2$, then $y(\ln 2)$ is equal to

(a) $\ln 2$ (b) $\ln 2+\dfrac{1}{2}$ (c) $\ln 2+\dfrac{3}{2}$ (d) $\ln 4$

2. If $(y^3-2x^2y)\,dx+(2xy^2-x^3)\,dy=0$, then the value of $xy\sqrt{y^2-x^2}$, is

(a) y^2+x (b) xy^2

(c) any constant (d) None of these

3. The solution of $dy/dx=\cos(x+y)+\sin(x+y)$, is given by

(a) $\log\left|1+\tan\left(\dfrac{x+y}{2}\right)\right|=x+C$

(b) $\log|1+\tan(x+y)|=x+C$

(c) $\log|1-\tan(x+y)|=x+C$

(d) None of the above

4. If the solution of differential equation $\frac{dy}{dx} = (x+y-1) + \frac{x+y}{\log(x+y)}, y(0) = 1$ is $p + \log(x+y) - \log[q + \log(x+y)] = x + r$, then the value of $3p + 4q + 5\log r$ is

(a) 7 (b) 12 (c) 9 (d) 8

5. The solution of $(2x^2 + 3y^2 - 7)\,xdx - (3x^2 + 2y^2 - 8)\,ydy = 0$, is given by

(a) $(x^2 + y^2 - 1) = (x^2 + y^2 - 3)^5\,C$
(b) $(x^2 + y^2 - 1)^2 = (x^2 + y^2 - 3)^5\,C$
(c) $(x^2 + y^2 - 3) = (x^2 + y^2 - 1)^5\,C$
(d) None of the above

6. The solution of $\frac{dy}{dx} = \left(\frac{x+2y-3}{2x+y+3}\right)^2$, is

(a) $(x+3)^3 - (y-3)^3 = C(x-y+6)^4$
(b) $(x+3)^3 - (y-3)^3 = C$
(c) $(x+3)^4 + (y-3)^4 = C$
(d) None of the above

7. The solution of $\frac{dy}{dx} = \frac{-\cos x(3\cos y - 7\sin x - 3)}{\sin y(3\sin x - 7\cos y + 7)}$, is

(a) $(\cos y - \sin x - 1)^2 (\sin x + \cos y - 1)^5 = C$
(b) $(\cos y - \sin x - 1)^2 (\sin x + \cos y - 1)^3 = C$
(c) $(\cos y - \sin x - 1)^2 (\sin x + \cos y - 1)^7 = C$
(d) None of the above

8. A curve C has the property that if the tangent drawn at any point P on C meets. The coordinate axes at A and B, then P is the mid-point of AB. The curve passes through the point (1, 1). Then, the equation of curve is

(a) $xy = 1$ (b) $\frac{x}{y} = 1$
(c) $2x = xy - 1$ (d) None of these

9. The family of curves whose tangent form an angle $\frac{\pi}{4}$ with the hyperbola $xy = 1$, is

(a) $y = x - 2\tan^{-1}(x) + K$ (b) $y = x + 2\tan^{-1}(x) + K$
(c) $y = 2x - \tan^{-1}(x) + K$ (d) $y = 2x + \tan^{-1}(x) + K$

10. A and B are two separate reservoires of water. The capacity of A is double that of B. Both the reservoir are filled completely with water. Their inlets are closed and then the water is released simultaneously from both the reservoirs. The rate of flow of water out of each reservoir at any instant of time is proportional to the quantity of water in the reservoir at that time. One hour after the water is released, the quantity of water in the reservoir A is $1\frac{1}{2}$ times the quantity of the water in reservoir B. The time after when do both the reservoirs have the same quantity of water, is

(a) $\log_{3/4}(2)$ (b) $\log_{3/4}\left(\frac{1}{2}\right)$
(c) $\log_{1/2}\left(\frac{1}{2}\right)$ (d) None of these

11. A curve passes through (2, 1) and is such that the square of the ordinate is twice the rectangle contained by the abscissa and the intercept of the normal. Then, the equation of curve is

(a) $x^2 + y^2 = 9x$ (b) $4x^2 + y^2 = 9x$
(c) $4x^2 + 2y^2 = 9x$ (d) None of these

12. A normal at $P(x,y)$ on a curve meets the X-axis at Q and N is the foot of the ordinate at P. If $NQ = \frac{x(1+y^2)}{(1+x^2)}$. Then, the equation of curve passing through (3, 1) is

(a) $5(1+y^2) = (1+x^2)$ (b) $(1+y^2) = 5(1+x^2)$
(c) $(1+x^2) = (1+y^2).x$ (d) None of these

13. The curve for which the ratio of the length of the segment intercepted by any tangent on the Y-axis to the length of the radius vector is constant (K), is

(a) $(y + \sqrt{x^2 - y^2})x^{K-1} = C$ (b) $(y + \sqrt{x^2 + y^2})x^{K-1} = C$
(c) $(y - \sqrt{x^2 - y^2})x^{K-1} = C$ (d) $(y - \sqrt{x^2 + y^2})x^{K-1} = C$

14. A point $P(x,y)$ nores on the curve $x^{2/3} + y^{2/3} = a^{2/3}$, $a > 0$ for each position (x,y) of P, perpendiculars are drawn from origin upon the tangent and normal at P, the length (absolute valve) of them being $P_1(x)$ and $P_2(x)$ respectively, then

(a) $\frac{dP_1}{dx}.\frac{dP_2}{dx} < 0$ (b) $\frac{dP_1}{dx}.\frac{dP_2}{dx} \le 0$
(c) $\frac{dP_1}{dx}.\frac{dP_2}{dx} > 0$ (d) $\frac{dP_1}{dx}.\frac{dP_2}{dx} \ge 0$

15. If $\frac{dy}{dx} = y + \int_0^1 y\,dx$ given $y = 1$, where $x = 0$, then the value of $y(1)$ is

(a) $\frac{e+1}{3-e}$ (b) $\frac{2e+1}{3-e}$ (c) $\frac{e+1}{3-2e}$ (d) $\frac{2e+1}{3-2e}$

Answer Key

1. (c)	2. (c)	3. (a)	4. (a)	5. (d)	6. (a)	7. (a)	8. (a)
9. (a)	10. (b)	11. (c)	12. (a)	13. (b)	14. (b)	15. (a)	

For Detailed Solution

Milestone 3 Linear Differential Equation

• First Order Linear Differential Equations • Bernoulli's Equation • Orthogonal Trajectory

4.8 First Order Linear Differential Equations

A differential equation is said to be linear if an unknown variable and its derivative occur only in the first degree.

An equation of the form

$$\frac{dy}{dx} + P(x) \cdot y = Q(x)$$

where, $P(x)$ and $Q(x)$ are functions of x only or constant is called a linear equation of the first order.

To get the general solution of the above equation we proceeds as follows. By multiplying both the sides of the above equation by $e^{\int Pdx}$, we get

$$e^{\int Pdx} \cdot \frac{dy}{dx} + yP \cdot e^{\int Pdx} = Q\, e^{\int Pdx}$$

i.e. $$e^{\int Pdx} \cdot \frac{dy}{dx} + y \frac{d}{dx}(e^{\int Pdx}) = Q\, e^{\int Pdx}$$

i.e. $$\frac{d}{dx}(y\, e^{\int Pdx}) = Q \cdot e^{\int Pdx}$$

∴ Integrating, we get

$$y\, e^{\int Pdx} = \int Q\, e^{\int Pdx} dx + C$$

Here, the term $e^{\int Pdx}$ which converts the left hand expression of the equation into a perfect differential is called an Integrating factor.

In short it is written as IF. Thus, we remember the solution of the above equation as

$$y\,(\text{IF}) = \int Q\,(\text{IF})\, dx + C.$$

Algorithm for Solving A Linear Differential Equation

Step I Write the differential equation in the form $dy / dx + Py = Q$ and obtain P and Q.

Step II Find integrating factor (IF) given by $\text{IF} = e^{\int Pdx}$.

Step III Multiply both sides of equation in Step I by IF.

Step IV Integrate both sides of the equation obtained in Step III w.r.t. x to obtain $y\,(\text{IF}) = \int Q.(\text{IF})\, dx + C$

In case, the first order linear differential equation is in the form $\frac{dx}{dy} + P_1 x = Q_1$, where P_1 and Q_1 are constant or function of y only. Then, $\text{IF} = e^{\int P_1 dy}$ and the solution of the differential equation is given by

$$x \cdot (\text{IF}) = \int Q_1 (\text{IF})\, dy + C$$

Example 23. Solve $\frac{dy}{dx} + 2y = \cos x.$

Sol. It is a linear equation of the form

$$\frac{dy}{dx} + Py = Q(x)$$

where $P = 2$ and $Q = \cos x$

Then, $\text{IF} = e^{\int Pdx} = e^{\int 2dx} = e^{2x}$

Hence, the general solution is $y\,(\text{IF}) = \int Q\,(\text{IF})\, dx$

i.e. $$y \cdot e^{2x} = \int e^{2x} \cos x\, dx + C$$

$$y \cdot e^{2x} = \frac{e^{2x}}{5}[2 \cos x + \sin x] + C$$

Example 24. Solve $\frac{dy}{dx} + \frac{y}{x} = \log x.$

Sol. It is a linear differential equation of the form

$$\frac{dy}{dx} + Py = Q(x)$$

Here, $P = \frac{1}{x}$ and $Q = \log x$

Then, $\text{IF} = e^{\int Pdx} = e^{\int 1/x\, dx} = e^{\log x} = x$

Hence, the general solution is

$$y\,(\text{IF}) = \int Q\,(\text{IF})\, dx + C$$

i.e. $$yx = \int (\log x)\, x\, dx + C$$

i.e. $$yx = (\log x) \cdot \frac{x^2}{2} - \int \frac{1}{x} \cdot \frac{x^2}{2} + C$$

i.e. $$yx = \frac{x^2}{2}(\log x) - \frac{x^2}{4} + C$$

JEE SCANNER

Example Similar to PYQ Asked in JEE Main 2023

If $y = y(x)$ is the solution of the differential equation $\cos^2 x \dfrac{dy}{dx} - y\tan 2x = \cos^4 x$, where $|x| < \dfrac{\pi}{4}$ and $y\left(\dfrac{\pi}{6}\right) = \dfrac{3\sqrt{3}}{8}$, then $y\left(\dfrac{\pi}{3}\right)$ is

(a) $\dfrac{\sqrt{3}}{8}$ (b) $\dfrac{3\sqrt{3}}{8}$ (c) $-\dfrac{\sqrt{3}}{8}$ (d) $\dfrac{-3\sqrt{3}}{8}$

Sol. (c) The given equation can be written as

$$\frac{dy}{dx} - \sec^2 x \cdot \tan 2x \cdot y = \cos^2 x$$

$$\text{IF} = e^{\int -\tan 2x \cdot \sec^2 x\, dx} = e^{\int + \frac{2\tan x}{\tan^2 x - 1}\sec^2 x\, dx}$$

$$= e^{\int \frac{dt}{t}}, \text{ where } t = \tan^2 x - 1$$

$$= e^{\ln|t|} = |t| = |\tan^2 x - 1|$$

It is given that $|x| < \dfrac{\pi}{4}$ and for this region $\tan^2 x < 1$.

$\therefore$ $\text{IF} = (1 - \tan^2 x)$

$\therefore$ The solution is

$$y(1 - \tan^2 x) = \int \cos^2 x (1 - \tan^2 x)\, dx$$

$$= \int (\cos^2 x - \sin^2 x)\, dx$$

$$= \int (\cos 2x)\, dx = \frac{\sin 2x}{2} + C$$

Now, when $x = \dfrac{\pi}{6}, y = \dfrac{3\sqrt{3}}{8}$

$$\therefore \quad \frac{3\sqrt{3}}{8}\left(1 - \frac{1}{3}\right) = \frac{1}{2} \cdot \frac{\sqrt{3}}{2} + C \Rightarrow C = 0$$

$$\therefore \quad y = \frac{\sin 2x}{2(1 - \tan^2 x)}$$

$$y\left(\frac{\pi}{3}\right) = \frac{\sin \frac{2\pi}{3}}{2\left(1 - \tan^2 \frac{\pi}{3}\right)} = \frac{\frac{\sqrt{3}}{2}}{2(1-3)} = -\frac{\sqrt{3}}{8}$$

Skill Builder

If $y = y(x)$ is the solution of the differential equation $\dfrac{dy}{dx} + 2y\tan x = \sin x$, given that $y = 0$ when $x = \dfrac{\pi}{3}$.

Then, $y(\pi/3)$ is

(a) 0 (b) -1

(c) $\dfrac{\sqrt{3}-3}{2}$ (d) $\dfrac{\sqrt{3}+3}{2}$

For Sol.

■ **For more practice** See Q.3 of Milestone Practice 4.3.

Example 25. Solve $\dfrac{dy}{dx} = \dfrac{y}{2y\ln y + y - x}$.

Sol. The equation can be written as

$$\frac{dx}{dy} = \frac{2y\ln y + y - x}{y} = (2\ln y + 1) - \frac{x}{y}$$

i.e. $$\frac{dx}{dy} + \frac{1}{y} \cdot x = (2\ln y + 1)$$

This equation is in the form of $\dfrac{dx}{dy} + P_1 x = Q_1$,

where $P_1 = \dfrac{1}{y}$ and $Q_1 = (2\ln y + 1)$

$$\text{IF} = e^{\int P_1 dy} = e^{\int 1/y\, dy} = e^{\ln y} = y$$

$\therefore$ The solution is, $x\,(\text{IF}) = \int (2\ln y + 1)(\text{IF})\, dy$

i.e. $$xy = \int (2\ln y + 1) \cdot y\, dy = y^2 \ln y + C$$

i.e. $$x = y\ln y + \frac{C}{y}$$

Example 26. Let $f: [2, \infty) \to R$ be a differentiable function such that $f(1) = \dfrac{1}{3}$ and $3\int_1^x f(t)\, dt = xf(x) - \dfrac{x^3}{3}$, $x \in [1, \infty)$. Let e denote the base of the natural logarithm, then find the value of $f(e)$.

Sol. Given, $f(1) = \dfrac{1}{3}$

and $3\int_1^x f(t)\, dt = xf(x) - \dfrac{x^3}{3}, x \in [1, \infty)$ ...(i)

On differentiating Eq. (i) w.r.t. x, we get

$$3 \cdot f(x) \times 1 = f(x) \times 1 + xf'(x) - \frac{1}{3} \times 3x^2$$

$$\Rightarrow \quad 3f(x) = f(x) + xf'(x) - x^2$$

$$\Rightarrow \quad xf'(x) = x^2 + 2f(x)$$

$$\Rightarrow \quad f'(x) - 2\left(\frac{f(x)}{x}\right) = \frac{x^2}{x}$$

[we can divide by x because $x \neq 0$ i.e. $x \in [1, \infty)$]

$$\Rightarrow \quad \frac{dy}{dx} - 2\left(\frac{y}{x}\right) = x$$

which is linear differential equation of the form $\dfrac{dy}{dx} + Py = Q$.

$$\text{IF} = e^{\int P dx} = e^{-\int \frac{2}{x} dx} = e^{-2\log x} = e^{\log x^{-2}} = \frac{1}{x^2}$$

$\therefore$ Solution is,

$$y \times (\text{IF}) = \int Q \times (\text{IF})\, dx$$

$$\Rightarrow \quad y \times \frac{1}{x^2} = \int x \times \left(\frac{1}{x^2}\right) dx \Rightarrow \frac{y}{x^2} = \log x + C$$

Given, $y(1) = \frac{1}{3}$

So, $\frac{1/3}{1} = \log(1) + C \Rightarrow C = \frac{1}{3}$

Hence, $y = x^2(\log x) + Cx^2 = x^2 \log x + \frac{x^2}{3}$ $\left[\because C = \frac{1}{3}\right]$

Thus, $y(e) = e^2 \log e + \frac{e^2}{3} = \frac{4e^2}{3}$

4.9 Bernoulli's Equation

Some differential equation can be reduced to linear differential equation using proper substitution. General form of such differential is

$$f'(y)\frac{dy}{dx} + f(y)\,P(x) = Q(x) \quad \text{...(i)}$$

Now, substituting $f(y) = z$ we have

$$f'(y)\frac{dy}{dx} = \frac{dz}{dx}$$

Eq. (i) becomes reduced to $\frac{dz}{dx} + zP(x) = Q(x)$ which is linear differential equation.

An equation of the form

$$\frac{dy}{dx} + Py = Q\,y^n. \quad (n \neq 0, 1)$$

where, P and Q are functions of x only, is known as **Bernoulli's equation** (for $n = 0$ the equation is linear.)

It is easy to reduce the above equation into linear form as below :

Dividing both the sides by y^n, we get

$$y^{-n}\frac{dy}{dx} + P\,y^{1-n} = Q$$

Putting $y^{1-n} = z$ and hence $(1-n)\,y^{-n}\frac{dy}{dx} = \frac{dz}{dx}$ the equation becomes $\frac{dz}{dx} + (1-n)\,Pz = (1-n)\,Q$ which is linear in z.

Here, $\text{IF} = e^{\int (1-n)\,P\,dx}$

$\therefore$ The solution is,

$$z\,e^{\int (1-n)\,Pdx} = \int \{(1-n)\cdot Q\cdot e^{\int (1-n)\,Pdx}\}\,dx$$

Example 27. Solve $(y \log x - 1)\,y\,dx = x\,dy$.

Sol. The given differential equation can be written as

$$x\frac{dy}{dx} + y = y^2 \log x \quad \text{...(i)}$$

Dividing by xy^2, hence

$$\frac{1}{y^2}\cdot\frac{dy}{dx} + \frac{1}{xy} = \frac{1}{x}\log x$$

Let $\frac{1}{y} = v \Rightarrow -\frac{1}{y^2}\cdot\frac{dy}{dx} = \frac{dv}{dx}$

So that $\frac{dv}{dx} - \frac{1}{x}v = -\frac{1}{x}\log x$

which is the standard linear differential equations, with

$$P = -\frac{1}{x},\ Q = -\frac{1}{x}\log x$$

$$\text{IF} = e^{\int -1/x\,dx} = e^{-\log x} = e^{\log x^{-1}} = \frac{1}{x}$$

The solution is given by

$$v\cdot\frac{1}{x} = \int \frac{1}{x}\left(-\frac{1}{x}\log x\right)dx = -\int \frac{\log x}{x^2}\,dx$$

$$= \frac{\log x}{x} - \int \frac{1}{x}\cdot\frac{1}{x}\,dx = \frac{\log x}{x} + \frac{1}{x} + C$$

$\Rightarrow$ $v = 1 + \log x + Cx = \log(ex) + Cx$

or $\frac{1}{y} = \log(ex) + Cx$

or $y\,\{\log(ex) + Cx\} = 1$

Example 28. Solve $\frac{dy}{dx} = \frac{y\,\phi'(x) - y^2}{\phi(x)}$, where $\phi(x)$ is a given function.

Sol. The equation can be written as

$$\frac{dy}{dx} - \frac{\phi'(x)}{\phi(x)}y = -\frac{y^2}{\phi(x)}$$

i.e. $-y^{-2}\frac{dy}{dx} + \frac{\phi'(x)}{\phi(x)}\cdot\frac{1}{y} = \frac{1}{\phi(x)}$

Let $\frac{1}{y} = z$. So that, $-\frac{1}{y^2}\frac{dy}{dx} = \frac{dz}{dx}$

$\therefore$ $\frac{dz}{dx} + \frac{\phi'(x)}{\phi(x)}\cdot z = \frac{1}{\phi(x)}$

$$\text{IF} = e^{\int \frac{\phi'(x)}{\phi(x)}dx} = e^{\ln \phi(x)} = \phi(x)$$

$\therefore$ The solution is $z\cdot\phi(x) = \int \frac{1}{\phi(x)}\cdot\phi(x)\,dx = x + C$

i.e. $\frac{\phi(x)}{y} = x + C$ i.e. $\frac{\phi(x)}{x + C} = y$

Example 29. If the solution curve $f(x, y) = 0$ of the differential equation $(1 + \log_e x)\frac{dx}{dy} - x\log_e x = e^y$, $x > 0$, passes through the points $(1, 0)$, and $(\alpha, 2)$, then find the value of α^α.

Sol. Given, $(1+\log_e x)\dfrac{dx}{dy} - x\log_e x = e^y,\ x>0$

Let $\qquad x\log_e x = t$

$\Rightarrow \left(x\cdot\dfrac{1}{x}+\log_e x\right)\dfrac{dx}{dy} = \dfrac{dt}{dy} \Rightarrow (1+\log_e x)\dfrac{dx}{dy} = \dfrac{dt}{dy}$

$\therefore \qquad \dfrac{dt}{dy} - t = e^y \Rightarrow \text{IF} = e^{\int(-1)dy} = e^{-y}$

$\therefore$ General solution

$$t(e^{-y}) = \int (e^y\cdot e^{-y})dy + C \Rightarrow te^{-y} = \int dy + C$$

$\Rightarrow \qquad te^{-y} = y + C \Rightarrow (x\log_e x)e^{-y} = y + C \quad$ ...(i)

Eq. (i) passes through the point (1, 0),

$\therefore \qquad 0 = 0 + C \Rightarrow C = 0$

$\therefore \qquad (x\log_e x)e^{-y} = y \Rightarrow x\log_e x = ye^y$

which pass through $(\alpha, 2)$.

$\therefore \qquad \alpha\log_e\alpha = 2e^2 \Rightarrow \log_e\alpha^\alpha = 2e^2 \Rightarrow \alpha^\alpha = e^{2e^2}$

Example 30. Solve $\dfrac{dy}{dx} + x(x+y) = x^3(x+y)^3 - 1$.

Sol. The given equation can be written as

$$\left(\frac{dy}{dx}+1\right) + x(x+y) = x^3(x+y)^3$$

i.e. $\qquad \dfrac{d(x+y)}{dx} + x(x+y) = x^3(x+y)^3$

i.e. $(x+y)^{-3}\cdot\dfrac{d(x+y)}{dx} + x(x+y)^{-2} = x^3$

Let $(x+y)^{-2} = z$ so that $-2(x+y)^{-3}\dfrac{d(x+y)}{dx} = \dfrac{dz}{dx}$

The given equation reduces to

$$-\frac{1}{2}\frac{dz}{dx} + xz = x^3$$

i.e. $\qquad \dfrac{dz}{dx} - 2xz = -2x^3 \Rightarrow \text{IF} = e^{\int -2x\,dx} = e^{-x^2}$

$\therefore$ The solution is

$$z\cdot e^{-x^2} = \int -2x^3\cdot e^{-x^2}dx = (x^2+1)e^{-x^2} + C$$

$$\frac{1}{(x+y)^2} = Ce^{x^2} + x^2 + 1$$

Example 31. Solve $\sin y\cdot\dfrac{dy}{dx} = \cos y(1 - x\cos y)$.

Sol. The given differential equation is

$$\sin y\frac{dy}{dx} = \cos y(1 - x\cos y)$$

or $\qquad \sin y\dfrac{dy}{dx} - \cos y = -x\cos^2 y$

Dividing by $\cos^2 y$, we get

$$\tan y\cdot\sec y\cdot\frac{dy}{dx} - \sec y = -x$$

Let $\sec y = v \Rightarrow \sec y\tan y\cdot\dfrac{dy}{dx} = \dfrac{dv}{dx}$

So that $\dfrac{dv}{dx} - v = -x$

which is linear differential equation with $P=-1, Q=-x$

$$\text{IF} = e^{\int Pdx} = e^{\int -1\,dx} = e^{-x}$$

The solution is given by

$v\cdot e^{-x} = \int -x\cdot e^{-x}dx = xe^{-x} + e^{-x} + C = e^{-x}(x+1) + C$

or $\qquad v = (1+x) + Ce^x$ or $\sec y = (1+x) + Ce^x$

4.10 Orthogonal Trajectory

Any curve, which cuts every member of a given family of curves at right angles, is called an orthogonal trajectory of the family. For example, each straight line passing through the origin i.e. $y = mx$ is an orthogonal trajectory of the family of the circles $x^2 + y^2 = a^2$.

Procedure for Finding the Orthogonal Trajectory

(i) Let $f(x, y, c) = 0$ be the equation of the given family of curves, where c is an arbitrary parameter.

(ii) Differentiate $f = 0$; w.r.t. 'x' and eliminate 'c', i.e. form a differential equation.

(iii) Substitute $-\dfrac{dx}{dy}$ for $\dfrac{dy}{dx}$ in the above differential equation. This will give the differential equation of the orthogonal trajectories.

(iv) By solving this differential equation, we get the required orthogonal trajectories.

Example 32. Find the orthogonal trajectories of the curves $y = cx^2$.

Sol. Here, $\qquad y = cx^2 \qquad$ ...(i)

Differentiating w.r.t. x, we get

$$\frac{dy}{dx} = 2cx \qquad \text{...(ii)}$$

Eliminating c from Eqs. (i) and (ii),

$$y = \left(\frac{1}{2x}\frac{dy}{dx}\right)x^2 \Rightarrow 2y = x\frac{dy}{dx} \qquad \text{...(iii)}$$

This is the differential equation of the family of curves given in Eq. (i).

Now, to obtain orthogonal trajectory replace $\dfrac{dy}{dx}$ by $-\dfrac{dx}{dy}$ in Eq. (iii).

$\Rightarrow \qquad 2y = -x\dfrac{dx}{dy}$ or $2y\,dy = -x\,dx$

Integrating both the sides, we get

$$y^2 = -\frac{x^2}{2} + C_1 \Rightarrow x^2 + 2y^2 = C_1,$$

is the required family of orthogonal trajectory.

Milestone Practice 4.3

1. The solution of $(1 + x^2)\dfrac{dy}{dx} + y = e^{\tan^{-1} x}$, is given by
   (a) $2ye^{\tan^{-1} x} = e^{2\tan^{-1} x} + C$
   (b) $ye^{\tan^{-1} y} = e^{2\tan^{-1} x} + C$
   (c) $2ye^{\tan^{-1} y} = e^{2\tan^{-1} y} + C$
   (d) None of the above

2. The solution of $\dfrac{dy}{dx} + \dfrac{x}{1 - x^2} y = x\sqrt{y}$, is given by
   (a) $3\sqrt{y} + (1 - x^2) = C(1 - x^2)^{1/4}$
   (b) $\dfrac{3}{2}\sqrt{y} + (1 - x^2) = C(1 - x^2)^{3/2}$
   (c) $3\sqrt{y} - (1 - x^2) = C(1 - x^2)^{3/2}$
   (d) None of the above

3. If $y = y(x)$ is the solution of differential equation $\dfrac{dy}{dx} + x\sin 2y = x^3\cos^2 y$, given that $y = \dfrac{\pi}{4}$ when $x = 0$, then $y(1)$ is
   (a) $\tan^{-1}\left(\dfrac{1}{e}\right)$ (b) $\tan^{-1}\left(\dfrac{3}{2e}\right)$
   (c) $\tan^{-1}\left(\dfrac{1}{2e}\right)$ (d) None of these

4. The solution of $3x(1 - x^2)y^2\, dy/dx + (2x^2 - 1)y^3 = ax^3$ is
   (a) $y^3 = ax + C\sqrt{1 - x^2}$
   (b) $y^3 = ax + Cx\sqrt{1 - x^2}$
   (c) $y^2 = ax + C\sqrt{1 - x^2}$
   (d) None of the above

5. The solution of $\dfrac{dy}{dx} + \dfrac{y}{x}\log y = \dfrac{y}{x^2}(\log y)^2$, is
   (a) $x = \dfrac{1}{2x}\log y + C$ (b) $x^2 + \log y = C$
   (c) $\dfrac{1}{x\log y} = \dfrac{1}{2x^2} + C$ (d) None of these

6. The solution of $\dfrac{dy}{dx} + y f'(x) - f(x)\cdot f'(x) = 0, y \neq f(x)$ is
   (a) $y = f(x) + 1 + Ce^{-f(x)}$ (b) $y - Ce^{-f(x)}$
   (c) $y = f(x) - 1 + Ce^{-f(x)}$ (d) None of these

7. The solution of $(x^2 - 1)\, dy/dx \cdot \sin y - 2x\cdot\cos y = 2xt - 2x^3$, is
   (a) $y = x^2 - 1 + Ce^{-x^2}$ (b) $y = x^2 + 1 + Ce^{-x^2}$
   (c) $y = x^2 + 1 + Ce^{x}$ (d) None of these

8. Let $x(t)$ be the solution of $t(1 + t^2)dx = (x + xt^2 - t^2)dt$, given that $x(1) = -\dfrac{\pi}{4}, t > 0$, then $-\dfrac{4}{\pi}\lim\limits_{t \to \infty} x'(t)$ equals
   (a) 2 (b) -2 (c) 1 (d) -1

9. If $\int_a^x t y(t)\, dt = x^2 + y(x)$, then y as a function of x is
   (a) $y = 2 - (2 + a^2)\, e^{\frac{x^2 - a^2}{2}}$ (b) $y = 1 - (2 + a^2)\, e^{\frac{x^2 - a^2}{2}}$
   (c) $y = 2 - (1 + a^2)\, e^{\frac{x^2 - a^2}{2}}$ (d) None of these

10. Let $y(x)$ be the solution of the differential equation $\dfrac{1}{x}\left(\dfrac{dy}{dx}\right) + ye^x = e^{(1 - x)e^x}$, $y(1) = 0$, then $y(0) + \dfrac{e}{2}$ equals
    (a) 0 (b) 1 (c) 2 (d) 3

11. If $y(x)$ is the solution of the differential equation $x\dfrac{dy}{dx} + 2y = xe^x$, $y(1) = 1$, then the local maximum value of the function $Z(x) = x^2 y(x) - e^x$, $x \in R$ is
    (a) $1 - e$ (b) 0 (c) $\dfrac{1}{2}$ (d) $\dfrac{4}{e} - e + 1$

12. If the solution of the differential equation $\dfrac{dy}{dx} + e^x(x^2 - 2)y = (x^2 - 2x)(x^2 - 2)e^{2x}$ satisfies $y(0) = 0$, then the value of $y(2)$ is
    (a) -1 (b) 1 (c) 0 (d) e

13. The curve possessing the property that the intercept made by the tangent at any point of the curve on the Y-axis is equal to square of the abscissa of the point of tangency, is given by
    (a) $y^2 = x + C$ (b) $y = 2x^2 + Cx$
    (c) $y = -x^2 + Cx$ (d) None of these

14. The tangent at a point P of a curve meets the Y-axis at A, and the line parallel to Y-axis at A, and the line parallel to Y-axis through P meets the X-axis at B. If area of ΔOAB is constant (O being the origin). Then, the curve is
    (a) $Cx^2 - xy = K_1$ (b) $x^2 + y^2 = cx$
    (c) $3x^2 + 4y^2 = k$ (d) $xy - x^2y^2 + kx = 0$

15. The value of k such that the family of parabolas $y = cx^2 + k$ is the orthogonal trajectory of the family of ellipse $x^2 + 2y^2 - y = C$ is
    (a) $\dfrac{1}{2}$ (b) $\dfrac{1}{3}$ (c) $\dfrac{1}{4}$ (d) $\dfrac{1}{5}$

Answer Key

1. (a)	2. (a)	3. (b)	4. (b)	5. (c)	6. (c)	7. (a)	8. (a)
9. (a)	10. (a)	11. (d)	12. (c)	13. (c)	14. (a)	15. (c)	

For Detailed Solution

Milestone 4 Exact Differential Equations

A differential equation of the form
$M(x, y)\, dx + N(x, y)\, dy = 0$ is said to be exact (or total) if its left hand expression is the exact differential of some function $u(x, y)$.

i.e. $$du = M \cdot dx + N \cdot dy$$

Hence, its solution is $u(x, y) = c$ (where c is an arbitrary constant). But then there is a question that how do we confirm whether the above mentioned equation is exact. The answer to this question is the following theorem.

Theorem The necessary and sufficient condition for the differential equation $M\, dx + N\, dy = 0$ to be exact is $\dfrac{\partial M}{\partial y} = \dfrac{\partial N}{\partial x}$.

The solution of $M\, dx + N\, dy = 0$ is ,

$$\int_{y-\text{constant}} M\, dx + \int (\text{terms of } N \text{ not containing } x)\, dy = C$$

provided $\dfrac{\partial M}{\partial y} = \dfrac{\partial N}{\partial x}$.

Example 33. Solve $(x^2 - ay)\, dx + (y^2 - ax)\, dy = 0$.

Sol. Here, we have $M = x^2 - ay$ and $N = y^2 - ax$

$$\therefore \quad \frac{\partial M}{\partial y} = -a = \frac{\partial N}{\partial x}$$

Thus, the equation is exact.

$\therefore$ The solution is, $\displaystyle\int_{y-\text{constant}} (x^2 - ay)\, dx + \int y^2\, dy = C$

$$\Rightarrow \quad \frac{x^3}{3} - axy + \frac{y^3}{3} = C$$

Example 34. Solve $(2x \log y)\, dx + \left(\dfrac{x^2}{y} + 3y^2\right) dy = 0$.

Sol. Here, we have $M = 2x \log y$ and $N = \dfrac{x^2}{y} + 3y^2$

$\therefore \quad \dfrac{\partial M}{\partial y} = \dfrac{2x}{y}$ and $\dfrac{\partial N}{\partial x} = \dfrac{2x}{y}$ and hence the equation is exact.

$\therefore$ The solution is,

$$\int_{y-\text{constant}} (2x \log y)\, dx + \int 3y^2\, dy = C$$

$$\Rightarrow \quad x^2 \log y + y^3 = C$$

Equations Reducible to the Exact Form

Sometimes a differential equation of the form $M\, dx + N\, dy = 0$ which is not exact can be reduced to an exact form by multiplying by a suitable function $f(x, y)$ which is not identically zero. This function $f(x, y)$ which then multiplied to a non-exact differential equation makes it exact is known as integrating factor.

One can find integrating factors by inspection but for that some experience and practice is required.

For finding the integrating factors by inspection, the following identities must be remembered.

1. $x\, dy + y\, dx = d(xy)$
2. $x\, dx + y\, dy = \dfrac{1}{2} d(x^2 + y^2)$
3. $\dfrac{x\, dy - y\, dx}{x^2} = d\left(\dfrac{y}{x}\right)$
4. $\dfrac{y\, dx - x\, dy}{y^2} = d\left(\dfrac{x}{y}\right)$
5. $\dfrac{x\, dy - y\, dx}{xy} = \dfrac{dy}{y} - \dfrac{dx}{x} = d\left[\log\left(\dfrac{y}{x}\right)\right]$
6. $\dfrac{y\, dx - x\, dy}{xy} = d\left[\log\left(\dfrac{x}{y}\right)\right]$
7. $\dfrac{x\, dy - y\, dx}{x^2 + y^2} = \dfrac{\dfrac{x\, dy - y\, dx}{x^2}}{1 + \dfrac{y^2}{x^2}} = \dfrac{d\left(\dfrac{y}{x}\right)}{1 + \left(\dfrac{y}{x}\right)^2}$
   $= d\left[\tan^{-1}\left(\dfrac{y}{x}\right)\right]$
8. $\dfrac{dx + dy}{x + y} = d[\ln(x + y)]$
9. $d(\ln(xy)) = \dfrac{x\, dy + y\, dx}{xy}$
10. $d\left(\dfrac{1}{2}\ln(x^2 + y^2)\right) = \dfrac{x\, dx + y\, dy}{x^2 + y^2}$

11. $d\left(-\frac{1}{xy}\right)=\frac{x\,dy+y\,dx}{x^2y^2}$

12. $d\left(\frac{e^y}{x}\right)=\frac{x\,e^y\,dy-e^y\,dx}{x^2}$

13. $d\left(\frac{e^x}{y}\right)=\frac{ye^x dx-e^x dy}{y^2}$

14. $d\,(x^m\,y^n)=x^{m-1}\,y^{n-1}\,(my\,dx+nx\,dy)$

15. $\frac{d\,[f(x,y)]^{1-n}}{1-n}=\frac{f\,'(x,y)}{(f(x,y))^n}$

Example 35. Solve $x\,dx+y\,dy=x\,dy-y\,dx$.

Sol. The given equation can be written as

$$\frac{1}{2}d\,(x^2+y^2)=x^2\,d\left(\frac{y}{x}\right)$$

$$\Rightarrow \quad \frac{d\,(x^2+y^2)}{x^2+y^2}=\frac{2x^2\,d\left(\frac{y}{x}\right)}{x^2+y^2}$$

$$\Rightarrow \quad \frac{d\,(x^2+y^2)}{x^2+y^2}=\frac{2d\,(y/x)}{1+(y/x)^2}$$

$$\Rightarrow \quad \log\,(x^2+y^2)=2\tan^{-1}\left(\frac{y}{x}\right)+C$$

Example 36. Solve

$$\frac{y+\sin x\cos^2(xy)}{\cos^2(xy)}dx+\left(\frac{x}{\cos^2(xy)}+\sin y\right)dy=0.$$

Sol. The given differential equation can be written as

$$\frac{y\,dx+x\,dy}{\cos^2(xy)}+\sin x\,dx+\sin y\,dy=0$$

$$\Rightarrow \quad \sec^2(xy)\,d\,(xy)+\sin x\,dx+\sin y\,dy=0$$

$$d\,(\tan\,(xy))+d\,(-\cos x)+d\,(-\cos y)=0$$

$$\Rightarrow \quad \tan\,(xy)-\cos x-\cos y=C$$

Example 37. Solve $\dfrac{x+y\dfrac{dy}{dx}}{y-x\dfrac{dy}{dx}}=x^2+2y^2+\dfrac{y^4}{x^2}$.

Sol. The given equation can be written as

$$\frac{x\,dx+y\,dy}{(x^2+y^2)^2}=\frac{y\,dx-x\,dy}{y^2}\cdot\frac{y^2}{x^2}$$

$$\Rightarrow \quad \frac{1}{2}\int\frac{d\,(x^2+y^2)}{(x^2+y^2)^2}=\int\frac{1}{x^2/y^2}\,d\left(\frac{x}{y}\right)$$

Integrating both the sides, we get

$$-\frac{1}{2(x^2+y^2)}=-\frac{1}{(x/y)}+C$$

$$\Rightarrow \quad \frac{y}{x}-\frac{1}{2(x^2+y^2)}=C$$

JEE SCANNER

Example Similar to PYQ Asked in JEE Main 2023

If the solution curve $y=y(x)$ of the differential equation $y^2dx+(x^2-xy+y^2)dy=1$ which passes through the point (1, 1) and intersects the line $y=\sqrt{3}x$ at the point $(\alpha,\sqrt{3}\alpha)$, then the value of $\ln(\sqrt{3}\alpha)$ is equal to

(a) $\frac{\pi}{3}$ (b) $\frac{\pi}{2}$ (c) $\frac{\pi}{12}$ (d) $\frac{\pi}{6}$

Sol. (c) $y^2dx-xydy=-(x^2+y^2)dy$

$$\Rightarrow \quad y(ydx-xdy)=-(x^2+y^2)dy$$

$$\Rightarrow -y(xdy-ydx)=-(x^2+y^2)dy$$

$$\Rightarrow \quad \frac{xdy-ydx}{x^2}=\left(1+\frac{y^2}{x^2}\right)\frac{dy}{y}$$

$$\Rightarrow \quad \frac{d(y/x)}{1+\frac{y^2}{x^2}}=\frac{dy}{y}\Rightarrow \tan^{-1}\left(\frac{y}{x}\right)=\ln y+C$$

when $x=1\Rightarrow y=1$

$$\tan^{-1}(1)=\ln(1)+C\Rightarrow C=\frac{\pi}{4}$$

when $x=\alpha\Rightarrow y=\sqrt{3}\alpha$

$$\frac{\pi}{3}=\ln(\sqrt{3}\alpha)+\frac{\pi}{4}$$

$$\therefore \quad \ln(\sqrt{3}\alpha)=\frac{\pi}{12}$$

Skill Builder

If the solution curve $y=y(x)$ of the differential equation $y(1+xy)\,dx=xdy$ which passes through the point $(1,-1)$ and intersects the line $y=5x$ at the point $(\alpha,5\alpha)$, then the value of $-5\alpha^2+2$ is

For Sol.

(a) 9 (b) 7

(c) 11 (d) −9

■ **For more practice** See Q.8 of Milestone Practice 4.4.

Example 38. Solve

$$e^{x\frac{(y^2-1)}{y}}\{xy^2\,dy + y^3dx\} + \{ydx - xdy\} = 0.$$

Sol. Here, $\quad e^{x\frac{(y^2-1)}{y}} \cdot y^2\,\{xdy + ydx\} + \{ydx - xdy\} = 0$

$$\Rightarrow \quad e^{xy} \cdot y^2 \cdot \{xdy + ydx\} + e^{x/y}\,\{ydx - xdy\} = 0$$

or $$e^{xy} \cdot \{xdy + ydx\} + e^{x/y}\,\frac{\{ydx - xdy\}}{y^2} = 0$$

or $$e^{xy} \cdot d\,(xy) + e^{x/y} \cdot d\left(\frac{x}{y}\right) = 0$$

or $$d\,(e^{xy}) + d\,(e^{x/y}) = 0$$

Integrating both the sides, we get

$$e^{xy} + e^{x/y} = C$$

Example 39. Solve $x^2dy - y^2dx + xy^2\,(x - y)\,dy = 0.$

Sol. Here, $x^2y^2\left(\frac{dy}{y^2} - \frac{dx}{x^2}\right) + x^2y^3\left(\frac{1}{y} - \frac{1}{x}\right)dy = 0$

$$\Rightarrow \quad -d\left(\frac{1}{y} - \frac{1}{x}\right) + y\left(\frac{1}{y} - \frac{1}{x}\right)dy = 0$$

$$\Rightarrow \quad -\frac{d\left(\frac{1}{y} - \frac{1}{x}\right)}{\left(\frac{1}{y} - \frac{1}{x}\right)} + ydy = 0 \text{ or } \frac{d\left(\frac{1}{y} - \frac{1}{x}\right)}{\left(\frac{1}{y} - \frac{1}{x}\right)} = d\left(\frac{y^2}{2}\right)$$

Integrating both the sides, we get

$$\log\left|\frac{1}{x} - \frac{1}{y}\right| = \frac{y^2}{2} + C$$

Example 40. Solve differential equation

$xdy\,(y^2e^{xy} + e^{x/y}) = ydx\,(e^{x/y} - y^2e^{xy})$

Sol. The given equation is

$$(xy^2e^{xy})\,dy + (xe^{x/y})\,dy = (ye^{x/y})\,dx - (y^3e^{xy})\,dx$$

$$\Rightarrow \quad y^2e^{xy}\,(xdy + ydx) = e^{x/y}\,(ydx - xdy)$$

$$\Rightarrow \quad e^{xy}\,(d\,(xy)) = e^{x/y} \cdot \left(\frac{ydx - xdy}{y^2}\right)$$

$$\Rightarrow \quad e^{xy}\,(d\,(xy)) = e^{x/y} \cdot d\left(\frac{x}{y}\right)$$

$$\Rightarrow \quad d\,(e^{xy}) = d\,(e^{x/y})$$

Integrating both the sides, we get

$$e^{xy} = e^{x/y} + C$$

$$\Rightarrow \quad xy = \log\,(e^{x/y} + C)$$

JEE SCANNER

Example Similar to PYQ Asked in JEE Main 2022

Let the solution curve $y = y(x)$ of the differential equation $\left[\frac{x}{\sqrt{x^2 - y^2}} + e^{y/x}\right]x\frac{dy}{dx} = x + \left[\frac{x}{\sqrt{x^2 - y^2}} + e^{y/x}\right]y$ pass through the point (1, 0) and $(2\alpha, \alpha)$, $\alpha > 0$, then α is equal to

(a) $\frac{1}{2}\exp\left(\frac{\pi}{6} + \sqrt{e} - 1\right)$ (b) $\frac{1}{2}\exp\left(\frac{\pi}{3} + \sqrt{e} - 1\right)$

(c) $\exp\left(\frac{\pi}{6} + \sqrt{e} + 1\right)$ (d) $2\exp\left(\frac{\pi}{3} + \sqrt{e} - 1\right)$

Sol. (a) $\left(\frac{x}{\sqrt{x^2 + (-y^2)}} + e^{y/x}\right)x\frac{dy}{dx} = x + \left(\frac{x}{\sqrt{x^2 - y^2}} + e^{y/x}\right)y$

$$\Rightarrow e^{y/x}(xdy - ydx) + \frac{x}{\sqrt{x^2 - y^2}}(xdy - ydx) = xdx$$

Dividing both side by x^2,

$$\Rightarrow e^{y/x}\left(\frac{xdy - ydx}{x^2}\right) + \frac{1}{\sqrt{1 - \left(\frac{y}{x}\right)^2}}\left(\frac{xdy - ydx}{x^2}\right) = \frac{dx}{x}$$

$$\Rightarrow \quad e^{y/x}d\left(\frac{y}{x}\right) + \frac{1}{\sqrt{1 - \left(\frac{y}{x}\right)^2}}d\left(\frac{y}{x}\right) = \frac{dx}{x}$$

Integrating both side,

$$\int e^{y/x}d\left(\frac{y}{x}\right) + \int\frac{1}{\sqrt{1 - \left(\frac{y}{x}\right)^2}}d\left(\frac{y}{x}\right) = \int\frac{dx}{x}$$

$$\Rightarrow \quad e^{y/x} + \sin^{-1}\left(\frac{y}{x}\right) = \ln x + C$$

It passes through (1, 0) $\quad 1 + 0 = 0 + C \Rightarrow C = 1$

It passes through $(2\alpha, \alpha)$

$$e^{1/2} + \sin^{-1}\frac{1}{2} = \ln 2\alpha + 1 \Rightarrow \ln 2\alpha = \sqrt{e} + \frac{\pi}{6} - 1$$

$$\Rightarrow \quad 2\alpha = e^{\left(\sqrt{e} + \frac{\pi}{6} - 1\right)} \Rightarrow \alpha = \frac{1}{2}e^{\left(\frac{\pi}{6} + \sqrt{e} - 1\right)}$$

Skill Builder

Let the solution curve $y = y(x)$ of the differential equation $e^xdy - y^3dx = -y^2dy$ passes through the point (0, 2) and the line $x = \ln(5)$ intersects it at points $y = \alpha$ and $y = \beta$, then the value of $\frac{2}{3}|\alpha + \beta|$ is

For Sol.

(a) 5 (b) $\frac{15}{2}$ (c) 15 (d) 10

■ **For more practice** See Q.10 of Milestone Practice 4.4.

Milestone Practice 4.4

1. The solution of $xdy + ydx + 2x^3dx = 0$, is
   (a) $xy + x^4 = C$
   (b) $xy + \frac{1}{2}x^4 = C$
   (c) $\frac{x^2}{y} + \frac{x^4}{4} = C$
   (d) None of these

2. The solution of
   $ydx - xdy + (1 + x^2)\,dx + x^2 \sin y\,dy = 0$, is given by
   (a) $x + 1 - y^2 + \cos y + C = 0$
   (b) $y + 1 - x^2 + \cos y + C = 0$
   (c) $\frac{x}{y} + \frac{1}{y} - y + \cos y + C = 0$
   (d) $\frac{y}{x} + \frac{1}{x} - x + \cos y + C = 0$

3. The solution of
   $(1 + x\sqrt{x^2 + y^2})\,dx + (-1 + \sqrt{x^2 + y^2})\,ydy = 0$, is
   (a) $2x - y^2 + \frac{2}{3}(x^2 + y^2)^{3/2} = K$
   (b) $2x - y + \frac{2}{3}(x^2 + y^2)^{3/2} = K$
   (c) $2y - x^2 + \frac{2}{3}(x^2 + y^2)^{3/2} = K$
   (d) None of the above

4. The solution of $\frac{xdy}{x^2 + y^2} = \left(\frac{y}{x^2 + y^2} - 1\right) dx$, is given by
   (a) $\tan^{-1}\left(\frac{x}{y}\right) + x = C$
   (b) $\tan^{-1}\left(\frac{y}{x}\right) + x = C$
   (c) $\tan^{-1}\left(\frac{y}{x}\right) + xy = C$
   (d) $\tan^{-1}\left(\frac{y}{x}\right) + x^2 = C$

5. The solution of $ye^{x/y}\,dx = (xe^{x/y} + y^2 \sin y)\,dy$, is given by
   (a) $e^{x/y} = -\cos y + C$
   (b) $e^{x/y} + 2\cos y = C$
   (c) $e^{x/y} = x\cos y + C$
   (d) $e^{x/y} = 2\cos y\, e^{x/y} + C$

6. The solution of
   $x \sin\left(\frac{y}{x}\right) dy = \left\{ y \sin\left(\frac{y}{x}\right) - x \right\} dx$, is given by
   (a) $\log x - \cos\left(\frac{y}{x}\right) = \log C$
   (b) $\log x - \sin\left(\frac{y}{x}\right) = C$
   (c) $\log\left(\frac{x}{y}\right) - \cos\left(\frac{y}{x}\right) = \log C$
   (d) None of these

7. The solution of $\frac{xdx + ydy}{xdy - ydx} = \sqrt{\frac{a^2 - x^2 - y^2}{x^2 + y^2}}$, is given by
   (a) $\sin^{-1}(\sqrt{x^2 + y^2}) = a\tan^{-1}\left(\frac{y}{x}\right) + C$
   (b) $\sin^{-1}(\sqrt{x^2 + y^2}) = \frac{1}{a}\tan^{-1}\left(\frac{y}{x}\right) + C$
   (c) $\sin^{-1}\left(\frac{\sqrt{x^2 + y^2}}{a}\right) = \tan^{-1}\left(\frac{y}{x}\right) + C$
   (d) None of the above

8. The solution of $(1 + e^{x/y})\,dx + e^{x/y}\left(1 - \frac{x}{y}\right) dy = 0$, which passes through the point (0, 4). If $y(3) = \alpha$, then the value of $\alpha \ln(\alpha)$ is
   (a) 3
   (b) −3
   (c) 4
   (d) −4

9. The solution of $\frac{x + y\,dy/dx}{y - x\,dy/dx} = \frac{x\sin^2(x^2 + y^2)}{y^3}$, is given by
   (a) $-\cot(x^2 + y^2) = \left(\frac{x}{y}\right)^2 + C$
   (b) $\tan(x^2 + y^2) = x^2y^2 + C$
   (c) $\cot(x^2 + y^2) = \frac{x}{y} + C$
   (d) None of the above

10. Let the solution of differential equation $\frac{dy}{dx} + \frac{y}{x} = \frac{1}{(1 + \log x + \log y)^2}$ passes through the point (1, 1) and (1, e), then $4e$ is equal to
    (a) $\frac{1}{2}$
    (b) 4
    (c) e
    (d) 2

Answer Key

1. (b)	2. (d)	3. (a)	4. (b)	5. (a)
6. (a)	7. (c)	8. (b)	9. (a)	10. (d)

For Detailed Solution

Milestone 5 Application of First Order Differential Equations

• Growth of Decay Problems • Geometrical Applications

Differential equations have applications in various fields of science like physics (dynamics, heat) chemistry (rate of chemical reaction, physical chemistry in mathematics population explosion, radioactive decay, in geometric application to find the slope of tangent, equation of tangent and normal length of tangent and normal, length of subtangent and subnormal.

4.11 Growth and Decay Problems

Let $N(t)$ denotes the amount of substance (or population) that is either growing or decaying. If we assume that dN/dt, the time rate of change of this amount of substance, is proportional to the amount of substance present, then

$$\frac{dN}{dt} = kN \quad \text{or} \quad \frac{dN}{dt} - kN = 0 \qquad \text{...(i)}$$

Where k is the constant of proportionality. We are assuming that $N(t)$ is a differentiable, hence continuous, function of time.

Example 41. The population of a certain country is known to increase at a rate proportional to the number of people presently living in the country. If after two years the population has doubled and after three years the population is 20000, estimate the number of people initially living in the country.

Sol. Let N denotes the number of people living in the country at any time t, and let N_0 denote the number of people initially living in the country. Then,

$$\frac{dN}{dt} - kN = 0$$

Which has the solution $N = Ce^{kt}$ ...(i)

At $t = 0$, $N = N_0$; hence it follows from Eq. (i) that $N_0 = Ce^{k(0)}$ or that $C = N_0$.

Thus, $$N = N_0 e^{kt} \qquad \text{...(ii)}$$

At $t = 2$, $N = 2N_0$. Substituting these values into Eq. (ii), we have

$$2N_0 = N_0 e^{2k} \text{ from which } k = \frac{1}{2} \ln 2 = 0.347$$

Substituting this value into Eq. (i) gives

$$N = N_0 e^{(0.347)\,t} \qquad \text{...(iii)}$$

At $t = 3$, $N = 20000$. Substituting these values into Eq. (iii), we obtain

$$20000 = N_0 e^{(0.347)(3)} \Rightarrow N_0 = \frac{20000}{e^{(0.347)(3)}}$$

Example 42. A certain radioactive material is known to decay at a rate proportional to the amount present. If initially there is 50 mg of the material present and after two hours it is observed that the material has lost 10% of its original mass, find (a) an expression for the mass of the material remaining at any time t, (b) the mass of the material after four hours, and
(c) the time at which the material has decayed to one half of its initial mass.

Sol. (a) Let N denotes the amount of material present at time t.

Then, $$\frac{dN}{dt} - kN = 0$$

This differential equation is separable and linear, its solution is

$$N = Ce^{kt} \qquad \text{...(i)}$$

At $t = 0$, we are given that $N = 50$.

Therefore, from Eq. (i), $50 = Ce^{k(0)}$ or $C = 50$.

Thus, $$N = 50\, e^{kt} \qquad \text{...(ii)}$$

At $t = 2$, 10% of the original mass of 50 mg or 5 mg has decayed. Hence, at $t = 2$, $N = 50 - 5 = 45$. Substituting these values into Eq. (ii) and solving for k, we have

$$45 = 50e^{2k} \quad \text{or} \quad k = \frac{1}{2} \ln \frac{45}{50} = -0.053$$

Substituting this value into Eq. (ii), we obtain the amount of mass present at any time t as

$$N = 50e^{-0.053\,t} \qquad \text{...(iii)}$$

Where t is measured in hours.

(b) We require N at $t = 4$. Substituting $t = 4$ into Eq. (iii) and then solving for N, we find $N = 50e^{(-0.053)(4)}$

(c) We require t when $N = 50/2 = 25$. Substituting $N = 25$ into Eq. (iii) and solving for t, we find $25 = 50e^{-0.053t}$

$$\text{or} \quad -0.053\, t = \ln \frac{1}{2} \quad \text{or} \quad t = 13\text{ h}$$

JEE SCANNER

Example Similar to PYQ Asked in JEE Main 2022

The volume of spherical balloon being inflated changes at a constant rate, if initially its radius is 3 units and after 3 sec it is 6 units, then radius of balloon after 8 sec is

(a) $(504)^{1/3}$ (b) $(531)^{1/3}$

(c) $(527)^{1/3}$ (d) 9

Sol. (b) Let the rate of change of volume of the bottom be k.

$$\therefore \quad \frac{dv}{dt} = k$$

$$dv = k\,dt$$

Integrating both side, we get

$$v = kt + C$$

$$\frac{4}{3}\pi r^3 = kt + C \quad \text{...(i)}$$

At $t = 0$, $r = 3$

$$\frac{4\pi(3)^3}{3} = C \Rightarrow C = 36\pi$$

At $t = 3$, $r = 6$

$$\frac{4}{3}\pi(6)^3 = 3k + 36\pi \Rightarrow k = 84\pi$$

Substituting the value of k and C in Eq. (i), we get

$$r = (63t + 27)^{1/3}$$

At $t = 8$,

$$r = (63 \times 8 + 27)^{1/3}$$

$$= (504 + 27)^{1/3} = (531)^{1/3} \text{ units}$$

Skill Builder

The population of a country is known to increase at a rate proportional to the number of people presently living there. If after two years the population has doubled and after three years the population is 20000. Thus the estimated number of people currently living in the country is

(a) 7071 (b) 7075

(c) 7080 (d) 7090

For Sol.

■ **For more practice** See Q.3 of Milestone Practice 4.5.

Example 43. Five mice in a stable population of 500 are intentionally infected with a contagious disease to test a theory of epidemic spread that postulates the rate of change in the infected population is proportional to the product of the number of mice who have the disease with the number that are disease free. Assuming the theory is correct, how long will it take half the population to contract the disease?

Sol. Let $N(t)$ denotes the number of mice with the disease at time t. We are given that $N(0) = 5$, and it follows that $500 - N(t)$ is the number of mice without the disease at time t. The theory predicts that

$$\frac{dN}{dt} = kN(500 - N) \quad \text{...(i)}$$

Where k is a constant of proportionality. This equation is different from Eq. (i) because the rate of change is no longer proportional to just the number of mice who have the disease.

Eq. (i) has the differential form

$$\frac{dN}{N(500 - N)} - k\,dt = 0 \quad \text{...(ii)}$$

Which is separable. Using partial fraction decomposition, we have

$$\frac{1}{N(500 - N)} = \frac{1/500}{N} + \frac{1/500}{500 - N}$$

Hence, Eq. (ii) may be rewritten as

$$\frac{1}{500}\left(\frac{1}{N} + \frac{1}{500 - N}\right)dN - k\,dt = 0$$

It solution is $\frac{1}{500}\int\left(\frac{1}{N} + \frac{1}{500 - N}\right)dN - \int k\,dt = C$

or $$\frac{1}{500}(\ln|N| - \ln|500 - N|) - kt = C$$

Which may be rewritten as

$$\ln\left|\frac{N}{500 - N}\right| = 500(C + kt)$$

$$\frac{N}{500 - N} = e^{500(C + kt)} \quad \text{...(iii)}$$

But $e^{500(C + kt)} = e^{500C}e^{500kt}$.

Putting $C_1 = e^{500C}$, we can write Eq. (iii) as

$$\frac{N}{500 - N} = C_1 e^{500kt} \quad \text{...(iv)}$$

At $t = 0$, $N = 5$.

Substituting these values into Eq. (iv), we find

$$\frac{5}{495} = C_1\, e^{500k(0)} = C_1$$

So, $C_1 = 1/99$ and Eq. (iv) becomes

$$\frac{N}{500 - N} = \frac{1}{99}e^{500kt} \quad \text{...(v)}$$

We could solve Eq. (v) for N, but this is not necessary. We seek a value of t when $N = 250$, one half the population. Substituting $N = 250$ into Eq. (v) and solving for t, we obtain

$$1 = \frac{1}{99}e^{500kt}; \qquad \ln 99 = 500kt$$

or $t = 0.0091/k$ time units. Without additional information, we cannot obtain a numerical value for the constant of proportionality k or be more definitive about t.

4.12 Geometrical Applications

Let $P(x_1, y_1)$ be any point on the curve $y = f(x)$, then slope of the tangent at $P (= \tan \psi) = \left(\dfrac{dy}{dx}\right)_{(x_1, y_1)}$ and hence we find the following facts.

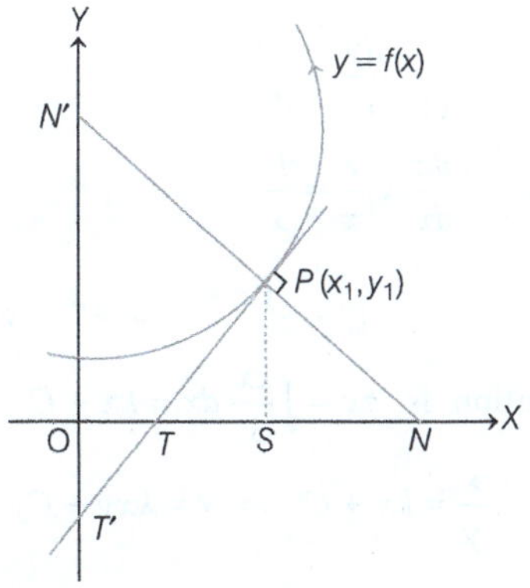

(i) The equation of the tangent at P is

$$y - y_1 = \frac{dy}{dx}(x - x_1).$$

When it cuts X-axis, $y = 0$

$\therefore$ x-intercept of the tangent $= x_1 - y_1 \left(\dfrac{dx}{dy}\right)$

When it cuts Y-axis, $x = 0$

$\therefore$ y-intercept of the tangent $= y_1 - x_1 \dfrac{dy}{dx}$

(ii) The equation of normal at P is,

$y - y_1 = -\dfrac{1}{(dy/dx)}(x - x_1)$ x and y-intercepts of normal are; $x_1 + y_1 \dfrac{dy}{dx}$ and $y_1 + x_1 \dfrac{dx}{dy}$

(iii) Length of tangent $= PT = |y_1| \sqrt{1 + (dx/dy)^2_{(x_1, y_1)}}$

(iv) Length of normal $= PN = |y_1| \sqrt{1 + (dy/dx)^2_{(x_1, y_1)}}$

(v) Length of subtangent $= ST = \left| y_1 \left(\dfrac{dx}{dy}\right)_{(x_1, y_1)} \right|$

(vi) Length of subnormal $= SN = \left| y_1 \left(\dfrac{dy}{dx}\right)_{(x_1, y_1)} \right|$

(vii) Length of radius vector $= \sqrt{x_1^2 + y_1^2}$

Example 44. Find the curve for which the area of the triangle formed by the X-axis, tangent drawn at any point on the curve and radius vector of the point of tangency is constant equal to a^2.

Sol. Tangent drawn at any point (x, y) is

$$Y - y = \frac{dy}{dx}(X - x)$$

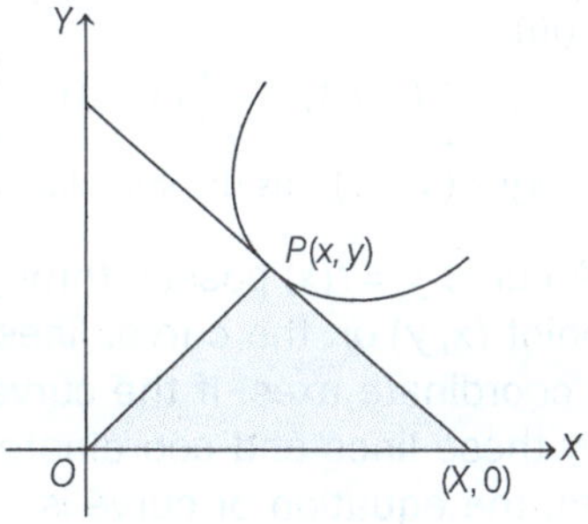

When $Y = 0$, $\quad X = x - y\dfrac{dx}{dy}$

Area of $\Delta = a^2$ [given]

i.e. $\left| \dfrac{1}{2} \cdot X \cdot y \right| = a^2$

i.e. $\left| xy - y^2 \dfrac{dx}{dy} \right| = 2a^2$

i.e. $xy - y^2 \dfrac{dx}{dy} = \pm 2a^2$

i.e. $\dfrac{dx}{dy} - \dfrac{x}{y} = \pm \dfrac{2a^2}{y^2}$

$$\text{IF} = e^{\int -\frac{1}{y} dy} = \frac{1}{y}$$

$\therefore$ The solution is $x \cdot \dfrac{1}{y} = \displaystyle\int \pm \dfrac{2a^2}{y^2} \cdot \dfrac{1}{y}\, dy$

$$\frac{x}{y} = \pm \frac{2a^2 \cdot y^{-2}}{-2} + C, \text{ i.e. } x = Cy \pm \frac{a^2}{y}$$

Example 45. The solution of $y = x\dfrac{dy}{dx} + \dfrac{dy}{dx} - \left(\dfrac{dy}{dx}\right)^2$, is

(a) $y = (x-1)^2$ (b) $4y = (x+1)^2$
(c) $(y-1)^2 = 4x$ (d) None of these

Sol. (b) The given equation can be written as

$$y = xp + p - p^2, \text{ where } p = \frac{dy}{dx} \quad \text{...(i)}$$

Differentiating both the sides w.r.t. x, we get

$$p = p + \frac{xdp}{dx} + \frac{dp}{dx} - 2p\frac{dp}{dx}$$

$\therefore$ $\dfrac{dp}{dx}(x + 1 - 2p) = 0$

$\therefore$ Either $\dfrac{dp}{dx} = 0$ i.e. $p = C$ ...(ii)

or $x + 1 - 2p = 0$ i.e. $p = \dfrac{1}{2}(x + 1)$ ...(iii)

Eliminating p between Eqs. (i) and (ii), we get

$$y = Cx + C - C^2$$

As the complete solution and eliminating p between Eqs. (i) and (iii),

$$y = \frac{1}{2}(x+1)\,x + \frac{1}{2}(x+1) - \frac{1}{4}(x+1)^2$$

i.e. $\quad 4y = (x+1)^2$ as the singular solution.

Example 46. A curve $y = f(x)$ passes through the origin. Through any point (x, y) on the curve, lines are drawn parallel to the coordinate axes. If the curve divides the area formed by these lines and coordinate axes in the ratio $m : n$. Then, the equation of curve is

(a) $y = Cx^{m/n}$ (b) $my^2 = Cx^{m/n}$

(c) $y^3 = Cx^{m/n}$ (d) None of these

Sol. (a) $\dfrac{\text{Area of } OBPO}{\text{Area of } OPAO} = \dfrac{m}{n}$

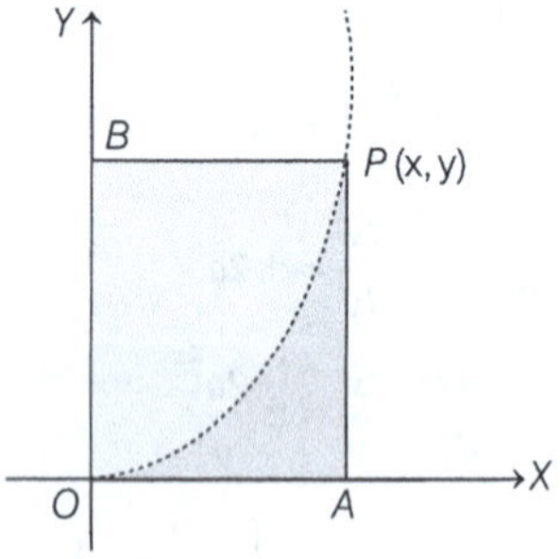

$$\Rightarrow \quad \frac{xy - \int_0^x y\,dx}{\int_0^x y\,dx} = \frac{m}{n} \Rightarrow nxy = (m+n)\int_0^x y\,dx$$

Differentiating w.r.t. x, we get

$$n\left(x\frac{dy}{dx} + y\right) = (m+n)\,y \Rightarrow nx\frac{dy}{dx} = my$$

$$\Rightarrow \quad \frac{m}{n}\cdot\frac{dx}{x} = \frac{dy}{y}$$

Integrating both the sides, we get

$$\Rightarrow \quad y = Cx^{m/n}$$

Example 47. Find the curve for which the intercept cut off by any tangent on Y-axis is proportional to the square of the ordinate of the point of tangency.

Sol. The equation of tangent at any point (x, y) is

$$Y - y = \frac{dy}{dx}(X - x)$$

When $X = 0$; $Y = y - x\dfrac{dy}{dx} = y$-intercept

It is given $Y \propto y^2$. i.e. $Y = ky^2$

[k being constant of proportionality]

i.e. $$y - x\frac{dy}{dx} = ky^2$$

i.e. $$\frac{dy}{dx} - \frac{1}{x}y = -\frac{ky^2}{x}$$

i.e. $$-y^{-2}\frac{dy}{dx} + \frac{1}{x}\cdot\frac{1}{y} = \frac{k}{x}$$

Let $\dfrac{1}{y} = z$ so that,

$$-\frac{1}{y^2}\cdot\frac{dy}{dx} = \frac{dz}{dx}$$

$$\therefore \quad \frac{dz}{dx} + \frac{z}{x} = \frac{k}{x}$$

$$\text{IF} = e^{\int \frac{1}{x}dx} = e^{\log x} = x$$

$\therefore$ The solution is $zx = \displaystyle\int \frac{kx}{x}\,dx = kx + C$

$$\Rightarrow \quad \frac{x}{y} = kx + C \Rightarrow x = kxy + Cy$$

$$\Rightarrow \quad x - Cy = kxy \Rightarrow \frac{1}{ky} + \frac{-C}{k}\cdot\frac{1}{x} = 1$$

$$\Rightarrow \quad \frac{C_1}{x} + \frac{C_2}{y} = 1 \quad \left[\text{where } \frac{1}{k} = C_2 \text{ and } -\frac{C}{k} = C_1\right]$$

Example 48. Find the family of curves, the subtangent at any point of which is the arithmetic mean of the coordinates of the point of tangency is given by

(a) $(x-y)^2 = Cy$ (b) $(y-x)^2 = Cx$

(c) $(x-y)^2 = Cxy$ (d) None of these

Sol. (a) Let the family of curves be $y = f(x)$

$$\tan\theta = \frac{l(PP')}{l(TP')}$$

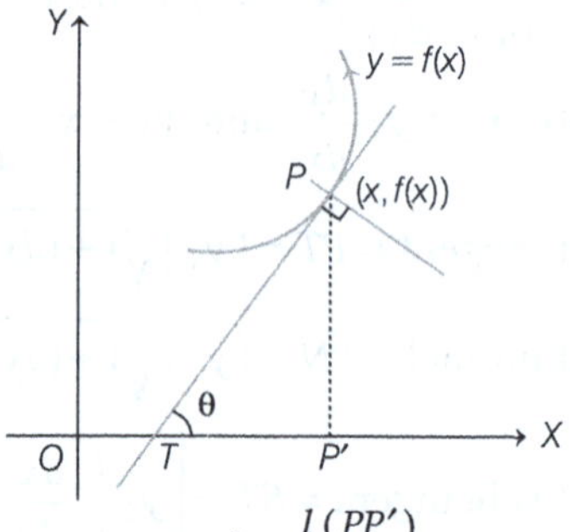

$$\tan\theta = \frac{l(PP')}{l(TP')}$$

$$\therefore \quad l\,(\text{subtangent}) = \frac{f(x)}{f'(x)}$$

$$\therefore \quad \frac{y}{y'} = \frac{x+y}{2} \text{ (given)}$$

$$\therefore \quad y' = \frac{2y}{x+y}$$

$$\Rightarrow \quad \frac{dy}{dx} = \frac{2y}{x+y} \quad \therefore \quad \frac{dx}{dy} = \frac{x+y}{2xy} \quad \text{...(i)}$$

It is a homogeneous differential equation.

$\therefore$ Put $x = vy$

Differentiating w.r.t. y, we get

$$\frac{dx}{dy} = v + y\frac{dv}{dy} \quad \text{...(ii)}$$

In Eq. (i) replacing $\frac{dx}{dy}$ by Eq. (ii), we get

$$v + y\frac{dv}{dy} = \frac{vy + y}{2y} = \frac{1+v}{2}$$

$$\Rightarrow y\frac{dv}{dy} = \frac{1+v}{2} - v = \frac{1+v-2v}{2} = \frac{1-v}{2} \Rightarrow \frac{2}{1-v}dv = \frac{dy}{y}$$

Integrating, $\frac{2\log|1-v|}{-1} = \log|y| + \log C_1 \; (C_1 > 0)$

$\therefore \quad -2\log|y-x| + 2\log|y| = \log|y| + \log C_1$

$\Rightarrow \quad \log|y-x|^2 = \log|y| - \log C_1$

$\Rightarrow \quad \log|y-x|^2 = \log|y| + \log C,$

where, $\log C = -\log C_1$

$\Rightarrow \quad \log|y-x|^2 = \log|yC|$

$\Rightarrow (x-y)^2 = Cy$, is the required equation of family of curves.

JEE SCANNER

Example Similar to PYQ Asked in JEE Main 2023

Let the tangent at any point P on a curve passing through the points (1, 2), and $\left(\frac{1}{10}, 200\right)$, intersects positive X-axis and Y-axis at the points A and B, respectively. If $PA : PB = 1 : k$ and $y = y(x)$ is the solution of the differential equation $e^{dy/dx} = kx + \frac{k}{2}$, $y(0) = k$, if $y(2) = \lambda \log_e 5$, then value of λ is ....

Sol. (2.5) Let the coordinates of a point P be (x, y).

Let the tangent intersects X-axis and Y-axis at a point $A(\alpha, 0)$ and $B(0, \beta)$, respectively.

Point P divides AB in the ratio $1 : k$.

$$x = \frac{k\alpha}{k+1} \text{ and } y = \frac{\beta}{k+1} \Rightarrow \alpha = \frac{x(k+1)}{k}$$

and $\beta = y(k+1)$

$$\text{Slope of tangent} = \frac{0-\beta}{\alpha - 0}$$

$$\frac{dy}{dx} = \frac{-y(k+1)}{\frac{x(k+1)}{k}} \Rightarrow \frac{dy}{dx} = \frac{-ky}{x}$$

$$\frac{1}{y}dy = \frac{-k}{x}dx$$

$$\log y = -k\log x + \log C$$

$$y \cdot x^k = C$$

The curve passes through (1, 2) $\Rightarrow C = 2$

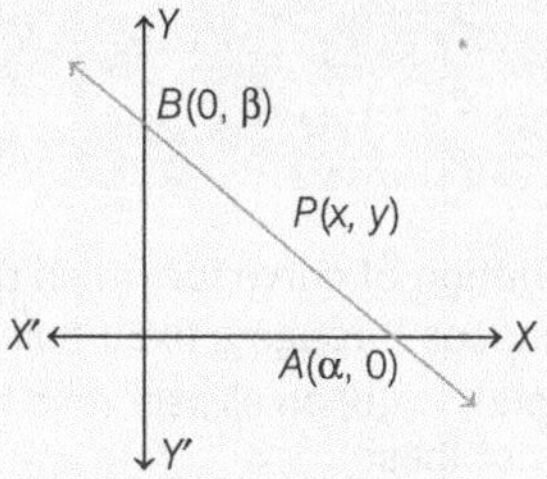

The curve also passes through $\left(\frac{1}{10}, 200\right)$

$$200 \times \left(\frac{1}{10}\right)^k = 2$$

$\Rightarrow \quad k = 2$

Also, $\quad e^{\frac{dy}{dx}} = 2x + 1$

$\Rightarrow \quad \frac{dy}{dx} = \log_e(2x+1)$

$\Rightarrow \quad dy = \log_e(2x+1)dx$

Let $\quad t = 2x + 1 \Rightarrow \frac{1}{2}dt = dx$

$\Rightarrow \int dy = \frac{1}{2}\int \log_e t \, dt$

$\Rightarrow \quad y = \frac{1}{2}[t\log_e t - t] \Rightarrow y = \frac{2x+1}{2}[\log_e(2x+1) - 1] + C$

$y(0) = 2$ is its solution,

$\Rightarrow \quad 2 = \frac{1}{2}[\log 1 - 1] + C \Rightarrow C = \frac{5}{2}$

$\therefore \quad y = \frac{2x+1}{2}[\log_e(2x+1) - 1] + \frac{5}{2}$

$$y(2) = \frac{5}{2}[\log_e 5 - 1] + \frac{5}{2}$$

$\therefore \quad y(2) = \frac{5}{2}\log_e 5$

$\therefore \quad \lambda = \frac{5}{2} = 2.5$

Skill Builder

Let the tangent is drawn at any point P of a curve which passes through the points (1, 1) and $\left(\frac{1}{8}, 2\right)$ cutting X-axis and Y-axis at A and B, respectively. If $BP; AP = k : 1$ and $y = y(x)$ is the solution of the differential equation $\frac{1x}{k}\frac{dy}{dx} + y = 0$, $y(1) = \frac{1}{k}$.

If $y(8) = \frac{\lambda}{8^2}$, then value of λ is ....

For Sol.

- **For more practice** See Q.10 of Milestone Practice 4.5.

Milestone Practice 4.5

1. The equation of curve for which the normal at every point passes through a fixed point, is
(a) a circle (b) an ellipse (c) a hyperbola
(d) None of these

2. If the tangent at any point P of a curve meets the axis of x at T. Then, the curve for which $OP = PT$, O being the origin is
(a) $x = Cy^2$ (b) $x = Cy^2$ or $x = C/y^2$
(c) $x = Cy$ or $x = C/y$ (d) None of these

3. According to Newton's law, the rate of cooling is proportional to the difference between the temperature of the body and the temperature of the air. If the temperature of the air is 20°C and body cools for 20 min from 100°C to 60°C, then the time it will take for the temperature to drop to 30°C, is
(a) 30 min (b) 40 min (c) 60 min (d) 80 min

4. Let $f(x, y)$ be a curve in the XY-plane having the property that distance from the origin of any tangent to the curve is equal to distance of point of contact from the Y-axis. If $f(1, 2) = 0$, then all such possible curves are
(a) $x^2 + y^2 = 5x$ (b) $x^2 - y^2 = 5x$
(c) $x^2y^2 = 5x$ (d) All of these

5. Given the curves $y = f(x)$ passing through the point $(0, 1)$ and $y = \int_{-\infty}^{x} f(t)$ passing through the point $\left(0, \frac{1}{2}\right)$. The tangents drawn to both the curves at the points with equal abscissae intersect on the X-axis. Then, the curve $y = f(x)$, is
(a) $f(x) = x^2 + x + 1$ (b) $f(x) = \dfrac{x^2}{e^x}$
(c) $f(x) = e^{2x}$ (d) $f(x) = x - e^x$

6. A curve passing through (1, 0) is such that the ratio of the square of the intercept cut by any tangent on the Y-axis to the sub-normal is equal to the ratio of the product of the coordinates of the point of tangency to the product of square of the slope of the tangent and the sub-tangent at the same point, is given by
(a) $x = e^{\pm 2\sqrt{y/x}}$
(b) $x = e^{\pm\sqrt{y/x}}$
(c) $y = e^{\pm\sqrt{y/x}} - 1$
(d) $xy + e^{y/x} - 1 = 0$

7. Consider a curve $y = f(x)$ in XY-plane. The curve passes through (0, 0) and has the property that a segment of tangent drawn at any point $P(x, f(x))$ and the line $y = 3$ gets bisected by the line $x + y = 1$, then the equation of curve, is
(a) $y^2 = 9(x - y)$
(b) $(y - 3)^2 = 9(1 - x - y)$
(c) $(y + 3)^2 = 9(1 - x - y)$
(d) $(y - 3)^2 = 9(1 + x + y)$

8. Let $y = f(x)$ be a curve such that y-intercept of tangent at any point P on the curve is equal to slope of line OP, where O being origin. If $y(1) = e$, then $\lim_{x \to 0^+} \frac{1}{y}$ is equal to (assume curve lies in first quadrant)
(a) 1 (b) 0
(c) ∞ (d) None of these

9. Let $y = y(x)$ be the solution of $\frac{dy}{dx} - 2xy = x^3$ with $y(0) = \frac{1}{2}$, then
(a) $y(x)$ has local maximum at $x = 0$
(b) $y(x)$ has local minimum at $x = 1$
(c) $y(x) = 0$ has exactly 1 root in R
(d) $y(x) = 0$ has no real root in R

10. Let the tangent at any point P on a curve passing through the points (1, 1) and $\left(\frac{1}{10}, 100\right)$ intersects positive X-axis and Y-axis at the points A and B respectively. If $PA : PB = 1 : k$ and $y = y(x)$ is the solution of the differential equation $(x \log x)\frac{dy}{dx} + y = kx \log x$, $y(2) = k$, if $y(4) = \lambda$, then the value of λ is
(a) 6 (b) 8
(c) 4 (d) 10

Answer Key

1. (a)	2. (c)	3. (c)	4. (a)	5. (c)
6. (a)	7. (b)	8. (b)	9. (d)	10. (a)

For Detailed Solution

JEE Pattern EXAMPLES

Single Option Correct Type Questions

Example 1 *The order of the differential equation of family of curves*

$y = C_1 \sin^{-1} x + C_2 \cos^{-1} x + C_3 \tan^{-1} x + C_4 \cot^{-1} x$

(where C_1, C_2, C_3 and C_4 are arbitrary constants) is

(a) 2 (b) 3

(c) 4 (d) None of these

> **Decoding the Question**
>
> Instead of counting arbitrary constants directly, first simplify the given equation and reduced the number of arbitrary constant to the lowest, then comment on order and degree.

Sol. (b) Here,

$$y = C_1 \sin^{-1} x + C_2 \cos^{-1} x + C_3 \tan^{-1} x + C_4 \cot^{-1} x$$

$$\Rightarrow y = C_1 \sin^{-1} x + C_2\left(\frac{\pi}{2} - \sin^{-1} x\right) + C_3 \tan^{-1} x + C_4\left(\frac{\pi}{2} - \tan^{-1} x\right)$$

$$= (C_1 - C_2)\sin^{-1} x + (C_3 - C_4)\tan^{-1} x + (C_2 + C_4)\frac{\pi}{2}$$

$$= a\sin^{-1} x + b\tan^{-1} x + C,$$

where $a = C_1 - C_2, b = C_3 - C_4, c = C_2 - C_4$

There are only three arbitrary constant.

$\therefore$ Order of the differential equation is 3.

Example 2 *The curve satisfying the differential equation* $\frac{dy}{dx} = \frac{y(x+y^3)}{x(y^3 - x)}$ *and passing through* $(4, -2)$ *is*

(a) $y^2 = -2x$ (b) $y = -2x$

(c) $y^3 = -2x$ (d) None of these

Sol. (c) Here, $(xy^3 - x^2)dy = (xy + y^4)dx$

$$\Rightarrow \quad y^3(xdy - ydx) - x(xdy + ydx) = 0$$

$$\Rightarrow \quad x^2y^3 d\left(\frac{y}{x}\right) - x\,d(xy) = 0$$

Dividing by x^3y^2, we get

$$\frac{y}{x}\, d\left(\frac{y}{x}\right) - \frac{1}{x^2y^2}\cdot d(xy) = 0$$

Now integrating, we get

$$\frac{1}{2}\left(\frac{y}{x}\right)^2 + \frac{1}{xy} = C$$

It passes through $(4, -2)$

$$\Rightarrow \quad \frac{1}{8} - \frac{1}{8} = C \Rightarrow C = 0$$

$\therefore y^3 = -2x$ is required curve.

Example 3 *Spherical rain drop evaporates at a rate proportional to its surface area. The differential equation corresponding to the rate of change of the radius of the rain drop, if the constant of proportionality is $k > 0$, is*

(a) $\frac{dr}{dt} + k = 0$ (b) $\frac{dr}{dt} - k = 0$

(c) $\frac{dr}{dt} = kr$ (d) None of these

Sol. (a) $\frac{dV}{dt} = -k4\pi r^2$ ...(i)

But $V = \frac{4}{3}\pi r^3 \Rightarrow \frac{dV}{dt} = 4\pi r^2 \frac{dr}{dt}$ ...(ii)

Therefore, $\frac{dr}{dt} = -k \Rightarrow \frac{dr}{dt} + k = 0$

Example 4 *A function $y = f(x)$ satisfies the differential equation $f(x) \cdot \sin 2x - \cos x + (1 + \sin^2 x) f'(x) = 0$ with initial condition $y(0) = 0$. The value of $f(\pi/6)$ is equal to*

(a) 1/5 (b) 3/5 (c) 4/5 (d) 2/5

Sol. (d) $y \sin 2x - \cos x + (1 + \sin^2 x)\frac{dy}{dx} = 0$, where $y = f(x)$

$$\frac{dy}{dx} + \left(\frac{\sin 2x}{1 + \sin^2 x}\right)y = \frac{\cos x}{1 + \sin^2 x}$$

$$\text{IF} = e^{\int \frac{\sin 2x}{1 + \sin^2 x}dx} = e^{\int \frac{dt}{t}} = e^{\ln(1 + \sin^2 x)}$$

$$= 1 + \sin^2 x \quad (\text{by putting } 1 + \sin^2 x = t)$$

$\therefore$ The solution is $y(1 + \sin^2 x) = \int \cos x\, dx$

$$y(1 + \sin^2 x) = \sin x + C;\ y(0) = 0 \Rightarrow C = 0$$

Therefore, $y = \frac{\sin x}{1 + \sin^2 x} \Rightarrow y\left(\frac{\pi}{6}\right) = \frac{2}{5}$

JEE SCANNER

Example 5 Similar to PYQ Asked in JEE Main 2022

Let $y = y(x)$ be the solution of the differential equation $\frac{dy}{dx} + (\sec x)y = \tan x, \left(0 \le x < \frac{\pi}{2}\right)$ satisfying the condition $y\left(\frac{\pi}{4}\right) = 1$. Then, $y(0)$ is equal to

(a) $\frac{\pi}{4} + 1$ (b) $\frac{\pi}{4} - 1$ (c) $\frac{\pi}{2}$ (d) $\frac{\pi}{2} - 1$

Sol. (a) Given differential equation is

$$\frac{dy}{dx} + (\sec x)y = \tan x$$

This is of the form $\frac{dy}{dx} + Py = Q$

Here, $P = \sec x$ and $Q = \tan x$

Now, integrating factor,

$$\text{IF} = e^{\int P dx} = e^{\int \sec x \, dx} = e^{\log|\sec x + \tan x|}$$
$$= \sec x + \tan x$$

and the solution of differential equation is given by

$$y \times \text{IF} = \int (Q \times \text{IF}) dx + C$$

$$\Rightarrow y \cdot (\sec x + \tan x) = \int \tan x (\sec x + \tan x) dx + C$$
$$= \int \tan x \sec x dx + \int \tan^2 x \, dx + C$$
$$= \sec x + \int (\sec^2 x - 1) dx + C$$
$$[\because \sec^2 x - \tan^2 x = 1]$$

$$\Rightarrow y \cdot (\sec x + \tan x) = \sec x + \tan x - x + C$$

Given, $y\left(\frac{\pi}{4}\right) = 1$

$$\Rightarrow \quad 1 \cdot \left(\sec\frac{\pi}{4} + \tan\frac{\pi}{4}\right) = \left(\sec\frac{\pi}{4} + \tan\frac{\pi}{4}\right) - \frac{\pi}{4} + C$$

$$\Rightarrow \quad \sqrt{2} + 1 = \sqrt{2} + 1 - \frac{\pi}{4} + C$$

$$\Rightarrow \quad C = \frac{\pi}{4}$$

$$\therefore \quad y[\sec(0) + \tan 0] = \sec(0) + \tan(0) - 0 + \frac{\pi}{4}$$

$$\Rightarrow \quad y[1 + 0] = 1 + 0 + \frac{\pi}{4} = \frac{\pi}{4} + 1$$

$$\Rightarrow \quad y = \frac{\pi}{4} + 1$$

Skill Builder

Let $y = y(t)$ is a solution of $(1 + t)\frac{dy}{dt} - ty = 1$ and $y(0) = -1$, then $y(1)$ is

(a) $-\frac{1}{2}$ (b) $-\frac{1}{4}$ (c) $-\frac{1}{6}$ (d) $-\frac{1}{8}$

For Sol.

Example 6 *The general solution of the differential equation* $\frac{dy}{dx} = \frac{1 - x}{y}$ *is a family of curves which looks most like which of the following?*

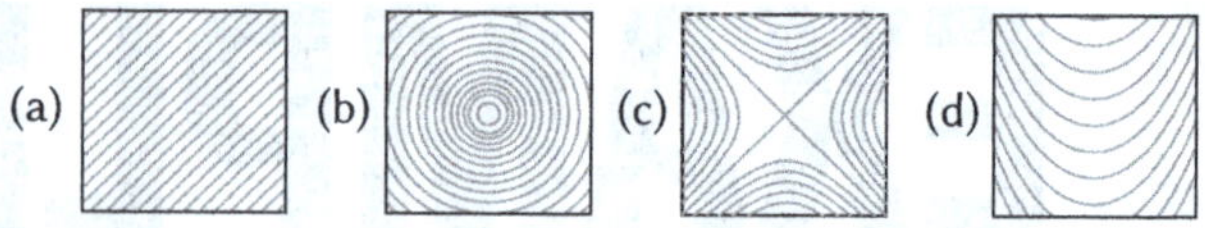

Sol. (b)

$$\int y dy = \int (1 - x) \, dx$$

$$\frac{y^2}{2} = x - \frac{x^2}{2} + C$$

$$x^2 + y^2 - 2x = C$$

$$(x - 1)^2 + y^2 = C + 1 = C$$

Remark Family of concentric circles with (1, 0) as the centre and variable radius.

Example 7 *Water is drained from a vertical cylindrical tank by opening a valve at the base of the tank. It is known that the rate at which the water level drops is proportional to the square root of water depth y, where the constant of proportionality $k > 0$ depends on the acceleration due to gravity and the geometry of the hole. If t is measured in minutes and $k = \frac{1}{15}$, then the time to drain the tank, if the water is 4 m deep to start with is*

(a) 30 min (b) 45 min (c) 60 min (d) 80 min

Sol. (c) $\frac{dy}{dt} = -k\sqrt{y}$; when $t = 0$; $y = 4$

$$\int_4^0 \frac{dy}{\sqrt{y}} = -k\int_0^t dt \Rightarrow [2\sqrt{y}]_4^0 = -kt = -\frac{t}{15}$$

$$\Rightarrow \quad 0 - 4 = -\frac{t}{15} \Rightarrow t = 60 \text{ min}$$

Example 8 *If* $y = \frac{x}{\ln|cx|}$ *(where c is an arbitrary constant) is the general solution of the differential equation* $\frac{dy}{dx} = \frac{y}{x} + \phi\left(\frac{x}{y}\right)$*, then the function* $\phi\left(\frac{x}{y}\right)$ *is*

(a) $\frac{x^2}{y^2}$ (b) $-\frac{x^2}{y^2}$ (c) $\frac{y^2}{x^2}$ (d) $-\frac{y^2}{x^2}$

Sol. (d) $\ln c + \ln|x| = \frac{x}{y}$

Differentiating w.r.t. x, we get

$$\frac{1}{x} = \frac{y - xy_1}{y^2} \Rightarrow \frac{y^2}{x} = y - x\frac{dy}{dx}$$

$$\Rightarrow \quad \frac{dy}{dx} = \frac{y}{x} - \frac{y^2}{x^2} \Rightarrow \phi\left(\frac{x}{y}\right) = -\frac{y^2}{x^2}$$

JEE SCANNER

Example 9 Similar to PYQ Asked in JEE Main 2024

Let $y = y(x)$ be the solution of the differential equation $\frac{dy}{dx} = 1 + x + y + xy$ such that $y = 0$, when $x = 1$.

Then, $y(2)$ is equal to

(a) $e^{5/2}$ (b) $e^{5/2} + 1$

(c) $e^{5/2} - 1$ (d) $\frac{e^{5/2}}{5}$

Sol. (c) Given, $\frac{dy}{dx} = 1 + x + y + xy$

$$\Rightarrow \frac{dy}{dx} = 1(1+x) + y(1+x)$$

$$\Rightarrow \frac{dy}{dx} = (1+x)(1+y) \quad \text{...(i)}$$

On separating the variables, we get

$$\frac{1}{(1+y)} dy = (1+x)dx \quad \text{...(ii)}$$

On integrating both sides of Eq. (ii), we get

$$\int \frac{1}{1+y} dy = \int (1+x)dx$$

$$\Rightarrow \log|1+y| = x + \frac{x^2}{2} + C \quad \text{...(iii)}$$

On substituting $x = 1, y = 0$ in Eq. (iii), we get

$$\log|1+0| = 1 + \frac{1}{2} + C$$

$$\Rightarrow C = -\frac{3}{2} \quad [\because \log 1 = 0]$$

Now, substituting the value of C in Eq. (iii), we get

$$\log|1+y| = x + \frac{x^2}{2} - \frac{3}{2}$$

which is the particular solution of differential equation.

$$\Rightarrow \log|1+y| = 2 + \frac{4}{2} - \frac{3}{2} = \frac{5}{2}$$

$$\Rightarrow y = e^{5/2} - 1$$

$$\therefore y(2) = e^{5/2} - 1$$

Skill Builder

Let $y = y(x)$ be the solution of differential equation $\frac{dy}{dx} = -4xy^2$ such that $y = 1$, when $x = 0$.

Then, $y(5)$ is equal to

(a) $\frac{1}{50}$ (b) $\frac{1}{51}$

(c) $\frac{1}{53}$ (d) $\frac{1}{49}$

For Sol.

Example 10 *Consider the two statements :*

Statement I $y = \sin kt$ *satisfy the differential equation* $y'' + 9y = 0$.

Statement II $y = e^{kt}$ *satisfy the differential equation* $y'' + y' - 6y = 0$.

The value of k for which both the statements are correct is

(a) −3 (b) 0 (c) 2 (d) 3

Sol. (a) **Statement I** $y = \sin kt, y' = k \cos kt; y'' = -k^2 \sin kt$

$$\therefore -k^2 \sin kt + 9 \sin kt = 0$$

$$\sin kt\,[9 - k^2] = 0 \Rightarrow k = 0, k = 3, k = -3$$

Statement II $y = e^{kt}, y' = ke^{kt}; y'' = k^2 e^{kt}$

$$\therefore k^2 e^{kt} + ke^{kt} - 6e^{kt} = 0$$

$$e^{kt}[k^2 + k - 6] = 0 \Rightarrow (k+3)(k-2) = 0$$

$$k = -3 \text{ or } 2$$

Common value is $k = -3$.

Example 11 *The differential equation* $\frac{dy}{dx} = \frac{\sqrt{1-y^2}}{y}$ *determines a family of circles with*

(a) variable radii and a fixed centre at (0, 1)

(b) variable radii and fixed centre at (0, −1)

(c) fixed radius 1 and variable centres along the X-axis

(d) fixed radius 1 and variable centres along the Y-axis

Sol. (c) $\because \frac{dy}{dx} = \frac{\sqrt{1-y^2}}{y} \Rightarrow \int \frac{y}{\sqrt{1-y^2}} dy = \int dx$

$$\Rightarrow -\frac{1}{2} \cdot 2\sqrt{1-y^2} = x + C \Rightarrow -\sqrt{1-y^2} = x + C$$

$$\Rightarrow 1 - y^2 = (x+C)^2 \Rightarrow (x+C)^2 + y^2 = 1$$

Therefore, the differential equation represents a circle of fixed radius 1 and variable centres along the X-axis.

Example 12 *Let* $f(x) = e^x + \sin x + x \ \forall \ x \in [-\pi, 0]$ *and* $f(0) = 0$. *If* $f(x)$ *satisfies* $f(x+y) = f(x) - f(y) \ \forall \ x, y \in R$, *then the number of solution of the equation* $f(x) = |x|$ *in* $[-\pi, \pi]$ *is*

(a) 0 (b) 1 (c) 2 (d) 3

Sol. (d) $f(x) = e^x + \sin x + x \Rightarrow f'(x) = e^x + \cos x + 1$

$\Rightarrow f'(x) > 0, x \in R$

$\Rightarrow f(x)$ is increasing

$$f(x+y) = f(x) - f(y)$$

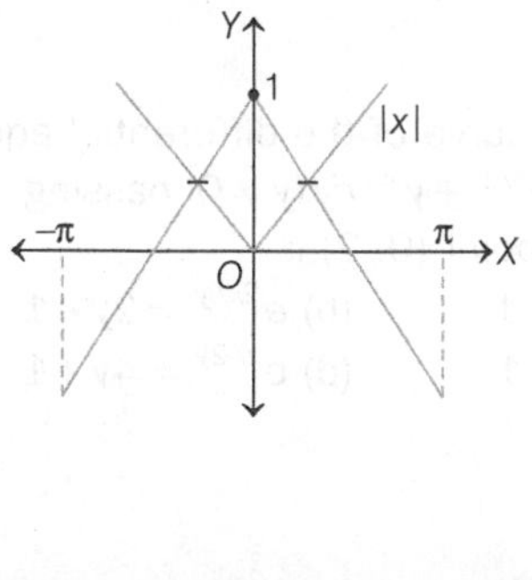

Put $y = -x$

$\Rightarrow \quad f(0) = f(x) - f(-x)$

$\Rightarrow \quad f(-x) = f(x) \Rightarrow \quad f(-x) = f(x)$

$\therefore$ From the graph it is clear that $f(x) = |x|$ has 3 solutions.

JEE SCANNER

Example 13 Similar to PYQ Asked in JEE Main 2022

The solution of the differential equation

$\frac{dy}{dx} - \frac{y}{x} + \text{cosec}\left(\frac{y}{x}\right) = 0$, $y = 0$ *when* $x = 1$ *is*

(a) $\cos\left(\frac{x}{y}\right) = \log|x| + 1$ (b) $\cos\left(\frac{y}{x}\right) = \log|x| - 1$

(c) $\cos\left(\frac{x}{y}\right) = \log|x| - 1$ (d) $\cos\left(\frac{y}{x}\right) = \log|x| + 1$

Sol. (d) Given differential equation is

$$\frac{dy}{dx} - \frac{y}{x} + \text{cosec}\left(\frac{y}{x}\right) = 0 \Rightarrow \frac{dy}{dx} = \frac{y}{x} - \text{cosec}\left(\frac{y}{x}\right) \quad \text{...(i)}$$

which is a homogeneous differential equation as $\frac{dy}{dx} = f\left(\frac{y}{x}\right)$.

On putting $y = vx$ and $\frac{dy}{dx} = v + x\frac{dv}{dx}$ in Eq. (i), we get

$$v + x\frac{dv}{dx} = v - \text{cosec } v$$

$$\Rightarrow \quad x\frac{dv}{dx} = -\text{cosec } v \Rightarrow \sin v \, dv = -\frac{dx}{x}$$

On integrating both sides, we get

$$\int \sin v \, dv = -\int \frac{dx}{x}$$

$$\Rightarrow \quad -\cos v = -\log|x| + C$$

$$\Rightarrow \quad \cos v = \log|x| - C$$

$$\Rightarrow \quad \cos\left(\frac{y}{x}\right) = \log|x| - C \quad \left[\text{put } v = \frac{y}{x}\right] \quad \text{...(ii)}$$

Also, given $y = 0$, when $x = 1$

Then, $\quad \cos 0 = \log 1 - C$

$\Rightarrow \quad 1 = 0 - C \Rightarrow C = -1$

So, Eq. (ii) becomes $\cos\left(\frac{y}{x}\right) = \log|x| + 1$

which is the required equation.

Skill Builder

The solution curve of the differential equation $ye^{x/y}dx = (xe^{x/y} + y^2)\,dy \; (y \neq 0)$ passing through the point (0, 2) is

(a) $e^{x/y} = y - 1$ (b) $e^{2x/y} = 2y - 1$

(c) $e^{y/x} = y + 1$ (d) $e^{x/2y} = 4y + 1$

For Sol.

Example 14 *Let* $y = y(x)$ *be the solution of the differential equation* $e^x \tan y \, dx + (2 - e^x)\sec^2 y \, dy = 0$*, given that* $y = \frac{\pi}{4}$ *when* $x = 0$*. Then,* $[\pi/3 - y(1)]$ *is*

(a) $\frac{\pi}{3} - \tan^{-1}(2 + e)$ (b) $\frac{\pi}{3} - \tan^{-1}(1 - e)$

(c) $\frac{\pi}{3} - \tan^{-1}(2 - e)$ (d) $\frac{\pi}{3} - \tan^{-1}(1 + e)$

Sol. (c) Given differential equation is

$$e^x \tan y \, dx + (2 - e^x)\sec^2 y \, dy = 0$$

which can be rewritten as

$$e^x \tan y \, dx = (e^x - 2)\sec^2 y \, dy$$

$$\Rightarrow \quad \frac{\sec^2 y}{\tan y}dy = \frac{e^x}{e^x - 2}dx$$

$$\Rightarrow \quad \int \frac{\sec^2 y}{\tan y}dy = \int \frac{e^x}{e^x - 2}dx$$

Let $\tan y = t \Rightarrow \sec^2 y \, dy = dt$

and $\quad e^x - 2 = u$

$\Rightarrow \quad e^x \, dx = du$

$$\Rightarrow \quad \log|\tan y| = \log|e^x - 2| + C \quad \left[\because \int \frac{f'(x)}{f(x)}dx = \log|f(x)| + C\right]$$

$$\Rightarrow \quad \log|\tan y| - \log|e^x - 2| = C$$

$$\Rightarrow \quad \log\left|\frac{\tan y}{e^x - 2}\right| = C \quad \left[\because \log m - \log n = \log\left(\frac{m}{n}\right)\right]$$

$$\Rightarrow \quad \frac{\tan y}{e^x - 2} = e^C \quad [\because \log m = n \Rightarrow m = e^n]$$

$$\Rightarrow \quad \tan y = e^C(e^x - 2)$$

Now, it is given that $y = \frac{\pi}{4}$ when $x = 0$

$$\therefore \quad \tan\frac{\pi}{4} = e^C(e^0 - 2)$$

$$\Rightarrow \quad 1 = e^C(1 - 2)$$

$$\Rightarrow \quad e^C = -1$$

Thus, the particular solution of the given differential equation is $\tan y = 2 - e^x$.

At $x = 1$,

$$\tan y = 2 - e^1$$

$$\Rightarrow \quad y = \tan^{-1}(2 - e)$$

$$\therefore \quad \left[\frac{\pi}{3} - y(1)\right] = \frac{\pi}{3} - \tan^{-1}(2 - e)$$

More than One Correct Option Type Questions

Example 15 *A curve $y = f(x)$ has the property that the perpendicular distance of the origin from the normal at any point P of the curve is equal to the distance of the point P from the X-axis. Then, the differential equation of the curve*

(a) is homogeneous

(b) can be converted into linear differential equation with some suitable substitution

(c) is the family of circles touching the X-axis at the origin

(d) the family of circles touching the Y-axis at the origin

Sol. (a,b,d) Equation of normal

$$Y - y = -\frac{1}{m}(X - x)$$

$\Rightarrow$ $$-mY + my = X - x$$

$\Rightarrow$ $$X + mY - (x + my) = 0$$

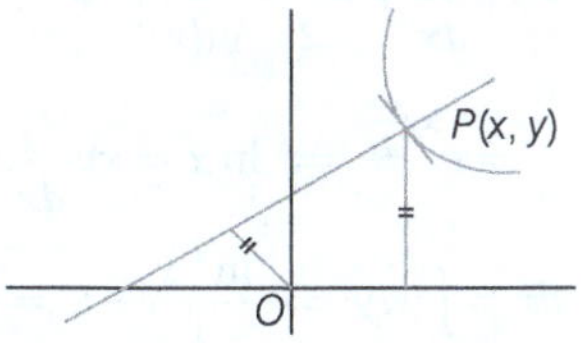

Perpendicular from (0, 0) $= \left|\frac{x + my}{\sqrt{1 + m^2}}\right| = y$

$\Rightarrow$ $$x^2 + 2xym = y^2$$

$$\frac{dy}{dx} = \frac{y^2 - x^2}{2xy} \Rightarrow \text{Homogeneous}$$

Also, $$x \cdot 2y \cdot \frac{dy}{dx} + x^2 = y^2$$

Put $y^2 = t \Rightarrow 2y\frac{dy}{dx} = \frac{dt}{dx}$

$$x \cdot \frac{dt}{dx} + x^2 = t$$

$$\frac{dt}{dx} - \frac{1}{x}t = -x,$$

which is linear differential equation.

Example 16 *A differentiable function satisfies $f(x) = \int_0^x \{f(t)\cos t - \cos(t - x)\}\,dt$. Which is of the following hold good?*

(a) $f(x)$ has a minimum value $1 - e$

(b) $f(x)$ has a maximum value $1 - e^{-1}$

(c) $f''\left(\frac{\pi}{2}\right) = e$

(d) $f'(0) = 1$

Sol. (a,b,c) $f(x) = \int_0^x \{f(t)\cos t - \cos(t - x)\}\,dt$

$$= \int_0^x f(t)\cos t\,dt - \int_0^x \cos(-t)\,dt$$

$$\left[\int_0^a f(x)dx = \int_0^a f(a - x)\,dx\right]$$

$$f(x) = \int_0^x f(t)\cos t\,dt - \sin x$$

Differentiating both the sides, we get

$$f'(x) = f(x)\cos x - \cos x$$

Let $$f(x) = y;\ f'(x) = \frac{dy}{dx}$$

$$\frac{dy}{dx} - y\cos x = -\cos x \qquad \text{(L.D.E.)}$$

$$\text{IF} = e^{-\int \cos x\,dx} = e^{-\sin x}$$

Therefore, $y \cdot e^{-\sin x} = -\int e^{-\sin x}\cos x\,dx;$

$$y \cdot e^{-\sin x} = C + e^{-\sin x}$$

$\Rightarrow$ $$y = Ce^{\sin x} + 1$$

If $x = 0$; $y = 0$ [from the given relation]

$\Rightarrow$ $$C = -1$$

Therefore, $f(x) = 1 - e^{\sin x}$

Now, minimum value $= 1 - e$ [when $x = \pi/2$]

Maximum value $= 1 - e^{-1}$ [when $x = -\pi/2$]

$$f'(x) = -e^{\sin x}\cos x$$

Therefore, $f'(0) = -1$

$$f''(x) = -[\cos^2 x \cdot e^{\sin x} - e^{\sin x} \cdot \sin x]$$

$$f''\left(\frac{\pi}{2}\right) = e$$

Example 17 *Let $\frac{dy}{dx} + y = f(x)$ where y is a continuous function of x with $y(0) = 1$ and $f(x) = \begin{cases} e^{-x}, & \text{if } 0 \le x \le 2 \\ e^{-2}, & \text{if } x > 2 \end{cases}$.*

Which is of the following hold(s) good?

(a) $y(1) = 2e^{-1}$ (b) $y'(1) = -e^{-1}$

(c) $y(3) = -2e^{-3}$ (d) $y'(3) = -2e^{-3}$

Sol. (a,b,d) $\frac{dy}{dx} + y = f(x)$

$\Rightarrow$ $$\text{IF} = e^x$$

$$ye^x = \int e^x f(x)\,dx + C$$

Now, if $0 \le x \le 2$, then $ye^x = \int e^x e^{-x}\,dx + C$

$\Rightarrow$ $$ye^x = x + C$$

At $x = 0$, $y(0) = 1 \Rightarrow C = 1$

$\therefore$ $$ye^x = x + 1 \qquad \text{...(i)}$$

$$y = \frac{x + 1}{e^x};\ y(1) = \frac{2}{e}$$

$\Rightarrow$ $$y' = \frac{e^x - (x + 1)e^x}{e^{2x}}$$

$$y'(1) = \frac{e - 2e}{e^2} = \frac{-e}{e^2} = -\frac{1}{e}$$

If $x > 2$, $ye^x = \int e^{x-2}\,dx$

$$ye^x = e^{x-2} + C$$
$$y = e^{-2} + Ce^{-x}$$

As y is continuous.

$$\therefore \quad \lim_{x \to 2} \frac{x+1}{e^x} = \lim_{x \to 2} (e^{-2} + Ce^{-x})$$
$$3e^{-2} = e^{-2} + Ce^{-2}$$
$$\Rightarrow \quad C = 2$$

$\therefore$ For $x > 2$

$$y = e^{-2} + 2e^{-x}$$

Hence, $y(3) = 2e^{-3} + e^{-2} = e^{-2}(2e^{-1} + 1)$

$$y' = -2e^{-x}$$
$$y'(3) = -2e^{-3}$$

Example 18 *A curve $y = f(x)$ passes through (1, 1) and tangent at $P(x, y)$ cuts the X-axis and Y-axis at A and B respectively such that $BP : AP = 3 : 1$, then*

(a) equation of curve is $xy' - 3y = 0$
(b) normal at (1, 1) is $x + 3y = 4$
(c) curve passes through $\left(2, \frac{1}{8}\right)$
(d) equation of curve is $xy' + 3y = 0$

Sol. (c,d) Equation of the tangent to the curve $y = f(x)$ at (x, y) is

$$Y - y = \frac{dy}{dx}(X - x)$$

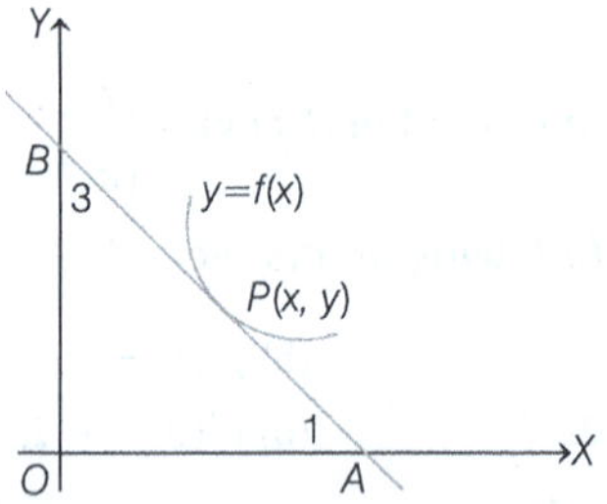

$\because$ Thus, cuts the X-axis at A and Y-axis at B.

$$\therefore \quad A\left(\frac{x\frac{dy}{dx} - y}{\frac{dy}{dx}}, 0\right) \text{ and } B\left(0, -x\frac{dy}{dx} + y\right)$$

$$\because \quad BP : PA = 3 : 1$$

$$\Rightarrow \quad x = \frac{\frac{3\left(x\frac{dy}{dx} - y\right)}{(dy/dx)} + 1 \times 0}{4}$$

$$\Rightarrow \quad x\frac{dy}{dx} + 3y = 0$$

$$\Rightarrow \quad \int \frac{dy}{y} = \int -3\frac{dx}{x}$$

$$\Rightarrow \quad \log y = -3\log x + \log C$$

$$\Rightarrow \quad y = \frac{C}{x^3}$$

$\because$ Curve passes through (1, 1)

$\therefore C = 1$

$\therefore$ Curve is $x^3 y = 1$ which also passes through $\left(2, \frac{1}{8}\right)$.

Example 19 *If $y = f(x)$ pass through (1, 0) and satisfy $x - 1 = xy\frac{dy}{dx} + \frac{x^2y^2}{2!}\left(\frac{dy}{dx}\right)^2 + \frac{x^3y^3}{3!}\left(\frac{dy}{dx}\right)^3 + \dots$, then*

(a) $f(x) = \ln x$
(b) $f(x) = \ln(1/x)$
(c) $f(x) = (\ln x)^2$
(d) $f(x) = \frac{1}{x}\ln x$

Sol. (a, b) $x = 1 + xy\frac{dy}{dx} + \frac{x^2y^2}{2!}\left(\frac{dy}{dx}\right)^2 + \dots$

$$x = e^{xy\frac{dy}{dx}} \Rightarrow \ln x = xy\frac{dy}{dx}$$

$$\int \frac{\ln x}{x}\,dx = \int y\,dy \Rightarrow \frac{\ln^2 x}{2} + C = \frac{y^2}{2}$$

At point, $(1, 0) \Rightarrow 0 + C = 0 \Rightarrow C = 0$

$$y = \pm \ln x$$

Example 20 *The equation of the curve such that the distance between the origin and the tangent line at an arbitrary point is equal to the distance between the origin and the normal at the same point is*

(a) $x^2 + y^2 = ce^{\arctan(y/x)}$
(b) $\sqrt{x^2 + y^2} = c \cdot e^{-\arctan(y/x)}$
(c) $\sqrt{x^2 + y^2} = c \cdot e^{\arctan(y/x)}$
(d) $x^2 + y^2 = c \cdot e^{\arctan(y/x)}$

Decoding the Question

We know that normal is a line perpendicular to the tangent at the point of contact.

Sol. (b, c) Equation of tangent $y - y_1 = m(x - x_1)$

$$\Rightarrow \quad mx - y + y_1 - mx_1 = 0$$

Equation of normal $y - y_1 = \frac{-1}{m}(x - x_1)$

$$my - my_1 + x - x_1 = 0$$
$$\Rightarrow \quad x + my - my_1 - x_1 = 0$$

$$\left|\frac{0 - 0 + y_1 - mx_1}{\sqrt{m^2 + 1}}\right| = \left|\frac{0 + 0 - my_1 - x_1}{\sqrt{1 + m^2}}\right|$$

$$y_1 - mx_1 = \pm(my_1 + x_1)$$

Taking positive sign, $y_1 - mx_1 = my_1 + x_1$

$$y_1 - x_1 = m(y_1 + x_1)$$

$$\Rightarrow \quad \frac{dy}{dx} = \frac{y/x - 1}{y/x + 1}$$

Put $\frac{y}{x} = t \Rightarrow y = tx$

$$\Rightarrow \quad \frac{dy}{dx} = t + x\frac{dt}{dx}$$

$$\Rightarrow \quad \frac{xdt}{dx} = \frac{t-1}{t+1} - t = \frac{t-1-t^2-t}{t+1}$$

$$\Rightarrow \quad \frac{t+1}{t^2+1}dt = \frac{-dx}{x}$$

$$\Rightarrow \quad \frac{1}{2}\ln(t^2+1) + \tan^{-1}t = -\ln x + \ln k$$

$$\Rightarrow \quad \tan^{-1}t = \frac{\ln k}{x} - \ln\sqrt{t^2+1}$$

$$\Rightarrow \quad \tan^{-1}t = \ln\frac{k}{x\sqrt{\frac{y^2+x^2}{x^2}}}$$

$$\Rightarrow \quad \tan^{-1}\frac{y}{x} = \ln\frac{k}{\sqrt{x^2+y^2}}$$

$$\Rightarrow \quad k = \sqrt{x^2+y^2}\,e^{\tan^{-1}\frac{y}{x}}$$

Now, taking negative sign,

$$y_1 - mx_1 = -my_1 - x_1$$

$$\Rightarrow \quad y_1 + x_1 = m(x_1 - y_1)$$

$$\Rightarrow \quad \frac{dy}{dx} = \frac{y/x+1}{1-y/x}$$

$$\Rightarrow \quad t + \frac{xdt}{dx} = \frac{t+1}{-t+1}$$

$$\Rightarrow \quad \frac{xdt}{dx} = \frac{t+1}{-t+1} - t = \frac{t+1-t+t^2}{1-t}$$

$$\Rightarrow \quad \frac{1-t}{1+t^2}dt = \frac{dx}{x}$$

$$\Rightarrow \quad \tan^{-1}t - \frac{1}{2}\ln(1+t^2) = \ln x + \ln k$$

$$\Rightarrow \quad \tan^{-1}t = \ln xk\sqrt{1+t^2}$$

$$\Rightarrow \quad \tan^{-1}\frac{y}{x} = \ln k\sqrt{x^2+y^2}$$

$$\Rightarrow \quad k\sqrt{x^2+y^2} = e^{\tan^{-1}\frac{y}{x}}$$

Example 21 *If function $y = f(x)$ satisfying the differential equation $\frac{dy}{dx}\cdot\sin x - y\cos x + \frac{\sin^2 x}{x^2} = 0$ is such that $y \to 0$ as $x \to \infty$, then which of the statement is correct?*

(a) $\lim_{x\to 0} f(x) = 1$

(b) $\int_0^{\pi/2} f(x)\,dx$ is less than $\frac{\pi}{2}$

(c) $\int_0^{\pi/2} f(x)dx$ is greater than unity

(d) $f(x)$ is an odd function.

Sol. (a, b, c) $\frac{dy}{dx} - y\cot x = \frac{-\sin x}{x^2}$

Integrating factor $= e^{-\int \cot x dx} = e^{-\ln \sin x} = \text{cosec } x$

$$\Rightarrow \quad y\,\text{cosec } x = \int \frac{-\sin x\,\text{cosec } x}{x^2}dx$$

$$\Rightarrow \quad \frac{y}{\sin x} = \frac{1}{x} + C$$

As $x \to \infty$; $y \to 0$

We have, $0 = 0 + C,\ C = 0$

$\Rightarrow y = \frac{\sin x}{x}$ is an even function

$$\lim_{x\to 0}\frac{\sin x}{x} = 1$$

$$\Rightarrow \quad f(0^{-1}) > f(x) > f\left(\frac{\pi}{2}\right)$$

$$\Rightarrow \quad 1 > \frac{\sin x}{x} > \frac{2}{\pi}$$

$$\Rightarrow \quad \int_0^{\pi/2} 1\,dx > \int_0^{\pi/2}\frac{\sin x}{x}dx > \int_0^{\pi/2}\frac{2}{\pi}dx$$

$$\Rightarrow \quad \frac{\pi}{2} > I > 1$$

Example 22 *If function $y = f(x)$ satisfies the differential equation $x^2\frac{dy}{dx} = y^2e^{1/x}(x \neq 0)$ and $\lim_{x\to 0^-} f(x) = 1$. Identify the correct statement(s)?*

(a) Range of $f(x)$ is $(0, 1) - \left\{\frac{1}{2}\right\}$

(b) $f(x)$ is bounded

(c) $\lim_{x\to 0^+} f(x) = 1$

(d) $\int_0^e f(x)\,dx > \int_0^1 f(x)\,dx$

Decoding the Question

A bounded function is a function that is bounded by some range, i.e. $a \le f(x) \le b$

Sol. (a, b, d) $\frac{x^2dy}{dx} = y^2e^{1/x}(x \neq 0)$

$$\Rightarrow \quad \int\frac{dy}{y^2} = \int\frac{1}{x^2}e^{1/x}dx$$

Let $\frac{1}{x} = t \Rightarrow \frac{-1}{x^2}dx = dt$

$$\frac{-1}{y} = \int e^t(-dt) = \frac{1}{y} = e^t + C$$

$$\Rightarrow \quad \frac{1}{y} = e^{1/x} + C$$

$$\lim_{x\to 0^-} f(x) = 1$$

$$\Rightarrow \quad \frac{1}{1} = e^{-\infty} + C$$

$$\Rightarrow \quad 1 = 0 + C$$

$$\frac{1}{y} = e^{1/x} + 1, \; y = \frac{1}{e^{1/x} + 1}$$

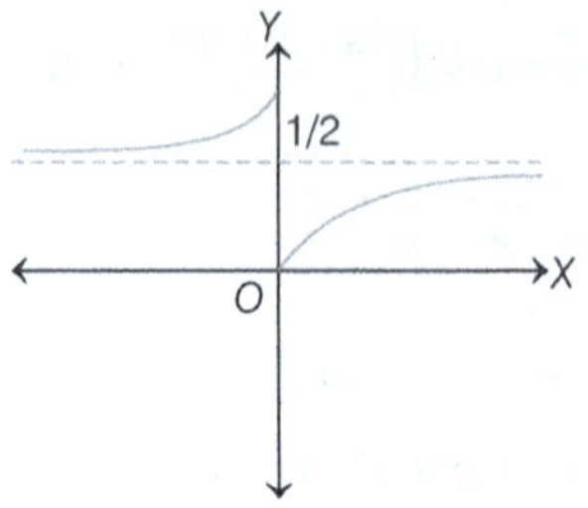

Range $(0, 1) - \left\{\frac{1}{2}\right\}$

Bounded $\lim_{x \to 0^+} f(x) = 0$

$$\int_0^e f(x)dx > \int_0^1 f(x)\,dx$$

True as RHS covers more area.

Example 23 *Let C be the family of curves $f(x, y, c) = 0$ (no member of C is X-axis) such that length of sub-normal at any point $P(x, y)$ on the curve C is equal to four times that of the length of sub-tangent at the same point. Which of the following statement(s) is (are) correct?*

(a) Equation of the line with position y-intercept passing through (4, 2) and perpendicular to the curve C is $x + 2y = 8$.
(b) Orthogonal trajectory of C is family of parallel lines having gradient ± 2.
(c) Order and degree of the differential equation of family of curves C are 1 and 2, respectively.
(d) Differential equation of family of curves is $2y' \pm x = 0$

Sol. (a, c) Given that

$$ym = 4\frac{y}{m} \Rightarrow m^2 = 4 \Rightarrow m = \pm 2$$

$$\Rightarrow \quad \frac{dy}{dx} = \pm 2 \Rightarrow y = \pm 2x + C$$

(a) $m = \pm\frac{1}{2} \Rightarrow y - 2 = \pm\frac{1}{2}(x - 4)$

$$2y - 4 = \pm(x - 4) \Rightarrow 2y = \pm(x - 4) + 4$$

Taking positive sign, $2y = x - 4 + 4 \Rightarrow x = 2y$

Taking negative sign, $2y = -x + 4 + 4$

$$\Rightarrow \quad x + 2y = 8$$

(b) Orthogonal $m = \pm\frac{1}{2}$

(c) $m = \pm 2 \Rightarrow m^2 = 4$

Order = 1 and degree = 2

(d) $\left(\frac{dy}{dx}\right)^2 = 4$

Passage Based Questions

Passage I

(Ex. Nos. 24 to 26)

A curve $y = f(x)$ satisfies the differential equation $(1 + x^2)\frac{dy}{dx} + 2yx = 4x^2$ and passes through the origin.

Example 24 *The function $y = f(x)$*

(a) is strictly increasing, $\forall\, x \in R$
(b) is such that it has a minima but no maxima
(c) is such that it has a maxima but no minima
(d) has no inflection point

Example 25 *The area enclosed by $y = f^{-1}(x)$, the X-axis and the ordinate at $x = 2/3$ is*

(a) $2\ln 2$ (b) $\frac{4}{3}\ln 2$ (c) $\frac{2}{3}\ln 2$ (d) $\frac{1}{3}\ln 2$

Example 26 *For the function $y = f(x)$ which one of the following does not hold good?*

(a) $f(x)$ is a rational function
(b) $f(x)$ has the same domain and same range
(c) $f(x)$ is a transcendental function
(d) $y = f(x)$ is a bijective mapping

Sol. (Q. Nos. 24 to 26)

$$\frac{dy}{dx} + \left(\frac{2x}{1 + x^2}\right)y = \frac{4x^2}{1 + x^2}$$

$$\text{IF} = e^{\int \frac{2x}{1+x^2}dx} = e^{\ln(1 + x^2)} = (1 + x^2)$$

$$\therefore \quad y(1 + x^2) = \int 4x^2\,dx = \frac{4x^3}{3} + C$$

Passing through $(0, 0) \Rightarrow C = 0$

$$\therefore \quad y = \frac{4x^3}{3(1 + x^2)}$$

$$\frac{dy}{dx} = \frac{4}{3}\left[\frac{(1 + x^2)3x^2 - x^3 \cdot 2x}{(1 + x^2)^2}\right]$$

$$= \frac{4}{3}\left[\frac{3x^2 + x^4}{(1 + x^2)^2}\right] = \frac{4x^2(3 + x^2)}{3(1 + x^2)^2}$$

Hence, $\frac{dy}{dx} > 0, \forall\, x \neq 0; \frac{dy}{dx} = 0$ at $x = 0$

and it does not change sign $\Rightarrow x = 0$ is the point of inflection. $y = f(x)$ is increasing for all $x \in R$.

$$x \to \infty;\; y \to \infty;\; x \to -\infty;\; y \to -\infty$$

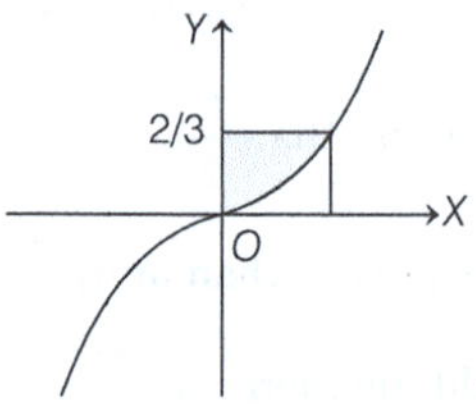

Area enclosed by $y = f^{-1}(x)$, X-axis and ordinate at $x = \frac{2}{3}$

$$A = \frac{2}{3} - \frac{4}{3}\int_0^1 \frac{x^3}{1+x^2}\,dx$$

Put $\quad 1 + x^2 = t \Rightarrow 2x\,dx = dt$

$$A = \frac{2}{3} - \frac{2}{3}\int_1^2 \frac{(t-1)}{t}\,dt$$

$$= \frac{2}{3} - \frac{2}{3}\int_1^2 \left(1 - \frac{1}{t}\right) dt$$

$$= \frac{2}{3} - \frac{2}{3}[t - \ln t]_1^2 = \frac{2}{3} - \frac{2}{3}[(2 - \ln 2) - 1]$$

$$= \frac{2}{3} - \frac{2}{3}[1 - \ln 2] = \frac{2}{3}\ln 2$$

Ans. 24. (a) **25.** (c) **26.** (c)

Stem Based Questions

Stem I

(Q. Nos. 27 to 28)

$y = f_1(x)$ and $y = f_2(x)$ are two solutions of the equation $ydx + dy = -e^x y^2 dy$, where $f_1(0) = 1$ and $f_2(0) = -1$.

The number of solution of the equation $f_1(x) \cdot f_2(x) + x^2 = 0$ is $\frac{100}{M}$ and the area enclosed by $y = f_1(x)$, $y = e^x$ and the X-axis is A_1 and $y = f_2(x)$, $y = -e^x$ and the X-axis is A_2.

Example 27 *The value of M is ....*

Sol. (100) $ydx + dy = -e^x y^2 dy$

$$\Rightarrow \quad \frac{ydx + dy}{e^x y^2} = -dy$$

$$\Rightarrow \quad \frac{e^{-x}}{y}dx + e^{-x}\frac{dy}{y^2} = -dy \Rightarrow -d\left(\frac{e^{-x}}{y}\right) = -dy$$

$$\Rightarrow \quad \int d\left(\frac{e^{-x}}{y}\right) = \int dy \Rightarrow \frac{e^{-x}}{y} = y + C$$

$$\therefore \quad f_1(x) = e^{-x/2} \text{ and } f_2(x) = -e^{-x/2}$$

$$[\because f_1(0) = 1 \text{ and } f_2(0) = -1]$$

$$f_1(x) \cdot f_2(x) + x^2 = 0$$

$$\Rightarrow \quad e^{-x/2} \cdot (-e^{-x/2}) + x^2 = 0$$

$$\Rightarrow \quad -e^{-x} + x^2 = 0$$

$$\Rightarrow \quad x^2 = e^{-x}$$

$$\Rightarrow \quad x^2 e^x = 1$$

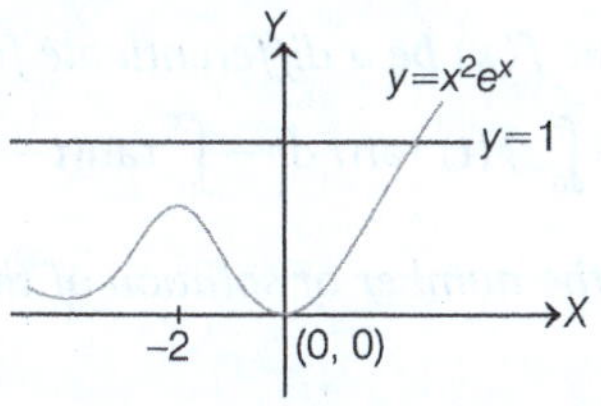

Both curves intersect each other at only one point.

$$\therefore \quad \frac{100}{M} = 1$$

$$\Rightarrow \quad M = 100$$

Example 28 *The value of $A_1 + A_2$ is ....*

Sol. (6) Area enclosed by $y = f_1(x)$, $y = e^x$ and the X-axis.

$$A_1 = \int_{-\infty}^0 e^x dx + \int_0^\infty e^{-x/2} dx$$

$$= [e^x]_{-\infty}^0 + [-2e^{-x/2}]_0^\infty$$

$$= 1 - 0 - 2(0 - 1) = 3$$

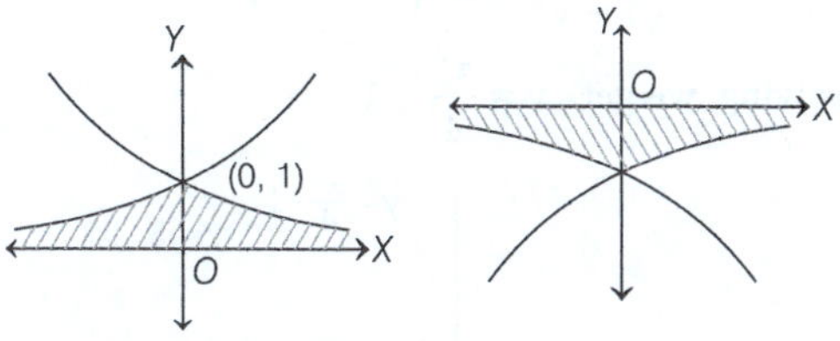

$$A_2 = \left| \int_{-\infty}^0 (-e^x)\,dx + \int_0^\infty \left(-e^{\frac{-x}{2}}\right) dx \right|$$

$$= \left| [-e^x]_{-\infty}^0 - \left[\frac{e^{-x/2}}{-1/2}\right]_0^\infty \right|$$

$$= |-(e^0 - e^{-\infty}) + 2(e^{-\infty} - e^{-0})|$$

$$= |-(1 - 0) + 2(0 - 1)|$$

$$= |-1 - 2| = |-3|$$

$$\therefore \quad A_1 + A_2 = 3 + 3 = 6$$

Single Integer Answer Type Questions

Example 29 *Let $y = f(x)$ be a curve passing through (4, 3) such that slope of normal at any point lying in the first quadrant is negative and the normal and tangent at any point P cuts the Y-axis at A and B respectively such that the mid-point of AB is origin, then the number of solutions of $y = f(x)$ and $y = |5 - |x||$, is*

Sol. (2) Equation of tangent at any point (x_1, y_1) of curve

$y = f(x)$ is $(y - y_1) = f'(x_1)(x - x_1)$, so $B(0, y_1 - x_1 f'(x_1))$

Equation of normal at (x_1, y_1) is $(y - y_1) = -\frac{1}{f'(x_1)}(x - x_1)$

so, $A = \left(0, y_1 + \frac{x_1}{f'(x_1)}\right)$ mid-point of AB is origin, so

$$2y_1 - x_1\left(f'(x_1) - \frac{1}{f'(x_1)}\right) = 0$$

Thus, differential equation of curve $y = f(x)$, is

$$x\left(\frac{dy}{dx}\right)^2 - 2y\frac{dy}{dx} - x = 0$$

Thus, $\dfrac{dy}{dx} = \dfrac{y \pm \sqrt{x^2 + y^2}}{x}$

In first quadrant, $x > 0, y > 0, \dfrac{dy}{dx} > 0$,

So, $\dfrac{dy}{dx} = \dfrac{y + \sqrt{x^2 + y^2}}{x}$,

Put $y = vx$,

$\Rightarrow \quad v + x\dfrac{dv}{dx} = \dfrac{vx + x\sqrt{1 + v^2}}{x}$

$\Rightarrow \quad \displaystyle\int \frac{dv}{\sqrt{1 + v^2}} = \int \frac{dx}{x}$

on solving, we get $y = \dfrac{x^2}{4} - 1$

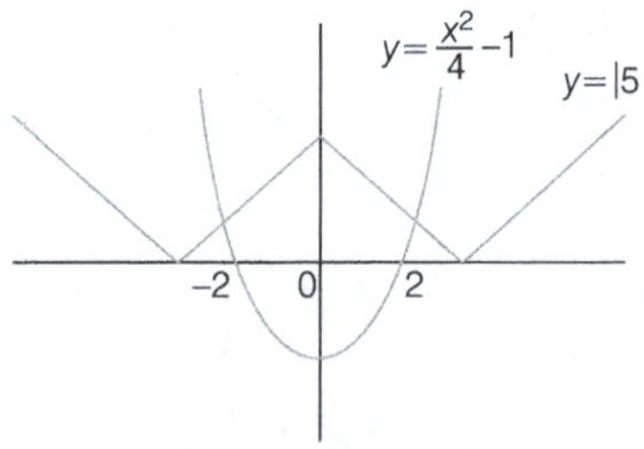

$\therefore$ Number of solutions for $y = f(x)$ and $y = |5 - |x||$

$\therefore$ Number of solutions are 2.

Example 30 *A real valued function, $f(x)$, $f : \left(0, \dfrac{\pi}{2}\right) \to R^+$ satisfies the differential equation $xf'(x) = 1 + f(x)\{x^2 f(x) - 1\}$ and $f\left(\dfrac{\pi}{4}\right) = \dfrac{4}{\pi}$, then $\lim\limits_{x \to 0} f(x)$, is*

Sol. (1) Here, $xf'(x) = 1 + x^2 f^2(x) - f(x)$

$\Rightarrow \quad \dfrac{x\, f'(x) + f(x)}{1 + x^2 f^2(x)} = 1$

Integrating both sides, we get

$$\int \frac{(x\, f'(x) + f(x))dx}{1 + (x\, f(x))^2} = x + C$$

$\Rightarrow \quad \tan^{-1}(xf(x)) = x + C$, as $f\left(\dfrac{\pi}{4}\right) = \dfrac{4}{\pi}$.

$\Rightarrow \quad \tan^{-1} 1 = \dfrac{\pi}{4} + C$

$\Rightarrow \quad C = 0$

$\therefore \quad x\, f(x) = \tan x$

$\Rightarrow \quad f(x) = \dfrac{\tan x}{x}$

and $\quad \lim\limits_{x \to 0} f(x) = \lim\limits_{x \to 0} \dfrac{\tan x}{x} = 1$

Example 31 *If the area bounded by $y = f(x)$, $x = \dfrac{1}{2}$, $x = \dfrac{\sqrt{3}}{2}$ and the X-axis is A sq units, where $f(x) = x + \dfrac{2}{3}x^3 + \dfrac{2}{3}\cdot\dfrac{4}{5}x^5 + \dfrac{2}{3}\cdot\dfrac{4}{5}\cdot\dfrac{6}{7}x^7 + \ldots \infty$, $|x| < 1$, then the value of $[4A]$ is (where $[\cdot]$ is G.I.F)*

Sol. (1) Here, $f'(x) = 1 + 2x^2 + \dfrac{2}{3}\cdot 4x^4 + \dfrac{2}{3}\cdot\dfrac{4}{5}\cdot 6x^6 + \ldots \infty$

$= 1 + x\left(\dfrac{d}{dx}(xf(x))\right)$

$\Rightarrow \quad f'(x) = 1 + x\,|xf'(x) + f(x)|$

$\Rightarrow (1 - x^2)f'(x) = 1 + xf(x)$

$\Rightarrow \quad \dfrac{dy}{dx} - \dfrac{x}{1 - x^2}\cdot y = \dfrac{1}{1 - x^2}$,

$\text{IF} = e^{\int \frac{-x}{1-x^2}dx} = e^{\frac{1}{2}\log|1 - x^2|} = \sqrt{1 - x^2}$

$\therefore \quad y \cdot \sqrt{1 - x^2} = \displaystyle\int \frac{1}{1 - x^2}\cdot\sqrt{1 - x^2}\,dx + C$

$\Rightarrow \quad y\sqrt{1 - x^2} = \sin^{-1} x + C$,

As, $f(0) = 0 \Rightarrow C = 0$

$\Rightarrow \quad y = \dfrac{\sin^{-1} x}{\sqrt{1 - x^2}}$

$\Rightarrow \quad A = \displaystyle\int_{1/2}^{\sqrt{3}/2} \frac{\sin^{-1} x}{\sqrt{1 - x^2}}dx = \int_{\pi/6}^{\pi/3} t\,dt = \left(\frac{t^2}{2}\right)_{\frac{\pi}{6}}^{\frac{\pi}{3}}$

$= \dfrac{1}{2}\left[\dfrac{\pi^2}{9} - \dfrac{\pi^2}{36}\right]$

$\therefore \quad [4A] = 1$

Example 32 *If $y = f(x)$ satisfies the differential equation $(1 + x^2)f'(x) = x(1 - f(x))$, $f(0) = \dfrac{4}{3}$, then find the value of $f(\sqrt{8}) + \dfrac{8}{9}$.*

Sol. (2) $f'(x) + \dfrac{x}{1 + x^2}\cdot f(x) = \dfrac{x}{1 + x^2}$

$\text{IF} = \sqrt{1 + x^2}$

$\therefore \quad f(x) = 1 + \dfrac{1}{3\sqrt{1 + x^2}}$

$\therefore \quad f(\sqrt{8}) + \dfrac{8}{9} = 2$

Example 33 *Let $f(x)$ be a differentiable function satisfying $f(x) + \int_0^x f(t)\tan t\,dt - \int_0^x \tan(t - x)dt = 0$ $\left(|x| < \dfrac{\pi}{2}\right)$. Find the number of solution of the equation $f(x) = 0$.*

Sol. (1) $f(x)+\int_0^x f(t)\tan t\,dt - \int_0^x \underbrace{\tan(t-x)}_{\text{using king property}} dt = 0$

$$f(x)+\int_0^x f(t)\tan t\,dt + \int_0^x \tan t\,dt = 0$$

Differentiable w.r.t. x, we get

$$f'(x)+(f(x)+1)\tan x = 0$$

$$\Rightarrow \quad \frac{f'(x)}{f(x)+1}+\tan x = 0$$

Integrate w.r.t. x, we get

$$\ln(f(x)+1)+\ln(\sec x) = C$$

$$\Rightarrow \quad f(0)=0 \Rightarrow C=0$$

Hence, $\dfrac{(f(x)+1)}{\cos x} = 1$

$\Rightarrow \quad f(x) = \cos x - 1$

$\therefore \quad f(x) = 0$

$\Rightarrow \quad \cos x = 1$

$\Rightarrow \quad x = 2n\pi, n \in I$

Number of solution is 1.

Example 34 *A function $y=f(x)$ satisfies $xf'(x)-2f(x)=x^4 f^2(x), \forall\, x>0$ and $f(1)=-6$. Find the value of $f'(3^{1/5})$.*

Sol. (8) Given, $\dfrac{xdy}{dx}-2y = x^4y^2$ or $\dfrac{dy}{dx}-\dfrac{2}{x}y = x^3y^2$

Now, dividing by y^2, we get

$$\frac{1}{y^2}\frac{dy}{dx}-\frac{2}{y}\frac{1}{x} = x^3 \quad \text{...(i)}$$

This is a Bernoulli's differential equation, substituting $\dfrac{-2}{y}=t$, we get

$$\frac{2}{y^2}\frac{dy}{dx} = \frac{dt}{dx}$$

So, Eq. (i) becomes,

$$\frac{1}{2}\frac{dt}{dx}+\frac{t}{x} = x^3 \Rightarrow \frac{dt}{dx}+\frac{2}{x}t = 2x^3$$

$$\text{IF} = e^{\int \frac{2}{x}dx} = e^{2\ln x} = e^{\ln x^2} = x^2$$

So, general solution is given by

$$x^2 t = \frac{2x^6}{6}+C \Rightarrow \frac{-2}{y} = \frac{x^4}{3}+\frac{C}{x^2}$$

If $x=1, y=-6 \Rightarrow C=0$

$$\therefore \quad \frac{-2}{y} = \frac{x^4}{3} \Rightarrow y = \frac{-6}{x^4}, f(x) = \frac{-6}{x^4}$$

Now, $\dfrac{dy}{dx} = 24x^{-5} = \dfrac{24}{x^5}$

Hence, $\left.\dfrac{dy}{dx}\right]_{x=3^{1/5}} = \dfrac{24}{3} = 8$

Example 35 *Let c_1 and c_2 be two curves which satisfies the differential equation $\left|x-y\cdot\dfrac{dx}{dy}\right| = 2\left|\dfrac{dy}{dx}\right|$ and passes through (1, 1). If the area enclosed by curves c_1, c_2 and coordinates axes is $\dfrac{m}{n}(m, n \in N)$, then find the least value of $(m+n)$.*

Sol. (9) We have, $\left|x-y\cdot\dfrac{dx}{dy}\right| = 2\left|\dfrac{dy}{dx}\right|$

$$\Rightarrow \quad x-y\frac{dx}{dy} = \pm 2\frac{dy}{dx}$$

Taking positive sign,

$$2\left(\frac{dy}{dx}\right)^2 - x\left(\frac{dy}{dx}\right)+y = 0$$

$$\Rightarrow \quad \frac{dy}{dx} = \frac{x \pm \sqrt{x^2-8y}}{4}$$

But no solution exist, as it does not pass through (1, 1).

Now, taking negative sign,

$$2\left(\frac{dy}{dx}\right)^2 + x\left(\frac{dy}{dx}\right)-y = 0 \Rightarrow \frac{dy}{dx} = \frac{-x \pm \sqrt{x^2+8y}}{4}$$

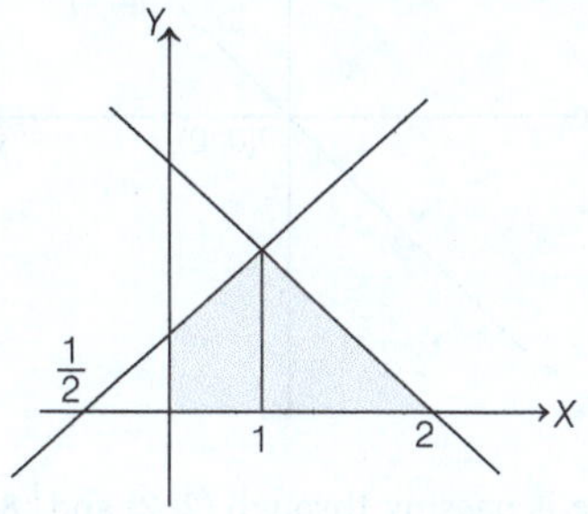

Let $x^2+8y = v^2 \Rightarrow 2x+8\dfrac{dy}{dx} = 2v\dfrac{dv}{dx}$

So, $\quad v\dfrac{dv}{dx}-x = -x \pm v$

$\Rightarrow \quad \dfrac{dv}{dx} = \pm 1$

$\Rightarrow \quad v = \pm x + C$

$\Rightarrow \quad \sqrt{x^2+8y} = \pm x + C$

So, curves are $\sqrt{x^2+8y} = x+2$

and $\quad \sqrt{x^2+8y} = (4-x)$

On squaring, we get

$$2y = x+1$$

and $\quad x+y = 2$

$\therefore$ Clearly, required area $= \dfrac{3}{4}+\dfrac{1}{2} = \dfrac{5}{4} = \dfrac{m}{n}$ (given)

So, least value of $(m+n) = 5+4 = 9$

Numerical Value Type Questions

Example 36 *Let $y = f(x)$ be a curve c_1 passing through $(2, 2)$ and $\left(8, \frac{1}{2}\right)$ and satisfying a differential equation $y\left(\frac{d^2y}{dx^2}\right) = 2\left(\frac{dy}{dx}\right)^2$. Curve c_2 is the director circle of the circle $x^2 + y^2 = 2$. If the shortest distance between the curves c_1 and c_2 is $\sqrt{p} - q$, where $p, q \in N$, then find the value of $(p^2 - q)$.*

Sol. (62) Given, $y\left(\frac{d^2y}{dx^2}\right) = 2\left(\frac{dy}{dx}\right)^2 \Rightarrow \frac{y''}{y'} = \frac{2y'}{y}$

$$\Rightarrow \quad \ln y' = 2\ln y + \ln a \Rightarrow \frac{y'}{y^2} = a$$

$$\Rightarrow \quad \int \frac{dy}{y^2} = \int a\,dx \Rightarrow \frac{-1}{y} = ax + b$$

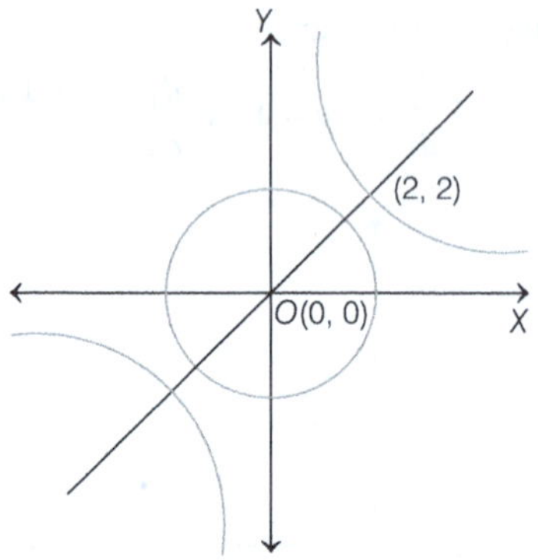

Since, curve is passing through (2, 2) and $\left(8, \frac{1}{2}\right)$, so

$$2a + b = \frac{-1}{2} \quad \text{...(i)}$$

$$8a + b = -2 \quad \text{...(ii)}$$

$\therefore$ On solving Eqs. (i) and (ii), we get

$$a = \frac{-1}{4} \text{ and } b = 0$$

Hence, $c_1 : xy = 4$ and curve c_2 is $x^2 + y^2 = 2$

$\therefore$ Shortest distance between c_1 and c_2 is

$$= 2\sqrt{2} - 2 = \sqrt{8} - 2$$

Hence, $(p^2 - q) = 64 - 2 = 62$

Example 37 *A function $y = f(x)$ satisfies $f''(x) = \frac{-1}{x^2} - \pi^2 \sin(\pi x)$ such that $f'(2) = \pi + \frac{1}{2}$ and $f(1) = 0$, if $I = \int_0^1 f(x)\,dx$, then the value of $16\pi(I + 1)$ is ....*

Sol. (32) $f'(x) = \frac{1}{x} + \pi\cos(\pi x) + C$

$$f'(2) = \frac{1}{2} + \pi + C = \frac{1}{2} + \pi \Rightarrow C = 0$$

$$\therefore \quad f(x) = \ln|x| + \sin(\pi x)$$

Now, $I = \int_0^1 (\ln|x| + \sin \pi x)\,dx$

$$= [x \ln x - x]_0^1 - \left[\frac{1}{\pi}\cos \pi x\right]_0^1$$

$$I = -1 + \frac{2}{\pi}$$

$\therefore \pi(I + 1) = 2$

$16\pi(I + 1) = 16 \times 2 = 32$

Example 38 *If solution of the differential equation $\frac{dy}{dx} + \frac{\cos x(3\cos y - 7\sin x - 3)}{\sin y(3\sin x - 7\cos y + 7)} = 0$ is $(\sin x + \cos y - 1)^{\lambda}(\sin x - \cos y + 1)^{\mu} = c$, where c is arbitrary constant, then find the value of $\lambda^2 + \mu^2$.*

Sol. (29) Since, $\sin y(3\sin x - 7\cos y + 7)dy$

$$+ \cos x(3\cos y - 7\sin x - 3)\,dx = 0$$

$\Rightarrow \sin y[(5 - 2)\sin x - (5 + 2)\cos y + (5 + 2)]dy$

$+ \cos x[(5 - 2)\cos y - (5 + 2)\sin x - (5 - 2)]dx = 0$

$\Rightarrow 5\sin y(\sin x - \cos y + 1)dy + 5\cos x \times (\cos y - \sin x - 1)dx$
$- 2\sin y(\sin x + \cos y - 1)$
$dy - 2\cos x(\cos y + \sin x - 1)dx = 0$

$\Rightarrow 5(\sin x - \cos y + 1)(\sin y\,dy - \cos x\,dx)$
$-2(\sin x + \cos y - 1)(\sin y\,dy + \cos x\,dx) = 0$

$$\Rightarrow \quad \frac{5(\cos x\,dx - \sin y\,dy)}{(\sin x + \cos y - 1)} + \frac{2(\cos x\,dx + \sin y\,dy)}{(\sin x - \cos y + 1)} = 0$$

On integrating, we get

$5\ln(\sin x + \cos y - 1) + 2\ln(\sin x - \cos y + 1) = \ln c$

$\Rightarrow \quad (\sin x + \cos y - 1)^5(\sin x - \cos y + 1)^2 = c$

$\therefore \quad \lambda = 5$ and $\mu = 2$

$\lambda^2 + \mu^2 = (5)^2 + (2)^2 = 29$

Example 39 *Let $f : R^+ \to R$ be a differentiable function satisfying $f(x) = e + (1 - x)\ln\left(\frac{x}{e}\right) + \int_1^x f(t)\,dt \;\forall\; x \in R$. If the area enclosed by the curve $g(x) = x(f(x) - e^x)$ lying in the fourth quadrant is A, then find the value of $|A|$.*

Sol. (0.25) We have, $f(x) = e + (1 - x)\ln\left(\frac{x}{e}\right) + \int_1^x f(t)dt$ ...(i)

Differentiable both sides w.r.t. x, we get

$$f'(x) = (1 - x)\frac{1}{x} + \ln\left(\frac{x}{e}\right)(-1) + f(x)$$

$$\Rightarrow \quad f'(x) - f(x) = \left(\frac{1}{x} - 1 - \ln\left(\frac{x}{e}\right)\right)$$

On multiplying both sides by e^{-x}, we get

$$e^{-x} f'(x) - e^{-x} f(x) = e^{-x}\left(\frac{1}{x} - 1 - \ln\left(\frac{x}{e}\right)\right)$$

$$\Rightarrow \quad \frac{d}{dx}(e^{-x} \cdot f(x)) = e^{-x}\left(\frac{1}{x} - 1 - \ln\left(\frac{x}{e}\right)\right)$$

On integrating both sides w.r.t. x, we get

$$e^{-x} f(x) = \int e^{-x}\left(\frac{1}{x} - \ln x\right) dx$$

$$= e^{-x} \ln x + C$$

$$\Rightarrow \quad f(x) = \ln x + Ce^{x} \quad \text{...(ii)}$$

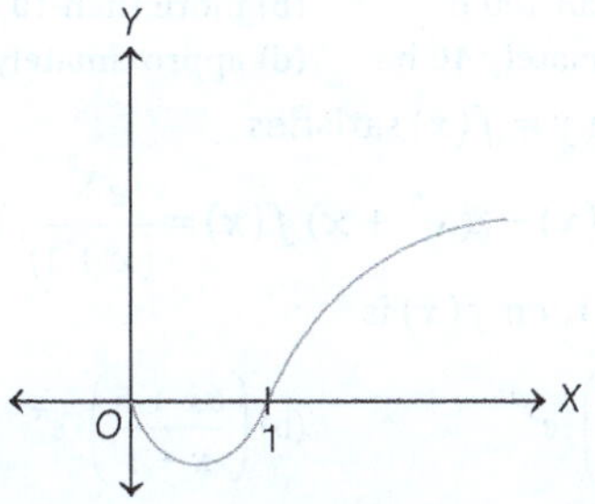

Now, putting $x = 1$ in Eq. (i) we get

$$f(1) = e \quad \text{...(iii)}$$

Using Eqs. (ii) and (iii), we get

$$C = 1$$

Thus, $\quad f(x) = e^{x} + \ln x$

Hence, $g(x) = x \ln x$;

Now, $\quad A = \int_0^1 x \ln x dx = -\frac{1}{4}$

$$|A| = \frac{1}{4} = 0.25$$

Example 40 *Let f be a differentiable function on R and satisfying $f(x) = -(x^2 - x + 1)\, e^{x} + \int_0^x e^{x-y},\, f'(y)\, dy$. If $f(1) + f'(1) + f''(1) = ke$, where $k \in N$, then find $k^2 - 1$.*

Sol. (80) Given, $f(x) = e^{x} \cdot \left[\int_0^x e^{-y} f'(y)\, dy - (x^2 - x + 1)\right]$ ...(i)

Differentiating both the sides, we get

$$f'(x) = e^{x} \cdot e^{-x} \cdot f'(x) +$$
$$e^{x} \int_0^x e^{-y} \cdot f'(y)\, dy - [(x^2 - x + 1)e^{x} + e^{x}(2x - 1)]$$

$$f'(x) = f'(x) + \int_0^x e^{x-y} \cdot f'(y)\, dy - e^{x}(x^2 + x)$$

$$\Rightarrow \quad 0 = f(x) + (x^2 - x + 1)e^{x} - e^{x}(x^2 + x)$$

[substituting $\int_0^x e^{x-y} f'(y) dy = f(x) + (x^2 - x + 1)e^{x}$ from Eq. (i)]

$$f(x) = e^{x}(x^2 + x - x^2 + x - 1)$$

$$\therefore \quad f(x) = e^{x} \cdot (2x - 1) \Rightarrow f(1) = e$$

Also, $\quad f'(x) = e^{x} \cdot 2 + (2x - 1)e^{x}$

$$\Rightarrow \quad f'(1) = 2e + e = 3e$$

And $\quad f''(x) = 2e^{x} + (2x\ 1)e^{x} + 2e^{x}$

$$\Rightarrow \quad f''(1) = 2e + e + 2e = 5e$$

Hence, $\quad f(1) + f'(1) + f'(1) = 9e$

$$\Rightarrow \quad k = 9$$

$$\because \quad k^2 - 1 = (9)^2 - 1 = 80$$

EXERCISE 1

JEE Main Pattern

Single Option Correct Type Questions

1. A curve passes through the point $\left(1, \frac{\pi}{4}\right)$ and its slope at any point is given by $\frac{y}{x} - \cos^2\left(\frac{y}{x}\right)$. Then, the curve has the equation

(a) $y = x\tan^{-1}\left(\ln \frac{e}{x}\right)$ (b) $y = x\tan^{-1}(\ln 2)$

(c) $y = \frac{1}{x}\tan^{-1}\left(\ln \frac{e}{x}\right)$ (d) None of these

2. A curve is such that the area of the region bounded by the coordinate axes, the curve and the ordinate of any point on it is equal to the cube of that ordinate. The curve represents

(a) a pair of straight lines (b) a circle

(c) a parabola (d) an ellipse

3. The value of the constant 'm' and 'c' for which $y = mx + c$ is a solution of the differential equation $D^2y - 3Dy - 4y = -4x$.

(a) is $m = -1; c = 3/4$ (b) is $m = 1; c = -3/4$

(c) no such real m, c (d) is $m = 1; c = 3/4$

4. The real value of m for which the substitution, $y = u^m$ will transform the differential equation, $2x^4 y\frac{dy}{dx} + y^4 = 4x^6$ into a homogeneous equation is

(a) $m = 0$ (b) $m = 1$

(c) $m = 3/2$ (d) No value of m

5. The solution of the differential equation,

$$x^2\frac{dy}{dx}\cdot\cos\frac{1}{x} - y\sin\frac{1}{x} = -1,$$

where $y \to -1$ as $x \to \infty$ is

(a) $y = \sin\frac{1}{x} - \cos\frac{1}{x}$ (b) $y = \frac{x+1}{x\sin\frac{1}{x}}$

(c) $y = \sin\frac{1}{x} + \cos\frac{1}{x}$ (d) $y = \frac{x+1}{x\cos\frac{1}{x}}$

6. A wet porous substance in the open air loses its moisture at a rate proportional to the moisture content. If a sheet hung in the wind loses half its moisture during the first hour, then the time when it would have lost 99.9% of its moisture is (weather conditions remaining same)

(a) more than 100 h (b) more than 10 h

(c) approximately 10 h (d) approximately 9 h

7. A function $y = f(x)$ satisfies

$$(x+1)\cdot f'(x) - 2(x^2 + x)\, f(x) = \frac{e^{x^2}}{(x+1)}, \forall\, x > -1.$$

If $f(0) = 5$, then $f(x)$ is

(a) $\left(\frac{3x+5}{x+1}\right)\cdot e^{x^2}$ (b) $\left(\frac{6x+5}{x+1}\right)\cdot e^{x^2}$

(c) $\left(\frac{6x+5}{(x+1)^2}\right)\cdot e^{x^2}$ (d) $\left(\frac{5-6x}{x+1}\right)\cdot e^{x^2}$

8. The substitution $y = z^\alpha$ transforms the differential equation $(x^2y^2 - 1)\,dy + 2xy^3\,dx = 0$ into a homogeneous differential equation for

(a) $\alpha = -1$ (b) 0 (c) $\alpha = 1$ (d) No value of α

9. Suppose that the quadratic function $f(x) = ax^2 + bx + c$ is non-negative on the interval $[-1, 1]$. Then, the area under the graph of f over the interval $[-1, 1]$ and the X-axis is given by the formula

(a) $A = f(-1) + f(1)$

(b) $A = f\left(-\frac{1}{2}\right) + f\left(\frac{1}{2}\right)$

(c) $A = \frac{1}{2}[f(-1) + 2f(0) + f(1)]$

(d) $A = \frac{1}{3}[f(-1) + 4f(0) + f(1))]$

10. Let $y'(x) + \frac{g'(x)}{g(x)}\cdot y(x) = \frac{g'(x)}{1 + g^2(x)}$, where $f'(x)$ denotes $\frac{df(x)}{dx}$ and $g(x)$ is a given non-constant differentiable function an R. If $g(1) = y(1) = 1$ and $g(e) = \sqrt{(2e-1)}$, then $y(e)$ equals

(a) $\frac{3}{2g(e)}$ (b) $\frac{1}{2g(e)}$ (c) $\frac{1}{g(e)}$ (d) $\frac{2}{3g(e)}$

11. A function $y = f(x)$ satisfies the equation
$$x = \frac{dy}{dx} - \frac{1}{2}\left(\frac{dy}{dx}\right)^2 + \frac{1}{3}\left(\frac{dy}{dx}\right)^3 - \ldots \infty \text{ and } y(0') = 1,\ x \le \ln 2,$$
then the value of $f'\left(\ln\frac{1}{2}\right) + f\left(\ln\frac{1}{2}\right)$ is equal to

(a) $-\ln 2$ (b) $\ln 2$
(c) $1 + \ln 2$ (d) $1 - \ln 2$

12. If the differential equation of a curve, passing through $\left(0, -\frac{\pi}{4}\right)$ and $(t, 0)$ is $\cos y\left(\frac{dy}{dx} + e^{-x}\right) + \sin y\left(e^{-x} - \frac{dy}{dx}\right) = e^{e^{-x}}$, then the value of $t \cdot e^{e^{-t}}$ is

(a) -1 (b) 1
(c) 2 (d) -2

13. Let f be a twice differentiable function satisfying $\frac{e^x f''(x) - e^x f'(x)}{e^{2x}} = 1$ and $f(0) = 0$, $f'(0) = 1$, then the value of $\int_0^1 \frac{f(x)}{x}\, dx$ is

(a) e (b) $e - 1$ (c) 1 (d) 0

14. Solution to the differential equation,
$$\frac{x + \frac{x^3}{3!} + \frac{x^5}{5!} + \ldots}{1 + \frac{x^2}{2!} + \frac{x^4}{4!} + \ldots} = \frac{dx - dy}{dx + dy} \text{ is}$$
(a) $2ye^{2x} = c \cdot e^{2x} + 1$ (b) $2ye^{2x} = c \cdot e^{2x} - 1$
(c) $ye^{2x} = c \cdot e^{2x} + 2$ (d) $2xe^{2y} = c \cdot e^{x} - 1$

15. It conic C satisfies the differential equation $(1 + y^2)\, dx - xydy = 0$ and passes through the point $(1, 0)$. An ellipse E which is confocal with C has its eccentric $\sqrt{2/3}$. The angle of intersection of the curves C and E is

(a) $\frac{\pi}{6}$ (b) $\frac{\pi}{4}$ (c) $\frac{\pi}{3}$ (d) $\frac{\pi}{2}$

16. Let $y = y(x)$ be the solution of the differential equation $\sin x \frac{dy}{dx} + y \cos x = 4x$, $x \in (0, \pi)$. If $y\left(\frac{\pi}{2}\right) = 0$, then $y\left(\frac{\pi}{6}\right)$ is equal to

(a) $\frac{4}{9\sqrt{3}}\pi^2$ (b) $\frac{-8}{9\sqrt{3}}\pi^2$ (c) $-\frac{8}{9}\pi^2$ (d) $-\frac{4}{9}\pi^2$

17. If a curve $y = f(x)$ passes through the point $(1, -1)$ and satisfies the differential equation,
$y(1 + xy)dx = x\, dy$, then $f\left(-\frac{1}{2}\right)$ is equal to

(a) $-\frac{2}{5}$ (b) $-\frac{4}{5}$ (c) $\frac{2}{5}$ (d) $\frac{4}{5}$

18. Let $y(x)$ be the solution of the differential equation $(x \log x)\frac{dy}{dx} + y = 2x \log x, (x \ge 1)$. Then, $y(e)$ is equal to

(a) e (b) 0 (c) 2 (d) $2e$

19. If $y\frac{dy}{dx} = x\left[\frac{y^2}{x^2} + \frac{\phi\left(\frac{y^2}{x^2}\right)}{\phi'\left(\frac{y^2}{x^2}\right)}\right]$, $x > 0$, $\phi > 0$ and $y(1) = -1$,

then $\phi\left(\frac{y^2}{4}\right)$ is equal to

(a) $4\phi(2)$ (b) $4\phi(1)$ (c) $2\phi(1)$ (d) $\phi(1)$

20. The curve such that the square of the intercept cut by any tangent of the Y-axis is equal to the product of the coordinates of the point of tangency, is

(a) $\sqrt{\frac{y}{x}} + \log x = C$ (b) $\sqrt{\frac{y}{x}} - \log x = C$
(c) $2\sqrt{\frac{y}{x}} + \log x = C$ (d) $2\sqrt{\frac{y}{x}} - \log x = C$

Numerical Value Type Questions

21. The general solution of the differential equation $(2x^2y - 2y^4)\, dx + (2x^3 + 3xy^3)\, dy = 0$ if curve passes through (1, 1), then the constant of integration is ....

22. Slope of the tangent at any point (x, y) on the curve $y = f(x)$ is $\frac{y}{x^2}$ and the curve passes through the point (1, 3), then $\lim_{x \to \infty} f(x) = ke$, where k is ....

23. Let $f(x)$ be a differentiable function and satisfy $f(0) = 2$, $f'(0) = 3$ and $f''(x) = f(x)$. If the value of $f(x)$ at $x = \ln 2$ is k, then the value of $\frac{[k]}{8}$ is ....

(where $[\cdot]$ denotes the greatest integer function)

24. Let $y = y(x)$ be solution of the differential equation $\log\left(\frac{dy}{dx}\right) = 3x + 4y$, with $y(0) = 0$. If $y\left(-\frac{2}{3}\log 2\right) = -\frac{1}{k}\log 2$, then the value of k is ....

25. If $y = y(x)$ satisfies the differential equation $8\sqrt{x}(\sqrt{9 + \sqrt{x}})dy = (\sqrt{4 + \sqrt{9 + \sqrt{x}}})^{-1}\, dx$, $x > 0$ and $y(0) = \sqrt{7}$, then the value of $y(256)$ is ....

26. Solution of differential equation
$$\frac{dy}{dx} = \frac{x^2 + y^2 + 3x + 3y + 2xy + 1}{x^2 + y^2 - 3x - 3y + 2xy + 1} \text{ is}$$
$y - \frac{m}{n}\log|(x + y)^2 + 1| = x + C$, then the value of $(m - n)$ is ....

27. If the curve $y = y(x)$ represented by the solution of the differential equation $(2xy^2 - y)dx + x\,dy = 0$ passes through the intersection of the lines $2x - 3y = 1$ and $3x + 2y = 8$, then $|y(1)|$ is equal to ....

28. Let f be a real valued differentiable function on R such that $f(1) = 1$. If the y-intercept of the tangent at any point $P(x, y)$ on the curve $y = f(x)$ is equal to the cube of the abcissa of P, then the value of $f(-3)$ is equal to ....

29. The rate of growth of bacteria culture is proportional to the number of bacteria present and the bacteria count is 1000 at initial time. The number of bacteria is increased by 20% in 2 h. If the population of bacteria is 2000 after $\dfrac{k}{\log\left(\dfrac{6}{5}\right)}$ h, then $\left(\dfrac{k}{\log 2}\right)^2$ is equal to ....

30. Let $y'(x) + y(x)g'(x) = g(x)g'(x)$, $y(0) = 0$, $x \in R$, where $g'(x)$ denotes $\dfrac{d}{dx}\{g(x)\}$ and $g(x)$ is a given non-constant differentiable function on R with $g(0) = g(2) = 0$, then $y(2)$ is equal to ....

31. A function $y = f(x)$ satisfies the differential equation $f(x)\sin 2x - \cos x + (1 + \sin^2 x)f'(x) = 0$ with initial condition $y(0) = 0$. The value of $f\left(\dfrac{\pi}{6}\right)$ is $\dfrac{A}{B}$, then $|A - B|$ is equal to ....

32. Let $f : [3, 5] \to R$ be a twice differentiable function on $(3, 5)$ such that $f(x) = e^{-x}\int_3^x (3t^2 + 2t + 4f'(t))\,dt$. If $f'(4) = \dfrac{\alpha e^{\beta} - 224}{(e^{\beta} - 4)^2}$, then $\alpha + \beta$ is equal to ......

Previous Year Questions

33. If $y = y(x)$ is the solution curve of the differential equation $(x^2 - 4)dy - (y^2 - 3y)dx = 0$, $x > 2$, $y(4) = \dfrac{3}{2}$ and the slope of the curve is never zero, then the value of $y(10)$ equals. **[Single Correct Type, 2024 Main]**

(a) $\dfrac{3}{1 - (8)^{1/4}}$ (b) $\dfrac{3}{1 + 2\sqrt{2}}$

(c) $\dfrac{3}{1 - 2\sqrt{2}}$ (d) $\dfrac{3}{1 + (8)^{1/4}}$

34. Let $y = y(x)$ be the solution of the differential equation $\sec x\,dy + [2(1 - x)\tan x + x(2 - x)]\,dx = 0$ such that $y(0) = 2$. Then, $y(2)$ is equal to **[Single Correct Type, 2024 Main]**

(a) 2 (b) $2\{1 - \sin(2)\}$

(c) 1 (d) $2\{\sin(2) + 1\}$

35. Let $y = y(x)$ be the solution of the differential equation $\dfrac{dy}{dx} = \dfrac{(\tan x) + y}{\sin x(\sec x - \sin x \tan x)}$, $x \in \left(0, \dfrac{\pi}{2}\right)$ satisfying the condition $y\left(\dfrac{\pi}{4}\right) = 2$. Then, $y\left(\dfrac{\pi}{3}\right)$ is **[Single Correct Type, 2024 Main]**

(a) $\sqrt{3}\,(2 + \log_e \sqrt{3})$ (b) $\sqrt{3}(1 + 2\log_e 3)$

(c) $\dfrac{\sqrt{3}}{2}(2 + \log_e 3)$ (d) $\sqrt{3}(2 + \log_e 3)$

36. The solution curve of the differential equation $y\dfrac{dx}{dy} = x(\log_e x - \log_e y + 1)$, $x > 0$, $y > 0$ passing through the point $(e, 1)$ is **[Single Correct Type, 2024 Main]**

(a) $\left|\log_e \dfrac{y}{x}\right| = x$ (b) $\left|\log_e \dfrac{x}{y}\right| = y$

(c) $\left|\log_e \dfrac{y}{x}\right| = y^2$ (d) $2\left|\log_e \dfrac{x}{y}\right| = y + 1$

37. If the solution of the differential equation $(2x + 3y - 2)dx + (4x + 6y - 7)dy = 0$, $y(0) = 3$, is $\alpha x + \beta y + 3\log_e|2x + 3y - \gamma| = 6$, then $\alpha + 2\beta + 3\gamma$ is equal to .... **[Numerical Value Type, 2024 Main]**

38. If the solution curve of the differential equation $\dfrac{dy}{dx} = \dfrac{x + y - 2}{x - y}$ passing through the point $(2, 1)$ is

$$\tan^{-1}\left(\frac{y-1}{x-1}\right) - \frac{1}{\beta}\log_e\left(\alpha + \left(\frac{y-1}{x-1}\right)^2\right) = \log_e|x - 1|,$$

then $5\beta + \alpha$ is equal to .... **[Numerical Value Type, 2024 Main]**

39. If the solution curve $y = y(x)$ of the differential equation $(1 + y^2)(1 + \log_e x)\,dx + x\,dy = 0$, $x > 0$ passes through the point $(1, 1)$ and $y(e) = \dfrac{\alpha - \tan\left(\dfrac{3}{2}\right)}{\beta + \tan\left(\dfrac{3}{2}\right)}$, then $\alpha + 2\beta$ is .... . **[Numerical Value Type, 2024 Main]**

40. Let $y = y(x)$ be the solution of the differential equation $\sec^2 x\,dx + (e^{2y}\tan^2 x + \tan x)\,dy = 0$, $0 < x < \dfrac{\pi}{2}$, $y(\pi/4) = 0$. If $y(\pi/6) = \alpha$, then $e^{8\alpha}$ is equal to .... **[Numerical Value Type, 2024 Main]**

41. If $x = x(t)$ is the solution of the differential equation $(t + 1)dx = (2x + (t + 1)^4)dt$, $x(0) = 2$, then, $x(1)$ equals .... **[Numerical Value Type, 2024 Main]**

42. If $\dfrac{dx}{dy} = \dfrac{1 + x - y^2}{y}$, $x(1) = 1$, then $5x(2)$ is equal to .... **[Numerical Value Type, 2024 Main]**

43. Let $y = y_1(x)$ and $y = y_2(x)$ be the solution curves of the differential equation $\frac{dy}{dx} = y + 7$ with initial conditions $y_1(0) = 0$ and $y_2(0) = 1$ respectively. Then, the curves $y = y_1(x)$ and $y = y_2(x)$ intersect at **[Single Correct Type, 2023 Main]**

(a) infinite number of points (b) two points
(c) one point (d) no point

44. Let $y = y(x)$ be the solution of the differential equation $\frac{dy}{dx} + \frac{5}{x(x^5+1)} y = \frac{(x^5+1)^2}{x^7}$, $x > 0$. If $y(1) = 2$, then $y(2)$ is equal to **[Single Correct Type, 2023 Main]**

(a) $\frac{693}{128}$ (b) $\frac{697}{128}$ (c) $\frac{637}{128}$ (d) $\frac{679}{128}$

45. Let $y = y(x)$ be a solution curve of the differential equation $(1 - x^2y^2)dx = ydx + xdy$. If the line $x = 1$ intersects the curve $y = y(x)$ at $y = 2$ and the line $x = 2$ intersects the curve $y = y(x)$ at $y = \alpha$, then a value of α is **[Single Correct Type, 2023 Main]**

(a) $\frac{3e^2}{2(3e^2+1)}$ (b) $\frac{3e^2}{2(3e^2-1)}$
(c) $\frac{1-3e^2}{2(3e^2+1)}$ (d) $\frac{1+3e^2}{2(3e^2-1)}$

46. If the solution curve $f(x, y) = 0$ of the differential equation $(1 + \log_e x)\frac{dx}{dy} - x\log_e x = e^y$, $x > 0$, passes through the points $(1, 0)$ and $(\alpha, 2)$, then α^α is equal to **[Single Correct Type, 2023 Main]**

(a) $e^{2e^{\sqrt{2}}}$ (b) $e^{\sqrt{2}e^2}$ (c) e^{2e^2} (d) e^{e^2}

47. Let $y = y(x)$ be the solution of the differential equation $(3y^2 - 5x^2)y\,dx + 2x(x^2 - y^2)\,dy = 0$ such that $y(1) = 1$. Then, $|(y(2))^3 - 12y(2)|$ is equal to **[Single Correct Type, 2023 Main]**

(a) $16\sqrt{2}$ (b) 32 (c) $32\sqrt{2}$ (d) 64

48. The solution of the differential equation $\frac{dy}{dx} = -\left(\frac{x^2+3y^2}{3x^2+y^2}\right)$, $y(1) = 0$ is **[Single Correct Type, 2023 Main]**

(a) $\log_e|x+y| - \frac{2xy}{(x+y)^2} = 0$
(b) $\log_e|x+y| - \frac{xy}{(x+y)^2} = 0$
(c) $\log_e|x+y| + \frac{2xy}{(x+y)^2} = 0$
(d) $\log_e|x+y| + \frac{xy}{(x+y)^2} = 0$

49. Let $y = f(x)$ be the solution of the differential equation $y(x+1)dx - x^2dy = 0$, $y(1) = e$. Then, $\lim_{x \to 0^+} f(x)$ is equal to **[Single Correct Type, 2023 Main]**

(a) 0 (b) e^2 (c) $\frac{1}{e^2}$ (d) $\frac{1}{e}$

50. Let $y = y(x)$ be the solution of the differential equation $(x^2 - 3y^2)dx + 3xy\,dy = 0$, $y(1) = 1$. Then, $6y^2(e)$ is equal to **[Single Correct Type, 2023 Main]**

(a) e^2 (b) $2e^2$ (c) $3e^2$ (d) $\frac{3}{2}e^2$

51. Let $x = x(y)$ be the solution of the differential equation $2(y+2)\log_e(y+2)\,dx + (x + 4 - 2\log_e(y+2))dy = 0$, $y > -1$ with $x(e^4 - 2) = 1$. Then, $x(e^9 - 2)$ is equal to **[Single Correct Type, 2023 Main]**

(a) 4/9 (b) 10/3
(c) 32/9 (d) 3

52. Let $y = y(x)$, $y > 0$, be a solution curve of the differential equation $(1 + x^2)dy = y(x - y)\,dx$. If $y(0) = 1$ and $y(2\sqrt{2}) = \beta$, then **[Single Correct Type, 2023 Main]**

(a) $e^{\beta^{-1}} = e^{-2}(5 + \sqrt{2})$ (b) $e^{\beta^{-1}} = e^{-2}(3 + 2\sqrt{2})$
(c) $e^{3\beta^{-1}} = e(3 + 2\sqrt{2})$ (d) $e^{3\beta^{-1}} = e(5 + \sqrt{2})$

53. Let f be a differentiable function such that $x^2 f(x) - x = 4\int_0^x tf(t)dt$, $f(1) = \frac{2}{3}$. Then, $18f(3)$ is equal to **[Single Correct Type, 2023 Main]**

(a) 210 (b) 160
(c) 180 (d) 130

54. If $y = y(x)$ is the solution curve of the differential equation $\frac{dy}{dx} + y\tan x = x\sec x$, $0 \le x \le \frac{\pi}{3}$, $y(0) = 1$, then $y\left(\frac{\pi}{6}\right)$ is equal to **[Single Correct Type, 2023 Main]**

(a) $\frac{\pi}{12} + \frac{\sqrt{3}}{2}\log_e\left(\frac{2}{e\sqrt{3}}\right)$ (b) $\frac{\pi}{12} - \frac{\sqrt{3}}{2}\log_e\left(\frac{2\sqrt{3}}{e}\right)$
(c) $\frac{\pi}{12} - \frac{\sqrt{3}}{2}\log_e\left(\frac{2}{e\sqrt{3}}\right)$ (d) $\frac{\pi}{12} + \frac{\sqrt{3}}{2}\log_e\left(\frac{2\sqrt{3}}{e}\right)$

55. Let $\alpha x = \exp(x^\beta y^\gamma)$ be the solution of the differential equation $2x^2y\,dy - (1 - xy^2)\,dx = 0$, $x > 0$, $y(2) = \sqrt{\log_e 2}$. Then, $\alpha + \beta - \gamma$ equals **[Single Correct Type, 2023 Main]**

(a) −1 (b) 3
(c) 0 (d) 1

56. Let the solution curve $y = y(x)$ of the differential equation $\frac{dy}{dx} - \frac{3x^5\tan^{-1}(x^3)}{(1+x^6)^{\frac{3}{2}}}y = 2x\exp\left\{\frac{x^3 - \tan^{-1}x^3}{\sqrt{(1+x^6)}}\right\}$ pass through the origin. Then, $y(1)$ is equal to **[Single Correct Type, 2023 Main]**

(a) $\exp\left(\frac{4+\pi}{4\sqrt{2}}\right)$ (b) $\exp\left(\frac{1-\pi}{4\sqrt{2}}\right)$
(c) $\exp\left(\frac{4-\pi}{4\sqrt{2}}\right)$ (d) $\exp\left(\frac{\pi-4}{4\sqrt{2}}\right)$

57. Let $y = y(x)$ be the solution of the differential equation $x \log_e x \dfrac{dy}{dx} + y = x^2 \log_e x, (x > 1)$. If $y(2) = 2$, then $y(e)$ is equal to **[Single Correct Type, 2023 Main]**

(a) $\dfrac{1+e^2}{2}$ (b) $\dfrac{2+e^2}{2}$

(c) $\dfrac{4+e^2}{4}$ (d) $\dfrac{1+e^2}{4}$

58. Let $y = y(t)$ be a solution of the differential equation $\dfrac{dy}{dt} + \alpha y = \gamma e^{-\beta t}$, where $\alpha > 0, \beta > 0$ and $\gamma > 0$. Then, $\lim\limits_{t \to \infty} y(t)$ **[Single Correct Type, 2023 Main]**

(a) does not exist (b) is 0

(c) is 1 (d) is -1

59. Let $y = y(x)$ be the solution curve of the differential equation $\dfrac{dy}{dx} = \dfrac{y}{x}(1 + xy^2(1 + \log_e x)), x > 0, y(1) = 3$. Then, $\dfrac{y^2(x)}{9}$ is equal to **[Single Correct Type, 2023 Main]**

(a) $\dfrac{x^2}{3x^3(1 + \log_e x^2) - 2}$ (b) $\dfrac{x^2}{2x^3(2 + \log_e x^3) - 3}$

(c) $\dfrac{x^2}{5 - 2x^3(2 + \log_e x^3)}$ (d) $\dfrac{x^2}{7 - 3x^3(2 + \log_e x^2)}$

60. Let $y = y(x)$ be the solution of the differential equation $x^3 dy + (xy - 1)dx = 0, x > 0, y\left(\dfrac{1}{2}\right) = 3 - e$. Then, $y(1)$ is equal to **[Single Correct Type, 2023 Main]**

(a) e (b) $2 - e$ (c) 1 (d) 3

61. Let the tangent at any point P on a curve passing through the points $(1, 1)$ and $\left(\dfrac{1}{10}, 100\right)$, intersect positive X-axis and Y-axis at the points A and B respectively. If $PA : PB = 1 : k$ and $y = y(x)$ is the solution of the differential equation $e^{dy/dx} = kx + \dfrac{k}{2}, y(0) = k$, then $4y(1) - 5 \log_e 3$ is equal to......... **[Numerical Value Type, 2023 Main]**

62. Let the solution curve $x = x(y), 0 < y < \dfrac{\pi}{2}$ of the differential equation $(\log_e(\cos y))^2 \cos y \, dx - (1 + 3x \log_e(\cos y)) \sin y \, dy = 0$ satisfy $x\left(\dfrac{\pi}{3}\right) = \dfrac{1}{2 \log_e 2}$. If $x\left(\dfrac{\pi}{6}\right) = \dfrac{1}{\log_e m - \log_e n}$, where m and n are coprime, then mn is equal to...... . **[Numerical Value Type, 2023 Main]**

63. If $y = y(x)$ is the solution of the differential equation $\dfrac{dy}{dx} + \dfrac{4x}{(x^2 - 1)} y = \dfrac{x + 2}{(x^2 - 1)^{5/2}}, x > 1$ such that $y(2) = \dfrac{2}{9} \log_e(2 + \sqrt{3})$ and $y(\sqrt{2}) = \alpha \log_e(\sqrt{\alpha} + \beta) + \beta - \sqrt{\gamma}, \alpha, \beta, \gamma \in N$, then $\alpha\beta\gamma$ is equal to .... **[Numerical Value Type, 2023 Main]**

64. If the solution curve of the differential equation $(y - 2 \log_e x)dx + (x \log_e x^2)dy = 0, x > 1$ passes through the points $\left(e, \dfrac{4}{3}\right)$ and (e^4, α), then a is equal to .... **[Numerical Value Type, 2023 Main]**

65. Let $y = y(x)$ be a solution of the differential equation $(x \cos x)dy + (xy \sin x + y \cos x - 1)dx = 0, 0 < x < \dfrac{\pi}{2}$. If $\dfrac{\pi}{3} y\left(\dfrac{\pi}{3}\right) = \sqrt{3}$, then $\left|\dfrac{\pi}{6} y''\left(\dfrac{\pi}{6}\right) + 2y'\left(\dfrac{\pi}{6}\right)\right|$ is equal to .... **[Numerical Value Type, 2023 Main]**

66. Let $f : R \to R$ be a differentiable function such that $f'(x) + f(x) = \int_0^2 f(t)dt$. If $f(0) = e^{-2}$, then $2f(0) - f(2)$ is equal to .... **[Numerical Value Type, 2023 Main]**

67. If the solution curve of the differential equation $\dfrac{dy}{dx} = \dfrac{x + y - 2}{x - y}$ passes through the point $(2, 1)$ and $(k + 1, 2), k > 0$, then **[Single Correct Type, 2022 Main]**

(a) $2 \tan^{-1}\left(\dfrac{1}{k}\right) = \log_e(k^2 + 1)$

(b) $\tan^{-1}\left(\dfrac{1}{k}\right) = \log_e(k^2 + 1)$

(c) $2 \tan^{-1}\left(\dfrac{1}{k + 1}\right) = \log_e(k^2 + 2k + 2)$

(d) $2 \tan^{-1}\left(\dfrac{1}{k}\right) = \log_e\left(\dfrac{k^2 + 1}{k^2}\right)$

68. If $\dfrac{dy}{dx} + 2y \tan x = \sin x, 0 < x < \dfrac{\pi}{2}$ and $y\left(\dfrac{\pi}{3}\right) = 0$, then the maximum value of $y(x)$ is **[Single Correct Type, 2022 Main]**

(a) $\dfrac{1}{8}$ (b) $\dfrac{3}{4}$ (c) $\dfrac{1}{4}$ (d) $\dfrac{3}{8}$

69. The general solution of the differential equation $(x - y^2)dx + y(5x + y^2)dy = 0$ is **[Single Correct Type, 2022 Main]**

(a) $(y^2 + x)^4 = C|(y^2 + 2x)^3|$

(b) $(y^2 + 2x)^4 = C|(y^2 + x)^3|$

(c) $|(y^2 + x)^3| = C(2y^2 + x)^4$

(d) $|(y^2 + 2x)^3| = C(2y^2 + x)^4$

70. Let the solution curve $y = y(x)$ of the differential equation,

$$\left[\frac{x}{\sqrt{x^2 - y^2}} + e^{\frac{y}{x}}\right] x\frac{dy}{dx} = x + \left[\frac{x}{\sqrt{x^2 - y^2}} + e^{\frac{y}{x}}\right] y$$ passes

through the points (1, 0) and $(2\alpha, \alpha)\, \alpha > 0$. Then, α is equal to **[Single Correct Type, 2022 Main]**

(a) $\frac{1}{2}\exp\left(\frac{\pi}{6} + \sqrt{e} - 1\right)$

(b) $\frac{1}{2}\exp\left(\frac{\pi}{3} + \sqrt{e} - 1\right)$

(c) $\exp\left(\frac{\pi}{6} + \sqrt{e} + 1\right)$

(d) $2\exp\left(\frac{\pi}{3} + \sqrt{e} - 1\right)$

71. If $y = y(x)$, $x \in \left(0, \frac{\pi}{2}\right)$ be the solution curve of the differential equation $(\sin^2 2x)\frac{dy}{dx} + (8\sin^2 2x + 2\sin 4x)y = 2e^{-4x}(2\sin 2x + \cos 2x)$, with $y\left(\frac{\pi}{4}\right) = e^{-\pi}$, then $y\left(\frac{\pi}{6}\right)$ is equal to **[Single Correct Type, 2022 Main]**

(a) $\frac{2}{\sqrt{3}}e^{-\frac{2\pi}{3}}$ (b) $\frac{2}{\sqrt{3}}e^{\frac{2\pi}{3}}$

(c) $\frac{1}{\sqrt{3}}e^{-\frac{2\pi}{3}}$ (d) $\frac{1}{\sqrt{3}}e^{\frac{2\pi}{3}}$

72. Let $y = y(x)$ be the solution of the differential equation $\frac{dy}{dx} = \frac{4y^3 + 2yx^2}{3xy^2 + x^3}$, $y(1) = 1$. If for some $n \in N$, $y(2) \in [n - 1, n)$, then n is equal to .... **[Numerical Value Type, 2022 Main]**

73. A hostel has 100 students. On a certain day (consider it day zero) it was found that two students are infected with some virus. Assume that the rate at which the virus spreads is directly proportional to the product of the number of infected students and the number of non-infected students. If the number of infected students on 4th day is 30, then number of infected students on 8th day will be .... **[Numerical Value Type, 2022 Main]**

74. If $\frac{dy}{dx} = \frac{2^{x+y} - 2^x}{2^y}$, $y(0) = 1$, then $y(1)$ is equal to **[Single Correct Type, 2021 Main]**

(a) $\log_2(2 + e)$

(b) $\log_2(1 + e)$

(c) $\log_2(2e)$

(d) $\log_2(1 + e^2)$

75. If $y^{\frac{1}{4}} + y^{-\frac{1}{4}} = 2x$, $(x^2 - 1)\frac{d^2y}{dx^2} + \alpha x\frac{dy}{dx} + \beta y = 0$, then $|\alpha - \beta|$ is equal to .... **[Numerical Value Type, 2021 Main]**

76. The differential equation of the family of curves, $x^2 = 4b(y + b)$, $b \in R$, is **[Single Correct Type, 2020 Main]**

(a) $x(y')^2 = x + 2yy'$

(b) $x(y')^2 = 2yy' - x$

(c) $xy'' = y'$

(d) $x(y')^2 = x - 2yy'$

77. If a curve $y = f(x)$, passing through the point (1, 2), is the solution of the differential equation, $2x^2 dy = (2xy + y^2)dx$, then $f\left(\frac{1}{2}\right)$ is equal to **[Single Correct Type, 2020 Main]**

(a) $\frac{1}{1 + \log_e 2}$ (b) $\frac{1}{1 - \log_e 2}$

(c) $1 + \log_e 2$ (d) $\frac{-1}{1 + \log_e 2}$

EXERCISE 2

JEE Advanced Pattern

Single Option Correct Type Questions

1. The x-intercept of the tangent to a curve is equal to the ordinate of the point of contact. The equation of the curve through the point (1, 1) is

(a) $ye^{\frac{x}{y}} = e$ (b) $xe^{\frac{x}{y}} = e$

(c) $xe^{\frac{y}{x}} = e$ (d) $ye^{\frac{y}{x}} = e$

2. A function $y = f(x)$ satisfies the condition $f'(x)\sin x + f(x)\cos x = 1$, $f(x)$ being bounded when $x \to 0$. If $I = \int_0^{\pi/2} f(x)\,dx$, then

(a) $\frac{\pi}{2} < I < \frac{\pi^2}{4}$ (b) $\frac{\pi}{4} < I < \frac{\pi^2}{2}$

(c) $1 < I < \frac{\pi}{2}$ (d) $0 < I < 1$

3. A curve C passes through origin and has the property that at each point (x, y) on it, the normal line at that point passes through (1, 0). The equation of a common tangent to the curve C and the parabola $y^2 = 4x$ is

(a) $x = 0$ (b) $y = 0$

(c) $y = x + 1$ (d) $x + y + 1 = 0$

4. The curve, with the property that the projection of the ordinate on the normal is constant and has a length equal to a, is

(a) $x - a\ln(\sqrt{y^2 - a^2} + y) = C$

(b) $x + \sqrt{a^2 - y^2} = C$

(c) $(y - a)^2 = Cx$

(d) $ay = \tan^{-1}(x + C)$

5. A function $f(x)$ satisfying $\int_0^1 f(tx)\,dt = n\,f(x)$, where $x > 0$, is

(a) $f(x) = C \cdot x^{\frac{1-n}{n}}$ (b) $f(x) = C \cdot x^{\frac{n}{n-1}}$

(c) $f(x) = C \cdot x^{\frac{1}{n}}$ (d) $f(x) = C \cdot x^{(1-n)}$

6. Which one of the following curves represents the solution of the initial value problem $Dy = 100 - y$, where $y(0) = 50$?

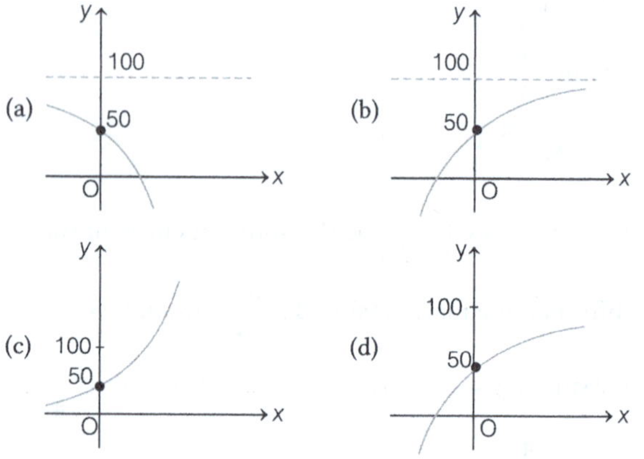

7. A continuous function $f : R \to R$ satisfy the differential equation $f(x) = (1 + x^2)\left[1 + \int_0^x \frac{f^2(t)}{1 + t^2}\,dt\right]$, then the value of $f(-2)$ is

(a) 0 (b) $\frac{17}{15}$

(c) $\frac{-17}{15}$ (d) $\frac{15}{17}$

8. Let the curve $y = f(x)$ passes through origin and satisfies the differential equation $\frac{dy}{dx} + \int_0^5 y\,dx = 27$. If a and b are chosen randomly from the set $s = \{1, 2, 3, 4\}$ with replacement. The probability that the above curve passes through (a, b) is

(a) $\frac{1}{2}$ (b) $\frac{1}{6}$ (c) $\frac{1}{8}$ (d) $\frac{1}{12}$

9. The largest value of c such that there exists a differential function $h(x)$ for $-c < x < c$ that is a solution of $y' = 1 + y^2$ with $h(0) = 0$ is

(a) 2π (b) π

(c) $\frac{\pi}{2}$ (d) $\frac{\pi}{4}$

10. The equation of the trajectories which is orthogonal to the family of curves $\cos y = ae^{-x}$ is

(a) $\sin y = ce^{x}$ (b) $\cos y = ce^{x}$

(c) $\sin y = ce^{-x}$ (d) None of these

11. Let $f(x)$ be differentiable on the interval $(0, \infty)$ such that $f(1)=1$ and $\lim\limits_{t\to x}\dfrac{t^2 f(x)-x^2 f(t)}{t-x}=1$ for each $x>0$.

Then, $f(x)$ is

(a) $\dfrac{1}{3x}+\dfrac{2x^2}{3}$ (b) $\dfrac{-1}{3x}+\dfrac{4x^2}{3}$

(c) $\dfrac{-1}{x}+\dfrac{2}{x^2}$ (d) $\dfrac{1}{x}$

12. Let $y=f(x)\cdot g(x)\cdot h(x)$ be the solution of the differential equation $xdy-ydx=xe^x(x\ln x+1)dx$ and $y(1)=0$. If $f(x)$ and $h(x)$ are images of each other in the mirror $y=g(x)$, then least distance between $f(x)$ and $h(x)$ is

(a) $\sqrt{2}$ (b) $2\sqrt{2}$ (c) $3\sqrt{2}$ (d) 2

13. A curve $y=f(x)$ passing through the point $\left(1,\dfrac{1}{\sqrt{e}}\right)$ satisfies the differential equation $\dfrac{dy}{dx}+xe^{-x^2/2}=0$, then which of the following does not hold good ?

(a) $f(x)$ is differentiable at $x=0$

(b) $f(x)$ is symmetric w.r.t the origin.

(c) $f(x)$ is increasing for $x<0$, and decreasing for $x>0$.

(d) $f(x)$ has two inflection points.

14. If for a curve ratio of the distance between the normal at any of its point and the origin to the distance between the same normal and the point (a, b) is equal to the constant $k\ (k>0, k\neq 1)$, then the curve is a

(a) Circle (b) Parabola

(c) Ellipse (d) Hyperbola

15. Let a function $f(x)$ be such that $f''(x)=f'(x)+e^x$ and $f(0)=0$, $f'(0)=1$, then $\ln\left(\dfrac{(f(2))^2}{4}\right)$ is equal to

(a) $\dfrac{1}{2}$ (b) 1 (c) 2 (d) 4

16. If $f(x)$ is a function such that $x\int_0^x(1-t)f(t)\,dt=\int_0^x t\,f(t)dt$, $f(1)=1$, then $f(x)$ is equal to

(a) $y=x^3e^{\left(\frac{x-1}{x}\right)}$ (b) $yx^3=e^{\left(\frac{x-1}{x}\right)}$

(c) $y=\dfrac{1}{x^3}e^{\left(\frac{1-x}{x}\right)}$ (d) $y=x^3e^{\frac{1}{x}}$

17. Solution of the given differential equation $y\cos\left(\dfrac{y}{x}\right)(x\,dy-y\,dx)+x\sin\left(\dfrac{y}{x}\right)(x\,dy+y\,dx)=0$, $y(1)=\dfrac{\pi}{2}$, is

(a) $xy\sin\left(\dfrac{x}{y}\right)=\dfrac{\pi}{4}$ (b) $xy\sin\left(\dfrac{y}{x}\right)=\dfrac{\pi}{2}$

(c) $xy\sin\left(\dfrac{y}{x}\right)=\pi$ (d) $2xy\sin\left(\dfrac{y}{x}\right)=0$

18. Let C_1 be the curve obtained by the solution of differential equation $2xy\dfrac{dy}{dx}=y^2-x^2$, $x>0$. Let the curve C_2 be the solution of $\dfrac{2xy}{x^2-y^2}=\dfrac{dy}{dx}$. If both the curves passes through (1, 1), then the area enclosed by the curves C_1 and C_2 is equal to

(a) $\dfrac{\pi}{4}+1$ (b) $\pi+1$

(c) $\pi-1$ (d) $\dfrac{\pi}{2}-1$

19. The integral curve of the differential equation $x(1-x\ln y)\dfrac{dy}{dx}+y=0$, which passes through the point $\left(e,\dfrac{1}{e}\right)$ is

(a) $\{(\ln y-1)+ey\}x=1$ (b) $\{(\ln y+1)+ey\}x=1$

(c) $\{(\ln y+1)+y\}x=2$ (d) $\{(\ln y+1)+y\}x=1$

20. A differentiable function f satisfies the relation $f(xy)=xf(y)+yf(x)$ for every x, y in R.

If $f'(1)=1$, then the function f is

(a) $y=x\log|x|+3$ (b) $y=x\log|x|$

(c) $2y=x\log x$ (d) $2y=x\log x-3$

More than One Correct Option Type Questions

21. Which of the following pair(s) is/are orthogonal?

(a) $16x^2+y^2=C$ and $y^{16}=kx$

(b) $y=x+Ce^{-x}$ and $x+2=y+ke^{-y}$

(c) $y=Cx^2$ and $x^2+2y^2=k$

(d) $x^2-y^2=C$ and $xy=k$

22. Family of curves whose tangent at a point with its intersection with the curve $xy=c^2$ form an angle of $\dfrac{\pi}{4}$ is

(a) $y^2-2xy-x^2=k$ (b) $y^2+2xy-x^2=k$

(c) $y=x-2c\tan^{-1}\left(\dfrac{x}{c}\right)+k$ (d) $y=c\ln\left|\dfrac{c+x}{c-x}\right|-x+k$

23. The general solution of the differential equation, $x\left(\dfrac{dy}{dx}\right)=y\cdot\log\left(\dfrac{y}{x}\right)$ is

(a) $y=xe^{1-Cx}$ (b) $y=xe^{1+Cx}$

(c) $y=ex\cdot e^{Cx}$ (d) $y=xe^{Cx}$

where C is an arbitrary constant.

24. Identify the statement(s) which is/are true?

(a) $f(x, y) = e^{y/x} + \tan\frac{y}{x}$ is homogeneous of degree zero.

(b) $x \cdot \log\frac{y}{x}\,dx + \frac{y^2}{x}\sin^{-1}\frac{y}{x}\,dy = 0$ is homogeneous differential equation.

(c) $f(x, y) = x^2 + \sin x \cdot \cos y$ is not homogeneous.

(d) $(x^2 + y^2)\,dx - (xy^2 - y^3)\,dy = 0$ is a homogeneous differential equation.

25. A function $y = f(x)$ satisfying the differential equation $\frac{dy}{dx}\cdot\sin x - y\cos x + \frac{\sin^2 x}{x^2} = 0$ is such that, $y \to 0$ as $x \to \infty$, then the statement which is correct?

(a) $\lim_{x \to 0} f(x) = 1$

(b) $\int_0^{\pi/2} f(x)\,dx$ is less than $\frac{\pi}{2}$

(c) $\int_0^{\pi/2} f(x)\,dx$ is greater than unity

(d) $f(x)$ is an odd function

26. Identify the statement(s) which is/are true?

(a) The order of differential equation $\sqrt{1 + \frac{d^2y}{dx^2}} = x$ is 1.

(b) Solution of the differential equation $xdy - ydx = \sqrt{x^2 + y^2}\,dx$ is $y + \sqrt{x^2 + y^2} = Cx^2$.

(c) $\frac{d^2y}{dx^2} = 2\left(\frac{dy}{dx} - y\right)$ is differential equation of family of curves $y = e^x\,(A\cos x + B\sin x)$.

(d) The solution of differential equation $(1 + y^2) + (x - 2e^{\tan^{-1} y})\frac{dy}{dx} = 0$ is $xe^{\tan^{-1} y} = e^{2\tan^{-1} y} + k$.

27. If curve passes through (2, 0) and the slope of tangent at $P(x, y)$ equals $\frac{(x+1)^2 + y - 3}{x+1}$, then

(a) curve is $y = x^2 - 2x$

(b) curve is $y = x^3 - 8$

(c) area bounded by the curve and X-axis in fourth quadrant is $\frac{2}{3}$ sq units.

(d) area bounded by the curve and X-axis in fourth quadrant is $\frac{4}{3}$ sq units.

28. Let C be a curve such that the normal at any point P on it meets X-axis and Y-axis at A and B, respectively. If $BP : PA = 1 : 2$ (internally) and the curve passes through the point (0, 4), then which of the following alternatives is/are correct?

(a) The curve passes through $(\sqrt{10}, -6)$

(b) The equation of tangent at $(4, 4\sqrt{3})$ is $2x + \sqrt{3}y = 20$

(c) The differential equation for the curve is $yy' + 2x = 0$

(d) The curve represent a hyperbola.

29. The normal at a general point (a, b) on curve makes an angle θ, with X-axis which satisfies $b(a^2 \tan\theta - \cot\theta) = a(b^2 + 1)$. The equation of curve can be

(a) $y = e^{x^2/2} + C$

(b) $\log(ky^2) = x^2$

(c) $y = ke^{x^2/2}$

(d) $x^2 - y^2 = C$

30. If $y(x)$ satisfies the differential equation $\frac{dy}{dx} = \sin 2x + 3y\cot x$ and $y\left(\frac{\pi}{2}\right) = 2$, then which of the following statement(s) is (are) correct?

(a) $y\left(\frac{\pi}{6}\right) = 0$

(b) $y'\left(\frac{\pi}{3}\right) = \frac{9 - 3\sqrt{2}}{2}$

(c) $y(x)$ is increases in interval $\left(\frac{\pi}{6}, \frac{\pi}{3}\right)$

(d) The value of definite integral $\int_{-\pi/2}^{\pi/2} y(x)\,dx$ is equal to π.

31. Let $y = f(x)$ defined on R satisfies the differential equation $(1 + x^2)\frac{dy}{dx} + 2xy = 2x$ and $f(0) = 2$, then which of the following statement(s) is (are) correct?

(a) $f(x)$ is neither even nor odd function.

(b) $f(x)$ increases on $(-\infty, 0)$ and decreases $(0, \infty)$.

(c) The x-intercept of normal on the graph of $y = f(x)$ at $x = 1$ equals $\frac{1}{4}$.

(d) The area bounded by $y = f(x)$ with X-axis between ordinates at $x = 0$ and $x = 1$ equals $\left(\frac{\pi + 4}{4}\right)$.

32. The solution of differential equation $2x^3y\,dy + (1 - y^2)(x^2y^2 + y^2 - 1)dx = 0$ is $x^m y^m = (cx + k)(1 - y^2)$, then

(a) $m + n + k = 3$

(b) $m + n + k = 4$

(c) $m \cdot n + k = 3$

(d) $m + n - k = 5$

33. Let f be a differentiable function on k satisfying $f'(t) = e^t(\cos^2 t - \sin^2 t)$ and $f(0) = 1$, then which of the following is/are correct?

(a) f is bounded in $(-\infty, 0)$.

(b) Number of solution satisfying the equation $f(t) - e^t = 0$ in $[0, 2\pi]$ is 3.

(c) The value of $\lim_{t \to 0}(f(t))^{\frac{1}{t}} = 1$.

(d) f is neither odd nor even.

34. If a function f satisfies the relation $f(x)f''(x)-f(x)f'(x)=(f'(x))^2\ \forall\ x\in R$ and $f(0)=f'(x)=1$, then identify which of the following statement(s) is (are) correct?

(a) Equation $f(x)=e^x$ has two solutions

(b) Equation $f(x)=e^x$ has exactly one solution

(c) $\lim_{x\to-\infty} f(x)=\frac{1}{e}$

(d) $\lim_{x\to 0}\frac{f(x)-1}{x}=1$

35. Let $f(x)$ be differentiable function on the interval $(-\infty,\infty)$ such that $f(1)=5$ and $\lim_{a\to x}\frac{af(x)-xf(a)}{a-x}=2$ for each $x\in R$, then which of the alternatives is/are correct?

(a) Area bounded by $f(x)$ with coordinate axes is $\frac{2}{3}$.

(b) $\int_0^2 f(x)\,dx=10$

(c) $f'(x)=3\ \forall\ x\in R$

(d) $f(x)$ has no inflection point

Passage Based Questions

Passage I

(Q. Nos. 36 to 37)

■ Let $y=f(x)$ satisfies the equation
$$f(x)=(e^{-x}+e^x)\cos x-2x-\int_0^x (x-t)\,f'(t)dt.$$

36. y satisfies the differential equation

(a) $\frac{dy}{dx}+y=e^x(\cos x-\sin x)-e^{-x}(\cos x+\sin x)$

(b) $\frac{dy}{dx}-y=e^x(\cos x-\sin x)+e^{-x}(\cos x+\sin x)$

(c) $\frac{dy}{dx}+y=e^x(\cos x+\sin x)-e^{-x}(\cos x-\sin x)$

(d) $\frac{dy}{dx}-y=e^x(\cos x-\sin x)+e^{-x}(\cos x-\sin x)$

37. $f(x)$ as a function of x equals to

(a) $e^{-x}(\cos x-\sin x)+\frac{e^x}{5}(3\cos x+\sin x)+\frac{2}{5}e^{-x}$

(b) $e^{-x}(\cos x+\sin x)+\frac{e^x}{5}(3\cos x-\sin x)-\frac{2}{5}e^{-x}$

(c) $e^{-x}(\cos x-\sin x)+\frac{e^x}{5}(3\cos x-\sin x)+\frac{2}{5}e^{-x}$

(d) $e^{-x}(\cos x+\sin x)+\frac{e^x}{5}(3\cos x-\sin x)-\frac{2}{5}e^{-x}$

Passage II

(Q. Nos. 38 to 39)

■ If any differential equation in the form
$$f(f_1(x,y))\,d(f_1(x,y))+\phi(f_2(x,y))\,d(f_2(x,y))+\ldots=0,$$
then each term can be integrated separately.

e.g. $\int \sin xy\, d(xy)+\int\left(\frac{x}{y}\right)d\left(\frac{x}{y}\right)$
$$=-\cos xy+\frac{1}{2}\left(\frac{x}{y}\right)^2+C$$

38. The solution of the differential equation $(xy^4+y)\,dx-xdy=0$ is

(a) $\frac{x^3}{4}+\frac{1}{2}\left(\frac{x}{y}\right)^2=C$

(b) $\frac{x^4}{4}+\frac{1}{3}\left(\frac{x}{y}\right)^3=C$

(c) $\frac{x^4}{4}-\frac{1}{2}\left(\frac{x}{y}\right)^3=C$

(d) $\frac{x^3}{4}-\frac{1}{2}\left(\frac{x}{y}\right)^2=C$

39. Solution of differential equation
$(2x\cos y+y^2\cos x)\,dx+(2y\sin x-x^2\sin y)\,dy=0$ is

(a) $x^2\cos y+y^2\sin x=C$

(b) $x\cos y-y\sin x=C$

(c) $x^2\cos^2 y+y^2\sin^2 x=C$

(d) None of the above

Passage III

(Q. Nos. 40 to 41)

■ Differential equation $\frac{dy}{dx}=f(x)\,g(x)$ can be solved by separating variable $\frac{dy}{g(y)}=f(x)\,dx$.

40. The equation of the curve to the point (1, 0) which satisfies the differential equation $(1+y^2)\,dx-xy\,dy=0$ is

(a) $x^2+y^2=1$

(b) $x^2-y^2=1$

(c) $x^2+y^2=2$

(d) $x^2-y^2=2$

41. Solution of the differential equation $\frac{dy}{dx}+\frac{1+y^2}{\sqrt{1-x^2}}=0$ is

(a) $\tan^{-1}y+\sin^{-1}x=C$

(b) $\tan^{-1}x+\sin^{-1}y=C$

(c) $\tan^{-1}y\cdot\sin^{-1}x=C$

(d) $\tan^{-1}y-\sin^{-1}x=C$

Passage IV

(Q. Nos. 42 to 43)

- Let C be the set of curves having the property that the point of intersection of tangent with Y-axis is equidistant from the point of tangency and origin (0, 0).

42. If $C_1, C_2 \in C$

C_1: Curve is passing through (1, 0)

C_2: Curve is passing through $(-1, 0)$

The number of common tangents for C_1 and C_2 is

(a) 1 (b) 2

(c) 3 (d) None of these

43. If common tangents of C_1 and C_2 form an equilateral triangle, where $C_1, C_2 \in C$ and C_1: Curve passes through (2, 0), then C_2 may passes through

(a) $(-1/3, 1/3)$ (b) $(-1/3, 1)$

(c) $(-2/3, 4)$ (d) $(-2/3, 2)$

Stem Based Questions

Stem I

(Q. Nos. 44 to 45)

- Consider the differential equation $e^x(ydx - dy) = e^{-x}(ydx + dy)$. Let $y = f(x)$ be a particular solution to this differential equation which passes through the point (0, 2).

Let curve c be $y = \log_{1/4}\left(x - \frac{1}{4}\right) + \frac{1}{2}\log_4(16x^2 - 8x + 1)$.

The range of the function $g(x) = \log_2(f(x))$ is $\left[\frac{2023}{\lambda}, \infty\right)$

and the area bounded by the curve $y = f(x)$, curve c, ordinate $x = \frac{1}{4}$ and the ordinate $x = a$ is

$4 - \log_e 4 + \frac{1}{e^{1/4}} - e^{1/4}$.

44. The value of λ is ....

45. The value of $\frac{100a}{\log_e 4}$ is ....

Stem II

(Q. Nos. 46 to 47)

- General solution of the differential equation $f(x)\,dx + g(y)\,dy = 0$ is $\int f(x)\,dx + f(y)\,dy = 0$.

46. General solution of the equation $\frac{dy}{dx} = \sin(x + y) + \cos(x + y)$ is $1 + \tan\left(\frac{x + y}{k}\right) = Ce^x$, then k is equal to ....

47. Solution of $\frac{dy}{dx} + \frac{y}{x} = \frac{1}{(1 + \log x + \log y)^2}$ is $xy[1 + \{\log(xy)\}^2] = \frac{x^k}{k} + C$, then k is equal to ....

Single Integer Type Questions

48. A tank initially contains 50 gallons of fresh water. Brine contains 2 pounds per gallon of salt, flows into the tank at the rate of 2 gallons per minutes and the mixture kept uniform by stirring, runs out at the same rate. If it will take for the quantity of salt in the tank to increase from 40 to 80 pounds (in seconds) is 206λ, then find λ is equal to ....

49. If $f : R - \{-1\} \to$ and f is differentiable function which satisfies :

$f\{x + f(y) + xf(y)\} = y + f(x) + yf(x)\ \forall\ x, y \in R - \{-1\}$,

then the value of $2010\,[1 + f(2009)]$ is ....

50. The degree of the differential equation satisfied by the curves $\sqrt{1 + x} - a\sqrt{1 + y} = 1$, is ....

51. Let $f(x)$ be a twice differentiable bounded function satisfayi $2f^5(x) \cdot f'(x) + 2(f'(x))^3 \cdot f^5(x) = f''(x)$. If $f(x)$ is bounded in between $y = k$, and $y = k_2$, Then, the number of integers between k_1 and k_2 is/are .... (where $f(0) = f'(0) = 0$)

52. Let $y(x)$ be a function satisfying $d^2y/dx^2 - dy/dx + e^{2x} = 0$, $y(0) = 2$ and $y'(0) = 1$. If maximum value of $y(x)$ is $y(\alpha)$, Then, integral part of (2α) is ....

Numerical Value Type Questions

53. If $f : R^+ \to R$ be a differentiable function satisfying $f(x) = x\ln x + x - \int_1^x \frac{f(t)}{t \cdot \ln t}\,dt\ x\ R^x$, then the value of $f'(e) + f''\left(\frac{1}{4}\right)^2$ is ....

54. Let f be a differentiable function satisfying $f'(x) = f^2(x)$ and $f(0) = -1$. If $\frac{\sqrt{2}}{\pi}\int_0^1\left(\frac{1 - x}{f(x)(x^4 + 1)} + \frac{2}{x^4 + 1}\right)dx = \frac{p}{q}$, where $p, q \in N$, then find least value of $(p + q)^3$ is ....

55. Let f_1, f_2 and f_3 be three curves satisfying the differential equation $y(1 - y^2)\,dx = x(y^2 + 1)\,dy$. If f_3 cuts the curve f_1 and f_2 at A and B, respectively and one of the curve is passing through $C(2, -1)$, find then the area of $\frac{\Delta ABC}{4}$ is equal to ....

56. Let $\frac{dy}{dx} - y\frac{\phi'(x)}{\phi(x)} = \frac{-y^2}{\phi(x)}$, where $\phi(x)$ is a specified function satisfying $\phi(1) = 1$, $\phi(4) = 1296$. If $y(1) = 1$, then the value of $\sqrt{y(4)}$ is ....

57. The differential equation $dy = x\tan y(\sin y - 1)dx$ has solution $y = \sin^{-1}\left(\frac{1}{k + ce^{x^2/2}}\right)$, then the value of $\frac{k}{3}$ is equal to ....

58. Let $f : R \to R$ be a differentiable function with $f(0) = 0$. If $y = f(x)$ satisfies the differential equation $\frac{dy}{dx} = (2 + 5y)(5y - 2)$, then the value of $\lim_{x \to -\infty} f(x)$ is ....

59. Let $f : R \to R$ be a differentiable function with $f(0) = 1$ and satisfying the equation $f(x + y) = f(x)f'(y) + f'(x)f(y), \forall x, y \in R$. Then, the value of $\log_e(f(4))$ is ....

Matching Type Questions

60. Match the following :

	Column I		Column II
(A)	$\frac{xdx + ydy}{xdy - ydx} = \sqrt{\frac{a^2 - x^2 - y^2}{x^2 + y^2}}$	(p)	$y = \frac{C}{x^3}e^{-1/x}$
(B)	Solution of $\cos^2 x\frac{dy}{dx} - \tan 2x \cdot y = \cos^4 x$, where $\lvert x\rvert < \frac{\pi}{4}$ and $y\left(\frac{\pi}{6}\right) = \frac{3\sqrt{3}}{8}$	(q)	$\sqrt{x^2 + y^2} = a\sin\left\{C + \tan^{-1}\left(\frac{y}{x}\right)\right\}$
(C)	The equation of all possible curves that will cut each member of the family of circles $x^2 + y^2 - 2cx = 0$ at right angle	(r)	$x^2 + y^2 + Cy = 0$
(D)	Solution of the equation $x\int_0^x y(t)\,dt = (x + 1)\int_0^x ty(t)\,dt,\ x > 0$ is	(s)	$y = \frac{\sin 2x}{2(1 - \tan^2 x)}$

61. Match the following

	Column I		Column II
(A)	Circular plate is expanded by heat from radius 5 cm to 5.06 cm. Approximate increase in area is	(p)	4
(B)	Side of cube increasing by 1%, then percentage increase in volume is	(q)	0.6π
(C)	If the rate of decrease of $\frac{x^2}{2} - 2x + 5$ is twice the rate of decrease of x, then x is equal to	(r)	3
(D)	Rate of increase in area of equilateral triangle of side 15 cm, when each side is increasing at the rate of 0.1 cm/s; is	(s)	$\frac{3\sqrt{3}}{4}$

62. Match the following :

	Column I		Column II
(A)	The differential equation of the family of curves $y = e^x(A\cos x + B\sin x)$, where A, B are arbitrary constants, has the degree n and order m. Then, the values of n and m are, respectively	(p)	2, 1
(B)	The degree and order of the differential equation of the family of all parabolas whose axis is the X-axis, are respectively	(q)	1, 1
(C)	The order and degree of the differential equations of the family of circles touching the X-axis at the origin, are respectively	(r)	2, 2
(D)	The degree and order of the differential equation of the family of ellipse having the same foci, are respectively.	(s)	1, 2

Previous Years Question's

63. Let $f : [1, \infty) \to R$ be a differentiable function such that $f(1) = \frac{1}{3}$ and $3\int_1^x f(t)dt = xf(x) - \frac{x^3}{3}$, $x \in [1, \infty)$. Let e denote the base of the natural logarithm . Then, the value of $f(e)$ is **[Single Correct Type, 2023 Adv.]**

(a) $\frac{e^2 + 4}{3}$
(b) $\frac{\log_e 4 + e}{3}$
(c) $\frac{4e^2}{3}$
(d) $\frac{e^2 - 4}{3}$

64. For $x \in R$, let $y(x)$ be a solution of the differential equation $(x^2-5)\frac{dy}{dx}-2xy=-2x(x^2-5)^2$ such that $y(2)=7$. Then, the maximum value of the function $y(x)$ is …… .

[Numerical Value Type, 2023 Adv.]

65. If $y(x)$ is the solution of the differential equation $xdy-(y^2-4y)dx=0$ for $x>0, y(1)=2$,
and the slope of the curve $y=y(x)$ is never zero, then the value of $10y(\sqrt{2})$ is ………

[Numerical Value Type, 2022 Adv.]

66. For $x \in R$, let the function $y(x)$ be the solution of the differential equation $\frac{dy}{dx}+12y=\cos\left(\frac{\pi x}{12}\right)$, $y(0)=0$.

Then, which of the following statements is/are true?

[More Than One Correct, 2022 Adv.]

(a) $y(x)$ is an increasing function
(b) $y(x)$ is a decreasing function
(c) There exists a real number β such that the line $y=\beta$ intersects the curve $y=y(x)$ at infinitely many points
(d) $y(x)$ is a periodic function

67. For any real numbers α and β, let $y_{\alpha,\beta}(x)$, $x \in R$, be the solution of the differential equation $\frac{dy}{dx}+\alpha y=xe^{\beta x}$, $y(1)=1$. Let $S=\{y_{\alpha,\beta}(x):\alpha,\beta \in R\}$.
Then, which of the following functions belong(s) to the set S?

[More Than One Correct, 2021 Adv.]

(a) $f(x)=\frac{x^2}{2}e^{-x}+\left(e-\frac{1}{2}\right)e^{-x}$
(b) $f(x)=-\frac{x^2}{2}e^{-x}+\left(e+\frac{1}{2}\right)e^{-x}$
(c) $f(x)=\frac{e^x}{2}\left(x-\frac{1}{2}\right)+\left(e-\frac{e^2}{4}\right)e^{-x}$
(d) $f(x)=\frac{e^x}{2}\left(\frac{1}{2}-x\right)+\left(e+\frac{e^2}{4}\right)e^{-x}$

68. Let b be a non-zero real number. Suppose $f:R\to R$ is a differentiable function such that $f(0)=1$. If the derivative f' of f satisfies the equation

$$f'(x)=\frac{f(x)}{b^2+x^2}, \forall x \in R,$$

then which of the following statements is/are TRUE?

[More Than One Correct, 2020 Adv.]

(a) If $b>0$, then f is an increasing function
(b) If $b<0$, then f is a decreasing function
(c) $f(x)f(-x)=1, \forall x \in R$
(d) $f(x)-f(-x)=0, \forall x \in R$

69. Let P denote a curve $y=y(x)$ which is in the first quadrant and let the point $(1, 0)$ lie on it. Let the tangent to P at a point P intersect the Y-axis at Y_P. If PY_P has length 1 for each point P on P, then which of the following options is/are correct?

[More Than One Correct, 2019 Adv.]

(a) $xy'+\sqrt{1-x^2}=0$
(b) $xy'-\sqrt{1-x^2}=0$
(c) $y=\log_e\left(\frac{1+\sqrt{1-x^2}}{x}\right)-\sqrt{1-x^2}$
(d) $y=-\log_e\left(\frac{1+\sqrt{1-x^2}}{x}\right)+\sqrt{1-x^2}$

EXERCISE 3

Challenging Problems

1. For a certain curve $y=f(x)$ satisfying $\frac{d^2y}{dx^2}=6x-4$; $f(x)$ has a local minimum value 5 when $x=1$. Find the equation of the curve and also the global maximum and global minimum values of $f(x)$ given that $0 \le x \le 2$.

2. If $\phi(x)$ is a differentiable real-valued function satisfying $\phi'(x)+2\phi(x)\le 1$, prove that $\phi(x)-\frac{1}{2}$ is a non-increasing function of x.

3. Determine all curve for which the ratios of the length of the segment intercepted by any tangent on the Y-axis to the length of the radius vector is a constant.

4. A normal is drawn at a point $P(x, y)$ of a curve. It meets the X-axis at Q. If PQ is of constant length k, then show that the differential equation describing such curves is, $y\frac{dy}{dx}=\pm\sqrt{k^2-y^2}$ and the equation of such a curve passing through $(0, k)$.

5. A curve passing through the point (1, 1) has the property that the perpendicular distance of the normal at any point P on the curve from the origin is equal to the distance of P from X-axis. Determine the equation of the curve.

6. A country has a food deficit of 10%. Its population grows continuously at a rate of 3% per year. Its annual food production every year is 4% more than that of the last year. Assuming that the average food requirement per person remains constant, prove that the country will become self-sufficient in food after n years, where n is the smallest integer bigger than or equal to $\dfrac{\log_e 10 - \log_e 9}{(\log_e 1.04) - 0.03}$.

7. Solve the equation
$$x \int_0^x y(t)\, dt = (x+1) \int_0^x t\, y(t)\, dt,\ x > 0.$$

8. If (y_1, y_2) are two solutions of the differential equation
$$\frac{dy}{dx} + P(x) \cdot y = Q(x)$$
Then, prove that $y = y_1 + C(y_1 - y_2)$ is the general solution of the equation where C is any constant. For what relation between the constant α, β will the linear combination $\alpha y_1 + \beta y_2$ also be a solution.

9. Given two curves $y = f(x)$ passing through (0, 1) and $y = \int_{-\infty}^{x} f(t)\, dt$ passing through $(0, 1/n)$. The tangents drawn to both the curves at the points with equal abscissae intersect on the X-axis find the curve $y = f(x)$.

10. A normal is drawn at a point $P(x, y)$ of a curve. It meets the X-axis and the Y-axis in point A and B, respectively, such that $\dfrac{1}{OA} + \dfrac{1}{OB} = 1$, where O is the origin, find the equation of such a curve passing through (5, 4).

11. A line is drawn from a point $P(x, y)$ on curve $y = f(x)$, making an angle with the X-axis which is supplementary to the one made by the tangent to the curve at $P(x, y)$. The line meets the X-axis at A. Another line perpendicular to the first, is drawn from $P(x, y)$ meeting the Y-axis at B. If $OA = OB$, where O is origin, find all curve which passes through (1, 1).

Answer Key

Exercise 1

1. (a)	2. (c)	3. (b)	4. (c)	5. (a)	6. (c)	7. (b)	8. (a)	9. (d)	10. (a)
11. (b)	12. (b)	13. (b)	14. (b)	15. (d)	16. (c)	17. (d)	18. (c)	19. (b)	20. (c)
21. (1)	22. (3)	23. (0.5)	24. (4)	25. (3)	26. (1)	27. (1)	28. (9)	29. (4)	30. (0)
31. (3)	32. (16)	33. (d)	34. (a)	35. (a)	36. (b)	37. (29)	38. (11)	39. (3)	40. (9)
41. (14)	42. (5)	43. (d)	44. (a)	45. (d)	46. (c)	47. (c)	48. (c)	49. (a)	50. (b)
51. (c)	52. (c)	53. (b)	54. (c)	55. (d)	56. (c)	57. (c)	58. (b)	59. (c)	60. (c)
61. (5)	62. (12)	63. (6)	64. (3)	65. (2)	66. (1)	67. (a)	68. (a)	69. (a)	70. (a)
71. (a)	72. (3)	73. (90)	74. (b)	75. (17)	76. (a)	77. (a)			

Exercise 2

1. (a)	2. (a)	3. (a)	4. (a)	5. (a)	6. (b)	7. (d)	8. (c)	9. (c)	10. (c)
11. (a)	12. (a)	13. (b)	14. (a)	15. (d)	16. (b)	17. (b)	18. (d)	19. (b)	20. (b)
21. (a,b,c,d)	22. (b,c,d)	23. (b,c)	24. (a,b,c)	25. (a,b,c)	26. (b,c,d)	27. (a,d)	28. (a,d)	29. (b,c,d)	30. (a,c)
31. (b,c,d)	32. (a,c,d)	33. (a,b,c,d)	34. (b,c,d)	35. (a,b,c,d)	36. (a)	37. (c)	38. (b)	39. (a)	40. (b)
41. (a)	42. (c)	43. (a)	44. (2023)	45. (100)	46. (2)	47. (2)	48. (8)	49. (1)	50. (1)
51. (3)	52. (1)	53. (18)	54. (27)	55. (0.5)	56. (18)	57. (0.33)	58. (0.4)	59. (2)	

60. (A) $\to$ (q), (B) $\to$ (s), (C) $\to$ (r), (D) $\to$ (p)
61. (A) $\to$ (q), (B) $\to$ (r), (C) $\to$ (p), (D) $\to$ (s)
62. (A) $\to$ (s), (B) $\to$ (s), (C) $\to$ (q), (D) $\to$ (p)

63. (c) 64. (16) 65. (8) 66. (c) 67. (a,c) 68. (a,c) 69. (a,c)

Solutions

Exercise 1 - JEE Main Pattern

1. $\dfrac{dy}{dx} = \dfrac{y}{x} - \cos^2 \dfrac{y}{x}$

Let $y = vx \Rightarrow v + x\dfrac{dv}{dx} = v - \cos^2 v$

$$\int \frac{dv}{\cos^2 v} + \int \frac{dx}{x} = C \Rightarrow \quad \tan v + \ln x = C$$

$$\tan \frac{y}{x} + \ln x = C$$

If $x = 1, y = \dfrac{\pi}{4} \Rightarrow \; C = 1 \; \Rightarrow \; \tan \dfrac{y}{x} = 1 - \ln x = \ln \dfrac{e}{x}$

$$y = x \tan^{-1}\left(\ln \frac{e}{x}\right)$$

2. $\int_0^x f(x)\, dx = y^3$

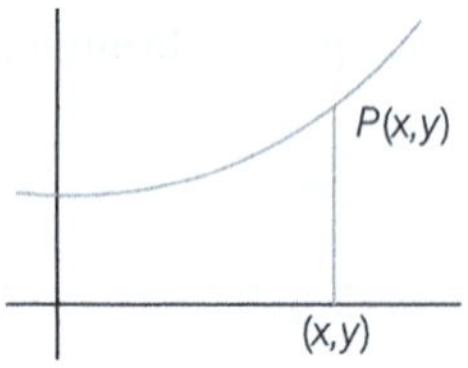

On differentiating $f(x) = 3y^2 \cdot \dfrac{dy}{dx}$, we get

$\Rightarrow \qquad y = 3y^2 \dfrac{dy}{dx} \; \Rightarrow \; y = 0 \qquad$ (rejected)

or $\qquad 3y\, dy = dx \Rightarrow \dfrac{3y^2}{2} = x + C \; \Rightarrow \;$ Parabola

3. $y = mx + c; \; \dfrac{dy}{dx} = m; \; \dfrac{d^2y}{dx^2} = 0$

Substituting in $\dfrac{d^2y}{dx^2} - 3\dfrac{dy}{dx} - 4y = -4x$

$\Rightarrow \qquad 0 - 3m - 4(mx + c) = -4x$

$\Rightarrow \qquad -3m - 4c - 4mx = -4x$

$\Rightarrow \qquad -(3m + 4c) = 4x(m - 1) \qquad$ ...(i)

Eq. (i) is true for all real x, if $m = 1$ and $c = -3/4$.

4. $y = u^m \Rightarrow \dfrac{dy}{dx} = mu^{m-1}\dfrac{du}{dx}$

Since, $2x^4 \cdot u^m \cdot mu^{m-1} \cdot \dfrac{du}{dx} + u^{4m} = 4x^6$

$$\frac{du}{dx} = \frac{4x^6 - u^{4m}}{2m\, x^4\, u^{2m-1}}$$

$\Rightarrow \qquad 4m = 6 \; \Rightarrow \; m = \dfrac{3}{2}$

and $\qquad 2m - 1 = 2 \; \Rightarrow \; m = \dfrac{3}{2}$

5. $\dfrac{dy}{dx} - \dfrac{y}{x^2}\tan\dfrac{1}{x} = -\sec\dfrac{1}{x} \cdot \dfrac{1}{x^2}$

$\text{IF} = e^{-\int \frac{1}{x^2}\tan\frac{1}{x}\, dx} = \sec\dfrac{1}{x}$

$\Rightarrow y \cdot \sec\dfrac{1}{x} = -\int \sec^2\left(\dfrac{1}{x}\right)\dfrac{1}{x^2}\, dx = \tan\dfrac{1}{x} + C$

If $y \to -1$, then $x \to \infty$

$\Rightarrow \qquad C = -1 \; \Rightarrow \; y = \sin\dfrac{1}{x} - \cos\dfrac{1}{x}$

6. $\dfrac{dM}{dt} = -KM \; \Rightarrow \; M = Ce^{-kt}$ when $t = 0$; $M = M_0$

$\Rightarrow \qquad C = M_0$

$\Rightarrow \qquad M = M_0 e^{-kt}$

when $t = 1$, $M = \dfrac{M_0}{2} \Rightarrow k = \ln 2$

Therefore, $M = M_0 e^{-t\ln 2}$

when $M = \dfrac{M_0}{1000}$, then $t = \log_2 1000 = 9.98$

$= 10\,\text{h}$ approximately

7. $f'(x) - \dfrac{2x(x+1)}{x+1} f(x) = \dfrac{e^{x^2}}{(x+1)^2}$

$$\text{IF} = e^{\int -2x\, dx} = e^{-x^2}$$

$\therefore \qquad f(x) \cdot e^{-x^2} = \int \dfrac{dx}{(x+1)^2} \Rightarrow f(x) \cdot e^{-x^2} = -\dfrac{1}{x+1} + C$

At $x = 0$, $f(0) = 5 \Rightarrow C = 6$

$\therefore \qquad f(x) = \left(\dfrac{6x+5}{x+1}\right) \cdot e^{x^2}$

8. $(x^2 z^{2\alpha} - 1)\, \alpha z^{\alpha - 1}\, dz + 2x\, z^{3\alpha}\, dx = 0$

or $\qquad \alpha(x^2 z^{3\alpha - 1} - z^{\alpha - 1})\, dz + 2x\, z^{3\alpha}\, dx = 0$

for homogeneous every term must be of the same degree,

$$3\alpha + 1 = \alpha - 1$$

$\Rightarrow \qquad \alpha = -1$

9. $f(-1) = a - b + c$; $f(1) = a + b + c$; $f(0) = c$

$$A = \int_{-1}^{1} (ax^2 + bx + c)\, dx = \left.\frac{ax^3}{3} + \frac{bx^2}{2} + cx\right|_{-1}^{1}$$

$$A = 2\left(\frac{a}{3} + c\right)$$

$$= \frac{1}{3}(2a + 6c)$$

$$= \frac{1}{3}(f(-1) + 4f(0) + f(1))$$

10. $\text{IF} = e^{\int \frac{g'(x)}{g(x)}} = e^{\ln g(x)} = g(x)$

$$\Rightarrow \quad yg(x) = \frac{1}{2}\int \frac{2g(x)g'(x)}{1+g^2(x)}\,dx = \frac{1}{2}\ln(1+g^2(x)) + C$$

Here, $\quad C = 1 - \dfrac{\ln 2}{2}$

$$\therefore \; y(e)g(e) = \frac{1}{2}\ln(1+2e-1) + 1 - \frac{\ln 2}{2} = \frac{3}{2}$$

$$\therefore \quad y(e) = \frac{3}{2g(e)}$$

11. $x = \ln\left(1 + \dfrac{dy}{dx}\right)$

$$\Rightarrow \quad 1 + \frac{dy}{dx} = e^x \Rightarrow \frac{dy}{dx} = e^x - 1$$

$$\Rightarrow \quad y = e^x - x + C$$

At $x = 0$, $y = 1$

$$\therefore \quad 1 = 1 - 0 + C \Rightarrow C = 0$$

$$\Rightarrow \quad y = e^x - x$$

$$\therefore f'\left(\ln\frac{1}{2}\right) + f\left(\ln\frac{1}{2}\right) = \frac{1}{2} - 1 + \frac{1}{2} + \ln 2 = \ln 2$$

12. $(\cos y - \sin y)\dfrac{dy}{dx} + (\cos y + \sin y)e^{-x} = e^{e^{-x}}$

$$\Rightarrow \quad \cos y + \sin y = u$$

$$\Rightarrow \quad \frac{du}{dx} + e^{-x}u = e^{e^{-x}}$$

$$\Rightarrow \quad ue^{-e^{-x}} = x + C$$

$$\Rightarrow \quad (\cos y + \sin y)e^{-e^{-x}} = x + C$$

$$\left(0, \frac{-\pi}{4}\right) \Rightarrow C = 0$$

$$\Rightarrow \quad e^{-e^{-t}} = t \qquad \text{[putting } (t, 0)\text{]}$$

$$\Rightarrow \quad t \cdot e^{e^{-t}} = 1$$

13. Given, $\dfrac{d}{dx}\left(\dfrac{f'(x)}{e^x}\right) = 1$

$$\therefore \quad \frac{f'(x)}{e^x} = x + C$$

Put $x = 0 \Rightarrow \dfrac{1}{1} = 0 + C$

$$\therefore \quad C = 1$$

$$\therefore \quad f'(x) = e^x(x+1) \Rightarrow f(x) = xe^x + k$$

Put $x = 0 \Rightarrow k = 0 \Rightarrow f(x) = xe^x$

$$\therefore \quad \frac{f(x)}{x} = e^x$$

$$\therefore \quad \int_0^1 e^x dx = e - 1$$

14. Applying C and D, we get

$$\frac{dy}{dx} = \frac{e^{-x}}{e^x} = e^{-2x}$$

$$\Rightarrow \quad 2y = -e^{-2x} + c$$

or $\quad 2ye^{2x} = c \cdot e^{2x} - 1$

15. $\displaystyle\int \frac{dx}{x} = \int \frac{y\,dy}{1+y^2} \Rightarrow \log x = \frac{1}{2}\log(1+y^2) + C$

$$\Rightarrow \quad 0 = \frac{1}{2}\log 1 + c \Rightarrow c = 0$$

$$\Rightarrow \quad x^2 - y^2 = 1$$

For $\dfrac{Cdy}{dx} = \dfrac{y}{x}$ and for $\dfrac{Edy}{dx} = \dfrac{-x}{3y}$

For point of intersection,

$$x^2 = \frac{3}{2} \text{ and } y^2 = \frac{1}{2}$$

$$m_1 \cdot m_2 = -1$$

The conic C is $x^2 - y^2 = 1$ and E is $x^2 + 3y^2 = 3$

Angle of intersection is $\pi/2$.

16. We have, $\sin x\dfrac{dy}{dx} + y\cos x = 4x$

$$\Rightarrow \quad \frac{dy}{dx} + y\cot x = 4x\,\text{cosec}\,x$$

This is a linear differential equation of form

$$\frac{dy}{dx} + Py = Q$$

where $P = \cot x$, $Q = 4x\,\text{cosec}\,x$

Now, $\text{IF} = e^{\int P dx} = e^{\int \cot x dx} = e^{\log_e \sin x} = \sin x$

Solution of the differential equation is

$$y \cdot \sin x = \int 4x\,\text{cosec}\,x \sin x\,dx + C$$

$$\Rightarrow \quad y\sin x = \int 4x dx + C = 2x^2 + C$$

Put $x = \dfrac{\pi}{2}, y = 0$, we get

$$C = -\frac{\pi^2}{2}$$

$$\Rightarrow \quad y\sin x = 2x^2 - \frac{\pi^2}{2}$$

Put $x = \dfrac{\pi}{6}$,

$$\therefore \quad y\left(\frac{1}{2}\right) = 2\left(\frac{\pi^2}{36}\right) - \frac{\pi^2}{2}$$

$$\Rightarrow \quad y = \frac{\pi^2}{9} - \pi^2 \Rightarrow y = -\frac{8\pi^2}{9}$$

17. Given differential equation is

$$y(1 + xy)\,dx = x\,dy$$

$$\Rightarrow \quad y\,dx + xy^2\,dx = x\,dy$$

$$\Rightarrow \quad \frac{x\,dy - y\,dx}{y^2} = x\,dx$$

$$\Rightarrow \quad -\frac{(y\,dx - x\,dy)}{y^2} = x\,dx$$

$$\Rightarrow \quad -d\left(\frac{x}{y}\right) = x\,dx$$

On integrating both sides, we get

$$-\frac{x}{y}=\frac{x^2}{2}+C \quad ...(i)$$

$\because$ It passes through $(1, -1)$.

$$\therefore \quad 1=\frac{1}{2}+C \Rightarrow C=\frac{1}{2}$$

Now, from Eq. (i) $-\frac{x}{y}=\frac{x^2}{2}+\frac{1}{2}$

$$\Rightarrow \quad x^2+1=-\frac{2x}{y} \Rightarrow y=-\frac{2x}{x^2+1}$$

$$\therefore \quad f\left(-\frac{1}{2}\right)=\frac{4}{5}$$

18. Given differential equation is

$$(x\log x)\frac{dy}{dx}+y=2x\log x$$

$$\Rightarrow \quad \frac{dy}{dx}+\frac{y}{x\log x}=2$$

This is a linear differential equation.

$$\therefore \ \text{IF}=e^{\int \frac{1}{x\log x}dx}=e^{\ln(\log x)}=\log x$$

Now, the solution of given differential equation is given by

$$y\cdot\log x=\int \log x\cdot 2dx$$

$$\Rightarrow y\cdot\log x=2\int \log x dx \Rightarrow y\cdot\log x=2\,[x\log x-x]+c$$

At $x=1, \ c=2$

$\Rightarrow y\cdot\log x=2\,[x\log x-x]+2$

At $x=e, \ y=2(e-e)+2 \Rightarrow y=2$

19. We have, $y\frac{dy}{dx}=x\left[\frac{y^2}{x^2}+\frac{\phi\left(\frac{y^2}{x^2}\right)}{\phi'\left(\frac{y^2}{x^2}\right)}\right]$

Let $y=tx \Rightarrow \frac{dy}{dx}=t+x\frac{dt}{dx}$

$$\therefore \quad tx\left(t+x\frac{dt}{dx}\right)=x\left[t^2+\frac{\phi(t^2)}{\phi'(t^2)}\right]$$

$$\int \frac{t\phi'(t^2)}{\phi(t^2)}dt=\int\frac{dx}{x}$$

Let $\phi(t^2)=P \Rightarrow \phi'(t^2)2t\,dt=dP$

$$\therefore \quad \frac{1}{2}\int\frac{1}{P}dP=\int\frac{dx}{x} \Rightarrow \frac{1}{2}\ln P=\ln x+\ln C$$

$$\Rightarrow \quad \ln P=\ln(xC)^2$$

$$\Rightarrow \quad \phi(t^2)=x^2K \quad [\text{where } K=C^2]$$

$$\Rightarrow \quad \phi\left(\frac{y^2}{x^2}\right)=x^2K$$

Now, $y(1)=-1 \Rightarrow \phi(1)=K$

Then, $\phi\left(\frac{y^2}{4}\right)=4K \Rightarrow \phi\left(\frac{y^2}{4}\right)=4\phi(1)$

20. The equation of tangent to the curve at (x, y), is

$$Y-y=\frac{dy}{dx}(X-x)$$

Putting $X=0$, we get

$$Y=y-x\frac{dy}{dx}$$

It is given that

$$\left(y-x\frac{dy}{dx}\right)^2=xy$$

$$\Rightarrow \quad \left(y-x\frac{dy}{dx}\right)=\sqrt{xy}$$

$$\Rightarrow \quad x\frac{dy}{dx}+\sqrt{xy}=y \Rightarrow \frac{dy}{dx}+\sqrt{\frac{y}{x}}=\frac{y}{x}$$

Putting $y=vx$,

$$\frac{dy}{dx}=v+x\frac{dv}{dx}$$

$$\therefore \quad v+x\frac{dv}{dx}+\sqrt{v}=v \Rightarrow x\frac{dv}{dx}=-\sqrt{v}$$

$$\Rightarrow \quad \frac{1}{\sqrt{v}}dv=-\frac{1}{x}dx$$

Integrating both sides, we get

$$2\sqrt{v}=-\log|x|+C \Rightarrow 2\sqrt{\frac{y}{x}}+\log|x|=C$$

21. $2x^2y\,dx-2y^4\,dx+2x^3dy+3xy^3\,dy=0$

Dividing throughout by x^3y, we get

$$2\frac{dx}{x}-\frac{2y^3}{x^3}dx+2\cdot\frac{dy}{y}+\frac{3y^2}{x^2}dy=0$$

$$\Rightarrow \quad 2\frac{dx}{x}+2\frac{dy}{y}+\frac{3y^2x^4\,dy-2y^3x^3dx}{x^6}=0$$

$$\Rightarrow \quad 2\frac{dx}{x}+2\frac{dy}{y}+\frac{3y^2x^2\,dy-2y^3x\,dx}{x^4}=0$$

$$\Rightarrow \quad 2d(\ln x)+2d(\ln y)+d\left(\frac{y^3}{x^2}\right)=0$$

$$\Rightarrow \quad 2\ln|x|+2\ln|y|+\frac{y^3}{x^2}=C$$

when $x=1, y=1$.

So, $\quad C=1$

22. $\frac{dy}{dx}=\frac{y}{x^2} \Rightarrow \frac{dy}{y}=\frac{dx}{x^2} \Rightarrow \log y=\frac{-1}{x}+k+\log c$

$\Rightarrow y=ce^{\frac{-1}{x}}$ which passes through $(1, 3)$

$$\Rightarrow \quad ce^{-1}=3 \Rightarrow c=3e$$

$\therefore \ y=3e^{1-\frac{1}{x}}$ is the curve.

Hence, $f(x)=3e^{1-\frac{1}{x}}$

$$\Rightarrow \quad f'(x)=3e^{1-\frac{1}{x}}\left(\frac{1}{x^2}\right)>0\ \forall\ x\in R-\{0\}$$

Also, $\lim_{x\to+\infty} f(x)=3e$

$$\therefore \quad k=3$$

23. $\dfrac{d^2y}{dx^2} = y$

$$y = Ae^x + Be^{-x}$$

$$A + B = 2$$

$$A - B = 3$$

On solving $y = \dfrac{1}{2}(5e^x - e^{-x})$

$$f(\ln 2) = \frac{1}{2}\left(5 \times 2 - \frac{1}{2}\right) = 5 - \frac{1}{4}$$

$$[f(\ln 2)] = \left[5 - \frac{1}{4}\right] = 4$$

$$\frac{[k]}{8} = \frac{4}{8} = 0.5$$

24. Given that

$$\log\left(\frac{dy}{dx}\right) = 3x + 4y$$

$$\Rightarrow \quad \frac{dy}{dx} = e^{3x+4y}$$

$$\Rightarrow \quad \frac{dy}{dx} = e^{3x} \cdot e^{4y}$$

$$[\because e^{a+b} = e^a \cdot e^b, \forall\ a, b \in R]$$

$$\Rightarrow \quad \int e^{-4y} dy = \int e^{3x} dx$$

$$\Rightarrow \quad \frac{e^{-4y}}{-4} = \frac{e^{3x}}{3} + C$$

$$y = 0, \text{ when } x = 0$$

$$\Rightarrow \quad -\frac{1}{4} = \frac{1}{3} + C \Rightarrow C = \frac{-7}{12}$$

So, $$\frac{e^{-4y}}{-4} = \frac{e^{3x}}{3} - \frac{7}{12}$$

$$\Rightarrow \quad e^{-4y} = \frac{4e^{3x} - 7}{-3}$$

$$\Rightarrow \quad 4y = \ln\left(\frac{3}{7 - 4e^{3x}}\right)$$

when $x = -\dfrac{2}{3}\ln 2$, then

$$4y = \ln\left(\frac{3}{6}\right) \Rightarrow y = \frac{1}{4}\ln\left(\frac{1}{2}\right) \Rightarrow y = -\frac{1}{4}\ln 2$$

Hence, $k = 4$

25. The given differential equation is

$$8\sqrt{x}(\sqrt{9+\sqrt{x}})dy = (\sqrt{4+\sqrt{9+\sqrt{x}}})^{-1}dx \quad [x > 0]$$

$$\Rightarrow \quad dy = \frac{1}{\{8\sqrt{x}(\sqrt{9+\sqrt{x}})\}(\sqrt{4+\sqrt{9+\sqrt{x}}})}dx$$

Let $4 + \sqrt{9+\sqrt{x}} = t$

$$\Rightarrow \quad \frac{1}{2\sqrt{9+\sqrt{x}}} \times \frac{1}{2\sqrt{x}}dx = dt$$

$$\therefore \quad dy = \frac{1}{2\sqrt{t}}dt$$

On integrating both sides, we get

$$y = \sqrt{t} + C \Rightarrow y = \sqrt{4+\sqrt{9+\sqrt{x}}} + C$$

It is given that $y = \sqrt{7}$ when $x = 0$.

Then, $C = 0$

So, $y = \sqrt{4+\sqrt{9+\sqrt{x}}}$

When $x = 256$, then

$$y = \sqrt{4+\sqrt{9+\sqrt{256}}} = 3 \quad [\text{since, } x > 0 \text{ given so, } y > 0]$$

Hence, $y(256) = 3$

26. The given differential equation is

$$\frac{dy}{dx} = \frac{x^2 + y^2 + 3x + 3y + 2xy + 1}{x^2 + y^2 - 3x - 3y + 2xy + 1}$$

$$\frac{dy}{dx} = \frac{(x+y)^2 + 3(x+y) + 1}{(x+y)^2 - 3(x+y) + 1}$$

Let $x + y = v \Rightarrow 1 + \dfrac{dy}{dx} = \dfrac{dv}{dx}$

$$\therefore \quad \frac{dv}{dx} - 1 = \frac{v^2 + 3v + 1}{v^2 - 3v + 1} \Rightarrow \frac{dv}{dx} = \frac{2v^2 + 2}{v^2 - 3v + 1}$$

$$\Rightarrow \quad \frac{v^2 - 3v + 1}{v^2 + 1}dv = 2dx$$

$$\Rightarrow \quad \left(1 - \frac{3}{2}\left(\frac{2v}{v^2+1}\right)\right)dv = 2dx$$

Integrating both sides, we get

$$v - \frac{3}{2}\log|v^2 + 1| = 2x + C$$

$$\Rightarrow \quad y - \frac{3}{2}\log|(x+y)^2 + 1| = x + C$$

Hence, $m - n = 3 - 2 = 1$

27. Given, $(2xy^2 - y)dx + x\,dy = 0$

$$\Rightarrow \quad \frac{dy}{dx} + 2y^2 - \frac{y}{x} = 0 \Rightarrow -\frac{1}{y^2}\frac{dy}{dx} + \frac{1}{y}\left(\frac{1}{x}\right) = 2$$

Let $\dfrac{1}{y} = t \Rightarrow -\dfrac{1}{y^2}\dfrac{dy}{dx} = \dfrac{dt}{dx}$

$$\therefore \quad \frac{dt}{dx} + \frac{1}{x}t = 2$$

$$\text{IF} = e^{\int \frac{1}{x}dx} = x$$

So, the solution is

$$t \cdot x = \int 2x\,dx + C$$

$$\frac{x}{y} = x^2 + C \quad \text{...(i)}$$

It passes through the point of intersection of lines $2x - 3y = 1$ and $3x + 2y = 8$ i.e. $(2, 1)$.

$$\therefore \quad \frac{2}{1} = 4 + C \Rightarrow C = -2$$

So, $\dfrac{x}{y} = x^2 - 2$

Put $x = 1$, then $\dfrac{1}{y} = 1 - 2 = -1$

$$\Rightarrow \quad y(1) = -1$$

$$|y(1)| = 1$$

28. Let equation of tangent at $P(x, y)$ is

$$Y - y = m(X - x)$$

For y-intercept, $X = 0$

$$Y = y - mx$$

Given that

$$y - mx = x^3$$

$$\Rightarrow \quad x\frac{dy}{dx} - y = -x^3 \quad \left[\because m = \frac{dy}{dx}\right]$$

$$\Rightarrow \quad \frac{dy}{dx} - \frac{1}{x}y = -x^2$$

$$\text{IF} = e^{-\int \frac{1}{x}dx} = e^{-\log x} = \frac{1}{x}$$

So, solution of given linear differential equation is

$$y\frac{1}{x} = \int \frac{1}{x}(-x^2)dx \Rightarrow y = -\frac{x^3}{2} + Cx$$

Given that $f(1) = 1 \Rightarrow C = \frac{3}{2}$

Hence, $y = -\frac{x^3}{2} + \frac{3}{2}x \Rightarrow f(-3) = 9$

29. Given that $\frac{dx}{dt} \propto x$

$$\Rightarrow \quad \frac{dx}{dt} = \lambda x \quad [\lambda = \text{constant}]$$

$$\Rightarrow \quad \frac{dx}{x} = \lambda dt$$

$$\Rightarrow \quad \int_{1000}^{x} \frac{dx}{x} = \int_0^t \lambda dt$$

$$\Rightarrow \log x - \log 1000 = \lambda t$$

$$\Rightarrow \quad \log\left(\frac{x}{1000}\right) = \lambda t$$

Put $t = 2$, $x = 1200$

$$\log\left(\frac{12}{10}\right) = 2\lambda$$

$$\lambda = \frac{1}{2}\ln\left(\frac{6}{5}\right)$$

Now, $\log\left(\frac{x}{1000}\right) = \frac{t}{2}\log\left(\frac{6}{5}\right)$

$$x = 1000e^{t/2\ln\left(\frac{6}{5}\right)}$$

when $x = 2000$ at $t = \dfrac{k}{\ln\left(\frac{6}{5}\right)}$

$$\Rightarrow \quad 2000 = 1000\, e^{\left(\frac{k}{2\ln(6/5)} \times \ln\left(\frac{6}{5}\right)\right)} \Rightarrow 2 = e^{k/2}$$

$$\Rightarrow \quad \frac{k}{2} = \ln 2 \Rightarrow k = 2\ln 2$$

$$\Rightarrow \quad \left(\frac{k}{\ln 2}\right) = 2$$

Hence, $\left(\frac{k}{\ln 2}\right)^2 = 4$

30. Given that

$$y'(x) + y(x)g'(x) = g(x)g'(x),\ y(0) = 0,\ x \in R$$

$$\frac{d}{dx}\{y(x)\} + g'(x)y(x) = g(x)g'(x)$$

$\text{IF} = e^{\int g'(x)dx} = e^{g(x)}$

So, $y(x)\cdot e^{g(x)} = \int e^{g(x)}\cdot g(x)\cdot g'(x)dx + C$

Let $g(x) = t$

$$\Rightarrow \quad g'(x)dx = dt$$

$$y(x)e^{g(x)} = \int t\cdot e^t dt + C = t\cdot e^t - e^t + C$$

$$\Rightarrow \quad y(x)e^{g(x)} = e^{g(x)}\{g(x) - 1\} + C$$

$$\Rightarrow \quad y(x) = (g(x) - 1) + Ce^{-g(x)}$$

Put $x = 0$, then

$$y(0) = (g(0) - 1) + Ce^{-g(0)}$$

$$\Rightarrow \quad C = 1$$

$$\Rightarrow \quad y(x) = (g(x) - 1) + e^{-g(x)}$$

When $x = 2$, then

$$y(2) = (g(2) - 1) + e^{-g(2)}$$

$$\Rightarrow \quad y(2) = (0 - 1) + e^{-(0)} = -1 + 1 = 0$$

31. $y\cdot\sin 2x - \cos x + (1 + \sin^2 x)\frac{dy}{dx} = 0$ [let $f(x) = y$, $f'(x) = \frac{dy}{dx}$]

$$\Rightarrow \quad (1 + \sin^2 x)\frac{dy}{dx} + (\sin 2x)y = \cos x$$

$$\Rightarrow \quad \frac{dy}{dx} + \left(\frac{\sin 2x}{1 + \sin^2 x}\right)y = \frac{\cos x}{1 + \sin^2 x}$$

This is a linear differential equation.

$$\therefore \quad \text{IF} = e^{\int P dx} = e^{\int \frac{\sin 2x}{1 + \sin^2 x}dx}$$

Let $1 + \sin^2 x = t \Rightarrow \sin 2x dx = dt$

$$\text{IF} = e^{\int \frac{dt}{t}} = e^{\ln t} = t$$

$$\text{IF} = (1 + \sin^2 x)$$

Here, solution is

$$y\cdot(1 + \sin^2 x) = \int \frac{\cos x}{(1 + \sin^2 x)}(1 + \sin^2 x)dx$$

$$\Rightarrow \quad y(1 + \sin^2 x) = \sin x + C \quad \text{...(i)}$$

Given that $y(0) = 0$

$$\Rightarrow \quad C = 0$$

Substituting in Eq. (i),

$$y = \frac{\sin x}{1 + \sin^2 x}$$

Now, when $x = \frac{\pi}{6}$, then $y = \dfrac{\sin\frac{\pi}{6}}{1 + \sin^2\frac{\pi}{6}} = \dfrac{2}{5}$

Hence, $|A - B| = |2 - 5| = 3$

32. Given that

$$f(x) = e^{-x}\int_3^x \{3t^2 + 2t + 4f'(t)\}dt$$

$\therefore f(3) = 0$

Now, $e^x f(x) = \int_3^x \{3t^2 + 2t + 4f'(t)\}dt$

$\Rightarrow e^x f(x) + e^x f'(x) = 3x^2 + 2x + 4f'(x)$

$\Rightarrow (e^x - 4)\dfrac{dy}{dx} + e^x y = (3x^2 + 2x)$

This is a linear differential equation.

So, IF $= e^{\int P\,dx} = e^{\int \frac{e^x}{e^x - 4}dx} = e^{\ln(e^x - 4)} = e^x - 4$

Solution is $y \cdot (e^x - 4) = \int \left(\dfrac{3x^2 + 2x}{(e^x - 4)} \cdot (e^x - 4)\right) dx$

$\Rightarrow \quad y(e^x - 4) = x^3 + x^2 + C$

Put $x = 3$

Then, $y = 0 \Rightarrow C = -36$

$$y = \frac{x^3 + x^2 - 36}{e^x - 4}$$

$$f'(x) = \frac{(3x^2 + 2x)(e^x - 4) - (x^3 + x^2 - 36)e^x}{(e^x - 4)^2}$$

Put $x = 4$, then $f'(4) = \dfrac{12e^4 - 224}{(e^4 - 4)^2}$

$\therefore \quad \alpha = 12$ and $\beta = 4$

Hence, $\alpha + \beta = 12 + 4 = 16$

33. Given, differential equation is

$(x^2 - 4)dy - (y^2 - 3y)dx = 0$, where $x > 2$ and $y(4) = \dfrac{3}{2}$

$\Rightarrow \quad (x^2 - 4)dy = (y^2 - 3y)\,dx = y(y - 3)dx$

$\Rightarrow \quad \dfrac{1}{y(y-3)}dy = \dfrac{1}{x^2 - 4}dx = \dfrac{1}{(x-2)(x+2)}dx$

$\Rightarrow \quad \dfrac{1}{3}\left[\dfrac{y - (y-3)}{y(y-3)}\right]dy = \dfrac{1}{4}\left[\dfrac{(x+2) - (x-2)}{(x+2)(x-2)}\right]dx$

$\Rightarrow \quad \dfrac{1}{3}\left[\dfrac{1}{y-3} - \dfrac{1}{y}\right]dy = \dfrac{1}{4}\left[\dfrac{1}{x-2} - \dfrac{1}{x+2}\right]dx$

On integrating both sides, we get

$\dfrac{1}{3}[\ln|y-3| - \ln|y|] = \dfrac{1}{4}[\ln|x-2| - \ln|x+2|] + C$

$\Rightarrow \quad \dfrac{1}{3}\ln\left|\dfrac{y-3}{y}\right| = \dfrac{1}{4}\ln\left|\dfrac{x-2}{x+2}\right| + C \quad$ ...(i)

As given, $y(4) = \dfrac{3}{2}$, i.e. we put $x = 4$ and $y = \dfrac{3}{2}$ in Eq. (i), we get

$$\frac{1}{3}\ln\left|\frac{\frac{3}{2} - 3}{\frac{3}{2}}\right| = \frac{1}{4}\ln\left|\frac{4-2}{4+2}\right| + C$$

$\Rightarrow \quad \dfrac{1}{3}\ln|-1| = \dfrac{1}{4}\ln\left|\dfrac{1}{3}\right| + C$

$\Rightarrow \quad \dfrac{1}{3}\ln(1) = -\dfrac{1}{4}\ln(3) + C$

$\Rightarrow \quad C = \dfrac{1}{4}\ln(3) \quad [\because \ln(1) = 0]$

From Eq. (i),

$\dfrac{1}{3}\ln\left|\dfrac{y-3}{y}\right| = \dfrac{1}{4}\ln\left|\dfrac{x-2}{x+2}\right| + \dfrac{1}{4}\ln(3) \quad$ ...(ii)

We have to find $y(10)$, i.e when $x = 10$, then $y = ?$

From Eq. (ii),

$$\frac{1}{3}\ln\left|\frac{y-3}{y}\right| = \frac{1}{4}\ln\left|\frac{2}{3}\right| + \frac{1}{4}\ln(3)$$

$\Rightarrow \quad \dfrac{1}{3}\ln\left|\dfrac{y-3}{y}\right| = \dfrac{1}{4}\ln(2) - \dfrac{1}{4}\ln(3) + \dfrac{1}{4}\ln(3) = \dfrac{1}{4}\ln(2)$

$\Rightarrow \quad \ln\left|\dfrac{y-3}{y}\right| = \ln(2)^{\frac{3}{4}}$

$\Rightarrow \quad \left|\dfrac{y-3}{y}\right| = 2^{\frac{3}{4}}, \forall\, x > 2, \dfrac{dy}{dx} < 0$

As, $\quad y(4) = \dfrac{3}{2} \Rightarrow y \in (0, 3)$

So, $\quad -y + 3 = 8^{\frac{1}{4}} \cdot y \Rightarrow y = \dfrac{3}{1 + (8)^{\frac{1}{4}}}$

34. We have, $\sec x\,dy + \{2(1-x)\tan x + x(2-x)\}\,dx = 0$

$\Rightarrow \quad \dfrac{dy}{dx} = -[2(1-x)\sin x + x(2-x)\cos x]$

On variable separable and integration,

$\int dy = -\int (2(1-x)\sin x + x(2-x)\cos x)\,dx$

$y = 2\int (x-1)\sin x\,dx + \int (x-2)x\cos x\,dx$

$= 2[-(x-1)\cos x + \int \cos x\,dx] + \int (x-2)x\cos x\,dx$

$= 2[\sin x - (x-1)\cos x] + (x-2)x\sin x - \int (2x-2)\sin x\,dx$

$= 2(\sin x - (x-1)\cos x) + (x-2)x\sin x$

$\quad -2[-(x-1)\cos x + \sin x] + C$

$y = (x-2)x\sin x + C$

Given, $y(0) = 2 \Rightarrow 2 = c$

$\therefore \quad y(x) = (x-2)x\sin x + 2$

So, $\quad y(2) = 2$

35. $\dfrac{dy}{dx} = \dfrac{\tan x + y}{\sin x(\sec x - \sin x \cdot \tan x)}$

$= \dfrac{\sin x + y\cos x}{\sin x(1 - \sin^2 x)} = \dfrac{\sin x + y\cos x}{\sin x \cdot \cos^2 x}$

$\dfrac{dy}{dx} = \sec^2 x + \dfrac{y}{\sin x \cos x}$

$\dfrac{dy}{dx} = \sec^2 x + \dfrac{2y}{\sin 2x}$

$\dfrac{dy}{dx} - (2\operatorname{cosec} 2x)y = \sec^2 x$

IF $= e^{-\int 2\operatorname{cosec} 2x\,dx} = e^{-\frac{2\ln|\operatorname{cosec} 2x - \cot 2x|}{2}}$

$= \dfrac{1}{\operatorname{cosec} 2x - \cot 2x} = \operatorname{cosec} 2x + \cot 2x$

$= \dfrac{1}{\sin 2x} + \dfrac{\cos 2x}{\sin 2x}$

$= \dfrac{1 + \cos 2x}{\sin 2x} = \dfrac{2\cos^2 x}{2\sin x\cos x} = \cot x$

Then, $y(\cot x) = \int (\cot x) \sec^2 x \, dx$

$\Rightarrow \quad \dfrac{y}{\tan x} = \int \dfrac{\sec^2 x}{\tan x} dx$

$\Rightarrow \quad \dfrac{y}{\tan x} = \ln|\tan x| + C$

$\Rightarrow \quad y = \tan x \ln|\tan x| + C \tan x$

Given, $y\left(\dfrac{\pi}{4}\right) = 2$

When $x = \dfrac{\pi}{4}$, $y = 2$

$\therefore \quad 2 = 1 \times 0 + C,\ C = 2$

$\because \quad y\left(\dfrac{\pi}{3}\right) = \tan\dfrac{\pi}{3} \ln \tan\dfrac{\pi}{3} + 2\tan\dfrac{\pi}{3}$

$= \sqrt{3} \ln\sqrt{3} + 2\sqrt{3} = \sqrt{3}(\ln\sqrt{3} + 2)$

36. **Decoding the Question**

The given differential equation is a homogenous differential equation. To find the solution of such type of differential equation substitute $x = vy$

Then, solve it by integration.

Given, $y\dfrac{dx}{dy} = x(\ln x - \ln y + 1)\ x > 0, y > 0$

$\Rightarrow \quad \dfrac{dx}{dy} = \dfrac{x}{y}\left(\ln\dfrac{x}{y} + 1\right)$

$\Rightarrow \quad \dfrac{x}{y} = v$

$x = vy \Rightarrow \dfrac{dx}{dy} = v + y\dfrac{dv}{dy}$

$\therefore$ Equation becomes,

$v + y\dfrac{dv}{dy} = v(\ln v + 1) \Rightarrow y\dfrac{dv}{dy} = v \ln v$

Integrating both sides, we get

$\int \dfrac{dv}{v \ln v} = \int \dfrac{dy}{y}$

$\ln(\ln v) = \ln y + C$

$\ln v = ky$

$\because \ln\left(\dfrac{x}{y}\right) = ky$

$\Rightarrow \quad x = e$ when $y = 1$ [given]

$\therefore \ln e = k \Rightarrow k = 1$

$\ln\dfrac{x}{y} = y$ or $\left|\ln\dfrac{x}{y}\right| = y$

37. Given, differential equation is

$(2x + 3y - 2)dx + (4x + 6y - 7)dy = 0$ ...(i)

$\dfrac{dy}{dx} = \dfrac{-(2x + 3y - 2)}{(4x + 6y - 7)}$

Put $2x + 3y - 2 = z \Rightarrow 2 + 3\dfrac{dy}{dx} = \dfrac{dz}{dx}$ ...(ii)

$\Rightarrow 4x + 6y - 4 = 2z \Rightarrow 4x + 6y - 7 = 2z - 3$

Eq. (i) becomes,

$\dfrac{dz}{dx} = \dfrac{-3z + 4z - 6}{2z - 3} = \dfrac{z - 6}{2z - 3}$ [from Eq. (ii)]

$\Rightarrow \quad \int \dfrac{2z - 3}{z - 6} dz = \int dx$

$\Rightarrow \quad \int \left(\dfrac{2z - 12}{z - 6} + \dfrac{9}{z - 6}\right) dz = x$

$\Rightarrow \quad 2z + 9\ln(z - 6) = x + C,$

where C = constant of integration.

$\Rightarrow 2(2x + 3y - 2) + 9\ln(2x + 3y - 8) = x + C$

According to condition given,

$x = 0,\ y = 3$

So, $C = 14$

Hence, $4x + 6y - 4 + 9\ln(2x + 3y - 8) = x + 14$

$\Rightarrow \quad x + 2y + 3\ln(2x + 3y - 8) = 6$

$\Rightarrow \quad \alpha = 1, \beta = 2, \gamma = 8$ [on comparing]

Therefore, $\alpha + 2\beta + 3\gamma = 1 + 4 + 24 = 29$

38. Given differential equation is

$\dfrac{dy}{dx} = \dfrac{x + y - 2}{x - y}$

Let $X = x - 1$ and $Y = y - 1$

$\Rightarrow \quad \dfrac{dY}{dX} = \dfrac{X + Y}{X - Y}$

Now, let $Y = VX$

$\Rightarrow \quad \dfrac{dY}{dX} = V + X \cdot \dfrac{dV}{dX}$

$\Rightarrow \quad V + X\dfrac{dV}{dX} = \dfrac{1 + V}{1 - V}$

$\Rightarrow \quad \dfrac{(1 - V)dV}{(1 + V^2)} = \dfrac{dX}{X}$

On integrating, we have

$\tan^{-1} V - \ln(\sqrt{1 + V^2}) = \ln|X| + C$

$\Rightarrow \quad \tan^{-1}\left(\dfrac{y - 1}{x - 1}\right) - \ln\sqrt{1 + \left(\dfrac{y - 1}{x - 1}\right)^2} = \ln|(x - 1)| + C$

$\Rightarrow \tan^{-1}\left(\dfrac{y - 1}{x - 1}\right) - \dfrac{1}{2}\ln\left[1 + \left(\dfrac{y - 1}{x - 1}\right)^2\right] = \ln|x - 1| + C$ ...(i)

Since, Eq. (i) passes through (2, 1).

i.e. when $x = 2$, then $y = 1$

So, put in Eq. (i), we get $C = 0$

Thus, $\tan^{-1}\left(\dfrac{y - 1}{x - 1}\right) - \dfrac{1}{2}\ln\left[1 + \left(\dfrac{y - 1}{x - 1}\right)^2\right] = \ln|x - 1|$

On comparing with

$\tan^{-1}\left(\dfrac{y - 1}{x - 1}\right) - \dfrac{1}{\beta}\log_e\left[\alpha + \left(\dfrac{y - 1}{x - 1}\right)^2\right] = \log_e|x - 1|$, we get

$\beta = 2$

and $\alpha = 1$

Hence, $5\beta + \alpha = 5 \times 2 + 1 = 11$

39. We have,

$$(1 + y^2)(1 + \log_e x)\,dx + x\,dy = 0$$

$$\Rightarrow \quad (1 + y^2)\left(\frac{1}{x} + \frac{\log x}{x}\right)dx + dy = 0$$

$$\Rightarrow \quad \int\left(\frac{1}{x} + \frac{\log x}{x}\right)dx + \int\frac{dy}{1 + y^2} = 0$$

$$\Rightarrow \quad \log x + \frac{(\log x)^2}{2} + \tan^{-1} y = c$$

On putting $x = y = 1$, we get

$$c = \frac{\pi}{4}$$

$$\therefore \quad \log x + \frac{(\log x)^2}{2} + \tan^{-1} y = \frac{\pi}{4}$$

At $x = e$, $\quad y = \tan\left(\frac{\pi}{4} - \frac{3}{2}\right) = \dfrac{1 - \tan\frac{3}{2}}{1 + \tan\frac{3}{2}}$

$\therefore \quad \alpha = 1, \beta = 1$

$\therefore \quad \alpha + 2\beta = 1 + 2 = 3$

40. $\sec^2 x \dfrac{dx}{dy} + e^{2y}\tan^2 x + \tan x = 0$

Put $\tan x = t \Rightarrow \sec^2 x \dfrac{dx}{dy} = \dfrac{dt}{dy}$

$$\therefore \quad \frac{dt}{dy} + t^2 e^{2y} + t = 0$$

$$\Rightarrow \quad \frac{dt}{dy} + t = -t^2 e^{2y} \Rightarrow \frac{1}{t^2}\frac{dt}{dy} + \frac{1}{t} = -e^{2y}$$

$$\Rightarrow \quad \frac{1}{t} = z \Rightarrow \frac{1}{t^2}\frac{dt}{dy} = -\frac{dz}{dy}$$

$$\Rightarrow \quad -\frac{dz}{dy} + z = -e^{2y} \Rightarrow \frac{dz}{dy} - z = e^{2y}$$

$$P = -1, Q = e^{2y}$$

$$\text{IF} = e^{\int P\,dy} = e^{-\int dy} = e^{-y}$$

General solution

$$z \cdot \text{IF} = \int Q \cdot \text{IF}\,dy$$

$$z \cdot e^{-y} = \int e^{2y} e^{-y} dy = e^y + C$$

$$z e^{-y} = e^y + C$$

$$\frac{1}{\tan x} \cdot e^{-y} = e^y + C$$

Given, $y\left(\dfrac{\pi}{4}\right) = 0$

$$\frac{1}{1} e^0 = e^0 + C \Rightarrow C = 0$$

Curve, $\tan x \cdot e^{2y} = 1$

At $x = \dfrac{\pi}{6}$, $y = \alpha$

$$\tan\frac{\pi}{6} e^{2\alpha} = 1 \Rightarrow e^{2\alpha} = \sqrt{3} \Rightarrow e^{8\alpha} = 9$$

41. **Decoding the Question**

First, form the linear differential equation in x. Then, conclude the solution of differential equation by equating integrating factors.

$$\frac{dx}{dt} = \frac{2x}{(t+1)} + (t+1)^3$$

$$\Rightarrow \quad \frac{dx}{dt} - \frac{2x}{t+1} = (t+1)^3 \text{ [LDE]}$$

$$\text{IF} \Rightarrow e^{-2\int\frac{dt}{t+1}} = e^{-2\ln(t+1)} = \frac{1}{(t+1)^2}$$

$$\Rightarrow \quad x \cdot \frac{1}{(1+t)^2} = \int (t+1)^3 \cdot \frac{1}{(t+1)^2}\,dt$$

$$\Rightarrow \quad \frac{x}{(t+1)^2} = \frac{(t+1)^2}{2} + c$$

$$\Rightarrow \quad = \frac{(t+1)^4}{2} + c(t+1)^2$$

Put $t = 0$, $x = 2$

$$2 = \frac{1}{2} + c \Rightarrow c = \frac{3}{2} \Rightarrow x = \frac{(t+1)^4}{2} + \frac{3}{2}(t+1)^2$$

Put $t = 1$, $x = \dfrac{16}{2} + \dfrac{3}{2} \cdot 4 = 14$

42. We have, $\dfrac{dx}{dy} = \dfrac{1 + x - y^2}{y} \Rightarrow \dfrac{dx}{dy} - \dfrac{x}{y} = \dfrac{1}{y} - y$ ...(i)

This form of

$$\frac{dx}{dy} + Px = Q(y) \quad \text{...(ii)}$$

So, IF $e^{\int P dy} = e^{-\int\frac{1}{y}dy} = e^{-\ln y} = \dfrac{1}{y}$

Now, solution of Eq. (i) is given by

$$x \cdot \text{IF} = \int Q \cdot \text{IF}\,dy = \int\left(\frac{1}{y^2} - 1\right)dy$$

$$\frac{x}{y} = -\frac{1}{y} - y + c$$

$x = -1 - y^2 + cy$ [use $x(1) = 1$]

$\Rightarrow \quad 1 = -1 - 1 + c$

$\Rightarrow \quad c = 3$

$\therefore \quad x = 3y - y^2 - 1$

$\Rightarrow \quad 5x(2) = 5(3 \times 2 - 4 - 1) = 5$

43. Given, $\dfrac{dy}{dx} = y + 7$ with initial conditions $y_1(0) = 0, y_2(0) = 1$

$\Rightarrow \quad \displaystyle\int\frac{dy}{y+7} = \int dx$ [taking integration on both sides]

$\Rightarrow \quad \log(y + 7) = x + \log c$

$\Rightarrow \quad (y + 7) = ce^x$ [c is constant]

Since, $y_1(x)$ and $y_2(x)$ satisfied the given equation, we get

$$y_1 + 7 = c_1 e^x$$

and $\quad y_2 + 7 = c_2 e^x$

Given, $y_1(0) = 0, y_2(0) = 1$

$\therefore \quad 0 + 7 = c_1$ and $1 + 7 = c_2$

$c_1 = 7$ and $c_2 = 8$

$\therefore \quad y_1(x) = 7(e^x - 1)$

and $\quad y_2(x) = 8e^x - 7$

Hence, its point of intersection at $7e^x - 7 = 8e^x - 7$

$\Rightarrow e^x = 0$, which is impossible.

Thus, $y_1(x)$ and $y_2(x)$ curves does not intersect at any point. So, no point.

44. Given, $\dfrac{dy}{dx} + \dfrac{5}{x(x^5+1)}y = \dfrac{(x^5+1)^2}{x^7}$ $x > 0$ and $y(1) = 2$

$\therefore$ Given differential equation is linear

$$\text{IF} = e^{\int \frac{5}{x(x^5+1)}dx} = e^{\int \frac{5x^4 dx}{x^5(x^5+1)}}$$

Let $x^5 = t$, then $5x^4 dx = dt$

$$\text{IF} = e^{\int \frac{dt}{t(t+1)}} = e^{\int\left(\frac{1}{t} - \frac{1}{t+1}\right)dt}$$

$$= e^{\ln\left(\frac{t}{t+1}\right)} = e^{\ln\left(\frac{x^5}{x^5+1}\right)}$$

$$\text{IF} = \frac{x^5}{x^5+1}$$

Now, $\left(\dfrac{x^5}{x^5+1}\right) y(x) = \displaystyle\int \frac{x^5}{(x^5+1)} \cdot \frac{(x^5+1)^2}{x^7}\,dx$

$$= \int \frac{x^5+1}{x^2}\,dx = \int\left(x^3 + \frac{1}{x^2}\right)dx$$

$$\Rightarrow \quad \left(\frac{x^5}{x^5+1}\right) y(x) = \frac{x^4}{4} - \frac{1}{x} + C$$

When $x = 1$ and $y = 2$, then $C = \dfrac{7}{4}$

$$\therefore \quad \left(\frac{x^5}{x^5+1}\right) y(x) = \frac{x^4}{4} - \frac{1}{x} + \frac{7}{4} \qquad \text{...(i)}$$

On putting $x = 2$ in Eq. (i), we get

$$\left(\frac{32}{33}\right) y(2) = \frac{21}{4} \Rightarrow y(2) = \frac{693}{128}$$

45. We have, $(1 - x^2y^2)dx = ydx + xdy$, $y(1) = 2$

$$\Rightarrow \quad dx = \frac{ydx + xdy}{1-(xy)^2}$$

On integrating both sides, we get

$$\int dx = \int \frac{d(xy)}{1-(xy)^2}$$

$$x = \frac{1}{2}\log\left|\frac{1+xy}{1-xy}\right| + C$$

As $y(1) = 2$,

$$1 = \frac{1}{2}\log\left|\frac{1+2}{1-2}\right| + C \Rightarrow C = 1 - \frac{1}{2}\log 3$$

Now, substituting $x = 2$ as $y(2) = \alpha$

$$2 = \frac{1}{2}\log\left|\frac{1+2\alpha}{1-2\alpha}\right| + 1 - \frac{1}{2}\log 3$$

$$\Rightarrow 1 + \frac{1}{2}\log 3 = \frac{1}{2}\log\left|\frac{1+2\alpha}{1-2\alpha}\right|$$

$$\Rightarrow \quad 2 + \log 3 = \log\left|\frac{1+2\alpha}{1-2\alpha}\right|$$

$$\Rightarrow \quad \left|\frac{1+2\alpha}{1-2\alpha}\right| = 3e^2 \Rightarrow \frac{1+2\alpha}{1-2\alpha} = \pm\frac{3e^2}{1}$$

$$\Rightarrow \quad \frac{1}{2\alpha} = \frac{\pm 3e^2 + 1}{\pm 3e^2 - 1} \Rightarrow 2\alpha = \frac{\pm 3e^2 - 1}{\pm 3e^2 + 1}$$

$$\Rightarrow \quad \alpha = \frac{1}{2}\left(\frac{\pm 3e^2 - 1}{1 \pm 3e^2}\right)$$

$$\therefore \quad \alpha = \frac{3e^2 - 1}{2(1+3e^2)} \text{ or } \frac{3e^2+1}{2(3e^2-1)}$$

46. We have, $(1 + \log_e x)\dfrac{dx}{dy} - x\log_e x = e^y$, $x > 0$

Let $x \log_e x = t$

$$\Rightarrow \quad \left(x \cdot \frac{1}{x} + \log_e x\right)\frac{dx}{dy} = \frac{dt}{dy} \Rightarrow (1 + \log_e x)\frac{dx}{dy} = \frac{dt}{dy}$$

$$\therefore \quad \frac{dt}{dy} - t = e^y$$

$$\text{IF} = e^{\int(-1)dy} = e^{-y}$$

$\therefore$ General solution, $t(e^{-y}) = \displaystyle\int (e^y \cdot e^{-y})\,dy + c$

$$\Rightarrow \quad te^{-y} = \int dy + c \Rightarrow te^{-y} = y + c$$

$$\Rightarrow \quad (x \log_e x)\,e^{-y} = y + c \qquad \text{...(i)}$$

Eq. (i) passes through the point (1, 0).

$$\therefore \quad 0 = 0 + c \Rightarrow c = 0$$

$$\therefore \quad (x \log_e x)\,e^{-y} = y \Rightarrow x\log_e x = ye^y$$

which passes through $(\alpha, 2)$.

$$\therefore \quad \alpha \log_e \alpha = 2e^2$$

$$\Rightarrow \quad \log_e \alpha^\alpha = 2e^2 \Rightarrow \alpha^\alpha = e^{2e^2}$$

47. We have, $(3y^2 - 5x^2)y\,dx + 2x(x^2 - y^2)dy = 0$

$$\Rightarrow \quad \frac{dy}{dx} = \frac{y(5x^2 - 3y^2)}{2x(x^2 - y^2)} \qquad \text{...(i)}$$

which is a homogeneous differential equation.

On putting $y = vx$ and $\dfrac{dy}{dx} = v + x\dfrac{dv}{dx}$ in Eq. (i), we get

$$v + x\frac{dv}{dx} = \frac{vx(5x^2 - 3v^2x^2)}{2x(x^2 - v^2x^2)}$$

$$\Rightarrow \quad v + x\frac{dv}{dx} = \frac{v(5 - 3v^2)}{2(1 - v^2)}$$

$$\Rightarrow \quad x\frac{dv}{dx} = \frac{3v - v^3}{2(1 - v^2)} \Rightarrow \frac{2(1-v^2)}{3v - v^3}\,dv = \frac{dx}{x}$$

On integrating both the sides, we get

$$2\int \frac{(1-v^2)}{3v - v^3}\,dv = \int \frac{dx}{x}$$

$$\Rightarrow \quad \frac{2}{3}\int\frac{3-3v^2}{3v-v^3}dv = \int\frac{dx}{x}$$

$$\Rightarrow \quad \log|3v-v^3| = \log(cx)^{3/2}$$

$$\Rightarrow \quad 3v-v^3 = c^{3/2}x^{3/2}$$

$$\Rightarrow \quad \frac{3y}{x}-\frac{y^3}{x^3} = c^{3/2}x^{3/2} \qquad [\because y = vx]$$

When, $x=1, y=1$

$$\therefore \quad 3-1 = c^{3/2} \Rightarrow c^{3/2} = 2$$

$$\therefore \quad \frac{3y}{x}-\frac{y^3}{x^3} = 2x^{3/2} \Rightarrow 3x^2y - y^3 = 2x^{9/2}$$

Now, putting $x = 2$, we get

$$12y(2) - y^3(2) = 2\times 2^{9/2}$$

$$\Rightarrow \quad -(y^3(2)-12y(2)) = 2^{11/2}$$

$$\Rightarrow \quad |y^3(2)-12y(2)| = 32\sqrt{2}$$

48. The given differential equation is

$$\frac{dy}{dx} = -\left(\frac{x^2+3y^2}{3x^2+y^2}\right) \qquad \text{...(i)}$$

On substituting $y = vx$

$$\Rightarrow \quad \frac{dy}{dx} = v + x\frac{dv}{dx}$$

Then, $$v + x\frac{dv}{dx} = -\left(\frac{x^2+3v^2x^2}{3x^2+v^2x^2}\right)$$

$$\Rightarrow \quad v + x\frac{dv}{dx} = -\left[\frac{1+3v^2}{3+v^2}\right] \Rightarrow x\frac{dv}{dx} = -\frac{(1+3v^2)}{3+v^2} - v$$

$$\Rightarrow \quad x\frac{dy}{dx} = \frac{-(1+3v^2+3v+v^3)}{3+v^2}$$

On variables separable and integrating,

$$\int\frac{3+v^2}{(1+v)^3}dv = -\int\frac{1}{x}\,dx$$

We can write on using partial fraction

$$\frac{3+v^2}{(1+v)^3} = \frac{1}{v+1} - \frac{2}{(v+1)^2} + \frac{4}{(v+1)^3}$$

$$\therefore \quad \int\left[\frac{1}{v+1} - \frac{2}{(v+1)^2} + \frac{4}{(v+1)^3}\right]dv = -\int\frac{1}{x}dx$$

$$\Rightarrow \quad \ln|v+1| + \frac{2}{(v+1)} - \frac{2}{(v+1)^2} = -\ln x + C$$

$$\Rightarrow \quad \ln\left|\frac{y}{x}+1\right| + \frac{2\,[y/x+1-1]}{(y/x+1)^2} = -\ln x + C$$

$$\Rightarrow \quad \ln\left(\frac{y+x}{x}\right) + \frac{2xy}{(x+y)^2} = -\ln x + C$$

or $$\ln(x+y) + \frac{2xy}{(x+y)^2} = C \qquad \text{...(ii)}$$

Given, $y(1) = 0$, put in Eq. (ii), we get

$$c = 0$$

Hence, $\ln|x+y| + \dfrac{2xy}{(x+y)^2} = 0$

49. We have, $y(x+1)dx = x^2dy \Rightarrow \left(\dfrac{x+1}{x^2}\right)dx = \dfrac{dy}{y}$

On integrating both the sides, we get

$$\log x - \frac{1}{x} = \log y + c$$

When $\quad x = 1, y = e$, then

$$c = 0-1-1 = -2$$

$$\therefore \quad \log y = \log x - \frac{1}{x} + 2 \Rightarrow y = xe^{2-\frac{1}{x}}$$

$$\therefore \quad \lim_{x\to 0^+} y = 0\times e^{-\infty} = 0$$

50. Given differential equation is

$$(x^2-3y^2)dx + 3xy\,dy = 0,\ y(1) = 1$$

$$\frac{3y^2-x^2}{3xy} = \frac{dy}{dx} \qquad \text{...(i)}$$

which is a homogeneous type.

Let $$y = vx$$

$$\therefore \quad \frac{dy}{dx} = v + x\frac{dv}{dx}$$

From Eq. (i),

$$\frac{3(vx)^2-x^2}{3x(vx)} = v + x\frac{dv}{dx}$$

$$\Rightarrow \quad \frac{3v^2-1}{3v} - v = \frac{xdv}{dx} \Rightarrow \frac{-1}{3v} = \frac{xdv}{dx}$$

$$\Rightarrow \quad \int\frac{dx}{x} = -\int 3v\,dv$$

On integrating both sides, we get

$$\ln x = -3\,.\frac{v^2}{2} + c$$

which satisfies $y(1) = 1$

$$\therefore \quad \ln(1) = -\frac{3}{2}\left(\frac{1}{1}\right)^2 + c \Rightarrow c = \frac{3}{2}$$

$\therefore$ Equation is

$$\ln x = \frac{-3}{2}\left(\frac{y}{x}\right)^2 + \frac{3}{2}$$

$$\Rightarrow \quad 3y^2 = 2x^2\left(\frac{3}{2} - \ln x\right)$$

$$\Rightarrow \quad 6y^2 = 6x^2 - 4x^2\ln x$$

$\therefore$ For $x = e$

$$6y^2(e) = 6e^2 - 4e^2\cdot\ln e = 6e^2 - 4e^2\times 1 = 2e^2$$

51. The given differential equation is

$$2(y+2)\log_e(y+2)\,dx + (x+4-2\log_e(y+2))\,dy = 0$$

$$\Rightarrow \quad 2\ln(y+2) + \frac{(x+4-2\ln(y+2))}{y+2}\frac{dy}{dx} = 0$$

Let $\ln(y+2) = z$

$$\Rightarrow \quad \frac{1}{y+2}\cdot\frac{dy}{dx} = \frac{dz}{dx} \Rightarrow 2z + (x+4-2z)\frac{dz}{dx} = 0$$

$$\Rightarrow \quad \frac{dz}{dx} = -\frac{2z}{x+4-2z}$$

$$\Rightarrow \quad \frac{dx}{dz} = -\frac{x+4-2z}{2z}$$

$$\Rightarrow \quad \frac{dx}{dz} + \frac{x}{2z} = \frac{2z-4}{2z}$$

On comparing $\frac{dx}{dz} + Px = Q$, whose

$$P = \frac{1}{2z}, Q = \frac{2z-4}{2z}$$

$$\text{IF} = e^{\int \frac{1}{2z} dz} = z^{1/2}$$

Thus, solution is

$$x \cdot z^{1/2} = \int \left\{ \frac{2z-4}{2z} \cdot z^{1/2} \right\} dt$$

$$= \int \left\{ \frac{2z-4}{2z^{1/2}} \right\} dt = \int z^{1/2} dz - 2 \int z^{-1/2} dz$$

$$\Rightarrow \quad x \cdot z^{1/2} = \frac{2}{3} z^{3/2} - 4z^{1/2} + c$$

$$\Rightarrow \quad x(z) = \frac{2z}{3} - 4 + cz^{-1/2}$$

On putting $z = \ln(y+2)$, we get

$$x(z) = \frac{2}{3} \ln(y+2) - 4 + c(\ln(y+2))^{-1/2}$$

$$\Rightarrow \quad x(e^4 - 2) = 1$$

$$\Rightarrow \quad 1 = \frac{2}{3} \ln(e^4) - 4 + c \cdot (4)^{-1/2}$$

$$\Rightarrow \quad 1 = \frac{8}{3} - 4 + \frac{c}{2} \Rightarrow c = \frac{14}{3}$$

$$\therefore \quad x(y) = \frac{2}{3} \ln(y+2) - 4 + \frac{14}{3} \{\ln(y+2)\}^{-1/2}$$

$$\Rightarrow \quad x(e^9 - 2) = \frac{2}{3} \times 9 - 4 + \frac{14}{3} \times \frac{1}{3}$$

$$= 6 - 4 + \frac{14}{9} = 2 + \frac{14}{9} = \frac{32}{9}$$

$$\therefore \quad x(e^9 - 2) = \frac{32}{9}$$

52. We have, $(1+x^2)dy = y(x-y)dx$ ...(i)

Let $y = \frac{1}{t} \Rightarrow dy = \frac{-1}{t^2} dt$

So, Eq. (i) becomes

$$\frac{-(1+x^2)}{t^2} dt = \frac{1}{t}\left(x - \frac{1}{t}\right) dx$$

$$\Rightarrow \quad \frac{-(1+x^2)}{t^2} dt = \frac{1}{t^2}(tx-1)dx$$

$$\Rightarrow \quad \frac{dt}{dx} + \frac{tx}{1+x^2} = \frac{1}{1+x^2} \quad \text{...(ii)}$$

Let $P(x) = \frac{x}{1+x^2} \Rightarrow \int P(x)dx = \frac{1}{2}\int \frac{2x\,dx}{1+x^2}$

$$= \frac{1}{2} \ln(1+x^2) = \ln\sqrt{1+x^2}$$

Now, integrating factor in Eq. (ii) is

$$e^{\int P(x)dx} = e^{\ln\sqrt{1+x^2}} = \sqrt{1+x^2}$$

$\therefore$ Solution of Eq. (ii) is

$$t \cdot \sqrt{1+x^2} = \int \frac{1}{1+x^2} \cdot \sqrt{1+x^2}\, dx$$

$$\Rightarrow \quad t \cdot \sqrt{1+x^2} = \int \frac{1}{1+x^2} \cdot \sqrt{1+x^2} dx$$

$$\Rightarrow \quad t \cdot \sqrt{1+x^2} = \int \frac{1}{\sqrt{1+x^2}} dx \quad \text{...(iii)}$$

$$\Rightarrow \quad \frac{\sqrt{1+x^2}}{y} = \ln|x + \sqrt{1+x^2}| + c$$

Now, $y(0) = 1$

$$\frac{\sqrt{1+0^2}}{1} = \ln|0 + \sqrt{1+0^2}| + c$$

$$\Rightarrow \quad c = 1$$

$$\therefore \quad y = \frac{\sqrt{1+x^2}}{\ln|x + \sqrt{1+x^2}| + 1}$$

Now, $y(2\sqrt{2}) = \beta$

$$\Rightarrow \quad \beta = \frac{\sqrt{1+(2\sqrt{2})^2}}{\ln|2\sqrt{2} + \sqrt{1+(2\sqrt{2})^2}| + 1} = \frac{3}{\ln|3+2\sqrt{2}|+1}$$

$$\Rightarrow \quad \ln|3+2\sqrt{2}| + 1 = 3\beta^{-1}$$

$$\Rightarrow \quad \ln(3+2\sqrt{2}) + \ln e = 3\beta^{-1}$$

$$\Rightarrow \quad \ln[(e)(3+2\sqrt{2})] = 3\beta^{-1}$$

$$\Rightarrow \quad e^{3\beta^{-1}} = e(3+2\sqrt{2})$$

53. Given, $x^2 f(x) - x = 4\int_0^x t f(t)dt$

Differentiating both side w.r.t. x, we get

$$2xf(x) + x^2 f'(x) - 1 = 4xf(x)$$

$$\Rightarrow \quad x^2 f'(x) - 2xf(x) - 1 = 0$$

$$\Rightarrow \quad x^2 \frac{dy}{dx} - 2xy = 1 \quad [\text{let } y = f(x)]$$

Comparing above equation with

$$\frac{dy}{dx} + Py = Q$$

where $P = -\frac{2}{x}, Q = \frac{1}{x^2}$

Now, If $= e^{\int(-2/x)dx} = e^{-2\log x} = 1/x^2$

Solution is $y \cdot \left(\frac{1}{x^2}\right) = \int \left(\frac{1}{x^2}\right) \frac{1}{x^2} dx$

$$\Rightarrow \quad \frac{y}{x^2} = \int \frac{1}{x^4} dx = -\frac{1}{3x^3} + C \Rightarrow y = -\frac{1}{3x} + Cx^2$$

Given, $f(1) = \frac{2}{3}$

So, $\frac{2}{3} = -\frac{1}{3} + C$

$\Rightarrow \quad C = 1$

Thus, $y = f(x) = -\frac{1}{3x} + x^2$

$$\therefore \quad 18f(3) = 18\left\{9 - \frac{1}{9}\right\} = 18 \times \frac{80}{9} = 160$$

54. We have, $\dfrac{dy}{dx} + y\tan x = x\sec x$

which is a linear differential equation.

Now, IF $= e^{\int \tan x\,dx} = e^{\log \sec x} = \sec x$

$\therefore$ Solution of differential equation is given by

$$y\cdot\sec x = \int x\sec x\cdot\sec x\,dx + c$$

$$y\sec x = \int x\sec^2 x\,dx + c$$

$$y\sec x = x\tan x - \int 1\cdot\tan x\,dx + c$$

$$y\sec x = x\tan x - \log\sec x + c$$

Now, $y(0) = 1$

$\therefore 1\times\sec 0 = 0\times\tan 0 - \log\sec 0 + c \Rightarrow 1 = c$

$\therefore \quad y\sec x = x\tan x - \log\sec x + 1$

$\Rightarrow \quad y = x\sin x - \cos x\log\sec x + \cos x$

$\therefore \quad y\left(\dfrac{\pi}{6}\right) = \dfrac{\pi}{6}\sin\dfrac{\pi}{6} - \cos\dfrac{\pi}{6}\log\sec\dfrac{\pi}{6} + \cos\dfrac{\pi}{6}$

$$= \frac{\pi}{12} - \frac{\sqrt{3}}{2}\log_e\left(\frac{2}{\sqrt{3}}\right) + \frac{\sqrt{3}}{2}$$

$$= \frac{\pi}{12} - \frac{\sqrt{3}}{2}\left(\log_e\left(\frac{2}{\sqrt{3}}\right) - 1\right) = \frac{\pi}{12} - \frac{\sqrt{3}}{2}\log_e\left(\frac{2}{\sqrt{3}e}\right)$$

55. We have, $2x^2y\,dy - (1 - xy^2)dx = 0$

$\Rightarrow \quad 2x^2y\,dy = (1 - xy^2)dx$

$\Rightarrow \quad 2x^2y\dfrac{dy}{dx} = 1 - xy^2$

$\Rightarrow \quad 2y\dfrac{dy}{dx} + \dfrac{1}{x}y^2 = \dfrac{1}{x^2}$

Let $y^2 = v \Rightarrow 2y\dfrac{dy}{dx} = \dfrac{dv}{dx}$

$\therefore \quad \dfrac{dv}{dx} + \dfrac{1}{x}v = \dfrac{1}{x^2}$

which is a linear differential equation.

$\therefore \quad$ IF $= e^{\int\frac{1}{x}dx} = e^{\log_e x} = x$

Now, solution of differential equation is

$$vx = \int\frac{1}{x^2}\cdot x\,dx + C$$

$\Rightarrow \quad vx = \int\dfrac{1}{x}dx + C \Rightarrow y^2x = \log x + C$

Now, we have $\quad y(2) = \sqrt{\log 2}$

$\therefore \quad 2\log 2 = \log 2 + c \Rightarrow c = \log 2$

$\therefore$ Solution is $y^2x = \log x + \log 2$

$\Rightarrow \quad y^2x = \log 2x \Rightarrow 2x = e^{xy^2}$

But solution given is $\alpha x = e^{x^\beta y^\gamma}$

$\therefore \quad \alpha = 2, \beta = 1, \gamma = 2$

So, $\alpha + \beta - \gamma = 2 + 1 - 2 = 1$

56. Given differential equation is

$$\frac{dy}{dx} - \frac{3x^5\tan^{-1}(x^3)}{(1 + x^6)^{3/2}}y = 2x\exp\left(\frac{x^3 - \tan^{-1}(x^3)}{\sqrt{1 + x^6}}\right)$$

$$\Rightarrow \frac{dy}{dx} + \left(\frac{-3x^5\tan^{-1}(x^3)}{(1 + x^6)^{3/2}}\right)y = 2xe^{\left[\frac{x^3 - \tan^{-1}(x^3)}{\sqrt{1 + x^6}}\right]}$$

which is a linear differential equation of the form $\dfrac{dy}{dx} + Py = Q$, whose integrating factor (IF) is $e^{\int P dx}$ and its solution is

$$y \times (\text{IF}) = \int Q \times (\text{IF})\,dx \qquad \text{...(i)}$$

So, IF $= e^{\int\frac{-3x^5\tan^{-1}(x^3)}{(1 + x^6)^{3/2}}dx} = e^{\frac{\tan^{-1}(x^3) - x^3}{\sqrt{1 + x^6}}}$

[you can solve it by setting $x^3 = z$ and then again putting $\tan^{-1}z = u$ and then proceed]

From Eq. (i),

$$y \times e^{\frac{\tan^{-1}(x^3) - x^3}{\sqrt{1 + x^6}}} = \int 2x\,e^{\left(\frac{x^3 - \tan^{-1}x^3}{\sqrt{1 + x^6}}\right)}\cdot e^{\left(\frac{\tan^{-1}(x^3) - x^3}{\sqrt{1 + x^6}}\right)}dx$$

$$\Rightarrow \quad y \times e^{\left(\frac{\tan^{-1}x^3 - x^3}{\sqrt{1 + x^6}}\right)} = \int 2x\,dx$$

$$\Rightarrow \quad y \times e^{\left(\frac{\tan^{-1}(x^3) - x^3}{\sqrt{1 + x^6}}\right)} = 2\cdot\frac{x^2}{2} + C = x^2 + C \qquad \text{... (ii)}$$

Also, Eq. (ii) passes through origin as question said.

So, put $x = y = 0$ in Eq. (ii), we get

$$C = 0$$

Hence, $y\cdot e^{(\tan^{-1}x^3 - x^3/\sqrt{1 + x^6})} = x^2$

$\therefore \quad y(1)\cdot e^{\tan^{-1}(1) - 1/\sqrt{1 + 1}} = 1 \Rightarrow y(1)\cdot e^{\frac{\pi}{4} - 1/\sqrt{2}} = 1$

$\Rightarrow \quad y(1) = \dfrac{1}{e^{\pi - 4/4\sqrt{2}}} = e^{4 - \pi/4\sqrt{2}} = \exp\left(\dfrac{4 - \pi}{4\sqrt{2}}\right)$

57. $x\log x\dfrac{dy}{dx} + y = x^2\log x \Rightarrow \dfrac{dy}{dx} + \dfrac{y}{x\log x} = x$

$$\text{IF} = e^{\int\frac{dx}{x\log x}} = e^{\log|\log x|} = |\log x|$$

Solution of equation is

$$y\cdot(\text{IF}) = \int x|\log x|\,dx$$

$\Rightarrow \quad y|\log x| = |\log x|\dfrac{x^2}{2} - \dfrac{x^2}{4} + c$

Put $x = 2$ and $y = 2 \Rightarrow 2\log 2 = \log 2\cdot 2 - 1 + c \Rightarrow c = 1$

Put $x = e, y = \dfrac{e^2}{2} - \dfrac{e^2}{4} + 1 \Rightarrow y(e) = 1 + \dfrac{e^2}{4} = \dfrac{4 + e^2}{4}$

58. Let $y = y(t)$, $\dfrac{dy}{dt} + \alpha y = \gamma e^{-\beta t}$, where $\alpha > 0, \beta > 0, \gamma > 0$,

where IF $= e^{\int P\,dx}$

So, $\quad$ IF $= e^{\int\alpha\,dt} = e^{\alpha t}$

Thus, solution is

$$y\cdot(e^{\alpha t}) = \int(e^{\alpha t})\cdot\gamma e^{-\beta t}\,dt$$

$$y\cdot e^{\alpha t} = \gamma\int e^{(\alpha - \beta)t}\cdot dt$$

Now, let $(\alpha - \beta)t = x \Rightarrow (\alpha - \beta)dt = dx \Rightarrow dt = \dfrac{dx}{\alpha - \beta}$

$$\therefore \quad ye^{\alpha t} = \gamma \int e^x \frac{dx}{(\alpha - \beta)}$$

$$\Rightarrow \quad ye^{\alpha t} = \frac{\gamma}{\alpha - \beta}(e^x) + C$$

$$\Rightarrow \quad ye^{\alpha t} = \frac{\gamma}{(\alpha - \beta)} e^{(\alpha - \beta)t} + C$$

On dividing both the sides by $(e^{\alpha t})$, we get

$$y = \left(\frac{\gamma}{\alpha - \beta}\right) e^{-\beta t} + c \cdot e^{-\alpha t} = y(t)$$

Now, $\lim_{t \to \infty} y(t) = \lim_{t \to \infty} \left[\left(\frac{\gamma}{\alpha - \beta}\right) e^{-\beta t} + c \cdot e^{-\alpha t}\right]$

$$\left[\because \lim_{x \to \infty} e^{-x} = 0\right]$$

So, $\lim_{t \to \infty} y(t) = 0 + 0 = 0$

59. $\frac{dy}{dx} = \frac{y}{x}(1 + xy^2(1 + \log x_e)), x > 0, y(1) = 3$

$$\frac{dy}{dx} - \frac{y}{x} = y^3(1 + \log_e x)$$

$$\frac{1}{y^3}\frac{dy}{dx} - \frac{1}{y^2}\frac{1}{x} = 1 + \log_e x$$

Let $-\frac{1}{y^2} = t$

On differentiating w.r.t. x, we get

$$\frac{2}{y^3}\frac{dy}{dx} = \frac{dt}{dx} \Rightarrow \frac{1}{y^3}\frac{dy}{dx} = \frac{1}{2}\frac{dt}{dx}$$

Differential equation becomes,

$$\frac{1}{2}\frac{dt}{dx} + \frac{t}{x} = 1 + \log_e x \Rightarrow \frac{dt}{dx} + \frac{2}{x}t = 2(1 + \log_e x)$$

On comparing with standard equation of linear differential equation, $\frac{dy}{dx} + Py = Q$

$$P = \frac{2}{x}, Q = 2(1 + \log_e x)$$

⇒ Integrating factor,

$$\text{IF} = e^{\int P\,dx} = e^{2\int \frac{1}{x}dx}$$

$$\text{IF} = e^{2\ln x} = e^{\ln x^2} = x^2$$

General solution $t \cdot \text{IF} = \int Q \cdot \text{IF}\, dx$

$$\therefore \quad t \cdot x^2 = \int 2(1 + \log_e x)\, x^2 dx$$

$$\Rightarrow \quad \frac{-x^2}{y^2} = 2\left[(1 + \log_e x)\frac{x^3}{3} - \int \frac{1}{x} \cdot \frac{x^3}{3} dx\right]$$

$$\Rightarrow \quad \frac{-x^2}{y^2} = \frac{2}{3}[x^3(1 + \log_e x) - \int x^2 dx]$$

$$\frac{-x^2}{y^2} = \frac{2}{3}\left[x^3(1 + \log_e x) - \frac{x^3}{3}\right] + C$$

Given, $y(1) = 3$

$$\frac{-1}{9} = \frac{2}{3}\left[1\,(1 + \log_e 1) - \frac{1}{3}\right] + C$$

$$\frac{-1}{9} = \frac{4}{9} + C \Rightarrow C = \frac{-5}{9}$$

Solution becomes,

$$-\frac{x^2}{y^2} = \frac{2}{3}\left[x^3(1 + \log_e x) - \frac{x^3}{3}\right] - \frac{5}{9}$$

$$\Rightarrow -\frac{x^2}{y^2} = \frac{2x^3}{9}[2 + \log_e x^3] - \frac{5}{9}$$

$$\Rightarrow \frac{9}{y^2} = -2x[2 + \log_e x^3] + \frac{5}{x^2}$$

$$\Rightarrow \frac{9}{y^2} = \frac{5 - 2x^3[2 + \log_e x^3]}{x^2} \Rightarrow \frac{y^2}{9} = \frac{x^2}{5 - 2x^3(2 + \log_e x^3)}$$

60. Given differential equation is

$$x^3 dy + (xy - 1)dx = 0, x > 0$$

and $$y\left(\frac{1}{2}\right) = 3 - e \quad \text{...(i)}$$

We have to find $y(1)$.

For this, we can write $x^3 dy + (xy - 1)dx = 0$ as

$$\frac{dy}{dx} = \frac{1 - xy}{x^3} = \frac{1}{x^3} - \frac{y}{x^2}$$

⇒ $\frac{dy}{dx} + \left(\frac{1}{x^2}\right)y = \frac{1}{x^3}$, which is linear differential equation of the form $\frac{dy}{dx} + Py = Q$, where P and Q are either constants or functions of x.

So, integrating factor (IF) $= e^{\int P dx} = e^{\int \frac{1}{x^2} dx} = e^{-\frac{1}{x}}$

Its solution is

$$y \times (\text{IF}) = \int Q \times (\text{IF})\, dx$$

$$\Rightarrow \quad y \times e^{-\frac{1}{x}} = \int \frac{1}{x^3} \times e^{-\frac{1}{x}} dx \Rightarrow ye^{-\frac{1}{x}} = -\int e^t \cdot t\,dt$$

[where, $-\frac{1}{x} = t$, so that $\frac{1}{x^2}dx = dt$]

$$\Rightarrow \quad y = \frac{1}{x} + 1 + Ce^{\frac{1}{x}} \quad \text{...(ii)}$$

where, C is constant

From Eq. (i), we put $x = \frac{1}{2}$ and $y = 3 - e$ in Eq. (ii), we get

$$3 - e = 2 + 1 + Ce^2 \Rightarrow C = -\frac{1}{e}$$

$$\therefore \quad y(1) = 1$$

61. Let the coordinate of a point P be (x, y).

Let the tangent intersect X-axis and Y-axis at a point $A(\alpha, 0)$ and $(0, \beta)$ respectively.

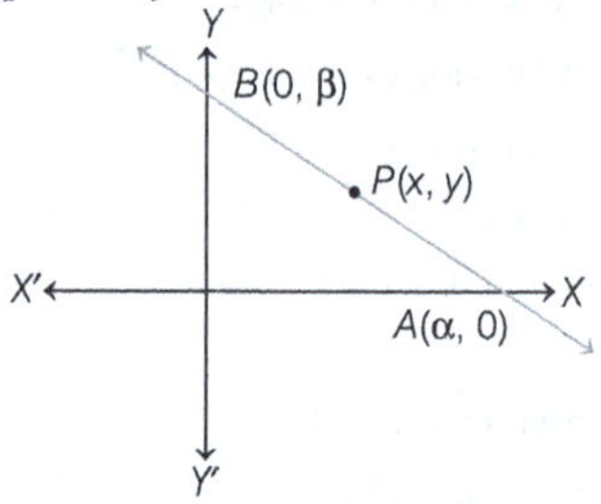

Point P divides AB in the ratio $1 : K$.

$$x=\frac{K\alpha}{K+1} \text{ and } y=\frac{\beta}{K+1}$$

$$\Rightarrow \quad \alpha=\frac{x(K+1)}{K} \text{ and } \beta = y(K+1)$$

Slope of tangent $= \dfrac{0-\beta}{\alpha-0}$

$$\frac{dy}{dx} = -\frac{y(K+1)}{\frac{x(K+1)}{K}} \Rightarrow \frac{dy}{dx} = -\frac{Ky}{x}$$

$$\frac{1}{y}dy = -\frac{K}{x}dx$$

$$\log y = -K\log x + \log C$$

$$y\cdot x^K = C$$

The curve passes through (1, 1) $\Rightarrow C = 1$

The curve also passes through $\left(\dfrac{1}{10}, 100\right)$

$$\Rightarrow \quad 100\times\left(\frac{1}{10}\right)^K = 1 \Rightarrow K = 2$$

Also, $\quad e^{\frac{dy}{dx}} = 2x+1$

$$\Rightarrow \quad \frac{dy}{dx} = \log_e(2x+1) \Rightarrow dy = \log_e(2x+1)dx$$

Let $t = 2x+1 \Rightarrow \dfrac{1}{2}dt = dx$

$$\Rightarrow \quad \int dy = \frac{1}{2}\int \log_e t\, dt$$

$$\Rightarrow \quad y = \frac{1}{2}[t\log_e t - t]$$

$$\Rightarrow \quad y = \frac{2x+1}{2}[\log_e(2x+1)-1]+C$$

$y(0) = 2$ is its solution

$$\Rightarrow \quad 2 = \frac{1}{2}[\log 1 - 1] + C \Rightarrow C = \frac{5}{2}$$

$$\therefore \quad y = \frac{2x+1}{2}[\log_e(2x+1)-1]+\frac{5}{2}$$

$$y(1) = \frac{3}{2}[\log_e 3 - 1] + \frac{5}{2} = \frac{3}{2}\log_e 3 + 1$$

$$\therefore\ 4y(1) - 5\log_e 3 = 6\log_e 3 + 4 - 5\log_e 3$$

$$= \log_e 3 + 4 = 1.09 + 4 = 5.09 \approx 5$$

62. Given, $(\ln(\cos y))^2 \cos y\,dx = (1 + 3x\ln\cos y)\sin y\,dy$

$$\frac{dx}{dy} = \tan y\left(\frac{1}{\ln^2\cos y} + \frac{3\ln\cos y}{\ln^2\cos y}x\right)$$

$$\Rightarrow \quad \frac{dx}{dy} - \left(\frac{3\tan y}{\ln\cos y}\right)x = \frac{\tan y}{\ln^2\cos y}$$

$$\therefore \quad \text{IF} = e^{\int\frac{-3\tan y}{\ln\cos y}dy} = e^{\int -\frac{3}{\ln\cos y}\frac{\sin y}{\cos y}dy}$$

On putting $\ln\cos y = t \Rightarrow \dfrac{1}{\cos y}(-\sin y)dy = dt$

$$\therefore \quad \text{IF} = e^{\int\frac{3}{t}dt} = e^{\ln t^3} = t^3 = \ln^3(\cos y)$$

Solution : $x\cdot\ln^3\cos y$

$$= \int\left[\frac{\sin y}{\cos y}\cdot\frac{1}{\ln^2\cos y}\times\ln^3\cos y\right]dy$$

$$\Rightarrow x\ln^3\cos y = \int(\ln\cos y)\frac{\sin y}{\cos y}\cdot dy$$

$$\Rightarrow x\ln^3\cos y = -\frac{\ln^2\cos y}{2} + C$$

$$\because \quad x\left(\frac{\pi}{3}\right) = \frac{1}{2\ln 2}$$

$$\therefore \quad \frac{1}{2\ln 2}\times\ln^3\cos\frac{\pi}{3} = -\frac{1}{2}\ln^2\cos\frac{\pi}{3} + C$$

$$\Rightarrow \quad \frac{1}{2\ln 2}\times\left(\ln\left(\frac{1}{2}\right)\right)^3 = -\frac{1}{2}\left(\ln\frac{1}{2}\right)^2 + C$$

$$\Rightarrow -\frac{1}{2}\cdot\frac{1}{\ln\left(\frac{1}{2}\right)}\cdot\left(\ln\left(\frac{1}{2}\right)\right)^3 = -\frac{1}{2}\left(\ln\frac{1}{2}\right)^2 + C \Rightarrow C = 0$$

When $y = \dfrac{\pi}{6} \Rightarrow x\ln^3\left(\dfrac{\sqrt{3}}{2}\right) = -\dfrac{1}{2}\ln^2\left(\dfrac{\sqrt{3}}{2}\right) + 0$

$$\Rightarrow \quad x = -\frac{1}{2\ln\left(\frac{\sqrt{3}}{2}\right)} = -\frac{1}{\ln\frac{3}{4}} = \frac{1}{\ln\left(\frac{4}{3}\right)} \Rightarrow x = \frac{1}{\ln 4 - \ln 3}$$

$$\Rightarrow \quad m = 4 \text{ and } n = 3 \Rightarrow mn = 12$$

63. The given differential equation is

$$\frac{dy}{dx} + \frac{4x}{x^2-1}y = \frac{x+2}{(x^2-1)^{5/2}}, x > 1$$

$$\text{IF} = e^{\int\frac{4x}{x^2-1}dx} = e^{2\int\frac{2x}{x^2-1}dx} = e^{2\log(x^2-1)} = (x^2-1)^2$$

The solution is $y\cdot(x^2-1)^2 = \int(x^2-1)^2\dfrac{x+2}{(x^2+1)^{5/2}}dx$

$$= \int\frac{x+2}{\sqrt{x^2-1}}dx$$

$$= \frac{1}{2}\int\frac{2x\,dx}{\sqrt{x^2-1}} + 2\int\frac{dx}{\sqrt{x^2-1}}$$

$$y\cdot(x^2-1)^2 = \sqrt{x^2-1} + 2\ln(x+\sqrt{x^2-1}) + C$$

Given, $y(2) = \dfrac{2}{9}\log_e(2+\sqrt{3})$

$$\Rightarrow \quad \frac{2}{9}\log_e(2+\sqrt{3})(3)^2 = \sqrt{3} + 2\ln|2+\sqrt{3}| + C$$

$$\Rightarrow \quad 2\ln(2+\sqrt{3}) = \sqrt{3} + 2\ln|2+\sqrt{3}| + C$$

$$\Rightarrow \quad C = -\sqrt{3}$$

Hence, $y(x^2-1)^2 = \sqrt{x^2-1} + 2\ln|x+\sqrt{x^2-1}| - \sqrt{3}$

Put $x = \sqrt{2}$

$$y(\sqrt{2}) = 1 + 2\ln|\sqrt{2}+1| - \sqrt{3}$$

$$\Rightarrow \quad y(\sqrt{2}) = 2\ln(\sqrt{2}+1) + 1 - \sqrt{3}$$

$$\because \quad y(\sqrt{2}) = \alpha\log_e(\sqrt{\alpha}+\beta) + \beta - \sqrt{\gamma}$$

$$\therefore \quad \alpha = 2, \beta = 1, \gamma = 3$$

Thus, $\alpha\beta\gamma = 6$

64. Given, differential equation

$$(y - 2\log_e x)\,dx + (x\log_e x^2)\,dy = 0$$

$$\Rightarrow \quad 2x\log x\frac{dy}{dx} + y = 2\log_e x$$

$$\Rightarrow \quad \frac{dy}{dx} + \frac{y}{2x\log_e x} = \frac{1}{x}$$

$$\text{IF} = e^{\int \frac{1}{2x\log_e x}dx} = e^{\frac{1}{2}\log(\log x)} = \sqrt{\log x}$$

$\therefore$ Solution of differential equation is

$$y\cdot\sqrt{\log_e x} = \int \frac{1}{x}\sqrt{\log x}\,dx + C$$

$$\Rightarrow \quad y\sqrt{\log_e x} = \frac{(\log x)^{3/2}}{3/2} + C$$

It passes through $\left(e, \frac{4}{3}\right)$

$$\Rightarrow \quad \frac{4}{3} = \frac{2}{3} + C \Rightarrow C = \frac{2}{3}$$

It also passes through (e^4, α),

$$\therefore \quad \alpha\cdot(2) = \frac{16}{3} + \frac{2}{3} = 6 \Rightarrow \alpha = 3$$

65. Given, differential equation

$$(x\cos x)\,dy + (xy\sin x + y\cos x - 1)\,dx = 0,\ 0 < x < \frac{\pi}{2}$$

$$\Rightarrow \frac{dy}{dx} + \frac{xy\sin x + y\cos x - 1}{x\cos x} = 0$$

$$\Rightarrow \frac{dy}{dx} + \left(\frac{xy\sin x + y\cos x}{x\cos x}\right) = \frac{1}{x\cos x}$$

$$\Rightarrow \quad \frac{dy}{dx} + \left(\tan x + \frac{1}{x}\right)y = \frac{1}{x\cos x}$$

which is linear differential equation in the form of $\frac{dy}{dx} + Py = Q$

$$\therefore \quad \text{IF} = e^{\int\left(\tan x + \frac{1}{x}\right)dx} = e^{(\log\sec x + \log x)}$$

$$= e^{\log(x\sec x)} = x\sec x$$

$\therefore$ The general solution of the given differential equation $y\cdot\text{IF} = \int(Q\times\text{IF})\,dx + c$

$$\Rightarrow \quad y\,(x\sec x) = \int\left(\frac{1}{x\cos x}x\sec x\right)dx + c$$

$$\Rightarrow \quad xy\sec x = \int\sec^2 x\,dx + c$$

$$\Rightarrow \quad xy\sec x = \tan x + c \qquad \text{...(i)}$$

Since, $\frac{\pi}{3}y\left(\frac{\pi}{3}\right) = \sqrt{3} \Rightarrow y\left(\frac{\pi}{3}\right) = \frac{3\sqrt{3}}{\pi}$

$$\therefore \quad \frac{\pi}{3}\left(\frac{3\sqrt{3}}{\pi}\right)\sec\left(\frac{\pi}{3}\right) = \tan\left(\frac{\pi}{3}\right) + c$$

$$\Rightarrow \quad \sqrt{3}\,(2) = \sqrt{3} + c \Rightarrow c = \sqrt{3}$$

On putting value of c in Eq. (i), we get

$$xy\sec x = \tan x + \sqrt{3}$$

$$\Rightarrow \quad y = \frac{1}{x}(\sin x + \sqrt{3}\cos x)$$

$$\Rightarrow \quad y' = \frac{1}{x}(\cos x - \sqrt{3}\sin x) - \frac{1}{x^2}(\sin x + \sqrt{3}\cos x)$$

and

$$y'' = \frac{1}{x}(-\sin x - \sqrt{3}\cos x) - \frac{1}{x^2}(\cos x - \sqrt{3}\sin x) - \frac{1}{x^2}(\cos x - \sqrt{3}\sin x) + \frac{2}{x^3}(\sin x - \sqrt{3}\cos x)$$

$$\therefore \quad \left|\frac{\pi}{6}y''\left(\frac{\pi}{6}\right) + 2y'\left(\frac{\pi}{6}\right)\right| = |-2| = 2$$

66. We have, $f'(x) + f(x) = \int_0^2 f(t)\,dt$

Let $\int_0^2 f(t)\,dt = k$

Then, $f'(x) + f(x) = k \Rightarrow \frac{d}{dx}f(x) + f(x) = k$

which is a linear differential equation.

Now, $\text{IF} = e^{\int 1\,dx} = e^x$

The solution is

$$e^x f(x) = \int k.e^x dx + c$$

$$\Rightarrow \quad e^x f(x) = ke^x + c$$

Now, $\quad f(0) = e^{-2}$

$$\therefore \quad e^0 f(0) = ke^0 + c$$

$$\Rightarrow \quad e^{-2} = k + c \Rightarrow c = e^{-2} - k$$

$$\therefore \quad e^x f(x) = ke^x + e^{-2} - k \Rightarrow f(x) = k + (e^{-2} - k)e^{-x}$$

Now, $\quad \int_0^2 f(t)\,dt = k$

$$\Rightarrow \quad \int_0^2 (k + (e^{-2} - k)e^{-t})\,dt = k$$

$$\Rightarrow \quad [kt - (e^{-2} - k)e^{-t}]_0^2 = k$$

$$\Rightarrow \quad [2k - (e^{-2} - k)e^{-2}] - [-(e^{-2} - k)] = k \Rightarrow k = e^{-2} - 1$$

Now, $\quad 2f(0) - f(2) = 2e^{-2} - [k + (e^{-2} - k)e^{-2}]$

$$= 2e^{-2} + 1 - 2e^{-2} = 1$$

67. Given differential equations is

$$\frac{dy}{dx} = \frac{x + y - 2}{x - y} = \frac{(x - 1) + (y - 1)}{(x - 1) - (y - 1)}$$

Put $x - 1 = h$, $y - 1 = k$

$$\frac{dy}{dx} = \frac{h + k}{h - k} \Rightarrow \frac{dk}{dh} = V + h\frac{dV}{dh} \text{ let } k = Vh,$$

$$V + h\frac{dV}{dh} = \frac{1 + V}{1 - V} \Rightarrow h\frac{dV}{dh} = \frac{V^2 + 1}{1 - V}$$

$$\Rightarrow \int\frac{1 - V}{1 + V^2}dV = \int\frac{dh}{h} \Rightarrow \int\frac{dV}{1 + V^2} - \frac{1}{2}\int\frac{2VdV}{1 + V^2} = \int\frac{dh}{h}$$

$$\Rightarrow \quad \tan^{-1}V - \frac{1}{2}\ln(1 + V^2) = \ln h + c$$

$$\Rightarrow \tan^{-1}\left(\frac{k}{h}\right) - \frac{1}{2}\ln\left(1 + \frac{k^2}{h^2}\right) = \ln h + c$$

Replace h and k by $(x-1)$ and $(y-1)$ respectively

$$\tan^{-1}\left(\frac{y-1}{x-1}\right)-\frac{1}{2}\ln\left(1+\frac{(y-1)^2}{(x-1)^2}\right)=\ln(x-1)+c$$

Satisfy (2, 1),

$$0-\frac{1}{2}\ln 1=\ln 1+C \Rightarrow C=0$$

Satisfy $(k+1, 2)$,

$$\tan^{-1}\left(\frac{1}{k}\right)-\frac{1}{2}\ln\left(1+\frac{1}{k^2}\right)=\ln k$$

$$\Rightarrow \quad 2\tan^{-1}\left(\frac{1}{k}\right)=\ln\left(\frac{1+k^2}{k^2}\right)+2\ln k$$

$$\Rightarrow \quad 2\tan^{-1}\left(\frac{1}{k}\right)=\ln(1+k^2)$$

68. Given, $\frac{dy}{dx}+2y\tan x=\sin x,\ 0<x<\frac{\pi}{2}$

Here, $P=2\tan x$ and $Q=\sin x$

$$\text{IF}=e^{\int P dx}=e^{\int 2\tan x\, dx}=e^{2\log|\sec x|}=\sec^2 x$$

General Solution

$$\Rightarrow \quad y\times \text{IF}=\int Q\times \text{IF}\, dx$$

$$y\times\sec^2 x=\int \sin x\times\sec^2 x\, dx=\int \tan x\sec x\, dx$$

$$\therefore \quad y\times\sec^2 x=\sec x+c$$

As, $y\left(\frac{\pi}{3}\right)=0$

$$0\times\sec^2\frac{\pi}{3}=\sec\frac{\pi}{3}+c$$

$$\Rightarrow \quad 0=2+c \Rightarrow c=-2$$

$$\therefore \quad y\sec^2 x=\sec x-2$$

$$\therefore \quad y=\cos x-2\cos^2 x$$

$$\Rightarrow \quad y=-2\left(\cos^2 x-\frac{1}{2}\cos x\right)$$

$$\Rightarrow \quad y=-2\left[\cos^2 x-\frac{1}{2}\cos x+\left(\frac{1}{4}\right)^2-\left(\frac{1}{4}\right)^2\right]$$

$$\Rightarrow \quad y=-2\left[\left(\cos x-\frac{1}{4}\right)^2-\frac{1}{16}\right]$$

$$\Rightarrow \quad y=\frac{1}{8}-2\left(\cos x-\frac{1}{4}\right)^2$$

Minimum value of $\cos x-\frac{1}{4}$ is 0.

$\therefore$ Maximum value of $y=\frac{1}{8}-0=\frac{1}{8}$

69. $(x-y^2)dx+y(5x+y^2)dy=0$

$$\frac{dy}{dx}=\frac{y^2-x}{y(5x+y^2)}$$

Let $\quad y^2=t$

$$\frac{2y\,dy}{dx}=2\left(\frac{y^2-x}{5x+y^2}\right)$$

$$\Rightarrow \quad \frac{dt}{dx}=2\left(\frac{t-x}{5x+t}\right) \qquad [t=kx]$$

$$\Rightarrow \quad k+x\frac{dk}{dx}=2\left(\frac{kx-x}{5x+kx}\right)\Rightarrow x\frac{dk}{dx}=-\frac{(k^2+3k+2)}{k+5}$$

$$\Rightarrow \quad \int\frac{(5+k)}{(k+1)(k+2)}dk=\int-\frac{dx}{x}$$

$$\Rightarrow \int\left(\frac{4}{k+1}-\frac{3}{k+2}\right)dk=-\int\frac{dx}{x}$$

$$\Rightarrow 4\ln(k+1)-3\ln(k+2)=-\ln x+\ln C$$

$$\Rightarrow \quad \frac{(k+1)^4}{(k+2)^3}=-\ln x+\ln C$$

$$\Rightarrow \quad C(y^2+2x)^3=(y^2+x)^4$$

70. Given differential equation is

$$\left(\frac{x}{\sqrt{x^2-y^2}}+e^{\frac{y}{x}}\right)x\frac{dy}{dx}=x+\left(\frac{x}{\sqrt{x^2-y^2}}+e^{\frac{y}{x}}\right)y$$

$$\left(\frac{1}{\sqrt{1-\left(\frac{y}{x}\right)^2}}+e^{\frac{y}{x}}\right)\frac{dy}{dx}=1+\left(\frac{1}{\sqrt{1-\left(\frac{y}{x}\right)^2}}+e^{\frac{y}{x}}\right)\frac{y}{x}$$

Put $y=vx$ then, $\frac{dy}{dx}=v+x\frac{dv}{dx}$

So, $\left(\frac{1}{\sqrt{1-v^2}}+e^v\right)\left(v+x\frac{dv}{dx}\right)=1+\left(\frac{1}{\sqrt{1-v^2}}+e^v\right)v$

$$\Rightarrow \quad x\left(\frac{1}{\sqrt{1-v^2}}+e^v\right)\frac{dv}{dx}=1$$

Take integral on both sides, we get

$$e^{\frac{y}{x}}+\sin^{-1}\left(\frac{y}{x}\right)=\ln x+C$$

It passes through (1, 0)

$$1+0=0+C\Rightarrow C=1$$

It passes through $(2\alpha, \alpha)$

$$e^{\frac{1}{2}}+\sin^{-1}\frac{1}{2}=\ln 2\alpha+1$$

$$\Rightarrow \quad \ln 2\alpha=\sqrt{e}+\frac{\pi}{6}-1$$

$$\Rightarrow \quad 2\alpha=e^{\left(\sqrt{e}+\frac{\pi}{6}-1\right)}\Rightarrow \alpha=\frac{1}{2}e^{\left(\frac{\pi}{6}+\sqrt{e}-1\right)}$$

71. Given differential equation can be written as

$$\frac{dy}{dx}+(8+4\cot 2x)y=\frac{2e^{-4x}}{\sin^2 2x}(2\sin 2x+\cos 2x) \qquad \text{...(i)}$$

Now, Eq. (i) is linear differential equation.

Now, $\quad \text{IF}=e^{\int(8+4\cot 2x)dx}$

$$=e^{8x+2\ln(\sin 2x)}=e^{8x}\cdot\sin^2 2x$$

$\therefore$ Solution is given by

$$y(e^{8x}\cdot\sin^2 2x)=\int 2e^{4x}(2\sin 2x+\cos 2x)dx+C$$

$$=e^{4x}\cdot\sin 2x+C$$

We have given that $y\left(\frac{\pi}{4}\right)=e^{-\pi}\Rightarrow C=0\Rightarrow y=\frac{e^{-4x}}{\sin 2x}$

Now, $y\left(\frac{\pi}{6}\right)=\frac{e^{-4\frac{\pi}{6}}}{\sin\left(2\cdot\frac{\pi}{6}\right)}=\frac{2}{\sqrt{3}}e^{-\frac{2\pi}{3}}$

72. Given differential equations is

$$\frac{dy}{dx}=\frac{y}{x}\frac{(4y^2+2x^2)}{(3y^2+x^2)}$$

Put $y=vx\Rightarrow\frac{dy}{dx}=v+x\frac{dv}{dx}$

$$\Rightarrow\quad v+x\frac{dv}{dx}=\frac{v(4v^2+2)}{(3v^2+1)}\Rightarrow x\frac{dv}{dx}=v\left(\frac{4v^2+2-3v^2-1}{3v^2+1}\right)$$

Take integral on both sides, we get

$$\int(3v^2+1)\frac{dv}{v^3+v}=\int\frac{dx}{x}$$

$$\Rightarrow\quad \ln|v^3+v|=\ln x+C$$

$$\Rightarrow\quad \ln\left|\left(\frac{y}{x}\right)^3+\left(\frac{y}{x}\right)\right|=\ln x+C$$

Here, $y(1)=1\Rightarrow C=\ln 2$

Here, $y(2)\in[n-1,n)$

$$\ln\left(\frac{y^3}{8}+\frac{y}{2}\right)=2\ln 2\Rightarrow\frac{y^3}{8}+\frac{y}{2}=4\Rightarrow y\in[2,3)=2$$

Therefore, $n=3$

73. Let the number of infected students be n.

Non-infected students be $(100-n)$.

$$\frac{dn}{dt}\propto n(100-n)$$

$$\Rightarrow\quad \frac{dn}{dt}=kn(100-n)\Rightarrow\frac{dn}{n(100-n)}=kdt$$

$$\Rightarrow\quad \frac{1}{100}\left[\frac{(n+100-n)dn}{n(100-n)}\right]=k\,dt$$

$$\Rightarrow\quad \frac{1}{100}\left[\frac{dn}{n}+\frac{dn}{100-n}\right]=k\,dt$$

Take integral on both sides, we get

$$\frac{1}{100}\int\frac{dn}{n}+\frac{1}{100}\int\frac{dn}{(100-n)}=k\int dt$$

$$\Rightarrow\quad \frac{1}{100}\ln(n)-\frac{1}{100}\ln(100-n)=kt+C$$

$$\Rightarrow\quad \frac{1}{100}\ln\left(\frac{n}{100-n}\right)=kt+C$$

$$\Rightarrow\quad \ln\left(\frac{n}{100-n}\right)=100kt+100C$$

$$\Rightarrow\quad \left(\frac{n}{100-n}\right)=e^{100kt}\cdot C' \qquad ...(i)$$

At $t=0$, $n=2$,

$$\left(\frac{2}{100-2}\right)=e^0\cdot C'\Rightarrow C'=\frac{2}{98}=\frac{1}{49}$$

At $t=4$, $n=30$,

$$\left(\frac{30}{100-30}\right)=e^{400k}\cdot\frac{1}{49}$$

$$\Rightarrow\quad \frac{30\times 49}{70}=e^{400k}\Rightarrow e^{400k}=21$$

$$\Rightarrow\quad 400k=\ln(21)\Rightarrow k=\frac{1}{400}\ln(21)$$

$$\Rightarrow\quad \left(\frac{n}{100-n}\right)=e^{100\times\frac{1}{400}\ln(21)t}\times\frac{1}{49}$$

[from Eq. (i)]

Put $t=8$ in the above equation,

$$\left(\frac{n}{100-n}\right)=\frac{e^{\left(\frac{1}{4}\ln(21)\right)8}}{49}$$

$$\Rightarrow\quad \left(\frac{n}{100-n}\right)=\frac{(21)^{\frac{1}{4}\times 8}}{49}\Rightarrow\left(\frac{n}{100-n}\right)=\frac{441}{49}$$

$$\Rightarrow\quad n=90$$

74. Given, $\frac{dy}{dx}=\frac{2^{x+y}-2^x}{2^y}$

$$\Rightarrow\quad \frac{dy}{dx}=\frac{2^x2^y-2^x}{2^y}\Rightarrow 2^y\frac{dy}{dx}=2^x(2^y-1)$$

$$\Rightarrow\quad \int\frac{2^y}{2^y-1}dy=\int 2^x\,dx\Rightarrow\frac{\log_e(2^y-1)}{\log_e 2}=\frac{2^x}{\log_e 2}+C$$

$\therefore\quad \log_2(2^y-1)=2^x\log_2 e+C$

$\because\quad y(0)=1$

$\Rightarrow\quad 0=\log_2 e+C\Rightarrow C=-\log_2 e$

$\therefore\quad \log_2(2^y-1)=(2^x-1)\log_2 e$

Put $x=1$, $\log_2(2^y-1)=\log_2 e$

$\Rightarrow\quad 2^y=e+1\Rightarrow y=\log_2(e+1)$

75. It is given that, $y^{1/4}+\frac{1}{y^{\frac{1}{4}}}=2x$

$$\Rightarrow\quad y^{1/4}=x+\sqrt{x^2-1}\text{ or }x-\sqrt{x^2-1}$$

So, $\frac{1}{4}\frac{1}{y^{\frac{3}{4}}}\frac{dy}{dx}=1+\frac{x}{\sqrt{x^2-1}}$

$$\Rightarrow\quad \frac{1}{4}\frac{1}{y^{\frac{3}{4}}}\frac{dy}{dx}=\frac{y^{1/4}}{\sqrt{x^2-1}}\Rightarrow\frac{dy}{dx}=\frac{4y}{\sqrt{x^2-1}} \qquad ....(i)$$

Now, $\frac{d^2y}{dx^2}=4\frac{(\sqrt{x^2-1})y'-\frac{yx}{\sqrt{x^2-1}}}{x^2-1}$

$$\Rightarrow(x^2-1)y''=4\left(\sqrt{x^2-1}y'-\frac{xy}{\sqrt{x^2-1}}\right)$$

$$\Rightarrow (x^2 - 1)y'' = 4\left(4y - \frac{xy'}{4}\right) \quad \text{[from Eq. (i)]}$$

$$\Rightarrow \quad (x^2 - 1)y'' + xy' - 16y = 0$$

$$\because \ (x^2 - 1)\frac{d^2y}{dx^2} + \alpha x\frac{dy}{dx} + \beta y = 0$$

$\therefore \ \alpha = 1$ and $\beta = -16$

So, $\ |\alpha - \beta| = 17$

76. Since, $x^2 = 4b(y + b)$

$$x^2 = 4by + 4b^2$$

On differentiating both sides w.r.t. x, we get

$$2x = 4by' \Rightarrow b = \frac{x}{2y'}$$

So, differential equation is

$$x^2 = \frac{2x}{y'} \cdot y + \left(\frac{x}{y'}\right)^2$$

$$\therefore \quad x(y')^2 = 2yy' + x$$

77. Given differential equation is

$$2x^2 dy = (2xy + y^2)\, dx$$

$$\Rightarrow \quad \frac{dy}{dx} = \frac{2xy + y^2}{2x^2}$$

[homogeneous differential equation]

Let $y = vx \Rightarrow \dfrac{dy}{dx} = v + x\dfrac{dv}{dx}$

$\therefore$ The differential equation becomes

$$v + x\frac{dv}{dx} = \frac{2vx^2 + v^2x^2}{2x^2}$$

$$\Rightarrow \quad x\frac{dv}{dx} = \frac{2v + v^2 - 2v}{2}$$

$$\Rightarrow \quad x\frac{dv}{dx} = \frac{v^2}{2}$$

$$\Rightarrow \quad 2\frac{dv}{v^2} = \frac{dx}{x}$$

$$\Rightarrow \quad 2\left(\frac{-1}{v}\right) = \log_e x + C$$

$$\Rightarrow \quad \log_e x + \frac{2x}{y} + C = 0 \quad \text{...(i)}$$

as $\quad v = y / x$

$\because$ The curve (i) passes through the point (1, 2).

So, $c = -1$

$$\therefore \quad \log_e x + \frac{2x}{y} = 1$$

Now, at $x = \dfrac{1}{2}$, $\ \log_e\left(\dfrac{1}{2}\right) + \dfrac{1}{y} = 1$

$$\Rightarrow \quad \frac{1}{y} = 1 + \log_e 2$$

$$\Rightarrow \quad y = f\left(\frac{1}{2}\right) = \frac{1}{1 + \log_e 2}$$

Exercise 2 - JEE Advanced Pattern

1. $Y - y = m(X - x)$. For X-intercept $Y = 0$

$$X = x - \frac{y}{m}$$

Therefore, $x - \dfrac{y}{m} = y$

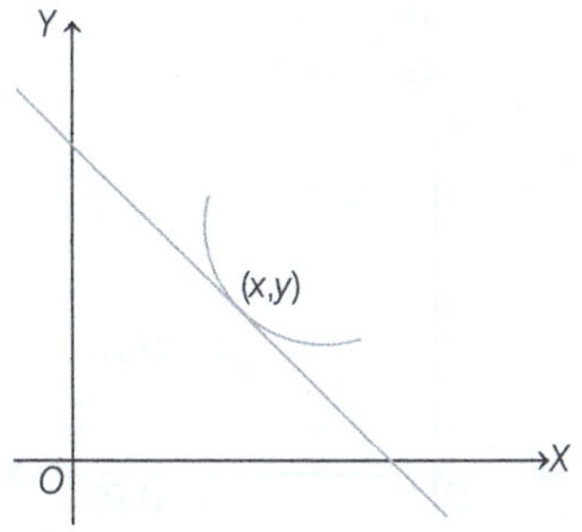

or $\quad \dfrac{dy}{dx} = \dfrac{y}{x - y} \quad \left[\because m = \dfrac{dy}{dx}\right]$

Put $y = vx \quad v + x\dfrac{dv}{dx} = \dfrac{v}{1 - v}$

$$x\frac{dv}{dx} = \frac{v}{1 - v} - v = \frac{v - v + v^2}{1 - v}$$

$$\int \frac{1 - v}{v^2}\, dv = \int \frac{dx}{x} \quad -\frac{1}{v} - \ln v = \ln x + C$$

$$-\frac{x}{y} - \ln\frac{y}{x} = \ln x + C \Rightarrow -\frac{x}{y} = \ln y + C$$

$x = 1, y = 1 \Rightarrow C = -1$

$$1 - \frac{x}{y} = \ln y \Rightarrow y = e \cdot e^{-x/y}$$

$$e^{-x/y} = \frac{e}{y} \quad \Rightarrow \quad ye^{x/y} = e$$

2. $\sin x \dfrac{dy}{dx} + y \cos x = 1$

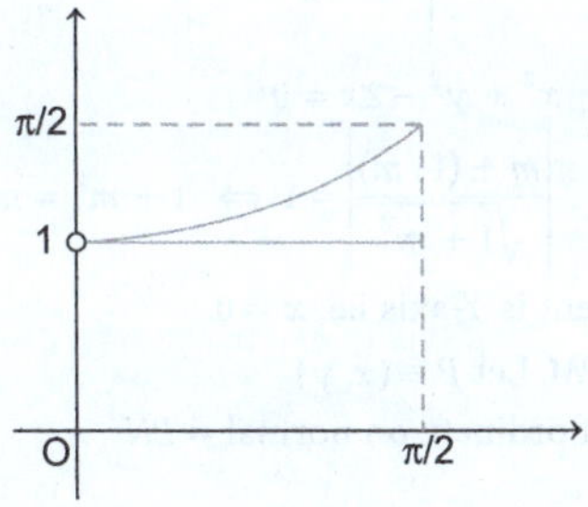

$$\frac{dy}{dx} + y \cot x = \operatorname{cosec} x$$

$$\text{IF} = e^{\int \cot x\, dx} = e^{\ln (\sin x)} = \sin x$$

$$y \sin x = \int \operatorname{cosec} x \cdot \sin x\, dx$$

$$y \sin x = x + C$$

If $x = 0$, y is finite $\therefore \ C = 0$

$$y = x\,(\operatorname{cosec} x) = \frac{x}{\sin x}$$

Now, $I < \dfrac{\pi^2}{4}$ and $I > \dfrac{\pi}{2}$

Hence, $\dfrac{\pi}{2} < I < \dfrac{\pi^2}{4}$

3. Slope of the normal $= \dfrac{y}{x-1}$

$\therefore \quad \dfrac{dx}{dy} = \dfrac{-y}{x-1}$

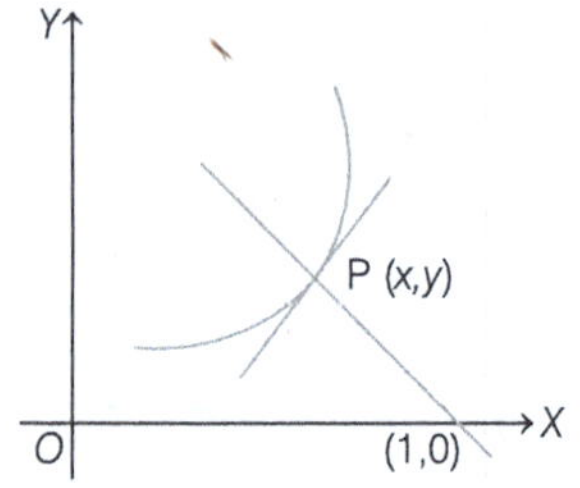

$\Rightarrow \quad \dfrac{dy}{dx} = \dfrac{1-x}{y} \Rightarrow y\,dy = (1-x)\,dx$

$\Rightarrow \quad \dfrac{y^2}{2} = x - \dfrac{x^2}{2} + C \qquad \text{...(ii)}$

Eq. (ii) passes through (0, 0).
Thus, $C = 0$

$$x^2 + y^2 - 2x = 0$$

Now, tangent to $y^2 = 4x$

$$y = mx + \frac{1}{m} \qquad \text{...(iii)}$$

If it touches the circle

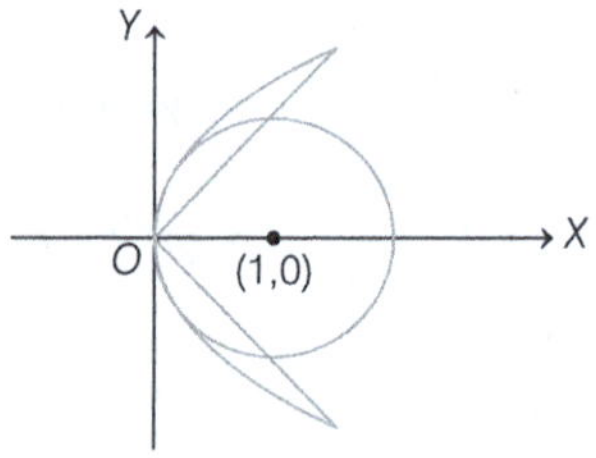

$$x^2 + y^2 - 2x = 0$$

Then, $\left|\dfrac{m + (1/m)}{\sqrt{1+m^2}}\right| = 1 \Rightarrow 1 + m^2 = m^2 \Rightarrow m \to \infty$

Hence, tangent is Y-axis i.e. $x = 0$.

4. Ordinate $= PM$. Let $P \equiv (x, y)$
Projection of ordinate on normal $= PN$

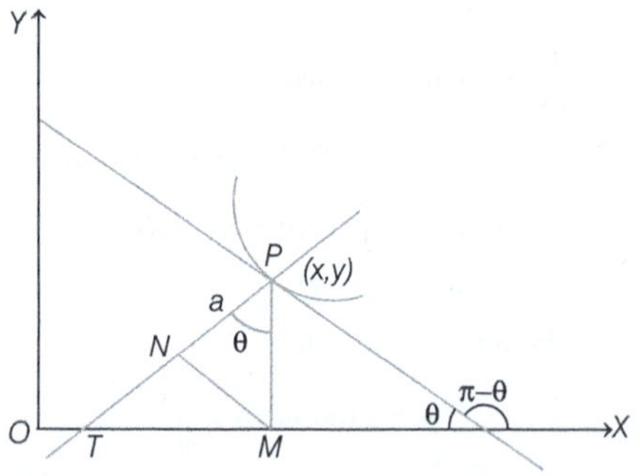

$\therefore \quad PN = PN\cos\theta = a \qquad \text{(given)}$

$\therefore \quad \dfrac{y}{\sqrt{1+\tan^2\theta}} = a \Rightarrow y = a\sqrt{1+(y_1)^2}$

$\Rightarrow \quad \dfrac{dy}{dx} = \dfrac{\sqrt{y^2-a^2}}{a} \Rightarrow \displaystyle\int \frac{a\,dy}{\sqrt{y^2-a^2}} = \int dx$

$\Rightarrow \quad a\ln|y + \sqrt{y^2-a^2}| = x + C$

5. $\displaystyle\int_0^1 f(tx)\,dt = n\cdot f(x)$

Put $tx = y \Rightarrow dt = \dfrac{1}{x}dy$

$\therefore \quad \dfrac{1}{x}\displaystyle\int_0^x f(y)\,dy = nf(x)$

$\therefore \quad \displaystyle\int_0^x f(y)\,dy = x\cdot n\cdot f(x)$

On differentiating, $\quad f(x) = n\,[f(x) + xf'(x)]$

$$f(x)(1-n) = nx\,f'(x)$$

$\therefore \quad \dfrac{f'(x)}{f(x)} = \dfrac{1-n}{nx}$

On integrating, $\ln f(x) = \left(\dfrac{1-n}{n}\right)\ln Cx = \ln (Cx)^{\frac{1-n}{n}}$;

$\therefore \quad f(x) = Cx^{\frac{1-n}{n}}$

6. $\displaystyle\int \frac{dy}{100-y} = \int dx$

$$-\ln(100-y) = x + C$$

$$\ln(100-y) = -x + C$$

Also, $\quad x = 0,\ y = 50$

$\therefore \quad C = \ln 50$

$$x = \ln 50 - \ln(100-y)$$

$\Rightarrow \quad \ln\dfrac{50}{100-y} = x \Rightarrow \dfrac{50}{100-y} = e^x$

$\Rightarrow \quad 100 - y = 50e^{-x} \Rightarrow y = 100 - 50e^{-x}$

7. $\dfrac{f(x)}{1+x^2} = 1 + \displaystyle\int_0^x \frac{f^2(t)}{1+t^2}\,dt \qquad$ [Note : $f(0) = 1$]

Differentiate both sides w.r.t. x, we get

$$\frac{(1+x^2)f'(x) - f(x)(2x)}{(1+x^2)^2} = \frac{f^2(x)}{(1+x^2)}$$

$$\frac{dy}{dx} - \left(\frac{2x}{1-x^2}\right)y = y^2$$

$$\frac{1}{y^2}dy - \left(\frac{2x}{1-x^2}\right)\frac{1}{y} = 1$$

Let $\dfrac{-1}{y} = t \Rightarrow \dfrac{dt}{dx} + \left(\dfrac{2x}{1-x^2}\right)t = 1$

$\therefore$ Solving the above equation, we get

$$f(x) = \frac{-3(1+x^2)}{x^3+3x-3}$$

$$f(-2) = \frac{-3(5)}{-8-6-3} = \frac{15}{17}$$

8. $\dfrac{dy}{dx} + \int_0^5 y\,dx = 27$

Let $k = \int_0^5 y dx$

$\Rightarrow \dfrac{dy}{dx} = 27 - k$

On integrating, we get

$$y = 27x - kx + \lambda,$$

origin (0, 0) lies on it so, we get

$$\lambda = 0$$

$$y = (27 - k)x$$

$$\Rightarrow \quad k = \int_0^5 y\,dx = (27 - k)\left.\frac{x^2}{2}\right|_0^5 \Rightarrow k = (27 - k)\frac{25}{2}$$

$$\Rightarrow \quad 2k = (27 - k)\,25$$

$$\Rightarrow \quad 27k = 27 \times 25$$

$$k = 25, \text{ curve } y = 2x$$

$a, b \in \{1, 2, 3, 4\}$

a	*b*
1	2
2	4

Required probability $P = \dfrac{2}{4 \times 4} = \dfrac{1}{8}$

9. We have, $y_1 = 1 + y^2$

$$\Rightarrow \quad \frac{dy}{dx} = 1 + y^2 \Rightarrow \frac{dy}{1 + y^2} = dx$$

On integrating, we get

$$\tan^{-1} y = x + c \Rightarrow an^{-1}(h(x)) = x + c$$

Given, $h(0) = 0$

$\therefore \quad 0 = 0 + c$

$\therefore \quad c = 0$

Then, $\tan^{-1} h(x) = x$

Since, the range of $\tan^{-1} h(x)$ is $(-\pi/2, \pi/2)$

$$\therefore \quad -\frac{\pi}{2} < x < \frac{\pi}{2}$$

But given, $-c < x < c$

Hence, the largest value of c such that $f(x)$ is differentiable is $\pi/2$.

10. $\cos y = ae^{-x}$

$$\Rightarrow \quad -\sin y\frac{dy}{dx} = -ae^{-x}$$

$$\Rightarrow \quad -\sin y\frac{dy}{dx} = -\cos y \Rightarrow \tan y\frac{dy}{dx} = 1$$

For orthogonal trajectory, replace $\dfrac{dy}{dx}$ by $\dfrac{-dy}{dx}$ $\tan y\left(\dfrac{-dx}{dy}\right) = 1$

$$\Rightarrow \quad \int -dx = \int \cot y\,dy$$

$$\Rightarrow \quad -x + C = \ln \sin y$$

$$\Rightarrow \quad \sin y = e^{-x+c} \Rightarrow \sin y = Ce^{-x}$$

11. $\displaystyle\lim_{t \to x} \frac{t^2 f(x) - x^2 f(t)}{t - x} = 1$

Using L' Hospital rule, differentiate w.r.t. t, we get

$$\lim_{t \to x} \frac{2tf(x) - x^2 f'(t)}{1} = 1 \Rightarrow 2xf(x) - x^2 f'(x) = 1$$

Let $f(x) = y \Rightarrow x^2\dfrac{dy}{dx} - 2xy = 1 \Rightarrow \dfrac{dy}{dx} - \dfrac{2}{x}y = -\dfrac{1}{x^2}$

$$\therefore \quad \text{IF} = e^{-\int \frac{2}{x}dx} = e^{-2\ln x} \Rightarrow y\frac{1}{x^2} = -\int \frac{1}{x^4}\,dx$$

As, $\quad y(1) = 1 \cdot c = \dfrac{2}{3}$

$$\therefore \quad \frac{y}{x^2} = \frac{1}{3x^3} + \frac{2}{3} \Rightarrow y = \frac{1}{3x} + \frac{2x^2}{3}$$

12. $\dfrac{xdy - ydx}{x^2} = e^x\left(\ln x + \dfrac{1}{x}\right)dx$

$$\int d\left(\frac{y}{x}\right) = \int e^x\left(\ln x + \frac{1}{x}\right)dx \Rightarrow \frac{y}{x} = e^x \ln x + C$$

$y(-1) = 0 \Rightarrow C = 0$

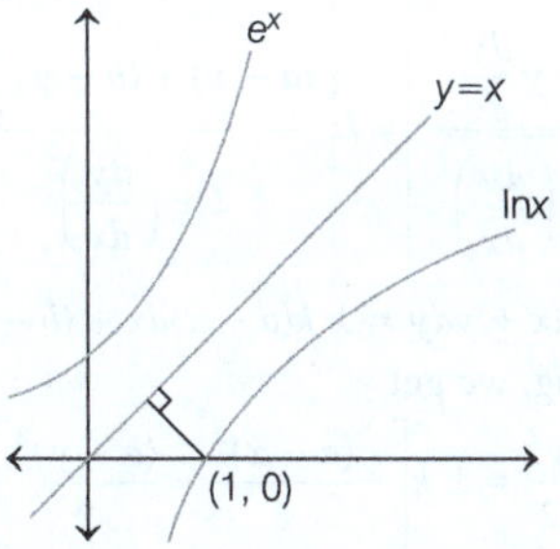

$$\therefore \quad y = xe^x \ln x$$

$$h(x) = \ln x$$

$$g(x) = x$$

Hence, least distance $= 2 \cdot \left(\dfrac{1}{\sqrt{2}}\right) = \sqrt{2}$

13. $\dfrac{dy}{dx} = -xe^{-x^2/2} \int dy = \int -xe^{-x^2/2}dx$

$$\frac{d^2y}{dx^2} = -e^{-x^2/2} - x(e^{-x^2/2}(-x) = e^{-x^2/2}[x^2 - 1] = 0$$

Put $\dfrac{-x^2}{2} = t - xdx = dt \Rightarrow x = 1, -1$

2 point infection $- xdx = dt$

$$y = \int e^t dt \Rightarrow y = e^t + C \Rightarrow y = e^{-x^2/2} + C$$

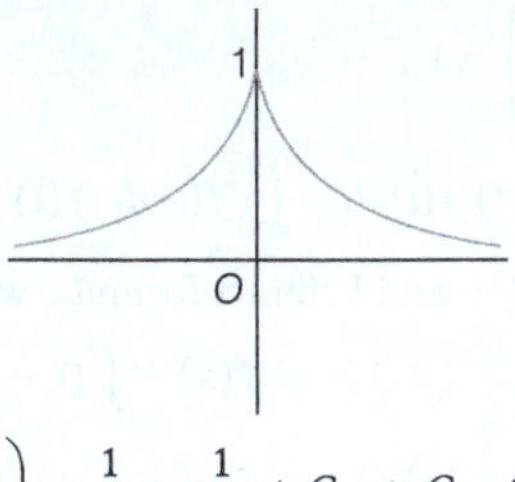

At point $\left(1, \dfrac{1}{\sqrt{e}}\right)$, $\dfrac{1}{\sqrt{e}} = \dfrac{1}{\sqrt{e}} + C \Rightarrow C = 0 \Rightarrow y = e^{-x^2/2}$

Differentiable not symmetric about origin but it is symmetric about Y-axis.

14. Let $y = f(x)$ be the curve and let $P(x, y)$ be any point on the curve. The equation of the normal at $P(x, y)$, to the given curves is

$$Y - y = \frac{-1}{\frac{dy}{dx}}(X - x)$$

The distance of (1) from the origin is,

$$d_1 = \left|\frac{y + \frac{x}{\frac{dy}{dx}}}{\sqrt{1 + \frac{1}{(dy/dx)^2}}}\right| = \left|\frac{x + y\frac{dy}{dx}}{\sqrt{1 + \left(\frac{dy}{dx}\right)^2}}\right|$$

$$d_2 = \left|\frac{(a - x) + (b - y)\frac{dy}{dx}}{\sqrt{1 + \left(\frac{dy}{dx}\right)^2}}\right|$$

Now, $d_1 = kd_2$

$$\left|\frac{x + y\frac{dy}{dx}}{\sqrt{1 + \left(\frac{dy}{dx}\right)^2}}\right| = k\left|\frac{(a - x) + (b - y)\frac{dy}{dx}}{1 + \left(\frac{dy}{dx}\right)^2}\right|$$

$$xdx + ydy = \pm k(a - x)dx + (b - y)dy$$

On integrating, we get

$$\frac{x^2}{2} + \frac{y^2}{2} = \pm k\left[-\frac{(a - x)^2}{2} - \frac{(b - y)^2}{2}\right] + C$$

15. $f''(x) = f'(x) + e^x$

Put $f'(x) = v \Rightarrow \frac{dy}{dx} + v(-1) = e^x$

$\Rightarrow \quad ve^{-x} = \int e^x \cdot e^{-x} dx$

$\Rightarrow \quad ve^{-x} = x + C_1,\ f'(0) = 1 \Rightarrow C_1 = 1$

$f'(x) = xe^x + e^x$

$f(x) = xe^x + C_2$

$\Rightarrow \quad f(0) = 0$

$\Rightarrow \quad C_2 = 0$

$\Rightarrow \quad f(x) = xe^x$

$\Rightarrow \quad f(2) = 2e^2$

$$\ln\left(\frac{(f(2))^2}{4}\right) = 4$$

16. Given, $x\int_0^x (1 - t)\, f(t)\, dt = \int_0^x t\, f(t)\, dt,\ f(1) = 1$

Applying Newton and Leibnitz formula, we get

$$\Rightarrow \quad x(1 - x)\, f(x) + \int_0^x (1 - t)\, f(t)\, dt = x\, f(x)$$

$$\Rightarrow \quad x\, f(x) - x^2 f(x) - x\, f(x) + \int_0^x (1 - t)\, f(t)\, dt = 0$$

$$\Rightarrow \quad -x^2 f(x) + \int_0^x (1 - t)\, f(t)\, dt = 0$$

$$\Rightarrow \quad -2x\, f(x) - x^2 f'(x) + (1 - x)\, f(x) = 0$$

$$\Rightarrow \quad -x^2 f'(x) - 3x\, f(x) + f(x) = 0$$

$$\Rightarrow \quad x^2 f'(x) + (3x - 1)\, f(x) = 0$$

$$\Rightarrow \quad f'(x) + \left(\frac{3x - 1}{x^2}\right) y = 0 \qquad [\because y = f(x)]$$

$$\Rightarrow \quad \frac{dy}{y} + \left(\frac{3x - 1}{x^2}\right) dx = 0$$

Integrating on both sides, we get

$$\Rightarrow \quad \int \frac{dy}{y} + \int \left[\frac{3}{x} - \frac{1}{x^2}\right] dx = C$$

$$\Rightarrow \quad \log|y| + 3\log|x| + \frac{1}{x} = C \Rightarrow \log|y \cdot x^3| + \frac{1}{x} = C$$

When $x = 1$, $y = 1$, then $C = 1$

Hence, the solution is

$$\log|y \cdot x^3| + \frac{1}{x} = 1$$

$$\Rightarrow \quad \log|y \cdot x^3| = \left(1 - \frac{1}{x}\right) = \left(\frac{x - 1}{x}\right) \Rightarrow y \cdot x^3 = e^{\left(\frac{x-1}{x}\right)}$$

17. The given differential equation is

$$y\cos\left(\frac{y}{x}\right)(x\,dy - y\,dx) + x\sin\left(\frac{y}{x}\right)(x\,dy + y\,dx) = 0$$

$$\Rightarrow \quad \frac{y}{x}\cos\left(\frac{y}{x}\right)\left(\frac{dy}{dx} - \frac{y}{x}\right) + \sin\left(\frac{y}{x}\right)\left(\frac{dy}{dx} + \frac{y}{x}\right) = 0$$

$$\Rightarrow \quad v\cos v\left(v + x\frac{dv}{dx} - v\right) + \sin v\left(v + x\frac{dv}{dx} + v\right) = 0 \quad \left[\text{let } \frac{y}{x} = v\right]$$

$$\Rightarrow \quad xv\cos v\frac{dv}{dx} + \sin v\left(2v + x\frac{dv}{dx}\right) = 0$$

$$\Rightarrow \quad x(v\cos v + \sin v)\frac{dv}{dx} = -2v\sin v$$

$$\Rightarrow \quad x\frac{dv}{dx} = -\frac{2v\sin v}{(v\cos v + \sin v)}$$

$$\Rightarrow \quad \frac{(v\cos v + \sin v)}{v\sin v}dv = -\frac{2dx}{x}$$

$$\Rightarrow \quad \left(\cot v + \frac{1}{v}\right)dv = -\frac{2dx}{x}$$

Integrating both sides, we get

$$\log|\sin v| + \log|v| = \log C - 2\log x$$

$$\Rightarrow \quad v\sin v = \frac{C}{x^2}$$

$$\Rightarrow \quad \left(\frac{y}{x}\right)\sin\left(\frac{y}{x}\right) = \frac{C}{x^2} \Rightarrow (xy)\sin\left(\frac{y}{x}\right) = C$$

When $x = 1$, $y = \frac{\pi}{2}$, then $C = \frac{\pi}{2}$

Hence, the solution is $(xy)\sin\left(\frac{y}{x}\right) = \frac{\pi}{2}$

18. We have,

$$2xy\frac{dy}{dx} = y^2 - x^2$$

$$\frac{dy}{dx} = \frac{y^2 - x^2}{2xy}$$

Put $y = vx \Rightarrow \dfrac{dy}{dx} = v + x\dfrac{dv}{dx}$

$\therefore \quad v + x\dfrac{dv}{dx} = \dfrac{v^2 - 1}{2v}$

$\Rightarrow \quad x\dfrac{dv}{dx} = \dfrac{v^2 - 1 - 2v^2}{2v} = \dfrac{-(v^2+1)}{2v} \Rightarrow \dfrac{2v}{v^2+1}dv = -\dfrac{dx}{x}$

Integrating both sides, we get

$$\ln(v^2+1) = -\ln x + \ln C \Rightarrow v^2 + 1 = \frac{C}{x}$$

$\Rightarrow \quad \dfrac{y^2}{x^2} + 1 = \dfrac{C}{x} \Rightarrow x^2 + y^2 = Cx$

It passes through (1, 1).

$\therefore \quad x^2 + y^2 - 2x = 0$

Similarly for second differential equation

$$\frac{dy}{dx} = \frac{2xy}{x^2 - y^2}$$

Equation of curve is $x^2 + y^2 - 2y = 0$.

Now, required area is

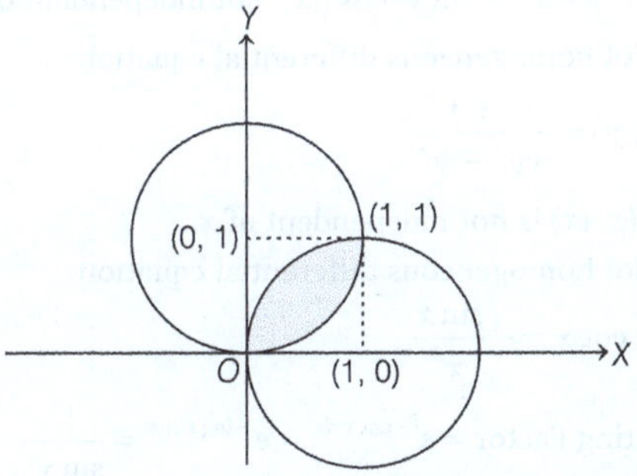

$$= 2\int_0^1 (\sqrt{2x - x^2} - x)\,dx = \left(\frac{\pi}{2} - 1\right) \text{ sq units}$$

19. We have, $x(1 - x\ln y)\dfrac{dy}{dx} + y = 0$

Let $\ln y = z$

$\Rightarrow \quad \dfrac{1}{y}\dfrac{dy}{dx} = \dfrac{dz}{dx} \Rightarrow y\dfrac{dx}{dy} = \dfrac{dx}{dz}$

$\therefore \quad \dfrac{dx}{dz} + x = x^2 z \Rightarrow \dfrac{1}{x^2}\dfrac{dx}{dz} + \dfrac{1}{x} = z$

which is a linear differential equation.

Let $\dfrac{1}{x} = v \Rightarrow -\dfrac{1}{x^2}\dfrac{dx}{dz} = \dfrac{dv}{dz}$

$\therefore \quad -\dfrac{dv}{dz} + v = z \Rightarrow \dfrac{dv}{dz} - v = -z$

which is a linear differential equation.

$\therefore$ IF $= e^{-\int dz} = e^{-z}$

Hence, the solution is

$$v \cdot e^{-z} = \int -ze^{-z}dz + C$$

$\Rightarrow \quad v \cdot e^{-z} = (z+1)e^{-z} + C \Rightarrow v = (z+1) + Ce^{z}$

$\Rightarrow \quad \dfrac{1}{x} = (\ln y + 1) + Ce^{\ln y}$

$\Rightarrow \quad \dfrac{1}{x} = (\ln y + 1) + Cy$

which is passing through $\left(e, \dfrac{1}{e}\right)$, so $C = e$

Hence, the required integral curve is

$$\frac{1}{x} = (\ln y + 1) + ey$$

$\Rightarrow \quad \{(\ln y + 1) + ey\}x = 1$

20. Put $x = 1, y = 1$, then $f(1) = 0$

Put $y = 1 + h$

Now, $f\{x(1+h)\} = xf(1+h) + (1+h)f(x)$

$\Rightarrow \quad f(x + xh) - f(x) = xf(1+h) + hf(x)$

$\Rightarrow \quad f(x + xh) - f(x) = x\{f(1+h) - f(1)\} + hf(x)$

$\Rightarrow \quad \left(\dfrac{f(xh + x) - f(x)}{xh}\right) \cdot x = \dfrac{x(f(1+h) - f(1))}{h} + \dfrac{hf(x)}{h}$

$\Rightarrow \quad \lim\limits_{h \to 0}\left(\dfrac{f(xh+x) - f(x)}{xh}\right)x = \lim\limits_{h \to 0}\left(\dfrac{f(1+h) - f(1)}{h}\right)x + f(x)$

$\Rightarrow \quad xf'(x) = xf'(1) + f(x)$

$\Rightarrow \quad xf'(x) = x + f(x) \qquad [\because f'(1) = 1]$

$\Rightarrow \quad x\dfrac{dy}{dx} = x + y$

$\Rightarrow \quad \dfrac{dy}{dx} = 1 + \dfrac{y}{x} \Rightarrow \dfrac{dy}{dx} + \left(-\dfrac{1}{x}\right)y = 1$

which is a linear differential equation.

$\therefore \quad$ IF $= e^{-\int \frac{dx}{x}} = e^{-\log x} = \dfrac{1}{x}$

Hence, the solution is

$$\frac{y}{x} = \int \frac{dx}{x} + C \Rightarrow \frac{y}{x} = \log|x| + C$$

When $x = 1, y = 0$, then $c = 0$

Thus, the equation of the given curve is

$$y = x\log|x|$$

21. $32x + 2y\dfrac{dy}{dx} = 0 \Rightarrow \dfrac{dy}{dx} = m_1 = -\dfrac{16x}{y}$

and $16y^{15}\dfrac{dy}{dx} = k \Rightarrow \dfrac{dy}{dx} = m_2 = \dfrac{k}{16y^{15}}$

$$m_1 m_2 = -\frac{16x}{y} \cdot \frac{k}{16y^{15}} = -\frac{x}{y^{16}} \cdot k = -\frac{x}{y^{16}} \cdot \frac{y^{16}}{x} = -1$$

(b) $\dfrac{dy}{dx} = 1 - ce^{-x} = 1 - (y - x) = -(y - x - 1) \quad$ [using $ce^{-x} = y - x$]

and $\quad \dfrac{dy}{dx} - k \cdot \dfrac{dy}{dx}e^{-y} = 1$

$\dfrac{dy}{dx}[1 - ke^{-y}] = 1$

or $\quad [1 - (x + 2 - y)]\dfrac{dy}{dx} = 1 \qquad$ [using $ke^{-y} = x - y + 2$]

$\dfrac{dy}{dx} = m_2 = \dfrac{1}{y - x - 1} \Rightarrow m_1 m_2 = -1$

(c) $\dfrac{dy}{dx} = 2cx = 2x \cdot \dfrac{y}{x^2} = \dfrac{2y}{x} = m_1$

Also, $2x + 4y\dfrac{dy}{dx} = 0 \Rightarrow \dfrac{dy}{dx} = -\dfrac{x}{2y} = m_2$

Hence, $\quad m_1 m_2 = -1$

(d) $x^2 - y^2 = c$

$$2x - 2y\frac{dy}{dx} = 0 \Rightarrow \frac{dy}{dx} = \frac{x}{y} = m_1$$

$$xy = k$$

$$x\frac{dy}{dx} + y = 0 \Rightarrow \frac{dy}{dx} = -\frac{y}{x} = m_2$$

$\therefore \quad m_1 m_2 = -1$

Hence, (a), (b), (c) and (d) are all correct.

22. Let $m = \frac{dy}{dx}$ be the slope of tangent (x, y) to the required curve.

m_1 = slope of the tangent at $xy = c^2$

$$= -\frac{c^2}{x^2} = -\frac{y}{x}$$

Hence, $$\frac{m + \frac{c^2}{x^2}}{1 - \frac{c^2}{x^2}m} = \pm 1 \quad \text{or} \quad \frac{m + \frac{y}{x}}{1 - \frac{y}{x}m} = \pm 1 \qquad \text{...(i)}$$

Consider $y^2 - 2xy - x^2 = k$

$$\Rightarrow 2y\frac{dy}{dx} - 2\left(y + x\frac{dy}{dx}\right) - 2x = 0$$

$$\Rightarrow \frac{dy}{dx}(y - x) = x + y$$

$$\Rightarrow \frac{dy}{dx} = \frac{x + y}{y - x} = m \qquad \text{(say)}$$

From Eq. (i),

$$\text{LHS} = \frac{\frac{x+y}{y-x} + \frac{y}{x}}{1 - \frac{y}{x}\left(\frac{x+y}{y-x}\right)} = \frac{x^2 + y^2}{x^2 + y^2} = 1 = \text{RHS}$$

Similarly, option (b), (c) and (d) satisfy.

23. $x\frac{dy}{dx} = y\log\left(\frac{y}{x}\right)\frac{dy}{dx} = \frac{y}{x}\log\left(\frac{y}{x}\right)$, put $y = vx$

$$\Rightarrow \frac{dy}{dx} = v + x\frac{dv}{dx}$$

$$\therefore \quad v + x\frac{dv}{dx} = v\log v \Rightarrow x\frac{dv}{dx} = v(\log v - 1)$$

$$\Rightarrow \int\frac{dv}{v(\log v - 1)} = \int\frac{dx}{x} \Rightarrow \int\frac{dt}{t-1} = \int\frac{dx}{x},$$

let $\log v = t$

$$\Rightarrow \log(t-1) = \log(x) + \log C$$

$$\Rightarrow \log(t-1) = \log(xC)$$

$$\Rightarrow t = 1 + xC$$

$$\Rightarrow \log\frac{y}{x} = 1 + xC$$

$$\Rightarrow y = x \cdot e^{1 + Cx}$$

or $$y = x \cdot e^{1 - Cx}$$

and $$\log\frac{y}{x} = \log e + Cx$$

$$\Rightarrow y = ex \cdot e^{Cx}$$

24. (a) $f(x, tx) = e^t + \tan^{-1}(t)$, independent of x.

$\Rightarrow$ Homogeneous differential equation.

(b) $\log\left(\frac{y}{x}\right)dx + \frac{y^2}{x^2}\sin^{-1}\frac{y}{x} \cdot dy = 0$

$$\Rightarrow \frac{dy}{dx} = \frac{\log\left(\frac{y}{x}\right)}{\frac{y^2}{x^2}\sin^{-1}\left(\frac{y}{x}\right)}$$

$$f(x, y) = \frac{\log\left(\frac{y}{x}\right)}{\frac{y^2}{x^2}\sin^{-1}\left(\frac{y}{x}\right)}$$

$$\therefore \quad f(x, tx) = \frac{\log(t)}{t^2\sin^{-1}(t)}, \text{ independent of } x$$

$\Rightarrow$ Homogeneous differential equation.

(c) $f(x, y) = x^2 + \sin x \cdot \cos y$

$f(x, tx) = x^2 + \sin x \cdot \cos(tx)$, not independent of x.

$\Rightarrow$ Not homogeneous differential equation.

(d) $f(x, y) = \frac{x^2 + y^2}{xy^2 - y^3}$

$\Rightarrow f(x, tx)$ is not independent of x.

$\Rightarrow$ Not homogeneous differential equation.

25. $\frac{dy}{dx} - y\cot x = -\frac{\sin x}{x^2}$

Integrating Factor $= e^{\int -\cot x\, dx} = e^{-\log\sin x} = \frac{1}{\sin x}$

$\therefore$ Required solution is $y \cdot \frac{1}{\sin x} = \int -\frac{\sin x}{x^2} \cdot \frac{1}{\sin x}dx + C$

$$y \cdot \frac{1}{\sin x} = \frac{1}{x} + C$$

As $x \to \infty$, $y \to 0 \Rightarrow C = 0$

$$\therefore \quad y = \frac{\sin x}{x} \Rightarrow \lim_{x \to 0} f(x) = 1 \qquad \text{...(i)}$$

$$\therefore \quad I = \int_0^{\pi/2}\frac{\sin x}{x}dx$$

Since, $\frac{\sin x}{x}$ is decreasing, when $x > 0$

$$\Rightarrow f(x) < f(0)$$

$$\Rightarrow \int_0^{\pi/2} f(x) < \frac{\pi}{2} \text{ and } x < \frac{\pi}{2}$$

$$\Rightarrow f(x) > \int\left(\frac{\pi}{2}\right) \Rightarrow \int_0^{\pi/2} f(x)\,dx > 1$$

26. (a) Order of the differential equation is 2.

(b) $$\frac{xdy - ydx}{\sqrt{x^2 + y^2}} = dx \Rightarrow \frac{\frac{xdy - ydx}{x^2}}{\sqrt{\left(1 + \frac{y^2}{x^2}\right)}} = \frac{dx}{x}$$

$$\therefore \qquad \ln\left|\frac{y}{x} + \sqrt{1 + \frac{y^2}{x^2}}\right| = \ln|Cx|$$

$$\therefore \qquad \frac{y}{x} + \frac{\sqrt{x^2 + y^2}}{x} = Cx$$

i.e. $\quad y + \sqrt{x^2 + y^2} = Cx^2$

(c) $y = e^x (A\cos x + B\sin x)$

$$\frac{dy}{dx} = e^x (A\cos x + B\sin x) + e^x(-A\sin x + B\cos x)$$

$$= y + e^x (-A\sin x + B\cos x)$$

$$\therefore \quad \frac{d^2y}{dx^2} = \frac{dy}{dx} + e^x (-A\sin x + B\cos x)$$

$$+ e^x (-A\cos x - B\sin x)$$

$$\therefore \quad \frac{d^2y}{dx^2} = \frac{dy}{dx} + e^x (-A\sin x + B\cos x) - y$$

$$\frac{dy}{dx} + \frac{dy}{dx} - y - y = 2\left(\frac{dy}{dx} - y\right)$$

(d) $(1 + y^2)\dfrac{dy}{dx} + x = 2e^{\tan^{-1} y}$

$$\Rightarrow \quad \frac{dx}{dy} + \frac{1}{1 + y^2} x = \frac{e^{\tan^{-1} y}}{1 + y^2}$$

$$\text{IF} = e^{\int \frac{1}{1+y^2}} = e^{\tan^{-1} y}$$

$$\Rightarrow \quad xe^{\tan^{-1} y} = 2\int e^{\tan^{-1} y} \cdot \frac{e^{\tan^1 y}}{1 + y^2} dy$$

$$\Rightarrow \quad xe^{\tan^{-1} y} = e^{2\tan^{-1} y} + k$$

27. $\dfrac{dy}{dx} = \dfrac{(x+1)^2 + y - 3}{x+1} = x + 1 + \dfrac{y-3}{x+1}$

On putting $x + 1 = X$ and $y - 3 = Y$,

$$\frac{dY}{dX} = X + \frac{Y}{X}$$

$$\Rightarrow \quad \frac{dY}{dX} - \frac{Y}{X} = X$$

Solution is $\dfrac{Y}{X} = X + C$

$$\Rightarrow \quad y - 3 = (x + 1)^2 + C(x + 1)$$

It passes through (2, 0)

$$c = -4$$

Equation of curve is $y = x^2 - 2x$

Area bounded $= \int_0^2 (2x - x^2)dx$

$$= \frac{4}{3} \text{ sq units}$$

28. The equation of normal of $P(x, y)$ is

$$(Y - y) = \frac{-1}{\frac{dy}{dx}}(X - x)$$

$P(x, y)$ is $(Y - y) = \dfrac{-1}{\frac{dy}{dx}}(X - x)$

$$\therefore A\left(x + y\frac{dy}{dx}, 0\right) \text{ and } B\left(0, y + \frac{x}{\frac{dy}{dx}}\right)$$

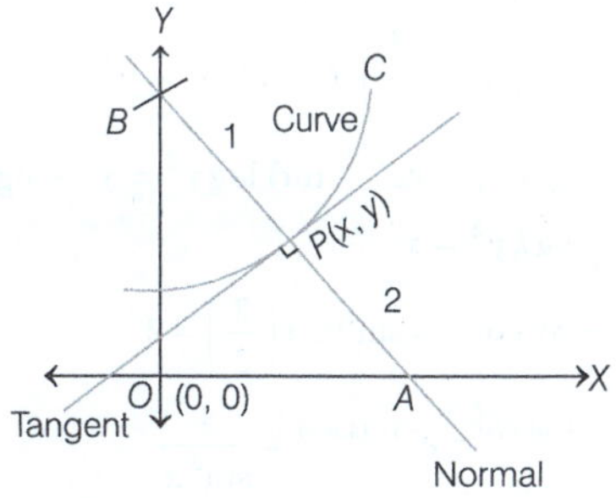

P divides BA in 1 : 2.

$$\therefore \quad \frac{1\left(x + y\frac{dy}{dx}\right) + 2(0)}{1 + 2} = x$$

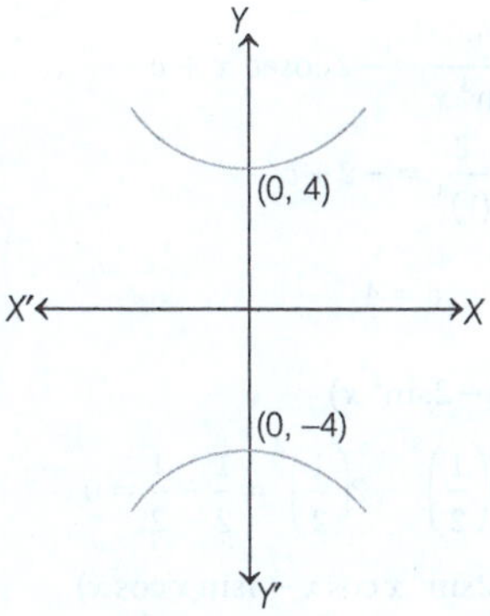

$$\Rightarrow \quad x + y\frac{dy}{dx} = 3x$$

$$\Rightarrow \quad y\frac{dy}{dx} = 2x \qquad \text{...(i)}$$

$$\Rightarrow \quad \int y dy = \int 2x\, dx \Rightarrow \frac{y^2}{2} = x^2 + C$$

Also, (0, 4) satisfy it, so $C = 8$

Equation of curve, $y^2 - 2x^2 = 16$

$\therefore$ Curve passes through $(\sqrt{10}, -6)$,

which represent a hyperbola.

Also, $\left.\dfrac{dy}{dx}\right]_{(4,\, 4\sqrt{3})} = \dfrac{2(4)}{4\sqrt{3}} = \dfrac{2}{\sqrt{3}}$

29. Slope of normal $\tan\theta = \dfrac{-dx}{dy}$

$\therefore$ The given equation becomes at a general point (x, y) is

$$y\left(x^2\left(\frac{-dx}{dy}\right) + \frac{dy}{dx}\right) = x(y^2 + 1)$$

$$-yx^2 + y\left(\frac{dy}{dx}\right)^2 = \frac{dy}{dx}x(y^2 + 1)$$

$$y\left(\frac{dy}{dx}\right)^2 - x(y^2+1)\frac{dy}{dx} - yx^2 = 0$$

$$yy'^2 - xy^2y' - xy' - yx^2 = 0$$

$$yy'(y'-xy) - x(y'-xy) = 0$$

$$\therefore \quad \frac{dy}{dx} = xy \text{ or } \frac{dy}{dx} = \frac{x}{y}$$

$$\log y = \frac{x^2}{2} + C \text{ (or) } x^2 - y^2 = C$$

$$y = ke^{x^2/2} \text{ (or) } \log y^2 = x^2 - \log k$$

$$\log ky^2 = x^2$$

30. Given, $\frac{dy}{dx} - 3y\cot x = \sin 2x,\ y\left(\frac{\pi}{2}\right) = 2$

$$\therefore \quad \text{IF} = e^{-\int 3\cot x dx} = e^{-3\ln(\sin x)} = \frac{1}{\sin^3 x}$$

$\therefore$ General solution is

$$y\left(\frac{1}{\sin^3 x}\right) = \int \frac{2\sin x\cos x}{\sin^3 x}dx + c$$

$$= 2\int \operatorname{cosec} x \cot x dx + c$$

$$\Rightarrow \quad \frac{y}{\sin^3 x} = -2\operatorname{cosec} x + c$$

$$\Rightarrow \quad \frac{2}{(1)^3} = -2 + c$$

$$\Rightarrow \quad c = 4 \qquad \left[\text{as, } y\left(\frac{\pi}{2}\right) = 2\right]$$

$$\therefore y = (4\sin^3 x - 2\sin^2 x)$$

(a) $y\left(\frac{\pi}{6}\right) = 4\left(\frac{1}{2}\right)^3 - 2\left(\frac{1}{2}\right)^2 = \frac{1}{2} - \frac{1}{2} = 0$

(b) $y'(x) = (12\sin^2 x\cos x - 4\sin x\cos x)$

As, $y'(x) = (4\sin x\cos x)(3\sin x - 1)$

$= 2\sin 2x(3\sin x - 1)$

So, $y'\left(\frac{\pi}{3}\right) = \left(\frac{12\times 3}{4}\times\frac{1}{2} - 4\times\frac{\sqrt{3}}{2}\times\frac{1}{2}\right)$

$= \frac{9}{2} - \frac{2\sqrt{3}}{2} = \left(\frac{9-2\sqrt{3}}{2}\right)$

(c) $\therefore y(x)$ increases in $\left(\frac{\pi}{6}, \frac{\pi}{3}\right)$.

(d) $\int_{-\pi/2}^{\pi/2}\left\{\underbrace{4\sin^3 x}_{\text{odd function}} - \underbrace{2\sin^3 x}_{\text{even function}}\right\}dx$

$= 0 - 4\int_0^{\pi/2}\sin^2 x dx$

$= -4\left(\frac{\pi}{4}\right) = -\pi$

31. We have, $\frac{dy}{dx} + \left(\frac{2x}{1+x^2}\right)y = \left(\frac{2x}{1+x^2}\right)$

So, IF $= e^{\int \frac{2x}{1+x^2}dx} = e^{\ln(1+x^2)} = (1+x^2)$

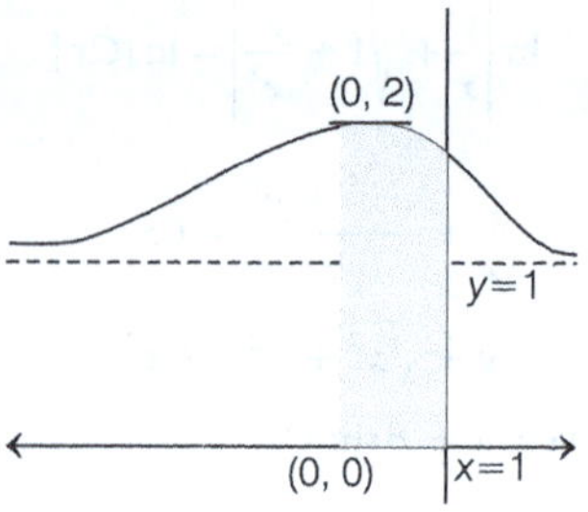

Now, general solution is

$$y(1+x^2) = \int\left(\frac{2x}{1+x^2}\right)\cdot(1+x^2)\,dx + C$$

$$\therefore \quad y(1+x^2) = x^2 + C \qquad \text{...(i)}$$

As, $\quad y(0) = 2 \Rightarrow 2 = C$

$$\therefore \quad f(x) = \left(\frac{x^2+2}{x^2+1}\right) = 1 + \frac{1}{x^2+1} \qquad \text{[even function]}$$

Range of $f(x) = (1, 2]$

Also, area $= \int_0^1\left(1 + \frac{1}{1+x^2}\right)dx$

$= (x + \tan^{-1} x)_0^1$

$= 1 + \frac{\pi}{4} = \frac{\pi+4}{4}$

Now, verify alternatives.

32. $2x^3ydy + (1-y^2)(x^2y^2 + y^2 - 1)dx = 0$

$$\Rightarrow \quad \frac{2y}{(1-y^2)^2}\frac{dy}{dx} + \frac{y^2}{1-y^2}\frac{1}{x} = \frac{1}{x^3} \qquad \text{...(i)}$$

Put $\frac{y^2}{1-y^2} = u \Rightarrow \frac{1}{1-y^2} - 1 = u$

$$\Rightarrow \quad \frac{2y}{(1-y^2)^2}\frac{dy}{dx} = \frac{dy}{dx}$$

From Eq. (i), we have

$$\frac{dy}{dx} + \frac{u}{x} = \frac{1}{x^3}$$

Integrating factor $= e^{\int \frac{1}{x}dx}$

$= e^{\ln x} = x$

$$u\cdot x = \int \frac{1}{x^2}dx = c - \frac{1}{x}$$

$$\Rightarrow \quad x^2y^2 = [(x-1)(1-y^2)]$$

We have, $m = 2, n = 2$ and $k = -1$

33. Given, $f'(t) = e^t(\cos^2 t - \sin 2t)$

On integrating both sides w.r.t. t, we get

$$f(t) = e^t\cos^2 t + C$$

But $f(0) = 1 \Rightarrow C = 0$

So, $\quad f(t) = e^t\cos^2 t$

Clearly, f is bounded in $(-\infty, 0)$.

Note that f is neither odd nor even function.

Also, $f(t) = e^t$

$\Rightarrow \quad e^t \cos^2 t = e^t$

$\Rightarrow \quad \cos^2 t = 1$

$\therefore \quad t = 0, \pi, 2\pi \in [0, 2\pi]$

Also, $\lim_{t \to 0} (f(t))^{1/t} = (1^\infty \text{ form}) = e^L$,

where L

$$= \lim_{t \to 0} \left(\frac{e^t \cos^2 t - 1}{t} \right)$$

$$= \lim_{t \to 0} \frac{e^t (1 - \sin^2 t)}{t} = 1$$

34. $f(x) \cdot f''(x) - f(x) \cdot f'(x) = (f'(x))^2$

$$f(x) \cdot f''(x) - f'(x) = (f'(x))^2$$

$$\therefore \quad \frac{f''(x) - f'(x)}{f'(x)} = \frac{f'(x)}{f(x)}$$

$$\frac{f''(x)}{f'(x)} - 1 = \frac{f'(x)}{f(x)}$$

On integrating w.r.t. x, we get

$$\ln(f'(x)) - x = \ln(f(x)) + C$$

At $x = 0$, $f(0) = 1, f'(0) + 1$

$\therefore \quad C = 0$

$$\therefore \quad \frac{f'(x)}{f(x)} = e^x$$

On integrating w.r.t. x, we get

$$\ln(f(x)) = e^x + C$$

At $x = 0$, $f(0) = 1$

$\therefore \quad C = -1$

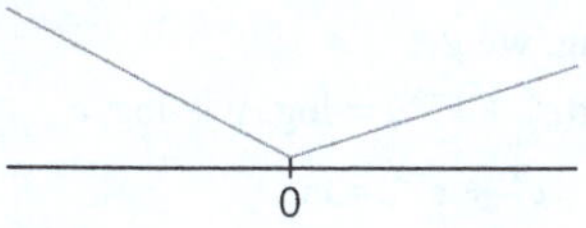

$$f(x) = e^{e^x - 1}$$

Hence, $\lim_{x \to -\infty} f(x) = e^{-1} = \frac{1}{e}$

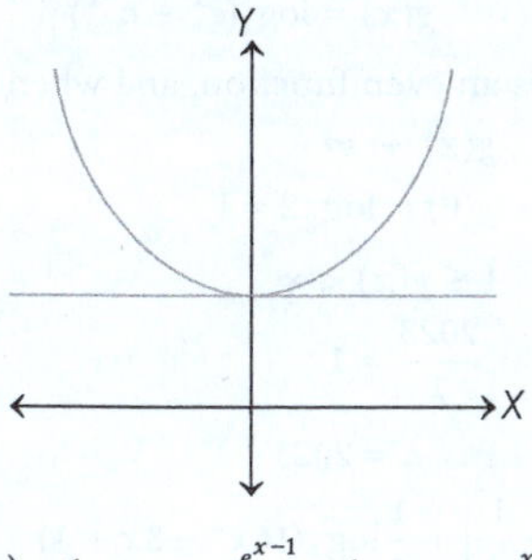

Also, $\lim_{x \to 0} \frac{f(x) - 1}{x} = \lim_{x \to 0} \frac{e^{e^x - 1} - 1}{x} = \lim_{x \to 0} \frac{e^x - 1}{x} = 1$

Now, $f(x) = e^x$

$\Rightarrow \quad e^x - x = 1$

$\Rightarrow \quad e^x - x = 1$

$$f(x) = e^x - x$$

$$f'(x) = e^x - 1$$

Hence, $f(x) = e^x$ has exactly one solution.

35. We have, $\lim_{a \to x} \frac{af(x) - xf(a)}{a - x} \left(\frac{0}{0} \right) = 2$

$$\Rightarrow \quad \lim_{a \to x} \frac{f(x) - xf'(a)}{1 - 0} = 2$$

$$\Rightarrow \quad f(x) - xf'(x) = 2$$

$$\Rightarrow \quad \frac{f'(x)}{f(x) - 2} = \frac{1}{x}$$

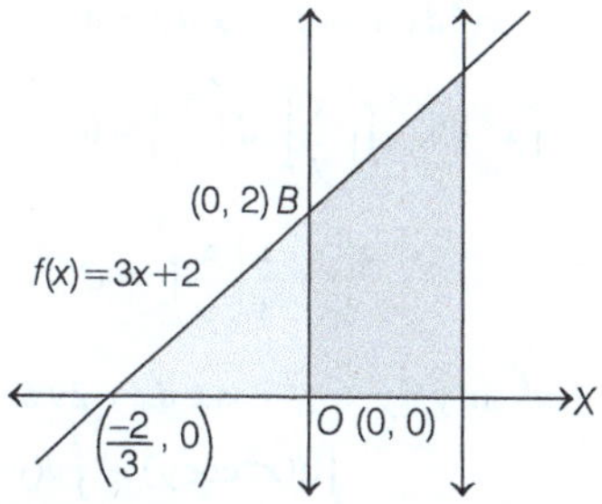

On integrating w.r.t. x, we get

$$\int \frac{f'(x)}{f(x) - 2} dx = \int \frac{1}{x} dx$$

$$\Rightarrow \quad \ln(f(x) - 2) = \ln x + \ln C$$

$$\Rightarrow \quad f(x) = Cx + 2$$

As, $f(1) = 5$

So $\quad 5 = C + 2 \Rightarrow C = 3$

Hence, $f(x) = 3x + 2$

Clearly, $\text{ar}(\Delta OAB) = \frac{1}{2}\left(\frac{2}{3}\right)(2) = \frac{2}{3}$ sq units

Also, $\int_0^2 (3x + 2) dx = \left(\frac{3x^2}{2} + 2x \right)_0^2 = 6 + 4 = 10$

36. $f(0) = 2$

$$f(x) = (e^x + e^{-x}) \cos x - 2x - \left[x \int_0^x f'(t)\, dt - \int_0^x \underset{\text{I}}{t}\, \underset{\text{II}}{f'(t)}\, dt \right]$$

$$f(x) = (e^x + e^{-x}) \cos x - 2x - [x(f(x) - f(0)) - \{t \cdot f(t)|_0^x - \int_0^x f(t) dt\}]$$

$$f(x) = (e^x + e^{-x}) \cos x - 2x - xf(x) + 2x + \left[x\, f(x) - \int_0^x f(t)\, dt \right]$$

$$f(x) = (e^x + e^{-x}) \cos x - \int_0^x f(t)\, dt \quad \text{...(i)}$$

On differentiating Eq. (i),

$$f'(x) + f(x) = \cos x\, (e^x - e^{-x}) - (e^x + e^{-x}) \sin x \quad \text{...(ii)}$$

Hence, $\frac{dy}{dx} + y = e^x (\cos x - \sin x) - e^{-x} (\cos x + \sin x)$

37. IF of Eq. (i) is e^x

$$y \cdot e^x = \int e^{2x} (\cos x - \sin x)\, dx - \int (\cos x + \sin x)\, dx$$

$$y \cdot e^x = \int e^{2x} (\cos x - \sin x)\, dx - (\sin x - \cos x) + C$$

Let $I = \int e^{2x}(\cos x - \sin x)\, dx = e^{2x}(A\cos x + B\sin x)$

Solving, $A = 3/5$ and $B = -1/5$ and $C = 2/5$

$\therefore \quad y = e^x\left(\frac{3}{5}\cos x - \frac{1}{5}\sin x\right) - (\sin x - \cos x)\, e^{-x} + \frac{2}{5}e^{-x}$

Also, $f(1) = 5$, $f\left(\frac{1}{3}\right) = \frac{157}{27}$, $f(0) = 5$, $f(2) = 7$

Hence, the global maximum value = 7.
and the global minimum value = 5.

38. $$(xy^4 + y)\, dx - x\, dy = 0$$

$$\Rightarrow \quad xy^4 dx + y\, dx - x\, dy = 0$$

$$\Rightarrow \quad \int x^3\, dx - \int \left(\frac{x}{y}\right)^2 d\left(\frac{x}{y}\right) = 0$$

$$\Rightarrow \quad \frac{x^4}{4} + \frac{1}{3}\left(\frac{x}{y}\right)^3 = C$$

39. $2x\cos y\, dx - x^2 \sin y\, dy + y^2 \cos x\, dx + 2y\sin x\, dy = 0$

$$\Rightarrow \quad \int d(x^2\cos y) + \int d(y^2 \sin x) = 0$$

$$\Rightarrow \quad x^2\cos y + y^2 \sin x = C$$

40. $$\frac{dx}{x} = \frac{y dy}{1 + y^2}$$

$$\Rightarrow \quad \ln x = \frac{1}{2}\cdot \ln(1 + y^2) + C$$

From the given condition, $C = 0$

$$\therefore \quad x^2 - y^2 = 1$$

41. $$\frac{dy}{dx} + \frac{1 + y^2}{\sqrt{1 - x^2}} = 0$$

$$\Rightarrow \quad \frac{dy}{1 + y^2} + \frac{dx}{\sqrt{1 - x^2}} = 0$$

$$\Rightarrow \quad \tan^{-1} y + \sin^{-1} x = C$$

42. Tangent at point $P(x, y)$, is $y - y = f'(x)(x - x)$

$Q{:}(0, y - x f'(x))$

Then, $PQ = OQ$

$\Rightarrow x^2 + x^2(f'(x))^2 = y^2 + x^2(f'(x))^2 - 2xy(f'(x))$

$\Rightarrow x^2 = y^2 - 2xy \cdot f'(x)$

or $dy / dx = \frac{y^2 - x^2}{2xy}$, put $y = tx$

$$\Rightarrow \quad t + x\frac{dt}{dx} = \frac{dy}{dx}$$

$$\therefore \quad t + x\frac{dt}{dx} = \frac{t^2 - 1}{2t}$$

$$\Rightarrow \quad x\frac{dt}{dx} = \frac{-(1 + t^2)}{2t}$$

$$\Rightarrow \quad \int \frac{2t}{1 + t^2}\, dt = -\int \frac{dx}{x}$$

$$\Rightarrow \quad \frac{c}{x} = 1 + \frac{y^2}{x^2} \Rightarrow x^2 + y^2 - cx = 0$$

$$\therefore \quad C_1{:} x^2 + y^2 - x = 0$$

$$C_2{:} x^2 + y^2 + x = 0$$

C_1 and C_2 touch externally $\Rightarrow$ number of common tangents = 3.

43. $C_1{:} x^2 + y^2 - 2x = 0$

$C_2{:} x^2 + y^2 - Cx = 0$

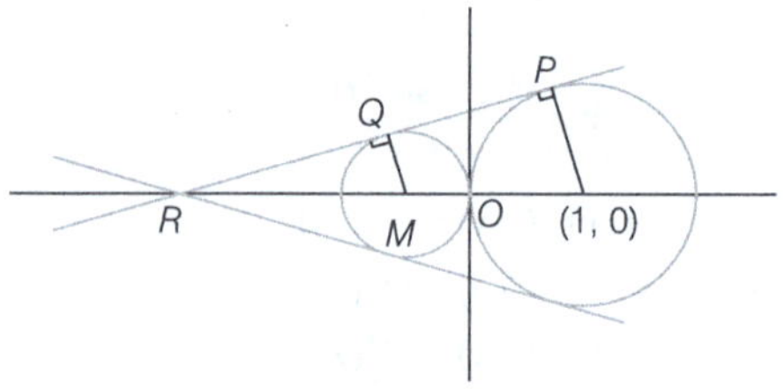

$\angle QRM = 30°$

$\sin 30° = \frac{1}{1 + OR} \Rightarrow OR = 1$

$\sin 30° = \frac{QM}{1 - QM} \Rightarrow QM = 1/3$

radius of $C_2 = 1/3 \Rightarrow C = -2/3, C_2{:} x^2 + y^2 + \frac{2}{3}x = 0$

Point $(-1/3, 1/3)$ will satisfy C_2.

44. We have, $e^x(ydx - dy) = e^{-x}(ydx + dy)$

$$\Rightarrow \quad ydx(e^x - e^{-x}) = (e^x + e^{-x})dy$$

$$\Rightarrow \quad \frac{dy}{y} = \left(\frac{e^x - e^{-x}}{e^x + e^{-x}}\right)dx$$

On integrating, we get

$$\log(e^x + e^{-x}) = \log_e y + \log_e c$$

$$\Rightarrow \quad e^x + e^{-x} = cy$$

Since, the curve passes through (0, 2)

$$\therefore \quad c = 1$$

$$\therefore \quad f(x) = e^x + e^{-x}$$

$$\Rightarrow \quad g(x) = \log_2(e^x + e^{-x})$$

Clearly, $g(x)$ is an even function, and when $x \to \pm\infty$,

$$g(x) \to \infty$$

$$g(0) = \log_2 2 = 1$$

$$\therefore \quad 1 \le g(x) < \infty$$

$$\Rightarrow \quad \frac{2023}{\lambda} = 1$$

$$\Rightarrow \quad \lambda = 2023$$

45. $y = \log_{1/4}\left(x - \frac{1}{4}\right) + \frac{1}{2}\log_4(16x^2 - 8x + 1)$

$$= \log_{1/4}\left(x - \frac{1}{4}\right) - \log_{1/4}(4x - 1),\ x > \frac{1}{4}$$

$$= \log_{1/4}\frac{\left(x - \frac{1}{4}\right)}{(4x - 1)}$$

$$= \log_{1/4} \frac{\left(x - \frac{1}{4}\right)}{4\left(x - \frac{1}{4}\right)}, x > \frac{1}{4}$$

$$= \log_{1/4} 1/4 = 1$$

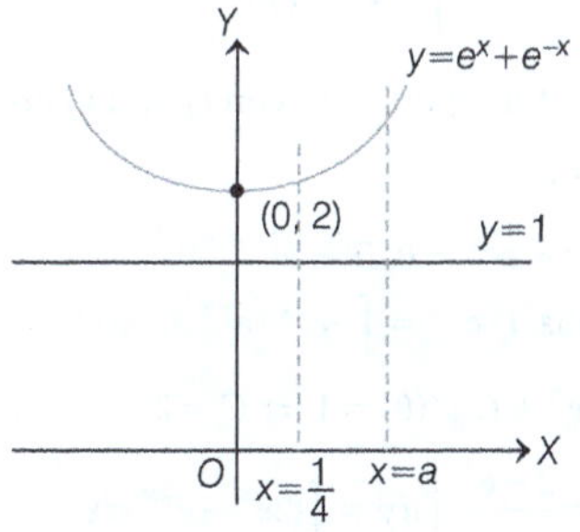

$$\text{Required area} = \int_{1/4}^{a} (e^x + e^{-x} - 1)dx$$

$$= 4 - \log_e 4 + \frac{1}{e^{1/4}} - e^{1/4} \quad \text{[given]}$$

$$\Rightarrow (e^x - e^{-x} - x)_{1/4}^{a} = 4 - \log_e 4 + \frac{1}{e^{1/4}} - e^{1/4}$$

$$\Rightarrow e^a - e^{-a} - a - e^{1/4} + \frac{1}{e^{1/4}} + \frac{1}{4} = 4 - \log_e 4 + \frac{1}{e^{1/4}} - e^{1/4}$$

$$\Rightarrow e^a - e^{-a} - a + \frac{1}{4} = 4 - \log_e 4 \Rightarrow a = \log_e 4$$

$$\therefore \frac{100a}{\log_e 4} = 100$$

46. The given equation is

$$\frac{dy}{dx} = \sin(x+y) + \cos(x+y)$$

Put $x + y = u$

$$\frac{du}{dx} = 1 + \sin u + \cos u = (1 + \cos u) + \sin u$$

$$= 2\cos^2\frac{u}{2} + 2\sin\frac{u}{2}\cos\frac{u}{2}$$

Therefore, $\dfrac{1}{2\cos^2\frac{u}{2} + 2\sin\frac{u}{2}\cos\frac{u}{2}} du = dx$

$$\Rightarrow \frac{\frac{1}{2}\sec^2\frac{u}{2}}{1 + \tan\frac{u}{2}} du = dx$$

Integrating both sides, we get

$$\int \frac{\frac{1}{2}\sec^2\frac{u}{2}}{1 + \tan\frac{u}{2}} du = x + C_1$$

$$\Rightarrow \log\left(1 + \tan\frac{u}{2}\right) = x + C_1$$

$$\Rightarrow 1 + \tan\left(\frac{x+y}{2}\right) = e^{x+C_1}$$

$$\Rightarrow 1 + \tan\left(\frac{x+y}{2}\right) = Ce^x \quad [C = e^{C_1}]$$

$$\Rightarrow k = 2$$

47. We have,

$$\frac{dy}{dx} + \frac{y}{x} = \frac{1}{(1 + \log x + \log y)^2} = \frac{1}{(1 + \log xy)^2}$$

Put $xy = u$, so that

$$\frac{du}{dx} = \frac{x}{(1 + \log u)^2}$$

Therefore, $(1 + \log u)^2 du = x\,dx$

$$\Rightarrow \int (1 + \log u)^2 du = \int x\,dx + C$$

$$\Rightarrow u(1 + \log u)^2 - \int \frac{2(1 + \log u)}{u} \cdot u\,du = \frac{x^2}{2} + C$$

$$\Rightarrow u(1 + \log u)^2 - 2u - 2\left[u \log u - \int 1\,du\right] = \frac{x^2}{2} + C$$

$$\Rightarrow u[1 + 2\log u + (\log u)^2] - 2u\log u = \frac{x^2}{2} + C$$

$$\Rightarrow u[(1 + (\log u)^2] = \frac{x^2}{2} + C$$

$$\Rightarrow xy[1 + \{\log(xy)\}^2] = \frac{x^2}{2} + C$$

$$\Rightarrow k = 2$$

48. Let the salt content at time t be u lb, so that its rate of change is du/dt.

$$= 2 \text{ gal} \times 2 \text{ lb} = 4 \text{ lb / min}$$

If c be the concentration of the brine at time t, the rate at which the salt content decreases due to the out flow

$$= 2 \text{ gal} \times \text{c lb / min}$$
$$= 2\text{c lb / min}$$

$$\therefore \frac{du}{dt} = 4 - 2c \quad \text{...(i)}$$

Also, since there is no increase in the volume of the liquid, the concentrations $\quad c = \dfrac{u}{50}$

$\therefore$ Eq. (i) becomes $\dfrac{du}{dt} = 4 - \dfrac{2u}{50}$

Separating the variables and integrating, we have

$$\int dt = 25 \int \frac{du}{100 - u}$$

or $\quad t = -25 \ln(100 - u) + K \quad$ ...(ii)

Initially when $t = 0$, $u = 0$

$$0 = -25 \ln 100 + K \quad \text{...(iii)}$$

Eliminating K from Eqs. (ii) and (iii), we get

$$t = 25 \ln\left(\frac{100}{100 - u}\right)$$

Taking $t = t_1$ when $u = 40$ and $t = t_2$ when $u = 80$, we have

$$t_1 = 25 \ln\left(\frac{100}{60}\right) \text{ and } t_2 = 25 \ln\left(\frac{100}{20}\right)$$

$\therefore$ The required time $(t_2 - t_1) = 25\left(\ln 5 - \ln\dfrac{5}{3}\right) = 25 \ln 3$

$$= 25 \times 1.0986 = 26 \text{ min } 28 \text{ s}$$
$$= 1648 \text{ s} = 206 \times 8 = 206 \times \lambda$$

$$\therefore \lambda = 8$$

49. $f(x + f(y) + xf(y)) = y + f(x) + yf(x)$ ...(i)

Differentiating w.r.t. x and y is constant

$$f'(x + f(y) + xf(y))(1 + f(y)) = f'(x) + yf'(x) \quad ...(ii)$$

From Eq. (i) again differentiating w.r.t. y as x is constant

$$f'(x + f(y) + xf(y))(1 + x) f'(y) = 1 + f(x) \quad ...(iii)$$

From Eqs. (ii) and (iii), we get

$$\frac{1 + f(y)}{(1 + x) f'(y)} = \frac{(1 + y) f'(x)}{1 + f(x)}$$

$$\frac{(1 + y) f'(y)}{1 + f(y)} = \frac{1 + f(x)}{(1 + x) f'(x)} = \lambda$$

$$\therefore \quad f'(y) = \frac{1 + f(y)}{1 + y}\lambda \text{ and } f'(x) = \frac{1 + f(x)}{\lambda(1 + x)}$$

$$\therefore \quad \lambda = \frac{1}{\lambda} \Rightarrow \lambda = \pm 1$$

$$\therefore \quad \frac{f'(x)}{1 + f(x)} = \pm\frac{1}{1 + x}$$

Integrating both the sides, $f(x) = C(1 + x)^{\pm 1} - 1$

From Eq. (i), put $x = y = 0$

$$f(f(0)) = f(0)$$

From Eq. (ii), $f(0) = C - 1$

So, $\quad f(C - 1) = C - 1$

$\therefore \quad C = 0, 1 \quad$ (taking +ve sign)

So, $f(x) = -1$ and $f(x) = (1 + x) - 1 = x$ and $C = 1$

$$\therefore \quad f(x) = (1 + x)^{-1} - 1 = \frac{-x}{1 + x}$$

$$1 + f(x) = \frac{1}{1 + x}$$

$$\therefore \quad 1 + f(2009) = \frac{1}{2010}$$

$\therefore$ (2010) $(1 + f(2009)) = 1$

50. $\frac{1}{2}(1 + x)^{-1/2} - \frac{a}{2}(1 + y)^{-1/2}\frac{dy}{dx} = 0$

$$\Rightarrow \frac{1}{\sqrt{1 + x}} = \frac{a}{\sqrt{1 + y}} \cdot \frac{dy}{dx} \Rightarrow a = \frac{\sqrt{1 + y}}{\sqrt{1 + x}} \cdot \frac{1}{dy/dx}$$

Putting this value in the given equation,

$$\frac{dy}{dx}\sqrt{1 + x} - \frac{1 + y}{\sqrt{1 + x}} = \frac{dy}{dx}$$

$$\Rightarrow \quad (1 + x)\frac{dy}{dx} = 1 + y + \sqrt{1 + x}\frac{dy}{dx}$$

$$\Rightarrow (1 + x - \sqrt{1 + x})\frac{dy}{dx} = 1 + y$$

$\therefore$ Degree of the given equation is 1.

51. Here, $2f^5(x) \cdot f'(x) \cdot |1 + (f'(x))^2| = f''(x)$

$$\Rightarrow \quad f^4(x)d(f^2(x)) = \frac{f''(x)}{1 + (f'(x))^2}$$

$$\Rightarrow \quad |f^4(x)d(f^2(x))| = \int d(\tan^{-1}(f'(x)))$$

$$\Rightarrow \frac{f^6(x)}{3} + C = \tan^{-1}(f'(x)), \text{ as } f(0) = f'(0) = 0 \Rightarrow c = 0$$

$$\Rightarrow \quad \frac{f^6(x)}{3} = \tan^{-1}(f'(x))$$

$$\Rightarrow \quad -\frac{\pi}{2} < \frac{f^6(x)}{3} < \frac{\pi}{2}$$

$$\therefore \quad -\left(\frac{3\pi}{2}\right)^{1/6} < f(x) < \left(\frac{3\pi}{2}\right)^{1/6}$$

$\Rightarrow$ Number of integers between k_1 and k_2 are 3.

52. Put $dy / dx = t$

$\therefore \quad dt / dx - t + e^{2x} = 0$, IF $= e^{\int -dx = e^{-x}}$

$\therefore \quad$ Solution is, $t \cdot e^{-x} = \int -e^{2x} \cdot e^{-x} dx + C$

$\Rightarrow te^{-x} = -e^x + C\, y'(0) = 1 \Rightarrow C = 2$

$\therefore \quad dy / dx = \frac{2 - e^x}{e - x} \int dy = \int (2e^x - e^{2x})dx$

$$\Rightarrow \quad y = 2^{ex} - \frac{e^{2x}}{2} + C^1, y(0) = 2 \Rightarrow C^1 = 1/2$$

$$\therefore \quad y(x) = 2e^x - \frac{e^{2x}}{2} + \frac{1}{2} \Rightarrow y(x) \le \frac{5}{2} \text{ for } x = \log 2$$

$\therefore \quad [2x] = [2\log 2] = [\log 4] = 1$

53. $\quad f(x) = x\ln x + x - \int_1^x \frac{f(t)}{t\ln t}dt$

$$\therefore f'(x) = \frac{x}{x} + \ln x + 1 - \frac{f(x)}{x\ln x}$$

$$\therefore f'(x) \neq \frac{f(x)}{x\ln x} = 2 + \ln x$$

$$\Rightarrow \frac{dy}{dx} + \frac{y}{x\ln x} = 2 + \ln x$$

This is linear differentiable equation

$$\text{IF} = e^{\int \frac{dx}{x\ln x}} = e\ln^{\ln x} = \ln x$$

Solution is $y\ln x = \int (2 + \ln x)\ln x dx$

$\therefore y\ln x = \int (\ln^2 x + 2\ln x)dx = x\ln^2 x + C$

On putting $x = 1$, we get $C = 0$

$$y\ln x = x\ln^2 x$$

$$\therefore \quad y = f(x) = x\ln x$$

$$f'(x) = 1 + \ln x$$

$$\therefore \quad f''(x) = \frac{1}{x}$$

$$f'(e) + f''\left(\frac{1}{4}\right)^2 = (1 + \ln e) + (4)^2 = 2 + 16 = 18$$

54. $f'(x) = f^2(x)$

$$\Rightarrow \quad \frac{f'(x)}{f^2(x)} = 1$$

$$\Rightarrow \int \frac{f'(x)}{f^2(x)}dx = \int 1dx + c$$

$$\Rightarrow \quad \frac{-1}{f(x)} = x + c$$

At $x = 0$, $f(0) = -1 \Rightarrow c = 1$

$\therefore \quad f(x) = \dfrac{-1}{x+1}$

$$I = \frac{\sqrt{2}}{\pi}\int_0^1 \left(\frac{1-x}{-\frac{1}{x+1}(x^4+1)} + \frac{2}{x^4+1} \right) dx$$

$$= \frac{\sqrt{2}}{\pi}\int_0^1 \left(\frac{x^2-1}{x^4+1} + \frac{2}{x^4+1} \right) dx$$

$$= \frac{\sqrt{2}}{\pi}\int_0^1 \frac{x^2+1}{x^4+1}$$

$$= \frac{\sqrt{2}}{\pi}\int_0^1 \frac{1+\frac{1}{x^2}}{x^2+\frac{1}{x^2}}$$

$$= \frac{\sqrt{2}}{\pi}\int_0^1 \frac{\left(1+\frac{1}{x^2}\right)dx}{\left(x-\frac{1}{x}\right)^2+2}, \; x - \frac{1}{x} = t$$

$$\Rightarrow \left(1+\frac{1}{x^2}\right) dx = dt$$

$$= \frac{\sqrt{2}}{\pi}\int_{-\infty}^0 \frac{dt}{t^2+2}$$

$$= \frac{\sqrt{2}}{\pi}\frac{1}{\sqrt{2}}\left[\tan^{-1}\left(\frac{t}{\sqrt{2}}\right)\right]_{-\infty}^0$$

$$= \frac{1}{\pi}\left[0 - \left(-\frac{\pi}{2}\right)\right]$$

$$= \frac{1}{2} = \frac{p}{q}$$

$$\Rightarrow \quad (p+q)^3 = (3)^3 = 27$$

55. $y(1-y^2)\,dx = x(y^2+1)dy$

$$\Rightarrow \quad \frac{dx}{x} = \frac{(1+y^2)\,dy}{y(1-y^2)} \Rightarrow x(y^2-1) = 0$$

$$\Rightarrow \quad x = 0, y = \pm 1$$

$f_3 : x = 0$ (Y-axis)

$f_1 : y = 1;\ f_2 : y = -1$

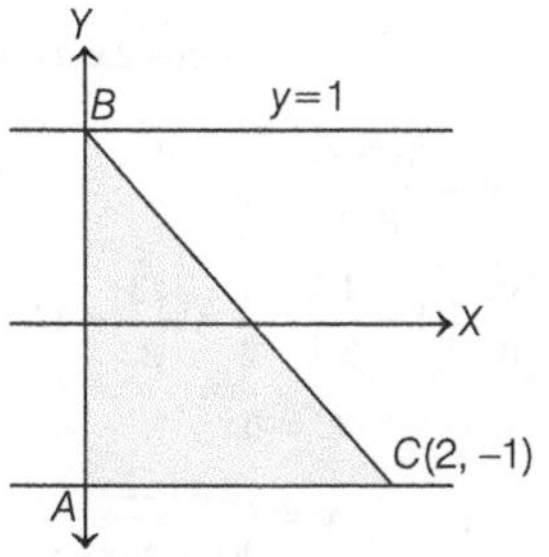

$$\text{Area of } \Delta ABC = \frac{1}{2} \times 2 \times 2 = 2$$

$$\frac{\Delta\text{Area of }\Delta ABC}{4} = \frac{2}{4} = 0.5$$

56. The given equation can be written as

$$\frac{dy}{dx} - y\frac{\phi'(x)}{\phi(x)} = \frac{-y^2}{\phi(x)}$$

$$\Rightarrow \quad -\frac{1}{y^2}\frac{dy}{dx} + \frac{1}{y}\frac{\phi'(x)}{\phi(x)} = \frac{1}{\phi(x)} \quad \ldots\text{(i)}$$

Put $\dfrac{1}{y} = u$ so that $-\dfrac{1}{y^2}\dfrac{dy}{dx} = \dfrac{du}{dx}$

Now, Eq. (i) becomes $\dfrac{du}{dx} + \dfrac{u\phi'(x)}{\phi(x)} = \dfrac{1}{\phi(x)}$

This is a linear equation in u, so its integrating factor is

$$\text{IF} = e^{\int \frac{\phi'(x)}{\phi(x)}} = e^{\log \phi(x)} = \phi(x)$$

Multiplying both sides by the integrating factor, we get

$$\frac{d}{dx}[u\phi(x)] = 1$$

$$\Rightarrow \quad u\phi(x) = x + C$$

$$\Rightarrow \quad \frac{1}{y} = \frac{x+C}{\phi(x)} \quad \left[\because \frac{1}{y} = u\right]$$

$$\Rightarrow \quad y = \frac{\phi(x)}{x+c} \Rightarrow y(1) = \frac{1}{1+c} \Rightarrow c = 0$$

Thus, $y = \dfrac{\phi(x)}{x}$

Hence, $y(4) = \dfrac{1296}{4} = 324$

$$\Rightarrow \quad \sqrt{y(4)} = \sqrt{3 \times 3 \times 36} = 3 \times 6 = 18$$

57. $dy = x\tan y(\sin y - 1)$

$$\frac{dy}{dx} + x\tan y = x\tan y \sin y$$

$$\cos y\frac{dy}{dx} + x\sin y = x\sin^2 y$$

Let $\sin y = t$, $\dfrac{dt}{dx} + xt = xt^2$

$$\frac{1}{t^2}\frac{dt}{dx} + x\left(\frac{1}{t}\right) = x$$

Put $\dfrac{1}{t} = u \Rightarrow \dfrac{-1}{t^2}\dfrac{dt}{dx} = \dfrac{du}{dx} \Rightarrow \dfrac{-du}{dx} + xu = x$

$$\frac{du}{dx} + (-x)u = -x;\ ue^{-\int x dx} = \int -xe^{-\int x dx}dx$$

$$ue^{-x^2/2} = -\int xe^{x^2/2}dx = e^{x^2/2} + c$$

$$u = 1 + ce^{x^2/2};\ t = \frac{1}{1+ce^{x^2/2}}$$

$$\sin y = \frac{1}{1+ce^{x^2/2}}$$

$$\frac{k}{3} = 0.33$$

58. We have, $\dfrac{dy}{dx} = (2+5y)(5y-2)$

$$\Rightarrow \quad \frac{dy}{25y^2-4} = dx \Rightarrow \frac{1}{25}\left(\frac{dy}{y^2-\frac{4}{25}}\right) = dx$$

On integrating both sides, we get

$$\frac{1}{25}\int \frac{dy}{y^2-\left(\frac{2}{5}\right)^2}=\int dx$$

$$\Rightarrow \frac{1}{25}\times\frac{1}{2\times\frac{2}{5}}\log\left|\frac{y-2/5}{y+2/5}\right|=x+C$$

$$\Rightarrow \log\left|\frac{5y-2}{5y+2}\right|=20(x+C)$$

$$\Rightarrow \left|\frac{5y-2}{5y+2}\right|=Ae^{20x} \qquad [\because e^{20C}=A]$$

when $x=0\Rightarrow y=0$, then $A=1$

$$\therefore \left|\frac{5y-2}{5y+2}\right|=e^{20x}$$

$$\Rightarrow \lim_{x\to-\infty}\left|\frac{5f(x)-2}{5f(x)+2}\right|=\lim_{x\to-\infty}e^{20x}$$

$$\Rightarrow \lim_{n\to-\infty}\left|\frac{5f(x)-2}{5f(x)+2}\right|=0$$

$$\Rightarrow \lim_{n\to-\infty}5f(x)-2=0$$

$$\Rightarrow \lim_{n\to-\infty}f(x)=\frac{2}{5}=0.4$$

59. $f(x+y)=f(x)f'(y)+f'(x)f(y)$ ...(i)

On putting $x=y=0$, we get

$$f(0)=2f'(0)f(0)$$

$$\Rightarrow f'(0)=\frac{1}{2} \qquad [\because f(0)=1]$$

On putting $y=0$ in Eq. (i), we get

$$f(x)=f(x)f'(0)+f'(x)f(0)$$

$$\Rightarrow f'(x)=\frac{f(x)}{2}$$

$$\Rightarrow \int\frac{f'(x)}{f(x)}dx=\frac{1}{2}\int dx$$

$$\left[\because f(0)=1 \text{ and } f'(0)=\frac{1}{2}\right]$$

$$\Rightarrow \log_e f(x)=\frac{x}{2}+\log_e c$$

$$\Rightarrow f(x)=ce^{x/2}$$

$$\Rightarrow f(x)=e^{x/2} \qquad [\because f(0)=1]$$

$$\Rightarrow \log_e(f(x))=\frac{x}{2}$$

$$\Rightarrow \log_e(f(4))=2$$

60. (A) Let $x=r\cos\theta$, $y=r\sin\theta$

$$\therefore x^2+y^2=r^2(\sin^2\theta+\cos^2\theta)=r^2 \qquad \text{...(i)}$$

$$\text{and} \quad \tan\theta=\frac{y}{x} \qquad \text{...(ii)}$$

$$\therefore d(x^2+y^2)=d(r^2)$$

From Eq. (i), $x\,dx+y\,dy=rdr$ ...(iii)

From Eq. (ii),

$$d\left(\frac{y}{x}\right)=d(\tan\theta)$$

$$\Rightarrow \frac{xdy-ydx}{x^2}=\sec^2\theta\,d\theta$$

$$\therefore x\,dy-y\,dx=x^2\sec^2\theta\,d\theta$$

$$=r^2\cos^2\theta\sec^2\theta\,d\theta=r^2d\theta \qquad \text{...(iv)}$$

From Eqs. (iii) and (iv), we get

$$\frac{rdr}{r^2d\theta}=\sqrt{\frac{a^2-r^2}{r^2}}$$

$$\text{or} \quad \frac{dr}{\sqrt{a^2-r^2}}=d\theta$$

$$\sin^{-1}\left(\frac{r}{a}\right)=\theta+C$$

$$\Rightarrow r=a\sin(\theta+C)$$

$$\Rightarrow \sqrt{x^2+y^2}=a\sin\left\{C+\tan^{-1}\left(\frac{y}{x}\right)\right\}$$

(B) $\dfrac{dy}{dx}-\sec^2x\tan 2xy=\cos^2x$

$$\text{IF}=e^{\int\tan 2x\sec^2x\,dx}=e^{\int\frac{2\tan x}{\tan^2x-1}\times\sec^2x\,dx}$$

$$=e^{\int\frac{dt}{t}},$$

where $t=\tan^2x-1$

$$=e^{\ln|t|}=|t|=|\tan^2x-1|$$

Given that $|x|<\dfrac{\pi}{4}$

$$\therefore \tan^2x<1$$

$$\therefore \text{IF}=1-\tan^2x$$

Solution is $y(1-\tan^2x)=\int\cos^2x(1-\tan^2x)\,dx$

$$=\int(\cos^2x-\sin^2x)\,dx$$

$$=\int\cos 2x\,dx=\frac{\sin 2x}{2}+C$$

when $x=\dfrac{\pi}{6}$, $y=\dfrac{3\sqrt{3}}{8}$

$$\therefore \frac{3\sqrt{3}}{8}\left(1-\frac{1}{3}\right)=\frac{1}{2}\times\frac{\sqrt{3}}{2}+C$$

$$\therefore C=0$$

$$\Rightarrow y=\frac{\sin 2x}{2(1-\tan^2x)}$$

(C) $\quad x^2+y^2-2cx=0$ ...(i)

$$\therefore 2x+2y\frac{dy}{dx}-2c=0$$

or $\qquad C = x + \dfrac{ydy}{dx}$ ...(ii)

From Eqs. (i) and (ii), $x^2 + y^2 - 2\left(x + \dfrac{ydy}{dx}\right)x = 0$

or $-x^2 + y^2 - 2xy\dfrac{dy}{dx} = 0$ is the differential equation representing the given family of circles. To find the orthogonal trajectories.

$$y^2 - x^2 = -2xy\frac{dx}{dy}$$

or $\qquad y^2\,dy = x^2\,dy - 2xy\,dx$

or $\qquad -dy = \dfrac{yd(x^2) - x^2\,dy}{y^2}$

or $\qquad -dy = d\left(\dfrac{x^2}{y}\right)$

or $\qquad -y = \dfrac{x^2}{y} + C \Rightarrow x^2 + y^2 + Cy = 0$

$\Rightarrow$ Orthogonal trajectory.

(D) Differentiating the equation w.r.t. x, we get

$$xy(x) + 1\int_0^x y(t)\,dt = (x+1)\,xy(x) + 1\int_0^x ty(t)\,dt$$

Again, differentiating, w.r.t. x, we get

$$y(x) = x^2y'(x) + 2xy(x) + xy(x)$$

or $\qquad (1-3x)\,y(x) = \dfrac{x^2dy(x)}{dx}$

or $\qquad \dfrac{(1-3x)\,dx}{x^2} = \dfrac{dy(x)}{y(x)}$ or $y = \dfrac{C}{x^3}e^{-1/x}$

61. (A) $r = 5$ cm, $\delta r = 0.06$, $A = \pi r^2$

$\delta A = 2\pi r\,\delta r = 10\pi \times 0.06 = 0.6\pi$

(B) $v = x^3$

$\delta v = 3x^2\,\delta x$

$\dfrac{\delta v}{v}\times 100 = 3\dfrac{\delta x}{x}\times 100 = 3\times 1 = 3$

(C) $(x-2)\dfrac{dx}{dt} = 2\dfrac{dx}{dt} \Rightarrow x = 4$

(D) $\qquad A = \dfrac{\sqrt{3}}{4}x^2$

$$\frac{dA}{dt} = \frac{\sqrt{3}}{2}x\frac{dx}{dt} = \frac{\sqrt{3}}{2}\cdot 15\cdot\frac{1}{10} = \frac{3\sqrt{3}}{4}$$

62. (A) $\dfrac{dy}{dx} = e^x(A\cos x + B\sin x) + e^x(-A\sin x + B\cos x)$

$= y + e^x(-A\sin x + B\cos x)$

$\therefore\ \dfrac{d^2y}{dx^2} = \dfrac{dy}{dx} + e^x(-A\sin x + B\cos x) + e^x(-A\cos x - B\sin x)$

$= \dfrac{dy}{dx} + \left(\dfrac{dy}{dx} - y\right) - y = 2\left(\dfrac{dy}{dx} - y\right)$

So, degree = 1 and order = 2

(B) The equation of the family is $y^2 = 4a(x-b)$ where a, b are arbitrary constants.

$\therefore \qquad 2y\dfrac{dy}{dx} = 4a$ or $\left(\dfrac{dy}{dx}\right)^2 + y\dfrac{d^2y}{dx^2} = 0$

So, degree = 1 and order = 2

(C) The equation of the family is

$$(x-c)^2 + y^2 = c^2$$

or $\qquad x^2 + y^2 - 2cx = 0$ or $\dfrac{x^2+y^2}{x} = 2c$

$\Rightarrow \qquad \dfrac{\left(2x + 2y\dfrac{dy}{dx}\right)x - (x^2+y^2)\cdot 1}{x^2} = 0$

So, degree = 1 and order = 1

(D) The equation of the family is $\dfrac{x^2}{a^2+\lambda} + \dfrac{y^2}{b^2+\lambda} = 1$ because they have the same foci $(\pm\sqrt{a^2-b^2}, 0)$.

On differentiating, $\dfrac{2x}{d^2+\lambda} + \dfrac{2y}{b^2+\lambda}\cdot\dfrac{dy}{dx} = 0$

or $\qquad \dfrac{x}{a^2+\lambda} + \dfrac{yp}{b^2+\lambda} = 0 \qquad \left(\text{Let } p = \dfrac{dy}{dx}\right)$

or $\quad x(b^2+\lambda) + yp(a^2+\lambda) = 0$

$\Rightarrow \qquad \lambda = \dfrac{-b^2x - a^2yp}{x+yp}$

$\therefore$ The differential equation is

$$\frac{x^2}{a^2 + \dfrac{-b^2x - a^2yp}{x+yp}} + \frac{y^2}{b^2 + \dfrac{-b^2x - a^2yp}{x+yp}} = 1$$

or $\qquad \dfrac{x(x+yp)}{a^2-b^2} + \dfrac{y(x+yp)}{(b^2-a^2)p} = 1$

So, order = 1 and degree = 2

63. Given, $f(1) = \dfrac{1}{3}$

and $3\int_1^x f(t)\,dt = xf(x) - \dfrac{x^3}{3}$, $x \in [1, \infty)$ ...(i)

On differentiating Eq. (i) w.r.t. x, we get

$$3\cdot f(x)\times 1 = f(x)\times 1 + xf'(x) - \frac{1}{3}\times 3x^2$$

$\Rightarrow \qquad 3f(x) = f(x) + xf'(x) - x^2$

$\Rightarrow \quad xf'(x) - 2f(x) = x^2$

$\Rightarrow \quad f'(x) - 2\left(\dfrac{f(x)}{x}\right) = \dfrac{x^2}{x}$

[we can divide by x be $2x \neq 0$, i.e. $x \in [1, \infty)$]

$\Rightarrow \qquad \dfrac{dy}{dx} - 2\left(\dfrac{y}{x}\right) = x,$

which is linear differential equation of the form

$$\frac{dy}{dx} + Py = Q$$

$$\text{IF} = e^{\int P dx} = e^{-\int \frac{2}{x}dx} = e^{-2\log x} = e^{\log x^{-2}} = \frac{1}{x^2}$$

Solution is

$$y \times (\text{IF}) = \int Q \times (\text{IF}) dx$$

$$\Rightarrow \quad y \times \frac{1}{x^2} = \int x \times \left(-\frac{1}{x^2}\right) dx$$

$$\Rightarrow \quad \frac{y}{x^2} = \log x + c$$

Given, $y(1) = \frac{1}{3}$

So, $\frac{1/3}{1} = \log(1) + c$

$$\Rightarrow \quad c = \frac{1}{3}$$

Hence, $y = x^2(\log x) + cx^2 = x^2 \log x + \frac{x^2}{3}$ $\left[\because c = \frac{1}{3}\right]$

Thus, $y(e) = e^2 \log e + \frac{e^2}{3} = \frac{4e^2}{3}$

64. Given differential equation is

$$(x^2 - 5)\frac{dy}{dx} - 2xy = -2x(x^2 - 5)^2 \quad \text{...(i)}$$

and $y(2) = 7$, i.e. when $x = 2$, then $y = 7$

From Eq. (i), $\frac{dy}{dx} = \left(\frac{-2x}{x^2 - 5}\right) y = -2x(x^2 - 5)$

$$\text{IF} = e^{-\int \frac{2x}{x^2 - 5} dx} = e^{-\ln|x^2 - 5|} = \frac{1}{|x^2 - 5|}$$

$\therefore$ Solution of differential equation

$$y \times \text{IF} = \int Q \times \text{IF}\, dx$$

$$\Rightarrow \quad y \times \frac{1}{|x^2 - 5|} = \int (-2x) \cdot \frac{x^2 - 5}{|x^2 - 5|} dx$$

$$\Rightarrow \quad \frac{y}{|x^2 - 5|} = \frac{x^2 - 5}{|x^2 - 5|}(-x^2) + c,$$

where, c = constant of integration.

$\because \quad y(2) = 7$

$$\therefore \quad \frac{7}{|2^2 - 5|} = \frac{2^2 - 5}{|2^2 - 5|}(-2)^2 + c \Rightarrow c = 3$$

Hence, $y = -x^2(x^2 - 5) + 3|x^2 - 5|$ ...(i)

Case I When $0 < x < \sqrt{5}$

$$\text{(A)} \Rightarrow y = -x^4 + 5x^2 - 3x^2 + 15$$
$$= -x^4 + 2x^2 + 15$$

For function to be increasing,

$$\frac{dy}{dx} > 0$$

$$\Rightarrow \quad -4x^3 + 4x > 0$$

$$\Rightarrow \quad -4x(x^2 - 1) > 0$$

$$\Rightarrow \quad x(x - 1)(x + 1) < 0$$

$-\infty$ — + — + ∞ (points -1, 0, 1)

$x \in (-\infty, -1) \cup (0, 1)$ but $0 < x < \sqrt{5}$

Hence, $x \in (0, 1)$

Case II When $x > \sqrt{5}$

$$\text{(A)} \Rightarrow y = -x^4 + 5x^2 + 3x^2 - 15 = -x^4 + 8x^2 - 15$$

For increasing, $\frac{dy}{dx} > 0$

$$\Rightarrow \quad -4x^3 + 16x > 0$$

$$\Rightarrow \quad -4x(x^2 - 4) > 0 \Rightarrow x(x - 2)(x + 2) < 0$$

$-\infty$ — + — + ∞ (points -2, 0, 2)

$\Rightarrow x \in (-\infty, -2) \cup (0, 2)$ but $x > \sqrt{5}$

So, $x \in \phi$.

Finally, we can say that $y(x)$ is increasing over (0, 1).

Also, from (A), we can say that $y(x)$ is an even function.

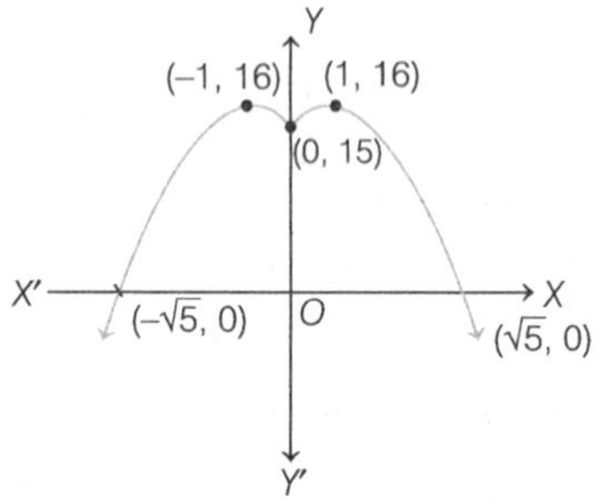

Thus, $f(x)|_{\max} = 16$

65. $x\,dy - (y^2 - 4y)\,dx = 0,\ x > 0,\ y(1) = 2$

$$\int \frac{dy}{y(y - 4)} = \int \frac{dx}{x}$$

$$\Rightarrow \quad \frac{1}{4}\int \frac{y - (y - 4)}{y(y - 4)} dy = \int \frac{1}{x} dx$$

$$\Rightarrow \quad \int \left(\frac{1}{y - 4} - \frac{1}{y}\right) dy = 4\int \frac{1}{x} dx$$

$$\Rightarrow \quad \ln|y - 4| - \ln|y| = 4\ln x + \ln c$$

$$\Rightarrow \quad \ln\left|\frac{y - 4}{y}\right| = \ln(x^4 c) \Rightarrow |y - 4| = |y|\, x^4 c$$

Given, $x = 1, y = 2$

$$2 = 2c \Rightarrow c = 1$$

Curve $|y - 4| = x^4|y| \Rightarrow y - 4 = \pm y \cdot x^4$

Case I

$$y - 4 = yx^4 \Rightarrow y = \frac{4}{1 - x^4}$$

$$\therefore \quad y(1) = \frac{4}{1 - 1} = \text{Not defined}$$

This case will be rejected.

Case II

$$y - 4 = -yx^4 \Rightarrow y = \frac{4}{1 + x^4}$$

Now, $y(1) = \frac{4}{1 + 1} = 2$

$$10y(\sqrt{2}) = 10 \times \frac{4}{1 + 4} = 8$$

66. Given, $\frac{dy}{dx} + 12y = \cos\left(\frac{\pi x}{12}\right)$

$$P = 12, Q = \cos\left(\frac{\pi x}{12}\right)$$

$$\text{IF} = e^{\int P\,dx} = e^{\int 12\,dx} = e^{12x}$$

$$\therefore y \times \text{IF} = \int Q \cdot \text{IF}\,dx + C$$

$$y \cdot e^{12x} = \int e^{12x} \cos\left(\frac{\pi x}{12}\right) dx + C$$

Using $\int e^{ax} \cos bx\,dx = \frac{e^{ax}}{a^2 + b^2}(a \cos bx + b \sin bx) + C$

Now, $a = 12, b = \pi/12$

$$y \cdot e^{12x} = \frac{e^{12x}}{12^2 + \left(\frac{\pi}{12}\right)^2}\left(12 \cos\frac{\pi x}{12} + \frac{\pi}{12} \sin\frac{\pi x}{12}\right) + C$$

$y(0) = 0$ [given]

$$\Rightarrow \quad 0 = \frac{1}{12^2 + \frac{\pi^2}{12^2}}(12) + C$$

$$\Rightarrow \quad C = \frac{-12}{12^2 + \frac{\pi^2}{12^2}}$$

Now, $y \cdot e^{12x} = \frac{e^{12x}}{12^2 + \left(\frac{\pi}{12}\right)^2}\left(12 \cos\frac{\pi x}{12} + \frac{\pi}{12} \sin\frac{\pi x}{12}\right) - \frac{12}{12^2 + \frac{\pi^2}{12^2}}$

$$\Rightarrow \quad y = \frac{1}{12^2 + \frac{\pi^2}{12^2}} \times \left(12 \cos\frac{\pi x}{12} + \frac{\pi}{12} \sin\frac{\pi x}{12} - 12e^{-12x}\right)$$

$$\Rightarrow \frac{dy}{dx} = \frac{1}{12^2 + \frac{\pi^2}{12^2}}\left[-\pi \sin\left(\frac{\pi x}{12}\right) + \frac{\pi^2}{12^2} \cos\left(\frac{\pi x}{12}\right) + 12^2 e^{-12x}\right]$$

Now, for $\forall x \le 0, \frac{dy}{dx} > 0$

and for $x > 0$, $\frac{dy}{dx}$ may be negative or positive.

So, $f(x)$ is neither increasing nor decreasing.

Now, $12 \cos\left(\frac{\pi x}{12}\right) + \frac{\pi}{12} \sin\left(\frac{\pi x}{12}\right)$ can be written as $\sin\left(\frac{\pi x}{12} + \alpha\right)$ where α is some angle and $y = \beta$ will cut $y = f(x)$ at infinite many points.

67. Given, $\frac{dy}{dx} + \alpha y = x \cdot e^{\beta x}$ which is a linear differential equation.

Integrating factor (IF) $= e^{\int \alpha\,dx} = e^{\alpha x}$

So, the solution is $y \times e^{\alpha x} = \int x e^{\beta x} \cdot e^{\alpha x} dx$

$$\Rightarrow \quad y \times e^{\alpha x} = \int x e^{(\alpha + \beta)x} dx \quad \text{... (i)}$$

Case I If $\alpha + \beta = 0$

From Eq. (i), we get

$$y e^{\alpha x} = \int x e^{0 \cdot x} dx = \int x\,dx = \frac{x^2}{2} + C \quad \text{...(ii)}$$

Given, $y(1) = 1$ i.e. when $x = 1$, then $y = 1$

From Eq. (ii), we get

$$1 \cdot e^{\alpha} = \frac{1}{2} + C \Rightarrow C = e^{\alpha} - \frac{1}{2}$$

From Eq. (ii), we get

$$y e^{\alpha x} = \frac{x^2 - 1}{2} + e^{\alpha}$$

For $\alpha = 1$, $\quad ye^x = \frac{x^2 - 1}{2} + e \Rightarrow y = \frac{x^2}{2} e^{-x} + \left(e - \frac{1}{2}\right) e^{-x}$

Option (a) is correct.

Case II If $\alpha + \beta \ne 0$

$$\Rightarrow \quad ye^{\alpha x} = x \cdot \frac{e^{(\alpha + \beta)x}}{(\alpha + \beta)} - \int 1 \times \frac{e^{(\alpha + \beta)x}}{(\alpha + \beta)} dx$$

$$\Rightarrow \quad ye^{\alpha x} = x \cdot \frac{e^{(\alpha + \beta)x}}{(\alpha + \beta)} - \frac{e^{(\alpha + \beta)x}}{(\alpha + \beta)^2} + c_1$$

$$\Rightarrow \quad y = \frac{x \cdot e^{\beta x}}{\alpha + \beta} - \frac{e^{\beta x}}{(\alpha + \beta)^2} + c_1 e^{-\alpha x}$$

[Cancelling $e^{\alpha x}$ from both sides]

$$\Rightarrow \quad y = \frac{e^{\beta x}}{\alpha + \beta}\left(x - \frac{1}{\alpha + \beta}\right) + c_1 e^{-\alpha x} \quad \text{...(iii)}$$

Putting $\alpha = \beta = 1$ in Eq. (iii), we get

$$y = \frac{e^x}{2}\left(x - \frac{1}{2}\right) + c_1 e^{-x}$$

Given, $y(1) = 1$

$$\therefore \quad 1 = \frac{e}{2} \times \frac{1}{2} + \frac{c_1}{e} \Rightarrow c_1 = e - \frac{e^2}{4}$$

So, $y = \frac{e^x}{2}\left(x - \frac{1}{2}\right) + \left(e - \frac{e^2}{4}\right) e^{-x}$

Option (c) is correct.

68. Given differential equation

$$f'(x) = \frac{f(x)}{b^2 + x^2} \Rightarrow \int \frac{f'(x)}{f(x)} dx = \int \frac{dx}{b^2 + x^2}$$

$$\Rightarrow \quad \log_e |f(x)| = \frac{1}{b} \tan^{-1}\left(\frac{x}{b}\right) + c$$

$$\because \quad f(0) = 1, \text{ so } c = 0$$

$$\therefore \quad |f(x)| = e^{\frac{1}{b} \tan^{-1}\left(\frac{x}{b}\right)}$$

$$\Rightarrow \quad f(x) = e^{\frac{1}{b} \tan^{-1}\left(\frac{x}{b}\right)} \text{ or } -e^{\frac{1}{b} \tan^{-1}\left(\frac{x}{b}\right)}$$

$$\because \quad f(0) = 1$$

$$\therefore \quad f(x) = e^{\frac{1}{b} \tan^{-1}\left(\frac{x}{b}\right)} \text{ and } f'(x) = \frac{1}{b^2} \frac{e^{\frac{1}{b} \tan^{-1}\left(\frac{x}{b}\right)}}{1 + \left(\frac{x}{b}\right)^2} = \frac{e^{\frac{1}{b} \tan^{-1}\left(\frac{x}{b}\right)}}{b^2 + x^2}$$

$\therefore f'(x) > 0 \ \forall x \in R$ and $b \in R_0$.

Therefore, $f(x)$ is an increasing function $\forall\ b \in R_0$.

and $f(x)\, f(-x) = e^{\frac{1}{b}\tan^{-1}\left(\frac{x}{b}\right)} \cdot e^{-\frac{1}{b}\tan^{-1}\left(\frac{x}{b}\right)} = 1$

69. Let a point $P(h, k)$ on the curve $y = y(x)$, so equation of tangent to the curve at point P is

$$y - k = \left(\frac{dy}{dx}\right)_{h,k}(x - h) \qquad \text{...(i)}$$

Now, the tangent (i) intersect the Y-axis at Y_p, so coordinates Y_p is $\left(0, k - h\dfrac{dy}{dx}\right)$, where $\dfrac{dy}{dx} = \left(\dfrac{dy}{dx}\right)_{(h, k)}$

So, $PY_p = 1$ [given]

$$\Rightarrow \sqrt{h^2 + h^2\left(\frac{dy}{dx}\right)^2} = 1 \Rightarrow \frac{dy}{dx} = \pm\frac{\sqrt{1-x^2}}{x} \text{ [on replacing } h \text{ by } x]$$

$$\Rightarrow \qquad dy = \pm\frac{\sqrt{1-x^2}}{x}dx$$

On putting $x = \sin\theta$, $dx = \cos\theta\, d\theta$, we get

$$dy = \pm\frac{\sqrt{1-\sin^2\theta}}{\sin\theta}\cos\theta d\theta$$

$$= \pm\frac{\cos^2\theta}{\sin\theta}d\theta$$

$$= \pm(\text{cosec}\theta - \sin\theta)d\theta$$

$$\Rightarrow \qquad y = \pm[\ln(\text{cosec}\theta - \cot\theta) + \cos\theta] + C$$

$$\Rightarrow \qquad y = \pm\left[\ln\left(\frac{1-\cos\theta}{\sin\theta}\right) + \cos\theta\right] + C$$

$$\Rightarrow \qquad y = \pm\left[\ln\left(\frac{1-\sqrt{1-\sin^2\theta}}{\sin\theta}\right) + \sqrt{1-\sin^2\theta}\right] + C$$

$$\Rightarrow \qquad y = \pm\left[\ln\left(\frac{1-\sqrt{1-x^2}}{x}\right) + \sqrt{1-x^2}\right] + C \quad [\because x = \sin\theta]$$

$$= \pm\left[-\ln\frac{1+\sqrt{1-x^2}}{x} + \sqrt{1-x^2}\right] + C$$

[on rationalisation]

$\because$ The curve is in the first quadrant so y must be positive, so

$$y = \ln\left(\frac{1+\sqrt{1-x^2}}{x}\right) - \sqrt{1-x^2} + C$$

As curve passes through (1, 0), so

$0 = 0 - 0 + c \Rightarrow c = 0$, so required curve is

$$y = \ln\left(\frac{1+\sqrt{1-x^2}}{x}\right) - \sqrt{1-x^2}$$

and required differential equation is

$$\frac{dy}{dx} = -\frac{\sqrt{1-x^2}}{x}$$

$$\Rightarrow \qquad xy' + \sqrt{1-x^2} = 0$$

Exercise 3 - Challenging Problems

1. Integrating, $\dfrac{d^2y}{dx^2} = 6x - 4$, we get $\dfrac{dy}{dx} = 3x^2 - 4x + C$

when $x = 1$, $\dfrac{dy}{dx} = 0$. So that $C = 1$

$$\text{Hence,} \qquad \frac{dy}{dx} = 3x^2 - 4x + 1 \qquad \text{...(i)}$$

Integrating, we get

$$y = x^3 - 2x^2 + x + C_1, \text{ when } x = 1, y = 5,$$

so that $C_1 = 5$

Thus, we have $y = x^3 - 2x^2 + x + 5$

Form Eq. (i), we get the critical points $x = \dfrac{1}{3}$, $x = 1$

At the critical point $x = \dfrac{1}{3}$, $\dfrac{d^2y}{dx^2}$ is (–ve).

Therefore, at $x = \dfrac{1}{3}$, y has a local maximum.

At $x = 1$, $\dfrac{d^2y}{dx^2}$ is (+ ve).

Therefore, at $x = 1$, y has a local minimum.

$$\text{Also,} \qquad f(1) = 5 \Rightarrow f\left(\frac{1}{3}\right) = \frac{139}{27}$$

$$f(0) = 5,\ f(2) = 7$$

Hence, the global maximum value = 7, the global minimum value = 5.

2. $\phi'(x) + 2\,\phi(x) \le 1$

$$\Rightarrow \qquad e^{2x}\,\phi'(x) + 2\,\phi(x)\,e^{2x} \le e^{2x}$$

$$\Rightarrow \qquad \frac{d}{dx}\left(e^{2x}\,\phi(x) - \frac{1}{2}e^{2x}\right) \le 0$$

$\Rightarrow e^{2x}\left(\phi(x) - \dfrac{1}{2}\right)$ is a non-increasing function of x.

$\Rightarrow \phi(x) - \dfrac{1}{2}$ is a non-increasing function of x.

3. Let $y = f(x)$ be the equation of the required curve.

$$\text{Given that} \quad \frac{\left|y - x\dfrac{dy}{dx}\right|}{\sqrt{x^2 + y^2}} = k \text{ (a constant)}$$

$$\Rightarrow \qquad \frac{dy}{dx} = \frac{y}{x} \pm k\sqrt{1 + \left(\frac{y}{x}\right)^2}$$

Let $y = vx$, then $v + x\dfrac{dv}{dx} = v \pm k\sqrt{1 + v^2}$

$$\Rightarrow \qquad \frac{dv}{\sqrt{1+v^2}} = \pm k\frac{dx}{x}, \text{ integrating we get}$$

$$\Rightarrow \qquad \log\left|v + \sqrt{1+v^2}\right| = \pm k\ln x + C$$

$$\Rightarrow \qquad \log\left|\frac{xy + \sqrt{x^2+y^2}}{x}\right| = \pm k\ln x + C$$

which are the equations of the required curves.

4. Let $y = f(x)$ be the curve such that the normal at $P(x, y)$ to this curve meets X-axis at Q.
Then,

$$PQ = \text{length of the normal at } P$$

$$= y\sqrt{1+\left(\frac{dy}{dx}\right)^2}$$

But $PQ = k$

$$\therefore \quad y\sqrt{1+\left(\frac{dy}{dx}\right)^2} = k$$

$$\Rightarrow \quad y^2 + y^2\left(\frac{dy}{dx}\right)^2 = k^2 \text{ or } y\frac{dy}{dx} = \pm\sqrt{k^2 - y^2}$$

$$\Rightarrow \quad \frac{y\,dy}{\sqrt{k^2 - y^2}} = \pm\, dx$$

Integrating both the sides, we get

$-\sqrt{k^2 - y^2} = \pm\, x + C$, since it passes through $(0, k) \rightarrow C = 0$.

$$\therefore \quad -\sqrt{k^2 - y^2} = \pm\, x$$

or $\quad k^2 - y^2 = x^2$

$\Rightarrow \quad x^2 + y^2 = k^2$, is required equation of the curve.

5. Let $P(x, y)$ be any point on the curve $y = f(x)$. Then, the equation of the normal at P is,

$$Y - y = -\frac{1}{(dy/dx)}(X - x)$$

or $$X + Y\frac{dy}{dx} - \left(y\frac{dy}{dx} + x\right) = 0 \quad \text{...(i)}$$

It is given that distance of Eq. (i) from origin = Distance from X-axis (i.e. y)

i.e. $$\left|\frac{0 - \left(y\frac{dy}{dx} + x\right)}{\sqrt{1+\left(\frac{dy}{dx}\right)^2}}\right| = y$$

$$\Rightarrow \quad \left(y\frac{dy}{dx} + x\right)^2 = y^2\left[1+\left(\frac{dy}{dx}\right)^2\right]$$

$$\Rightarrow \quad x^2 + 2xy\frac{dy}{dx} = y^2 \text{ or } \frac{dy}{dx} = \frac{y^2 - x^2}{2xy}$$

which is homogeneous differential equation and we can solve by homogeneous or by total differential.
Here, using total differential,

$$2xy\,dy - y^2\,dx = -\,x^2\,dx$$

$$\Rightarrow \quad \frac{x\,d(y^2) - y^2\,dx}{x^2} = -\,dx \Rightarrow d\left(\frac{y^2}{x}\right) = -\,dx$$

Integrating both the sides, we get

$$\Rightarrow \quad \frac{y^2}{x} = -\,x + C \quad \text{...(ii)}$$

It passes through $(1, 1) \Rightarrow C = 2$

$$\therefore \quad \frac{y^2}{x} = -\,x + 2 \text{ or } y^2 = -\,x^2 + 2x$$

$\Rightarrow \quad x^2 + y^2 - 2x = 0$, is required equation of curve.

6. Let P_0 be the initial population, Q_0 be its initial food production.
Let P be the population of the country in year t and Q be its food production in year t.

$$\Rightarrow \quad \frac{dP}{dt} = \frac{3P}{100} \text{ or } \frac{dP}{P} = \frac{3}{100}\,dt$$

Integrating, we get

$$\log P = \frac{3}{100}t + C$$

At $t = 0$, we have $P = P_0$

$$\Rightarrow \quad C = \log P_0 \Rightarrow P = P_0\,e^{0.03\,t} \quad \text{...(i)}$$

It is given that the annual food production every year is 4% more than that of last year.

$$\Rightarrow \quad Q = Q_0\left(1 + \frac{4}{100}\right)^t$$

Let the average consumption per person be k units.

$$\Rightarrow \quad Q_0 = kP_0\left(\frac{90}{100}\right) = 0.9\,kP_0$$

$$\therefore \quad Q = 0.9\,kP_0\,(1.04)^t \quad \text{...(ii)}$$

This gives quantity of food available in year t.
The population in year t is

$$P = P_0\,e^{0.03\,t} \quad \text{[from Eq. (i)]}$$

$\therefore$ Consumption in year, $t = kP_0e^{0.03\,t}$ ...(iii)

The country will be self sufficient, if

$$Q \geq P$$

$$\Rightarrow \quad 0.9k\,P_0\,(1.04)^t \geq kP_0e^{0.03\,t}$$

$$\Rightarrow \quad \frac{9}{10}(1.04)^t \geq e^{0.03\,t} \Rightarrow (1.04)^t\,e^{-0.03\,t} \geq \frac{10}{9}$$

$$\Rightarrow \quad t\log(1.04) - 0.03\,t \geq \log\left(\frac{10}{9}\right)$$

$$\Rightarrow \quad t\,\{\log(1.04) - 0.03\} \geq \log\left(\frac{10}{9}\right) \Rightarrow t \geq \frac{\log 10 - \log 9}{\log(1.04) - 0.03}$$

Thus, the least number of year in which country becomes self sufficient.

$$\Rightarrow \quad t = \frac{\log 10 - \log 9}{\log(1.04) - 0.03}$$

7. Differentiating the equation w.r.t. x, we get

$$xy(x) + 1\cdot\int_0^x y(t)\,dt = (x+1)\,xy(x) + 1\cdot\int_0^x t\,y(t)\,dt$$

i.e. $$\int_0^x y(t)\,dt = x^2\,y(x) + \int_0^x t\,y(t)\,dt$$

Again, differentiating w.r.t. x, we get

$$y(x) = x^2\,y'(x) + 2xy(x) + xy(x)$$

i.e. $$(1 - 3x)\,y(x) = \frac{x^2\,dy(x)}{dx}$$

i.e. $$\frac{(1 - 3x)\,dx}{x^2} = \frac{dy(x)}{y(x)}$$

Integrating, we get $y = \dfrac{C}{x^3}\,e^{-1/x}$

8. As y_1, y_2 are the solutions of the differential equation;

$$\frac{dy}{dx} + P(x) \cdot y = Q(x) \quad ...(i)$$

$$\therefore \quad \frac{dy_1}{dx} + P(x) \cdot y_1 = Q(x) \quad ...(ii)$$

$$\text{and} \quad \frac{dy_2}{dx} + P(x) \cdot y_2 = Q(x) \quad ...(iii)$$

From Eqs. (i) and (ii),

$$\left(\frac{dy}{dx} - \frac{dy_1}{dx}\right) + P(x)(y - y_1) = 0$$

$$\therefore \quad \frac{d}{dx}(y - y_1) + P(x) \cdot (y - y_1) = 0 \quad ...(iv)$$

From Eqs. (ii) and (iii),

$$\frac{d}{dx}(y_1 - y_2) + P(x)(y_1 - y_2) = 0 \quad ...(v)$$

From Eqs. (iv) and (v),

$$\frac{\frac{d}{dx}(y - y_1)}{\frac{d}{dx}(y_1 - y_2)} = \frac{y - y_1}{y_1 - y_2} \Rightarrow \frac{\frac{d}{dx}(y - y_1)}{y - y_1} = \frac{\frac{d}{dx}(y_1 - y_2)}{y_1 - y_2}$$

Integrating both the sides, we get

$$\log(y - y_1) = \log(y_1 - y_2)$$

$$\therefore \quad y = y_1 + C(y_1 - y_2)$$

Now, $y = \alpha y_1 + \beta y_2$ will be a solutions, if

$$\frac{d}{dx}(\alpha y_1 + \beta y_2) + P(x)(\alpha y_1 + \beta y_2) = Q(x)$$

$$\text{or} \quad \alpha\left(\frac{dy_1}{dx} + P(x) y_1\right) + \beta\left(\frac{dy_2}{dx} + P(x) y_2\right) = Q(x)$$

$$\text{or} \quad \alpha Q(x) + \beta Q(x) = Q(x) \quad \text{[using Eqs. (ii) and (iii)]}$$

$$\therefore \quad (\alpha + \beta) Q(x) = Q(x)$$

Hence, $\alpha + \beta = 1$

9. Equation of the tangent to the curve; $y = f(x)$ is

$$(Y - y) = f'(x)(X - x)$$

Equation of tangent to the curve $g(x) = y_1 = \int_{-\infty}^{x} f(t)\, dt$ is

$$(Y - y_1) = g'(x)(X - x) = f(x)(X - x)$$

Given that tangent with equal abscissas intersect on the X-axis.

$$\Rightarrow \quad x - \frac{y}{f'(x)} = x - \frac{y_1}{f(x)}$$

$$\Rightarrow \quad \frac{f(x)}{f'(x)} = \frac{y_1}{f(x)} \quad [\because y = f(x)]$$

$$\Rightarrow \quad \frac{f(x)}{y_1} = \frac{f'(x)}{f(x)} \Rightarrow \frac{g'(x)}{g(x)} = \frac{f'(x)}{f(x)}$$

$$\Rightarrow \quad \frac{g'(x)}{g(x)} = k \quad \Rightarrow g(x) = Ce^{kx}$$

$$\Rightarrow \quad g'(x) = k\,Ce^{kx} \Rightarrow f(x) = k\,Ce^{kx}$$

$y = f(x)$ passes through $(0, 1) \Rightarrow kC = 1$

$y_1 = g(x)$ passes through

$(0, 1/n) \Rightarrow C = \frac{1}{n} \Rightarrow k = n \Rightarrow f(x) = e^{nx}$

10. The equation of the normal at (x, y) is

$$(X - x) + (Y - y)\frac{dy}{dx} = 0$$

$$\Rightarrow \quad \frac{X}{x + y\frac{dy}{dx}} + \frac{Y}{\frac{(x + y\, dy/dx)}{dy/dx}} = 1$$

$$\Rightarrow \quad OA = x + y\frac{dy}{dx},\ OB = \frac{\left(x + y\frac{dy}{dx}\right)}{\frac{dy}{dx}}$$

Also, $\frac{1}{OA} + \frac{1}{OB} = 1 \Rightarrow 1 + \frac{dy}{dx} = x + y\frac{dy}{dx}$

$$\Rightarrow \quad (y - 1)\frac{dy}{dx} + (x - 1) = 0$$

Integrating, we get

$$(y - 1)^2 + (x - 1)^2 = C$$

Since, the curve passes through $(5, 4)$, $C = 25$.

Hence, the curve is $(x - 1)^2 + (y - 1)^2 = 25$.

11. The equation of the line through $P(x, y)$ making an angle with the X-axis which is supplementary to the angle made by the tangent at $P(x, y)$ is

$$Y - y = -\frac{dy}{dx}(X - x) \quad ...(i)$$

where, it meets the X-axis.

$$Y = 0, \quad X = x + \frac{y}{dy/dx}$$

$$\Rightarrow \quad OA = x + y\frac{dx}{dy} \quad ...(ii)$$

The line through $P(x, y)$ and perpendicular to Eq. (i) is

$$Y - y = \frac{dx}{dy}(X - x)$$

where, it meets the Y-axis.

$$X = 0,\ Y = y - x\frac{dx}{dy} \Rightarrow OB = y - x\frac{dx}{dy} \quad ...(iii)$$

Since, $OA = OB$

$$\Rightarrow \quad x + y\frac{dx}{dy} = y - x\frac{dx}{dy}$$

$$\text{or} \quad (y - x) = (y + x)\frac{dx}{dy}$$

$$\text{or} \quad \frac{dy}{dx} = \frac{y + x}{y - x}, \text{ put } y = vx$$

$$\Rightarrow \quad x\frac{dv}{dx} = \frac{1 + 2v - v^2}{v - 1} \Rightarrow \frac{(1 - v)\, dv}{1 + 2v - v^2} + \frac{dx}{x} = 0$$

$$\Rightarrow \quad \log(1 + 2v - v^2) + \log x = C_1 \Rightarrow x^2 + 2xy - y^2 = C$$

where $C_1 = \log\sqrt{C}$

Since, curve passes through $(1, 1) \rightarrow C = 2$

$\therefore$ Required curve, $\quad x^2 - y^2 + 2xy = 2$